THE TIMES

ATLAS
OF THE
WORLD

REFERENCE EDITION

TIMES BOOKS
London

THE ⚜ TIMES
ATLAS
OF THE
WORLD
REFERENCE EDITION

Times Books, 77-85 Fulham Palace Road, London W6 8JB

The Times is a registered trademark of Times Newspapers Ltd

First published 1995
Published as The Times Atlas of the World New Generation Edition 1997
Second Edition 2002

Third Edition 2005

Copyright © Times Books Group Ltd 2005

Maps © Collins Bartholomew Ltd 2005

Printed and bound in Singapore by Imago

British Library Cataloguing in Publication Data
A catalogue record for this book is available from the British Library

ISBN 0 00 715728 2

QH11457 Imp 001

All mapping in this atlas is generated from Collins Bartholomew digital databases. Collins Bartholomew, the UK's leading independent geographical information supplier, can provide a digital, custom, and premium mapping service to a variety of markets. For further information:
Tel: +44 (0) 141 306 3752
e-mail: collinsbartholomew@harpercollins.co.uk

or visit our website at: www.collinsbartholomew.com

www.harpercollins.co.uk
visit the book lover's website

OCEANIA

Total land area: 8 844 516 sq km / 3 414 887 sq miles
(including New Guinea and Pacific Island nations)

HIGHEST MOUNTAINS

	Location	m	ft
Puncak Jaya	Indonesia	5 030	16 502
Puncak Trikora	Indonesia	4 730	15 518
Puncak Mandala	Indonesia	4 700	15 420
Puncak Yamin	Indonesia	4 595	15 075
Mt Wilhelm	Papua New Guinea	4 509	14 793
Mt Kubor	Papua New Guinea	4 359	14 301

LARGEST ISLANDS

	sq km	sq miles
New Guinea	808 510	312 167
South Island, New Zealand	151 215	58 384
North Island, New Zealand	115 777	44 702
Tasmania	67 800	26 178

LONGEST RIVERS

	km	miles
Murray-Darling	3 750	2 330
Darling	2 739	1 702
Murray	2 589	1 608
Murrumbidgee	1 690	1 050
Lachlan	1 480	919
Macquarie	950	590

LARGEST LAKES

	sq km	sq miles
Lake Eyre	0–8 900	0–3 436
Lake Torrens	0–5 780	0–2 232

DRAINAGE BASINS

	sq km	sq miles
Murray-Darling	1 058 000	408 000

Data from the 1km AVHRR Global Land dataset project by
ESA, CEOS, IGBP, NASA, NOAA, USGS, IONIA processed
by ESA/ESRIN distributed by Eurimage S.p.A.

See pages 66–67 for a map of Oceania.

ASIA

Total land area: 45 036 492 sq km / 17 388 686 sq miles

HIGHEST MOUNTAINS

	Location	m	ft
Mt Everest	China/Nepal	8 848	29 028
K2	China/Jammu and Kashmir	8 611	28 251
Kangchenjunga	India/Nepal	8 586	28 169
Lhotse	China/Nepal	8 516	27 939
Makalu	China/Nepal	8 463	27 765
Cho Oyu	China/Nepal	8 201	26 906

LARGEST ISLANDS

	sq km	sq miles
Borneo	745 561	287 863
Sumatra	473 606	182 860
Honshū	227 414	87 805
Celebes	189 216	73 057
Java	132 188	51 038
Luzon	104 690	40 421

LONGEST RIVERS

	km	miles
Yangtze	6 380	3 965
Ob'-Irtysh	5 568	3 460
Yenisey-Angara-Selenga	5 550	3 448
Yellow	5 464	3 395
Irtysh	4 440	2 759
Mekong	4 425	2 749

LARGEST LAKES

	sq km	sq miles
Caspian Sea	371 000	143 244
Aral Sea	28 687	11 076
Lake Baikal	30 500	11 776
Lake Balkhash	17 400	6 718
Ysyk-Köl	6 200	2 393

DRAINAGE BASINS

	sq km	sq miles
Ob'-Irtysh	2 990 000	1 154 000
Yenisey-Angara-Selenga	2 580 000	996 000
Lena-Kirenga	2 490 000	961 000
Yangtze	1 959 000	756 000
Heilong Jiang (Amur)-Argun'	1 855 000	716 000
Ganges-Brahmaputra	1 621 000	626 000

Data from the 1km AVHRR Global Land dataset project by ESA, CEOS, IGBP, NASA, NOAA, USGS, IONIA processed by ESA/ESRIN distributed by Eurimage S.p.A.

See pages 74–75 for a map of Asia.

EUROPE

Total land area: 9 908 599 sq km / 3 825 731 sq miles

HIGHEST MOUNTAINS

	Location	metres	feet
Elbrus	Russian Federation	5 642	18 510
Gora Dykh-Tau	Russian Federation	5 204	17 073
Shkhara	Georgia/Russian Federation	5 201	17 063
Kazbek	Georgia/Russian Federation	5 047	16 558
Mont Blanc	France/Italy	4 808	15 774
Dufourspitze	Italy/Switzerland	4 634	15 203

LARGEST ISLANDS

	sq km	sq miles
Great Britain	218 476	84 354
Iceland	102 820	39 699
Novaya Zemlya	90 650	35 000
Ireland	83 045	32 064
Spitsbergen	37 814	14 600
Sicily	25 426	9 817

LONGEST RIVERS

	km	miles
Volga	3 688	2 291
Danube	2 850	1 770
Dnieper	2 285	1 419
Kama	2 028	1 260
Don	1 931	1 199
Pechora	1 802	1 119

LARGEST LAKES

	sq km	sq miles
Caspian Sea	371 000	143 243
Lake Ladoga	18 390	7 100
Lake Onega	9 600	3 706
Vänern	5 585	2 156
Rybinskoye Vodokhranilishche	5 180	2 000

DRAINAGE BASINS

	sq km	sq miles
Volga	1 380 000	533 000

Data from the 1km AVHRR Global Land dataset project by ESA, CEOS, IGBP, NASA, NOAA, USGS, IONIA processed by ESA/ESRIN distributed by Eurimage S.p.A.

See pages 100–101 for a map of Europe.

AFRICA

Total land area: 30 343 578 sq km / 11 715 721 sq miles

HIGHEST MOUNTAINS

	Location	m	ft
Kilimanjaro	Tanzania	5 892	19 331
Mt Kenya	Kenya	5 199	17 057
Margherita Peak	Democratic Republic of Congo/Uganda	5 110	16 765
Meru	Tanzania	4 565	14 977
Ras Dejen	Ethiopia	4 533	14 872
Mt Karisimbi	Rwanda	4 510	14 796

LARGEST ISLAND

	sq km	sq miles
Madagascar	587 040	226 657

LONGEST RIVERS

	km	miles
Nile	6 695	4 160
Congo	4 667	2 900
Niger	4 184	2 599
Zambezi	2 736	1 700
Webi Shabeelle	2 490	1 547
Ubangi	2 250	1 398

LARGEST LAKES

	sq km	sq miles
Lake Victoria	68 800	26 564
Lake Tanganyika	32 900	12 702
Lake Nyasa	30 044	11 600
Lake Volta	8 485	3 276
Lake Turkana	6 475	2 500
Lake Albert	5 600	2 162

DRAINAGE BASINS

	sq km	sq miles
Congo	3 700 000	1 429 000
Nile	3 349 000	1 293 000
Niger	1 890 000	730 000
Zambezi	1 330 000	514 000

Data from the 1km AVHRR Global Land dataset project by ESA, CEOS, IGBP, NASA, NOAA, USGS, IONIA processed by ESA/ESRIN distributed by Eurimage S.p.A.

See pages 118–119 for a map of Africa.

NORTH AMERICA

Total land area: 24 680 331 sq km / 9 529 129 sq miles

HIGHEST MOUNTAINS

	Location	m	ft
Mt McKinley	USA	6 194	20 321
Mt Logan	Canada	5 959	19 550
Pico de Orizaba	Mexico	5 747	18 855
Mt St Elias	USA	5 489	18 008
Volcán Popocatépetl	Mexico	5 452	17 887
Mt Foraker	USA	5 303	17 398

LARGEST ISLANDS

	sq km	sq miles
Greenland	2 175 600	840 004
Baffin Island	507 451	195 927
Victoria Island	217 291	83 897
Ellesmere Island	196 236	75 767
Cuba	110 860	42 803
Newfoundland	108 860	42 031
Hispaniola	76 192	29 418

LONGEST RIVERS

	km	miles
Mississippi-Missouri	5 969	3 709
Mackenzie-Peace-Finlay	4 241	2 635
Missouri	4 086	2 539
Mississippi	3 765	2 339
Yukon	3 185	1 979
Rio Grande	3 057	1 899

LARGEST LAKES

	sq km	sq miles
Lake Superior	82 100	31 699
Lake Huron	59 600	23 012
Lake Michigan	57 800	22 317
Great Bear Lake	31 328	12 095
Great Slave Lake	28 568	11 030
Lake Erie	25 700	9 922

DRAINAGE BASINS

	sq km	sq miles
Mississippi-Missouri	3 250 000	1 255 000
Mackenzie-Peace-Finlay	1 805 000	697 000
St Lawrence-St Louis	1 463 000	565 000
Nelson-Saskatchewan	1 150 000	444 000

Data from the 1km AVHRR Global Land dataset project by
ESA, CEOS, IGBP, NASA, NOAA, USGS, IONIA processed
by ESA/ESRIN distributed by Eurimage S.p.A.

See pages 126–127 for a map of North America.

SOUTH AMERICA

Total land area: 17 815 420 sq km / 6 878 572 sq miles

HIGHEST MOUNTAINS

	Location	m	ft
Cerro Aconcagua	Argentina	6 959	22 831
Nevado Ojos del Salado	Argentina/Chile	6 908	22 664
Cerro Bonete	Argentina	6 872	22 546
Cerro Pissis	Argentina	6 858	22 500
Cerro Tupungato	Argentina/Chile	6 800	22 309
Cerro Mercedario	Argentina	6 770	22 211

LARGEST ISLANDS

	sq km	sq miles
Isla Grande de Tierra del Fuego	47 000	18 147
Isla de Chiloé	8 394	3 240
East Falkland	6 760	2 610
West Falkland	5 413	2 090

LONGEST RIVERS

	km	miles
Amazon	6 516	4 049
Río de la Plata-Paraná	4 500	2 796
Purus	3 218	1 999
Madeira	3 200	1 988
São Francisco	2 900	1 802
Tocantins	2 750	1 708

LARGEST LAKE

	sq km	sq miles
Lake Titicaca	8 340	3 220

DRAINAGE BASINS

	sq km	sq miles
Amazon	7 050 000	2 722 000
Río de la Plata-Paraná	3 100 000	1 197 000

Data from the 1km AVHRR Global Land dataset project by
ESA, CEOS, IGBP, NASA, NOAA, USGS, IONIA processed
by ESA/ESRIN distributed by Eurimage S.p.A.

See pages 152–153 for a map of South America.

ANTARCTICA

Total land area: 12 093 000 sq km / 4 669 133 sq miles
(excluding ice shelves)

AREA

	sq km	sq miles
Total land area (excluding ice shelves)	12 093 000	4 669 133
Ice shelves	1 559 000	601 933
Exposed rock	49 000	18 919

HIGHEST MOUNTAINS

	m	ft
Vinson Massif	4 897	16 066
Mt Tyree	4 852	15 918
Mt Kirkpatrick	4 528	14 855
Mt Markham	4 351	14 275
Mt Jackson	4 190	13 747
Mt Sidley	4 181	13 717

HEIGHTS

	m	ft
Lowest bedrock elevation (Bentley Subglacial Trench)	-2 496	-8 189
Maximum ice thickness (Astrolabe Subglacial Basin)	4 776	15 669
Mean ice thickness (including ice shelves)	1 859	6 099

VOLUME

	cubic km	cubic miles
Ice sheet (including ice shelves)	25 400 000	10 160 000

See page 73 for a map of Antarctica.

All 193 independent countries and all populated dependent and disputed territories are included in this list of the states and territories of the world; the list is arranged in alphabetical order by the conventional name form. For independent states, the full name is given below the conventional name, if this is different; for territories, the status is given. The capital city name is given in conventional English form with selected alternative, usually local, form in brackets.

Area and population statistics are the latest available and include estimates. The information on languages and religions is based on the latest information on 'de facto' speakers of the language or 'de facto' adherents of the religion. This varies greatly from country to country because some countries include questions in censuses while others do not, in which case best estimates are used. The order of the languages and religions reflects their relative importance within the country; generally, languages or religions are included when more than one per cent of the population are estimated to be speakers or adherents.

ABBREVIATIONS

CURRENCIES

CFA	Communauté Financière Africaine
CFP	Comptoirs Français du Pacifique

Membership of selected international organizations is shown by the abbreviations below; dependent territories do not normally have separate memberships of these organizations.

ORGANIZATIONS

APEC	Asia-Pacific Economic Cooperation
ASEAN	Association of Southeast Asian Nations
CARICOM	Caribbean Community
CIS	Commonwealth of Independent States
Comm.	The Commonwealth
EU	European Union
NATO	North Atlantic Treaty Organization
OECD	Organization of Economic Cooperation and Development
OPEC	Organization of Petroleum Exporting Countries
SADC	Southern African Development Community
UN	United Nations

AFGHANISTAN
Islamic Republic of Afghanistan

Area Sq Km	652 225	Languages	Dari, Pushtu, Uzbek, Turkmen
Area Sq Miles	251 825	Religions	Sunni Muslim, Shi'a Muslim
Population	23 897 000	Currency	Afghani
Capital	Kābul	Organizations	UN

Map page 85

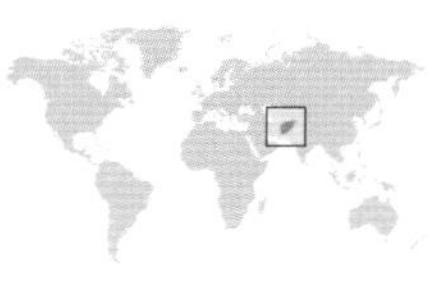

A landlocked country in central Asia with central highlands bordered by plains in the north and southwest, and by the Hindu Kush mountains in the northeast. The climate is dry continental. Over the last twenty-five years war has disrupted the economy, which is highly dependent on farming and livestock rearing. Most trade is with the former USSR, Pakistan and Iran.

ALBANIA
Republic of Albania

Area Sq Km	28 748	Languages	Albanian, Greek
Area Sq Miles	11 100	Religions	Sunni Muslim, Albanian Orthodox, Roman Catholic
Population	3 166 000	Currency	Lek
Capital	Tirana (Tiranë)	Organizations	UN

Map page 115

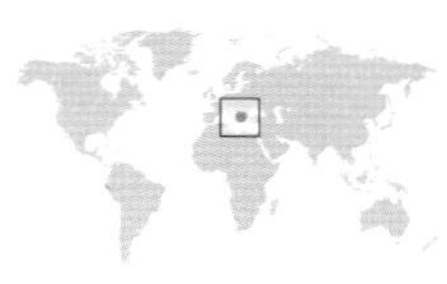

Albania lies in the western Balkan Mountains in southeastern Europe, bordering the Adriatic Sea. It is mountainous, with coastal plains where half the population lives. The economy is based on agriculture and mining. Albania is one of the poorest countries in Europe and relies heavily on foreign aid.

ALGERIA
People's Democratic Republic of Algeria

Area Sq Km	2 381 741	Languages	Arabic, French, Berber
Area Sq Miles	919 595	Religions	Sunni Muslim
Population	31 800 000	Currency	Algerian dinar
Capital	Algiers (Alger)	Organizations	OPEC, UN

Map page 120

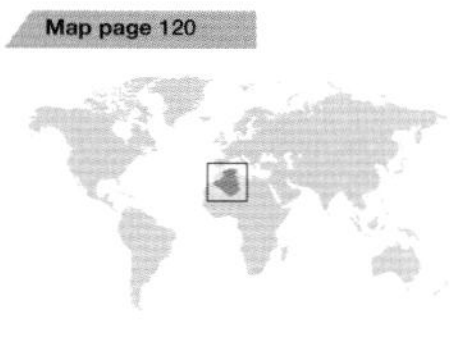

Algeria, the second largest country in Africa, lies on the Mediterranean coast of northwest Africa and extends southwards to the Atlas Mountains and the dry sandstone plateau and desert of the Sahara. The climate ranges from Mediterranean on the coast to semi-arid and arid inland. The most populated areas are the coastal plains and the fertile northern slopes of the Atlas Mountains. Oil, natural gas and related products account for over ninety-five per cent of export earnings. Agriculture employs about a quarter of the workforce, producing mainly food crops. Algeria's main trading partners are Italy, France and the USA.

American Samoa
United States Unincorporated Territory

Area Sq Km	197	Languages	Samoan, English
Area Sq Miles	76	Religions	Protestant, Roman Catholic
Population	67 000	Currency	United States dollar
Capital	Fagatogo		

Map page 67

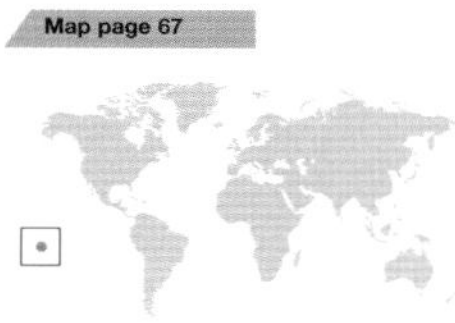

Lying in the south Pacific Ocean, American Samoa consists of five main islands and two coral atolls. The largest island is Tutuila. Tuna and tuna products are the main exports, and the main trading partner is the USA.

ANDORRA
Principality of Andorra

Area Sq Km	465	Languages	Spanish, Catalan, French
Area Sq Miles	180	Religions	Roman Catholic
Population	71 000	Currency	Euro
Capital	Andorra la Vella	Organizations	UN

Map page 111

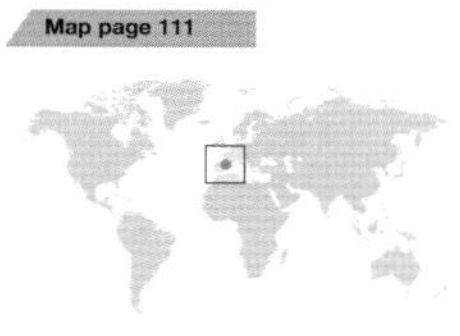

A landlocked state in southwest Europe, Andorra lies in the Pyrenees mountain range between France and Spain. It consists of deep valleys and gorges, surrounded by mountains. Tourism, encouraged by the development of ski resorts, is the mainstay of the economy. Banking is also an important economic activity.

ANGOLA
Republic of Angola

Area Sq Km	1 246 700	Languages	Portuguese, Bantu, local languages
Area Sq Miles	481 354	Religions	Roman Catholic, Protestant, traditional beliefs
Population	13 625 000	Currency	Kwanza
Capital	Luanda	Organizations	SADC, UN

Map page 120–121

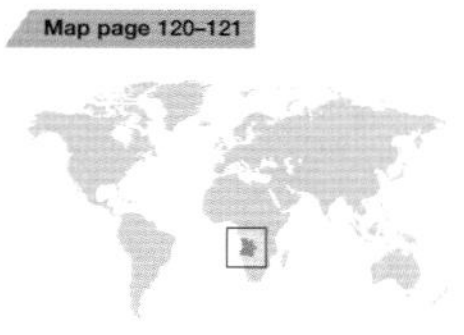

Angola lies on the Atlantic coast of south central Africa. Its small northern province, Cabinda, is separated from the rest of the country by part of the Democratic Republic of Congo. Much of Angola is high plateau. In the west is a narrow coastal plain and in the southwest is desert. The climate is equatorial in the north but desert in the south. Over eighty per cent of the population relies on subsistence agriculture. Angola is rich in minerals (particularly diamonds), and oil accounts for approximately ninety per cent of export earnings. The USA, South Korea and Portugal are its main trading partners.

Anguilla
United Kingdom Overseas Territory

Area Sq Km	155	Languages	English
Area Sq Miles	60	Religions	Protestant, Roman Catholic
Population	12 000	Currency	East Caribbean dollar
Capital	The Valley		

Map page 149

Anguilla lies at the northern end of the Leeward Islands in the eastern Caribbean. Tourism and fishing form the basis of the economy.

ANTIGUA AND BARBUDA

Area Sq Km	442	Languages	English, Creole
Area Sq Miles	171	Religions	Protestant, Roman Catholic
Population	73 000	Currency	East Caribbean dollar
Capital	St John's	Organizations	CARICOM, Comm., UN

Map page 149

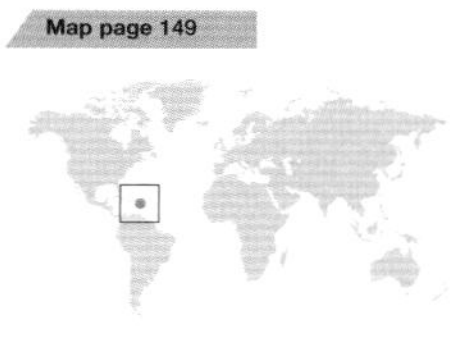

The state comprises the islands of Antigua, Barbuda and the tiny rocky outcrop of Redonda, in the Leeward Islands in the eastern Caribbean. Antigua, the largest and most populous island, is mainly hilly scrubland, with many beaches. The climate is tropical, and the economy relies heavily on tourism. Most trade is with other eastern Caribbean states and the USA.

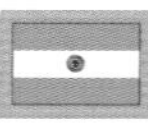

ARGENTINA
Argentine Republic

Area Sq Km	2 766 889	Languages	Spanish, Italian, Amerindian languages
Area Sq Miles	1 068 302	Religions	Roman Catholic, Protestant
Population	38 428 000	Currency	Argentinian peso
Capital	Buenos Aires	Organizations	UN

Map page 156

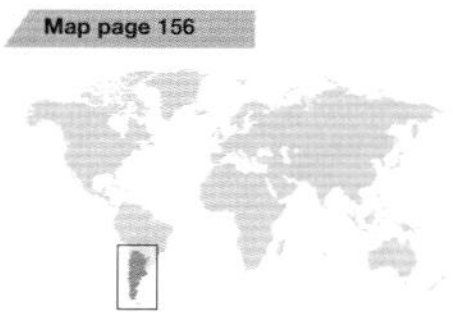

Argentina, the second largest state in South America, extends from Bolivia to Cape Horn and from the Andes mountains to the Atlantic Ocean. It has four geographical regions: subtropical forests and swampland in the northeast; temperate fertile plains or Pampas in the centre; the wooded foothills and valleys of the Andes in the west; and the cold, semi-arid plateaus of Patagonia in the south. The highest mountain in South America, Cerro Aconcagua, is in Argentina. Nearly ninety per cent of the population lives in towns and cities. The country is rich in natural resources including petroleum, natural gas, ores and precious metals. Agricultural products dominate exports, which also include motor vehicles and crude oil. Most trade is with Brazil and the USA.

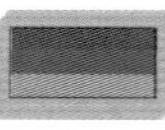

ARMENIA
Republic of Armenia

Area Sq Km	29 800	Languages	Armenian, Azeri
Area Sq Miles	11 506	Religions	Armenian Orthodox
Population	3 061 000	Currency	Dram
Capital	Yerevan (Erevan)	Organizations	CIS, UN

Map page 81

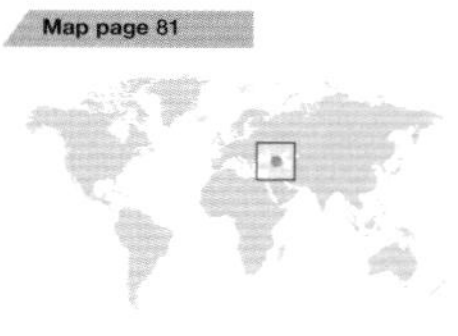

A landlocked state in southwest Asia, Armenia lies in the south of the Lesser Caucasus mountains. It is a mountainous country with a continental climate. One-third of the population lives in the capital, Yerevan. Exports include diamonds, scrap metal and machinery. Many Armenians depend on remittances from abroad.

Aruba
Self-governing Netherlands Territory

Area Sq Km	193	Languages	Papiamento, Dutch, English
Area Sq Miles	75	Religions	Roman Catholic, Protestant
Population	100 000	Currency	Aruban florin
Capital	Oranjestad		

Map page 157

The most southwesterly of the islands in the Lesser Antilles in the Caribbean, Aruba lies just off the coast of Venezuela. Tourism, offshore finance and oil refining are the most important sectors of the economy. The USA is the main trading partner.

AUSTRALIA
Commonwealth of Australia

Area Sq Km	7 692 024	Languages	English, Italian, Greek
Area Sq Miles	2 969 907	Religions	Protestant, Roman Catholic, Orthodox
Population	19 731 000	Currency	Australian dollar
Capital	Canberra	Organizations	APEC, Comm., OECD, UN

Map page 68

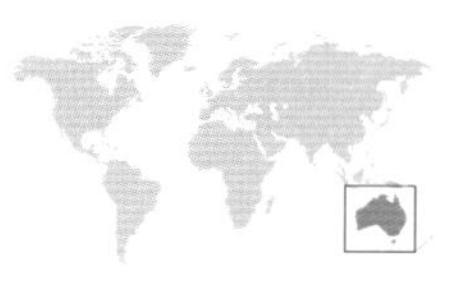

Australia, the world's sixth largest country, occupies the smallest, flattest and driest continent. The western half of the continent is mostly arid plateaus, ridges and vast deserts. The central eastern area comprises the lowlands of river systems draining into Lake Eyre, while to the east is the Great Dividing Range, a belt of ridges and plateaus running from Queensland to Tasmania. Climatically, more than two-thirds of the country is arid or semi-arid. The north is tropical monsoon, the east subtropical, and the southwest and southeast temperate. The majority of Australia's highly urbanized population lives along the east, southeast and southwest coasts. Australia has vast mineral deposits and various sources of energy. It is among the world's leading producers of iron ore, bauxite, nickel, copper and uranium. It is a major producer of coal, and oil and natural gas are also being exploited. Although accounting for only five per cent of the workforce, agriculture continues to be an important sector of the economy, with food and agricultural raw materials making up most of Australia's export earnings. Fuel, ores and metals, and manufactured goods, account for the remainder of exports. Japan and the USA are Australia's main trading partners.

Australian Capital Territory (Federal Territory)
Area Sq Km (Sq Miles) 2 358 (910) | Population 321 680 | Capital Canberra

Jervis Bay Territory (Territory)
Area Sq Km (Sq Miles) 73 (28) | Population 611

New South Wales (State)
Area Sq Km (Sq Miles) 800 642 (309 130) | Population 6 609 304 | Capital Sydney

Northern Territory (Territory)
Area Sq Km (Sq Miles) 1 349 129 (520 902) | Population 200 019 | Capital Darwin

Queensland (State)
Area Sq Km (Sq Miles) 1 730 648 (668 207) | Population 3 635 121 | Capital Brisbane

South Australia (State)
Area Sq Km (Sq Miles) 983 482 (379 725) | Population 1 514 854 | Capital Adelaide

Tasmania (State)
Area Sq Km (Sq Miles) 68 401 (26 410) | Population 472 931 | Capital Hobart

Victoria (State)
Area Sq Km (Sq Miles) 227 416 (87 806) | Population 4 822 663 | Capital Melbourne

Western Australia (State)
Area Sq Km (Sq Miles) 2 529 875 (976 790) | Population 1 906 114 | Capital Perth

AUSTRIA
Republic of Austria

Area Sq Km	83 855	Languages	German, Croatian, Turkish
Area Sq Miles	32 377	Religions	Roman Catholic, Protestant
Population	8 116 000	Currency	Euro
Capital	Vienna (Wien)	Organizations	EU, OECD, UN

Map page 112

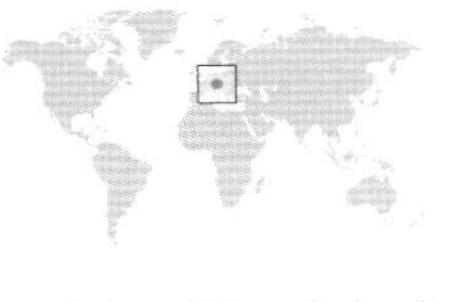

Two-thirds of Austria, a landlocked state in central Europe, lies within the Alps, with lower mountains to the north. The only lowlands are in the east. The Danube river valley in the northeast contains almost all the agricultural land and most of the population. Although the climate varies with altitude, in general summers are warm and winters cold with heavy snowfalls. Manufacturing industry and tourism are the most important sectors of the economy. Exports are dominated by manufactured goods. Germany is Austria's main trading partner.

AZERBAIJAN
Republic of Azerbaijan

Area Sq Km	86 600	Languages	Azeri, Armenian, Russian, Lezgian
Area Sq Miles	33 436	Religions	Shi'a Muslim, Sunni Muslim, Russian and Armenian Orthodox
Population	8 370 000	Currency	Azerbaijani manat
Capital	Baku	Organizations	CIS, UN

Map page 81

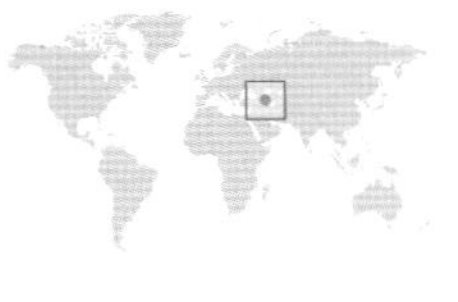

Azerbaijan lies to the southeast of the Caucasus mountains, on the Caspian Sea. Its region of Naxçivan is separated from the rest of the country by part of Armenia. It has mountains in the northeast and west, valleys in the centre, and a low coastal plain. The climate is continental. It is rich in energy and mineral resources. Oil production, onshore and offshore, is the main industry and the basis of heavy industries. Agriculture is important, with cotton and tobacco the main cash crops.

THE BAHAMAS
Commonwealth of the Bahamas

Area Sq Km	13 939	Languages	English, Creole
Area Sq Miles	5 382	Religions	Protestant, Roman Catholic
Population	314 000	Currency	Bahamian dollar
Capital	Nassau	Organizations	CARICOM, Comm., UN

Map page 149

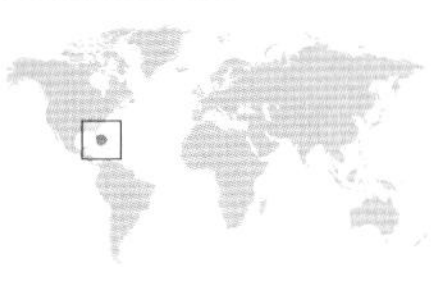

The Bahamas, an archipelago made up of approximately seven hundred islands and over two thousand cays, lies to the northeast of Cuba and east of the Florida coast of the USA. Twenty-two islands are inhabited, and two-thirds of the population lives on the main island of New Providence. The climate is warm for much of the year, with heavy rainfall in the summer. Tourism is the islands' main industry. Offshore banking, insurance and ship registration are also major foreign exchange earners.

BAHRAIN
Kingdom of Bahrain

Area Sq Km	691	Languages	Arabic, English
Area Sq Miles	267	Religions	Shi'a Muslim, Sunni Muslim, Christian
Population	724 000	Currency	Bahraini dinar
Capital	Manama (Al Manāmah)	Organizations	UN

Map page 84

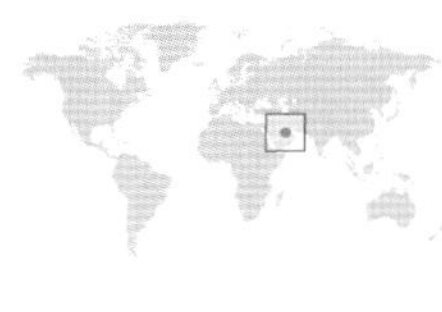

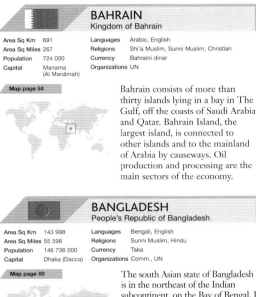

Bahrain consists of more than thirty islands lying in a bay in The Gulf, off the coasts of Saudi Arabia and Qatar. Bahrain Island, the largest island, is connected to other islands and to the mainland of Arabia by causeways. Oil production and processing are the main sectors of the economy.

BANGLADESH
People's Republic of Bangladesh

Area Sq Km	143 998	Languages	Bengali, English
Area Sq Miles	55 598	Religions	Sunni Muslim, Hindu
Population	146 736 000	Currency	Taka
Capital	Dhaka (Dacca)	Organizations	Comm., UN

Map page 89

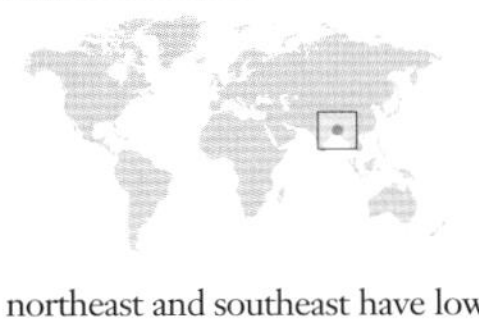

The south Asian state of Bangladesh is in the northeast of the Indian subcontinent, on the Bay of Bengal. It consists almost entirely of the low-lying alluvial plains and deltas of the Ganges and Brahmaputra rivers. The southwest is swampy, with mangrove forests in the delta area. The north, northeast and southeast have low forested hills. Bangladesh is one of the world's most densely populated and least developed countries. The economy is based on agriculture, though the garment industry is the main export sector. Storms during the summer monsoon season often cause devastating flooding and crop destruction. The country relies on large-scale foreign aid and remittances from workers abroad.

BARBADOS

Area Sq Km	430	Languages	English, Creole
Area Sq Miles	166	Religions	Protestant, Roman Catholic
Population	270 000	Currency	Barbados dollar
Capital	Bridgetown	Organizations	CARICOM, Comm., UN

Map page 149

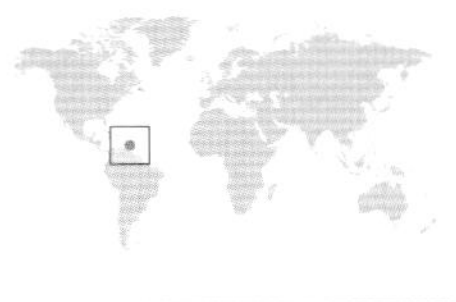

The most easterly of the Caribbean islands, Barbados is small and densely populated. It has a tropical climate and is subject to hurricanes. The economy is based on tourism, financial services, light industries and sugar production.

BELARUS
Republic of Belarus

Area Sq Km	207 600	Languages	Belorussian, Russian
Area Sq Miles	80 155	Religions	Belorussian Orthodox, Roman Catholic
Population	9 895 000	Currency	Belarus rouble
Capital	Minsk	Organizations	CIS, UN

Map page 113

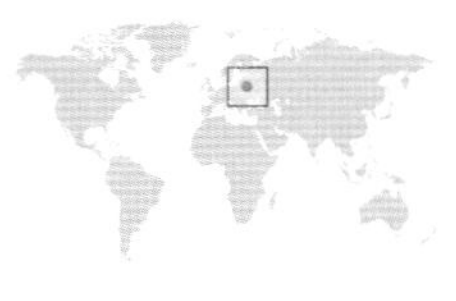

Belarus, a landlocked state in eastern Europe, consists of low hills and plains, with many lakes, rivers and, in the south, extensive marshes. Forests cover approximately one-third of the country. It has a continental climate. Agriculture contributes one-third of national income, with beef cattle and grains as the major products. Manufacturing industries produce a range of items, from construction equipment to textiles. The Russian Federation and Ukraine are the main trading partners.

BELGIUM
Kingdom of Belgium

Area Sq Km	30 520	Languages	Dutch (Flemish), French (Walloon), German
Area Sq Miles	11 784	Religions	Roman Catholic, Protestant
Population	10 318 000	Currency	Euro
Capital	Brussels (Bruxelles)	Organizations	EU, OECD, UN

Map page 108

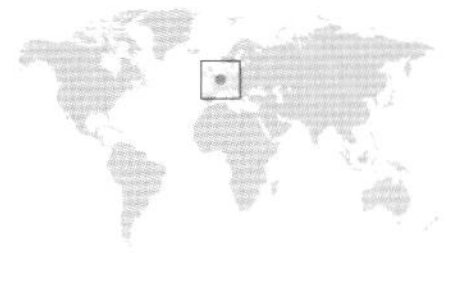

Belgium lies on the North Sea coast of western Europe. Beyond low sand dunes and a narrow belt of reclaimed land, fertile plains extend to the Sambre-Meuse river valley. The land rises to the forested Ardennes plateau in the southeast. Belgium has mild winters and cool summers. It is densely populated and has a highly urbanized population. With few mineral resources, Belgium imports raw materials for processing and manufacture. The agricultural sector is small, but provides for most food needs. A large services sector reflects Belgium's position as the home base for over eight hundred international institutions. The headquarters of the European Union are in the capital, Brussels.

BELIZE

Area Sq Km	22 965	Languages	English, Spanish, Mayan, Creole
Area Sq Miles	8 867	Religions	Roman Catholic, Protestant
Population	256 000	Currency	Belize dollar
Capital	Belmopan	Organizations	CARICOM, Comm., UN

Map page 151

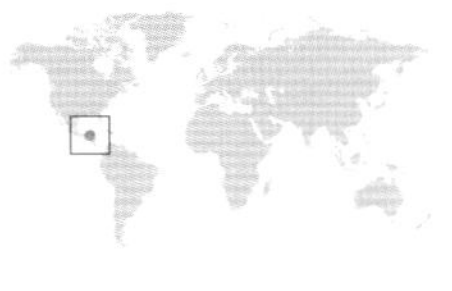

Belize lies on the Caribbean coast of central America and includes numerous cays and a large barrier reef offshore. The coastal areas are flat and swampy. To the southwest are the Maya Mountains. Tropical jungle covers much of the country and the climate is humid tropical, but tempered by sea breezes. A third of the population lives in the capital. The economy is based primarily on agriculture, forestry and fishing, and exports include raw sugar, orange concentrate and bananas.

BENIN
Republic of Benin

Area Sq Km	112 620	Languages	French, Fon, Yoruba, Adja, local languages
Area Sq Miles	43 483	Religions	Traditional beliefs, Roman Catholic, Sunni Muslim
Population	6 736 000	Currency	CFA franc
Capital	Porto-Novo	Organizations	UN

Map page 120

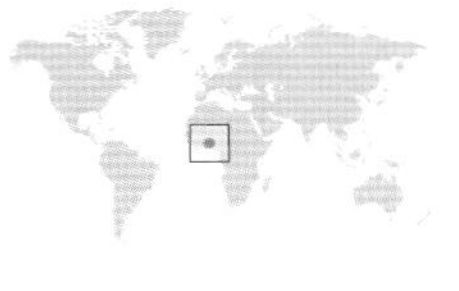

Benin is in west Africa, on the Gulf of Guinea. The climate is tropical in the north, equatorial in the south. The economy is based mainly on agriculture and transit trade. Agricultural products account for two-thirds of export earnings. Oil, produced offshore, is also a major export.

Bermuda
United Kingdom Overseas Territory

Area Sq Km	54	Languages	English
Area Sq Miles	21	Religions	Protestant, Roman Catholic
Population	82 000	Currency	Bermuda dollar
Capital	Hamilton		

Map page 149

In the Atlantic Ocean to the east of the USA, Bermuda comprises a group of small islands with a warm and humid climate. The economy is based on tourism, insurance and shipping.

BHUTAN
Kingdom of Bhutan

Area Sq Km	46 620	Languages	Dzongkha, Nepali, Assamese
Area Sq Miles	18 000	Religions	Buddhist, Hindu
Population	2 257 000	Currency	Ngultrum, Indian rupee
Capital	Thimphu	Organizations	UN

Map page 89

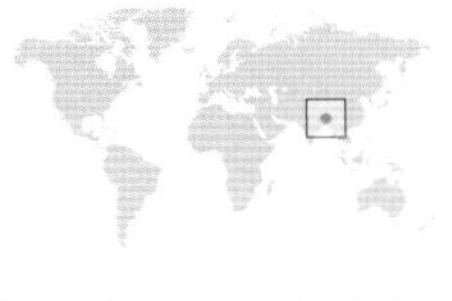

Bhutan lies in the eastern Himalaya mountains, between China and India. It is mountainous in the north, with fertile valleys. The climate ranges between permanently cold in the far north and subtropical in the south. Most of the population is involved in livestock rearing and subsistence farming. Bhutan is the world's largest producer of cardamom. Tourism is an increasingly important foreign currency earner.

BOLIVIA
Republic of Bolivia

Area Sq Km	1 098 581	Languages	Spanish, Quechua, Aymara
Area Sq Miles	424 164	Religions	Roman Catholic, Protestant, Baha'i
Population	8 808 000	Currency	Boliviano
Capital	La Paz/Sucre	Organizations	UN

Map page 154

Bolivia is a landlocked state in central South America. Most Bolivians live on the high plateau within the Andes mountains. The lowlands range between dense rainforest in the northeast and semi-arid grasslands in the southeast. Bolivia is rich in minerals (zinc, tin and gold), and sales generate approximately half of export income. Natural gas, timber and soya beans are also exported. The USA is the main trading partner.

BOSNIA-HERZEGOVINA
Republic of Bosnia and Herzegovina

Area Sq Km	51 130	Languages	Bosnian, Serbian, Croatian
Area Sq Miles	19 741	Religions	Sunni Muslim, Serbian Orthodox, Roman Catholic, Protestant
Population	4 161 000	Currency	Marka
Capital	Sarajevo	Organizations	UN

Map page 114–115

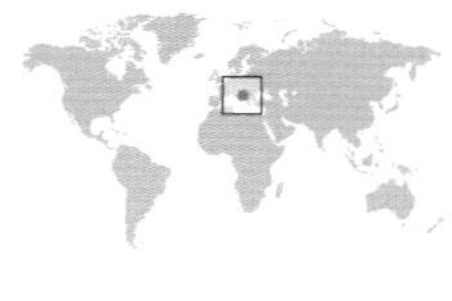

Bosnia-Herzegovina lies in the western Balkan Mountains of southern Europe, on the Adriatic Sea. It is mountainous, with ridges running northwest-southeast. The main lowlands are around the Sava valley in the north. Summers are warm, but winters can be very cold. The economy relies heavily on overseas aid.

BOTSWANA
Republic of Botswana

Area Sq Km	581 370	Languages	English, Setswana, Shona, local languages
Area Sq Miles	224 468	Religions	Traditional beliefs, Protestant, Roman Catholic
Population	1 785 000	Currency	Pula
Capital	Gaborone	Organizations	Comm., SADC, UN

Map page 123

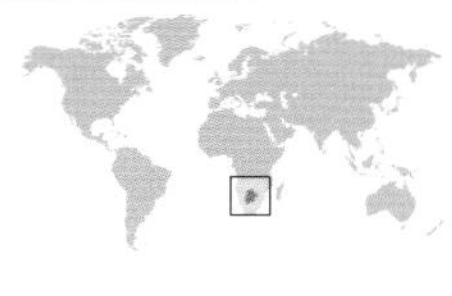

Botswana is a landlocked state in southern Africa. Over half of the country lies within the Kalahari Desert, with swamps to the north and salt-pans to the northeast. Most of the population lives near the eastern border. The climate is subtropical, but drought-prone. The economy was founded on cattle rearing, and although beef remains an important export, the economy is now based on mining. Diamonds account for seventy per cent of export earnings. Copper-nickel matte is also exported. Most trade is with other members of the Southern African Customs Union.

BRAZIL
Federative Republic of Brazil

Area Sq Km	8 514 879	Languages	Portuguese
Area Sq Miles	3 287 613	Religions	Roman Catholic, Protestant
Population	178 470 000	Currency	Real
Capital	Brasília	Organizations	UN

Map page 154–155

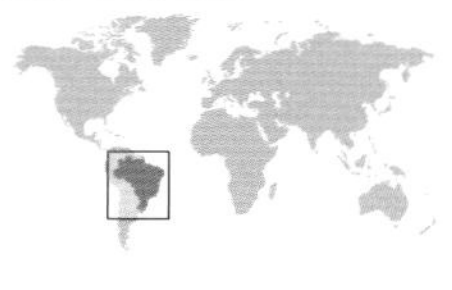

Brazil, in eastern South America, covers almost half of the continent, and is the world's fifth largest country. The northwest contains the vast basin of the Amazon, while the centre-west is largely a vast plateau of savanna and rock escarpments. The northeast is mostly semi-arid plateaus, while to the east and south are rugged mountains, fertile valleys and narrow, fertile coastal plains. The Amazon basin is hot, humid and wet; the rest of the country is cooler and drier, with seasonal variations. The northeast is drought-prone. Most Brazilians live in urban areas along the coast and on the central plateau. Brazil has well-developed agricultural, mining, and service sectors, and the economy is larger than that of all other South American countries combined. Brazil is the world's biggest producer of coffee, and other agricultural crops include grains and sugar cane. Mineral production includes iron, aluminium and gold. Manufactured goods include food products, transport equipment, machinery and industrial chemicals. The main trading partners are the USA and Argentina. Despite its natural wealth, Brazil has a large external debt and a growing poverty gap.

BRUNEI
Brunei Darussalam

Area Sq Km	5 765	Languages	Malay, English, Chinese
Area Sq Miles	2 226	Religions	Sunni Muslim, Buddhist, Christian
Population	358 000	Currency	Brunei dollar
Capital	Bandar Seri Begawan	Organizations	APEC, ASEAN, Comm., UN

Map page 99

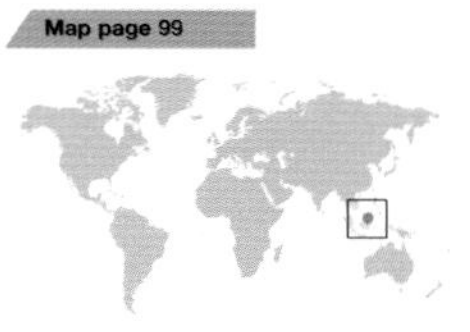

The southeast Asian oil-rich state of Brunei lies on the northwest coast of the island of Borneo, on the South China Sea. Its two enclaves are surrounded by the Malaysian state of Sarawak. Tropical rainforest covers over two-thirds of the country. The economy is dominated by the oil and gas industries.

BULGARIA
Republic of Bulgaria

Area Sq Km	110 994	Languages	Bulgarian, Turkish, Romany, Macedonian
Area Sq Miles	42 855	Religions	Bulgarian Orthodox, Sunni Muslim
Population	7 897 000	Currency	Lev
Capital	Sofia (Sofiya)	Organizations	NATO, UN

Map page 115

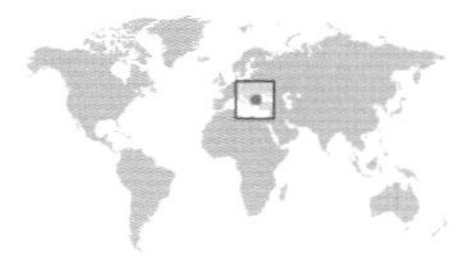

Bulgaria, in southern Europe, borders the western shore of the Black Sea. The Balkan Mountains separate the Danube plains in the north from the Rhodope Mountains and the lowlands in the south. The economy has a strong agricultural base. Manufacturing industries include machinery, consumer goods, chemicals and metals. Most trade is with the Russian Federation, Italy and Germany.

BURKINA
Democratic Republic of Burkina Faso

Area Sq Km	274 200	Languages	French, Moore (Mossi), Fulani, local languages
Area Sq Miles	105 869	Religions	Sunni Muslim, traditional beliefs, Roman Catholic
Population	13 002 000	Currency	CFA franc
Capital	Ouagadougou	Organizations	UN

Map page 120

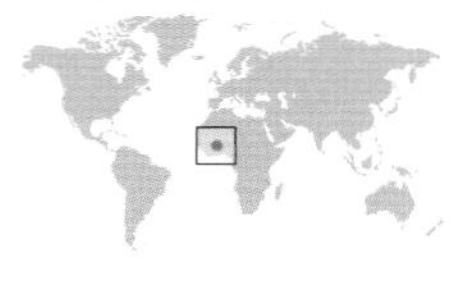

Burkina, a landlocked country in west Africa, lies within the Sahara desert to the north and semi-arid savanna to the south. Rainfall is erratic, and droughts are common. Livestock rearing and farming are the main activities, and cotton, livestock, groundnuts and some minerals are exported. Burkina relies heavily on foreign aid, and is one of the poorest and least developed countries in the world.

BURUNDI
Republic of Burundi

Area Sq Km	27 835	Languages	Kirundi (Hutu, Tutsi), French
Area Sq Miles	10 747	Religions	Roman Catholic, traditional beliefs, Protestant
Population	6 825 000	Currency	Burundian franc
Capital	Bujumbura	Organizations	UN

Map page 122

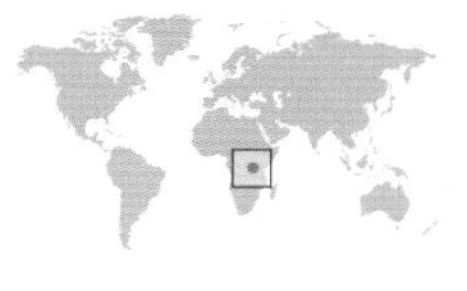

The densely populated east African state of Burundi consists of high plateaus rising from the shores of Lake Tanganyika in the southwest. It has a tropical climate and depends on subsistence farming. Coffee is its main export, and its main trading partners are Germany and Belgium. The country has been badly affected by internal conflict since the early 1990s.

CAMBODIA
Kingdom of Cambodia

Area Sq Km	181 000	Languages	Khmer, Vietnamese
Area Sq Miles	69 884	Religions	Buddhist, Roman Catholic, Sunni Muslim
Population	14 144 000	Currency	Riel
Capital	Phnom Penh	Organizations	ASEAN, UN

Map page 98

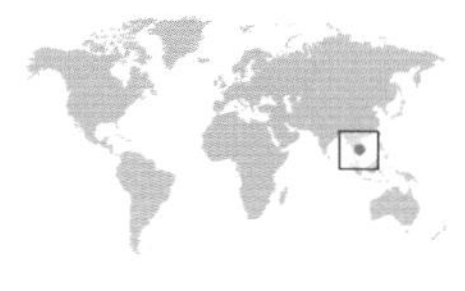

Cambodia lies in southeast Asia on the Gulf of Thailand, and occupies the Mekong river basin, with the Tônlé Sap (Great Lake) at its centre. The climate is tropical monsoon. Forests cover half the country. Most of the population lives on the plains and is engaged in farming (chiefly rice growing), fishing and forestry. The economy is recovering slowly following the devastation of civil war in the 1970s.

CAMEROON
Republic of Cameroon

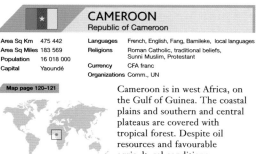

Area Sq Km	475 442	Languages	French, English, Fang, Bamileke, local languages
Area Sq Miles	183 569	Religions	Roman Catholic, traditional beliefs, Sunni Muslim, Protestant
Population	16 018 000	Currency	CFA franc
Capital	Yaoundé	Organizations	Comm., UN

Map page 120–121

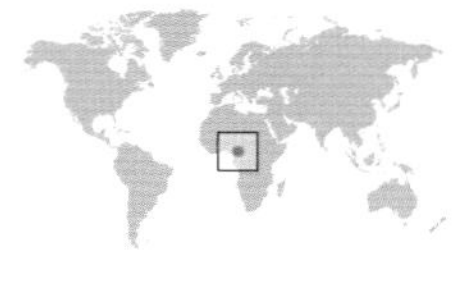

Cameroon is in west Africa, on the Gulf of Guinea. The coastal plains and southern and central plateaus are covered with tropical forest. Despite oil resources and favourable agricultural conditions Cameroon still faces problems of underdevelopment. Oil, timber and cocoa are the main exports. France is the main trading partner.

CANADA

Area Sq Km	9 984 670	Languages	English, French
Area Sq Miles	3 855 103	Religions	Roman Catholic, Protestant, Eastern Orthodox, Jewish
Population	31 510 000	Currency	Canadian dollar
Capital	Ottawa	Organizations	APEC, Comm., OECD, UN

Map page 128–129

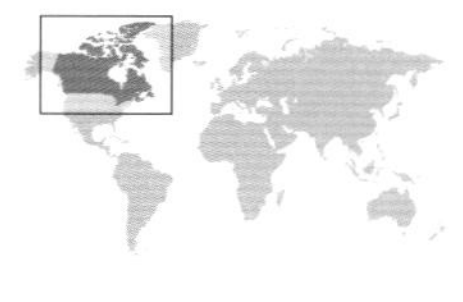

The world's second largest country, Canada covers the northern two-fifths of North America and has coastlines on the Atlantic, Arctic and Pacific Oceans. In the west are the Coast Mountains, the Rocky Mountains and interior plateaus. In the centre lie the fertile Prairies. Further east, covering about half the total land area, is the Canadian Shield, a relatively flat area of infertile lowlands around Hudson Bay, extending to Labrador on the east coast. The Shield is bordered to the south by the fertile Great Lakes-St Lawrence lowlands. In the far north climatic conditions are polar, while the rest has a continental climate. Most Canadians live in the urban areas of the Great Lakes-St Lawrence basin. Canada is rich in mineral and energy resources. Only five per cent of land is arable . Canada is among the world's leading producers of wheat, of wood from its vast coniferous forests, and of fish and seafood from its Atlantic and Pacific fishing grounds. It is a major producer of nickel, uranium, copper, iron ore, zinc and other minerals, as well as oil and natural gas. Its abundant raw materials are the basis for many manufacturing industries. Main exports are machinery, motor vehicles, oil, timber, newsprint and paper, wood pulp and wheat. Since the 1989 free trade agreement with the USA and the 1994 North America Free Trade Agreement, trade with the USA has grown and now accounts for around seventy-five per cent of imports and around eighty-five per cent of exports.

Province / Territory	Area Sq Km (Sq Miles)	Population	Capital
Alberta (Province)	661 848 (255 541)	3 113 600	Edmonton
British Columbia (Province)	944 735 (364 764)	4 141 300	Victoria
Manitoba (Province)	647 797 (250 116)	1 150 800	Winnipeg
New Brunswick (Province)	72 908 (28 150)	756 700	Fredericton
Newfoundland and Labrador (Province)	405 212 (156 453)	531 600	St John's
Northwest Territories (Territory)	1 346 106 (519 734)	41 400	Yellowknife
Nova Scotia (Province)	55 284 (21 345)	944 800	Halifax
Nunavut (Territory)	2 093 190 (808 185)	28 700	Iqaluit
Ontario (Province)	1 076 395 (415 598)	12 068 300	Toronto
Prince Edward Island (Province)	5 660 (2 185)	139 900	Charlottetown
Québec (Province)	1 542 056 (595 391)	7 455 200	Québec
Saskatchewan (Province)	651 036 (251 366)	1 011 800	Regina
Yukon Territory (Territory)	482 443 (186 272)	29 900	Whitehorse

CAPE VERDE
Republic of Cape Verde

Area Sq Km	4 033	Languages	Portuguese, Creole
Area Sq Miles	1 557	Religions	Roman Catholic, Protestant
Population	463 000	Currency	Cape Verde escudo
Capital	Praia	Organizations	UN

Map page 120

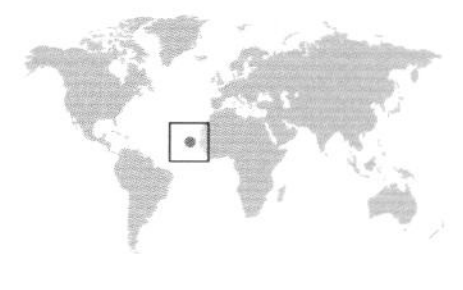

Cape Verde is a group of semi-arid volcanic islands lying off the coast of west Africa. The economy is based on fishing and subsistence farming but relies on emigrant workers' remittances and foreign aid.

Cayman Islands
United Kingdom Overseas Territory

Area Sq Km	259	Languages	English
Area Sq Miles	100	Religions	Protestant, Roman Catholic
Population	40 000	Currency	Cayman Islands dollar
Capital	George Town		

Map page 149 A group of islands in the Caribbean, northwest of Jamaica. There are three main islands: Grand Cayman, Little Cayman and Cayman Brac. The Cayman Islands are one of the world's major offshore financial centres. Tourism is also important to the economy.

CENTRAL AFRICAN REPUBLIC

Area Sq Km	622 436	Languages	French, Sango, Banda, Baya, local languages
Area Sq Miles	240 324	Religions	Protestant, Roman Catholic, traditional beliefs, Sunni Muslim
Population	3 865 000	Currency	CFA franc
Capital	Bangui	Organizations	UN

Map page 121

A landlocked country in central Africa, the Central African Republic is mainly savanna plateau, drained by the Ubangi and Chari river systems, with mountains to the east and west. The climate is tropical, with high rainfall. Most of the population lives in the south and west, and a majority of the workforce is involved in subsistence farming. Some cotton, coffee, tobacco and timber are exported, but diamonds account for around half of export earnings.

CHAD
Republic of Chad

Area Sq Km	1 284 000	Languages	Arabic, French, Sara, local languages
Area Sq Miles	495 755	Religions	Sunni Muslim, Roman Catholic, Protestant, traditional beliefs
Population	8 598 000	Currency	CFA franc
Capital	Ndjamena	Organizations	UN

Map page 121

Chad is a landlocked state of north-central Africa. It consists of plateaus, the Tibesti mountains in the north and the Lake Chad basin in the west. Climatic conditions range between desert in the north and tropical forest in the southwest. With few natural resources, Chad relies on subsistence farming, exports of raw cotton, and foreign aid. The main trading partners are France, Portugal and Cameroon.

CHILE
Republic of Chile

Area Sq Km	756 945	Languages	Spanish, Amerindian languages
Area Sq Miles	292 258	Religions	Roman Catholic, Protestant
Population	15 805 000	Currency	Chilean peso
Capital	Santiago	Organizations	APEC, UN

Map page 156

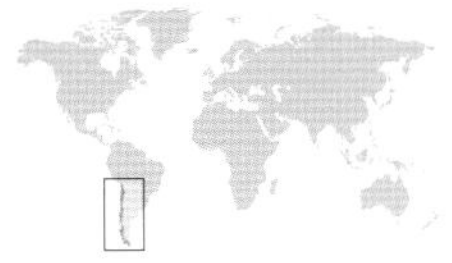

Chile lies along the Pacific coast of the southern half of South America. Between the Andes in the east and the lower coastal ranges is a central valley, with a mild climate, where most Chileans live. To the north is the arid Atacama Desert and to the south is cold, wet forested grassland. Chile has considerable mineral resources and is the world's leading exporter of copper. Nitrates, molybdenum, gold and iron ore are also mined. Agriculture (particularly viticulture), forestry and fishing are also important to the economy.

CHINA
People's Republic of China

Area Sq Km	9 584 492	Languages	Mandarin, Wu, Cantonese, Hsiang, regional languages
Area Sq Miles	3 700 593	Religions	Confucian, Taoist, Buddhist, Christian, Sunni Muslim
Population	1 289 161 000	Currency	Yuan, Hong Kong dollar, Macau pataca
Capital	Beijing (Peking)	Organizations	APEC, UN

Map page 90

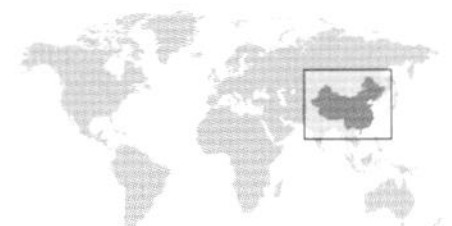

China, the world's most populous and fourth largest country, occupies a large part of east Asia, borders fourteen states and has coastlines on the Yellow, East China and South China Seas. It has a huge variety of landscapes. The southwest contains the high Plateau of Tibet, flanked by the Himalaya and Kunlun Shan mountains. The north is mountainous with arid basins and extends from the Tien Shan and Altai Mountains and the vast Taklimakan Desert in the west to the plateau and Gobi Desert in the centre-east. Eastern China is predominantly lowland and is divided broadly into the basins of the Huang He (Yellow River) in the north, the Chang Jiang (Yangtze) in the centre and the Xi Jiang (Pearl River) in the southeast. Climatic conditions and vegetation are as diverse as the topography: much of the country experiences temperate conditions, while the southwest has an extreme mountain climate and the southeast enjoys a moist, warm subtropical climate. Nearly seventy per cent of China's huge population lives in rural areas, and agriculture employs around half of the working population. The main crops are rice, wheat, soya beans, peanuts, cotton, tobacco and hemp. China is rich in coal, oil and natural gas and has the world's largest potential in hydroelectric power. It is a major world producer of iron ore, molybdenum, copper, asbestos and gold. Economic reforms from the early 1980's led to an explosion in manufacturing development concentrated on the 'coastal economic open region'. The main exports are machinery, textiles, footwear, toys and sports goods. Japan and the USA are China's main trading partners.

Anhui (Province)
Area Sq Km (Sq Miles) 139 000 (53 668) Population 59 860 000 Capital Hefei

Beijing (Municipality)
Area Sq Km (Sq Miles) 16 800 (6 487) Population 13 820 000 Capital Beijing (Peking)

Chongqing (Municipality)
Area Sq Km (Sq Miles) 23 000 (8 880) Population 30 900 000 Capital Chongqing

Fujian (Province)
Area Sq Km (Sq Miles) 121 400 (46 873) Population 34 710 000 Capital Fuzhou

Gansu (Province)
Area Sq Km (Sq Miles) 453 700 (175 175) Population 25 620 000 Capital Lanzhou

Guangdong (Province)
Area Sq Km (Sq Miles) 178 000 (68 726) Population 86 420 000 Capital Guangzhou (Canton)

Guangxi Zhuangzu Zizhiqu (Autonomous Region)
Area Sq Km (Sq Miles) 236 000 (91 120) Population 44 890 000 Capital Nanning

Guizhou (Province)
Area Sq Km (Sq Miles) 176 000 (67 954) Population 35 250 000 Capital Guiyang

Hainan (Province)
Area Sq Km (Sq Miles) 34 000 (13 127) Population 7 870 000 Capital Haikou

Hebei (Province)
Area Sq Km (Sq Miles) 187 700 (72 471) Population 67 440 000 Capital Shijiazhuang

Heilongjiang (Province)
Area Sq Km (Sq Miles) 454 600 (175 522) Population 36 890 000 Capital Harbin

Henan (Province)
Area Sq Km (Sq Miles) 167 000 (64 479) Population 92 560 000 Capital Zhengzhou

Hong Kong (Special Administrative Region)
Area Sq Km (Sq Miles) 1 075 (415) Population 6 780 000 Capital Hong Kong

Hubei (Province)
Area Sq Km (Sq Miles) 185 900 (71 776) Population 60 280 000 Capital Wuhan

Hunan (Province)
Area Sq Km (Sq Miles) 210 000 (81 081) Population 64 400 000 Capital Changsha

Jiangsu (Province)
Area Sq Km (Sq Miles) 102 600 (39 614) Population 74 380 000 Capital Nanjing

Jiangxi (Province)
Area Sq Km (Sq Miles) 166 900 (64 440) Population 41 400 000 Capital Nanchang

Jilin (Province)
Area Sq Km (Sq Miles) 187 000 (72 201) Population 27 280 000 Capital Changchun

Liaoning (Province)
Area Sq Km (Sq Miles) 147 400 (56 911) Population 42 380 000 Capital Shenyang

Macau (Special Administrative Region)
Area Sq Km (Sq Miles) 17 (7) Population 440 000 Capital Macau

Nei Mongol Zizhiqu Inner Mongolia (Autonomous Region)
Area Sq Km (Sq Miles) 1 183 000 (456 759) Population 23 760 000 Capital Hohhot

Ningxia Huizu Zizhiqu (Autonomous Region)
Area Sq Km (Sq Miles) 66 400 (25 637) Population 5 620 000 Capital Yinchuan

Qinghai (Province)
Area Sq Km (Sq Miles) 721 000 (278 380) Population 5 180 000 Capital Xining

Shaanxi (Province)
Area Sq Km (Sq Miles) 205 600 (79 383) Population 36 050 000 Capital Xi'an

Shandong (Province)
Area Sq Km (Sq Miles) 153 300 (59 189) Population 90 790 000 Capital Jinan

Shanghai (Municipality)
Area Sq Km (Sq Miles) 6 300 (2 432) Population 16 740 000 Capital Shanghai

Shanxi (Province)
Area Sq Km (Sq Miles) 156 300 (60 348) Population 32 970 000 Capital Taiyuan

Sichuan (Province)
Area Sq Km (Sq Miles) 569 000 (219 692) Population 83 290 000 Capital Chengdu

Tianjin (Municipality)
Area Sq Km (Sq Miles) 11 300 (4 363) Population 10 010 000 Capital Tianjin

Xinjiang Uygur Zizhiqu Sinkiang (Autonomous Region)
Area Sq Km (Sq Miles) 1 600 000 (617 763) Population 19 250 000 Capital Ürümqi

Xizang Zizhiqu Tibet (Autonomous Region)
Area Sq Km (Sq Miles) 1 228 400 (474 288) Population 2 620 000 Capital Lhasa

Yunnan (Province)
Area Sq Km (Sq Miles) 394 000 (152 124) Population 42 880 000 Capital Kunming

Zhejiang (Province)
Area Sq Km (Sq Miles) 101 800 (39 305) Population 46 770 000 Capital Hangzhou

Christmas Island
Australian External Territory

Area Sq Km	135	Languages	English
Area Sq Miles	52	Religions	Buddhist, Sunni Muslim, Protestant, Roman Catholic
Population	1 560	Currency	Australian dollar
Capital	The Settlement		

Map page 91 The island is situated in the east of the Indian Ocean, to the south of Indonesia. The economy was formerly based on phosphate extraction, although reserves are now nearly depleted. Tourism is developing and is a major employer.

Cocos Islands (Keeling Islands)
Australian External Territory

Area Sq Km	14	Languages	English
Area Sq Miles	5	Religions	Sunni Muslim, Christian
Population	632	Currency	Australian dollar
Capital	West Island		

Map page 91 The Cocos Islands consist of numerous islands on two coral atolls in the eastern Indian Ocean between Sri Lanka and Australia. Most of the population lives on West Island or Home Island. Coconuts are the only cash crop, and the main export.

COLOMBIA
Republic of Colombia

Area Sq Km	1 141 748	Languages	Spanish, Amerindian languages
Area Sq Miles	440 831	Religions	Roman Catholic, Protestant
Population	44 222 000	Currency	Colombian peso
Capital	Bogotá	Organizations	APEC, UN

Map page 157

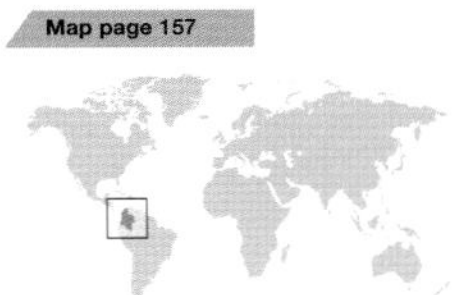

A state in northwest South America, Colombia has coastlines on the Pacific Ocean and the Caribbean Sea. Behind coastal plains lie three ranges of the Andes mountains, separated by high valleys and plateaus where most Colombians live. To the southeast are grasslands and the forests of the Amazon. The climate is tropical, although temperatures vary with altitude. Only five per cent of land is cultivable. Coffee (Colombia is the world's second largest producer), sugar, bananas, cotton and flowers are exported. Coal, nickel, gold, silver, platinum and emeralds (Colombia is the world's largest producer) are mined. Oil and its products are the main export. Industries include the processing of minerals and crops. The main trade partner is the USA. Internal violence - both politically motivated and relating to Colombia's leading role in the international trade in illegal drugs - continues to hinder development.

COMOROS
Union of the Comoros

Area Sq Km	1 862	Languages	Comorian, French, Arabic
Area Sq Miles	719	Religions	Sunni Muslim, Roman Catholic
Population	768 000	Currency	Comoros franc
Capital	Moroni	Organizations	UN

Map page 123

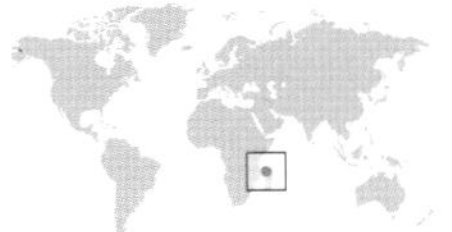

This state, in the Indian Ocean off the east African coast, comprises three volcanic islands of Njazidja (Grande Comore), Nzwani (Anjouan) and Mwali (Mohéli), and some coral atolls. These tropical islands are mountainous, with poor soil and few natural resources. Subsistence farming predominates. Vanilla, cloves and ylang-ylang (an essential oil) are exported, and the economy relies heavily on workers' remittances from abroad.

© Collins Bartholomew Ltd

CONGO
Republic of the Congo

Area Sq Km	342 000
Area Sq Miles	132 047
Population	3 724 000
Capital	Brazzaville
Languages	French, Kongo, Monokutuba, local languages
Religions	Roman Catholic, Protestant, traditional beliefs, Sunni Muslim
Currency	CFA franc
Organizations	UN

Map page 122

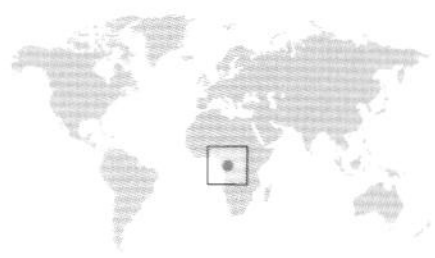

Congo, in central Africa, is mostly a forest or savanna-covered plateau drained by the Ubangi-Congo river systems. Sand dunes and lagoons line the short Atlantic coast. The climate is hot and tropical. Most Congolese live in the southern third of the country. Half of the workforce are farmers, growing food and cash crops including sugar, coffee, cocoa and oil palms. Oil and timber are the mainstays of the economy, and oil generates over fifty per cent of the country's export revenues.

CONGO, DEMOCRATIC REPUBLIC OF

Area Sq Km	2 345 410
Area Sq Miles	905 568
Population	52 771 000
Capital	Kinshasa
Languages	French, Lingala, Swahili, Kongo, local languages
Religions	Christian, Sunni Muslim
Currency	Congolese franc
Organizations	SADC, UN

Map page 122–123

This central African state, formerly Zaire, consists of the basin of the Congo river flanked by plateaus, with high mountain ranges to the east and a short Atlantic coastline to the west. The climate is tropical, with rainforest close to the Equator and savanna to the north and south. Fertile land allows a range of food and cash crops to be grown, chiefly coffee. The country has vast mineral resources, with copper, cobalt and diamonds being the most important.

Cook Islands
New Zealand Overseas Territory

Area Sq Km	293
Area Sq Miles	113
Population	18 000
Capital	Avarua
Languages	English, Maori
Religions	Protestant, Roman Catholic
Currency	New Zealand dollar

Map page 67 These consist of groups of coral atolls and volcanic islands in the southwest Pacific Ocean. The main island is Rarotonga. Distance from foreign markets and restricted natural resources hinder development.

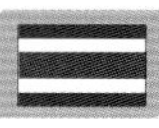

COSTA RICA
Republic of Costa Rica

Area Sq Km	51 100
Area Sq Miles	19 730
Population	4 173 000
Capital	San José
Languages	Spanish
Religions	Roman Catholic, Protestant
Currency	Costa Rican colón
Organizations	UN

Map page 150

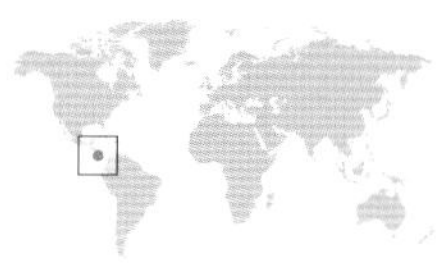

Costa Rica, in central America, has coastlines on the Caribbean Sea and Pacific Ocean. From tropical coastal plains, the land rises to mountains and a temperate central plateau, where most of the population lives. The economy depends on agriculture and tourism, with ecotourism becoming increasingly important. Main exports are textiles, coffee and bananas, and almost half of all trade is with the USA.

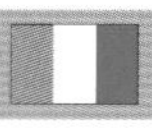

CÔTE D'IVOIRE (Ivory Coast)
Republic of Côte d'Ivoire

Area Sq Km	322 463
Area Sq Miles	124 504
Population	16 631 000
Capital	Yamoussoukro
Languages	French, Creole, Akan, local languages
Religions	Sunni Muslim, Roman Catholic, traditional beliefs, Protestant
Currency	CFA franc
Organizations	UN

Map page 120

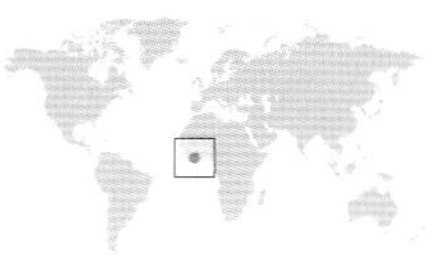

Côte d'Ivoire (Ivory Coast) is in west Africa, on the Gulf of Guinea. In the north are plateaus and savanna; in the south are low undulating plains and rainforest, with sand-bars and lagoons on the coast. Temperatures are warm, and rainfall is heavier in the south. Most of the workforce is engaged in farming. Côte d'Ivoire is a major producer of cocoa and coffee, and agricultural products (also including cotton and timber) are the main exports. Oil and gas have begun to be exploited.

CROATIA
Republic of Croatia

Area Sq Km	56 538
Area Sq Miles	21 829
Population	4 428 000
Capital	Zagreb
Languages	Croatian, Serbian
Religions	Roman Catholic, Serbian Orthodox, Sunni Muslim
Currency	Kuna
Organizations	UN

Map page 114

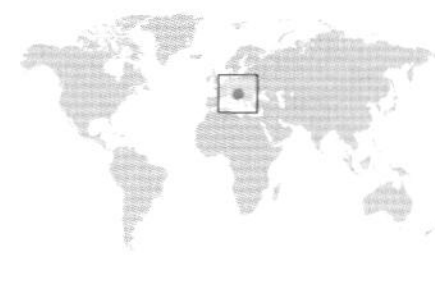

The southern European state of Croatia has a long coastline on the Adriatic Sea, with many offshore islands. Coastal areas have a Mediterranean climate; inland is cooler and wetter. Croatia was once strong agriculturally and industrially, but conflict in the early 1990s, and associated loss of markets and a fall in tourist revenue, caused economic difficulties from which recovery has been slow.

CUBA
Republic of Cuba

Area Sq Km	110 860
Area Sq Miles	42 803
Population	11 300 000
Capital	Havana (La Habana)
Languages	Spanish
Religions	Roman Catholic, Protestant
Currency	Cuban peso
Organizations	UN

Map page 149

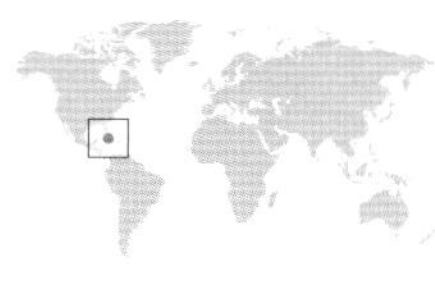

The country comprises the island of Cuba (the largest island in the Caribbean), and many islets and cays. A fifth of Cubans live in and around Havana. Cuba is slowly recovering from the withdrawal of aid and subsidies from the former USSR. Sugar remains the basis of the economy, although tourism is developing and is, together with remittances from workers abroad, an important source of revenue.

CYPRUS
Republic of Cyprus

Area Sq Km	9 251
Area Sq Miles	3 572
Population	802 000
Capital	Nicosia (Lefkosia)
Languages	Greek, Turkish, English
Religions	Greek Orthodox, Sunni Muslim
Currency	Cyprus pound
Organizations	Comm., UN

Map page 80

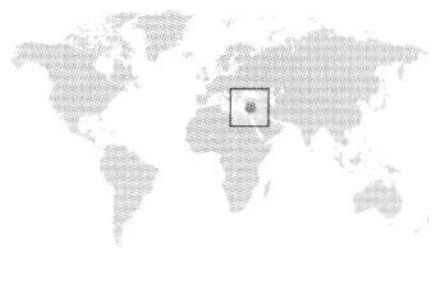

The eastern Mediterranean island of Cyprus has effectively been divided into two since 1974. The economy of the Greek-speaking south is based mainly on specialist agriculture and tourism, with shipping and offshore banking. The ethnically Turkish north depends on agriculture, tourism and aid from Turkey. The island has hot dry summers and mild winters. Cyprus joined the European Union in May 2004.

CZECH REPUBLIC

Area Sq Km	78 864
Area Sq Miles	30 450
Population	10 236 000
Capital	Prague (Praha)
Languages	Czech, Moravian, Slovakian
Religions	Roman Catholic, Protestant
Currency	Czech koruna
Organizations	Comm., EU, UN

Map page 112

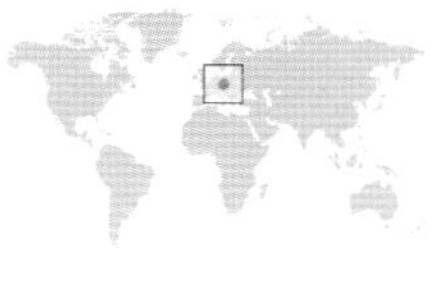

The landlocked Czech Republic in central Europe consists of rolling countryside, wooded hills and fertile valleys. The climate is continental. The country has substantial reserves of coal and lignite, timber and some minerals, chiefly iron ore. It is highly industrialized, and major manufactured goods include industrial machinery, consumer goods, cars, iron and steel, chemicals and glass. Germany is the main trading partner. The Czech Republic joined the European Union in May 2004.

DENMARK
Kingdom of Denmark

Area Sq Km	43 075
Area Sq Miles	16 631
Population	5 364 000
Capital	Copenhagen (København)
Languages	Danish
Religions	Protestant
Currency	Danish krone
Organizations	EU, NATO, OECD, UN

Map page 103

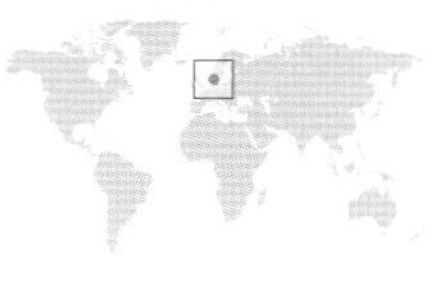

In northern Europe, Denmark occupies the Jutland (Jylland) peninsula and nearly five hundred islands in and between the North and Baltic Seas. The country is low-lying, with long, indented coastlines. The climate is cool and temperate, with rainfall throughout the year. A fifth of the population lives in and around the capital, Copenhagen (København), on the largest of the islands, Zealand (Sjælland). The country's main natural resource is its agricultural potential: two-thirds of the total area is fertile farmland or pasture. Agriculture is high-tech, and with forestry and fishing employs only around six per cent of the workforce. Denmark is self-sufficient in oil and natural gas, produced from fields in the North Sea. Manufacturing, largely based on imported raw materials, accounts for over half of all exports, which include machinery, food, furniture, and pharmaceuticals. The main trading partners are Germany and Sweden.

DJIBOUTI
Republic of Djibouti

Area Sq Km	23 200
Area Sq Miles	8 958
Population	703 000
Capital	Djibouti
Languages	Somali, Afar, French, Arabic
Religions	Sunni Muslim, Christian
Currency	Djibouti franc
Organizations	UN

Map page 122

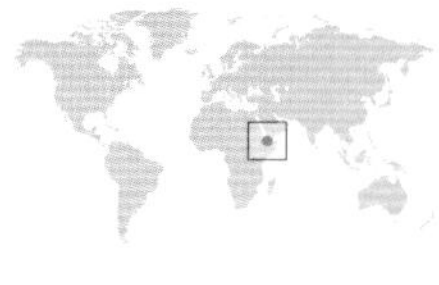

Djibouti lies in northeast Africa, on the Gulf of Aden at the entrance to the Red Sea. Most of the country is semi-arid desert with high temperatures and low rainfall. More than two-thirds of the population lives in the capital. There is some camel, sheep and goat herding, but with few natural resources the economy is based on services and trade. Djibouti serves as a free trade zone for northern Africa, and the capital's port is a major transhipment and refuelling destination. It is linked by rail to Addis Ababa in Ethiopia.

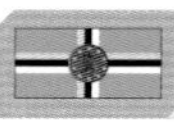

DOMINICA
Commonwealth of Dominica

Area Sq Km	750
Area Sq Miles	290
Population	79 000
Capital	Roseau
Languages	English, Creole
Religions	Roman Catholic, Protestant
Currency	East Caribbean dollar
Organizations	CARICOM, Comm., UN

Map page 149

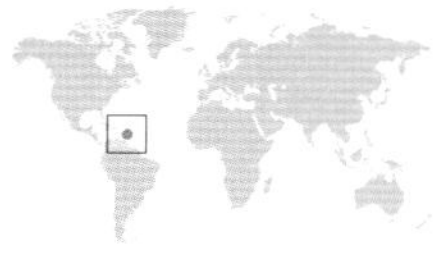

Dominica is the most northerly of the Windward Islands, in the eastern Caribbean. It is very mountainous and forested, with a coastline of steep cliffs. The climate is tropical and rainfall is abundant. Approximately a quarter of Dominicans live in the capital. The economy is based on agriculture, with bananas (the major export), coconuts and citrus fruits the most important crops. Tourism is a developing industry.

DOMINICAN REPUBLIC

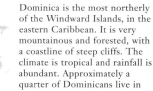

Area Sq Km	48 442
Area Sq Miles	18 704
Population	8 745 000
Capital	Santo Domingo
Languages	Spanish, Creole
Religions	Roman Catholic, Protestant
Currency	Dominican peso
Organizations	UN

Map page 149

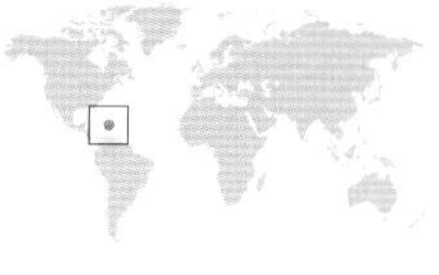

The state occupies the eastern two-thirds of the Caribbean island of Hispaniola (the western third is Haiti). It has a series of mountain ranges, fertile valleys and a large coastal plain in the east. The climate is hot tropical, with heavy rainfall. Sugar, coffee and cocoa are the main cash crops. Nickel (the main export), and gold are mined, and there is some light industry. The USA is the main trading partner. Tourism is the main foreign exchange earner.

EAST TIMOR
Democratic Republic of Timor-Leste

Area Sq Km	14 874
Area Sq Miles	5 743
Population	778 000
Capital	Dili
Languages	Portuguese, Tetun, English
Religions	Roman Catholic
Currency	United States dollar
Organizations	UN

Map page 91

The island of Timor is part of the Indonesian archipelago, to the north of western Australia. East Timor occupies the eastern section of the island, and a small coastal enclave (Ocussi) to the west. A referendum in 1999 ended Indonesia's occupation, after which the country was under UN transitional administration until full independence was achieved in 2002. The economy is in a poor state and East Timor is heavily dependent on foreign aid.

ECUADOR
Republic of Ecuador

Area Sq Km	272 045
Area Sq Miles	105 037
Population	13 003 000
Capital	Quito
Languages	Spanish, Quechua, and other Amerindian languages
Religions	Roman Catholic
Currency	United States dollar
Organizations	APEC, UN

Map page 154

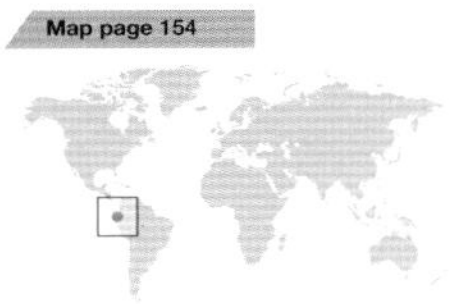

Ecuador is in northwest South America, on the Pacific coast. It consists of a broad coastal plain, high mountain ranges in the Andes, and part of the forested upper Amazon basin to the east. The climate is tropical, moderated by altitude. Most people live on the coast or in the mountain valleys. Ecuador is one of South America's main oil producers, and mineral reserves include gold. Most of the workforce depends on agriculture. Petroleum, bananas, shrimps, coffee and cocoa are exported. The USA is the main trading partner.

EGYPT
Arab Republic of Egypt

Area Sq Km	1 000 250
Area Sq Miles	386 199
Population	71 931 000
Capital	Cairo (Al Qāhirah)
Languages	Arabic
Religions	Sunni Muslim, Coptic Christian
Currency	Egyptian pound
Organizations	UN

Map page 121

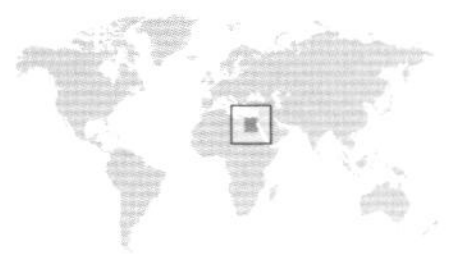

Egypt, on the eastern Mediterranean coast of north Africa, is low-lying, with areas below sea level in the Qattara depression. It is a land of desert and semi-desert, except for the Nile valley, where ninety-nine per cent of Egyptians live. The Sinai peninsula in the northeast of the country forms the only land bridge between Africa and Asia. The summers are hot, the winters mild and rainfall is negligible. Less than four per cent of land (chiefly around the Nile floodplain and delta) is cultivated. Farming employs about one-third of the workforce; cotton is the main cash crop. Egypt imports over half its food needs. There are oil and natural gas reserves, although nearly a quarter of electricity comes from hydroelectric power. Main exports are oil and oil products, cotton, textiles and clothing.

EL SALVADOR
Republic of El Salvador

Area Sq Km	21 041
Area Sq Miles	8 124
Population	6 515 000
Capital	San Salvador
Languages	Spanish
Religions	Roman Catholic, Protestant
Currency	El Salvador colón, United States dollar
Organizations	UN

Map page 151

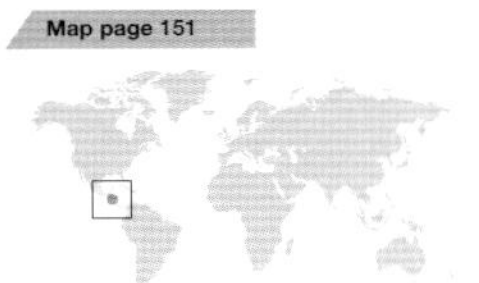

Located on the Pacific coast of central America, El Salvador consists of a coastal plain and volcanic mountain ranges which enclose a densely populated plateau area. The coast is hot, with heavy summer rainfall; the highlands are cooler. Coffee (the chief export), sugar and cotton are the main cash crops. The main trading partners are the USA and Guatemala.

EQUATORIAL GUINEA
Republic of Equatorial Guinea

Area Sq Km	28 051
Area Sq Miles	10 831
Population	494 000
Capital	Malabo
Languages	Spanish, French, Fang
Religions	Roman Catholic, traditional beliefs
Currency	CFA franc
Organizations	UN

Map page 120

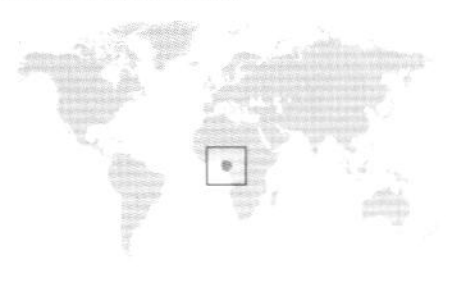

The state consists of Rio Muni, an enclave on the Atlantic coast of central Africa, and the islands of Bioco, Annobón and the Corisco group. Most of the population lives on the coastal plain and upland plateau of Rio Muni. The capital city, Malabo, is on the fertile volcanic island of Bioco. The climate is hot, humid and wet. Oil production started in 1992, and oil is now the main export, along with timber. The economy depends heavily on foreign aid.

ERITREA
State of Eritrea

Area Sq Km	117 400
Area Sq Miles	45 328
Population	4 141 000
Capital	Asmara
Languages	Tigrinya, Tigre
Religions	Sunni Muslim, Coptic Christian
Currency	Nakfa
Organizations	UN

Map page 122

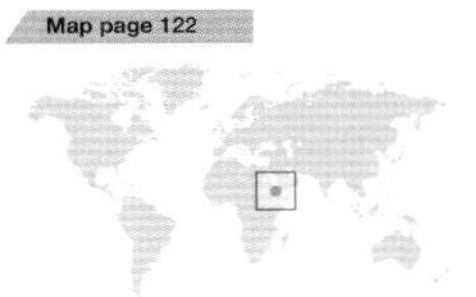

Eritrea, on the Red Sea coast of northeast Africa, consists of a high plateau in the north with a coastal plain which widens to the south. The coast is hot; inland is cooler. Rainfall is unreliable. The agriculture-based economy has suffered from over thirty years of war and occasional poor rains. Eritrea is one of the least developed countries in the world.

ESTONIA
Republic of Estonia

Area Sq Km	45 200
Area Sq Miles	17 452
Population	1 323 000
Capital	Tallinn
Languages	Estonian, Russian
Religions	Protestant, Estonian and Russian Orthodox
Currency	Kroon
Organizations	EU, NATO, UN

Map page 103

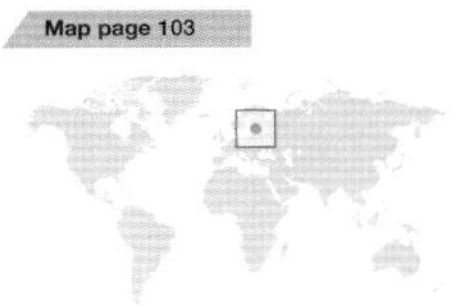

Estonia is in northern Europe, on the Gulf of Finland and the Baltic Sea. The land, over one-third of which is forested, is generally low-lying with many lakes. Approximately one-third of Estonians live in the capital, Tallinn. Exported goods include machinery, wood products, textiles and food products. The main trading partners are the Russian Federation, Finland and Sweden. Estonia joined the European Union in May 2004.

ETHIOPIA
Federal Democratic Republic of Ethiopia

Area Sq Km	1 133 880
Area Sq Miles	437 794
Population	70 678 000
Capital	Addis Ababa (Ādīs Ābeba)
Languages	Oromo, Amharic, Tigrinya, local languages
Religions	Ethiopian Orthodox, Sunni Muslim, traditional beliefs
Currency	Birr
Organizations	UN

Map page 122

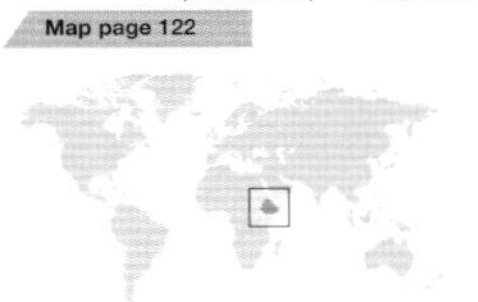

A landlocked country in northeast Africa, Ethiopia comprises a mountainous region in the west which is traversed by the Great Rift Valley. The east is mostly arid plateau land. The highlands are warm with summer rainfall. Most people live in the central–northern area. In recent years civil war, conflict with Eritrea and poor infrastructure have hampered economic development. Subsistence farming is the main activity, although droughts have led to frequent famines. Coffee is the main export and there is some light industry. Ethiopia is one of the least developed countries in the world.

Falkland Islands
United Kingdom Overseas Territory

Area Sq Km	12 170
Area Sq Miles	4 699
Population	3 000
Capital	Stanley
Languages	English
Religions	Protestant, Roman Catholic
Currency	Falkland Islands pound

Map page 156 Lying in the southwest Atlantic Ocean, northeast of Cape Horn, two main islands, West Falkland and East Falkland and many smaller islands, form the territory of the Falkland Islands. The economy is based on sheep farming and the sale of fishing licences.

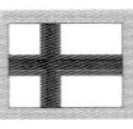

Faroe Islands
Self-governing Danish Territory

Area Sq Km	1 399
Area Sq Miles	540
Population	47 000
Capital	Thorshavn (Tórshavn)
Languages	Faroese, Danish
Religions	Protestant
Currency	Danish krone

Map page 102 A self-governing territory, the Faroe Islands lie in the north Atlantic Ocean between the UK and Iceland. The islands benefit from the North Atlantic Drift, which has a moderating effect on the climate. The economy is based on deep-sea fishing.

FIJI
Sovereign Democratic Republic of Fiji

Area Sq Km	18 330
Area Sq Miles	7 077
Population	839 000
Capital	Suva
Languages	English, Fijian, Hindi
Religions	Christian, Hindu, Sunni Muslim
Currency	Fiji dollar
Organizations	Comm., UN

Map page 69

The southwest Pacific republic of Fiji comprises two mountainous and volcanic islands, Vanua Levu and Viti Levu, and over three hundred smaller islands. The climate is tropical and the economy is based on agriculture (chiefly sugar, the main export), fishing, forestry, gold mining and tourism.

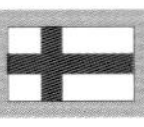

FINLAND
Republic of Finland

Area Sq Km	338 145
Area Sq Miles	130 559
Population	5 207 000
Capital	Helsinki (Helsingfors)
Languages	Finnish, Swedish
Religions	Protestant, Greek Orthodox
Currency	Euro
Organizations	EU, OECD, UN

Map page 102–103

Finland is in northern Europe, and nearly one-third of the country lies north of the Arctic Circle. Forests cover over seventy per cent of the land area, and ten per cent is covered by lakes. Summers are short and warm, and winters are long and severe, particularly in the north. Most of the population lives in the southern third of the country, along the coast or near the lakes. Timber is a major resource and there are important minerals, chiefly chromium. Main industries include metal working, electronics, paper and paper products, and chemicals. The main trading partners are Germany, Sweden and the UK.

FRANCE
French Republic

Area Sq Km	543 965
Area Sq Miles	210 026
Population	60 144 000
Capital	Paris
Languages	French, Arabic
Religions	Roman Catholic, Protestant, Sunni Muslim
Currency	Euro
Organizations	EU, NATO, OECD, UN

Map page 110

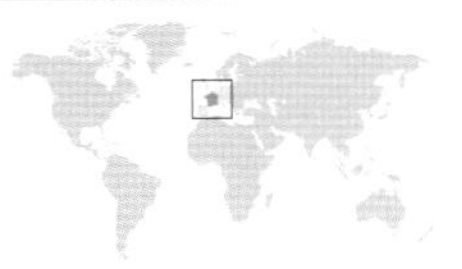

France lies in western Europe and has coastlines on the Atlantic Ocean and the Mediterranean Sea. It includes the Mediterranean island of Corsica. Northern and western regions consist mostly of flat or rolling countryside, and include the major lowlands of the Paris basin, the Loire valley and the Aquitaine basin, drained by the Seine, Loire and Garonne river systems respectively. The centre-south is dominated by the hill region of the Massif Central. To the east are the Vosges and Jura mountains and the Alps. In the southwest, the Pyrenees form a natural border with Spain. The climate is temperate with warm summers and cool winters, although the Mediterranean coast has hot, dry summers and mild winters. Over seventy per cent of the population lives in towns, with almost a sixth of the population living in the Paris area. The French economy has a substantial and varied agricultural base. It is a major producer of both fresh and processed food. There are relatively few mineral resources; it has coal reserves, and some oil and natural gas, but it relies heavily on nuclear and hydroelectric power and imported fuels. France is one of the world's major industrial countries. Main industries include food processing, iron, steel and aluminium production, chemicals, cars, electronics and oil refining. The main exports are transport equipment, plastics and chemicals. Tourism is a major source of revenue and employment. Trade is predominantly with other European Union countries.

French Guiana
French Overseas Department

Area Sq Km	90 000
Area Sq Miles	34 749
Population	178 000
Capital	Cayenne
Languages	French, Creole
Religions	Roman Catholic
Currency	Euro

Map page 155 French Guiana, on the north coast of South America, is densely forested. The climate is tropical, with high rainfall. Most people live in the coastal strip, and agriculture is mostly subsistence farming. Forestry and fishing are important, but mineral resources are largely unexploited and industry is limited. French Guiana depends on French aid. The main trading partners are France and the USA.

French Polynesia
French Overseas Country

Area Sq Km	3 265
Area Sq Miles	1 261
Population	244 000
Capital	Papeete
Languages	French, Tahitian, Polynesian languages
Religions	Protestant, Roman Catholic
Currency	CFP franc

Map page 67 Extending over a vast area of the southeast Pacific Ocean, French Polynesia comprises more than one hundred and thirty islands and coral atolls. The main island groups are the Marquesas Islands, the Tuamotu Archipelago and the Society Islands. The capital, Papeete, is on Tahiti in the Society Islands. The climate is subtropical, and the economy is based on tourism. The main export is cultured pearls.

GABON
Gabonese Republic

Area Sq Km	267 667	Languages	French, Fang, local languages
Area Sq Miles	103 347	Religions	Roman Catholic, Protestant, traditional beliefs
Population	1 329 000	Currency	CFA franc
Capital	Libreville	Organizations	UN

Map page 122

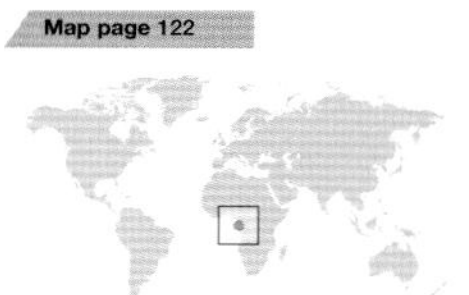

Gabon, on the Atlantic coast of central Africa, consists of low plateaus and a coastal plain lined by lagoons and mangrove swamps. The climate is tropical and rainforests cover over three-quarters of the land area. Over seventy per cent of the population lives in towns. The economy is heavily dependent on oil, which accounts for around seventy-five per cent of exports; manganese, uranium and timber are the other main exports. Agriculture is mainly at subsistence level.

THE GAMBIA
Republic of the Gambia

Area Sq Km	11 295	Languages	English, Malinke, Fulani, Wolof
Area Sq Miles	4 361	Religions	Sunni Muslim, Protestant
Population	1 426 000	Currency	Dalasi
Capital	Banjul	Organizations	Comm., UN

Map page 120

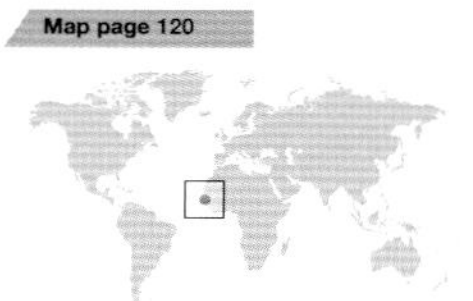

The Gambia, on the coast of west Africa, occupies a strip of land along the lower Gambia river. Sandy beaches are backed by mangrove swamps, beyond which is savanna. The climate is tropical, with most rainfall in the summer. Over seventy per cent of Gambians are farmers, growing chiefly groundnuts (the main export), cotton, oil palms and food crops. Livestock rearing and fishing are important, while manufacturing is limited. Re-exports, mainly from Senegal, and tourism are major sources of income.

Gaza
Semi-autonomous region

Area Sq Km	363	Languages	Arabic
Area Sq Miles	140	Religions	Sunni Muslim, Shi'a Muslim
Population	1 203 591	Currency	Israeli shekel
Capital	Gaza		

Map page 80 Gaza is a narrow strip of land on the southeast corner of the Mediterranean Sea, between Egypt and Israel. This Palestinian territory has limited autonomy from Israel, but hostilities between Israel and the indigenous Arab population continue to restrict its economic development.

GEORGIA
Republic of Georgia

Area Sq Km	69 700	Languages	Georgian, Russian, Armenian, Azeri, Ossetian, Abkhaz
Area Sq Miles	26 911	Religions	Georgian Orthodox, Russian Orthodox, Sunni Muslim
Population	5 126 000	Currency	Lari
Capital	T'bilisi	Organizations	CIS, UN

Map page 117

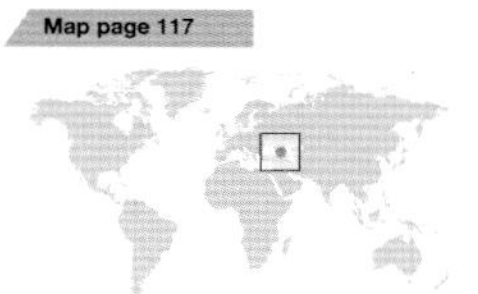

Georgia is in the northwest Caucasus area of southwest Asia, on the eastern coast of the Black Sea. Mountain ranges in the north and south flank the Kura and Rioni valleys. The climate is generally mild, and along the coast it is subtropical. Agriculture is important, with tea, grapes, and citrus fruits the main crops. Mineral resources include manganese ore and oil, and the main industries are steel, oil refining and machine building. The main trading partners are the Russian Federation and Turkey.

GERMANY
Federal Republic of Germany

Area Sq Km	357 022	Languages	German, Turkish
Area Sq Miles	137 847	Religions	Protestant, Roman Catholic
Population	82 476 000	Currency	Euro
Capital	Berlin	Organizations	EU, NATO, OECD, UN

Map page 112

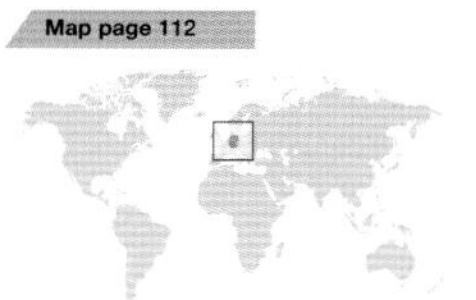

The central European state of Germany borders nine countries and has coastlines on the North and Baltic Seas. Behind the indented coastline, and covering about one-third of the country, is the north German plain, a region of fertile farmland and sandy heaths drained by the country's major rivers. The central highlands are a belt of forested hills and plateaus which stretch from the Eifel region in the west to the Erzgebirge mountains along the border with the Czech Republic. Farther south the land rises to the Swabian Alps (Schwäbische Alb), with the high rugged and forested Black Forest (Schwarzwald) in the southwest. In the far south the Bavarian Alps form the border with Austria. The climate is temperate, with continental conditions in eastern areas. The population is highly urbanized, with over eighty-five per cent living in cities and towns. With the exception of coal, lignite, potash and baryte, Germany lacks minerals and other industrial raw materials. It has a small agricultural base, although a few products (chiefly wines and beers) enjoy an international reputation. Germany is the world's third ranking economy after the USA and Japan. Its industries are amongst the world's most technologically advanced. Exports include machinery, vehicles and chemicals. The majority of trade is with other countries in the European Union, the USA and Japan.

Baden-Württemberg (State)
Area Sq Km (Sq Miles) 35 752 (13 804) Population 10 601 000 Capital Stuttgart

Bayern (State)
Area Sq Km (Sq Miles) 70 550 (27 240) Population 12 330 000 Capital Munich (München)

Berlin (State)
Area Sq Km (Sq Miles) 892 (344) Population 3 388 000 Capital Berlin

Brandenburg (State)
Area Sq Km (Sq Miles) 29 476 (11 381) Population 2 593 000 Capital Potsdan

Bremen
Area Sq Km (Sq Miles) 404 (156) Population 660 000 Capital Bremen

Hamburg (State)
Area Sq Km (Sq Miles) 755 (292) Population 1 726 000 Capital Hamburg

Hessen (State)
Area Sq Km (Sq Miles) 21 114 (8 152) Population 6 078 000 Capital Wiesbaden

Mecklenburg-Vorpommern (State)
Area Sq Km (Sq Miles) 23 173 (8 947) Population 1 760 000 Capital Schwerin

Niedersachsen (State)
Area Sq Km (Sq Miles) 47 616 (18 385) Population 7 956 000 Capital Hannover

Nordrhein-Westfalen (State)
Area Sq Km (Sq Miles) 34 082 (13 159) Population 18 052 000 Capital Düsseldorf

Rheinland-Pfalz (State)
Area Sq Km (Sq Miles) 19 847 (7 663) Population 4 049 000 Capital Mainz

Saarland (State)
Area Sq Km (Sq Miles) 2 568 (992) Population 1 066 000 Capital Saarbrücken

Sachsen (State)
Area Sq Km (Sq Miles) 18 413 (7 109) Population 4 384 000 Capital Dresden

Sachsen-Anhalt (State)
Area Sq Km (Sq Miles) 20 447 (7 895) Population 2 581 000 Capital Magdeburg

Schleswig-Holstein (State)
Area Sq Km (Sq Miles) 15 761 (6 085) Population 2 804 000 Capital Kiel

Thüringen (State)
Area Sq Km (Sq Miles) 16 172 (6 244) Population 2 411 000 Capital Erfurt

GHANA
Republic of Ghana

Area Sq Km	238 537	Languages	English, Hausa, Akan, local languages
Area Sq Miles	92 100	Religions	Christian, Sunni Muslim, traditional beliefs
Population	20 922 000	Currency	Cedi
Capital	Accra	Organizations	Comm., UN

Map page 120

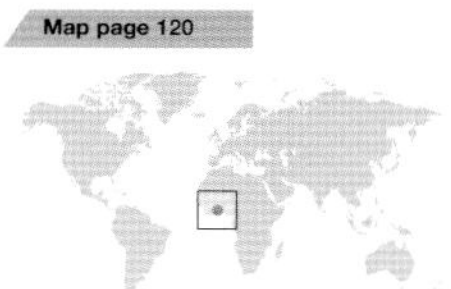

A west African state on the Gulf of Guinea, Ghana is a land of plains and low plateaus covered with savanna and rainforest. In the east is the Volta basin and Lake Volta. The climate is tropical, with the highest rainfall in the south, where most of the population lives. Agriculture employs around sixty per cent of the workforce. Main exports are gold, timber, cocoa, bauxite and manganese ore.

Gibraltar
United Kingdom Overseas Territory

Area Sq Km	7	Languages	English, Spanish
Area Sq Miles	3	Religions	Roman Catholic, Protestant, Sunni Muslim
Population	27 000	Currency	Gibraltar pound
Capital	Gibraltar		

Map page 111 Gibraltar lies on the south coast of Spain at the western entrance to the Mediterranean Sea. The economy depends on tourism, offshore banking and shipping services.

GREECE
Hellenic Republic

Area Sq Km	131 957	Languages	Greek
Area Sq Miles	50 949	Religions	Greek Orthodox, Sunni Muslim
Population	10 976 000	Currency	Euro
Capital	Athens (Athina)	Organizations	EU, NATO, OECD, UN

Map page 115

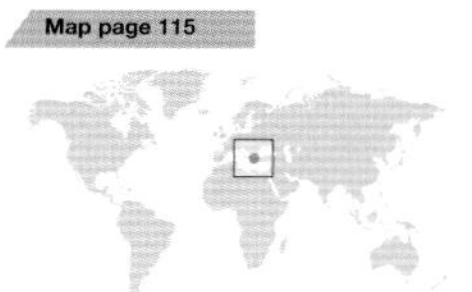

Greece comprises a mountainous peninsula in the Balkan region of southeastern Europe and many islands in the Ionian, Aegean and Mediterranean Seas. The islands make up over one-fifth of its area. Mountains and hills cover much of the country. The main lowland areas are the plains of Thessaly in the centre and around Thessaloniki in the northeast. Summers are hot and dry while winters are mild and wet, but colder in the north with heavy snowfalls in the mountains. One-third of Greeks live in the Athens area. Employment in agriculture accounts for approximately twenty per cent of the workforce, and exports include citrus fruits, raisins, wine, olives and olive oil. Aluminium and nickel are mined and a wide range of manufactures are produced, including food products and tobacco, textiles, clothing, and chemicals. Tourism is an important industry and there is a large services sector. Most trade is with other European Union countries.

Greenland
Self-governing Danish Territory

Area Sq Km	2 175 600	Languages	Greenlandic, Danish
Area Sq Miles	840 004	Religions	Protestant
Population	57 000	Currency	Danish krone
Capital	Nuuk (Godthåb)		

Map page 129

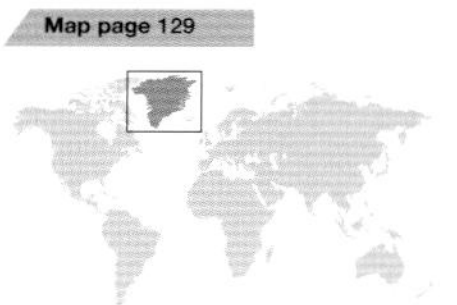

Situated to the northeast of North America between the Atlantic and Arctic Oceans, Greenland is the largest island in the world. It has a polar climate and over eighty per cent of the land area is covered by permanent ice cap. The economy is based on fishing and fish processing.

GRENADA

Area Sq Km	378	Languages	English, Creole
Area Sq Miles	146	Religions	Roman Catholic, Protestant
Population	80 000	Currency	East Caribbean dollar
Capital	St George's	Organizations	CARICOM, Comm., UN

Map page 157

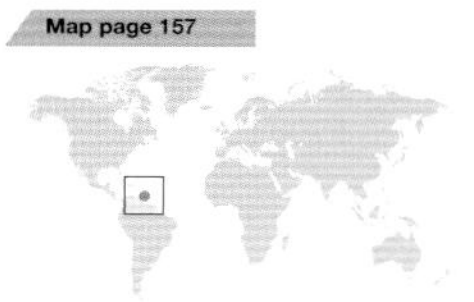

The Caribbean state comprises Grenada, the most southerly of the Windward Islands, and the southern islands of the Grenadines. Grenada has wooded hills, with beaches in the southwest. The climate is warm and wet. Agriculture is the main activity, with bananas, nutmeg and cocoa the main exports. Tourism is the main foreign exchange earner.

Guadeloupe
French Overseas Department

Area Sq Km	1 780	Languages	French, Creole
Area Sq Miles	687	Religions	Roman Catholic
Population	440 000	Currency	Euro
Capital	Basse-Terre		

Map page 149 Guadeloupe, in the Leeward Islands in the Caribbean, consists of two main islands (Basse-Terre and Grande-Terre, connected by a bridge), Marie-Galante, and a few outer islands. The climate is tropical, but moderated by trade winds. Bananas, sugar and rum are the main exports and tourism is a major source of income.

Guam
United States Unincorporated Territory

Area Sq Km	541	Languages	Chamorro, English, Tagalog
Area Sq Miles	209	Religions	Roman Catholic
Population	163 000	Currency	United States dollar
Capital	Hagåtña		

Map page 91 Lying at the south end of the Northern Mariana Islands in the western Pacific Ocean, Guam has a humid tropical climate. The island has a large US military base and the economy relies on that and on tourism.

GUATEMALA
Republic of Guatemala

Area Sq Km	108 890	Languages	Spanish, Mayan languages
Area Sq Miles	42 043	Religions	Roman Catholic, Protestant
Population	12 347 000	Currency	Quetzal, United States dollar
Capital	Guatemala City	Organizations	UN

Map page 151

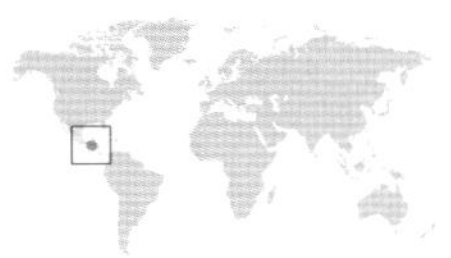

The most populous country in Central America after Mexico, Guatemala has long Pacific and short Caribbean coasts separated by a mountain chain which includes several active volcanoes. The climate is hot tropical in the lowlands and cooler in the highlands, where most of the population lives. Farming is the main activity and coffee, sugar and bananas are the main exports. There is some manufacturing of clothing and textiles. The main trading partner is the USA.

Guernsey
United Kingdom Crown Dependency

Area Sq Km	78	Languages	English, French
Area Sq Miles	30	Religions	Protestant, Roman Catholic
Population	62 701	Currency	Pound sterling
Capital	St Peter Port		

Map page 110 Guernsey is one of the Channel Islands, lying off northern France. The dependency also includes the nearby islands of Alderney, Sark and Herm. Financial services are an important part of the island's economy.

GUINEA
Republic of Guinea

Area Sq Km	245 857	Languages	French, Fulani, Malinke, local languages
Area Sq Miles	94 926	Religions	Sunni Muslim, traditional beliefs, Christian
Population	8 480 000	Currency	Guinea franc
Capital	Conakry	Organizations	UN

Map page 120

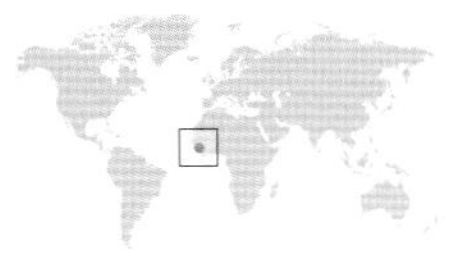

Guinea is in west Africa, on the Atlantic Ocean. There are mangrove swamps along the coast, while inland are lowlands and the Fouta Djallon mountains and plateaus. To the east are savanna plains drained by the upper Niger river system. The southeast is hilly. The climate is tropical, with high coastal rainfall. Agriculture is the main activity, employing nearly eighty per cent of the workforce, with coffee, bananas and pineapples the chief cash crops. There are huge reserves of bauxite, which accounts for more than seventy per cent of exports. Other exports include aluminium oxide, gold, coffee and diamonds.

GUINEA-BISSAU
Republic of Guinea-Bissau

Area Sq Km	36 125	Languages	Portuguese, Crioulo, local languages
Area Sq Miles	13 948	Religions	Traditional beliefs, Sunni Muslim, Christian
Population	1 493 000	Currency	CFA franc
Capital	Bissau	Organizations	UN

Map page 120

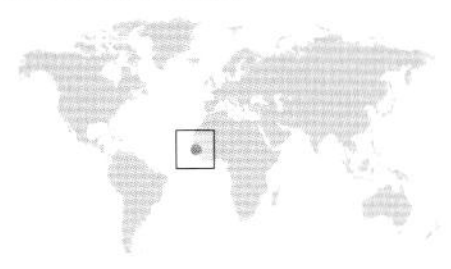

Guinea-Bissau is on the Atlantic coast of west Africa. The mainland coast is swampy and contains many estuaries. Inland are forested plains, and to the east are savanna plateaus. The climate is tropical. The economy is based mainly on subsistence farming. There is little industry, and timber and mineral resources are largely unexploited. Cashews account for seventy per cent of exports. Guinea-Bissau is one of the least developed countries in the world.

GUYANA
Co-operative Republic of Guyana

Area Sq Km	214 969	Languages	English, Creole, Amerindian languages
Area Sq Miles	83 000	Religions	Protestant, Hindu, Roman Catholic, Sunni Muslim
Population	765 000	Currency	Guyana dollar
Capital	Georgetown	Organizations	CARICOM, Comm., UN

Map page 154–155

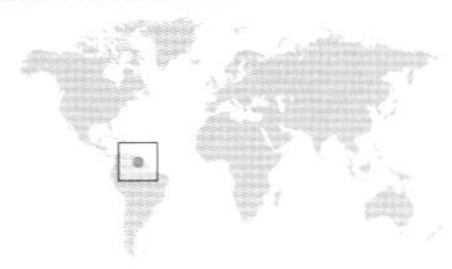

Guyana, on the northeast coast of South America, consists of highlands in the west and savanna uplands in the southwest. Most of the country is densely forested. A lowland coastal belt supports crops and most of the population. The generally hot, humid and wet conditions are modified along the coast by sea breezes. The economy is based on agriculture, bauxite, and forestry. Sugar, bauxite, gold, rice and timber are the main exports.

HAITI
Republic of Haiti

Area Sq Km	27 750	Languages	French, Creole
Area Sq Miles	10 714	Religions	Roman Catholic, Protestant, Voodoo
Population	8 326 000	Currency	Gourde
Capital	Port-au-Prince	Organizations	CARICOM, UN

Map page 149

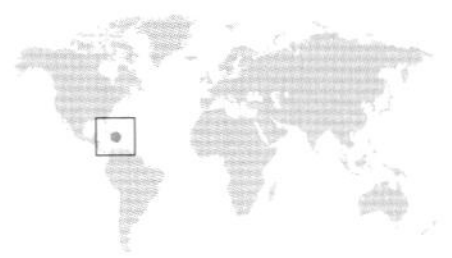

Haiti, occupying the western third of the Caribbean island of Hispaniola, is a mountainous state with small coastal plains and a central valley. The Dominican Republic occupies the rest of the island. The climate is tropical, and is hottest in coastal areas. Haiti has few natural resources, is densely populated and relies on exports of local crafts and coffee, and remittances from workers abroad.

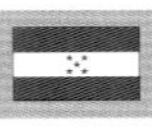

HONDURAS
Republic of Honduras

Area Sq Km	112 088	Languages	Spanish, Amerindian languages
Area Sq Miles	43 277	Religions	Roman Catholic, Protestant
Population	6 941 000	Currency	Lempira
Capital	Tegucigalpa	Organizations	UN

Map page 150

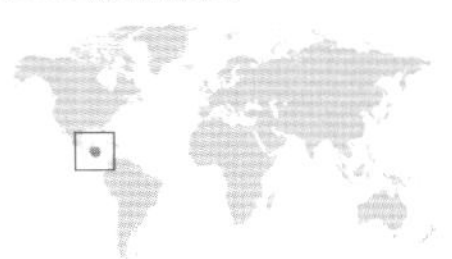

Honduras, in central America, is a mountainous and forested country with lowland areas along its long Caribbean and short Pacific coasts. Coastal areas are hot and humid with heavy summer rainfall; inland is cooler and drier. Most of the population lives in the central valleys. Coffee and bananas are the main exports, along with shellfish and zinc. Industry involves mainly agricultural processing.

HUNGARY
Republic of Hungary

Area Sq Km	93 030	Languages	Hungarian
Area Sq Miles	35 919	Religions	Roman Catholic, Protestant
Population	9 877 000	Currency	Forint
Capital	Budapest	Organizations	EU, NATO, OECD, UN

Map page 112–113

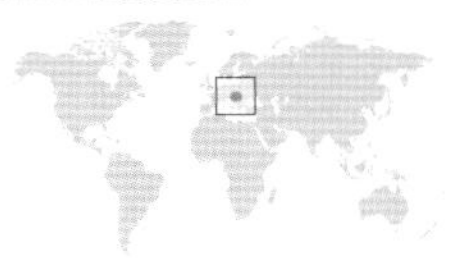

The Danube river flows north-south through central Hungary, a landlocked country in eastern Europe. In the east lies a great plain, flanked by highlands in the north. In the west low mountains and Lake Balaton separate a smaller plain and southern uplands. The climate is continental. Sixty per cent of the population lives in urban areas, and one-fifth lives in the capital, Budapest. Some minerals and energy resources are exploited, chiefly bauxite, coal and natural gas. Hungary has an industrial economy based on metals, machinery, transport equipment, chemicals and food products. The main trading partners are Germany and Austria. Hungary joined the European Union in May 2004.

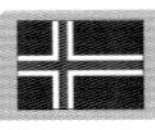

ICELAND
Republic of Iceland

Area Sq Km	102 820	Languages	Icelandic
Area Sq Miles	39 699	Religions	Protestant
Population	290 000	Currency	Icelandic króna
Capital	Reykjavík	Organizations	NATO, OECD, UN

Map page 102

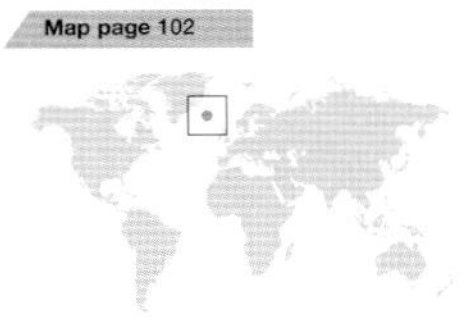

Iceland lies in the north Atlantic Ocean near the Arctic Circle, to the northwest of Scandinavia. The landscape is volcanic, with numerous hot springs, geysers, and approximately two hundred volcanoes. One-tenth of the country is covered by ice caps. Only coastal lowlands are cultivated and settled, and over half the population lives in the Reykjavik area. The climate is mild, moderated by the North Atlantic Drift ocean current and by southwesterly winds. The mainstays of the economy are fishing and fish processing, which account for seventy per cent of exports. Agriculture involves mainly sheep and dairy farming. Hydroelectric and geothermal energy resources are considerable. The main industries produce aluminium, ferro-silicon and fertilizers. Tourism, including ecotourism, is growing in importance.

INDIA
Republic of India

Area Sq Km	3 064 898	Languages	Hindi, English, many regional languages
Area Sq Miles	1 183 364	Religions	Hindu, Sunni Muslim, Shi'a Muslim, Sikh, Christian
Population	1 065 462 000	Currency	Indian rupee
Capital	New Delhi	Organizations	Comm., UN

Map page 78–79

The south Asian country of India occupies a peninsula that juts out into the Indian Ocean between the Arabian Sea and Bay of Bengal. The heart of the peninsula is the Deccan plateau, bordered on either side by ranges of hills, the western Ghats and the lower eastern Ghats, which fall away to narrow coastal plains. To the north is a broad plain, drained by the Indus, Ganges and Brahmaputra rivers and their tributaries. The plain is intensively farmed and is the most populous region. In the west is the Thar Desert. The mountains of the Himalaya form India's northern border, together with parts of the Karakoram and Hindu Kush ranges in the northwest. The climate shows marked seasonal variation: a hot season from March to June; a monsoon season from June to October; and a cold season from November to February. Rainfall ranges between very high in the northeast Assam region to negligible in the Thar Desert. Temperatures range from very cold in the Himalaya to tropical heat over much of the south. Over seventy per cent of the huge population – the second largest in the world – is rural, although Delhi, Mumbai (Bombay) and Kolkata (Calcutta) all rank among the ten largest cities in the world. Agriculture, forestry and fishing account for a quarter of national output and two-thirds of employment. Much of the farming is on a subsistence basis and involves mainly rice and wheat. India is a major world producer of tea, sugar, jute, cotton and tobacco. Livestock is reared mainly for dairy products and hides. There are major reserves of coal, reserves of oil and natural gas, and many minerals, including iron, manganese, bauxite, diamonds and gold. The manufacturing sector is large and diverse – mainly chemicals and chemical products, textiles, iron and steel, food products, electrical goods and transport equipment; software and pharmaceuticals are also important. All the main manufactured products are exported, together with diamonds and jewellery. The USA, Germany, Japan and the UK are the main trading partners.

INDONESIA
Republic of Indonesia

Area Sq Km	1 919 445	Languages	Indonesian, local languages
Area Sq Miles	741 102	Religions	Sunni Muslim, Protestant, Roman Catholic, Hindu, Buddhist
Population	219 883 000	Currency	Rupiah
Capital	Jakarta	Organizations	APEC, ASEAN, OPEC, UN

Map page 91

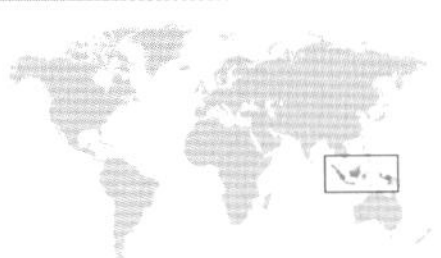

Indonesia, the largest and most populous country in southeast Asia, consists of over thirteen thousand islands extending between the Pacific and Indian Oceans. Sumatra, Java, Sulawesi (Celebes), Kalimantan (two-thirds of Borneo) and Papua (formerly Irian Jaya, western New Guinea) make up ninety per cent of the land area. Most of Indonesia is mountainous and covered with rainforest or mangrove swamps, and there are over three hundred volcanoes, many active. Two-thirds of the population lives in the lowland areas of the islands of Java and Madura. The climate is tropical monsoon. Agriculture is the largest sector of the economy and Indonesia is among the world's top producers of rice, palm oil, tea, coffee, rubber and tobacco. Many goods are produced, including textiles, clothing, cement, tin, fertilizers and vehicles. Main exports are oil, natural gas, timber products and clothing. Main trading partners are Japan, the USA and Singapore. Indonesia is a relatively poor country, and ethnic tensions and civil unrest often hinder economic development.

IRAN
Islamic Republic of Iran

Area Sq Km	1 648 000	Languages	Farsi, Azeri, Kurdish, regional languages
Area Sq Miles	636 296	Religions	Shi'a Muslim, Sunni Muslim
Population	68 920 000	Currency	Iranian rial
Capital	Tehrān	Organizations	OPEC, UN

Map page 84–85

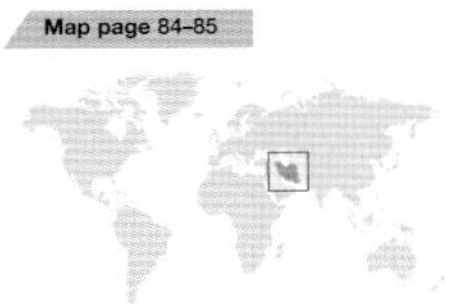

Iran is in southwest Asia, and has coasts on The Gulf, the Caspian Sea and the Gulf of Oman. In the east is a high plateau, with large salt pans and a vast sand desert. In the west the Zagros Mountains form a series of ridges, and to the north lie the Elburz Mountains. Most farming and settlement is on the narrow plain along the Caspian Sea and in the foothills of the north and west. The climate is one of extremes, with hot summers and very cold winters. Most of the light rainfall is in the winter months. Agriculture involves approximately one-third of the workforce. Wheat is the main crop, but fruit (especially dates) and pistachio nuts are grown for export. Petroleum (the main export) and natural gas are Iran's leading natural resources. Manufactured goods include carpets, clothing, food products and construction materials.

© Collins Bartholomew Ltd

IRAQ
Republic of Iraq

Area Sq Km	438 317	Languages	Arabic, Kurdish, Turkmen
Area Sq Miles	169 235	Religions	Shi'a Muslim, Sunni Muslim, Christian
Population	25 175 000	Currency	Iraqi dinar
Capital	Baghdād	Organizations	OPEC, UN

Map page 81

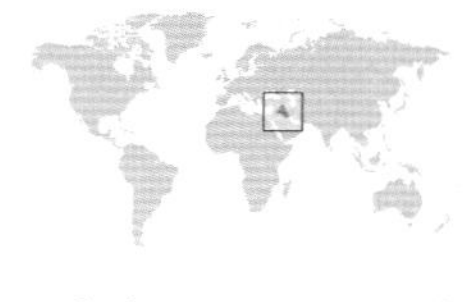

Iraq, in southwest Asia, has at its heart the lowland valley of the Tigris and Euphrates rivers. In the southeast, where the two rivers join, are the Mesopotamian marshes and the Shaṭṭ al Arab waterway leading to The Gulf. The north is hilly, while the west is mostly desert. Summers are hot and dry, and winters are mild with light, unreliable rainfall. The Tigris-Euphrates valley contains most of the country's arable land. One in five of the population lives in the capital, Baghdad. Oil is normally the main export, but the economy suffered as a result of defeat in the 1991 Gulf War and subsequent sanctions. In 2003 the country was occupied and became administered by a US-led coalition. Control was transferred to an interim government in June 2004 with further plans to move the country towards democratic elections.

IRELAND, REPUBLIC OF

Area Sq Km	70 282	Languages	English, Irish
Area Sq Miles	27 136	Religions	Roman Catholic, Protestant
Population	3 956 000	Currency	Euro
Capital	Dublin (Baile Átha Cliath)	Organizations	EU, OECD, UN

Map page 107

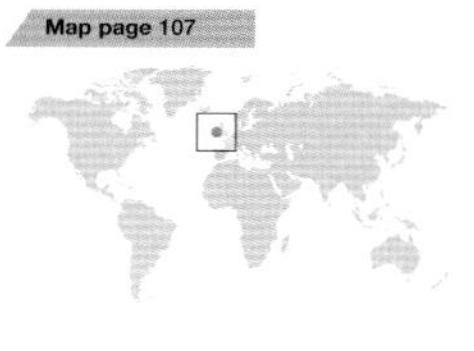

The Irish Republic occupies some eighty per cent of the island of Ireland, in northwest Europe. It is a lowland country of wide valleys, lakes and peat bogs, with isolated mountain ranges around the coast. The west coast is rugged and indented with many bays. The climate is mild due to the modifying effect of the North Atlantic Drift ocean current and rainfall is plentiful, although highest in the west. Nearly sixty per cent of the population lives in urban areas, Dublin and Cork being the main cities. Resources include natural gas, peat, lead and zinc. Agriculture, the traditional mainstay, now employs less than ten per cent of the workforce, while industry employs nearly thirty per cent. The main industries are electronics, pharmaceuticals and engineering as well as food processing, brewing and textiles. Service industries are expanding, with tourism a major earner. The UK is the main trading partner.

Isle of Man
United Kingdom Crown Dependency

Area Sq Km	572	Languages	English
Area Sq Miles	221	Religions	Protestant, Roman Catholic
Population	75 000	Currency	Pound sterling
Capital	Douglas		

Map page 104

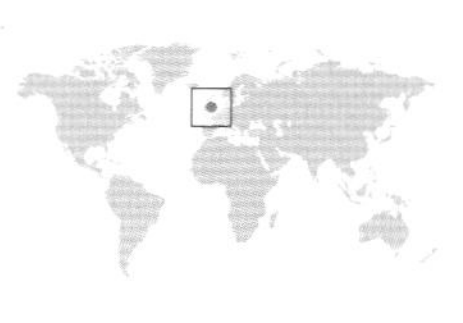

The Isle of Man lies in the Irish Sea between England and Northern Ireland. The island is self-governing, although the UK is responsible for its defence and foreign affairs. It is not part of the European Union, but has a special relationship with the EU which allows for free trade. Eighty per cent of the economy is based on the service sector, particularly financial services.

ISRAEL
State of Israel

Area Sq Km	20 770	Languages	Hebrew, Arabic
Area Sq Miles	8 019	Religions	Jewish, Sunni Muslim, Christian, Druze
Population	6 433 000	Currency	Shekel
Capital	Jerusalem (Yerushalayim) (El Quds) De facto capital. Disputed.	Organizations	UN

Map page 80

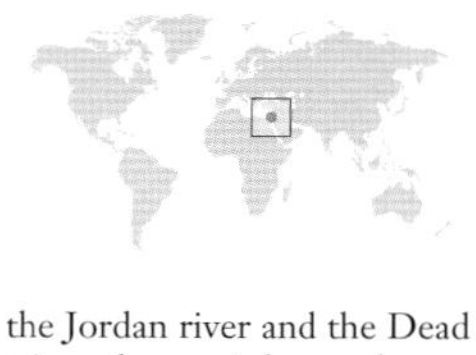

Israel lies on the Mediterranean coast of southwest Asia. Beyond the coastal Plain of Sharon are the hills and valleys of Samaria, with the Galilee highlands to the north. In the east is a rift valley, which extends from Lake Tiberias (Sea of Galilee) to the Gulf of Aqaba and contains the Jordan river and the Dead Sea. In the south is the Negev, a triangular semi-desert plateau. Most of the population lives on the coastal plain or in northern and central areas. Much of Israel has warm summers and mild, wet winters. The south is hot and dry. Agricultural production was boosted by the occupation of the West Bank in 1967. Manufacturing makes the largest contribution to the economy, and tourism is also important. Israel's main exports are machinery and transport equipment, software, diamonds, clothing, fruit and vegetables. The country relies heavily on foreign aid. Security issues relating to territorial disputes over the West Bank and Gaza have still to be resolved.

ITALY
Italian Republic

Area Sq Km	301 245	Languages	Italian
Area Sq Miles	116 311	Religions	Roman Catholic
Population	57 423 000	Currency	Euro
Capital	Rome (Roma)	Organizations	EU, NATO, OECD, UN

Map page 114–115

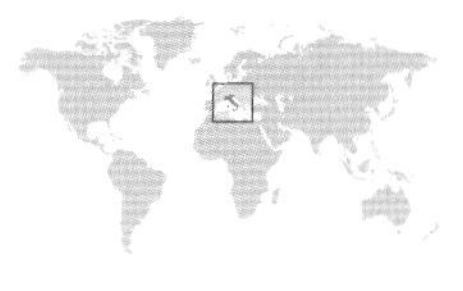

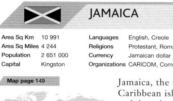

Most of the southern European state of Italy occupies a peninsula that juts out into the Mediterranean Sea. It includes the islands of Sicily and Sardinia and approximately seventy much smaller islands in the surrounding seas. Italy is mountainous, dominated by the Alps, which form its northern border, and the various ranges of the Apennines, which run almost the full length of the peninsula. Many of Italy's mountains are of volcanic origin, and its active volcanoes are Vesuvius, near Naples, Etna and Stromboli. The main lowland area, the Po river valley in the northeast, is the main agricultural and industrial area and is the most populous region. Italy has a Mediterranean climate, although the north experiences colder, wetter winters, with heavy snow in the Alps. Natural resources are limited, and only about twenty per cent of the land is suitable for cultivation. The economy is fairly diversified. Some oil, natural gas and coal are produced, but most fuels and minerals used by industry are imported. Agriculture is important, with cereals, vines, fruit and vegetables the main crops. Italy is the world's largest wine producer. The north is the centre of Italian industry, especially around Turin, Milan and Genoa. Leading manufactures include industrial and office equipment, domestic appliances, cars, textiles, clothing, leather goods, chemicals and metal products. There is a strong service sector, and with over twenty-five million visitors a year, tourism is a major employer and accounts for five per cent of the national income. Finance and banking are also important. Most trade is with other European Union countries.

JAMAICA

Area Sq Km	10 991	Languages	English, Creole
Area Sq Miles	4 244	Religions	Protestant, Roman Catholic
Population	2 651 000	Currency	Jamaican dollar
Capital	Kingston	Organizations	CARICOM, Comm., UN

Map page 149

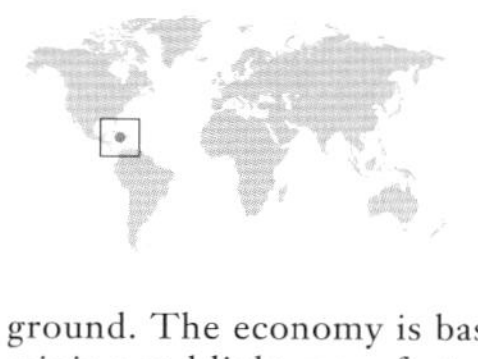

Jamaica, the third largest Caribbean island, has beaches and densely populated coastal plains traversed by hills and plateaus rising to the forested Blue Mountains in the east. The climate is tropical, but cooler and wetter on high ground. The economy is based on tourism, agriculture, mining and light manufacturing. Bauxite, aluminium oxide, sugar and bananas are the main exports. The USA is the main trading partner. Foreign aid is also significant.

Jammu and Kashmir
Disputed territory (India/Pakistan/China)

Area Sq Km	222 236	Population	13 000 000
Area Sq Miles	85 806	Capital	Srinagar

Map page 88 A disputed region in the north of the Indian subcontinent, to the west of the Karakoram and Himalaya mountains. The 'Line of Control' separates the northwestern, Pakistani-controlled area and the southeastern, Indian-controlled area. China occupies the Himalayan section known as the Aksai Chin, which is also claimed by India.

JAPAN

Area Sq Km	377 727	Languages	Japanese
Area Sq Miles	145 841	Religions	Shintoist, Buddhist, Christian
Population	127 654 000	Currency	Yen
Capital	Tōkyō	Organizations	APEC, OECD, UN

Map page 94–95

Japan lies in the Pacific Ocean off the coast of eastern Asia and consists of four main islands – Hokkaidō, Honshū, Shikoku and Kyūshū – and more than three thousand smaller islands in the surrounding Sea of Japan, East China Sea and Pacific Ocean. The central island of Honshū accounts for sixty per cent of the total land area and contains eighty per cent of the population. Behind the long and deeply indented coastline, nearly three-quarters of the country is mountainous and heavily forested. Japan has over sixty active volcanoes, and is subject to frequent earthquakes and typhoons. The climate is generally temperate maritime, with warm summers and mild winters, except in western Hokkaidō and northwest Honshū, where the winters are very cold with heavy snow. Only fourteen per cent of the land area is suitable for cultivation, and its few raw materials (coal, oil, natural gas, lead, zinc and copper) are insufficient for its industry. Most materials must be imported, including about ninety per cent of energy requirements. Yet Japan has the world's second largest industrial economy, with a range of modern heavy and light industries centred mainly around the major ports of Yokohama, Ōsaka and Tōkyō. It is the world's largest manufacturer of cars, motorcycles and merchant ships, and a major producer of steel, textiles, chemicals and cement. It is also a leading producer of many consumer durables, such as washing machines, and electronic equipment, chiefly office equipment and computers. Japan has a strong service sector, banking and finance being particularly important, and Tōkyō has one of the world's major stock exchanges. Owing to intensive agricultural production, Japan is seventy per cent self-sufficient in food. The main food crops are rice, barley, fruit, wheat and soya beans. Livestock rearing (chiefly cattle, pigs and chickens) and fishing are also important, and Japan has one of the largest fishing fleets in the world. A major trading nation, Japan has trade links with many countries in southeast Asia and in Europe, although its main trading partner is the USA.

Jersey
United Kingdom Crown Dependency

Area Sq Km	116	Languages	English, French
Area Sq Miles	45	Religions	Protestant, Roman Catholic
Population	87 186	Currency	Pound sterling
Capital	St Helier		

Map page 110 One of the Channel Islands lying off the west coast of the Cherbourg peninsula in northern France. Financial services are the most important part of the economy.

JORDAN
Hashemite Kingdom of Jordan

Area Sq Km	89 206	Languages	Arabic
Area Sq Miles	34 443	Religions	Sunni Muslim, Christian
Population	5 473 000	Currency	Jordanian dinar
Capital	'Ammān	Organizations	UN

Map page 80–81

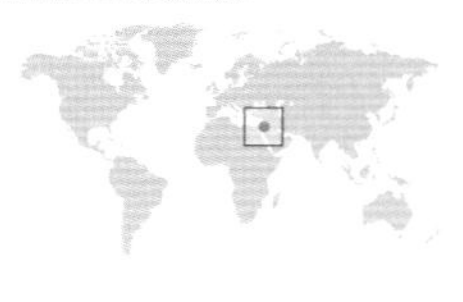

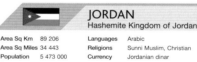

Jordan, in southwest Asia, is landlocked apart from a short coastline on the Gulf of Aqaba. Much of the country is rocky desert plateau. To the west of the mountains, the land falls below sea level to the Dead Sea and the Jordan river. The climate is hot and dry. Most people live in the northwest. Phosphates, potash, pharmaceuticals, fruit and vegetables are the main exports. The tourist industry is important, and the economy relies on workers' remittances from abroad and foreign aid.

KAZAKHSTAN
Republic of Kazakhstan

Area Sq Km	2 717 300	Languages	Kazakh, Russian, Ukrainian, German, Uzbek, Tatar
Area Sq Miles	1 049 155	Religions	Sunni Muslim, Russian Orthodox, Protestant
Population	15 433 000	Currency	Tenge
Capital	Astana (Akmola)	Organizations	CIS, UN

Map page 82–83

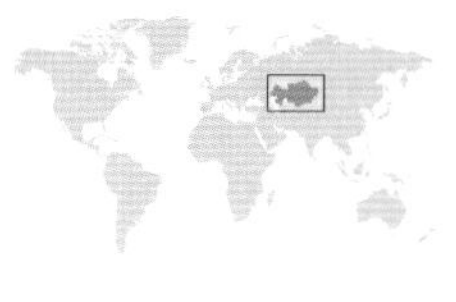

Stretching across central Asia, Kazakhstan covers a vast area of steppe land and semi-desert. The land is flat in the west, with large lowlands around the Caspian Sea, rising to mountains in the southeast. The climate is continental. Agriculture and livestock rearing are important, and cotton and tobacco are the main cash crops. Kazakhstan is very rich in minerals, including coal, chromium, gold, molybdenum, lead and zinc, and has substantial reserves of oil and gas. Mining, metallurgy, machine building and food processing are major industries. Oil, gas and minerals are the main exports, and the Russian Federation is the dominant trading partner.

KENYA
Republic of Kenya

Area Sq Km	582 646	Languages	Swahili, English, local languages
Area Sq Miles	224 961	Religions	Christian, traditional beliefs
Population	31 987 000	Currency	Kenyan shilling
Capital	Nairobi	Organizations	Comm., UN

Map page 122

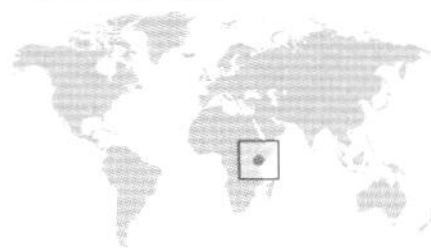

Kenya is in east Africa, on the Indian Ocean. Inland beyond the coastal plains the land rises to plateaus interrupted by volcanic mountains. The Great Rift Valley runs north-south to the west of the capital, Nairobi. Most of the population lives in the central area. Conditions are tropical on the coast, semi-desert in the north and savanna in the south. Hydroelectric power from the Upper Tana river provides most of the country's electricity. Agricultural products, mainly tea, coffee, fruit and vegetables, are the main exports. Light industry is important, and tourism, oil refining and re-exports for landlocked neighbours are major foreign exchange earners.

KIRIBATI
Republic of Kiribati

Area Sq Km	717	Languages	Gilbertese, English
Area Sq Miles	277	Religions	Roman Catholic, Protestant
Population	88 000	Currency	Australian dollar
Capital	Bairiki	Organizations	Comm., UN

Map page 67

Kiribati, in the Pacific Ocean, straddles the Equator and comprises coral islands in the Gilbert, Phoenix and Line Island groups and the volcanic island of Banaba. Most people live on the Gilbert Islands, and the capital, Bairiki, is on Tarawa island in this group. The climate is hot, and wetter in the north. Copra and fish are exported. Kiribati relies on remittances from workers abroad and foreign aid.

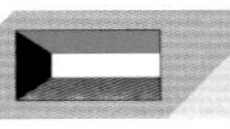

KUWAIT
State of Kuwait

Area Sq Km	17 818	Languages	Arabic
Area Sq Miles	6 880	Religions	Sunni Muslim, Shi'a Muslim, Christian, Hindu
Population	2 521 000	Currency	Kuwaiti dinar
Capital	Kuwait (Al Kuwayt)	Organizations	OPEC, UN

Map page 81

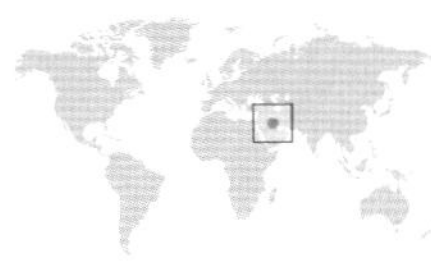

Kuwait lies on the northwest shores of The Gulf in southwest Asia. It is mainly low-lying desert, with irrigated areas along the bay, Kuwait Jun, where most people live. Summers are hot and dry, and winters are cool with some rainfall. The oil industry, which accounts for eighty per cent of exports, has largely recovered from the damage caused by the Gulf War in 1991. Income is also derived from extensive overseas investments. Japan and the USA are the main trading partners.

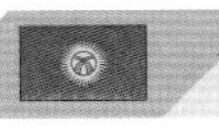

KYRGYZSTAN
Kyrgyz Republic

Area Sq Km	198 500	Languages	Kyrgyz, Russian, Uzbek
Area Sq Miles	76 641	Religions	Sunni Muslim, Russian Orthodox
Population	5 138 000	Currency	Kyrgyz som
Capital	Bishkek (Frunze)	Organizations	CIS, UN

Map page 83

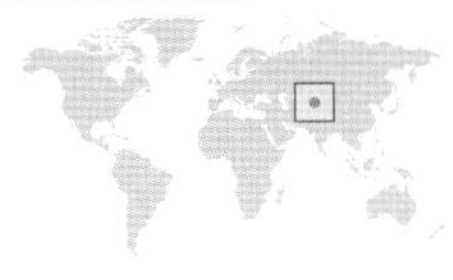

A landlocked central Asian state, Kyrgyzstan is rugged and mountainous, lying to the west of the Tien Shan mountain range. Most of the population lives in the valleys of the north and west. Summers are hot and winters cold. Agriculture (chiefly livestock farming) is the main activity. Some oil and gas, coal, gold, antimony and mercury are produced. Manufactured goods include machinery, metals and metal products, which are the main exports. Most trade is with Germany, the Russian Federation, Kazakhstan and Uzbekistan.

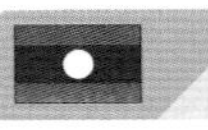

LAOS
Lao People's Democratic Republic

Area Sq Km	236 800	Languages	Lao, local languages
Area Sq Miles	91 429	Religions	Buddhist, traditional beliefs
Population	5 657 000	Currency	Kip
Capital	Vientiane (Viangchan)	Organizations	ASEAN, UN

Map page 91

A landlocked country in southeast Asia, Laos is a land of mostly forested mountains and plateaus. The climate is tropical monsoon. Most of the population lives in the Mekong valley and the low plateau in the south, where food crops, chiefly rice, are grown. Hydroelectricity from a plant on the Mekong river, timber, coffee and tin are exported. Laos relies heavily on foreign aid.

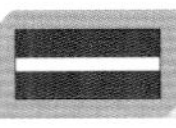

LATVIA
Republic of Latvia

Area Sq Km	63 700	Languages	Latvian, Russian
Area Sq Miles	24 595	Religions	Protestant, Roman Catholic, Russian Orthodox
Population	2 307 000	Currency	Lats
Capital	Rīga	Organizations	EU, NATO, UN

Map page 103

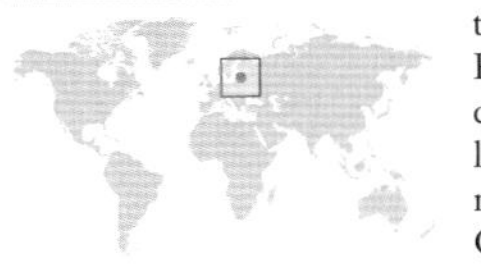

Latvia is in northern Europe, on the Baltic Sea and the Gulf of Riga. The land is flat near the coast but hilly with woods and lakes inland. The country has a modified continental climate. One-third of the people live in the capital, Rīga. Crop and livestock farming are important. There are few natural resources. Industries and main exports include food products, transport equipment, wood and wood products and textiles. The main trading partners are the Russian Federation and Germany. Latvia joined the European Union in May 2004.

LEBANON
Republic of Lebanon

Area Sq Km	10 452	Languages	Arabic, Armenian, French
Area Sq Miles	4 036	Religions	Shi'a Muslim, Sunni Muslim, Christian
Population	3 653 000	Currency	Lebanese pound
Capital	Beirut (Beyrouth)	Organizations	UN

Map page 80

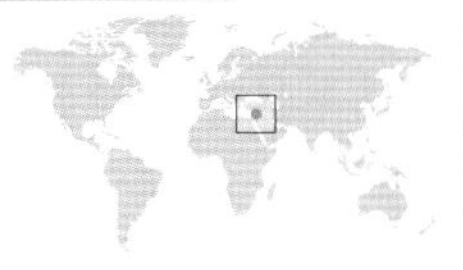

Lebanon lies on the Mediterranean coast of southwest Asia. Beyond the coastal strip, where most of the population lives, are two parallel mountain ranges, separated by the Bekaa Valley (El Beq'a). The economy and infrastructure have been recovering since the 1975–1991 civil war crippled the traditional sectors of financial services and tourism. Italy, France and the UAE are the main trading partners.

LESOTHO
Kingdom of Lesotho

Area Sq Km	30 355	Languages	Sesotho, English, Zulu
Area Sq Miles	11 720	Religions	Christian, traditional beliefs
Population	1 802 000	Currency	Loti, South African rand
Capital	Maseru	Organizations	Comm., SADC, UN

Map page 125

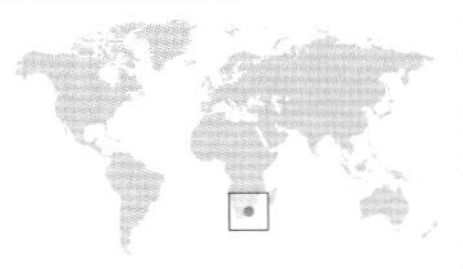

Lesotho is a landlocked state surrounded by the Republic of South Africa. It is a mountainous country lying within the Drakensberg mountain range. Farming and herding are the main activities. The economy depends heavily on South Africa for transport links and employment. A major hydroelectric plant completed in 1998 allows the sale of water to South Africa. Exports include manufactured goods (mainly clothing and road vehicles), food, live animals, wool and mohair.

LIBERIA
Republic of Liberia

Area Sq Km	111 369	Languages	English, Creole, local languages
Area Sq Miles	43 000	Religions	Traditional beliefs, Christian, Sunni Muslim
Population	3 367 000	Currency	Liberian dollar
Capital	Monrovia	Organizations	UN

Map page 120

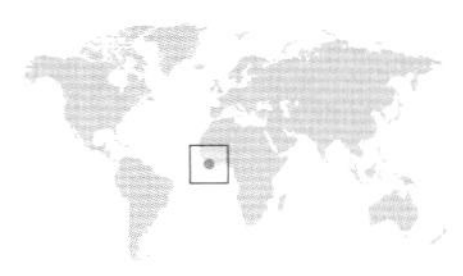

Liberia is on the Atlantic coast of west Africa. Beyond the coastal belt of sandy beaches and mangrove swamps the land rises to a forested plateau and highlands along the Guinea border. A quarter of the population lives along the coast. The climate is hot with heavy rainfall. Liberia is rich in mineral resources and forests. The economy is based on the production and export of basic products. Exports include diamonds, iron ore, rubber and timber. Liberia has a huge international debt and relies heavily on foreign aid.

LIBYA
Great Socialist People's Libyan Arab Jamahiriya

Area Sq Km	1 759 540	Languages	Arabic, Berber
Area Sq Miles	679 362	Religions	Sunni Muslim
Population	5 551 000	Currency	Libyan dinar
Capital	Tripoli (Ṭarābulus)	Organizations	OPEC, UN

Map page 120–121

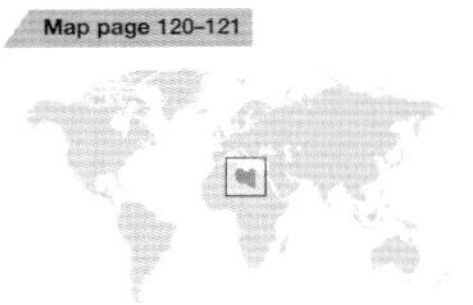

Libya lies on the Mediterranean coast of north Africa. The desert plains and hills of the Sahara dominate the landscape and the climate is hot and dry. Most of the population lives in cities near the coast, where the climate is cooler with moderate rainfall. Farming and herding, chiefly in the northwest, are important but the main industry is oil. Libya is a major producer, and oil accounts for virtually all of its export earnings. Italy and Germany are the main trading partners.

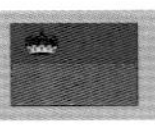

LIECHTENSTEIN
Principality of Liechtenstein

Area Sq Km	160	Languages	German
Area Sq Miles	62	Religions	Roman Catholic, Protestant
Population	34 000	Currency	Swiss franc
Capital	Vaduz	Organizations	UN

Map page 110

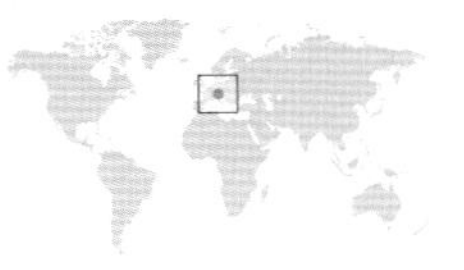

A landlocked state between Switzerland and Austria, Liechtenstein has an industrialized, free-enterprise economy. Low business taxes have attracted companies to establish offices which provide approximately one-third of state revenues. Banking is also important. Major products include precision instruments, ceramics and textiles.

LITHUANIA
Republic of Lithuania

Area Sq Km	65 200	Languages	Lithuanian, Russian, Polish
Area Sq Miles	25 174	Religions	Roman Catholic, Protestant, Russian Orthodox
Population	3 444 000	Currency	Litas
Capital	Vilnius	Organizations	EU, NATO, UN

Map page 103

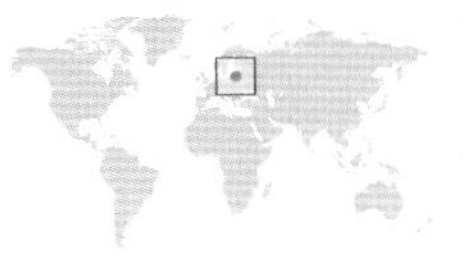

Lithuania is in northern Europe on the eastern shores of the Baltic Sea. It is mainly lowland with many lakes, rivers and marshes. Agriculture, fishing and forestry are important, but manufacturing dominates the economy. The main exports are machinery, mineral products and chemicals. The Russian Federation and Germany are the main trading partners. Lithuania joined the European Union in May 2004.

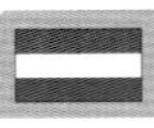

LUXEMBOURG
Grand Duchy of Luxembourg

Area Sq Km	2 586	Languages	Letzeburgish, German, French
Area Sq Miles	998	Religions	Roman Catholic
Population	453 000	Currency	Euro
Capital	Luxembourg	Organizations	EU, NATO, OECD, UN

Map page 108

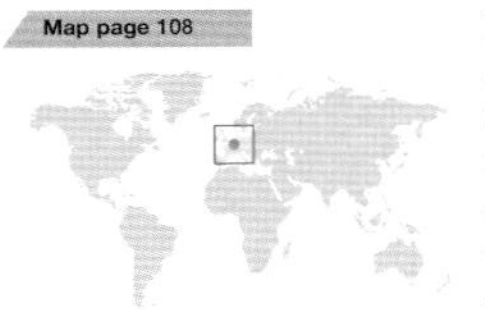

Luxembourg, a small landlocked country in western Europe, borders Belgium, France and Germany. The hills and forests of the Ardennes dominate the north, with rolling pasture to the south, where the main towns, farms and industries are found. The iron and steel industry is still important, but light industries (including textiles, chemicals and food products) are growing. Luxembourg is a major banking centre. Main trading partners are Belgium, Germany and France.

MACEDONIA (F.Y.R.O.M.)
Republic of Macedonia

Area Sq Km	25 713	Languages	Macedonian, Albanian, Turkish
Area Sq Miles	9 928	Religions	Macedonian Orthodox, Sunni Muslim
Population	2 056 000	Currency	Macedonian denar
Capital	Skopje	Organizations	UN

Map page 115

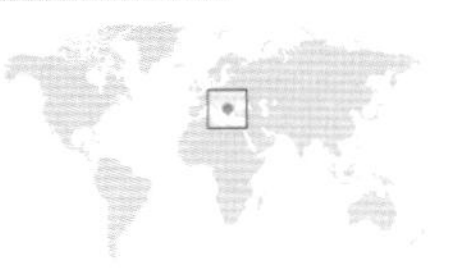

The Former Yugoslav Republic of Macedonia is a landlocked state in southern Europe. Lying within the southern Balkan Mountains, it is traversed northwest-southeast by the Vardar valley. The climate is continental. The economy is based on industry, mining and agriculture, but conflicts in the region have reduced trade and caused economic difficulties. Foreign aid and loans are now assisting in modernization and development of the country.

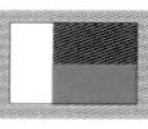

MADAGASCAR
Republic of Madagascar

Area Sq Km	587 041	Languages	Malagasy, French
Area Sq Miles	226 658	Religions	Traditional beliefs, Christian, Sunni Muslim
Population	17 404 000	Currency	Malagasy franc
Capital	Antananarivo	Organizations	UN

Map page 123

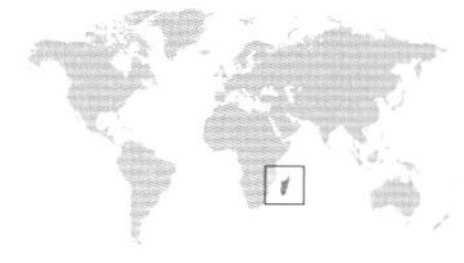

Madagascar lies off the east coast of southern Africa. The world's fourth largest island, it is mainly a high plateau, with a coastal strip to the east and scrubby plain to the west. The climate is tropical, with heavy rainfall in the north and east. Most of the population lives on the plateau. Although the amount of arable land is limited, the economy is based on agriculture. The main industries are agricultural processing, textile manufacturing and oil refining. Foreign aid is important. Exports include coffee, vanilla, cotton cloth, sugar and shrimps. France is the main trading partner.

MALAWI
Republic of Malawi

Area Sq Km	118 484	Languages	Chichewa, English, local languages
Area Sq Miles	45 747	Religions	Christian, traditional beliefs, Sunni Muslim
Population	12 105 000	Currency	Malawian kwacha
Capital	Lilongwe	Organizations	Comm., SADC, UN

Map page 123

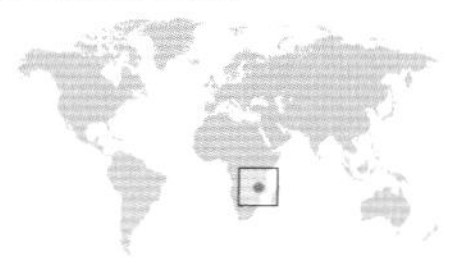

Landlocked Malawi in central Africa is a narrow hilly country at the southern end of the Great Rift Valley. One-fifth is covered by Lake Nyasa. Most of the population lives in rural areas in the southern regions. The climate is mainly subtropical, with varying rainfall. The economy is predominantly agricultural, with tobacco, tea and sugar the main exports. Malawi is one of the world's least developed countries and relies heavily on foreign aid. South Africa is the main trading partner.

MALAYSIA
Federation of Malaysia

Area Sq Km	332 965	Languages	Malay, English, Chinese, Tamil, local languages
Area Sq Miles	128 559	Religions	Sunni Muslim, Buddhist, Hindu, Christian, traditional beliefs
Population	24 425 000	Currency	Ringgit
Capital	Kuala Lumpur/ Putrajaya	Organizations	APEC, ASEAN, Comm., UN

Map page 99

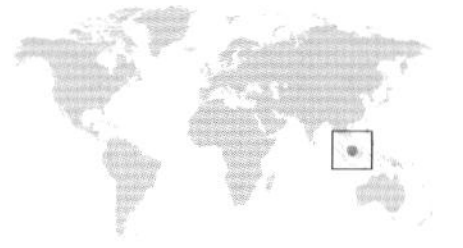

Malaysia, in southeast Asia, comprises two regions, separated by the South China Sea. The western region occupies the southern Malay Peninsula, which has a chain of mountains dividing the eastern coastal strip from wider plains to the west. East Malaysia, consisting of the states of Sabah and Sarawak in the north of the island of Borneo, is mainly rainforest-covered hills and mountains with mangrove swamps along the coast. Both regions have a tropical climate with heavy rainfall. About eighty per cent of the population lives in Peninsular Malaysia. The country is rich in natural resources and has reserves of minerals and fuels. It is an important producer of tin, oil, natural gas and tropical hardwoods. Agriculture remains a substantial part of the economy, but industry is the most important sector. The main exports are transport and electronic equipment, oil, chemicals, palm oil, wood and rubber. The main trading partners are Japan, the USA and Singapore.

MALDIVES
Republic of the Maldives

Area Sq Km	298	Languages	Divehi (Maldivian)
Area Sq Miles	115	Religions	Sunni Muslim
Population	318 000	Currency	Rufiyaa
Capital	Male	Organizations	Comm., UN

Map page 74

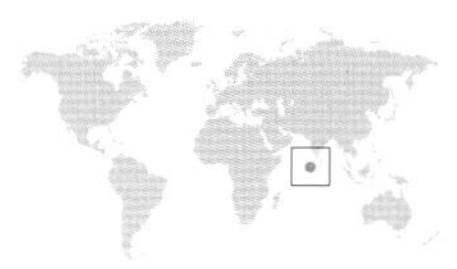

The Maldive archipelago comprises over a thousand coral atolls (around two hundred of which are inhabited), in the Indian Ocean, southwest of India. Over eighty per cent of the land area is less than one metre above sea level. The main atolls are North and South Male and Addu. The climate is hot, humid and monsoonal. There is little cultivation and almost all food is imported. Tourism has expanded rapidly and is the most important sector of the economy.

MALI
Republic of Mali

Area Sq Km	1 240 140	Languages	French, Bambara, local languages
Area Sq Miles	478 821	Religions	Sunni Muslim, traditional beliefs, Christian
Population	13 007 000	Currency	CFA franc
Capital	Bamako	Organizations	UN

Map page 120

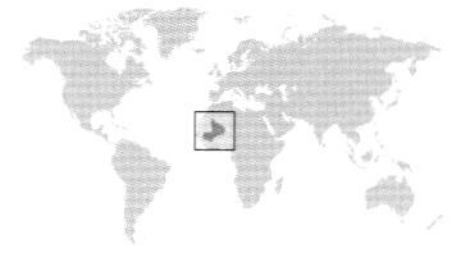

A landlocked state in west Africa, Mali is low-lying, with a few rugged hills in the northeast. Northern regions lie within the Sahara desert. To the south, around the Niger river, are marshes and savanna grassland. Rainfall is unreliable. Most of the population lives along the Niger and Falémé rivers. Exports include cotton, livestock and gold. Mali is one of the least developed countries in the world and relies heavily on foreign aid.

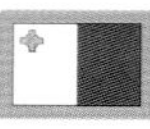

MALTA
Republic of Malta

Area Sq Km	316	Languages	Maltese, English
Area Sq Miles	122	Religions	Roman Catholic
Population	394 000	Currency	Maltese lira
Capital	Valletta	Organizations	Comm., EU, UN

Map page 114

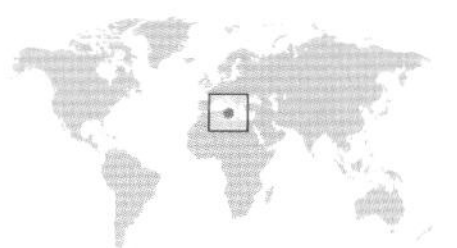

The islands of Malta and Gozo lie in the Mediterranean Sea, off the coast of southern Italy. The islands have hot, dry summers and mild winters. The economy depends on foreign trade, tourism and the manufacture of electronics and textiles. Main trading partners are the USA, France and Italy. Malta joined the European Union in May 2004.

MARSHALL ISLANDS
Republic of the Marshall Islands

Area Sq Km	181	Languages	English, Marshallese
Area Sq Miles	70	Religions	Protestant, Roman Catholic
Population	53 000	Currency	United States dollar
Capital	Delap-Uliga-Djarrit	Organizations	UN

Map page 67

The Marshall Islands consist of over a thousand atolls, islands and islets, within two chains in the north Pacific Ocean. The main atolls are Majuro (home to half the population), Kwajalein, Jaluit, Enewetak and Bikini. The climate is tropical, with heavy autumn rainfall. About half the workforce is employed in farming or fishing. Tourism is a small source of foreign exchange and the islands depend heavily on aid from the USA.

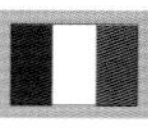

Martinique
French Overseas Department

Area Sq Km	1 079	Languages	French, Creole
Area Sq Miles	417	Religions	Roman Catholic, traditional beliefs
Population	393 000	Currency	Euro
Capital	Fort-de-France		

Map page 149

Martinique, one of the Caribbean Windward Islands, has volcanic peaks in the north, a populous central plain, and hills and beaches in the south. Tourism is a major source of foreign exchange, and substantial aid is received from France. The main trading partners are France and Guadeloupe.

MAURITANIA
Islamic Arab and African Republic of Mauritania

Area Sq Km	1 030 700	Languages	Arabic, French, local languages
Area Sq Miles	397 955	Religions	Sunni Muslim
Population	2 893 000	Currency	Ouguiya
Capital	Nouakchott	Organizations	UN

Map page 120

Mauritania is on the Atlantic coast of northwest Africa and lies almost entirely within the Sahara desert. Oases and a fertile strip along the Senegal river to the south are the only areas suitable for cultivation. The climate is generally hot and dry. About a quarter of Mauritanians live in the capital, Nouakchott. Most of the workforce depends on livestock rearing and subsistence farming. There are large deposits of iron ore which account for more than half of total exports. Mauritania's coastal waters are among the richest fishing grounds in the world. The main trading partners are France, Japan and Italy.

MAURITIUS
Republic of Mauritius

Area Sq Km	2 040	Languages	English, Creole, Hindi, Bhojpurī, French
Area Sq Miles	788	Religions	Hindu, Roman Catholic, Sunni Muslim
Population	1 221 000	Currency	Mauritius rupee
Capital	Port Louis	Organizations	Comm., SADC, UN

Map page 119

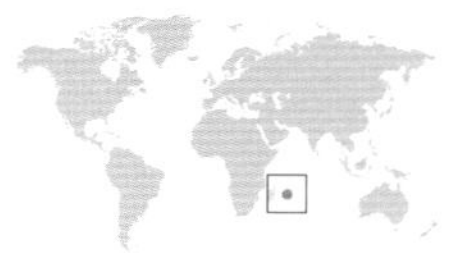

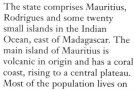

The state comprises Mauritius, Rodrigues and some twenty small islands in the Indian Ocean, east of Madagascar. The main island of Mauritius is volcanic in origin and has a coral coast, rising to a central plateau. Most of the population lives on the north and west sides of the island. The climate is warm and humid. The economy is based on sugar production, light manufacturing (chiefly clothing) and tourism.

Mayotte
French Departmental Collectivity

Area Sq Km	373	Languages	French, Mahorian
Area Sq Miles	144	Religions	Sunni Muslim, Christian
Population	170 879	Currency	Euro
Capital	Dzaoudzi		

Map page 123

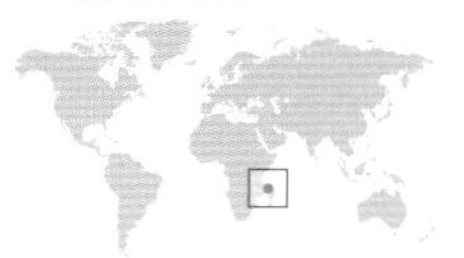

Lying in the Indian Ocean off the east coast of central Africa, Mayotte is geographically part of the Comoro archipelago. The economy is based on agriculture, but Mayotte depends heavily on aid from France.

MEXICO
United Mexican States

Area Sq Km	1 972 545	Languages	Spanish, Amerindian languages
Area Sq Miles	761 604	Religions	Roman Catholic, Protestant
Population	103 457 000	Currency	Mexican peso
Capital	Mexico City	Organizations	APEC, OECD, UN

Map page 150–151

The largest country in Central America, Mexico extends south from the USA to Guatemala and Belize, and from the Pacific Ocean to the Gulf of Mexico. The greater part of the country is high plateau flanked by the western and eastern ranges of the Sierra Madre mountains. The principal lowland is the Yucatán peninsula in the southeast. The climate varies with latitude and altitude: hot and humid in the lowlands, warm on the plateau and cool with cold winters in the mountains. The north is arid, while the far south has heavy rainfall. Mexico City is the second largest conurbation in the world and the country's centre of trade and industry. Agriculture involves a fifth of the workforce; crops include grains, coffee, cotton and vegetables. Mexico is rich in minerals, including copper, zinc, lead, tin, sulphur, and silver. It is one of the world's largest producers of oil, from vast reserves in the Gulf of Mexico. The oil and petrochemical industries still dominate the economy, but a variety of manufactured goods are produced, including iron and steel, motor vehicles, textiles, chemicals and food and tobacco products. Tourism is growing in importance. Over three-quarters of all trade is with the USA.

MICRONESIA, FEDERATED STATES OF

Area Sq Km	701	Languages	English, Chuukese, Pohnpeian, local languages
Area Sq Miles	271	Religions	Roman Catholic, Protestant
Population	109 000	Currency	United States dollar
Capital	Palikir	Organizations	UN

Map page 66–67

Micronesia comprises over six hundred atolls and islands of the Caroline Islands in the north Pacific Ocean. A third of the population lives on Pohnpei. The climate is tropical, with heavy rainfall. Fishing and subsistence farming are the main activities. Fish, garments and bananas are the main exports. Income is also derived from tourism and the licensing of foreign fishing fleets. The islands depend heavily on aid from the USA.

MOLDOVA
Republic of Moldova

Area Sq Km	33 700	Languages	Romanian, Ukrainian, Gagauz, Russian
Area Sq Miles	13 012	Religions	Romanian Orthodox, Russian Orthodox
Population	4 267 000	Currency	Moldovan leu
Capital	Chişinău (Kishinev)	Organizations	CIS, UN

Map page 117

Moldova lies between Romania and Ukraine in eastern Europe. It consists of hilly steppe land, drained by the Prut and Dniester rivers. Moldova has no mineral resources, and the economy is mainly agricultural, with sugar beet, tobacco, wine and fruit the chief products. Food processing, machinery and textiles are the main industries. The Russian Federation is the main trading partner.

MONACO
Principality of Monaco

Area Sq Km	2	Languages	French, Monégasque, Italian
Area Sq Miles	1	Religions	Roman Catholic
Population	34 000	Currency	Euro
Capital	Monaco-Ville	Organizations	UN

Map page 110

The principality occupies a rocky peninsula and a strip of land on France's Mediterranean coast. Monaco's economy depends on service industries (chiefly tourism, banking and finance) and light industry.

MONGOLIA

Area Sq Km	1 565 000	Languages	Khalka (Mongolian), Kazakh, local languages
Area Sq Miles	604 250	Religions	Buddhist, Sunni Muslim
Population	2 594 000	Currency	Tugrik (tögrög)
Capital	Ulan Bator (Ulaanbaatar)	Organizations	UN

Map page 90

Mongolia is a landlocked country in eastern Asia between the Russian Federation and China. Much of it is high steppe land, with mountains and lakes in the west and north. In the south is the Gobi desert. Mongolia has long, cold winters and short, mild summers. A quarter of the population lives in the capital, Ulaanbaatar. Livestock breeding and agricultural processing are important. There are substantial mineral resources. Copper and textiles are the main exports. China and the Russian Federation are the main trading partners.

Montserrat
United Kingdom Overseas Territory

Area Sq Km	100	Languages	English
Area Sq Miles	39	Religions	Protestant, Roman Catholic
Population	4 000	Currency	East Caribbean dollar
Capital	Plymouth	Organizations	CARICOM

Map page 149

An island in the Leeward Islands group in the Lesser Antilles, in the Caribbean. From 1995 to 1997 the volcanoes in the Soufrière Hills erupted for the first time since 1630. Over sixty per cent of the island was covered in volcanic ash and the capital was virtually destroyed. Many people emigrated, and the remaining population moved to the north of the island. Reconstruction is being funded by aid from the UK.

MOROCCO
Kingdom of Morocco

Area Sq Km	446 550	Languages	Arabic, Berber, French
Area Sq Miles	172 414	Religions	Sunni Muslim
Population	30 566 000	Currency	Moroccan dirham
Capital	Rabat	Organizations	UN

Map page 120

Lying in the northwest corner of Africa, Morocco has both Atlantic and Mediterranean coasts. The Atlas Mountains separate the arid south and disputed region of western Sahara from the fertile regions of the west and north, which have a milder climate. Most Moroccans live on the Atlantic coastal plain. The economy is based on agriculture, phosphate mining and tourism; the most important industries are food processing, textiles and chemicals. France is the main trading partner.

MOZAMBIQUE
Republic of Mozambique

Area Sq Km	799 380	Languages	Portuguese, Makua, Tsonga, local languages
Area Sq Miles	308 642	Religions	Traditional beliefs, Roman Catholic, Sunni Muslim
Population	18 863 000	Currency	Metical
Capital	Maputo	Organizations	Comm., SADC, UN

Map page 123

Mozambique lies on the east coast of southern Africa. The land is mainly a savanna plateau drained by the Zambezi and Limpopo rivers, with highlands to the north. Most of the population lives on the coast or in the river valleys. In general the climate is tropical with winter rainfall, but droughts occur. The economy is based on subsistence agriculture. Exports include shrimps, cashews, cotton and sugar, but Mozambique relies heavily on aid, and remains one of the least developed countries in the world.

MYANMAR (Burma)
Union of Myanmar

Area Sq Km	676 577	Languages	Burmese, Shan, Karen, local languages
Area Sq Miles	261 228	Religions	Buddhist, Christian, Sunni Muslim
Population	49 485 000	Currency	Kyat
Capital	Rangoon (Yangôn)	Organizations	ASEAN, UN

Map page 91

Myanmar (Burma) is in southeast Asia, bordering the Bay of Bengal and the Andaman Sea. Most of the population lives in the valley and delta of the Irrawaddy river, which is flanked by mountains and high plateaus. The climate is hot and monsoonal, and rainforest covers much of the land. Most of the workforce is employed in agriculture. Myanmar is rich in minerals, including zinc, lead, copper and silver. Political and social unrest and lack of foreign investment have affected economic development.

NAMIBIA
Republic of Namibia

Area Sq Km	824 292	Languages	English, Afrikaans, German, Ovambo, local languages
Area Sq Miles	318 261	Religions	Protestant, Roman Catholic
Population	1 987 000	Currency	Namibian dollar
Capital	Windhoek	Organizations	Comm., SADC, UN

Map page 123

Namibia lies on the Atlantic coast of southern Africa. Mountain ranges separate the coastal Namib Desert from the interior plateau, bordered to the south and east by the Kalahari Desert. The country is hot and dry, but some summer rain in the north supports crops and livestock. Most of the workforce is employed in agriculture, although the economy is based on mineral extraction – predominantly diamonds, but also uranium, lead, zinc and silver. Fishing is increasingly important. The economy is closely linked to that of the Republic of South Africa.

NAURU
Republic of Nauru

Area Sq Km	21	Languages	Nauruan, English
Area Sq Miles	8	Religions	Protestant, Roman Catholic
Population	13 000	Currency	Australian dollar
Capital	Yaren	Organizations	Comm., UN

Map page 69

Nauru is a coral island near the Equator in the Pacific Ocean. It has a fertile coastal strip and a barren central plateau. The climate is tropical. The economy is based on phosphate mining, but reserves are near exhaustion and replacement of this income is a serious long-term problem.

NEPAL
Kingdom of Nepal

Area Sq Km	147 181	Languages	Nepali, Maithili, Bhojpuri, English, local languages
Area Sq Miles	56 827	Religions	Hindu, Buddhist, Sunni Muslim
Population	25 164 000	Currency	Nepalese rupee
Capital	Kathmandu	Organizations	UN

Map page 88–89

Nepal lies in the eastern Himalaya mountains between India and China. High mountains (including Everest) dominate the north. Most people live in the temperate central valleys and subtropical southern plains. The economy is based largely on agriculture and forestry. There is some manufacturing, chiefly of textiles and carpets, and tourism is important. Nepal relies heavily on foreign aid.

NETHERLANDS
Kingdom of the Netherlands

Area Sq Km	41 526	Languages	Dutch, Frisian
Area Sq Miles	16 033	Religions	Roman Catholic, Protestant, Sunni Muslim
Population	16 149 000	Currency	Euro
Capital	Amsterdam/ The Hague	Organizations	EU, OECD, UN

Map page 108

The Netherlands lies on the North Sea coast of western Europe. Apart from low hills in the far southeast, the land is flat and low-lying, much of it below sea level. The coastal region includes the delta of five rivers and dykes (reclaimed land), protected by sand dunes, dykes and canals. The climate is temperate, with cool summers and mild winters. Rainfall is spread evenly throughout the year. The Netherlands is a densely populated and highly urbanized country, with the majority of the population living in the cities of Amsterdam, Rotterdam and The Hague. Horticulture and dairy farming are important activities, although they employ less than four per cent of the workforce. The Netherlands ranks as the world's third agricultural exporter, and is a leading producer and exporter of natural gas from reserves in the North Sea. The economy is based mainly on international trade and manufacturing industry. The main industries produce food products, chemicals, machinery, electrical and electronic goods and transport equipment. Germany is the main trading partner, followed by other European Union countries.

Netherlands Antilles
Self-governing Netherlands Territory

Area Sq Km	800	Languages	Dutch, Papiamento, English
Area Sq Miles	309	Religions	Roman Catholic, Protestant
Population	221 000	Currency	Netherlands Antilles guilder
Capital	Willemstad		

Map page 157

The territory comprises two separate island groups: Curaçao and Bonaire off the northern coast of Venezuela, and Saba, Sint Eustatius and the southern part of St Martin (Sint Maarten) in the Lesser Antilles. Tourism, oil refining and offshore finance are the mainstays of the economy. The main trading partners are the USA, Venezuela and Mexico.

New Caledonia
French Overseas Country

Area Sq Km	19 058	Languages	French, local languages
Area Sq Miles	7 358	Religions	Roman Catholic, Protestant, Sunni Muslim
Population	228 000	Currency	CFP franc
Capital	Nouméa		

Map page 69

An island group lying in the southwest Pacific, with a sub-tropical climate. New Caledonia has over one-fifth of the world's nickel reserves, and the main economic activity is metal mining. Tourism is also important. New Caledonia relies on aid from France.

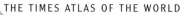

NEW ZEALAND

Area Sq Km	270 534	Languages	English, Maori
Area Sq Miles	104 454	Religions	Protestant, Roman Catholic
Population	3 875 000	Currency	New Zealand dollar
Capital	Wellington	Organizations	APEC, Comm., OECD, UN

Map page 72

New Zealand comprises two main islands separated by the narrow Cook Strait, and a number of smaller islands. North Island, where three-quarters of the population lives, has mountain ranges, broad fertile valleys and a central plateau with hot springs and active volcanoes. South Island is also mountainous, with the Southern Alps running its entire length. The only major lowland area is the Canterbury Plains in the centre-east. The climate is generally temperate, although South Island has colder winters. Farming is the mainstay of the economy. New Zealand is one of the world's leading producers of meat (beef, lamb and mutton), wool and dairy products; fruit and fish are also important. Hydroelectric and geothermal power provide much of the country's energy needs. Other industries produce timber, wood pulp, iron, aluminium, machinery and chemicals. Tourism is the fastest growing sector of the economy. The main trading partners are Australia, the USA and Japan.

NICARAGUA
Republic of Nicaragua

Area Sq Km	130 000	Languages	Spanish, Amerindian languages
Area Sq Miles	50 193	Religions	Roman Catholic, Protestant
Population	5 466 000	Currency	Córdoba
Capital	Managua	Organizations	UN

Map page 150

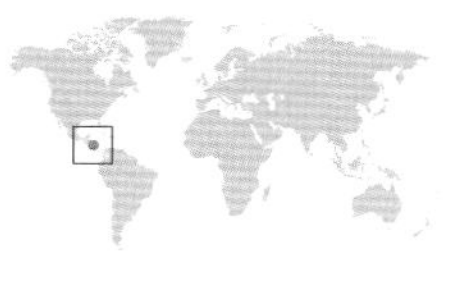

Nicaragua lies at the heart of Central America, with both Pacific and Caribbean coasts. Mountain ranges separate the east, which is largely rainforest, from the more developed western regions, which include Lake Nicaragua and some active volcanoes. The highest land is in the north. The climate is tropical. Nicaragua is one of the western hemisphere's poorest countries, and the economy is largely agricultural. Exports include coffee, seafood, cotton and bananas. The USA is the main trading partner. Nicaragua has a huge national debt, and relies heavily on foreign aid.

NIGER
Republic of Niger

Area Sq Km	1 267 000	Languages	French, Hausa, Fulani, local languages
Area Sq Miles	489 191	Religions	Sunni Muslim, traditional beliefs
Population	11 972 000	Currency	CFA franc
Capital	Niamey	Organizations	UN

Map page 120–121

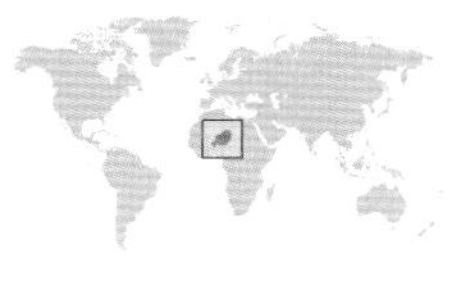

A landlocked state of west Africa, Niger lies mostly within the Sahara desert, but with savanna in the south and in the Niger valley area. The mountains of the Massif de l'Aïr dominate central regions. Much of the country is hot and dry. The south has some summer rainfall, although droughts occur. The economy depends on subsistence farming and herding, and uranium exports, but Niger is one of the world's least developed countries and relies heavily on foreign aid. France is the main trading partner.

NIGERIA
Federal Republic of Nigeria

Area Sq Km	923 768	Languages	English, Hausa, Yoruba, Ibo, Fulani, local languages
Area Sq Miles	356 669	Religions	Sunni Muslim, Christian, traditional beliefs
Population	124 009 000	Currency	Naira
Capital	Abuja	Organizations	Comm., OPEC, UN

Map page 120–121

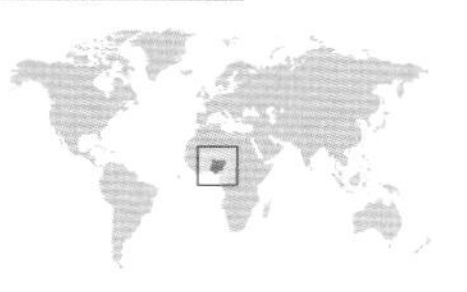

Nigeria is in west Africa, on the Gulf of Guinea, and is the most populous country in Africa. The Niger delta dominates coastal areas, fringed with sandy beaches, mangrove swamps and lagoons. Inland is a belt of rainforest which gives way to woodland or savanna on high plateaus. The far north is the semi-desert edge of the Sahara. The climate is tropical, with heavy summer rainfall in the south but low rainfall in the north. Most of the population lives in the coastal lowlands or in the west. About half the workforce is involved in agriculture, mainly growing subsistence crops. Agricultural production, however, has failed to keep up with demand, and Nigeria is now a net importer of food. Cocoa and rubber are the only significant export crops. The economy is heavily dependent on vast oil resources in the Niger delta and in shallow offshore waters, and oil accounts for over ninety per cent of export earnings. Nigeria also has natural gas reserves and some mineral deposits, but these are largely undeveloped. Industry involves mainly oil refining, chemicals (chiefly fertilizers), agricultural processing, textiles, steel manufacture and vehicle assembly. Political instability in the past has left Nigeria with heavy debts, poverty and unemployment.

Niue
Self-governing New Zealand Territory

Area Sq Km	258	Languages	English, Polynesian
Area Sq Miles	100	Religions	Christian
Population	2 000	Currency	New Zealand dollar
Capital	Alofi		

Map page 69

Niue, one of the largest coral islands in the world, lies in the south Pacific Ocean about 500 kilometres (300 miles) east of Tonga. The economy depends on aid and remittances from New Zealand. The population is declining because of migration to New Zealand.

Norfolk Island
Australian External Territory

Area Sq Km	35	Languages	English
Area Sq Miles	14	Religions	Protestant, Roman Catholic
Population	2 037	Currency	Australian dollar
Capital	Kingston		

Map page 69

In the south Pacific Ocean, Norfolk Island lies between Vanuatu and New Zealand. Tourism has increased steadily and is the mainstay of the economy and provides revenues for agricultural development.

Northern Mariana Islands
United States Commonwealth

Area Sq Km	477	Languages	English, Chamorro, local languages
Area Sq Miles	184	Religions	Roman Catholic
Population	79 000	Currency	United States dollar
Capital	Capitol Hill		

Map page 91

A chain of islands in the northwest Pacific Ocean, extending over 550 kilometres (350 miles) north to south. The main island is Saipan. Tourism is a major industry, employing approximately half the workforce.

NORTH KOREA
People's Democratic Republic of Korea

Area Sq Km	120 538	Languages	Korean
Area Sq Miles	46 540	Religions	Traditional beliefs, Chondoist, Buddhist
Population	22 664 000	Currency	North Korean won
Capital	P'yŏngyang	Organizations	UN

Map page 96

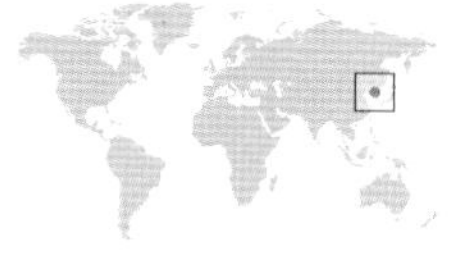

Occupying the northern half of the Korean peninsula in eastern Asia, North Korea is a rugged and mountainous country. The principal lowlands and the main agricultural areas are the plains in the southwest. More than half the population lives in urban areas, mainly on the coastal plains. North Korea has a continental climate, with cold, dry winters and hot, wet summers. Approximately one-third of the workforce is involved in agriculture, mainly growing food crops on cooperative farms. Various minerals, notably iron ore, are mined and are the basis of the country's heavy industries. Exports include minerals (lead, magnesite and zinc) and metal products (chiefly iron and steel). The economy declined after 1991, when ties to the former USSR and eastern bloc collapsed, and there have been serious food shortages

NORWAY
Kingdom of Norway

Area Sq Km	323 878	Languages	Norwegian
Area Sq Miles	125 050	Religions	Protestant, Roman Catholic
Population	4 533 000	Currency	Norwegian krone
Capital	Oslo	Organizations	NATO, OECD, UN

Map page 102–103

Norway stretches along the north and west coasts of Scandinavia, from the Arctic Ocean to the North Sea. Its extensive coastline is indented with fjords and fringed with many islands. Inland, the terrain is mountainous, with coniferous forests and lakes in the south. The only major lowland areas are along the southern North Sea and Skagerrak coasts, where most of the population lives. The climate is modified by the effect of the North Atlantic Drift ocean current. Norway has vast petroleum and natural gas resources in the North Sea. It is one of western Europe's leading producers of oil and gas, and exports of oil account for approximately half of total export earnings. Related industries include engineering (oil and gas platforms) and petrochemicals. More traditional industries process local raw materials, particularly fish, timber and minerals. Agriculture is limited, but fishing and fish farming are important. Norway is the world's leading exporter of farmed salmon. Merchant shipping and tourism are major sources of foreign exchange.

OMAN
Sultanate of Oman

Area Sq Km	309 500	Languages	Arabic, Baluchi, Indian languages
Area Sq Miles	119 499	Religions	Ibadhi Muslim, Sunni Muslim
Population	2 851 000	Currency	Omani riyal
Capital	Muscat (Masqaṭ)	Organizations	UN

Map page 86

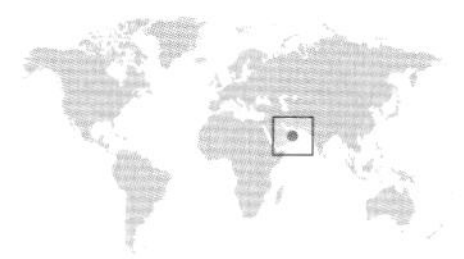

In southwest Asia, Oman occupies the east and southeast coasts of the Arabian Peninsula and an enclave north of the United Arab Emirates. Most of the land is desert, with mountains in the north and south. The climate is hot and mainly dry. Most of the population lives on the coastal strip on the Gulf of Oman. The majority depend on farming and fishing, but the oil and gas industries dominate the economy with around eighty per cent of export revenues coming from oil.

PAKISTAN
Islamic Republic of Pakistan

Area Sq Km	803 940	Languages	Urdu, Punjabi, Sindhi, Pushtu, English
Area Sq Miles	310 403	Religions	Sunni Muslim, Shi'a Muslim, Christian, Hindu
Population	153 578 000	Currency	Pakistani rupee
Capital	Islamabad	Organizations	Comm., UN

Map page 85

Pakistan is in the northwest part of the Indian subcontinent in south Asia, on the Arabian Sea. The east and south are dominated by the great basin of the Indus river system. This is the main agricultural area and contains most of the predominantly rural population. To the north the land rises to the mountains of the Karakoram, Hindu Kush and Himalaya mountains. The west is semi-desert plateaus and mountain ranges. The climate ranges between dry desert, and arctic tundra on the mountain tops. Temperatures are generally warm and rainfall is monsoonal. Agriculture is the main sector of the economy, employing approximately half of the workforce, and is based on extensive irrigation schemes. Pakistan is one of the world's leading producers of cotton and a major exporter of rice. Pakistan produces natural gas and has a variety of mineral deposits including coal and gold, but they are little developed. The main industries are textiles and clothing manufacture and food processing, with fabrics and ready-made clothing the leading exports. Pakistan also produces leather goods, fertilizers, chemicals, paper and precision instruments. The country depends heavily on foreign aid and remittances from workers abroad.

PALAU
Republic of Palau

Area Sq Km	497	Languages	Palauan, English
Area Sq Miles	192	Religions	Roman Catholic, Protestant, traditional beliefs
Population	20 000	Currency	United States dollar
Capital	Koror	Organizations	UN

Map page 91

Palau comprises over three hundred islands in the western Caroline Islands, in the west Pacific Ocean. The climate is tropical. The economy is based on farming, fishing and tourism, but Palau is heavily dependent on aid from the USA.

PANAMA
Republic of Panama

Area Sq Km	77 082	Languages	Spanish, English, Amerindian languages
Area Sq Miles	29 762	Religions	Roman Catholic, Protestant, Sunni Muslim
Population	3 120 000	Currency	Balboa
Capital	Panama City	Organizations	UN

Map page 150

Panama is the most southerly state in central America and has Pacific and Caribbean coasts. It is hilly, with mountains in the west and jungle near the Colombian border. The climate is tropical. Most of the population lives on the drier Pacific side. The economy is based mainly on services related to the Panama Canal: shipping, banking and tourism. Exports include bananas, shrimps, coffee, clothing and fish products. The USA is the main trading partner.

PAPUA NEW GUINEA
Independent State of Papua New Guinea

Area Sq Km	462 840	Languages	English, Tok Pisin (Creole), local languages
Area Sq Miles	178 704	Religions	Protestant, Roman Catholic, traditional beliefs
Population	5 711 000	Currency	Kina
Capital	Port Moresby	Organizations	Comm., UN

Map page 68

Papua New Guinea occupies the eastern half of the island of New Guinea and includes many island groups. It has a forested and mountainous interior, bordered by swampy plains, and a tropical monsoon climate. Most of the workforce are farmers. Timber, copra, coffee and cocoa are important, but exports are dominated by minerals, chiefly gold and copper. The country depends on foreign aid. Australia, Japan and Singapore are the main trading partners.

PARAGUAY
Republic of Paraguay

Area Sq Km	406 752	Languages	Spanish, Guaraní
Area Sq Miles	157 048	Religions	Roman Catholic, Protestant
Population	5 878 000	Currency	Guaraní
Capital	Asunción	Organizations	UN

Map page 156

Paraguay is a landlocked country in central South America, bordering Bolivia, Brazil and Argentina. The Paraguay river separates a sparsely populated western zone of marsh and flat alluvial plains from a more developed, hilly and forested region to the east and south. The climate is subtropical. Virtually all electricity is produced by hydroelectric plants, and surplus power is exported to Brazil and Argentina. The hydroelectric dam at Itaipú is one of the largest in the world. The mainstay of the economy is agriculture and related industries. Exports include cotton, soya bean and edible oil products, timber and meat. Brazil and Argentina are the main trading partners.

PERU
Republic of Peru

Area Sq Km	1 285 216	Languages	Spanish, Quechua, Aymara
Area Sq Miles	496 225	Religions	Roman Catholic, Protestant
Population	27 167 000	Currency	Sol
Capital	Lima	Organizations	APEC, UN

Map page 154

Peru lies on the Pacific coast of South America. Most Peruvians live on the coastal strip and on the plateaus of the high Andes mountains. East of the Andes is the Amazon rainforest. The coast is temperate with low rainfall while the east is hot, humid and wet. Agriculture involves one-third of the workforce and fishing is also important. Agriculture and fishing have both been disrupted by the El Niño climatic effect in recent years. Sugar, cotton, coffee and, illegally, coca are the main cash crops. Copper and copper products, fishmeal, zinc products, coffee, petroleum and its products, and textiles are the main exports. The USA and the European Union are the main trading partners.

PHILIPPINES
Republic of the Philippines

Area Sq Km	300 000	Languages	English, Filipino, Tagalog, Cebuano, local languages
Area Sq Miles	115 831	Religions	Roman Catholic, Protestant, Sunni Muslim, Aglipayan
Population	79 999 000	Currency	Philippine peso
Capital	Manila	Organizations	APEC, ASEAN, UN

Map page 97

The Philippines, in southeast Asia, consists of over seven thousand islands and atolls lying between the South China Sea and the Pacific Ocean. The islands of Luzon and Mindanao account for two-thirds of the land area. They and nine other fairly large islands are mountainous and forested. There are active volcanoes, and earthquakes and tropical storms are common. Most of the population lives in the plains on the larger islands or on the coastal strips. The climate is hot and humid with heavy monsoonal rainfall. Rice, coconuts, sugar cane, pineapples and bananas are the main agricultural crops, and fishing is also important. Main exports are electronic equipment, machinery and transport equipment, garments and coconut products. Foreign aid and remittances from workers abroad are important to the economy, which faces problems of high population growth rate and high unemployment. The USA and Japan are the main trading partners.

Pitcairn Islands
United Kingdom Overseas Territory

Area Sq Km	45	Languages	English
Area Sq Miles	17	Religions	Protestant
Population	51	Currency	New Zealand dollar
Capital	Adamstown		

Map page 67

An island group in the southeast Pacific Ocean consisting of Pitcairn Island and three uninhabited islands. It was originally settled by mutineers from HMS Bounty in 1790.

POLAND
Polish Republic

Area Sq Km	312 683	Languages	Polish, German
Area Sq Miles	120 728	Religions	Roman Catholic, Polish Orthodox
Population	38 587 000	Currency	Złoty
Capital	Warsaw (Warszawa)	Organizations	EU, NATO, OECD, UN

Map page 112–113

Poland lies on the Baltic coast of eastern Europe. The Oder (Odra) and Vistula (Wisła) river deltas dominate the coast. Inland, much of the country is low-lying, with woods and lakes. In the south the land rises to the Sudeten Mountains and the western part of the Carpathian Mountains, which form the borders with the Czech Republic and Slovakia respectively. The climate is continental. Around a quarter of the workforce is involved in agriculture, and exports include livestock products and sugar. The economy is heavily industrialized, with mining and manufacturing accounting for forty per cent of national income. Poland is one of the world's major producers of coal, and also produces copper, zinc, lead, sulphur and natural gas. The main industries are machinery and transport equipment, shipbuilding, and metal and chemical production. Exports include machinery and transport equipment, manufactured goods, food and live animals. Germany is the main trading partner. Poland joined the European Union in May 2004.

PORTUGAL
Portuguese Republic

Area Sq Km	88 940	Languages	Portuguese
Area Sq Miles	34 340	Religions	Roman Catholic, Protestant
Population	10 062 000	Currency	Euro
Capital	Lisbon (Lisboa)	Organizations	EU, NATO, OECD, UN

Map page 111

Portugal lies in the western part of the Iberian peninsula in southwest Europe, has an Atlantic coastline and is bordered by Spain to the north and east. The island groups of the Azores and Madeira are parts of Portugal. On the mainland, the land north of the river Tagus (Tejo) is mostly highland, with extensive forests of pine and cork. South of the river is undulating lowland. The climate in the north is cool and moist; the south is warmer, with dry, mild winters. Most Portuguese live near the coast, and more than one-third of the total population lives around the capital, Lisbon (Lisboa). Agriculture, fishing and forestry involve approximately ten per cent of the workforce. Mining and manufacturing are the main sectors of the economy. Portugal produces kaolin, copper, tin, zinc, tungsten and salt. Exports include textiles, clothing and footwear, electrical machinery and transport equipment, cork and wood products, and chemicals. Service industries, chiefly tourism and banking, are important to the economy, as are remittances from workers abroad. Most trade is with other European Union countries.

Puerto Rico
United States Commonwealth

Area Sq Km	9 104	Languages	Spanish, English
Area Sq Miles	3 515	Religions	Roman Catholic, Protestant
Population	3 879 000	Currency	United States dollar
Capital	San Juan		

Map page 149

The Caribbean island of Puerto Rico has a forested, hilly interior, coastal plains and a tropical climate. Half of the population lives in the San Juan area. The economy is based on manufacturing (chiefly chemicals, electronics and food), tourism and agriculture. The USA is the main trading partner.

QATAR
State of Qatar

Area Sq Km	11 437	Languages	Arabic
Area Sq Miles	4 416	Religions	Sunni Muslim
Population	610 000	Currency	Qatari riyal
Capital	Doha (Ad Dawḥah)	Organizations	OECD, UN

Map page 84

Qatar occupies a peninsula in southwest Asia that extends northwards from east-central Saudi Arabia into The Gulf. The land is flat and barren with sand dunes and salt pans. The climate is hot and mainly dry. Most people live in the area of the capital, Doha. The economy is heavily dependent on oil and natural gas production and the oil-refining industry. Income also comes from overseas investment. Japan is the largest trading partner.

Réunion
French Overseas Department

Area Sq Km	2 551	Languages	French, Creole
Area Sq Miles	985	Religions	Roman Catholic
Population	756 000	Currency	Euro
Capital	St-Denis		

Map page 119

The Indian Ocean island of Réunion is mountainous, with coastal lowlands and a warm climate. The economy depends on tourism, French aid, and exports of sugar. Several widely-dispersed and uninhabited islets to the west are administered from Réunion.

ROMANIA

Area Sq Km	237 500	Languages	Romanian, Hungarian
Area Sq Miles	91 699	Religions	Romanian Orthodox, Protestant, Roman Catholic
Population	22 334 000	Currency	Romanian leu
Capital	Bucharest (Bucureşti)	Organizations	NATO, UN

Map page 115

Romania lies in eastern Europe, on the northwest coast of the Black Sea. Mountains separate the Transylvanian Basin in the centre of the country from the populous plains of the east and south and from the Danube delta. The climate is continental. Romania has mineral resources (zinc, lead, silver and gold) and oil and natural gas reserves. Economic development has been slow and sporadic, but measures to accelerate change were introduced in 1999. Agriculture employs over one-third of the workforce. The main exports are textiles, mineral products, chemicals, machinery and footwear. The main trading partners are Germany and Italy.

RUSSIAN FEDERATION

Area Sq Km	17 075 400	Languages	Russian, Tatar, Ukrainian, local languages
Area Sq Miles	6 592 849	Religions	Russian Orthodox, Sunni Muslim, Protestant
Population	143 246 000	Currency	Russian rouble
Capital	Moscow (Moskva)	Organizations	APEC, CIS, UN

Map page 76–77

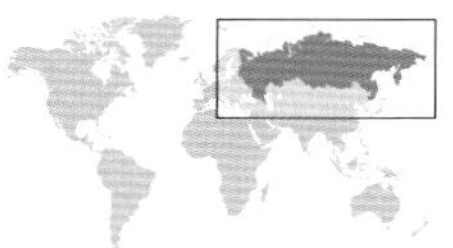

The Russian Federation occupies much of eastern Europe and all of northern Asia, and is the world's largest country. It borders fourteen countries to the west and south and has long coastlines on the Arctic and Pacific Oceans to the north and east. European Russia lies west of the Ural Mountains. To the south the land rises to uplands and the Caucasus mountains on the border with Georgia and Azerbaijan. East of the Urals lies the flat West Siberian Plain and the Central Siberian Plateau. In the south-east is Lake Baikal, the world's deepest lake, and the Sayan ranges on the border with Kazakhstan and Mongolia. Eastern Siberia is rugged and mountainous, with many active volcanoes in the Kamchatka Peninsula. The country's major rivers are the Volga in the west and the Ob', Irtysh, Yenisey, Lena and Amur in Siberia. The climate and vegetation range between arctic tundra in the north and semi-arid steppe towards the Black and Caspian Sea coasts in the south. In general, the climate is continental with extreme temperatures. The majority of the population (the eighth largest in the world), and industry and agriculture are concentrated in European Russia. The economy is dependent on exploitation of raw materials and on heavy industry. Russia has a wealth of mineral resources, although they are often difficult to exploit because of climate and remote locations. It is one of the world's leading producers of petroleum, natural gas and coal as well as iron ore, nickel, copper, bauxite, and many precious and rare metals. Forests cover over forty per cent of the land area and supply an important timber, paper and pulp industry. Approximately eight per cent of the land is suitable for cultivation, but farming is generally inefficient and food, especially grains, must be imported. Fishing is important and Russia has a large fleet operating around the world. The transition to a market economy has been slow and difficult, with considerable underemployment. As well as mining and extractive industries there is a wide range of manufacturing industry, from steel mills to aircraft and space vehicles, shipbuilding, synthetic fabrics, plastics, cotton fabrics, consumer durables, chemicals and fertilizers. Exports include fuels, metals, machinery, chemicals and forest products. The most important trading partners include Germany, the USA and Belarus.

RWANDA
Republic of Rwanda

Area Sq Km	26 338	Languages	Kinyarwanda, French, English
Area Sq Miles	10 169	Religions	Roman Catholic, traditional beliefs, Protestant
Population	8 387 000	Currency	Rwandan franc
Capital	Kigali	Organizations	UN

Map page 122

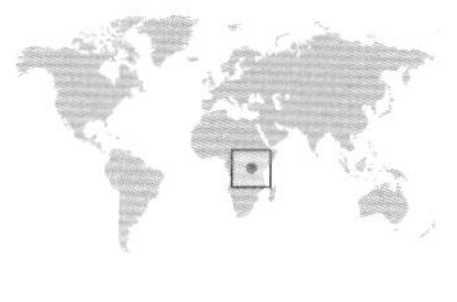

Rwanda, the most densely populated country in Africa, is situated in the mountains and plateaus to the east of the western branch of the Great Rift Valley in east Africa. The climate is warm with a summer dry season. Rwanda depends on subsistence farming, coffee and tea exports, light industry and foreign aid. The country is slowly recovering from serious internal conflict which caused devastation in the early 1990s.

St Helena and Dependencies
United Kingdom Overseas Territory

Area Sq Km	307	Languages	English
Area Sq Miles	119	Religions	Protestant, Roman Catholic
Population	7 050	Currency	St Helena pound, Pound sterling
Capital	Jamestown		

Map page 118 St Helena and its dependencies Ascension and Tristan da Cunha are isolated island groups lying in the south Atlantic Ocean. St Helena is a rugged island of volcanic origin. The main activity is fishing, but the economy relies on financial aid from the UK. Main trading partners are the UK and South Africa.

ST KITTS AND NEVIS
Federation of St Kitts and Nevis

Area Sq Km	261	Languages	English, Creole
Area Sq Miles	101	Religions	Protestant, Roman Catholic
Population	42 000	Currency	East Caribbean dollar
Capital	Basseterre	Organizations	CARICOM, Comm., UN

Map page 149

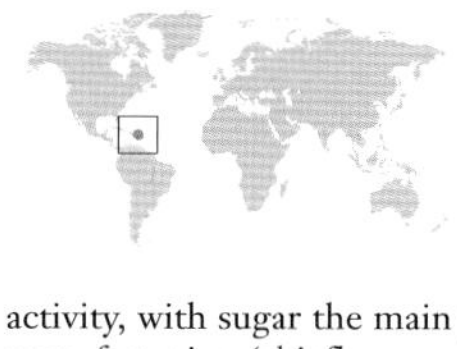

St Kitts and Nevis are in the Leeward Islands, in the Caribbean. Both volcanic islands are mountainous and forested, with sandy beaches and a warm, wet climate. About three-quarters of the population lives on St Kitts. Agriculture is the main activity, with sugar the main product. Tourism and manufacturing (chiefly garments and electronic components) and offshore banking are important activities.

ST LUCIA

Area Sq Km	616	Languages	English, Creole
Area Sq Miles	238	Religions	Roman Catholic, Protestant
Population	149 000	Currency	East Caribbean dollar
Capital	Castries	Organizations	CARICOM, Comm., UN

Map page 149

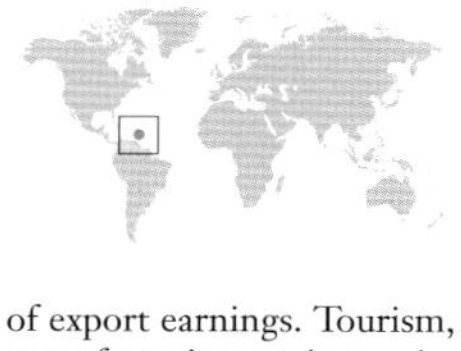

St Lucia, one of the Windward Islands in the Caribbean Sea, is a volcanic island with forested mountains, hot springs, sandy beaches and a wet tropical climate. Agriculture is the main activity, with bananas accounting for approximately forty per cent of export earnings. Tourism, agricultural processing and light manufacturing are increasingly important.

St Pierre and Miquelon
French Territorial Collectivity

Area Sq Km	242	Languages	French
Area Sq Miles	93	Religions	Roman Catholic
Population	6 000	Currency	Euro
Capital	St-Pierre		

Map page 129

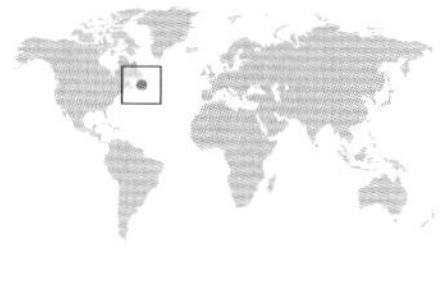

A group of islands off the south coast of Newfoundland in eastern Canada. The islands are largely unsuitable for agriculture, and fishing and fish processing are the most important activities. The islands rely heavily on financial assistance from France.

ST VINCENT AND THE GRENADINES

Area Sq Km	389	Languages	English, Creole
Area Sq Miles	150	Religions	Protestant, Roman Catholic
Population	120 000	Currency	East Caribbean dollar
Capital	Kingstown	Organizations	CARICOM, Comm., UN

Map page 149

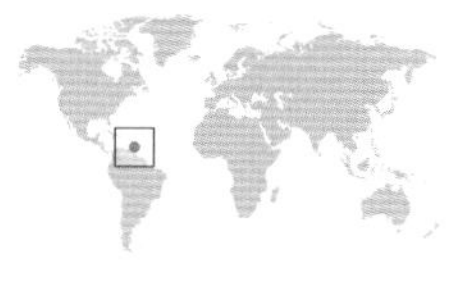

St Vincent, whose territory includes islets and cays in the Grenadines, is in the Windward Islands, in the Caribbean. St Vincent itself is forested and mountainous, with an active volcano, Soufrière. The climate is tropical and wet. The economy is based mainly on agriculture and tourism. Bananas account for approximately one-third of export earnings and arrowroot is also important. Most trade is with the USA and other CARICOM countries.

SAMOA
Independent State of Samoa

Area Sq Km	2 831	Languages	Samoan, English
Area Sq Miles	1 093	Religions	Protestant, Roman Catholic
Population	178 000	Currency	Tala
Capital	Apia	Organizations	Comm., UN

Map page 69

Samoa consists of two larger mountainous and forested islands, Savai'i and Upolu, and seven smaller islands, in the south Pacific Ocean. Over half the population lives on Upolu. The climate is tropical. The economy is based on agriculture, with some fishing and light manufacturing. Traditional exports are coconut products, fish and beer. Tourism is increasing, but the islands depend on workers' remittances and foreign aid.

SAN MARINO
Republic of San Marino

Area Sq Km	61	Languages	Italian
Area Sq Miles	24	Religions	Roman Catholic
Population	28 000	Currency	Euro
Capital	San Marino	Organizations	UN

Map page 114

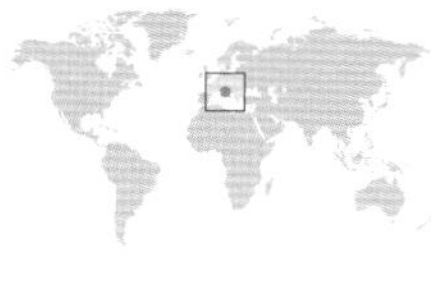

Landlocked San Marino lies in northeast Italy. A third of the people live in the capital. There is some agriculture and light industry, but most income comes from tourism. Italy is the main trading partner.

SÃO TOMÉ AND PRÍNCIPE
Democratic Republic of São Tomé and Príncipe

Area Sq Km	964	Languages	Portuguese, Creole
Area Sq Miles	372	Religions	Roman Catholic, Protestant
Population	161 000	Currency	Dobra
Capital	São Tomé	Organizations	UN

Map page 120

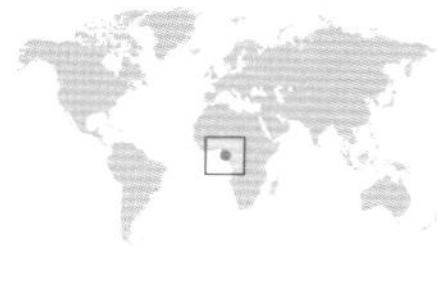

The two main islands and adjacent islets lie off the coast of west Africa in the Gulf of Guinea. São Tomé is the larger island, with over ninety per cent of the population. Both São Tomé and Príncipe are mountainous and tree-covered, and have a hot and humid climate. The economy is heavily dependent on cocoa, which accounts for around ninety per cent of export earnings.

SAUDI ARABIA
Kingdom of Saudi Arabia

Area Sq Km	2 200 000	Languages	Arabic
Area Sq Miles	849 425	Religions	Sunni Muslim, Shi'a Muslim
Population	24 217 000	Currency	Saudi Arabian riyal
Capital	Riyadh (Ar Riyāḍ)	Organizations	OPEC, UN

Map page 86

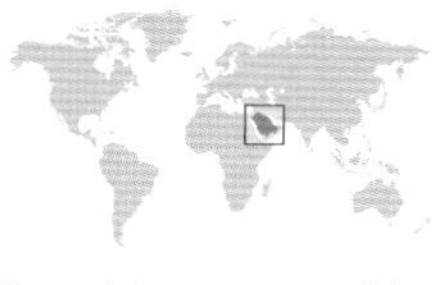

Saudi Arabia occupies most of the Arabian Peninsula in southwest Asia. The terrain is desert or semi-desert plateaus, which rise to mountains running parallel to the Red Sea in the west and slope down to plains in the southeast and along The Gulf in the east. Over eighty per cent of the population lives in urban areas. There are around four million foreign workers in Saudi Arabia, employed mainly in the oil and service industries. Summers are hot, winters are warm and rainfall is low. Saudi Arabia has the world's largest reserves of oil and significant natural gas reserves, both onshore and in The Gulf. Crude oil and refined products account for over ninety per cent of export earnings. Other industries and irrigated agriculture are being encouraged, but most food and raw materials are imported. Saudi Arabia has important banking and commercial interests. Japan and the USA are the main trading partners.

SENEGAL
Republic of Senegal

Area Sq Km	196 720	Languages	French, Wolof, Fulani, local languages
Area Sq Miles	75 954	Religions	Sunni Muslim, Roman Catholic, traditional beliefs
Population	10 095 000	Currency	CFA franc
Capital	Dakar	Organizations	UN

Map page 120

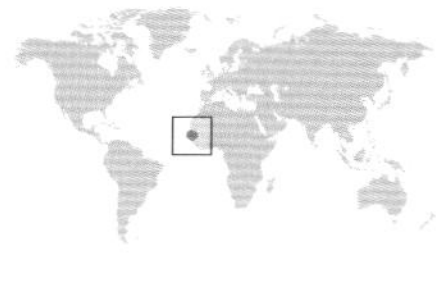

Senegal lies on the Atlantic coast of west Africa. The north is arid semi-desert, while the south is mainly fertile savanna bushland. The climate is tropical with summer rains, although droughts occur. One-fifth of the population lives in and around Dakar, the capital and main port. Fish, groundnuts and phosphates are the main exports. France is the main trading partner.

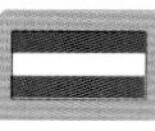

SERBIA AND MONTENEGRO
Federal Republic of Yugoslavia

Area Sq Km	102 173	Languages	Serbian, Albanian, Hungarian
Area Sq Miles	39 449	Religions	Serbian Orthodox, Montenegrin Orthodox, Sunni Muslim
Population	10 527 000	Currency	Serbian dinar, Euro
Capital	Belgrade (Beograd)	Organizations	UN

Map page 115

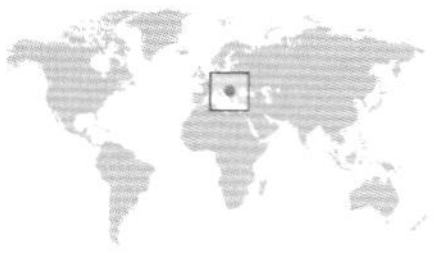

The southern European state comprises two of the former Yugoslav republics: Serbia and the much smaller Montenegro. It dropped the name Yugoslavia in 2003. The landscape is for the most part rugged, mountainous and forested. Northern Serbia is low-lying and is drained by the Danube river system. The climate is Mediterranean on the coast and continental inland. After 1991 the economy was seriously affected for some years by civil war, trade embargoes and economic sanctions. The southern province of Kosovo is under UN administration.

SEYCHELLES
Republic of the Seychelles

Area Sq Km	455	Languages	English, French, Creole
Area Sq Miles	176	Religions	Roman Catholic, Protestant
Population	81 000	Currency	Seychelles rupee
Capital	Victoria	Organizations	Comm., SADC, UN

Map page 119

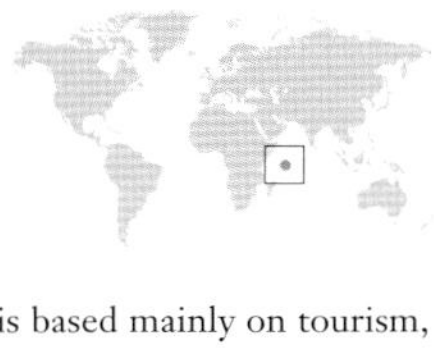

The Seychelles comprises an archipelago of over one hundred granitic and coral islands in the western Indian Ocean. Over ninety per cent of the population lives on the main island, Mahé. The climate is hot and humid with heavy rainfall. The economy is based mainly on tourism, fishing and light manufacturing.

SIERRA LEONE
Republic of Sierra Leone

Area Sq Km	71 740	Languages	English, Creole, Mende, Temne, local languages
Area Sq Miles	27 699	Religions	Sunni Muslim, traditional beliefs
Population	4 971 000	Currency	Leone
Capital	Freetown	Organizations	Comm., UN

Map page 120

Sierra Leone lies on the Atlantic coast of west Africa. Its coastline is heavily indented and is lined with mangrove swamps. Inland is a forested area rising to savanna plateaus, with mountains to the northeast. The climate is tropical and rainfall is heavy. Most of the workforce is involved in subsistence farming. Cocoa and coffee are the main cash crops. Diamonds and rutile (titanium ore) are the main exports. Sierra Leone is one of the world's poorest countries, and the economy relies on substantial foreign aid.

SINGAPORE
Republic of Singapore

Area Sq Km	639	Languages	Chinese, English, Malay, Tamil
Area Sq Miles	247	Religions	Buddhist, Taoist, Sunni Muslim, Christian, Hindu
Population	4 253 000	Currency	Singapore dollar
Capital	Singapore	Organizations	APEC, ASEAN, Comm., UN

Map page 94

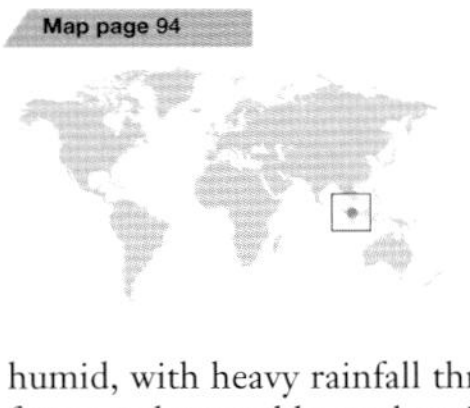

The state comprises the main island of Singapore and over fifty other islands, lying off the southern tip of the Malay Peninsula in southeast Asia. Singapore is generally low-lying and includes land reclaimed from swamps and the sea. It is hot and humid, with heavy rainfall throughout the year. There are fish farms and vegetable gardens in the north and east of the island, but most food is be imported. Singapore also lacks mineral and energy resources. Manufacturing industries and services are the main sectors of the economy. Their rapid development has fuelled the nation's impressive economic growth during recent decades. Main industries include electronics, oil refining, chemicals, pharmaceuticals, ship repair, food processing and textiles. Singapore is also a major financial centre. Its port is one of the world's largest and busiest and acts as an entrepôt for neighbouring states. Tourism is also important. Japan, the USA and Malaysia are the main trading partners.

SLOVAKIA
Slovak Republic

Area Sq Km	49 035	Languages	Slovakian, Hungarian, Czech
Area Sq Miles	18 933	Religions	Roman Catholic, Protestant, Orthodox
Population	5 402 000	Currency	Slovakian koruna
Capital	Bratislava	Organizations	EU, NATO, OECD, UN

Map page 112–113

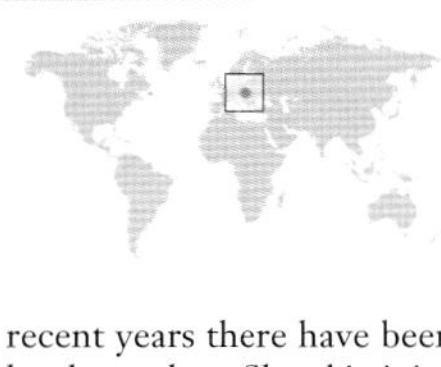

A landlocked country in central Europe, Slovakia is mountainous in the north, but low-lying in the southwest. The climate is continental. There is a range of manufacturing industries, and the main exports are machinery and transport equipment, but in recent years there have been economic difficulties and growth has been slow. Slovakia joined the European Union in May 2004. Most trade is with other EU countries, especially the Czech Republic.

SLOVENIA
Republic of Slovenia

Area Sq Km	20 251	Languages	Slovenian, Croatian, Serbian
Area Sq Miles	7 819	Religions	Roman Catholic, Protestant
Population	1 984 000	Currency	Tólar
Capital	Ljubljana	Organizations	EU, NATO, UN

Map page 114

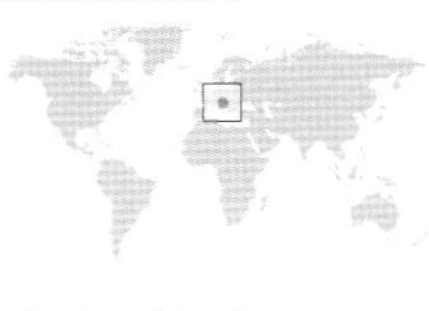

Slovenia lies in the northwest Balkan Mountains of southern Europe and has a short coastline on the Adriatic Sea. It is mountainous and hilly, with lowlands on the coast and in the Sava and Drava river valleys. The climate is generally continental inland and Mediterranean nearer the coast. The main agricultural products are potatoes, grain and sugar beet; the main industries include metal processing, electronics and consumer goods. Trade has been re-orientated towards western markets and the main trading partners are Germany and Italy. Slovenia joined the European Union in May 2004.

SOLOMON ISLANDS

Area Sq Km	28 370	Languages	English, Creole, local languages
Area Sq Miles	10 954	Religions	Protestant, Roman Catholic
Population	477 000	Currency	Solomon Islands dollar
Capital	Honiara	Organizations	Comm., UN

Map page 69

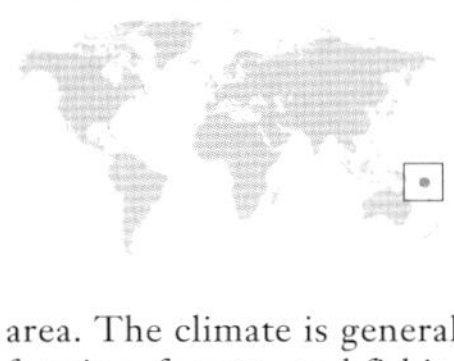

The state consists of the Solomon, Santa Cruz and Shortland Islands in the southwest Pacific Ocean. The six main islands are volcanic, mountainous and forested, although Guadalcanal, the most populous, has a large lowland area. The climate is generally hot and humid. Subsistence farming, forestry and fishing predominate. Exports include timber products, fish, copra and palm oil. The islands depend on foreign aid.

SOMALIA
Somali Republic

Area Sq Km	637 657	Languages	Somali, Arabic
Area Sq Miles	246 201	Religions	Sunni Muslim
Population	9 890 000	Currency	Somali shilling
Capital	Mogadishu (Muqdisho)	Organizations	UN

Map page 122

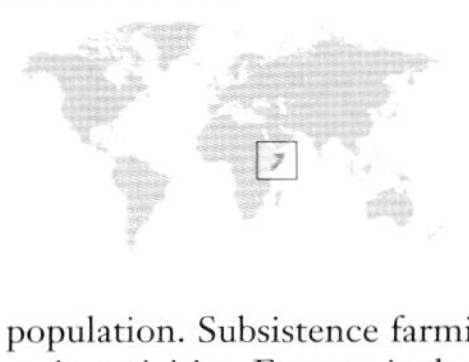

Somalia is in northeast Africa, on the Gulf of Aden and Indian Ocean. It consists of a dry scrubby plateau, rising to highlands in the north. The climate is hot and dry, but coastal areas and the Jubba and Webi Shabeelle river valleys support crops and most of the population. Subsistence farming and livestock rearing are the main activities. Exports include livestock and bananas. Frequent drought and civil war have prevented economic development. Somalia is one of the poorest, most unstable and least developed countries in the world.

SOUTH AFRICA, REPUBLIC OF

Area Sq Km	1 219 090	Languages	Afrikaans, English, nine other official languages
Area Sq Miles	470 693	Religions	Protestant, Roman Catholic, Sunni Muslim, Hindu
Population	45 026 000	Currency	Rand
Capital	Pretoria/ Cape Town	Organizations	Comm., SADC, UN

Map page 124–125

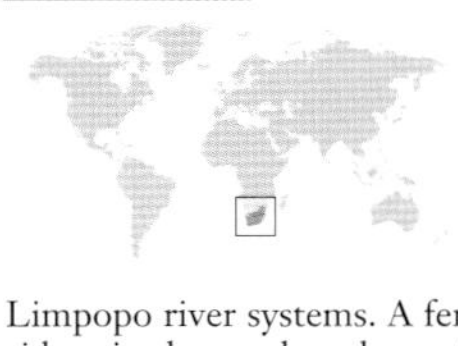

The Republic of South Africa occupies most of the southern part of Africa. It surrounds Lesotho and has a long coastline on the Atlantic and Indian Oceans. Much of the land is a vast plateau, covered with grassland or bush and drained by the Orange and Limpopo river systems. A fertile coastal plain rises to mountain ridges in the south and east, including Table Mountain near Cape Town and the Drakensberg range in the east. Gauteng is the most populous province, with Johannesburg and Pretoria its main cities. South Africa has warm summers and mild winters. Most of the country has the majority of its rainfall in summer, but the coast around Cape Town has winter rains. South Africa has the largest economy in Africa, although wealth is unevenly distributed and unemployment is very high. Agriculture employs approximately one-third of the workforce, and crops include fruit, wine, wool and maize. The country is the world's leading producer of gold and chromium and an important producer of diamonds. Many other minerals are also mined. The main industries are mineral and food processing, chemicals, electrical equipment, textiles and motor vehicles. Financial services are also important.

SOUTH KOREA
Republic of Korea

Area Sq Km	99 274	Languages	Korean
Area Sq Miles	38 330	Religions	Buddhist, Protestant, Roman Catholic
Population	47 700 000	Currency	South Korean won
Capital	Seoul (Sŏul)	Organizations	APEC, UN

Map page 96

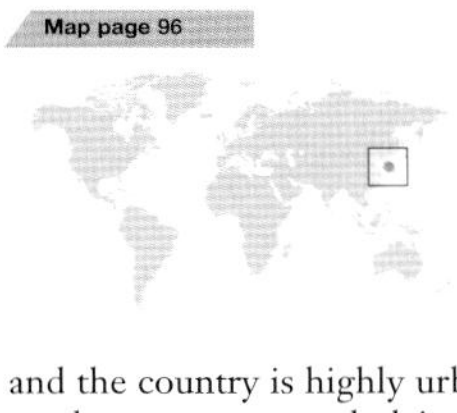

The state consists of the southern half of the Korean Peninsula in eastern Asia and many islands lying off the western and southern coasts in the Yellow Sea. The terrain is mountainous, although less rugged than that of North Korea. Population density is high and the country is highly urbanized; most of the population lives on the western coastal plains and in the river basins of the Han-gang in the northwest and the Naktong-gang in the southeast. The climate is continental, with hot, wet summers and dry, cold winters. Arable land is limited by the mountainous terrain, but because of intensive farming South Korea is nearly self-sufficient in food. Sericulture (silk) is important, as is fishing, which contributes to exports. South Korea has few mineral resources, except for coal and tungsten. It has achieved high economic growth based mainly on export manufacturing. The main manufactured goods are cars, electronic and electrical goods, ships, steel, chemicals and toys, as well as textiles, clothing, footwear and food products. The USA and Japan are the main trading partners.

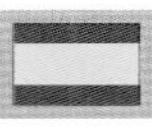

SPAIN
Kingdom of Spain

Area Sq Km	504 782	Languages	Spanish, Castilian, Catalan, Galician, Basque
Area Sq Miles	194 897	Religions	Roman Catholic
Population	41 060 000	Currency	Euro
Capital	Madrid	Organizations	EU, NATO, OECD, UN

Map page 111

Spain occupies the greater part of the Iberian peninsula in southwest Europe, with coastlines on the Atlantic Ocean and Mediterranean Sea. It includes the Balearic Islands in the Mediterranean, the Canary Islands in the Atlantic, and two enclaves in north Africa (Ceuta and Melilla). Much of the mainland is a high plateau drained by the Douro (Duero), Tagus (Tajo) and Guadiana rivers. The plateau is interrupted by a low mountain range and bounded to the east and north also by mountains, including the Pyrenees, which form the border with France and Andorra. The main lowland areas are the Ebro basin in the northeast, the eastern coastal plains and the Guadalquivir basin in the southwest. Over three-quarters of the population lives in urban areas. The plateau experiences hot summers and cold winters. Conditions are cooler and wetter to the north, and warmer and drier to the south. Agriculture involves about ten per cent of the workforce, and fruit, vegetables and wine are exported. Fishing is an important industry, and Spain has a large fishing fleet. Mineral resources include lead, copper, mercury and fluorspar. Some oil is produced, but Spain has to import most energy needs. The economy is based mainly on manufacturing and services. The principal products are machinery, transport equipment, motor vehicles and food products, with a wide variety of other manufactured goods. With approximately fifty million visitors a year, tourism is a major industry. Banking and commerce are also important. Approximately seventy per cent of trade is with other European Union countries.

SRI LANKA
Democratic Socialist Republic of Sri Lanka

Area Sq Km	65 610	Languages	Sinhalese, Tamil, English
Area Sq Miles	25 332	Religions	Buddhist, Hindu, Sunni Muslim, Roman Catholic
Population	19 065 000	Currency	Sri Lankan rupee
Capital	Sri Jayewardenepura Kotte	Organizations	Comm., UN

Map page 87

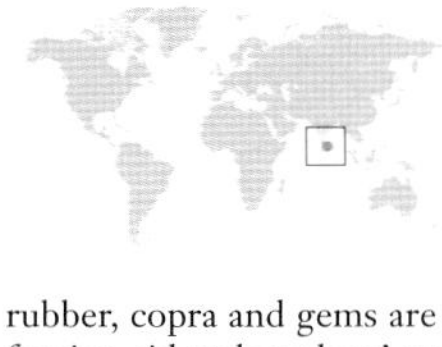

Sri Lanka lies in the Indian Ocean off the southeast coast of India in south Asia. It has rolling coastal plains, with mountains in the centre-south. The climate is hot and monsoonal. Most people live on the west coast. Manufactures (chiefly textiles and clothing), tea, rubber, copra and gems are exported. The economy relies on foreign aid and workers' remittances. The USA and the UK are the main trading partners.

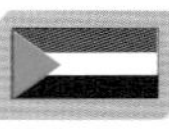

SUDAN
Republic of the Sudan

Area Sq Km	2 505 813	Languages	Arabic, Dinka, Nubian, Beja, Nuer, local languages
Area Sq Miles	967 500	Religions	Sunni Muslim, traditional beliefs, Christian
Population	33 610 000	Currency	Sudanese dinar
Capital	Khartoum	Organizations	UN

Map page 121

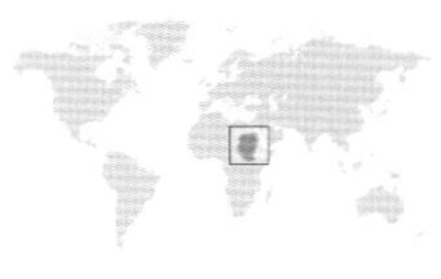

Africa's largest country, the Sudan is in the northeast of the continent, on the Red Sea. It lies within the upper Nile basin, much of which is arid plain but with swamps to the south. Mountains lie to the northeast, west and south. The climate is hot and arid with light summer rainfall, and droughts occur. Most people live along the Nile and are farmers and herders. Cotton, gum arabic, livestock and other agricultural products are exported. The government is working with foreign investors to develop oil resources, but civil war in the south and ethnic cleansing in Darfur continue to restrict the growth of the economy. Main trading partners are Saudi Arabia, China and Libya.

SURINAME
Republic of Suriname

Area Sq Km	163 820	Languages	Dutch, Surinamese, English, Hindi
Area Sq Miles	63 251	Religions	Hindu, Roman Catholic, Protestant, Sunni Muslim
Population	436 000	Currency	Suriname guilder
Capital	Paramaribo	Organizations	CARICOM, UN

Map page 155

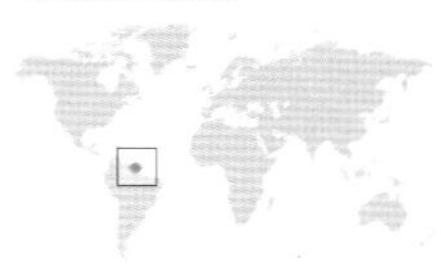

Suriname, on the Atlantic coast of northern South America, consists of a swampy coastal plain (where most of the population lives), central plateaus, and highlands in the south. The climate is tropical, and rainforest covers much of the land. Bauxite mining is the main industry, and alumina and aluminium are the chief exports, with shrimps, rice, bananas and timber also exported. The main trading partners are the Netherlands, Norway and the USA.

SWAZILAND
Kingdom of Swaziland

Area Sq Km	17 364	Languages	Swazi, English
Area Sq Miles	6 704	Religions	Christian, traditional beliefs
Population	1 077 000	Currency	Emalangeni, South African rand
Capital	Mbabane	Organizations	Comm., SADC, UN

Map page 125

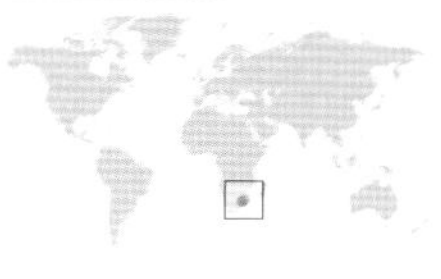

Landlocked Swaziland in southern Africa lies between Mozambique and the Republic of South Africa. Savanna plateaus descend from mountains in the west towards hill country in the east. The climate is subtropical, but temperate in the mountains. Subsistence farming predominates. Asbestos and diamonds are mined. Exports include sugar, fruit and wood pulp. Tourism and workers' remittances are important to the economy. Most trade is with South Africa.

SWEDEN
Kingdom of Sweden

Area Sq Km	449 964	Languages	Swedish
Area Sq Miles	173 732	Religions	Protestant, Roman Catholic
Population	8 876 000	Currency	Swedish krona
Capital	Stockholm	Organizations	EU, OECD, UN

Map page 102–103

Sweden occupies the eastern part of the Scandinavian peninsula in northern Europe and borders the Baltic Sea, the Gulf of Bothnia, and the Kattegat and Skagerrak, connecting with the North Sea. Forested mountains cover the northern half, part of which lies within the Arctic Circle. The southern part of the country is a lowland lake region where most of the population lives. Sweden has warm summers and cold winters, which are more severe in the north. Natural resources include coniferous forests, mineral deposits and water resources. Some dairy products, meat, cereals and vegetables are produced in the south. The forests supply timber for export and for the important pulp, paper and furniture industries. Sweden is an important producer of iron ore and copper. Zinc, lead, silver and gold are also mined. Machinery and transport equipment, chemicals, pulp and wood, and telecommunications equipment are the main exports. The majority of trade is with other European Union countries.

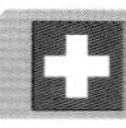

SWITZERLAND
Swiss Confederation

Area Sq Km	41 293	Languages	German, French, Italian, Romansch
Area Sq Miles	15 943	Religions	Roman Catholic, Protestant
Population	7 169 000	Currency	Swiss franc
Capital	Bern	Organizations	OECD, UN

Map page 110

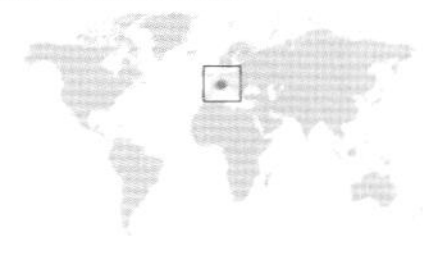

Switzerland is a mountainous landlocked country in west central Europe. The southern regions lie within the Alps, while the northwest is dominated by the Jura mountains. The rest of the land is a high plateau, where most of the population lives. The climate varies greatly, depending on altitude and relief, but in general summers are mild and winters are cold with heavy snowfalls. Switzerland has one of the highest standards of living in the world, yet it has few mineral resources, and most food and industrial raw materials are imported. Manufacturing makes the largest contribution to the economy. Engineering is the most important industry, producing precision instruments and heavy machinery. Other important industries are chemicals and pharmaceuticals. Banking and financial services are very important, and Zürich is one of the world's leading banking cities. Tourism, and international organizations based in Switzerland, are also major foreign currency earners. Germany is the main trading partner.

SYRIA
Syrian Arab Republic

Area Sq Km	185 180	Languages	Arabic, Kurdish, Armenian
Area Sq Miles	71 498	Religions	Sunni Muslim, Shi'a Muslim, Christian
Population	17 800 000	Currency	Syrian pound
Capital	Damascus (Dimashq)	Organizations	UN

Map page 80–81

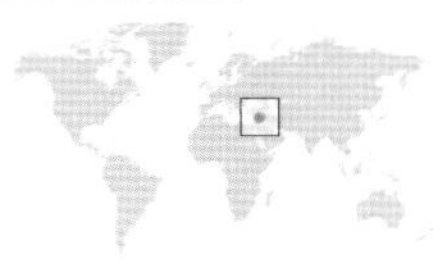

Syria is in southwest Asia, has a short coastline on the Mediterranean Sea, and stretches inland to a plateau traversed northwest-southeast by the Euphrates river. Mountains flank the southwest borders with Lebanon and Israel. The climate is Mediterranean in coastal regions, hotter and drier inland. Most Syrians live on the coast or in the river valleys. Cotton, cereals and fruit are important products, but the main exports are petroleum and related products, and textiles.

TAIWAN
Republic of China

Area Sq Km	36 179	Languages	Mandarin, Min, Hakka, local languages
Area Sq Miles	13 969	Religions	Buddhist, Taoist, Confucian, Christian
Population	22 548 009	Currency	Taiwan dollar
Capital	T'aipei	Organizations	APEC

Map page 103

The east Asian state consists of the island of Taiwan, separated from mainland China by the Taiwan Strait, and several much smaller islands. Much of Taiwan is mountainous and forested. Densely populated coastal plains in the west contain the bulk of the population and most economic activity. Taiwan has a tropical monsoon climate, with warm, wet summers and mild winters. Agriculture is highly productive. The country is virtually self-sufficient in food and exports some products. Coal, oil and natural gas are produced and a few minerals are mined, but none of them are of great significance to the economy. Taiwan depends heavily on imports of raw materials and exports of manufactured goods. The main manufactures are electrical and electronic goods, including television sets, personal computers and calculators, textiles, fertilizers, clothing, footwear and toys. The main trading partners are the USA, Japan and Germany.

TAJIKISTAN
Republic of Tajikistan

Area Sq Km	143 100	Languages	Tajik, Uzbek, Russian
Area Sq Miles	55 251	Religions	Sunni Muslim
Population	6 245 000	Currency	Somoni
Capital	Dushanbe	Organizations	CIS, UN

Map page 83

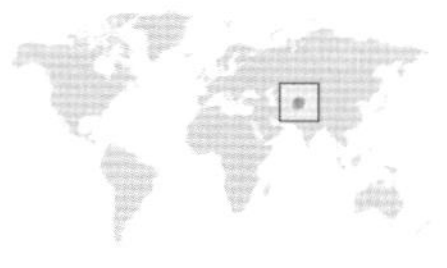

Landlocked Tajikistan in central Asia is a mountainous country, dominated by the mountains of the Alai Range and the Pamir. In the less mountainous western areas summers are warm, although winters are cold. Agriculture is the main sector of the economy, chiefly cotton growing and cattle breeding. Mineral deposits include lead, zinc, and uranium. Metal processing, textiles and clothing are the main manufactured goods; the main exports are aluminium and cotton. Uzbekistan, Kazakhstan and the Russian Federation are the main trading partners.

TANZANIA
United Republic of Tanzania

Area Sq Km	945 087	Languages	Swahili, English, Nyamwezi, local languages
Area Sq Miles	364 900	Religions	Shi'a Muslim, Sunni Muslim, traditional beliefs, Christian
Population	36 977 000	Currency	Tanzanian shilling
Capital	Dodoma	Organizations	Comm., SADC, UN

Map page 122–123

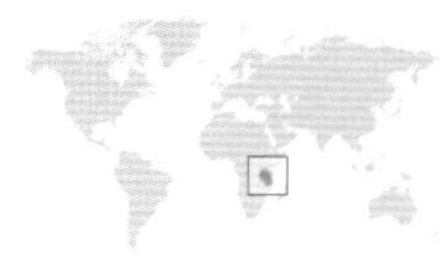

Tanzania lies on the coast of east Africa and includes the island of Zanzibar in the Indian Ocean. Most of the mainland is a savanna plateau lying east of the Great Rift Valley. In the north, near the border with Kenya, is Kilimanjaro, the highest mountain in Africa. The climate is tropical. The economy is predominantly based on agriculture, which employs an estimated ninety per cent of the workforce. Agricultural processing and gold and diamond mining are the main industries, although tourism is growing. Coffee, cotton, cashew nuts and tobacco are the main exports, with cloves from Zanzibar. Most export trade is with India and the UK. Tanzania depends heavily on foreign aid.

THAILAND
Kingdom of Thailand

Area Sq Km	513 115	Languages	Thai, Lao, Chinese, Malay, Mon-Khmer languages
Area Sq Miles	198 115	Religions	Buddhist, Sunni Muslim
Population	62 833 000	Currency	Baht
Capital	Bangkok (Krung Thep)	Organizations	APEC, ASEAN, UN

Map page 98

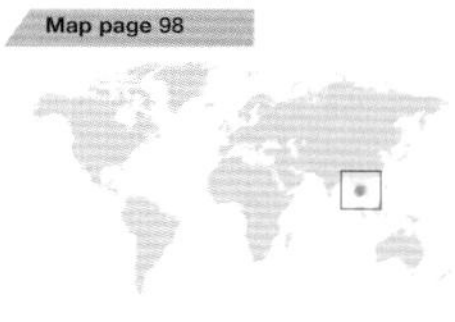

The largest country in the Indo-China peninsula, Thailand has coastlines on the Gulf of Thailand and Andaman Sea. Central Thailand is dominated by the Chao Phraya river basin, which contains Bangkok, the capital city and centre of most economic activity. To the east is a dry plateau drained by tributaries of the Mekong river, while to the north, west and south, extending down most of the Malay peninsula, are forested hills and mountains. Many small islands line the coast. The climate is hot, humid and monsoonal. About half the workforce is involved in agriculture. Fishing and fish processing are important. Thailand produces natural gas, some oil and lignite, minerals (chiefly tin, tungsten and baryte) and gemstones. Manufacturing is the largest contributor to national income, with electronics, textiles, clothing and footwear, and food processing the main industries. With around seven million visitors a year, tourism is the major source of foreign exchange. Thailand is one of the world's leading exporters of rice and rubber, and a major exporter of maize and tapioca. Japan and the USA are the main trading partners.

TOGO
Republic of Togo

Area Sq Km	56 785	Languages	French, Ewe, Kabre, local languages
Area Sq Miles	21 925	Religions	Traditional beliefs, Christian, Sunni Muslim
Population	4 909 000	Currency	CFA franc
Capital	Lomé	Organizations	UN

Map page 120

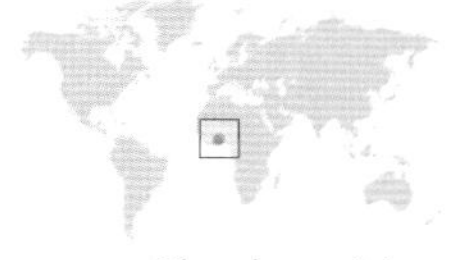

Togo is a long narrow country in west Africa with a short coastline on the Gulf of Guinea. The interior consists of plateaus rising to mountainous areas. The climate is tropical, and is drier inland. Agriculture is the mainstay of the economy. Phosphate mining and food processing are the main industries. Cotton, phosphates, coffee and cocoa are the main exports. Lomé, the capital, is an entrepôt trade centre.

Tokelau
New Zealand Overseas Territory

Area Sq Km	10	Languages	English, Tokelauan
Area Sq Miles	4	Religions	Christian
Population	2 000	Currency	New Zealand dollar

Map page 69

Tokelau consists of three atolls, Atafu, Nukunonu and Fakaofa, lying in the Pacific Ocean north of Samoa. Subsistence agriculture is the main activity, and the islands rely on aid from New Zealand and remittances from workers overseas.

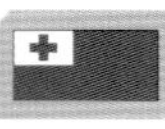

TONGA
Kingdom of Tonga

Area Sq Km	748	Languages	Tongan, English
Area Sq Miles	289	Religions	Protestant, Roman Catholic
Population	104 000	Currency	Pa'anga
Capital	Nuku'alofa	Organizations	Comm., UN

Map page 69

Tonga comprises some one hundred and seventy islands in the south Pacific Ocean, northeast of New Zealand. The three main groups are Tongatapu (where sixty per cent of Tongans live), Ha'apai and Vava'u. The climate is warm and wet, and the economy relies heavily on agriculture. Tourism and light industry are also important to the economy. Exports include squash, fish, vanilla beans and root crops. Most trade is with New Zealand, Japan and Australia.

TRINIDAD AND TOBAGO
Republic of Trinidad and Tobago

Area Sq Km	5 130	Languages	English, Creole, Hindi
Area Sq Miles	1 981	Religions	Roman Catholic, Hindu, Protestant, Sunni Muslim
Population	1 303 000	Currency	Trinidad and Tobago dollar
Capital	Port of Spain	Organizations	CARICOM, Comm., UN

Map page 157

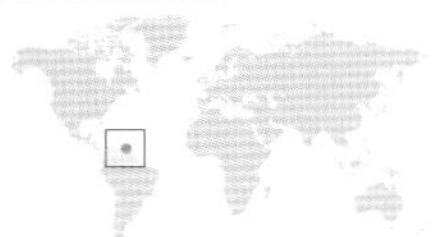

Trinidad, the most southerly Caribbean island, lies off the Venezuelan coast. It is hilly in the north, with a central plain. Tobago, to the northeast, is smaller, more mountainous and less developed. The climate is tropical. The main crops are cocoa, sugar cane, coffee, fruit and vegetables. Oil and petrochemical industries dominate the economy. Tourism is also important. The USA is the main trading partner.

TUNISIA
Tunisian Republic

Area Sq Km	164 150	Languages	Arabic, French
Area Sq Miles	63 379	Religions	Sunni Muslim
Population	9 832 000	Currency	Tunisian dinar
Capital	Tunis	Organizations	UN

Map page 120

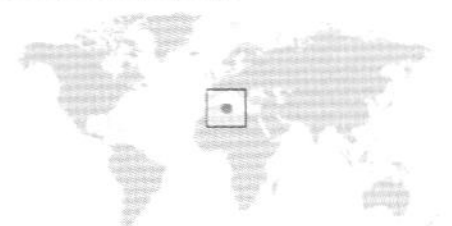

Tunisia is on the Mediterranean coast of north Africa. The north is mountainous with valleys and coastal plains, has a Mediterranean climate and is the most populous area. The south is hot and arid. Oil and phosphates are the main resources, and the main crops are olives and citrus fruit. Tourism is an important industry. Exports include petroleum products, textiles, fruit and phosphorus. Most trade is with European Union countries.

TURKEY
Republic of Turkey

Area Sq Km	779 452	Languages	Turkish, Kurdish
Area Sq Miles	300 948	Religions	Sunni Muslim, Shi'a Muslim
Population	71 325 000	Currency	Turkish lira
Capital	Ankara	Organizations	NATO, OECD, UN

Map page 80–81

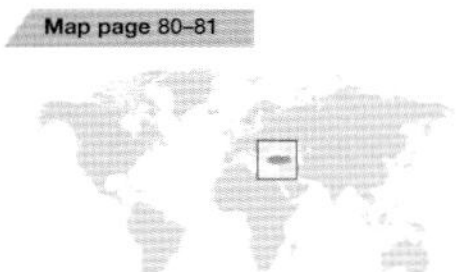

Turkey occupies a large peninsula of southwest Asia and has coastlines on the Black, Mediterranean and Aegean Seas. It includes eastern Thrace, which is in southeastern Europe and separated from the rest of the country by the Bosporus, the Sea of Marmara and the Dardanelles. The Asian mainland consists of the semi-arid Anatolian plateau, flanked to the north, south and east by mountains. Over forty per cent of Turks live in central Anatolia and on the Marmara and Aegean coastal plains. The coast has a Mediterranean climate, but inland conditions are more extreme with hot, dry summers and cold, snowy winters. Agriculture involves about forty per cent of the workforce, and products include cotton, grain, tobacco, fruit, nuts and livestock. Turkey is a leading producer of chromium, iron ore, lead, tin, borate, and baryte. Coal is also mined. The main manufactured goods are clothing, textiles, food products, steel and vehicles. Tourism is a major industry, with nine million visitors a year. Germany and the USA are the main trading partners. Remittances from workers abroad are important to the

TURKMENISTAN
Republic of Turkmenistan

Area Sq Km	488 100	Languages	Turkmen, Uzbek, Russian
Area Sq Miles	188 456	Religions	Sunni Muslim, Russian Orthodox
Population	4 867 000	Currency	Turkmen manat
Capital	Ashgabat (Ashkhabad)	Organizations	CIS, UN

Map page 82

Turkmenistan, in central Asia, comprises the plains of the Karakum Desert, the foothills of the Kopet Dag mountains in the south, the Amudar'ya valley in the north and the Caspian Sea plains in the west. The climate is dry, with extreme temperatures. The economy is based mainly on irrigated agriculture (chiefly cotton growing), and natural gas and oil. Main exports are natural gas, oil and cotton fibre. Ukraine, Iran, Turkey and the Russian Federation are the main trading partners.

Turks and Caicos Islands
United Kingdom Overseas Territory

Area Sq Km	430	Languages	English
Area Sq Miles	166	Religions	Protestant
Population	21 000	Currency	United States dollar
Capital	Grand Turk (Cockburn Town)		

Map page 149

The state consists of over forty low-lying islands and cays in the northern Caribbean. Only eight islands are inhabited, and two-fifths of the people live on Grand Turk and Salt Cay. The climate is tropical, and the economy is based on tourism, fishing and offshore banking.

TUVALU

Area Sq Km	25	Languages	Tuvaluan, English
Area Sq Miles	10	Religions	Protestant
Population	11 000	Currency	Australian dollar
Capital	Vaiaku	Organizations	Comm., UN

Map page 69

Tuvalu comprises nine low-lying coral atolls in the south Pacific Ocean. One-third of the population lives on Funafuti, and most people depend on subsistence farming and fishing. The islands export copra, stamps and clothing, but rely heavily on foreign aid. Most trade is with Fiji, Australia and New Zealand.

UGANDA
Republic of Uganda

Area Sq Km	241 038	Languages	English, Swahili, Luganda, local languages
Area Sq Miles	93 065	Religions	Roman Catholic, Protestant, Sunni Muslim, traditional beliefs
Population	25 827 000	Currency	Ugandan shilling
Capital	Kampala	Organizations	Comm., UN

Map page 122

A landlocked country in east Africa, Uganda consists of a savanna plateau with mountains and lakes. The climate is warm and wet. Most people live in the southern half of the country. Agriculture employs around eighty per cent of the workforce and dominates the economy. Coffee, tea, fish and fish products are the main exports. Uganda relies heavily on aid.

UKRAINE

Area Sq Km	603 700	Languages	Ukrainian, Russian
Area Sq Miles	233 090	Religions	Ukrainian Orthodox, Ukrainian Catholic, Roman Catholic
Population	48 523 000	Currency	Hryvnia
Capital	Kiev (Kyiv)	Organizations	CIS, UN

Map page 117

The country lies on the Black Sea coast of eastern Europe. Much of the land is steppe, generally flat and treeless, but with rich black soil, and it is drained by the river Dnieper. Along the border with Belarus are forested, marshy plains. The only uplands are the Carpathian Mountains in the west and smaller ranges on the Crimean peninsula. Summers are warm and winters are cold, with milder conditions in the Crimea. About a quarter of the population lives in the mainly industrial areas around Donets'k, Kiev and Dnipropetrovs'k. The Ukraine is rich in natural resources: fertile soil, substantial mineral and natural gas deposits, and forests. Agriculture and livestock rearing are important, but mining and manufacturing are the dominant sectors of the economy. Coal, iron and manganese mining, steel and metal production, machinery, chemicals and food processing are the main industries. The Russian Federation is the main trading partner.

UNITED ARAB EMIRATES
Federation of Emirates

Area Sq Km	77 700	Languages	Arabic, English
Area Sq Miles	30 000	Religions	Sunni Muslim, Shi'a Muslim
Population	2 995 000	Currency	United Arab Emirates dirham
Capital	Abu Dhabi (Abū Ẓabī)	Organizations	OPEC, UN

Map page 84

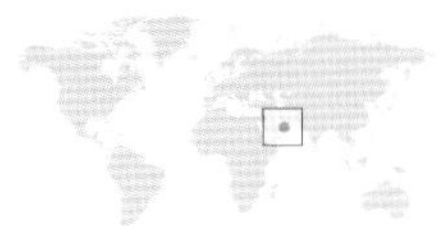

The UAE lies on the Gulf coast of the Arabian Peninsula. Six emirates are on The Gulf, while the seventh, Fujairah, is on the Gulf of Oman. Most of the land is flat desert with sand dunes and salt pans. The only hilly area is in the northeast. Over eighty per cent of the population lives in three of the emirates - Abu Dhabi, Dubai and Sharjah. Summers are hot and winters are mild, with occasional rainfall in coastal areas. Fruit and vegetables are grown in oases and irrigated areas, but the Emirates' wealth is based on hydrocarbons found in Abu Dhabi, Dubai, Sharjah and Ras al Khaimah. The UAE is one of the major oil producers in the Middle East. Dubai is an important entrepôt trade centre The main trading partner is Japan.

Abu Dhabi (Emirate)
Area Sq Km (Sq Miles) 67 340 (26 000) Population 1 248 000 Capital Abu Dhabi (Abū Ẓabī)

Ajman (Emirate)
Area Sq Km (Sq Miles) 259 (100) Population 189 000 Capital Ajman

Dubai (Emirate)
Area Sq Km (Sq Miles) 3 885 (1 500) Population 971 000 Capital Dubai

Fujairah (Emirate)
Area Sq Km (Sq Miles) 1 165 (450) Population 103 000 Capital Fujairah

Ra's al Khaymah (Emirate)
Area Sq Km (Sq Miles) 1 684 (650) Population 179 000 Capital Ra's al Khaymah

Sharjah (Emirate)
Area Sq Km (Sq Miles) 2 590 (1 000) Population 551 000 Capital Sharjah

Umm al Qaywayn (Emirate)
Area Sq Km (Sq Miles) 777 (300) Population 49 000 Capital Umm al Qaywayn

UNITED KINGDOM
United Kingdom of Great Britain and Northern Ireland

Area Sq Km	243 609	Languages	English, Welsh, Gaelic
Area Sq Miles	94 058	Religions	Protestant, Roman Catholic, Muslim
Population	58 789 194	Currency	Pound sterling
Capital	London	Organizations	Comm., EU, NATO, OECD, UN

Map page 104–107

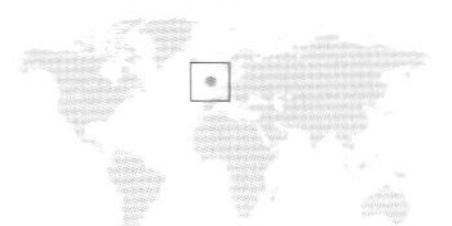

The United Kingdom, in northwest Europe, occupies the island of Great Britain, part of Ireland, and many small adjacent islands. Great Britain comprises England, Scotland and Wales. England covers over half the land area and supports over four-fifths of the population, at its densest in the southeast. The English landscape is flat or rolling with some uplands, notably the Cheviot Hills on the Scottish border, the Pennines in the centre-north, and the hills of the Lake District in the northwest. Scotland consists of southern uplands, central lowlands, the Highlands (which include the UK's highest peak) and many islands. Wales is a land of hills, mountains and river valleys. Northern Ireland contains uplands, plains and the UK's largest lake, Lough Neagh. The climate of the UK is mild, wet and variable. There are few mineral deposits, but important energy resources. Agricultural activities involve sheep and cattle rearing, dairy farming, and crop and fruit growing in the east and southeast. Productivity is high, but approximately one-third of food is imported. The UK produces petroleum and natural gas from reserves in the North Sea and is self-sufficient in energy in net terms. Major manufactures are food and drinks, motor vehicles and parts, aerospace equipment, machinery, electronic and electrical equipment, and chemicals and chemical products. However, the economy is dominated by service industries, including banking, insurance, finance and business services. London, the capital, is one of the world's major financial centres. Tourism is also a major industry, with approximately twenty-five million visitors a year. International trade is also important, equivalent to one-third of national income. Over half of the UK's trade is with other European Union countries.

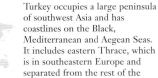

England (Constituent country)
Area Sq Km (Sq Miles) 130 433 (50 360)   Population 49 138 831   Capital London

Northern Ireland (Province)
Area Sq Km (Sq Miles) 13 576 (5 242)   Population 1 685 267   Capital Belfast

Scotland (Constituent country)
Area Sq Km (Sq Miles) 78 822 (30 433)   Population 5 062 011   Capital Edinburgh

Wales (Principality)
Area Sq Km (Sq Miles) 20 778 (8 022)   Population 2 903 085   Capital Cardiff

UNITED STATES OF AMERICA
Federal Republic

Area Sq Km	9 826 635	Languages	English, Spanish
Area Sq Miles	3 794 085	Religions	Protestant, Roman Catholic, Sunni Muslim, Jewish
Population	294 043 000	Currency	United States dollar
Capital	Washington D.C.	Organizations	APEC, NATO, OECD, UN

Map page 136–137

The USA comprises forty-eight contiguous states in North America, bounded by Canada and Mexico, plus the states of Alaska, to the northwest of Canada, and Hawaii, in the north Pacific Ocean. The populous eastern states cover the Atlantic coastal plain (which includes the Florida peninsula and the Gulf of Mexico coast) and the Appalachian Mountains. The central states occupy a vast interior plain drained by the Mississippi-Missouri river system. To the west lie the Rocky Mountains, separated from the Pacific coastal ranges by intermontane plateaus. The Pacific coastal zone is also mountainous, and prone to earthquakes. Hawaii is a group of some twenty volcanic islands. Climatic conditions range between arctic in Alaska to desert in the intermontane plateaus. Most of the USA has a temperate climate, although the interior has continental conditions. There are abundant natural resources, including major reserves of minerals and energy resources. The USA has the largest and most technologically advanced economy in the world, based on manufacturing and services. Although agriculture accounts for approximately two per cent of national income, productivity is high and the USA is a net exporter of food, chiefly grains and fruit. Cotton is the major industrial crop. The USA produces iron ore, copper, lead, zinc, and many other minerals. It is a major producer of coal, petroleum and natural gas, although being the world's biggest energy user it imports significant quantities of petroleum and its products. Manufacturing is diverse. The main industries are petroleum, steel, motor vehicles, aerospace, telecommunications, electronics, food processing, chemicals and consumer goods. Tourism is a major foreign currency earner, with approximately forty-five million visitors a year. Other important service industries are banking and finance, Wall Street in New York being one of the world's major stock exchanges. Canada and Mexico are the main trading partners.

Alabama (State)
Area Sq Km (Sq Miles) 135 765 (52 419)   Population 4 486 508   Capital Montgomery

Alaska (State)
Area Sq Km (Sq Miles) 1 717 854 (663 267)   Population 643 786   Capital Juneau

Arizona (State)
Area Sq Km (Sq Miles) 295 253 (113 998)   Population 5 456 453   Capital Phoenix

Arkansas (State)
Area Sq Km (Sq Miles) 137 733 (53 179)   Population 2 710 079   Capital Little Rock

California (State)
Area Sq Km (Sq Miles) 423 971 (163 696)   Population 35 116 033   Capital Sacramento

Colorado (State)
Area Sq Km (Sq Miles) 269 602 (104 094)   Population 4 506 542   Capital Denver

Connecticut (State)
Area Sq Km (Sq Miles) 14 356 (5 543)   Population 3 460 503   Capital Hartford

Delaware (State)
Area Sq Km (Sq Miles) 6 446 (2 489)   Population 807 385   Capital Dover

District of Columbia (District)
Area Sq Km (Sq Miles) 176 (68)   Population 570 898   Capital Washington

Florida (State)
Area Sq Km (Sq Miles) 170 305 (65 755)   Population 16 713 149   Capital Tallahassee

Georgia (State)
Area Sq Km (Sq Miles) 69 700 (26 911)   Population 5 126 000   Capital Atlanta

Hawaii (State)
Area Sq Km (Sq Miles) 28 311 (10 931)   Population 1 244 898   Capital Honolulu

Idaho (State)
Area Sq Km (Sq Miles) 216 445 (83 570)   Population 1 341 131   Capital Boise

Illinois (State)
Area Sq Km (Sq Miles) 149 997 (57 914)   Population 12 600 620   Capital Springfield

Indiana (State)
Area Sq Km (Sq Miles) 94 322 (36 418)   Population 6 159 068   Capital Indianapolis

Iowa (State)
Area Sq Km (Sq Miles) 145 744 (56 272)   Population 2 936 760   Capital Des Moines

Kansas (State)
Area Sq Km (Sq Miles) 213 096 (82 277)   Population 2 715 884   Capital Topeka

Kentucky (State)
Area Sq Km (Sq Miles) 104 659 (40 409)   Population 4 092 891   Capital Frankfort

Louisiana (State)
Area Sq Km (Sq Miles) 134 265 (51 840)   Population 4 482 646   Capital Baton Rouge

Maine (State)
Area Sq Km (Sq Miles) 91 647 (35 385)   Population 1 294 464   Capital Augusta

Maryland (State)
Area Sq Km (Sq Miles) 32 134 (12 407)   Population 5 458 137   Capital Annapolis

Massachusetts (State)
Area Sq Km (Sq Miles) 27 337 (10 555)   Population 6 427 801   Capital Boston

Michigan (State)
Area Sq Km (Sq Miles) 250 493 (96 716)   Population 10 050 446   Capital Lansing

Minnesota (State)
Area Sq Km (Sq Miles) 225 171 (86 939)   Population 5 019 720   Capital St Paul

Mississippi (State)
Area Sq Km (Sq Miles) 125 433 (48 430)   Population 2 871 782   Capital Jackson

Missouri (State)
Area Sq Km (Sq Miles) 180 533 (69 704)   Population 5 672 579   Capital Jefferson City

Montana (State)
Area Sq Km (Sq Miles) 380 837 (147 042)   Population 909 453   Capital Helena

Nebraska (State)
Area Sq Km (Sq Miles) 200 346 (77 354)   Population 1 729 180   Capital Lincoln

Nevada (State)
Area Sq Km (Sq Miles) 286 352 (110 561)   Population 2 173 491   Capital Carson City

New Hampshire (State)
Area Sq Km (Sq Miles) 24 216 (9 350)   Population 1 275 056   Capital Concord

New Jersey (State)
Area Sq Km (Sq Miles) 22 587 (8 721)   Population 8 590 300   Capital Trenton

New Mexico (State)
Area Sq Km (Sq Miles) 314 914 (121 589)   Population 1 855 059   Capital Santa Fe

New York (State)
Area Sq Km (Sq Miles) 141 299 (54 556)   Population 19 157 532   Capital Albany

North Carolina (State)
Area Sq Km (Sq Miles) 139 391 (53 819)   Population 8 320 146   Capital Raleigh

North Dakota (State)
Area Sq Km (Sq Miles) 183 112 (70 700)   Population 634 110   Capital Bismarck

Ohio (State)
Area Sq Km (Sq Miles) 116 096 (44 825)   Population 11 421 267   Capital Columbus

Oklahoma (State)
Area Sq Km (Sq Miles) 181 035 (69 898)   Population 3 493 714   Capital Oklahoma City

Oregon (State)
Area Sq Km (Sq Miles) 254 806 (98 381)   Population 3 521 515   Capital Salem

Pennsylvania (State)
Area Sq Km (Sq Miles) 119 282 (46 055)   Population 12 335 091   Capital Harrisburg

Rhode Island (State)
Area Sq Km (Sq Miles) 4 002 (1 545)   Population 1 069 725   Capital Providence

South Carolina (State)
Area Sq Km (Sq Miles) 82 931 (32 020)   Population 4 107 183   Capital Columbia

South Dakota (State)
Area Sq Km (Sq Miles) 199 730 (77 116)   Population 761 063   Capital Pierre

Tennessee (State)
Area Sq Km (Sq Miles) 109 150 (42 143)   Population 5 797 289   Capital Nashville

Texas (State)
Area Sq Km (Sq Miles) 695 622 (268 581)   Population 21 779 893   Capital Austin

Utah (State)
Area Sq Km (Sq Miles) 219 887 (84 899)   Population 2 316 256   Capital Salt Lake City

Vermont (State)
Area Sq Km (Sq Miles) 24 900 (9 614)   Population 616 592   Capital Montpelier

Virginia (State)
Area Sq Km (Sq Miles) 110 784 (42 774)   Population 7 293 542   Capital Richmond

Washington (State)
Area Sq Km (Sq Miles) 184 666 (71 300)   Population 6 068 996   Capital Olympia

West Virginia (State)
Area Sq Km (Sq Miles) 62 755 (24 230)   Population 1 801 873   Capital Charleston

Wisconsin (State)
Area Sq Km (Sq Miles) 169 639 (65 498)   Population 5 441 196   Capital Madison

Wyoming (State)
Area Sq Km (Sq Miles) 253 337 (97 814)   Population 498 703   Capital Cheyenne

URUGUAY
Oriental Republic of Uruguay

Area Sq Km	176 215	Languages	Spanish
Area Sq Miles	68 037	Religions	Roman Catholic, Protestant, Jewish
Population	3 415 000	Currency	Uruguayan peso
Capital	Montevideo	Organizations	UN

Map page 159

Uruguay, on the Atlantic coast of central South America, is a low-lying land of prairies. The coast and the River Plate estuary in the south are fringed with lagoons and sand dunes. Almost half the population lives in the capital, Montevideo. Uruguay has warm summers and mild winters. The economy is based on cattle and sheep ranching, and the main industries produce food products, textiles, and petroleum products. Meat, wool, hides, textiles and agricultural products are the main exports. Brazil and Argentina are the main trading partners.

UZBEKISTAN
Republic of Uzbekistan

Area Sq Km	447 400	Languages	Uzbek, Russian, Tajik, Kazakh
Area Sq Miles	172 742	Religions	Sunni Muslim, Russian Orthodox
Population	26 093 000	Currency	Uzbek som
Capital	Tashkent	Organizations	CIS, UN

Map page 82–83

A landlocked country of central Asia, Uzbekistan consists mainly of the flat Kyzylkum Desert. High mountains and valleys are found towards the southeast borders with Kyrgyzstan and Tajikistan. Most settlement is in the Fergana basin. The climate is hot and dry. The economy is based mainly on irrigated agriculture, chiefly cotton production. Uzbekistan is rich in minerals, including gold, copper, lead, zinc and uranium, and it has one of the largest gold mines in the world. Industry specializes in fertilizers and machinery for cotton harvesting and textile manufacture. The Russian Federation is the main trading partner.

VANUATU
Republic of Vanuatu

Area Sq Km	12 190	Languages	English, Bislama (Creole), French
Area Sq Miles	4 707	Religions	Protestant, Roman Catholic, traditional beliefs
Population	212 000	Currency	Vatu
Capital	Port Vila	Organizations	Comm., UN

Map page 69

Vanuatu occupies an archipelago of approximately eighty islands in the southwest Pacific. Many of the islands are mountainous, of volcanic origin and densely forested. The climate is tropical, with heavy rainfall. Half of the population lives on the main islands of Éfaté and Espíritu Santo, and the majority of people are employed in agriculture. Copra, beef, timber, vegetables, and cocoa are the main exports. Tourism is becoming important to the economy. Australia, Japan and Germany are the main trading partners.

VATICAN CITY
Vatican City State or Holy See

Area Sq Km	0.5	Languages	Italian
Area Sq Miles	0.2	Religions	Roman Catholic
Population	472	Currency	Euro
Capital	Vatican City		

Map page 114

The world's smallest sovereign state, the Vatican City occupies a hill to the west of the river Tiber within the Italian capital, Rome. It is the headquarters of the Roman Catholic church, and income comes from investments, voluntary contributions and tourism.

VENEZUELA
Republic of Venezuela

Area Sq Km	912 050	Languages	Spanish, Amerindian languages
Area Sq Miles	352 144	Religions	Roman Catholic, Protestant
Population	25 699 000	Currency	Bolívar
Capital	Caracas	Organizations	OPEC, UN

Map page 157

Venezuela is in northern South America, on the Caribbean. Its coast is much indented, with the oil-rich area of Lake Maracaibo at the western end, and the swampy Orinoco Delta to the east. Mountain ranges run parallel to the coast, and turn southwestwards to form a northern extension of the Andes. Central Venezuela is an area of lowland grasslands drained by the Orinoco river system. To the south are the Guiana Highlands, which contain the Angel Falls, the world's highest waterfall. Almost ninety per cent of the population lives in towns, mostly in the coastal mountain areas. The climate is tropical, with most rainfall in summer. Farming is important, particularly cattle ranching and dairy farming; coffee, maize, rice and sugar cane are the main crops. Venezuela is a major oil producer, and oil accounts for about seventy-five per cent of export earnings. Aluminium, iron ore, copper and gold are also mined, and manufactures include petrochemicals, aluminium, steel, textiles and food products. The USA and Puerto Rico are the main trading partners.

VIETNAM
Socialist Republic of Vietnam

Area Sq Km	329 565	Languages	Vietnamese, Thai, Khmer, Chinese, local languages
Area Sq Miles	127 246		
Population	81 377 000	Religions	Buddhist, Taoist, Roman Catholic, Cao Dai, Hoa Hao
Capital	Ha Nôi	Currency	Dong
		Organizations	APEC, ASEAN, UN

Map page 91

Vietnam lies in southeast Asia on the west coast of the South China Sea. The Red River delta lowlands in the north are separated from the huge Mekong delta in the south by long, narrow coastal plains backed by the mountainous and forested terrain of the Annam Highlands. Most of the population lives in the river deltas. The climate is tropical, with summer monsoon rains. Over three-quarters of the workforce is involved in agriculture, forestry and fishing. Coffee, tea and rubber are important cash crops, but Vietnam is the world's second largest rice exporter. Oil, coal and copper are produced, and other main industries are food processing, clothing and footwear, cement and fertilizers. Exports include oil, coffee, rice, clothing, fish and fish products. Japan and Singapore are the main trading partners.

Virgin Islands (U.K.)
United Kingdom Overseas Territory

Area Sq Km	153	Languages	English
Area Sq Miles	59	Religions	Protestant, Roman Catholic
Population	21 000	Currency	United States dollar
Capital	Road Town		

Map page 149

The Caribbean territory comprises four main islands and over thirty islets at the eastern end of the Virgin Islands group. Apart from the flat coral atoll of Anegada, the islands are volcanic in origin and hilly. The climate is subtropical, and tourism is the main industry.

Virgin Islands (U.S.A.)
United States Unincorporated Territory

Area Sq Km	352	Languages	English, Spanish
Area Sq Miles	136	Religions	Protestant, Roman Catholic
Population	111 000	Currency	United States dollar
Capital	Charlotte Amalie		

Map page 149

The territory consists of three main islands and over fifty islets in the Caribbean's western Virgin Islands. The islands are hilly, of volcanic origin, and the climate is subtropical. The economy is based on tourism, with some manufacturing, including a major oil refinery on St Croix.

Wallis and Futuna Islands
French Overseas Territory

Area Sq Km	274	Languages	French, Wallisian, Futunian
Area Sq Miles	106	Religions	Roman Catholic
Population	15 000	Currency	CFP franc
Capital	Matā'utu		

Map page 69

The south Pacific territory comprises the volcanic islands of the Wallis archipelago and the Hoorn Islands. The climate is tropical. The islands depend on subsistence farming, the sale of licences to foreign fishing fleets, workers' remittances from abroad and French aid.

West Bank
Disputed territory

Area Sq Km	5 860	Languages	Arabic, Hebrew
Area Sq Miles	2 263	Religions	Sunni Muslim, Jewish, Shi'a Muslim, Christian
Population	2 303 660	Currency	Jordanian dinar, Isreali shekel

Map page 80

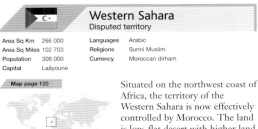

The territory consists of the west bank of the river Jordan and parts of Judea and Samaria. The land was annexed by Israel in 1967, but some areas have been granted autonomy under agreements between Israel and the Palestinian Authority. Conflict between the Israelis and the Palestinians continues to restrict economic development.

Western Sahara
Disputed territory

Area Sq Km	266 000	Languages	Arabic
Area Sq Miles	102 703	Religions	Sunni Muslim
Population	308 000	Currency	Moroccan dirham
Capital	Laâyoune		

Map page 120

Situated on the northwest coast of Africa, the territory of the Western Sahara is now effectively controlled by Morocco. The land is low, flat desert with higher land in the northeast. There is little cultivation and only about twenty per cent of the land is pasture. Livestock herding, fishing and phosphate mining are the main activities. All trade is controlled by Morocco.

YEMEN
Republic of Yemen

Area Sq Km	527 968	Languages	Arabic
Area Sq Miles	203 850	Religions	Sunni Muslim, Shi'a Muslim
Population	20 010 000	Currency	Yemeni riyal
Capital	San'ā'	Organizations	UN

Map page 86

Yemen occupies the southwestern part of the Arabian Peninsula, on the Red Sea and the Gulf of Aden. Beyond the Red Sea coastal plain the land rises to a mountain range and then descends to desert plateaus. Much of the country is hot and arid, but there is more rainfall in the west, where most of the population lives. Farming and fishing are the main activities, with cotton the main cash crop. The main exports are crude oil, fish, coffee and dried fruit. Despite some oil resources Yemen is one of the poorest countries in the Arab world. Main trading partners are Thailand, China, South Korea and Saudi Arabia.

ZAMBIA
Republic of Zambia

Area Sq Km	752 614	Languages	English, Bemba, Nyanja, Tonga, local languages
Area Sq Miles	290 586	Religions	Christian, traditional beliefs
Population	10 812 000	Currency	Zambian kwacha
Capital	Lusaka	Organizations	Comm., SADC, UN

Map page 123

A landlocked state in south central Africa, Zambia consists principally of high savanna plateaus and is bordered by the Zambezi river in the south. Most people live in the Copperbelt area in the centre-north. The climate is tropical, with a rainy season from November to May. Agriculture employs approximately eighty per cent of the workforce, but is mainly at subsistence level. Copper mining is the mainstay of the economy, although reserves are declining. Copper and cobalt are the main exports. Most trade is with South Africa.

ZIMBABWE
Republic of Zimbabwe

Area Sq Km	390 759	Languages	English, Shona, Ndebele
Area Sq Miles	150 873	Religions	Christian, traditional beliefs
Population	12 891 000	Currency	Zimbabwean dollar
Capital	Harare	Organizations	SADC, UN

Map page 123

Zimbabwe, a landlocked state in south-central Africa, consists of high plateaus flanked by the Zambezi river valley and Lake Kariba in the north and the Limpopo river in the south. Most of the population lives in the centre of the country. There are significant mineral resources, including gold, nickel, copper, asbestos, platinum and chromium. Agriculture is a major sector of the economy, with crops including tobacco, maize, sugar cane and cotton. Beef cattle are also important. Exports include tobacco, gold, ferroalloys, nickel and cotton. South Africa is the main trading partner. The economy has suffered recently through significant political unrest and instability.

DISTRIBUTION OF MAJOR EARTHQUAKES AND VOLCANOES

Winkel Tripel Projection
scale approximately 1:95 000 000

●	'Deadliest' earthquakes
●	Earthquakes of magnitude >=7.5
○	Earthquakes of magnitude 5.5–7.5
▲	'Major' Volcanoes
▲	Other volcanoes

DEADLIEST EARTHQUAKES 1900–2004

Year	Location	Deaths
1905	Kangra, India	19 000
1907	west of Dushanbe, Tajikistan	12 000
1908	Messina, Italy	110 000
1915	Abruzzo, Italy	35 000
1917	Bali, Indonesia	15 000
1920	Ningxia Province, China	200 000
1923	Tōkyō, Japan	142 807
1927	Qinghai Province, China	200 000
1932	Gansu Province, China	70 000
1933	Sichuan Province, China	10 000
1934	Nepal/India	10 700
1935	Quetta, Pakistan	30 000
1939	Chillán, Chile	28 000
1939	Erzincan, Turkey	32 700
1948	Ashgabat, Turkmenistan	19 800
1962	northwest Iran	12 225
1970	Huánuco Province, Peru	66 794
1974	Yunnan and Sichuan Provinces, China	20 000
1975	Liaoning Province, China	10 000
1976	central Guatemala	22 778
1976	Hebei Province, China	242 000
1978	Khorāsān Province, Iran	20 000
1980	Ech Chélif, Algeria	11 000
1988	Spitak, Armenia	25 000
1990	Manjil, Iran	50 000
1999	Kocaeli (Izmit), Turkey	17 000
2001	Gujarat, India	20 000
2003	Bam, Iran	26 271

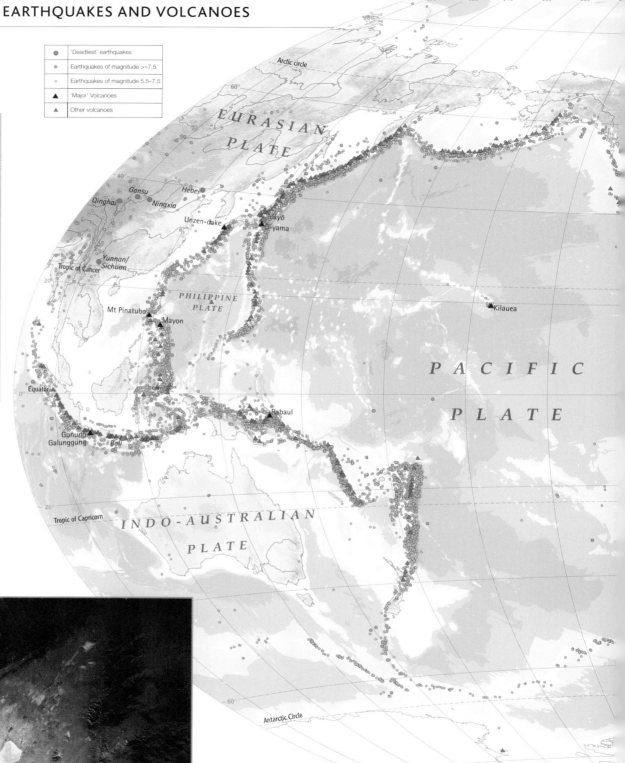

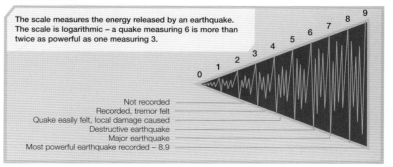

The San Andreas fault (top left) and the Garlock fault (right side of image) in California, USA are two major earthquake producing fault lines.

RICHTER SCALE

The scale measures the energy released by an earthquake. The scale is logarithmic – a quake measuring 6 is more than twice as powerful as one measuring 3.

Not recorded
Recorded, tremor felt
Quake easily felt, local damage caused
Destructive earthquake
Major earthquake
Most powerful earthquake recorded – 8.9

NORTH
AMERICAN
PLATE

EURASIAN
PLATE

Hekla

Arctic Circle

Helens

Izmit
(Kocaeli) Spitak
Erzincan Ashgabat
Monte Etna Messina Manjil Khorāsān Kangra
Bam Quetta

El Chichónal
Guatemala

CARIBBEAN
PLATE

Soufrière Hills

Gujarat Tropic of Cancer

ARABIAN
PLATE

COCOS
PLATE

Nevado del Ruiz

Volcán Galeras

AFRICAN
PLATE

Nyiragongo

Equator

Huánuco

SOUTH
AMERICAN
PLATE

NAZCA
PLATE

Chillán

Volcán Llaima

Tropic of Capricorn

SCOTIA
PLATE

ANTARCTIC
PLATE

Mount Bromo, Java, Indonesia, one of the many active volcanoes that have formed around the edge of the Pacific Ocean.

MAJOR VOLCANIC ERUPTIONS SINCE 1980

Date	Volcano	Country
1980	Mt St Helens	USA
1982	El Chichónal	Mexico
1982	Gunung Galunggung	Indonesia
1983	Kilauea	Hawaii
1983	Ō-yama	Japan
1985	Nevado del Ruiz	Colombia
1991	Hekla	Iceland
1991	Mt Pinatubo	Philippines
1991	Unzen-dake	Japan
1993	Mayon	Philippines
1993	Volcán Galeras	Colombia
1994	Volcán Llaima	Chile
1994	Rabaul	Papua New Guinea
1997	Soufrière Hills	Montserrat
2000	Hekla	Iceland
2001	Monte Etna	Italy
2002	Nyiragongo	Democratic Republic of Congo

Virgin rainforest, Borneo, Malaysia, with a deforested hillside in the background.

A sand dune in Libya threatens to engulf an oasis highlighting the threat of desertification in the Sahel region.

LAND COVER GRAPHS – CLASSIFICATION

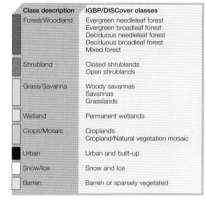

Class description	IGBP/DISCover classes
Forest/Woodland	Evergreen needleleaf forest Evergreen broadleaf forest Deciduous needleleaf forest Deciduous broadleaf forest Mixed forest
Shrubland	Closed shrublands Open shrublands
Grass/Savanna	Woody savannas Savannas Grasslands
Wetland	Permanent wetlands
Crops/Mosaic	Croplands Cropland/Natural vegetation mosaic
Urban	Urban and built-up
Snow/Ice	Snow and ice
Barren	Barren or sparsely vegetated

CONTINENTAL LAND COVER COMPOSITION

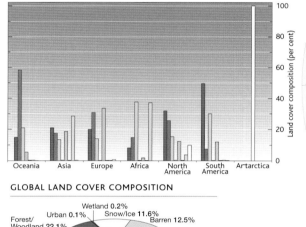

Land cover composition (per cent)

Oceania · Asia · Europe · Africa · North America · South America · Antarctica

GLOBAL LAND COVER COMPOSITION

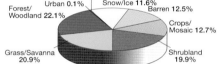

Wetland 0.2%
Urban 0.1%
Snow/Ice 11.6%
Barren 12.5%
Forest/Woodland 22.1%
Crops/Mosaic 12.7%
Shrubland 19.9%
Grass/Savanna 20.9%

MAJOR CLIMATIC REGIONS AND SUB-TYPES

Köppen classification system
Winkel Tripel Projection
scale 1:170 000 000

• Weather extreme location

A Rainy climate with no winter: coolest month above 18°C (64.4°F).

B Dry climates: limits are defined by formulae based on rainfall effectiveness:
BS Steppe or semi-arid climate.
BW Desert or arid climate.

*C Rainy climates with mild winters: coolest month above 0°C (32°F), but below 18°C (64.4°F); warmest month above 10°C (50°F).

*D Rainy climates with severe winters: coolest month below 0°C (32°F); warmest month above 10°C (50°F).

E Polar climates with no warm season: warmest month below 10°C (50°F).
ET Tundra climate: warmest month below 10°C (50°F) but above 0°C (32°F).
EF Perpetual frost: all months below 0°C (32°F).

a Warmest month above 22°C (71.6°F).

b Warmest month below 22°C (71.6°F).

c Less than four months over 10°C (50°F).

d As 'c', but with severe cold: coldest month below -38°C (-36.4°F).

f Constantly moist rainfall throughout the year.

*h Warmer dry: all months above 0°C (32°F).

*k Cooler dry: at least one month below 0°C (32°F).

m Monsoon rain: short dry season, but is compensated by heavy rains during rest of the year.

n Frequent fog.

s Dry season in summer.

w Dry season in winter.

* Modification of Köppen definition

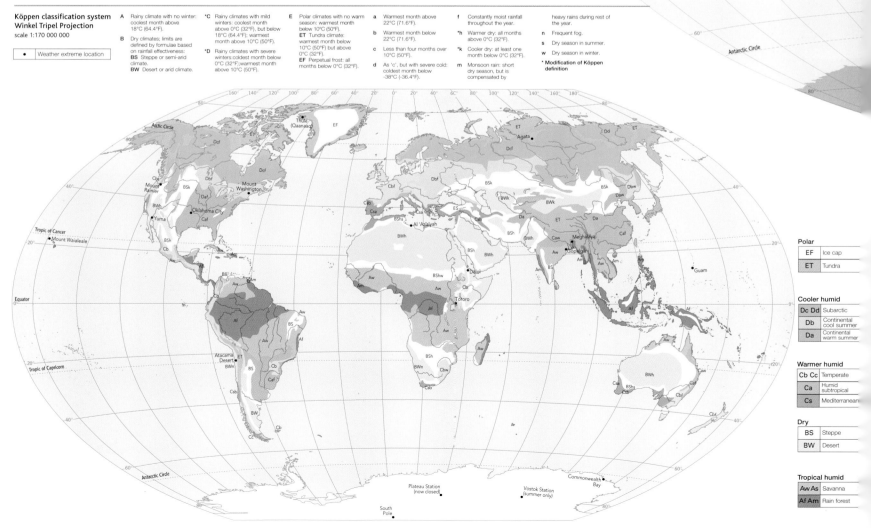

Polar
EF	Ice cap
ET	Tundra

Cooler humid
Dc Dd	Subarctic
Db	Continental cool summer
Da	Continental warm summer

Warmer humid
Cb Cc	Temperate
Ca	Humid subtropical
Cs	Mediterranean

Dry
BS	Steppe
BW	Desert

Tropical humid
Aw As	Savanna
Af Am	Rain forest

WORLD LAND COVER

Winkel Tripel Projection
scale 1:107 000 000

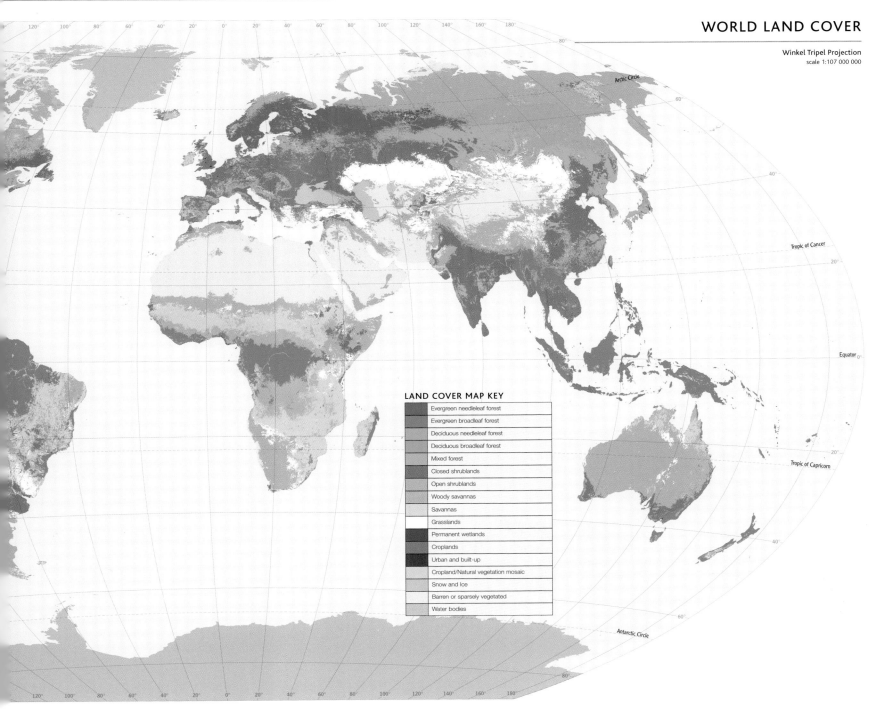

LAND COVER MAP KEY

- Evergreen needleleaf forest
- Evergreen broadleaf forest
- Deciduous needleleaf forest
- Deciduous broadleaf forest
- Mixed forest
- Closed shrublands
- Open shrublands
- Woody savannas
- Savannas
- Grasslands
- Permanent wetlands
- Croplands
- Urban and built-up
- Cropland/Natural vegetation mosaic
- Snow and ice
- Barren or sparsely vegetated
- Water bodies

WORLD WEATHER EXTREMES

Highest shade temperature	57.8°C/136°F Al 'Azīzīyah, Libya (13th September 1922)
Hottest place – Annual mean	34.4°C/93.9°F Dalol, Ethiopia
Driest place – Annual mean	0.1 mm/0.004 inches Atacama Desert, Chile
Most sunshine – Annual mean	90% Yuma, Arizona, USA (over 4 000 hours)
Least sunshine	Nil for 182 days each year, South Pole
Lowest screen temperature	-89.2°C/-128.6°F Vostok Station, Antarctica (21st July 1983)
Coldest place – Annual mean	-56.6°C/-69.9°F Plateau Station, Antarctica
Wettest place – Annual mean	11 873 mm/467.4 inches Meghalaya, India
Most rainy days	Up to 350 per year Mount Waialeale, Hawaii, USA
Windiest place	322 km per hour/200 miles per hour in gales, Commonwealth Bay, Antarctica

Highest surface wind speed		
– High altitude		372 km per hour/231 miles per hour Mount Washington, New Hampshire, USA (12th April 1934)
– Low altitude		333 km per hour/207 miles per hour Thule (Qaanaaq), (Greenland 8th March 1972)
– Tornado		512 km per hour/318 miles per hour Oklahoma City, Oklahoma, USA (3rd May 1999)
Greatest snowfall		31 102 mm/1 224.5 inches Mount Rainier, Washington, USA (19th February 1971 – 18th February 1972)
Heaviest hailstones		1 kg/2.21 lb Gopalganj, Bangladesh (14th April 1986)
Thunder-days – Average		251 days per year Tororo, Uganda
Highest barometric pressure		1 083.8 mb Agata, Siberia, Russian Federation (31st December 1968)
Lowest barometric pressure		870 mb 483 km/300 miles west of Guam, Pacific Ocean (12th October 1979)

PRECIPITATION IN THE 2080s

Predicted average precipitation change

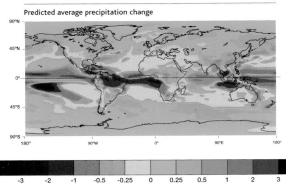

Average precipitation change (mm per day)

-3 -2 -1 -0.5 -0.25 0 0.25 0.5 1 2 3

TEMPERATURE IN THE 2080s

Predicted annual mean temperature change

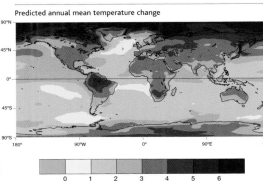

Annual mean temperature change (°C)

0 1 2 3 4 5 6

GLOBAL TEMPERATURE DIFFERENCES, 1950–2080

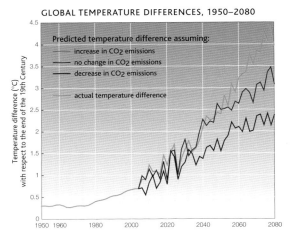

Predicted temperature difference assuming:
— increase in CO_2 emissions
— no change in CO_2 emissions
— decrease in CO_2 emissions

actual temperature difference

Temperature difference (°C) with respect to the end of the 19th Century

WORLD POPULATION DISTRIBUTION AND THE WORLD'S MAJOR CITIES

Winkel Tripel Projection
scale approximately 1:109 000 000

TOP TWENTY COUNTRIES BY POPULATION AND POPULATION DENSITY 2003

TOTAL POPULATION 2003	COUNTRY	RANK	POPULATION DENSITY 2003 (countries with populations over 10 million) COUNTRY	per sq mile	per sq km
1 289 161 000	China	1	Bangladesh	2 639	1 019
1 065 462 000	India	2	Taiwan	1 614	623
294 043 000	United States of America	3	South Korea	1 244	480
219 883 000	Indonesia	4	Netherlands	1 007	389
178 470 000	Brazil	5	India	900	348
153 578 000	Pakistan	6	Belgium	876	338
146 736 000	Bangladesh	7	Japan	875	338
143 246 000	Russian Federation	8	Sri Lanka	753	291
127 654 000	Japan	9	Philippines	691	267
124 009 000	Nigeria	10	Vietnam	640	247
103 457 000	Mexico	11	United Kingdom	625	241
82 476 000	Germany	12	Germany	598	231
81 377 000	Vietnam	13	Pakistan	495	191
79 999 000	Philippines	14	Italy	494	191
71 931 000	Egypt	15	North Korea	487	188
71 325 000	Turkey	16	Nepal	443	171
70 678 000	Ethiopia	17	China	348	135
68 920 000	Iran	18	Nigeria	348	134
62 833 000	Thailand	19	Czech Republic	336	130
60 144 000	France	20	Poland	320	123

WORLD POPULATION GROWTH BY CONTINENT 1750–2050

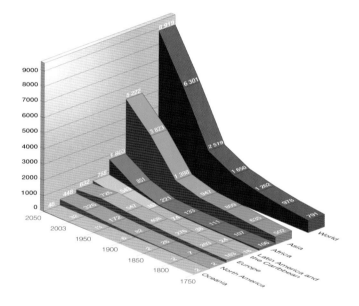

POPULATION CHANGE 2000–2005

Average annual rate of population change

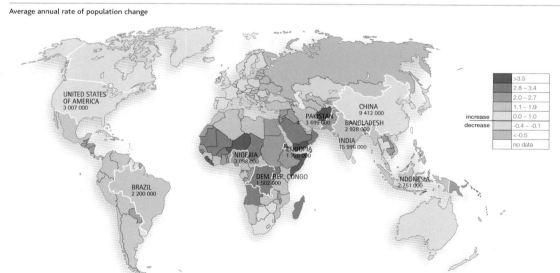

	increase / decrease
>3.5	
2.8 – 3.4	
2.0 – 2.7	increase
1.1 – 1.9	
0.0 – 1.0	
-0.4 – -0.1	decrease
<-0.5	
no data	

THE WORLD'S LARGEST CITIES 2005

City	Country	Population
Tōkyō	Japan	35 327 000
Mexico City	Mexico	19 013 000
New York	United States of America	18 498 000
Mumbai	India	18 336 000
São Paulo	Brazil	18 333 000
Delhi	India	15 334 000
Kolkata	India	14 299 000
Buenos Aires	Argentina	13 349 000
Jakarta	Indonesia	13 194 000
Shanghai	China	12 665 000
Dhaka	Bangladesh	12 560 000
Los Angeles	United States of America	12 146 000
Karachi	Pakistan	11 819 000
Rio de Janeiro	Brazil	11 469 000
Ōsaka	Japan	11 286 000
Cairo	Egypt	11 146 000
Lagos	Nigeria	11 135 000
Beijing	China	10 849 000
Manila	Philippines	10 677 000
Moscow	Russian Federation	10 672 000
Paris	France	9 854 000
İstanbul	Turkey	9 760 000
Seoul	South Korea	9 592 000
Tianjin	China	9 346 000
Chicago	United States of America	8 711 000
Lima	Peru	8 180 000
London	United Kingdom	7 615 000
Bogotá	Colombia	7 594 000
Tehrān	Iran	7 352 000
Hong Kong	China	7 182 000
Chennai	India	6 915 000
Bangkok	Thailand	6 604 000
Essen	Germany	6 566 000
Bangalore	India	6 532 000
Lahore	Pakistan	6 373 000
Hyderabad	India	6 145 000
Wuhan	China	6 003 000
Baghdād	Iraq	5 910 000
Kinshasa	Dem. Rep. of Congo	5 717 000
Santiago	Chile	5 623 000
Riyadh	Saudi Arabia	5 514 000
Miami	United States of America	5 380 000
Philadelphia	United States of America	5 325 000
St Petersburg	Russian Federation	5 315 000
Belo Horizonte	Brazil	5 304 000
Ahmadabad	India	5 171 000
Madrid	Spain	5 145 000
Toronto	Canada	5 060 000
Ho Chi Minh City	Vietnam	5 030 000
Chongqing	China	4 975 000

KEY POPULATION STATISTICS FOR MAJOR REGIONS

	Population (millions) 2003	Growth (per cent)	Infant mortality rate	Total fertility rate	Life expectancy (years)
World	6 301	1.2	56	2.7	65
More developed regions	1 203	0.3	8	1.6	76
Less developed regions	5 098	1.5	61	2.9	63
Africa	851	2.2	89	4.9	49
Asia	3 823	1.3	53	2.6	67
Europe	726	-0.1	9	1.4	74
Latin America and the Caribbean	543	1.4	32	2.5	70
North America	326	1.0	7	2.1	77
Oceania	32	1.2	26	2.3	74

Infant mortality rate: Number of deaths of children under 5 per 1 000 live births, 2000–2005.
Total fertility rate: The average number of children that would be born to a woman during her child-bearing years, 2000–2005.

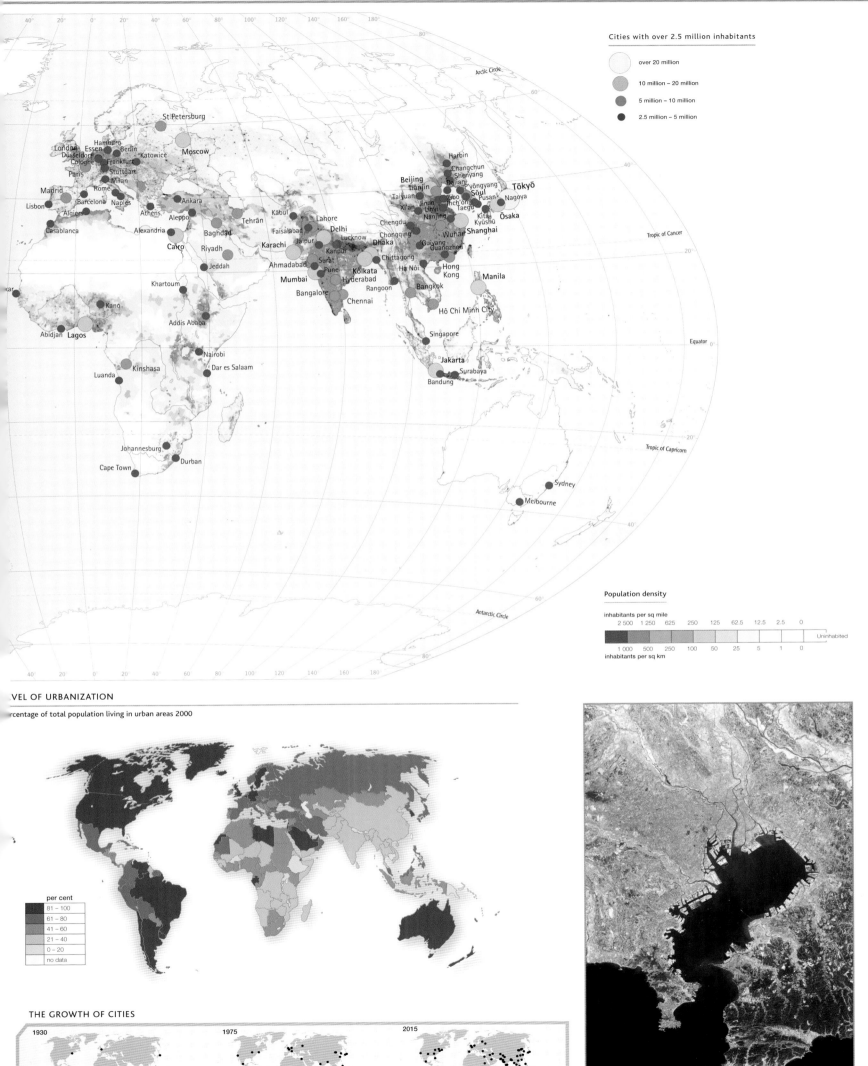

Cities with over 2.5 million inhabitants

- over 20 million
- 10 million – 20 million
- 5 million – 10 million
- 2.5 million – 5 million

Population density

inhabitants per sq mile

| 2 500 | 1 250 | 625 | 250 | 125 | 62.5 | 12.5 | 2.5 | 0 | Uninhabited |

| 1 000 | 500 | 250 | 100 | 50 | 25 | 5 | 1 | 0 |

inhabitants per sq km

VEL OF URBANIZATION

rcentage of total population living in urban areas 2000

per cent

- 81 – 100
- 61 – 80
- 41 – 60
- 21 – 40
- 0 – 20
- no data

THE GROWTH OF CITIES

1930   1975   2015

Each dot on the map represents a city with over 5 million inhabitants

Tōkyō, the world's largest city, has grown to incorporate neighbouring towns and has been restricted only by hills surrounding the city

© Collins Bartholomew Ltd

INTERNATIONAL TELECOMMUNICATIONS TRAFFIC 2003

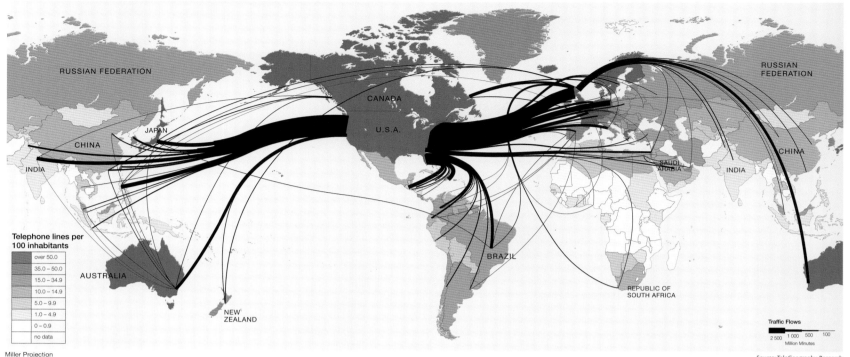

Telephone lines per
100 inhabitants

	over 50.0
	35.0 – 50.0
	15.0 – 34.9
	10.0 – 14.9
	5.0 – 9.9
	1.0 – 4.9
	0 – 0.9
	no data

Miller Projection

Traffic Flows

2 500 1 000 500 100
Million Minutes

Source: TeleGeography Research
© Primetrica, Inc

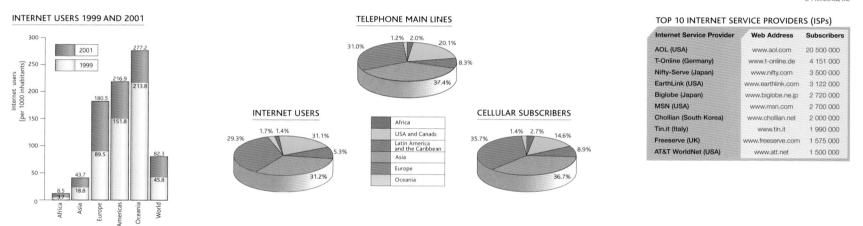

INTERNET USERS 1999 AND 2001

Internet users (per 1000 inhabitants)

- 2001
- 1999

Africa: 8.5 / 3.7
Asia: 43.7 / 18.8
Europe: 180.5 / 89.5
Americas: 216.9 / 151.8
Oceania: 277.2 / 213.8
World: 82.3 / 45.8

TELEPHONE MAIN LINES

31.0% · 1.2% · 2.0% · 20.1% · 8.3% · 37.4%

INTERNET USERS

29.3% · 1.7% · 1.4% · 31.1% · 5.3% · 31.2%

- Africa
- USA and Canada
- Latin America and the Caribbean
- Asia
- Europe
- Oceania

CELLULAR SUBSCRIBERS

35.7% · 1.4% · 2.7% · 14.6% · 8.9% · 36.7%

TOP 10 INTERNET SERVICE PROVIDERS (ISPs)

Internet Service Provider	Web Address	Subscribers
AOL (USA)	www.aol.com	20 500 000
T-Online (Germany)	www.t-online.de	4 151 000
Nifty-Serve (Japan)	www.nifty.com	3 500 000
EarthLink (USA)	www.earthlink.com	3 122 000
Biglobe (Japan)	www.biglobe.ne.jp	2 720 000
MSN (USA)	www.msn.com	2 700 000
Chollian (South Korea)	www.chollian.net	2 000 000
Tin.it (Italy)	www.tin.it	1 990 000
Freeserve (UK)	www.freeserve.com	1 575 000
AT&T WorldNet (USA)	www.att.net	1 500 000

GEOSTATIONARY COMMUNICATIONS SATELLITES

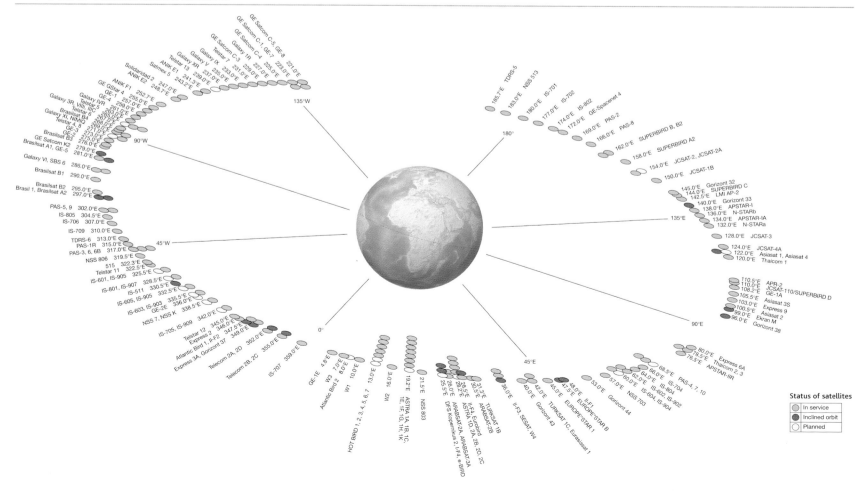

Status of satellites
- In service
- Inclined orbit
- Planned

KEY TO CITY PLANS

Built-up area	Cemetery	Marsh	Road
Park/Open space	Water	River/Canal	Railway

Administrative boundary	General place of interest	Academic/Municipal building	
Airport	Place of worship	Transport location	

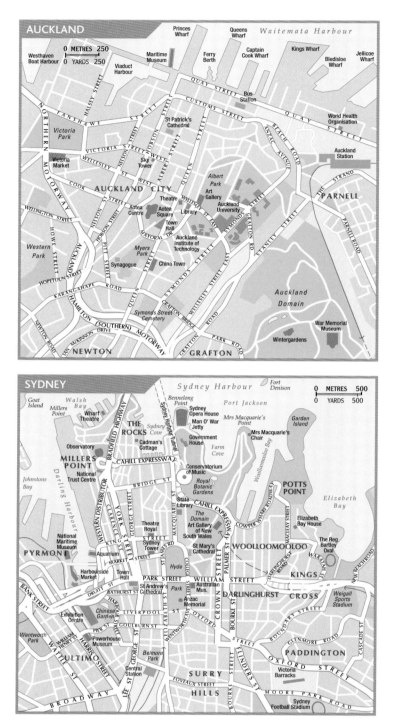

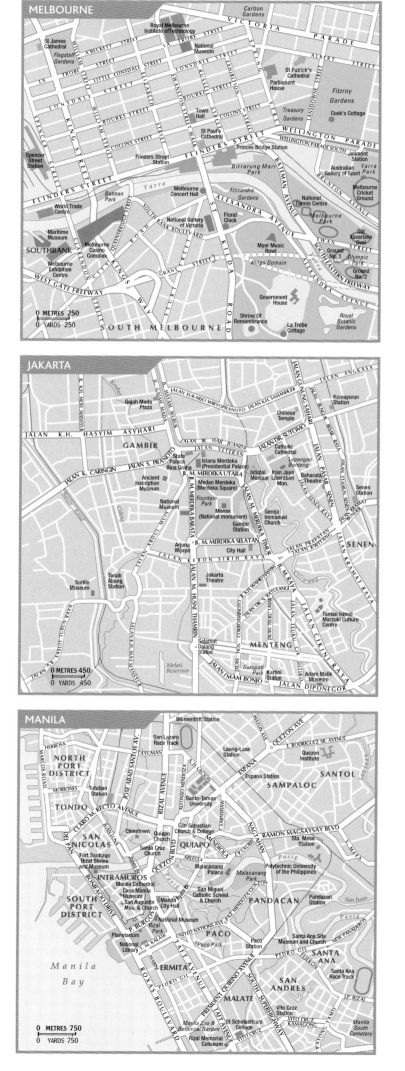

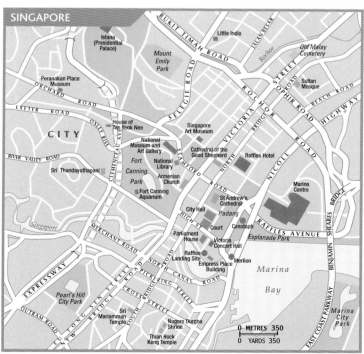

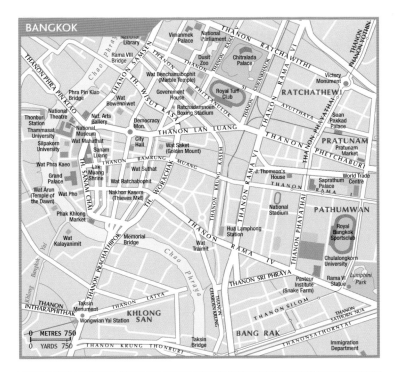

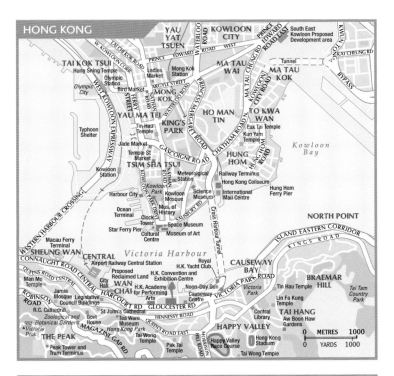

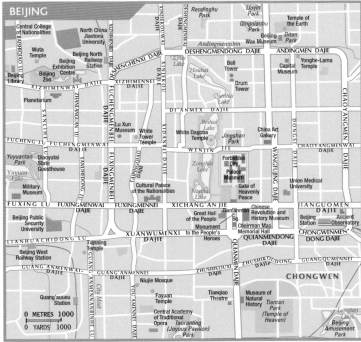

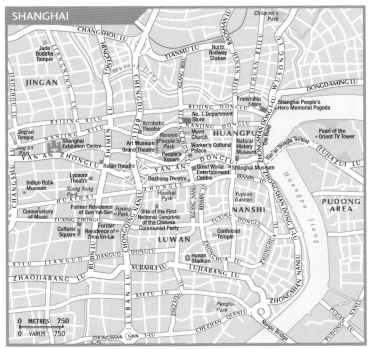

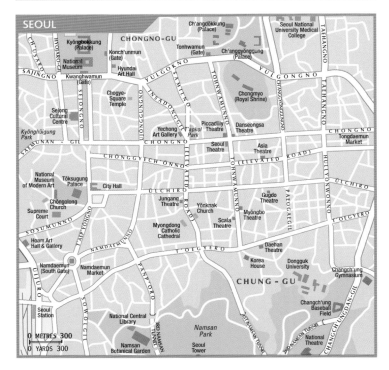

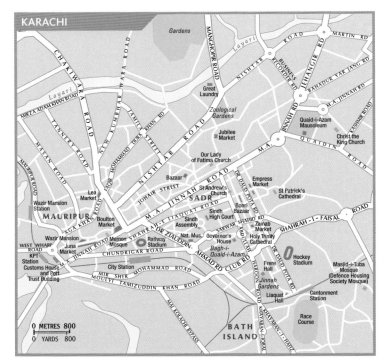

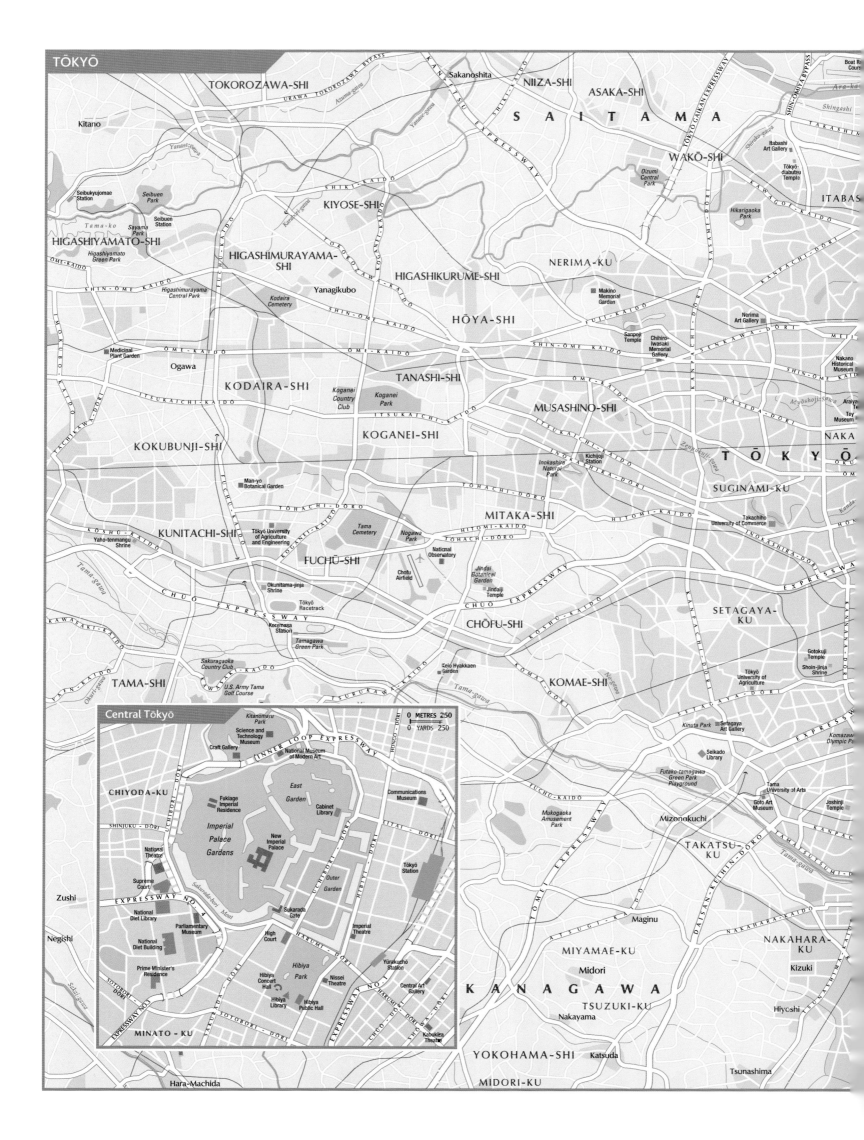

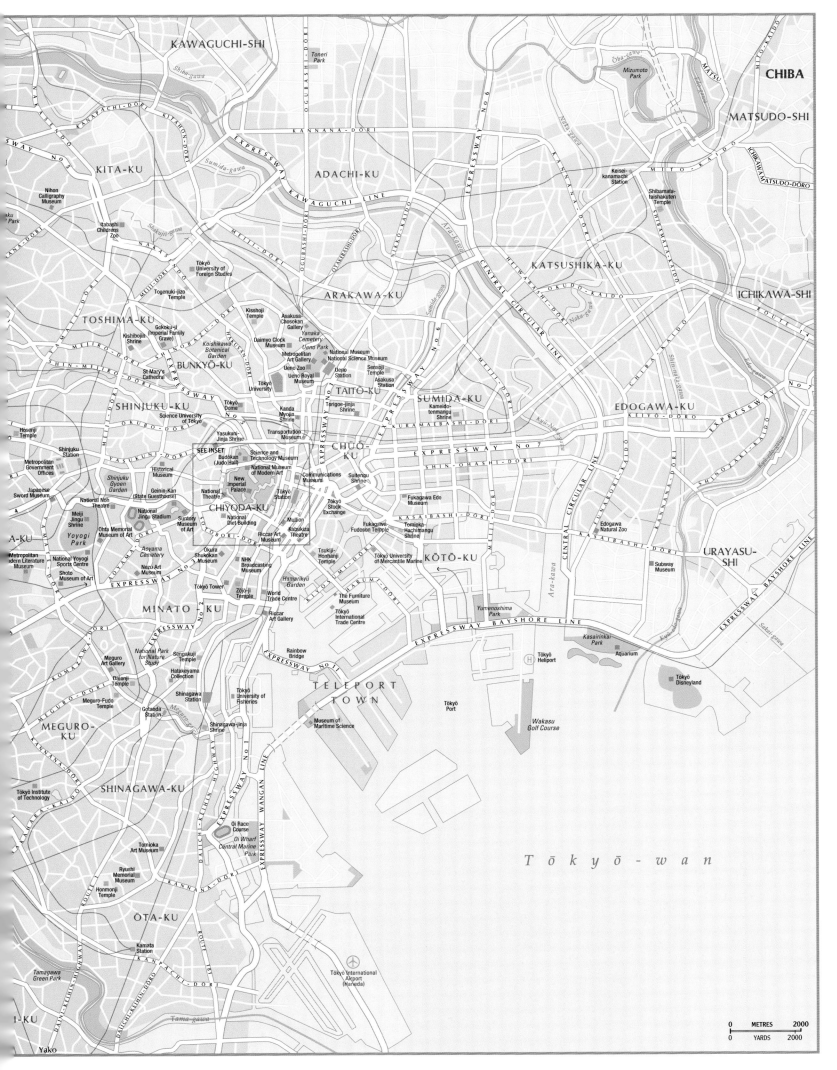

CHIBA

MATSUDO-SHI

ICHIKAWA-SHI

KAWAGUCHI-SHI

KITA-KU

KATSUSHIKA-KU

ADACHI-KU

ARAKAWA-KU

TOSHIMA-KU

BUNKYŌ-KU

SUMIDA-KU

EDOGAWA-KU

TAITŌ-KU

SHINJUKU-KU

CHŪŌ-KU

CHIYODA-KU

URAYASU-SHI

KŌTŌ-KU

MINATO-KU

TELEPORT TOWN

MEGURO-KU

SHINAGAWA-KU

ŌTA-KU

Tōkyō-wan

Yoyogi Park

Nihon Calligraphy Museum

Itabashi Childrens Zoo

Tōkyō University of Foreign Studies

Togenuki-jizo Temple

Kisshoji Temple

Asakusa-Chosokan Gallery

Daimyo Clock Museum

Yanaka Cemetery

Ueno Park

National Museum

Gokoku-ji (Imperial Family Grave)

Koishikawa Botanical Garden

Metropolitan Art Gallery

National Science Museum

Kishibojin Shrine

St Mary's Cathedral

Ueno Zoo

Ueno Royal Museum

Depo Station

Sensōji Temple

Asakusa Station

Tōkyō University

Science University of Tokyo

Tōkyō Dome

Kanda Myojin Shrine

Torigoe-jinja Shrine

Kameido-tenmangu Shrine

Hosenji Temple

Yasukuni-Jinja Shrine

Transportation Museum

SEE INSET

Budōkan (Judo Hall)

Science and Technology Museum

KURAMAEBASHI-DORI

Metropolitan Government Offices

Historical Museum

National Museum of Modern Art

Communications Museum

Fukagawa Edo Museum

Shinjuku Station

New Imperial Palace

Suitengu Shrine

Japanese Sword Museum

National Noh Theatre

Geinin-Kan (State Guesthouse)

National Theatre

Tōkyō Station

National Diet Building

Tōkyō Stock Exchange

Fukagawa-Fudoson Temple

Shinjuku Gyoen Garden

Mullion

Suntory Museum of Art

Riccar Art Museum

Kabukiza Theatre

Tomioka-Hachimangu Shrine

Edogawa Natural Zoo

Meiji Jingu Shrine

Ohta Memorial Museum of Art

National Jingu Stadium

Okura Shukokan Museum

Tsukiji-Honhanji Temple

Tōkyō University of Mercantile Marine

Metropolitan Modern Literature Museum

Nezu Art Museum

NHK Broadcasting Museum

Aoyama Cemetery

Subway Museum

Shoto Museum of Art

Tōkyō Tower

Hamarikyū Garden

Tōkyō Heliport

Kasairinkai Park

National Yoyogi Sports Centre

Zōjō-ji Temple

World Trade Centre

The Furniture Museum

Aquarium

Meguro Art Gallery

Sengakuji Temple

Riccar Art Gallery

Tōkyō International Trade Centre

Yumenoshima Park

Tōkyō Disneyland

National Park for Nature Study

Hatakeyama Collection

Rainbow Bridge

Daienji Temple

Shinagawa Station

Tōkyō University of Fisheries

Tōkyō Port

Meguro-Fudo Temple

Gotanda Station

Wakasu Golf Course

Tōkyō Institute of Technology

Shinagawa-jinja Shrine

Museum of Maritime Science

Tomioka Art Museum

Ōi Race Course

Ryushi Memorial Museum

Ōi Wharf Central Marine Park

Honmonji Temple

Kamata Station

Tōkyō International Airport (Haneda)

Tamagawa Green Park

Yako

MIZUMOTO Park

Keisei-kanamachi Station

Shibamata-taishakuten Temple

Toneri Park

0 METRES 2000
0 YARDS 2000

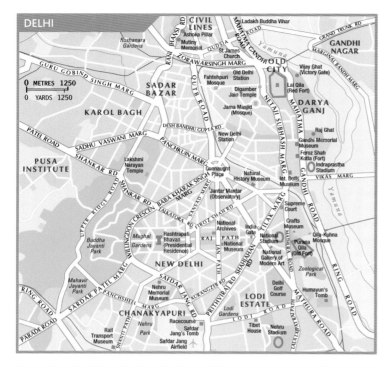

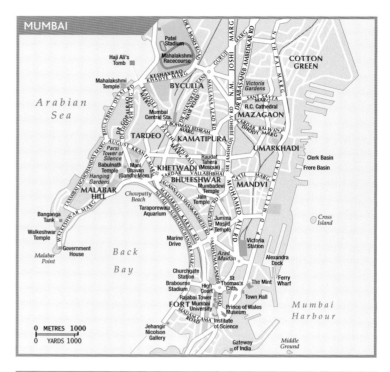

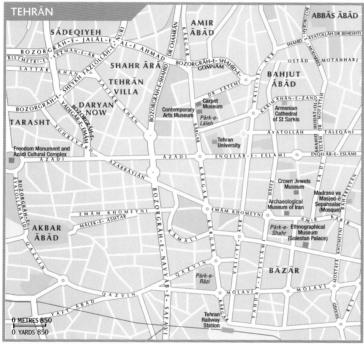

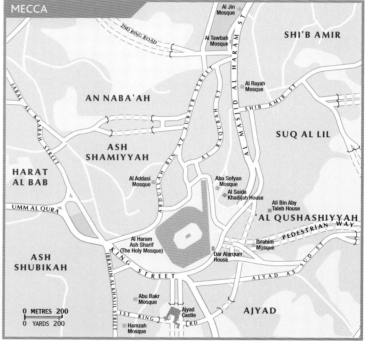

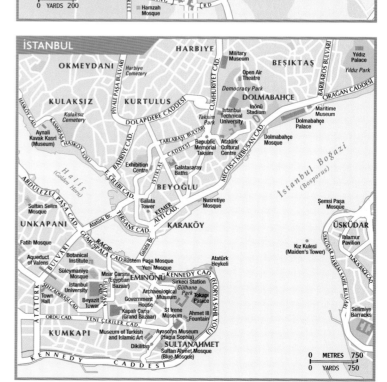

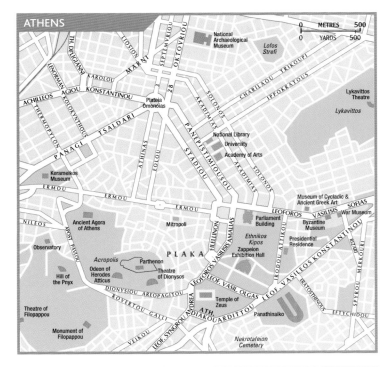

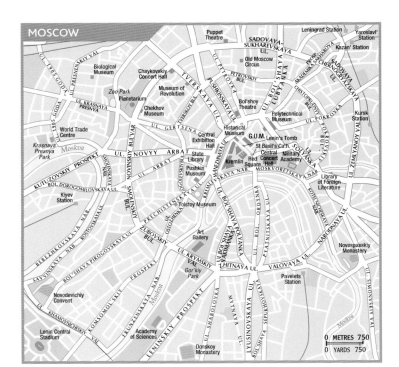

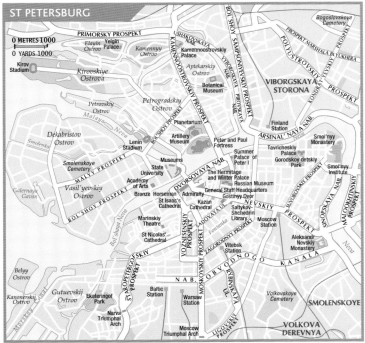

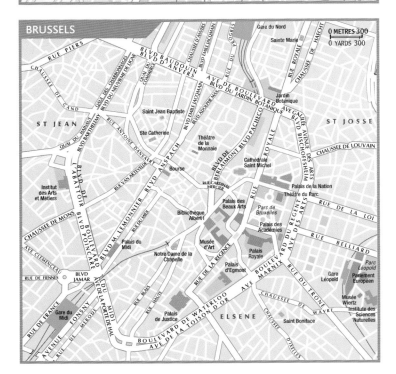

© Collins Bartholomew Ltd

LONDON

Central London

The Wigmore Hall
Dominion Theatre
British Museum
HIGH HOLBORN
Holborn
Lincoln's Inn Fields
Lincoln's Inn
KINGSWAY
Royal Courts of Justice
OXFORD STREET
REGENT STREET
Palladium
Soho
CHARING CROSS ROAD
SHAFTESBURY AVE
Royal Opera House
Theatre Royal
ALDWYCH
STRAND
NEW BOND STREET
Royal Academy of Arts
PICCADILLY CIRCUS
National Gallery
REGENT ST
HAYMARKET
London Transport Museum
STRAND
King's College
Somerset House
Mayfair
PICCADILLY
St James's
ST JAMES'S ST
TRAFALGAR SQUARE
Charing Cross Station
CHARING EMBANKMENT
VICTORIA EMBANKMENT
Royal National Theatre
PICCADILLY
PALL MALL
Admiralty Arch
WHITEHALL
HUNGERFORD BRIDGE
WATERLOO BR
Queen Elizabeth Hall
Royal Festival Hall
WATERLOO RD
Green Park
St James's Palace
Marlborough House
THE MALL
Government Buildings
BA London Eye
Waterloo Station
CONSTITUTION HILL
DOWNING ST
PARLIAMENT STREET
Treasury
Thames
Old County Hall
Buckingham Palace
BIRDCAGE WALK
St James's Park
PARLIAMENT SQUARE
WESTMINSTER BR
Big Ben
LAMBETH
GROSVENOR PLACE
WESTMINSTER
Houses of Parliament
WESTMINSTER BRIDGE ROAD
VICTORIA STREET
Westminster Abbey
Lambeth Palace Gardens
Victoria Station
Lambeth Palace

| 0 | METRES | 500 |
| 0 | YARDS | 500 |

Belmont
RAF Museums
A1
GREAT N. WAY
Holders Hill
Pinner Park
Copse Wood
Ruislip Lido
Pinner Green
Queensbury
EDGWARE ROAD
Hendon
HENDON
Golders Green
Bayhurst Wood Country Park
Pinner
Kingsbury
Fryent Country Park
FRYENT WAY
Brent Reservoir
A41
A406
Dollis Hill
Cricklewood
Ickenham
Northwick Park
Wembley Park
BRENT
Wembley Stadium
Gladstone Park
NORTH CIRCULAR ROAD
Mayfair
North Hillingdon
Wembley
Willesden
Willesden Green
Hillingdon
Sunbury Golf Course
EALING
Alperton
Harlesden
Grand Union Canal
Kilburn
HARROW ROAD
Perivale
Park Royal
North Acton
WESTERN AVENUE
HANGER LANE
Wormwood Scrubs
North Kensington
Ealing Golf Course
EALING
Ealing
WESTWAY
A40(M)
A40
Notting Hill
Holland Park
Hayes
Yiewsley
Acton
East Acton
THE VALE
Shepherd's Bush
Southall
Hanwell
Gunnersbury
HAMMERSMITH
Olympia
West Drayton
Norwood Green
M4
Gunnersbury Park
CHISWICK HIGH ROAD
AND FULHAM
M4
Brentford
Chiswick
Earls Court Exhibition Centre
Earls Court
North Hyde
Osterley Park
A4
Chiswick House
Hammersmith Bridge
Castelnau
BATH ROAD
Heston
Osterley
Syon House
Royal Botanic Gardens Kew
A316
Barn Elms Wildfowl Reserve
Football Stadium
FULHAM ROAD
Harlington
A4
Cranford
GREAT WEST ROAD
Syon Park
KEW ROAD
Barnes
Putney Bridge
KING
Pa G
Heathrow Airport (London)
A30
Hounslow West
Isleworth
Mortlake
SOUTH CIRCULAR ROAD
A205
Putney
A316
Hounslow
Richmond
Putney Heath
WA
South
Stanwell
GREAT SOUTH WEST ROAD
HOUNSLOW
Hounslow Heath
Rugby Ground
Richmond
ROEHAMPTON LANE
East Bedfont
A316
RICHMOND UPON
Richmond Park
Feltham
Crane
Twickenham
Thames
THAMES
A3
All England Lawn Tennis and Croquet Club
Wimbledon Park
Ashford
Hanworth
Teddington
Wimbledon Common
Wimbled
A308
KINGSTON HILL
Coombe Hill Golf Course
COOMBE BYPASS
Kempton Park Racecourse
Bushy Park
KINGSTON
Sunbury
M3
Hampton
Norbiton
New Malden
Bushy Mead
Queen Mary Reservoir
Molesey Reservoirs
A308
Kingston Upon Thames
Mo
West Molesey
East Molesey
Hampton Court Palace
Hampton Court Park
West Barnes
Morden Park
Shepperton
Queen Elizabeth II Reservoir
Island Barn Reservoir
Mole
Thames Ditton
A309
KINGSTON UPON THAMES
Motspur Park
Surbiton

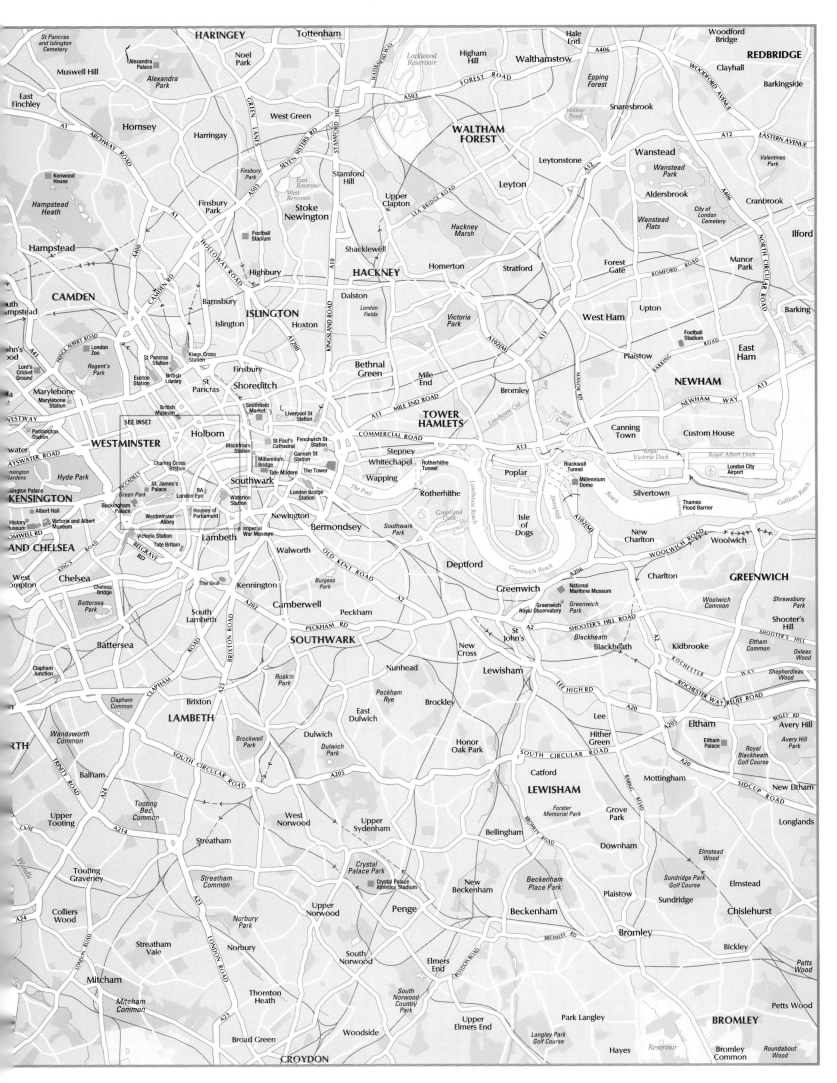

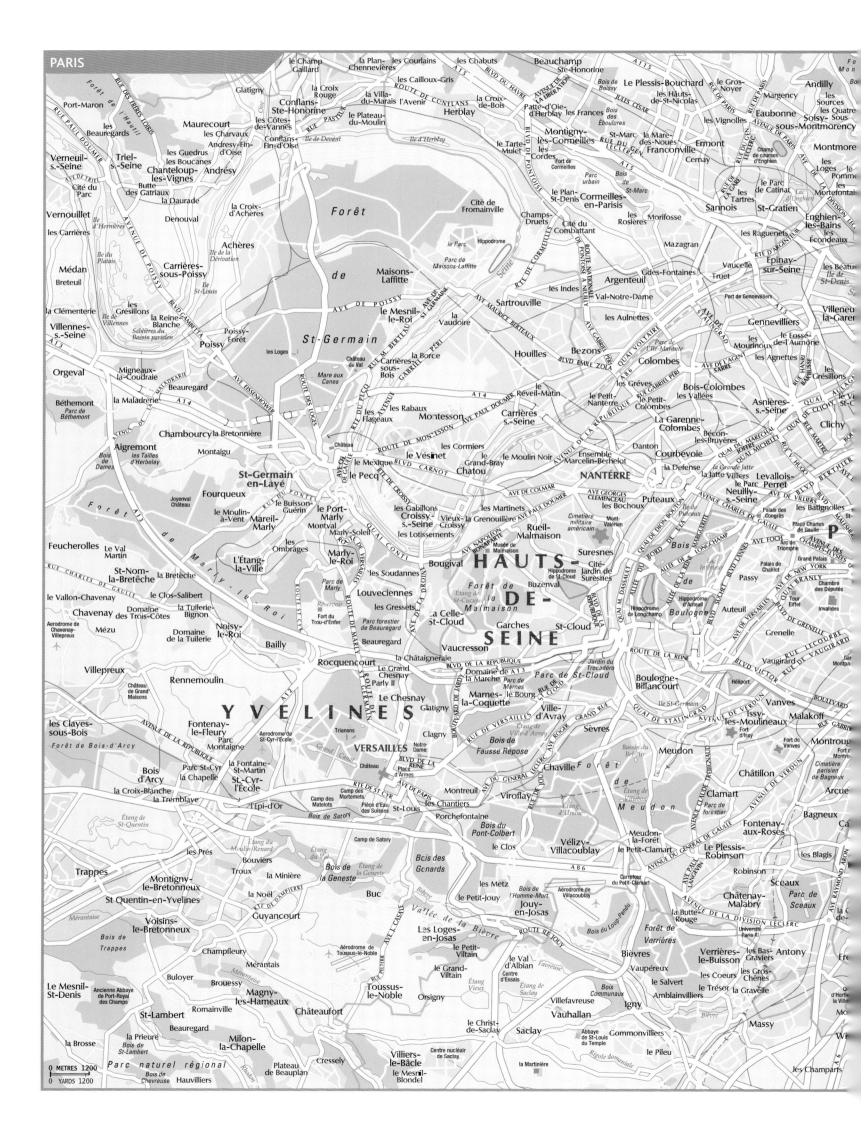

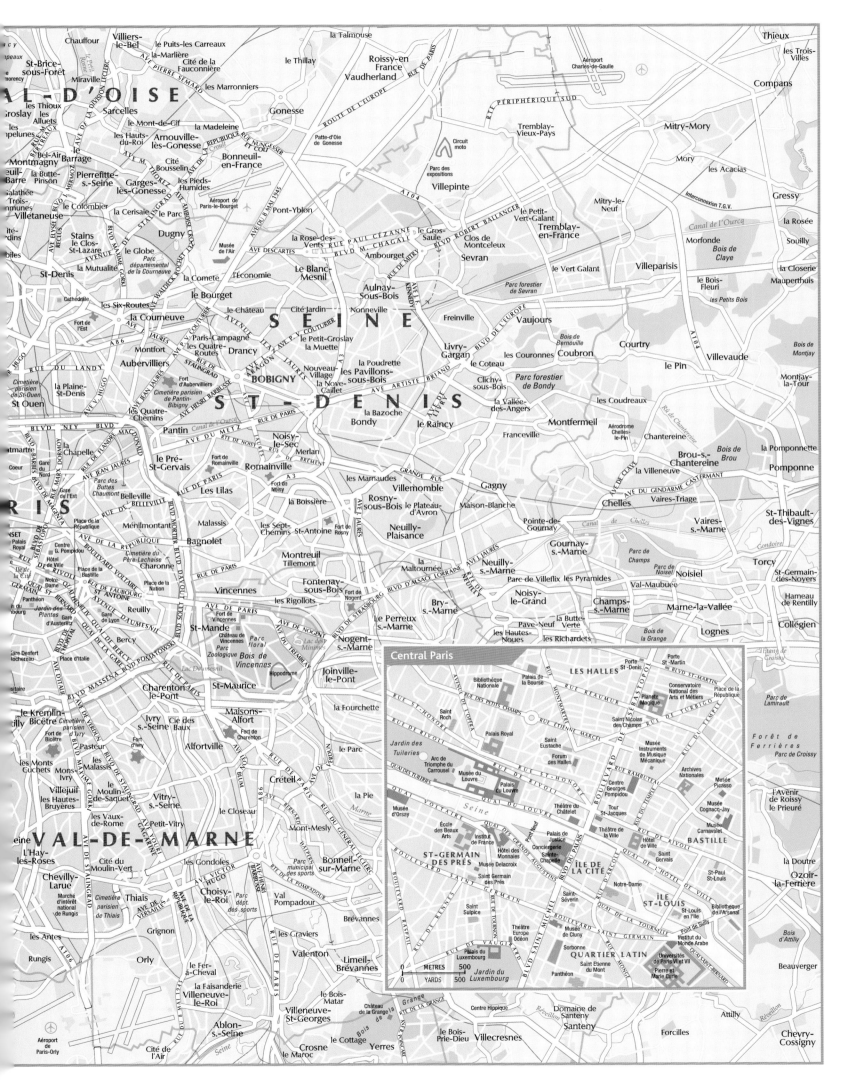

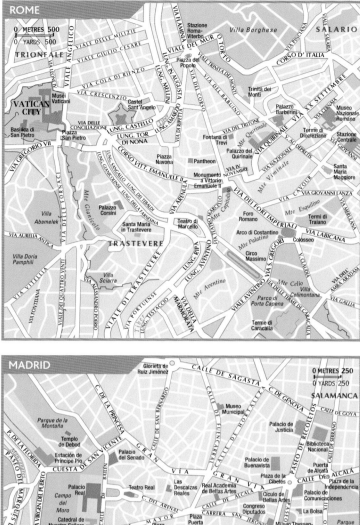

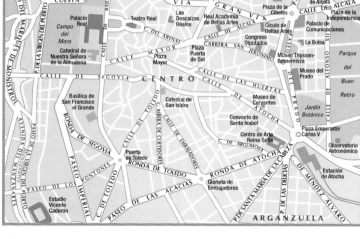

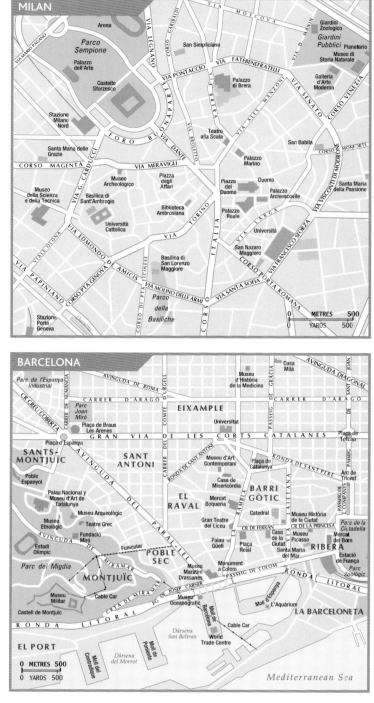

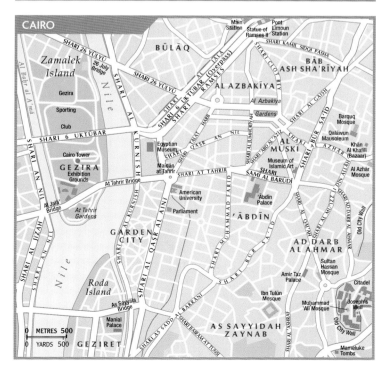

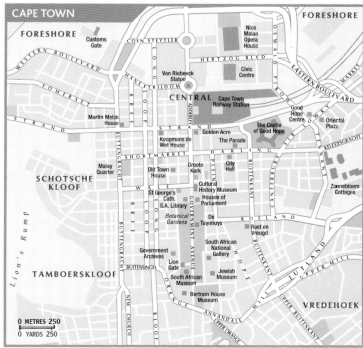

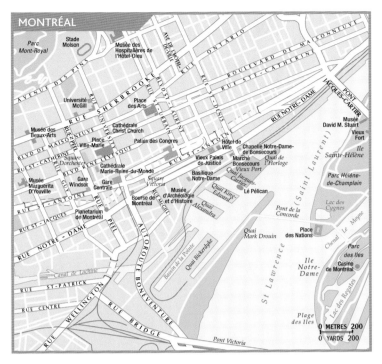

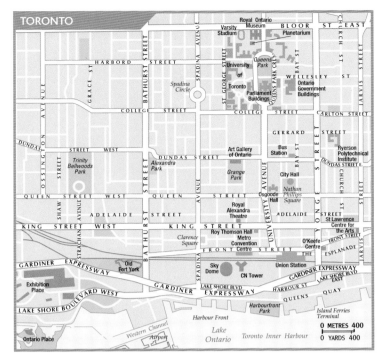

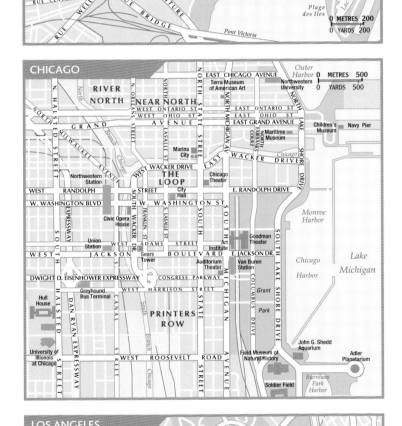

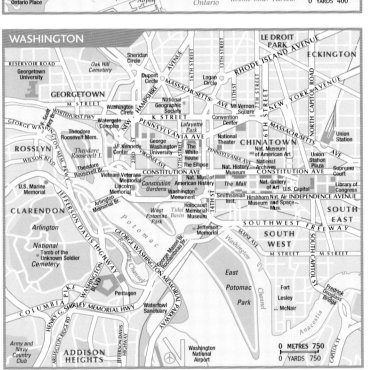

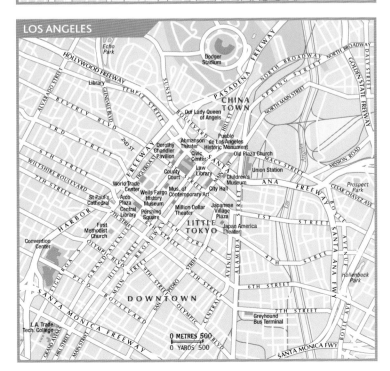

© Collins Bartholomew Ltd

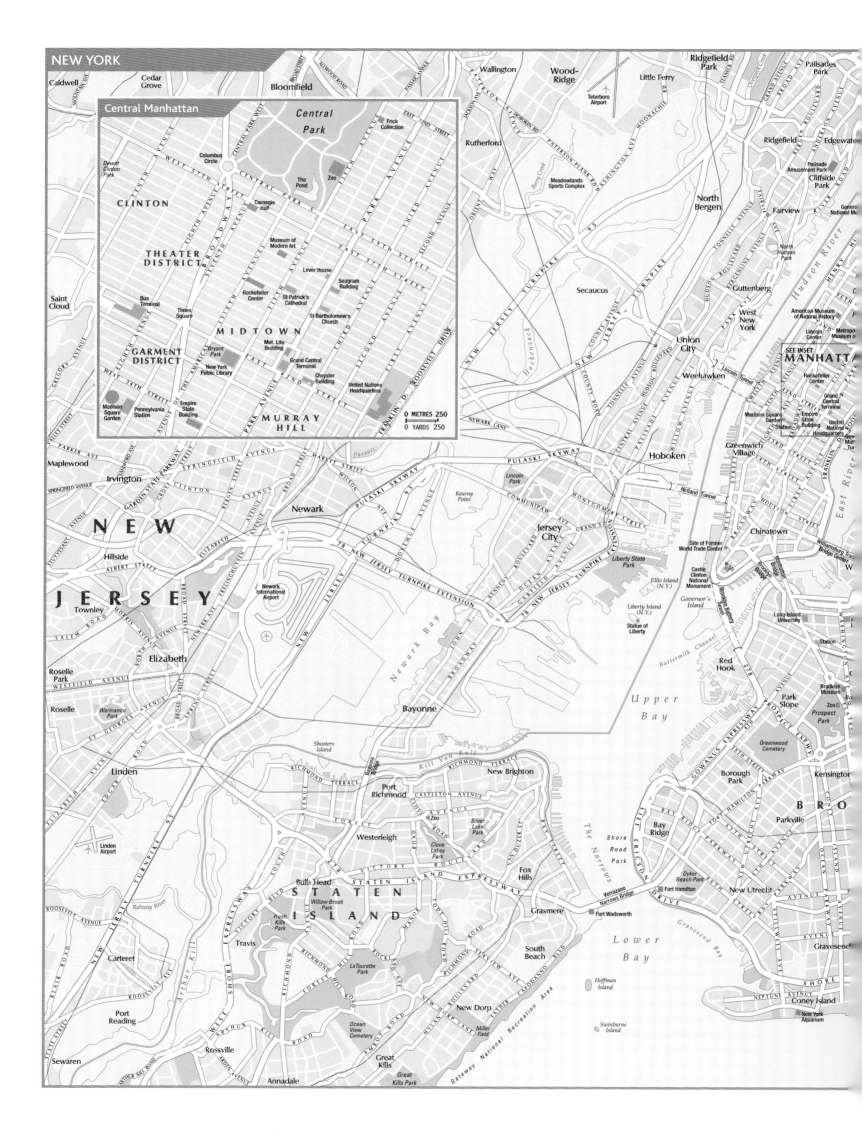

NEW YORK

Central Manhattan

Caldwell · Cedar Grove · Bloomfield · Wallington · Wood-Ridge · Little Ferry · Ridgefield Park · Palisades Park

CLINTON · THEATER DISTRICT · MIDTOWN · GARMENT DISTRICT · MURRAY HILL

Central Park · Frick Collection · Columbus Circle · Dewitt Clinton Park · Carnegie Hall · The Pond · Zoo · Museum of Modern Art · Lever House · Seagram Building · Rockefeller Center · St Patrick's Cathedral · St Bartholomew's Church · Bus Terminal · Times Square · Met. Life Building · Bryant Park · New York Public Library · Grand Central Terminal · Chrysler Building · Saint Cloud · Empire State Building · Pennsylvania Station · Madison Square Garden · United Nations Headquarters

0 METRES 250
0 YARDS 250

Rutherford · North Bergen · Teterboro Airport · Meadowlands Sports Complex · Ridgefield · Edgewater · Palisade Amusement Park · Cliffside Park · Fairview · North Hudson Park

Secaucus · Guttenberg · West New York · American Museum of Natural History · Lincoln Center · Metropolitan Museum

Union City · Weehawken · SEE INSET MANHATTAN · Rockefeller Center · Grand Central Terminal · Empire State Building · United Nations Headquarters · Madison Square Garden · Station · Lincoln Tunnel

Maplewood · Irvington · Newark · Kearny Point · Lincoln Park · Pulaski Skyway · Hoboken · Greenwich Village · Holland Tunnel

NEW · Passaic

JERSEY · Townley · Hillside · Newark International Airport · Jersey City · Liberty State Park · Ellis Island · Site of Former World Trade Center · Chinatown · Long Island University

Elizabeth · Roselle Park · Roselle · Warinanco Park · Liberty Island (N.Y.) · Statue of Liberty · Governor's Island · Castle Clinton National Monument · Buttermilk Channel · Red Hook · Brooklyn Museum · Park Slope · Zoo · Prospect Park

Linden · Bayonne · Upper Bay · Greenwood Cemetery · Borough Park · Kensington · BRO

Shooters Island · Bayonne Bridge · Kill Van Kull · New Brighton · Port Richmond · Bay Ridge Park · Bay Ridge · Parkville

Linden Airport · Richmond Terrace · Castleton Avenue · Zoo · Silver Lake Park · Clove Lakes Park · Westerleigh · The Narrows · Shore Road Park · Dyker Beach Park · New Utrecht

Fox Hills · Verrazano Narrows Bridge · Fort Hamilton

Bulls Head · STATEN ISLAND EXPRESSWAY · Willow Brook Park · Fresh Kills Park · Grasmere · Fort Wadsworth · Gravesend

Travis · Carteret · Rahway River · LaTourette Park · South Beach · Lower Bay · Hoffman Island · Gravesend Bay

Port Reading · Ocean View Cemetery · Miller Field · New Dorp · Swinburne Island · Coney Island · New York Aquarium

Sewaren · Rossville · Annadale · Great Kills · Great Kills Park · Gateway National Recreation Area

Ridgefield Park · Palisades Park
Hudson River

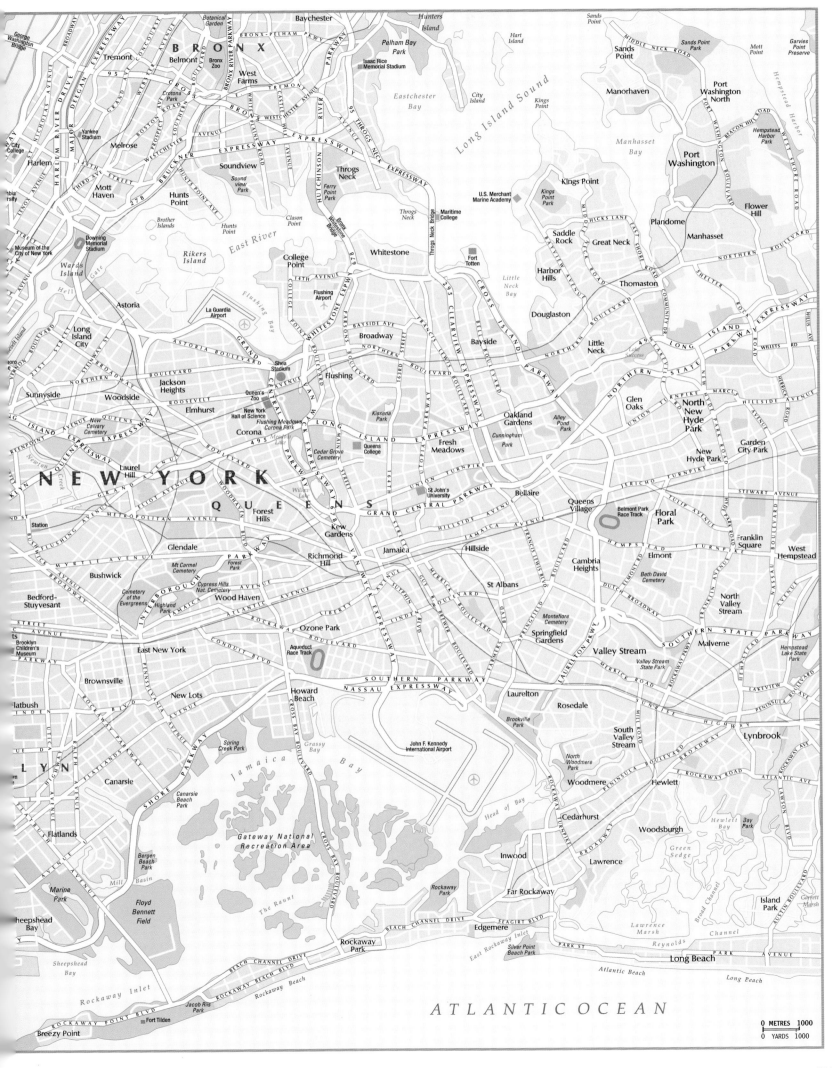

ATLANTIC OCEAN

0 METRES 1000
0 YARDS 1000

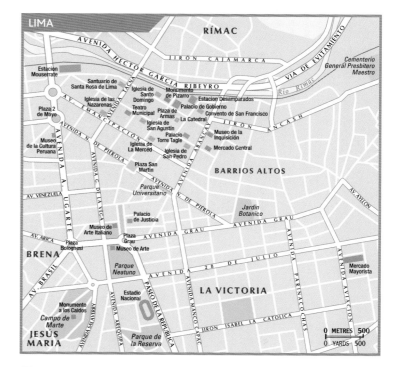

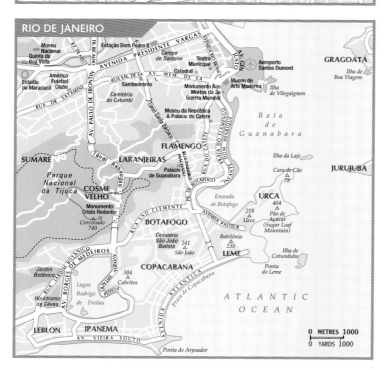

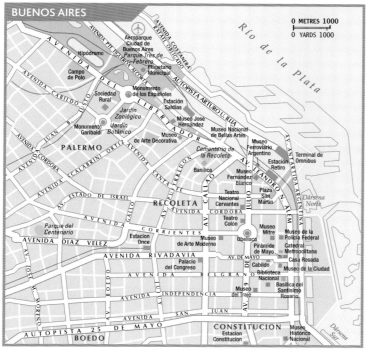

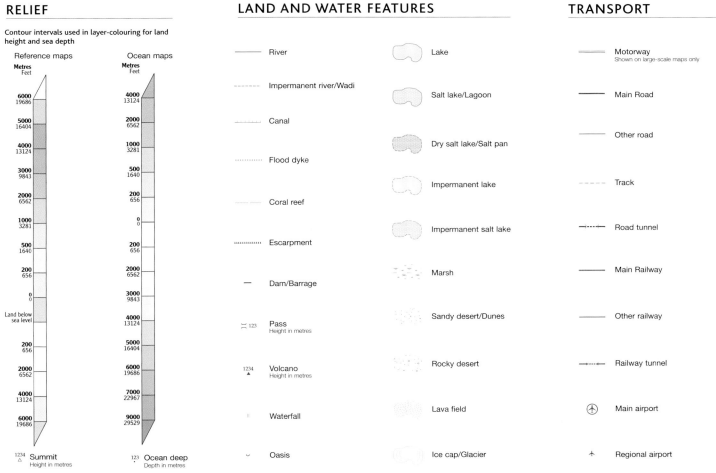

RELIEF

Contour intervals used in layer-colouring for land height and sea depth

Reference maps	Ocean maps
Metres / Feet	Metres / Feet

Reference maps:
- 6000 / 19686
- 5000 / 16404
- 4000 / 13124
- 3000 / 9843
- 2000 / 6562
- 1000 / 3281
- 500 / 1640
- 200 / 656
- 0 / 0
- Land below sea level
- 200 / 656
- 2000 / 6562
- 4000 / 13124
- 6000 / 19686

Ocean maps:
- 4000 / 13124
- 2000 / 6562
- 1000 / 3281
- 500 / 1640
- 200 / 656
- 0 / 0
- 200 / 656
- 2000 / 6562
- 3000 / 9843
- 4000 / 13124
- 5000 / 16404
- 6000 / 19686
- 7000 / 22967
- 9000 / 29529

1234 △ Summit
Height in metres

123 • Ocean deep
Depth in metres

LAND AND WATER FEATURES

- River
- Impermanent river/Wadi
- Canal
- Flood dyke
- Coral reef
- Escarpment
- Dam/Barrage
- ⊐⊏ 123 Pass — Height in metres
- 1234 ▲ Volcano — Height in metres
- Waterfall
- Oasis

- Lake
- Salt lake/Lagoon
- Dry salt lake/Salt pan
- Impermanent lake
- Impermanent salt lake
- Marsh
- Sandy desert/Dunes
- Rocky desert
- Lava field
- Ice cap/Glacier

TRANSPORT

- Motorway — Shown on large-scale maps only
- Main Road
- Other road
- Track
- Road tunnel
- Main Railway
- Other railway
- Railway tunnel
- ⊕ Main airport
- ✦ Regional airport

CITIES AND TOWNS

Population	National Capital	Administrative Capital (Shown for selected countries only)	Other City or Town
over 10 million	**Tōkyō** ▣	**Karachi** ⊙	**New York** ⊙
5 million to 10 million	**Santiago** ▣	**Tianjin** ⊙	**Hong Kong** ⊙
1 million to 5 million	**Seoul** ▣	**Lagos** ⊙	**Barranquilla** ⊙
500 000 to 1 million	**Bangui** ▣	**Douala** ◎	**Memphis** ◎
100 000 to 500 000	Wellington ▢	Mansa ○	Mara ○
50 000 to 100 000	Port of Spain ▢	Lubango ○	Arecibo ○
10 000 to 50 000	Malabo ▫	Chinhoyi ○	El Tigre ○
under 10 000	Roseau ▫	Ati ○	Soledad ○

BOUNDARIES

- International boundary
- Disputed international boundary/ alignment unconfirmed
- Ceasefire line
- Administrative boundary

STYLES OF LETTERING

Cities and towns are explained above

Country	**FRANCE**
Overseas Territory/Dependency	**Guadeloupe**
Disputed Territory	AKSAI CHIN
Administrative name — Shown for selected countries only	SCOTLAND
Area name	PATAGONIA

Island	*Gran Canaria*
Lake	*Lake Erie*
Mountain	*Mont Blanc*
River	*Thames*
Region	*LAPPLAND*

MISCELLANEOUS SYMBOLS

- National park
- Reserve
- Ancient wall
- ∴ Site of specific interest
- Built-up area

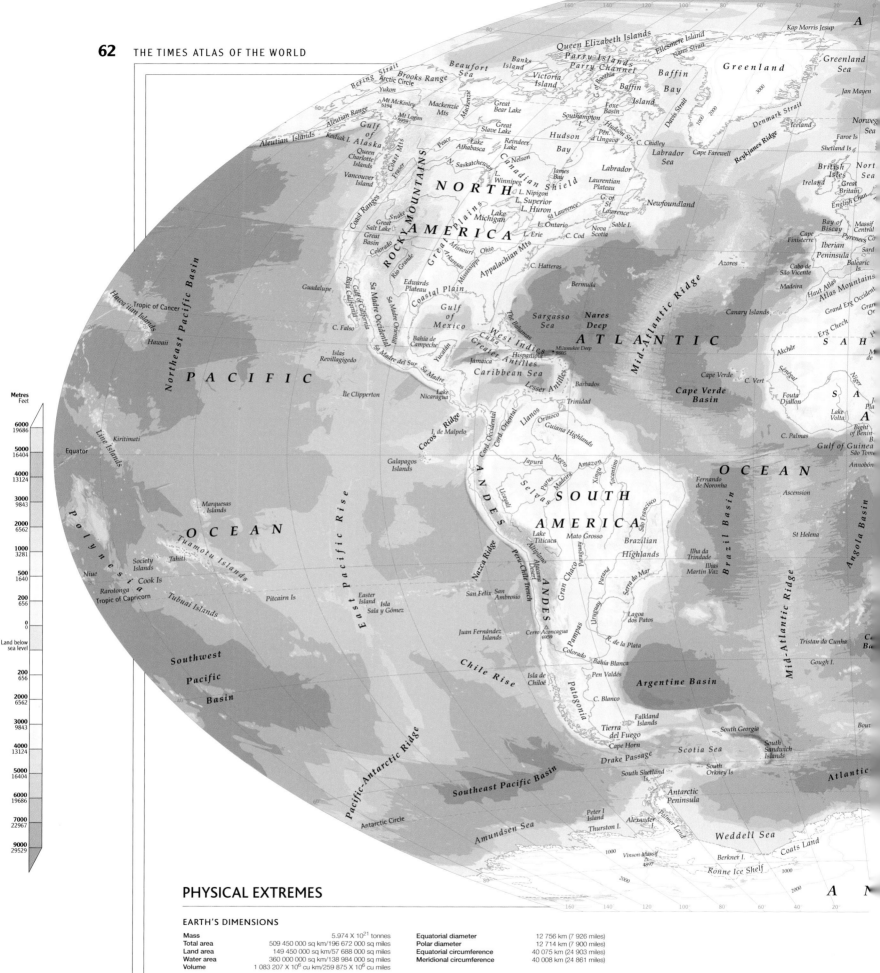

PHYSICAL EXTREMES

EARTH'S DIMENSIONS

Mass	5.974×10^{21} tonnes	Equatorial diameter	12 756 km (7 926 miles)
Total area	509 450 000 sq km/196 672 000 sq miles	Polar diameter	12 714 km (7 900 miles)
Land area	149 450 000 sq km/57 688 000 sq miles	Equatorial circumference	40 075 km (24 903 miles)
Water area	360 000 000 sq km/138 984 000 sq miles	Meridional circumference	40 008 km (24 861 miles)
Volume	$1 083 207 \times 10^{6}$ cu km/$259 875 \times 10^{6}$ cu miles		

HIGHEST MOUNTAINS

	Location	Height metres	feet
Mt Everest	China/Nepal	8 848	29 028
K2	China/Jammu and Kashmir	8 611	28 251
Kangchenjunga	India/Nepal	8 586	28 169
Lhotse	China/Nepal	8 516	27 939
Makalu	China/Nepal	8 463	27 765
Cho Oyu	China/Nepal	8 201	26 906
Dhaulagiri	Nepal	8 167	26 794
Manaslu	Nepal	8 163	26 781
Nanga Parbat	Jammu and Kashmir	8 126	26 660
Annapurna I	Nepal	8 091	26 545

LONGEST RIVERS

	Location	Length km	miles
Nile	Africa	6 695	4 160
Amazon	South America	6 516	4 049
Yangtze	Asia	6 380	3 965
Mississippi-Missouri	North America	5 969	3 709
Ob'-Irtysh	Asia	5 568	3 460
Yenisey-Angara-Selenga	Asia	5 550	3 449
Yellow	Asia	5 464	3 395
Congo	Africa	4 667	2 900
Rio de la Plata-Paraná	South America	4 500	2 796
Irtysh	Asia	4 440	2 759

LARGEST ISLANDS

	Location	Area sq km	sq miles
Greenland	North America	2 175 600	840 004
New Guinea	Oceania	808 510	312 167
Borneo	Asia	745 561	287 863
Madagascar	Africa	587 040	226 657
Baffin Island	North America	507 451	195 927
Sumatra	Asia	473 606	182 860
Honshū	Asia	227 414	87 805
Great Britain	Europe	218 476	84 354
Victoria Island	North America	217 291	83 897
Ellesmere Island	North America	196 236	75 767

LARGEST LAKES

	Location
Caspian Sea	Asia/Europe
Lake Superior	North America
Lake Victoria	Africa
Lake Huron	North America
Lake Michigan	North America
Lake Tanganyika	Africa
Great Bear Lake	North America
Lake Baikal	Asia
Lake Nyasa	Africa
Aral Sea	Asia

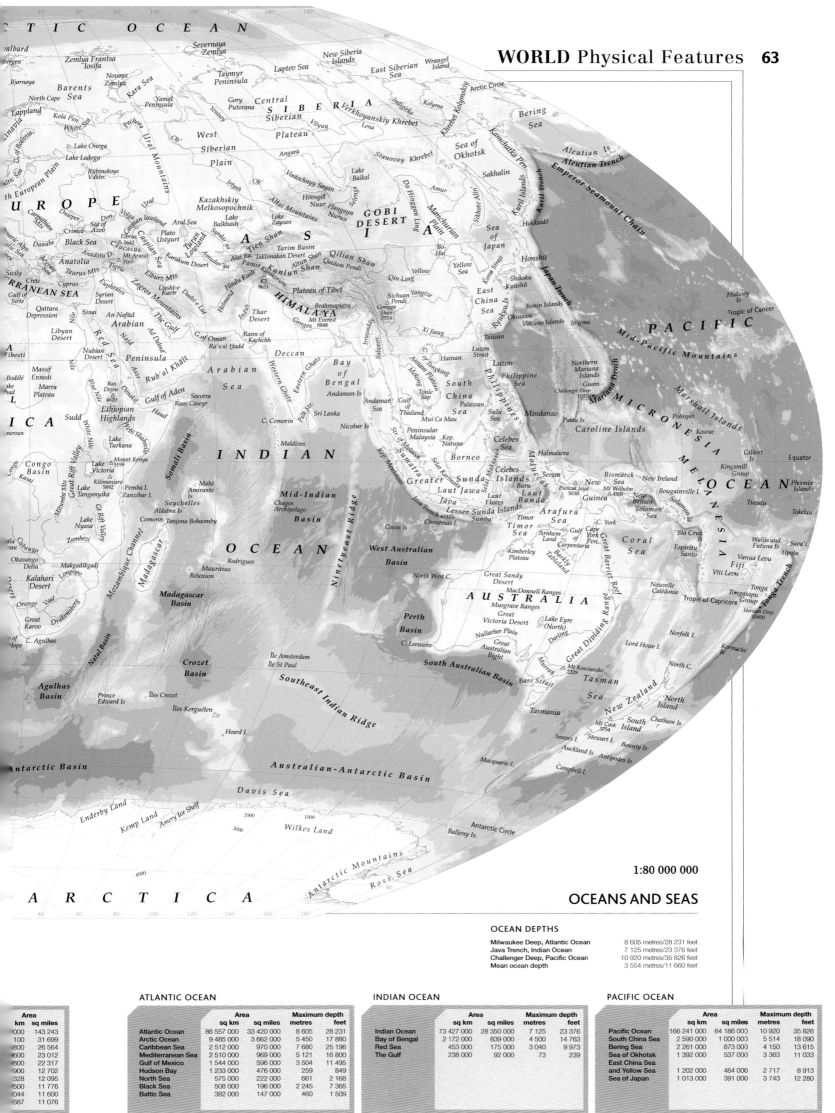

1:80 000 000

OCEANS AND SEAS

OCEAN DEPTHS

Milwaukee Deep, Atlantic Ocean	8 605 metres/28 231 feet
Java Trench, Indian Ocean	7 125 metres/23 376 feet
Challenger Deep, Pacific Ocean	10 920 metres/35 826 feet
Mean ocean depth	3 554 metres/11 660 feet

ATLANTIC OCEAN

	Area		Maximum depth	
	sq km	sq miles	metres	feet
Atlantic Ocean	86 557 000	33 420 000	8 605	28 231
Arctic Ocean	9 485 000	3 662 000	5 450	17 880
Caribbean Sea	2 512 000	970 000	7 680	25 196
Mediterranean Sea	2 510 000	969 000	5 121	16 800
Gulf of Mexico	1 544 000	596 000	3 504	11 495
Hudson Bay	1 233 000	476 000	259	849
North Sea	575 000	222 000	661	2 168
Black Sea	508 000	196 000	2 245	7 365
Baltic Sea	382 000	147 000	460	1 509

Area				
km	sq miles			
000	143 243			
100	31 699			
800	26 564			
600	23 012			
800	22 317			
900	12 702			
328	12 095			
500	11 776			
044	11 600			
687	11 076			

INDIAN OCEAN

	Area		Maximum depth	
	sq km	sq miles	metres	feet
Indian Ocean	73 427 000	28 350 000	7 125	23 376
Bay of Bengal	2 172 000	839 000	4 500	14 763
Red Sea	453 000	175 000	3 040	9 973
The Gulf	238 000	92 000	73	239

PACIFIC OCEAN

	Area		Maximum depth	
	sq km	sq miles	metres	feet
Pacific Ocean	166 241 000	64 186 000	10 920	35 826
South China Sea	2 590 000	1 000 000	5 514	18 090
Bering Sea	2 261 000	873 000	4 150	13 615
Sea of Okhotsk	1 392 000	537 000	3 363	11 033
East China Sea and Yellow Sea	1 202 000	464 000	2 717	8 913
Sea of Japan	1 013 000	391 000	3 743	12 280

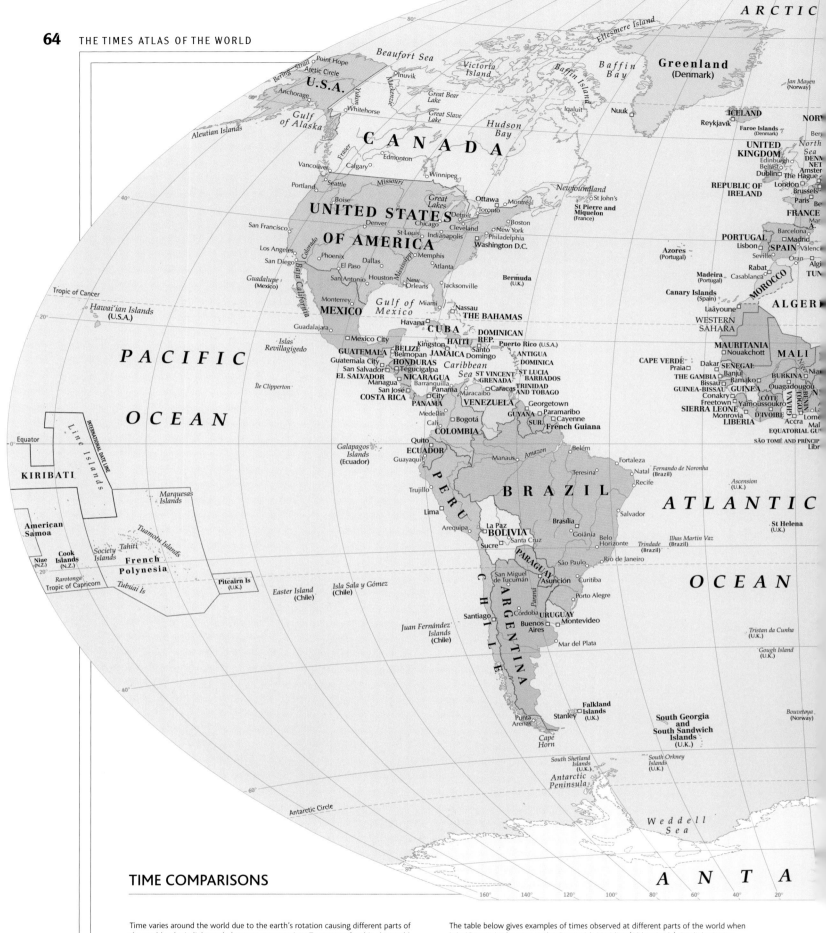

TIME COMPARISONS

Time varies around the world due to the earth's rotation causing different parts of the world to be in light or darkness at any one time. To account for this, the world is divided into twenty-four Standard Time Zones based on 15° intervals of longitude.

The table below gives examples of times observed at different parts of the world when it is 12 noon in the zone at the Greenwich Meridian (0° longitude). Daylight Saving Time, normally one hour ahead of local Standard Time, observed by certain countries for parts of the year, is not considered.

01:00	02:00	03:00	04:00	05:00	06:00	07:00	08:00	09:00	10:00	11:00	12:00
Samoa American Samoa	Cook Islands Hawaiian Islands Society Islands Tahiti	Anchorage	Vancouver Seattle San Francisco Los Angeles Pitcairn Islands	Edmonton Denver	Winnipeg Chicago Dallas Houston Monterrey Mexico City San Salvador San José Easter Island	Ottawa Toronto New York Philadelphia Washington D.C. Havana Bogotá Quito Lima	Puerto Rico Caracas Manaus La Paz Sucre Asunción	Nuuk Recife Brasília Rio de Janeiro São Paulo Montevideo Buenos Aires	South Georgia and South Sandwich Islands	Azores Cape Verde	Reykjavik Dublin London Rabat Nouakchott Dakar Freetown Accra Lomé

Winkel Tripel Projection

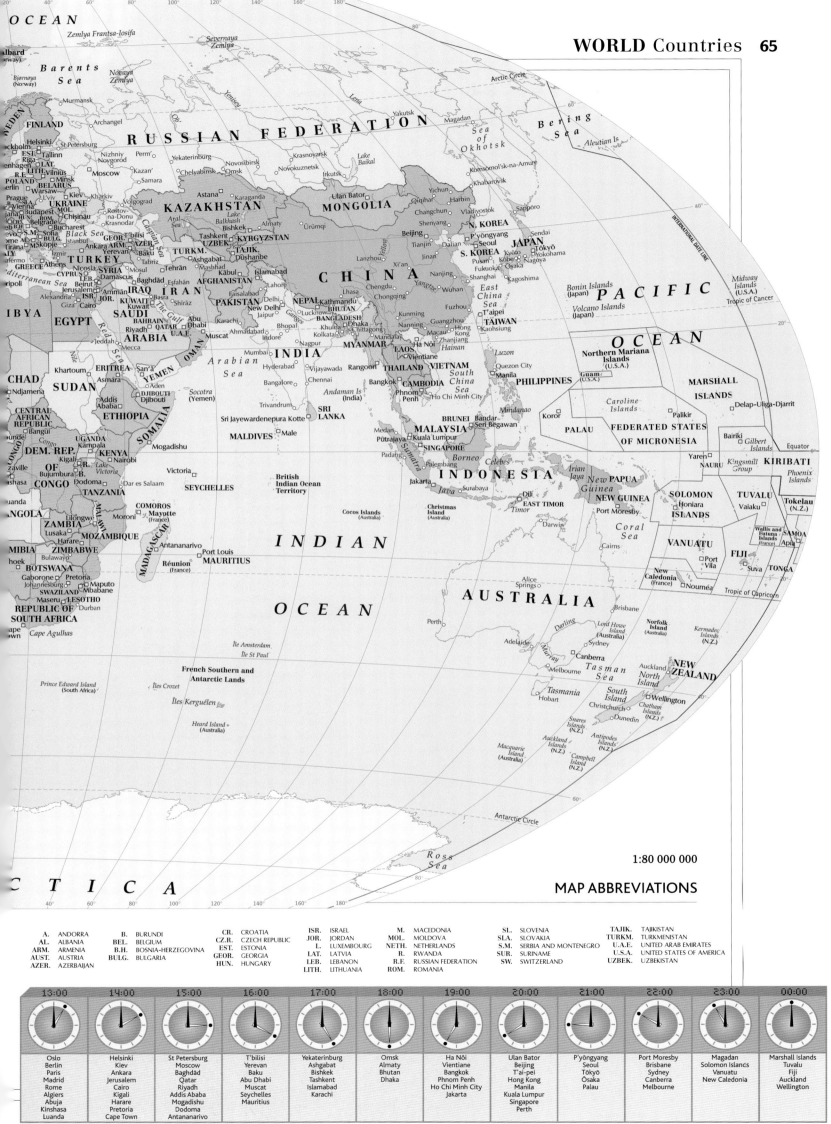

1:80 000 000

MAP ABBREVIATIONS

A.	ANDORRA	B.	BURUNDI	CR.	CROATIA	ISR.	ISRAEL	M.	MACEDONIA	SL.	SLOVENIA	TAJIK.	TAJIKISTAN
AL.	ALBANIA	BEL.	BELGIUM	CZ.R.	CZECH REPUBLIC	JOR.	JORDAN	MOL.	MOLDOVA	SLA.	SLOVAKIA	TURKM.	TURKMENISTAN
ARM.	ARMENIA	B.H.	BOSNIA-HERZEGOVINA	EST.	ESTONIA	L.	LUXEMBOURG	NETH.	NETHERLANDS	S.M.	SERBIA AND MONTENEGRO	U.A.E.	UNITED ARAB EMIRATES
AUST.	AUSTRIA	BULG.	BULGARIA	GEOR.	GEORGIA	LAT.	LATVIA	R.	RWANDA	SUR.	SURINAME	U.S.A.	UNITED STATES OF AMERICA
AZER.	AZERBAIJAN			HUN.	HUNGARY	LEB.	LEBANON	R.F.	RUSSIAN FEDERATION	SW.	SWITZERLAND	UZBEK.	UZBEKISTAN
						LITH.	LITHUANIA	ROM.	ROMANIA				

13:00	14:00	15:00	16:00	17:00	18:00	19:00	20:00	21:00	22:00	23:00	00:00
Oslo	Helsinki	St Petersburg	T'bilisi	Yekaterinburg	Omsk	Ha Nôi	Ulan Bator	P'yŏngyang	Port Moresby	Magadan	Marshall Islands
Berlin	Kiev	Moscow	Yerevan	Ashgabat	Almaty	Vientiane	Beijing	Seoul	Brisbane	Solomon Islancs	Tuvalu
Paris	Ankara	Baghdad	Baku	Bishkek	Bhutan	Bangkok	T'ai-pei	Tōkyō	Sydney	Vanuatu	Fiji
Madrid	Jerusalem	Qatar	Abu Dhabi	Tashkent	Dhaka	Phnom Penh	Hong Kong	Ōsaka	Canberra	New Caledonia	Auckland
Rome	Cairo	Riyadh	Muscat	Islamabad		Ho Chi Minh City	Manila	Palau	Melbourne		Wellington
Algiers	Kigali	Addis Ababa	Seychelles	Karachi		Jakarta	Kuala Lumpur				
Abuja	Harare	Mogadishu	Mauritius				Singapore				
Kinshasa	Pretoria	Dodoma					Perth				
Luanda	Cape Town	Antananarivo									

A B C D E

1

2

3

4

5

6

7

Hokkaidō
Kuril Island
Sea of Japan
Honshū
East China Sea
Shikoku
Kyūshū
Bonin Islands
Volcano Islands
Pagan
Northern Mariana Islands (U.S.A.)
Tinian Saipan
Rota
Guam (U.S.A.) Hagåtña

A S I A
Yangtze
Taiwan Strait
Ryukyu Islands
Luzon Strait
Luzon
Hainan
Samar
Tropic of Cancer
Mekong

Ulithi Fais
Yap Sorol Faraulep
Ngulu Eauripik
Caroline Islands
Pikelot Hall Is
Chuuk
FEDERATED STAT
Mort
Islan

Bay of Bengal
Gulf of Thailand
South China Sea
Palawan Panay
Negros
Sulu Sea
Mindanao
Palau Islands
Admiralty Islands
New Hanover
Bismarck Sea
Vanimo Wewak Rabaul New Britain
New Irela
Sepik Madang
New Guinea Mt Wilhelm Goroka PAPUA
4509 Lae
Kerema NEW GUINEA
Balimo Gulf
Daru of Papua Port Moresby
Louisiade Archipelago
So

Borneo
Celebes Sea
Laut Maluku
Halmahera
Selat Makassar
Celebes

Strait of Malacca
Sumatra
Laut Jawa
Laut Flores
Laut Banda
Timor
Sumbawa
Sumba Flores
Bali
Java (Jawa)
Kepulauan Mentawai

Arafura Sea
Wessel Islands
Cape Arnhem
Melville I.
Bathurst I.
Darwin
Arnhem Land
Timor Sea
Cape Londonderry
Ashmore and Cartier Islands (Australia)

Torres Strait
Cape York
Cape York Peninsula
Gulf of Carpentaria
Cooktown
Cairns
Normanton
Townsville

Coral Sea Islands Territory (Australia)
Great Barrier Reef
Cora
Sea

Christmas Island (Australia)

INDIAN OCEAN
Equator

Cocos Islands (Australia)

Wyndham
Halls Creek
Broome
Cape Lévêque

NORTHERN TERRITORY
Mount Isa
Cloncurry
Mackay
Rockhamp
Gladst

QUEENSLAND
Longreach
Great Sandy Desert
Mount Liebig 1524
Alice Springs
Charleville
Toowoomba
Brisb

Port Hedland
Karratha
Newman
AUSTRALIA
WESTERN AUSTRALIA
Great Victoria Desert
Oodnadatta
SOUTH AUSTRALIA
Darling
Marybor
C

Barrow Island
North West Cape
Paraburdoo
Meekatharra
Mount Magnet
Leonora
Kalgoorlie
Woomera
Port Augusta
Whyalla Port Pirie
Ceduna
Broken Hill
Orange
NEW SOUTH
Newcastle
Lithgow
Sydn
Wollongo
Tamw

Geraldton
Great Australian Bight
Esperance
Port Lincoln
Adelaide
Kangaroo Island
Bendigo
Wagga Wagga
Murray Albury
A.C.T. Canberra
WALES
VICTORIA

Perth
Fremantle
Bunbury
Albany
Mount Gambier
Geelong
Melbourne
Bass Strait
Flinders Islan

Cape Leeuwin
King Island
Devonport Launceston
TASMANIA
Hobart
South East Cape

Tropic of Capricorn

60° 30° 75° 90° 45° 105° 120° 135°
A B C D E

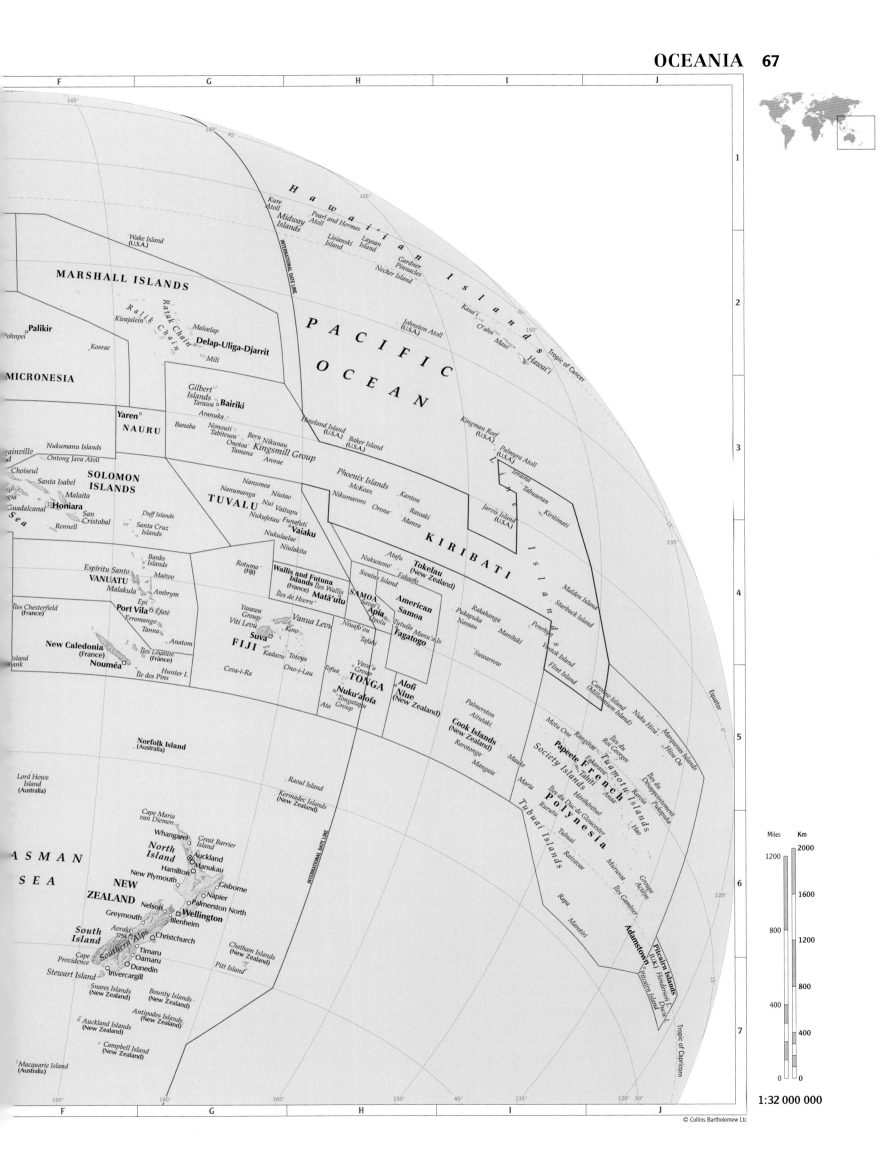

F G H I J

Hawaiian Islands

PACIFIC
OCEAN

Kure Atoll
Pearl and Hermes Atoll
Midway Islands
Lisianski Island
Laysan Island
Gardner Pinnacles
Necker Island

Wake Island (U.S.A.)

MARSHALL ISLANDS

Palikir
Pohnpei
Kosrae

Kwajalein
Ralik Chain
Ratak Chain
Maloelap
Delap-Uliga-Djarrit
Mili

INTERNATIONAL DATE LINE

Johnston Atoll (U.S.A.)

Kaua'i
O'ahu Maui
Hawai'i

Tropic of Cancer

MICRONESIA

Gilbert Islands
Tarawa **Bairiki**
Aranuka

Yaren
NAURU

Banaba
Nonouti
Tabiteuea
Beru Nikunau
Onotoa Nikunau
Tamana
Arorae
Kingsmill Group

Howland Island (U.S.A.)
Baker Island (U.S.A.)

Kingman Reef (U.S.A.)
Palmyra Atoll (U.S.A.)

Nukumanu Islands
Ontong Java Atoll

SOLOMON
ISLANDS

ainville
ad
Choiseul
Santa Isabel
gia
Malaita
Guadalcanal **Honiara**
San Cristobal
Rennell

Nanumea
Nanumanga
Niutao
Nanumanga
Nui Vaitupu
Nukufetau Funafuti
Vaiaku
Nukulaelae
Niulakita

TUVALU

Phoenix Islands
McKean
Nikumaroro Kanton
Orona Rawaki
Manra

Jarvis Island (U.S.A.)

Teraina
Tabuaeran
Kiritimati

KIRIBATI

Malden Island
Starbuck Island

Banks Islands
Duff Islands
Santa Cruz Islands

Rotuma (Fiji)
Nukunono
Atafu
Tokelau
(New Zealand)
Swains Island
Fakaofo

Espíritu Santo
Maéwo
VANUATU
Malakula Ambrym
Epi
Port Vila Efaté
Erromango
Tanna Anatom

Îles Chesterfield (France)

Wallis and Futuna Islands
(France) Îles Wallis
Îles de Hoorn
Matā'utu

Yasawa Group
Viti Levu
Suva
Vanua Levu
Koro
Niuafo'ou
Tafahi
SAMOA
Savai'i
Apia
Upolu
American Samoa
Tutuila Manu'a Is
Fagatogo

Pukapuka
Nassau
Rakahanga
Manihiki
Penrhyn
Suwarrow

Vostok Island
Flint Island
Caroline Island (Millennium Island)

Nuku Hiva
Marquesas Islands
Hiva Oa

New Caledonia
(France)
Nouméa
Îles Loyauté (France)
Hunter I.
Île des Pins

FIJI
Kadavu Totoya
Ceva-i-Ra Ono-i-Lau
Tofua
Vava'u Group
TONGA
Nuku'alofa
Tongatapu Group
Ata

Alofi
Niue
(New Zealand)

Palmerston
Aitutaki
Cook Islands
(New Zealand)
Rarotonga
Mangaia
Mauke
Maria

Îles du Roi Georges
Rangiroa
Fakarava
Takaroa
Papeete
Society Islands
Tahiti
Huahiné
Raiatea
Mo'orea

Îles du Duc de Gloucester
Hao

**French
Polynesia**

Îles du Roi Georges
Anaa
Tuamotu Islands

Rurutu
Tubuai Islands
Tubuai
Raivavae
Rapa
Marotiri

Marutea
Îles Gambier
Groupe Actéon

Norfolk Island
(Australia)

Lord Howe Island (Australia)

Raoul Island
Kermadec Islands
(New Zealand)

INTERNATIONAL DATE LINE

Adamstown
Pitcairn Islands
(UK)
Henderson I.
Pitcairn Island
Ducie I.

T A S M A N
S E A

Cape Maria van Diemen
Whangarei
Great Barrier Island
North Island
Auckland
Manukau
Hamilton
New Plymouth
Gisborne
Napier
**NEW
ZEALAND**
Palmerston North
Nelson
Wellington
Greymouth
Blenheim
South Island
Aoraki 3754
Southern Alps
Christchurch
Cape Providence
Timaru
Oamaru
Dunedin
Invercargill
Stewart Island

Chatham Islands (New Zealand)
Pitt Island

Snares Islands (New Zealand)
Bounty Islands (New Zealand)
Antipodes Islands (New Zealand)
Auckland Islands (New Zealand)

Campbell Island (New Zealand)

Macquarie Island (Australia)

Tropic of Capricorn

Equator

Miles Km
2000
1200
1600
1200
800
800
400
400
0 0

1:32 000 000

© Collins Bartholomew Ltd

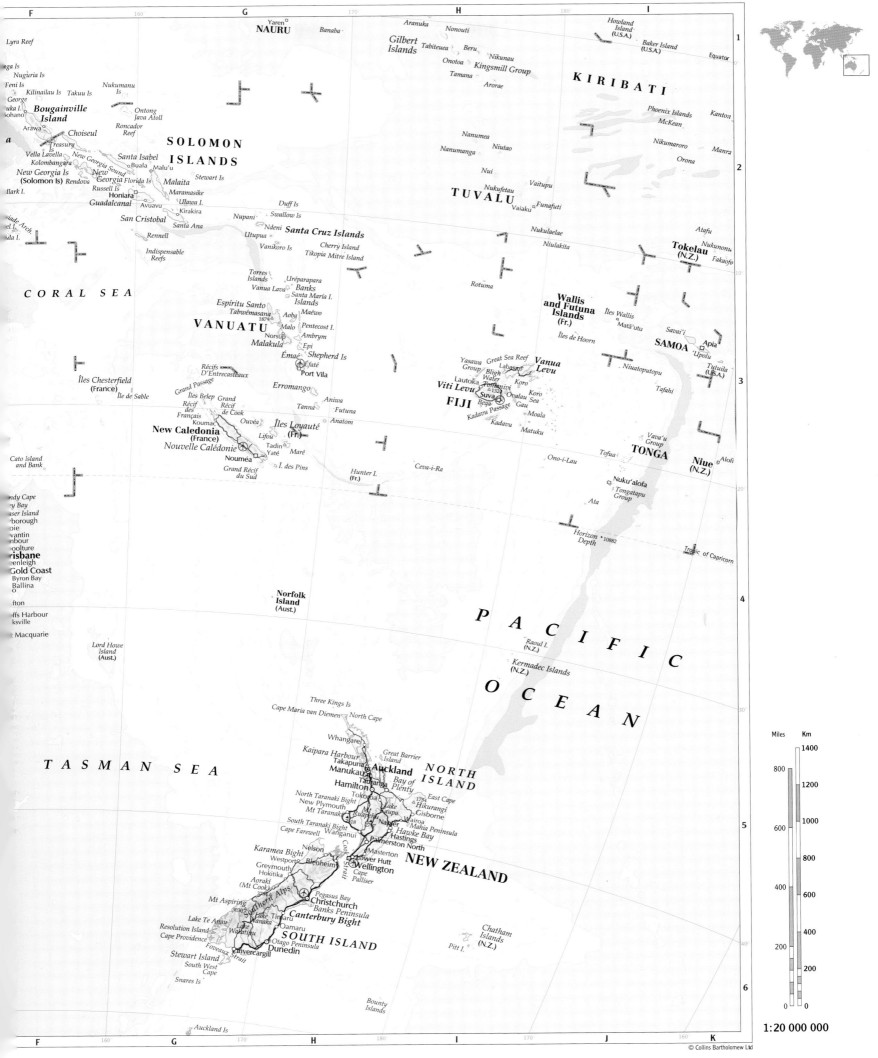

1:20 000 000

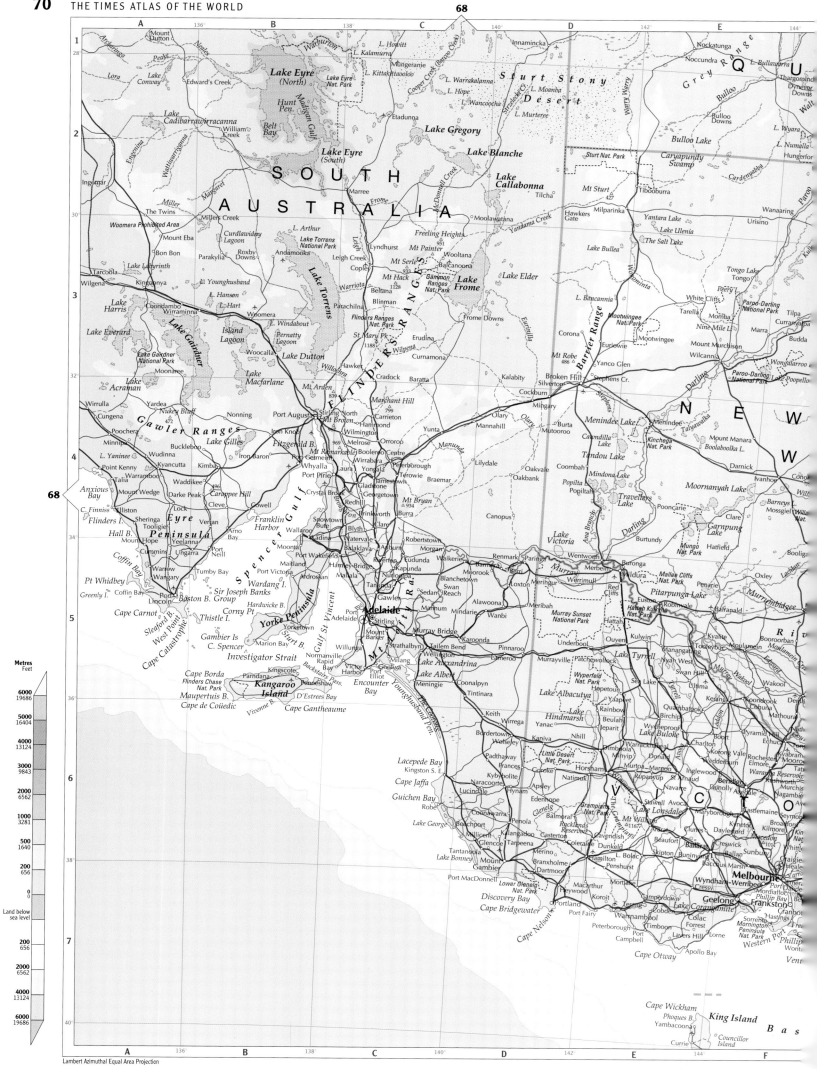

TASMANIA 1:5 000 000

1:5 000 000

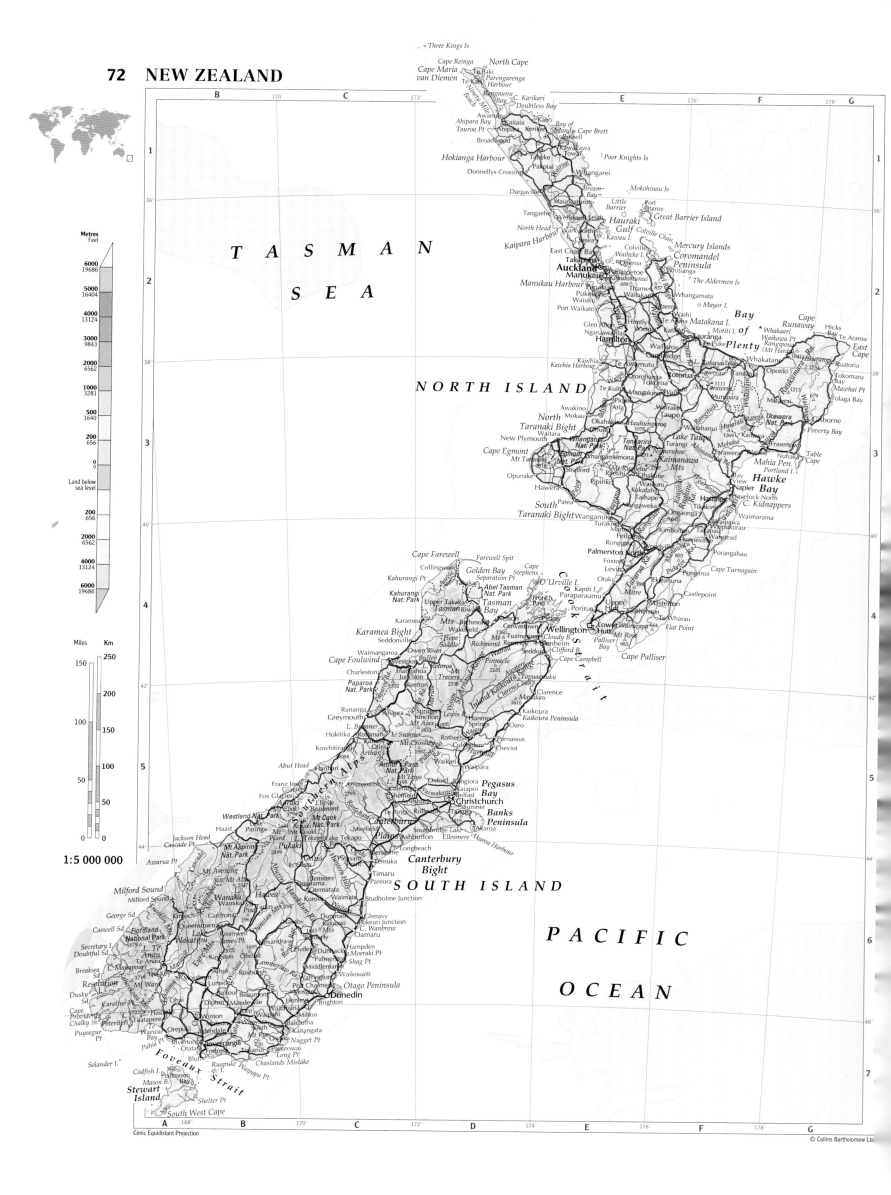

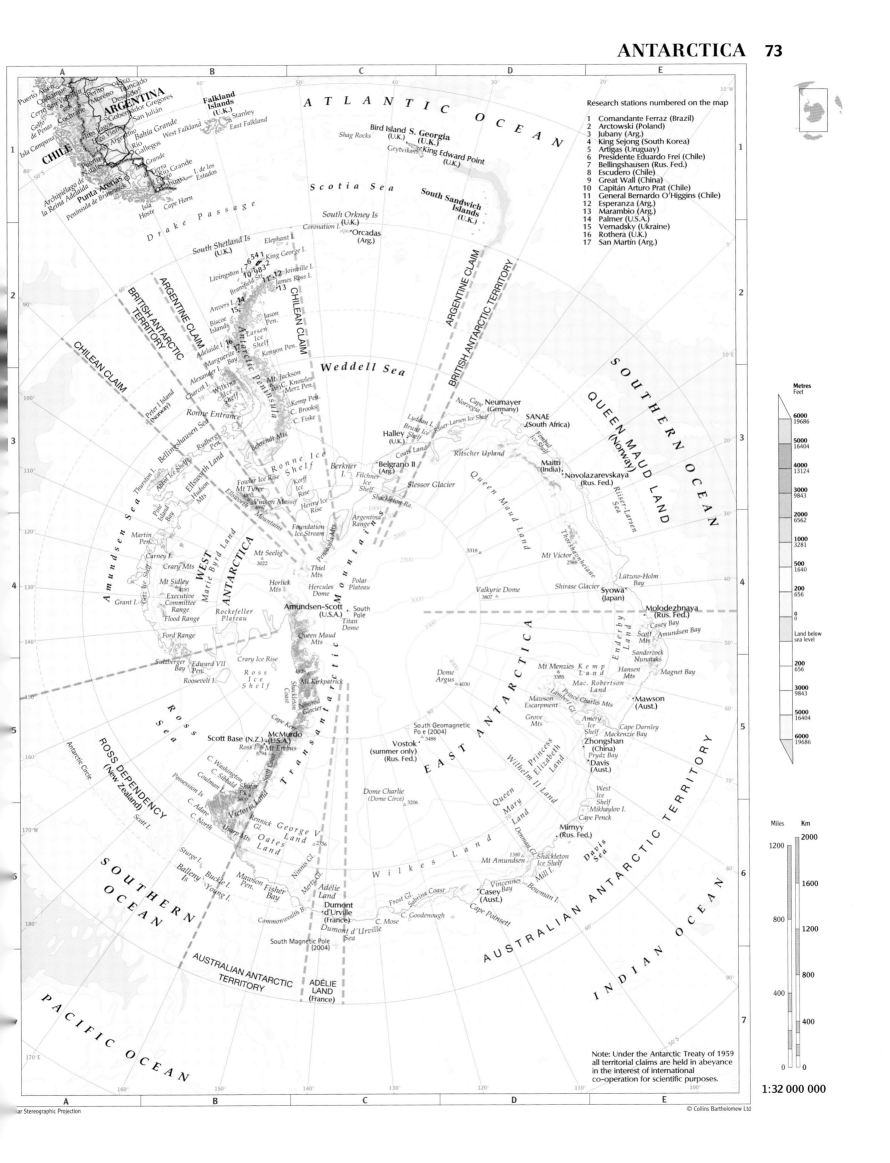

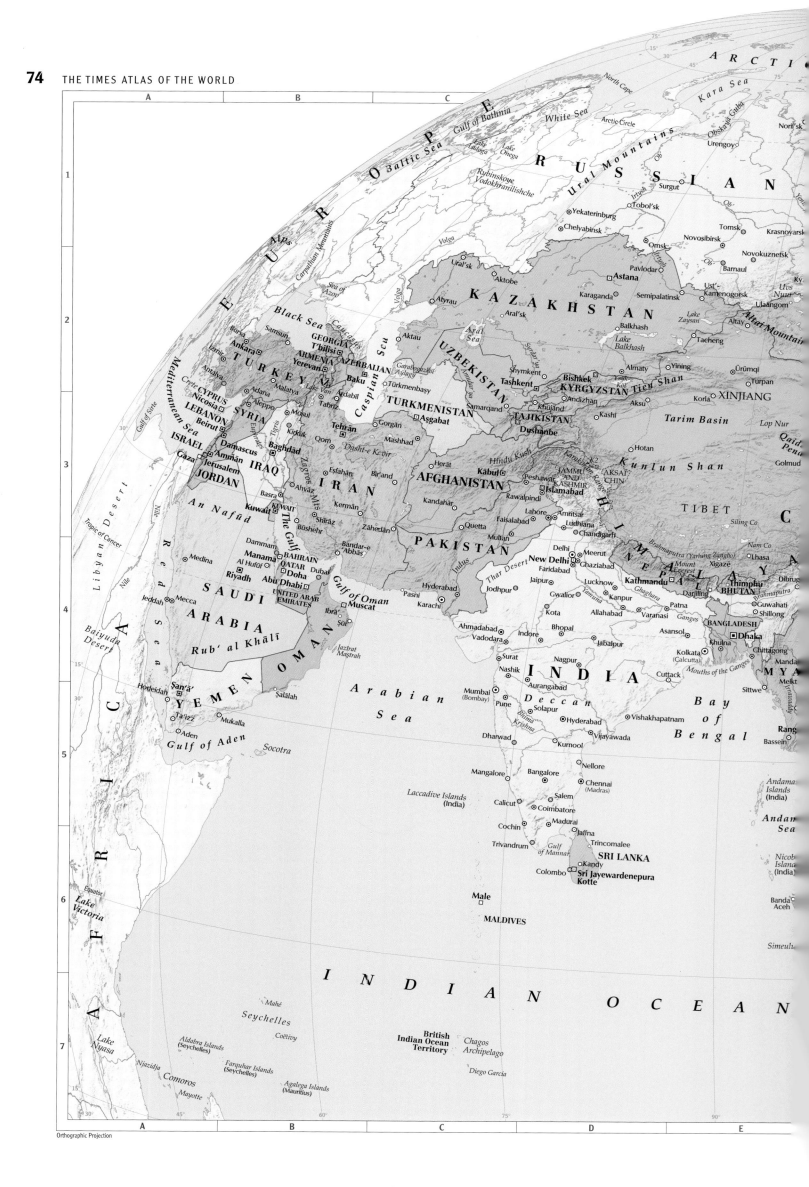

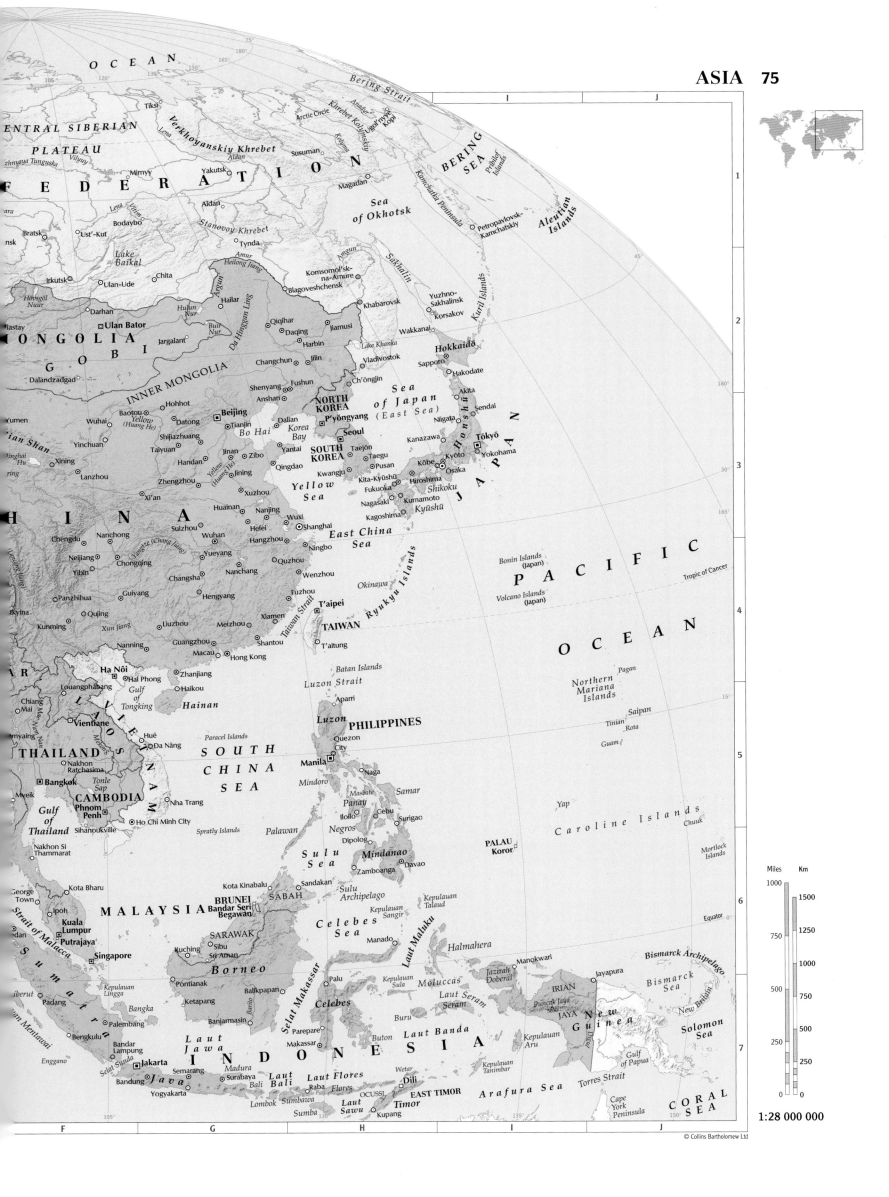

OCEAN

ENTRAL SIBERIAN

PLATEAU

zhnyaya Tunguska

Vilyuy

Lena

Tiksi

Arctic Circle

Bering Strait

Khrebet Kolymskiy

Anadyr'

Ogoľnyye Kopi

BERING SEA

Verkhoyanskiy Khrebet

Suntar

Aldan

Susuman

Kolyma

Magadan

Kamchatka Peninsula

Pribilof Islands

1

ara

FEDERATION

Bratsk

nsk

Irkutsk

Lake Baikal

Hövsgöl Nuur

Ulan-Ude

Darhan

MONGOLIA

Dalandzadgad

Ust'-Kut

Bodaybo

Lena

Vitim

Mirnyy

Aldan

Yakutsk

Stanovoy Khrebet

Tynda

Chita

Amur

Heilong Jiang

Argun

Hailar

Hulun Nur

Komsomoľsk-na-Amure

Blagoveshchensk

Amgun

Khabarovsk

Sea of Okhotsk

Sakhalin

Aleutian Islands

Petropavlovsk-Kamchatskiy

45

2

Ulan Bator

Jargalant

GOBI

Buir Nur

Da Hinggan Ling

Qiqihar

Daqing

Jiamusi

Lake Khanka

Vladivostok

Yuzhno-Sakhalinsk

Korsakov

Wakkanai

Kuril Islands

Hokkaidō

tastay

INNER MONGOLIA

Harbin

Changchun

Jilin

Ch'ŏngjin

Sapporo

Hakodate

Yumen

ian Shan

Baotou

Hohhot

Shenyang

Fushun

Anshan

NORTH KOREA

Sea of Japan (East Sea)

Akita

Sendai

Honshū

180°

inghai Hu

ring

Yinchuan

Wuhai

Datong

Beijing

Tianjin

Dalian

Shijiazhuang

Bo Hai

Korea Bay

P'yŏngyang

Seoul

SOUTH KOREA

Niigata

Kanazawa

Tōkyō

Yokohama

30°

3

Xining

Lanzhou

Taiyuan

Handan

Jinan

Zibo

Yantai

Qingdao

Taejŏn

Taegu

Pusan

Kōbe

Kyōto

Osaka

CHINA

Xi'an

Zhengzhou

Jining

Xuzhou

Huaian

Nanjing

Wuxi

Yellow (Huang He)

Yellow (Huang He)

Yellow Sea

Kwangju

Kita-Kyūshū

Fukuoka

Nagasaki

Kumamoto

Hiroshima

Shikoku

JAPAN

Chengdu

Nanchong

Suizhou

Wuhan

Hefei

Hangzhou

Shanghai

East China Sea

Kagoshima

Kyūshū

165°

Neijiang

Chongqing

Yangtze (Chang Jiang)

Yueyang

Nanchang

Ningbo

Yibin

Changsha

Quzhou

Panzhihua

Guiyang

Hengyang

Wenzhou

Bonin Islands (Japan)

PACIFIC

4

Qujing

Xun Jiang

Liuzhou

Meizhou

Fuzhou

Okinawa

Ryukyu Islands

Volcano Islands (Japan)

Tropic of Cancer

Kunming

Nanning

Guangzhou

Shantou

Xiamen

Taiwan Strait

T'aipei

TAIWAN

T'aitung

OCEAN

15°

Ha Nôi

Hai Phong

Zhanjiang

Hong Kong

Macau

Hainan

Haikou

Batan Islands

Luzon Strait

Northern Mariana Islands

Pagan

Louangphabang

Gulf of Tongking

Aparri

Saipan

Chiang Mai

Mae Nam Nan

LAOS

VIETNAM

Vientiane

Huê

Da Năng

Paracel Islands

Luzon

PHILIPPINES

Quezon City

Tinian

Rota

Guam

nmyaing

THAILAND

Nakhon Ratchasima

SOUTH CHINA SEA

Manila

Naga

Mindoro

5

Myeik

Bangkok

Tonle Sap

CAMBODIA

Mekong

Nha Trang

Masbate

Panay

Samar

Iloilo

Cebu

Surigao

Yap

Caroline Islands

Chuuk

Phnom Penh

Ho Chi Minh City

Spratly Islands

Palawan

Negros

Dipolog

PALAU

Koror

Mortlock Islands

Gulf of Thailand

Sihanoukville

Sulu Sea

Mindanao

Davao

Nakhon Si Thammarat

Zamboanga

Kota Bharu

Kota Kinabalu

Sandakan

Sulu Archipelago

Kepulauan Talaud

6

George Town

Ipoh

MALAYSIA

BRUNEI

Bandar Seri Begawan

SABAH

Celebes Sea

Kepulauan Sangir

Equator

0°

edan

Kuala Lumpur

Putrajaya

SARAWAK

Kuching

Sibu

Sri Aman

Manado

Halmahera

Bismarck Archipelago

Strait of Malacca

Singapore

Borneo

Laut Maluku

Manokwari

Bismarck Sea

New Britain

Sumatra

Pontianak

Balikpapan

Palu

Kepulauan Sula

Moluccas

Jazirah Doberai

Jayapura

berut

Kepulauan Lingga

Ketapang

Barito

Celebes

Laut Seram

Laut Seram

IRIAN

Padang

Bangka

Banjarmasin

Parepare

Buru

JAYA

New Guinea

Solomon Sea

Mentawai

Palembang

Laut Jawa

INDONESIA

Celebes

Buton

Laut Banda

Puncak Jaya

Bengkulu

Bandar Lampung

7

Enggano

Selat Sunda

Jakarta

Semarang

Surabaya

Madura

Bali

Laut Bali

Laut Flores

Wetar

Kepulauan Aru

Kepulauan Tanimbar

Gulf of Papua

on Mentawai

Bandung

Java

Yogyakarta

Lombok

Sumbawa

Raba

Flores

Dili

OCUSSI

EAST TIMOR

Arafura Sea

Cape York Peninsula

Torres Strait

CORAL SEA

Sumba

Laut Sawu

Kupang

Timor

F

G

H

I

J

Miles

Km

1000

1500

750

1250

1000

500

750

250

500

250

0

0

1:28 000 000

© Collins Bartholomew Ltd

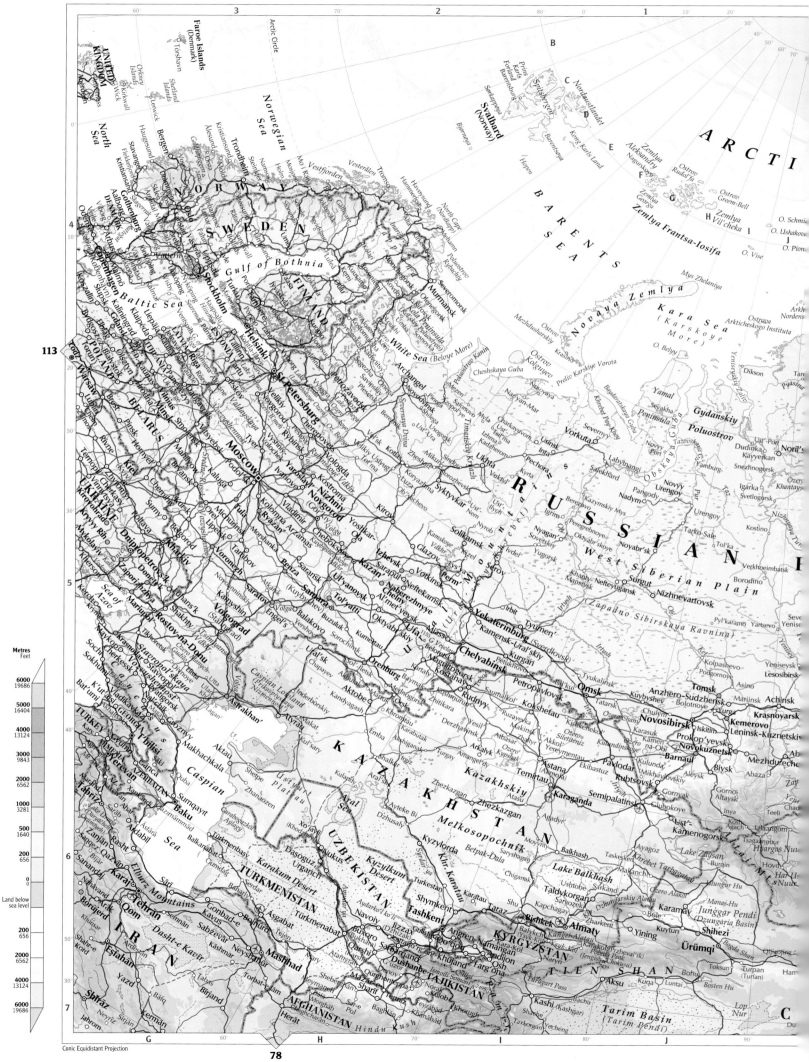

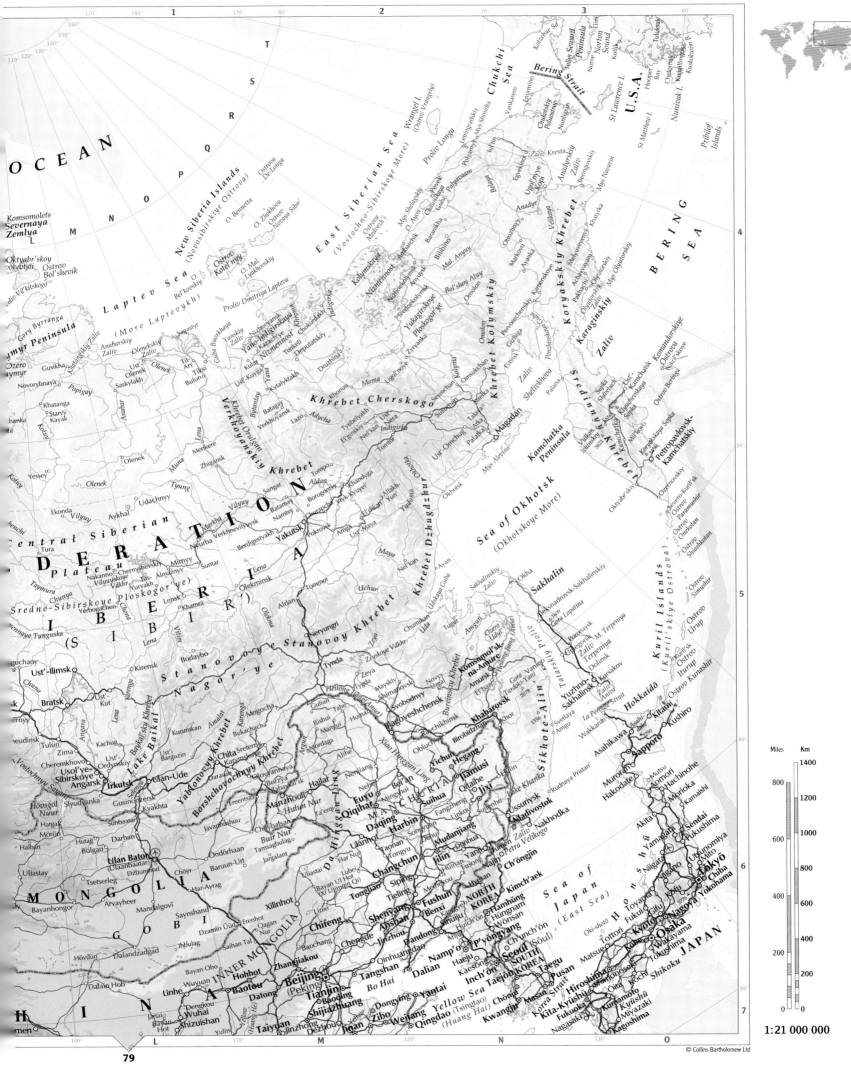

© Collins Bartholomew Ltd

1:21 000 000

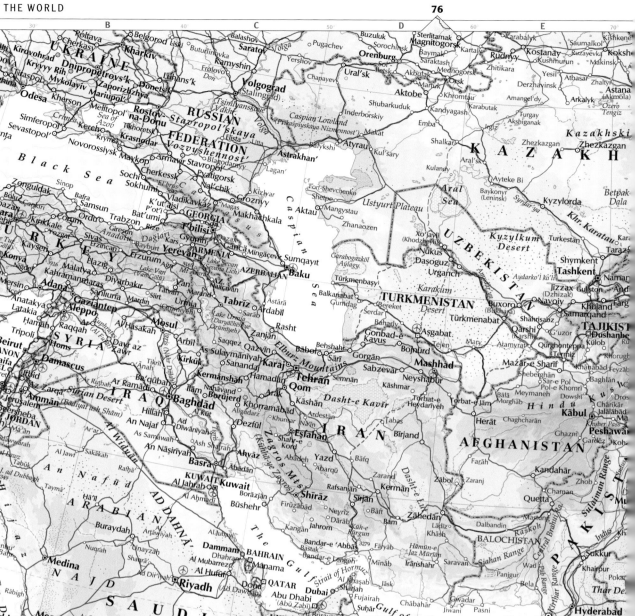

Albers Equal Area Conic Projection

90

91

99

Miles   Km

1400

800   1200

1000

600

800

400   600

400

200

200

0   0

1:20 000 000

© Collins Bartholomew Ltd

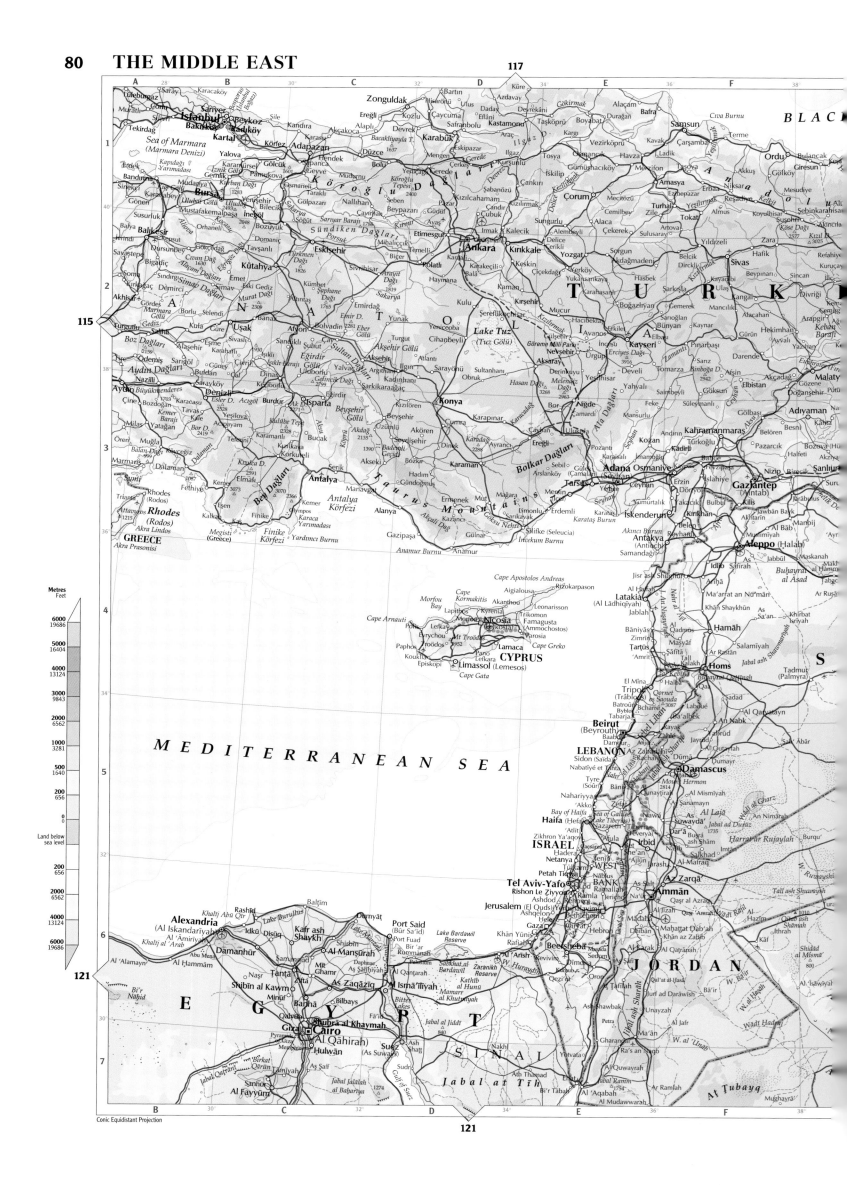

Conic Equidistant Projection

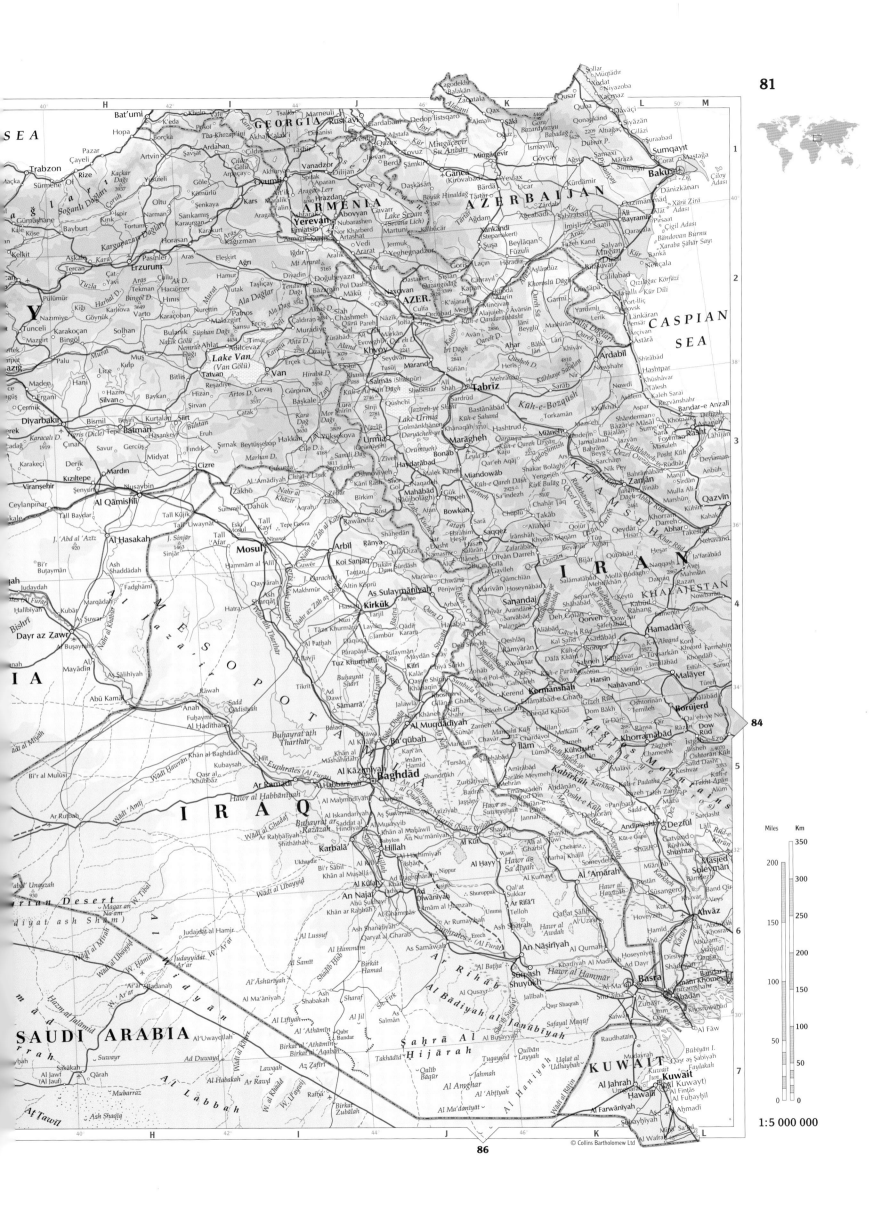

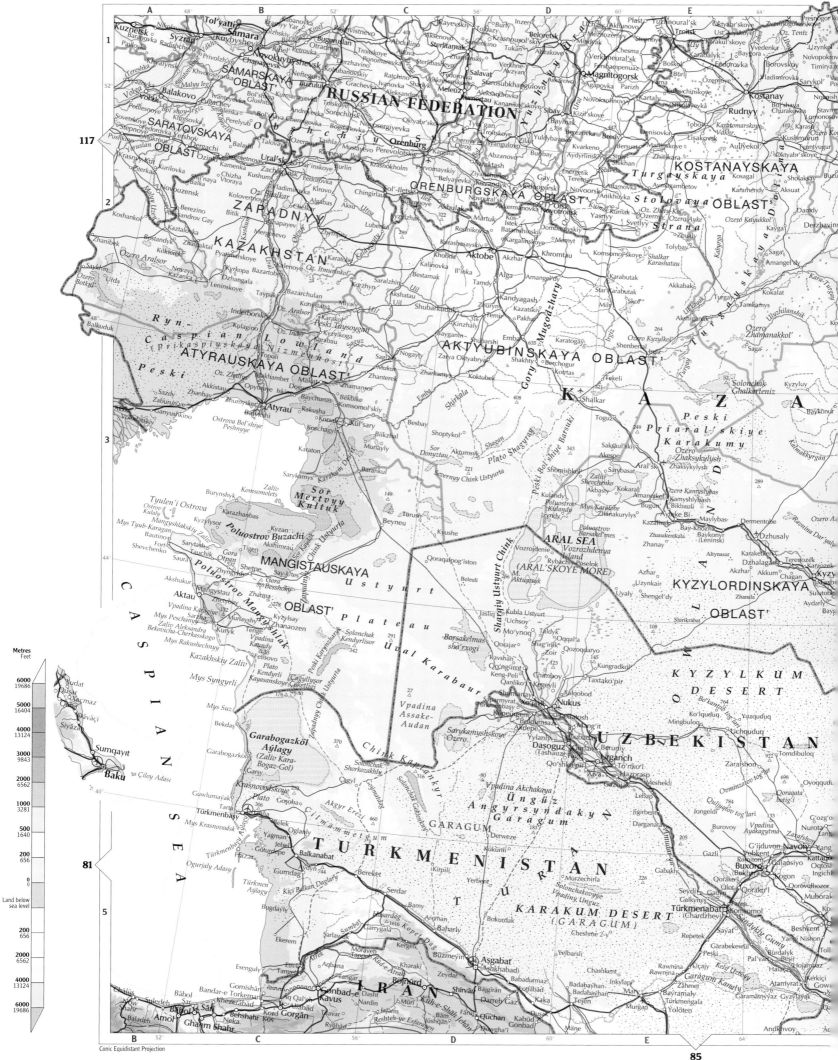

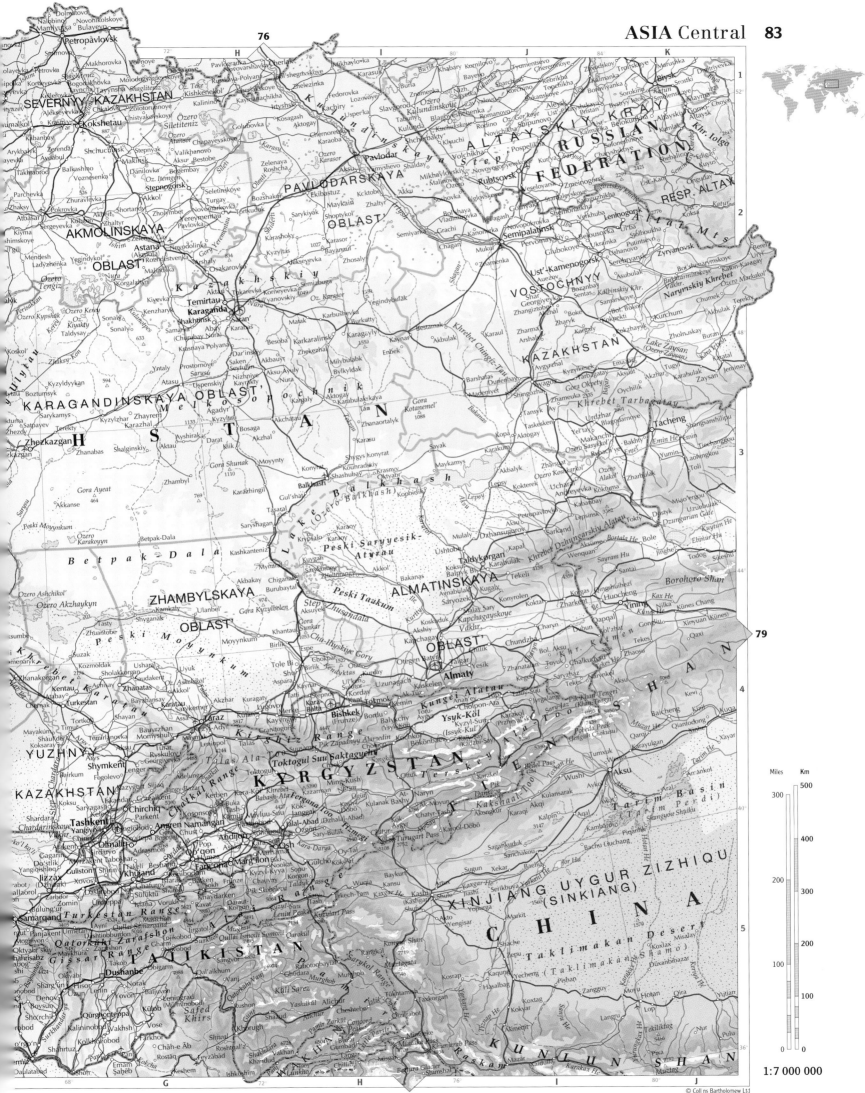

1:7 000 000

© Collins Bartholomew Ltd

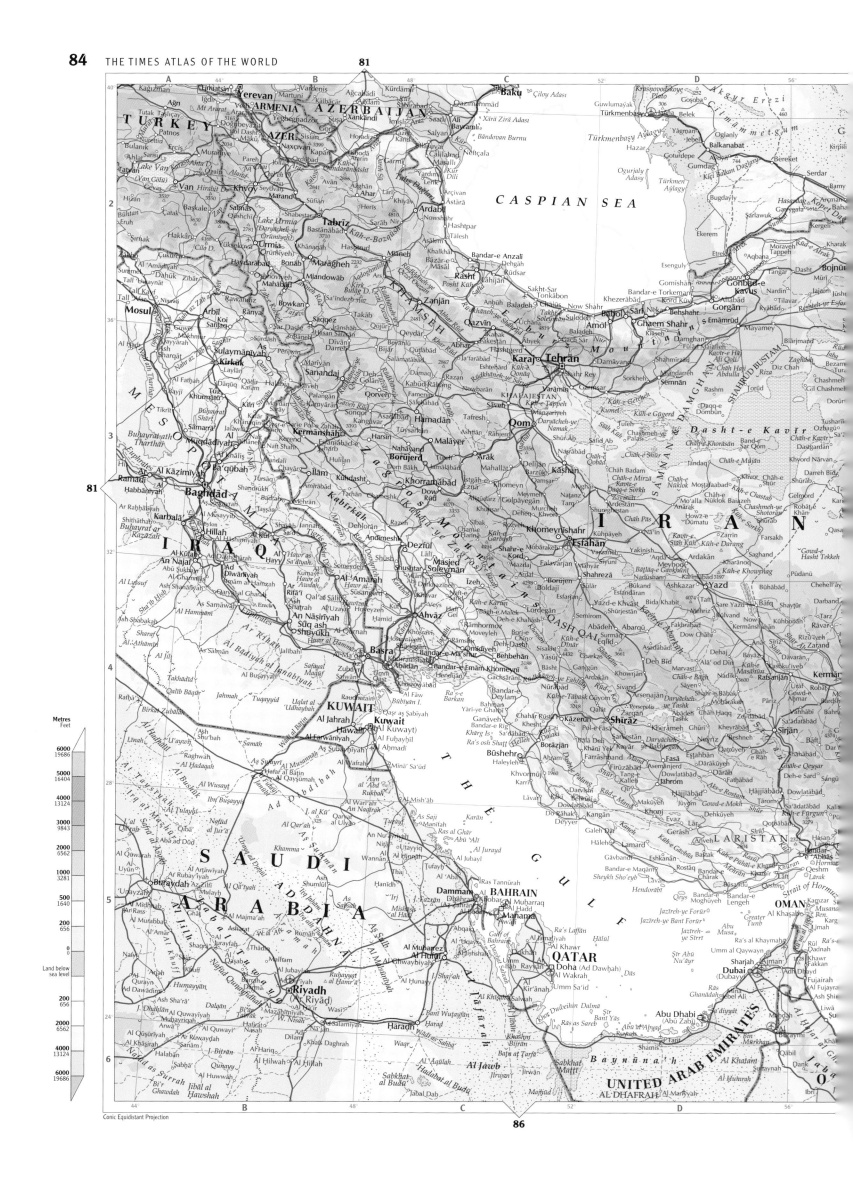

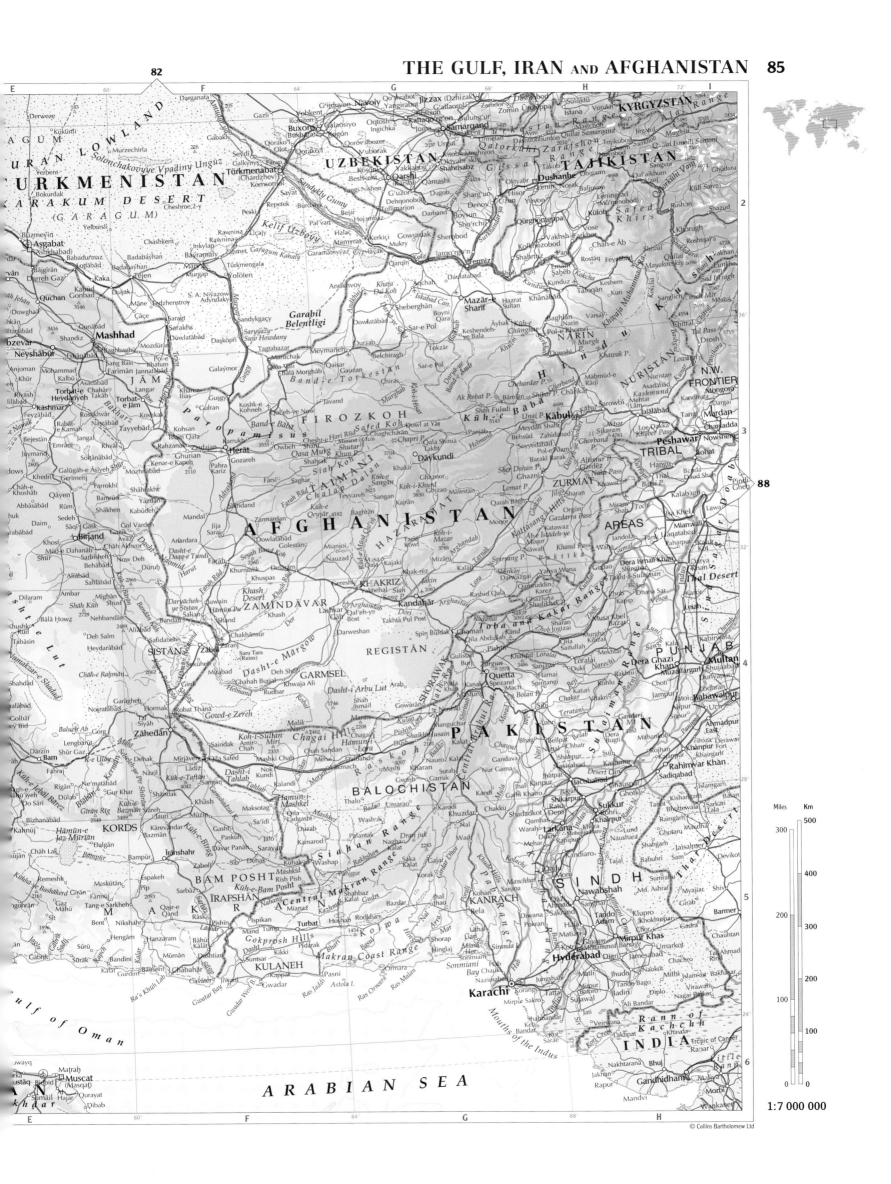

TURKMENISTAN

URAN LOWLAND

KARAKUM DESERT
(G A R A G U M)

Asgabat
Ashkhabad

UZBEKISTAN

Buxoro
(Bukhara)

TAJIKISTAN

KYRGYZSTAN

Dushanbe

Türkmenabat
(Chardzhev)

Samarqand

Mazār-e
Sharīf

Mashhad

Neyshābūr

JĀM

FIROZKOH

AFGHANISTAN

Herāt

Kābul

N.W.
FRONTIER

Peshāwar

TRIBAL

ZURMAT

AREAS

Daykundi

HAZARAJAT

Ghazni

PUNJAB

Birjand

ZAMINDĀVAR

KHAKRIZ

Kandahār

Multan

REGISTĀN

GARMSEL

SISTĀN

Zābol

Zāhedān

PAKISTAN

Quetta

Bahāwalpur

Chagai Hills

Hamun-i-
Mashkel

BALOCHISTAN

Sukkur

KORDS

Larkana

Rahīmyār Khān

Īrānshahr

Jacobabad

Shikārpur

MAKRĀN

BAM POSHT

ĪRAFSHĀN

KANRACH

SINDH

Nawabshah

Kuh-e-Bam Posht

Mīrpur Khās

Makran Coast Range

KULANEH

Hyderābad

Karachi

Mouths of the Indus

Gulf of Oman

Muscat
(Masqat)

A R A B I A N   S E A

INDIA

Rann of
Kachchh

Tropic of Cancer

Gandhidham

Miles   Km

300   500

     400

200   300

     200

100   100

0   0

1:7 000 000

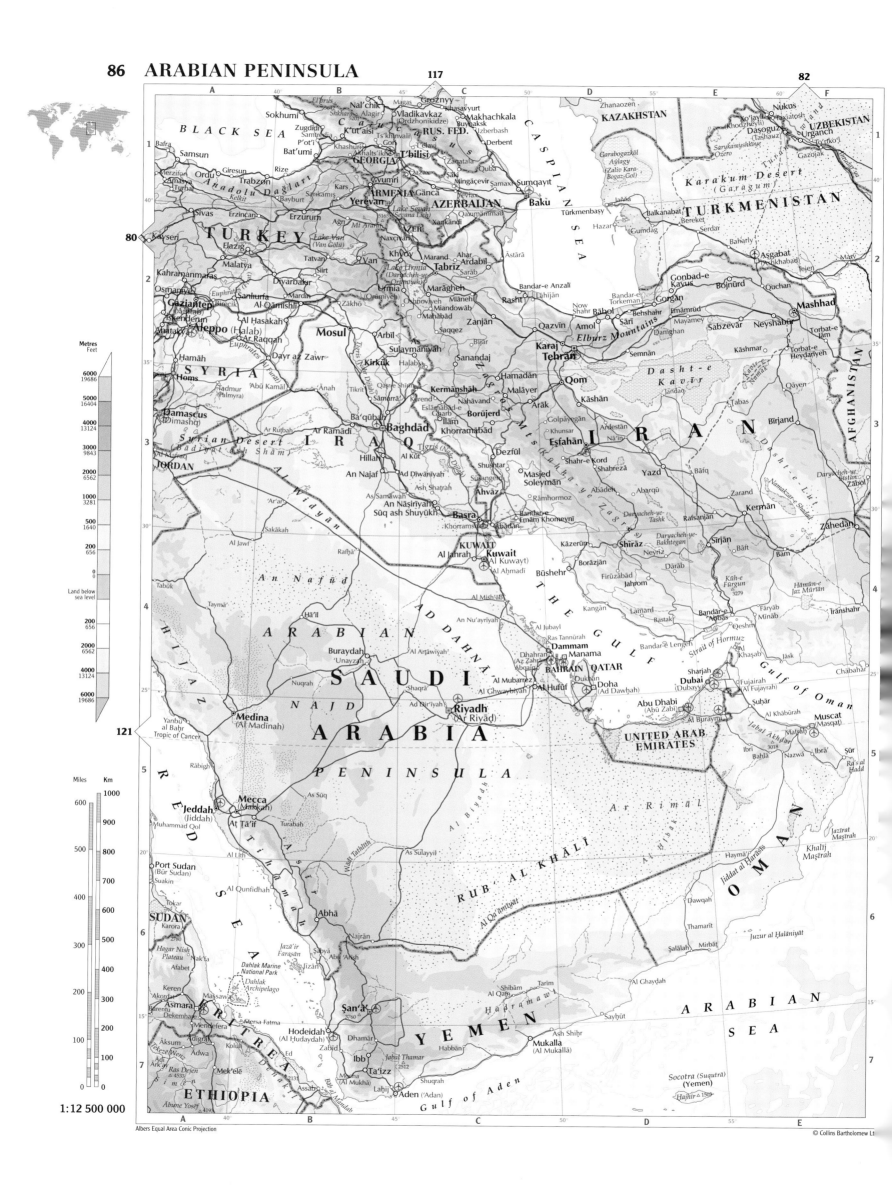

117

82

80

121

Metres
Feet

6000
19686

5000
16404

4000
13124

3000
9843

2000
6562

1000
3281

500
1640

200
656

0
0

Land below
sea level

200
656

2000
6562

4000
13124

6000
19686

Miles   Km

600   1000

900

500   800

700

400   600

300   500

400

200   300

200

100

100   100

0   0

1:12 500 000

Albers Equal Area Conic Projection

© Collins Bartholomew Lt

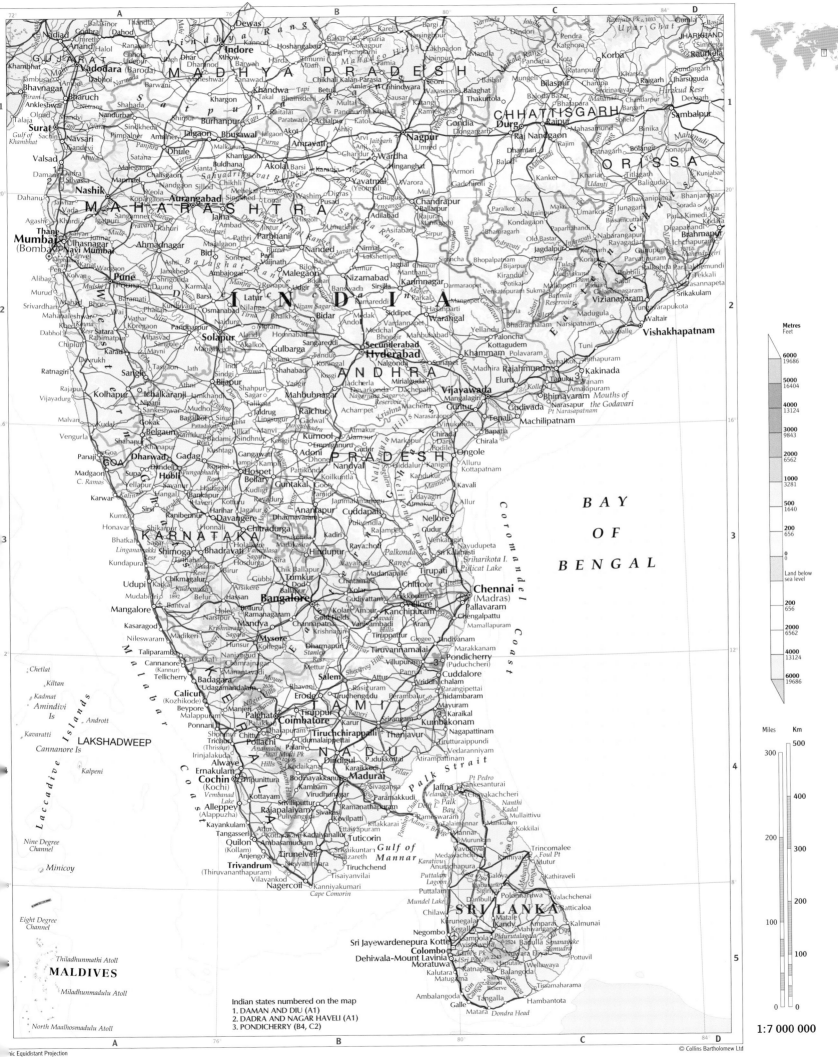

B A Y

O F

B E N G A L

Metres
Feet

6000	19686
5000	16404
4000	13124
3000	9843
2000	6562
1000	3281
500	1640
200	656
0	

Land below
sea level

200	656
2000	6562
4000	13124
6000	19686

Miles   Km

300 — 500

— 400

200 — 300

— 200

100 — 100

0 — 0

1:7 000 000

Indian states numbered on the map
1. DAMAN AND DIU (A1)
2. DADRA AND NAGAR HAVELI (A1)
3. PONDICHERRY (B4, C2)

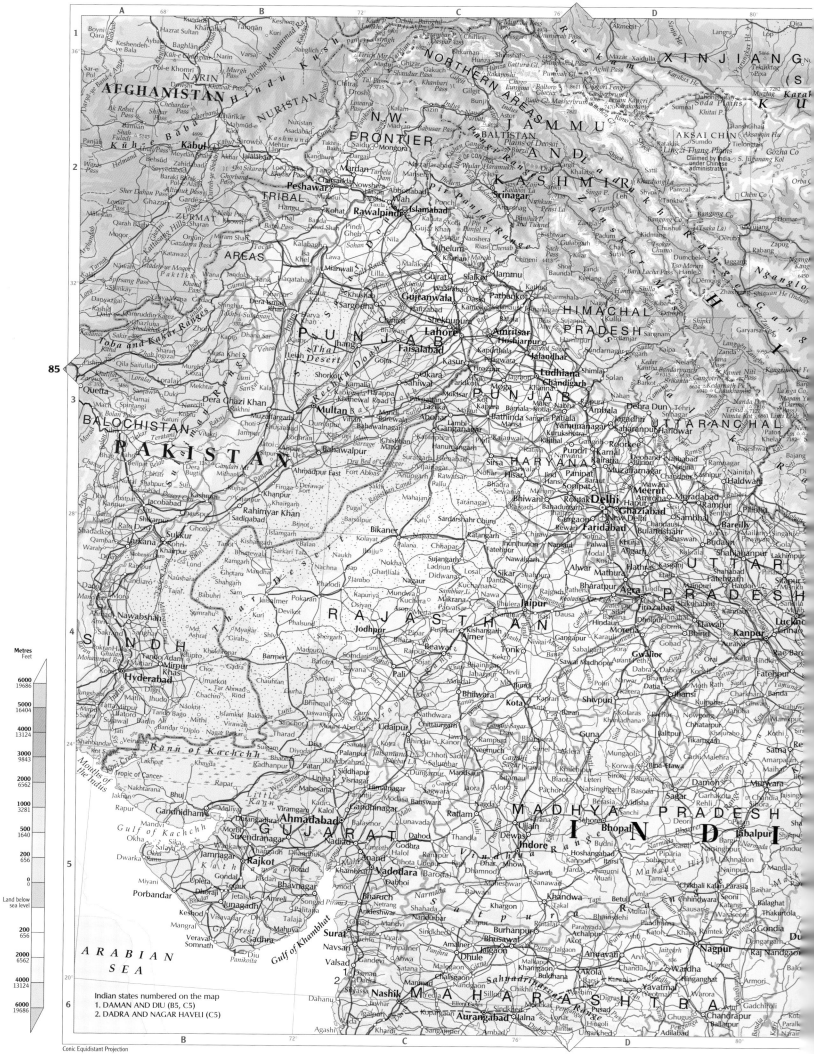

Metres
Feet

6000
19686

5000
16404

4000
13124

3000
9843

2000
6562

1000
3281

500
1640

200
656

0
0

Land below
sea level

200
656

2000
6562

4000
13124

6000
19686

Indian states numbered on the map
1. DAMAN AND DIU (B5, C5)
2. DADRA AND NAGAR HAVELI (C5)

Conic Equidistant Projection

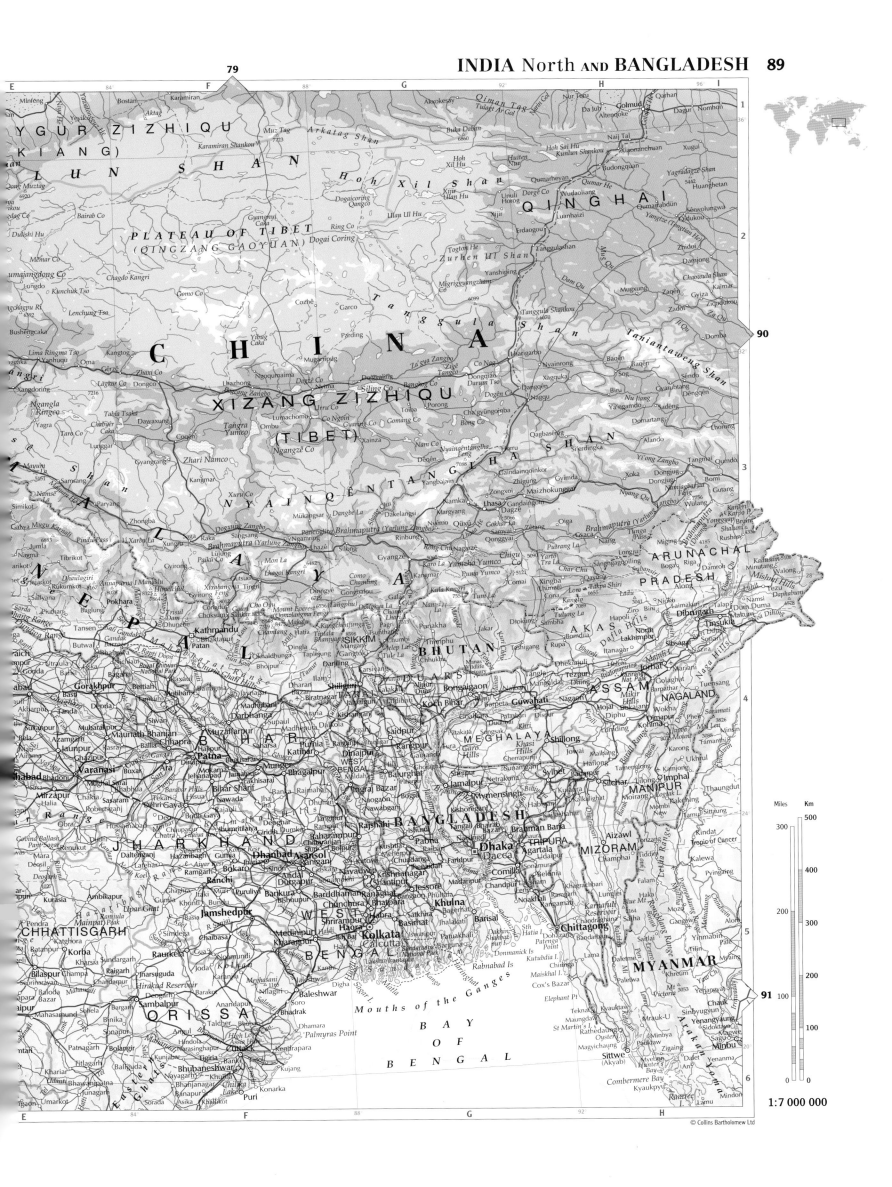

1:7 000 000

© Collins Bartholomew Ltd

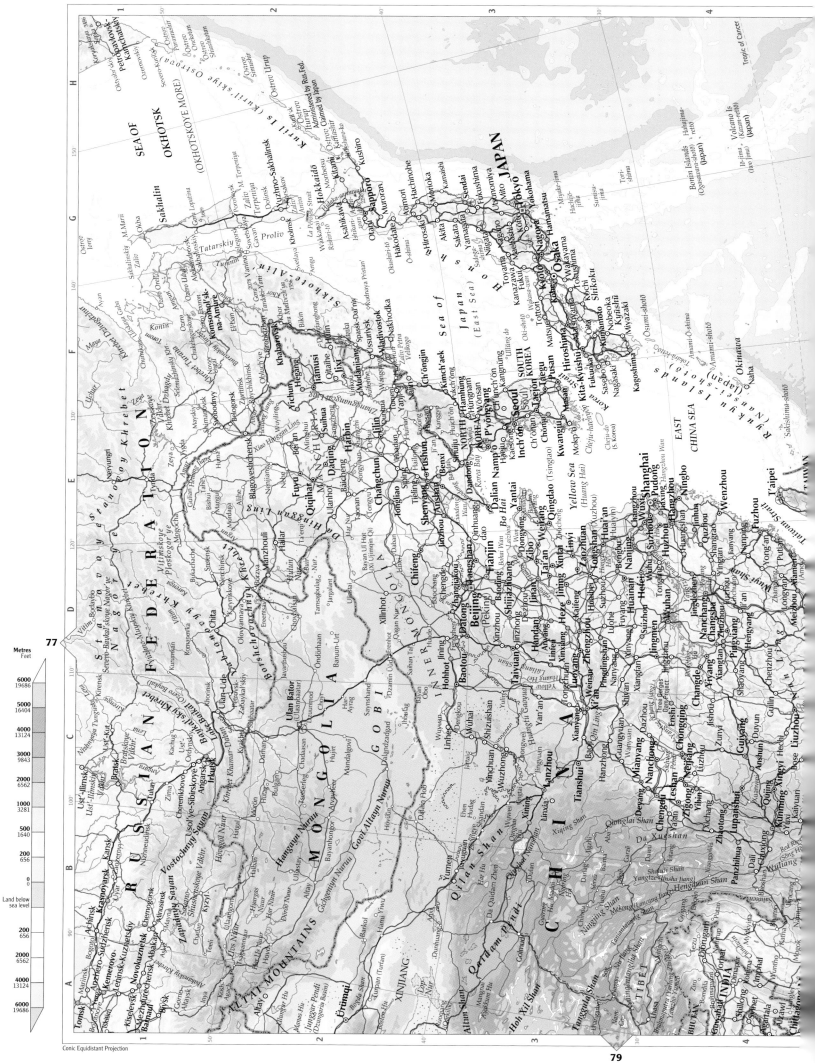

Metres / Feet

6000 / 19686
5000 / 16404
4000 / 13124
3000 / 9843
2000 / 6562
1000 / 3281
500 / 1640
200 / 656
0 / 0
Land below sea level
200 / 656
2000 / 6562
4000 / 13124
6000 / 19686

Conic Equidistant Projection

77
79

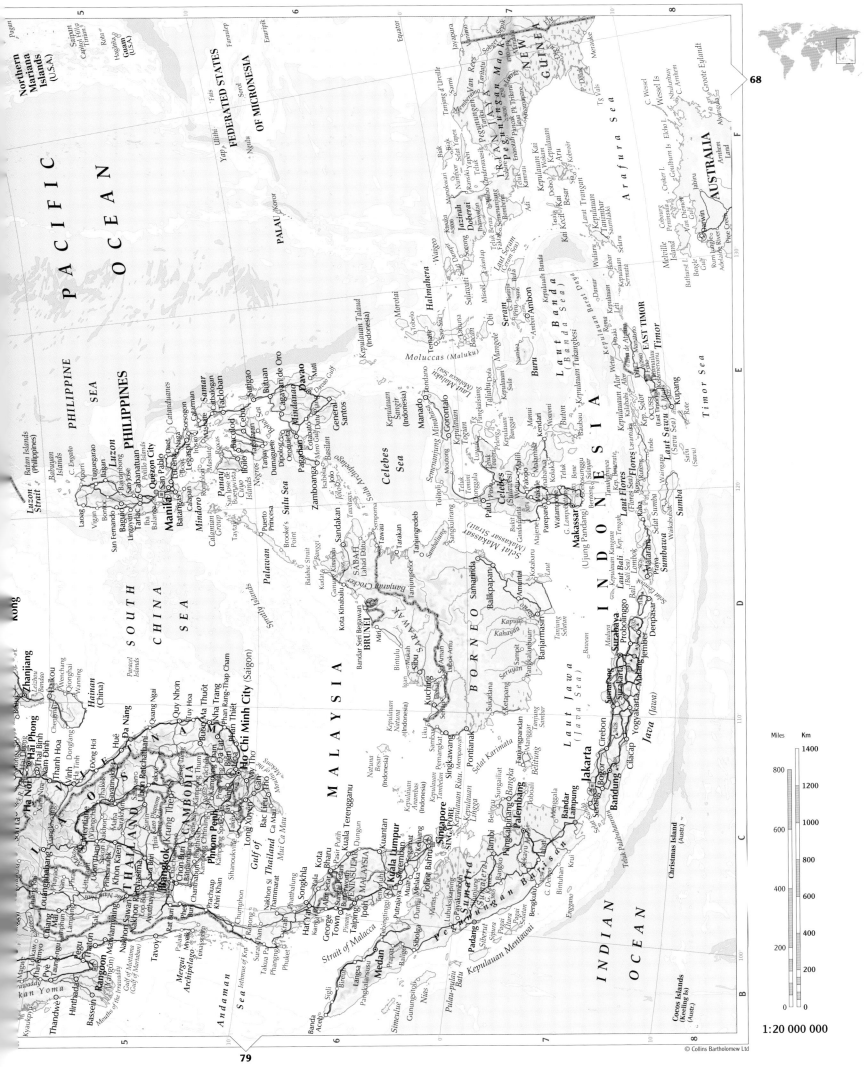

PACIFIC OCEAN

Northern Mariana Islands (U.S.A.)

Batan Islands (Philippines)

PHILIPPINE SEA

FEDERATED STATES OF MICRONESIA

PALAU

NEW GUINEA

IRIAN JAYA

AUSTRALIA

Arafura Sea

Timor Sea

EAST TIMOR

Timor

Halmahera

Moluccas (Maluku)

Seram

Buru

Ambon

Laut Banda (Banda Sea)

Celebes Sea

Celebes (Sulawesi)

Manado

Makassar (Ujung Pandang)

Selat Makassar (Makassar Strait)

PHILIPPINES

Luzon

Manila

Quezon City

Samar

Mindanao

Davao

General Santos

Zamboanga

Sulu Sea

Palawan

SABAH

BRUNEI

Bandar Seri Begawan

SARAWAK

BORNEO

Kuching

Banjarmasin

Balikpapan

Samarinda

I N D O N E S I A

Makassar

Laut Flores (Flores Sea)

Laut Jawa (Java Sea)

Sumbawa

Sumba

Kupang

Laut Sawu

SOUTH CHINA SEA

Spratly Islands

Paracel Islands (China)

Hainan (China)

Zhanjiang

Haikou

Hải Phòng

Hà Nội

Đà Nẵng

Ho Chi Minh City (Saigon)

V I E T N A M

L A O S

THAILAND

Bangkok

CAMBODIA

Phnom Penh

Gulf of Thailand

M A L A Y S I A

Kuala Lumpur

PENINSULAR MALAYSIA

Singapore

SINGAPORE

Kepulauan Riau (Indonesia)

Kepulauan Lingga

Kepulauan Natuna (Indonesia)

Kepulauan Anambas (Indonesia)

Pontianak

Palembang

Bandar Lampung

Jakarta

Bandung

Java (Jawa)

Surabaya

Yogyakarta

Semarang

Denpasar

Laut Bali

Strait of Malacca

Medan

S u m a t r a

B a r i s a n

Padang

INDIAN OCEAN

Christmas Island (Austr.)

Cocos Islands (Keeling Is) (Austr.)

Andaman Sea

Rangoon

PEGU YOMA

Gulf of Mottama (Gulf of Martaban)

1:20 000 000

Miles Km

800

1400

1200

600

1000

800

400

600

200

400

200

0 0

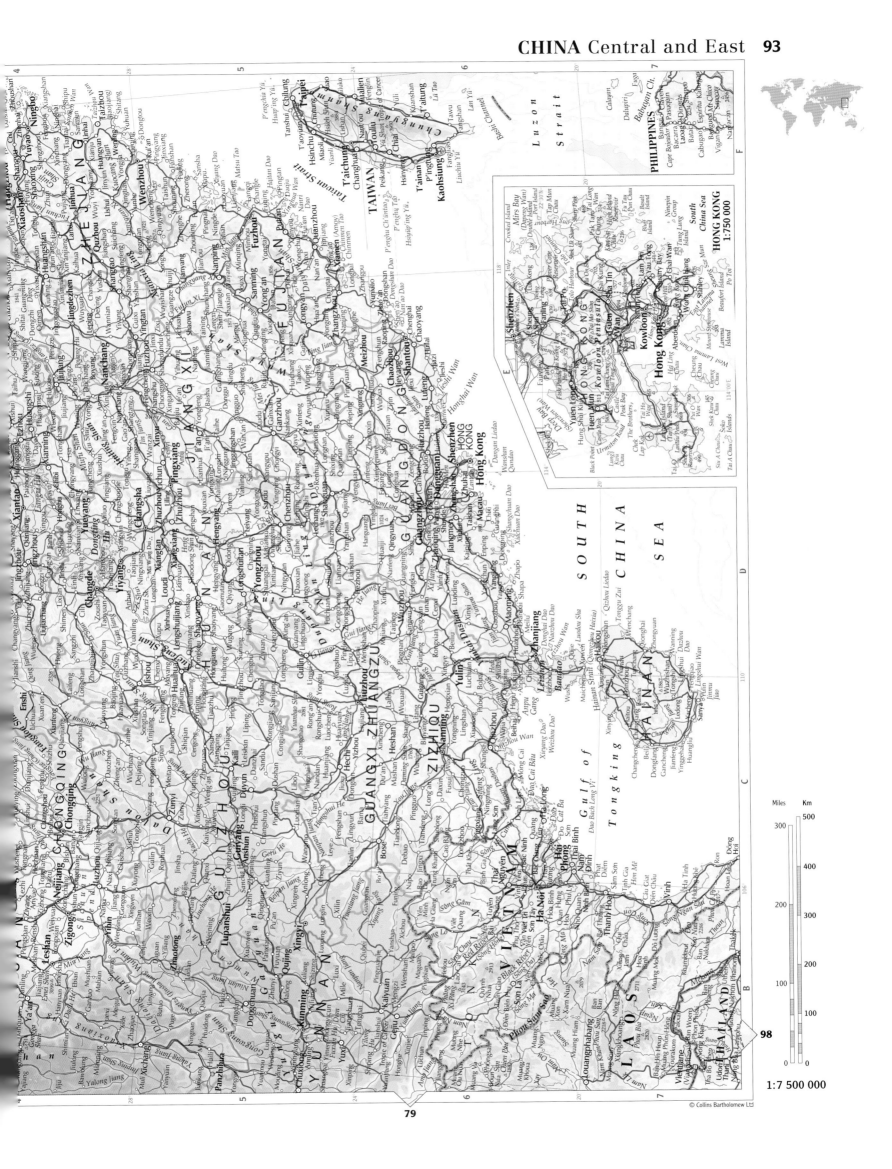

PHILIPPINES

Luzon Strait

TAIWAN

Taipei
Hsinchu
T'aichung
Changhua
Tainan
Kaohsiung
T'aitung

HONG KONG
1:750 000

Shenzhen
Kowloon
Hong Kong

SOUTH CHINA SEA

ZHEJIANG
Ningbo
Wenzhou

FUJIAN
Fuzhou
Quanzhou
Xiamen

JIANGXI
Nanchang

HUNAN
Changsha
Yiyang
Loudi
Hengyang
Yongzhou

GUIZHOU
Guiyang
Anshun
Zunyi
Lupanshui

CHONGQING
Chongqing

YUNNAN
Kunming
Qujing
Xingyi

GUANGDONG
Guangzhou
Shantou
Chaozhou
Shenzhen
Zhongshan
Macau
Zhuhai

GUANGXI ZHUANGZU ZIZHIQU
Nanning
Liuzhou
Guilin
Yulin

HAINAN
Haikou
Sanya

Gulf of Tongking

VIETNAM
Ha Nôi
Hai Phong
Nam Dinh
Vinh

LAOS
Louangphabang
THAILAND

Miles Km
300   500
       400
200   300
100   200
       100
0   0

1:7 500 000

79

98

© Collins Bartholomew Ltd

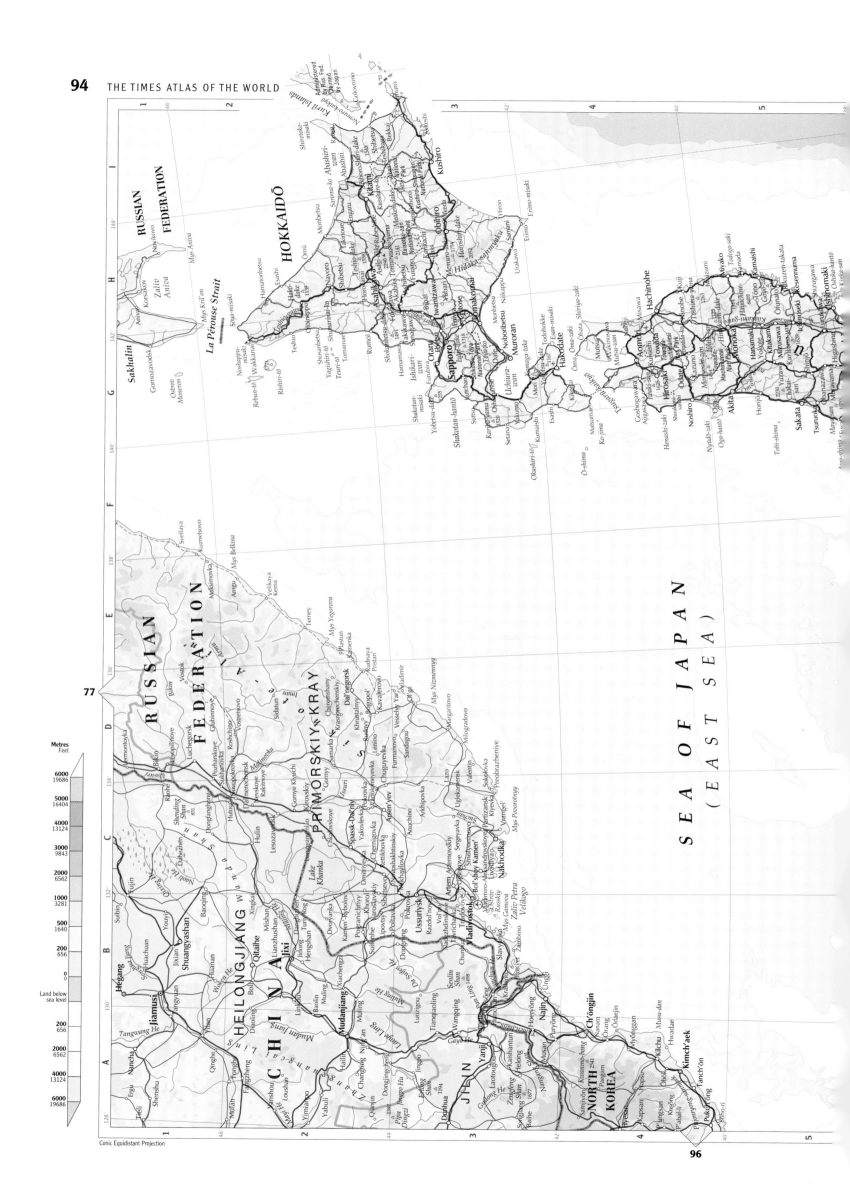

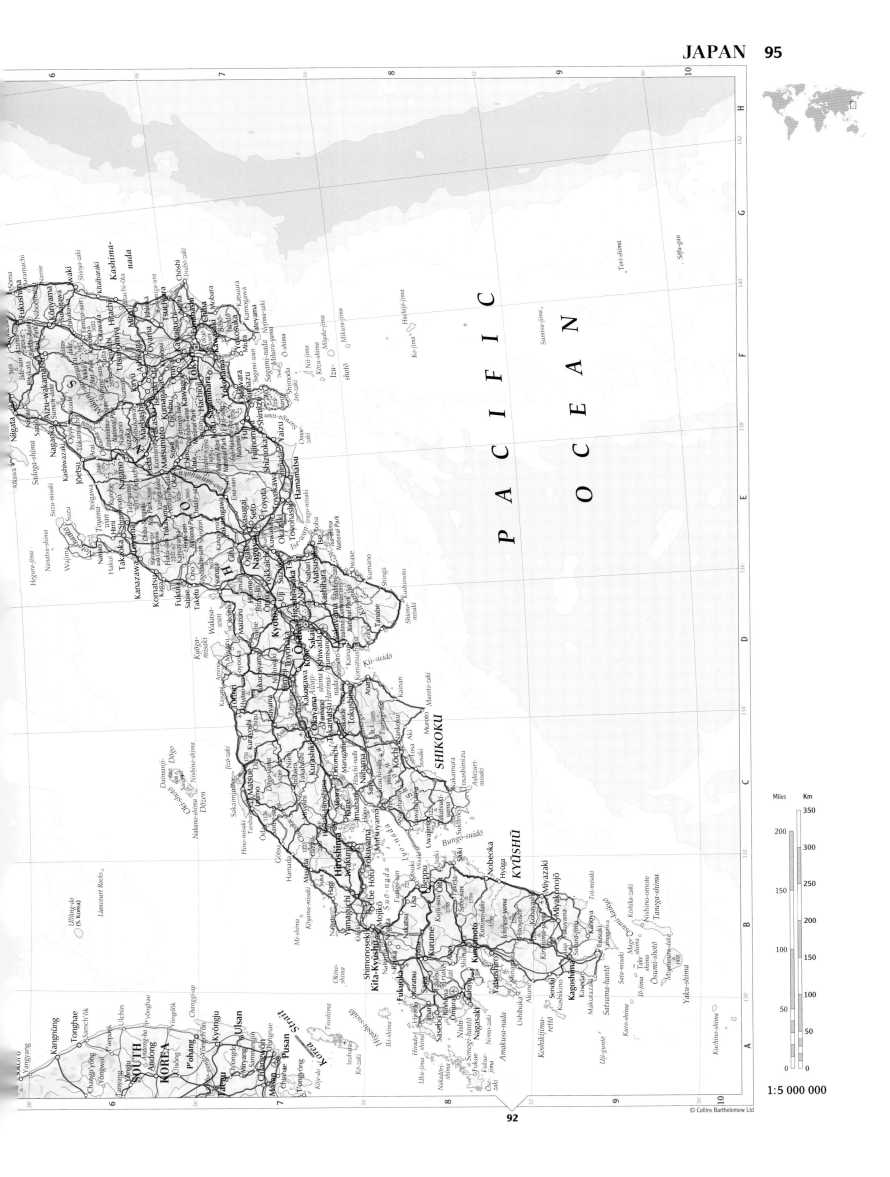

PACIFIC

OCEAN

KYŪSHŪ

SHIKOKU

SOUTH KOREA

Korea Strait

© Collins Bartholomew Ltd

1:5 000 000

Miles   Km

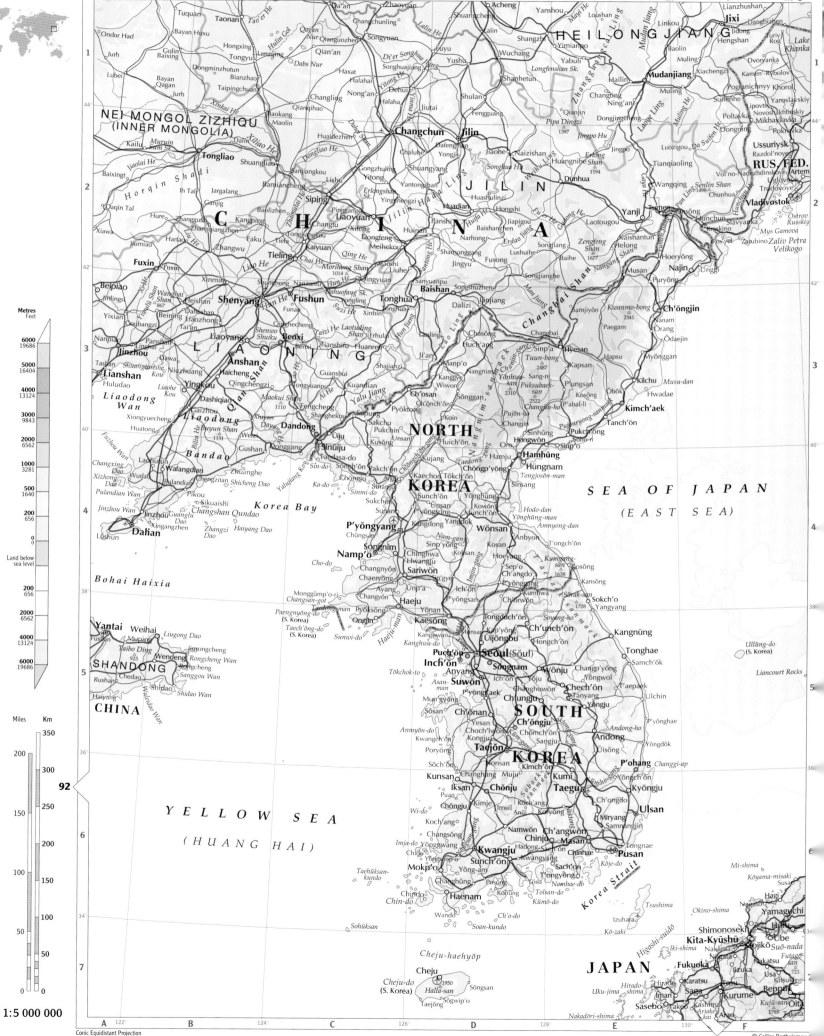

1:5 000 000

Conic Equidistant Projection

© Collins Bartholomew

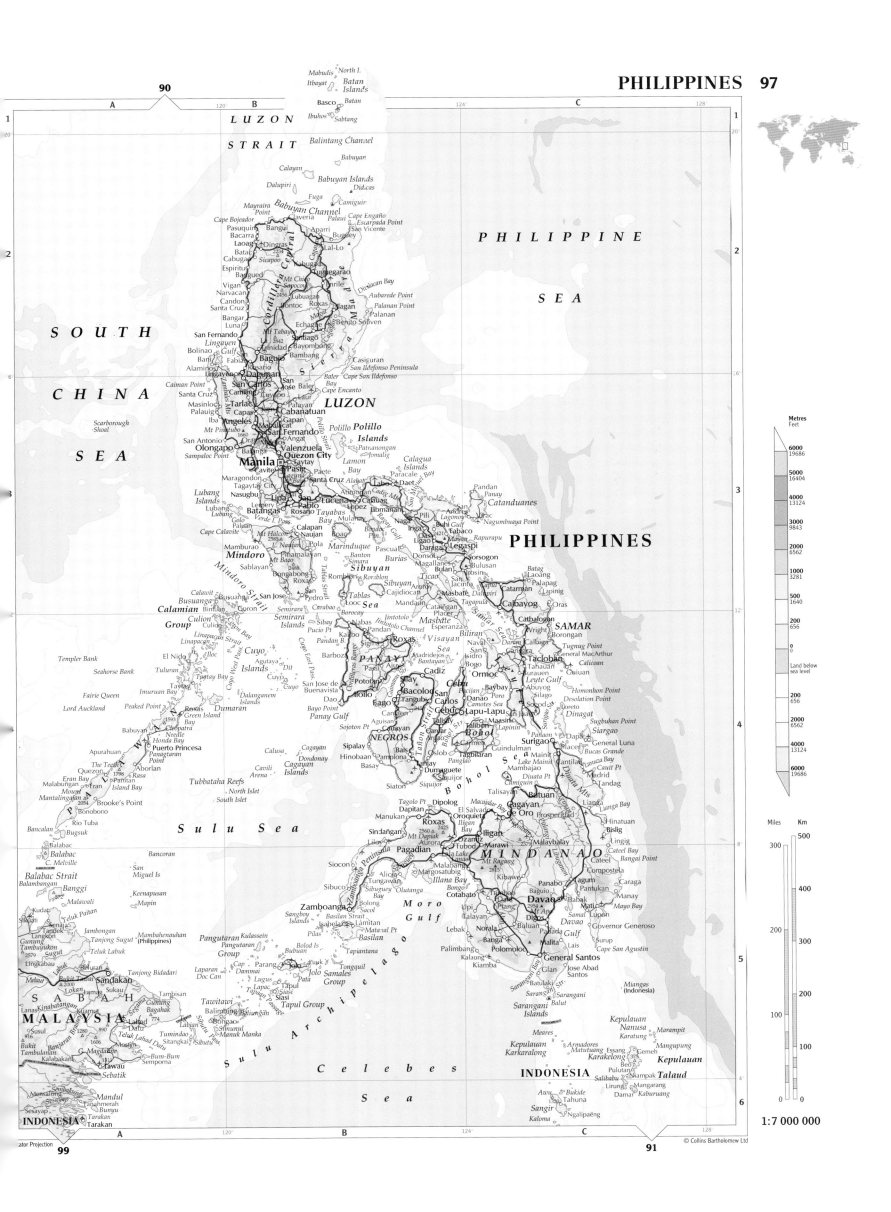

THAILAND, CAMBODIA AND PENINSULAR MALAYSIA

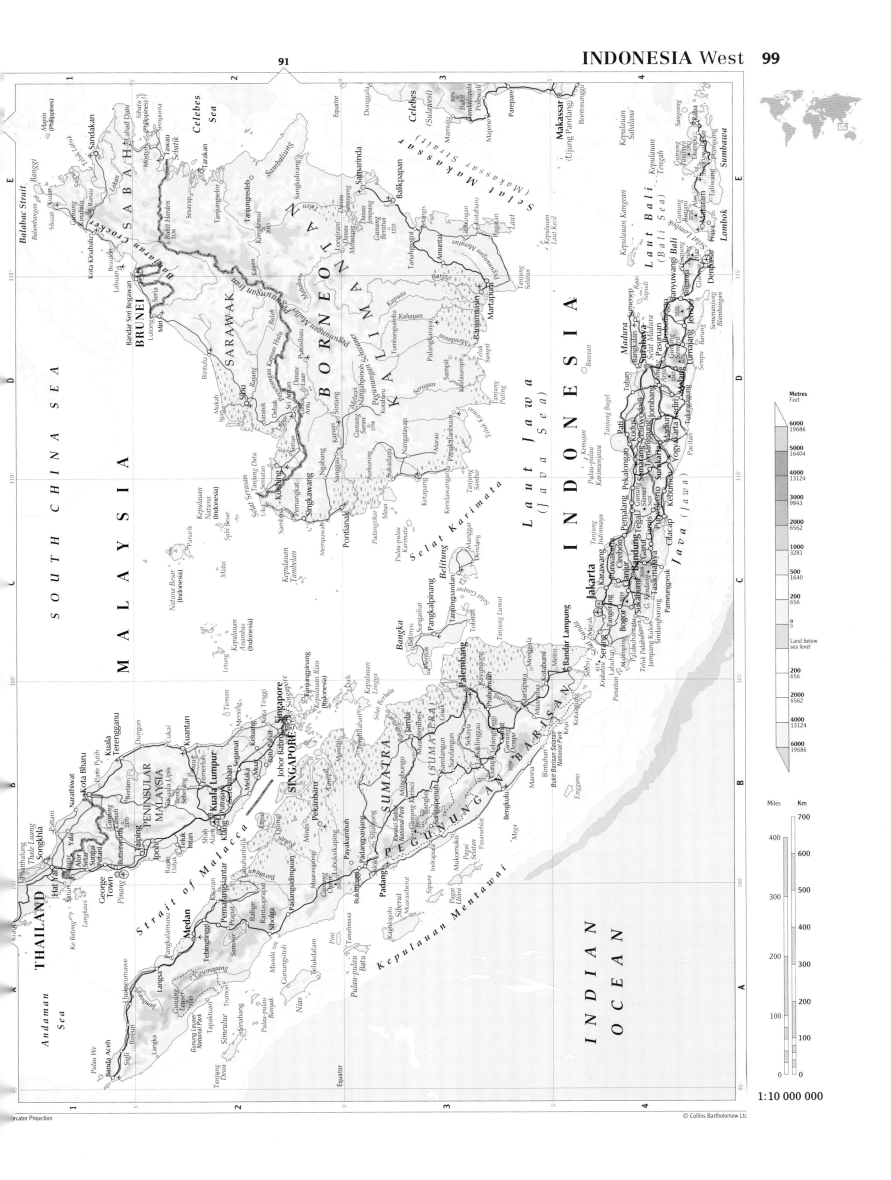

NORTH AMERICA

Baffin Bay

Greenland

Arctic Circle

Greenland Sea

Spitsbergen

Longyearbyen

Nordaustlandet

Svalbard
(Norway)

Zemlya
Frantsa-Iosifa

BARENTS SEA

Bjørnøya
(Norway)

North Cape

Jan Mayen
(Norway)

Denmark Strait

ICELAND

Reykjavík

NORWEGIAN
SEA

Trondheim

Faroe Islands
(Denmark)
Tórshavn

Shetland
Islands

Bergen

Oslo

Vänern

Stockh

Vä

Gothenbur

Orkney
Islands

Skagerrak

Kattegat

Aalborg

DENMARK

Copenhagen

Outer Hebrides

SCOTLAND

Glasgow Edinburgh

NORTH
SEA

Odense

Bors

NORTHERN
IRELAND
Belfast

UNITED
KINGDOM

Leeds

Hamburg

Dublin

Manchester

REPUBLIC
OF IRELAND

Liverpool

Birmingham

WALES

Cardiff

ENGLAND

NETHERLANDS
Amsterdam
The Hague

Rotterdam

Essen
Düsseldorf
Cologne

Hannover

Ber

GERMAN

Leip

London

English Channel

Channel Islands

Brussels

Lille

BELGIUM

LUXEMBOURG
Luxembourg

Frankfurt

Nurem

Mannheim

Stuttga

Brest

Rennes

Paris

Orléans

Strasbourg

Dijon

Mur

ATLANTIC

OCEAN

Nantes

Loire

FRANCE

Seine

Rhine

Zürich

LIECHTEN
STEIN

Bern

SWITZERLAND

Innsb

Bay of
Biscay

Geneva

Mont
Blanc

Lyon

Rhône

Milan

Turin

MONACO
Nice

Ge

Bordeaux

Toulouse

Marseille

Pyrenees

A Coruña

Bilbao

Corsica

Andorra
la Vella

ANDORRA

Ebro

Flores

Azores
(Portugal)

São Jorge

Terceira

Pico **Ponta**
Delgada

São
Miguel

Santa
Maria

Arquipélago dos Açores

Oporto

Zaragoza

Barcelona

PORTUGAL

Salamanca

Madrid

Balearic Islands

Minorca

Majorca

SPAIN

Valencia

Ibiza

M E D

Lisbon

Tagus

Sardinia

Córdoba

Cartagena

Seville

Cádiz

Málaga

Gibraltar (U.K.)
Ceuta (Spain)

Melilla
(Spain)

Madeira
(Portugal)
Funchal

Ilha de
Porto Santo

A

F

1:17 500 000

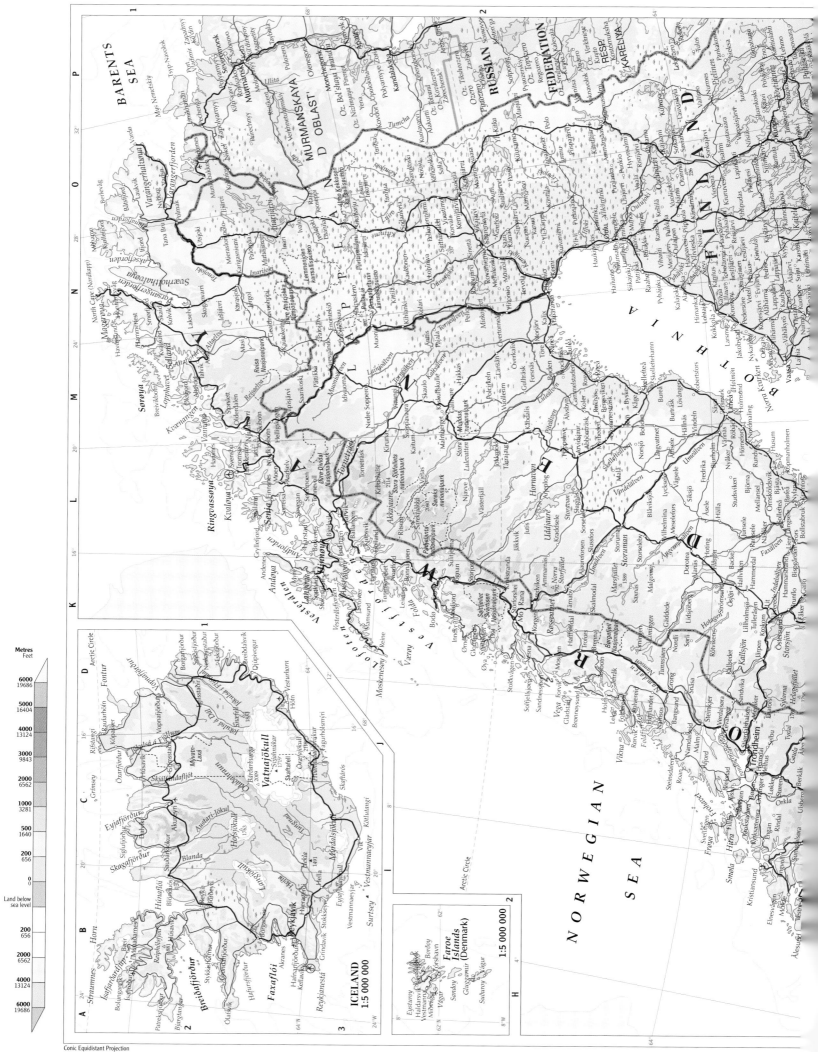

Conic Equidistant Projection

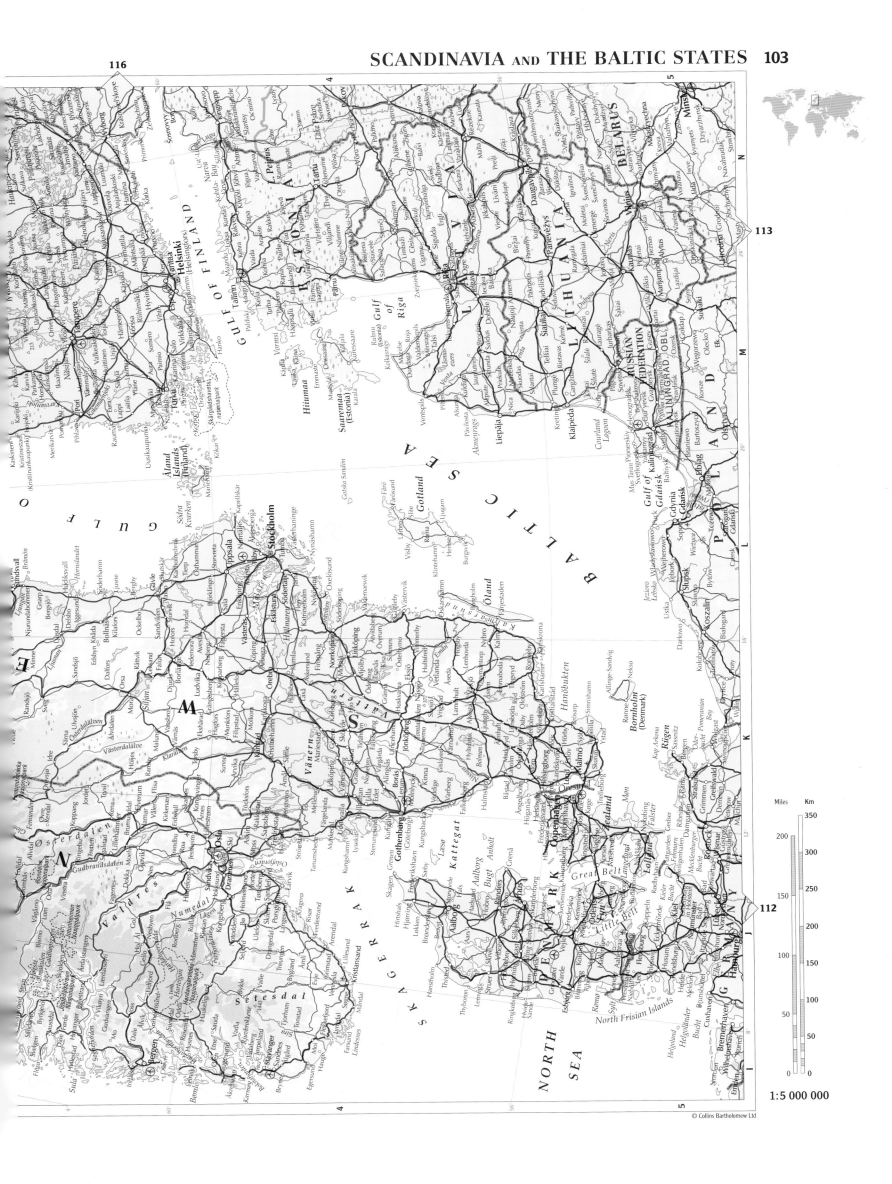

1:5 000 000

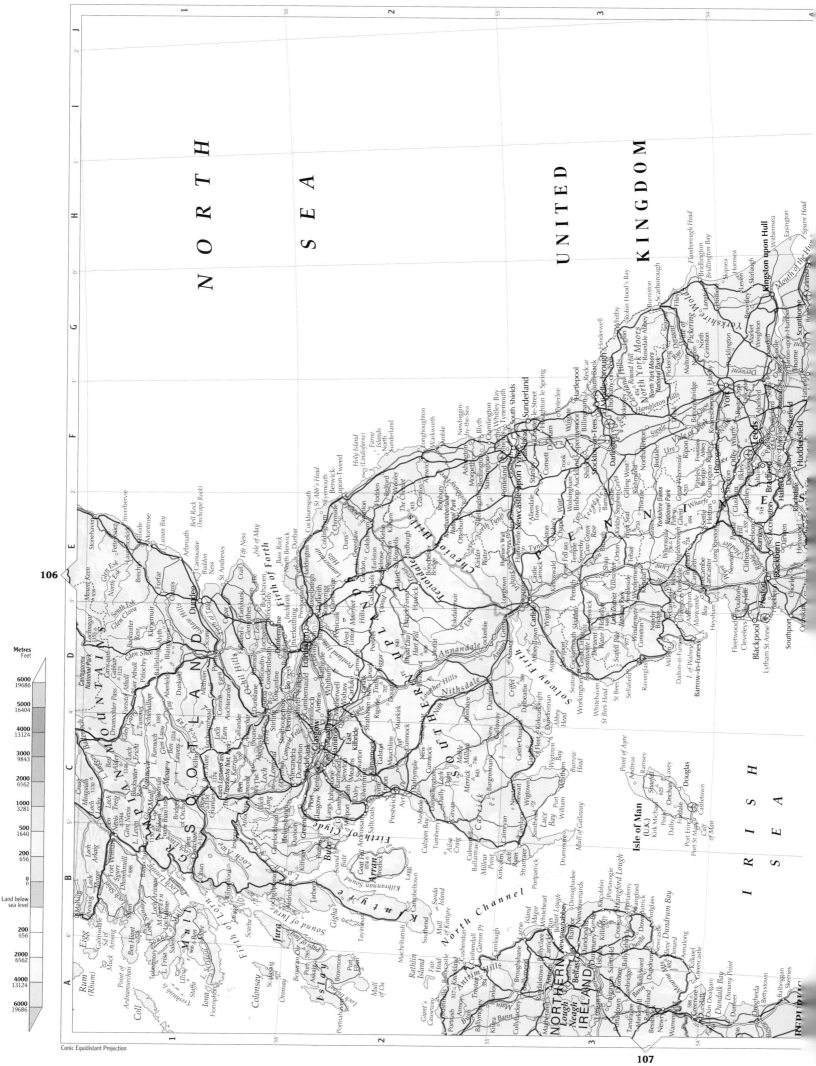

Metres
Feet

6000
19686

5000
16404

4000
13124

3000
9843

2000
6562

1000
3281

500
1640

200
656

0

Land below
sea level

200
656

2000
6562

4000
13124

6000
19686

Conic Equidistant Projection

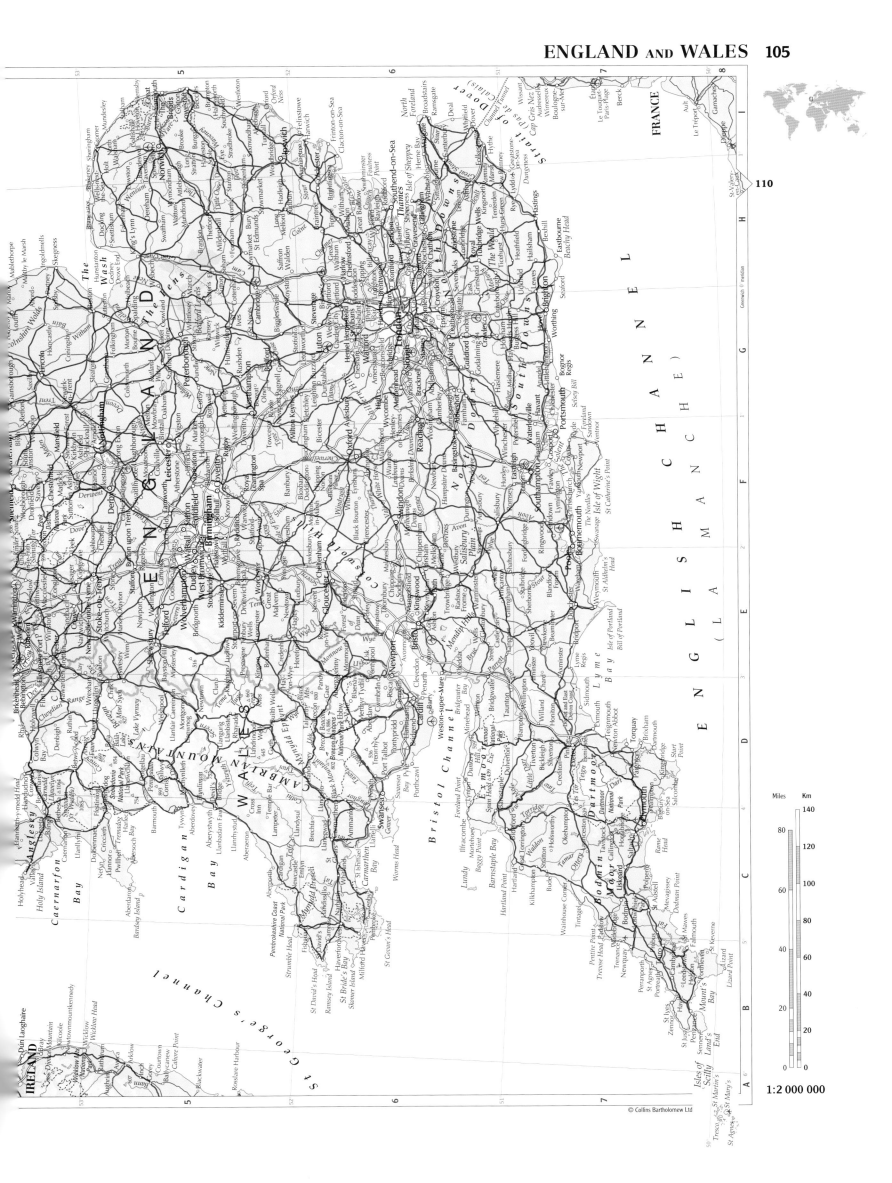

FRANCE

110

1:2 000 000

Miles Km

IRELAND

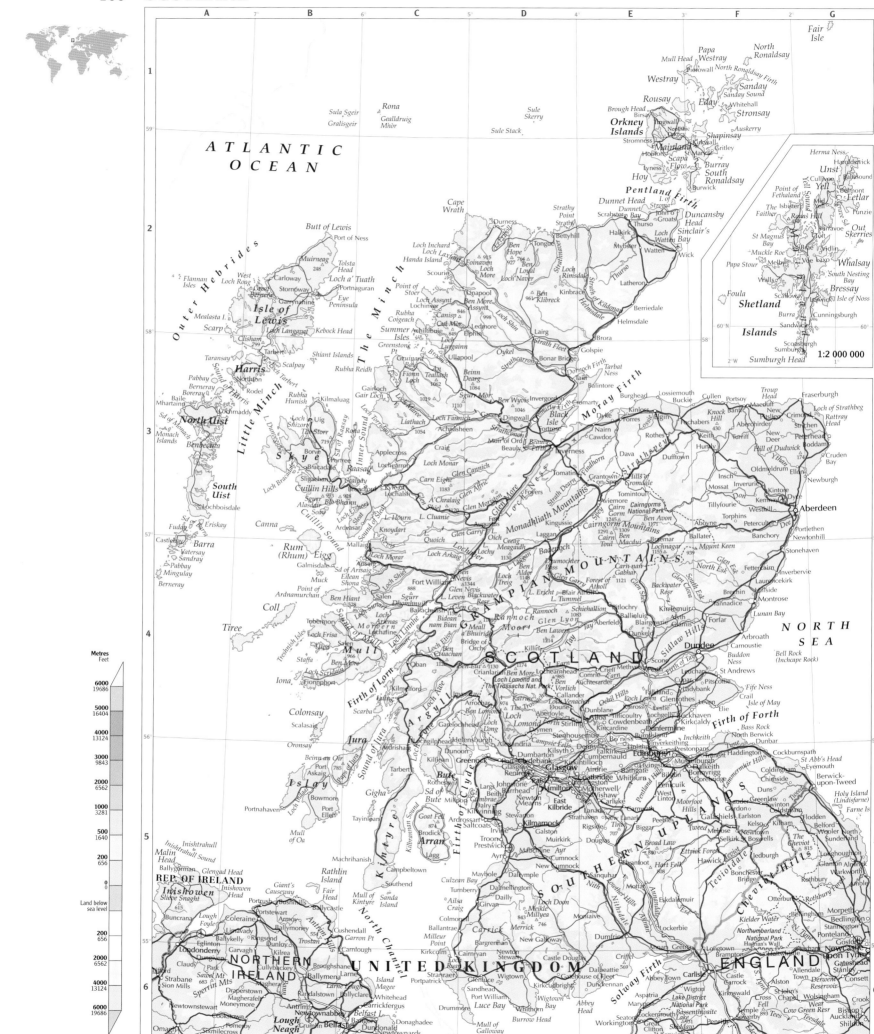

Metres
Feet

6000 / 19686
5000 / 16404
4000 / 13124
3000 / 9843
2000 / 6562
1000 / 3281
500 / 1640
200 / 656
0
Land below sea level
200 / 656
2000 / 6562
4000 / 13124
6000 / 19686

1:2 000 000

Conic Equidistant Projection

© Collins Bartholomew

A L A N T I C

O C E A N

SCOTLAND

UNITED

KINGDOM

NORTHERN

IRELAND

Belfast

Londonderry

Lough
Neagh

Donegal Bay

Sligo Bay

IRISH

SEA

REPUBLIC

OF

IRELAND

Dublin
Dún Laoghaire

Galway Bay

Lough
Ree

Lough
Corrib

Connemara

Limerick

Mouth of the Shannon

Golden Vale

WALES

Dingle Bay

Bantry Bay

Cork

St George's Channel

106

105

Miles	Km
	140
80	120
	100
60	80
	60
40	40
20	20
0	0

1:2 000 000

© Collins Bartholomew Ltd

Conic Equidistant Projection

NORTH

SEA

East Frisian Islands

West Frisian Islands

NETHERLANDS

Amsterdam

Haarlem

The Hague
(s'-Gravenhage)

Rotterdam

BELGIUM

Brussels
(Bruxelles)

Antwerp

Ghent

Lille

LUXEMBOURG

FRANCE

Paris

Reims

Metres / Feet

Metres	Feet
6000	19686
5000	16404
4000	13124
3000	9843
2000	6562
1000	3281
500	1640
200	656
0	0

Land below sea level

200	656
2000	6562
4000	13124
6000	19686

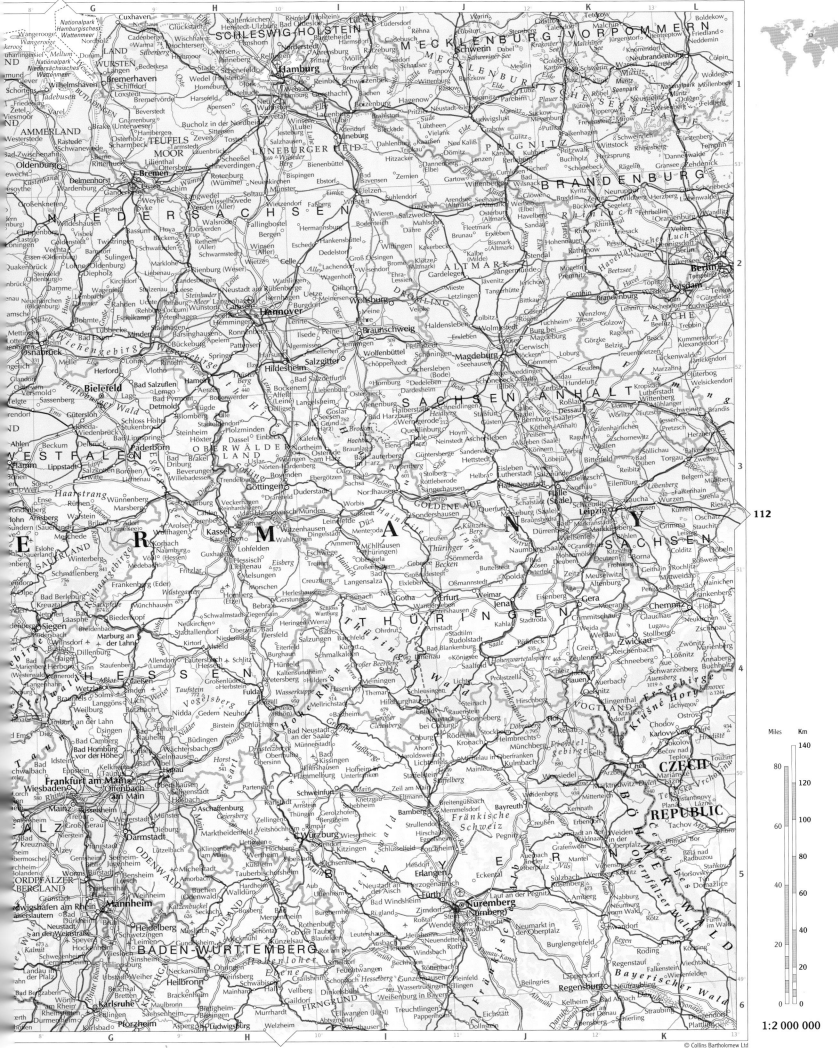

1:2 000 000

© Collins Bartholomew Ltd

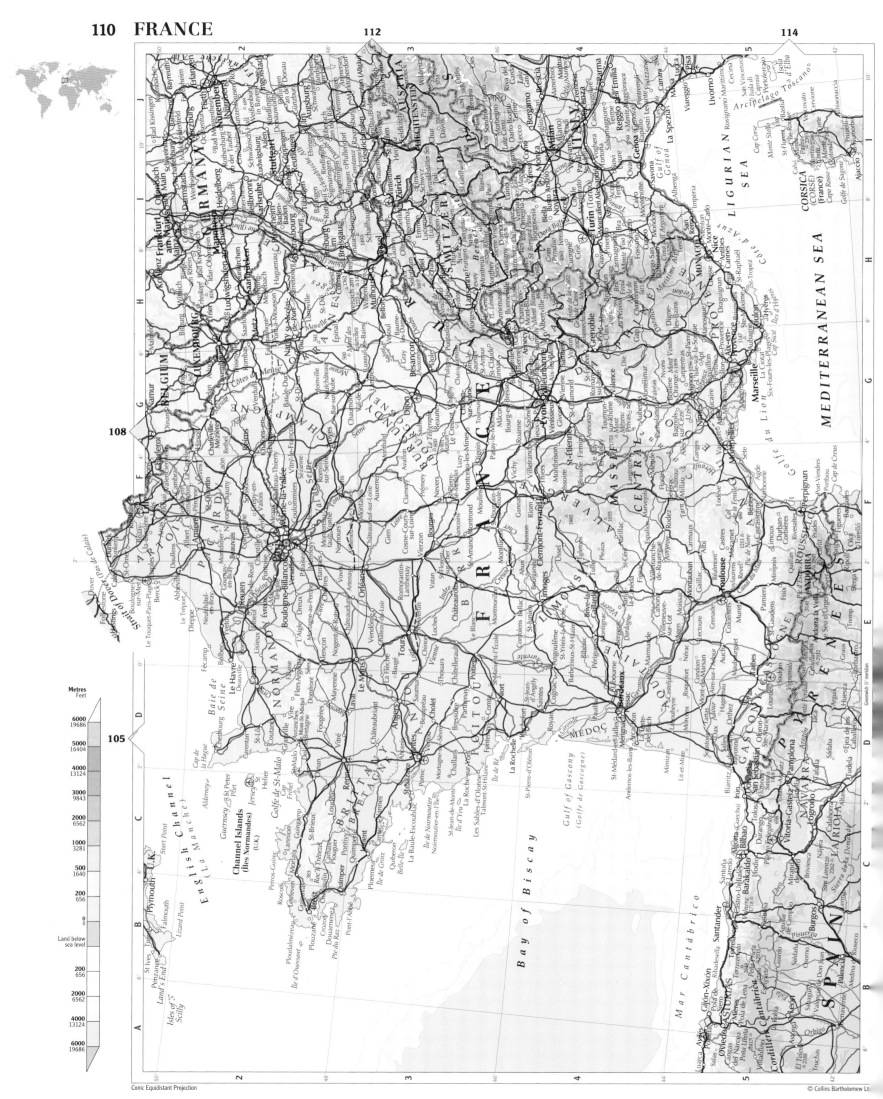

Conic Equidistant Projection

© Collins Bartholomew Lt

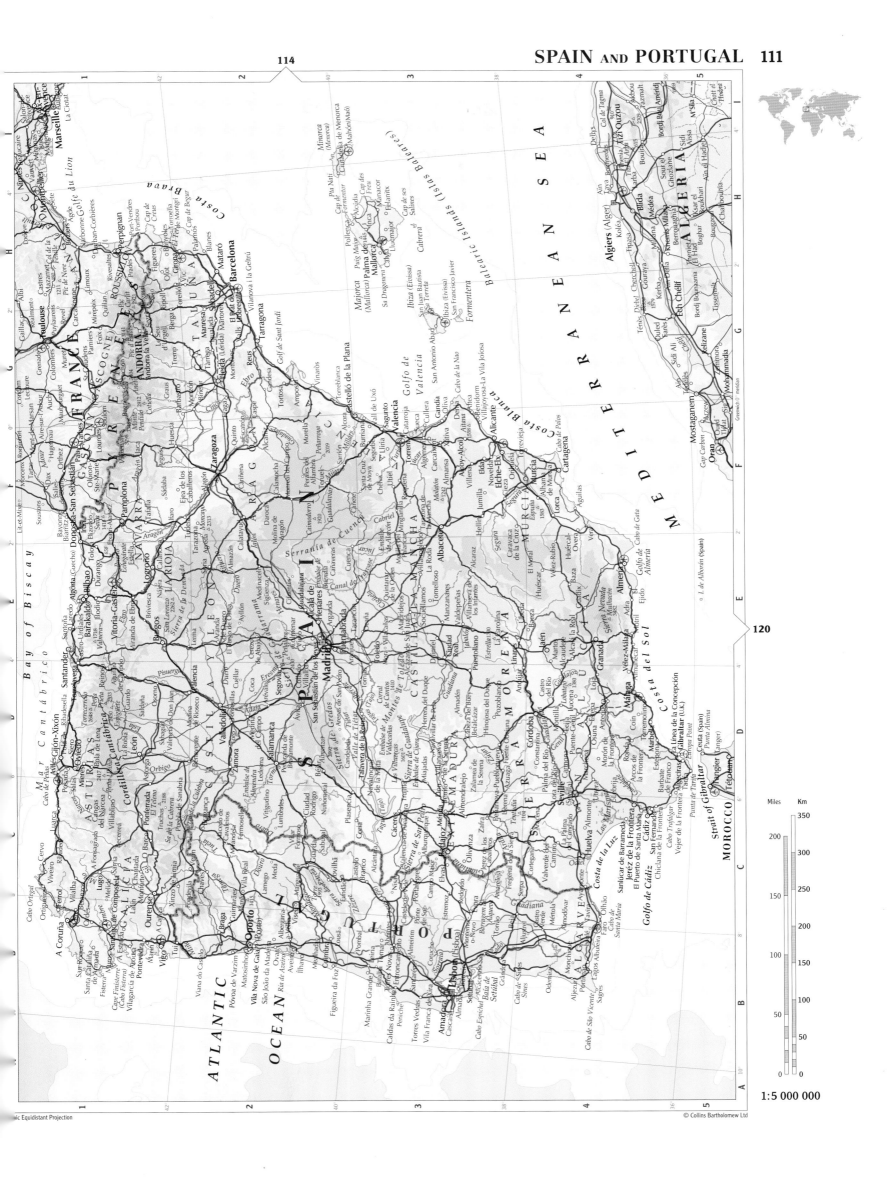

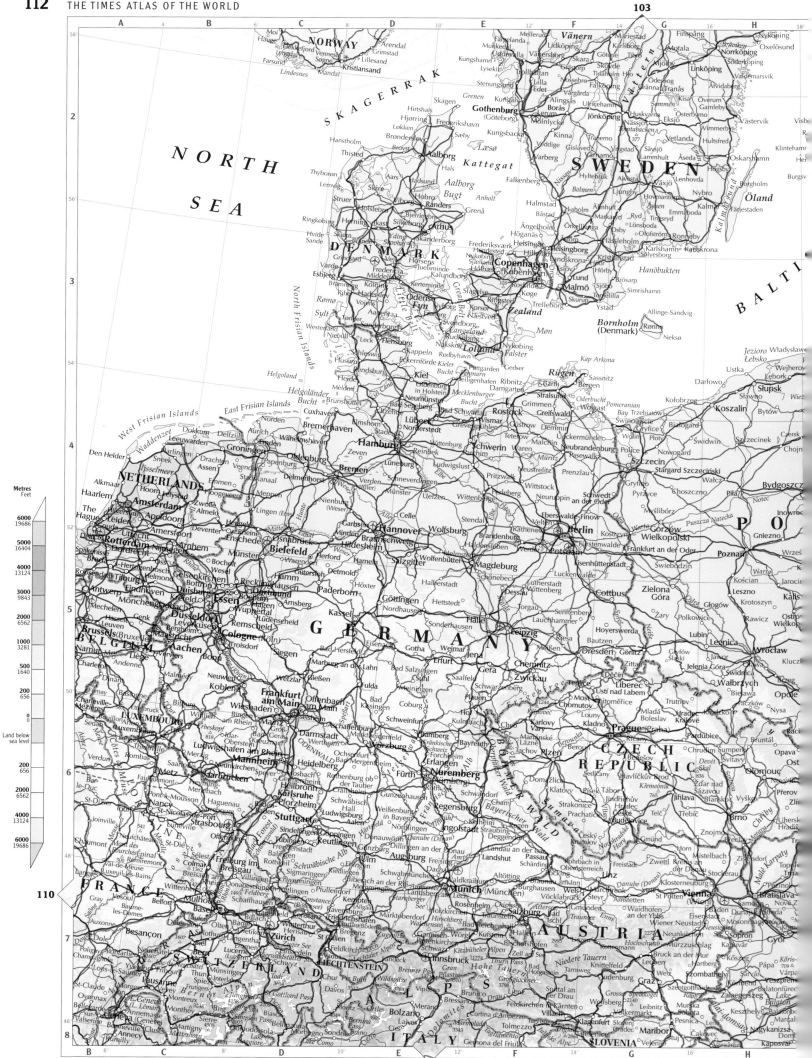

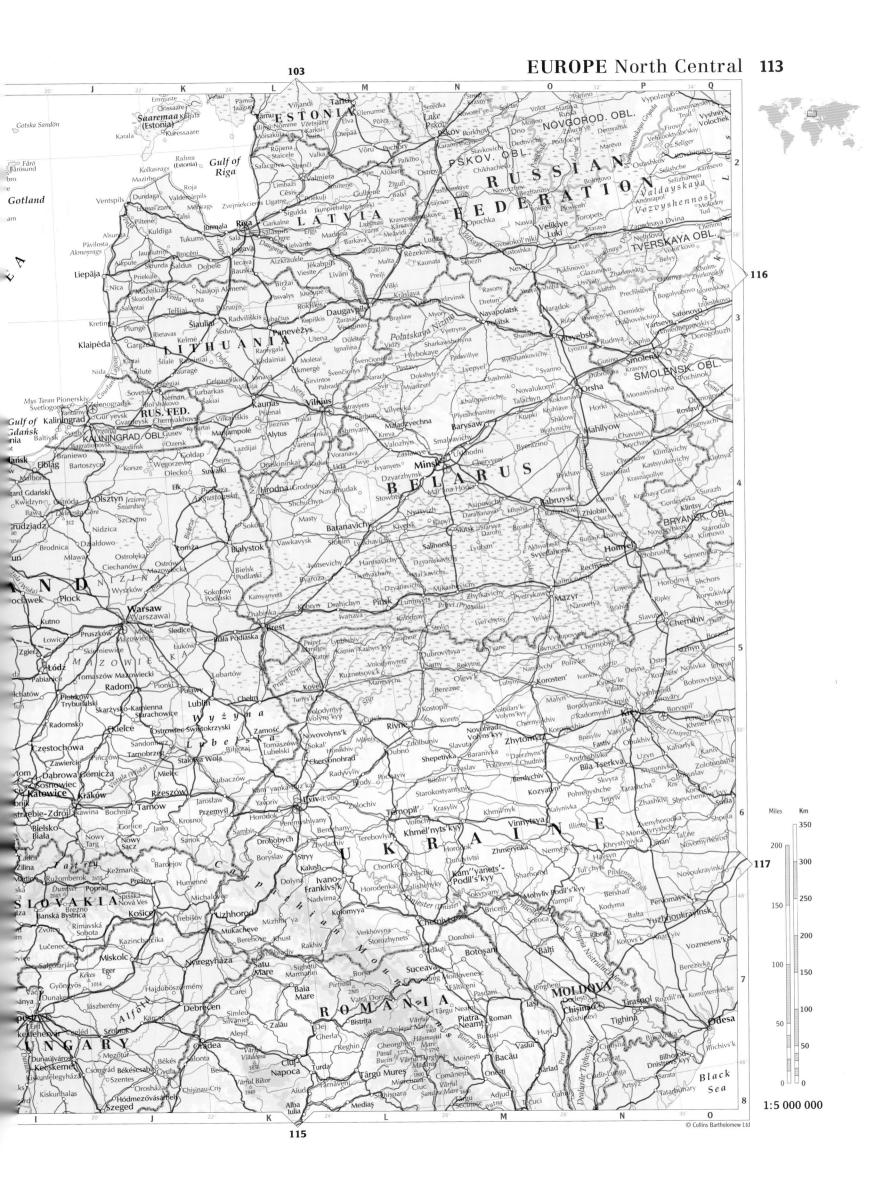

1:5 000 000

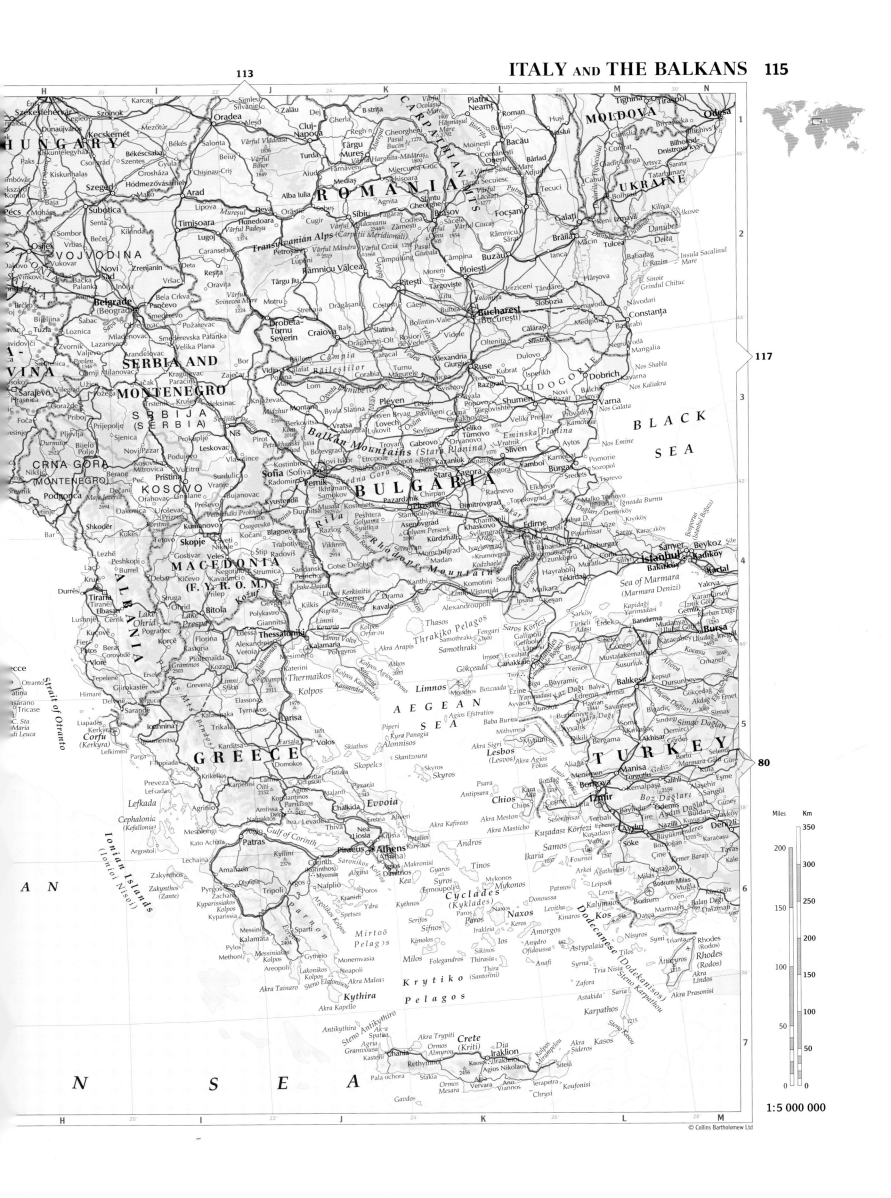

Metres
Feet

6000
19686

5000
16404

4000
13124

3000
9843

2000
6562

1000
3281

500
1640

200
656

0

Land below
sea level

200
656

2000
6562

4000
13124

6000
19686

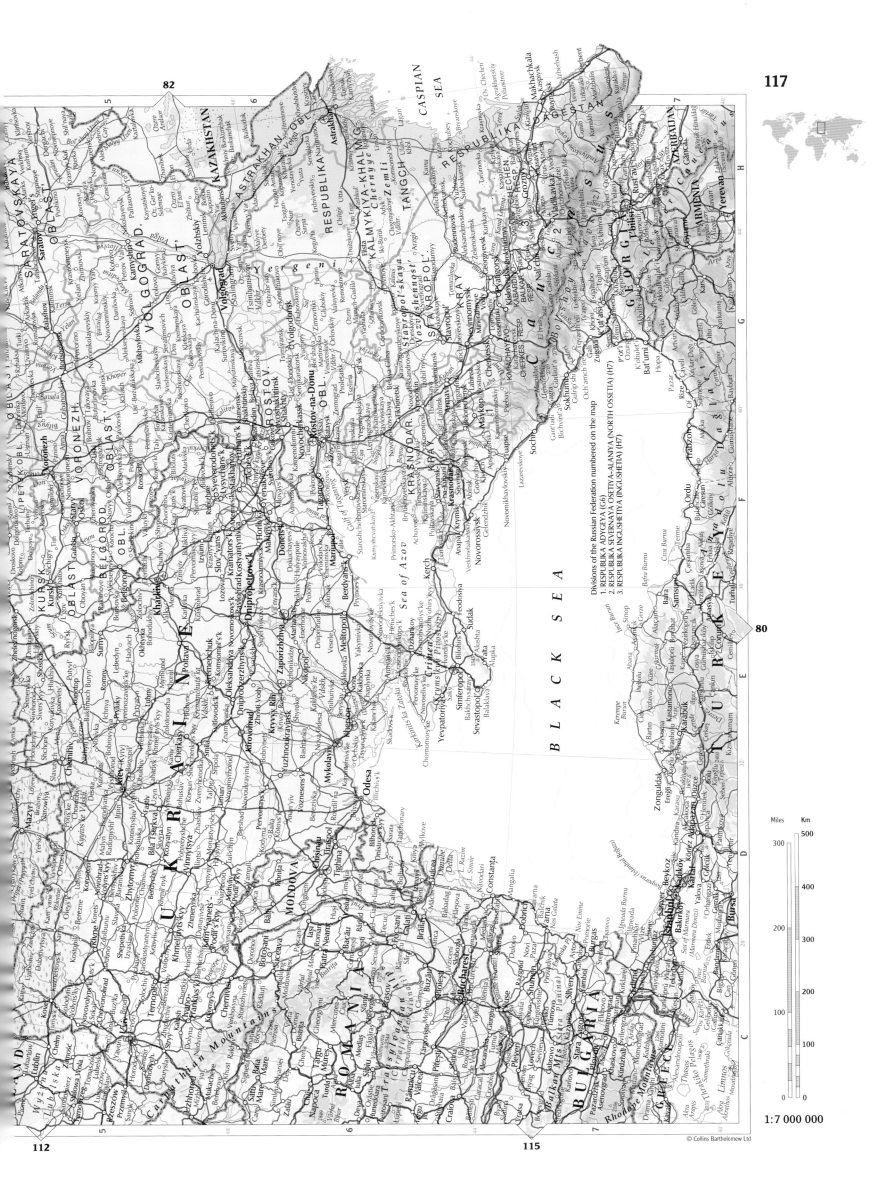

82

80

112

115

1:7 000 000

© Collins Bartholomew Ltd

Divisions of the Russian Federation numbered on the map
1. RESPUBLIKA ADYGEYA (G6)
2. RESPUBLIKA SEVERNAYA OSETIYA-ALANIYA (NORTH OSSETIA) (H7)
3. RESPUBLIKA INGUSHETIYA (INGUSHETIA) (H7)

CASPIAN SEA

BLACK SEA

Sea of Azov

KAZAKHSTAN

SARATOVSKAYA OBLAST'

VOLGOGRAD OBLAST'

ASTRAKHAN OBLAST'

RESPUBLIKA KALMYKIYA-KHALM'G

VORONEZH OBLAST'

ROSTOV OBL.

KRASNODAR KRAY

STAVROPOL' KRAY

DAGESTAN RESPUBLIKA

CHECHEN RESP.

GEORGIA

ARMENIA

AZERBAIJAN

UKRAINE

MOLDOVA

ROMANIA

BULGARIA

TURKEY

GREECE

Miles Km
300   500
       400
200   300
       200
100   100
0   0

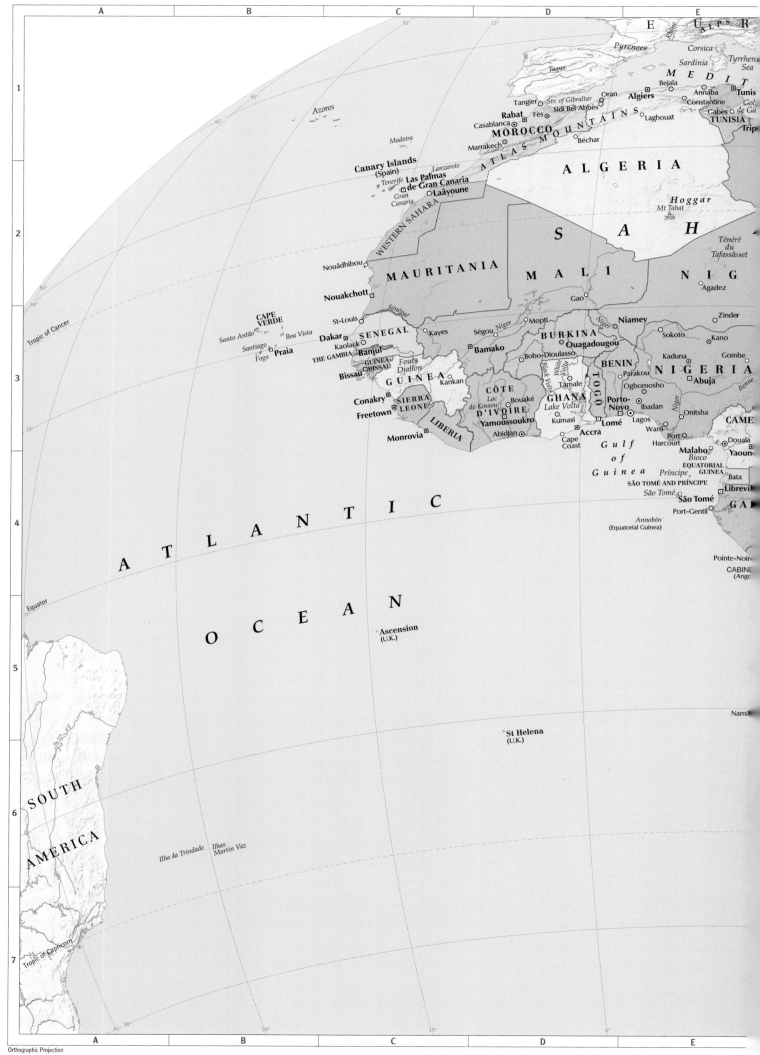

A B C D E

1

Azores

Pyrenees

Corsica

Tagus

Sardinia *Tyrrhen Sea*

M E D I T

Bejaïa

Tangier *Str. of Gibraltar* Oran **Algiers** Constantine **Tunis**
Sidi Bel Abbès Annaba *Col de Ga*
Rabat Fès Gabes
Casablanca Laghouat **TUNISIA** *Trip*
MOROCCO
Marrakech Béchar

Madeira

Canary Islands
(Spain)

A L G E R I A

Lanzarote

Tenerife **Las Palmas**
□**de Gran Canaria** *Hoggar*
Gran □**Laâyoune** *Mt Tahat*
Canaria 2918

Ténéré du Tafassâsset

S A H

2

Nouâdhibou

WESTERN SAHARA

S

Agadez

MAURITANIA **M A L I** **N I G**

Nouakchott Gao

Zinder

30° Tropic of Cancer

CAPE VERDE

St-Louis *Sénégal*

Santo Antão *Boa Vista*

Santiago **Dakar** **SENEGAL** Kayes Ségou *Niger* Mopti **Niamey** Sokoto Kano

Fogo **Praia** Kaolack **BURKINA**

Bamako **Ouagadougou**

THE GAMBIA **Banjul** Bobo-Dioulasso Kaduna Gombe

3 **Bissau** GUINEA-□**BISSAU** *Fouta Djallon* **BENIN** Parakou **NIGERIA**

GUINEA Kankan Ogbomosho

CÔTE Tamale **Abuja**

Conakry *Lac* **D'IVOIRE** Bouaké **GHANA** **Porto-** Ibadan Onitsha **CAME**

Freetown **SIERRA LEONE** *de Kossou* **Yamoussoukro** *Lake Volta* **Novo** Lagos Douala

Monrovia LIBERIA Kumasi **Lomé** Warri **Yaoun**

Abidjan *Cape* **Accra** Port Harcourt **Malabo** □

Coast *Gulf* *Bioco* **EQUATORIAL**

of **GUINEA** Bata

Guinea Príncipe **SÃO TOMÉ AND PRÍNCIPE** **Librevi**

São Tomé

São Tomé **GA**

4

A T L A N T I C

Annobón
(Equatorial Guinea)

Port-Gentil

Pointe-Noire

CABIN
(Ango

O C E A N

Ascension
(U.K.)

5 Equator Namib

St Helena
(U.K.)

SOUTH

6

Ilha da Trindade *Ilhas Martin Vaz*

AMERICA

7 Tropic of Capricorn

A B C D E

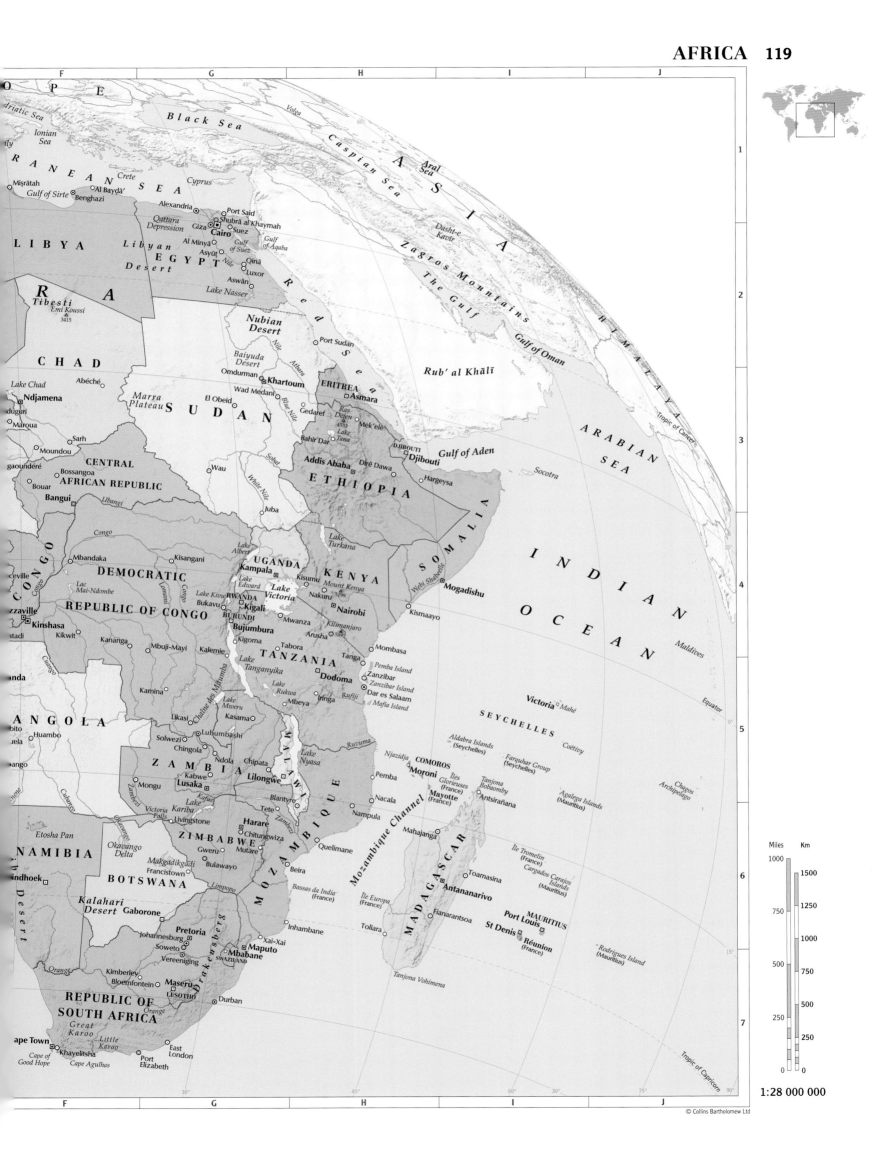

F G H I J

OPE

Adriatic Sea
Ionian Sea
Sily

Crete
Cyprus

Black Sea

Caspian Sea

Volga

Aral Sea

A S I A

Mişrātah
Gulf of Sirte
Al Baydā'
Benghazi

MEDITERRANEAN SEA

Alexandria
Port Said
Giza □ Shubrā al Khaymah
Cairo
Suez
Qattara Depression
Al Minyā
Asyūţ
Qinā
Luxor
Aswān
Lake Nasser

Gulf of Suez
Gulf of Aqaba

Zagros Mountains

Dasht-e Kavir

The Gulf

Gulf of Oman

HIMALAYA

LIBYA
Libyan Desert
EGYPT

Nile

Red Sea

Rub' al Khālī

ARABIAN SEA

Tropic of Cancer

R A
Tibesti
Emi Koussi
3415

CHAD

Nubian Desert

Baiyuda Desert
Port Sudan

Lake Chad
Abéché
Marra Plateau

Ndjamena
duguri
Maroua

SUDAN
El Obeid
Omdurman
Khartoum
Wad Medani

Nile
Atbara
Blue Nile

ERITREA
Asmara

Ras Dejen 4533
Mek'elē

Moundou
Sarh

CENTRAL
AFRICAN REPUBLIC

Bossangoa
Bangui

Wau

Gedaref
Bahir Dar
Lake Tana

DJIBOUTI
Djibouti

Gulf of Aden

gaoundéré
Bouar

Ubangi

Sebat
White Nile
Juba

Addis Ababa
Dire Dawa

ETHIOPIA

Hargeysa

Socotra

CONGO
ville
zzaville
Kinshasa
atadi

Mbandaka
Kisangani

DEMOCRATIC
REPUBLIC OF CONGO

Congo
Lac Mai-Ndombe

Lake Albert

UGANDA
Kampala
Lake Edward
Bukavu
RWANDA
Kigali
BURUNDI
Bujumbura

Lake Kivu

Lake Victoria

Kisumu
Nakuru
Mwanza

Arusha

KENYA

Nairobi
Kilimanjaro 5895

Mount Kenya 5199

Lake Turkana

SOMALIA

Mogadishu

INDIAN
OCEAN

Kikwit
Kananga
Mbuji-Mayi
Kalemie
Kigoma

Kamina

Likasi
Solwezi

Kamina

Lualaba

Lomami

TANZANIA
Tabora
Dodoma

Lake Tanganyika
Lake Rukwa

Iringa
Mbeya

Rufiji

Mombasa
Tanga
Pemba Island
Zanzibar
Zanzibar Island
Dar es Salaam
Mafia Island

Kismaayo

SEYCHELLES

Victoria ○ Mahé

Equator

Maldives

Chagos Archipelago

ANGOLA

ito
uela
ango
nda

Cuango

Chaîne de Mitumba

Lubumbashi
Chingola
Ndola

ZAMBIA
Mongu
Lusaka

Lake Mweru

Chipata
MALAWI
Lake Nyasa
Lilongwe
Pemba
Blantyre

Ruvuma

Njazidja
COMOROS
Moroni

Iles Glorieuses (France)
Mayotte (France)

Aldabra Islands
(Seychelles)

Farquhar Group (Seychelles)

Tanjona Bobaomby

Antsiranana

Agalega Islands (Mauritius)

Coëtivy

NAMIBIA
ndhoek

Etosha Pan

Okavango Delta

BOTSWANA

Mongu
Kabwe
Kafue
Lake Kariba
Victoria Falls
Livingstone

Tete
Chitungwiza
ZIMBABWE
Harare
Gweru
Mutare
Bulawayo

Nacala
Nampula

Quelimane
Beira

MOZAMBIQUE

Mahajanga

MADAGASCAR
Antananarivo

Ile Tromelin (France)

Cargados Carajos Islands (Mauritius)

Makgadikgadi
Francistown

Kalahari Desert
Gaborone

Limpopo

Bassas da India (France)

Ile Europa (France)

Mozambique Channel

Toamasina

Fianarantsoa

Port Louis
MAURITIUS
St Denis
Réunion (France)

Rodrigues Island (Mauritius)

esert

REPUBLIC OF SOUTH AFRICA
Johannesburg
Pretoria
Soweto
Vereeniging
SWAZILAND
Mbabane
Maseru
LESOTHO

Xai-Xai
Maputo

Inhambane
Toliara

Tanjona Vohimena

Kimberley
Bloemfontein
Orange

ape Town
Khayelitsha
Cape of Good Hope
Cape Agulhas
Port Elizabeth
East London

Great Karoo
Little Karoo
Durban

Drakensberg

Tropic of Capricorn

Miles Km
1000 1500
750   1250
      1000
500   750
250   500
      250
0   0

1:28 000 000

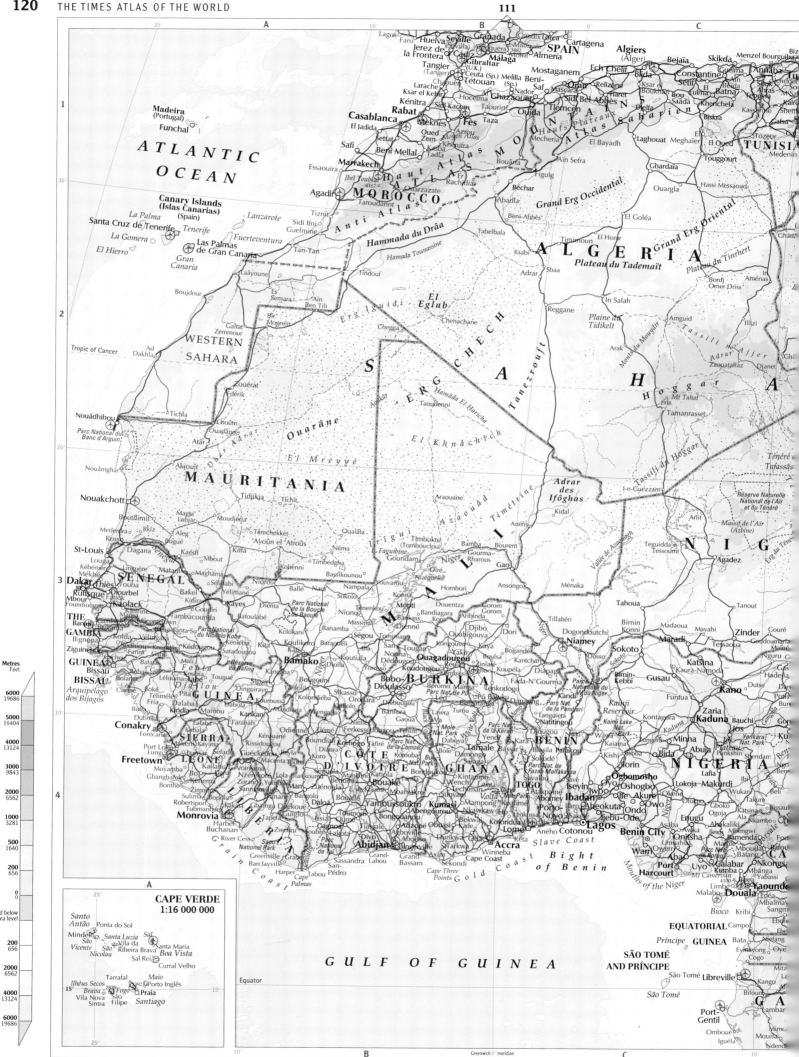

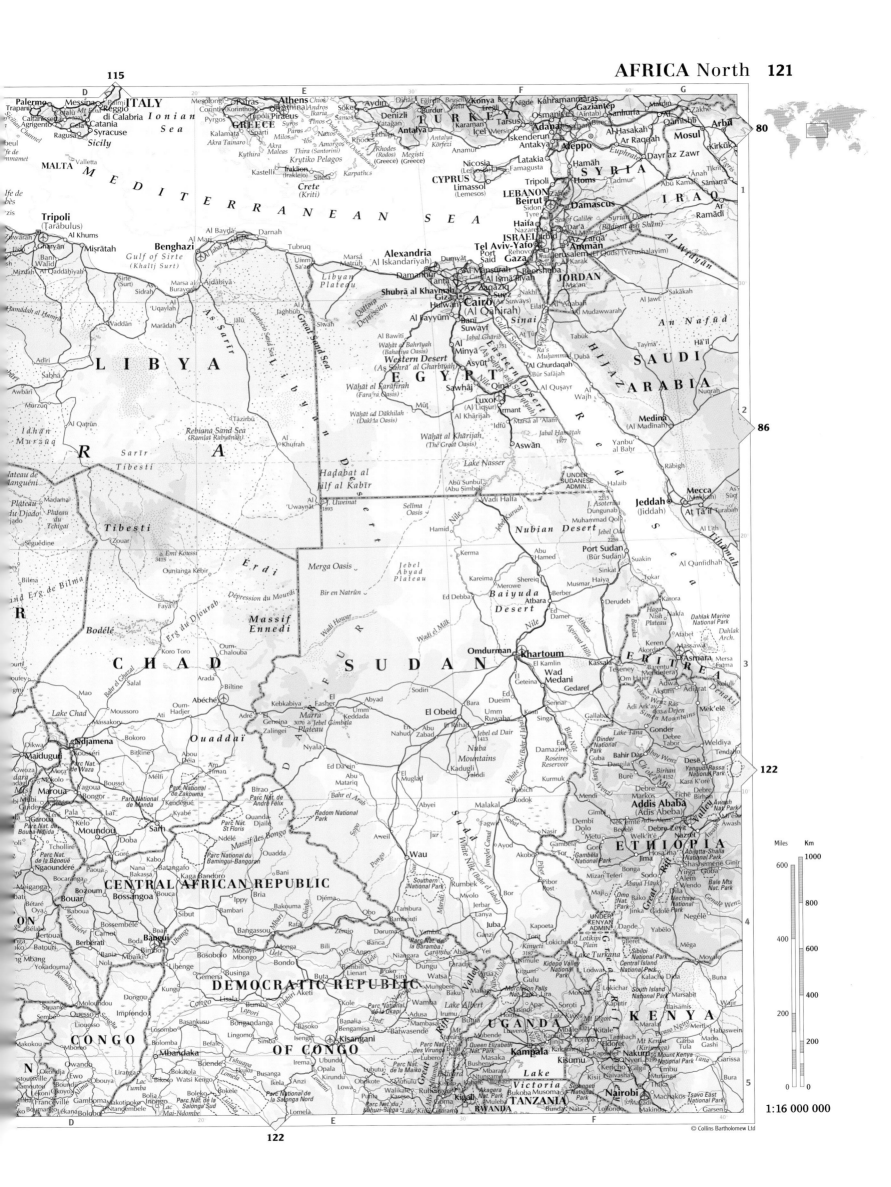

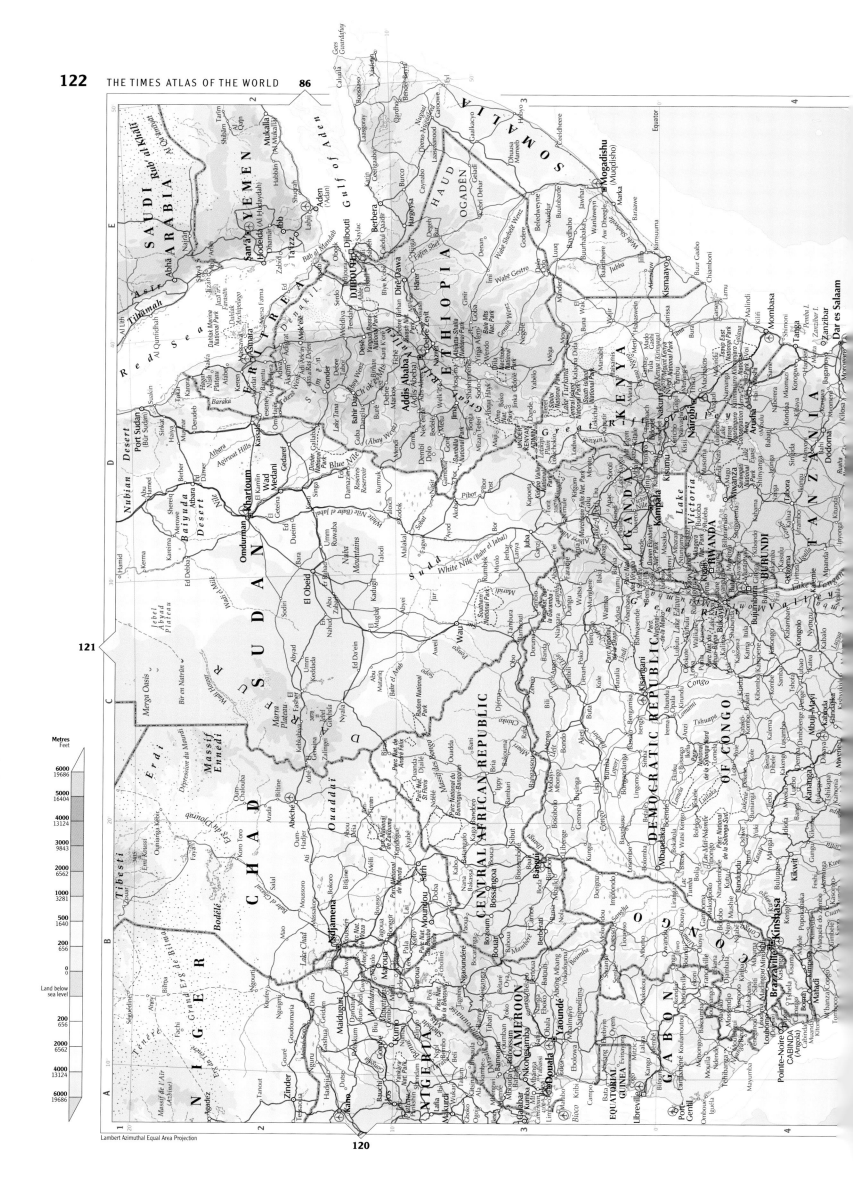

Metres / Feet

6000	19686
5000	16404
4000	13124
3000	9843
2000	6562
1000	3281
500	1640
200	656
0	0

Land below sea level

200	656
2000	6562
4000	13124
6000	19686

Lambert Azimuthal Equal Area Projection

120
121

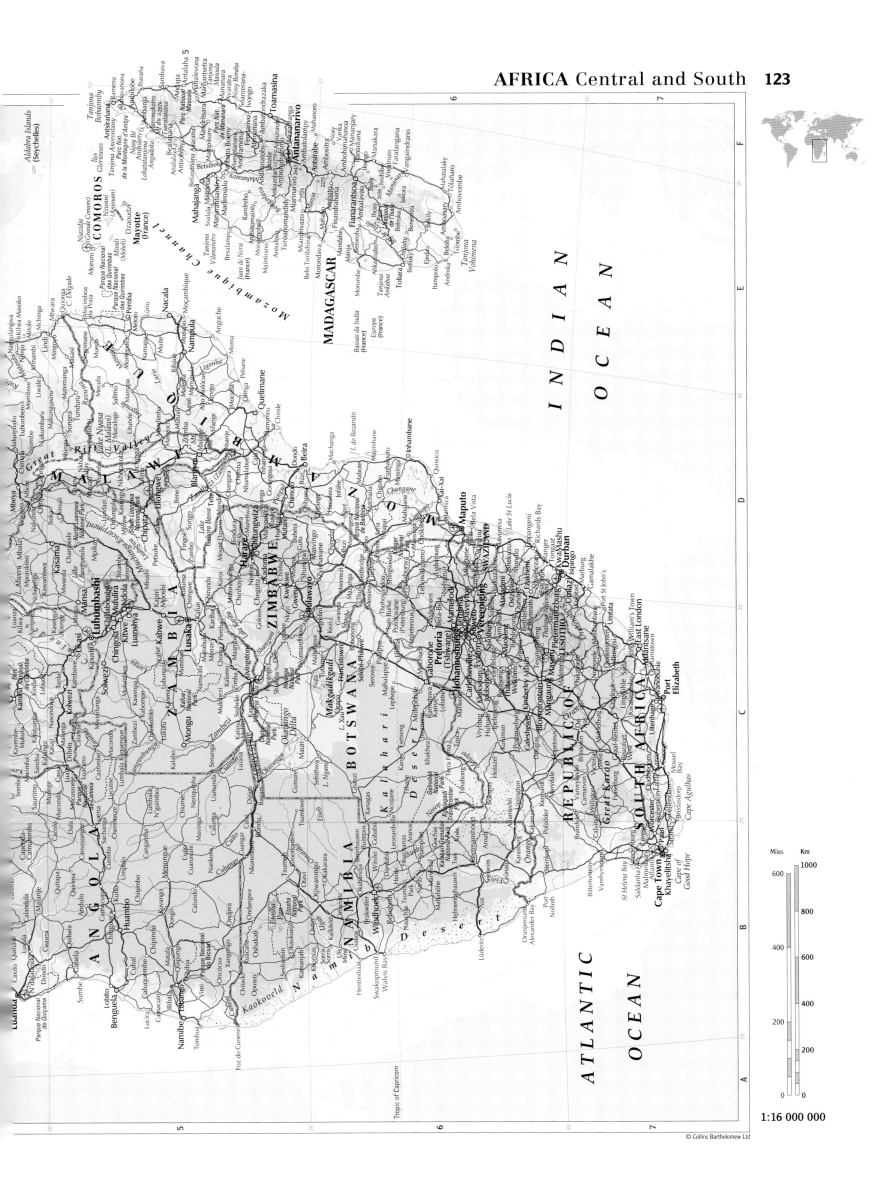

1:16 000 000

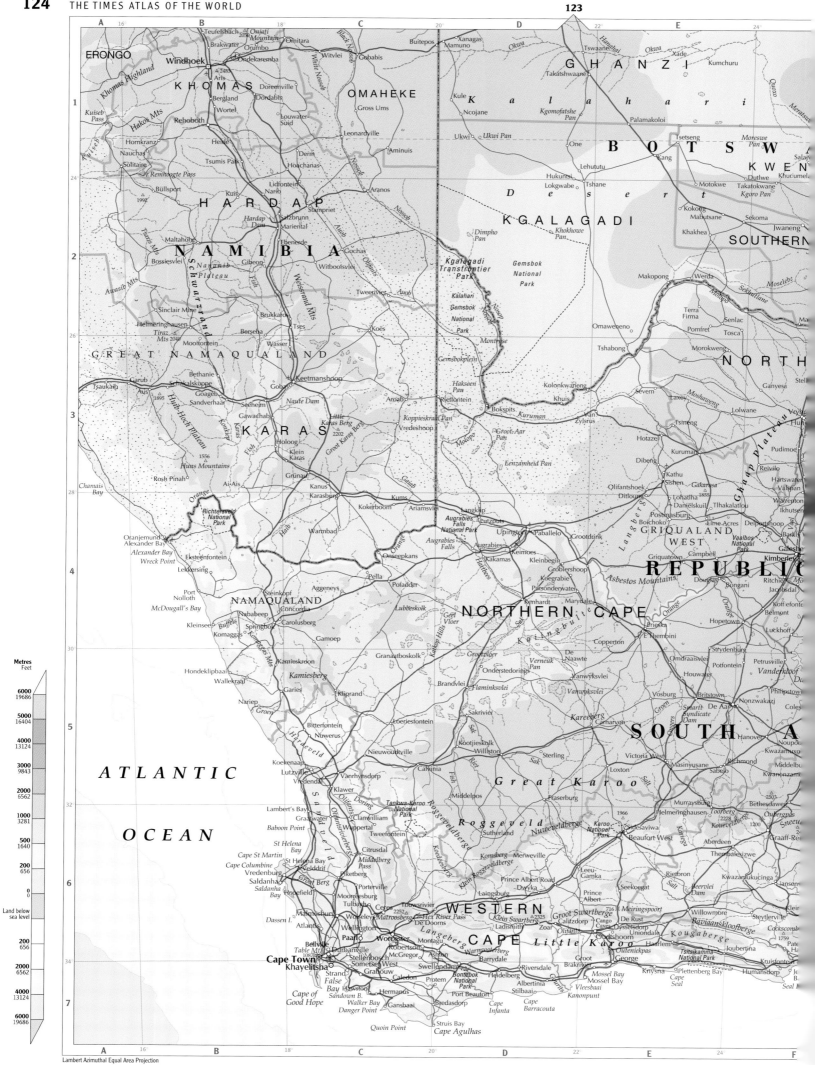

Metres
Feet

6000
19686

5000
16404

4000
13124

3000
9843

2000
6562

1000
3281

500
1640

200
656

0

Land below
sea level

200
656

2000
6562

4000
13124

6000
19686

Lambert Azimuthal Equal Area Projection

1:5 000 000

© Collins Bartholomew Ltd

	A	B	C	D	E

ASIA

ARCTIC OCEAN

Arctic Circle

Chukchi Sea

Point Hope

Barrow

Beaufort Sea

BERING SEA

St Matthew Island

St Lawrence Island

Bering Strait

Nunivak Island

Nome

Norton Sound

Yukon

Brooks Range

Mackenzie Bay

Sachs Harbour

Amundsen Gulf

Banks Island

Prince Patrick Island

McClure Strait

Melville Isla

Viscount Mel Sound

Parr

Queen

Pribilof Islands

Andreanof Islands

Aleutian Islands

Fox Islands

Attu Island

ALASKA

Mount McKinley Range

Alaska Ra.

Anchorage

Mount Logan

Victoria Island

Coronation Gulf

N U

Bathurst Inlet

Bristol Bay

Aleutian Range

Kodiak Island

Gulf of Alaska

YUKON TERRITORY

Whitehorse

Inuvik

Great Bear Lake

Déline

Mackenzie Mountains

NORTHWEST TERRITORIES

Yellowknife

Fort Simpson

Great Slave Lake

Juneau

Fort Nelson

Watson Lake

C A

N

Uranium Ci

Tropic of Cancer

Alexander Archipelago

Coast Mountains

Queen Charlotte Islands

Prince Rupert

Hecate Str.

BRITISH COLUMBIA

Dawson Creek

Prince George

Lake Athabasca

Fort McMurray

Lynn L

ALBERTA

Grande Prairie

Edmonton

SASKATCHEWA

Midway Islands (U.S.A.)

Vancouver Island

Kamloops

Jasper

Lloydminster

Prince Albert

Saskatoo

Vancouver

Calgary

Victoria

Medicine Hat

Regi

Seattle

Lethbridge

N

Olympia

WASHINGTON

Spokane

Great Falls

PACIFIC

Portland

Salem

Columbia

Bitterroot Ra.

Helena

MONTANA

Billings

Bism

Eugene

OREGON

IDAHO

Boise

R O C K

Snake

Twin Falls

Rapid City

Casper

OCEAN

Cascade Range

Great Salt Lake

WYOMING

Kaua'i

O'ahu

Honolulu

Maui

HAWAII

Sacramento

Reno

NEVADA

Salt Lake City

Cheyenne

N

No Pl.

San Francisco

Carson City

UTAH

Denver

Hawai'ian Islands (U.S.A.)

Hawai'i

San Jose

Sierra Nevada

Mount Whitney 4418

COLORADO

UNITED STA

CALIFORNIA

Las Vegas

Albuquerque

Santa Fe

Ama

Los Angeles

ARIZONA

NEW MEXICO

Lubboc

San Diego

Phoenix

Tijuana

Mexicali

Tucson

El Paso

Ensenada

Mexicali

Ciudad Juárez

Rio Grande

T

Equator

Guadalupe (Mexico)

Gulf of California

Hermosillo

Chihuahua

Sierra Madre

MEXIC

Baja California

Los Mochis

Mont

Villa Insurgentes

Durango

La Paz

Mazatlán

Sierra Madre Occidental

Line Islands

Tepic

León

Guadalajara

Islas Revillagigedo (Mexico)

Morel

Administrative divisions abbreviated on the map:

U.S.A.		CANADA	
CONN.	CONNECTICUT	P.E.I.	PRINCE EDWARD ISLAND
DEL.	DELAWARE		
MD	MARYLAND		
MASS.	MASSACHUSETTS		
N.H.	NEW HAMPSHIRE		
N.J.	NEW JERSEY		
R.I.	RHODE ISLAND		
VER.	VERMONT		

Île Clipperton (France)

	A	B	C	D	E

Orthographic Projection

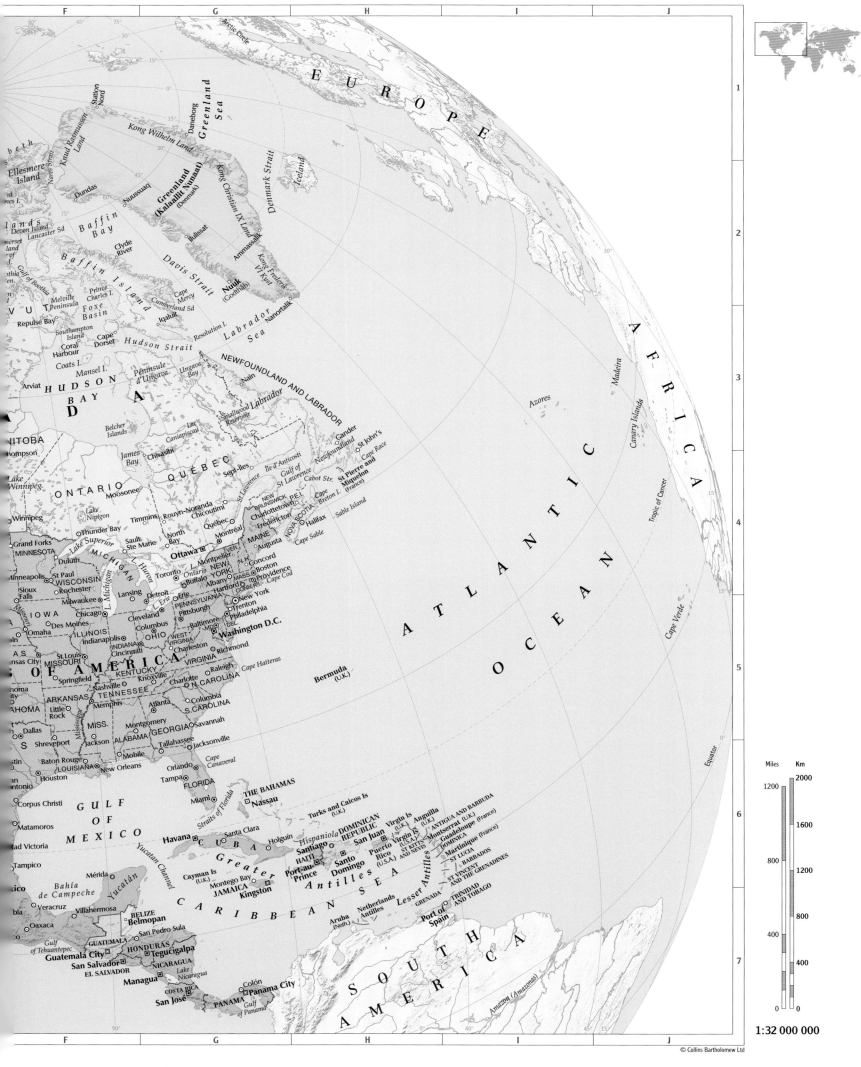

EUROPE

AFRICA

ATLANTIC

OCEAN

SOUTH AMERICA

Arctic Circle

Station Nord
Daneborg
Kong Wilhelm Land
Greenland Sea
Greenland
(Kalaallit Nunaat)
(Denmark)
Kong Christian IX Land
Iceland
Denmark Strait

Kong Frederik VI Kyst
Ammassalik
Nuuk
(Godthåb)

Nanortalik

Labrador Sea

Madeira

Canary Islands

Azores

Tropic of Cancer

Cape Verde

NEWFOUNDLAND AND LABRADOR

Nain

Shallwood Labrador Reservoir

Gander
St John's
Cape Race
Newfoundland
Cabot Str.
St Pierre and Miquelon (France)
Gulf of St Lawrence
Île d'Anticosti
NEW BRUNSWICK
P.E.I.
Cape Breton I.
NOVA SCOTIA
Sable Island
Halifax
Cape Sable

Sept-Îles

QUEBEC

Chisasibi
James Bay

Chicoutimi
Rouyn-Noranda
Timmins
North Bay
Québec
Montréal
MAINE
Augusta
VER.
Montpelier
N.H.
Concord
MASS.
Boston
Providence
CONN.
Cape Cod
Hartford
Ottawa
Toronto
L. Ontario
NEW YORK
Albany
Buffalo
R.I.
L. Erie
New York
PENNSYLVANIA
Trenton
N.J.
Pittsburgh
Philadelphia
DEL.
Baltimore
MD.
Washington D.C.
WEST VIRGINIA
Richmond
Charleston
VIRGINIA
Cape Hatteras
Raleigh
N.CAROLINA

Bermuda (U.K.)

Belcher Islands
Lac Caniapiscau

ONTARIO

Moosonee

Lake Nipigon

Thunder Bay
Sault Ste Marie
MICHIGAN
Lansing
Detroit
Lake Huron
Cleveland
Columbus
OHIO
Cincinnati
KENTUCKY
Knoxville
TENNESSEE
Nashville
Charlotte
S.CAROLINA
Columbia

Lake Superior
Duluth
WISCONSIN
St Paul
Milwaukee
L. Michigan
Chicago
Rochester
Minneapolis
Sioux Falls
IOWA
Des Moines
ILLINOIS
Indianapolis
INDIANA
Springfield
St Louis
MISSOURI
OF AMERICA
Omaha

Lake Winnipeg
Winnipeg
Grand Forks
MINNESOTA

MANITOBA
Thompson
Lake Winnipeg

HUDSON BAY

CANADA

Arviat

Coral Harbour
Coats I.
Southampton Island
Repulse Bay
NUNAVUT
Foxe Basin
Melville Peninsula
Prince Charles I.
Cape Dorset
Mansel I.
Peninsule d'Ungava
Ungava Bay
Resolution I.

Baffin Island
Iqaluit
Cumberland Sd
Cape Mercy
Davis Strait

Baffin Bay

Clyde River
Gulf of Boothia
Lancaster Sd
Devon Island
Somerset Island
Dundas
Nuussuaq

Ellesmere Island
Knud Rasmussen Land
Iceland
Kong Christian IX Land
Kong Frederik VI Kyst

Arkansas
Little Rock
Memphis
MISS.
ARKANSAS
Jackson
ALABAMA
Montgomery
GEORGIA
Atlanta
Savannah
Tallahassee
Mobile
Jacksonville
LOUISIANA
Baton Rouge
New Orleans
Shreveport
Dallas
Orlando
Tampa
FLORIDA
Cape Canaveral
Miami

Houston
Corpus Christi
Matamoros
Victoria
Tampico
Veracruz
Villahermosa
Oaxaca
Gulf of Tehuantepec

GULF OF MEXICO

Mérida
Bahía de Campeche
Yucatán

Yucatán Channel

Straits of Florida

THE BAHAMAS
Nassau

Turks and Caicos Is (U.K.)

Santa Clara
Holguín
Havana
CUBA
Greater Antilles
Cayman Is (U.K.)
Montego Bay
JAMAICA
Kingston

Hispaniola
HAITI
Port-au-Prince
Santiago
DOMINICAN REPUBLIC
Santo Domingo
Puerto Rico (U.S.A.)
San Juan
Virgin Is (U.K.)
Virgin Is (U.S.A.)
Anguilla (U.K.)
ANTIGUA AND BARBUDA
Montserrat (U.K.)
Guadeloupe (France)
DOMINICA
Martinique (France)
ST LUCIA
BARBADOS
ST VINCENT AND THE GRENADINES
GRENADA
TRINIDAD AND TOBAGO
Port of Spain

ST KITTS AND NEVIS

Lesser Antilles

CARIBBEAN SEA

Netherlands Antilles
Aruba (Neth.)

BELIZE
Belmopan
San Pedro Sula
GUATEMALA
HONDURAS
Guatemala City
Tegucigalpa
San Salvador
EL SALVADOR
NICARAGUA
Managua
Lake Nicaragua
Colón
COSTA RICA
Panama City
San José
PANAMA
Gulf of Panama

Equator

Amazon (Amazonas)

Miles	Km
1200	2000
	1600
800	1200
	800
400	400
0	0

1:32 000 000

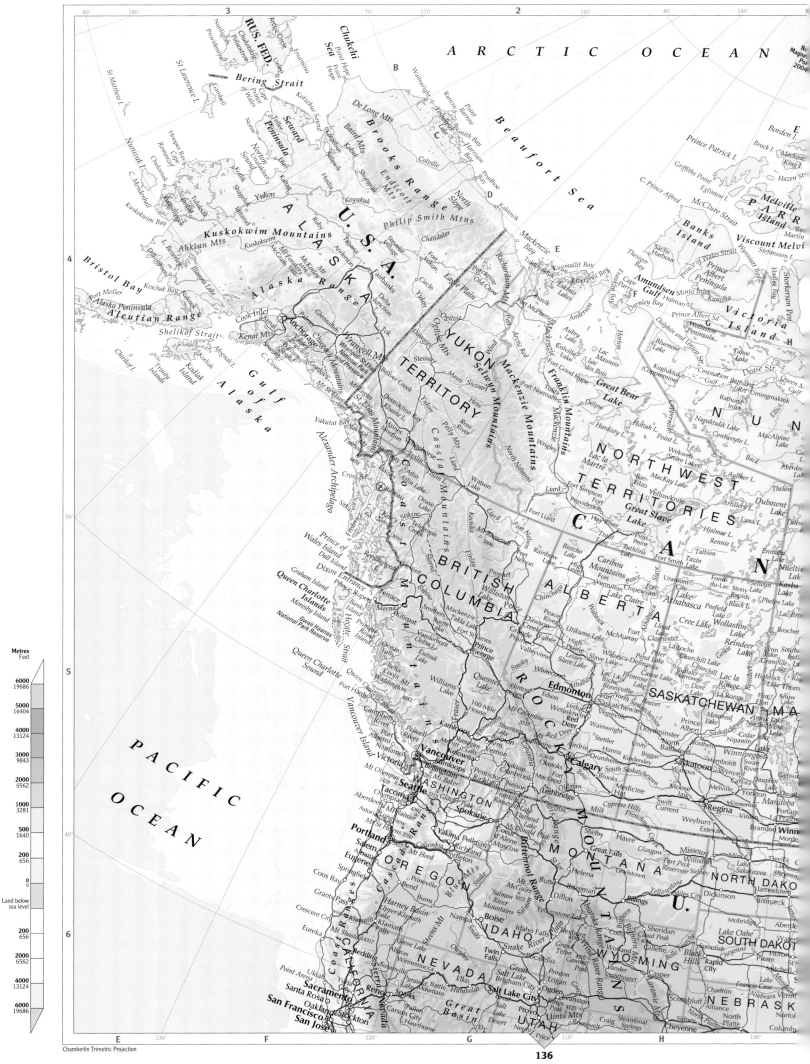

Metres
Feet

6000
19686

5000
16404

4000
13124

3000
9843

2000
6562

1000
3281

500
1640

200
656

0

Land below
sea level

200
656

2000
6562

4000
13124

6000
19686

Chamberlin Trimetric Projection

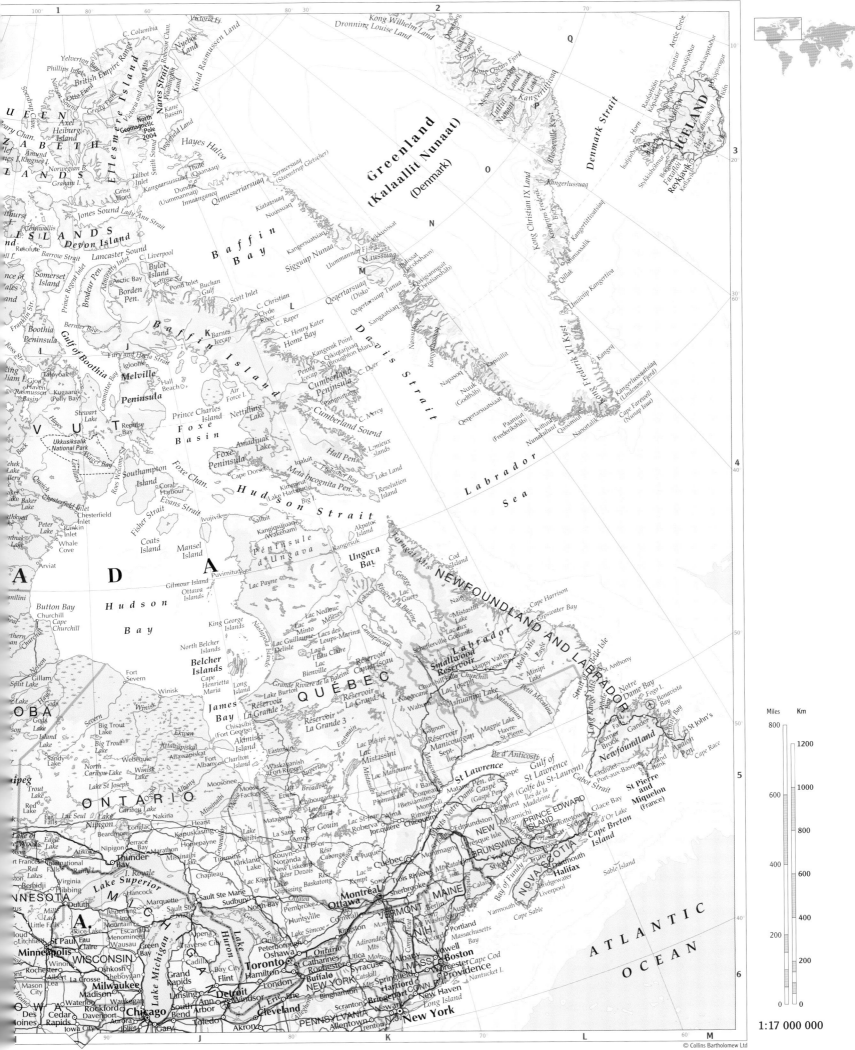

1:17 000 000

© Collins Bartholomew Ltd

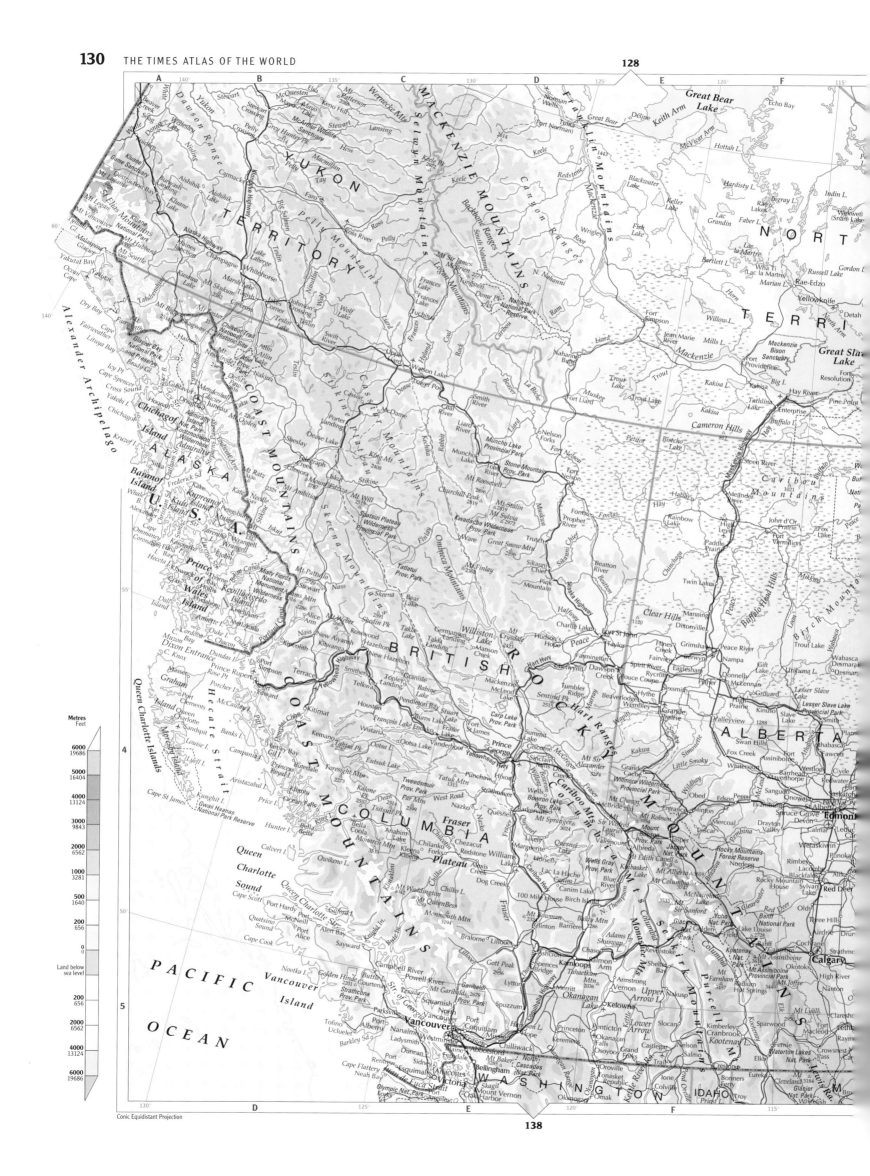

Conic Equidistant Projection

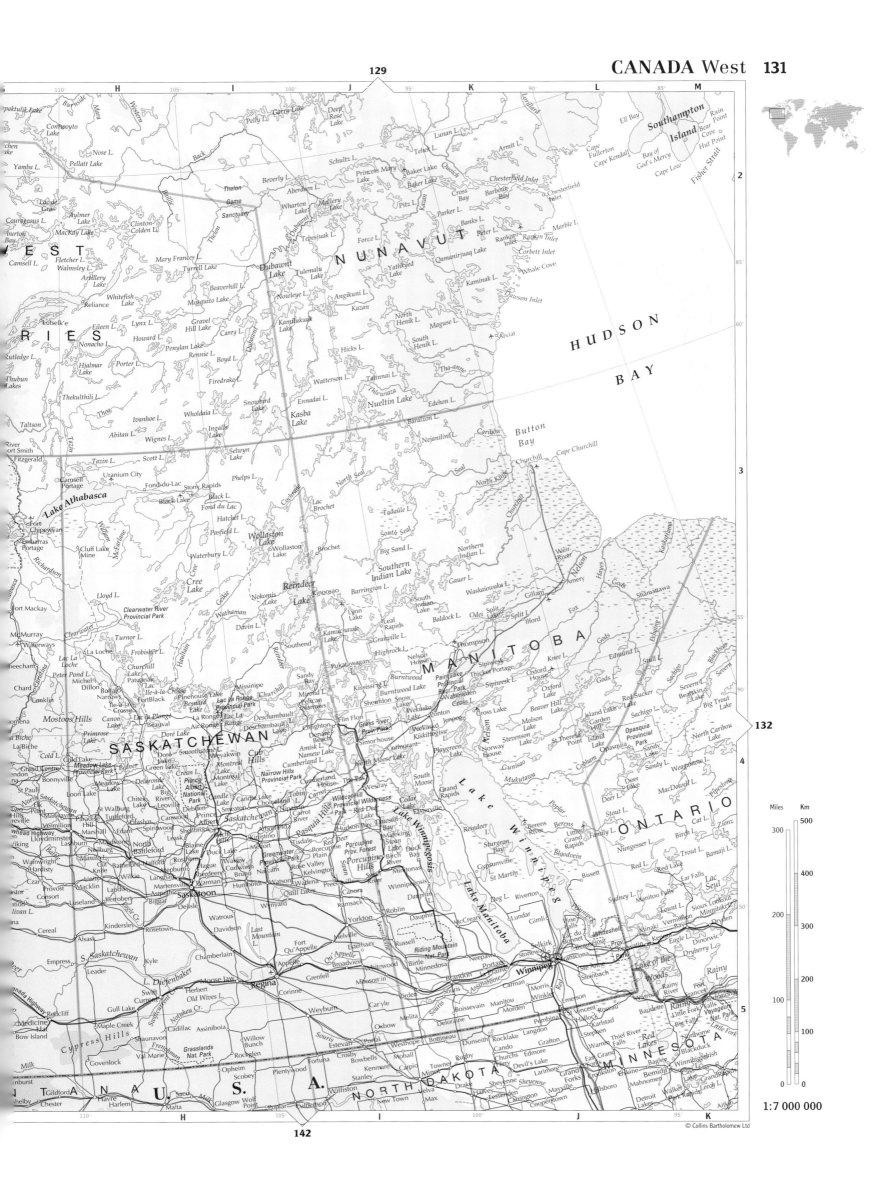

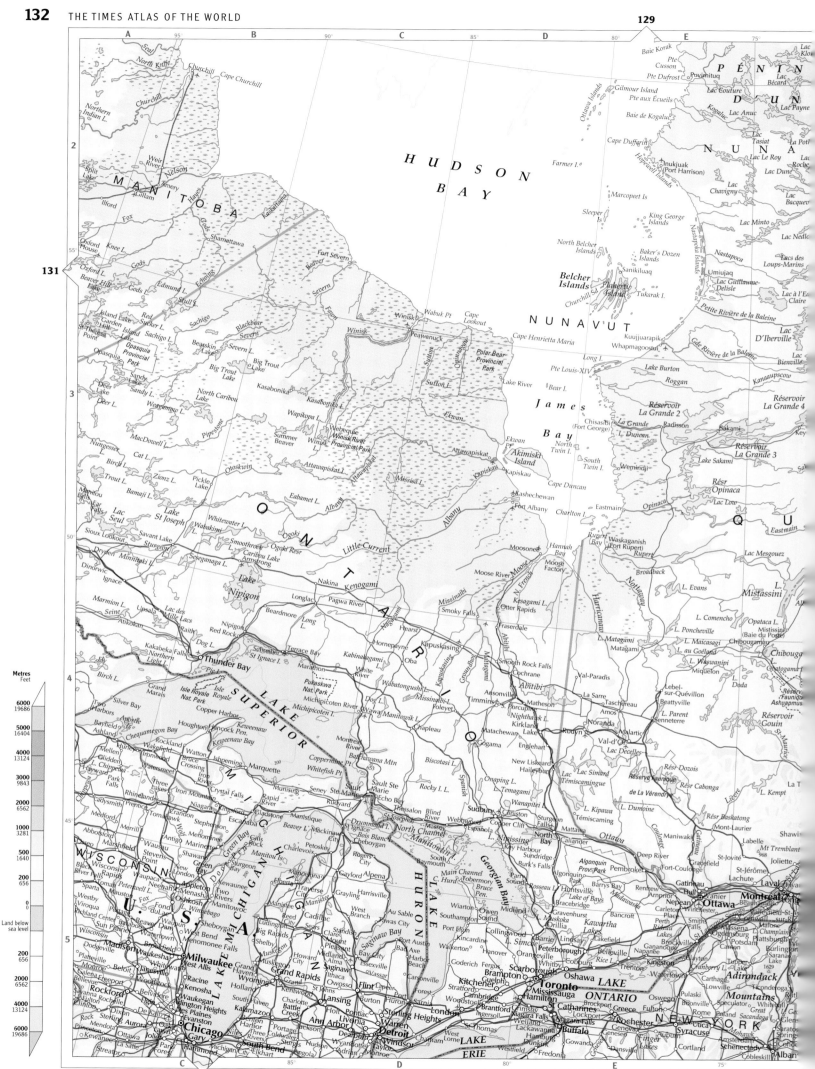

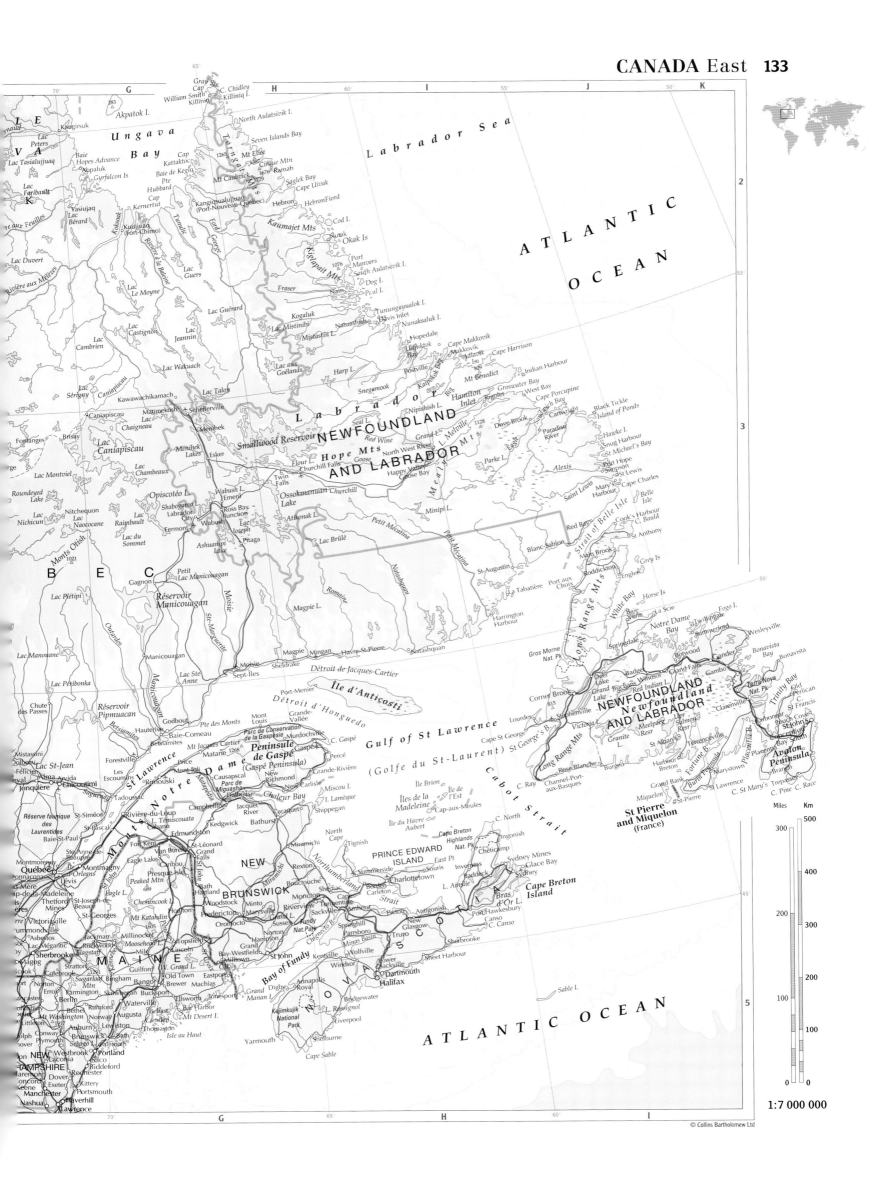

1:7 000 000

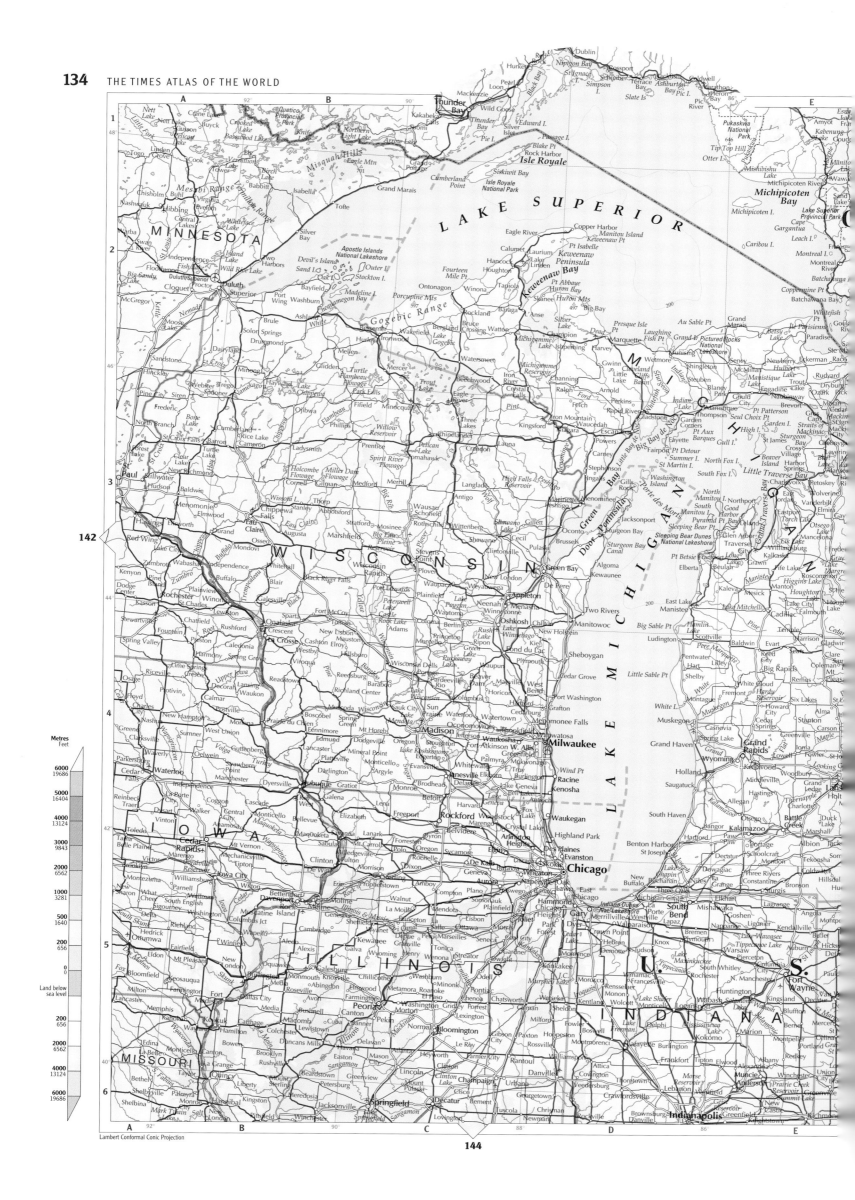

Lambert Conformal Conic Projection

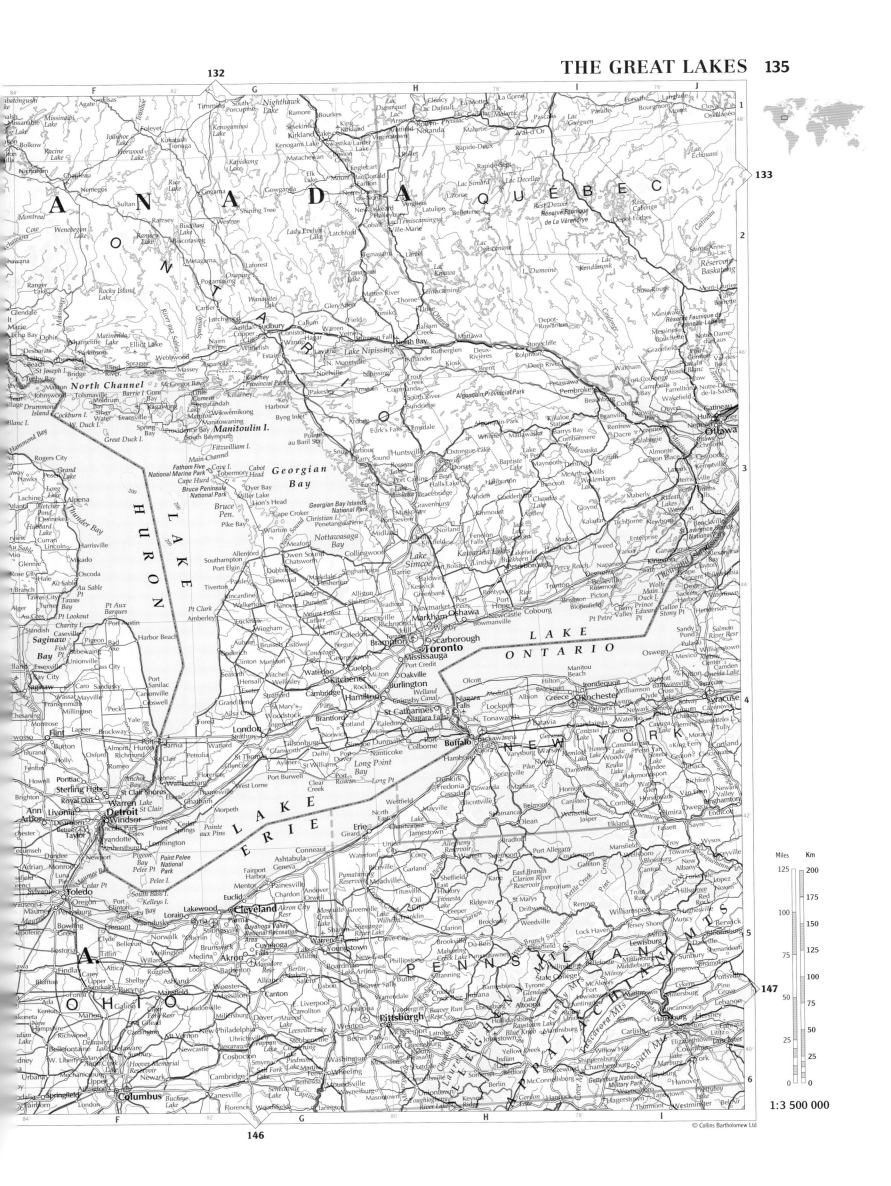

1:3 500 000

© Collins Bartholomew Ltd

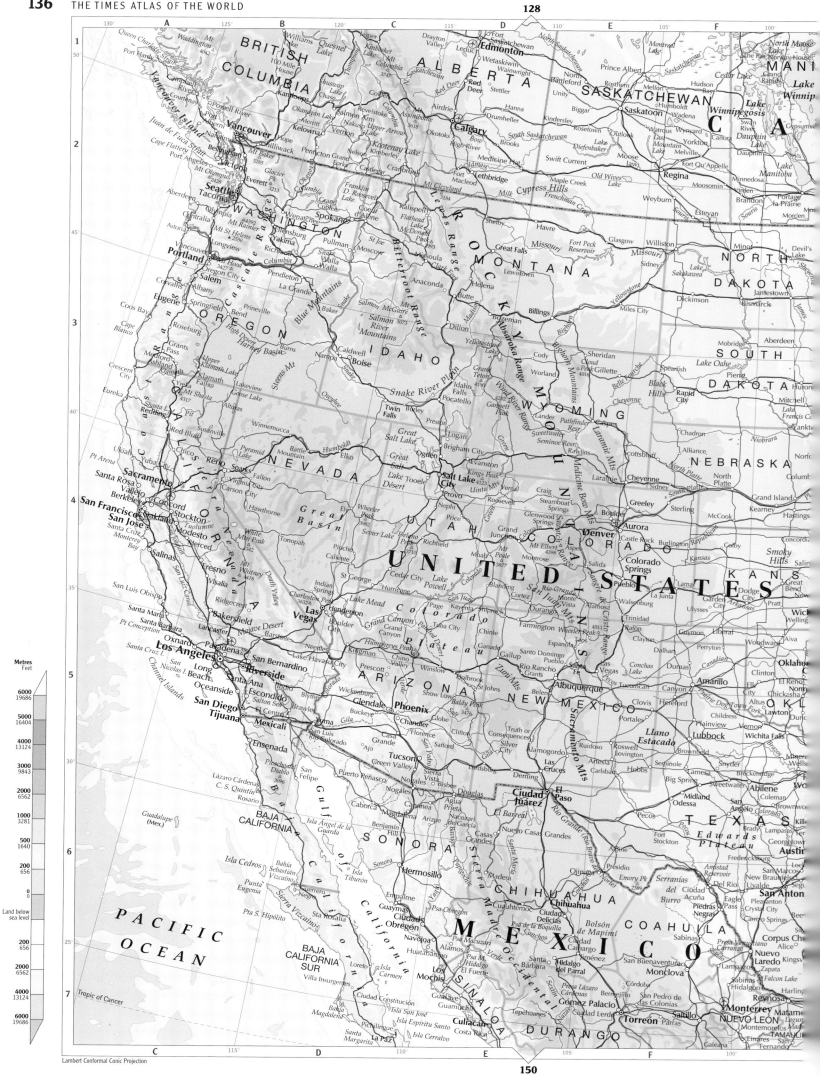

Lambert Conformal Conic Projection

1:12 000 000

© Collins Bartholomew Ltd

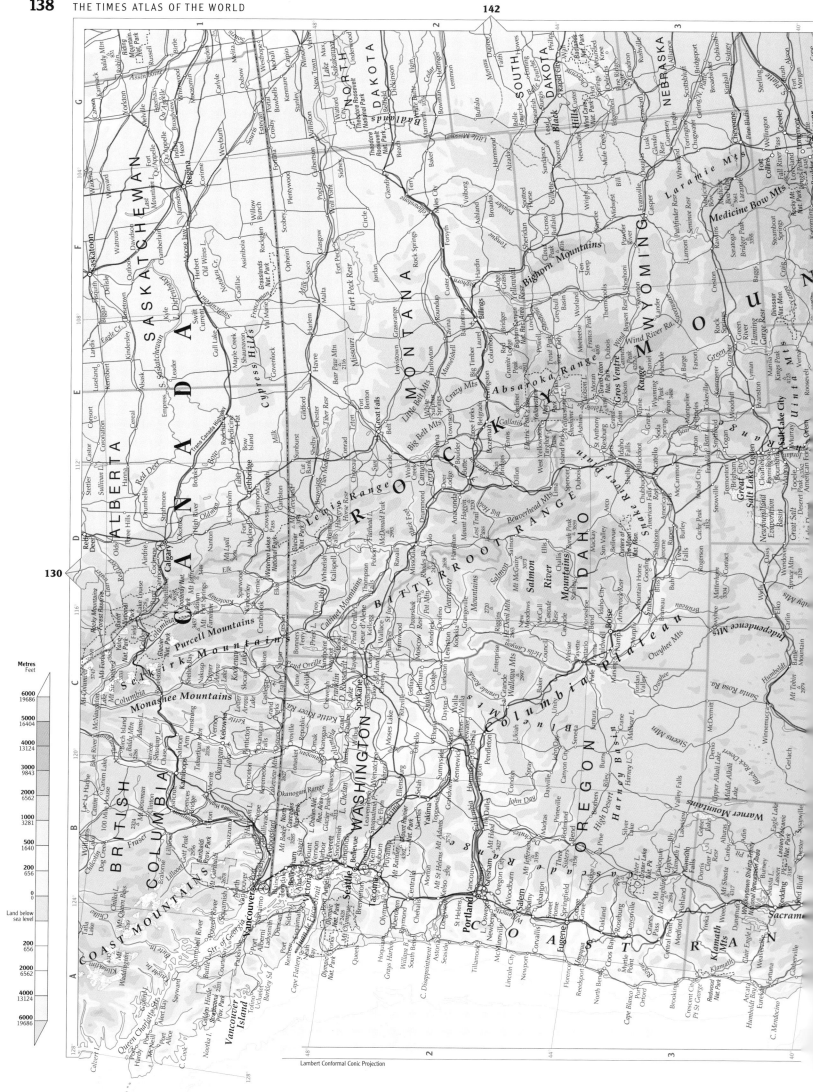

Metres
Feet

6000
19686

5000
16404

4000
13124

3000
9843

2000
6562

1000
3281

500
1640

200
656

0
0

Land below
sea level

200
656

2000
6562

4000
13124

6000
19686

Lambert Conformal Conic Projection

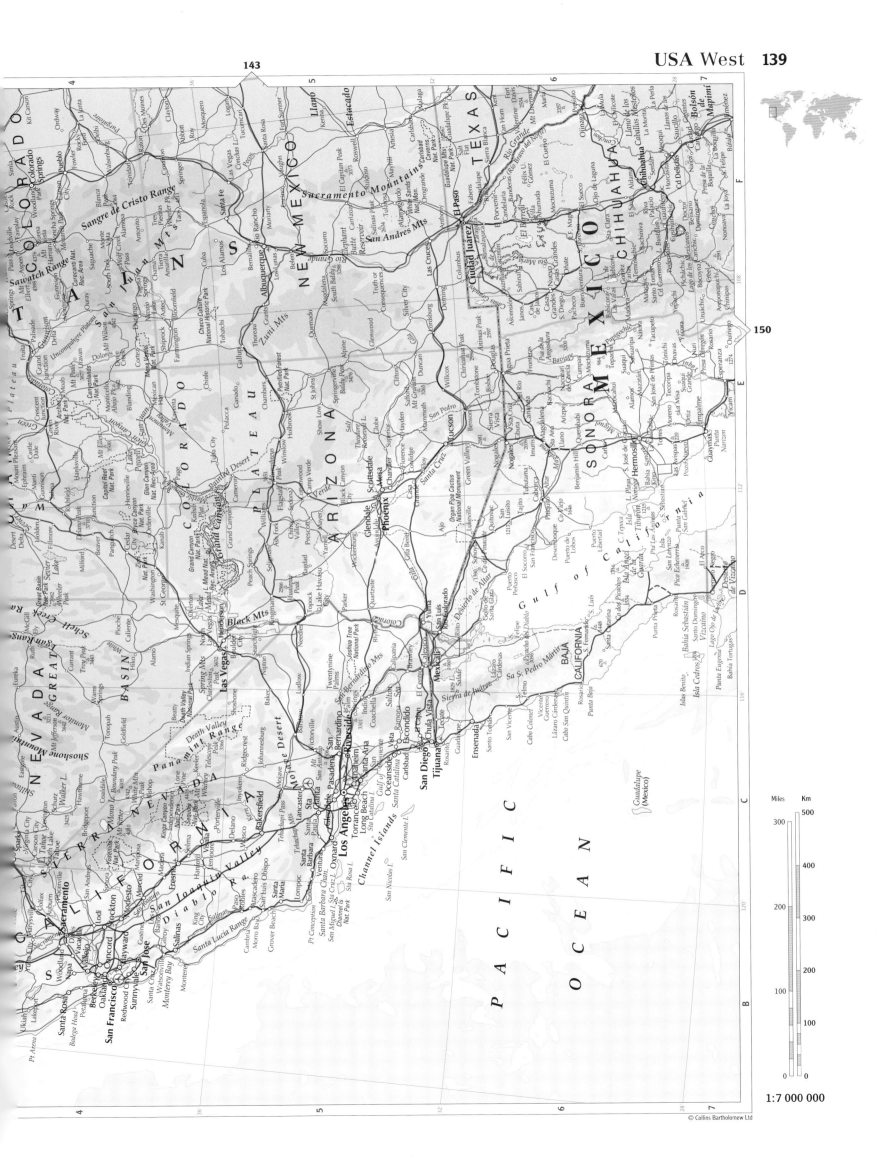

143

150

P A C I F I C

O C E A N

Gulf of California

BAJA CALIFORNIA

SONORA

CHIHUAHUA

M E X I C O

TEXAS

NEW MEXICO

COLORADO

ARIZONA

NEVADA

CALIFORNIA

GREAT BASIN

COLORADO PLATEAU

1:7 000 000

© Collins Bartholomew Ltd

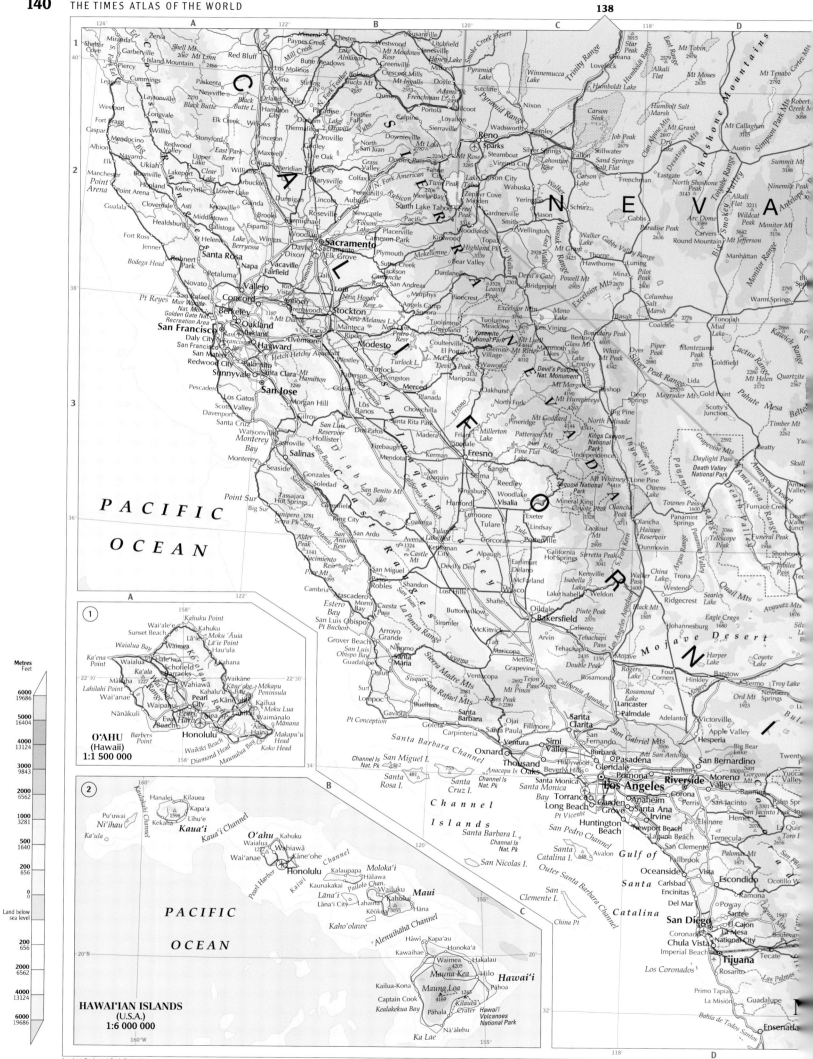

Lambert Conformal Conic Projection

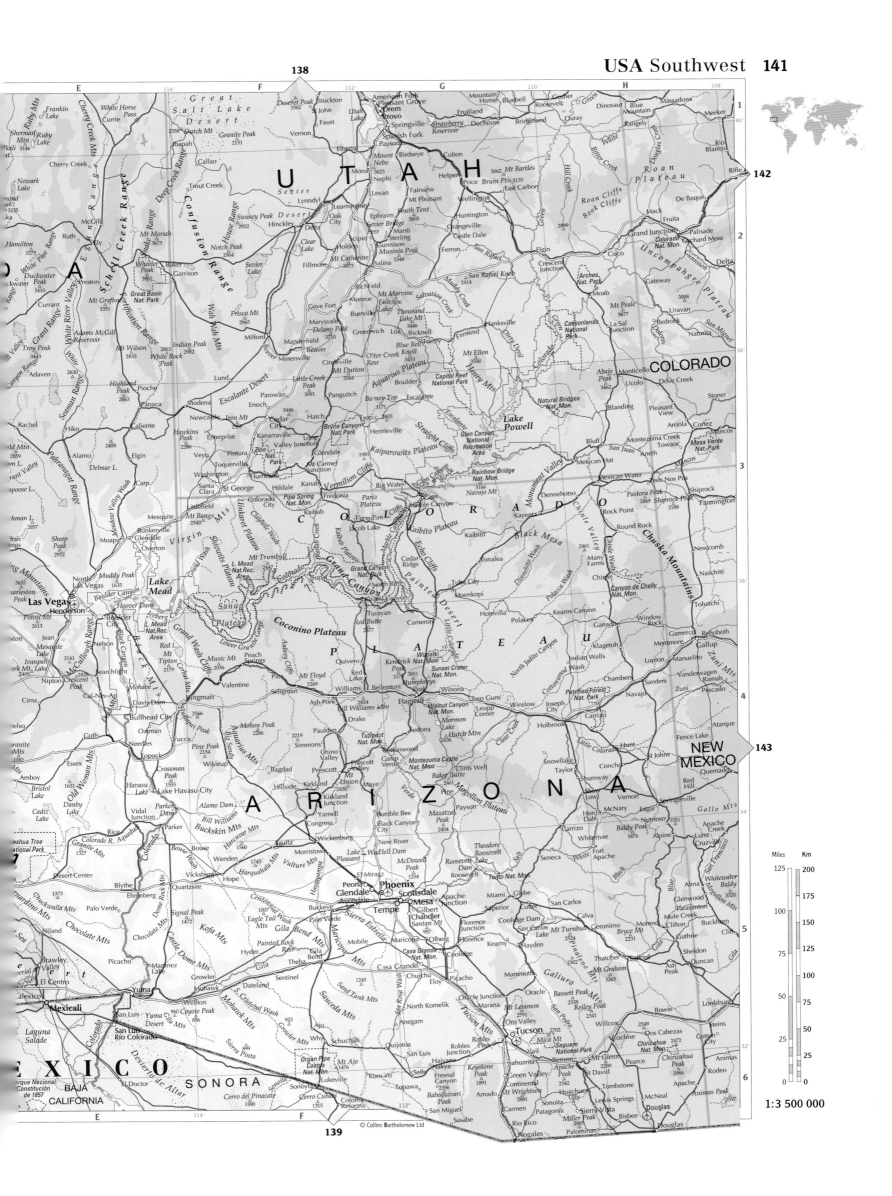

142

143

139

© Collins Bartholomew Ltd

Miles   Km

125 — 200

100 — 175

— 150

75 — 125

— 100

50 — 75

— 50

25 — 25

0 — 0

1:3 500 000

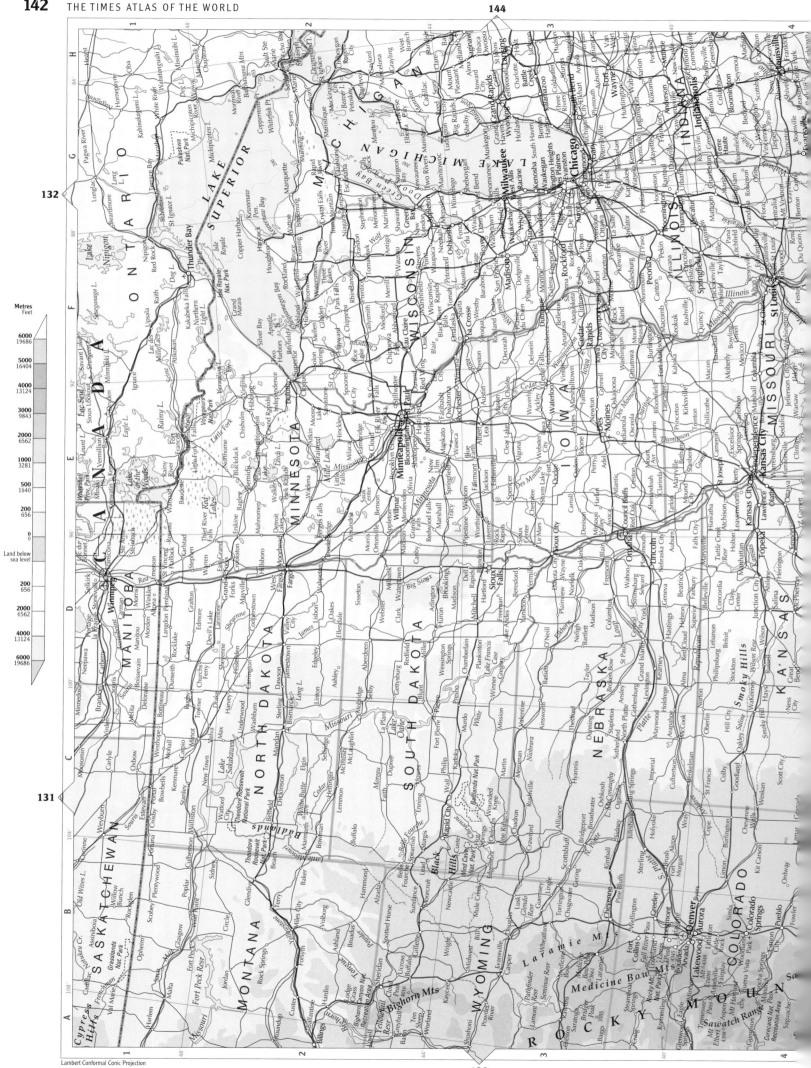

Metres
Feet

6000
19686

5000
16404

4000
13124

3000
9843

2000
6562

1000
3281

500
1640

200
656

0

Land below
sea level

200
656

2000
6562

4000
13124

6000
19686

Lambert Conformal Conic Projection

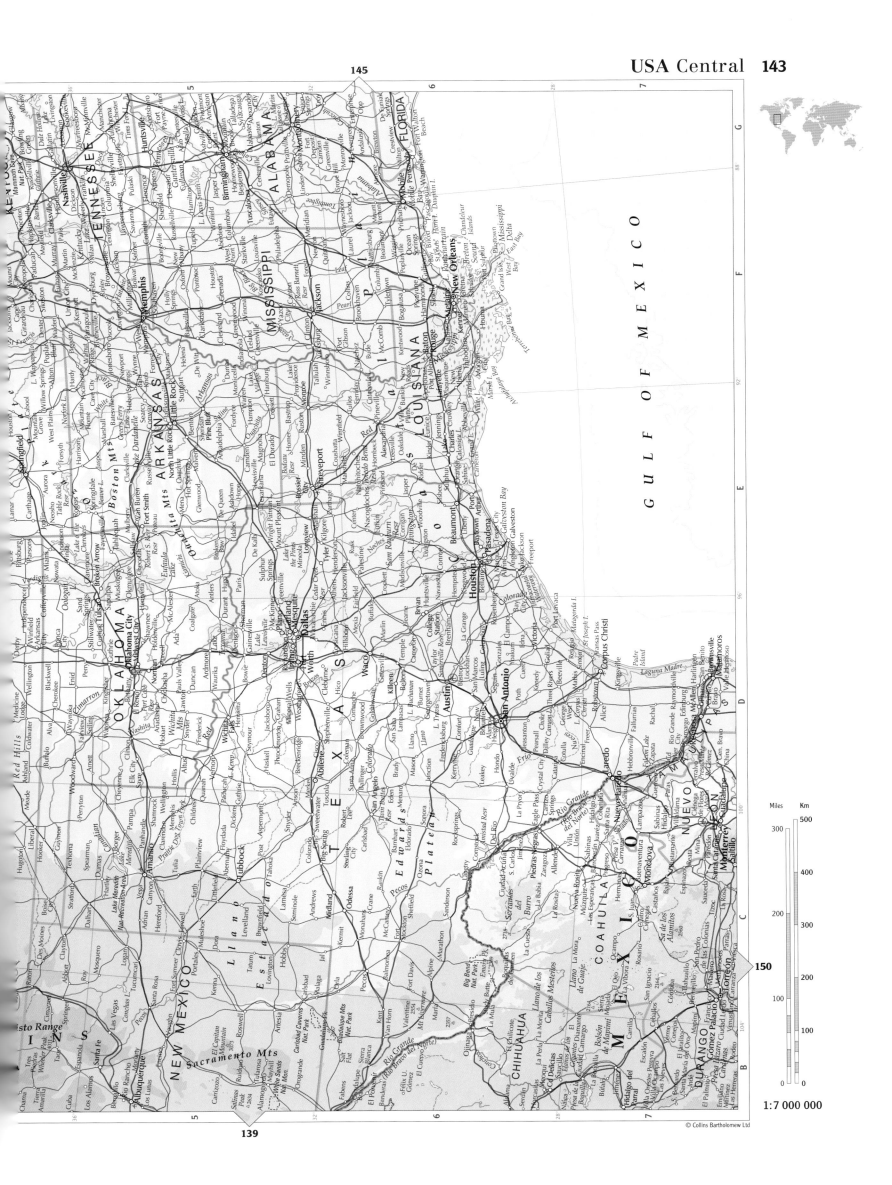

1:7 000 000

© Collins Bartholomew Ltd

Metres
Feet

6000
19686

5000
16404

4000
13124

3000
9843

2000
6562

1000
3281

500
1640

200
656

0

Land below
sea level

200
656

2000
6562

4000
13124

6000
19686

Lambert Conformal Conic Projection

1:7 000 000

© Collins Bartholomew Ltd

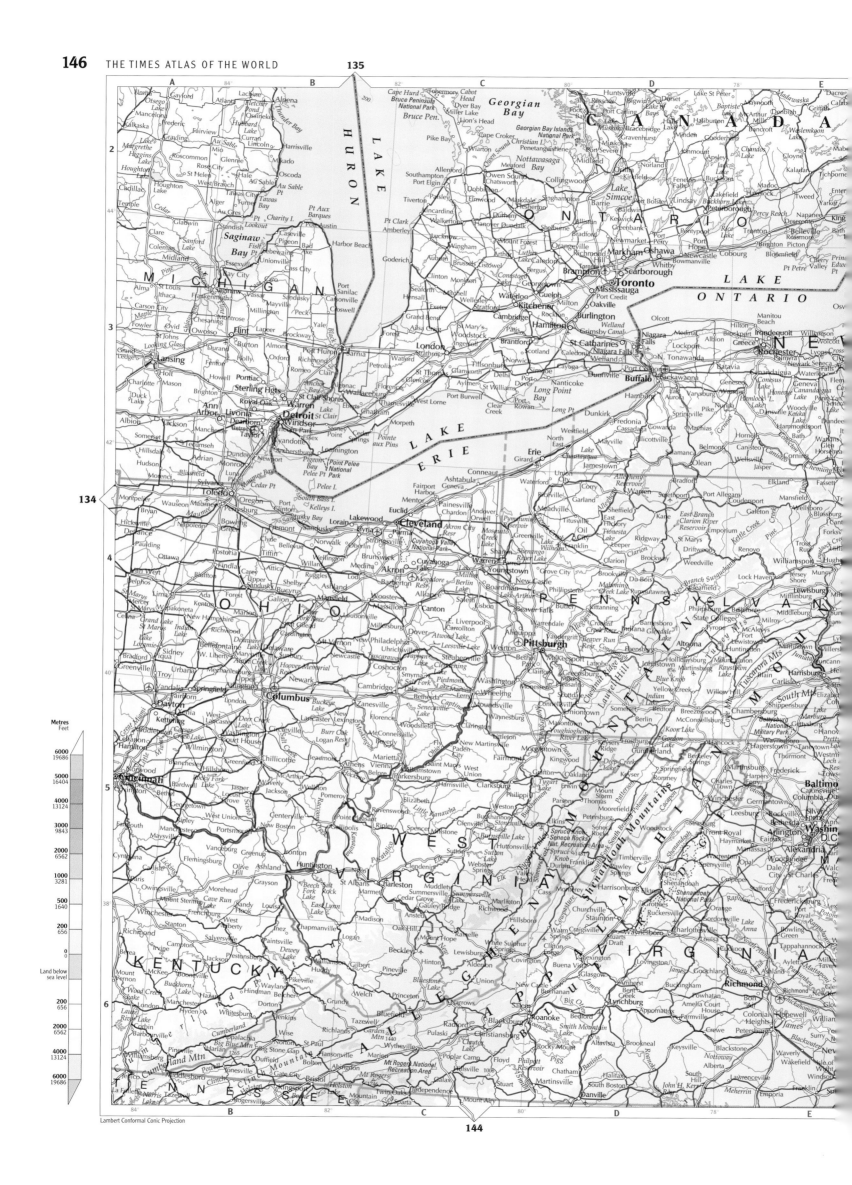

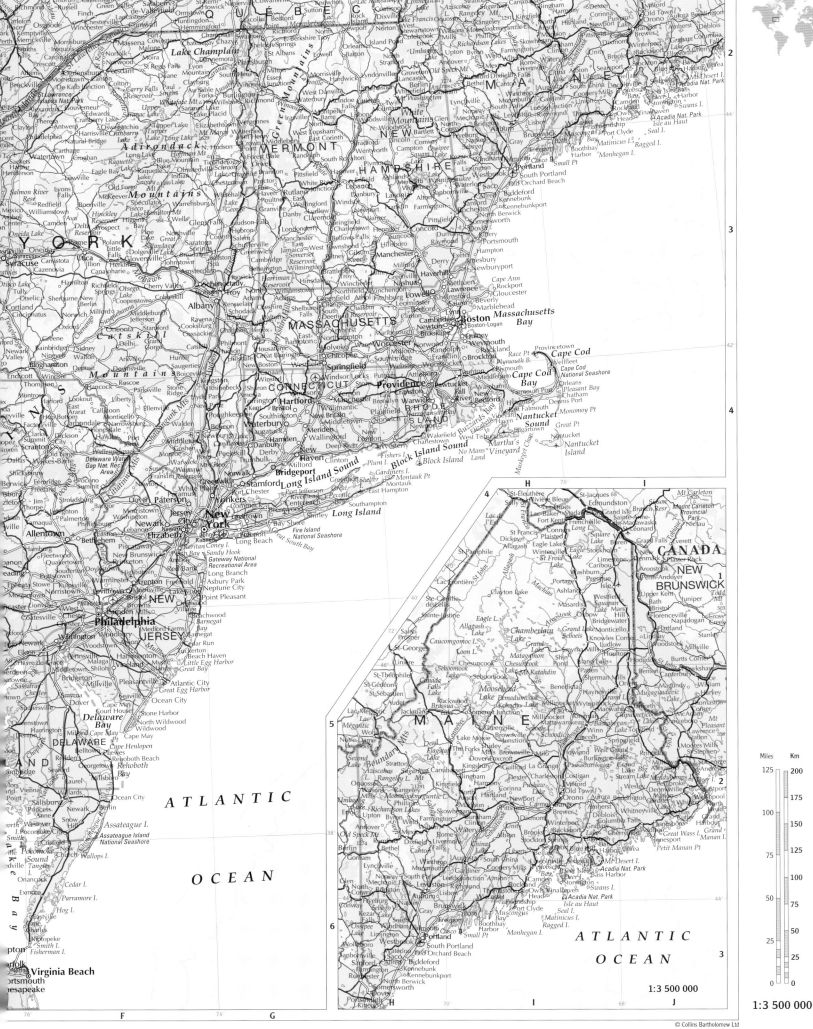

1:3 500 000

1:3 500 000

Miles   Km
125   200
  175
100   150
  125
75   100
50   75
  50
25   25
0   0

Metres
Feet

6000
19686

5000
16404

4000
13124

3000
9843

2000
6562

1000
3281

500
1640

200
656

0

Land below
sea level

200
656

2000
6562

4000
13124

6000
19686

Lambert Azimuthal Equal Area Projection

ATLANTIC

OCEAN

Bermuda
(U.K.) Hamilton

THE BAHAMAS

Havana
(La Habana)

CUBA

GREATER

Cayman Islands
(U.K.)
George Town
Grand Cayman

JAMAICA
Kingston

Turks and Caicos Islands
(U.K.)
Grand Turk
(Cockburn Town)
Turks Is

HISPANIOLA

HAITI
Port-au-Prince
DOMINICAN
REPUBLIC
Santo
Domingo

Puerto
Rico
(U.S.A.)

San
Juan

Virgin Is
(U.S.A.) Virgin Is
(U.K.)

LEEWARD ISLANDS

ANGUILLA

St-Martin (Fr.)
St Maarten (Neth.)
St-Barthélemy (Fr.)

ANTIGUA
AND
BARBUDA

ST KITTS AND NEVIS
Montserrat
(U.K.)
Basse-Terre

Guadeloupe
(Fr.)
Marie-
Galante
Roseau

DOMINICA

Martinique
(Fr.)
Fort-de-
France

ST LUCIA
Castries

ST VINCENT &
THE GRENADINES

Kingstown
Bridgetown
BARBADOS

GRENADA
St George's

TRINIDAD
AND
TOBAGO
Scarborough
Port of
Spain

WINDWARD ISLANDS

Lesser Antilles

CARIBBEAN SEA

LESSER ANTILLES

Netherlands
Antilles

Aruba
(Neth.)
Oranjestad
Curaçao
Willemstad
Bonaire

I. Orchila
(Ven.)

I. La Tortuga

I. de Margarita
(Ven.)
Porlamar

Islas Los Roques
(Ven.)

NICARAGUA
COSTA RICA
San
José

PANAMA
Panama
City
David

Gulf of
Panama

COLOMBIA

Barranquilla
Cartagena

Santa Marta

Maracaibo

Caracas

VENEZUELA

Medellín

Bogotá

Cali

BRAZIL

Miles Km
500   800

400   600

200   400

200

0   0

1:14 000 000

© Collins Bartholomew Ltd

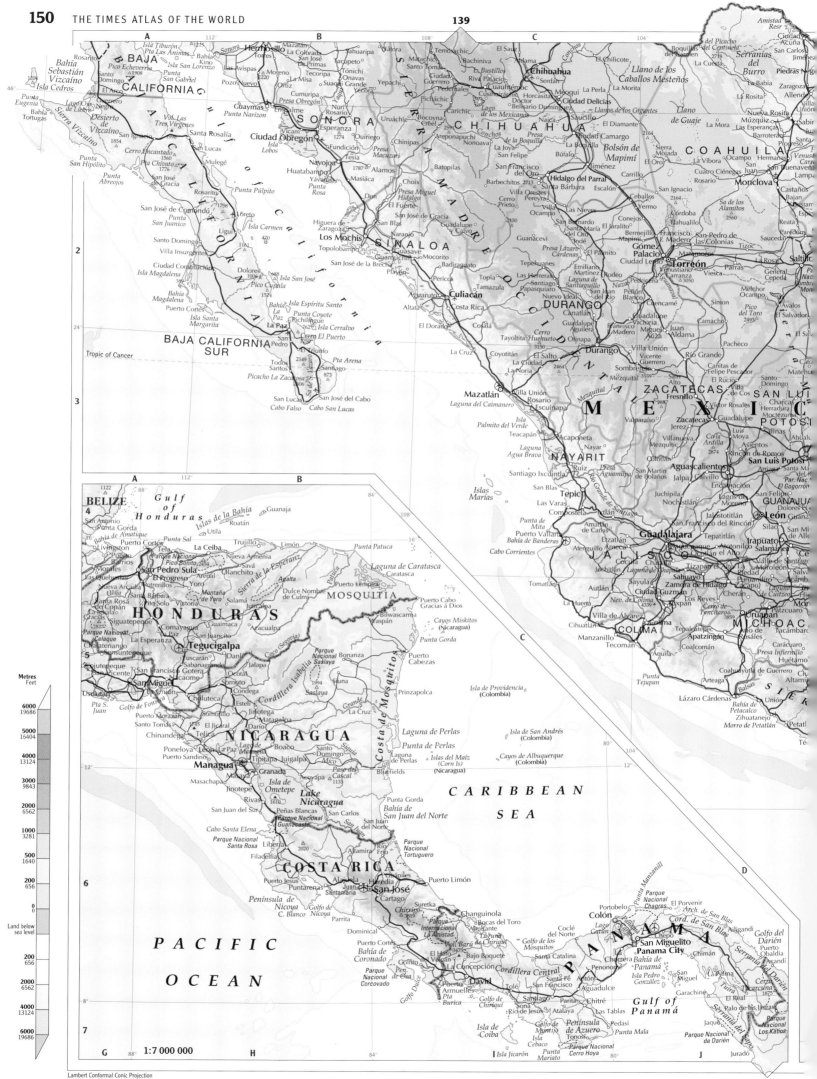

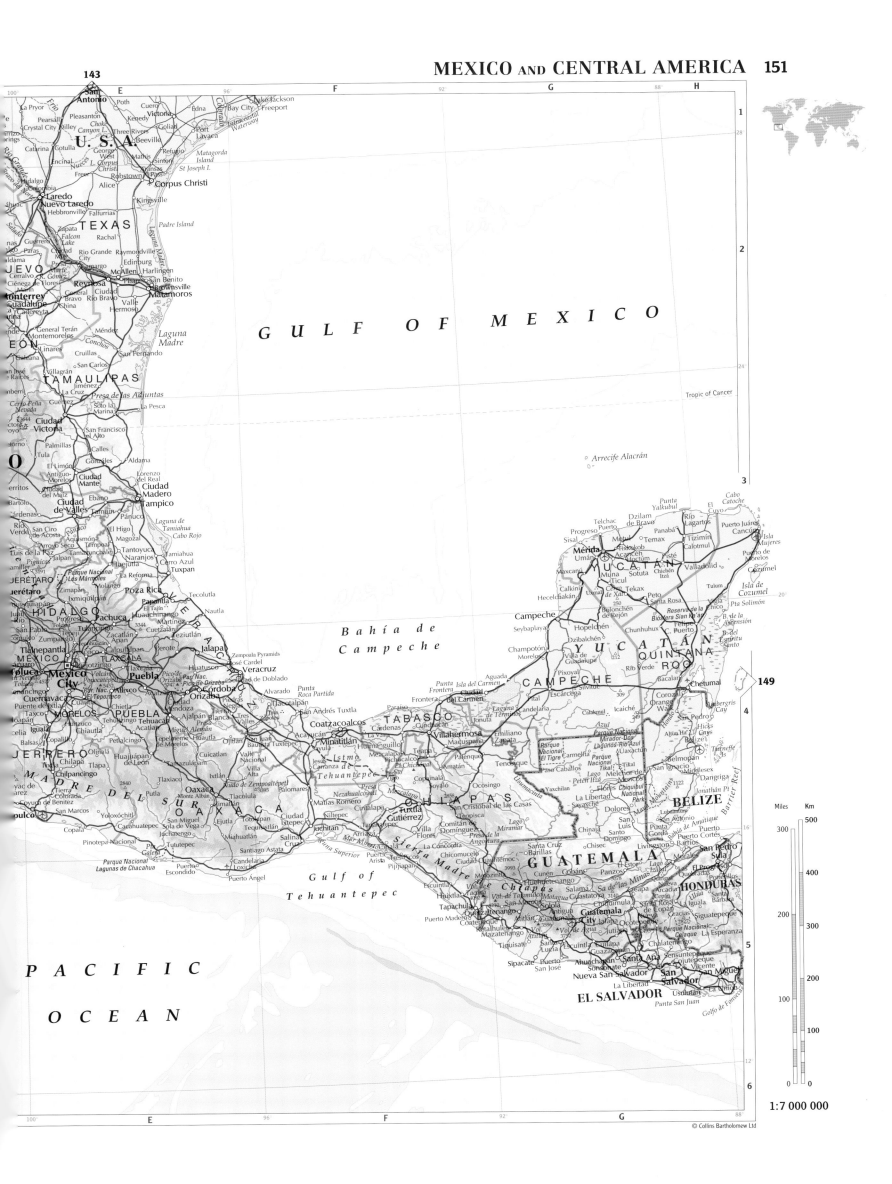

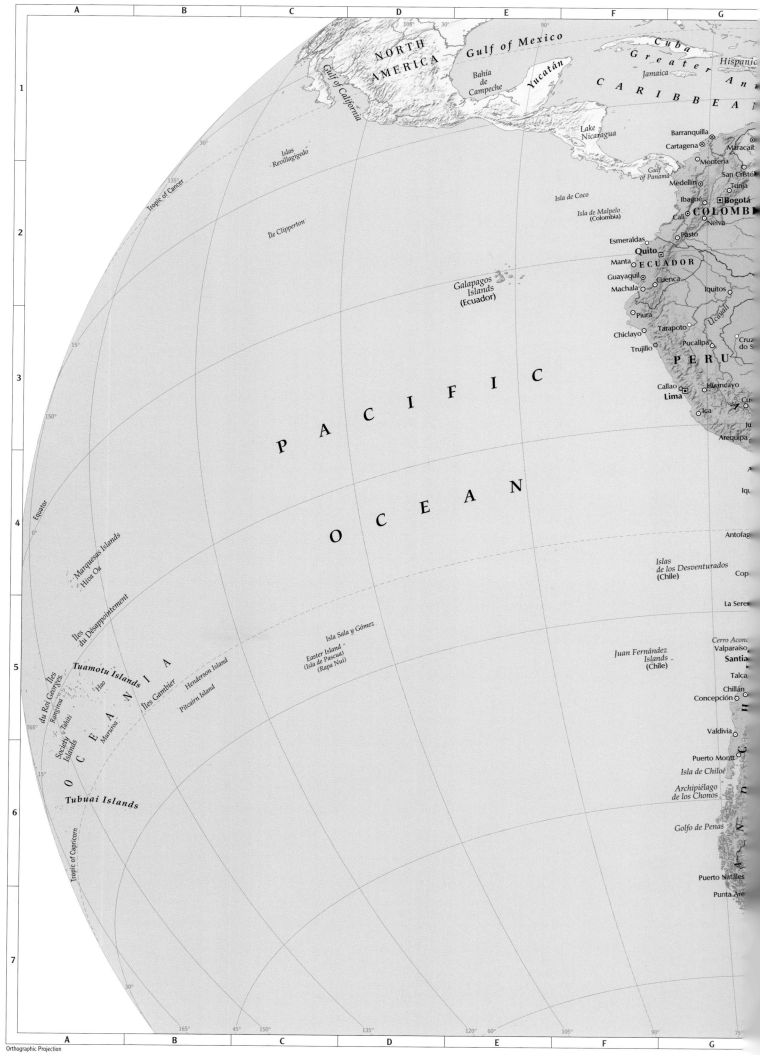

Puerto Rico
Anguilla
Antigua
Guadeloupe
Dominica
Martinique
St Lucia
Barbados
St Vincent
and the Grenadines
Grenada
Tobago
Trinidad

les
S E A
Lesser Antilles
ruba
laracay **Caracas**
Valencia
Cumaná

Madeira
Canary
Islands
Gran
Canaria

Ciudad Bolívar
V E N E Z U E L A
Orinoco
Puerto Ayacucho
Georgetown
Paramaribo
Cayenne
G U Y A N A
S U R I N A M E
French
Guiana
Boa Vista

Santo Antão
Cape Verde
Boa Vista
São Tiago

Tropic of Cancer

Senegal

Negro
Japurá
Tonantins
Macapá
Manaus
Amazon
Santarém
Belém
São Luís
Parnaíba
Carauari
L V A S
Madeira
Tapajós
Marabá
Araguaína
Teresina
Fortaleza

Niger

o Branco
Porto
Velho
B R A Z I L
Xingu
Palmas
Teófilo
Natal
João Pessoa
Floresta
Juàzeiro
Recife
Maceió
Aracaju

Fernando
de Noronha
(Brazil)

A
F
R
I
C
A

Gulf
of
Guinea

Puerto Maldonado
Trinidad
Lake
Titicaca
Mamoré
La Paz
B O L I V I A
Cochabamba
Santa Cruz
Potosí
Sucre
Tarija
P A R A G U A Y
Cuiabá
Brasília
Goiânia
Barragem
de Sobradinho
São Francisco
Araguaia
Paraná
Campo
Grande
Uberaba
Patos
de Minas
Teófilo
Otóni
Salvador
Ilhéus

Ascension

Equator

San Salvador
de Jujuy
Pedro Juan
Caballero
Araçatuba
Ribeirão
Preto
Belo
Horizonte
Vitória

Ilha da Trindade
(Brazil)
Ilhas
Martin Vaz
(Brazil)

A
T
L
A
N
T
I
C

San Miguel
de Tucumán
Nevado
Ojos del Salado
Asunción
Coronel
Oviedo
Formosa
Resistencia
Maringá
Paraná
Campinas
São Paulo
Santos
Rio
de Janeiro

amarca
Corrientes
Encarnación
Posadas
Curitiba

La Rioja
Santa Maria
Florianópolis

St Helena

Córdoba
Santa Fé
Concordia
Paraná
Porto Alegre
Lagoa
dos Patos

O
C
E
A
N

Mendoza
Rosario
U R U G U A Y
Santa María
Rio Grande

San Luis
Buenos
Aires
Rio de la Plata
Montevideo

San Rafael
R G E N T I N A
La
Plata

Santa Rosa

Tropic of Capricorn

uquén
Bahía Blanca
Mar del Plata

Viedma
Golfo San Matías

Trelew

Comodoro Rivadavia
Golfo de San Jorge

Tristan
da Cunha

hía
ande
Gallegos

Falkland
Islands
(U.K.)
Stanley

a Grande
Tierra del Fuego
shuaia
Isla de los Estados
ape Horn
ake Passage

Shag
Rocks

South Georgia

Cape of Good Hope

Orange

South Shetland
Islands

South Orkney
Islands

South Georgia
and
South Sandwich
Islands
(U.K.)

Traversay Islands
Candlemas Island
Saunders Island
Montagu Island
Bristol Island

South
Sandwich
Islands

Southern Thule
Island

ntarctic Peninsula

Miles	Km
1200	2000
	1600
800	1200
	800
400	400
0	0

1:32 000 000

© Collins Bartholomew Ltd

CARIBBEAN
SEA

PACIFIC OCEAN

VENEZUELA

COLOMBIA

PANAMA

COSTA RICA

NICARAGUA

ECUADOR

PERU

BOLIVIA

ARGENTINA

Metres
Feet

6000
19686

5000
16404

4000
13124

3000
9843

2000
6562

1000
3281

500
1640

200
656

0
0

Land below
sea level

200
656

2000
6562

4000
13124

6000
19686

GALAPAGOS IS
(Ecuador)

I. Culpepper
I. Wenman

I. Pinta
I. Marchena
Pta Albemarle
Vol. Wolf
I. Fernandina
I. San Salvador
Isla Isabela
I. Santa Cruz
Cabo Rosa
Puerto
Baquerizo
Moreno
I. San Cristóbal
I. Santa María
I. Española

Equator

Tropic of Capricorn

1:15 000 000

Lambert Azimuthal Equal Area Projection

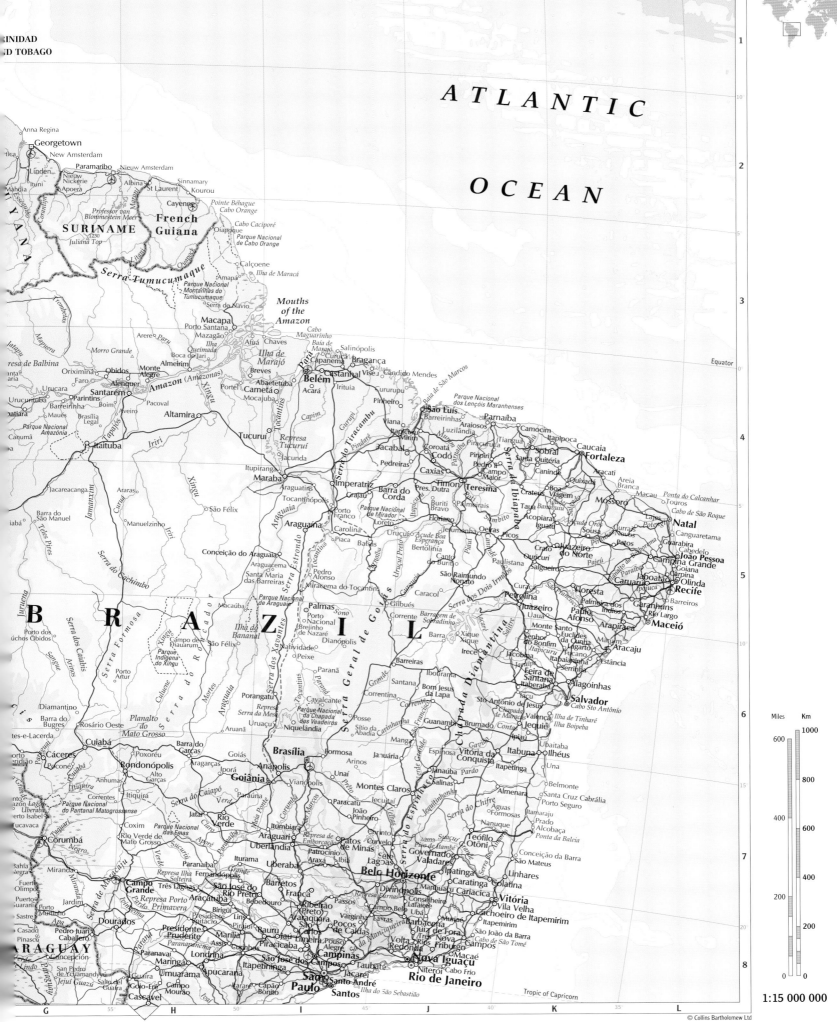

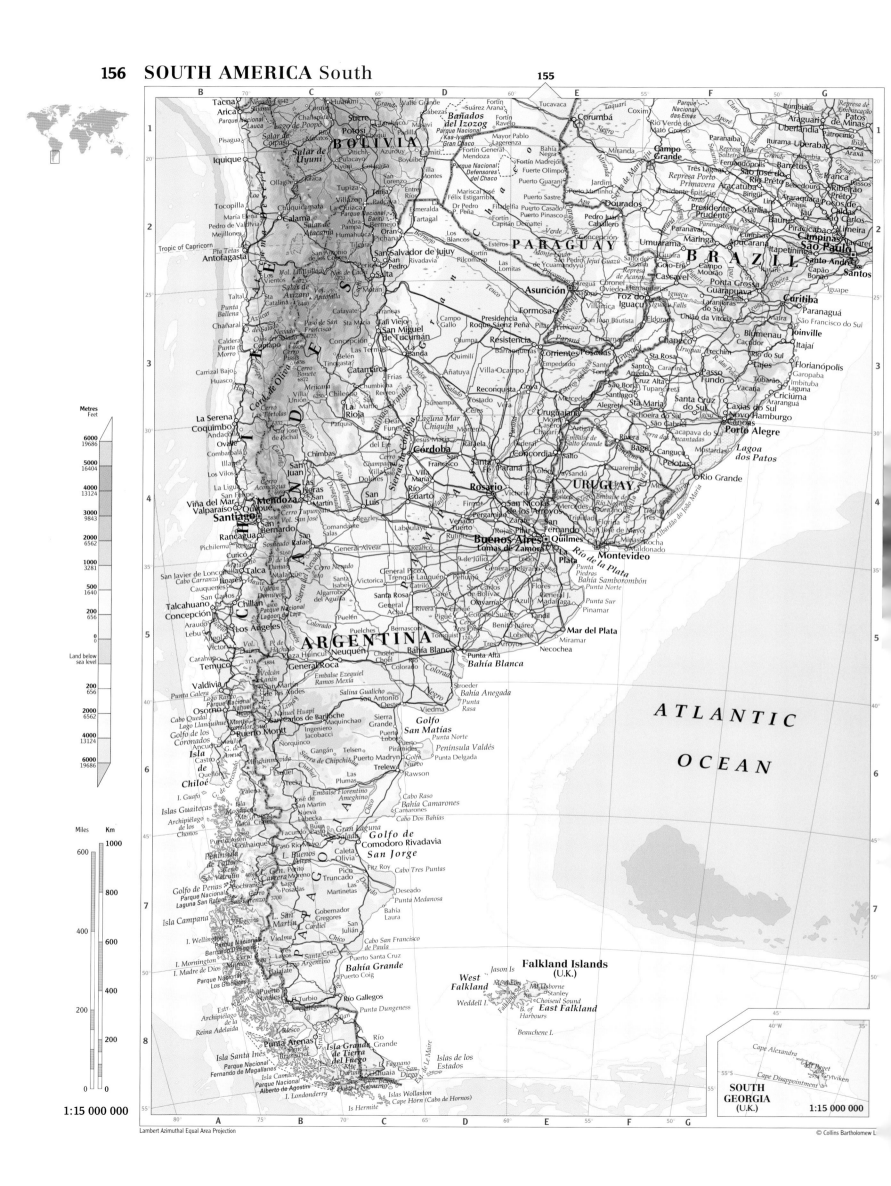

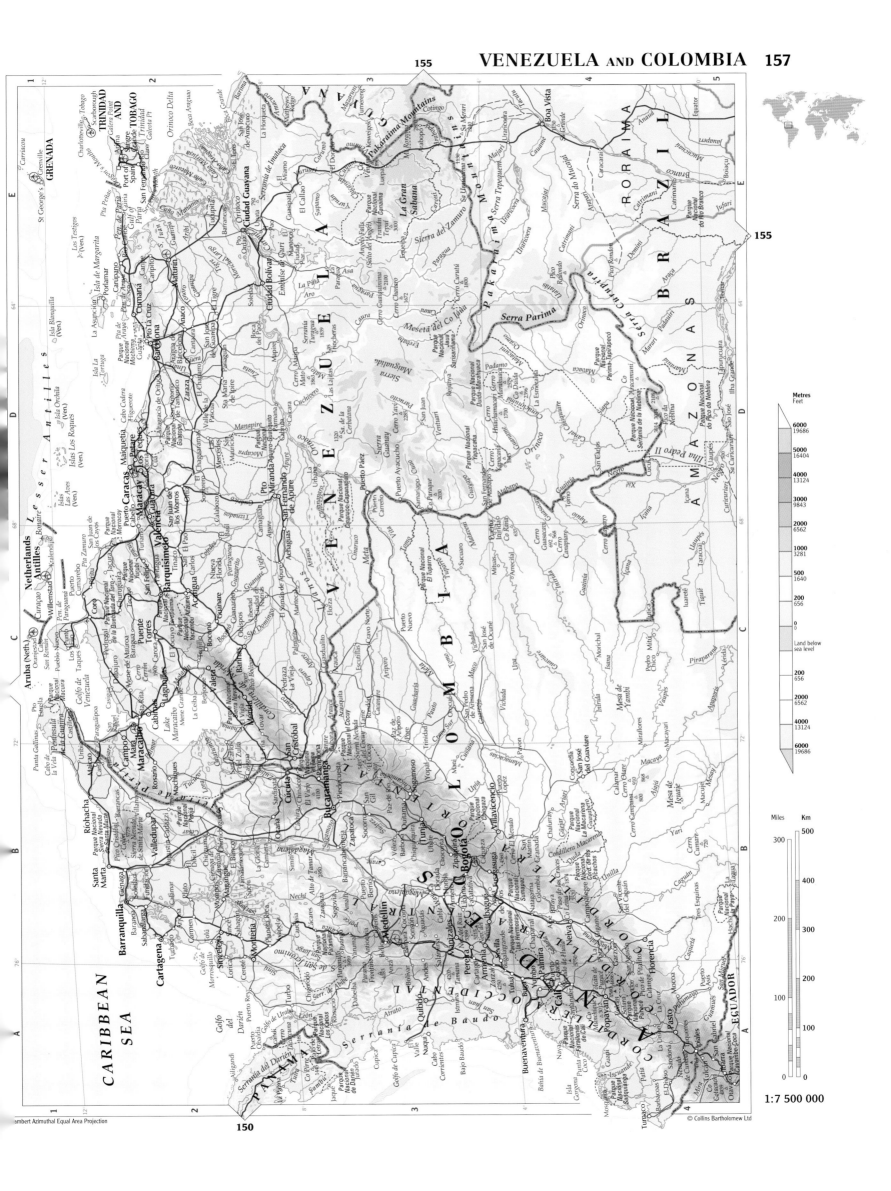

155

155

150

1:7 500 000

© Collins Bartholomew Ltd

Lambert Azimuthal Equal Area Projection

Metres
Feet

6000	19686
5000	16404
4000	13124
3000	9843
2000	6562
1000	3281
500	1640
200	656
0	

Land below
sea level

200	656
2000	6562
4000	13124
6000	19686

Miles   Km

300   500

400

200   300

200

100

100

0   0

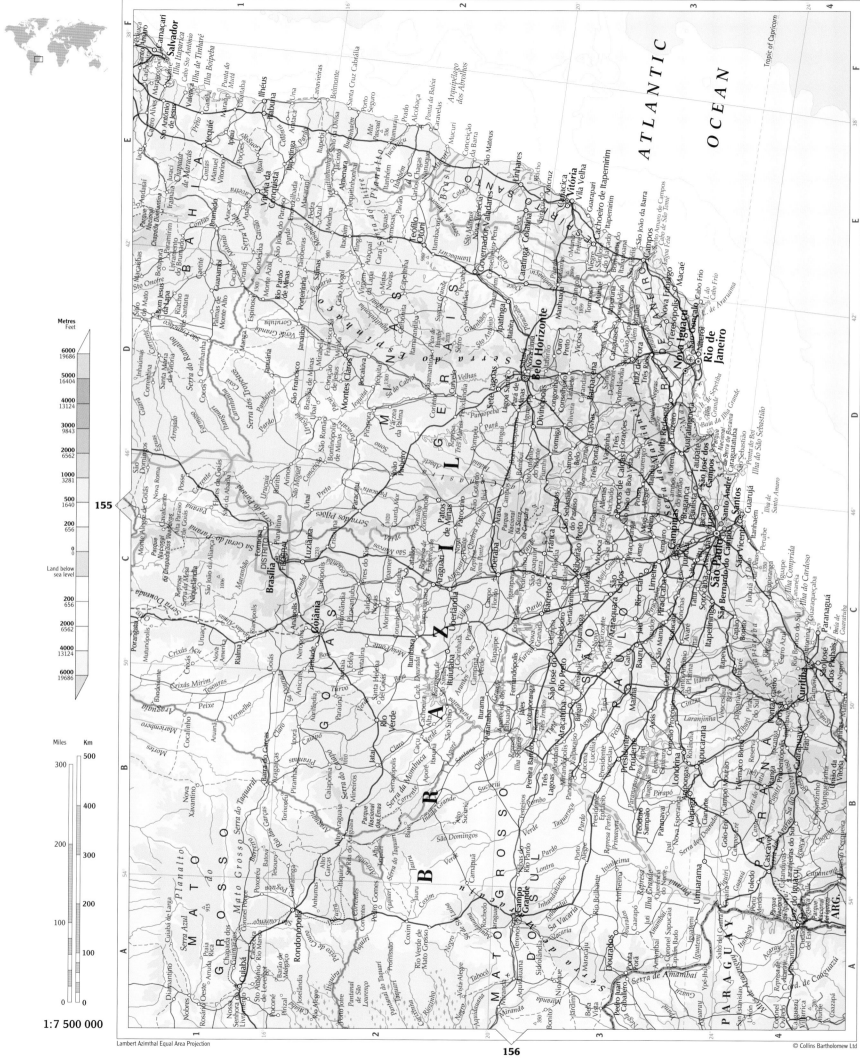

Metres
Feet

6000
19686

5000
16404

4000
13124

3000
9843

2000
6562

1000
3281

500
1640

200
656

0

Land below
sea level

200
656

2000
6562

4000
13124

6000
19686

Miles   Km

300   500

400

200   300

200

100

100

0   0

1:7 500 000

Lambert Azimuthal Equal Area Projection

ATLANTIC   OCEAN

Tropic of Capricorn

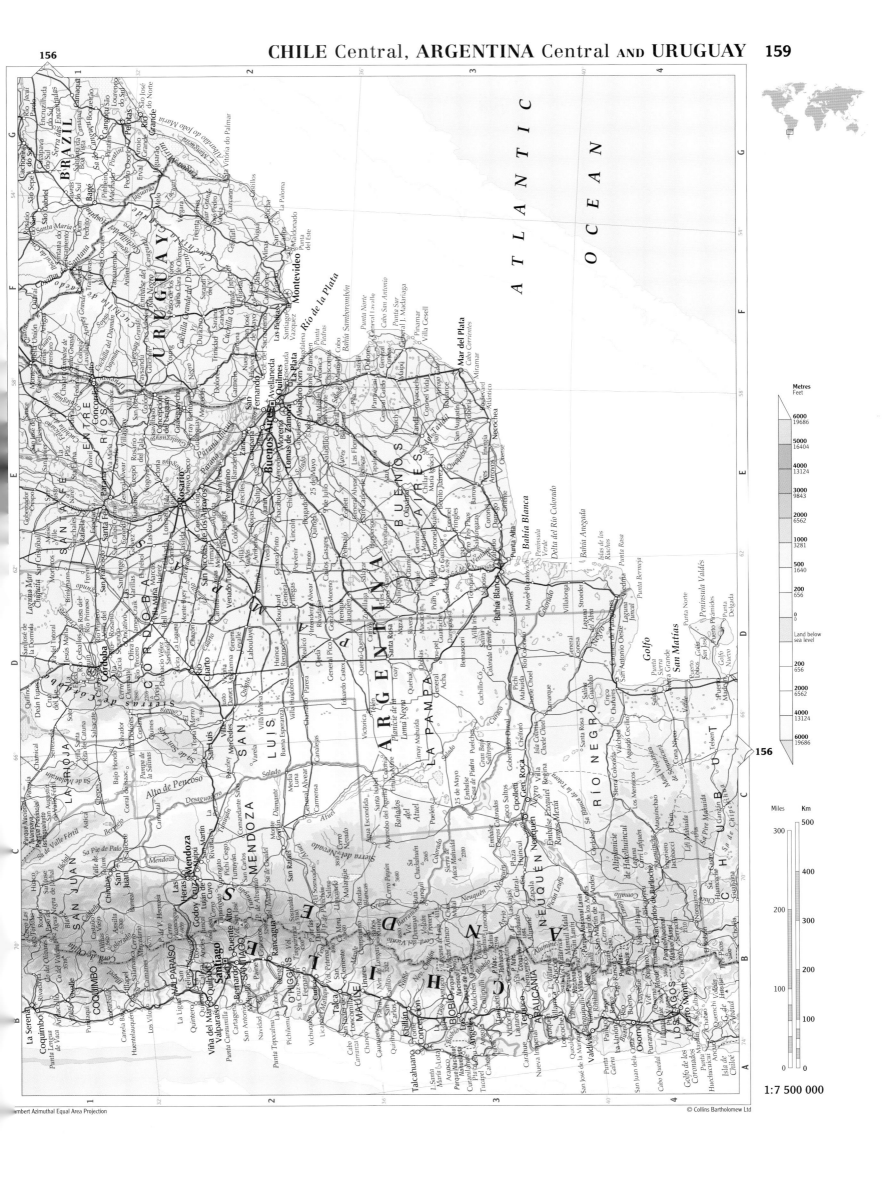

1:7 500 000

© Collins Bartholomew Ltd

Lambert Azimuthal Equal Area Projection

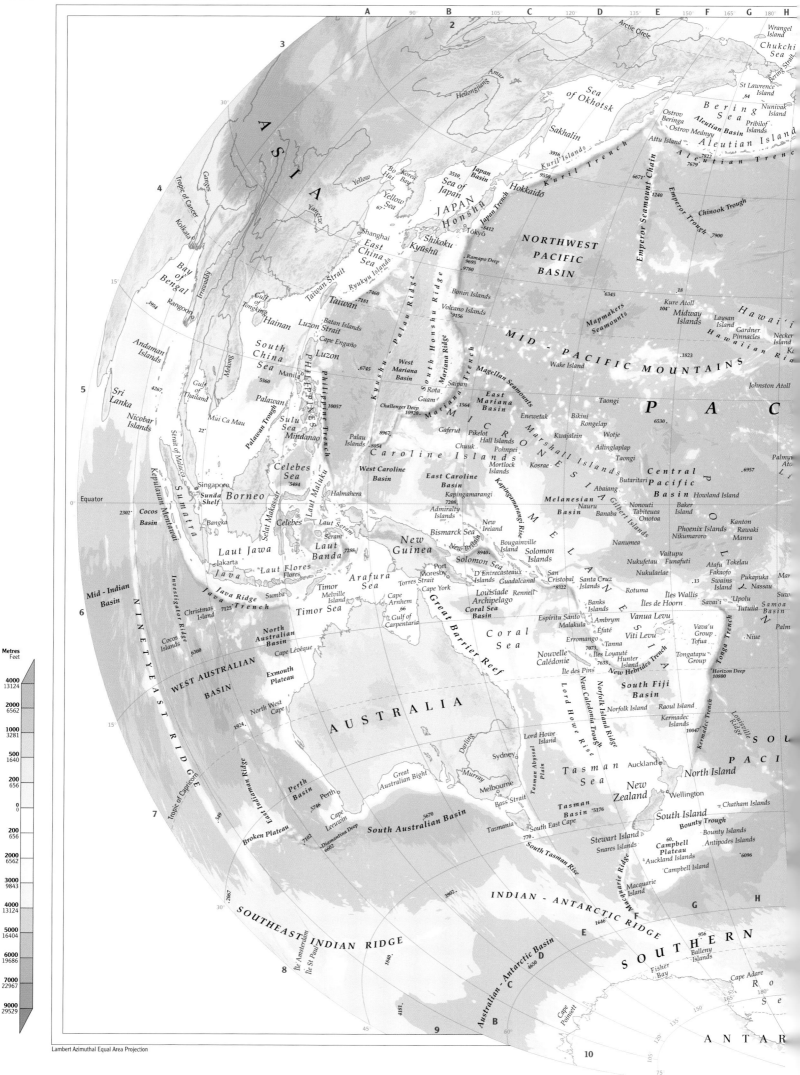

Metres
Feet

4000
13124

2000
6562

1000
3281

500
1640

200
656

0
0

200
656

2000
6562

3000
9843

4000
13124

5000
16404

6000
19686

7000
22967

9000
29529

Lambert Azimuthal Equal Area Projection

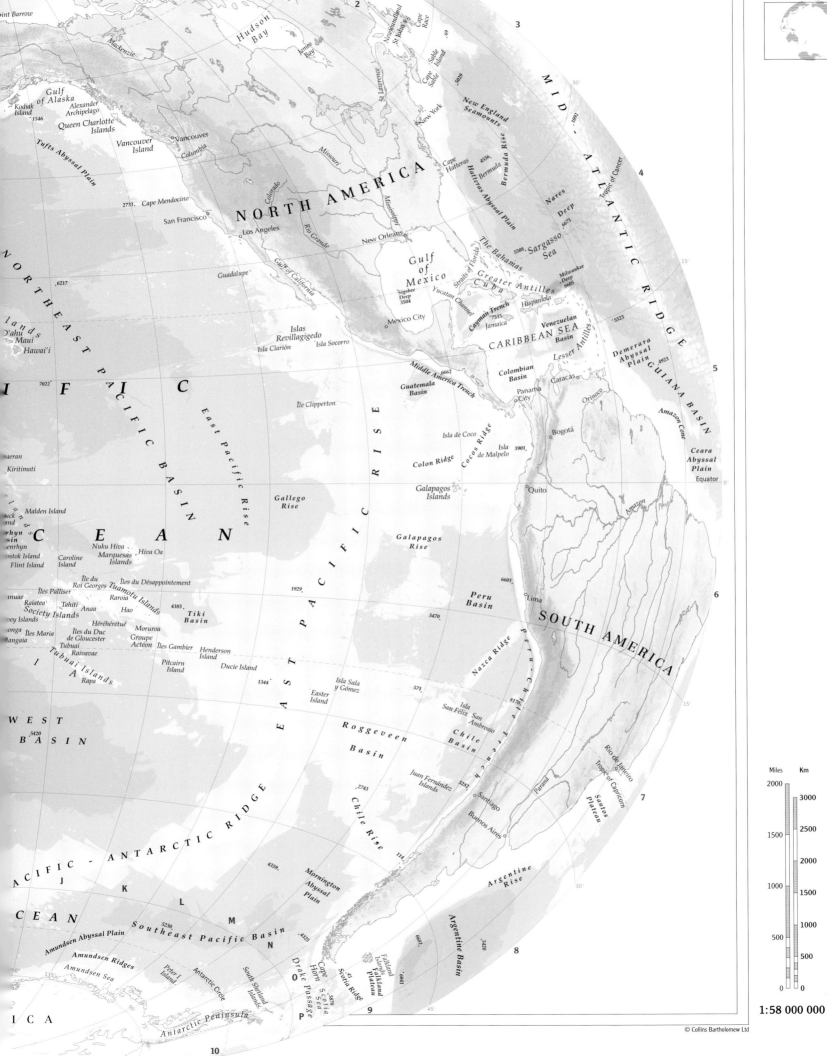

1:58 000 000

© Collins Bartholomew Ltd

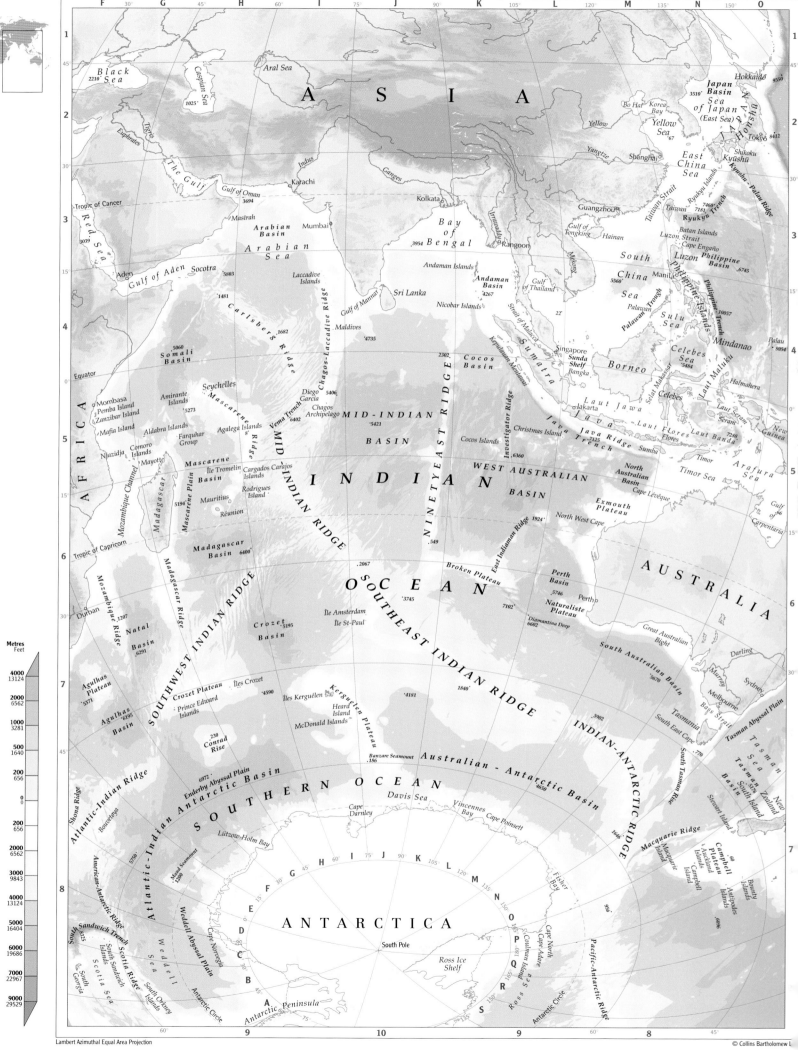

Metres
Feet

4000
13124

2000
6562

1000
3281

500
1640

200
656

0
0

200
656

2000
6562

3000
9843

4000
13124

5000
16404

6000
19686

7000
22967

9000
29529

Lambert Azimuthal Equal Area Projection

© Collins Bartholomew L

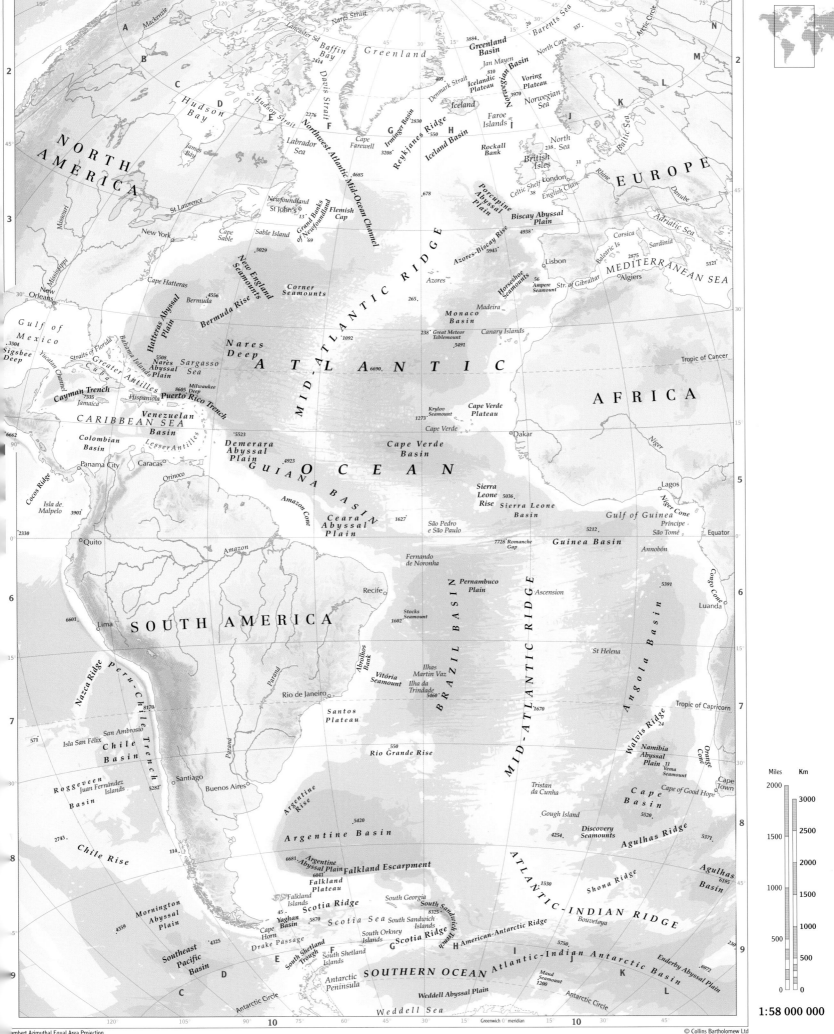

1:58 000 000

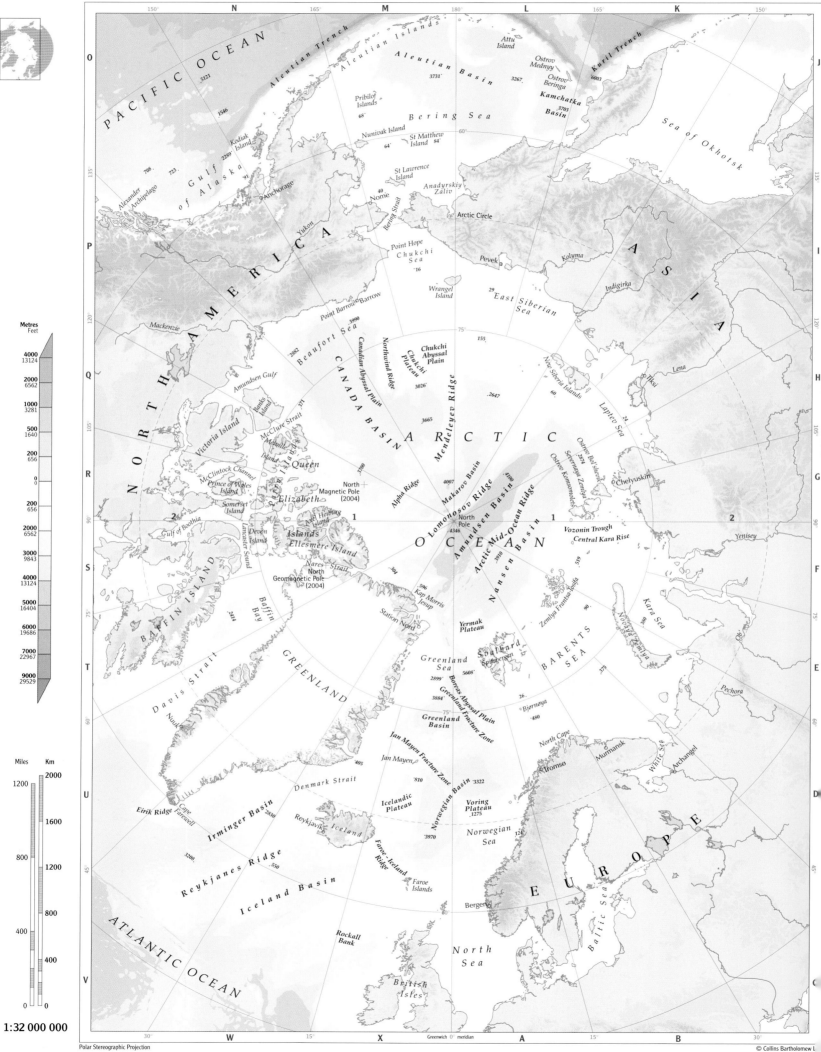

Metres
Feet

4000	13124
2000	6562
1000	3281
500	1640
200	656
0	0
200	656
2000	6562
3000	9843
4000	13124
5000	16404
6000	19686
7000	22967
9000	29529

Miles   Km

1200   2000

          1600

800   1200

          800

400

          400

0   0

1:32 000 000

Polar Stereographic Projection

© Collins Bartholomew L

INTRODUCTION TO THE INDEX

The index includes all names shown on the reference maps in the atlas. Each entry includes the country or geographical area in which the feature is located, a page number and an alphanumeric reference. Additional entry details and aspects of the index are explained below.

REFERENCING

Names are referenced by page number and by grid reference. The grid reference relates to the alphanumeric values which appear in the margin of each map. These reflect the graticule on the map – the letter relates to longitude divisions, the number to latitude divisions.

Names are generally referenced to the largest scale map page on which they appear. For large geographical features, including countries, the reference is to the largest scale map on which the feature appears in its entirety, or on which the majority of it appears.

Rivers are referenced to their lowest downstream point – either their mouth or their confluence with another river. The river name will generally be positioned as close to this point as possible.

Entries relating to names appearing on insets are indicated by a small box symbol: □ followed by a grid reference if the inset has its own alphanumeric values.

ALTERNATIVE NAMES

Alternative names appear as cross-references and refer the user to the index entry for the form of the name used on the map.

For rivers with multiple names – for example those which flow through several countries – all alternative name forms are included within the main index entries, with details of the countries in which each form applies.

ADMINISTRATIVE QUALIFIERS

Administrative divisions are included in an entry to differentiate duplicate names – entries of exactly the same name and feature type within the one country – where these division names are shown on the maps. In such cases, duplicate names are alphabetized in the order of the administrative division names. Additional qualifiers are included for names within selected geographical areas, to indicate more clearly their location.

DESCRIPTORS

Entries, other than those for towns and cities, include a descriptor indicating the type of geographical feature. Descriptors are not included where the type of feature is implicit in the name itself, unless there is a town or city of exactly the same name.

NAME FORMS AND ALPHABETICAL ORDER

Name forms are as they appear on the maps, with additional alternative forms included as cross-references. Names appear in full in the index, although they may appear in abbreviated form on the maps.

The German character ß is alphabetized as 'ss'. Names beginning with Mac or Mc are alphabetized exactly as they appear. The terms Saint, Sainte, etc, are abbreviated to St, Ste, etc, but alphabetized as if in the full form.

NUMERICAL ENTRIES

Entries beginning with numerals appear at the beginning of the index, in numerical order. Elsewhere, numerals are alphabetized before 'a'.

PERMUTED TERMS

Names beginning with generic, geographical terms are permuted – the descriptive term is placed after, and the index alphabetized by, the main part of the name. For example, Lake Superior is indexed as Superior, Lake; Mount Everest as Everest, Mount. This policy is applied to all languages. Permuting has not been applied to names of towns, cities or administrative divisions beginning with such geographical terms. These remain in their full form, for example, Lake Isabella, USA.

INDEX ABBREVIATIONS

admin. dist.	administrative district	IN	Indiana	plat.	plateau
admin. div.	administrative division	Indon.	Indonesia	P.N.G.	Papua New Guinea
admin. reg.	administrative region	is	islands	Port.	Portugal
Afgh.	Afghanistan	Kazakh.	Kazakhstan	prov.	province
AK	Alaska	KS	Kansas	pt	point
AL	Alabama	KY	Kentucky	Qld	Queensland
Alg.	Algeria	Kyrg.	Kyrgyzstan	Que.	Québec
Alta	Alberta	l.	lake	r.	river
AR	Arkansas	LA	Louisiana	reg.	region
Arg.	Argentina	lag.	lagoon	Rep. of Ireland	Republic of Ireland
aut. comm.	autonomous community	Lith.	Lithuania	res.	reserve
aut. reg.	autonomous region	Lux.	Luxembourg	resr	reservoir
aut. rep.	autonomous republic	MA	Massachusetts	RI	Rhode Island
AZ	Arizona	Madag.	Madagascar	r. mouth	river mouth
Azer.	Azerbaijan	Man.	Manitoba	Rus. Fed.	Russian Federation
b.	bay	MD	Maryland	S.	South
Bangl.	Bangladesh	ME	Maine	S.A.	South Australia
B.C.	British Columbia	Mex.	Mexico	S. Africa	Republic of South Africa
Bol.	Bolivia	MI	Michigan	salt l.	salt lake
Bos.-Herz.	Bosnia-Herzegovina	MN	Minnesota	Sask.	Saskatchewan
Bulg.	Bulgaria	MO	Missouri	SC	South Carolina
c.	cape	Moz.	Mozambique	SD	South Dakota
CA	California	MS	Mississippi	sea chan.	sea channel
Cent. Afr. Rep.	Central African Republic	MT	Montana	Serb. and Mont.	Serbia and Montenegro
CO	Colorado	mt.	mountain	Sing.	Singapore
Col.	Colombia	mts	mountains	Switz.	Switzerland
CT	Connecticut	N.	North, Northern	Tajik.	Tajikistan
Czech Rep.	Czech Republic	nat. park	national park	Tanz.	Tanzania
DC	District of Columbia	N.B.	New Brunswick	Tas.	Tasmania
DE	Delaware	NC	North Carolina	terr.	territory
Dem. Rep. Congo	Democratic Republic of Congo	ND	North Dakota	Thai.	Thailand
depr.	depression	NE	Nebraska	TN	Tennessee
des.	desert	Neth.	Netherlands	Trin. and Tob.	Trinidad and Tobago
Dom. Rep.	Dominican Republic	Neth. Antilles	Netherlands Antilles	Turkm.	Turkmenistan
Equat. Guinea	Equatorial Guinea	Nfld.	Newfoundland	TX	Texas
esc.	escarpment	NH	New Hampshire	U.A.E.	United Arab Emirates
est.	estuary	NJ	New Jersey	U.K.	United Kingdom
Eth.	Ethiopia	NM	New Mexico	Ukr.	Ukraine
Fin.	Finland	N.S.	Nova Scotia	U.S.A.	United States of America
FL	Florida	N.S.W.	New South Wales	UT	Utah
for.	forest	N.W.T.	Northwest Territories	Uzbek.	Uzbekistan
Fr. Guiana	French Guiana	N.Z.	New Zealand	VA	Virginia
Fr. Polynesia	French Polynesia	NV	Nevada	Venez.	Venezuela
g.	gulf	NY	New York	Vic.	Victoria
GA	Georgia	OH	Ohio	vol.	volcano
Guat.	Guatemala	OK	Oklahoma	vol. crater	volcanic crater
h.	hill	Ont.	Ontario	VT	Vermont
hd	headland	OR	Oregon	W.	Western
HI	Hawaii	PA	Pennsylvania	WA	Washington
Hond.	Honduras	Pak.	Pakistan	W.A.	Western Australia
i.	island	Para.	Paraguay	WI	Wisconsin
IA	Iowa	P.E.I.	Prince Edward Island	WV	West Virginia
ID	Idaho	pen.	peninsula	WY	Wyoming
IL	Illinois	Phil.	Philippines	Y.T.	Yukon Territory

166 9 de Julio

1

159 E2 9 de Julio Arg.
159 E2 25 de Mayo Arg.
159 C3 25 de Mayo Arg.
130 E4 100 Mile House Canada

A

103 J5 Aabenraa Denmark
108 E4 Aachen Germany
103 J4 Aalborg Denmark
103 J4 Aalborg Bugt b. Denmark
112 E6 Aalen Germany
108 C4 Aalst Belgium
103 J4 Aars Denmark
108 C4 Aarschot Belgium
92 A3 Aba China
122 D3 Aba Dem. Rep. Congo
120 C4 Aba Nigeria
84 B5 Abā ad Dūd Saudi Arabia
84 C4 Ābādān Iran
84 D4 Ābādeh Iran
84 D4 Ābādeh Ţashk Iran
120 B1 Abadla Alg.
158 D2 Abaeté r. Brazil
155 I4 Abaetetuba Brazil
160 G6 Abaiang atoll Kiribati
139 E4 Abajo Peak U.S.A.
120 C4 Abakaliki Nigeria
90 B1 Abakan Rus. Fed.
90 A1 Abakanskiy Khrebet mts Rus. Fed.
117 E7 Abana Turkey
154 D6 Abancay Peru
84 D4 Abarkūh, Kavīr-e des. Iran
84 D4 Abarqū Iran
94 I2 Abashiri Japan
94 I2 Abashiri-wan b. Japan
68 E3 Abau P.N.G.
83 H2 Abay Kazakh.
122 D3 Abaya, Lake Eth.
Ābaya Hāyk' l. Eth. see Abaya, Lake
121 F3 Ābay Wenz r. Eth. alt. Azraq, Bahr el (Sudan), conv. Blue Nile
76 K4 Abaza Rus. Fed.
85 E3 Abbāsābād Iran
114 C4 Abbasanta Sardinia Italy
134 C2 Abbaye, Point U.S.A.
108 A5 Abbaye de Chaalis tourist site France
108 D5 Abbaye d'Orval tourist site Belgium
122 E2 Abbe, Lake Eth.
110 E1 Abbeville France
143 E6 Abbeville LA U.S.A.
145 D5 Abbeville SC U.S.A.
107 B5 Abbeyfeale Rep. of Ireland
106 E6 Abbey Head U.K.
107 D5 Abbeyleix Rep. of Ireland
104 D3 Abbey Town U.K.
102 L2 Abborrträsk Sweden
73 B3 Abbot Ice Shelf ice feature Antarctica
130 E5 Abbotsford Canada
134 B3 Abbotsford U.S.A.
139 F4 Abbott U.S.A.
88 C2 Abbottabad Pak.
81 H3 'Abd al 'Azīz, Jabal h. Syria
81 K5 Ābdānān Iran
82 C1 Abdulino Rus. Fed.
121 E3 Abéché Chad
72 D4 Abel Tasman National Park N.Z.
120 B4 Abengourou Côte d'Ivoire
Åbenrå Denmark see Aabenraa
109 J6 Abensberg Germany
120 C4 Abeokuta Nigeria
105 C5 Aberaeron U.K.
106 F3 Aberchirder U.K.
71 H5 Abercrombie r. Australia
105 D6 Aberdare U.K.
105 C5 Aberdaron U.K.
71 I4 Aberdeen Australia
131 H4 Aberdeen Canada
93 □ Aberdeen Hong Kong China
124 F6 Aberdeen S. Africa
106 F3 Aberdeen U.K.
147 E5 Aberdeen MD U.S.A.
143 F5 Aberdeen MS U.S.A.
142 D2 Aberdeen SD U.S.A.
138 B2 Aberdeen WA U.S.A.
131 I2 Aberdeen Lake Canada
105 C5 Aberdovey U.K.
Aberdyfi U.K. see Aberdovey
106 E4 Aberfeldy U.K.
104 F4 Aberford U.K.
106 D4 Aberfoyle U.K.
105 D6 Abergavenny U.K.
143 C5 Abernathy U.S.A.
105 C5 Aberporth U.K.
105 C5 Abersoch U.K.
105 C5 Aberystwyth U.K.
86 B6 Abhā Saudi Arabia
84 C2 Abhar Iran
84 C2 Abhar Rūd r. Iran
121 F3 Abiad, Bahr el r. Sudan/Uganda alt. Jebel, Bahr el, conv. White Nile
Ab-i Bazuft r. Iran see Bāzoft, Āb-e
157 A2 Abibe, Serranía de mts Col.
120 B4 Abidjan Côte d'Ivoire
Ab-i-Istada l. Afgh. see Īstādeh-ye Moqor, Āb-e
122 D3 Abijatta-Shalla National Park Eth.
84 E3 Ab-i-Kavīr salt flat Iran
142 D4 Abilene KS U.S.A.
143 D5 Abilene TX U.S.A.
105 F6 Abingdon U.K.
134 B5 Abingdon IL U.S.A.
146 C6 Abingdon VA U.S.A.
117 F6 Abinsk Rus. Fed.
Ab-i-Safed r. Afgh. see Safīd, Daryā-ye
Abiseo, Parque Nacional nat. park Peru see Río Abiseo, Parque Nacional
131 H2 Abitau Lake Canada
132 D4 Abitibi r. Canada
132 E4 Abitibi, Lake Canada
88 C3 Abohar India
120 B4 Aboisso Côte d'Ivoire
120 C4 Abomey Benin
121 D4 Abong Mbang Cameroon
97 A4 Aborlan Phil.
121 D3 Abou Déia Chad
81 J1 Abovyan Armenia
106 F3 Aboyne U.K.
86 C4 Abqaiq Saudi Arabia
Abra, Lago del l. Arg. see Abra, Laguna del
159 D4 Abra, Laguna del l. Arg.
111 B3 Abrantes Port.
156 C2 Abra Pampa Arg.
150 A2 Abreojos, Punta pt Mex.
158 E2 Abrolhos, Arquipélago dos is Brazil
163 G7 Abrolhos Bank sea feature S. Atlantic Ocean
138 E2 Absaroka Range mts U.S.A.
109 H6 Abtsgmünd Germany
84 D5 Abū al Abyaḑ i. U.A.E.
84 C5 Abū 'Alī i. Saudi Arabia
Abu al Jirab i. U.A.E. see Abū al Abyaḑ
86 B6 Abū 'Arīsh Saudi Arabia
86 D5 Abu Dhabi U.A.E.
121 F3 Abu Hamed Sudan
120 C4 Abuja Nigeria
81 H4 Abū Kamāl Syria
121 E3 Abu Matariq Sudan
80 B6 Abu Mena tourist site Egypt
84 D5 Abu Musa i. U.A.E.
154 E6 Abunã r. Bol.
154 E5 Abunã Brazil
86 A7 Ābune Yosēf mt. Eth.
80 C6 Abū Qīr, Khalīj b. Egypt
79 F4 Abu Road India
Abu Simbel Egypt see Abū Sunbul
81 J6 Abū Şukhayr Iraq
121 F2 Abū Sunbul Egypt
72 C5 Abut Head N.Z.
97 C4 Abuyog Phil.
121 E3 Abu Zabad Sudan
Abū Ẓabī U.A.E. see Abu Dhabi
81 L6 Abūzam Iran
121 E3 Abyad Sudan
121 E4 Abyei Sudan
84 C2 Ābyek Iran
82 D1 Abzakovo Rus. Fed.
82 D2 Abzanovo Rus. Fed.
147 I2 Acadia National Park U.S.A.
150 D3 Acambaro Mex.
151 G3 Acancéh Mex.
157 A2 Acandí Col.
111 B1 A Cañiza Spain
150 C3 Acaponeta Mex.
151 E4 Acapulco Mex.
155 I4 Acará Brazil
155 J4 Acaraú r. Brazil
158 A4 Acaray r. Para.
156 E3 Acaray, Represa de resr Para.
157 C2 Acarigua Venez.
151 E4 Acatlan Mex.
151 E4 Acatzingo Mex.
151 F4 Acayucán Mex.
120 B4 Accra Ghana
104 E4 Accrington U.K.
157 C3 Achaguas Venez.
88 D5 Achalpur India
87 B2 Achampet India
77 S3 Achayvayam Rus. Fed.
96 D1 Acheng China
108 A4 Achicourt France
107 B4 Achill Rep. of Ireland
107 A4 Achill Island Rep. of Ireland
106 C2 Achiltibuie U.K.
109 H1 Achim Germany
90 B1 Achinsk Rus. Fed.
83 G4 Achisay Kazakh.
106 C3 Achnasheen U.K.
106 C3 A'Chralaig mt. U.K.
117 F6 Achuyevo Rus. Fed.
80 B3 Acıgöl l. Turkey
80 B3 Acıpayam Turkey
114 F6 Acireale Sicily Italy
142 E3 Ackley U.S.A.
149 J4 Acklins Island Bahamas
105 I5 Acle U.K.
159 B2 Aconcagua r. Chile
159 B2 Aconcagua, Cerro mt. Arg.
155 K5 Acopiara Brazil
100 A6 Açores, Arquipélago dos is N. Atlantic Ocean
111 B1 A Coruña Spain
150 H6 Acoyapa Nicaragua
114 C2 Acqui Terme Italy
70 A4 Acraman, Lake salt flat Australia
Acre Israel see 'Akko
114 G5 Acri Italy
112 I7 Ács Hungary
67 J6 Actéon, Groupe is Fr. Polynesia
146 B4 Ada OH U.S.A.
143 D5 Ada OK U.S.A.
111 D2 Adaja r. Spain
156 E8 Adam, Mount h. Falkland Is
71 H6 Adaminaby Australia
82 D2 Adamovka Rus. Fed.
147 G3 Adams MA U.S.A.
134 C4 Adams WI U.S.A.
138 B2 Adams, Mount U.S.A.
87 B4 Adam's Bridge sea feature India/Sri Lanka
130 F4 Adams Lake Canada
141 E2 Adams McGill Reservoir U.S.A.
130 C3 Adams Mountain U.S.A.
140 B2 Adams Peak U.S.A.
87 C5 Adam's Peak Sri Lanka
'Adan Yemen see Aden
80 E3 Adana Turkey
80 C1 Adapazarı Turkey
107 C5 Adare Rep. of Ireland
73 B6 Adare, Cape c. Antarctica
141 E2 Adaven U.S.A.
81 J5 Ad Daghghārah Iraq
86 C5 Ad Dahnā' des. Saudi Arabia
120 A2 Ad Dakhla W. Sahara
Ad Dammām Saudi Arabia see Dammam
84 B5 Ad Dawādimī Saudi Arabia
Ad Dawḩah Qatar see Doha
81 I4 Ad Dawr Iraq
81 K6 Ad Dayr Iraq
84 B5 Ad Dibdibah plain Saudi Arabia
84 B6 Ad Dilam Saudi Arabia
86 C5 Ad Dir'īyah Saudi Arabia
122 D3 Addis Ababa Eth.
147 J2 Addison U.S.A.
81 J6 Ad Dīwānīyah Iraq
105 G6 Addlestone U.K.
125 F6 Addo Elephant National Park S. Africa
81 I6 Ad Duwayd well Saudi Arabia
145 D6 Adel GA U.S.A.
142 E3 Adel IA U.S.A.
70 C5 Adelaide Australia
145 E7 Adelaide Bahamas
125 G6 Adelaide S. Africa
73 B2 Adelaide Island i. Antarctica
68 D3 Adelaide River Australia
140 D4 Adelanto U.S.A.
73 C6 Adélie Land reg. Antarctica
73 C7 Adélie Land reg. Antarctica
71 H5 Adelong Australia
83 G4 Adelunga Uzbek.
86 C7 Aden Yemen
86 C7 Aden, Gulf of Somalia/Yemen
108 E4 Adenau Germany
109 I1 Adendorf Germany
84 D5 Adh Dhayd U.A.E.
91 F7 Adi i. Indon.
122 D2 Ādī Ārk'ay Eth.
122 D2 Ādīgrat Eth.
88 D6 Adilabad India
81 I2 Adilcevaz Turkey
138 B3 Adin U.S.A.
121 D2 Adīrī Libya
147 F2 Adirondack Mountains U.S.A.
Ādīs Ābeba Eth. see Addis Ababa
122 D3 Ādīs Alem Eth.
80 G3 Adıyaman Turkey
113 M7 Adjud Romania
133 I3 Adlavik Islands Canada
68 C3 Admiralty Gulf Australia
129 J2 Admiralty Inlet Canada
130 C3 Admiralty Island U.S.A.
130 C3 Admiralty Island National Monument-Kootznoowoo Wilderness nat. park U.S.A.
68 E2 Admiralty Islands P.N.G.
87 B3 Adoni India
109 K4 Adorf Germany
109 G3 Adorf (Diemelsee) Germany
110 D5 Adour r. France
111 E4 Adra Spain
114 F6 Adrano Sicily Italy
120 B2 Adrar Alg.
120 A2 Adrar mts Alg.
85 F3 Adraskand r. Afgh.
83 G4 Adrasmon Tajik.
121 E3 Adré Chad
135 E5 Adrian MI U.S.A.
143 C5 Adrian TX U.S.A.
114 E2 Adriatic Sea Europe
87 B4 Adur India
122 C3 Adusa Dem. Rep. Congo
122 D2 Ādwa Eth.
77 O3 Adycha r. Rus. Fed.
117 F6 Adygeya, Respublika aut. rep. Rus. Fed.
117 F6 Adygeysk Rus. Fed.
117 H6 Adyk Rus. Fed.
120 B4 Adzopé Côte d'Ivoire
115 K5 Aegean Sea Greece/Turkey
109 H2 Aerzen Germany
111 B1 A Estrada Spain
122 D2 Afabet Eritrea
81 J3 Afan Iran
85 F3 Afghanistan country Asia
102 J3 Åfjord Norway
122 E3 Afmadow Somalia
128 C4 Afognak Island U.S.A.
111 C1 A Fonsagrada Spain
118 Africa
80 F3 'Afrīn, Nahr r. Syria/Turkey
80 F2 Afşin Turkey
108 D2 Afsluitdijk barrage Neth.
138 E3 Afton U.S.A.
155 H4 Afuá Brazil
80 E5 'Afula Israel
80 C2 Afyon Turkey
109 K4 Aga Germany
120 C3 Agadez Niger
120 B1 Agadir Morocco
83 H2 Agadyr' Kazakh.
119 I5 Agalega Islands Mauritius
150 H5 Agalta nat. park Hond.
82 D1 Agapovka Rus. Fed.
89 G5 Agartala India
88 C6 Agashi India
135 F2 Agate Canada
115 L6 Agathonisi i. Greece
120 B4 Agboville Côte d'Ivoire
81 K1 Ağcabädi Azer.
81 K2 Ağdam Azer.
110 F5 Agde France
110 E4 Agen France
124 C4 Aggeneys S. Africa
108 F4 Agger r. Germany
88 D1 Aghil Pass China
107 C3 Aghla Mountain h. Rep. of Ireland
115 K7 Agia Vervara Greece
80 G2 Ağın Turkey
115 J6 Agios Dimitrios Greece
115 K5 Agios Efstratios i. Greece
115 L5 Agios Fokas, Akra pt Greece
115 J5 Agios Konstantinos Greece
115 K7 Agios Nikolaos Greece
115 J4 Agiou Orous, Kolpos b. Greece
121 F3 Agirwat Hills Sudan
125 F3 Agisanang S. Africa
120 B4 Agnibilékrou Côte d'Ivoire
115 K2 Agnita Romania
92 A2 Agong China
88 D4 Agra India
117 H7 Agrakhanskiy Poluostrov pen. Rus. Fed.
111 F2 Agreda Spain
81 I2 Ağrı Turkey
115 J7 Agria Gramvousa i. Greece
114 E6 Agrigento Sicily Italy
115 I5 Agrinio Greece
159 B3 Agrio r. Arg.
114 F4 Agropoli Italy
81 J1 Ağstafa Azer.
81 L1 Ağsu Azer.
151 G5 Agua, Volcán de vol. Guat.
150 C3 Agua Brava, Laguna lag. Mex.
151 G4 Aguada Mex.
157 B3 Aguadas Col.
157 B3 Agua de Dios Col.
149 K5 Aguadilla Puerto Rico
159 D4 Aguado Cecilio Arg.
150 I6 Aguadulce Panama
159 C3 Agua Escondida Arg.
150 C3 Aguamilpa, Presa l. Mex.
148 D4 Aguanaval r. Mex.
159 C1 Agua Negra, Paso del pass Arg./Chile
158 B3 Aguapeí r. Brazil
148 C2 Agua Prieta Mex.
158 A3 Aguaray Guazú r. Para.
157 D2 Aguaro-Guariquito, Parque Nacional nat. park Venez.
150 C2 Aguaruto Mex.
150 D3 Aguascalientes Mex.
150 D3 Aguascalientes state Mex.
158 E2 Águas Formosas Brazil
158 C3 Agudos Brazil
141 F5 Aguila U.S.A.
111 D1 Aguilar de Campóo Spain
111 F4 Águilas Spain
97 B4 Aguisan Phil.
124 D7 Agulhas, Cape S. Africa
163 K9 Agulhas Basin sea feature Southern Ocean
158 D3 Agulhas Negras mt. Brazil
162 F7 Agulhas Plateau sea feature Southern Ocean
163 J8 Agulhas Ridge sea feature S. Atlantic Ocean
99 E4 Agung, Gunung vol. Indon.
97 C4 Agusan r. Phil.
97 B4 Agutaya Phil.
84 B2 Ahar Iran
72 C5 Ahaura N.Z.
108 F2 Ahaus Germany
72 F3 Ahimanawa Range mts N.Z.
72 D1 Ahipara N.Z.
72 D1 Ahipara Bay N.Z.
128 B4 Ahklun Mountains U.S.A.
81 I2 Ahlat Turkey
109 F3 Ahlen Germany
88 C5 Ahmadabad India
87 A2 Ahmadnagar India
88 B3 Ahmadpur East Pak.
109 I4 Ahorn Germany
84 C4 Ahram Iran
109 I1 Ahrensburg Germany
81 I2 Ahta Dağı mt. Turkey
102 N3 Ähtäri Fin.
103 N4 Ahtme Estonia
81 L6 Āhū Iran
151 G5 Ahuachapán El Salvador
150 D3 Ahualulco Mex.
110 F3 Ahun France
72 B6 Ahuriri r. N.Z.
84 C4 Ahvāz Iran
88 C5 Ahwa India
124 B3 Ai-Ais Namibia
92 D1 Aibag Gol r. China
Aidin Turkm. see Aýdyň
Aiea U.S.A. see 'Aiea
140 □1 'Aiea U.S.A.
80 E4 Aigialousa Cyprus
115 J6 Aigina i. Greece
115 J5 Aigio Greece
110 H4 Aigle de Chambeyron mt. France
159 F2 Aiguá Uruguay
96 C3 Ai He r. China
95 F5 Aikawa Japan
145 D5 Aiken U.S.A.
150 J6 Ailigandi Panama
Ailinglapalap atoll Marshall Is see Ailinglaplap
160 G6 Ailinglaplap atoll Marshall Is
108 A5 Ailly-sur-Noye France
135 G4 Ailsa Craig Canada
106 C5 Ailsa Craig i. U.K.
158 E2 Aimorés, Serra dos hills Brazil
140 □1 'Āina Haina U.S.A.
120 C1 Aïn Beïda Alg.
120 B2 'Aïn Ben Tili Mauritania
111 H4 Aïn Defla Alg.
111 H5 Aïn el Hadjel Alg.
120 B1 Aïn Sefra Alg.
133 H4 Ainslie, Lake Canada
142 D3 Ainsworth U.S.A.
Aintab Turkey see Gaziantep
111 H4 Aïn Taya Alg.
111 G5 Aïn Tédélès Alg.
157 B4 Aipe Col.
98 C5 Air i. Indon.
130 G4 Airdrie Canada
106 E5 Airdrie U.K.
108 D6 Aire r. France
110 D5 Aire-sur-l'Adour France
120 C3 Aïr et du Ténéré, Réserve Naturelle Nationale de l' nature res. Niger
129 K3 Air Force Island Canada
92 D1 Airgin Sum China
131 H3 Air Ronge Canada
92 F2 Ai Shan h. China
130 B2 Aishihik Canada
130 B2 Aishihik Lake Canada
110 G2 Aisne r. France
111 F3 Aitana mt. Spain
68 E2 Aitape P.N.G.
142 E2 Aitkin U.S.A.
82 C1 Aitova Rus. Fed.
67 I5 Aitutaki i. Pacific Ocean
113 K7 Aiud Romania
110 G5 Aix-en-Provence France
110 G4 Aix-les-Bains France
89 F5 Aiyar Reservoir India
89 H5 Aizawl India
103 N4 Aizkraukle Latvia
103 M4 Aizpute Latvia
95 F6 Aizu-wakamatsu Japan
114 C4 Ajaccio Corsica France
157 B4 Ajajú r. Col.
151 E4 Ajalpán Mex.
87 A1 Ajanta India
102 K2 Ajaureforsen Sweden
72 D5 Ajax, Mount N.Z.
121 E1 Ajdābiyā Libya
94 G4 Ajigasawa Japan
80 E5 'Ajlūn Jordan
84 D5 'Ajman U.A.E.
88 C4 Ajmer India
141 F5 Ajo U.S.A.
141 F5 Ajo, Mount U.S.A.
97 B4 Ajuy Phil.
94 H3 Akabira Japan
122 D4 Akagera National Park Rwanda
87 B2 Akalkot India
94 I3 Akan National Park Japan
80 D4 Akanthou Cyprus
72 D5 Akaroa N.Z.
72 D5 Akaroa Harbour N.Z.
89 H4 Akas reg. India
83 H3 Akbakay Kazakh.
83 I3 Akbalyk Kazakh.
85 H3 Akbar Afgh.
89 E4 Akbarpur India
82 E3 Akbasty Kazakh.
83 H2 Akbauyr Kazakh.
83 G2 Akbeit Kazakh.
111 I4 Akbou Alg.
83 I2 Akbulak Vostochnyy Kazakhstan Kazakh.
83 K2 Akbulak Vostochnyy Kazakhstan Kazakh.
82 C2 Akbulak Rus. Fed.
80 F2 Akçadağ Turkey
81 G3 Akçakale Turkey
80 C1 Akçakoca Turkey
80 D3 Akçali Dağ mt. Turkey
82 D4 Akchakaya, Vpadina depr. Turkm.
83 H3 Akchatau Kazakh.
80 C3 Akdağ mt. Turkey
80 C3 Ak Dağı mt. Turkey
81 H2 Ak Dağı mts Turkey
80 E2 Akdağmadeni Turkey
82 D4 Akdepe Turkm.
103 L4 Åkersberga Sweden
108 C2 Akersloot Neth.
82 E3 Akespe Kazakh.
122 C3 Aketi Dem. Rep. Congo
82 C4 Akgyr Erezi hills Turkm.
81 I1 Akhalk'alak'i Georgia
117 G7 Akhalts'ikhe Georgia
89 G5 Akhaura Bangl.
121 E1 Akhḑar, Al Jabal al mts Libya
86 E5 Akhḑar, Jabal mts Oman
80 A2 Akhisar Turkey
80 F3 Akhtarīn Syria
117 H5 Akhtubinsk Rus. Fed.
82 D1 Akhunovo Rus. Fed.
81 I1 Akhuryan Armenia
95 C8 Aki Japan
132 D3 Akimiski Island Canada
80 E3 Akıncı Burun pt Turkey
80 G1 Akıncılar Turkey
94 G5 Akita Japan
120 A3 Akjoujt Mauritania
82 E2 Akkabak Kazakh.
102 L2 Akkajaure l. Sweden
Akkala Uzbek. see Oqqal'a
83 G3 Akkanse Kazakh.
82 D2 Akkermanovka Rus. Fed.
94 I3 Akkeshi Japan
82 B3 Akkistau Kazakh.
80 E5 'Akko Israel
83 G2 Akkol' Akmolinskaya Oblast' Kazakh.
83 H3 Akkol' Almatinskaya Oblast' Kazakh.
82 B3 Akkol' Atyrauskaya Oblast' Kazakh.
83 G4 Akkol' Zhambylskaya Oblast' Kazakh.
83 I2 Akku Kazakh.
82 F3 Akkum Kazakh.
80 F1 Akkuş Turkey
Akkyr, Gory hills Turkm. see Akgyr Erezi
88 D4 Aklera India
103 M4 Akmeņrags pt Latvia
88 D1 Akmeqit China
Akmola Kazakh. see Astana
83 G2 Akmolinskaya Oblast' admin. div. Kazakh.
83 I4 Ak-Moyun Kyrg.
95 D7 Akō Japan
121 F4 Akobo Sudan
88 D5 Akola India
83 I4 Akongkür China
122 D2 Akordat Eritrea
80 D3 Akören Turkey
88 D5 Akot India
133 G1 Akpatok Island Canada
83 I4 Akqi China
102 B2 Akranes Iceland
117 C7 Akrathos, Akra pt Greece
103 I4 Åkrehamn Norway
85 G3 Ak Robat Pass Afgh.
138 G3 Akron CO U.S.A.
146 C4 Akron OH U.S.A.
146 C4 Akron City Reservoir U.S.A.
88 D2 Aksai Chin terr. Asia
80 E2 Aksaray Turkey
83 H4 Ak-Say r. Kyrg.
117 F6 Aksay Rus. Fed.
88 D2 Aksayqin Hu l. China/Jammu and Kashmir
80 C2 Akşehir Turkey
80 C2 Akşehir Gölü l. Turkey
80 C3 Akseki Turkey
82 C1 Aksenovo Rus. Fed.
84 D4 Aks-e Rostam r. Iran
82 C2 Akshatau Kazakh.
82 E2 Akshiganak Kazakh.
82 C3 Akshimrau Kazakh.
83 I4 Akshiy Kazakh.
82 B4 Akshukur Kazakh.
83 J4 Aksu Xinjiang China
83 J4 Aksu Xinjiang China
83 I3 Aksu Almatinskaya Oblast' Kazakh.
83 I1 Aksu Pavlodarskaya Oblast' Kazakh.
83 G1 Aksu Severnyy Kazakhstan Kazakh.
83 G4 Aksu Yuzhnyy Kazakhstan Kazakh.
82 C2 Aksu Zapadnyy Kazakhstan Kazakh.
83 I3 Aksu r. Kazakh.
80 C3 Aksu r. Turkey
82 F2 Aksuat Kustanayskaya Oblast' Kazakh.
83 J3 Aksuat Vostochnyy Kazakhstan Kazakh.
83 H2 Aksu-Ayuly Kazakh.
83 J4 Aksu He r. China
122 D2 Āksum Eth.
83 F3 Aksumbe Kazakh.
83 J3 Aksüme China
83 H3 Aksuyek Kazakh.
89 F1 Aktag mt. China
82 F2 Aktas Kazakh.
81 J2 Aktas Dağı mt. Turkey
Aktash Uzbek. see Oqtosh
83 G3 Aktau Karagandinskaya Oblast' Kazakh.
83 H2 Aktau Karagandinskaya Oblast' Kazakh.
82 B4 Aktau Mangistauskaya Oblast' Kazakh.
83 I5 Akto China
82 D2 Aktobe Kazakh.
83 H2 Aktogay Karagandinskaya Oblast' Kazakh.
83 H1 Aktogay Pavlodarskaya Oblast' Kazakh.
83 I3 Aktogay Vostochnyy Kazakhstan Kazakh.
113 N4 Aktsyabrski Belarus
83 F2 Aktuma Kazakh.
82 D3 Aktumsyk Kazakh.
82 D3 Aktumsyk, Mys pt Uzbek.
83 H4 Ak-Tüz Kyrg.
82 D2 Aktyubinskaya Oblast' admin. div. Kazakh.
95 B8 Akune Japan
120 C4 Akure Nigeria
102 C2 Akureyri Iceland
89 G1 Akxokesay China
Akyab Myanmar see Sittwe
83 H3 Akzhal Karagandinskaya Oblast' Kazakh.
83 J2 Akzhal Vostochnyy Kazakhstan Kazakh.
82 D2 Akzhar Aktyubinskaya Oblast' Kazakh.
82 F3 Akzhar Kzyl-Ordinskaya Oblast' Kazakh.
83 J3 Akzhar Vostochnyy Kazakhstan Kazakh.
83 G4 Akzhar Zhambylskaya Oblast' Kazakh.
83 F3 Akzhaykyn, Ozero salt l. Kazakh.
80 G3 Akziyaret Turkey
103 J3 Ål Norway
84 C5 Al 'Abā Saudi Arabia
145 C6 Alabama r. U.S.A.
145 C5 Alabama state U.S.A.
145 C5 Alabaster U.S.A.
97 B3 Alabat i. Phil.
81 J7 Al 'Abţīyah well Iraq
83 G4 Ala-Buka Kyrg.
80 E1 Alaca Turkey
80 F2 Alacahan Turkey
80 E1 Alaçam Turkey
80 B2 Alaçam Dağları mts Turkey
151 G3 Alacrán, Arrecife rf Mex.
81 I2 Ala Dag mt. Turkey
81 I2 Ala Dağlar mts Turkey
80 E3 Ala Dağları mts Turkey
117 H7 Alagir Rus. Fed.
155 K6 Alagoinhas Brazil
111 F2 Alagón Spain
97 C5 Alah r. Phil.
102 M3 Alahärmä Fin.
81 K7 Al Aḩmadī Kuwait
83 G5 Alai Range mts Asia
102 M3 Alajärvi Fin.
150 H6 Alajuela Costa Rica
81 K2 Alajujeh Iran
88 D3 Alaknanda r. India
83 J3 Alakol', Ozero salt l. Kazakh.
102 O2 Alakurtti Rus. Fed.
80 B6 Al 'Alamayn Egypt
154 F4 Alalaú r. Brazil
81 I3 Al 'Amādīyah Iraq
84 B5 Al'Amār Saudi Arabia
81 K6 Al 'Amārah Iraq
Alamdo China see Alando
83 H4 Alamedin, Pik Zapadnyy mt. Kyrg.
81 J7 Al Amghar waterhole Iraq
97 A2 Alaminos Phil.
80 B6 Al 'Āmirīyah Egypt
141 E3 Alamo U.S.A.
141 F4 Alamo Dam U.S.A.
139 F5 Alamogordo U.S.A.
143 D6 Alamo Heights U.S.A.
139 E6 Alamos Sonora Mex.
150 B2 Alamos Sonora Mex.
139 F4 Alamosa U.S.A.
87 B3 Alampur India
102 K2 Alanäs Sweden
Åland is Fin. see Åland Islands
109 J1 Aland r. Germany
87 B2 Aland India
84 B2 Aland r. Iran
103 L3 Åland Islands Fin.
89 H3 Alando China
98 B5 Alang Besar i. Indon.
134 E3 Alanson U.S.A.
80 D3 Alanya Turkey
84 D4 'Alā' od Dīn Iran
80 C1 Alaplı Turkey
Alappuzha India see Alleppey
80 E7 Al 'Aqabah Jordan
84 C6 Al 'Āqūlah well Saudi Arabia
111 E3 Alarcón, Embalse de resr Spain
80 D6 Al 'Arīsh Egypt
86 C4 Al Arţāwīyah Saudi Arabia
99 E4 Alas Indon.
80 B2 Alaşehir Turkey
81 I6 Al 'Āshūrīyah well Iraq
128 D3 Alaska state U.S.A.
128 D4 Alaska, Gulf of U.S.A.
130 E3 Alaska Highway Canada/U.S.A.
128 B4 Alaska Peninsula U.S.A.
128 D3 Alaska Range mts U.S.A.
81 L2 Älät Azer.
Alat Uzbek. see Olot
81 I6 Al 'Athāmīn hills Iraq
116 H4 Alatyr' Rus. Fed.
116 H4 Alatyr' r. Rus. Fed.
154 C4 Alausí Ecuador
81 J1 Alaverdi Armenia
102 N2 Alavieska Fin.
102 M3 Alavus Fin.
70 D5 Alawoona Australia
81 K1 Alazani r. Azer./Georgia
81 J5 Al 'Azīzīyah Iraq
114 C2 Alba Italy
80 F3 Al Bāb Syria
111 F3 Albacete Spain
70 D5 Albacutya, Lake dry lake Australia
81 J6 Al Bādiyah al Janūbīyah des. Iraq
115 J1 Alba Iulia Romania
132 F3 Albanel, Lac Canada
115 I4 Albania country Europe
68 B5 Albany Australia
132 C3 Albany r. Canada
145 C6 Albany GA U.S.A.
134 E5 Albany IN U.S.A.
144 C4 Albany KY U.S.A.
147 G3 Albany NY U.S.A.
138 B2 Albany OR U.S.A.
71 H1 Albany Downs Australia
159 G2 Albardão do João Maria coastal area Brazil
84 B5 Al Barrah Saudi Arabia
81 J6 Al Baţḩa' marsh Iraq
68 E3 Albatross Bay Australia
71 F8 Albatross Island Australia
121 E2 Al Bawītī Egypt
Al Bawiti Egypt see Al Bawītī
121 E1 Al Bayḑā' Libya
154 □ Albemarle, Punta pt Galapagos Is Ecuador
145 E5 Albemarle Sound sea chan. U.S.A.
114 C2 Albenga Italy
111 D3 Alberche r. Spain
68 D4 Alberga watercourse Australia
111 B2 Albergaria-a-Velha Port.
71 G4 Albert Australia
110 F2 Albert France
70 C5 Albert, Lake Australia
122 D3 Albert, Lake Dem. Rep. Congo/Uganda
130 F4 Alberta prov. Canada
146 E6 Alberta U.S.A.
130 F4 Alberta, Mount Canada
124 D7 Albertinia S. Africa
108 D4 Albert Kanaal canal Belgium
142 E3 Albert Lea U.S.A.
122 D3 Albert Nile r. Sudan/Uganda
156 B8 Alberto de Agostini, Parque Nacional nat. park Chile
125 H3 Alberton S. Africa
110 H4 Albertville France
108 E6 Albestroff France
110 F5 Albi France
155 H2 Albina Suriname
140 A2 Albion CA U.S.A.
147 I2 Albion ME U.S.A.
134 E4 Albion MI U.S.A.
146 D3 Albion NY U.S.A.
111 E5 Alborán, Isla de i. Spain
Ålborg Denmark see Aalborg
Ålborg Bugt b. Denmark see Aalborg Bugt
Alborz, Reshteh-ye mts Iran see Elburz Mountains
130 F4 Albreda Canada
84 C5 Al Budayyi' Bahrain
111 B4 Albufeira Port.
139 F5 Albuquerque U.S.A.
150 I5 Albuquerque, Cayos de is Col.
86 E5 Al Buraymī Oman
111 C3 Alburquerque Spain
71 G6 Albury Australia
81 H4 Al Buşayrah Syria
80 G7 Al Busayţā' plain Saudi Arabia
81 K6 Al Buşayyah Iraq
84 B4 Al Bushūk well Saudi Arabia
111 B3 Alcácer do Sal Port.
111 E2 Alcalá de Henares Spain
111 E4 Alcalá la Real Spain
114 E6 Alcamo Sicily Italy
111 F2 Alcañiz Spain
111 C3 Alcántara Spain
111 E3 Alcaraz Spain
111 D4 Alcaudete Spain
111 E3 Alcázar de San Juan Spain
117 F5 Alchevs'k Ukr.
159 D2 Alcira Arg.
158 E2 Alcobaça Brazil
111 F2 Alcora Spain
159 E2 Alcorta Arg.
Alcoy Spain see Alcoy-Alcoi
111 F3 Alcoy-Alcoi Spain
111 H3 Alcúdia Spain
123 E4 Aldabra Islands Seychelles
150 C1 Aldama Chihuahua Mex.
151 E3 Aldama Tamaulipas Mex.
77 N4 Aldan Rus. Fed.
77 O3 Aldan r. Rus. Fed.
108 D1 Aldeboarn Neth.
105 I5 Aldeburgh U.K.
110 D2 Alderney i. U.K.
140 B4 Alder Peak U.S.A.
105 G6 Aldershot U.K.
146 C6 Alderson U.S.A.
84 D6 Al Dhafrah reg. U.A.E.
104 D3 Aldingham U.K.
105 F5 Aldridge U.K.
134 B5 Aledo U.S.A.
120 A3 Aleg Mauritania
158 E3 Alegre Brazil
156 E3 Alegrete Brazil
159 E2 Alejandro Korn Arg.
156 □ Alejandro Selkirk, Isla i. Atlantic Ocean
116 E2 Alekhovshchina Rus. Fed.
82 B4 Aleksandra Bekovicha-Cherkasskoga, Zaliv b. Kazakh.
116 F3 Aleksandrov Rus. Fed.
117 I5 Aleksandrov Gay Rus. Fed.
82 C1 Aleksandrovka Orenburgskaya Oblast' Rus. Fed.
82 D1 Aleksandrovka Respublika Bashkortostan Rus. Fed.
117 H6 Aleksandrovskoye Rus. Fed.
77 P4 Aleksandrovsk-Sakhalinskiy Rus. Fed.
76 F1 Aleksandry, Zemlya i. Rus. Fed.
83 G1 Alekseyevka Kokshetauskaya Oblast' Kazakh.
83 H2 Alekseyevka Pavlodarskaya Oblast' Kazakh.
117 F5 Alekseyevka Belgorodskaya Oblast' Rus. Fed.
117 F5 Alekseyevka Belgorodskaya Oblast' Rus. Fed.
117 G5 Alekseyevskaya Rus. Fed.
116 F4 Aleksin Rus. Fed.
115 I3 Aleksinac Serb. and Mont.
122 B4 Alèmbé Gabon
80 E1 Alembeyli Turkey
158 D3 Além Paraíba Brazil
102 J3 Ålen Norway
110 E2 Alençon France
155 H4 Alenquer Brazil
140 □2 'Alenuihāhā Channel U.S.A.
80 F3 Aleppo Syria
129 M1 Alert Canada
154 D6 Alerta Peru
130 D4 Alert Bay Canada
110 G4 Alès France
113 K7 Aleşd Romania
114 C2 Alessandria Italy
102 I3 Ålesund Norway
160 G2 Aleutian Basin sea feature Bering Sea
126 C2 Aleutian Islands AK U.S.A.
128 C4 Aleutian Range mts U.S.A.
160 H2 Aleutian Trench sea feature N. Pacific Ocean
77 Q4 Alevina, Mys c. Rus. Fed.
147 J2 Alexander U.S.A.
130 B3 Alexander Archipelago is U.S.A.
124 B4 Alexander Bay b. Namibia/S. Africa
124 B4 Alexander Bay S. Africa
145 C5 Alexander City U.S.A.
73 B3 Alexander Island i. Antarctica
71 F6 Alexandra Australia
72 B6 Alexandra N.Z.
156 □ Alexandra, Cape Atlantic Ocean
115 J4 Alexandreia Greece
147 F2 Alexandria Canada
121 E1 Alexandria Egypt
115 K3 Alexandria Romania
125 G6 Alexandria S. Africa
106 D5 Alexandria U.K.
134 E5 Alexandria IN U.S.A.
143 E6 Alexandria LA U.S.A.
142 E2 Alexandria MN U.S.A.
146 E5 Alexandria VA U.S.A.
147 F2 Alexandria Bay U.S.A.
70 C5 Alexandrina, Lake Australia
115 K4 Alexandroupoli Greece
133 I3 Alexis r. Canada
134 B5 Alexis U.S.A.
130 E4 Alexis Creek Canada
83 J1 Aley r. Rus. Fed.
83 J1 Aleysk Rus. Fed.
108 F4 Alf Germany
111 F1 Alfaro Spain
81 K7 Al Farwānīyah Kuwait
81 I4 Al Fatḩah Iraq
81 L7 Al Fāw Iraq
121 F2 Al Fayyūm Egypt
109 H3 Alfeld (Leine) Germany
158 D3 Alfenas Brazil
81 L7 Al Finţās Kuwait
113 J7 Alföld plain Hungary
105 H4 Alford U.K.
147 F2 Alfred Canada
147 H3 Alfred U.S.A.
81 L7 Al Fuḩayḩīl Kuwait

Barpeta 169

80 A2 Aydın Dağları mts Turkey
82 C5 Aýdyň Turkm.
82 D2 Aydyrlinskiy Rus. Fed.
83 G3 Ayeat, Gora h. Kazakh.
98 □ Ayer Chawan, Pulau i. Sing.
98 □ Ayer Merbau, Pulau i. Sing.
Ayers Rock h. Australia see Uluṟu
83 J2 Aygyrzhal Kazakh.
82 E2 Ayke, Ozero l. Kazakh.
77 M3 Aykhal Rus. Fed.
116 I2 Aykino Rus. Fed.
83 J4 Aykol China
72 D5 Aylesbury N.Z.
105 G6 Aylesbury U.K.
146 E6 Aylett U.S.A.
111 E2 Ayllón Spain
135 G4 Aylmer Canada
131 H2 Aylmer Lake Canada
82 E2 Aymagambetov Kazakh.
83 I3 Aynabulak Kazakh.
84 C4 'Ayn al 'Abd well Saudi Arabia
83 G5 Ayní Tajik.
80 G3 'Ayn 'Īsá Syria
121 F4 Ayod Sudan
77 R3 Ayon, Ostrov i. Rus. Fed.
120 B3 'Ayoûn el 'Atroûs Mauritania
68 E3 Ayr Australia
106 D5 Ayr U.K.
106 D5 Ayr r. U.K.
80 D3 Ayrancı Turkey
104 C3 Ayre, Point of Isle of Man
83 G3 Ayshirak Kazakh.
82 E3 Ayteke Bi Kazakh.
115 L3 Aytos Bulg.
98 D2 A Yun Pa Vietnam
98 B2 Ayutthaya Thai.
115 L5 Ayvacık Turkey
80 F2 Ayvalı Turkey
115 L5 Ayvalık Turkey
150 H5 Azacualpa Hond.
89 E4 Azamgarh India
120 B3 Azaouâd reg. Mali
120 C3 Azaouagh, Vallée de watercourse Mali/Niger
Azbine mts Niger see L'Aïr, Massif de
80 D1 Azdavay Turkey
81 K1 Azerbaijan country Asia
84 B2 Āzghān Iran
82 E3 Azhar Kazakh.
135 G2 Azilda Canada
147 H2 Aziscohos Lake U.S.A.
154 C4 Azogues Ecuador
76 F3 Azopol'ye Rus. Fed.
100 A6 Azores terr. N. Atlantic Ocean
163 H3 Azores-Biscay Rise sea feature N. Atlantic Ocean
117 F6 Azov Rus. Fed.
117 F6 Azov, Sea of Rus. Fed./Ukr.
121 F3 Azraq, Bahr el r. Sudan alt. Ābay Wenz (Ethiopia), conv. Blue Nile
120 B1 Azrou Morocco
139 F4 Aztec U.S.A.
111 D3 Azuaga Spain
156 B3 Azúcar r. Chile
150 I7 Azuero, Península de pen. Panama
159 E3 Azul Arg.
Azúl r. Mex. see Azul
151 G4 Azul r. Mex.
159 B4 Azul, Cerro mt. Arg.
154 C5 Azul, Cordillera mts Peru
158 A1 Azul, Serra hills Brazil
95 G6 Azuma-san vol. Japan
154 F8 Azurduy Bol.
114 B6 Azzaba Alg.
80 F5 Az Zabadānī Syria
81 I6 Aẓ Ẓafīrī reg. Iraq
Aẓ Ẓahrān Saudi Arabia see Dhahran
121 F1 Az Zaqāzīq Egypt
80 F5 Az Zarqā' Jordan
84 B5 Az Zilfī Saudi Arabia
81 K6 Az Zubayr Iraq

B

98 D2 Ba, Sông r. Vietnam
80 E5 Baabda Lebanon
80 F4 Ba'albek Lebanon
71 H3 Baan Baa Australia
122 E3 Baardheere Somalia
85 F3 Bābā, Band-e mts Afgh.
85 H3 Bābā, Kūh-e mts Afgh.
115 L5 Baba Burnu pt Turkey
81 L1 Babadağ mt. Azer.
115 M2 Babadag Romania
Babadaykhan Turkm. see Badabaýhan
Babadaykhan Turkm. see Badabaýhan
82 D5 Babadurmaz Turkm.
117 C7 Babaeski Turkey
154 C4 Babahoyo Ecuador
87 B1 Babai India
89 E3 Babai r. Nepal
92 B1 Babai Gaxun China
81 K2 Bābā Jān Iran
97 C5 Babak Phil.
122 E2 Bāb al Mandab str. Africa/Asia
91 E7 Babar i. Indon.
83 H4 Babash-Ata, Khrebet mt. Kyrg.
122 D4 Babati Tanz.
116 E3 Babayevo Rus. Fed.
117 H7 Babayurt Rus. Fed.
134 B2 Babbitt U.S.A.
71 H7 Babel Island Australia
128 F4 Babine r. Canada
130 D4 Babine Lake Canada
91 F7 Babo Indon.
84 D2 Bābol Iran
82 C5 Bābol Sar Iran
124 C6 Baboon Point S. Africa
141 G6 Baboquivari Peak U.S.A.
122 B3 Baboua Centr. Afr. Rep.
116 D4 Babruysk Belarus
88 B4 Babuhri India
88 C2 Babusar Pass Pak.
97 A4 Babuyan Phil.
97 B2 Babuyan i. Phil.
93 F7 Babuyan Channel Phil.
97 B2 Babuyan Islands Phil.
81 J5 Babylon tourist site Iraq
155 J4 Bacabal Brazil
80 C1 Bacakliyayla Tepesi mt. Turkey
151 G4 Bacalar Mex.
91 E7 Bacan i. Indon.
97 B2 Bacarra Phil.
113 M7 Bacău Romania
70 F6 Bacchus Marsh Australia
93 C6 Băc Giang Vietnam
150 C1 Bachiniva Mex.
93 C6 Bach Long Vi, Đao i. Vietnam
83 I5 Bachu China
83 I5 Bachu Liuchang China
131 I1 Back r. Canada
115 H2 Bačka Palanka Serb. and Mont.
130 D2 Backbone Ranges mts Canada
102 L3 Backe Sweden
70 B5 Backstairs Passage sea chan. Australia
106 E4 Backwater Reservoir U.K.
Bac Lac Vietnam see Bao Lac
98 C3 Bac Liêu Vietnam
93 C6 Băc Ninh Vietnam
97 B3 Baco, Mount Phil.
97 B4 Bacolod Phil.
Băc Quang Vietnam see Viêt Quang
132 F2 Bacqueville, Lac l. Canada
82 E5 Badabaýhan Turkm.
82 E5 Badabaýhan Turkm.
109 K6 Bad Abbach Germany
87 A4 Badagara India
92 A1 Badain Jaran Shamo des. China
154 F4 Badajós, Lago l. Brazil
111 C3 Badajoz Spain
87 A3 Badami India
81 H6 Badanah Saudi Arabia
89 H4 Badarpur India
135 F4 Bad Axe U.S.A.
109 F5 Bad Bergzabern Germany
109 G3 Bad Berleburg Germany
109 I1 Bad Bevensen Germany
109 J4 Bad Blankenburg Germany
109 G4 Bad Camberg Germany
133 H4 Baddeck Canada
85 G4 Baddo r. Pak.
109 H3 Bad Driburg Germany
109 K3 Bad Düben Germany
109 G5 Bad Dürkheim Germany
109 K3 Bad Dürrenberg Germany
80 C3 Bademli Geçidi pass Turkey
109 F4 Bad Ems Germany
112 H6 Baden Austria
112 D7 Baden Switz.
112 D6 Baden-Baden Germany
106 D4 Badenoch reg. U.K.
109 G5 Baden-Württemberg land Germany
109 G2 Bad Essen Germany
133 I4 Badger Canada
109 I3 Bad Grund (Harz) Germany
109 I3 Bad Harzburg Germany
109 H4 Bad Hersfeld Germany
112 F7 Bad Hofgastein Austria
109 G4 Bad Homburg vor der Höhe Germany
114 D2 Badia Polesine Italy
88 B4 Badin Pak.
150 C2 Badiraguato Mex.
112 F7 Bad Ischl Austria
Bādiyat ash Shām des. Asia see Syrian Desert
109 I4 Bad Kissingen Germany
109 J3 Bad Kösen Germany
109 F5 Bad Kreuznach Germany
109 G4 Bad Laasphe Germany
142 C2 Badlands reg. U.S.A.
142 C3 Badlands National Park U.S.A.
109 I3 Bad Langensalza Germany
109 I3 Bad Lauterberg im Harz Germany
109 G3 Bad Lippspringe Germany
109 F4 Bad Marienberg (Westerwald) Germany
109 H5 Bad Mergentheim Germany
109 G4 Bad Nauheim Germany
108 F4 Bad Neuenahr-Ahrweiler Germany
109 I4 Bad Neustadt an der Saale Germany
109 I1 Bad Oldesloe Germany
92 D4 Badong China
98 C3 Ba Đông Vietnam
109 H3 Bad Pyrmont Germany
81 J5 Badrah Iraq
112 F7 Bad Reichenhall Germany
109 I3 Bad Sachsa Germany
109 I2 Bad Salzdetfurth Germany
109 G2 Bad Salzuflen Germany
109 I4 Bad Salzungen Germany
109 G4 Bad Schwalbach Germany
112 E4 Bad Schwartau Germany
112 E4 Bad Segeberg Germany
68 E3 Badu Island Australia
87 C5 Badulla Sri Lanka
109 G4 Bad Vilbel Germany
109 J2 Bad Wilsnack Germany
109 I5 Bad Windsheim Germany
109 G1 Bad Zwischenahn Germany
102 B1 Bæir Iceland
71 I4 Baerami Australia
108 E4 Baesweiler Germany
111 E4 Baeza Spain
120 D4 Bafang Cameroon
120 A3 Bafatá Guinea-Bissau
129 L2 Baffin Bay sea Canada/Greenland
129 K2 Baffin Island Canada
120 D4 Bafia Cameroon
120 A3 Bafing, Réserve du nature res. Mali
120 A3 Bafoulabé Mali
120 D4 Bafoussam Cameroon
84 D4 Bāfq Iran
80 E1 Bafra Turkey
117 E7 Bafra Burnu pt Turkey
84 E4 Bāft Iran
122 C3 Bafwasende Dem. Rep. Congo
89 F4 Bagaha India
97 A5 Bagahak, Gunung h. Sabah Malaysia
87 A2 Bagalkot India
122 D4 Bagamoyo Tanz.
99 B2 Bagan Datuk Malaysia
123 C5 Bagani Namibia
98 B4 Bagan Serai Malaysia
98 B5 Bagansiapiapi Indon.
83 J3 Bagar watercourse Kazakh.
141 F4 Bagdad U.S.A.
159 F1 Bagé Brazil
89 G5 Bagerhat Bangl.
88 D3 Bageshwar India
138 F3 Baggs U.S.A.
105 C6 Baggy Point U.K.
88 C5 Bagh India
84 D4 Bāgh, Chāh-e well Iran
85 F2 Baghbaghū Iran
81 J5 Baghdād Iraq
85 E4 Bāgh-e Bābū'īyeh Iran
84 C4 Bāgh-e Malek Iran
85 H2 Baghlān Afgh.
85 G3 Baghrān Afgh.
142 E2 Bagley U.S.A.
89 E3 Baglung Nepal
111 G1 Bagnères-de-Luchon France
110 G4 Bagnols-sur-Cèze France
89 F4 Bagnuiti r. Nepal
92 C2 Bag Nur l. China
97 B4 Bago Phil.
113 J3 Bagrationovsk Rus. Fed.
97 B2 Baguio Phil.
97 C5 Baguio Phil.
88 D3 Bahadurgarh India
89 G4 Baharampur India
Bahariya Oasis oasis Egypt see Bahrīyah, Wāḥāt al
82 D5 Baharly Turkm.
99 B2 Bahau Malaysia
88 C3 Bahawalnagar Pak.
88 B3 Bahawalpur Pak.
80 F3 Bahçe Turkey
92 C4 Ba He r. China
88 D3 Baheri India
122 D4 Bahi Tanz.
158 E1 Bahia state Brazil
159 D3 Bahía Blanca Arg.
150 B1 Bahía Kino Mex.
156 C7 Bahía Laura Arg.
156 E2 Bahía Negra Para.
150 A2 Bahía Tortugas Mex.
122 D2 Bahir Dar Eth.
86 E5 Bahlā Oman
84 C4 Bahman Yārī-ye Gharbī Iran
89 E4 Bahraich India
84 C5 Bahrain country Asia
84 C5 Bahrain, Gulf of Asia
81 L3 Bahrāmābād Iran
81 L3 Bahrām Beyg Iran
84 E4 Bahrāmjerd Iran
121 E2 Bahrīyah, Wāḥāt al oasis Egypt
154 E6 Bahuaja-Sonene, Parque Nacional nat. park Peru
85 F5 Bāhū Kālāt Iran
113 K7 Baia Mare Romania
84 D3 Baiazeh Iran
90 E2 Baicheng Jilin China
83 J4 Baicheng Xinjiang China
133 G4 Baie-Comeau Canada
Baie du Poste Canada see Mistissini
133 F4 Baie-St-Paul Canada
133 I4 Baie Verte Canada
92 E2 Baigou He r. China
88 E5 Baihar India
96 E2 Baihe Jilin China
92 D3 Baihe Shaanxi China
92 E1 Bai He r. China
90 C1 Baikal, Lake Rus. Fed.
106 A3 Baile Mhartainn U.K.
115 J2 Băileşti Romania
115 J2 Băileştilor, Câmpia plain Romania
107 E4 Bailieborough Rep. of Ireland
92 D1 Bailingmiao China
108 A4 Bailleul France
131 H2 Baillie r. Canada
92 B3 Bailong Jiang r. China
90 C3 Baima China
92 E4 Baima Jian mt. China
105 G4 Bain r. U.K.
145 C6 Bainbridge GA U.S.A.
147 F3 Bainbridge NY U.S.A.
Baingoin China see Porong
80 F6 Bā'ir Jordan
80 F6 Bā'ir, Wādī watercourse Jordan
89 E2 Bairab Co l. China
89 F4 Bairagnia India
128 C3 Baird Mountains U.S.A.
67 G3 Bairiki Kiribati
92 F1 Bairin Qiao China
83 G4 Bairkum Kazakh.
71 G6 Bairnsdale Australia
97 B4 Bais Phil.
93 C7 Baisha Hainan China
93 E5 Baisha Jiangxi China
92 C4 Baisha Sichuan China
96 D3 Baishan China
96 D2 Baishanzhen China
92 B3 Baishui Jiang r. China
93 B7 Bai Thương Vietnam
96 A2 Baixingt China
92 B2 Baiyin China
121 F3 Baiyuda Desert Sudan
115 H1 Baja Hungary
150 A2 Baja California pen. Mex.
136 C6 Baja California state Mex.
150 A2 Baja California Sur state Mex.
81 L3 Bājalān Iran
150 D2 Bajan Mex.
88 E3 Bajang Nepal
89 G5 Baj Baj India
85 E2 Bājgīrān Iran
157 A3 Bajo Baudó Col.
150 I6 Bajo Boquete Panama
159 D1 Bajo Hondo Arg.
83 I3 Bakanas Kazakh.
83 I3 Bakanas watercourse Kazakh.
120 A3 Bakel Senegal
140 D4 Baker CA U.S.A.
138 F2 Baker MT U.S.A.
141 E2 Baker NV U.S.A.
138 C2 Baker OR U.S.A.
138 B1 Baker, Mount vol. U.S.A.
141 G4 Baker Butte mt. U.S.A.
69 I1 Baker Island terr. Pacific Ocean
130 C3 Baker Island U.S.A.
131 J2 Baker Lake Canada
131 J2 Baker Lake l. Canada
132 E2 Baker's Dozen Islands Canada
140 C4 Bakersfield U.S.A.
98 C2 Bâ Kêv Cambodia
Bakhardok Turkm. see Bokurdak
85 F3 Bākharz mts Iran
88 B4 Bakhasar India
117 E6 Bakhchysaray Ukr.
Bakherden Turkm. see Baharly
117 E5 Bakhmach Ukr.
84 D4 Bakhtegan, Daryācheh-ye l. Iran
83 J3 Bakhty Kazakh.
80 B1 Bakırköy Turkey
122 D3 Bako Eth.
122 C3 Bakouma Centr. Afr. Rep.
122 B4 Bakoumba Gabon
117 G7 Baksan Rus. Fed.
81 L1 Baku Azer.
122 D3 Baku Dem. Rep. Congo
80 D2 Balâ Turkey
105 D5 Bala U.K.
154 E6 Bala, Cerros de mts Bol.
97 A4 Balabac Phil.
97 A5 Balabac i. Phil.
99 E1 Balabac Strait Malaysia/Phil.
81 J4 Balad Iraq
84 C2 Baladeh Iran
84 C2 Baladeh Iran
84 C4 Bālā Deh Iran
88 E5 Balaghat India
87 A2 Balaghat Range hills India
85 E4 Bālā Ḥowz Iran
81 K1 Balakän Azer.
116 G3 Balakhna Rus. Fed.
70 C5 Balaklava Australia
117 E6 Balaklava Ukr.
117 F5 Balakliya Ukr.
117 H4 Balakovo Rus. Fed.
105 D5 Bala Lake U.K.
99 E1 Balambangan i. Sabah Malaysia
85 F3 Bālā Morghāb Afgh.
88 B4 Balan India
117 H5 Balanda r. Rus. Fed.
80 B3 Balan Dağı h. Turkey
97 B3 Balanga Phil.
Balangir India see Bolangir
87 C5 Balangoda Sri Lanka
82 B2 Balashi Rus. Fed.
117 G5 Balashov Rus. Fed.
88 C5 Balasinor India
112 H7 Balaton, Lake Hungary
112 H7 Balatonboglár Hungary
112 H7 Balatonfüred Hungary
155 G4 Balbina, Represa de resr Brazil
107 E4 Balbriggan Rep. of Ireland
70 C3 Balcanoona Australia
159 E3 Balcarce Arg.
115 M3 Balchik Bulg.
72 B7 Balclutha N.Z.
143 F5 Bald Knob U.S.A.
141 E3 Bald Mountain U.S.A.
131 J3 Baldock Lake Canada
135 H3 Baldwin Canada
145 D6 Baldwin FL U.S.A.
134 E4 Baldwin MI U.S.A.
134 A3 Baldwin WI U.S.A.
147 E3 Baldwinsville U.S.A.
141 H5 Baldy Peak U.S.A.
Baleares, Islas is Spain see Balearic Islands
111 H3 Balearic Islands is Spain
99 D2 Baleh r. Sarawak Malaysia
158 E2 Baleia, Ponta da pt Brazil
122 D3 Bale Mountains National Park Eth.
97 B3 Baler Phil.
97 B3 Baler Bay Phil.
89 F5 Baleshwar India
103 I3 Balestrand Norway
114 C4 Balestrieri, Punta mt. Italy
72 B6 Balfour N.Z.
99 E4 Bali i. Indon.
99 E4 Bali, Laut sea Indon.
Balieborough Rep. of Ireland see Bailieborough
99 A2 Balige Indon.
87 C1 Baliguda India
92 F1 Balihan China
80 A2 Balıkesir Turkey
99 E3 Balikpapan Indon.
97 A5 Balimbing Phil.
87 C2 Balimila Reservoir India
68 E2 Balimo P.N.G.
112 D6 Balingen Germany
97 B2 Balintang Channel Phil.
106 E3 Balintore U.K.
Bali Sea sea Indon. see Bali, Laut
97 B5 Baliungan i. Phil.
83 G5 Baljuvon Tajik.
108 D2 Balk Neth.
82 C5 Balkanabat Turkm.
115 J3 Balkan Mountains Bulg./Serb. and Mont.
83 G1 Balkashino Kazakh.
85 G2 Balkhab r. Afgh.
83 H3 Balkhash Kazakh.
83 H3 Balkhash, Lake Kazakh.
82 A3 Balkuduk Kazakh.
106 C4 Ballachulish U.K.
68 C5 Balladonia Australia
71 H3 Balladoran Australia
107 C4 Ballaghaderreen Rep. of Ireland
70 F6 Ballan Australia
102 L1 Ballangen Norway
138 E2 Ballantine U.S.A.
106 D5 Ballantrae U.K.
70 E6 Ballarat Australia
68 C4 Ballard, Lake salt flat Australia
88 D6 Ballarpur India
106 E3 Ballater U.K.
120 B3 Ballé Mali
156 B3 Ballena, Punta pt Chile
73 B6 Balleny Islands is Antarctica
89 F4 Ballia India
71 J2 Ballina Australia
107 B3 Ballina Rep. of Ireland
107 C3 Ballinafad Rep. of Ireland
107 D4 Ballinalack Rep. of Ireland
107 D3 Ballinamore Rep. of Ireland
107 C4 Ballinasloe Rep. of Ireland
107 C4 Ballindine Rep. of Ireland
143 D6 Ballinger U.S.A.
106 E4 Ballinluig U.K.
107 B4 Ballinrobe Rep. of Ireland
147 G3 Ballston Spa U.S.A.
107 E3 Ballybay Rep. of Ireland
107 A6 Ballybrack Rep. of Ireland
107 B5 Ballybunnion Rep. of Ireland
107 E5 Ballycanew Rep. of Ireland
107 B3 Ballycastle Rep. of Ireland
107 E2 Ballycastle U.K.
107 F3 Ballyclare U.K.
107 A4 Ballyconneely Bay Rep. of Ireland
107 D3 Ballyconnell Rep. of Ireland
107 C4 Ballygar Rep. of Ireland
107 D3 Ballygawley U.K.
107 D2 Ballygorman Rep. of Ireland
107 C4 Ballyhaunis Rep. of Ireland
107 B5 Ballyheigue Rep. of Ireland
107 C5 Ballyhoura Mountains Rep. of Ireland
107 D2 Ballykelly U.K.
107 D5 Ballylynan Rep. of Ireland
107 D5 Ballymacmague Rep. of Ireland
107 D4 Ballymahon Rep. of Ireland
107 E3 Ballymena U.K.
107 E2 Ballymoney U.K.
107 C3 Ballymote Rep. of Ireland
107 F3 Ballynahinch U.K.
107 C3 Ballyshannon Rep. of Ireland
107 E5 Ballyteige Bay Rep. of Ireland
107 B4 Ballyvaughan Rep. of Ireland
107 E3 Ballyward U.K.
70 D6 Balmoral Australia
143 C6 Balmorhea U.S.A.
85 G4 Balochistan prov. Pak.
78 E4 Balochistan reg. Pak.
88 E5 Balod India
87 C1 Baloda Bazar India
71 H2 Balonne r. Australia
88 C4 Balotra India
83 I3 Balpyk Bi Kazakh.
89 E4 Balrampur India
70 E5 Balranald Australia
115 K2 Balş Romania
135 H2 Balsam Creek Canada
155 I5 Balsas Brazil
151 E4 Balsas Mex.
150 D4 Balsas r. Mex.
117 D6 Balta Ukr.
116 I3 Baltasi Rus. Fed.
106 □ Baltasound U.K.
117 C6 Bălţi Moldova
103 L5 Baltic Sea g. Europe
80 C6 Balṭīm Egypt
125 H1 Baltimore S. Africa
146 E5 Baltimore U.S.A.
107 E5 Baltinglass Rep. of Ireland
88 C2 Baltistan reg. Jammu and Kashmir
113 I3 Baltiysk Rus. Fed.
88 D2 Baltoro Glacier Pak.
85 E4 Baluch Ab well Iran
89 G4 Balurghat India
97 C5 Balut i. Phil.
109 F3 Balve Germany
103 N4 Balvi Latvia
115 L5 Balya Turkey
83 I4 Balykchy Kyrg.
82 B3 Balykshi Kazakh.
85 E2 Bām Iran
85 E4 Bam Iran
93 C5 Bama China
68 E3 Bamaga Australia
132 B3 Bamaji Lake Canada
120 B3 Bamako Mali
120 B3 Bamba Mali
97 B2 Bambang Phil.
122 C3 Bambari Centr. Afr. Rep.
98 A5 Bambel Indon.
109 I5 Bamberg Germany
145 D5 Bamberg U.S.A.
122 C3 Bambili Dem. Rep. Congo
125 G5 Bamboesberg mts S. Africa
122 C3 Bambouti Centr. Afr. Rep.
158 D3 Bambuí Brazil
81 L6 Bāmdezh Iran
120 D4 Bamenda Cameroon
Bami Turkm. see Bamy
85 G3 Bāmīān Afgh.
96 C2 Bamiancheng China
122 C3 Bamingui-Bangoran, Parc National du nat. park Centr. Afr. Rep.
85 F5 Bam Posht reg. Iran
85 F5 Bam Posht, Kūh-e mts Iran
105 D7 Bampton U.K.
85 F5 Bampūr Iran
85 E5 Bampūr watercourse Iran
85 F3 Bamrūd Iran
82 D5 Bamy Turkm.
69 G2 Banaba i. Kiribati
155 K5 Banabuiu, Açude resr Brazil
159 C3 Bañados del Atuel marsh Arg.
154 F7 Bañados del Izozog swamp Bol.
107 D4 Banagher Rep. of Ireland
122 C3 Banalia Dem. Rep. Congo
125 J1 Banamana, Lagoa l. Moz.
120 B3 Banamba Mali
93 C4 Banan China
155 H6 Bananal, Ilha do i. Brazil
87 D2 Banapur India
88 D4 Banas r. India
80 B2 Banaz Turkey
98 B1 Ban Ban Laos
Banbar China see Domartang
107 E3 Banbridge U.K.
98 B2 Ban Bua Yai Thai.
105 F5 Banbury U.K.
97 A4 Bancalan i. Phil.
70 D3 Bancannia Lake salt flat Australia
120 A2 Banc d'Arguin, Parc National du nat. park Mauritania
106 F3 Banchory U.K.
97 A5 Bancoran i. Phil.
135 I3 Bancroft Canada
85 E3 Band Iran
122 C3 Banda Dem. Rep. Congo
88 E4 Banda India
91 E7 Banda, Kepulauan is Indon.
91 F7 Banda, Laut sea Indon.
99 A1 Banda Aceh Indon.
71 J3 Banda Banda, Mount Australia
88 B2 Banda Daud Shah Pak.
98 A5 Bandahara, Gunung mt. Indon.
95 F6 Bandai-Asahi National Park Japan
85 F4 Bandān Iran
85 F4 Bandān Kūh mts Iran
89 H5 Bandarban Bangl.
84 E5 Bandar-e 'Abbās Iran
84 C2 Bandar-e Anzalī Iran
84 D5 Bandar-e Chārak Iran
84 C4 Bandar-e Deylam Iran
84 C4 Bandar-e Emām Khomeynī Iran
84 D5 Bandar-e Lengeh Iran
84 D5 Bandar-e Maqām Iran
84 C4 Bandar-e Ma'shur Iran
84 D5 Bandar-e Moghūyeh Iran
84 C4 Bandar-e Rīg Iran
84 D2 Bandar-e Torkeman Iran
99 C4 Bandar Lampung Indon.
88 D3 Bandarpunch mt. India
99 D1 Bandar Seri Begawan Brunei
Banda Sea Indon. see Banda, Laut
85 G3 Band-e Amīr, Daryā-ye r. Afgh.
158 B1 Bandeirante Brazil
158 E3 Bandeiras, Pico de mt. Brazil
125 H1 Bandelierkop S. Africa
150 C3 Banderas, Bahía de b. Mex.
84 D3 Band-e Sar Qom Iran
88 C4 Bandi r. Rajasthan India
88 C4 Bandi r. Rajasthan India
88 E6 Bandia r. India
120 B3 Bandiagara Mali
Band-i-Amir r. Afgh. see Band-e Amīr, Daryā-ye
Band-i-Baba mts Afgh. see Bābā, Band-e
85 E5 Bandīnī Iran
80 A1 Bandırma Turkey
Band-i-Turkestan mts Afgh. see Torkestān, Band-e
107 C6 Bandon Rep. of Ireland
107 C6 Bandon r. Rep. of Ireland
98 A3 Ban Don, Ao b. Thai.
81 L2 Bändovan Burnu pt Azer.
81 L6 Band Qīr Iran
122 B4 Bandundu Dem. Rep. Congo
99 C4 Bandung Indon.
84 B3 Bāneh Iran
149 I4 Banes Cuba
130 F4 Banff Canada
106 F3 Banff U.K.
130 F4 Banff National Park Canada
120 B3 Banfora Burkina
122 C4 Banga Dem. Rep. Congo
97 C5 Banga Phil.
97 C5 Bangai Point Phil.
87 B3 Bangalore India
88 D4 Banganga r. India
89 G5 Bangaon India
97 B2 Bangar Phil.
122 C3 Bangassou Centr. Afr. Rep.
89 E2 Bangdag Co salt l. China
98 C1 Bangfai, Xé r. Laos
68 C2 Banggai Indon.
91 E7 Banggai, Kepulauan is Indon.
99 E1 Banggi i. Sabah Malaysia
98 C1 Banghiang, Xé r. Laos
99 C3 Bangka i. Indon.
99 D4 Bangkalan Indon.
98 A5 Bangkaru i. Indon.
99 B3 Bangko Indon.
89 G3 Bangkog Co salt l. China
98 B2 Bangkok Thai. (City Plan 51)
98 B2 Bangkok, Bight of b. Thai.
89 G5 Bangladesh country Asia
98 D3 Ba Ngoi Vietnam
120 B4 Bangolo Côte d'Ivoire
88 D2 Bangong Co salt l. China
88 D2 Bangong Co l. India
107 F3 Bangor Northern Ireland U.K.
105 C4 Bangor Wales U.K.
147 I2 Bangor ME U.S.A.
134 D4 Bangor MI U.S.A.
147 F4 Bangor PA U.S.A.
107 B3 Bangor Erris Rep. of Ireland
141 F3 Bangs, Mount U.S.A.
98 A3 Bang Saphan Yai Thai.
102 J2 Bangsund Norway
97 B2 Bangued Phil.
122 B3 Bangui Centr. Afr. Rep.
97 B2 Bangui Phil.
98 A5 Bangunpurba Indon.
123 C5 Bangweulu, Lake Zambia
80 C6 Banhā Egypt
123 D6 Banhine, Parque Nacional de nat. park Moz.
98 B1 Ban Hin Heup Laos
122 C3 Bani Centr. Afr. Rep.
97 A2 Bani Phil.
122 B3 Bania Centr. Afr. Rep.
84 D5 Banī Forūr, Jazīreh-ye i. Iran
88 C2 Banihal Pass and Tunnel Jammu and Kashmir
146 D6 Banister r. U.S.A.
121 F2 Banī Suwayf Egypt
121 D1 Banī Walīd Libya
84 C5 Banī Wuṭayfān well Saudi Arabia
80 E4 Bāniyās Syria
80 E5 Bāniyās Syria
114 G2 Banja Luka Bos.-Herz.
88 D3 Banjar India
99 D3 Banjarmasin Indon.
120 A3 Banjul Gambia
81 L2 Bankä Azer.
89 F4 Banka India
87 A3 Bankapur India
120 B3 Bankass Mali
98 A2 Ban Khao Yoi Thai.
98 A3 Ban Khok Kloi Thai.
89 F5 Banki India
128 E4 Banks Island B.C. Canada
128 F2 Banks Island N.W.T. Canada
69 G3 Banks Islands Vanuatu
131 K2 Banks Lake Canada
138 C2 Banks Lake U.S.A.
72 D5 Banks Peninsula N.Z.
71 H8 Banks Strait Australia
89 F5 Bankura India
98 B1 Ban Mouang Laos
107 E5 Bann r. Rep. of Ireland
107 E3 Bann r. U.K.
98 C1 Ban Nakham Laos
98 A3 Ban Na San Thai.
134 C5 Banner U.S.A.
145 E7 Bannerman Town Bahamas
140 D5 Banning U.S.A.
159 B3 Baños Maule Chile
98 B1 Ban Pak-Leng Laos
98 C1 Ban Phaeng Thai.
98 B1 Ban Phai Thai.
Ban Phon Laos see Lamam
98 A2 Banphot Phisai Thai.
98 A2 Ban Pong Thai.
98 A3 Ban Sawi Thai.
89 E4 Bansi India
113 I6 Banská Bystrica Slovakia
85 F5 Bānsont Iran
98 A1 Ban Sut Ta Thai.
98 C2 Ban Suwan Wari Thai.
87 B2 Banswada India
88 C5 Banswara India
97 B4 Bantayan i. Phil.
107 C5 Banteer Rep. of Ireland
98 A3 Ban Tha Chang Thai.
98 A3 Ban Tha Kham Thai.
98 A1 Ban Tha Song Yang Thai.
98 B2 Ban Tha Tako Thai.
98 A1 Ban Tha Ton Thai.
98 B2 Ban Tha Tum Thai.
98 A2 Ban Thung Luang Thai.
97 B3 Banton i. Phil.
98 C1 Ban Tôp Laos
107 B6 Bantry Rep. of Ireland
107 B6 Bantry Bay Rep. of Ireland
87 A3 Bantval India
98 B1 Ban Woen Laos
99 A2 Banyak, Pulau-pulau is Indon.
120 D4 Banyo Cameroon
111 H1 Banyoles Spain
99 D4 Banyuwangi Indon.
162 J8 Banzare Seamount sea feature Indian Ocean
109 J1 Banzkow Germany
92 B3 Bao'an China
92 E1 Baochang China
92 E2 Baoding China
92 D3 Baofeng China
92 C3 Baoji China
93 C4 Baojing China
92 D4 Baokang Hubei China
96 B1 Baokang Nei Mongol China
93 B6 Bao Lac Vietnam
96 E1 Baolin China
96 B2 Baolizhen China
98 C3 Bao Lôc Vietnam
94 C1 Baoqing China
90 B4 Baoshan China
92 D1 Baotou China
93 B4 Baoxing China
92 F3 Baoying China
88 C4 Bap India
87 C3 Bapatla India
108 A4 Bapaume France
135 H3 Baptiste Lake Canada
89 H2 Baqên China
89 H3 Baqên China
93 E5 Baqiu China
81 J5 Ba'qūbah Iraq
Baquerizo Moreno Ecuador see Puerto Baquerizo Moreno
115 H3 Bar Serb. and Mont.
121 F3 Bara Sudan
122 E3 Baraawe Somalia
89 F4 Barabar Hills India
134 C4 Baraboo U.S.A.
134 B4 Baraboo r. U.S.A.
149 J4 Baracoa Cuba
159 E2 Baradero Arg.
71 H3 Baradine Australia
71 H3 Baradine r. Australia
134 C2 Baraga U.S.A.
157 C2 Baragua Venez.
149 J5 Barahona Dom. Rep.
89 H4 Barail Range mts India
89 H4 Barak r. India
121 F3 Baraka watercourse Eritrea/Sudan
111 E1 Barakaldo Spain
85 H3 Barakī Barak Afgh.
87 D1 Barakot India
88 D2 Bara Lacha Pass India
131 J3 Baralzon Lake Canada
87 A2 Baramati India
88 D4 Baran India
88 B4 Baran r. Pak.
85 F3 Bārān, Kūh-e mts Iran
116 C4 Baranavichy Belarus
77 R3 Baranikha Rus. Fed.
117 C5 Baranivka Ukr.
82 C3 Barankul Kazakh.
157 B2 Baranoa Col.
130 B3 Baranof Island U.S.A.
82 A1 Baranovka Rus. Fed.
158 A2 Barão de Melgaço Brazil
120 B3 Baraouéli Mali
108 D4 Baraque de Fraiture h. Belgium
91 E7 Barat Daya, Kepulauan is Indon.
70 C4 Baratta Australia
88 D3 Baraut India
157 B4 Baraya Col.
158 D3 Barbacena Brazil
157 A4 Barbacoas Col.
149 M6 Barbados country Caribbean Sea
111 G1 Barbastro Spain
111 D4 Barbate de Franco Spain
150 C2 Barbechitos Mex.
140 □1 Barbers Point U.S.A.
Barbers Pt U.S.A. see Barbers Point
125 I2 Barberton S. Africa
146 C4 Barberton U.S.A.
110 D4 Barbezieux-St-Hilaire France
157 B3 Barbosa Col.
131 K2 Barbour Bay Canada
146 B6 Barbourville U.S.A.
97 B4 Barboza Phil.
149 L5 Barbuda i. Antigua and Barbuda
109 J3 Barby (Elbe) Germany
68 E4 Barcaldine Australia
111 H2 Barcelona Spain (City Plan 60)
157 D2 Barcelona Venez.
154 F4 Barcelos Brazil
109 I4 Barchfeld Germany
120 B4 Barclayville Liberia
114 G2 Barcs Hungary
81 K1 Bärdä Azer.
102 C2 Bárðarbunga mt. Iceland
159 C2 Bardas Blancas Arg.
80 D6 Bardawīl, Sabkhat al lag. Egypt
89 F5 Barddhaman India
113 J6 Bardejov Slovakia
Bar Đôn Vietnam see Buôn Đôn
105 C5 Bardsey Island U.K.
84 E4 Bardsīr Iran
144 C4 Bardstown U.S.A.
146 B5 Bardwell U.S.A.
88 D3 Bareilly India
76 C2 Barentsburg Svalbard
76 D2 Barentsøya i. Svalbard
76 F2 Barents Sea Arctic Ocean
122 D2 Barentu Eritrea
88 E3 Barga China
87 C1 Bargarh India
88 D5 Bargi India
106 D5 Bargrennan U.K.
109 I1 Bargteheide Germany
89 G5 Barguna Bangl.
147 I2 Bar Harbor U.S.A.
114 G4 Bari Italy
98 C3 Ba Ria Vietnam
88 C3 Bari Doab lowland Pak.
89 E3 Barikot Nepal
157 E2 Barima r. Venez.
157 C2 Barinas Venez.
89 G5 Barisal Bangl.
99 B3 Barisan, Pegunungan mts Indon.
99 D3 Barito r. Indon.
154 F8 Baritú, Parque Nacional nat. park Arg.
85 E6 Barkā Oman
92 B4 Barkam China
84 C4 Barkan, Ra's-e pt Iran
103 N4 Barkava Latvia
130 E4 Barkerville Canada
144 C4 Barkley, Lake U.S.A.
130 D5 Barkley Sound inlet Canada
125 G5 Barkly East S. Africa
68 D3 Barkly Tableland reg. Australia
124 F4 Barkly West S. Africa
90 B2 Barkol China
88 D3 Barkot India
113 M7 Bârlad Romania
110 G2 Bar-le-Duc France
68 B4 Barlee, Lake salt flat Australia
114 G4 Barletta Italy
71 G5 Barmedman Australia
88 B4 Barmer India
70 D5 Barmera Australia
105 C5 Barmouth U.K.
88 C3 Barnala India
104 F3 Barnard Castle U.K.
71 F3 Barnato Australia
76 J4 Barnaul Rus. Fed.
147 F5 Barnegat U.S.A.
147 F5 Barnegat Bay U.S.A.
146 D4 Barnesboro U.S.A.
129 K2 Barnes Icecap Canada
108 D2 Barneveld Neth.
70 F4 Barneys Lake imp. l. Australia
141 G3 Barney Top mt. U.S.A.
143 C6 Barnhart U.S.A.
104 F4 Barnsley U.K.
105 C6 Barnstaple U.K.
105 C6 Barnstaple Bay U.K.
109 G2 Barnstorf Germany
145 D5 Barnwell U.S.A.
Baroda India see Vadodara
88 C1 Baroghil Pass Afgh.
89 H4 Barpathar India
89 G4 Barpeta India

Bosporus 171

89 E4 Bhairawa Nepal
89 F4 Bhaktapur Nepal
87 B2 Bhalki India
90 B4 Bhamo Myanmar
87 C2 Bhamragarh India
88 D4 Bhander India
89 F6 Bhanjanagar India
88 C4 Bhanpura India
88 D5 Bhanrer Range hills India
88 D4 Bharatpur India
89 H4 Bhareli r. India
85 F5 Bhari r. Pak.
88 C5 Bharuch India
87 C1 Bhatapara India
87 A3 Bhatkal India
89 G5 Bhatpara India
87 B4 Bhavani India
87 B4 Bhavani r. India
88 C5 Bhavnagar India
88 C3 Bhawana Pak.
87 C2 Bhawanipatna India
125 I3 Bhekuzulu S. Africa
89 E3 Bheri r. Nepal
88 C4 Bhilwara India
87 B2 Bhima r. India
87 C2 Bhimavaram India
88 D4 Bhind India
88 C4 Bhindar India
89 E4 Bhinga India
88 C4 Bhinmal India
88 D3 Bhiwani India
89 F4 Bhojpur Nepal
87 B2 Bhongir India
125 H5 Bhongweni S. Africa
88 D5 Bhopal India
87 C2 Bhopalpatnam India
87 A2 Bhor India
89 F5 Bhuban India
89 F5 Bhubaneshwar India
88 B5 Bhuj India
88 C5 Bhusawal India
89 G4 Bhutan country Asia
88 B4 Bhuttewala India
98 B1 Bia, Phou mt. Laos
84 E5 Bīabān mts Iran
88 C2 Biafo Glacier Pak.
91 F7 Biak Indon.
91 F7 Biak i. Indon.
113 K4 Biała Podlaska Poland
112 G4 Białogard Poland
113 K4 Białystok Poland
120 B4 Biankouma Côte d'Ivoire
96 B1 Bianzhao China
88 D5 Biaora India
84 D2 Biārjmand Iran
110 D5 Biarritz France
84 B5 Bi'ār Tabrāk well Saudi Arabia
112 D7 Biasca Switz.
94 G3 Bibai Japan
123 B5 Bibala Angola
71 H6 Bibbenluke Australia
114 D3 Bibbiena Italy
112 D6 Biberach an der Riß Germany
89 G4 Bibiyana r. Bangl.
109 G5 Biblis Germany
80 C2 Biçer Turkey
105 F6 Bicester U.K.
71 H8 Bicheno Australia
117 G7 Bichvint'a Georgia
68 D3 Bickerton Island Australia
105 D7 Bickleigh U.K.
141 G2 Bicknell U.S.A.
123 B5 Bicuari, Parque Nacional do nat. park Angola
87 A2 Bid India
120 C4 Bida Nigeria
97 A5 Bidadari, Tanjung pt Sabah Malaysia
84 D4 Bida Khabit Iran
87 B2 Bidar India
85 E6 Bidbid Oman
147 H3 Biddeford U.S.A.
108 D2 Biddinghuizen Neth.
106 C4 Bidean nam Bian mt. U.K.
105 C6 Bideford U.K.
Bideford Bay U.K. see Barnstaple Bay
113 K4 Biebrza r. Poland
109 G4 Biedenkopf Germany
112 C7 Biel Switz.
112 H5 Bielawa Poland
109 G2 Bielefeld Germany
114 C2 Biella Italy
113 I6 Bielsko-Biała Poland
113 K4 Bielsk Podlaski Poland
109 I1 Bienenbüttel Germany
98 C3 Biên Hoa Vietnam
132 F2 Bienville, Lac l. Canada
125 F3 Biesiesvlei S. Africa
109 H6 Bietigheim-Bissingen Germany
108 D5 Bièvre Belgium
122 B4 Bifoun Gabon
133 I3 Big r. Canada
140 A2 Big r. U.S.A.
117 C7 Biga Turkey
80 B2 Bigadiç Turkey
115 L5 Biga Yarımadası pen. Turkey
134 D2 Big Bay U.S.A.
134 D3 Big Bay de Noc U.S.A.
140 D4 Big Bear Lake U.S.A.
138 E2 Big Belt Mountains U.S.A.
125 I3 Big Bend Swaziland
143 C6 Big Bend National Park U.S.A.
143 F5 Big Black r. U.S.A.
105 D7 Bigbury-on-Sea U.K.
145 D7 Big Cypress National Preserve U.S.A.
134 C3 Big Eau Pleine Reservoir U.S.A.
131 K5 Big Falls U.S.A.
131 H4 Biggar Canada
106 E5 Biggar U.K.
130 B3 Bigger, Mount Canada
105 G5 Biggleswade U.K.
138 D2 Big Hole r. U.S.A.
138 F2 Bighorn r. U.S.A.
138 E2 Bighorn Canyon National Recreation Area park U.S.A.
138 F2 Bighorn Mountains U.S.A.
129 K3 Big Island Nunavut Canada
130 F2 Big Island N.W.T. Canada
147 J2 Big Lake U.S.A.
120 A3 Bignona Senegal
146 D6 Big Otter r. U.S.A.
140 C3 Big Pine U.S.A.
134 E4 Big Rapids U.S.A.
134 C3 Big Rib r. U.S.A.
131 H4 Big River Canada
134 D3 Big Sable Point U.S.A.
130 C2 Big Salmon r. Canada
131 J3 Big Sand Lake Canada
141 F4 Big Sandy watercourse U.S.A.
142 D2 Big Sioux r. U.S.A.
140 D2 Big Smokey Valley U.S.A.
143 C5 Big Spring U.S.A.
142 C3 Big Springs U.S.A.
146 B6 Big Stone Gap U.S.A.
140 B3 Big Sur U.S.A.
138 E2 Big Timber U.S.A.
132 C3 Big Trout Lake Canada
132 C3 Big Trout Lake l. Canada
141 G3 Big Water U.S.A.
135 H3 Bigwin Canada
114 F2 Bihać Bos.-Herz.
89 F4 Bihar state India
89 F4 Bihar Sharif India
113 K7 Bihor, Vârful mt. Romania
94 I3 Bihoro Japan
82 C3 Biikzhal Kazakh.
120 A3 Bijagós, Arquipélago dos is Guinea-Bissau
88 C4 Bijainagar India
87 A2 Bijapur India
84 B3 Bījār Iran
87 C2 Bijarpur India
115 H2 Bijeljina Bos.-Herz.
115 H3 Bijelo Polje Serb. and Mont.
93 B5 Bijie China
89 G4 Bijni India
88 D3 Bijnor India
88 B3 Bijnot Pak.
84 C5 Bijrān, Khashm h. Saudi Arabia
88 C3 Bikaner India
82 E3 Bikbauli Kazakh.
90 F2 Bikin Rus. Fed.
94 D1 Bikin r. Rus. Fed.
160 G5 Bikini atoll Marshall Is
122 B4 Bikoro Dem. Rep. Congo
92 B3 Bikou China
88 C4 Bilara India
87 C1 Bilaspur India
81 L2 Biläsuvar Azer.
117 D5 Bila Tserkva Ukr.
98 A2 Bilauktaung Range mts Myanmar/Thai.
111 E1 Bilbao Spain
80 C6 Bilbays Egypt
115 H3 Bileća Bos.-Herz.
80 B1 Bilecik Turkey
113 K5 Biłgoraj Poland
122 D4 Bilharamulo Tanz.
117 D6 Bilhorod-Dnistrovs'kyy Ukr.
122 C3 Bili Dem. Rep. Congo
77 R3 Bilibino Rus. Fed.
97 C4 Biliran i. Phil.
96 B4 Biliu He r. China
138 F3 Bill U.S.A.
105 H6 Billericay U.K.
163 J2 Billingford U.K.
104 F3 Billingham U.K.
138 E2 Billings U.S.A.
105 E7 Bill of Portland hd U.K.
141 F4 Bill Williams r. U.S.A.
141 F4 Bill Williams Mountain U.S.A.
121 D3 Bilma Niger
68 F4 Biloela Australia
117 E6 Bilohirs'k Ukr.
113 M5 Bilohir"ya Ukr.
87 B2 Biloli India
117 F5 Biloluts'k Ukr.
117 E5 Bilopillya Ukr.
117 F5 Bilovods'k Ukr.
145 B6 Biloxi U.S.A.
68 D4 Bilpa Morea Claypan salt flat Australia
106 E5 Bilston U.K.
121 E3 Biltine Chad
98 A1 Bilugyun Island Myanmar
150 I5 Bilwascarma Nicaragua
116 I4 Bilyarsk Rus. Fed.
117 D6 Bilyayivka Ukr.
108 D4 Bilzen Belgium
71 H5 Bimberi, Mount Australia
122 B3 Bimbo C.A.R.
145 E7 Bimini Islands Bahamas
81 L3 Bināb Iran
88 D4 Bina-Etawa India
91 E7 Binaija, Gunung mt. Indon.
80 F2 Binboğa Daği mt. Turkey
71 G1 Bindebango Australia
88 E4 Bindki India
71 H1 Bindle Australia
123 B4 Bindu Dem. Rep. Congo
123 D5 Bindura Zimbabwe
111 G2 Binefar Spain
71 I2 Bingara N.S.W. Australia
71 F2 Bingara Qld Australia
92 B2 Bingcaowan China
109 F5 Bingen am Rhein Germany
120 B4 Bingerville Côte d'Ivoire
147 I2 Bingham U.S.A.
147 F3 Binghamton U.S.A.
81 H2 Bingöl Turkey
81 H2 Bingol Dağı mt. Turkey
93 C6 Binh Gia Vietnam
Binh Sơn Vietnam see Châu Ô
89 H4 Bini India
87 C1 Binika India
98 A5 Binjai Indon.
84 D5 Bin Mūrkhan well U.A.E.
71 H3 Binnaway Australia
98 C5 Bintan i. Indon.
97 B3 Bintuan Phil.
99 B3 Bintuhan Indon.
99 D2 Bintulu Sarawak Malaysia
92 C3 Binxian China
71 G5 Binya Australia
93 C6 Binyang China
92 F2 Binzhou China
159 B3 Bíobío admin. reg. Chile
159 B3 Bíobío r. Chile
120 C4 Bioco i. Equat. Guinea
114 F3 Biograd na Moru Croatia
114 G3 Biokovo mts Croatia
85 F5 Bīrag, Kūh-e mts Iran
81 H5 Bi'r al Mulūsi Iraq
116 F2 Birandozero Rus. Fed.
122 C2 Birao Centr. Afr. Rep.
80 D6 Bi'r ar Rummānah Egypt
89 F4 Biratnagar Nepal
81 G3 Bi'r Buṭaymān Syria
130 G3 Birch r. Canada
131 H4 Birch Hills Canada
70 E5 Birchip Australia
130 F4 Birch Island Canada
132 B3 Birch Lake Canada
134 B2 Birch Lake U.S.A.
130 G3 Birch Mountains Canada
131 I4 Birch River Canada
Birdaard Neth. see Burdaard
73 C1 Bird Island i. S. Georgia
141 G2 Birdseye U.S.A.
68 D4 Birdsville Australia
80 F3 Birecik Turkey
121 E3 Bir en Natrûn well Sudan
99 A1 Bireun Indon.
84 B6 Bi'r Ghawdah well Saudi Arabia
122 D2 Birhan mt. Eth.
158 B3 Birigüi Brazil
85 E3 Bīrjand Iran
81 J6 Birkát Hamad well Iraq
108 F5 Birkenfeld Germany
105 D4 Birkenhead U.K.
81 J3 Bīrkim Iraq
114 F7 Birkirkara Malta
83 H3 Birlik Kazakh.
83 H4 Birlik Kazakh.
105 F5 Birmingham U.K.
145 C5 Birmingham U.S.A.
120 A2 Bîr Mogreïn Mauritania
80 B6 Bi'r Nāḥid oasis Egypt
120 C3 Birnin-Kebbi Nigeria
120 C3 Birnin Konni Niger
90 F2 Birobidzhan Rus. Fed.
107 D4 Birr Rep. of Ireland
71 G2 Birrie r. Australia
81 I5 Bi'r Sābil Iraq
106 E1 Birsay U.K.
105 F5 Birstall U.K.
109 H4 Birstein Germany
80 E7 Bi'r Tābah Egypt
131 I4 Birtle Canada
89 H3 Biru China
87 A3 Birur India
103 N4 Biržai Lith.
141 H6 Bisbee U.S.A.
110 B4 Biscay, Bay of sea France/Spain
163 I3 Biscay Abyssal Plain sea feature N. Atlantic Ocean
145 D7 Biscayne National Park U.S.A.
112 F7 Bischofshofen Austria
73 B2 Biscoe Islands is Antarctica
135 F2 Biscotasi Lake Canada
135 F2 Biscotasing Canada
93 C4 Bishan China
81 L5 Bīsheh Iran
83 H4 Bishkek Kyrg.
89 F5 Bishnupur India
125 G6 Bisho S. Africa
140 C3 Bishop U.S.A.
104 F3 Bishop Auckland U.K.
105 H6 Bishop's Stortford U.K.
81 G4 Bishrī, Jabal hills Syria
90 E1 Bishui China
120 C1 Biskra Alg.
97 C4 Bislig Phil.
142 C2 Bismarck U.S.A.
68 E2 Bismarck Archipelago is P.N.G.
68 E2 Bismarck Range mts P.N.G.
68 E2 Bismarck Sea P.N.G.
109 J2 Bismark (Altmark) Germany
81 H3 Bismil Turkey
103 J3 Bismo Norway
81 K4 Bīsotūn Iran
102 L3 Bispgården Sweden
109 I1 Bispingen Germany
111 G4 Bissa, Djebel mt. Alg.
87 C2 Bissamcuttak India
120 A3 Bissau Guinea-Bissau
120 D4 Bissaula Nigeria
131 J4 Bissett Canada
130 F3 Bistcho Lake Canada
113 L7 Bistriţa Romania
113 M7 Bistriţa r. Romania
108 E5 Bitburg Germany
108 F5 Bitche France
82 B2 Bitik Kazakh.
121 D3 Bitkine Chad
81 I2 Bitlis Turkey
115 I4 Bitola Macedonia
114 G4 Bitonto Italy
84 B6 Bitrān, Jabal h. Saudi Arabia
141 H2 Bitter Creek r. U.S.A.
109 K3 Bitterfeld Germany
124 C5 Bitterfontein S. Africa
80 D6 Bitter Lakes Egypt
138 D2 Bitterroot Range mts U.S.A.
109 J2 Bittkau Germany
117 G5 Bityug r. Rus. Fed.
121 D3 Biu Nigeria
95 D7 Biwa-ko l. Japan
83 K1 Biya r. Rus. Fed.
92 D3 Biyang China
122 E2 Bīye K'obē Eth.
83 K1 Biysk Rus. Fed.
125 H5 Bizana S. Africa
120 C1 Bizerte Tunisia
85 E5 Bīzhanābād Iran
102 A2 Bjargtangar hd Iceland
102 L3 Bjästa Sweden
114 G2 Bjelovar Croatia
102 L1 Bjerkvik Norway
103 J4 Bjerringbro Denmark
103 L3 Björklinge Sweden
103 J3 Bjorli Norway
102 L3 Björna Sweden
76 C2 Bjørnøya i. Svalbard
102 L3 Bjurholm Sweden
120 B3 Bla Mali
106 B3 Bla Bheinn h. U.K.
143 F5 Black r. AR U.S.A.
141 H5 Black r. AZ U.S.A.
135 F4 Black r. MI U.S.A.
134 B3 Black r. WI U.S.A.
68 E4 Blackall Australia
134 C1 Black Bay Canada
132 B3 Blackbear r. Canada
105 F6 Black Bourton U.K.
104 E4 Blackburn U.K.
71 J1 Blackbutt Australia
140 A2 Black Butte mt. U.S.A.
140 A2 Black Butte Lake U.S.A.
141 E4 Black Canyon gorge U.S.A.
141 F4 Black Canyon City U.S.A.
142 E2 Blackduck U.S.A.
130 G4 Blackfalds Canada
138 D3 Blackfoot U.S.A.
138 D2 Black Foot r. U.S.A.
112 D6 Black Forest mts Germany
142 C2 Black Hills U.S.A.
106 D3 Black Isle pen. U.K.
131 H3 Black Lake Canada
131 H3 Black Lake l. Canada
135 E3 Black Lake l. U.S.A.
141 G3 Black Mesa ridge U.S.A.
105 D6 Black Mountain hills U.K.
140 D4 Black Mountain U.S.A.
105 D6 Black Mountains U.K.
141 E4 Black Mountains U.S.A.
124 C1 Black Nossob watercourse Namibia
93 □ Black Point Hong Kong China
104 D4 Blackpool U.K.
93 B6 Black River r. Vietnam
134 B3 Black River Falls U.S.A.
138 C3 Black Rock Desert U.S.A.
146 C6 Blacksburg U.S.A.
117 E7 Black Sea Asia/Europe
107 A3 Blacksod Bay Rep. of Ireland
107 E5 Blackstairs Mountain h. Rep. of Ireland
107 E5 Blackstairs Mountains Rep. of Ireland
146 E6 Blackstone U.S.A.
71 I3 Black Sugarloaf mt. Australia
133 I3 Black Tickle Canada
120 B4 Black Volta r. Africa
107 E5 Blackwater Rep. of Ireland
107 D5 Blackwater r. Rep. of Ireland
107 E4 Blackwater r. Rep. of Ireland
107 E3 Blackwater r. Rep. of Ireland/U.K.
105 H6 Blackwater r. U.K.
146 E6 Blackwater r. U.S.A.
130 E2 Blackwater Lake Canada
106 D4 Blackwater Reservoir U.K.
143 D4 Blackwell U.S.A.
68 B5 Blackwood r. Australia
105 D6 Blaenavon U.K.
83 J3 Blagodarnoye Kazakh.
117 G6 Blagodarnyy Rus. Fed.
115 J3 Blagoevgrad Bulg.
83 I1 Blagoveshchenka Rus. Fed.
90 E1 Blagoveshchensk Rus. Fed.
146 E4 Blain U.S.A.
138 B1 Blaine U.S.A.
131 H4 Blaine Lake Canada
142 D3 Blair NE U.S.A.
134 B3 Blair WI U.S.A.
106 E4 Blair Atholl U.K.
106 E4 Blairgowrie U.K.
145 C6 Blakely U.S.A.
105 I5 Blakeney U.K.
134 C1 Blake Point U.S.A.
99 D4 Blambangan, Semenanjung pen. Indon.
110 H4 Blanc, Mont mt. France/Italy
159 E3 Blanca, Bahía b. Arg.
159 C3 Blanca de la Totora, Sierra hills Arg.
139 F4 Blanca Peak U.S.A.
70 C2 Blanche, Lake salt flat Australia
146 B5 Blanchester U.S.A.
70 C5 Blanchetown Australia
159 C1 Blanco r. Arg.
154 F6 Blanco r. Bol.
150 H6 Blanco, Cabo c. Costa Rica
138 A3 Blanco, Cape U.S.A.
133 I3 Blanc-Sablon Canada
71 G4 Bland r. Australia
102 B2 Blanda r. Iceland
105 E7 Blandford Forum U.K.
141 H3 Blanding U.S.A.
111 H2 Blanes Spain
134 E2 Blaney Park U.S.A.
98 □ Blangah, Telok Sing.
98 A5 Blangkejeren Indon.
108 B3 Blankenberge Belgium
108 E4 Blankenheim Germany
157 D2 Blanquilla, Isla i. Venez.
112 H6 Blansko Czech Rep.
123 D5 Blantyre Malawi
107 C6 Blarney Rep. of Ireland
109 H5 Blaufelden Germany
102 L2 Blåviksjön Sweden
71 H4 Blayney Australia
109 I1 Bleckede Germany
72 D4 Blenheim N.Z.
105 F6 Blenheim Palace tourist site U.K.
108 E3 Blerick Neth.
107 E4 Blessington Lakes Rep. of Ireland
105 G5 Bletchley U.K.
120 C1 Blida Alg.
108 F5 Blies r. Germany
69 H3 Bligh Water b. Fiji
135 F2 Blind River Canada
70 C3 Blinman Australia
138 D3 Bliss U.S.A.
135 F5 Blissfield U.S.A.
147 H4 Block Island U.S.A.
147 H4 Block Island Sound sea chan. U.S.A.
125 G4 Bloemfontein S. Africa
125 F3 Bloemhof S. Africa
125 F3 Bloemhof Dam S. Africa
109 H3 Blomberg Germany
102 B2 Blönduós Iceland
147 E5 Bloodsworth Island U.S.A.
131 J4 Bloodvein r. Canada
107 C2 Bloody Foreland pt Rep. of Ireland
135 I4 Bloomfield Canada
134 A5 Bloomfield IA U.S.A.
144 C4 Bloomfield IN U.S.A.
139 E4 Bloomfield NM U.S.A.
134 C5 Bloomington IL U.S.A.
144 C4 Bloomington IN U.S.A.
142 E2 Bloomington MN U.S.A.
147 E4 Bloomsburg U.S.A.
146 E4 Blossburg U.S.A.
129 P3 Blosseville Kyst coastal area Greenland
125 H1 Blouberg S. Africa
105 F5 Bloxham U.K.
141 H5 Blue watercourse U.S.A.
141 G1 Bluebell U.S.A.
141 G2 Blue Bell Knoll mt. U.S.A.
142 E3 Blue Earth U.S.A.
146 C6 Bluefield U.S.A.
150 I5 Bluefields Nicaragua
147 I2 Blue Hill U.S.A.
135 H5 Blue Knob h. U.S.A.
89 H5 Blue Mountain mt. India
141 H1 Blue Mountain U.S.A.
147 F3 Blue Mountain Lake U.S.A.
125 G4 Blue Mountain Pass Lesotho
71 I4 Blue Mountains Australia
138 C2 Blue Mountains U.S.A.
71 I4 Blue Mountains National Park Australia
121 F3 Blue Nile r. Sudan alt. Ābay Wenz (Ethiopia), alt. Azraq, Bahr el (Sudan)
128 G3 Bluenose Lake Canada
145 C5 Blue Ridge U.S.A.
146 D6 Blue Ridge mts U.S.A.
130 F4 Blue River Canada
140 D2 Blue Springs U.S.A.
107 C3 Blue Stack h. Rep. of Ireland
107 C3 Blue Stack Mountains Rep. of Ireland
146 C6 Bluestone Lake U.S.A.
72 B7 Bluff N.Z.
141 H3 Bluff U.S.A.
93 □ Bluff Island Hong Kong China
134 E5 Bluffton IN U.S.A.
146 B4 Bluffton OH U.S.A.
156 G3 Blumenau Brazil
142 C2 Blunt U.S.A.
138 B3 Bly U.S.A.
70 C4 Blyth Australia
104 F2 Blyth England U.K.
105 F4 Blyth England U.K.
141 E5 Blythe U.S.A.
143 F5 Blytheville U.S.A.
103 J4 Bø Norway
120 A4 Bo Sierra Leone
97 B3 Boac Phil.
150 H5 Boaco Nicaragua
155 J5 Boa Esperança, Açude resr Brazil
92 D3 Bo'ai China
93 C6 Bo'ai China
122 B3 Boali Centr. Afr. Rep.
125 J3 Boane Moz.
146 C4 Boardman U.S.A.
125 F1 Boatlaname Botswana
71 G1 Boatman Australia
155 K5 Boa Viagem Brazil
157 E4 Boa Vista Brazil
120 □ Boa Vista i. Cape Verde
71 G4 Bobadah Australia
93 D6 Bobai China
123 E5 Bobaomby, Tanjona c. Madag.
87 C2 Bobbili India
120 B3 Bobo-Dioulasso Burkina
123 C6 Bobonong Botswana
83 G4 Boboyob, Gora mt. Uzbek.
117 G5 Bobrov Rus. Fed.
117 D5 Bobrovytsya Ukr.
117 E5 Bobrynets' Ukr.
123 E6 Boby mt. Madag.
157 D2 Boca del Pao Venez.
149 L7 Boca de Macareo Venez.
154 E5 Boca do Acre Brazil
155 H4 Boca do Jari Brazil
157 E2 Boca Grande r. mouth Venez.
158 D2 Bocaiúva Brazil
157 C2 Bocanó r. Venez.
122 B3 Bocaranga Centr. Afr. Rep.
145 D7 Boca Raton U.S.A.
150 I6 Bocas del Toro Panama
113 J6 Bochnia Poland
108 E3 Bocholt Germany
108 F3 Bochum Germany
125 H1 Bochum S. Africa
109 I2 Bockenem Germany
157 C2 Boconó Venez.
150 C2 Bocoyna Mex.
122 B3 Boda Centr. Afr. Rep.
71 I6 Bodalla Australia
90 D1 Bodaybo Rus. Fed.
143 E5 Bodcau Reservoir U.S.A.
106 G3 Boddam U.K.
109 J3 Bode r. Germany
140 A2 Bodega Head U.S.A.
121 D3 Bodélé reg. Chad
102 M2 Boden Sweden
105 E5 Bodenham U.K.
Bodensee l. Germany/Switz. see Constance, Lake
109 I2 Bodenteich Germany
109 H3 Bodenwerder Germany
87 B2 Bodhan India
89 F4 Bodh Gaya India
87 B4 Bodinayakkanur India
105 C7 Bodmin U.K.
105 C7 Bodmin Moor moorland U.K.
102 K2 Bodø Norway
115 L6 Bodrum Turkey
115 L6 Bodrum-Milas airport Turkey
108 C3 Boechout Belgium
122 C4 Boende Dem. Rep. Congo
120 A3 Boffa Guinea
89 H3 Boga India
143 F6 Bogalusa U.S.A.
71 G3 Bogan r. Australia
120 B3 Bogandé Burkina
71 G4 Bogan Gate Australia
116 I3 Bogatye Saby Rus. Fed.
80 E2 Boğazlıyan Turkey
89 F3 Bogcang Zangbo r. China
82 C1 Bogdanovka Rus. Fed.
90 A2 Bogda Shan mts China
83 H1 Bogembay Kazakh.
71 I2 Boggabilla Australia
71 I3 Boggabri Australia
107 B5 Boggeragh Mountains Rep. of Ireland
111 H5 Boghar Alg.
105 G7 Bognor Regis U.K.
97 C4 Bogo Phil.
83 G1 Bogodukhovka Kazakh.
107 D4 Bog of Allen reg. Rep. of Ireland
116 E4 Bogolyubovo Rus. Fed.
71 G6 Bogong, Mount Australia
94 D2 Bogopol' Rus. Fed.
99 C4 Bogor Indon.
116 G3 Bogorodsk Rus. Fed.
116 I3 Bogorodskoye Rus. Fed.
157 B3 Bogotá Col.
90 A1 Bogotol Rus. Fed.
89 G4 Bogra Bangl.
77 K4 Boguchany Rus. Fed.
117 G5 Boguchar Rus. Fed.
120 A3 Bogué Mauritania
92 F2 Bo Hai g. China
96 A4 Bohai Haixia sea chan. China
110 F2 Bohain-en-Vermandois France
92 E2 Bohai Wan b. China
109 K3 Böhlen Germany
125 H4 Bohlokong S. Africa
109 K5 Böhmer Wald mts Germany
109 G2 Bohmte Germany
117 E5 Bohodukhiv Ukr.
97 C4 Bohol i. Phil.
97 C4 Bohol Sea Phil.
97 B4 Bohol Strait Phil.
79 G2 Bohu China
117 D5 Bohuslav Ukr.
158 D4 Boi, Ponta do pt Brazil
147 F4 Boiceville U.S.A.
124 E4 Boichoko S. Africa
125 G3 Boikhutso S. Africa
155 G4 Boim Brazil
89 H5 Boinu r. Myanmar
158 E1 Boipeba, Ilha i. Brazil
158 C2 Bois r. Brazil
128 F3 Bois, Lac des l. Canada
135 E3 Bois Blanc Island U.S.A.
138 C3 Boise U.S.A.
143 C4 Boise City U.S.A.
131 I5 Boissevain Canada
125 F3 Boitumelong S. Africa
109 I1 Boizenburg Germany
97 B2 Bojeador, Cape Phil.
84 E2 Bojnūrd Iran
89 H4 Bokajan India
82 E4 Bo'kantov tog'lari hills Uzbek.
89 F5 Bokaro India
122 B4 Bokatola Dem. Rep. Congo
120 A3 Boké Guinea
83 J2 Boke Kazakh.
122 C4 Bokele Dem. Rep. Congo
71 G2 Bokhara r. Australia
103 I4 Boknafjorden sea chan. Norway
83 I4 Bökönbaev Kyrg.
121 D3 Bokoro Chad
117 G5 Bokovskaya Rus. Fed.
116 E3 Boksitogorsk Rus. Fed.
124 D3 Bokspits Botswana
82 D5 Bokurdak Turkm.
122 C4 Bolaiti Dem. Rep. Congo
120 A3 Bolama Guinea-Bissau
88 A3 Bolan r. Pak.
87 C1 Bolangir India
88 A3 Bolan Pass Pak.
110 E2 Bolbec France
84 C4 Boldajī Iran
109 L1 Boldekow Germany
82 D4 Boldumsaz Turkm.
83 J3 Bole China
120 B4 Bole Ghana
122 B4 Boleko Dem. Rep. Congo
120 B3 Bolgatanga Ghana
117 D6 Bolhrad Ukr.
94 B2 Boli China
122 B4 Bolia Dem. Rep. Congo
102 M2 Boliden Sweden
97 A2 Bolinao Phil.
115 K2 Bolintin-Vale Romania
157 A3 Bolívar Col.
154 C5 Bolívar Peru
143 E4 Bolivar MO U.S.A.
145 B5 Bolivar TN U.S.A.
157 C2 Bolívar, Pico mt. Venez.
154 E7 Bolivia country S. America
80 E3 Bolkar Dağları mts Turkey
116 F4 Bolkhov Rus. Fed.
135 F1 Bolkow Canada
110 G4 Bollène France
103 L3 Bollnäs Sweden
71 G2 Bollon Australia
102 L3 Bollstabruk Sweden
103 K4 Bolmen l. Sweden
117 H7 Bolnisi Georgia
122 B4 Bolobo Dem. Rep. Congo
97 B5 Bolod Islands Phil.
114 D2 Bologna Italy
113 O2 Bologovo Rus. Fed.
116 E3 Bologoye Rus. Fed.
125 F4 Bolokanang S. Africa
122 B3 Bolomba Dem. Rep. Congo
151 G3 Bolonchén de Rejón Mex.
97 B5 Bolong Phil.
76 J4 Bolotnoye Rus. Fed.
98 C2 Bolovens, Phouphieng plat. Laos
89 F5 Bolpur India
114 D3 Bolsena, Lago di l. Italy
113 J3 Bol'shakovo Rus. Fed.
82 B1 Bol'shaya Chernigovka Rus. Fed.
82 F1 Bol'shaya Churakovka Kazakh.
82 B1 Bol'shaya Glushitsa Rus. Fed.
102 P2 Bol'shaya Imandra, Ozero l. Rus. Fed.
82 B1 Bol'shaya Kinel' r. Rus. Fed.
117 G6 Bol'shaya Martinovka Rus. Fed.
83 I2 Bol'shaya Vladimirovka Kazakh.
83 H1 Bol'shegrivskoye Rus. Fed.
83 K2 Bol'shenarymskoye Kazakh.
77 L2 Bol'shevik, Ostrov i. Rus. Fed.
82 D3 Bol'shiye Barsuki, Peski des. Kazakh.
116 H2 Bol'shiye Chirki Rus. Fed.
82 B3 Bol'shiye Peshnyye, Ostrova is Kazakh.
83 I4 Bol'shoy Aksu Kazakh.
77 R3 Bol'shoy Aluy r. Rus. Fed.
83 J2 Bol'shoy Bukon' Kazakh.
82 D2 Bol'shoy Ik r. Rus. Fed.
82 B2 Bol'shoy Irgiz r. Rus. Fed.
94 C3 Bol'shoy Kamen' Rus. Fed.
Bol'shoy Kavkaz mts Asia/Europe see Caucasus
117 I5 Bol'shoy Uzen' r. Rus. Fed.
108 D1 Bolsward Neth.
104 E4 Bolton U.K.
146 B6 Bolton U.S.A.
80 C1 Bolu Turkey
102 B1 Bolungarvík Iceland
93 E6 Boluo China
80 C2 Bolvadin Turkey
114 D1 Bolzano Italy
122 B4 Boma Dem. Rep. Congo
71 I5 Bomaderry Australia
71 H6 Bombala Australia
Bombay India see Mumbai
91 F7 Bomberai, Semenanjung pen. Indon.
154 E5 Bom Comércio Brazil
158 D2 Bom Despacho Brazil
89 H4 Bomdila India
89 H3 Bomi China
158 D1 Bom Jesus da Lapa Brazil
158 E3 Bom Jesus do Itabapoana Brazil
103 I4 Bømlo i. Norway
121 D1 Bon, Cap c. Tunisia
84 B2 Bonāb Iran
146 E6 Bon Air U.S.A.
149 K6 Bonaire i. Neth. Antilles
150 H5 Bonanza Nicaragua
68 C3 Bonaparte Archipelago is Australia
106 D3 Bonar Bridge U.K.
133 J4 Bonavista Canada
133 J4 Bonavista Bay Canada
70 A3 Bon Bon Australia
106 F5 Bonchester Bridge U.K.
122 C3 Bondo Dem. Rep. Congo
97 B3 Bondoc Peninsula Phil.
120 B4 Bondoukou Côte d'Ivoire
91 E7 Bone, Teluk b. Indon.
134 A3 Bone Lake U.S.A.
109 F3 Bönen Germany
91 E7 Bonerate, Kepulauan is Indon.
106 E4 Bo'ness U.K.
158 D2 Bonfinópolis de Minas Brazil
122 D3 Bonga Eth.
97 B3 Bongabong Phil.
89 G4 Bongaigaon India
122 C3 Bongandanga Dem. Rep. Congo
124 H3 Bongani S. Africa
97 A5 Bongao Phil.
89 G3 Bong Co l. China
97 C5 Bongo i. Phil.
122 C3 Bongo, Massif des mts Centr. Afr. Rep.
123 E5 Bongolava mts Madag.
121 D3 Bongor Chad
120 B4 Bongouanou Côte d'Ivoire
98 D2 Bông Sơn Vietnam
108 C3 Bonheiden Belgium
114 C4 Bonifacio Corsica France
114 C4 Bonifacio, Strait of France/Italy
90 G4 Bonin Islands Japan
158 A3 Bonito Brazil
108 F4 Bonn Germany
102 K2 Bonnåsjøen Norway
138 C1 Bonners Ferry U.S.A.
110 H3 Bonneville France
70 D6 Bonney, Lake Australia
68 B5 Bonnie Rock Australia
106 E5 Bonnyrigg U.K.
131 G4 Bonnyville Canada
97 A4 Bonobono Phil.
Bonom Mhai mt. Vietnam see S'Lung, B'Nom
114 C4 Bonorva Sardinia Italy
71 I2 Bonshaw Australia
124 D7 Bontebok National Park S. Africa
120 A4 Bonthe Sierra Leone
97 B2 Bontoc Phil.
99 E4 Bontosunggu Indon.
125 F6 Bontrug S. Africa
125 G1 Bonwapitse Botswana
141 H2 Book Cliffs ridge U.S.A.
70 E4 Boolaboolka Lake imp. l. Australia
70 C4 Booleroo Centre Australia
107 D5 Booley Hills Rep. of Ireland
70 F4 Booligal Australia
71 H2 Boomi Australia
71 J1 Boonah Australia
142 E3 Boone IA U.S.A.
145 D4 Boone NC U.S.A.
146 B6 Boone Lake U.S.A.
146 B6 Booneville KY U.S.A.
143 F5 Booneville MS U.S.A.
140 A2 Boonville CA U.S.A.
144 C4 Boonville IN U.S.A.
142 E4 Boonville MO U.S.A.
147 F3 Boonville NY U.S.A.
70 F5 Booroorban Australia
71 H5 Boorowa Australia
70 E6 Boort Australia
122 E2 Boosaaso Somalia
147 I3 Boothbay Harbor U.S.A.
129 I2 Boothia, Gulf of Canada
129 I2 Boothia Peninsula Canada
105 E4 Bootle U.K.
120 A4 Bopolu Liberia
108 F4 Boppard Germany
159 G1 Boqueirão Brazil
150 D1 Boquillas del Carmen Mex.
109 K5 Bor Czech Rep.
115 J2 Bor Serb. and Mont.
121 F4 Bor Sudan
80 E3 Bor Turkey
123 F5 Boraha, Nosy i. Madag.
138 D2 Borah Peak U.S.A.
98 B2 Boraphet, Bung l. Thai.
103 K4 Borås Sweden
84 C4 Borāzjān Iran
155 G4 Borba Brazil
155 K5 Borborema, Planalto da plat. Brazil
109 G3 Borchen Germany
81 H1 Borçka Turkey
70 B5 Borda, Cape Australia
80 B3 Bor Dağı mt. Turkey
110 D4 Bordeaux France
Borden Canada see Borden-Carleton
133 H4 Borden-Carleton Canada
128 G2 Borden Island Canada
129 J2 Borden Peninsula Canada
70 D6 Bordertown Australia
102 B2 Borðeyri Iceland
111 I4 Bordj Bou Arréridj Alg.
111 G5 Bordj Bounaama Alg.
120 C2 Bordj Omer Driss Alg.
102 □ Borðoy i. Faroe Is
83 H4 Bordu Kyrg.
106 A3 Boreray i. U.K.
102 D2 Borgarfjörður Iceland
102 B2 Borgarnes Iceland
102 K2 Børgefjell Nasjonalpark nat. park Norway
143 C5 Borger U.S.A.
103 L4 Borgholm Sweden
114 B2 Borgo San Dalmazzo Italy
114 D3 Borgo San Lorenzo Italy
114 C2 Borgosesia Italy
108 B4 Borinage reg. Belgium
117 G5 Borisoglebsk Rus. Fed.
117 F5 Borisovka Rus. Fed.
116 F3 Borisovo-Sudskoye Rus. Fed.
117 G7 Borjomi Georgia
108 E3 Borken Germany
102 L1 Borkenes Norway
108 E1 Borkum Germany
108 E1 Borkum i. Germany
103 K3 Borlänge Sweden
80 B2 Borlu Turkey
109 K3 Borna Germany
108 D1 Borndiep sea chan. Neth.
108 E2 Borne Neth.
99 D2 Borneo i. Asia
103 K5 Bornholm i. Denmark
115 L5 Bornova Turkey
97 B4 Borocay i. Phil.
76 J3 Borodino Rus. Fed.
103 O3 Borodinskoye Rus. Fed.
117 D5 Borodyanka Ukr.
77 O3 Borogontsy Rus. Fed.
83 J3 Borohoro Shan mts China
116 F3 Borok Rus. Fed.
120 B3 Boromo Burkina
97 C4 Borongan Phil.
104 F3 Boroughbridge U.K.
116 E3 Borovichi Rus. Fed.
83 K1 Borovlyanka Rus. Fed.
116 I3 Borovoy Kirovskaya Oblast' Rus. Fed.
116 E1 Borovoy Respublika Kareliya Rus. Fed.
116 J2 Borovoy Respublika Komi Rus. Fed.
82 F1 Borovskoy Kazakh.
107 C5 Borrisokane Rep. of Ireland
68 D3 Borroloola Australia
102 J3 Børsa Norway
113 L7 Borşa Romania
82 D4 Borsakelmas sho'rxogi salt marsh Uzbek.
117 C5 Borshchiv Ukr.
90 C2 Borshchovochnyy Khrebet mts Rus. Fed.
83 J3 Bortala He r. China
84 C4 Borūjen Iran
84 C3 Borūjerd Iran
106 B3 Borve U.K.
117 B5 Boryslav Ukr.
117 D5 Boryspil' Ukr.
117 E5 Borzna Ukr.
90 D1 Borzya Rus. Fed.
83 H3 Bosaga Kazakh.
114 G2 Bosanska Dubica Bos.-Herz.
114 G2 Bosanska Gradiška Bos.-Herz.
114 G2 Bosanska Krupa Bos.-Herz.
114 G2 Bosanski Novi Bos.-Herz.
114 G2 Bosansko Grahovo Bos.-Herz.
134 B4 Boscobel U.S.A.
93 C6 Bose China
125 F4 Boshof S. Africa
82 E1 Boskol' Kazakh.
114 G2 Bosnia-Herzegovina country Europe
122 B3 Bosobolo Dem. Rep. Congo
95 G7 Bōsō-hantō pen. Japan
80 B1 Bosporus str. Turkey

172 Bossangoa

122 B3 **Bossangoa** Centr. Afr. Rep.
122 B3 **Bossembélé** Centr. Afr. Rep.
143 E5 **Bossier City** U.S.A.
124 B2 **Bossiesvlei** Namibia
89 F1 **Bostan** China
81 K6 **Bostān** Iran
82 B2 **Bostandyk** Kazakh.
90 A2 **Bosten Hu** *l.* China
105 G5 **Boston** U.K.
147 H3 **Boston** U.S.A.
70 A5 **Boston Bay** Australia
135 H1 **Boston Creek** Canada
147 H3 **Boston-Logan** *airport* U.S.A.
143 E5 **Boston Mountains** U.S.A.
104 F4 **Boston Spa** U.K.
134 D5 **Boswell** U.S.A.
88 B5 **Botad** India
71 I4 **Botany Bay** Australia
102 L3 **Boteå** Sweden
115 K3 **Botev** *mt.* Bulg.
115 J3 **Botevgrad** Bulg.
125 G3 **Bothaville** S. Africa
102 L3 **Bothnia, Gulf of** Fin./Sweden
71 G9 **Bothwell** Australia
117 H5 **Botkul', Ozero** *l.* Kazakh./Rus. Fed.
113 M7 **Botoşani** Romania
92 E2 **Botou** China
Bô Trach Vietnam *see* **Hoan Lao**
125 G4 **Botshabelo** S. Africa
123 C6 **Botswana** *country* Africa
114 G5 **Botte Donato, Monte** *mt.* Italy
102 M2 **Bottenviken** *g.* Fin./Sweden
104 G4 **Bottesford** U.K.
142 C1 **Bottineau** U.S.A.
108 E3 **Bottrop** Germany
158 C3 **Botucatu** Brazil
158 D1 **Botuporã** Brazil
133 J4 **Botwood** Canada
120 B4 **Bouaflé** Côte d'Ivoire
120 B4 **Bouaké** Côte d'Ivoire
122 B3 **Bouar** Centr. Afr. Rep.
120 B1 **Bouârfa** Morocco
121 D4 **Bouba Ndjida, Parc National de** *nat. park* Cameroon
122 B3 **Bouca** Centr. Afr. Rep.
108 B4 **Bouchain** France
147 G2 **Boucherville** Canada
135 J2 **Bouchette** Canada
133 H4 **Bouctouche** Canada
69 F2 **Bougainville Island** P.N.G.
120 B3 **Bougouni** Mali
108 D5 **Bouillon** Belgium
111 H4 **Bouira** Alg.
120 A2 **Boujdour** W. Sahara
138 F3 **Boulder** *CO* U.S.A.
138 D2 **Boulder** *MT* U.S.A.
141 G3 **Boulder** *UT* U.S.A.
141 E3 **Boulder Canyon** *gorge* U.S.A.
141 E4 **Boulder City** U.S.A.
140 D5 **Boulevard** U.S.A.
159 E3 **Boulevard Atlántico** Arg.
68 D4 **Boulia** Australia
110 F2 **Boulogne-Billancourt** France
110 E1 **Boulogne-sur-Mer** France
120 B3 **Boulsa** Burkina
122 B4 **Boumango** Gabon
121 D4 **Boumba** *r.* Cameroon
111 H4 **Boumerdes** Alg.
120 B4 **Bouna** Côte d'Ivoire
147 H2 **Boundary Mountains** U.S.A.
140 C3 **Boundary Peak** U.S.A.
120 B4 **Boundiali** Côte d'Ivoire
122 B4 **Boundji** Congo
Boung *r.* Vietnam *see* **Thu Bôn, Sông**
93 A6 **Boun Nua** Laos
138 E3 **Bountiful** U.S.A.
69 H6 **Bounty Islands** N.Z.
160 G9 **Bounty Trough** *sea feature* S. Pacific Ocean
120 B3 **Bourem** Mali
110 E4 **Bourganeuf** France
110 G3 **Bourg-en-Bresse** France
110 F3 **Bourges** France
147 F2 **Bourget** Canada
135 J1 **Bourgmont** Canada
Bourgogne *reg.* France *see* **Burgundy**
71 F3 **Bourke** Australia
135 G1 **Bourkes** Canada
105 G5 **Bourne** U.K.
105 F7 **Bournemouth** U.K.
108 F2 **Bourtanger Moor** *reg.* Germany
120 C1 **Bou Saâda** Alg.
114 C6 **Bou Salem** Tunisia
141 E5 **Bouse** U.S.A.
141 E5 **Bouse Wash** *watercourse* U.S.A.
121 D3 **Bousso** Chad
108 B4 **Boussu** Belgium
120 A3 **Boutilimit** Mauritania
163 J9 **Bouvetøya** *terr.* Atlantic Ocean
108 C5 **Bouy** France
109 H3 **Bovenden** Germany
Boven Kapuas, Pegunungan *mts* Malaysia *see* **Kapuas Hulu, Pegunungan**
159 E1 **Bovril** Arg.
131 G4 **Bow** *r.* Canada
142 C1 **Bowbells** U.S.A.
68 E4 **Bowen** Australia
134 B5 **Bowen** U.S.A.
71 H6 **Bowen, Mount** Australia
71 I1 **Bowenville** Australia
160 G2 **Bowers Ridge** *sea feature* Bering Sea
141 H5 **Bowie** *AZ* U.S.A.
143 D5 **Bowie** *TX* U.S.A.
131 G5 **Bow Island** Canada
84 B2 **Bowkan** Iran
144 C4 **Bowling Green** *KY* U.S.A.
142 F4 **Bowling Green** *MO* U.S.A.
146 B4 **Bowling Green** *OH* U.S.A.
146 E5 **Bowling Green** *VA* U.S.A.
142 C2 **Bowman** U.S.A.
130 E4 **Bowman, Mount** Canada
73 D6 **Bowman Island** *i.* Antarctica
135 H4 **Bowmanville** Canada
106 B5 **Bowmore** U.K.
71 I5 **Bowral** Australia
71 J3 **Bowraville** Australia
130 E4 **Bowron** *r.* Canada
130 E4 **Bowron Lake Provincial Park** Canada
109 H5 **Boxberg** Germany
92 F2 **Boxing** China
108 D3 **Boxtel** Neth.
80 E1 **Boyabat** Turkey
115 J3 **Boyana** *tourist site* Bulg.
93 E4 **Boyang** China
71 J3 **Boyd** *r.* Australia
131 I2 **Boyd Lake** Canada
130 G4 **Boyle** Canada
107 C4 **Boyle** Rep. of Ireland
107 E4 **Boyne** *r.* Rep. of Ireland
85 G2 **Boyni Qara** Afgh.
145 D7 **Boynton Beach** U.S.A.
138 E3 **Boysen Reservoir** U.S.A.
83 F5 **Boysun** Uzbek.
154 F8 **Boyuibe** Bol.
81 J1 **Böyük Hinaldağ** *mt.* Azer.
83 J2 **Bozanbay** Kazakh.
115 L5 **Bozcaada** *i.* Turkey
115 L5 **Bozdağ** *mt.* Turkey
80 A2 **Boz Dağları** *mts* Turkey
80 B3 **Bozdoğan** Turkey
105 G5 **Bozeat** U.K.
138 E2 **Bozeman** U.S.A.
92 E3 **Bozhou** China
80 D3 **Bozkır** Turkey
122 B3 **Bozoum** Centr. Afr. Rep.
80 G3 **Bozova** Turkey
84 B2 **Bozqūsh, Kūh-e** *mts* Iran
83 H2 **Bozshakol'** Kazakh.
83 F2 **Boztumsyk** Kazakh.
80 C2 **Bozüyük** Turkey
114 B2 **Bra** Italy
114 G3 **Brač** *i.* Croatia
106 B3 **Bracadale** U.K.
106 B3 **Bracadale, Loch** *b.* U.K.
114 E3 **Bracciano, Lago di** *l.* Italy
135 H3 **Bracebridge** Canada
102 K3 **Bräcke** Sweden
109 H5 **Brackenheim** Germany
105 G6 **Bracknell** U.K.
114 G4 **Bradano** *r.* Italy
145 D7 **Bradenton** U.S.A.
135 H3 **Bradford** Canada
104 F4 **Bradford** U.K.
146 A4 **Bradford** *OH* U.S.A.
146 D4 **Bradford** *PA* U.S.A.
147 G3 **Bradford** *VT* U.S.A.
143 D6 **Brady** U.S.A.
130 B3 **Brady Glacier** U.S.A.
106 □ **Brae** U.K.
70 C4 **Braemar** Australia
106 E3 **Braemar** U.K.
111 B2 **Braga** Port.
159 E2 **Bragado** Arg.
155 I4 **Bragança** Brazil
111 C2 **Bragança** Port.
158 C3 **Bragança Paulista** Brazil
117 D5 **Brahin** Belarus
109 I1 **Brahlstorf** Germany
89 G5 **Brahmanbaria** Bangl.
87 D1 **Brahmani** *r.* India
87 D2 **Brahmapur** India
89 G4 **Brahmaputra** *r.* Asia *alt.* **Dihang (India),** *alt.* **Yarlung Zangbo (China)**
115 L2 **Brăila** Romania
108 B5 **Braine** France
108 C4 **Braine-le-Comte** Belgium
142 E2 **Brainerd** U.S.A.
105 H6 **Braintree** U.K.
125 H1 **Brak** *r.* S. Africa
109 G1 **Brake (Unterweser)** Germany
108 B4 **Brakel** Belgium
109 H3 **Brakel** Germany
123 B6 **Brakwater** Namibia
130 E4 **Bralorne** Canada
103 J5 **Bramming** Denmark
103 L3 **Brämön** *i.* Sweden
135 H4 **Brampton** Canada
104 E3 **Brampton** *England* U.K.
105 I5 **Brampton** *England* U.K.
109 G2 **Bramsche** Germany
105 H5 **Brancaster** U.K.
133 J4 **Branch** Canada
157 E4 **Branco** *r.* Brazil
103 J3 **Brandbu** Norway
103 J5 **Brande** Denmark
109 K2 **Brandenburg** Germany
109 K2 **Brandenburg** *land* Germany
125 G4 **Brandfort** S. Africa
109 L3 **Brandis** Germany
131 J5 **Brandon** Canada
105 H5 **Brandon** U.K.
142 D3 **Brandon** *SD* U.S.A.
147 G3 **Brandon** *VT* U.S.A.
107 A5 **Brandon Head** Rep. of Ireland
107 E5 **Brandon Hill** Rep. of Ireland
107 A5 **Brandon Mountain** Rep. of Ireland
124 D5 **Brandvlei** S. Africa
145 D6 **Branford** U.S.A.
113 I3 **Braniewo** Poland
73 B2 **Bransfield Strait** *str.* Antarctica
135 G4 **Brantford** Canada
70 D6 **Branxholme** Australia
133 H4 **Bras d'Or Lake** Canada
158 E2 **Brasil, Planalto do** *plat.* Brazil
154 E6 **Brasiléia** Brazil
158 C1 **Brasília** Brazil
158 D2 **Brasília de Minas** Brazil
155 G4 **Brasília Legal** Brazil
113 M3 **Braslaw** Belarus
115 K2 **Braşov** Romania
97 A5 **Brassey, Banjaran** *mts Sabah* Malaysia
147 I2 **Brassua Lake** U.S.A.
112 H6 **Bratislava** Slovakia
90 C1 **Bratsk** Rus. Fed.
90 C1 **Bratskoye Vodokhranilishche** *resr* Rus. Fed.
147 G3 **Brattleboro** U.S.A.
112 F6 **Braunau am Inn** Austria
109 G4 **Braunfels** Germany
109 I3 **Braunlage** Germany
109 J3 **Braunsbedra** Germany
109 I2 **Braunschweig** Germany
120 □ **Brava** *i.* Cape Verde
103 L4 **Bråviken** *inlet* Sweden
151 E2 **Bravo del Norte, Río** *r.* Mex./U.S.A. *alt.* **Rio Grande**
141 E5 **Brawley** U.S.A.
107 E4 **Bray** Rep. of Ireland
130 F4 **Brazeau** *r.* Canada
155 H6 **Brazil** *country* S. America
163 H7 **Brazil Basin** *sea feature* S. Atlantic Ocean
143 D5 **Brazos** *r.* U.S.A.
122 B4 **Brazzaville** Congo
115 H2 **Brčko** Bos.-Herz.
72 A6 **Breaksea Sound** *inlet* N.Z.
72 E1 **Bream Bay** N.Z.
72 E1 **Bream Head** N.Z.
105 C6 **Brechfa** U.K.
106 F4 **Brechin** U.K.
108 C3 **Brecht** Belgium
142 D2 **Breckenridge** *MN* U.S.A.
143 D5 **Breckenridge** *TX* U.S.A.
112 H6 **Břeclav** Czech Rep.
105 D6 **Brecon** U.K.
105 D6 **Brecon Beacons** *reg.* U.K.
105 D6 **Brecon Beacons National Park** U.K.
108 C3 **Breda** Neth.
124 D7 **Bredasdorp** S. Africa
71 H5 **Bredbo** Australia
109 K2 **Breddin** Germany
108 E3 **Bredevoort** Neth.
102 K2 **Bredviken** Norway
82 E1 **Bredy** Rus. Fed.
108 D3 **Bree** Belgium
146 D5 **Breezewood** U.S.A.
112 D7 **Bregenz** Austria
102 A2 **Breiðafjörður** *b.* Iceland
102 D2 **Breiðdalsvík** Iceland
109 G4 **Breidenbach** Germany
112 C6 **Breisach am Rhein** Germany
109 I1 **Breitenfelde** Germany
109 I5 **Breitengüßbach** Germany
102 M1 **Breivikbotn** Norway
155 I6 **Brejinho de Nazaré** Brazil
102 J3 **Brekstad** Norway
109 G1 **Bremen** Germany
145 C5 **Bremen** *GA* U.S.A.
134 D5 **Bremen** *IN* U.S.A.
109 G1 **Bremerhaven** Germany
138 B2 **Bremerton** U.S.A.
109 H1 **Bremervörde** Germany
108 F4 **Bremm** Germany
143 D6 **Brenham** U.S.A.
102 K2 **Brenna** Norway
112 E7 **Brenner Pass** Austria/Italy
135 H2 **Brent** Canada
114 D2 **Brenta** *r.* Italy
105 H6 **Brentwood** U.K.
140 B3 **Brentwood** *CA* U.S.A.
147 G4 **Brentwood** *NY* U.S.A.
114 D2 **Brescia** Italy
114 D1 **Bressanone** Italy
106 □ **Bressay** *i.* U.K.
110 D3 **Bressuire** France
117 B4 **Brest** Belarus
110 B2 **Brest** France
Bretagne *reg.* France *see* **Brittany**
108 A5 **Breteuil** France
143 F6 **Breton Sound** *b.* U.S.A.
72 E1 **Brett, Cape** N.Z.
109 G5 **Bretten** Germany
105 G5 **Bretton** U.K.
145 D5 **Brevard** U.S.A.
155 H4 **Breves** Brazil
134 E2 **Brevort** U.S.A.
71 G2 **Brewarrina** Australia
147 I2 **Brewer** U.S.A.
138 C1 **Brewster** U.S.A.
143 G6 **Brewton** U.S.A.
125 H3 **Breyten** S. Africa
113 I6 **Brezno** Slovakia
114 G2 **Brezovo Polje** *plain* Croatia
122 C3 **Bria** Centr. Afr. Rep.
110 H4 **Briançon** France
71 G5 **Bribbaree** Australia
71 J1 **Bribie Island** Australia
117 C5 **Briceni** Moldova
110 H4 **Bric Froid** *mt.* France/Italy
107 C5 **Bride** *r.* Rep. of Ireland
141 G1 **Bridgeland** U.S.A.
105 D6 **Bridgend** U.K.
106 D4 **Bridge of Orchy** U.K.
140 C2 **Bridgeport** *CA* U.S.A.
147 G4 **Bridgeport** *CT* U.S.A.
142 C3 **Bridgeport** *NE* U.S.A.
138 E2 **Bridger** U.S.A.
138 F3 **Bridger Peak** U.S.A.
147 F5 **Bridgeton** U.S.A.
149 M6 **Bridgetown** Barbados
71 G9 **Bridgewater** Australia
133 H5 **Bridgewater** Canada
147 J1 **Bridgewater** U.S.A.
70 D7 **Bridgewater, Cape** Australia
105 E5 **Bridgnorth** U.K.
147 H2 **Bridgton** U.S.A.
105 D6 **Bridgwater** U.K.
105 D6 **Bridgwater Bay** U.K.
104 G3 **Bridlington** U.K.
104 G3 **Bridlington Bay** U.K.
71 G8 **Bridport** Australia
105 E7 **Bridport** U.K.
112 C7 **Brig** Switz.
104 G4 **Brigg** U.K.
138 D3 **Brigham City** U.S.A.
71 G6 **Bright** Australia
105 I6 **Brightlingsea** U.K.
135 I3 **Brighton** Canada
72 C6 **Brighton** N.Z.
105 G7 **Brighton** U.K.
147 H3 **Brighton** U.S.A.
135 F4 **Brighton** U.S.A.
110 H5 **Brignoles** France
120 A3 **Brikama** Gambia
109 G3 **Brilon** Germany
114 G4 **Brindisi** Italy
159 D1 **Brinkmann** Arg.
70 C4 **Brinkworth** Australia
133 H4 **Brion, Île** *i.* Canada
110 F4 **Brioude** France
133 F3 **Brisay** Canada
71 J1 **Brisbane** Australia
147 J1 **Bristol** Canada
105 E6 **Bristol** U.K.
147 G4 **Bristol** *CT* U.S.A.
147 F4 **Bristol** *PA* U.S.A.
146 B6 **Bristol** *TN* U.S.A.
128 B4 **Bristol Bay** U.S.A.
105 C6 **Bristol Channel** *est.* U.K.
153 G7 **Bristol Island** S. Sandwich Is
141 E4 **Bristol Lake** U.S.A.
141 E4 **Bristol Mountains** U.S.A.
73 D3 **British Antarctic Territory** *reg.* Antarctica
130 D3 **British Columbia** *prov.* Canada
129 J1 **British Empire Range** *mts* Canada
74 C7 **British Indian Ocean Territory** *terr.* Indian Ocean
163 J6 **British Isles** N. Atlantic Ocean
125 G2 **Brits** S. Africa
124 E5 **Britstown** S. Africa
110 C2 **Brittany** *reg.* France
110 E4 **Brive-la-Gaillarde** France
111 E1 **Briviesca** Spain
105 D7 **Brixham** U.K.
Brlik Kazakh. *see* **Birlik**
112 H6 **Brno** Czech Rep.
145 D5 **Broad** *r.* U.S.A.
147 F3 **Broadalbin** U.S.A.
132 E3 **Broadback** *r.* Canada
70 F6 **Broadford** Australia
107 C5 **Broadford** Rep. of Ireland
106 C3 **Broadford** U.K.
106 E5 **Broad Law** *h.* U.K.
105 I6 **Broadstairs** U.K.
138 F2 **Broadus** U.S.A.
131 I4 **Broadview** Canada
71 J2 **Broadwater** Australia
142 C3 **Broadwater** U.S.A.
72 D1 **Broadwood** N.Z.
103 M4 **Broceni** Latvia
131 I3 **Brochet** Canada
131 I3 **Brochet, Lac** *l.* Canada
109 I3 **Brocken** *mt.* Germany
128 G2 **Brock Island** Canada
146 E3 **Brockport** U.S.A.
147 H3 **Brockton** U.S.A.
135 J3 **Brockville** Canada
135 F4 **Brockway** *MI* U.S.A.
146 D4 **Brockway** *PA* U.S.A.
129 J2 **Brodeur Peninsula** Canada
134 C4 **Brodhead** U.S.A.
106 C5 **Brodick** U.K.
113 I4 **Brodnica** Poland
117 C5 **Brody** Ukr.
143 E4 **Broken Arrow** U.S.A.
71 I4 **Broken Bay** Australia
142 D3 **Broken Bow** *NE* U.S.A.
143 E5 **Broken Bow** *OK* U.S.A.
70 D3 **Broken Hill** Australia
162 K7 **Broken Plateau** *sea feature* Indian Ocean
109 I2 **Brome** Germany
105 G6 **Bromley** U.K.
105 E5 **Bromsgrove** U.K.
103 J4 **Brønderslev** Denmark
125 H2 **Bronkhorstspruit** S. Africa
102 K2 **Brønnøysund** Norway
145 E5 **Bronson** U.S.A.
105 I5 **Brooke** U.K.
97 A4 **Brooke's Point** Phil.
134 C4 **Brookfield** U.S.A.
143 F6 **Brookhaven** U.S.A.
138 A3 **Brookings** *OR* U.S.A.
142 D2 **Brookings** *SD* U.S.A.
147 H3 **Brookline** U.S.A.
134 A5 **Brooklyn** *IA* U.S.A.
134 B5 **Brooklyn** *IL* U.S.A.
142 E2 **Brooklyn Center** U.S.A.
146 D6 **Brookneal** U.S.A.
131 G4 **Brooks** Canada
140 A2 **Brooks** *CA* U.S.A.
147 I2 **Brooks** *ME* U.S.A.
73 C3 **Brooks, Cape** *c.* Antarctica
128 D3 **Brooks Range** *mts* U.S.A.
145 D6 **Brooksville** U.S.A.
146 D4 **Brookville** U.S.A.
106 C3 **Broom, Loch** *inlet* U.K.
68 C3 **Broome** Australia
106 E2 **Brora** U.K.
103 K5 **Brösarp** Sweden
107 D4 **Brosna** *r.* Rep. of Ireland
138 B3 **Brothers** U.S.A.
93 □ **Brothers, The** *is* Hong Kong China
104 E3 **Brough** U.K.
106 E1 **Brough Head** U.K.
107 E3 **Broughshane** U.K.
70 C4 **Broughton** *r.* Australia
Broughton Island Canada *see* **Qikiqtarjuaq**
71 J4 **Broughton Islands** Australia
113 O5 **Brovary** Ukr.
103 J4 **Brovst** Denmark
70 C4 **Brown, Mount** *h.* Australia
143 C5 **Brownfield** U.S.A.
138 D1 **Browning** U.S.A.
134 D5 **Brownsburg** U.S.A.
147 F5 **Browns Mills** U.S.A.
145 B5 **Brownsville** *TN* U.S.A.
143 D7 **Brownsville** *TX* U.S.A.
147 I2 **Brownville** U.S.A.
147 I2 **Brownville Junction** U.S.A.
143 D6 **Brownwood** U.S.A.
113 N4 **Brozha** Belarus
110 F1 **Bruay-la-Bussière** France
134 C2 **Bruce Crossing** U.S.A.
132 D4 **Bruce Peninsula** Canada
135 G3 **Bruce Peninsula National Park** Canada
109 G5 **Bruchsal** Germany
109 K2 **Brück** Germany
112 G7 **Bruck an der Mur** Austria
105 E6 **Brue** *r.* U.K.
Bruges Belgium *see* **Brugge**
108 B3 **Brugge** Belgium
109 G5 **Brühl** Germany
108 E4 **Brühl** Germany
141 G2 **Bruin Point** *mt.* U.S.A.
89 I3 **Bruint** India
124 C3 **Brukkaros** Namibia
134 B2 **Brule** U.S.A.
133 H3 **Brûlé, Lac** *l.* Canada
108 C5 **Brûly** Belgium
158 E1 **Brumado** Brazil
103 J3 **Brumunddal** Norway
107 E4 **Brú Na Bóinne** *tourist site* Rep. of Ireland
109 J2 **Brunau** Germany
138 D3 **Bruneau** U.S.A.
138 D3 **Bruneau** *r.* U.S.A.
99 D2 **Brunei** *country* Asia
102 K3 **Brunflo** Sweden
114 D1 **Brunico** Italy
72 C5 **Brunner, Lake** N.Z.
131 H4 **Bruno** Canada
112 D4 **Brunsbüttel** Germany
108 D4 **Brunssum** Neth.
145 D6 **Brunswick** *GA* U.S.A.
147 I3 **Brunswick** *ME* U.S.A.
146 C4 **Brunswick** *OH* U.S.A.
156 B8 **Brunswick, Península de** *pen.* Chile
71 J2 **Brunswick Heads** Australia
112 H6 **Bruntál** Czech Rep.
73 C3 **Brunt Ice Shelf** *ice feature* Antarctica
125 I4 **Bruntville** S. Africa
71 G9 **Bruny Island** Australia
138 G3 **Brush** U.S.A.
108 C4 **Brussels** Belgium (City Plan **55**)
135 G4 **Brussels** Canada
134 D3 **Brussels** U.S.A.
113 N5 **Brusyliv** Ukr.
71 G6 **Bruthen** Australia
Bruxelles Belgium *see* **Brussels**
146 A4 **Bryan** *OH* U.S.A.
143 D6 **Bryan** *TX* U.S.A.
70 C4 **Bryan, Mount** *h.* Australia
116 E4 **Bryansk** Rus. Fed.
116 E4 **Bryanskaya Oblast'** *admin. div.* Rus. Fed.
117 H6 **Bryanskoye** Rus. Fed.
141 F3 **Bryce Canyon National Park** U.S.A.
141 H5 **Bryce Mountain** U.S.A.
103 I4 **Bryne** Norway
117 F6 **Bryukhovetskaya** Rus. Fed.
112 H5 **Brzeg** Poland
69 F2 **Buala** Solomon Is
120 A3 **Buba** Guinea-Bissau
81 L7 **Būbiyān Island** Kuwait
97 B5 **Bubuan** *i.* Phil.
80 C3 **Bucak** Turkey
157 B3 **Bucaramanga** Col.
97 C4 **Bucas Grande** *i.* Phil.
70 A5 **Buchanan** Australia
120 A4 **Buchanan** Liberia
134 D5 **Buchanan** *MI* U.S.A.
146 D6 **Buchanan** *VA* U.S.A.
143 D6 **Buchanan, Lake** U.S.A.
129 K2 **Buchan Gulf** Canada
133 I4 **Buchans** Canada
115 L2 **Bucharest** Romania
109 I1 **Büchen** Germany
109 H5 **Buchen (Odenwald)** Germany
109 K1 **Buchholz** Germany
109 H1 **Buchholz in der Nordheide** Germany
140 B4 **Buchon, Point** U.S.A.
113 L7 **Bucin, Pasul** *pass* Romania
71 F3 **Buckambool Mountain** *h.* Australia
109 H2 **Bückeburg** Germany
109 H2 **Bücken** Germany
141 G5 **Buckeye** U.S.A.
146 B5 **Buckeye Lake** U.S.A.
146 C5 **Buckhannon** U.S.A.
146 C5 **Buckhannon** *r.* U.S.A.
106 E4 **Buckhaven** U.K.
135 H3 **Buckhorn** Canada
141 H5 **Buckhorn** U.S.A.
135 H3 **Buckhorn Lake** Canada
146 B6 **Buckhorn Lake** U.S.A.
106 F3 **Buckie** U.K.
135 J3 **Buckingham** Canada
105 G5 **Buckingham** U.K.
146 D6 **Buckingham** U.S.A.
68 D3 **Buckingham Bay** Australia
68 E4 **Buckland Tableland** *reg.* Australia
70 B4 **Buckleboo** Australia
73 B6 **Buckle Island** *i.* Antarctica
141 F4 **Buckskin Mountains** U.S.A.
140 D2 **Bucks Mountain** U.S.A.
147 I2 **Bucksport** U.S.A.
109 K2 **Bückwitz** Germany
București Romania *see* **Bucharest**
146 B4 **Bucyrus** U.S.A.
113 O4 **Buda-Kashalyova** Belarus
113 I7 **Budapest** Hungary
88 D3 **Budaun** India
70 F3 **Budda** Australia
106 F4 **Buddon Ness** *pt* U.K.
114 C4 **Buddusò** *Sardinia* Italy
105 C7 **Bude** U.K.
143 F6 **Bude** U.S.A.
117 H6 **Budennovsk** Rus. Fed.
71 J1 **Buderim** Australia
109 H4 **Büdingen** Germany
88 D5 **Budni** India
116 E3 **Budogoshch'** Rus. Fed.
89 H2 **Budongquan** China
114 C4 **Budoni** *Sardinia* Italy
84 C6 **Budū', Sabkhat al** *salt pan* Saudi Arabia
120 C4 **Buea** Cameroon
140 B4 **Buellton** U.S.A.
159 D2 **Buena Esperanza** Arg.
157 A4 **Buenaventura** Col.
148 C3 **Buenaventura** Mex.
157 A4 **Buenaventura, Bahía de** *b.* Col.
139 F4 **Buena Vista** *CO* U.S.A.
146 D6 **Buena Vista** *VA* U.S.A.
111 E2 **Buendía, Embalse de** *resr* Spain
159 B4 **Bueno** *r.* Chile
159 E2 **Buenos Aires** Arg. (City Plan **64**)
159 E3 **Buenos Aires** *prov.* Arg.
156 B7 **Buenos Aires, Lago** *l.* Arg./Chile
156 C7 **Buen Pasto** Arg.
150 C2 **Búfalo** Mex.
130 G3 **Buffalo** *r.* Canada
143 E4 **Buffalo** *MO* U.S.A.
146 D3 **Buffalo** *NY* U.S.A.
143 D4 **Buffalo** *OK* U.S.A.
142 C2 **Buffalo** *SD* U.S.A.
143 D6 **Buffalo** *TX* U.S.A.
134 B3 **Buffalo** *WI* U.S.A.
138 F2 **Buffalo** *WY* U.S.A.
134 B3 **Buffalo** *r.* U.S.A.
71 G6 **Buffalo, Mount** *h.* Australia
130 F3 **Buffalo Head Hills** Canada
130 F2 **Buffalo Lake** Canada
131 H3 **Buffalo Narrows** Canada
124 B4 **Buffels** *watercourse* S. Africa
125 G1 **Buffels Drift** S. Africa
145 D5 **Buford** U.S.A.
115 K2 **Buftea** Romania
113 J4 **Bug** *r.* Poland
157 A4 **Buga** Col.
157 A3 **Bugalagrande** Col.
71 H3 **Bugaldie** Australia
Bugdaýly Turkm. *see* **Bugdaýly**
82 C5 **Bugdaýly** Turkm.
99 D4 **Bugel, Tanjung** *pt* Indon.
108 C3 **Buggenhout** Belgium
114 G2 **Bugojno** Bos.-Herz.
97 A4 **Bugsuk** *i.* Phil.
97 B2 **Buguey** Phil.
82 E3 **Bugun'** Kazakh.
82 C1 **Buguruslan** Rus. Fed.
84 D4 **Būhābād** Iran
123 D5 **Buhera** Zimbabwe
97 B3 **Buhi** Phil.
138 D3 **Buhl** *ID* U.S.A.
134 A2 **Buhl** *MN* U.S.A.
81 I3 **Bühtan** *r.* Turkey
113 M7 **Buhuşi** Romania
105 D5 **Builth Wells** U.K.
120 B4 **Bui National Park** Ghana
116 I4 **Buinsk** Rus. Fed.
81 K4 **Bu'in Soflā** Iran
90 D2 **Buir Nur** *l.* Mongolia
123 B6 **Buitepos** Namibia
115 I3 **Bujanovac** Serb. and Mont.
122 C4 **Bujumbura** Burundi
90 D1 **Bukachacha** Rus. Fed.
89 G1 **Buka Daban** *mt.* China
69 F2 **Buka Island** P.N.G.
84 D4 **Būkand** Iran
83 J1 **Bukanskoye** Rus. Fed.
Bukantau, Gory *h.* Uzbek. *see* **Bo'kantov tog'lari**
122 C4 **Bukavu** Dem. Rep. Congo
Bukhara Uzbek. *see* **Buxoro**
83 K2 **Bukhtarminskoye Vodokhranilishche** *resr* Kazakh.
97 C6 **Bukide** *i.* Indon.
99 B4 **Bukit Barisan Selatan National Park** Indon.
98 B5 **Bukit Fraser** Malaysia
98 □ **Bukit Timah** Sing.
99 B3 **Bukittinggi** Indon.
122 D4 **Bukoba** Tanz.
98 □ **Bukum, Pulau** *i.* Sing.
91 F7 **Bula** Indon.
116 I4 **Bula** *r.* Rus. Fed.
112 D7 **Bülach** Switz.
71 J4 **Bulahdelah** Australia
Bulahdelal Australia *see* **Bulahdelah**
97 B3 **Bulan** Phil.
80 G1 **Bulancak** Turkey
88 D3 **Bulandshahr** India
81 I2 **Bulanık** Turkey
123 C6 **Bulawayo** Zimbabwe
83 G1 **Bulayevo** Kazakh.
80 F3 **Bulbul** Syria
80 B2 **Buldan** Turkey
88 D5 **Buldhana** India
125 I2 **Bulembu** Swaziland
90 C2 **Bulgan** Mongolia
92 B1 **Bulgan** Mongolia
115 K3 **Bulgaria** *country* Europe
70 E1 **Bullawarra, Lake** *salt flat* Australia
70 D3 **Bullea, Lake** *salt flat* Australia
72 D4 **Buller** *r.* N.Z.
71 G6 **Buller, Mount** Australia
141 E4 **Bullhead City** U.S.A.
140 D4 **Bullion Mountains** U.S.A.
70 E2 **Bulloo** *watercourse* Australia
70 E2 **Bulloo Downs** Australia
70 E2 **Bulloo Lake** *salt flat* Australia
124 B2 **Büllsport** Namibia
98 □ **Buloh, Pulau** *i.* Sing.
70 E6 **Buloke, Lake** *dry lake* Australia
125 G4 **Bultfontein** S. Africa
97 C5 **Buluan** Phil.
68 C2 **Bulukumba** Indon.
77 N2 **Bulun** Rus. Fed.
122 B4 **Bulungu** Dem. Rep. Congo
122 C4 **Bulungu** Dem. Rep. Congo
83 F5 **Bulung'ur** Uzbek.
Bulungur Uzbek. *see* **Bulung'ur**
97 C3 **Bulusan** Phil.
122 C3 **Bumba** Dem. Rep. Congo
92 B1 **Bumbat** China
141 F4 **Bumble Bee** U.S.A.
97 A5 **Bum-Bum** *i.* Malaysia
122 B4 **Buna** Dem. Rep. Congo
122 D3 **Buna** Kenya
122 D4 **Bunazi** Tanz.
107 C2 **Bunbeg** Rep. of Ireland
68 B5 **Bunbury** Australia
107 E5 **Bunclody** Rep. of Ireland
107 D2 **Buncrana** Rep. of Ireland
122 D4 **Bunda** Tanz.
68 F4 **Bundaberg** Australia
71 G2 **Bundaleer** Australia
71 I3 **Bundarra** Australia
88 C4 **Bundi** India
71 J2 **Bundjalung National Park** Australia
107 C3 **Bundoran** Rep. of Ireland
89 F5 **Bundu** India
105 I5 **Bungay** U.K.
71 H5 **Bungendore** Australia
95 C8 **Bungo-suidō** *sea chan.* Japan
122 D3 **Bunia** Dem. Rep. Congo
122 C4 **Bunianga** Dem. Rep. Congo
70 E6 **Buninyong** Australia
120 D3 **Buni-Yadi** Nigeria
88 C2 **Bunji** Jammu and Kashmir
141 E3 **Bunkerville** U.S.A.
143 E6 **Bunkie** U.S.A.
145 D6 **Bunnell** U.S.A.
80 E2 **Bünyan** Turkey
97 A6 **Bunyu** *i.* Indon.
98 C2 **Buôn Đôn** Vietnam
98 D2 **Buôn Hô** Vietnam
98 D2 **Buôn Ma Thuôt** Vietnam
77 O2 **Buorkhaya, Guba** *b.* Rus. Fed.
122 D4 **Bura** Kenya
83 K2 **Buran** Kazakh.
Burang China *see* **Jirang**
158 E2 **Buranhaém** *r.* Brazil
82 C2 **Burannoye** Rus. Fed.
Burao Somalia *see* **Burco**
97 C4 **Burauen** Phil.
86 B4 **Buraydah** Saudi Arabia
109 G4 **Burbach** Germany
140 C4 **Burbank** U.S.A.
71 G4 **Burcher** Australia
122 E3 **Burco** Somalia
108 D1 **Burdaard** Neth.
82 F5 **Burdalyk** Turkm.
80 C3 **Burdur** Turkey
122 D2 **Burē** Eth.
105 I5 **Bure** *r.* U.K.
102 M2 **Bureå** Sweden
90 F1 **Bureinskiy Khrebet** *mts* Rus. Fed.
Bûr Fu'ad Egypt *see* **Port Fuad**
115 L3 **Burgas** Bulg.
145 E5 **Burgaw** U.S.A.
109 J2 **Burg bei Magdeburg** Germany
109 I5 **Burgbernheim** Germany
109 I2 **Burgdorf** Germany
133 I4 **Burgeo** Canada
125 G5 **Burgersdorp** S. Africa
125 I2 **Burgersfort** S. Africa
105 G7 **Burgess Hill** U.K.
109 H4 **Burghaun** Germany
112 F6 **Burghausen** Germany
106 E3 **Burghead** U.K.
108 B3 **Burgh-Haamstede** Neth.
114 F6 **Burgio, Serra di** *h. Sicily* Italy
109 K5 **Burglengenfeld** Germany
111 E1 **Burgos** Spain
109 K4 **Burgstädt** Germany
103 L4 **Burgsvik** Sweden
108 E1 **Burgum** Neth.
110 G3 **Burgundy** *reg.* France
90 B3 **Burhan Budai Shan** *mts* China
115 L5 **Burhaniye** Turkey
88 D5 **Burhanpur** India
89 E5 **Burhar-Dhanpuri** India
89 F4 **Burhi Gandak** *r.* India
97 B3 **Burias** *i.* Phil.
82 D2 **Buribay** Rus. Fed.
150 I6 **Burica, Punta** *pt* Costa Rica
89 H4 **Buri Dihing** *r.* India
89 E4 **Buri Gandak** *r.* Nepal
133 I4 **Burin Peninsula** Canada
98 B2 **Buriram** Thai.
155 J5 **Buriti Bravo** Brazil
158 C1 **Buritis** Brazil
85 G4 **Burj** Pak.
68 D3 **Burketown** Australia
120 B3 **Burkina** *country* Africa
135 H3 **Burk's Falls** Canada
83 I2 **Burkutty** Kazakh.
83 I1 **Burla** Rus. Fed.
83 I1 **Burla** *r.* Rus. Fed.
138 D3 **Burley** U.S.A.
82 E1 **Burli** Kazakh.
82 C2 **Burlin** Kazakh.
135 H4 **Burlington** Canada
142 C4 **Burlington** *CO* U.S.A.
134 B5 **Burlington** *IA* U.S.A.
134 D5 **Burlington** *IN* U.S.A.
147 I2 **Burlington** *ME* U.S.A.
147 G2 **Burlington** *VT* U.S.A.
134 C4 **Burlington** *WI* U.S.A.
82 D1 **Burly** Rus. Fed.
Burma *country* Asia *see* **Myanmar**
143 D6 **Burnet** U.S.A.
138 B3 **Burney** U.S.A.
147 I2 **Burnham** U.S.A.
71 F8 **Burnie** Australia
104 G3 **Burniston** U.K.
104 E4 **Burnley** U.K.
138 C3 **Burns** U.S.A.
131 H1 **Burnside** *r.* Canada
128 F4 **Burns Lake** Canada
146 C5 **Burnsville Lake** U.S.A.
106 E4 **Burntisland** U.K.
131 J3 **Burntwood** *r.* Canada
131 I3 **Burntwood Lake** Canada
70 E5 **Buronga** Australia
82 E4 **Burovoy** Uzbek.
76 J5 **Burqin** China
80 G5 **Burqu'** Jordan
70 C4 **Burra** Australia
106 □ **Burra** *i.* U.K.
106 □ **Burravoe** U.K.
106 F2 **Burray** *i.* U.K.
115 I4 **Burrel** Albania
71 H4 **Burrendong, Lake** Australia
71 H3 **Burren Junction** Australia
71 I5 **Burrewarra Point** Australia
111 F3 **Burriana** Spain
71 H5 **Burrinjuck** Australia
71 H5 **Burrinjuck Reservoir** Australia
150 D1 **Burro, Serranías del** *mts* Mex.
146 B5 **Burr Oak Reservoir** U.S.A.
106 D6 **Burrow Head** U.K.
141 G2 **Burrville** U.S.A.
80 B1 **Bursa** Turkey
121 F2 **Būr Safājah** Egypt
Būr Sa'īd Egypt *see* **Port Said**
109 G5 **Bürstadt** Germany
Būr Sudan Sudan *see* **Port Sudan**
70 D4 **Burta** Australia
134 E3 **Burt Lake** U.S.A.
135 F4 **Burton** U.S.A.
132 E3 **Burton, Lac** *l.* Canada
107 C3 **Burtonport** Rep. of Ireland
105 F5 **Burton upon Trent** U.K.
102 M2 **Burträsk** Sweden
147 J1 **Burtts Corner** Canada
70 E4 **Burtundy** Australia
91 E7 **Buru** *i.* Indon.
83 H3 **Burubaytal** Kazakh.
80 C6 **Burullus, Lake** *lag.* Egypt
122 D4 **Burundi** *country* Africa
122 C4 **Bururi** Burundi
130 B2 **Burwash Landing** Canada
106 F2 **Burwick** U.K.
117 E5 **Buryn'** Ukr.
82 B3 **Burynshyk** Kazakh.
105 H5 **Bury St Edmunds** U.K.
88 C2 **Burzil Pass** Jammu and Kashmir
122 C4 **Busanga** Dem. Rep. Congo
107 E2 **Bush** *r.* U.K.
84 C4 **Būshehr** Iran
89 E2 **Bushêngcaka** China
122 D4 **Bushenyi** Uganda
107 E2 **Bushmills** U.K.
134 B5 **Bushnell** U.S.A.
98 □ **Busing, Pulau** *i.* Sing.
122 C3 **Businga** Dem. Rep. Congo
80 F5 **Buşrá ash Shām** Syria
68 B5 **Busselton** Australia
108 D2 **Bussum** Neth.
150 D2 **Bustamante** Mex.
150 C1 **Bustillos, Lago** Mex.
114 C2 **Busto Arsizio** Italy
97 A3 **Busuanga** Phil.
97 A3 **Busuanga** *i.* Phil.
122 C3 **Buta** Dem. Rep. Congo
159 C3 **Buta Ranquil** Arg.
122 C4 **Butare** Rwanda
160 G6 **Butaritari** *atoll* Kiribati
70 B4 **Bute** Australia
106 C5 **Bute** *i.* U.K.
106 C5 **Bute, Sound of** *sea chan.* U.K.
130 D4 **Butedale** Canada
130 D4 **Bute Inlet** Canada
125 H4 **Butha-Buthe** Lesotho
109 G1 **Butjadingen** *reg.* Germany
134 E5 **Butler** *IN* U.S.A.
146 D4 **Butler** *PA* U.S.A.
107 D3 **Butlers Bridge** Rep. of Ireland
91 E7 **Buton** *i.* Indon.
109 K1 **Bütow** Germany
138 D2 **Butte** U.S.A.
109 J3 **Buttelstedt** Germany
140 B1 **Butte Meadows** U.S.A.
99 B1 **Butterworth** Malaysia
125 H6 **Butterworth** S. Africa
107 C5 **Buttevant** Rep. of Ireland
130 D5 **Buttle Lake** Canada
106 B2 **Butt of Lewis** *hd* U.K.
129 I4 **Button Bay** Canada
140 C4 **Buttonwillow** U.S.A.
97 C4 **Butuan** Phil.
93 B5 **Butuo** China
117 G5 **Buturlinovka** Rus. Fed.
89 E4 **Butwal** Nepal
109 G4 **Butzbach** Germany
122 E3 **Buulobarde** Somalia
122 E4 **Buur Gaabo** Somalia
122 E3 **Buurhabaka** Somalia
89 F4 **Buxar** India
82 F5 **Buxoro** Uzbek.
109 H1 **Buxtehude** Germany
105 F4 **Buxton** U.K.
116 G3 **Buy** Rus. Fed.
134 A1 **Buyck** U.S.A.
117 H7 **Buynaksk** Rus. Fed.
Büyük Ağrı Dağı *mt.* Turkey *see* **Ararat, Mount**
80 A3 **Büyükmenderes** *r.* Turkey
96 B3 **Buyun Shan** *mt.* China
82 B3 **Buzachi, Poluostrov** *pen.* Kazakh.
83 H5 **Buzai Gumbad** Afgh.
108 C5 **Buzancy** France
115 L2 **Buzău** Romania
123 D5 **Búzi** Moz.
82 F2 **Buzuluk** Kazakh.
82 C1 **Buzuluk** Rus. Fed.
117 G5 **Buzuluk** *r.* Rus. Fed.
147 H4 **Buzzards Bay** U.S.A.
115 K3 **Byala** Bulg.
115 J3 **Byala Slatina** Bulg.
113 N4 **Byalynichy** Belarus
128 H2 **Byam Martin Island** Canada
116 D4 **Byarezina** *r.* Belarus
116 C4 **Byaroza** Belarus
80 E4 **Byblos** *tourist site* Lebanon
112 I4 **Bydgoszcz** Poland
116 D4 **Byerazino** Belarus
138 F4 **Byers** U.S.A.
113 N3 **Byeshankovichy** Belarus
103 I4 **Bygland** Norway
116 D4 **Bykhaw** Belarus
103 I4 **Bykle** Norway
83 H2 **Bylkyldak** Kazakh.
129 K2 **Bylot Island** Canada

Caucasia 173

135 G3 **Byng Inlet** Canada
103 I3 **Byrkjelo** Norway
71 G3 **Byrock** Australia
134 C4 **Byron** *IL* U.S.A.
147 H2 **Byron** *ME* U.S.A.
71 J2 **Byron, Cape** Australia
71 J2 **Byron Bay** Australia
77 L2 **Byrranga, Gory** *mts* Rus. Fed.
102 M2 **Byske** Sweden
83 K1 **Bystryy Istok** Rus. Fed.
77 O3 **Bytantay** *r.* Rus. Fed.
113 I5 **Bytom** Poland
112 H3 **Bytów** Poland
82 D5 **Byuzmeyin** Turkm.

C

156 E3 **Caacupé** Para.
158 A4 **Caaguazú** Para.
158 A4 **Caaguazú, Cordillera de** *hills* Para.
158 A3 **Caarapó** Brazil
158 A4 **Caazapá** Para.
154 C6 **Caballas** Peru
154 D4 **Caballococha** Peru
97 B3 **Cabanatuan** Phil.
133 G4 **Cabano** Canada
122 E2 **Cabdul Qaadir** Somalia
158 A1 **Cabeceira Rio Manso** Brazil
155 L5 **Cabedelo** Brazil
111 D3 **Cabeza del Buey** Spain
154 F7 **Cabezas** Bol.
159 E3 **Cabildo** Arg.
157 C2 **Cabimas** Venez.
122 B4 **Cabinda** Angola
122 B4 **Cabinda** *prov.* Angola
138 C1 **Cabinet Mountains** U.S.A.
157 B3 **Cable Way** *pass* Col.
158 D3 **Cabo Frio** Brazil
158 E3 **Cabo Frio, Ilha do** *i.* Brazil
132 E4 **Cabonga, Réservoir** *resr* Canada
143 E4 **Cabool** U.S.A.
71 J1 **Caboolture** Australia
155 H3 **Cabo Orange, Parque Nacional de** *nat. park* Brazil
154 C4 **Cabo Pantoja** Peru
123 D5 **Cabora Bassa, Lake** *resr* Moz.
148 B2 **Caborca** Mex.
135 G3 **Cabot Head** Canada
133 I4 **Cabot Strait** Canada
158 D2 **Cabral, Serra do** *mts* Brazil
81 K2 **Cäbrayıl** Azer.
111 H3 **Cabrera** *i.* Spain
111 F3 **Cabriel** *r.* Spain
157 D3 **Cabruta** Venez.
97 B2 **Cabugao** Phil.
156 F3 **Caçador** Brazil
151 E4 **Cacahuatepec** Mex.
115 I3 **Čačak** Serb. and Mont.
159 G1 **Cacapava do Sul** Brazil
146 D5 **Cacapon** *r.* U.S.A.
157 B3 **Cácares** Col.
114 C4 **Caccia, Capo** *c. Sardinia* Italy
85 F2 **Çäçe** Turkm.
155 G7 **Cáceres** Brazil
111 C3 **Cáceres** Spain
138 D3 **Cache Peak** U.S.A.
120 A3 **Cacheu** Guinea-Bissau
156 C3 **Cachi** *r.* Arg.
156 C2 **Cachi, Nevados de** *mts* Arg.
155 H5 **Cachimbo, Serra do** *hills* Brazil
157 B3 **Cáchira** Col.
158 E1 **Cachoeira** Brazil
158 B2 **Cachoeira Alta** Brazil
159 G1 **Cachoeira do Sul** Brazil
158 E3 **Cachoeiro de Itapemirim** Brazil
120 A3 **Cacine** Guinea-Bissau
155 H3 **Caciporé, Cabo** *c.* Brazil
123 B5 **Cacolo** Angola
122 B4 **Cacongo** Angola
140 D3 **Cactus Range** *mts* U.S.A.
158 B2 **Caçu** Brazil
158 D1 **Caculé** Brazil
113 I6 **Čadca** Slovakia
109 H1 **Cadenberge** Germany
151 D2 **Cadereyta** Mex.
70 A2 **Cadibarrawirracanna, Lake** *salt flat* Australia
97 B3 **Cadig Mountains** Phil.
135 H1 **Cadillac** *Que.* Canada
131 H5 **Cadillac** *Sask.* Canada
134 E3 **Cadillac** U.S.A.
97 B4 **Cadiz** Phil.
111 C4 **Cádiz** Spain
111 C4 **Cádiz, Golfo de** *g.* Spain
141 E4 **Cadiz Lake** U.S.A.
110 D2 **Caen** France
105 C4 **Caernarfon** U.K.
105 C4 **Caernarfon Bay** U.K.
105 D6 **Caerphilly** U.K.
146 B5 **Caesar Creek Lake** U.S.A.
80 E5 **Caesarea** *tourist site* Israel
158 D1 **Caetité** Brazil
156 C3 **Cafayate** Arg.
97 B4 **Cagayan** *i.* Phil.
97 B2 **Cagayan** *r.* Phil.
97 C4 **Cagayan de Oro** Phil.
97 B4 **Cagayan Islands** Phil.
114 E3 **Cagli** Italy
114 C5 **Cagliari** *Sardinia* Italy
114 C5 **Cagliari, Golfo di** *b. Sardinia* Italy
157 B4 **Caguán** *r.* Col.
82 C4 **Çagyl** Turkm.
82 C4 **Çagyllyşor Çöketligi** *depr.* Turkm.
107 B6 **Caha** *h.* Rep. of Ireland
145 C5 **Cahaba** *r.* U.S.A.
107 B6 **Caha Mountains** Rep. of Ireland
107 A6 **Cahermore** Rep. of Ireland
Cahersiveen Rep. of Ireland *see* Cahirciveen
107 D5 **Cahir** Rep. of Ireland
107 A6 **Cahirciveen** Rep. of Ireland
Cahora Bassa, Lago de *resr* Moz. *see* **Cabora Bassa, Lake**
107 E5 **Cahore Point** Rep. of Ireland
110 E4 **Cahors** France
154 C5 **Cahuapanas** Peru
117 D6 **Cahul** Moldova
123 D5 **Caia** Moz.
155 G6 **Caiabis, Serra dos** *hills* Brazil
123 C5 **Caianda** Angola
158 B2 **Caiapó** *r.* Brazil
158 B2 **Caiapó, Serra do** *mts* Brazil
158 B2 **Caiapônia** Brazil
149 I4 **Caibarién** Cuba
93 C6 **Cai Bầu, Đao** *i.* Vietnam
98 C3 **Cai Be** Vietnam
157 D3 **Caicara** Venez.
149 J4 **Caicos Islands** Turks and Caicos Is
93 E4 **Caidian** China
150 C3 **Caimanero, Laguna del** *lag.* Mex.
159 B1 **Caimanes** Chile
97 A3 **Caiman Point** Phil.
111 F2 **Caimodorro** *mt.* Spain
98 C3 **Cai Nươc** Vietnam
106 E3 **Cairn Gorm** *mt.* U.K.
106 E3 **Cairngorm Mountains** U.K.
106 D4 **Cairngorms National Park** U.K.
106 C6 **Cairnryan** U.K.
68 E3 **Cairns** Australia
106 E3 **Cairn Toul** *mt.* U.K.
121 F1 **Cairo** Egypt (City Plan **60)**
145 C6 **Cairo** U.S.A.
114 C2 **Cairo Montenotte** Italy
123 B5 **Caiundo** Angola
71 F2 **Caiwarro** Australia
154 C5 **Cajamarca** Peru
97 B3 **Cajidiocan** Phil.
114 G1 **Čakovec** Croatia
80 B2 **Çal** Turkey
125 G5 **Cala** S. Africa
120 C4 **Calabar** Nigeria
135 I3 **Calabogie** Canada
157 D2 **Calabozo** Venez.
115 J3 **Calafat** Romania
156 B8 **Calafate** Arg.
97 B3 **Calagua Islands** Phil.
111 F1 **Calahorra** Spain
123 B5 **Calai** Angola
110 E1 **Calais** France
147 J2 **Calais** U.S.A.
151 G4 **Calakmul** *tourist site* Mex.
154 F5 **Calama** Brazil
156 C2 **Calama** Chile
157 B2 **Calamar** Col.
157 B4 **Calamar** Col.
97 A4 **Calamian Group** *is* Phil.
111 F2 **Calamocha** Spain
123 B4 **Calandula** Angola
121 E2 **Calanscio Sand Sea** *des.* Libya
97 B3 **Calapan** Phil.
115 L2 **Călărași** Romania
111 F2 **Calatayud** Spain
97 B3 **Calauag** Phil.
97 B3 **Calavite, Cape** Phil.
97 A3 **Calawit** *i.* Phil.
97 B2 **Calayan** *i.* Phil.
97 C3 **Calbayog** Phil.
109 J3 **Calbe (Saale)** Germany
97 C4 **Calbiga** Phil.
159 B4 **Calbuco** Chile
155 K5 **Calcanhar, Ponta do** *pt* Brazil
143 E6 **Calcasieu Lake** U.S.A.
155 H3 **Calçoene** Brazil
Calcutta India *see* **Kolkata**
111 B3 **Caldas da Rainha** Port.
158 C2 **Caldas Novas** Brazil
109 H3 **Calden** Germany
156 B3 **Caldera** Chile
81 I2 **Çaldıran** Turkey
138 C3 **Caldwell** U.S.A.
146 D3 **Caledon** Canada
125 G5 **Caledon** *r.* Lesotho/S. Africa
124 C7 **Caledon** S. Africa
135 H4 **Caledonia** Canada
134 B4 **Caledonia** U.S.A.
156 C7 **Caleta Olivia** Arg.
141 E5 **Calexico** U.S.A.
104 C3 **Calf of Man** *i.* U.K.
130 G4 **Calgary** Canada
145 C5 **Calhoun** U.S.A.
157 A4 **Cali** Col.
97 C4 **Calicoan** *i.* Phil.
87 A4 **Calicut** India
140 C4 **Caliente** *CA* U.S.A.
141 E3 **Caliente** *NV* U.S.A.
140 B3 **California** *state* U.S.A.
California, Golfo de *g.* Mex. *see* **California, Gulf of**
150 B2 **California, Gulf of** Mex.
140 B3 **California Aqueduct** *canal* U.S.A.
140 C4 **California Hot Springs** U.S.A.
81 L2 **Cälilabad** Azer.
139 D5 **Calipatria** U.S.A.
140 A2 **Calistoga** U.S.A.
124 D6 **Calitzdorp** S. Africa
151 G3 **Calkiní** Mex.
70 D2 **Callabonna, Lake** *salt flat* Australia
140 D2 **Callaghan, Mount** U.S.A.
145 D6 **Callahan** U.S.A.
107 D5 **Callan** Rep. of Ireland
135 H2 **Callander** Canada
106 D4 **Callander** U.K.
154 C6 **Callao** Peru
141 F2 **Callao** U.S.A.
151 E3 **Calles** Mex.
147 F4 **Callicoon** U.S.A.
105 C7 **Callington** U.K.
135 G2 **Callum** Canada
130 G4 **Calmar** Canada
134 B4 **Calmar** U.S.A.
141 E4 **Cal-Nev-Ari** U.S.A.
145 D7 **Caloosahatchee** *r.* U.S.A.
151 G3 **Calotmul** Mex.
71 J1 **Caloundra** Australia
140 B2 **Calpine** U.S.A.
151 E4 **Calpulálpan** Mex.
114 F6 **Caltanissetta** *Sicily* Italy
134 C2 **Calumet** U.S.A.
123 B5 **Calunga** Angola
123 B5 **Caluquembe** Angola
97 B4 **Calusa** *i.* Phil.
122 F2 **Caluula** Somalia
141 G5 **Calva** U.S.A.
130 D4 **Calvert Island** Canada
114 C3 **Calvi** *Corsica* France
111 H3 **Calvià** Spain
150 D3 **Calvillo** Mex.
124 C5 **Calvinia** S. Africa
114 F4 **Calvo, Monte** *mt.* Italy
105 H5 **Cam** *r.* U.K.
158 E1 **Camaçari** Brazil
140 B2 **Camache Reservoir** U.S.A.
150 D2 **Camacho** Mex.
123 B5 **Camacuio** Angola
123 B5 **Camacupa** Angola
157 D2 **Camaguán** Venez.
149 I4 **Camagüey** Cuba
149 I4 **Camagüey, Archipiélago de** *is* Cuba
99 B1 **Camah, Gunung** *mt.* Malaysia
Çamalan Turkey *see* **Gülek**
154 D7 **Camana** Peru
123 C5 **Camanongue** Angola
158 B2 **Camapuã** Brazil
159 G1 **Camaquã** Brazil
159 G1 **Camaquã** *r.* Brazil
80 E3 **Çamardı** Turkey
151 E2 **Camargo** Mex.
156 C6 **Camarones** Arg.
156 C6 **Camarones, Bahía** *b.* Arg.
138 B2 **Camas** U.S.A.
98 C3 **Ca Mau** Vietnam
98 C3 **Ca Mau, Mui** *c.* Vietnam
105 G6 **Camberley** U.K.
98 C2 **Cambodia** *country* Asia
105 B7 **Camborne** U.K.
110 F1 **Cambrai** France
140 B4 **Cambria** U.S.A.
105 D5 **Cambrian Mountains** U.K.
135 G4 **Cambridge** Canada
72 E2 **Cambridge** N.Z.
105 H5 **Cambridge** U.K.
134 B5 **Cambridge** *IL* U.S.A.
147 H3 **Cambridge** *MA* U.S.A.
147 E5 **Cambridge** *MD* U.S.A.
142 E2 **Cambridge** *MN* U.S.A.
147 G3 **Cambridge** *NY* U.S.A.
146 C4 **Cambridge** *OH* U.S.A.
133 G2 **Cambrien, Lac** *l.* Canada
71 I5 **Camden** Australia
145 C5 **Camden** *AL* U.S.A.
143 E5 **Camden** *AR* U.S.A.
147 I2 **Camden** *ME* U.S.A.
147 F5 **Camden** *NJ* U.S.A.
147 F3 **Camden** *NY* U.S.A.
145 D5 **Camden** *SC* U.S.A.
156 B8 **Camden, Isla** *i.* Chile
123 C5 **Cameia, Parque Nacional da** *nat. park* Angola
141 G4 **Cameron** *AZ* U.S.A.
143 E6 **Cameron** *LA* U.S.A.
142 E4 **Cameron** *MO* U.S.A.
143 D6 **Cameron** *TX* U.S.A.
134 B3 **Cameron** *WI* U.S.A.
130 F3 **Cameron Hills** Canada
140 B2 **Cameron Park** U.S.A.
120 D4 **Cameroon** *country* Africa
120 C4 **Cameroun, Mont** *vol.* Cameroon
155 I4 **Cametá** Brazil
97 B2 **Camiguin** *i.* Phil.
97 C4 **Camiguin** *i.* Phil.
97 B3 **Camiling** Phil.
145 C6 **Camilla** U.S.A.
154 F8 **Camiri** Bol.
155 J4 **Camocim** Brazil
68 D3 **Camooweal** Australia
97 C4 **Camotes Sea** *g.* Phil.
159 E2 **Campana** Arg.
157 B4 **Campana, Cerro** *h.* Col.
156 A7 **Campana, Isla** *i.* Chile
159 B2 **Campanario** *mt.* Arg./Chile
130 D4 **Campania Island** Canada
124 E4 **Campbell** S. Africa
72 E4 **Campbell, Cape** N.Z.
67 F7 **Campbell Island** N.Z.
160 G9 **Campbell Plateau** *sea feature* S. Pacific Ocean
130 D4 **Campbell River** Canada
135 I3 **Campbells Bay** Canada
144 C4 **Campbellsville** U.S.A.
133 G4 **Campbellton** Canada
71 G8 **Campbell Town** Australia
106 C5 **Campbeltown** U.K.
151 G4 **Campeche** Mex.
151 G4 **Campeche** *state* Mex.
151 F4 **Campeche, Bahía de** *g.* Mex.
70 E7 **Camperdown** Australia
115 K2 **Câmpina** Romania
155 K5 **Campina Grande** Brazil
158 C3 **Campinas** Brazil
158 C2 **Campina Verde** Brazil
120 C4 **Campo** Cameroon
157 B4 **Campoalegre** Col.
114 F4 **Campobasso** Italy
158 D3 **Campo Belo** Brazil
155 H6 **Campo de Diauarum** Brazil
158 C2 **Campo Florido** Brazil
156 D3 **Campo Gallo** Arg.
158 A3 **Campo Grande** Brazil
155 J4 **Campo Maior** Brazil
111 C3 **Campo Maior** Port.
157 C2 **Campo Mara** Venez.
158 B4 **Campo Mourão** Brazil
158 E3 **Campos** Brazil
158 C2 **Campos Altos** Brazil
158 D3 **Campos do Jordão** Brazil
106 D4 **Campsie Fells** *hills* U.K.
146 B6 **Campton** *KY* U.S.A.
147 H3 **Campton** *NH* U.S.A.
115 K2 **Câmpulung** Romania
113 L7 **Câmpulung Moldovenesc** Romania
141 G4 **Camp Verde** U.S.A.
Cam Ranh Vietnam *see* **Ba Ngoi**
130 G4 **Camrose** Canada
105 B6 **Camrose** U.K.
131 G2 **Camsell Lake** Canada
131 H3 **Camsell Portage** Canada
117 C7 **Çan** Turkey
98 D3 **Ca Na, Mui** *hd* Vietnam
147 G3 **Canaan** U.S.A.
128 G3 **Canada** *country* N. America
164 O1 **Canada Basin** *sea feature* Arctic Ocean
159 E2 **Cañada de Gómez** Arg.
147 H2 **Canada Falls Lake** U.S.A.
143 C5 **Canadian** *r.* U.S.A.
157 E3 **Canaima, Parque Nacional** *nat. park* Venez.
147 F3 **Canajoharie** U.S.A.
117 C7 **Çanakkale** Turkey
Çanakkale Boğazı *str.* Turkey *see* **Dardanelles**
159 C2 **Canalejas** Arg.
146 E3 **Canandaigua** U.S.A.
146 E3 **Canandaigua Lake** U.S.A.
148 B2 **Cananea** Mex.
158 C4 **Cananéia** Brazil
157 C4 **Canapiare, Cerro** *h.* Col.
154 C4 **Cañar** Ecuador
118 C2 **Canarias, Islas** *aut. comm.* Atlantic Ocean
120 A2 **Canary Islands** *terr.* N. Atlantic Ocean
147 F3 **Canastota** U.S.A.
158 C2 **Canastra, Serra da** *mts* Brazil
150 C2 **Canatlán** Mex.
145 D6 **Canaveral, Cape** U.S.A.
111 E2 **Cañaveras** Spain
158 E1 **Canavieiras** Brazil
71 G3 **Canbelego** Australia
71 H5 **Canberra** Australia
138 B3 **Canby** *CA* U.S.A.
142 D2 **Canby** *MN* U.S.A.
151 H3 **Cancún** Mex.
151 G4 **Candelaria** *Campeche* Mex.
139 F6 **Candelaria** *Chihuahua* Mex.
151 E5 **Candelaria Loxicha** Mex.
111 D2 **Candeleda** Spain
71 H6 **Candelo** Australia
155 I4 **Cândido Mendes** Brazil
80 D1 **Çandır** Turkey
131 H4 **Candle Lake** Canada
131 H4 **Candle Lake** *l.* Canada
153 G7 **Candlemas Island** S. Sandwich Is
147 G4 **Candlewood, Lake** U.S.A.
142 D1 **Cando** U.S.A.
97 B2 **Candon** Phil.
159 B1 **Canela Baja** Chile
159 F2 **Canelones** Uruguay
159 B3 **Cañete** Chile
111 F2 **Cañete** Spain
154 D6 **Cangallo** Peru
123 B5 **Cangamba** Angola
111 C1 **Cangas del Narcea** Spain
124 E6 **Cango Caves** S. Africa
155 K5 **Canguaretama** Brazil
159 G1 **Canguçu** Brazil
159 G1 **Canguçu, Serra do** *hills* Brazil
93 D6 **Cangwu** China
92 E2 **Cangzhou** China
133 G3 **Caniapiscau** Canada
133 G2 **Caniapiscau** *r.* Canada
133 G3 **Caniapiscau, Lac** Canada
129 K4 **Caniapiscau, Lac** *l.* Canada
114 E6 **Canicattì** *Sicily* Italy
130 E4 **Canim Lake** Canada
130 E4 **Canim Lake** *l.* Canada
155 K4 **Canindé** Brazil
155 J5 **Canindé** *r.* Brazil
106 C2 **Canisp** *h.* U.K.
146 E3 **Canisteo** U.S.A.
146 E3 **Canisteo** *r.* U.S.A.
150 D3 **Cañitas de Felipe Pescador** Mex.
80 D1 **Çankırı** Turkey
97 B4 **Canlaon** Phil.
130 F4 **Canmore** Canada
106 B3 **Canna** *i.* U.K.
87 A4 **Cannanore** India
87 A4 **Cannanore Islands** India
110 H5 **Cannes** France
105 E5 **Cannock** U.K.
71 H6 **Cann River** Australia
156 F3 **Canoas** Brazil
131 H3 **Canoe Lake** Canada
158 B4 **Canoinhas** Brazil
139 F4 **Canon City** U.S.A.
70 D4 **Canopus** Australia
131 I4 **Canora** Canada
71 H4 **Canowindra** Australia
133 H4 **Canso, Cape** Canada
111 D1 **Cantábrica, Cordillera** *mts* Spain
110 B4 **Cantábrico, Mar** *sea* France/Spain
159 C2 **Cantantal** Arg.
157 D2 **Cantaura** Venez.
147 J2 **Canterbury** Canada
105 I6 **Canterbury** U.K.
72 C6 **Canterbury Bight** *b.* N.Z.
72 C5 **Canterbury Plains** N.Z.
98 C3 **Cân Thơ** Vietnam
97 C4 **Cantilan** Phil.
155 J5 **Canto do Buriti** Brazil
Canton China *see* **Guangzhou**
134 B5 **Canton** *IL* U.S.A.
147 H2 **Canton** *ME* U.S.A.
134 B5 **Canton** *MO* U.S.A.
143 F5 **Canton** *MS* U.S.A.
147 F2 **Canton** *NY* U.S.A.
146 C4 **Canton** *OH* U.S.A.
146 E4 **Canton** *PA* U.S.A.
158 B4 **Cantu** *r.* Brazil
158 B4 **Cantu, Serra do** *hills* Brazil
159 E2 **Cañuelas** Arg.
155 G4 **Canumã** Brazil
71 J2 **Canungra** Australia
154 F5 **Canutama** Brazil
72 D4 **Canvastown** N.Z.
105 H6 **Canvey Island** U.K.
131 H4 **Canwood** Canada
143 C5 **Canyon** U.S.A.
138 C2 **Canyon City** U.S.A.
141 H3 **Canyon de Chelly National Monument** *nat. park* U.S.A.
138 D2 **Canyon Ferry Lake** U.S.A.
141 H2 **Canyonlands National Park** U.S.A.
130 D2 **Canyon Ranges** *mts* Canada
138 B3 **Canyonville** U.S.A.
93 C6 **Cao Băng** Vietnam
96 C3 **Cao He** *r.* China
Cao Nguyên Đăc Lăc *plat.* Vietnam *see* **Đăk Lăk, Cao Nguyên**
96 C2 **Caoshi** China
92 E3 **Caoxian** China
97 B5 **Cap** *i.* Phil.
157 D3 **Capanaparo** *r.* Venez.
155 I4 **Capanema** Brazil
158 B4 **Capanema** *r.* Brazil
158 C4 **Capão Bonito** Brazil
157 C3 **Caparo** *r.* Venez.
157 C4 **Caparro, Cerro** *h.* Brazil
97 B3 **Capas** Phil.
133 H4 **Cap-aux-Meules** Canada
133 F4 **Cap-de-la-Madeleine** Canada
71 H8 **Cape Barren Island** Australia
163 J8 **Cape Basin** *sea feature* S. Atlantic Ocean
133 H4 **Cape Breton Highlands National Park** Canada
133 H4 **Cape Breton Island** Canada
133 I3 **Cape Charles** Canada
147 E6 **Cape Charles** U.S.A.
120 B4 **Cape Coast** Ghana
147 H4 **Cape Cod Bay** U.S.A.
147 I4 **Cape Cod National Seashore** *nature res.* U.S.A.
145 D7 **Cape Coral** U.S.A.
135 G3 **Cape Croker** Canada
129 K3 **Cape Dorset** Canada
145 E5 **Cape Fear** *r.* U.S.A.
143 F4 **Cape Girardeau** U.S.A.
158 D2 **Capelinha** Brazil
108 C3 **Capelle aan de IJssel** Neth.
147 F5 **Cape May** U.S.A.
147 F5 **Cape May Court House** U.S.A.
147 F5 **Cape May Point** U.S.A.
123 B4 **Capenda-Camulemba** Angola
133 I4 **Cape St George** Canada
133 H4 **Cape Tormentine** Canada
124 C6 **Cape Town** S. Africa (City Plan **60)**
120 □ **Cape Verde** *country* N. Atlantic Ocean
163 G5 **Cape Verde Basin** *sea feature* N. Atlantic Ocean
163 G4 **Cape Verde Plateau** *sea feature* N. Atlantic Ocean
147 E2 **Cape Vincent** U.S.A.
68 E3 **Cape York Peninsula** Australia
149 J5 **Cap-Haïtien** Haiti
155 I4 **Capim** *r.* Brazil
73 E2 **Capitán Arturo Prat** *research stn* Antarctica
158 A3 **Capitán Bado** Para.
91 G5 **Capitol Hill** N. Mariana Is
141 G2 **Capitol Reef National Park** U.S.A.
158 B3 **Capivara, Represa** *resr* Brazil
114 G3 **Čapljina** Bos.-Herz.
114 F5 **Capo d'Orlando** *Sicily* Italy
107 D5 **Cappoquin** Rep. of Ireland
114 C3 **Capraia, Isola di** *i.* Italy
114 F4 **Capri, Isola di** *i.* Italy
68 F4 **Capricorn Channel** Australia
123 C5 **Caprivi Strip** *reg.* Namibia
140 □2 **Captain Cook** U.S.A.
71 H5 **Captain's Flat** Australia
146 C5 **Captina** *r.* U.S.A.
97 C3 **Capul** *i.* Phil.
154 C3 **Caquetá** *r.* Col.
157 B3 **Cáqueza** Col.
97 B3 **Carabao** *i.* Phil.
115 K2 **Caracal** Romania
157 E4 **Caracarai** Brazil
157 D2 **Caracas** Venez. (City Plan **64)**
155 J5 **Caracol** Brazil
150 D4 **Carácuaro** Mex.
97 C5 **Caraga** Phil.
159 F2 **Caraguatá** *r.* Uruguay
158 D3 **Caraguatatuba** Brazil
159 B3 **Carahue** Chile
158 E2 **Caraí** Brazil
158 D3 **Carandaí** Brazil
158 D3 **Carangola** Brazil
115 J2 **Caransebeş** Romania
70 B4 **Carappee Hill** Australia
133 H4 **Caraquet** Canada
157 B3 **Carare** *r.* Col.
150 I5 **Caratasca** Hond.
150 I5 **Caratasca, Laguna de** *lag.* Hond.
158 D2 **Caratinga** Brazil
154 E4 **Carauari** Brazil
111 F3 **Caravaca de la Cruz** Spain
158 E2 **Caravelas** Brazil
156 F3 **Carazinho** Brazil
142 D1 **Carberry** Canada
114 C5 **Carbonara, Capo** *c. Sardinia* Italy
144 B4 **Carbondale** *IL* U.S.A.
147 F4 **Carbondale** *PA* U.S.A.
133 J4 **Carbonear** Canada
114 C5 **Carbonia** *Sardinia* Italy
158 D2 **Carbonita** Brazil
111 F3 **Carcaixent** Spain
97 B4 **Carcar** Phil.
159 E2 **Carcaraña** *r.* Arg.
110 F5 **Carcassonne** France
130 C2 **Carcross** Canada
87 B4 **Cardamom Hills** India
98 B2 **Cardamom Range** *mts* Cambodia
Cardamon Hills India *see* **Cardamom Hills**
151 E3 **Cárdenas** Mex.
151 F4 **Cárdenas** Mex.
70 E2 **Cardenyabba** *watercourse* Australia
156 B7 **Cardiel, Lago** *l.* Arg.
105 D6 **Cardiff** U.K.
105 C5 **Cardigan** U.K.
105 C5 **Cardigan Bay** U.K.
147 F2 **Cardinal** Canada
146 B4 **Cardington** U.S.A.
159 F2 **Cardona** Uruguay
158 C4 **Cardoso, Ilha do** *i.* Brazil
72 B6 **Cardrona** N.Z.
130 G5 **Cardston** Canada
113 K7 **Carei** Romania
110 D2 **Carentan** France
146 B4 **Carey** U.S.A.
68 C4 **Carey, Lake** *salt flat* Australia
131 I2 **Carey Lake** Canada
162 H6 **Cargados Carajos Islands** Mauritius
110 C2 **Carhaix-Plouguer** France
159 D3 **Carhué** Arg.
158 E3 **Cariacica** Brazil
157 E2 **Cariaco** Venez.
149 I5 **Caribbean Sea** Atlantic Ocean
130 E4 **Cariboo Mountains** Canada
131 J3 **Caribou** *r. Man.* Canada
130 D2 **Caribou** *r. N.W.T.* Canada
147 J1 **Caribou** U.S.A.
134 E2 **Caribou Island** Canada
129 J4 **Caribou Lake** Canada
130 F3 **Caribou Mountains** Canada
150 C2 **Carichic** Mex.
97 C4 **Carigara** Phil.
108 D5 **Carignan** France
71 G3 **Carinda** Australia
111 F2 **Cariñena** Spain
158 D1 **Carinhanha** Brazil
158 D1 **Carinhanha** *r.* Brazil
157 E2 **Caripe** Venez.
157 E2 **Caripito** Venez.
107 D3 **Cark Mountain** *h.* Rep. of Ireland
135 I3 **Carleton Place** Canada
125 G3 **Carletonville** S. Africa
138 C3 **Carlin** U.S.A.
107 E3 **Carlingford Lough** *inlet* Rep. of Ireland/U.K.
104 E3 **Carlisle** U.K.
146 A5 **Carlisle** *KY* U.S.A.
146 E4 **Carlisle** *PA* U.S.A.
110 E5 **Carlit, Pic** *mt.* France
159 E2 **Carlos Casares** Arg.
158 E2 **Carlos Chagas** Brazil
107 E5 **Carlow** Rep. of Ireland
106 B2 **Carloway** U.K.
140 D5 **Carlsbad** *CA* U.S.A.
139 F5 **Carlsbad** *NM* U.S.A.
143 C6 **Carlsbad** *TX* U.S.A.
139 F5 **Carlsbad Caverns National Park** U.S.A.
162 H4 **Carlsberg Ridge** *sea feature* Indian Ocean
106 E5 **Carluke** U.K.
131 I5 **Carlyle** Canada
130 B2 **Carmacks** Canada
114 B2 **Carmagnola** Italy
131 J5 **Carman** Canada
105 C6 **Carmarthen** U.K.
105 C6 **Carmarthen Bay** U.K.
110 F4 **Carmaux** France
147 I2 **Carmel** U.S.A.
105 C4 **Carmel Head** U.K.
151 G4 **Carmelita** Guat.
159 E2 **Carmelo** Uruguay
157 B2 **Carmen** Col.
97 C4 **Carmen** Phil.
141 G6 **Carmen** U.S.A.
150 B2 **Carmen, Isla** *i.* Mex.
151 G4 **Carmen, Isla del** *i.* Mex.
159 D4 **Carmen de Patagones** Arg.
159 C2 **Carmensa** Arg.
144 B4 **Carmi** U.S.A.
140 B2 **Carmichael** U.S.A.
111 D4 **Carmona** Spain
110 C3 **Carnac** France
124 E5 **Carnarvon** S. Africa
107 D2 **Carndonagh** Rep. of Ireland
105 D4 **Carnedd Llywelyn** *mt.* U.K.
68 C4 **Carnegie, Lake** *salt flat* Australia
161 N6 **Carnegie Ridge** *sea feature* S. Pacific Ocean
106 C3 **Carn Eighe** *mt.* U.K.
134 D3 **Carney** U.S.A.
73 B4 **Carney Island** *i.* Antarctica
104 E3 **Carnforth** U.K.
107 F3 **Carnlough** U.K.
106 E4 **Carn nan Gabhar** *mt.* U.K.
122 B3 **Carnot** Centr. Afr. Rep.
70 A5 **Carnot, Cape** Australia
106 F4 **Carnoustie** U.K.
107 E5 **Carnsore Point** Rep. of Ireland
106 E5 **Carnwath** U.K.
135 F4 **Caro** U.S.A.
145 D7 **Carol City** U.S.A.
155 I5 **Carolina** Brazil
125 I3 **Carolina** S. Africa
67 I5 **Caroline Island** *atoll* Kiribati
66 D2 **Caroline Islands** N. Pacific Ocean
72 A6 **Caroline Peak** N.Z.
124 B4 **Carolusberg** S. Africa
157 E2 **Caroní** *r.* Venez.
157 C2 **Carora** Venez.
141 E3 **Carp** U.S.A.
113 L6 **Carpathian Mountains** Romania/Ukr.
Carpații Meridionali *mts* Romania *see* **Transylvanian Alps**
68 D3 **Carpentaria, Gulf of** Australia
110 G4 **Carpentras** France
114 D2 **Carpi** Italy
155 K5 **Carpina** Brazil
140 C4 **Carpinteria** U.S.A.
131 I5 **Carpio** U.S.A.
130 E4 **Carp Lake Provincial Park** Canada
107 B4 **Carra, Lough** *l.* Rep. of Ireland
147 H2 **Carrabassett** U.S.A.
145 C6 **Carrabelle** U.S.A.
157 B2 **Carraipía** Col.
107 B6 **Carran** *h.* Rep. of Ireland
107 B6 **Carrantuohill** *mt.* Rep. of Ireland
159 B2 **Carranza, Cabo** *c.* Chile
150 D2 **Carranza, Presa Venustiano** *resr* Mex.
157 E3 **Carrao** *r.* Venez.
114 D2 **Carrara** Italy
71 F5 **Carrathool** Australia
159 C3 **Carrero, Cerro** *mt.* Arg.
157 E1 **Carriacou** *i.* Grenada
106 D5 **Carrick** *reg.* U.K.
107 F3 **Carrickfergus** U.K.
107 E4 **Carrickmacross** Rep. of Ireland
107 C4 **Carrick-on-Shannon** Rep. of Ireland
107 D5 **Carrick-on-Suir** Rep. of Ireland
70 C4 **Carrieton** Australia
107 D4 **Carrigallen** Rep. of Ireland
107 C6 **Carrigtwohill** Rep. of Ireland
159 C4 **Carri Lafquén, Laguna** *l.* Arg.
150 D2 **Carrillo** Mex.
142 D2 **Carrington** U.S.A.
156 B3 **Carrizal Bajo** Chile
141 G4 **Carrizo** *AZ* U.S.A.
141 H4 **Carrizo** *AZ* U.S.A.
140 D5 **Carrizo Creek** *watercourse* U.S.A.
143 D6 **Carrizo Springs** U.S.A.
139 F5 **Carrizozo** U.S.A.
142 E3 **Carroll** U.S.A.
145 C5 **Carrollton** *GA* U.S.A.
144 C4 **Carrollton** *KY* U.S.A.
142 E4 **Carrollton** *MO* U.S.A.
146 C4 **Carrollton** *OH* U.S.A.
131 I4 **Carrot** *r.* Canada
131 I4 **Carrot River** Canada
107 B3 **Carrowmore Lake** Rep. of Ireland
147 F2 **Carry Falls Reservoir** U.S.A.
80 F1 **Çarşamba** Turkey
134 E4 **Carson City** *MI* U.S.A.
140 C2 **Carson City** *NV* U.S.A.
140 C2 **Carson Lake** U.S.A.
140 C2 **Carson Sink** *l.* U.S.A.
135 F4 **Carsonville** U.S.A.
159 B2 **Cartagena** Chile
157 B2 **Cartagena** Col.
111 F4 **Cartagena** Spain
157 B3 **Cartago** Col.
150 I6 **Cartago** Costa Rica
145 C5 **Cartersville** U.S.A.
134 B5 **Carthage** *IL* U.S.A.
143 E4 **Carthage** *MO* U.S.A.
147 F2 **Carthage** *NY* U.S.A.
143 E5 **Carthage** *TX* U.S.A.
135 G2 **Cartier** Canada
104 E3 **Cartmel** U.K.
133 I3 **Cartwright** Canada
155 K5 **Caruarú** Brazil
157 E2 **Carúpano** Venez.
140 D2 **Carvers** U.S.A.
108 A4 **Carvin** France
145 E5 **Cary** U.S.A.
70 E2 **Caryapundy Swamp** Australia
120 B1 **Casablanca** Morocco
158 C3 **Casa Branca** Brazil
139 E6 **Casa de Janos** Mex.
159 C3 **Casa de Piedra, Embalse** *resr* Arg.
141 G5 **Casa Grande** U.S.A.
141 G5 **Casa Grande National Monument** *nat. park* U.S.A.
114 C2 **Casale Monferrato** Italy
114 D2 **Casalmaggiore** Italy
157 C3 **Casanare** *r.* Col.
115 H4 **Casarano** Italy
136 E5 **Casas Grandes** Mex.
72 B6 **Cascade** *r.* N.Z.
134 B4 **Cascade** *IA* U.S.A.
138 C2 **Cascade** *ID* U.S.A.
138 E2 **Cascade** *MT* U.S.A.
72 B6 **Cascade Point** N.Z.
138 B3 **Cascade Range** *mts* U.S.A.
138 D2 **Cascade Reservoir** U.S.A.
111 B3 **Cascais** Port.
150 H6 **Cascal, Paso del** *pass* Nicaragua
158 B4 **Cascavel** Brazil
147 I3 **Casco Bay** U.S.A.
114 F4 **Caserta** Italy
135 F4 **Caseville** U.S.A.
73 D6 **Casey** *research stn* Antarctica
73 E4 **Casey Bay** *b.* Antarctica
Caseyr, Raas *c.* Somalia *see* **Gwardafuy, Gees**
107 D5 **Cashel** Rep. of Ireland
71 H1 **Cashmere** Australia
134 B4 **Cashton** U.S.A.
157 C2 **Casigua** Venez.
157 B2 **Casigua** Venez.
97 B2 **Casiguran** Phil.
159 E2 **Casilda** Arg.
71 J2 **Casino** Australia
157 D4 **Casiquiare, Canal** *r.* Venez.
154 C5 **Casma** Peru
134 E4 **Casnovia** U.S.A.
140 A2 **Caspar** U.S.A.
111 F2 **Caspe** Spain
138 F3 **Casper** U.S.A.
82 B3 **Caspian Lowland** Kazakh./Rus. Fed.
76 C2 **Caspian Sea** *l.* Asia/Europe
146 D5 **Cass** U.S.A.
135 F4 **Cass** *r.* U.S.A.
146 D3 **Cassadaga** U.S.A.
123 C5 **Cassai** Angola
135 F4 **Cass City** U.S.A.
108 A4 **Cassel** France
147 F2 **Casselman** Canada
130 D3 **Cassiar** Canada
130 C3 **Cassiar Mountains** Canada
71 H4 **Cassilis** Australia
114 E4 **Cassino** Italy
142 E2 **Cass Lake** U.S.A.
155 I4 **Castanhal** Brazil
159 C1 **Castaño** *r.* Arg.
150 D2 **Castaños** Mex.
159 C1 **Castaño Viejo** Arg.
114 D2 **Castelfranco Veneto** Italy
110 E4 **Casteljaloux** France
114 F4 **Castellammare di Stabia** Italy
159 F3 **Castelli** Arg.
111 F3 **Castelló de la Plana** Spain
111 C3 **Castelo Branco** Port.
111 C3 **Castelo de Vide** Port.
114 C4 **Castelsardo** *Sardinia* Italy
114 E6 **Casteltermini** *Sicily* Italy
114 E6 **Castelvetrano** *Sicily* Italy
70 D6 **Casterton** Australia
133 G2 **Castignon, Lac** *l.* Canada
111 E3 **Castilla-La Mancha** *aut. comm.* Spain
111 D2 **Castilla y León** *aut. comm.* Spain
157 C2 **Castilletes** Col.
159 G2 **Castillos** Uruguay
107 B4 **Castlebar** Rep. of Ireland
106 A4 **Castlebay** U.K.
107 E4 **Castlebellingham** Rep. of Ireland
107 E3 **Castleblayney** Rep. of Ireland
107 E5 **Castlebridge** Rep. of Ireland
104 E3 **Castle Carrock** U.K.
105 E6 **Castle Cary** U.K.
141 G2 **Castle Dale** U.S.A.
107 D3 **Castlederg** U.K.
107 E5 **Castledermot** Rep. of Ireland
141 E5 **Castle Dome Mountains** U.S.A.
105 F5 **Castle Donington** U.K.
106 E6 **Castle Douglas** U.K.
104 F4 **Castleford** U.K.
130 F5 **Castlegar** Canada
107 A5 **Castlegregory** Rep. of Ireland
107 B5 **Castleisland** Rep. of Ireland
70 F6 **Castlemaine** Australia
107 B5 **Castlemaine** Rep. of Ireland
107 C6 **Castlemartyr** Rep. of Ireland
140 B4 **Castle Mountain** U.S.A.
93 □ **Castle Peak** *h. Hong Kong* China
93 □ **Castle Peak Bay** *Hong Kong* China
72 F4 **Castlepoint** N.Z.
107 D4 **Castlepollard** Rep. of Ireland
107 C4 **Castlerea** Rep. of Ireland
71 H3 **Castlereagh** *r.* Australia
139 F4 **Castle Rock** U.S.A.
134 B4 **Castle Rock Lake** U.S.A.
104 C3 **Castletown** Isle of Man
107 D5 **Castletown** Rep. of Ireland
131 G4 **Castor** Canada
110 F5 **Castres** France
108 C2 **Castricum** Neth.
149 L6 **Castries** St Lucia
158 C4 **Castro** Brazil
156 B6 **Castro** Chile
111 D4 **Castro del Río** Spain
111 E1 **Castro-Urdiales** Spain
111 B4 **Castro Verde** Port.
114 G5 **Castrovillari** Italy
140 B3 **Castroville** U.S.A.
72 A6 **Caswell Sound** *inlet* N.Z.
81 H2 **Çat** Turkey
154 B5 **Catacaos** Peru
158 D3 **Cataguases** Brazil
143 E6 **Catahoula Lake** U.S.A.
97 B3 **Cataiñgan** Phil.
81 I3 **Çatak** Turkey
158 C2 **Catalão** Brazil
111 G2 **Cataluña** *aut. comm.* Spain
156 C3 **Catamarca** Arg.
97 C3 **Catanduanes** *i.* Phil.
158 B4 **Catanduvas** Brazil
114 F6 **Catania** *Sicily* Italy
114 G5 **Catanzaro** Italy
143 D6 **Catarina** U.S.A.
97 C3 **Catarman** Phil.
111 F3 **Catarroja** Spain
70 A5 **Catastrophe, Cape** Australia
157 B2 **Catatumbo** *r.* Venez.
93 C6 **Cat Ba, Đao** *i.* Vietnam
97 C4 **Catbalogan** Phil.
145 E7 **Cat Cays** *is* Bahamas
97 C5 **Cateel** Phil.
97 C5 **Cateel Bay** Phil.
125 J3 **Catembe** Moz.
71 H6 **Cathcart** Australia
125 G6 **Cathcart** S. Africa
125 H4 **Cathedral Peak** S. Africa
107 A6 **Catherdaniel** Rep. of Ireland
141 F2 **Catherine, Mount** U.S.A.
159 B3 **Catillo** Chile
145 E7 **Cat Island** Bahamas
132 B3 **Cat Lake** Canada
151 H3 **Catoche, Cabo** Mex.
69 F4 **Cato Island and Bank** *rf* Australia
146 E5 **Catonsville** U.S.A.
150 D3 **Catorce** Mex.
159 D3 **Catriló** Arg.
157 E4 **Catrimani** Brazil
157 E4 **Catrimani** *r.* Brazil
108 A4 **Cats, Mont des** *h.* France
147 G3 **Catskill** U.S.A.
147 F4 **Catskill Mountains** U.S.A.
125 J3 **Catuane** Moz.
157 E4 **Cauamé** *r.* Brazil
97 B4 **Cauayan** Phil.
133 H2 **Caubvick, Mount** Canada
157 B3 **Cauca** *r.* Col.
155 K4 **Caucaia** Brazil
157 B3 **Caucasia** Col.

174 Caucasus

117 G7 Caucasus mts Asia/Europe
159 C1 Caucete Arg.
147 I1 Caucomgomoc Lake U.S.A.
108 B4 Caudry France
98 C1 Câu Giat Vietnam
97 C4 Cauit Point Phil.
159 B2 Cauquenes Chile
157 D3 Caura r. Venez.
133 G4 Causapscal Canada
110 G5 Cavaillon France
158 C1 Cavalcante Brazil
120 B4 Cavally r. Côte d'Ivoire
107 D4 Cavan Rep. of Ireland
143 F4 Cave City U.S.A.
158 E1 Caveira r. Brazil
70 E6 Cavendish Australia
158 B4 Cavernoso, Serra do mts Brazil
146 B5 Cave Run Lake U.S.A.
97 B4 Cavili rf Phil.
97 B3 Cavite Phil.
106 E3 Cawdor U.K.
70 D4 Cawndilla Lake imp. l. Australia
105 I5 Cawston U.K.
155 J4 Caxias Brazil
156 F3 Caxias do Sul Brazil
123 B4 Caxito Angola
80 C2 Çay Turkey
145 D5 Cayce U.S.A.
80 D1 Çaycuma Turkey
81 H1 Çayeli Turkey
155 H3 Cayenne Fr. Guiana
80 E3 Çayhan Turkey
80 C1 Çayırhan Turkey
149 I5 Cayman Brac i. Cayman Is
149 H5 Cayman Islands terr. Caribbean Sea
163 D4 Cayman Trench sea feature Caribbean Sea
122 E3 Caynabo Somalia
135 H4 Cayuga Canada
146 E3 Cayuga Lake U.S.A.
147 F3 Cazenovia U.S.A.
123 C5 Cazombo Angola
163 G6 Ceara Abyssal Plain sea feature S. Atlantic Ocean
150 I7 Cebaco, Isla i. Panama
150 C2 Ceballos Mex.
159 F2 Cebollatí r. Uruguay
97 B4 Cebu Phil.
97 B4 Cebu i. Phil.
134 C3 Cecil U.S.A.
71 I1 Cecil Plains Australia
114 D3 Cecina Italy
134 A4 Cedar r. IA U.S.A.
142 C2 Cedar r. ND U.S.A.
134 D4 Cedarburg U.S.A.
141 F3 Cedar City U.S.A.
143 D5 Cedar Creek Reservoir U.S.A.
134 A4 Cedar Falls U.S.A.
134 D4 Cedar Grove WI U.S.A.
146 C5 Cedar Grove WV U.S.A.
147 F6 Cedar Island U.S.A.
131 I4 Cedar Lake Canada
134 D5 Cedar Lake U.S.A.
146 B4 Cedar Point U.S.A.
134 B5 Cedar Rapids U.S.A.
141 G3 Cedar Ridge U.S.A.
147 F5 Cedar Run U.S.A.
135 F4 Cedar Springs Canada
134 E4 Cedar Springs U.S.A.
145 C5 Cedartown U.S.A.
125 H5 Cedarville S. Africa
134 E3 Cedarville U.S.A.
150 A1 Cedros, Isla i. Mex.
68 D5 Ceduna Australia
122 E3 Ceeldheere Somalia
122 E2 Ceerigaabo Somalia
114 F5 Cefalù Sicily Italy
113 I7 Cegléd Hungary
93 B5 Ceheng China
80 E1 Çekerek Turkey
150 G5 Celaque, Parque Nacional nat. park Hond.
150 D3 Celaya Mex.
107 E4 Celbridge Rep. of Ireland
99 E3 Celebes i. Indon.
91 E6 Celebes Sea Indon./Phil.
146 A4 Celina U.S.A.
114 F1 Celje Slovenia
109 I2 Celle Germany
163 I2 Celtic Shelf sea feature N. Atlantic Ocean
80 E1 Cemilbey Turkey
80 G2 Çemişgezek Turkey
91 F7 Cenderawasih, Teluk b. Indon.
93 C5 Cengong China
141 F5 Centennial Wash watercourse U.S.A.
143 E6 Center U.S.A.
147 G4 Centereach U.S.A.
145 C5 Center Point U.S.A.
146 B5 Centerville OH U.S.A.
Centerville U.S.A. see Centreville
125 G1 Central admin. dist. Botswana
157 A4 Central, Cordillera mts Col.
150 I6 Central, Cordillera mts Panama
154 C5 Central, Cordillera mts Peru
97 B2 Central, Cordillera mts Phil.
121 D4 Central African Republic country Africa
85 G4 Central Brahui Range mts Pak.
134 B4 Central City IA U.S.A.
142 D3 Central City NE U.S.A.
144 B4 Centralia IL U.S.A.
138 B2 Centralia WA U.S.A.
122 D2 Central Island National Park Kenya
134 A2 Central Lakes U.S.A.
85 G5 Central Makran Range mts Pak.
160 G5 Central Pacific Basin sea feature Pacific Ocean
138 B3 Central Point U.S.A.
68 E2 Central Range mts P.N.G.
76 E4 Central Russian Upland hills Rus. Fed.
77 L3 Central Siberian Plateau Rus. Fed.
145 C5 Centreville AL U.S.A.
93 D6 Cenxi China
115 I5 Cephalonia i. Greece
Ceram Sea sea Indon. see Seram, Laut
141 E4 Cerbat Mountains U.S.A.
131 G4 Cereal Canada
156 D3 Ceres Arg.
124 C6 Ceres S. Africa
157 B2 Cereté Col.
111 E2 Cerezo de Abajo Spain
114 F4 Cerignola Italy
80 D2 Çerikli Turkey
80 D1 Çerkeş Turkey
80 G3 Çermelik Deresi r. Syria
81 G2 Çermik Turkey
115 M2 Cernavodă Romania
151 E2 Cerralvo Mex.
150 B2 Cerralvo, Isla i. Mex.
115 H4 Cërrik Albania
151 D3 Cerritos Mex.
158 C4 Cerro Azul Brazil
151 E3 Cerro Azul Mex.
154 C6 Cerro de Pasco Peru
150 I7 Cerro Hoya, Parque Nacional nat. park Panama
157 D3 Cerro Jáua, Meseta del plat. Venez.
157 C2 Cerrón, Cerro mt. Venez.
150 C2 Cerro Prieto Mex.
159 C3 Cerros Colorados, Embalse resr Arg.
154 B4 Cerros de Amotape, Parque Nacional nat. park Peru
114 F4 Cervati, Monte mt. Italy
114 C3 Cervione Corsica France
111 C1 Cervo Spain
157 B2 César r. Col.
114 E2 Cesena Italy
103 N4 Cēsis Latvia
112 G6 České Budějovice Czech Rep.
112 G6 Český Krumlov Czech Rep.
109 K5 Český Les mts Czech Rep./Germany
115 L5 Çeşme Turkey
71 I4 Cessnock Australia
115 H3 Cetinje Serb. and Mont.
114 F5 Cetraro Italy
111 D5 Ceuta Spain
69 H4 Ceva-i-Ra rf Fiji
110 F4 Cévennes mts France
80 E3 Ceyhan Turkey
80 E3 Ceyhan r. Turkey
81 H3 Ceylanpınar Turkey
Chaacha Turkm. see Çäçe
85 F5 Chābahār Iran
89 E3 Chabyêr Caka salt l. China
159 E2 Chacabuco Arg.
159 B4 Chacao Chile
159 C3 Chachahuén, Sierra mts Arg.
154 C5 Chachapoyas Peru
116 D4 Chachersk Belarus
98 B2 Chachoengsao Thai.
88 B4 Chachro Pak.
139 F4 Chaco Culture National Historical Park nat. park U.S.A.
130 C4 Chacon, Cape U.S.A.
121 D3 Chad country Africa
121 D3 Chad, Lake Africa
79 H1 Chadan Rus. Fed.
125 G1 Chadibe Botswana
Chadileo r. Arg. see Salado
142 C3 Chadron U.S.A.
98 A1 Chae Hom Thai.
83 H4 Chaek Kyrg.
96 C4 Chaeryŏng N. Korea
157 B4 Chafurray Col.
85 G4 Chagai Pak.
85 F4 Chagai Hills Afgh./Pak.
82 F3 Chagan Kzyl-Ordinskaya Oblast' Kazakh.
83 I2 Chagan Vostochnyy Kazakhstan Kazakh.
89 F2 Chagdo Kangri mt. China
85 G3 Chaghcharān Afgh.
83 G1 Chaglinka r. Kazakh.
110 G3 Chagny France
75 C7 Chagos Archipelago is British Indian Ocean Terr.
162 I5 Chagos-Laccadive Ridge sea feature Indian Ocean
162 I5 Chagos Trench sea feature Indian Ocean
116 I4 Chagra r. Rus. Fed.
150 J6 Chagres, Parque Nacional nat. park Panama
157 D2 Chaguaramas Venez.
Chagyl Turkm. see Çagyl
89 G3 Cha'gyüngoinba China
85 F4 Chahah Burjal Afgh.
85 E3 Chāh Ākhvor Iran
84 C4 Chahār Rūstā'ī Iran
85 E3 Chahār Takāb Iran
81 K3 Chahār Ţāq Iran
84 D3 Chāh Badam Iran
85 H2 Chāh-e Āb Afgh.
85 E3 Chāh-e Khoshāb Iran
84 D3 Chāh-e Nūklok Iran
84 D4 Chāh-e Rāh Iran
84 D3 Chāh-e Shūr Iran
84 D4 Chāh Ḩaqq Iran
Chah-i-Ab Afgh. see Chāh-e Āb
Chah-i-Shurkh Iraq see Chiyā Surkh
85 E5 Chāh Lak Iran
85 F4 Chah Sandan Pak.
89 F5 Chaibasa India
133 G3 Chaigneau, Lac l. Canada
96 C2 Chai He r. China
98 B2 Chainat Thai.
98 B2 Chai Si r. Thai.
93 □ Chai Wan Hong Kong China
98 A3 Chaiya Thai.
98 B2 Chaiyaphum Thai.
159 F1 Chajarí Arg.
88 B3 Chakar r. Pak.
89 H5 Chakaria Bangl.
85 F4 Chakhānsūr Afgh.
89 E4 Chakia India
85 G5 Chakku Pak.
154 D7 Chala Peru
85 G3 Chalap Dalan mts Afgh.
150 G5 Chalatenango El Salvador
133 G4 Chaleur Bay inlet Canada
93 D5 Chaling China
88 C5 Chalisgaon India
115 J5 Chalkida Greece
83 I4 Chalkudysu Kazakh.
72 A7 Chalky Inlet N.Z.
110 D3 Challans France
154 E7 Challapata Bol.
160 E5 Challenger Deep sea feature N. Pacific Ocean
138 D2 Challis U.S.A.
110 G2 Châlons-en-Champagne France
110 G3 Chalon-sur-Saône France
96 C2 Chaluhe China
84 C2 Chālūs Iran
109 K5 Cham Germany
98 D2 Cham, Cu Lao i. Vietnam
139 F4 Chama U.S.A.
157 C2 Chama r. Venez.
123 D5 Chama Zambia
159 D2 Chamaico Arg.
124 A3 Chamais Bay Namibia
85 G4 Chaman Pak.
88 D4 Chambal r. India
133 G3 Chambeaux, Lac l. Canada
131 H4 Chamberlain Canada
142 D3 Chamberlain U.S.A.
147 I1 Chamberlain Lake U.S.A.
141 H4 Chambers U.S.A.
146 E5 Chambersburg U.S.A.
110 G4 Chambéry France
123 D5 Chambeshi Zambia
114 C7 Chambi, Jebel mt. Tunisia
110 G4 Chamechaude mt. France
84 C3 Cham-e Ḩannā Iran
84 C3 Chameshk Iran
159 C1 Chamical Arg.
89 F4 Chamlang mt. Nepal
98 B3 Châmnar Cambodia
110 H4 Chamonix-Mont-Blanc France
87 C1 Champa India
130 B2 Champagne Canada
110 G2 Champagne France
125 H4 Champagne Castle mt. S. Africa
110 G3 Champagnole France
134 C5 Champaign U.S.A.
159 D1 Champaqui, Cerro mt. Arg.
98 C2 Champasak Laos
89 H5 Champhai India
134 D2 Champion U.S.A.
147 G2 Champlain U.S.A.
147 G2 Champlain, Lake Canada/U.S.A.
151 G4 Champotón Mex.
87 B4 Chamrajnagar India
116 H4 Chamzinka Rus. Fed.
98 B4 Chana Thai.
156 B3 Chañaral Chile
157 E3 Chanaro, Cerro mt. Venez.
159 B2 Chanco Chile
128 D3 Chandalar r. U.S.A.
87 C1 Chandarpur India
88 D3 Chandausi India
143 F6 Chandeleur Islands U.S.A.
88 E5 Chandia India
88 D3 Chandigarh India
141 G5 Chandler U.S.A.
135 I3 Chandos Lake Canada
89 G5 Chandpur Bangl.
88 D3 Chandpur India
89 H5 Chandraghona Bangl.
88 D6 Chandrapur India
88 D5 Chandur India
98 B2 Chang, Ko i. Thai.
123 D6 Changane r. Moz.
123 D5 Changara Moz.
96 E3 Changbai China
96 D3 Changbai Shan mts China/N. Korea
93 C7 Changcheng China
96 C2 Changchun China
96 C1 Changchunling China
92 F2 Changdao China
93 D4 Changde China
96 D4 Ch'angdo N. Korea
92 E3 Changfeng China
96 E5 Changgi-ap pt S. Korea
96 D6 Changhang S. Korea
96 D5 Changhowŏn S. Korea
93 F5 Changhua Taiwan
98 D1 Changhua Jiang r. China
96 D6 Changhŭng S. Korea
98 □ Changi Sing.
93 C7 Changjiang China
93 E4 Chang Jiang r. China alt. Jinsha Jiang, alt. Tongtian He, alt. Zhi Qu, conv. Yangtze, long Yangtze Kiang
96 D3 Changjin N. Korea
96 D3 Changjin-gang r. N. Korea
96 D3 Changjin-ho resr N. Korea
93 F5 Changle China
92 F2 Changli China
96 B1 Changling China
93 D5 Changning China
96 C4 Changnyŏn N. Korea
92 E1 Changping China
96 E5 Changp'yŏng S. Korea
96 C4 Changsan-got pt N. Korea
93 D4 Changsha China
93 F4 Changshan China
96 B4 Changshan Qundao is China
93 C4 Changshou China
93 D4 Changshoujie China
92 F4 Changshu China
93 C5 Changshun China
96 D6 Changsŏng S. Korea
93 E5 Changtai China
93 E5 Changting Fujian China
96 E1 Changting Heilong. China
96 C2 Changtu China
150 I6 Changuinola Panama
96 E6 Ch'angwŏn S. Korea
92 C3 Changwu China
96 A4 Changxing Dao i. China
93 D4 Changyang China
92 F2 Changyi China
96 C4 Changyŏn N. Korea
92 E3 Changyuan China
92 D2 Changzhi China
92 F4 Changzhou China
115 K7 Chania Greece
92 B3 Chankou China
87 B3 Channapatna India
110 C2 Channel Islands English Chan.
140 C5 Channel Islands U.S.A.
140 B5 Channel Islands National Park U.S.A.
133 I4 Channel-Port-aux-Basques Canada
105 I6 Channel Tunnel France/U.K.
134 C2 Channing U.S.A.
111 C1 Chantada Spain
98 B2 Chanthaburi Thai.
110 F2 Chantilly France
143 E4 Chanute U.S.A.
76 I4 Chany, Ozero salt l. Rus. Fed.
92 E2 Chaobai Xinhe r. China
92 E4 Chaohu China
92 E4 Chao Hu l. China
98 B2 Chao Phraya r. Thai.
120 B1 Chaouèn Morocco
89 H2 Chaowula Shan mt. China
93 E6 Chaoyang Guangdong China
92 F1 Chaoyang Liaoning China
93 E6 Chaozhou China
158 E1 Chapada Diamantina, Parque Nacional nat. park Brazil
158 A1 Chapada dos Guimarães Brazil
158 C1 Chapada dos Veadeiros, Parque Nacional da nat. park Brazil
150 D3 Chapala Mex.
150 D3 Chapala, Laguna de l. Mex.
157 B4 Chaparral Col.
82 B2 Chapayev Kazakh.
116 I4 Chapayevsk Rus. Fed.
83 H1 Chapayevskoye Kazakh.
156 F3 Chapecó Brazil
156 F3 Chapecó r. Brazil
105 F4 Chapel-en-le-Frith U.K.
145 E5 Chapel Hill U.S.A.
108 C4 Chapelle-lez-Herlaimont Belgium
105 F4 Chapeltown U.K.
134 D5 Chapin, Lake U.S.A.
135 F2 Chapleau Canada
116 F4 Chaplygin Rus. Fed.
117 E6 Chaplynka Ukr.
146 B6 Chapmanville U.S.A.
71 G8 Chappell Islands Australia
85 G3 Chapri Pass Afgh.
154 E7 Chaqui Bol.
88 D2 Char Jammu and Kashmir
150 D3 Charcas Mex.
89 H3 Char Chu r. China
73 B3 Charcot Island i. Antarctica
131 G3 Chard Canada
105 E7 Chard U.K.
83 F4 Chardara, Step' plain Kazakh.
83 G4 Chardarinskoye Vodokhranilishche resr Kazakh./Uzbek.
81 K5 Chardāvol Iran
146 C4 Chardon U.S.A.
110 E3 Charente r. France
84 D4 Charg Iran
85 H3 Chārīkār Afgh.
142 E3 Chariton r. U.S.A.
135 F3 Charity Island U.S.A.
84 C4 Charkas Iran
76 G3 Charkayuvom Rus. Fed.
88 D4 Charkhari India
108 C4 Charleroi Belgium
137 K4 Charles, Cape U.S.A.
134 A4 Charles City U.S.A.
72 C4 Charleston N.Z.
144 B4 Charleston IL U.S.A.
147 I2 Charleston ME U.S.A.
143 F4 Charleston MO U.S.A.
145 E5 Charleston SC U.S.A.
146 C5 Charleston WV U.S.A.
141 E3 Charleston Peak U.S.A.
107 C4 Charlestown Rep. of Ireland
147 G3 Charlestown NH U.S.A.
147 H4 Charlestown RI U.S.A.
146 E5 Charles Town U.S.A.
68 E4 Charleville Australia
110 G2 Charleville-Mézières France
134 E3 Charlevoix U.S.A.
130 E3 Charlie Lake Canada
134 E4 Charlotte MI U.S.A.
145 D5 Charlotte NC U.S.A.
145 D7 Charlotte Harbor b. U.S.A.
146 D5 Charlottesville U.S.A.
133 H4 Charlottetown Canada
157 E2 Charlotteville Trin. and Tob.
70 E6 Charlton Australia
132 E3 Charlton Island Canada
116 F2 Charozero Rus. Fed.
88 B2 Charsadda Pak.
68 E4 Charters Towers Australia
110 E2 Chartres France
Charvakskoye Vdkhr. resr Kazakh./Uzbek. see Chorvoq suv ombori
83 I4 Charyn Kazakh.
83 I4 Charyn r. Kazakh.
83 J1 Charysh r. Rus. Fed.
83 J2 Charyshskoye Rus. Fed.
159 E2 Chascomús Arg.
130 F4 Chase Canada
82 E5 Chashkent Turkm.
84 E3 Chashmeh Nūrī Iran
84 D3 Chashmeh-ye Palasi Iran
116 D4 Chashniki Belarus
72 B7 Chaslands Mistake c. N.Z.
96 D3 Chasŏng N. Korea
84 D3 Chastab, Kūh-e mts Iran
110 D3 Châteaubriant France
110 E3 Château-du-Loir France
110 E2 Châteaudun France
147 F2 Chateaugay U.S.A.
147 G2 Châteauguay Canada
110 B2 Châteaulin France
110 F3 Châteauneuf-sur-Loire France
110 E3 Châteauroux France
108 E6 Château-Salins France
110 F2 Château-Thierry France
108 C4 Châtelet Belgium
110 E3 Châtellerault France
134 A4 Chatfield U.S.A.
135 F4 Chatham Canada
105 H6 Chatham U.K.
147 H4 Chatham MA U.S.A.
147 G3 Chatham NY U.S.A.
146 D6 Chatham VA U.S.A.
69 I6 Chatham Islands N.Z.
160 H8 Chatham Rise sea feature S. Pacific Ocean
130 C4 Chatham Sound sea chan. Canada
130 C3 Chatham Strait U.S.A.
83 G4 Chatkal r. Kyrg.
83 G4 Chatkal Range mts Kyrg.
89 F4 Chatra India
135 G3 Chatsworth Canada
134 C5 Chatsworth U.S.A.
145 C5 Chattanooga U.S.A.
105 H5 Chatteris U.K.
98 B2 Chatturat Thai.
83 H4 Chatyr-Köl l. Kyrg.
83 I4 Chatyr-Tash Kyrg.
98 C3 Châu Đôc Vietnam
88 B4 Chauhtan India
89 H5 Chauk Myanmar
88 E4 Chauka r. India
88 D3 Chaukhamba mts India
110 G2 Chaumont France
98 A2 Chaungwabyin Myanmar
77 R3 Chaunskaya Guba b. Rus. Fed.
110 F2 Chauny France
98 D2 Châu Ô Vietnam
89 F4 Chauparan India
146 D3 Chautauqua, Lake U.S.A.
83 H4 Chauvay Kyrg.
87 C4 Chavakachcheri Sri Lanka
84 B3 Chavār Iran
155 I4 Chaves Brazil
111 C2 Chaves Port.
132 E2 Chavigny, Lac l. Canada
116 D4 Chavusy Belarus
88 A3 Chawal r. Pak.
Chây r. Vietnam see Chay, Sông
93 B6 Chay, Sông r. Vietnam
159 D2 Chazón Arg.
147 G2 Chazy U.S.A.
105 F5 Cheadle U.K.
146 D5 Cheat r. U.S.A.
112 F5 Cheb Czech Rep.
114 D7 Chebba Tunisia
116 H3 Cheboksary Rus. Fed.
134 E3 Cheboygan U.S.A.
117 H7 Chechen', Ostrov i. Rus. Fed.
117 H7 Chechenskaya Respublika aut. rep. Rus. Fed.
Chechnia aut. rep. Rus. Fed. see Chechenskaya Respublika
96 E5 Chech'ŏn S. Korea
143 E5 Checotah U.S.A.
96 A5 Chedao China
105 E6 Cheddar U.K.
131 G3 Cheecham Canada
128 B3 Chefornak U.S.A.
125 J1 Chefu Moz.
120 B2 Chegga Mauritania
123 D5 Chegutu Zimbabwe
138 B2 Chehalis U.S.A.
85 H3 Chehardar Pass Afgh.
81 K5 Chehariz tourist site Iraq
84 E4 Chehell'āyeh Iran
96 D7 Cheju S. Korea
90 E3 Cheju do S. Korea
96 D7 Cheju-do i. S. Korea
96 D7 Cheju-haehyŏp sea chan. S. Korea
116 F4 Chekhov Rus. Fed.
138 B2 Chelan, Lake U.S.A.
Cheleken Turkm. see Hazar
159 C3 Chelforó Arg.
111 G4 Chélif, Oued r. Alg.
82 B2 Chelkar Kazakh.
113 K5 Chełm Poland
105 H6 Chelmer r. U.K.
113 I4 Chełmno Poland
105 H6 Chelmsford U.K.
147 H3 Chelmsford U.S.A.
105 E6 Cheltenham U.K.
111 F3 Chelva Spain
76 H4 Chelyabinsk Rus. Fed.
123 D5 Chemba Moz.
88 D2 Chêm Co l. China
109 K4 Chemnitz Germany
146 E3 Chemung r. U.S.A.
85 H4 Chenab r. India/Pak.
120 B2 Chenachane Alg.
147 F3 Chenango r. U.S.A.
138 C2 Cheney U.S.A.
143 D4 Cheney Reservoir U.S.A.
87 C3 Chengalpattu India
92 E2 Cheng'an China
93 D5 Chengbu China
92 E1 Chengde China
93 B4 Chengdu China
92 C3 Chenggu China
93 E6 Chenghai China
92 C4 Chengkou China
91 D5 Chengmai China
96 B4 Chengzitan China
92 F3 Cheniu Shan i. China
87 C3 Chennai India
134 C5 Chenoa U.S.A.
93 D5 Chenxi China
93 D5 Chenzhou China
Cheo Reo Vietnam see A Yun Pa
154 C5 Chepén Peru
159 C1 Chepes Arg.
150 J6 Chepo Panama
105 E6 Chepstow U.K.
116 I3 Cheptsa r. Rus. Fed.
81 K5 Cheqād Kabūd Iran
134 B2 Chequamegon Bay U.S.A.
110 F3 Cher r. France
150 D4 Cherán Mex.
145 E5 Cheraw U.S.A.
110 D2 Cherbourg France
111 H4 Cherchell Alg.
116 I4 Cherdakly Rus. Fed.
90 C1 Cheremkhovo Rus. Fed.
83 J1 Cheremnoye Rus. Fed.
94 D2 Cheremshany Rus. Fed.
116 F3 Cherepovets Rus. Fed.
116 H2 Cherevkovo Rus. Fed.
114 B7 Chéria Alg.
117 E5 Cherkasy Ukr.
117 G6 Cherkessk Rus. Fed.
87 C2 Cherla India
83 H1 Cherlak Rus. Fed.
83 H1 Cherlakskoye Rus. Fed.
123 C5 Chermenze Angola
83 G4 Chernak Kazakh.
116 I3 Chernaya Kholunitsa Rus. Fed.
94 C2 Chernigovka Rus. Fed.
117 D5 Chernihiv Ukr.
117 F6 Cherninivka Ukr.
117 C5 Chernivtsi Ukr.
90 B1 Chernogorsk Rus. Fed.
83 I1 Chernoretskoye Kazakh.
116 H3 Chernovskoye Rus. Fed.
117 D5 Chernyakhiv Ukr.
113 J3 Chernyakhovsk Rus. Fed.
117 F5 Chernyanka Rus. Fed.
77 M3 Chernyshevskiy Rus. Fed.
117 H6 Chernyye Zemli reg. Rus. Fed.
82 C2 Chernyy Otrog Rus. Fed.
117 H5 Chernyy Yar Rus. Fed.
142 E3 Cherokee IA U.S.A.
143 D4 Cherokee OK U.S.A.
143 E4 Cherokees, Lake o' the U.S.A.
145 E7 Cherokee Sound Bahamas
159 B3 Cherquenco Chile
89 G4 Cherrapunji India
141 E2 Cherry Creek U.S.A.
141 E1 Cherry Creek Mountains U.S.A.
147 J2 Cherryfield U.S.A.
69 G3 Cherry Island Solomon Is
135 I4 Cherry Valley Canada
147 F3 Cherry Valley U.S.A.
77 P3 Cherskogo, Khrebet mts Rus. Fed.
117 G5 Chertkovo Rus. Fed.
116 I2 Cherva Rus. Fed.
115 K3 Cherven Bryag Bulg.
117 C5 Chervonohrad Ukr.
117 E5 Chervonozavods'ke Ukr.
116 D4 Chervyen' Belarus
105 F6 Cherwell r. U.K.
116 D4 Cherykaw Belarus
135 E4 Chesaning U.S.A.
147 E6 Chesapeake U.S.A.
147 E5 Chesapeake Bay U.S.A.
105 G6 Chesham U.K.
147 G3 Cheshire U.S.A.
105 E4 Cheshire Plain U.K.
Cheshme Vtoroy Turkm. see Cheshme 2-y
82 E5 Cheshme 2-y Turkm.
76 F3 Cheshskaya Guba b. Rus. Fed.
83 H5 Cheshtebe Tajik.
85 F3 Chesht-e Sharīf Afgh.
105 G6 Cheshunt U.K.
82 E1 Chesma Rus. Fed.
105 E4 Chester U.K.
140 B1 Chester CA U.S.A.
144 B4 Chester IL U.S.A.
138 E1 Chester MT U.S.A.
147 F5 Chester PA U.S.A.
145 D5 Chester SC U.S.A.
147 E5 Chester r. U.S.A.
105 F4 Chesterfield U.K.
69 F3 Chesterfield, Îles is New Caledonia
131 K2 Chesterfield Inlet Canada
131 K2 Chesterfield Inlet inlet Canada
104 F3 Chester-le-Street U.K.
147 E5 Chestertown MD U.S.A.
147 G3 Chestertown NY U.S.A.
147 F2 Chesterville Canada
146 D4 Chestnut Ridge U.S.A.
147 I1 Chesuncook U.S.A.
147 I1 Chesuncook Lake U.S.A.
114 B6 Chetaïbi Alg.
133 H4 Chéticamp Canada
87 A4 Chetlat i. India
151 G4 Chetumal Mex.
130 E3 Chetwynd Canada
93 □ Cheung Chau Hong Kong China
93 □ Cheung Chau i. Hong Kong China
72 D5 Cheviot N.Z.
104 E2 Cheviot Hills U.K.
138 C1 Chewelah U.S.A.
143 D5 Cheyenne OK U.S.A.
138 F3 Cheyenne WY U.S.A.
142 C3 Cheyenne r. U.S.A.
142 C4 Cheyenne Wells U.S.A.
130 E4 Chezacut Canada
88 C4 Chhapar India
89 F4 Chhapra India
88 D4 Chhatarpur India
88 B3 Chhatr Pak.
89 E5 Chhattisgarh state India
88 D5 Chhindwara India
88 C5 Chhota Udepur India
88 C4 Chhoti Sadri India
89 G4 Chhukha Bhutan
98 C2 Chi, Lam r. Thai.
93 F6 Chiai Taiwan
122 E4 Chiamboni Kenya
98 A1 Chiang Dao Thai.
98 B1 Chiang Kham Thai.
98 B1 Chiang Khan Thai.
98 A1 Chiang Mai Thai.
98 A1 Chiang Rai Thai.
151 F4 Chiapas state Mex.
114 C2 Chiari Italy
151 E4 Chiautla Mex.
95 G7 Chiba Japan
93 D4 Chibi China
123 B5 Chibia Angola
123 D6 Chiboma Moz.
132 F4 Chibougamau Canada
132 F4 Chibougamau, Lac l. Canada
95 E6 Chibu-Sangaku National Park Japan
125 J2 Chibuto Moz.
Chibuzhang Hu l. China see Migriggyangzham Co
134 D5 Chicago U.S.A. (City Plan 61)
134 D5 Chicago Heights U.S.A.
134 C5 Chicago Ship Canal U.S.A.
157 B3 Chicamocha r. Col.
157 E3 Chicanán r. Venez.
130 B3 Chichagof U.S.A.
130 B3 Chichagof Island U.S.A.
92 E1 Chicheng China
151 G3 Chichén Itzá tourist site Mex.
105 G7 Chichester U.K.
68 B4 Chichester Range mts Australia
95 F7 Chichibu Japan
95 F7 Chichibu-Tama National Park Japan
146 E6 Chickahominy r. U.S.A.
145 C5 Chickamauga Lake U.S.A.
143 D5 Chickasha U.S.A.
111 C4 Chiclana de la Frontera Spain
154 C5 Chiclayo Peru
156 C6 Chico r. Chubut Arg.
159 B4 Chico r. Chubut/Río Negro Arg.
156 C7 Chico r. Arg.
140 B2 Chico U.S.A.
125 K2 Chicomo Moz.
151 F5 Chicomucelo Mex.
147 G3 Chicopee U.S.A.
97 B2 Chico Sapocoy, Mount Phil.
133 F4 Chicoutimi Canada
125 I1 Chicualacuala Moz.
87 B4 Chidambaram India
125 K2 Chidenguele Moz.
133 H1 Chidley, Cape Canada
96 D6 Chido S. Korea
125 K2 Chiducuane Moz.
145 D6 Chiefland U.S.A.
112 F7 Chiemsee l. Germany
108 D5 Chiers r. France
114 F3 Chieti Italy
151 E4 Chietla Mex.
92 F1 Chifeng China
158 E2 Chifre, Serra do mts Brazil
83 H3 Chiganak Kazakh.
133 G4 Chignecto Bay Canada
157 A3 Chigorodó Col.
123 D6 Chigubo Moz.
89 G3 Chigu Co l. China
150 C1 Chihuahua Mex.
150 C1 Chihuahua state Mex.
83 F3 Chiili Kazakh.
93 D6 Chikan China
87 B3 Chik Ballapur India
116 D3 Chikhachevo Rus. Fed.
88 D5 Chikhali Kalan Parasia India
88 D5 Chikhli India
87 A3 Chikmagalur India
95 F6 Chikuma-gawa r. Japan
130 E4 Chilanko Forks Canada
151 E4 Chilapa Mex.
79 F3 Chilas Jammu and Kashmir
87 B5 Chilaw Sri Lanka
140 B2 Chilcoot U.S.A.
130 E4 Chilcotin r. Canada
143 C5 Childress U.S.A.
156 B5 Chile country S. America
161 N8 Chile Basin sea feature S. Pacific Ocean
156 C3 Chilecito Arg.
161 N8 Chile Rise sea feature S. Pacific Ocean
117 H6 Chilgir Rus. Fed.
83 I4 Chilik Kazakh.
89 F6 Chilika Lake India
123 C5 Chililabombwe Zambia
130 E4 Chilko r. Canada
130 E4 Chilko Lake Canada
Chilkoot U.S.A. see Chilcoot
159 B3 Chillán Chile
159 B3 Chillán, Nevado mts Chile
159 E3 Chillar Arg.
134 C5 Chillicothe IL U.S.A.
142 E4 Chillicothe MO U.S.A.
146 B5 Chillicothe OH U.S.A.
88 C1 Chillinji Pak.
130 E5 Chilliwack Canada
Chil'mamedkum, Peski des. Turkm. see Çilmämmetgum
156 B6 Chiloé, Isla de i. Chile
138 B3 Chiloquin U.S.A.
151 E4 Chilpancingo Mex.
71 G6 Chiltern Australia
105 G6 Chiltern Hills U.K.
134 C3 Chilton U.S.A.
93 F5 Chilung Taiwan
Chilung Pass India see Pensi La
123 D4 Chimala Tanz.
150 J6 Chimán Panama
108 C4 Chimay Belgium
108 C4 Chimay, Bois de for. Belgium
159 C1 Chimbas Arg.
Chimbay Uzbek. see Chimboy
154 C4 Chimborazo mt. Ecuador
154 C5 Chimbote Peru
82 D4 Chimboy Uzbek.
157 B2 Chimichaguá Col.
123 D5 Chimoio Moz.
90 B3 China country Asia
151 E2 China Mex.
157 B3 Chinácota Col.
151 G4 Chinajá Guat.
140 D4 China Lake CA U.S.A.
147 I2 China Lake ME U.S.A.
150 H5 Chinandega Nicaragua
140 C5 China Point U.S.A.
Chinaz Uzbek. see Chinoz
154 C6 Chincha Alta Peru
130 F3 Chinchaga r. Canada
148 G5 Chinchorro, Banco sea feature Mex.
147 F6 Chincoteague Bay U.S.A.
123 D5 Chinde Moz.
96 D6 Chindo S. Korea
96 D6 Chin-do i. S. Korea
90 B3 Chindu China
89 H5 Chindwin r. Myanmar
88 C2 Chineni Jammu and Kashmir
157 B3 Chingaza, Parque Nacional nat. park Col.
96 C4 Chinghwa N. Korea
82 C2 Chingirlau Kazakh.
83 I2 Chingiz-Tau, Khrebet mts Kazakh.
123 C5 Chingola Zambia
123 B5 Chinguar Angola
96 E6 Chinhae S. Korea
123 D5 Chinhoyi Zimbabwe
88 C3 Chiniot Pak.
150 B2 Chinipas Mex.
98 C2 Chinit, Stœng r. Cambodia
96 E6 Chinju S. Korea
122 C3 Chinko r. Centr. Afr. Rep.
141 H3 Chinle U.S.A.
141 H3 Chinle Valley U.S.A.
141 H3 Chinle Wash watercourse U.S.A.
93 F5 Chinmen Taiwan
93 F5 Chinmen Tao i. Taiwan
87 B2 Chinnur India
95 F7 Chino Japan
110 E3 Chinon France
160 H3 Chinook Trough sea feature N. Pacific Ocean
141 F4 Chino Valley U.S.A.
83 G4 Chinoz Uzbek.
123 D5 Chinsali Zambia
87 B3 Chintamani India
114 E2 Chioggia Italy
115 L5 Chios Greece
115 K5 Chios i. Greece
123 D5 Chipata Zambia
159 C4 Chipchihua, Sierra de mts Arg.
123 B5 Chipindo Angola
123 D6 Chipinge Zimbabwe
87 A2 Chiplun India
105 E6 Chippenham U.K.
134 B3 Chippewa r. U.S.A.
134 B3 Chippewa, Lake U.S.A.
134 B3 Chippewa Falls U.S.A.
105 F6 Chipping Norton U.K.
105 E6 Chipping Sodbury U.K.
147 J2 Chiputneticook Lakes U.S.A.
151 G4 Chiquibul National Park Belize
151 G5 Chiquimula Guat.
157 B3 Chiquinquira Col.
117 G5 Chir r. Rus. Fed.
87 C3 Chirada India
87 A4 Chirakkal India
87 C3 Chirala India
85 G3 Chiras Afgh.
88 C3 Chirawa India
Chirchik Uzbek. see Chirchiq
83 G4 Chirchiq Uzbek.
123 D6 Chiredzi Zimbabwe
141 H5 Chiricahua National Monument nat. park U.S.A.
141 H6 Chiricahua Peak U.S.A.
157 B2 Chiriguaná Col.
128 C4 Chirikof Island U.S.A.
150 I6 Chiriquí, Golfo de b. Panama
150 I6 Chiriquí, Laguna de b. Panama
105 D5 Chirk U.K.
106 F5 Chirnside U.K.
115 K3 Chirpan Bulg.
150 I6 Chirripo mt. Costa Rica
123 C5 Chirundu Zambia
132 E3 Chisasibi Canada
151 G5 Chisec Guat.
134 A2 Chisholm U.S.A.
88 C3 Chishtian Mandi Pak.
93 B4 Chishui China
117 D6 Chişinău Moldova
113 J7 Chişineu-Criş Romania
116 I4 Chistopol' Rus. Fed.
83 G1 Chistyakovskoye Kazakh.
90 D1 Chita Rus. Fed.
123 B5 Chitado Angola
123 D5 Chitambo Zambia
122 C4 Chitato Angola
131 H4 Chitek Lake Canada
123 B5 Chitembo Angola
123 D4 Chitipa Malawi
123 C5 Chitokoloki Zambia
94 G3 Chitose Japan
87 B3 Chitradurga India
88 B2 Chitral Pak.
88 B2 Chitral r. Pak.
150 I7 Chitré Panama
89 G5 Chittagong Bangl.
89 F5 Chittaranjan India
88 C4 Chittaurgarh India
87 B3 Chittoor India
87 B4 Chittur India
123 D5 Chitungulu Zambia
123 D5 Chitungwiza Zimbabwe
123 C5 Chiume Angola
150 A2 Chívato, Punta pt Mex.
123 D5 Chivhu Zimbabwe
159 E2 Chivilcoy Arg.
93 D6 Chixi China
81 J4 Chiyā Surkh Iraq
82 B2 Chizha Vtoraya Kazakh.
93 E4 Chizhou China
95 D7 Chizu Japan
83 G1 Chkalovo Kazakh.
116 G3 Chkalovsk Rus. Fed.

178 Doreenville

124 C1 **Doreenville** Namibia
131 H4 **Doré Lake** Canada
131 H4 **Doré Lake** *l.* Canada
114 C4 **Dorgali** *Sardinia* Italy
89 H2 **Dorgê Co** *l.* China
85 G4 **Dori** *r.* Afgh.
120 B3 **Dori** Burkina
124 C5 **Doring** *r.* S. Africa
105 G6 **Dorking** U.K.
108 E3 **Dormagen** Germany
108 B5 **Dormans** France
106 D3 **Dornoch Firth** *est.* U.K.
92 C1 **Dornogovĭ** *prov.* Mongolia
108 F1 **Dornum** Germany
116 E4 **Dorogobuzh** Rus. Fed.
113 M7 **Dorohoi** Romania
90 B2 **Döröö Nuur** *salt l.* Mongolia
102 L2 **Dorotea** Sweden
68 B4 **Dorre Island** Australia
71 J3 **Dorrigo** Australia
138 B3 **Dorris** U.S.A.
120 D4 **Dorsale Camerounaise** *slope* Cameroon/Nigeria
135 H3 **Dorset** Canada
105 D7 **Dorset and East Devon Coast** *tourist site* U.K.
108 F3 **Dortmund** Germany
146 B6 **Dorton** U.S.A.
80 F3 **Dörtyol** Turkey
109 G1 **Dorum** Germany
122 C3 **Doruma** Dem. Rep. Congo
84 E3 **Dorūneh** Iran
109 H2 **Dörverden** Germany
85 E4 **Do Sārī** Iran
156 C6 **Dos Bahías, Cabo** *c.* Arg.
141 H5 **Dos Cabezas** U.S.A.
154 C5 **Dos de Mayo** Peru
Đo Son Vietnam *see* **Đo Sơn**
93 C6 **Đo Sơn** Vietnam
140 B3 **Dos Palos** U.S.A.
109 K2 **Dosse** *r.* Germany
120 C3 **Dosso** Niger
82 C3 **Dossor** Kazakh.
83 G4 **Do'stlik** Uzbek.
83 J3 **Dostyk** Kazakh.
145 C6 **Dothan** U.S.A.
110 F1 **Douai** France
120 C4 **Douala** Cameroon
110 B2 **Douarnenez** France
93 □ **Double Island** *Hong Kong* China
140 C4 **Double Peak** U.S.A.
110 H3 **Doubs** *r.* France
72 A6 **Doubtful Sound** *inlet* N.Z.
72 D1 **Doubtless Bay** N.Z.
120 B3 **Douentza** Mali
104 C3 **Douglas** Isle of Man
124 E4 **Douglas** S. Africa
106 E5 **Douglas** U.K.
130 C3 **Douglas** *AK* U.S.A.
141 H6 **Douglas** *AZ* U.S.A.
145 D6 **Douglas** *GA* U.S.A.
138 F3 **Douglas** *WY* U.S.A.
71 H8 **Douglas Apsley National Park** Australia
130 D4 **Douglas Channel** Canada
141 H2 **Douglas Creek** *r.* U.S.A.
110 F1 **Doullens** France
106 D4 **Doune** U.K.
158 C2 **Dourada, Cachoeira** *waterfall* Brazil
158 B2 **Dourada, Serra** *hills* Brazil
158 C1 **Dourada, Serra** *mts* Brazil
158 A3 **Dourados** Brazil
158 A3 **Dourados** *r.* Brazil
158 B3 **Dourados, Serra dos** *hills* Brazil
111 C2 **Douro** *r.* Port. *alt.* **Duero (Spain)**
108 D5 **Douzy** France
105 F4 **Dove** *r. England* U.K.
105 I5 **Dove** *r. England* U.K.
133 I3 **Dove Brook** Canada
141 H3 **Dove Creek** U.S.A.
71 G9 **Dover** Australia
105 I6 **Dover** U.K.
147 F5 **Dover** *DE* U.S.A.
147 H3 **Dover** *NH* U.S.A.
147 F4 **Dover** *NJ* U.S.A.
146 C4 **Dover** *OH* U.S.A.
105 I7 **Dover, Strait of** France/U.K.
147 I2 **Dover-Foxcroft** U.S.A.
84 B3 **Doveyrīch, Rūd-e** *r.* Iran/Iraq
134 D5 **Dowagiac** U.S.A.
84 D4 **Dow Chāhī** Iran
85 E2 **Dowgha'ī** Iran
98 A5 **Dowi, Tanjung** *pt* Indon.
85 F3 **Dowlatābād** Afgh.
85 G2 **Dowlatābād** Afgh.
84 D4 **Dowlatābād** Iran
84 D4 **Dowlatābād** Iran
84 E4 **Dowlatābād** Iran
85 F2 **Dowlatābād** Iran
85 G3 **Dowl at Yār** Afgh.
140 B2 **Downieville** U.S.A.
107 F3 **Downpatrick** U.K.
147 F3 **Downsville** U.S.A.
84 C3 **Dow Rūd** Iran
81 K4 **Dow Sar** Iran
85 H3 **Dowshī** Afgh.
140 B1 **Doyle** U.S.A.
147 F4 **Doylestown** U.S.A.
95 C6 **Dōzen** *is* Japan
135 I2 **Dozois, Réservoir** *resr* Canada
120 B2 **Drâa, Hammada du** *plat.* Alg.
158 B3 **Dracena** Brazil
108 E1 **Drachten** Neth.
115 K2 **Drăgănești-Olt** Romania
115 K2 **Drăgășani** Romania
157 E2 **Dragon's Mouths** *str.* Trin. and Tob./Venez.
103 M3 **Dragsfjärd** Fin.
110 H5 **Draguignan** France
117 C4 **Drahichyn** Belarus
71 J2 **Drake** Australia
141 F4 **Drake** *AZ* U.S.A.
131 I5 **Drake** *ND* U.S.A.
125 H5 **Drakensberg** *mts* Lesotho/S. Africa
125 I2 **Drakensberg** *mts* S. Africa
163 E9 **Drake Passage** *sea chan.* S. Atlantic Ocean
115 K4 **Drama** Greece
103 J4 **Drammen** Norway
103 J4 **Drangedal** Norway
85 G5 **Dranjuk** *h.* Pak.
109 H3 **Dransfeld** Germany
107 E3 **Draperstown** U.K.
88 C2 **Dras** Jammu and Kashmir
112 F7 **Drau** *r.* Austria
130 G4 **Drayton Valley** Canada
114 B6 **Dréan** Alg.
109 H4 **Dreistelzberge** *h.* Germany
112 F5 **Dresden** Germany
116 D4 **Dretun'** Belarus
110 E2 **Dreux** France
103 K3 **Drevsjø** Norway
104 G3 **Driffield** U.K.
146 D4 **Driftwood** U.S.A.
107 B6 **Drimoleague** Rep. of Ireland
114 G3 **Drniš** Croatia
109 H1 **Drochtersen** Germany
107 E4 **Drogheda** Rep. of Ireland
117 B5 **Drohobych** Ukr.
105 E5 **Droitwich Spa** U.K.
89 G4 **Drokung** India
109 I2 **Drömling** *reg.* Germany
107 D4 **Dromod** Rep. of Ireland
107 D3 **Dromore** *Northern Ireland* U.K.
107 E3 **Dromore** *Northern Ireland* U.K.
105 F4 **Dronfield** U.K.
129 P2 **Dronning Louise Land** *reg.* Greenland
108 D2 **Dronten** Neth.
88 B2 **Drosh** Pak.
117 F4 **Droskovo** Rus. Fed.
71 F7 **Drouin** Australia
130 G4 **Drumheller** Canada
138 D2 **Drummond** *MT* U.S.A.
134 B2 **Drummond** *WI* U.S.A.
135 F3 **Drummond Island** U.S.A.
133 F4 **Drummondville** Canada
106 D6 **Drummore** U.K.
106 D4 **Drumochter, Pass of** U.K.
103 N5 **Druskininkai** Lith.
77 P3 **Druzhina** Rus. Fed.
115 K3 **Dryanovo** Bulg.
130 B3 **Dry Bay** U.S.A.
131 K5 **Dryberry Lake** Canada
134 E2 **Dryburg** U.S.A.
132 B4 **Dryden** Canada
140 D2 **Dry Lake** U.S.A.
106 D4 **Drymen** U.K.
68 C3 **Drysdale** *r.* Australia
84 C3 **Dūāb** *r.* Iran
93 C6 **Du'an** China
147 F2 **Duane** U.S.A.
89 G4 **Duars** *reg.* India
149 J5 **Duarte, Pico** *mt.* Dom. Rep.
78 B4 **Ḍubā** Saudi Arabia
86 E4 **Dubai** U.A.E.
131 I2 **Dubawnt** *r.* Canada
131 I2 **Dubawnt Lake** Canada
Dubayy U.A.E. *see* **Dubai**
78 B4 **Dubbagh, Jabal ad** *mt.* Saudi Arabia
71 H4 **Dubbo** Australia
134 D1 **Dublin** Canada
107 E4 **Dublin** Rep. of Ireland
145 D5 **Dublin** U.S.A.
116 F3 **Dubna** Rus. Fed.
117 C5 **Dubno** Ukr.
138 D2 **Dubois** *ID* U.S.A.
138 E3 **Dubois** *WY* U.S.A.
146 D4 **Du Bois** U.S.A.
117 H5 **Dubovka** Rus. Fed.
117 G6 **Dubovskoye** Rus. Fed.
81 L1 **Dübrar Pass** Azer.
120 A4 **Dubréka** Guinea
115 H3 **Dubrovnik** Croatia
117 C5 **Dubrovytsya** Ukr.
116 D4 **Dubrowna** Belarus
83 J4 **Dubun** Kazakh.
134 B4 **Dubuque** U.S.A.
103 M5 **Dubysa** *r.* Lith.
98 C3 **Đưc Bôn** Vietnam
67 J6 **Duc de Gloucester, Îles du** *is* Fr. Polynesia
93 E4 **Duchang** China
141 G1 **Duchesne** U.S.A.
67 J7 **Ducie Island** *atoll* Pitcairn Is
145 C5 **Duck** *r.* U.S.A.
131 I4 **Duck Bay** Canada
131 H4 **Duck Lake** Canada
134 E4 **Duck Lake** U.S.A.
141 E2 **Duckwater** U.S.A.
141 E2 **Duckwater Peak** U.S.A.
98 C3 **Đưc Linh** Vietnam
98 D2 **Đưc Phô** Vietnam
98 C1 **Duc Tho** Vietnam
Đưc Trong Vietnam *see* **Liên Nghia**
157 B4 **Duda** *r.* Col.
108 E5 **Dudelange** Lux.
109 I3 **Duderstadt** Germany
89 E4 **Dudhi** India
89 G4 **Dudhnai** India
76 J3 **Dudinka** Rus. Fed.
105 E5 **Dudley** U.K.
88 D6 **Dudna** *r.* India
106 F3 **Dudwick, Hill of** U.K.
120 B4 **Duékoué** Côte d'Ivoire
111 C2 **Duero** *r.* Spain *alt.* **Douro (Portugal)**
135 H1 **Dufault, Lac** *l.* Canada
108 C3 **Duffel** Belgium
132 E2 **Dufferin, Cape** Canada
146 B6 **Duffield** U.S.A.
69 G2 **Duff Islands** Solomon Is
106 E3 **Dufftown** U.K.
132 E1 **Dufrost, Pointe** *pt* Canada
Dugab Uzbek. *see* **Dugob**
114 F3 **Dugi Otok** *i.* Croatia
83 F5 **Dugob** Uzbek.
92 C2 **Dugui Qarag** China
92 D3 **Du He** *r.* China
157 D4 **Duida, Cerro** *mt.* Venez.
154 E3 **Duida-Marahuaca, Parque Nacional** Venez.
108 E3 **Duisburg** Germany
157 B3 **Duitama** Col.
125 I1 **Duiwelskloof** S. Africa
92 B4 **Dujiangyan** China
81 J4 **Dukān Dam** Iraq
125 G5 **Dukathole** S. Africa
130 C4 **Duke Island** U.S.A.
84 C5 **Dukhān** Qatar
113 P3 **Dukhovshchina** Rus. Fed.
88 B3 **Duki** Pak.
103 N5 **Dūkštas** Lith.
85 E4 **Dūlab** Iran
90 B3 **Dulan** China
156 D3 **Dulce** *r.* Arg.
150 I6 **Dulce, Golfo** *b.* Costa Rica
150 H5 **Dulce Nombre de Culmí** Hond.
89 E2 **Dulishi Hu** *salt l.* China
125 I2 **Dullstroom** S. Africa
108 F3 **Dülmen** Germany
115 L3 **Dulovo** Bulg.
134 A2 **Duluth** U.S.A.
134 A2 **Duluth/Superior** *airport* U.S.A.
105 D6 **Dulverton** U.K.
80 F5 **Dūmā** Syria
97 B4 **Dumaguete** Phil.
99 B2 **Dumai** Indon.
97 B4 **Dumaran** *i.* Phil.
143 F5 **Dumas** *AR* U.S.A.
143 C5 **Dumas** *TX* U.S.A.
80 F5 **Ḍumayr** Syria
106 D5 **Dumbarton** U.K.
125 I3 **Dumbe** S. Africa
113 I6 **Ďumbier** *mt.* Slovakia
88 D2 **Dumchele** Jammu and Kashmir
89 H4 **Dum Duma** India
106 E5 **Dumfries** U.K.
89 F4 **Dumka** India
109 G2 **Dümmer** *l.* Germany
132 E4 **Dumoine, Lac** Canada
73 C6 **Dumont d'Urville** *research stn* Antarctica
73 C6 **Dumont d'Urville Sea** *sea* Antarctica
108 E4 **Dümpelfeld** Germany
121 F1 **Dumyāṭ** Egypt
109 I3 **Dün** *ridge* Germany
115 H1 **Duna** *r.* Hungary *alt.* **Donau (Austria/Germany),** *alt.* **Dunaj (Slovakia),** *alt.* **Dunărea (Romania),** *alt.* **Dunav (Yugoslavia),** *conv.* **Danube**
115 L3 **Dunaj** *r.* Slovakia *alt.* **Donau (Austria/Germany),** *alt.* **Duna (Hungary),** *alt.* **Dunărea (Romania),** *alt.* **Dunav (Yugoslavia),** *conv.* **Danube**
112 H7 **Dunajská Streda** Slovakia
113 I7 **Dunakeszi** Hungary
71 G9 **Dunalley** Australia
107 E4 **Dunany Point** Rep. of Ireland
115 L3 **Dunărea** *r.* Romania *alt.* **Donau (Austria/Germany),** *alt.* **Duna (Hungary),** *alt.* **Dunaj (Slovakia),** *alt.* **Dunav (Yugoslavia),** *conv.* **Danube**
113 I7 **Dunaújváros** Hungary
115 L3 **Dunav** *r.* Serb. and Mont. *alt.* **Donau (Austria/Germany),** *alt.* **Duna (Hungary),** *alt.* **Dunaj (Slovakia),** *alt.* **Dunărea (Romania),** *conv.* **Danube**
117 C5 **Dunayivtsi** Ukr.
72 C6 **Dunback** N.Z.
106 F4 **Dunbar** U.K.
106 E4 **Dunblane** U.K.
107 E4 **Dunboyne** Rep. of Ireland
130 E5 **Duncan** Canada
141 H5 **Duncan** *AZ* U.S.A.
143 D5 **Duncan** *OK* U.S.A.
132 D3 **Duncan, Cape** Canada
132 E3 **Duncan, Lac** *l.* Canada
146 E4 **Duncannon** U.S.A.
106 E2 **Duncansby Head** U.K.
134 B5 **Duncans Mills** U.S.A.
107 E5 **Duncormick** Rep. of Ireland
103 M4 **Dundaga** Latvia
135 G3 **Dundalk** Canada
107 E3 **Dundalk** Rep. of Ireland
146 E5 **Dundalk** U.S.A.
107 E4 **Dundalk Bay** Rep. of Ireland
129 L2 **Dundas** Greenland
130 C4 **Dundas Island** Canada
Dún Dealgan Rep. of Ireland *see* **Dundalk**
125 I4 **Dundee** S. Africa
106 F4 **Dundee** U.K.
135 F5 **Dundee** *MI* U.S.A.
146 E3 **Dundee** *NY* U.S.A.
92 E1 **Dund Hot** China
107 F3 **Dundonald** U.K.
71 F1 **Dundoo** Australia
106 E6 **Dundrennan** U.K.
107 F3 **Dundrum** U.K.
107 F3 **Dundrum Bay** U.K.
89 E4 **Dundwa Range** *mts* India/Nepal
132 F2 **Dune, Lac** *l.* Canada
72 C6 **Dunedin** N.Z.
145 D6 **Dunedin** U.S.A.
71 H4 **Dunedoo** Australia
83 J2 **Dunenbay** Kazakh.
106 E4 **Dunfermline** U.K.
107 E3 **Dungannon** U.K.
88 C5 **Dungarpur** India
107 D5 **Dungarvan** Rep. of Ireland
105 H7 **Dungeness** *hd* U.K.
156 C8 **Dungeness, Punta** *pt* Arg.
108 F4 **Düngenheim** Germany
107 E3 **Dungiven** U.K.
107 C3 **Dungloe** Rep. of Ireland
71 I4 **Dungog** Australia
122 C3 **Dungu** Dem. Rep. Congo
99 B2 **Dungun** Malaysia
121 F2 **Dungunab** Sudan
96 E2 **Dunhua** China
90 B2 **Dunhuang** China
70 E6 **Dunkeld** Australia
106 E4 **Dunkeld** U.K.
Dunkerque France *see* **Dunkirk**
105 D6 **Dunkery Hill** U.K.
110 F1 **Dunkirk** France
146 D3 **Dunkirk** U.S.A.
120 B4 **Dunkwa** Ghana
107 E4 **Dún Laoghaire** Rep. of Ireland
107 E4 **Dunlavin** Rep. of Ireland
107 E4 **Dunleer** Rep. of Ireland
107 E2 **Dunloy** U.K.
107 B6 **Dunmanus Bay** Rep. of Ireland
107 B6 **Dunmanway** Rep. of Ireland
107 C4 **Dunmore** Rep. of Ireland
145 E7 **Dunmore Town** Bahamas
140 D3 **Dunmovin** U.S.A.
107 F3 **Dunmurry** U.K.
145 E5 **Dunn** U.S.A.
106 E2 **Dunnet Bay** U.K.
106 E2 **Dunnet Head** U.K.
140 B2 **Dunnigan** U.S.A.
142 C3 **Dunning** U.S.A.
135 H4 **Dunnville** Canada
70 E6 **Dunolly** Australia
106 D5 **Dunoon** U.K.
106 F5 **Duns** U.K.
142 C1 **Dunseith** U.S.A.
138 B3 **Dunsmuir** U.S.A.
105 G6 **Dunstable** U.K.
72 B6 **Dunstan Mountains** N.Z.
108 D5 **Dun-sur-Meuse** France
72 C6 **Duntroon** N.Z.
106 B3 **Dunvegan, Loch** *b.* U.K.
88 B3 **Dunyapur** Pak.
92 E1 **Duolun** China
98 C3 **Dương Đông** Vietnam
93 D5 **Dupang Ling** *mts* China
135 H1 **Duparquet, Lac** *l.* Canada
115 J3 **Dupnitsa** Bulg.
142 C2 **Dupree** U.S.A.
144 B4 **Du Quoin** U.S.A.
68 C3 **Durack** *r.* Australia
80 E1 **Durağan** Turkey
110 G5 **Durance** *r.* France
135 F4 **Durand** *MI* U.S.A.
134 B3 **Durand** *WI* U.S.A.
150 C2 **Durango** Mex.
150 C2 **Durango** *state* Mex.
111 E1 **Durango** Spain
139 F4 **Durango** U.S.A.
143 D5 **Durant** U.S.A.
159 F2 **Durazno** Uruguay
159 F1 **Durazno, Cuchilla Grande del** *hills* Uruguay
125 I4 **Durban** S. Africa
110 F5 **Durban-Corbières** France
124 C6 **Durbanville** S. Africa
146 D5 **Durbin** U.S.A.
108 D4 **Durbuy** Belgium
108 E4 **Düren** Germany
88 E5 **Durg** India
89 F5 **Durgapur** India
135 G3 **Durham** Canada
104 F3 **Durham** U.K.
140 B2 **Durham** *CA* U.S.A.
145 E4 **Durham** *NC* U.S.A.
147 H3 **Durham** *NH* U.S.A.
117 D6 **Durlești** Moldova
109 G6 **Durmersheim** Germany
115 H3 **Durmitor** *mt.* Serb. and Mont.
106 D2 **Durness** U.K.
115 H4 **Durrës** Albania
105 F6 **Durrington** U.K.
107 A6 **Dursey Island** Rep. of Ireland
80 B2 **Dursunbey** Turkey
85 F3 **Dūruḥ** Iran
80 F5 **Durūz, Jabal ad** *mt.* Syria
68 D2 **D'Urville, Tanjung** *pt* Indon.
72 D4 **D'Urville Island** N.Z.
85 G3 **Durzab** Afgh.
82 D5 **Duşak** Turkm.
85 G4 **Dushai** Pak.
Dushak Turkm. *see* **Duşak**
93 C5 **Dushan** China
83 G5 **Dushanbe** Tajik.
117 H7 **Dushet'i** Georgia
72 A6 **Dusky Sound** *inlet* N.Z.
108 E3 **Düsseldorf** Germany
Dustlik Uzbek. *see* **Do'stlik**
141 F1 **Dutch Mountain** U.S.A.
124 E1 **Dutlwe** Botswana
120 C3 **Dutse** Nigeria
70 B3 **Dutton, Lake** *salt flat* Australia
141 F2 **Dutton, Mount** U.S.A.
116 H3 **Duvannoye** Rus. Fed.
133 F2 **Duvert, Lac** *l.* Canada
84 C5 **Duweihin, Khor** *b.* Saudi Arabia/U.A.E.
83 J5 **Düxanbibazar** China
93 C5 **Duyun** China
85 F5 **Duzab** Pak.
80 C1 **Düzce** Turkey
117 F5 **Dvorichna** Ukr.
94 B2 **Dvoryanka** Rus. Fed.
88 B5 **Dwarka** India
125 G2 **Dwarsberg** S. Africa
134 C5 **Dwight** U.S.A.
108 E2 **Dwingelderveld, Nationaal Park** *nat. park* Neth.
138 C2 **Dworshak Reservoir** U.S.A.
124 D6 **Dwyka** S. Africa
Dyanev Turkm. *see* **Galkynyş**
116 E4 **Dyat'kovo** Rus. Fed.
106 F3 **Dyce** U.K.
134 D5 **Dyer** *IN* U.S.A.
140 C3 **Dyer** *NV* U.S.A.
129 L3 **Dyer, Cape** Canada
135 G3 **Dyer Bay** Canada
145 B4 **Dyersburg** U.S.A.
134 B4 **Dyersville** U.S.A.
105 D5 **Dyfi** *r.* U.K.
106 E3 **Dyke** U.K.
Dykh Tau *mt.* Georgia/Rus. Fed. *see* **Gistola, Gora**
109 K5 **Dyleň** *h.* Czech Rep.
113 I4 **Dylewska Góra** *h.* Poland
70 F2 **Dynevor Downs** Australia
125 H5 **Dyoki** S. Africa
134 A4 **Dysart** U.S.A.
124 E6 **Dysselsdorp** S. Africa
90 D2 **Dzamīn Üüd** Mongolia
123 E5 **Dzaoudzi** Africa
116 G3 **Dzerzhinsk** Rus. Fed.
113 M5 **Dzerzhyns'k** Ukr.
90 E1 **Dzhagdy, Khrebet** *mts* Rus. Fed.
82 F3 **Dzhalagash** Kazakh.
Dzhalal-Abad Kyrg. *see* **Jalal-Abad**
Dzhanga Turkm. *see* **Jaňňa**
82 B2 **Dzhangala** Kazakh.
Dzhangel'dy Uzbek. *see* **Jongeldi**
117 E6 **Dzhankoy** Ukr.
83 I3 **Dzhansugurov** Kazakh.
Dzharkurgan Uzbek. *see* **Jarqo'rgo'n**
Dzhebel Turkm. *see* **Jebel**
Dzhigirbent Turkm. *see* **Jigerbent**
Dzhizak Uzbek. *see* **Jizzax**
90 F1 **Dzhugdzhur, Khrebet** *mts* Rus. Fed.
Dzhuma Uzbek. *see* **Juma**
79 F2 **Dzhungarskiy Alatau, Khrebet** *mts* China/Kazakh.
82 F3 **Dzhusaly** Kazakh.
113 J4 **Działdowo** Poland
151 G4 **Dzibalchén** Mex.
151 G3 **Dzilam de Bravo** Mex.
Dzungaria Basin *basin* China *see* **Junggar Pendi**
83 J3 **Dzungarian Gate** *pass* China/Kazakh.
90 C2 **Dzuunmod** Mongolia
116 C4 **Dzyaniskavichy** Belarus
116 C4 **Dzyarzhynsk** Belarus
113 M4 **Dzyatlavichy** Belarus

E

132 C3 **Eabamet Lake** Canada
141 H4 **Eagar** U.S.A.
133 I3 **Eagle** *r.* Canada
139 F4 **Eagle** U.S.A.
147 F3 **Eagle Bay** U.S.A.
140 D4 **Eagle Crags** *mt.* U.S.A.
131 H4 **Eagle Creek** *r.* Canada
131 K5 **Eagle Lake** *l.* Canada
147 I1 **Eagle Lake** U.S.A.
138 B3 **Eagle Lake** *l. CA* U.S.A.
147 I1 **Eagle Lake** *l.* U.S.A.
134 B2 **Eagle Mountain** *h.* U.S.A.
143 C6 **Eagle Pass** U.S.A.
128 D3 **Eagle Plain** Canada
134 C2 **Eagle River** *MI* U.S.A.
134 C3 **Eagle River** *WI* U.S.A.
130 F3 **Eaglesham** Canada
141 F5 **Eagle Tail Mountains** U.S.A.
132 B3 **Ear Falls** Canada
140 C4 **Earlimart** U.S.A.
106 F5 **Earlston** U.K.
135 H2 **Earlton** Canada
106 E4 **Earn** *r.* U.K.
106 D4 **Earn, Loch** *l.* U.K.
143 C5 **Earth** U.S.A.
104 H4 **Easington** U.K.
145 D5 **Easley** U.S.A.
73 D5 **East Antarctica** *reg.* Antarctica
147 F4 **East Ararat** U.S.A.
146 D3 **East Aurora** U.S.A.
143 F6 **East Bay** U.S.A.
147 G2 **East Berkshire** U.S.A.
105 H7 **Eastbourne** U.K.
146 D4 **East Branch Clarion River Reservoir** U.S.A.
147 H4 **East Brooklyn** U.S.A.
72 G2 **East Cape** N.Z.
141 G2 **East Carbon City** U.S.A.
160 E5 **East Caroline Basin** *sea feature* N. Pacific Ocean
134 D5 **East Chicago** U.S.A.
90 E3 **East China Sea** Asia
72 E2 **East Coast Bays** N.Z.
147 G2 **East Corinth** U.S.A.
East Dereham U.K. *see* **Dereham**
152 C5 **Easter Island** S. Pacific Ocean
125 G5 **Eastern Cape** *prov.* S. Africa
121 F2 **Eastern Desert** Egypt
87 C2 **Eastern Ghats** *mts* India
88 B4 **Eastern Nara** *canal* Pak.
Eastern Transvaal *prov.* S. Africa *see* **Mpumalanga**
131 J4 **Easterville** Canada
156 E8 **East Falkland** *i.* Falkland Is
147 H4 **East Falmouth** U.S.A.
108 E1 **East Frisian Islands** Germany
140 D2 **Eastgate** U.S.A.
142 D2 **East Grand Forks** U.S.A.
105 G6 **East Grinstead** U.K.
147 G3 **Easthampton** U.S.A.
147 G4 **East Hampton** U.S.A.
146 D4 **East Hickory** U.S.A.
162 K6 **East Indiaman Ridge** *sea feature* Indian Ocean
147 G3 **East Jamaica** U.S.A.
134 E3 **East Jordan** U.S.A.
106 D5 **East Kilbride** U.K.
134 D3 **East Lake** U.S.A.
93 □ **East Lamma Channel** *Hong Kong* China
105 F7 **Eastleigh** U.K.
146 C4 **East Liverpool** U.S.A.
106 B3 **East Loch Tarbert** *inlet* U.K.
125 G6 **East London** S. Africa
146 B5 **East Lynn Lake** U.S.A.
132 E3 **Eastmain** Canada
132 F3 **Eastmain** *r.* Canada
147 G2 **Eastman** Canada
145 D5 **Eastman** U.S.A.
160 F5 **East Mariana Basin** *sea feature* Pacific Ocean
147 I2 **East Millinocket** U.S.A.
134 B5 **East Moline** U.S.A.
134 C5 **Easton** *IL* U.S.A.
147 E5 **Easton** *MD* U.S.A.
147 F4 **Easton** *PA* U.S.A.
161 L8 **East Pacific Ridge** *sea feature* S. Pacific Ocean
161 L4 **East Pacific Rise** *sea feature* N. Pacific Ocean
140 A2 **East Park Reservoir** U.S.A.
133 H4 **East Point** *pt* Canada
145 C5 **East Point** U.S.A.
147 J2 **Eastport** *ME* U.S.A.
134 E3 **Eastport** *MI* U.S.A.
140 D1 **East Range** *mts* U.S.A.
144 B4 **East St Louis** U.S.A.
East Sea *sea* Pacific Ocean *see* **Japan, Sea of**
77 Q2 **East Siberian Sea** Rus. Fed.
71 H7 **East Sister Island** Australia
91 E7 **East Timor** *country* Asia
89 F4 **East Tons** *r.* India
71 F3 **East Toorale** Australia
134 C4 **East Troy** U.S.A.
147 F6 **Eastville** U.S.A.
140 C2 **East Walker** *r.* U.S.A.
147 G3 **East Wallingford** U.S.A.
145 D5 **Eatonton** U.S.A.
134 B3 **Eau Claire** U.S.A.
134 B3 **Eau Claire** *r.* U.S.A.
91 G6 **Eauripik** *atoll* Micronesia
160 E5 **Eauripik Rise-New Guinea Rise** *sea feature* N. Pacific Ocean
151 E3 **Ebano** Mex.
105 D6 **Ebbw Vale** U.K.
120 D4 **Ebebiyin** Equat. Guinea
124 B2 **Ebenerde** Namibia
146 D4 **Ebensburg** U.S.A.
80 C2 **Eber Gölü** *l.* Turkey
109 I3 **Ebergötzen** Germany
112 F4 **Eberswalde-Finow** Germany
135 F4 **Eberts** Canada
94 G3 **Ebetsu** Japan
93 B4 **Ebian** China
83 J3 **Ebinur Hu** *salt l.* China
114 F4 **Eboli** Italy
120 D4 **Ebolowa** Cameroon
81 J3 **Ebrāhim Ḥeṣār** Iran
111 G2 **Ebro** *r.* Spain
109 I1 **Ebstorf** Germany
115 L4 **Eceabat** Turkey
97 B2 **Echague** Phil.
120 C1 **Ech Chélif** Alg.
111 E1 **Echegárate, Puerto** *pass* Spain
150 A1 **Echeverria, Pico** *mt.* Mex.
71 G9 **Echo, Lake** Australia
130 F1 **Echo Bay** *N.W.T.* Canada
135 E2 **Echo Bay** *Ont.* Canada
141 G3 **Echo Cliffs** U.S.A.
132 B3 **Echoing** *r.* Canada
135 J2 **Échouani, Lac** *l.* Canada
108 D3 **Echt** Neth.
108 E5 **Echternach** Lux.
70 F6 **Echuca** Australia
109 G4 **Echzell** Germany
111 D4 **Écija** Spain
109 J5 **Eckental** Germany
134 E2 **Eckerman** U.S.A.
112 D3 **Eckernförde** Germany
129 K2 **Eclipse Sound** *sea chan.* Canada
154 C4 **Ecuador** *country* S. America
132 E2 **Écueils, Pointe aux** *pt* Canada
122 E2 **Ed** Eritrea
103 J4 **Ed** Sweden
131 H4 **Edam** Canada
108 D2 **Edam** Neth.
106 F1 **Eday** *i.* U.K.
121 E3 **Ed Da'ein** Sudan
121 F3 **Ed Damazin** Sudan
121 F3 **Ed Damer** Sudan
121 F3 **Ed Debba** Sudan
121 F3 **Ed Dueim** Sudan
71 H8 **Eddystone Point** Australia
108 D2 **Ede** Neth.
120 D4 **Edéa** Cameroon
131 J2 **Edehon Lake** Canada
158 C2 **Edéia** Brazil
71 H6 **Eden** Australia
104 E3 **Eden** *r.* U.K.
143 D6 **Eden** U.S.A.
125 F4 **Edenburg** S. Africa
72 B7 **Edendale** N.Z.
107 D4 **Edenderry** Rep. of Ireland
70 D6 **Edenhope** Australia
145 E4 **Edenton** U.S.A.
125 G3 **Edenville** S. Africa
115 J4 **Edessa** Greece
109 F1 **Edewecht** Germany
147 H4 **Edgartown** U.S.A.
142 D2 **Edgeley** U.S.A.
142 C3 **Edgemont** U.S.A.
134 C4 **Edgerton** U.S.A.
107 D4 **Edgeworthstown** Rep. of Ireland
83 K2 **Edigan** Rus. Fed.
134 A5 **Edina** U.S.A.
143 D7 **Edinburg** U.S.A.
106 E5 **Edinburgh** U.K.
117 C7 **Edirne** Turkey
130 F4 **Edith Cavell, Mount** Canada
138 B2 **Edmonds** U.S.A.
130 G4 **Edmonton** Canada
131 J5 **Edmore** U.S.A.
134 B4 **Edmund** U.S.A.
131 K4 **Edmund Lake** Canada
133 G4 **Edmundston** Canada
143 D6 **Edna** U.S.A.
130 C3 **Edna Bay** U.S.A.
115 L5 **Edremit** Turkey
103 K3 **Edsbyn** Sweden
130 F4 **Edson** Canada
159 D2 **Eduardo Castex** Arg.
70 F5 **Edward** *r.* Australia
122 C4 **Edward, Lake** Dem. Rep. Congo/Uganda
134 C1 **Edward Island** Canada
147 F2 **Edwards** U.S.A.
70 A2 **Edward's Creek** Australia
143 C6 **Edwards Plateau** U.S.A.
144 B4 **Edwardsville** U.S.A.
73 B5 **Edward VII Peninsula** *pen.* Antarctica
130 C3 **Edziza, Mount** Canada
108 B3 **Eeklo** Belgium
140 A1 **Eel** *r.* U.S.A.
140 A2 **Eel, South Fork** *r.* U.S.A.
108 E1 **Eemshaven** *pt* Neth.
108 E1 **Eenrum** Neth.
124 D3 **Eenzamheid Pan** *salt pan* S. Africa
69 G3 **Éfaté** *i.* Vanuatu
115 L6 **Efes** *tourist site* Turkey
144 B4 **Effingham** U.S.A.
80 D1 **Eflâni** Turkey
141 E2 **Egan Range** *mts* U.S.A.
135 I3 **Eganville** Canada
113 J7 **Eger** Hungary
103 I4 **Egersund** Norway
109 G3 **Eggegebirge** *hills* Germany
109 J5 **Eggolsheim** Germany
108 C4 **Eghezée** Belgium
102 D2 **Egilsstaðir** Iceland
80 C3 **Eğirdir** Turkey
80 C3 **Eğirdir Gölü** *l.* Turkey
110 F4 **Égletons** France
107 D2 **Eglinton** U.K.
128 F2 **Eglinton Island** Canada
108 C2 **Egmond aan Zee** Neth.
72 D3 **Egmont, Cape** N.Z.
Egmont, Mount *vol.* N.Z. *see* **Taranaki, Mount**
72 E3 **Egmont National Park** N.Z.
80 B2 **Eğrigöz Dağı** *mts* Turkey
104 G3 **Egton** U.K.
158 D1 **Éguas** *r.* Brazil
77 U3 **Egvekinot** Rus. Fed.
121 E2 **Egypt** *country* Africa
92 A2 **Ehen Hudag** China
112 D6 **Ehingen (Donau)** Germany
109 I2 **Ehra-Lessien** Germany
141 E5 **Ehrenberg** U.S.A.
109 I5 **Eibelstadt** Germany
108 E2 **Eibergen** Neth.
109 H4 **Eichenzell** Germany
109 J6 **Eichstätt** Germany
103 I3 **Eidfjord** Norway
103 J3 **Eidsvoll** Norway
108 E4 **Eifel** *hills* Germany
106 B4 **Eigg** *i.* U.K.
87 A4 **Eight Degree Channel** India/Maldives
68 C3 **Eighty Mile Beach** Australia
80 E7 **Eilat** Israel
71 F6 **Eildon** Australia
71 F6 **Eildon, Lake** Australia
131 H2 **Eileen Lake** Canada
109 K3 **Eilenburg** Germany
109 I2 **Eimke** Germany
109 H3 **Einbeck** Germany
108 D3 **Eindhoven** Neth.
112 D7 **Einsiedeln** Switz.
163 G2 **Eirik Ridge** *sea feature* N. Atlantic Ocean
154 E5 **Eirunepé** Brazil
109 H3 **Eisberg** *h.* Germany
123 C5 **Eiseb** *watercourse* Namibia
109 I4 **Eisenach** Germany
109 J4 **Eisenberg** Germany
112 G4 **Eisenhüttenstadt** Germany
112 H7 **Eisenstadt** Austria
109 I4 **Eisfeld** Germany
106 C3 **Eishort, Loch** *inlet* U.K.
109 J3 **Eisleben Lutherstadt** Germany
109 H4 **Eiterfeld** Germany
Eivissa Spain *see* **Ibiza**
Eivissa *i.* Spain *see* **Ibiza**
111 F1 **Ejea de los Caballeros** Spain
123 E6 **Ejeda** Madag.
81 J1 **Ejmiatsin** Armenia
151 E4 **Ejutla** Mex.
103 M4 **Ekenäs** Fin.
82 C5 **Ekerem** Turkm.
108 C3 **Ekeren** Belgium
72 E4 **Eketahuna** N.Z.
83 H2 **Ekibastuz** Kazakh.
77 L3 **Ekonda** Rus. Fed.
103 K3 **Ekshärad** Sweden
103 K4 **Eksjö** Sweden
124 B4 **Eksteenfontein** S. Africa
122 C4 **Ekuku** Dem. Rep. Congo
132 D3 **Ekwan** *r.* Canada
132 D3 **Ekwan Point** Canada
115 J6 **Elafonisou, Steno** *sea chan.* Greece
125 H2 **Elands** *r.* S. Africa
125 H2 **Elandsdoorn** S. Africa
114 B7 **El Aouinet** Alg.
150 A1 **El Arco** Mex.
115 J5 **Elassona** Greece
81 G2 **Elazığ** Turkey
114 D3 **Elba, Isola d'** *i.* Italy
90 F1 **El'ban** Rus. Fed.
157 B2 **El Banco** Col.
136 E5 **El Barreal** *salt l.* Mex.
115 I4 **Elbasan** Albania
80 E2 **Elbaşı** Turkey
157 C2 **El Baúl** Venez.
120 C1 **El Bayadh** Alg.
109 I1 **Elbe** *r.* Germany *alt.* **Labe (Czech Rep.)**
139 F4 **Elbert, Mount** U.S.A.
134 D3 **Elberta** *MI* U.S.A.
141 G2 **Elberta** *UT* U.S.A.
145 D5 **Elberton** U.S.A.
110 E2 **Elbeuf** France
80 F2 **Elbistan** Turkey
113 I3 **Elbląg** Poland
159 B4 **El Bolsón** Arg.
145 E7 **Elbow Cay** *i.* Bahamas
117 G7 **El'brus** *mt.* Rus. Fed.
108 D2 **Elburg** Neth.
111 E2 **El Burgo de Osma** Spain
84 C2 **Elburz Mountains** Iran
159 C4 **El Cain** Arg.
140 D5 **El Cajon** U.S.A.
157 E3 **El Callao** Venez.
143 D6 **El Campo** U.S.A.
139 F5 **El Capitan Mountain** U.S.A.
141 E5 **El Centro** U.S.A.
154 F7 **El Cerro** Bol.
157 D2 **El Chaparro** Venez.
Elche Spain *see* **Elche-Elx**
111 F3 **Elche-Elx** Spain
151 F4 **El Chichónal** *vol.* Mex.
150 C1 **El Chilicote** Mex.
68 D3 **Elcho Island** Australia
157 B3 **El Cocuy** Col.
157 B3 **El Cocuy, Parque Nacional** *nat. park* Col.
151 H3 **El Cuyo** Mex.
111 F3 **Elda** Spain
109 J1 **Elde** *r.* Germany
135 H2 **Eldee** Canada
70 D3 **Elder, Lake** Australia
150 D2 **El Diamante** Mex.
157 B2 **El Difícil** Col.
77 O3 **El'dikan** Rus. Fed.
157 A4 **El Diviso** Col.
141 E6 **El Doctor** Mex.
134 A5 **Eldon** *IA* U.S.A.
142 E4 **Eldon** *MO* U.S.A.
156 F3 **Eldorado** Arg.
150 C2 **El Dorado** Mex.
143 E5 **El Dorado** *AR* U.S.A.
143 D4 **El Dorado** *KS* U.S.A.
143 C6 **Eldorado** U.S.A.
157 E3 **El Dorado** Venez.
122 D3 **Eldoret** Kenya
138 E2 **Electric Peak** U.S.A.
120 B2 **El Eglab** *plat.* Alg.
111 E4 **El Ejido** Spain
116 F4 **Elektrostal'** Rus. Fed.
154 D4 **El Encanto** Col.
109 I3 **Elend** Germany
87 A2 **Elephanta Caves** *tourist site* India
139 F5 **Elephant Butte Reservoir** U.S.A.
73 B2 **Elephant Island** *i.* Antarctica
89 H5 **Elephant Point** Bangl.
81 I2 **Eleşkirt** Turkey
151 G5 **El Estor** Guat.
120 C1 **El Eulma** Alg.
145 E7 **Eleuthera** *i.* Bahamas
114 C6 **El Fahs** Tunisia
121 E3 **El Fasher** Sudan
109 H4 **Elfershausen** Germany
150 B2 **El Fuerte** Mex.
121 E3 **El Geneina** Sudan
121 F3 **El Geteina** Sudan
106 E3 **Elgin** U.K.
134 C4 **Elgin** *IL* U.S.A.
142 C2 **Elgin** *ND* U.S.A.
141 E3 **Elgin** *NV* U.S.A.
141 G2 **Elgin** *UT* U.S.A.
77 P3 **El'ginskiy** Rus. Fed.
150 D3 **El Gogorrón, Parque Nacional** *nat. park* Mex.
120 C1 **El Goléa** Alg.
121 F4 **Elgon, Mount** Uganda
114 B6 **El Hadjar** Alg.
150 I6 **El Hato del Volcán** Panama
120 A2 **El Hierro** *i.* Canary Is
151 E3 **El Higo** Mex.
120 C2 **El Homr** Alg.
106 F4 **Elie** U.K.
72 C5 **Elie de Beaumont** *mt.* N.Z.
128 B3 **Elim** U.S.A.
133 H2 **Eliot, Mount** Canada
117 H6 **Elista** Rus. Fed.
134 B4 **Elizabeth** *IL* U.S.A.
147 F4 **Elizabeth** *NJ* U.S.A.
146 C5 **Elizabeth** *WV* U.S.A.
145 E4 **Elizabeth City** U.S.A.
147 H4 **Elizabeth Islands** U.S.A.
145 D4 **Elizabethton** U.S.A.
144 C4 **Elizabethtown** *KY* U.S.A.
145 E5 **Elizabethtown** *NC* U.S.A.
147 G2 **Elizabethtown** *NY* U.S.A.
146 E4 **Elizabethtown** *PA* U.S.A.
111 F1 **Elizondo** Spain
120 B1 **El Jadida** Morocco
150 C2 **El Jaralito** Mex.
114 D7 **El Jem** Tunisia
150 H5 **El Jicaral** Nicaragua
130 G4 **Elk** *r.* Canada
113 K4 **Ełk** Poland
140 A2 **Elk** U.S.A.
146 C5 **Elk** *r.* U.S.A.
114 C6 **El Kala** Alg.
121 F3 **El Kamlin** Sudan
143 D5 **Elk City** U.S.A.
140 A2 **Elk Creek** U.S.A.
140 B2 **Elk Grove** U.S.A.
134 E5 **Elkhart** U.S.A.
120 B2 **El Khnâchîch** *esc.* Mali
134 C4 **Elkhorn** U.S.A.
142 D3 **Elkhorn** *r.* U.S.A.
115 L3 **Elkhovo** Bulg.
146 D5 **Elkins** U.S.A.
130 G4 **Elk Island National Park** Canada
135 G2 **Elk Lake** Canada
134 E3 **Elk Lake** *l.* U.S.A.
146 E4 **Elkland** U.S.A.
130 F5 **Elko** Canada
138 D3 **Elko** U.S.A.
131 G4 **Elk Point** Canada
142 E2 **Elk River** U.S.A.
147 F5 **Elkton** *MD* U.S.A.
146 D5 **Elkton** *VA* U.S.A.

Fermoy 179

131 L2 **Ell Bay** Canada
129 H2 **Ellef Ringnes Island** Canada
141 G2 **Ellen, Mount** U.S.A.
88 C3 **Ellenabad** India
142 D2 **Ellendale** U.S.A.
138 B2 **Ellensburg** U.S.A.
147 F4 **Ellenville** U.S.A.
71 H6 **Ellery, Mount** Australia
72 D5 **Ellesmere, Lake** N.Z.
129 J2 **Ellesmere Island** Canada
105 E4 **Ellesmere Port** U.K.
128 H3 **Ellice** *r.* Canada
146 D3 **Ellicottville** U.S.A.
151 E3 **El Limón** Mex.
109 I5 **Ellingen** Germany
125 G5 **Elliot** S. Africa
125 H5 **Elliotdale** S. Africa
135 F2 **Elliot Lake** Canada
138 D2 **Ellis** U.S.A.
Ellisras S. Africa *see* **Lephalale**
70 A4 **Elliston** Australia
106 F3 **Ellon** U.K.
88 C5 **Ellora Caves** *tourist site* India
147 I2 **Ellsworth** *ME* U.S.A.
134 A3 **Ellsworth** *WI* U.S.A.
73 B3 **Ellsworth Land** *reg.* Antarctica
73 B3 **Ellsworth Mountains** *mts* Antarctica
109 I6 **Ellwangen (Jagst)** Germany
80 B3 **Elmalı** Turkey
140 D6 **El Maneadero** Mex.
157 E3 **El Manteco** Venez.
120 C1 **El Meghaïer** Alg.
157 E3 **El Miamo** Venez.
El Mīna Lebanon *see* **El Mîna**
80 E4 **El Mîna** Lebanon
134 E3 **Elmira** *MI* U.S.A.
146 E3 **Elmira** *NY* U.S.A.
141 F5 **El Mirage** U.S.A.
111 E4 **El Moral** Spain
70 F6 **Elmore** Australia
159 D2 **El Morro** *mt.* Arg.
120 B2 **El Mreyyé** *reg.* Mauritania
109 H1 **Elmshorn** Germany
121 E3 **El Muglad** Sudan
135 G3 **Elmwood** Canada
134 C5 **Elmwood** *IL* U.S.A.
134 A3 **Elmwood** *WI* U.S.A.
102 I3 **Elnesvågen** Norway
157 B3 **El Nevado, Cerro** *mt.* Col.
97 A4 **El Nido** Phil.
121 F3 **El Obeid** Sudan
150 D2 **El Oro** Mex.
157 C3 **Elorza** Venez.
120 C1 **El Oued** Alg.
141 G5 **Eloy** U.S.A.
150 C2 **El Palmito** Mex.
157 E2 **El Pao** Venez.
157 C2 **El Pao** Venez.
134 C5 **El Paso** *IL* U.S.A.
139 F6 **El Paso** *TX* U.S.A.
106 C2 **Elphin** U.K.
140 C3 **El Portal** U.S.A.
150 J6 **El Porvenir** Panama
111 H2 **El Prat de Llobregat** Spain
El Progreso Guat. *see* **Guastatoya**
151 H5 **El Progreso** Hond.
150 B2 **El Puerto, Cerro** *mt.* Mex.
111 C4 **El Puerto de Santa María** Spain
El Quds Israel/West Bank *see* **Jerusalem**
150 J6 **El Real** Panama
143 D5 **El Reno** U.S.A.
151 D3 **El Retorno** Mex.
134 B4 **Elroy** U.S.A.
150 D3 **El Rucio** Mex.
130 B2 **Elsa** Canada
150 D2 **El Salado** Mex.
150 C3 **El Salto** Mex.
151 G5 **El Salvador** *country* Central America
150 D2 **El Salvador** Mex.
97 C4 **El Salvador** Phil.
157 C3 **El Samán de Apure** Venez.
135 F1 **Elsas** Canada
150 C1 **El Sauz** Mex.
109 G2 **Else** *r.* Germany
Elsen Nur *l.* China *see* **Dorgê Co**
140 D5 **Elsinore** U.S.A.
157 D2 **El Sombrero** Venez.
159 C2 **El Sosneado** Arg.
151 E3 **El Tajín** *tourist site* Mex.
157 B3 **El Tama, Parque Nacional** *nat. park* Venez.
114 C6 **El Tarf** Alg.
111 C1 **El Teleno** *mt.* Spain
151 E4 **El Tepozteco, Parque Nacional** *nat. park* Mex.
111 H1 **El Ter** *r.* Spain
157 D2 **El Tigre** Venez.
151 G4 **El Tigre, Parque Nacional** *nat. park* Guat.
109 I5 **Eltmann** Germany
157 C2 **El Tocuyo** Venez.
117 H5 **El'ton** Rus. Fed.
117 H5 **El'ton, Ozero** *l.* Rus. Fed.
138 C2 **Eltopia** U.S.A.
157 E2 **El Toro** Venez.
159 E2 **El Trébol** Arg.
150 B3 **El Triunfo** Mex.
157 C3 **El Tuparro, Parque Nacional** *nat. park* Col.
156 B8 **El Turbio** Chile
87 C2 **Eluru** India
103 N4 **Elva** Estonia
157 A3 **El Valle** Col.
106 E5 **Elvanfoot** U.K.
111 C3 **Elvas** Port.
103 J3 **Elverum** Norway
157 B3 **El Viejo** *mt.* Col.
157 C2 **El Vigía** Venez.
154 D5 **Elvira** Brazil
122 E3 **El Wak** Kenya
134 E5 **Elwood** U.S.A.
109 I3 **Elxleben** Germany
105 H5 **Ely** U.K.
134 B2 **Ely** *MN* U.S.A.
141 E2 **Ely** *NV* U.S.A.
146 B4 **Elyria** U.S.A.
109 G4 **Elz** Germany
109 H2 **Elze** Germany
69 G3 **Émaé** *i.* Vanuatu
84 D2 **Emāmrūd** Iran
85 H2 **Emām Şaḩēb** Afgh.
81 K5 **Emāmzādeh Naşrod Dīn** Iran
103 L4 **Emån** *r.* Sweden
158 B2 **Emas, Parque Nacional das** *nat. park* Brazil
83 J3 **Emazar** Kazakh.
82 D2 **Emba** Kazakh.
82 C3 **Emba** *r.* Kazakh.
125 H3 **Embalenhle** S. Africa
131 G3 **Embarras Portage** Canada
158 C2 **Emborcação, Represa de** *resr* Brazil
147 F2 **Embrun** Canada
122 D4 **Embu** Kenya
108 F1 **Emden** Germany
93 B4 **Emeishan** China
93 B4 **Emei Shan** *mt.* China
83 J3 **Emel'** *r.* Kazakh.
68 E4 **Emerald** *Qld* Australia
70 F6 **Emerald** *Vic.* Australia
133 G3 **Emeril** Canada
131 J5 **Emerson** Canada
80 B2 **Emet** Turkey
125 I2 **eMgwenya** S. Africa
141 E3 **Emigrant Valley** U.S.A.
eMijindini S. Africa *see* **eMjindini**
121 D3 **Emi Koussi** *mt.* Chad
150 C2 **Emiliano Martínez** Mex.
151 G4 **Emiliano Zapata** Mex.
83 J3 **Emin** China
115 L3 **Emine, Nos** *pt* Bulg.
83 J3 **Emin He** *r.* China
115 L3 **Eminska Planina** *hills* Bulg.
80 C2 **Emirdağ** Turkey
80 C2 **Emir Dağı** *mt.* Turkey
71 G8 **Emita** Australia
125 I2 **eMjindini** S. Africa
103 K4 **Emmaboda** Sweden
103 M4 **Emmaste** Estonia
71 I2 **Emmaville** Australia
108 D2 **Emmeloord** Neth.
108 F4 **Emmelshausen** Germany
108 E2 **Emmen** Neth.
112 D7 **Emmen** Switz.
108 E3 **Emmerich** Germany
87 B3 **Emmiganuru** India
143 C6 **Emory Peak** U.S.A.
150 B2 **Empalme** Mex.
125 I4 **Empangeni** S. Africa
156 E3 **Empedrado** Arg.
160 G2 **Emperor Seamount Chain** *sea feature* N. Pacific Ocean
160 G2 **Emperor Trough** *sea feature* N. Pacific Ocean
114 D3 **Empoli** Italy
142 D4 **Emporia** *KS* U.S.A.
146 E6 **Emporia** *VA* U.S.A.
146 D4 **Emporium** U.S.A.
131 G4 **Empress** Canada
85 E3 **'Emrānī** Iran
108 F2 **Ems** *r.* Germany
135 H3 **Emsdale** Canada
108 F2 **Emsdetten** Germany
108 F1 **Ems-Jade-Kanal** *canal* Germany
108 F2 **Emsland** *reg.* Germany
125 H3 **Emzinoni** S. Africa
102 K3 **Enafors** Sweden
91 F7 **Enarotali** Indon.
95 E7 **Ena-san** *mt.* Japan
83 I2 **Enbek** Kazakh.
159 G1 **Encantadas, Serra das** *hills* Brazil
150 A2 **Encantado, Cerro** *mt.* Mex.
97 B3 **Encanto, Cape** Phil.
150 D3 **Encarnación** Mex.
156 E3 **Encarnación** Para.
143 D6 **Encinal** U.S.A.
140 D5 **Encinitas** U.S.A.
139 F5 **Encino** U.S.A.
70 C5 **Encounter Bay** Australia
158 E1 **Encruzilhada** Brazil
159 G1 **Encruzilhada do Sul** Brazil
130 D4 **Endako** Canada
91 E7 **Ende** Indon.
68 E3 **Endeavour Strait** Australia
Endeh Indon. *see* **Ende**
163 L9 **Enderby Abyssal Plain** *sea feature* Southern Ocean
73 E4 **Enderby Land** *reg.* Antarctica
147 E3 **Endicott** U.S.A.
130 C3 **Endicott Arm** *est.* U.S.A.
128 C3 **Endicott Mountains** U.S.A.
82 D2 **Energetik** Rus. Fed.
159 E3 **Energía** Arg.
117 E6 **Enerhodar** Ukr.
160 G6 **Enewetak** *atoll* Marshall Is
114 D6 **Enfidaville** Tunisia
147 G3 **Enfield** U.S.A.
134 E2 **Engadine** U.S.A.
102 J3 **Engan** Norway
97 B2 **Engaño, Cape** Phil.
94 H2 **Engaru** Japan
125 G5 **Engcobo** S. Africa
145 F5 **Engelhard** U.S.A.
117 H5 **Engel's** Rus. Fed.
108 C1 **Engelschmangat** *sea chan.* Neth.
70 A2 **Engenina** *watercourse* Australia
99 B4 **Enggano** *i.* Indon.
108 C4 **Enghien** Belgium
105 E5 **England** *admin. div.* U.K.
133 I3 **Englee** Canada
135 H2 **Englehart** Canada
137 H1 **English** *r.* Canada
105 D7 **English Channel** France/U.K.
117 G7 **Enguri** *r.* Georgia
125 I4 **Enhlalakahle** S. Africa
143 D4 **Enid** U.S.A.
94 G3 **Eniwa** Japan
108 D2 **Enkhuizen** Neth.
103 L4 **Enköping** Sweden
114 F6 **Enna** *Sicily* Italy
131 I2 **Ennadai Lake** Canada
121 E3 **En Nahud** Sudan
121 E3 **Ennedi, Massif** *mts* Chad
107 D4 **Ennell, Lough** *l.* Rep. of Ireland
71 F2 **Enngonia** Australia
142 C2 **Enning** U.S.A.
107 C5 **Ennis** Rep. of Ireland
138 E2 **Ennis** *MT* U.S.A.
143 D5 **Ennis** *TX* U.S.A.
107 E5 **Enniscorthy** Rep. of Ireland
107 D3 **Enniskillen** U.K.
107 B5 **Ennistymon** Rep. of Ireland
112 G7 **Enns** *r.* Austria
102 O3 **Eno** Fin.
141 F3 **Enoch** U.S.A.
102 M1 **Enontekiö** Fin.
93 D6 **Enping** China
97 B2 **Enrile** Phil.
108 D2 **Ens** Neth.
71 G6 **Ensay** Australia
108 E2 **Enschede** Neth.
109 G3 **Ense** Germany
159 F2 **Ensenada** Arg.
148 A2 **Ensenada** Mex.
93 C4 **Enshi** China
130 F2 **Enterprise** *N.W.T.* Canada
135 I3 **Enterprise** *Ont.* Canada
145 C6 **Enterprise** *AL* U.S.A.
138 C2 **Enterprise** *OR* U.S.A.
141 F3 **Enterprise** *UT* U.S.A.
130 F4 **Entrance** Canada
159 E2 **Entre Ríos** *prov.* Arg.
154 F8 **Entre Ríos** Bol.
111 B3 **Entroncamento** Port.
120 C4 **Enugu** Nigeria
77 U3 **Enurmino** Rus. Fed.
154 D5 **Envira** Brazil
154 D5 **Envira** *r.* Brazil
72 C5 **Enys, Mount** N.Z.
95 F7 **Enzan** Japan
108 D2 **Epe** Neth.
108 B5 **Épernay** France
141 G2 **Ephraim** U.S.A.
147 E4 **Ephrata** *PA* U.S.A.
138 C2 **Ephrata** *WA* U.S.A.
69 G3 **Epi** *i.* Vanuatu
110 H2 **Épinal** France
80 D4 **Episkopi** Cyprus
114 E4 **Epomeo, Monte** *vol.* Italy
105 H6 **Epping** U.K.
109 G4 **Eppstein** Germany
105 D5 **Eppynt, Mynydd** *hills* U.K.
105 G6 **Epsom** U.K.
159 D3 **Epu-pel** Arg.
84 D4 **Eqlīd** Iran
120 C4 **Equatorial Guinea** *country* Africa
157 E3 **Equeipa** Venez.
97 A4 **Eran** Phil.
97 A4 **Eran Bay** Phil.
80 F1 **Erbaa** Turkey
109 K5 **Erbendorf** Germany
108 F5 **Erbeskopf** *h.* Germany
81 I2 **Erçek** Turkey
81 I2 **Erciş** Turkey
80 E2 **Erciyes Dağı** *mt.* Turkey
113 I7 **Érd** Hungary
89 H2 **Erdaogou** China
96 D2 **Erdao Jiang** *r.* China
80 A1 **Erdek** Turkey
80 E3 **Erdemli** Turkey
92 C1 **Erdenetsogt** Mongolia
121 E3 **Erdi** *reg.* Chad
117 H6 **Erdniyevskiy** Rus. Fed.
158 B4 **Eré, Campos** *hills* Brazil
157 D3 **Erebato** *r.* Venez.
73 B5 **Erebus, Mount** *vol.* Antarctica
81 J6 **Erech** *tourist site* Iraq
156 F3 **Erechim** Brazil
90 D2 **Ereentsav** Mongolia
80 E3 **Ereğli** Turkey
80 C1 **Ereğli** Turkey
114 F6 **Erei, Monti** *mts Sicily* Italy
Eréndira Mex. *see* **Carácuaro**
92 D1 **Erenhot** China
84 E3 **Eresk** Iran
111 D2 **Eresma** *r.* Spain
115 J5 **Eretria** Greece
109 J4 **Erfurt** Germany
81 G2 **Ergani** Turkey
120 B2 **'Erg Chech** *des.* Alg./Mali
92 C1 **Ergel** Mongolia
115 L4 **Ergene** *r.* Turkey
103 N4 **Ērgļi** Latvia
94 A1 **Ergu** China
96 C3 **Erhulai** China
106 D2 **Eriboll, Loch** *inlet* U.K.
106 D4 **Ericht, Loch** *l.* U.K.
134 B5 **Erie** *IL* U.S.A.
143 E4 **Erie** *KS* U.S.A.
146 C3 **Erie** *PA* U.S.A.
135 G4 **Erie, Lake** Canada/U.S.A.
94 H3 **Erimo** Japan
94 H4 **Erimo-misaki** *c.* Japan
106 A3 **Eriskay** *i.* U.K.
122 D2 **Eritrea** *country* Africa
83 H5 **Erkech-Tam** Kyrg.
80 E2 **Erkilet** Turkey
109 J5 **Erlangen** Germany
68 D4 **Erldunda** Australia
96 E2 **Erlong Shan** *mt.* China
96 C2 **Erlongshan Shuiku** *resr* China
108 D2 **Ermelo** Neth.
125 H3 **Ermelo** S. Africa
80 D3 **Ermenek** Turkey
115 K6 **Ermoupoli** Greece
87 B4 **Ernakulam** India
87 B4 **Erode** India
124 A1 **Erongo** *admin. reg.* Namibia
108 D3 **Erp** Neth.
120 B1 **Er Rachidia** Morocco
121 F3 **Er Rahad** Sudan
123 D5 **Errego** Moz.
114 D7 **Er Remla** Tunisia
107 C2 **Errigal** *h.* Rep. of Ireland
107 A3 **Erris Head** Rep. of Ireland
147 H2 **Errol** U.S.A.
69 G3 **Erromango** *i.* Vanuatu
115 I4 **Ersekë** Albania
142 D2 **Erskine** U.S.A.
102 M3 **Ersmark** Sweden
117 G5 **Ertil'** Rus. Fed.
70 C3 **Erudina** Australia
81 I3 **Eruh** Turkey
159 G2 **Erval** Brazil
146 D5 **Erwin** U.S.A.
109 G3 **Erwitte** Germany
109 J2 **Erxleben** *Sachsen-Anhalt* Germany
109 J2 **Erxleben** *Sachsen-Anhalt* Germany
109 K4 **Erzgebirge** *mts* Czech Rep./Germany
80 F3 **Erzin** Turkey
81 G2 **Erzincan** Turkey
81 H2 **Erzurum** Turkey
94 G4 **Esan-misaki** *pt* Japan
94 G4 **Esashi** Japan
94 H2 **Esashi** Japan
103 J5 **Esbjerg** Denmark
141 G3 **Escalante** U.S.A.
141 G3 **Escalante** *r.* U.S.A.
141 F3 **Escalante Desert** U.S.A.
150 C2 **Escalón** Mex.
134 D3 **Escanaba** U.S.A.
151 G4 **Escárcega** Mex.
97 B2 **Escarpada Point** Phil.
111 F2 **Escatrón** Spain
108 B4 **Escaut** *r.* Belgium
108 D3 **Esch** Neth.
108 E2 **Esche** Germany
109 I2 **Eschede** Germany
108 D5 **Esch-sur-Alzette** Lux.
109 I3 **Eschwege** Germany
108 E4 **Eschweiler** Germany
140 D5 **Escondido** U.S.A.
150 C3 **Escuinapa** Mex.
151 G5 **Escuintla** Guat.
151 F5 **Escuintla** Mex.
157 C3 **Escutillas** Col.
80 B3 **Eşen** Turkey
82 C5 **Esenguly** Turkm.
108 F1 **Esens** Germany
84 C3 **Eşfahān** Iran
84 D4 **Esfandāran** Iran
84 E2 **Esfarayen, Reshteh-ye** *mts* Iran
84 C4 **Esfarjan** Iran
85 E3 **Eshāqābād** Iran
84 D5 **Eshkanān** Iran
125 I4 **Eshowe** S. Africa
84 C3 **Eshtehārd** Iran
123 C6 **Esigodini** Zimbabwe
125 J4 **Esikhawini** S. Africa
71 J1 **Esk** Australia
71 G8 **Esk** *r.* Australia
104 D2 **Esk** *r.* U.K.
106 E5 **Eskdalemuir** U.K.
133 G3 **Esker** Canada
102 D2 **Eskifjörður** Iceland
80 B2 **Eski Gediz** Turkey
103 L4 **Eskilstuna** Sweden
128 E3 **Eskimo Lakes** Canada
81 I3 **Eski Mosul** Iraq
83 H4 **Eski-Nookat** Kyrg.
80 D1 **Eskipazar** Turkey
80 C2 **Eskişehir** Turkey
111 D1 **Esla** *r.* Spain
84 B3 **Eslāmābād-e Gharb** Iran
80 B3 **Esler Dağı** *mt.* Turkey
109 G3 **Eslohe (Sauerland)** Germany
103 K5 **Eslöv** Sweden
80 B2 **Eşme** Turkey
154 C3 **Esmeraldas** Ecuador
134 E1 **Esnagi Lake** Canada
108 B4 **Esnes** France
85 F5 **Espakeh** Iran
110 F4 **Espalion** France
135 G2 **Espanola** Canada
139 F4 **Espanola** U.S.A.
154 □ **Española, Isla** *i. Galapagos Is* Ecuador
140 A2 **Esparto** U.S.A.
83 H4 **Espe** Kazakh.
109 G2 **Espelkamp** Germany
68 C5 **Esperance** Australia
73 E2 **Esperanza** *research stn* Antarctica
159 E1 **Esperanza** Arg.
150 B2 **Esperanza** Mex.
97 C4 **Esperanza** Phil.
150 H5 **Esperanza, Sierra de la** *mts* Hond.
111 B3 **Espichel, Cabo** *c.* Port.
111 D1 **Espigüete** *mt.* Spain
150 D2 **Espinazo** Mex.
158 D2 **Espinhaço, Serra do** *mts* Brazil
158 D1 **Espinosa** Brazil
158 E2 **Espírito Santo** *state* Brazil
97 B2 **Espiritu** Phil.
69 G3 **Espíritu Santo** *i.* Vanuatu
151 H4 **Espíritu Santo, Bahía del** *b.* Mex.
150 B2 **Espíritu Santo, Isla** *i.* Mex.
103 N3 **Espoo** Fin.
111 F4 **Espuña** *mt.* Spain
156 B6 **Esquel** Arg.
130 E5 **Esquimalt** Canada
97 C5 **Essang** Indon.
120 B1 **Essaouira** Morocco
120 A2 **Es Semara** W. Sahara
108 C3 **Essen** Belgium
108 F3 **Essen** Germany
109 F2 **Essen (Oldenburg)** Germany
155 G3 **Essequibo** *r.* Guyana
135 F4 **Essex** Canada
141 E4 **Essex** U.S.A.
147 G2 **Essex Junction** U.S.A.
135 F4 **Essexville** U.S.A.
77 Q4 **Esso** Rus. Fed.
84 D4 **Eşţahbān** Iran
135 G2 **Estaire** Canada
155 K6 **Estância** Brazil
111 G1 **Estats, Pic d'** *mt.* France/Spain
125 H4 **Estcourt** S. Africa
109 H1 **Este** *r.* Germany
150 H5 **Estelí** Nicaragua
111 E1 **Estella** Spain
111 D4 **Estepa** Spain
111 D4 **Estepona** Spain
131 I4 **Esterhazy** Canada
140 B4 **Estero Bay** U.S.A.
156 D2 **Esteros** Para.
131 I5 **Estevan** Canada
142 E3 **Estherville** U.S.A.
145 D5 **Estill** U.S.A.
103 N4 **Estonia** *country* Europe
108 A5 **Estrées-St-Denis** France
111 C2 **Estrela, Serra da** *mts* Port.
111 E3 **Estrella** *mt.* Spain
141 F5 **Estrella, Sierra** *mts* U.S.A.
111 C3 **Estremoz** Port.
155 I5 **Estrondo, Serra** *hills* Brazil
81 L4 **Estūh** Iran
70 C2 **Etadunna** Australia
88 D4 **Etah** India
108 D5 **Étain** France
110 F2 **Étampes** France
110 E1 **Étaples** France
88 D4 **Etawah** India
125 I3 **eThandakukhanya** S. Africa
124 E4 **E'Thembini** S. Africa
122 D3 **Ethiopia** *country* Africa
80 D2 **Etimesğut** Turkey
106 C4 **Etive, Loch** *inlet* U.K.
114 F6 **Etna, Mount** *vol. Sicily* Italy
103 I4 **Etne** Norway
130 C3 **Etolin Island** U.S.A.
123 B5 **Etosha National Park** Namibia
123 B5 **Etosha Pan** *salt pan* Namibia
82 C5 **Etrek** Turkm.
115 K3 **Etropole** Bulg.
87 B4 **Ettaiyapuram** India
108 E5 **Ettelbruck** Lux.
108 C3 **Etten-Leur** Neth.
109 G6 **Ettlingen** Germany
106 E5 **Ettrick Forest** *reg.* U.K.
Etxarri Spain *see* **Etxarri-Aranatz**
111 E1 **Etxarri-Aranatz** Spain
150 C3 **Etzatlán** Mex.
71 G4 **Euabalong** Australia
68 C5 **Eucla** Australia
146 C4 **Euclid** U.S.A.
155 K6 **Euclides da Cunha** Brazil
71 H6 **Eucumbene, Lake** Australia
70 C5 **Eudunda** Australia
145 C6 **Eufaula** U.S.A.
143 E5 **Eufaula Lake** *resr* U.S.A.
138 B2 **Eugene** U.S.A.
150 A2 **Eugenia, Punta** *pt* Mex.
71 H4 **Eugowra** Australia
71 F2 **Eulo** Australia
71 H3 **Eumungerie** Australia
143 E6 **Eunice** U.S.A.
108 E4 **Eupen** Belgium
81 J6 **Euphrates** *r.* Asia *alt.* **Al Furāt (Iraq/Syria),** *alt.* **Fırat (Turkey)**
103 M3 **Eura** Fin.
110 E2 **Eure** *r.* France
138 A3 **Eureka** *CA* U.S.A.
138 D1 **Eureka** *MT* U.S.A.
141 E2 **Eureka** *NV* U.S.A.
70 D3 **Eurinilla** *watercourse* Australia
70 D3 **Euriowie** Australia
71 F6 **Euroa** Australia
123 E6 **Europa, Île** *i.* Indian Ocean
111 D4 **Europa Point** Gibraltar
100 **Europe**
108 E4 **Euskirchen** Germany
70 E5 **Euston** Australia
145 C5 **Eutaw** U.S.A.
130 D4 **Eutsuk Lake** Canada
109 K3 **Eutzsch** Germany
125 H3 **Evander** S. Africa
132 E3 **Evans, Lac** *l.* Canada
139 F4 **Evans, Mount** U.S.A.
130 F4 **Evansburg** Canada
71 J2 **Evans Head** Australia
129 J3 **Evans Strait** Canada
134 D4 **Evanston** *IL* U.S.A.
138 E3 **Evanston** *WY* U.S.A.
135 F3 **Evansville** Canada
144 C4 **Evansville** *IN* U.S.A.
134 C4 **Evansville** *WI* U.S.A.
138 F3 **Evansville** *WY* U.S.A.
134 E4 **Evart** U.S.A.
125 G3 **Evaton** S. Africa
84 D5 **Evaz** Iran
134 A2 **Eveleth** U.S.A.
77 Q3 **Evensk** Rus. Fed.
70 A3 **Everard, Lake** *salt flat* Australia
68 D4 **Everard Range** *hills* Australia
108 D3 **Everdingen** Neth.
89 F4 **Everest, Mount** China
147 J1 **Everett** Canada
138 B1 **Everett** U.S.A.
108 B3 **Evergem** Belgium
145 D7 **Everglades** *swamp* U.S.A.
145 D7 **Everglades National Park** U.S.A.
143 G6 **Evergreen** U.S.A.
105 F5 **Evesham** U.K.
105 F5 **Evesham, Vale of** *val.* U.K.
102 M3 **Evijärvi** Fin.
120 D4 **Evinayong** Equat. Guinea
103 I4 **Evje** Norway
111 C3 **Évora** Port.
90 F1 **Evoron, Ozero** *l.* Rus. Fed.
81 J2 **Evowghlī** Iran
110 E2 **Évreux** France
115 J6 **Evrotas** *r.* Greece
80 D4 **Evrychou** Cyprus
115 K5 **Evvoia** *i.* Greece
140 □1 **'Ewa Beach** U.S.A.
122 D3 **Ewaso Ngiro** *r.* Kenya
106 C3 **Ewe, Loch** *b.* U.K.
122 B4 **Ewo** Congo
154 E6 **Exaltación** Bol.
125 G4 **Excelsior** S. Africa
140 C2 **Excelsior Mountain** U.S.A.
140 C2 **Excelsior Mountains** U.S.A.
142 E4 **Excelsior Springs** U.S.A.
105 D6 **Exe** *r.* U.K.
73 B4 **Executive Committee Range** *mts* Antarctica
71 I5 **Exeter** Australia
135 G4 **Exeter** Canada
105 D7 **Exeter** U.K.
140 C3 **Exeter** *CA* U.S.A.
147 H3 **Exeter** *NH* U.S.A.
108 E2 **Exloo** Neth.
105 D7 **Exminster** U.K.
105 D6 **Exmoor** *hills* U.K.
105 D6 **Exmoor National Park** U.K.
147 F6 **Exmore** U.S.A.
105 D7 **Exmouth** U.K.
71 H3 **Exmouth, Mount** Australia
68 B4 **Exmouth Gulf** Australia
162 L6 **Exmouth Plateau** *sea feature* Indian Ocean
111 D3 **Extremadura** *aut. comm.* Spain
145 E7 **Exuma Sound** *sea chan.* Bahamas
117 F6 **Eya** *r.* Rus. Fed.
122 D4 **Eyasi, Lake** *salt l.* Tanz.
105 I5 **Eye** U.K.
106 F5 **Eyemouth** U.K.
106 B2 **Eye Peninsula** U.K.
102 C3 **Eyjafjallajökull** *ice cap* Iceland
102 C1 **Eyjafjörður** *inlet* Iceland
122 E3 **Eyl** Somalia
105 F6 **Eynsham** U.K.
70 B2 **Eyre (North), Lake** *salt flat* Australia
70 B2 **Eyre (South), Lake** *salt flat* Australia
72 B6 **Eyre Mountains** N.Z.
70 A4 **Eyre Peninsula** Australia
109 H2 **Eystrup** Germany
102 □ **Eysturoy** *i.* Faroe Is
125 I4 **Ezakheni** S. Africa
125 H3 **Ezenzeleni** S. Africa
159 C3 **Ezequiel Ramos Mexía, Embalse** *resr* Arg.
93 E4 **Ezhou** China
116 I2 **Ezhva** Rus. Fed.
115 L5 **Ezine** Turkey
80 F1 **Ezinepazar** Turkey

F

103 J5 **Faaborg** Denmark
143 B6 **Fabens** U.S.A.
98 □ **Faber, Mount** *h.* Sing.
130 F2 **Faber Lake** Canada
Fåborg Denmark *see* **Faaborg**
114 E3 **Fabriano** Italy
157 B3 **Facatativá** Col.
108 B4 **Faches-Thumesnil** France
120 D3 **Fachi** Niger
147 F4 **Factoryville** U.S.A.
156 B7 **Facundo** Arg.
120 C3 **Fada-N'Gourma** Burkina
81 H4 **Fadghāmī** Syria
114 D2 **Faenza** Italy
Faeroes *terr.* Atlantic Ocean *see* **Faroe Islands**
91 F7 **Fafanlap** Indon.
122 E3 **Fafen Shet'** *watercourse* Eth.
115 K2 **Făgăraş** Romania
103 J3 **Fagernes** Norway
103 K4 **Fagersta** Sweden
156 C8 **Fagnano, Lago** *l.* Arg./Chile
108 C4 **Fagne** *reg.* Belgium
120 B3 **Faguibine, Lac** *l.* Mali
102 C3 **Fagurhólsmýri** Iceland
121 F4 **Fagwir** Sudan
84 C4 **Fahlīān, Rūdkhāneh-ye** *watercourse* Iran
85 E4 **Fahraj** Iran
80 D6 **Fā'id** Egypt
128 D3 **Fairbanks** U.S.A.
146 B5 **Fairborn** U.S.A.
142 D3 **Fairbury** U.S.A.
146 E5 **Fairfax** U.S.A.
140 A2 **Fairfield** *CA* U.S.A.
134 B5 **Fairfield** *IA* U.S.A.
144 C4 **Fairfield** *OH* U.S.A.
143 D6 **Fairfield** *TX* U.S.A.
147 G3 **Fair Haven** U.S.A.
107 E2 **Fair Head** U.K.
97 A4 **Fairie Queen** *sea feature* Phil.
106 G1 **Fair Isle** *i.* U.K.
72 C7 **Fairlie** N.Z.
142 E3 **Fairmont** *MN* U.S.A.
146 C5 **Fairmont** *WV* U.S.A.
139 F4 **Fairplay** U.S.A.
134 D3 **Fairport** U.S.A.
146 C4 **Fairport Harbor** U.S.A.
130 F3 **Fairview** Canada
135 E3 **Fairview** *MI* U.S.A.
143 D4 **Fairview** *OK* U.S.A.
141 G2 **Fairview** *UT* U.S.A.
93 □ **Fairview Park** *Hong Kong* China
130 B3 **Fairweather, Cape** U.S.A.
130 B3 **Fairweather, Mount** Canada/U.S.A.
91 G6 **Fais** *i.* Micronesia
88 C3 **Faisalabad** Pak.
108 C5 **Faissault** France
142 C2 **Faith** U.S.A.
106 □ **Faither, The** *stack* U.K.
89 E4 **Faizabad** India
69 I2 **Fakaofo** *atoll* Tokelau
105 H5 **Fakenham** U.K.
102 K3 **Fåker** Sweden
91 F7 **Fakfak** Indon.
84 D4 **Fakhrabad** Iran
96 B2 **Faku** China
105 C7 **Fal** *r.* U.K.
120 A4 **Falaba** Sierra Leone
110 D2 **Falaise** France
89 G4 **Falakata** India
89 H5 **Falam** Myanmar
84 C3 **Falavarjan** Iran
143 D7 **Falcon Lake** Mex./U.S.A.
143 D7 **Falfurrias** U.S.A.
130 F3 **Falher** Canada
109 L3 **Falkenberg** Germany
103 K4 **Falkenberg** Sweden
109 K1 **Falkenhagen** Germany
109 K3 **Falkenhain** Germany
109 L2 **Falkensee** Germany
109 K5 **Falkenstein** Germany
106 E5 **Falkirk** U.K.
106 E4 **Falkland** U.K.
163 F9 **Falkland Escarpment** *sea feature* S. Atlantic Ocean
156 E8 **Falkland Islands** *terr.* Atlantic Ocean
163 F9 **Falkland Plateau** *sea feature* S. Atlantic Ocean
156 D8 **Falkland Sound** *sea chan.* Falkland Is
103 K4 **Falköping** Sweden
140 D5 **Fallbrook** U.S.A.
109 H2 **Fallingbostel** Germany
140 C2 **Fallon** U.S.A.
147 H4 **Fall River** U.S.A.
138 F3 **Fall River Pass** U.S.A.
142 E3 **Falls City** U.S.A.
105 B7 **Falmouth** U.K.
146 A5 **Falmouth** *KY* U.S.A.
147 H3 **Falmouth** *ME* U.S.A.
134 E3 **Falmouth** *MI* U.S.A.
124 C7 **False Bay** S. Africa
150 B3 **Falso, Cabo** *c.* Mex.
103 J5 **Falster** *i.* Denmark
113 M7 **Fălticeni** Romania
103 K3 **Falun** Sweden
80 D4 **Famagusta** Cyprus
108 E5 **Fameck** France
84 C3 **Famenin** Iran
108 D4 **Famenne** *val.* Belgium
131 J4 **Family Lake** Canada
92 F4 **Fanchang** China
107 E4 **Fane** *r.* Rep. of Ireland
98 A1 **Fang** Thai.
92 D3 **Fangcheng** China
93 C4 **Fangdou Shan** *mts* China
93 F6 **Fangliao** Taiwan
92 E2 **Fangshan** *Beijing* China
92 D2 **Fangshan** *Shanxi* China
93 F6 **Fangshan** Taiwan
92 D3 **Fangxian** China
94 A2 **Fangzheng** China
93 □ **Fanling** *Hong Kong* China
106 C3 **Fannich, Loch** *l.* U.K.
85 E5 **Fannūj** Iran
114 E3 **Fano** Italy
93 F5 **Fanshan** China
92 D2 **Fanshi** China
Fan Si Pan *mt.* Vietnam *see* **Phăng Xi Păng**
122 C3 **Faradje** Dem. Rep. Congo
123 E6 **Farafangana** Madag.
121 E2 **Farāfirah, Wāḩāt al** *oasis* Egypt
Farafra Oasis *oasis* Egypt *see* **Farāfirah, Wāḩāt al**
85 F3 **Farāh** Afgh.
85 F4 **Farah Rūd** *watercourse* Afgh.
157 A4 **Farallones de Cali, Parque Nacional** *nat. park* Col.
120 A3 **Faranah** Guinea
82 E5 **Farap** Turkm.
86 B6 **Farasān, Jazā'ir** *is* Saudi Arabia
91 G6 **Faraulep** *atoll* Micronesia
105 F7 **Fareham** U.K.
129 N4 **Farewell, Cape** Greenland
72 D4 **Farewell, Cape** N.Z.
72 D4 **Farewell Spit** N.Z.
103 K4 **Färgelanda** Sweden
142 D2 **Fargo** U.S.A.
83 G4 **Farg'ona** Uzbek.
142 E2 **Faribault** U.S.A.
133 F2 **Faribault, Lac** *l.* Canada
88 D3 **Faridabad** India
88 C3 **Faridkot** India
89 G5 **Faridpur** Bangl.
120 A3 **Farim** Guinea-Bissau
85 E3 **Farīmān** Iran
103 L4 **Färjestaden** Sweden
83 G5 **Farkhor** Tajik.
81 L4 **Farmahin** Iran
134 C5 **Farmer City** U.S.A.
132 D2 **Farmer Island** Canada
130 E3 **Farmington** Canada
134 B5 **Farmington** *IA* U.S.A.
134 B5 **Farmington** *IL* U.S.A.
147 H2 **Farmington** *ME* U.S.A.
147 H3 **Farmington** *NH* U.S.A.
141 H3 **Farmington** *NM* U.S.A.
138 E3 **Farmington** *UT* U.S.A.
130 D4 **Far Mountain** Canada
146 D6 **Farmville** U.S.A.
105 G6 **Farnborough** U.K.
104 F2 **Farne Islands** U.K.
105 G6 **Farnham** U.K.
130 F4 **Farnham, Mount** Canada
155 G4 **Faro** Brazil
130 C2 **Faro** Canada
111 C4 **Faro** Port.
103 L4 **Fårö** *i.* Sweden
102 □2 **Faroe Islands** *terr.* N. Atlantic Ocean
103 L4 **Fårösund** Sweden
119 I5 **Farquhar Group** *is* Seychelles
Farquhar Islands Seychelles *see* **Farquhar Group**
84 D4 **Farrāshband** Iran
146 C4 **Farrell** U.S.A.
135 J3 **Farrellton** Canada
85 E3 **Farrokhī** Iran
84 D3 **Farsakh** Iran
115 J5 **Farsala** Greece
85 F3 **Fārsī** Afgh.
138 E3 **Farson** U.S.A.
103 I4 **Farsund** Norway
82 D5 **Fārūj** Iran
Farvel, Kap *c.* Greenland *see* **Farewell, Cape**
143 C5 **Farwell** U.S.A.
84 E5 **Fāryāb** Iran
84 D4 **Fasā** Iran
114 G4 **Fasano** Italy
109 I2 **Faßberg** Germany
146 E4 **Fassett** U.S.A.
117 D5 **Fastiv** Ukr.
88 D4 **Fatehgarh** India
88 C4 **Fatehpur** *Rajasthan* India
88 E4 **Fatehpur** *Uttar Pradesh* India
88 D4 **Fatehpur Sikri** India
84 D4 **Fatḩābād** Iran
135 G3 **Fathom Five National Marine Park** Canada
120 A3 **Fatick** Senegal
110 H2 **Faulquemont** France
125 F4 **Fauresmith** S. Africa
102 K2 **Fauske** Norway
141 F1 **Faust** U.S.A.
114 E6 **Favignana, Isola** *i. Sicily* Italy
130 G4 **Fawcett** Canada
105 F7 **Fawley** U.K.
132 C3 **Fawn** *r.* Canada
102 B2 **Faxaflói** *b.* Iceland
102 L3 **Faxälven** *r.* Sweden
121 D3 **Faya** Chad
134 D3 **Fayette** U.S.A.
143 E4 **Fayetteville** *AR* U.S.A.
145 E5 **Fayetteville** *NC* U.S.A.
145 C5 **Fayetteville** *TN* U.S.A.
81 L7 **Faylakah** *i.* Kuwait
120 C4 **Fazao Malfakassa, Parc National de** *nat. park* Togo
88 C3 **Fazilka** India
84 C5 **Fazrān, Jabal** *h.* Saudi Arabia
120 A2 **Fdérik** Mauritania
107 B5 **Feale** *r.* Rep. of Ireland
145 E5 **Fear, Cape** U.S.A.
140 B2 **Feather, North Fork** *r.* U.S.A.
140 B2 **Feather Falls** U.S.A.
72 E4 **Featherston** N.Z.
71 G6 **Feathertop, Mount** Australia
110 E2 **Fécamp** France
159 F1 **Federación** Arg.
156 E4 **Federal** Arg.
82 E1 **Fedorovka** *Kustanayskaya Oblast'* Kazakh.
83 I1 **Fedorovka** *Pavlodarskaya Oblast'* Kazakh.
82 B2 **Fedorovka** *Zapadnyy Kazakhstan* Kazakh.
82 C1 **Fedorovka** Rus. Fed.
112 E3 **Fehmarn** *i.* Germany
109 K2 **Fehrbellin** Germany
158 E3 **Feia, Lagoa** *lag.* Brazil
92 E4 **Feidong** China
92 F3 **Feihuanghe Kou** *r. mouth* China
154 D5 **Feijó** Brazil
72 E4 **Feilding** N.Z.
155 K6 **Feira de Santana** Brazil
92 E4 **Feixi** China
80 E3 **Feke** Turkey
111 H3 **Felanitx** Spain
134 D3 **Felch** U.S.A.
109 L1 **Feldberg** Germany
112 D7 **Feldberg** *mt.* Germany
112 D7 **Feldkirch** Austria
112 G7 **Feldkirchen in Kärnten** Austria
159 E1 **Feliciano** *r.* Arg.
151 G4 **Felipe C. Puerto** Mex.
158 D2 **Felixlândia** Brazil
105 I6 **Felixstowe** U.K.
114 D1 **Feltre** Italy
103 J3 **Femunden** *l.* Norway
103 K3 **Femundsmarka Nasjonalpark** *nat. park* Norway
114 D3 **Fenaio, Punta del** *pt* Italy
141 H4 **Fence Lake** U.S.A.
135 H3 **Fenelon Falls** Canada
115 K4 **Fengari** *mt.* Greece
93 E4 **Fengcheng** *Jiangxi* China
96 C3 **Fengcheng** *Liaoning* China
93 C4 **Fengdu** China
93 C5 **Fenggang** China
96 D1 **Fengguang** China
93 F4 **Fenghua** China
93 C5 **Fenghuang** China
92 C4 **Fengjie** China
93 D6 **Fengkai** China
93 F6 **Fenglin** Taiwan
92 F2 **Fengnan** China
92 E1 **Fengning** China
92 E3 **Fengqiu** China
93 C5 **Fengshan** China
93 E6 **Fengshun** China
92 E3 **Fengtai** China
93 E4 **Fengxin** China
92 E3 **Fengyang** China
92 D1 **Fengzhen** China
92 D2 **Fen He** *r.* China
89 G5 **Feni** Bangl.
69 F2 **Feni Islands** P.N.G.
134 B4 **Fennimore** U.S.A.
123 E5 **Fenoarivo Atsinanana** Madag.
135 F4 **Fenton** U.S.A.
92 D2 **Fenxi** China
92 D2 **Fenyang** China
93 E5 **Fenyi** China
117 E6 **Feodosiya** Ukr.
114 B6 **Fer, Cap de** *c.* Alg.
85 E3 **Ferdows** Iran
Fergana Uzbek. *see* **Farg'ona**
83 H4 **Fergana Too Tizmegi** *mts* Kyrg.
135 G4 **Fergus** Canada
142 D2 **Fergus Falls** U.S.A.
68 F2 **Fergusson Island** P.N.G.
114 C7 **Fériana** Tunisia
120 B4 **Ferkessédougou** Côte d'Ivoire
114 E3 **Fermo** Italy
133 G3 **Fermont** Canada
111 C2 **Fermoselle** Spain
107 C5 **Fermoy** Rep. of Ireland

180 Fernandina, Isla

154 □ Fernandina, Isla i. Galapagos Is Ecuador
145 D6 Fernandina Beach U.S.A.
156 B8 Fernando de Magallanes, Parque Nacional nat. park Chile
163 G6 Fernando de Noronha i. Brazil
158 B3 Fernandópolis Brazil
138 B1 Ferndale U.S.A.
105 F7 Ferndown U.K.
130 F5 Fernie Canada
71 G2 Fernlee Australia
140 C2 Fernley U.S.A.
147 F4 Fernridge U.S.A.
107 E5 Ferns Rep. of Ireland
138 C2 Fernwood U.S.A.
114 D2 Ferrara Italy
158 B3 Ferreiros Brazil
143 F6 Ferriday U.S.A.
114 C4 Ferro, Capo c. Sardinia Italy
111 B1 Ferrol Spain
131 G2 Ferron U.S.A.
82 D1 Fershampenuaz Rus. Fed.
108 D1 Ferwert Neth.
120 B1 Fès Morocco
122 B4 Feshi Dem. Rep. Congo
131 J5 Fessenden U.S.A.
142 F4 Festus U.S.A.
106 □ Fethaland, Point of U.K.
107 D5 Fethard Rep. of Ireland
80 B3 Fethiye Turkey
82 C4 Fetisovo Kazakh.
106 □ Fetlar i. U.K.
106 F4 Fettercairn U.K.
109 J5 Feucht Germany
109 I5 Feuchtwangen Germany
133 F2 Feuilles, Rivière aux r. Canada
80 F3 Fevzipaşa Turkey
85 H2 Feyzābād Afgh.
85 E3 Feyẓābād Iran
105 D5 Ffestiniog U.K.
123 E6 Fianarantsoa Madag.
122 D3 Fichē Eth.
109 K4 Fichtelgebirge hills Germany
125 G4 Ficksburg S. Africa
130 F4 Field B.C. Canada
135 G2 Field Ont. Canada
115 H4 Fier Albania
134 E3 Fife Lake U.S.A.
106 F4 Fife Ness pt U.K.
71 G4 Fifield Australia
134 B3 Fifield U.S.A.
110 F4 Figeac France
111 B2 Figueira da Foz Port.
111 H1 Figueres Spain
120 B1 Figuig Morocco
69 H3 Fiji country Pacific Ocean
150 H6 Filadelfia Costa Rica
156 D2 Filadelfia Para.
73 C3 Filchner Ice Shelf ice feature Antarctica
104 G3 Filey U.K.
115 I5 Filippiada Greece
103 K4 Filipstad Sweden
102 J3 Fillan Norway
140 C4 Fillmore CA U.S.A.
141 F2 Fillmore UT U.S.A.
73 D3 Fimbull Ice Shelf ice feature Antarctica
147 F2 Finch Canada
106 E3 Findhorn r. U.K.
81 H3 Fındık Turkey
146 B4 Findlay U.S.A.
71 H8 Fingal Australia
132 E5 Finger Lakes U.S.A.
123 D5 Fingoè Moz.
80 C3 Finike Turkey
80 C3 Finike Körfezi b. Turkey
111 B1 Finisterre, Cape Spain
116 S5 Finland country Europe
103 M4 Finland, Gulf of Europe
130 D3 Finlay r. Canada
130 D3 Finlay, Mount Canada
71 F5 Finley Australia
109 J3 Finne ridge Germany
70 A4 Finniss, Cape Australia
102 L1 Finnsnes Norway
103 K4 Finspång Sweden
107 D3 Fintona U.K.
107 C3 Fintown Rep. of Ireland
106 C3 Fionn Loch l. U.K.
106 B4 Fionnphort U.K.
72 A6 Fiordland National Park N.Z.
81 J6 Fīrat r. Turkey alt. Al Furāt (Iraq/Syria), conv. Euphrates
140 B3 Firebaugh U.S.A.
131 I2 Firedrake Lake Canada
147 G4 Fire Island National Seashore nature res. U.S.A.
Firenze Italy see Florence
81 J6 Firk, Sha'īb watercourse Iraq
159 E2 Firmat Arg.
110 G4 Firminy France
109 I6 Firngrund reg. Germany
113 P2 Firovo Rus. Fed.
88 B3 Firoza Pak.
88 D4 Firozabad India
85 G3 Firozkoh reg. Afgh.
88 C3 Firozpur India
147 H2 First Connecticut Lake U.S.A.
84 D4 Fīrūzābād Iran
108 F5 Fischbach Germany
123 B6 Fish watercourse Namibia
124 D5 Fish r. S. Africa
73 B6 Fisher Bay b. Antarctica
147 F6 Fisherman Island U.S.A.
147 H4 Fishers Island U.S.A.
131 M2 Fisher Strait Canada
105 C6 Fishguard U.K.
130 E2 Fish Lake Canada
134 A2 Fish Lake MN U.S.A.
141 G2 Fish Lake UT U.S.A.
135 F4 Fish Point U.S.A.
73 C3 Fiske, Cape c. Antarctica
108 B5 Fismes France
111 B1 Fisterra Spain
Fisterra, Cabo c. Spain see Finisterre, Cape
147 H3 Fitchburg U.S.A.
131 G3 Fitzgerald Canada
145 D6 Fitzgerald U.S.A.
70 B4 Fitzgerald Bay Australia
156 C7 Fitz Roy Arg.
68 C3 Fitzroy Crossing Australia
135 G3 Fitzwilliam Island Canada
107 D3 Fivemiletown U.K.
114 D2 Fivizzano Italy
122 C4 Fizi Dem. Rep. Congo
103 J3 Flå Norway
125 H5 Flagstaff S. Africa
141 G4 Flagstaff U.S.A.
147 H2 Flagstaff Lake U.S.A.
132 E2 Flaherty Island Canada
134 B3 Flambeau r. U.S.A.
104 G3 Flamborough Head U.K.
109 K2 Fläming hills Germany
138 E3 Flaming Gorge Reservoir U.S.A.
124 D5 Flaminksvlei salt pan S. Africa
108 A3 Flanders reg. Europe
108 A4 Flandre reg. France
106 A2 Flannan Isles U.K.
102 K2 Flåsjön l. Sweden
134 E4 Flat r. U.S.A.
138 D2 Flathead Lake U.S.A.
72 E4 Flat Point N.Z.
68 E3 Flattery, Cape Australia
138 A1 Flattery, Cape U.S.A.
109 J2 Fleetmark Germany
104 D4 Fleetwood U.K.
147 F4 Fleetwood U.S.A.
103 I4 Flekkefjord Norway
146 E3 Fleming U.S.A.
146 B5 Flemingsburg U.S.A.
163 G2 Flemish Cap sea feature N. Atlantic Ocean
103 L4 Flen Sweden
112 D3 Flensburg Germany
110 D2 Flers France
135 G3 Flesherton Canada
131 H2 Fletcher Lake Canada
135 F3 Fletcher Pond l. U.S.A.
68 E3 Flinders r. Australia
68 B5 Flinders Bay Australia
70 B5 Flinders Chase National Park Australia
70 A4 Flinders Island S.A. Australia
71 H7 Flinders Island Tas. Australia
70 C3 Flinders Ranges mts Australia
70 C3 Flinders Ranges National Park Australia
131 I4 Flin Flon Canada
105 D4 Flint U.K.
135 F4 Flint U.S.A.
145 C6 Flint r. GA U.S.A.
135 F4 Flint r. MI U.S.A.
161 I5 Flint Island Kiribati
71 H1 Flinton Australia
103 K3 Flisa Norway
104 E2 Flodden U.K.
109 L4 Flöha Germany
109 L4 Flöha r. Germany
73 B4 Flood Range mts Antarctica
134 A2 Floodwood U.S.A.
144 B4 Flora U.S.A.
110 F4 Florac France
108 E5 Florange France
130 G4 Florence Canada
114 D3 Florence Italy
145 C5 Florence AL U.S.A.
141 G5 Florence AZ U.S.A.
142 D4 Florence KS U.S.A.
146 C5 Florence OH U.S.A.
138 A3 Florence OR U.S.A.
145 E5 Florence SC U.S.A.
141 G5 Florence Junction U.S.A.
147 J1 Florenceville Canada
157 B4 Florencia Col.
108 C4 Florennes Belgium
156 C6 Florentino Ameghino, Embalse resr Arg.
159 E2 Flores r. Arg.
100 A6 Flores i. Azores
151 G4 Flores Guat.
91 E7 Flores i. Indon.
91 D7 Flores, Laut sea Indon.
158 C1 Flores de Goiás Brazil
Flores Sea sea Indon. see Flores, Laut
155 K5 Floresta Brazil
155 J5 Floriano Brazil
156 G3 Florianópolis Brazil
159 F2 Florida Uruguay
145 D6 Florida state U.S.A.
149 H4 Florida, Straits of Bahamas/U.S.A.
145 D7 Florida Bay U.S.A.
145 D7 Florida City U.S.A.
69 G2 Florida Islands Solomon Is
137 J7 Florida Keys is U.S.A.
115 I4 Florina Greece
103 I3 Florø Norway
133 H3 Flour Lake Canada
134 A4 Floyd IA U.S.A.
146 C6 Floyd VA U.S.A.
141 G4 Floyd, Mount U.S.A.
143 C5 Floydada U.S.A.
108 D2 Fluessen l. Neth.
68 E2 Fly r. P.N.G.
146 C5 Fly U.S.A.
115 H3 Foča Bos.-Herz.
106 E3 Fochabers U.K.
125 G3 Fochville S. Africa
115 L2 Focşani Romania
93 D6 Fogang China
114 F4 Foggia Italy
120 □ Fogo i. Cape Verde
133 J4 Fogo Island Canada
83 G4 Fogolevo Kazakh.
106 D2 Foinaven h. U.K.
110 E5 Foix France
102 K2 Folda sea chan. Norway
102 K2 Foldereid Norway
102 J2 Foldfjorden sea chan. Norway
115 K6 Folegandros i. Greece
135 F1 Foleyet Canada
114 E3 Foligno Italy
105 I6 Folkestone U.K.
105 G5 Folkingham U.K.
145 D6 Folkston U.S.A.
103 J3 Folldal Norway
114 D3 Follonica Italy
140 B2 Folsom Lake U.S.A.
117 G6 Fomin Rus. Fed.
116 I2 Fominskiy Rus. Fed.
131 H3 Fond-du-Lac Canada
131 I3 Fond du Lac r. Canada
134 C4 Fond du Lac U.S.A.
111 D2 Fondevila Spain
114 E4 Fondi Italy
69 H2 Fongafale i. Tuvalu
114 C4 Fonni Sardinia Italy
150 H5 Fonseca, Golfo do b. Central America
133 F3 Fontanges Canada
130 E3 Fontas Canada
130 E3 Fontas r. Canada
154 E4 Fonte Boa Brazil
110 D3 Fontenay-le-Comte France
102 D1 Fontur pt Iceland
133 H3 Foot's Bay Canada
92 C3 Foping China
71 H4 Forbes Australia
138 C1 Forbes, Mount Canada
109 J5 Forchheim Germany
133 G2 Ford r. Canada
134 D2 Ford r. U.S.A.
103 I3 Førde Norway
131 J2 Forde Lake Canada
105 H5 Fordham U.K.
105 F7 Fordingbridge U.K.
73 B4 Ford Range mts Antarctica
71 F2 Fords Bridge Australia
143 E5 Fordyce U.S.A.
120 A4 Forécariah Guinea
105 F7 Foreland hd U.K.
105 D6 Foreland Point U.K.
130 D4 Foresight Mountain Canada
135 G4 Forest Canada
143 F5 Forest MS U.S.A.
146 B4 Forest OH U.S.A.
147 G3 Forest Dale U.S.A.
71 G5 Forest Hill Australia
140 B2 Foresthill U.S.A.
71 H9 Forestier, Cape Australia
71 H9 Forestier Peninsula Australia
134 A3 Forest Lake U.S.A.
145 C5 Forest Park U.S.A.
133 G4 Forestville Canada
106 F4 Forfar U.K.
138 A2 Forks U.S.A.
146 E4 Forksville U.S.A.
114 E2 Forlì Italy
104 D4 Formby U.K.
111 G3 Formentera i. Spain
111 H3 Formentor, Cap de c. Spain
158 D3 Formiga Brazil
156 E3 Formosa Arg.
158 C1 Formosa Brazil
155 G6 Formosa, Serra hills Brazil
158 D1 Formoso r. Brazil
106 E3 Forres U.K.
70 E7 Forrest Australia
134 C5 Forrest U.S.A.
143 F5 Forrest City U.S.A.
134 C4 Forreston U.S.A.
102 L3 Fors Sweden
68 E3 Forsayth Australia
102 M2 Forsnäs Sweden
103 M3 Forssa Fin.
71 J4 Forster Australia
143 E4 Forsyth MO U.S.A.
138 F2 Forsyth MT U.S.A.
135 I1 Forsythe Canada
88 C3 Fort Abbas Pak.
132 D3 Fort Albany Canada
155 K4 Fortaleza Brazil
141 H5 Fort Apache U.S.A.
130 G4 Fort Assiniboine Canada
134 C4 Fort Atkinson U.S.A.
106 D3 Fort Augustus U.K.
125 G6 Fort Beaufort S. Africa
138 E2 Fort Benton U.S.A.
131 H3 Fort Black Canada
140 A2 Fort Bragg U.S.A.
Fort-Chimo Canada see Kuujjuaq
131 G3 Fort Chipewyan Canada
143 D5 Fort Cobb Reservoir U.S.A.
138 F3 Fort Collins U.S.A.
135 I3 Fort-Coulonge Canada
147 F2 Fort Covington U.S.A.
143 C6 Fort Davis U.S.A.
149 L6 Fort-de-France Martinique
145 C5 Fort Deposit U.S.A.
142 E3 Fort Dodge U.S.A.
142 E1 Fort Frances U.S.A.
Fort George Canada see Chisasibi
128 F3 Fort Good Hope Canada
106 D4 Forth r. U.K.
106 F4 Forth, Firth of est. U.K.
141 E2 Fortification Range mts U.S.A.
156 D2 Fortín Capitán Demattei Para.
156 D2 Fortín General Mendoza Para.
156 D2 Fortín Madrejón Para.
156 E2 Fortín Pilcomayo Arg.
154 F7 Fortín Ravelo Bol.
154 F7 Fortín Suárez Arana Bol.
147 I1 Fort Kent U.S.A.
145 D7 Fort Lauderdale U.S.A.
130 E2 Fort Liard Canada
131 G3 Fort Mackay Canada
130 G5 Fort Macleod Canada
134 B5 Fort Madison U.S.A.
134 B3 Fort McCoy U.S.A.
131 G3 Fort McMurray Canada
128 E3 Fort McPherson Canada
138 G3 Fort Morgan U.S.A.
145 D7 Fort Myers U.S.A.
130 E3 Fort Nelson Canada
130 E3 Fort Nelson r. Canada
Fort Norman Canada see Tulita
145 C5 Fort Payne U.S.A.
138 F1 Fort Peck U.S.A.
138 F2 Fort Peck Reservoir U.S.A.
145 D7 Fort Pierce U.S.A.
142 C2 Fort Pierre U.S.A.
130 F2 Fort Providence Canada
131 I4 Fort Qu'Appelle Canada
130 G2 Fort Resolution Canada
72 B7 Fortrose N.Z.
106 D3 Fortrose U.K.
140 A2 Fort Ross U.S.A.
Fort Rupert Canada see Waskaganish
130 E4 Fort St James Canada
130 E3 Fort St John Canada
130 G4 Fort Saskatchewan Canada
143 E4 Fort Scott U.S.A.
132 C2 Fort Severn Canada
82 B3 Fort-Shevchenko Kazakh.
130 E2 Fort Simpson Canada
131 G2 Fort Smith Canada
143 E5 Fort Smith U.S.A.
143 C5 Fort Stockton U.S.A.
139 F5 Fort Sumner U.S.A.
138 A3 Fortuna CA U.S.A.
142 C1 Fortuna ND U.S.A.
133 I4 Fortune Bay Canada
130 F3 Fort Vermilion Canada
145 C6 Fort Walton Beach U.S.A.
134 E5 Fort Wayne U.S.A.
106 C4 Fort William U.K.
143 D5 Fort Worth U.S.A.
128 D3 Fort Yukon U.S.A.
84 D5 Forūr, Jazīreh-ye i. Iran
103 I4 Forvik Norway
93 D6 Foshan China
114 B2 Fossano Italy
71 G7 Foster Australia
130 B3 Foster, Mount Canada/U.S.A.
129 P2 Foster Bugt b. Greenland
146 B4 Fostoria U.S.A.
105 D4 Fotherby U.K.
110 D2 Fougères France
106 □ Foula i. U.K.
105 H6 Foulness Point U.K.
87 C4 Foul Point Sri Lanka
72 C4 Foulwind, Cape N.Z.
120 D4 Foumban Cameroon
73 C4 Foundation Ice Stream glacier Antarctica
120 A3 Foundiougne Senegal
134 A4 Fountain U.S.A.
104 F3 Fountains Abbey tourist site U.K.
110 G2 Fourches, Mont des h. France
140 D4 Four Corners U.S.A.
125 H4 Fouriesburg S. Africa
108 C4 Fourmies France
115 L6 Fournoi i. Greece
134 C2 Fourteen Mile Point U.S.A.
120 A3 Fouta Djallon reg. Guinea
72 A7 Foveaux Strait N.Z.
145 E7 Fowl Cay i. Bahamas
139 F4 Fowler CO U.S.A.
134 D5 Fowler IN U.S.A.
134 E4 Fowler MI U.S.A.
73 B3 Fowler Ice Rise ice feature Antarctica
68 D5 Fowlers Bay Australia
81 L3 Fowman Iran
131 K3 Fox r. Canada
134 C4 Fox r. U.S.A.
130 F4 Fox Creek Canada
104 C3 Foxdale U.K.
129 J3 Foxe Basin g. Canada
129 J3 Foxe Channel Canada
129 K3 Foxe Peninsula Canada
72 C5 Fox Glacier N.Z.
130 G3 Fox Lake Canada
134 C4 Fox Lake U.S.A.
72 E4 Foxton N.Z.
106 D3 Foyers U.K.
107 D3 Foyle r. Rep. of Ireland/U.K.
107 D2 Foyle, Lough b. Rep. of Ireland/U.K.
107 B5 Foynes Rep. of Ireland
123 B5 Foz do Cunene Angola
156 F3 Foz do Iguaçu Brazil
111 G2 Fraga Spain
158 C3 Franca Brazil
69 G3 Français, Récif des rf New Caledonia
110 F3 France country Europe
70 D6 Frances Australia
130 D2 Frances r. Canada
130 D2 Frances Lake Canada
130 D2 Frances Lake l. Canada
134 D5 Francesville U.S.A.
122 B4 Franceville Gabon
147 H2 Francis, Lake U.S.A.
142 D3 Francis Case, Lake U.S.A.
150 D2 Francisco I. Madero Mex.
150 C2 Francisco I. Madero Mex.
158 D2 Francisco Sá Brazil
123 C6 Francistown Botswana
130 D4 François Lake Canada
138 E3 Francs Peak U.S.A.
108 D1 Franeker Neth.
109 L4 Frankenberg Germany
109 G3 Frankenberg (Eder) Germany
135 F4 Frankenmuth U.S.A.
109 G5 Frankenthal (Pfalz) Germany
109 J4 Frankenwald mts Germany
125 H3 Frankfort S. Africa
134 D5 Frankfort IN U.S.A.
144 C4 Frankfort KY U.S.A.
134 D3 Frankfort MI U.S.A.
109 G4 Frankfurt am Main Germany
112 G4 Frankfurt an der Oder Germany
141 E1 Frankin Lake U.S.A.
109 J5 Fränkische Alb hills Germany
109 J5 Fränkische Schweiz reg. Germany
138 E3 Franklin ID U.S.A.
144 C4 Franklin IN U.S.A.
143 F6 Franklin LA U.S.A.
147 H3 Franklin MA U.S.A.
145 D5 Franklin NC U.S.A.
147 H3 Franklin NH U.S.A.
147 F4 Franklin NJ U.S.A.
146 D4 Franklin PA U.S.A.
145 C5 Franklin TN U.S.A.
146 E6 Franklin VA U.S.A.
146 D5 Franklin WV U.S.A.
128 F3 Franklin Bay Canada
138 C1 Franklin D. Roosevelt Lake resr U.S.A.
71 F9 Franklin-Gordon National Park Australia
70 B4 Franklin Harbor b. Australia
130 E2 Franklin Mountains Canada
72 A6 Franklin Mountains N.Z.
71 G8 Franklin Sound sea chan. Australia
129 I2 Franklin Strait Canada
70 F7 Frankston Australia
103 L3 Frånsta Sweden
76 G2 Frantsa-Iosifa, Zemlya is Rus. Fed.
134 E1 Franz Canada
72 C5 Franz Josef Glacier N.Z.
114 C5 Frasca, Capo della c. Sardinia Italy
114 E4 Frascati Italy
130 E4 Fraser r. B.C. Canada
133 H2 Fraser r. Nfld Canada
124 D5 Fraserburg S. Africa
106 F3 Fraserburgh U.K.
132 D4 Fraserdale Canada
69 F4 Fraser Island Australia
130 E4 Fraser Lake Canada
130 E4 Fraser Plateau Canada
72 F3 Frasertown N.Z.
134 E2 Frater Canada
112 D7 Frauenfeld Switz.
159 E2 Fray Bentos Uruguay
108 E4 Frechen Germany
104 E4 Freckleton U.K.
134 E3 Frederic MI U.S.A.
134 A3 Frederic WI U.S.A.
103 J5 Fredericia Denmark
146 E5 Frederick MD U.S.A.
143 D5 Frederick OK U.S.A.
143 D6 Fredericksburg TX U.S.A.
146 E5 Fredericksburg VA U.S.A.
130 C3 Frederick Sound sea chan. U.S.A.
143 F4 Fredericktown U.S.A.
133 G4 Fredericton Canada
Frederikshåb Greenland see Paamiut
103 J4 Frederikshavn Denmark
103 K5 Frederiksværk Denmark
141 F3 Fredonia AZ U.S.A.
146 D3 Fredonia NY U.S.A.
102 L2 Fredrika Sweden
103 J4 Fredrikstad Norway
147 F4 Freehold U.S.A.
147 F4 Freeland U.S.A.
70 C3 Freeling Heights h. Australia
140 C2 Freel Peak U.S.A.
142 D3 Freeman U.S.A.
134 D5 Freeman, Lake U.S.A.
142 F3 Freeport IL U.S.A.
147 H3 Freeport ME U.S.A.
147 G4 Freeport NY U.S.A.
143 E6 Freeport TX U.S.A.
145 E7 Freeport City Bahamas
143 D7 Freer U.S.A.
125 G4 Free State prov. S. Africa
120 A4 Freetown Sierra Leone
111 C3 Fregenal de la Sierra Spain
110 C2 Fréhel, Cap c. France
112 C6 Freiburg im Breisgau Germany
108 F5 Freisen Germany
112 E6 Freising Germany
112 F6 Freistadt Austria
110 H5 Fréjus France
68 B5 Fremantle Australia
134 E4 Fremont MI U.S.A.
142 D3 Fremont NE U.S.A.
146 B4 Fremont OH U.S.A.
141 G2 Fremont r. U.S.A.
146 B6 Frenchburg U.S.A.
146 C4 French Creek r. U.S.A.
155 H3 French Guiana terr. S. America
70 F7 French Island Australia
131 H5 Frenchman r. Canada/U.S.A.
140 C2 Frenchman U.S.A.
140 C3 Frenchman L. U.S.A.
140 B2 Frenchman Lake U.S.A.
71 F9 Frenchman's Cap mt. Australia
107 C4 Frenchpark Rep. of Ireland
72 D4 French Pass N.Z.
67 I5 French Polynesia terr. Pacific Ocean
65 French Southern and Antarctic Lands terr. Indian Ocean
147 I1 Frenchville U.S.A.
108 F2 Frenen Germany
107 D5 Freshford Rep. of Ireland
141 E4 Fresnal Canyon U.S.A.
150 D3 Fresnillo Mex.
140 C3 Fresno U.S.A.
140 C3 Fresno r. U.S.A.
111 H3 Freu, Cap des c. Spain
109 F4 Freudenberg Germany
112 D6 Freudenstadt Germany
108 A4 Frévent France
71 H9 Freycinet National Park Australia
71 H9 Freycinet Peninsula Australia
109 K1 Freyenstein Germany
110 H2 Freyming-Merlebach France
159 D1 Freyre Arg.
120 A3 Fria Guinea
140 C3 Friant U.S.A.
156 C3 Frias Arg.
112 C7 Fribourg Switz.
109 F1 Friedeburg Germany
109 L1 Friedland Germany
112 D7 Friedrichshafen Germany
147 I3 Friendship U.S.A.
109 K2 Friesack Germany
108 D1 Friese Wad tidal flat Neth.
109 F1 Friesoythe Germany
105 I6 Frinton-on-Sea U.K.
143 D6 Frio r. U.S.A.
106 B4 Frisa, Loch l. U.K.
141 F2 Frisco Mountain U.S.A.
109 H3 Fritzlar Germany
129 L3 Frobisher Bay Canada
131 H3 Frobisher Lake Canada
102 J3 Frohavet b. Norway
109 K3 Frohburg Germany
108 A5 Froissy France
117 G5 Frolovo Rus. Fed.
116 J2 Frolovskaya Rus. Fed.
70 C2 Frome watercourse Australia
105 E6 Frome U.K.
70 C3 Frome, Lake salt flat Australia
70 C3 Frome Downs Australia
109 F3 Fröndenberg Germany
151 F4 Frontera Mex.
151 F4 Frontera, Punta pt Mex.
146 D5 Front Royal U.S.A.
114 E4 Frosinone Italy
146 D5 Frostburg U.S.A.
73 C6 Frost Glacier glacier Antarctica
102 J3 Frøya i. Norway
108 A4 Fruges France
141 H2 Fruita U.S.A.
141 G1 Fruitland U.S.A.
83 G4 Frunze Kyrg.
Frunze Kyrg. see Bishkek
112 C7 Frutigen Switz.
113 I6 Frýdek-Místek Czech Rep.
147 H2 Fryeburg U.S.A.
93 F5 Fu'an China
93 D5 Fuchuan China
93 F4 Fuchun Jiang r. China
106 A3 Fuday i. U.K.
93 F5 Fuding China
111 E2 Fuenlabrada Spain
111 D3 Fuente Obejuna Spain
96 D2 Fu'er He r. China
156 E2 Fuerte Olimpo Para.
120 A2 Fuerteventura i. Canary Is
97 B2 Fuga i. Phil.
92 E3 Fugou China
92 D2 Fugu China
81 I4 Fuhaymī Iraq
86 E4 Fujairah U.A.E.
95 F7 Fuji Japan
93 E5 Fujian prov. China
92 C4 Fu Jiang r. China
95 F7 Fuji-Hakone-Izu National Park Japan
94 B1 Fujin China
95 F7 Fujinomiya Japan
95 F7 Fuji-san vol. Japan
94 H3 Fukagawa Japan
95 D7 Fukuchiyama Japan
95 A8 Fukue Japan
95 A8 Fukue-jima i. Japan
95 E6 Fukui Japan
95 B8 Fukuoka Japan
95 G6 Fukushima Japan
95 B9 Fukuyama Japan
84 D2 Fūlād Maīalleh Iran
109 H4 Fulda Germany
109 H3 Fulda r. Germany
105 G6 Fulham U.K.
92 E3 Fuliji China
93 C4 Fuling China
131 L2 Fullerton, Cape Canada
134 B5 Fulton IL U.S.A.
144 B4 Fulton KY U.S.A.
142 E4 Fulton MO U.S.A.
147 E3 Fulton NY U.S.A.
125 J2 Fumane Moz.
108 C5 Fumay France
95 F7 Funabashi Japan
69 H2 Funafuti atoll Tuvalu
96 B3 Funan China
120 A1 Funchal Madeira
157 B2 Fundación Col.
111 C2 Fundão Port.
150 B2 Fundición Mex.
133 G5 Fundy, Bay of g. Canada
133 G4 Fundy National Park Canada
140 D3 Funeral Peak U.S.A.
Fung Wong Shan h. Hong Kong China see Lantau Peak
123 D6 Funhalouro Moz.
92 F3 Funing Jiangsu China
93 B6 Funing Yunnan China
92 D3 Funiu Shan mts China
120 C3 Funtua Nigeria
106 □ Funzie U.K.
93 F5 Fuqing China
94 H3 Furano Japan
84 E5 Fūrgun, Kūh-e mt. Iran
116 G3 Furmanov Rus. Fed.
94 D3 Furmanovo Rus. Fed.
140 D3 Furnace Creek U.S.A.
158 C3 Furnas, Represa resr Brazil
68 E6 Furneaux Group is Australia
109 F2 Fürstenau Germany
109 L1 Fürstenberg Germany
112 G4 Fürstenwalde Germany
109 I5 Fürth Germany
109 K5 Furth im Wald Germany
94 G3 Furubira Japan
94 G5 Furukawa Japan
129 J3 Fury and Hecla Strait Canada
157 B3 Fusagasugá Col.
93 C7 Fushan Hainan China
96 A5 Fushan Shandong China
96 B3 Fushun Liaoning China
93 B4 Fushun Sichuan China
96 D2 Fusong China
93 C6 Fusui China
95 B8 Futago-san vol. Japan
69 H3 Futuna i. Vanuatu
93 E5 Futun Xi r. China
92 C3 Fuxian China
93 B5 Fuxian Hu l. China
96 A2 Fuxin Liaoning China
96 A2 Fuxin Liaoning China
94 F5 Fuya Japan
92 E3 Fuyang Anhui China
93 F4 Fuyang Zhejiang China
92 E2 Fuyang He r. China
90 E2 Fuyu Heilong. China
96 D1 Fuyu Jilin China
93 B5 Fuyuan China
93 F5 Fuzhou China
93 E5 Fuzhou China
96 A4 Fuzhou Wan b. China
81 K2 Füzuli Azer.
103 J5 Fyn i. Denmark
106 C5 Fyne, Loch inlet U.K.
F.Y.R.O.M. (Former Yugoslav Republic of Macedonia) country Europe see Macedonia

G

114 C6 Gaâfour Tunisia
122 E3 Gaalkacyo Somalia
82 E5 Gabakly Turkm.
125 F2 Gabane Botswana
140 D2 Gabbs U.S.A.
140 C2 Gabbs Valley Range mts U.S.A.
123 B5 Gabela Angola
120 D1 Gabès Tunisia
121 D1 Gabès, Golfe de g. Tunisia
71 H6 Gabo Island Australia
122 B4 Gabon country Africa
123 C6 Gaborone Botswana
85 E5 Gābrīk Iran
85 E5 Gābrīk watercourse Iran
115 K3 Gabrovo Bulg.
120 A3 Gabú Guinea-Bissau
84 C2 Gach Sār Iran
84 C4 Gachsārān Iran
87 A3 Gadag India
88 E5 Gadchiroli India
102 K2 Gäddede Sweden
109 J1 Gadebusch Germany
88 B5 Gadhra India
88 B4 Gadra Pak.
145 C5 Gadsden U.S.A.
87 B2 Gadwal India
82 E5 Gadyn Turkm.
Gæi'dnuvuop'pi Norway see Geaidnovuohppi
105 D6 Gaer U.K.
115 K2 Găeşti Romania
114 E4 Gaeta Italy
114 E4 Gaeta, Golfo di g. Italy
160 E5 Gaferut i. Micronesia
145 D5 Gaffney U.S.A.
120 C1 Gafsa Tunisia
116 E4 Gagarin Rus. Fed.
83 G4 Gagarin Uzbek.
116 H4 Gagino Rus. Fed.
120 B4 Gagnoa Côte d'Ivoire
133 G3 Gagnon Canada
117 G7 Gagra Georgia
81 K4 Gahvāreh Iran
124 C3 Gaiab watercourse Namibia
89 G4 Gaibandha Bangl.
109 H6 Gaildorf Germany
110 E5 Gaillac France
89 G3 Gaindainqoinkor China
145 D6 Gainesville FL U.S.A.
145 D5 Gainesville GA U.S.A.
143 D5 Gainesville TX U.S.A.
105 G4 Gainsborough U.K.
70 A3 Gairdner, Lake salt flat Australia
106 C3 Gairloch U.K.
106 C3 Gair Loch b. U.K.
96 B3 Gaizhou China
87 C2 Gajapatinagaram India
85 G5 Gajar Pak.
124 E3 Gakarosa mt. S. Africa
88 C1 Gakuch Jammu and Kashmir
89 G3 Gala China
Galaasiya Uzbek. see Galaosiyo
122 D4 Galana r. Kenya
82 F5 Galaosiyo Uzbek.
161 N6 Galapagos Islands Pacific Ocean
161 M6 Galapagos Rise sea feature Pacific Ocean
106 F5 Galashiels U.K.
115 L3 Galata, Nos pt Bulg.
115 M2 Galați Romania
115 H4 Galatina Italy
146 C6 Galax U.S.A.
85 F3 Galaýmor Turkm.
107 C5 Galbally Rep. of Ireland
103 J3 Galdhøpiggen mt. Norway
151 D2 Galeana Mex.
84 D5 Galeh Dār Iran
134 B4 Galena U.S.A.
157 E2 Galeota Point Trin. and Tob.
159 B4 Galera, Punta pt Chile
151 E5 Galera, Punta pt Mex.
157 E2 Galera Point Trin. and Tob.
134 B5 Galesburg U.S.A.
124 F4 Galeshewe S. Africa
134 B3 Galesville U.S.A.
146 E4 Galeton U.S.A.
117 G7 Gali Georgia
116 G3 Galich Rus. Fed.
116 G2 Galichskaya Vozvyshennost' hills Rus. Fed.
111 C1 Galicia aut. comm. Spain
80 E5 Galilee, Sea of l. Israel
146 B4 Galion U.S.A.
141 G5 Galiuro Mountains U.S.A.
85 F2 Galkynyş Turkm.
121 F3 Gallabat Sudan
83 F4 G'allaorol Uzbek.
145 C4 Gallatin U.S.A.
138 E2 Gallatin r. U.S.A.
87 C5 Galle Sri Lanka
161 L6 Gallego Rise sea feature Pacific Ocean
156 B8 Gallegos r. Arg.
157 C1 Gallinas, Punta pt Col.
115 L4 Gallipoli Turkey
146 B5 Gallipolis U.S.A.
102 M2 Gällivare Sweden
102 K3 Gällö Sweden
147 E3 Gallo Island U.S.A.
141 H4 Gallo Mountains U.S.A.
141 H4 Gallup U.S.A.
Gallyaaral Uzbek. see G'allaorol
106 B4 Galmisdale U.K.
71 H5 Galong Australia
87 C4 Galoya Sri Lanka
87 C5 Gal Oya r. Sri Lanka
106 D5 Galston U.K.
140 B2 Galt U.S.A.
120 A2 Galtat Zemmour W. Sahara
107 C5 Galtee Mountains Rep. of Ireland
107 C5 Galtymore h. Rep. of Ireland
85 E3 Galūgāh-e Āsīyeh Iran
134 B5 Galva U.S.A.
143 E6 Galveston U.S.A.
143 E6 Galveston Bay U.S.A.
159 E2 Galvez Arg.
89 E3 Galwa Nepal
107 B4 Galway Rep. of Ireland
107 B4 Galway Bay Rep. of Ireland
Gâm r. Vietnam see Gâm, Sông
93 B6 Gâm, Sông r. Vietnam
105 I8 Gamaches France
125 I5 Gamalakhe S. Africa
157 B2 Gamarra Col.
Gamba China see Gongbalou
122 D3 Gambēla Eth.
122 D3 Gambēla National Park Eth.
128 A3 Gambell U.S.A.
88 D4 Gambhir r. India
120 A3 Gambia r. Gambia
67 J6 Gambier, Îles is Fr. Polynesia
70 B5 Gambier Islands Australia
133 J4 Gambo Canada
122 B4 Gamboma Congo
141 H4 Gamerco U.S.A.
103 L4 Gamleby Sweden
102 M2 Gammelstaden Sweden
70 C3 Gammon Ranges National Park Australia
124 C4 Gamoep S. Africa
94 B3 Gamova, Mys pt Rus. Fed.
87 C5 Gampola Sri Lanka
85 F4 Gamshadzai Kūh mts Iran
92 A3 Gana China
141 H4 Ganado U.S.A.
135 I3 Gananoque Canada
84 C4 Ganāveh Iran
81 K1 Gäncä Azer.
93 C7 Gancheng China
99 E3 Gandadiwata, Bukit mt. Indon.
89 G3 Gandaingoin China
122 C4 Gandajika Dem. Rep. Congo
89 E4 Gandak Barrage dam Nepal
Gandak Dam Nepal see Gandak Barrage
88 B3 Gandari Mountain Pak.
88 A3 Gandava Pak.
133 J4 Gander Canada
109 G1 Ganderkesee Germany
111 G2 Gandesa Spain
88 C5 Gandevi India
88 B5 Gandhidham India
88 C5 Gandhinagar India
88 C4 Gandhi Sagar resr India
88 C4 Gandhi Sagar Dam India
111 F3 Gandía Spain
Gand-i-Zureh plain Afgh. see Zereh, Gowd-e
158 E1 Gandu Brazil
88 E4 Ganga r. Bangl./India alt. Padma, conv. Ganges
87 C5 Ganga r. Sri Lanka
159 C4 Gangán Arg.
88 C3 Ganganagar India
88 D4 Gangapur India
89 H5 Gangaw Myanmar
87 B3 Gangawati India
92 A2 Gangca China
89 E3 Gangdisê Shan mts China
79 G4 Ganges r. Bangl./India alt. Ganga, alt. Padma
110 F5 Ganges France
89 G5 Ganges, Mouths of the Bangl./India
162 J3 Ganges Cone sea feature Indian Ocean
88 D3 Gangoh India
88 D3 Gangotri Group mts India
89 G4 Gangtok India
92 B3 Gangu China
87 D2 Ganjam India
84 C4 Ganjgūn Iran
93 E4 Gan Jiang r. China
96 B2 Ganjig China
93 B4 Ganluo China
71 G5 Ganmain Australia
110 F3 Gannat France
138 E3 Gannett Peak U.S.A.
88 C5 Ganora India
92 C2 Ganquan China
124 C7 Gansbaai S. Africa
92 B3 Gansu prov. China
92 B2 Gantang China
70 B6 Gantheaume, Cape Australia
117 G7 Gant'iadi Georgia
93 E5 Ganxian China
124 F3 Ganyesa S. Africa
92 F3 Ganyu China
82 B3 Ganyushkino Kazakh.
93 E5 Ganzhou China
121 F4 Ganzi Sudan
120 B3 Gao Mali
93 E4 Gao'an China
92 E2 Gaocheng China
92 F4 Gaochun China
92 B2 Gaolan China
92 F2 Gaomi China
93 D5 Gaomutang China
92 D3 Gaoping China

182 Granada

142 C4 Granada U.S.A.
107 D4 Granard Rep. of Ireland
159 C3 Gran Bajo Salitroso salt flat Arg.
132 F4 Granby Canada
120 A2 Gran Canaria i. Canary Is
156 D3 Gran Chaco reg. Arg./Para.
134 D4 Grand MI U.S.A.
142 E3 Grand r. MO U.S.A.
145 E7 Grand Bahama i. Bahamas
133 I4 Grand Bank Canada
163 F3 Grand Banks of Newfoundland sea feature N. Atlantic Ocean
120 B4 Grand-Bassam Côte d'Ivoire
Grand Bay Canada see Grand Bay-Westfield
133 G4 Grand Bay-Westfield Canada
135 G4 Grand Bend Canada
Grand Canal canal China see Da Yunhe
107 D4 Grand Canal Rep. of Ireland
141 F3 Grand Canyon U.S.A.
141 F3 Grand Canyon gorge U.S.A.
141 F3 Grand Canyon National Park U.S.A.
149 H5 Grand Cayman i. Cayman Is
131 G4 Grand Centre Canada
138 C2 Grand Coulee U.S.A.
159 C3 Grande r. Arg.
154 F7 Grande r. Bol.
155 I6 Grande r. Bahia Brazil
158 B2 Grande r. São Paulo Brazil
159 F3 Grande, Arroyo r. Arg.
156 C8 Grande, Bahía b. Arg.
158 D3 Grande, Ilha i. Brazil
157 E4 Grande, Serra mt. Brazil
130 F4 Grande Cache Canada
Grande Comore i. Comoros see Njazidja
130 F3 Grande Prairie Canada
121 D3 Grand Erg de Bilma des. Niger
120 B1 Grand Erg Occidental des. Alg.
120 C2 Grand Erg Oriental des. Alg.
133 H4 Grande-Rivière Canada
138 C2 Grande Ronde r. U.S.A.
156 C4 Grandes, Salinas salt flat Arg.
133 G4 Grande-Vallée Canada
133 G4 Grand Falls N.B. Canada
133 I4 Grand Falls Nfld Canada
130 F5 Grand Forks Canada
142 D2 Grand Forks U.S.A.
147 F3 Grand Gorge U.S.A.
147 J2 Grand Harbour Canada
134 D4 Grand Haven U.S.A.
130 F2 Grandin, Lac l. Canada
142 D3 Grand Island NE U.S.A.
134 D2 Grand Island i. MI U.S.A.
143 F6 Grand Isle LA U.S.A.
147 I1 Grand Isle ME U.S.A.
141 H2 Grand Junction U.S.A.
120 B4 Grand-Lahou Côte d'Ivoire
133 H3 Grand Lake Nfld Canada
133 I4 Grand Lake Nfld Canada
143 E6 Grand Lake LA U.S.A.
147 J2 Grand Lake ME U.S.A.
135 F3 Grand Lake MI U.S.A.
147 I1 Grand Lake Matagamon U.S.A.
146 A4 Grand Lake St Marys U.S.A.
147 I1 Grand Lake Seboeis U.S.A.
147 J2 Grand Lake Stream U.S.A.
134 E4 Grand Ledge U.S.A.
133 G5 Grand Manan Island Canada
134 E2 Grand Marais MI U.S.A.
134 B2 Grand Marais MN U.S.A.
133 F4 Grand-Mère Canada
111 B3 Grândola Port.
69 G3 Grand Passage New Caledonia
134 C2 Grand Portage U.S.A.
131 J4 Grand Rapids Canada
134 E4 Grand Rapids MI U.S.A.
142 E2 Grand Rapids MN U.S.A.
138 E3 Grand Teton mt. U.S.A.
138 E3 Grand Teton National Park U.S.A.
134 E3 Grand Traverse Bay U.S.A.
149 J4 Grand Turk Turks and Caicos Is
138 C2 Grandview U.S.A.
141 F3 Grand Wash watercourse U.S.A.
141 E4 Grand Wash Cliffs mts U.S.A.
159 B2 Graneros Chile
107 D6 Grange Rep. of Ireland
138 E3 Granger U.S.A.
103 K3 Grängesberg Sweden
138 C2 Grangeville U.S.A.
130 D3 Granisle Canada
142 E2 Granite Falls U.S.A.
133 I4 Granite Lake Canada
141 E4 Granite Mountains U.S.A.
138 E2 Granite Peak MT U.S.A.
141 F1 Granite Peak UT U.S.A.
83 H4 Granitogorsk Kazakh.
114 E6 Granitola, Capo c. Sicily Italy
156 C6 Gran Laguna Salada l. Arg.
103 K4 Gränna Sweden
114 B2 Gran Paradiso mt. Italy
112 E7 Gran Pilastro mt. Austria/Italy
109 K3 Granschütz Germany
109 L1 Gransee Germany
140 C2 Grant, Mount NV U.S.A.
140 D2 Grant, Mount NV U.S.A.
105 G5 Grantham U.K.
73 A4 Grant Island i. Antarctica
106 E3 Grantown-on-Spey U.K.
141 E2 Grant Range mts U.S.A.
139 F5 Grants U.S.A.
138 B3 Grants Pass U.S.A.
110 D2 Granville France
134 C5 Granville IL U.S.A.
147 G3 Granville NY U.S.A.
131 I3 Granville Lake Canada
158 D2 Grão Mogol Brazil
140 C4 Grapevine U.S.A.
140 D3 Grapevine Mountains U.S.A.
147 G3 Graphite U.S.A.
131 G2 Gras, Lac de l. Canada
125 I2 Graskop S. Africa
147 F2 Grass r. U.S.A.
110 H5 Grasse France
104 F3 Grassington U.K.
131 H5 Grasslands National Park Canada
138 E2 Grassrange U.S.A.
131 I4 Grass River Provincial Park Canada
140 B2 Grass Valley U.S.A.
71 F8 Grassy Australia
145 E7 Grassy Creek r. Bahamas
103 K4 Grästorp Sweden
134 B4 Gratiot U.S.A.
111 G1 Graus Spain
131 I2 Gravel Hill Lake Canada
108 A4 Gravelines France
125 I1 Gravelotte S. Africa
135 H3 Gravenhurst Canada
71 I2 Gravesend Australia
105 H6 Gravesend U.K.
114 G4 Gravina in Puglia Italy
134 E3 Grawn U.S.A.
110 G3 Gray France
147 H3 Gray U.S.A.
134 E3 Grayling U.S.A.
105 H6 Grays U.K.
138 A2 Grays Harbor inlet U.S.A.
138 E3 Grays Lake U.S.A.
146 B5 Grayson U.S.A.
133 H1 Gray Strait Canada
144 B4 Grayville U.S.A.
112 G7 Graz Austria
145 E7 Great Abaco i. Bahamas
68 C5 Great Australian Bight g. Australia
105 H6 Great Baddow U.K.
149 I3 Great Bahama Bank sea feature Bahamas
72 E2 Great Barrier Island N.Z.
68 E3 Great Barrier Reef Australia
147 G3 Great Barrington U.S.A.
139 C4 Great Basin U.S.A.
141 E2 Great Basin National Park U.S.A.
147 F5 Great Bay U.S.A.
130 E1 Great Bear r. Canada
130 E1 Great Bear Lake Canada
103 J5 Great Belt sea chan. Denmark
142 D4 Great Bend U.S.A.
106 B2 Great Bernera i. U.K.
107 A5 Great Blasket Island Rep. of Ireland
104 D3 Great Clifton U.K.
106 D5 Great Cumbrae i. U.K.
68 E5 Great Dividing Range mts Australia
135 F3 Great Duck Island Canada
147 F5 Great Egg Harbor Inlet U.S.A.
149 H4 Greater Antilles is Caribbean Sea
125 J3 Greater St Lucia Wetland Park nature res. S. Africa
84 D5 Greater Tunb i. Iran
149 I4 Great Exuma i. Bahamas
138 E2 Great Falls U.S.A.
125 G6 Great Fish r. S. Africa
125 G6 Great Fish Point S. Africa
89 F4 Great Gandak r. India
145 E7 Great Guana Cay i. Bahamas
145 E7 Great Harbour Cay i. Bahamas
149 J4 Great Inagua i. Bahamas
124 D5 Great Karoo plat. S. Africa
125 H6 Great Kei r. S. Africa
71 G8 Great Lake Australia
125 I1 Great Limpopo Transfrontier Park nat. park Africa
105 E5 Great Malvern U.K.
163 H4 Great Meteor Tablemount sea feature N. Atlantic Ocean
146 A5 Great Miami r. U.S.A.
124 B3 Great Namaqualand reg. Namibia
Great Oasis, The oasis Egypt see Khārijah, Wāḥāt al
105 D4 Great Ormes Head U.K.
105 H5 Great Ouse r. U.K.
71 H9 Great Oyster Bay Australia
147 G4 Great Peconic Bay U.S.A.
147 H4 Great Point U.S.A.
105 D5 Great Rhos h. U.K.
122 D3 Great Rift Valley Africa
122 D3 Great Rift Valley Eth.
122 D4 Great Ruaha r. Tanz.
147 F3 Great Sacandaga Lake U.S.A.
114 B2 Great St Bernard Pass Italy/Switz.
145 E7 Great Sale Cay i. Bahamas
138 D3 Great Salt Lake U.S.A.
138 D3 Great Salt Lake Desert U.S.A.
121 E2 Great Sand Sea des. Egypt/Libya
68 C4 Great Sandy Desert Australia
69 H3 Great Sea Reef Fiji
128 G3 Great Slave Lake Canada
145 D5 Great Smoky Mountains U.S.A.
145 D5 Great Smoky Mountains National Park U.S.A.
130 E3 Great Snow Mountain Canada
147 G4 Great South Bay U.S.A.
105 H7 Greatstone-on-Sea U.K.
105 I6 Great Stour r. U.K.
105 C7 Great Torrington U.K.
68 C4 Great Victoria Desert Australia
73 E2 Great Wall research stn Antarctica
92 F1 Great Wall tourist site China
105 H6 Great Waltham U.K.
147 J2 Great Wass Island U.S.A.
71 G8 Great Western Tiers mts Australia
104 F3 Great Whernside h. U.K.
105 I5 Great Yarmouth U.K.
114 E4 Greco, Monte mt. Italy
111 D2 Gredos, Sierra de mts Spain
115 I5 Greece country Europe
138 F3 Greeley U.S.A.
129 J1 Greely Fiord inlet Canada
76 H1 Greem-Bell, Ostrov i. Rus. Fed.
144 C4 Green r. KY U.S.A.
141 H2 Green r. UT/WY U.S.A.
135 H3 Greenbank Canada
134 C3 Green Bay U.S.A.
134 D3 Green Bay b. U.S.A.
71 I6 Green Cape Australia
107 E3 Greencastle U.K.
144 C4 Greencastle U.S.A.
145 E7 Green Cay i. Bahamas
145 D6 Green Cove Springs U.S.A.
134 A4 Greene IA U.S.A.
147 F3 Greene NY U.S.A.
145 D4 Greeneville U.S.A.
140 B3 Greenfield CA U.S.A.
134 E6 Greenfield IN U.S.A.
147 G3 Greenfield MA U.S.A.
146 B5 Greenfield OH U.S.A.
134 C4 Greenfield WI U.S.A.
97 A4 Green Island Bay Phil.
131 H4 Green Lake Canada
134 C4 Green Lake l. U.S.A.
129 N2 Greenland terr. N. America
164 X2 Greenland Basin sea feature Arctic Ocean
164 X1 Greenland Sea Greenland/Svalbard
106 F5 Greenlaw U.K.
70 A5 Greenly Island Australia
147 G2 Green Mountains U.S.A.
106 D5 Greenock U.K.
107 E3 Greenore Rep. of Ireland
147 G4 Greenport U.S.A.
139 E4 Green River UT U.S.A.
138 E3 Green River WY U.S.A.
145 E4 Greensboro U.S.A.
144 C4 Greensburg IN U.S.A.
143 D4 Greensburg KS U.S.A.
146 D4 Greensburg PA U.S.A.
106 C3 Greenstone Point U.K.
137 K5 Green Swamp U.S.A.
146 B5 Greenup U.S.A.
147 F2 Green Valley Canada
141 G6 Green Valley U.S.A.
134 C5 Greenview U.S.A.
120 B4 Greenville Liberia
145 C6 Greenville AL U.S.A.
140 B1 Greenville CA U.S.A.
145 D6 Greenville FL U.S.A.
147 I2 Greenville ME U.S.A.
134 E4 Greenville MI U.S.A.
143 F5 Greenville MS U.S.A.
145 E5 Greenville NC U.S.A.
147 H3 Greenville NH U.S.A.
146 A4 Greenville OH U.S.A.
146 C4 Greenville PA U.S.A.
145 D5 Greenville SC U.S.A.
143 D5 Greenville TX U.S.A.
131 I4 Greenwater Provincial Park Canada
71 I5 Greenwell Point Australia
105 H6 Greenwich U.K.
147 G4 Greenwich CT U.S.A.
147 G3 Greenwich NY U.S.A.
141 G2 Greenwich UT U.S.A.
143 F5 Greenwood MS U.S.A.
145 D5 Greenwood SC U.S.A.
143 E5 Greers Ferry Lake U.S.A.
142 D3 Gregory U.S.A.
68 C4 Gregory, Lake salt flat Australia
70 C2 Gregory, Lake salt flat Australia
68 E3 Gregory Range hills Australia
112 F3 Greifswald Germany
109 K4 Greiz Germany
80 E4 Greko, Cape Cyprus
103 J4 Grenå Denmark
157 E1 Grenada country Caribbean Sea
143 F5 Grenada U.S.A.
110 E5 Grenade France
103 J4 Grenen spit Denmark
71 H4 Grenfell Australia
131 I4 Grenfell Canada
110 G4 Grenoble France
157 E1 Grenville Grenada
68 E3 Grenville, Cape Australia
138 B2 Gresham U.S.A.
104 F3 Greta r. U.K.
106 E6 Gretna U.K.
143 F6 Gretna U.S.A.
109 I3 Greußen Germany
108 B3 Grevelingen sea chan. Neth.
108 F2 Greven Germany
115 I4 Grevena Greece
108 D3 Grevenbicht Neth.
108 E3 Grevenbroich Germany
108 E5 Grevenmacher Lux.
112 E4 Grevesmühlen Germany
72 C5 Grey r. N.Z.
138 E2 Greybull U.S.A.
130 B2 Grey Hunter Peak Canada
133 I3 Grey Islands Canada
72 C5 Greymouth N.Z.
70 E2 Grey Range hills Australia
125 I4 Greytown S. Africa
108 C4 Grez-Doiceau Belgium
117 G5 Gribanovskiy Rus. Fed.
140 B2 Gridley CA U.S.A.
134 C5 Gridley IL U.S.A.
145 C5 Griffin U.S.A.
71 G5 Griffith Australia
135 I3 Griffith Canada
128 F2 Griffiths Point Canada
71 F8 Grim, Cape Australia
109 K3 Grimma Germany
112 F3 Grimmen Germany
135 H4 Grimsby Canada
104 G4 Grimsby U.K.
102 C1 Grímsey i. Iceland
130 F3 Grimshaw Canada
102 C2 Grímsstaðir Iceland
103 J4 Grimstad Norway
102 B3 Grindavík Iceland
103 J5 Grindsted Denmark
115 M2 Grindul Chituc spit Romania
142 E3 Grinnell U.S.A.
125 H5 Griqualand East reg. S. Africa
124 E4 Griqualand West reg. S. Africa
124 E4 Griquatown S. Africa
129 J2 Grise Fiord Canada
99 B3 Grisik Indon.
105 I7 Gris Nez, Cap c. France
106 F2 Gritley U.K.
114 G2 Grmeč mts Bos.-Herz.
108 C3 Grobbendonk Belgium
125 H2 Groblersdal S. Africa
124 E4 Groblershoop S. Africa
Grodekovo Rus. Fed. see Pogranichnyy
Grodno Belarus see Hrodna
124 B5 Groen watercourse N. Cape S. Africa
124 E5 Groen watercourse N. Cape S. Africa
110 C3 Groix, Île de i. France
114 D6 Grombalia Tunisia
108 F2 Gronau (Westfalen) Germany
102 K2 Grong Norway
108 E1 Groningen Neth.
108 E1 Groninger Wad tidal flat Neth.
141 E3 Groom Lake U.S.A.
124 D3 Groot-Aar Pan salt pan S. Africa
124 C6 Groot Berg r. S. Africa
124 E7 Groot Brakrivier S. Africa
125 H3 Grootdraaidam dam S. Africa
124 D4 Grootdrink S. Africa
68 D3 Groote Eylandt i. Australia
123 B5 Grootfontein Namibia
124 C3 Groot Karas Berg plat. Namibia
125 I1 Groot Letaba r. S. Africa
125 G2 Groot Marico S. Africa
124 D6 Groot Swartberge mts S. Africa
124 D5 Grootvloer salt pan S. Africa
125 G6 Groot Winterberg mt. S. Africa
134 E3 Gros Cap U.S.A.
133 I4 Gros Morne National Park Canada
109 G2 Große Aue r. Germany
109 I3 Großengottern Germany
109 G2 Großenkneten Germany
109 H4 Großenlüder Germany
109 I4 Großer Beerberg h. Germany
109 I4 Großer Gleichberg h. Germany
112 G7 Grosser Speikkogel mt. Austria
114 D3 Grosseto Italy
109 G5 Groß-Gerau Germany
114 E1 Großglockner mt. Austria
109 I2 Groß Oesingen Germany
109 J3 Großrudestedt Germany
109 L2 Groß Schönebeck Germany
124 C1 Gross Ums Namibia
138 E3 Gros Ventre Range mts U.S.A.
133 I3 Groswater Bay Canada
147 E3 Groton U.S.A.
146 D5 Grottoes U.S.A.
108 D1 Grou Neth.
130 F3 Grouard Canada
132 D4 Groundhog r. Canada
Grouw Neth. see Grou
146 C4 Grove City U.S.A.
145 C6 Grove Hill U.S.A.
140 B3 Groveland U.S.A.
73 D5 Grove Mountains mts Antarctica
140 B4 Grover Beach U.S.A.
147 H2 Groveton U.S.A.
141 F5 Growler U.S.A.
141 F5 Growler Mountains U.S.A.
117 H7 Groznyy Rus. Fed.
113 I4 Grudziądz Poland
106 C3 Gruinard Bay U.K.
123 B6 Grünau Namibia
102 B2 Grundarfjörður Iceland
146 B6 Grundy U.S.A.
109 G5 Grünstadt Germany
117 F4 Gryazi Rus. Fed.
116 G3 Gryazovets Rus. Fed.
112 G4 Gryfice Poland
112 G4 Gryfino Poland
112 G5 Gryfów Śląski Poland
102 L1 Gryllefjord Norway
156 □ Grytviken Atlantic Ocean
87 D1 Gua India
149 I4 Guacanayabo, Golfo de b. Cuba
157 D2 Guacara Venez.
157 C3 Guacharía r. Col.
111 D4 Guadajoz r. Spain
150 D3 Guadalajara Mex.
111 E2 Guadalajara Spain
111 F2 Guadalaviar r. Spain
69 G2 Guadalcanal i. Solomon Is
111 C4 Guadalete r. Spain
111 F2 Guadalope r. Spain
111 D4 Guadalquivir r. Spain
151 D2 Guadalupe Nuevo León Mex.
150 D3 Guadalupe Zacatecas Mex.
136 C6 Guadalupe i. Mex.
140 B4 Guadalupe U.S.A.
143 D6 Guadalupe r. U.S.A.
111 D3 Guadalupe, Sierra de mts Spain
150 C2 Guadalupe Aguilera Mex.
143 B6 Guadalupe Mountains National Park U.S.A.
143 B6 Guadalupe Peak U.S.A.
150 C2 Guadalupe Victoria Mex.
150 C2 Guadalupe y Calvo Mex.
111 D2 Guadarrama, Sierra de mts Spain
159 C2 Guadel, Sierra de mts Arg.
149 L5 Guadeloupe terr. Caribbean Sea
111 C4 Guadiana r. Port./Spain
111 E4 Guadix Spain
156 B6 Guafo, Isla i. Chile
150 H5 Guaimaca Hond.
157 D4 Guainía r. Col./Venez.
157 E3 Guaiquinima, Cerro mt. Venez.
158 A4 Guaíra Brazil
156 B6 Guaitecas, Islas is Chile
92 B1 Guaizihu China
150 D2 Guaje, Llano de plain Mex.
154 C4 Gualaceo Ecuador
140 A2 Gualala U.S.A.
159 E2 Gualeguay Arg.
159 E2 Gualeguay r. Arg.
159 E2 Gualeguaychu Arg.
159 D4 Gualicho, Salina salt flat Arg.
159 B4 Gualjaina Arg.
91 G5 Guam terr. Pacific Ocean
159 D3 Guamini Arg.
150 B2 Guamúchil Mex.
157 A4 Guamués r. Col.
98 B4 Gua Musang Malaysia
150 H6 Guanacaste, Parque Nacional nat. park Costa Rica
150 C2 Guanacevi Mex.
159 D3 Guanaco, Cerro h. Arg.
150 H4 Guanaja Hond.
150 D3 Guanajuato Mex.
150 D3 Guanajuato state Mex.
158 D1 Guanambi Brazil
157 D4 Guaname r. Venez.
157 C2 Guanare Venez.
157 C2 Guanare Viejo r. Venez.
157 C2 Guanarito Venez.
157 C2 Guanarito r. Venez.
157 D3 Guanay, Sierra mts Venez.
92 D2 Guandi Shan mt. China
149 H4 Guane Cuba
93 C4 Guang'an China
93 E5 Guangchang China
93 D6 Guangdong prov. China
93 F4 Guangfeng China
93 D6 Guanghai China
92 B4 Guanghan China
92 B3 Guanghe China
92 E2 Guangling China
96 B4 Guanglu Dao i. China
93 F4 Guangming Ding mt. China
93 B5 Guangnan China
93 D6 Guangning China
92 F2 Guangrao China
92 E4 Guangshan China
92 D4 Guangshui China
93 C6 Guangxi Zhuangzu Zizhiqu aut. reg. China
92 B3 Guangyuan China
93 E5 Guangze China
93 D6 Guangzhou China
158 D2 Guanhães Brazil
158 D2 Guanhães r. Brazil
157 E2 Guanipa r. Venez.
93 B5 Guanling China
92 C4 Guanmian Shan mts China
92 D3 Guanpo China
96 C3 Guanshui China
157 D2 Guanta Venez.
149 I4 Guantánamo Cuba
92 E1 Guanting Shuiku resr China
93 D5 Guanyang China
92 A4 Guanyinqiao China
92 F3 Guanyun China
157 A4 Guapí Col.
150 I6 Guápiles Costa Rica
154 F6 Guaporé r. Bol./Brazil
154 E7 Guaqui Bol.
158 D1 Guará r. Brazil
155 K5 Guarabira Brazil
158 E3 Guarapari Brazil
158 B4 Guarapuava Brazil
158 C4 Guaraqueçaba Brazil
158 D3 Guaratinguetá Brazil
158 C4 Guaratuba, Baía de b. Brazil
111 C2 Guarda Port.
158 C2 Guarda Mor Brazil
111 D1 Guardo Spain
157 D2 Guárico r. Venez.
157 C3 Guarrojo r. Col.
158 C4 Guarujá Brazil
157 D4 Guasacavi r. Col.
157 C4 Guasacavi, Cerro h. Col.
157 B2 Guasare r. Venez.
150 B2 Guasave Mex.
157 C3 Guasdualito Venez.
157 E3 Guasipati Venez.
158 B4 Guassú r. Brazil
151 G5 Guastatoya Guat.
151 G5 Guatemala country Central America
161 M5 Guatemala Basin sea feature Pacific Ocean
151 G5 Guatemala City Guat.
157 D2 Guatope, Parque Nacional nat. park Venez.
159 D3 Guatrache Arg.
157 C4 Guaviare r. Col.
158 C3 Guaxupé Brazil
157 B4 Guayabero r. Col.
157 D3 Guayapo r. Venez.
154 C4 Guayaquil Ecuador
154 B4 Guayaquil, Golfo de g. Ecuador
154 E6 Guayaramerín Bol.
150 B2 Guaymas Mex.
151 G5 Guazacapán Guat.
122 D2 Guba Eth.
82 D4 Gubadag Turkm.
87 B3 Gubbi India
114 E3 Gubbio Italy
117 F5 Gubkin Rus. Fed.
92 D3 Gucheng China
117 G7 Gudaut'a Georgia
103 J3 Gudbrandsdalen val. Norway
117 H7 Gudermes Rus. Fed.
87 C2 Gudivada India
87 B3 Gudiyattam India
96 E2 Gudong He r. China
85 G5 Gudri r. Pak.
80 D1 Güdül Turkey
87 B3 Gudur Andhra Pradesh India
87 B3 Gudur Andhra Pradesh India
103 I3 Gudvangen Norway
Guecho Spain see Algorta
120 A4 Guéckédou Guinea
135 I1 Guéguen, Lac l. Canada
157 B4 Güejar r. Col.
120 C1 Guelma Alg.
120 A2 Guelmine Morocco
135 G4 Guelph Canada
151 E3 Guémez Mex.
108 E5 Guénange France
157 D2 Güera r. Venez.
133 G2 Guérard, Lac l. Canada
110 E3 Guéret France
110 C2 Guernsey i. U.K.
138 F3 Guernsey U.S.A.
151 E2 Guerrero Mex.
151 D4 Guerrero state Mex.
150 A2 Guerrero Negro Mex.
129 L4 Guers, Lac l. Canada
84 D3 Gügerd, Kūh-e mts Iran
163 F5 Guiana Basin sea feature N. Atlantic Ocean
70 C6 Guichen Bay Australia
Guichi China see Chizhou
159 F2 Guichón Uruguay
92 A3 Guide China
121 D4 Guider Cameroon
93 C5 Guiding China
114 E4 Guidonia-Montecelio Italy
93 C6 Guigang China
120 B4 Guiglo Côte d'Ivoire
108 B5 Guignicourt France
125 J2 Guija Moz.
93 D6 Gui Jiang r. China
93 F4 Guiji Shan mts China
105 G6 Guildford U.K.
147 I2 Guilford U.S.A.
93 D5 Guilin China
132 E2 Guillaume-Delisle, Lac l. Canada
111 B2 Guimarães Port.
97 B4 Guimaras Strait Phil.
92 E3 Guimeng Ding mt. China
92 A3 Guinan China
140 A2 Guinda U.S.A.
97 C4 Guindulman Phil.
120 A3 Guinea country Africa
120 B4 Guinea, Gulf of Africa
163 I5 Guinea Basin sea feature N. Atlantic Ocean
120 A3 Guinea-Bissau country Africa
149 H4 Güines Cuba
110 C2 Guingamp France
110 B2 Guipavas France
93 D6 Guiping China
158 B2 Guiratinga Brazil
157 E2 Güiria Venez.
108 B5 Guiscard France
108 B5 Guise France
97 C4 Guiuan Phil.
93 E4 Guixi China
93 C5 Guiyang Guizhou China
93 D5 Guiyang Hunan China
93 C5 Guizhou prov. China
88 B5 Gujarat state India
88 C2 Gujar Khan Pak.
88 C2 Gujranwala Pak.
88 C2 Gujrat Pak.
117 F5 Gukovo Rus. Fed.
81 J3 Gūk Tappeh Iran
88 D2 Gulabgarh Jammu and Kashmir
Gulabie Uzbek. see Taxiatosh
92 B2 Gulang China
71 H3 Gulargambone Australia
87 B2 Gulbarga India
103 N4 Gulbene Latvia
83 H4 Gülchö Kyrg.
80 E3 Gülek Turkey
Gulf of Martaban g. Myanmar see Mottama, Gulf of
143 F6 Gulfport U.S.A.
71 H4 Gulgong Australia
90 E1 Gulian China
93 B5 Gulin China
85 G4 Gulistan Pak.
Gulistan Uzbek. see Guliston
83 G4 Guliston Uzbek.
109 J1 Gülitz Germany
134 E3 Gull Island U.S.A.
131 H4 Gull Lake Canada
102 M2 Gullträsk Sweden
80 D3 Gülnar Turkey
85 F3 Gulran Afgh.
117 G7 Gulrip'shi Georgia
80 E2 Gülşehir Turkey
83 H3 Gul'shat Kazakh.
122 D3 Gulu Uganda
88 B3 Gumal r. Pak.
123 C5 Gumare Botswana
82 C5 Gumdag Turkm.
89 F5 Gumia India
87 D1 Gumla India
108 F3 Gummersbach Germany
80 E1 Gümüşhacıköy Turkey
81 G1 Gümüşhane Turkey
88 D4 Guna India
71 F5 Gunbar Australia
71 H5 Gundagai Australia
109 H5 Gundelsheim Germany
80 D3 Gündoğmuş Turkey
80 B2 Güney Turkey
122 B4 Gungu Dem. Rep. Congo
117 H7 Gunib Rus. Fed.
131 J4 Gunisao r. Canada
71 I3 Gunnedah Australia
71 H5 Gunning Australia
139 F4 Gunnison CO U.S.A.
141 G2 Gunnison UT U.S.A.
139 E4 Gunnison r. U.S.A.
83 G5 Gunt r. Tajik.
87 B3 Guntakal India
109 I3 Güntersberge Germany
145 C5 Guntersville U.S.A.
145 C5 Guntersville Lake U.S.A.
87 C2 Guntur India
99 A2 Gunung Leuser National Park Indon.
99 A2 Gunungsitoli Indon.
98 A5 Gunungtua Indon.
87 C2 Gunupur India
112 E6 Günzburg Germany
109 I5 Gunzenhausen Germany
93 D4 Guojiaba China
92 E1 Guojiatun China
92 E3 Guoyang China
92 A2 Gurban Hudag China
92 D1 Gurban Obo China
85 F5 Gurdim Iran
80 B2 Güre Turkey
88 D3 Gurgaon India
155 J5 Gurgueia r. Brazil
88 B4 Gurha India
157 E3 Guri, Embalse de resr Venez.
158 C2 Gurinhatã Brazil
117 H7 Gurjaani Georgia
85 E4 Gur Khar Iran
82 E4 Gurlan Uzbek.
Gurlen Uzbek. see Gurlan
81 I2 Gürpınar Turkey
89 G3 Guru China
123 D5 Gurué Moz.
80 F2 Gürün Turkey
155 I4 Gurupi r. Brazil
88 C4 Guru Sikhar mt. India
116 B4 Gur'yevsk Rus. Fed.
120 C3 Gusau Nigeria
109 J2 Güsen Germany
116 B4 Gusev Rus. Fed.
96 B4 Gushan China
141 H1 Gusher U.S.A.
85 F3 Gushgy Turkm.
85 F3 Gushgy r. Turkm.
92 E3 Gushi China
77 L2 Gusikha Rus. Fed.
116 D4 Gusino Rus. Fed.
77 L4 Gusinoozersk Rus. Fed.
89 F5 Guskara India
116 G4 Gus'-Khrustal'nyy Rus. Fed.
114 C5 Guspini Sardinia Italy
130 B3 Gustavus U.S.A.
109 J3 Güsten Germany
140 B3 Gustine U.S.A.
109 K1 Güstrow Germany
89 H3 Gutang China
109 L2 Güterfelde Germany
109 G3 Gütersloh Germany
141 H5 Guthrie AZ U.S.A.
144 C4 Guthrie KY U.S.A.
143 D5 Guthrie OK U.S.A.
143 C5 Guthrie TX U.S.A.
93 E5 Gutian Fujian China
93 F5 Gutian Fujian China
108 E5 Gutland reg. Germany/Lux.
89 F3 Gutsuo China
134 B4 Guttenberg U.S.A.
123 D5 Gutu Zimbabwe
89 G4 Guwahati India
81 I3 Guwēr Iraq
82 C4 Guwlumaýak Turkm.
109 H3 Guxhagen Germany
155 G2 Guyana country S. America
92 D1 Guyang China
143 C4 Guymon U.S.A.
84 D4 Güyom Iran
71 I3 Guyra Australia
92 E1 Guyuan Hebei China
92 C3 Guyuan Ningxia China
Guzar Uzbek. see G'uzor
93 C4 Guzhang China
92 E3 Guzhen China
82 F5 G'uzor Uzbek.
113 J3 Gvardeysk Rus. Fed.
71 H3 Gwabegar Australia
85 F5 Gwadar Pak.
85 F5 Gwadar West Bay Pak.
128 E4 Gwaii Haanas National Park Reserve Canada
88 D4 Gwalior India
123 C6 Gwanda Zimbabwe
122 F2 Gwardafuy, Gees c. Somalia
85 G4 Gwash Pak.
85 F5 Gwatar Bay Pak.
107 C3 Gweebarra Bay Rep. of Ireland
107 C2 Gweedore Rep. of Ireland
123 C5 Gweru Zimbabwe
134 D2 Gwinn U.S.A.
121 D3 Gwoza Nigeria
71 H2 Gwydir r. Australia
89 H3 Gyaca China
92 B3 Gyagartang China
89 F2 Gyangnyi Caka salt l. China
89 F3 Gyangrang China
89 G3 Gyangzê China
89 G3 Gyaring Co l. China
90 B3 Gyaring Hu l. China
115 K6 Gyaros i. Greece
89 H3 Gyarubtang China
76 I2 Gydan Peninsula Rus. Fed.
Gydanskiy Poluostrov pen. Rus. Fed. see Gydan Peninsula
90 B4 Gyigang China
89 H3 Gyimda China
89 F3 Gyirong Xizang China
89 F3 Gyirong Xizang China
89 H2 Gyiza China
69 F4 Gympie Australia
113 I7 Gyöngyös Hungary
112 H7 Győr Hungary
131 J4 Gypsumville Canada
133 G2 Gyrfalcon Islands Canada
115 J6 Gytheio Greece
113 J7 Gyula Hungary
81 I1 Gyumri Armenia
Gyzylarbat Turkm. see Serdar
82 F5 Gyzylaýak Turkm.
Gyzyletrek Turkm. see Etrek

H

102 N3 Haapajärvi Fin.
102 N2 Haapavesi Fin.
103 M4 Haapsalu Estonia
108 C2 Haarlem Neth.
124 E6 Haarlem S. Africa
109 G3 Haarstrang ridge Germany
72 B5 Haast N.Z.
85 G5 Hab r. Pak.
87 C4 Habarane Sri Lanka
122 D3 Habaswein Kenya
130 F3 Habay Canada
86 C7 Habbān Yemen
81 I5 Ḥabbānīyah, Hawr al l. Iraq
85 G5 Hab Chauki Pak.
89 G4 Habiganj Bangl.
92 E1 Habirag China
89 G5 Habra India
157 B5 Hacha Col.
159 B3 Hachado, Paso de pass Arg./Chile
95 F8 Hachijō-jima i. Japan
94 G4 Hachinohe Japan
95 F7 Hachiōji Japan
80 E2 Hacıbektaş Turkey
81 H2 Hacıömer Turkey
70 C3 Hack, Mount Australia
123 D6 Hacufera Moz.
84 C6 Hadabat al Budū plain Saudi Arabia
87 A3 Hadagalli India
86 E5 Ḥadd, Ra's al pt Oman
106 F5 Haddington U.K.
120 D3 Hadejia Nigeria
80 E5 Ḥadera Israel
103 J5 Haderslev Denmark
80 D3 Hadım Turkey
105 H5 Hadleigh U.K.
128 H2 Hadley Bay Canada
96 D6 Hadong S. Korea
98 Ha Đông Vietnam
80 F6 Ḥadraj, Wādī watercourse Saudi Arabia
86 C6 Ḥaḍramawt reg. Yemen
104 E3 Hadrian's Wall tourist site U.K.
103 J4 Hadsund Denmark
117 E5 Hadyach Ukr.
159 F1 Haedo, Cuchilla de hills Uruguay
96 C4 Haeju N. Korea
96 C5 Haeju-man b. N. Korea
96 D6 Haenam S. Korea
125 H1 Haenertsburg S. Africa
84 B4 Ḥafar al Bāṭin Saudi Arabia
131 H4 Hafford Canada
80 F2 Hafik Turkey
84 B5 Hafirat Nasah Saudi Arabia
88 C2 Hafizabad Pak.
89 H4 Haflong India
102 B2 Hafnarfjörður Iceland
84 C4 Haft Gel Iran
102 B2 Hafursfjörður b. Iceland
135 G2 Hagar Canada
87 B3 Hagari r. India
122 D2 Hagar Nish Plateau Eritrea
91 G5 Hagåtña Guam
108 C4 Hageland reg. Belgium
108 F3 Hagen Germany
109 J1 Hagenow Germany
146 E5 Hagerstown U.S.A.
110 D5 Hagetmau France
103 K3 Hagfors Sweden
138 D2 Haggin, Mount U.S.A.
95 B7 Hagi Japan
93 B6 Ha Giang Vietnam
105 E5 Hagley U.K.
107 B5 Hag's Head Rep. of Ireland
131 H4 Hague Canada
110 H2 Haguenau France
90 G4 Hahajima-rettō is Japan
122 D4 Hai Tanz.
92 F3 Hai'an China
124 B4 Haib watercourse Namibia
96 B3 Haicheng China
109 J5 Haidenaab r. Germany
93 C6 Hai Dương Vietnam
80 E5 Haifa Israel
80 E5 Haifa, Bay of Israel
93 E6 Haifeng China
109 G4 Haiger Germany
92 E2 Hai He r. China
93 D6 Haikou China
86 B4 Ḥā'il Saudi Arabia
135 H2 Haileybury Canada
96 E1 Hailin China
105 H7 Hailsham U.K.
102 N2 Hailuoto Fin.
92 F4 Haimen China
93 D7 Hainan i. China
93 C7 Hainan prov. China
93 C6 Hainan Strait China
130 B3 Haines U.S.A.
130 B2 Haines Junction Canada
109 I3 Hainich ridge Germany
109 L4 Hainichen Germany
109 I3 Hainleite ridge Germany
93 C6 Hai Phong Vietnam
92 A2 Hairag China
Hairhan Namag China see Guaizihu
93 F5 Haitan Dao i. China
149 J5 Haiti country Caribbean Sea
93 C7 Haitou China
98 D2 Hai Triêu Vietnam
141 G5 Haivana Nakya U.S.A.
140 D3 Haiwee Reservoir U.S.A.
92 E2 Haixing China
121 F3 Haiya Sudan
92 A2 Haiyan Qinghai China
93 F4 Haiyan Zhejiang China
96 A5 Haiyang China
96 B4 Haiyang Dao i. China
92 B2 Haiyuan China
92 F3 Haizhou Wan b. China
84 D3 Hāj Ali Qoli, Kavīr-e salt l. Iran
113 J7 Hajdúböszörmény Hungary
114 C7 Hajeb El Ayoun Tunisia
86 D7 Ḥajhir mt. Yemen
84 D3 Haji Abdulla, Chāh well Iran
94 F5 Hajiki-zaki pt Japan
89 F4 Hajipur India
84 D4 Ḥājjīābād Iran
84 D4 Ḥājjīābād Iran
89 H5 Haka Myanmar
140 □2 Hakalau U.S.A.
159 C4 Hakelhuincul, Altiplanicie de plat. Arg.
81 I3 Hakkârı Turkey
102 M2 Hakkas Sweden
95 D7 Hakken-zan mt. Japan
94 H2 Hako-dake mt. Japan
94 G4 Hakodate Japan
124 B1 Hakos Mountains Namibia

Hodeidah 183

124 D3 **Hakseen Pan** *salt pan* S. Africa
95 E6 **Hakui** Japan
95 E6 **Haku-san** *vol.* Japan
95 E6 **Haku-san National Park** Japan
88 B4 **Hala** Pak.
Halab Syria *see* **Aleppo**
84 B6 **Halabān** Saudi Arabia
81 J4 **Halabja** Iraq
82 F5 **Halaç** Turkm.
96 C1 **Halaha** China
96 C1 **Halahai** China
121 F2 **Halaib** Sudan
98 D2 **Ha Lam** Vietnam
86 E6 **Ḥalāniyāt, Juzur al** *is* Oman
140 □2 **Hālawa** U.S.A.
80 F4 **Halba** Lebanon
90 B2 **Halban** Mongolia
109 J3 **Halberstadt** Germany
97 B3 **Halcon, Mount** Phil.
102 □ **Haldarsvik** Faroe Is
103 J4 **Halden** Norway
109 J2 **Haldensleben** Germany
89 G5 **Haldi** *r.* India
89 G5 **Haldia** India
89 G4 **Haldibari** India
88 D3 **Haldwani** India
135 F3 **Hale** U.S.A.
84 D5 **Hāleh** Iran
140 □1 **Hale'iwa** U.S.A.
105 E5 **Halesowen** U.K.
105 I5 **Halesworth** U.K.
84 C4 **Haleyleh** Iran
80 F3 **Halfeti** Turkey
72 B7 **Halfmoon Bay** N.Z.
130 E3 **Halfway** *r.* Canada
107 C6 **Halfway** Rep. of Ireland
108 C2 **Halfweg** Neth.
89 E4 **Halia** India
81 G4 **Ḥalībīyah** Syria
135 H3 **Haliburton** Canada
133 H5 **Halifax** Canada
104 F4 **Halifax** U.K.
146 D6 **Halifax** U.S.A.
92 C1 **Haliut** China
106 E2 **Halkirk** U.K.
102 L3 **Hälla** Sweden
96 D7 **Halla-san** *mt.* S. Korea
70 A5 **Hall Bay** Australia
129 J3 **Hall Beach** Canada
108 C4 **Halle** Belgium
108 E3 **Halle** Neth.
109 J3 **Halle (Saale)** Germany
103 K4 **Hällefors** Sweden
112 F7 **Hallein** Austria
109 J3 **Halle-Neustadt** Germany
73 C3 **Halley** *research stn* Antarctica
66 E2 **Hall Islands** Micronesia
102 L2 **Hällnäs** Sweden
142 D1 **Hallock** U.S.A.
129 L3 **Hall Peninsula** Canada
103 K4 **Hallsberg** Sweden
68 C3 **Halls Creek** Australia
135 H3 **Halls Lake** Canada
108 B4 **Halluin** France
102 K3 **Hallviken** Sweden
91 E6 **Halmahera** *i.* Indon.
103 K4 **Halmstad** Sweden
88 C5 **Halol** India
93 C6 **Ha Long** Vietnam
103 J4 **Hals** Denmark
102 N3 **Halsua** Fin.
108 F3 **Haltern** Germany
104 E3 **Haltwhistle** U.K.
84 D5 **Ḥālūl** *i.* Qatar
108 F3 **Halver** Germany
108 B5 **Ham** France
95 C7 **Hamada** Japan
84 C3 **Hamadān** Iran
80 F4 **Ḥamāh** Syria
94 G3 **Hamamasu** Japan
95 E7 **Hamamatsu** Japan
103 J3 **Hamar** Norway
102 K1 **Hamarøy** Norway
121 F2 **Ḥamāṭah, Jabal** *mt.* Egypt
Ḥamāṭah, Jabal *mt.* Egypt *see* **Ghārib, Jabal**
94 H2 **Hamatonbetsu** Japan
87 C5 **Hambantota** Sri Lanka
109 G1 **Hambergen** Germany
104 F3 **Hambleton Hills** U.K.
109 H1 **Hamburg** Germany
125 G6 **Hamburg** S. Africa
143 F5 **Hamburg** *AR* U.S.A.
146 D3 **Hamburg** *NY* U.S.A.
147 F4 **Hamburg** *PA* U.S.A.
109 G1 **Hamburgisches Wattenmeer, Nationalpark** *nat. park* Germany
147 G4 **Hamden** U.S.A.
103 N3 **Hämeenlinna** Fin.
109 H2 **Hameln** Germany
68 B4 **Hamersley Range** *mts* Australia
96 D4 **Hamhŭng** N. Korea
90 B2 **Hami** China
84 C4 **Ḥamīd** Iran
121 F2 **Hamid** Sudan
70 E6 **Hamilton** Australia
149 L2 **Hamilton** Bermuda
135 H4 **Hamilton** Canada
72 E2 **Hamilton** N.Z.
106 D5 **Hamilton** U.K.
145 C5 **Hamilton** *AL* U.S.A.
134 B5 **Hamilton** *IL* U.S.A.
138 D2 **Hamilton** *MT* U.S.A.
147 F3 **Hamilton** *NY* U.S.A.
146 A5 **Hamilton** *OH* U.S.A.
140 B3 **Hamilton, Mount** *CA* U.S.A.
141 E2 **Hamilton, Mount** *NV* U.S.A.
140 A2 **Hamilton City** U.S.A.
103 N3 **Hamina** Fin.
81 H6 **Ḥāmir, Wādī al** *watercourse* Saudi Arabia
88 D3 **Hamirpur** India
96 D4 **Hamju** N. Korea
70 C5 **Hamley Bridge** Australia
134 D3 **Hamlin Lake** U.S.A.
109 F3 **Hamm** Germany
81 I3 **Ḥammām al 'Alīl** Iraq
114 D6 **Hammamet** Tunisia
121 D1 **Hammamet, Golfe de** *g.* Tunisia
81 K6 **Ḥammār, Hawr al** *imp. l.* Iraq
102 L3 **Hammarstrand** Sweden
109 H4 **Hammelburg** Germany
102 K3 **Hammerdal** Sweden
102 M1 **Hammerfest** Norway
108 E3 **Hamminkeln** Germany
70 C4 **Hammond** Australia
134 D5 **Hammond** *IN* U.S.A.
143 F6 **Hammond** *LA* U.S.A.
138 F2 **Hammond** *MT* U.S.A.
135 E3 **Hammond Bay** U.S.A.
146 E3 **Hammondsport** U.S.A.
147 F5 **Hammonton** U.S.A.
108 D4 **Hamoir** Belgium
72 C6 **Hampden** N.Z.
87 B3 **Hampi** India
105 F6 **Hampshire Downs** *hills* U.K.
133 G4 **Hampton** Canada
143 E5 **Hampton** *AR* U.S.A.
147 H3 **Hampton** *NH* U.S.A.
147 E6 **Hampton** *VA* U.S.A.
121 D2 **Ḥamrā', Al Ḥamādah al** *plat.* Libya
81 J4 **Ḥamrīn, Jabal** *hills* Iraq
98 C3 **Ham Tân** Vietnam
88 D2 **Hamta Pass** India
81 I2 **Hamur** Turkey
83 G4 **Hamza** Uzbek.
108 D4 **Han, Grotte de** *tourist site* Belgium
140 □2 **Hāna** U.S.A.
124 E1 **Hanahai** *watercourse* Botswana/Namibia
140 □2 **Hanalei** U.S.A.
94 G5 **Hanamaki** Japan
109 G4 **Hanau** Germany
92 D3 **Hancheng** China
146 D5 **Hancock** *MD* U.S.A.
134 C2 **Hancock** *MI* U.S.A.
147 F4 **Hancock** *NY* U.S.A.
106 C2 **Handa Island** U.K.
92 E2 **Handan** China
122 D4 **Handeni** Tanz.
140 C3 **Hanford** U.S.A.
87 A3 **Hangal** India
96 D5 **Han-gang** *r.* S. Korea
90 B2 **Hangayn Nuruu** *mts* Mongolia
92 E2 **Hangu** China
88 B2 **Hangu** Pak.
93 D5 **Hanguang** China
93 F4 **Hangzhou** China
93 F4 **Hangzhou Wan** *b.* China
81 H2 **Hani** Turkey
84 C5 **Ḥanīdh** Saudi Arabia
Hanjiang China *see* **Yangzhou**
92 B2 **Hanjiaoshui** China
109 I2 **Hankensbüttel** Germany
124 F6 **Hankey** S. Africa
103 M4 **Hanko** Fin.
141 G2 **Hanksville** U.S.A.
88 D2 **Hanle** Jammu and Kashmir
72 D5 **Hanmer Springs** N.Z.
131 G4 **Hanna** Canada
132 D3 **Hannah Bay** Canada
134 B6 **Hannibal** U.S.A.
109 H2 **Hannover** Germany
109 H3 **Hannoversch Münden** Germany
108 D4 **Hannut** Belgium
103 K5 **Hanöbukten** *b.* Sweden
93 B6 **Ha Nôi** Vietnam
135 G3 **Hanover** Canada
124 F5 **Hanover** S. Africa
147 G3 **Hanover** *NH* U.S.A.
146 E5 **Hanover** *PA* U.S.A.
73 E5 **Hansen Mountains** Antarctica
93 D4 **Hanshou** China
92 E4 **Han Shui** *r.* China
88 D3 **Hansi** India
102 L1 **Hansnes** Norway
70 B3 **Hanson, Lake** *salt flat* Australia
146 B6 **Hansonville** U.S.A.
103 J4 **Hanstholm** Denmark
108 E6 **Han-sur-Nied** France
116 C4 **Hantsavichy** Belarus
88 C3 **Hanumangarh** India
71 G5 **Hanwood** Australia
92 C3 **Hanyin** China
93 B4 **Hanyuan** China
85 F5 **Hanzaram** Iran
92 C3 **Hanzhong** China
67 J6 **Hao** *atoll* Fr. Polynesia
89 G5 **Haora** India
102 N2 **Haparanda** Sweden
89 H4 **Hapoli** India
133 H3 **Happy Valley-Goose Bay** Canada
96 E3 **Hapsu** N. Korea
88 D3 **Hapur** India
87 C5 **Haputale** Sri Lanka
84 C5 **Ḥaraḍ** *well* Saudi Arabia
84 C5 **Ḥaraḍh** Saudi Arabia
116 D4 **Haradok** Belarus
95 G6 **Haramachi** Japan
88 C2 **Haramukh** *mt.* India
88 C3 **Harappa Road** Pak.
123 D5 **Harare** Zimbabwe
86 E6 **Ḥarāsīs, Jiddat al** *des.* Oman
90 C2 **Har-Ayrag** Mongolia
120 A4 **Harbel** Liberia
90 E2 **Harbin** China
135 F4 **Harbor Beach** U.S.A.
134 E3 **Harbor Springs** U.S.A.
133 I4 **Harbour Breton** Canada
156 E8 **Harbours, Bay of** Falkland Is
141 F5 **Harcuvar Mountains** U.S.A.
88 D5 **Harda** India
103 I4 **Hardangerfjorden** *sea chan.* Norway
103 I3 **Hardangervidda** *plat.* Norway
103 I3 **Hardangervidda Nasjonalpark** *nat. park* Norway
124 B2 **Hardap** *admin. reg.* Namibia
124 B2 **Hardap Dam** Namibia
99 E2 **Harden, Bukit** *mt.* Indon.
108 E2 **Hardenberg** Neth.
108 D2 **Harderwijk** Neth.
124 C5 **Hardeveld** *mts* S. Africa
109 H5 **Hardheim** Germany
138 F2 **Hardin** U.S.A.
125 H5 **Harding** S. Africa
131 G4 **Hardisty** Canada
130 F2 **Hardisty Lake** Canada
88 E4 **Hardoi** India
147 G2 **Hardwick** U.S.A.
70 B5 **Hardwicke Bay** Australia
143 F4 **Hardy** U.S.A.
Hardy, Mt *mt.* N.Z. *see* Rangipoua
134 E4 **Hardy Reservoir** U.S.A.
108 B4 **Harelbeke** Belgium
108 E1 **Haren** Neth.
108 F2 **Haren (Ems)** Germany
122 E3 **Härer** Eth.
147 F4 **Harford** U.S.A.
122 E3 **Hargeysa** Somalia
113 L7 **Harghita-Mădăraş, Vârful** *mt.* Romania
81 H2 **Harhal Dağları** *mts* Turkey
92 C2 **Harhatan** China
90 B3 **Har Hu** *l.* China
120 B2 **Ḥaricha, Ḥamâda El** *des.* Mali
88 D3 **Haridwar** India
87 A3 **Harihar** India
72 C5 **Harihari** N.Z.
95 D7 **Harima-nada** *b.* Japan
89 G5 **Haringhat** *r.* Bangl.
108 C3 **Haringvliet** *est.* Neth.
85 G3 **Hari Rūd** *r.* Afgh./Iran
103 M3 **Harjavalta** Fin.
142 E3 **Harlan** *IA* U.S.A.
146 B6 **Harlan** *KY* U.S.A.
105 C5 **Harlech** U.K.
138 E1 **Harlem** U.S.A.
105 I5 **Harleston** U.K.
108 D1 **Harlingen** Neth.
143 D7 **Harlingen** U.S.A.
105 H6 **Harlow** U.K.
138 E2 **Harlowton** U.S.A.
108 B5 **Harly** France
147 I2 **Harmony** *ME* U.S.A.
134 A4 **Harmony** *MN* U.S.A.
109 I1 **Harmsdorf** Germany
88 A3 **Harnai** Pak.
108 A4 **Harnes** France
138 B3 **Harney Basin** U.S.A.
138 C3 **Harney Lake** U.S.A.
103 L3 **Härnösand** Sweden
90 E2 **Har Nur** China
90 B2 **Har Nuur** *l.* Mongolia
106 □ **Haroldswick** U.K.
120 B4 **Harper** Liberia
140 D4 **Harper Lake** U.S.A.
146 E5 **Harpers Ferry** U.S.A.
133 H2 **Harp Lake** Canada
109 G2 **Harpstedt** Germany
81 G2 **Harput** Turkey
141 F5 **Harquahala Mountains** U.S.A.
81 G3 **Harran** Turkey
132 E3 **Harricanaw** *r.* Canada
145 C5 **Harriman** U.S.A.
147 G3 **Harriman Reservoir** U.S.A.
71 J3 **Harrington** Australia
147 F5 **Harrington** U.S.A.
133 I3 **Harrington Harbour** Canada
106 B3 **Harris** *reg.* U.K.
70 A3 **Harris, Lake** *salt flat* Australia
106 A3 **Harris, Sound of** *sea chan.* U.K.
144 B4 **Harrisburg** *IL* U.S.A.
146 E4 **Harrisburg** *PA* U.S.A.
125 H4 **Harrismith** S. Africa
143 E4 **Harrison** *AR* U.S.A.
134 E3 **Harrison** *MI* U.S.A.
133 I3 **Harrison, Cape** Canada
128 C2 **Harrison Bay** U.S.A.
146 D5 **Harrisonburg** U.S.A.
130 E5 **Harrison Lake** Canada
142 E4 **Harrisonville** U.S.A.
135 F3 **Harrisville** *MI* U.S.A.
147 F2 **Harrisville** *NY* U.S.A.
146 C5 **Harrisville** *WV* U.S.A.
104 F4 **Harrogate** U.K.
109 H1 **Harsefeld** Germany
84 B3 **Harsīn** Iran
80 G1 **Harşit** *r.* Turkey
115 L2 **Hârşova** Romania
102 L1 **Harstad** Norway
109 H2 **Harsum** Germany
134 D4 **Hart** U.S.A.
70 B3 **Hart, Lake** *salt flat* Australia
96 B2 **Hartao** China
124 D4 **Hartbees** *watercourse* S. Africa
112 G7 **Hartberg** Austria
103 I3 **Harteigan** *mt.* Norway
106 E5 **Hart Fell** *h.* U.K.
147 G4 **Hartford** *CT* U.S.A.
134 D4 **Hartford** *MI* U.S.A.
142 D3 **Hartford** *SD* U.S.A.
134 C4 **Hartford** *WI* U.S.A.
130 E3 **Hart Highway** Canada
133 G4 **Hartland** Canada
105 C7 **Hartland** U.K.
147 I2 **Hartland** U.S.A.
105 C6 **Hartland Point** U.K.
104 F3 **Hartlepool** U.K.
143 C5 **Hartley** U.S.A.
130 D4 **Hartley Bay** Canada
103 N3 **Hartola** Fin.
130 E4 **Hart Ranges** *mts* Canada
112 E6 **Härtsfeld** *hills* Germany
124 F3 **Hartswater** S. Africa
145 D5 **Hartwell Reservoir** U.S.A.
90 B2 **Har Us Nuur** *l.* Mongolia
85 F3 **Harut** *watercourse* Afgh.
134 C4 **Harvard** U.S.A.
139 F4 **Harvard, Mount** U.S.A.
147 J2 **Harvey** Canada
134 D2 **Harvey** *MI* U.S.A.
142 C2 **Harvey** *ND* U.S.A.
105 I6 **Harwich** U.K.
71 J2 **Harwood** Australia
88 C3 **Haryana** *state* India
109 I3 **Harz** *hills* Germany
80 F6 **Ḥaşāh, Wādī al** *watercourse* Jordan
83 I5 **Hasalbag** China
88 C2 **Hasan Abdal** Pak.
80 E2 **Hasan Dağı** *mts* Turkey
81 H3 **Hasankeyf** Turkey
84 E5 **Ḥasan Langī** Iran
87 B2 **Hasanparti** India
84 B2 **Ḥasan Sālārān** Iran
82 D5 **Hasardag** *mt.* Turkm.
80 E5 **Hasbani** *r.* Lebanon
80 E2 **Hasbek** Turkey
87 C1 **Hasdo** *r.* India
109 F2 **Hase** *r.* Germany
108 F2 **Haselünne** Germany
109 I4 **Hasenkopf** *h.* Germany
84 C3 **Hashtgerd** Iran
84 C2 **Hashtpar** Iran
84 B2 **Hashtrud** Iran
84 E3 **Hasht Tekkeh, Gowd-e** *waterhole* Iran
143 D5 **Haskell** U.S.A.
105 G6 **Haslemere** U.K.
113 L7 **Hăşmaşul Mare** *mt.* Romania
87 B3 **Hassan** India
81 J4 **Hassan** Iraq
141 F5 **Hassayampa** *watercourse* U.S.A.
109 I4 **Haßberge** *hills* Germany
108 D4 **Hasselt** Belgium
108 E2 **Hasselt** Neth.
120 C1 **Hassi Messaoud** Alg.
103 K4 **Hässleholm** Sweden
70 F7 **Hastings** Australia
71 J3 **Hastings** *r.* Australia
72 F3 **Hastings** N.Z.
105 H7 **Hastings** U.K.
134 E4 **Hastings** *MI* U.S.A.
134 A3 **Hastings** *MN* U.S.A.
142 D3 **Hastings** *NE* U.S.A.
141 F3 **Hatch** U.S.A.
131 I3 **Hatchet Lake** Canada
145 B5 **Hatchie** *r.* U.S.A.
70 E4 **Hatfield** Australia
104 G4 **Hatfield** U.K.
90 C1 **Hatgal** Mongolia
88 D4 **Hathras** India
89 F4 **Hatia** Nepal
98 C3 **Ha Tiên** Vietnam
98 C1 **Ha Tinh** Vietnam
81 I4 **Hatra** Iraq
70 E5 **Hattah** Australia
70 E5 **Hattah-Kulkyne National Park** Australia
145 F5 **Hatteras, Cape** U.S.A.
163 E4 **Hatteras Abyssal Plain** *sea feature* S. Atlantic Ocean
102 K2 **Hattfjelldal** Norway
87 C2 **Hatti** *r.* India
145 B6 **Hattiesburg** U.S.A.
108 F3 **Hattingen** Germany
98 B4 **Hat Yai** Thai.
98 C3 **Hâu, Sông** *r.* Vietnam
122 E3 **Haud** *reg.* Eth.
103 I4 **Hauge** Norway
103 I4 **Haugesund** Norway
Hâu Giang, Sông *r.* Vietnam *see* **Hâu, Sông**
72 E3 **Hauhungaroa** *mt.* N.Z.
103 I4 **Haukeligrend** Norway
102 N2 **Haukipudas** Fin.
103 O3 **Haukivesi** *l.* Fin.
131 H3 **Haultain** *r.* Canada
72 E2 **Hauraki Gulf** N.Z.
72 A7 **Hauroko, Lake** N.Z.
147 I3 **Haut, Isle au** *i.* U.S.A.
120 B1 **Haut Atlas** *mts* Morocco
133 G4 **Hauterive** Canada
120 B1 **Hauts Plateaux** Alg.
140 □1 **Hau'ula** U.S.A.
Hauula U.S.A. *see* **Hau'ula**
149 H4 **Havana** Cuba
134 B5 **Havana** U.S.A.
105 G7 **Havant** U.K.
141 E4 **Havasu, Lake** U.S.A.
109 K2 **Havel** *r.* Germany
108 D4 **Havelange** Belgium
109 K2 **Havelberg** Germany
109 K2 **Havelländisches Luch** *marsh* Germany
135 I3 **Havelock** Canada
145 E5 **Havelock** U.S.A.
72 F3 **Havelock North** N.Z.
105 C6 **Haverfordwest** U.K.
147 H3 **Haverhill** U.S.A.
87 A3 **Haveri** India
108 D4 **Haversin** Belgium
108 F3 **Havixbeck** Germany
112 G6 **Havlíčkův Brod** Czech Rep.
102 N1 **Havøysund** Norway
115 L5 **Havran** Turkey
138 E1 **Havre** U.S.A.
133 H4 **Havre Aubert, Île du** *i.* Canada
147 E5 **Havre de Grace** U.S.A.
133 H3 **Havre-St-Pierre** Canada
115 L4 **Havsa** Turkey
80 E1 **Havza** Turkey
140 □2 **Hawai'i** *i.* U.S.A.
Hawaii *i.* U.S.A. *see* **Hawai'i**
Hawaiian Islands N. Pacific Ocean *see* **Hawai'ian Islands**
140 □1 **Hawai'ian Islands** N. Pacific Ocean
160 H4 **Hawaiian Ridge** *sea feature* N. Pacific Ocean
Hawaii Volcanoes National Park U.S.A. *see* Hawai'i Volcanoes National Park
140 □2 **Hawai'i Volcanoes National Park** U.S.A.
81 K7 **Ḥawallī** Kuwait
105 D4 **Hawarden** U.K.
72 B6 **Hawea, Lake** N.Z.
72 E3 **Hawera** N.Z.
104 E3 **Hawes** U.K.
Hawi U.S.A. *see* **Hāwī**
140 □2 **Hāwī** U.S.A.
106 F5 **Hawick** U.K.
81 K6 **Ḥawīzah, Hawr al** *imp. l.* Iraq
72 B6 **Hawkdun Range** *mts* N.Z.
72 F3 **Hawke Bay** N.Z.
133 I3 **Hawke Island** Canada
70 C3 **Hawker** Australia
70 D2 **Hawkers Gate** Australia
147 F2 **Hawkesbury** Canada
141 F3 **Hawkins Peak** U.S.A.
135 F3 **Hawks** U.S.A.
147 J2 **Hawkshaw** Canada
147 F4 **Hawley** U.S.A.
81 I5 **Ḥawrān, Wādī** *watercourse* Iraq
84 B6 **Ḥawshah, Jibāl al** *mts* Saudi Arabia
124 C7 **Hawston** S. Africa
140 C2 **Hawthorne** U.S.A.
96 C1 **Haxat** China
104 F3 **Haxby** U.K.
70 F5 **Hay** Australia
130 F2 **Hay** *r.* Canada
134 B3 **Hay** *r.* U.S.A.
Haya China *see* **Yagan**
94 G5 **Hayachine-san** *mt.* Japan
84 B2 **Haydarābad** Iran
141 G5 **Hayden** *AZ* U.S.A.
138 C2 **Hayden** *ID* U.S.A.
131 K3 **Hayes** *r. Man.* Canada
129 I3 **Hayes** *r. Nunavut* Canada
129 L2 **Hayes Halvø** *pen.* Greenland
105 B7 **Hayle** U.K.
86 E6 **Haymā'** Oman
80 D2 **Haymana** Turkey
146 E5 **Haymarket** U.S.A.
147 I2 **Haynesville** U.S.A.
105 D5 **Hay-on-Wye** U.K.
117 C7 **Hayrabolu** Turkey
130 F2 **Hay River** Canada
142 D4 **Hays** U.S.A.
117 D5 **Haysyn** Ukr.
140 A3 **Hayward** *CA* U.S.A.
134 B2 **Hayward** *WI* U.S.A.
105 G7 **Haywards Heath** U.K.
82 C5 **Hazar** Turkm.
85 G3 **Hazarajat** *reg.* Afgh.
146 B6 **Hazard** U.S.A.
89 F5 **Hazaribagh** India
89 E5 **Hazaribagh Range** *mts* India
108 A4 **Hazebrouck** France
130 D3 **Hazelton** Canada
128 G2 **Hazen Strait** Canada
108 C2 **Hazerswoude-Rijndijk** Neth.
147 F4 **Hazleton** U.S.A.
82 E4 **Hazorasp** Uzbek.
85 G2 **Hazrat Sultan** Afgh.
81 H2 **Hazro** Turkey
159 D2 **H. Bouchard** Arg.
107 B4 **Headford** Rep. of Ireland
140 A2 **Healdsburg** U.S.A.
70 F6 **Healesville** Australia
105 F4 **Heanor** U.K.
162 I8 **Heard Island** Indian Ocean
143 D6 **Hearne** U.S.A.
132 D4 **Hearst** Canada
105 H7 **Heathfield** U.K.
147 E6 **Heathsville** U.S.A.
143 D7 **Hebbronville** U.S.A.
92 E2 **Hebei** *prov.* China
71 G2 **Hebel** Australia
136 D3 **Heber City** U.S.A.
143 E5 **Heber Springs** U.S.A.
92 E3 **Hebi** China
133 H2 **Hebron** Canada
134 D5 **Hebron** *IN* U.S.A.
142 D3 **Hebron** *NE* U.S.A.
147 G3 **Hebron** *NY* U.S.A.
80 E6 **Hebron** West Bank
133 H2 **Hebron Fiord** *inlet* Canada
130 C4 **Hecate Strait** Canada
151 G3 **Hecelchakán** Mex.
130 C3 **Heceta Island** U.S.A.
93 C5 **Hechi** China
93 C4 **Hechuan** China
103 K3 **Hede** Sweden
103 K3 **Hedemora** Sweden
138 C2 **He Devil Mountain** U.S.A.
93 D6 **Hedi Shuiku** *resr* China
134 A5 **Hedrick** U.S.A.
108 D2 **Heeg** Neth.
108 F2 **Heek** Germany
108 C4 **Heer** Belgium
108 E2 **Heerde** Neth.
108 D2 **Heerenveen** Neth.
108 C2 **Heerhugowaard** Neth.
108 D4 **Heerlen** Neth.
Ḥefa Israel *see* **Haifa**
92 E4 **Hefei** China
93 D4 **Hefeng** China
94 B1 **Hegang** China
95 E6 **Hegura-jima** *i.* Japan
109 J3 **Heidberg** *h.* Germany
112 D3 **Heide** Germany
123 B6 **Heide** Namibia
109 G5 **Heidelberg** Germany
125 H3 **Heidelberg** *Gauteng* S. Africa
124 D7 **Heidelberg** *W. Cape* S. Africa
125 G3 **Heilbron** S. Africa
109 H5 **Heilbronn** Germany
112 E3 **Heiligenhafen** Germany
93 □ **Hei Ling Chau** *i.* Hong Kong China
96 E1 **Heilongjiang** *prov.* China
90 E2 **Heilong Jiang** *r.* China/Rus. Fed. *alt.* **Amur**
109 I5 **Heilsbronn** Germany
102 J3 **Heimdal** Norway
103 N3 **Heinola** Fin.
98 A2 **Heinze Islands** Myanmar
96 B3 **Heishan** China
108 C3 **Heist-op-den-Berg** Belgium
92 E2 **Hejian** China
93 B4 **Hejiang** China
93 D6 **He Jiang** *r.* China
92 D3 **Hejin** China
80 F2 **Hekimhan** Turkey
102 C3 **Hekla** *vol.* Iceland
92 B2 **Hekou** *Gansu* China
93 B6 **Hekou** *Yunnan* China
102 K3 **Helagsfjället** *mt.* Sweden
92 B2 **Helan Shan** *mts* China
109 J3 **Helbra** Germany
89 H4 **Helem** India
140 D3 **Helen, Mount** U.S.A.
143 F5 **Helena** *AR* U.S.A.
138 E2 **Helena** *MT* U.S.A.
106 D4 **Helensburgh** U.K.
80 E6 **Ḥeleẓ** Israel
112 C3 **Helgoland** *i.* Germany
112 D3 **Helgoländer Bucht** *g.* Germany
71 J1 **Helidon** Australia
102 B3 **Hella** Iceland
102 L1 **Helland** Norway
84 C4 **Helleh** *r.* Iran
108 C3 **Hellevoetsluis** Neth.
102 M1 **Helligskogen** Norway
111 F3 **Hellín** Spain
138 C2 **Hells Canyon** *gorge* U.S.A.
85 F4 **Helmand** *r.* Afgh.
85 F4 **Helmand, Hāmūn** *salt flat* Afgh./Iran
109 J4 **Helmbrechts** Germany
109 I3 **Helme** *r.* Germany
123 B6 **Helmeringhausen** Namibia
108 D3 **Helmond** Neth.
106 E2 **Helmsdale** U.K.
106 E2 **Helmsdale** *r.* U.K.
109 J2 **Helmstedt** Germany
96 E2 **Helong** China
141 G2 **Helper** U.S.A.
103 K4 **Helsingborg** Sweden
Helsingfors Fin. *see* **Helsinki**
103 K4 **Helsingør** Denmark
103 N3 **Helsinki** Fin.
105 B7 **Helston** U.K.
104 D3 **Helvellyn** *h.* U.K.
107 D5 **Helvick Head** Rep. of Ireland
105 G6 **Hemel Hempstead** U.K.
140 D5 **Hemet** U.S.A.
146 E3 **Hemlock Lake** U.S.A.
109 H2 **Hemmingen** Germany
147 G2 **Hemmingford** Canada
109 H1 **Hemmoor** Germany
143 D6 **Hempstead** U.S.A.
105 I5 **Hemsby** U.K.
103 L4 **Hemse** Sweden
92 A3 **Henan** China
92 D3 **Henan** *prov.* China
111 E2 **Henares** *r.* Spain
94 F4 **Henashi-zaki** *pt* Japan
80 C1 **Hendek** Turkey
159 E3 **Henderson** Arg.
144 C4 **Henderson** *KY* U.S.A.
145 E4 **Henderson** *NC* U.S.A.
141 E3 **Henderson** *NV* U.S.A.
147 E3 **Henderson** *NY* U.S.A.
143 E5 **Henderson** *TX* U.S.A.
67 J7 **Henderson Island** Pitcairn Is
145 D5 **Hendersonville** *NC* U.S.A.
145 C4 **Hendersonville** *TN* U.S.A.
84 C4 **Hendījān** Iran
105 G6 **Hendon** U.K.
84 D5 **Hendorābī** *i.* Iran
85 E5 **Hengām** Iran
90 B4 **Hengduan Shan** *mts* China
108 E2 **Hengelo** Neth.
96 F1 **Hengshan** *Heilong.* China
93 D5 **Hengshan** *Hunan* China
92 C2 **Hengshan** *Shaanxi* China
93 D5 **Heng Shan** *mt. Hunan* China
92 D2 **Heng Shan** *mts Shanxi* China
92 E2 **Hengshui** China
93 C6 **Hengxian** China
93 D5 **Hengyang** *Hunan* China
93 D5 **Hengyang** *Hunan* China
117 E6 **Heniches'k** Ukr.
72 C6 **Henley** N.Z.
105 G6 **Henley-on-Thames** U.K.
147 F5 **Henlopen, Cape** U.S.A.
108 F4 **Hennef (Sieg)** Germany
125 G3 **Hennenman** S. Africa
109 L2 **Hennigsdorf Berlin** Germany
147 H3 **Henniker** U.S.A.
143 D5 **Henrietta** U.S.A.
132 D2 **Henrietta Maria, Cape** Canada
141 G3 **Henrieville** U.S.A.
134 C5 **Henry** U.S.A.
73 C3 **Henry Ice Rise** *ice feature* Antarctica
129 L3 **Henry Kater, Cape** Canada
141 G2 **Henry Mountains** U.S.A.
135 G4 **Hensall** Canada
109 H1 **Henstedt-Ulzburg** Germany
123 B6 **Hentiesbaai** Namibia
71 G5 **Henty** Australia
Henzada Myanmar *see* **Hinthada**
131 H4 **Hepburn** Canada
93 E5 **Heping** China
93 C6 **Hepu** China
92 D2 **Hequ** China
85 F3 **Herāt** Afgh.
110 F5 **Hérault** *r.* France
131 H4 **Herbert** Canada
109 G4 **Herborn** Germany
109 H4 **Herbstein** Germany
73 C4 **Hercules Dome** *ice feature* Antarctica
108 F3 **Herdecke** Germany
109 F4 **Herdorf** Germany
150 H6 **Heredia** Costa Rica
105 E5 **Hereford** U.K.
143 C5 **Hereford** U.S.A.
67 J6 **Héréhérétué** *atoll* Fr. Polynesia
108 C4 **Herent** Belgium
109 G2 **Herford** Germany
109 I4 **Heringen (Werra)** Germany
142 D4 **Herington** U.S.A.
84 B2 **Herīs** Iran
112 D7 **Herisau** Switz.
147 F3 **Herkimer** U.S.A.
109 I3 **Herleshausen** Germany
150 D2 **Hermanas** Mex.
106 □ **Herma Ness** *hd* U.K.
109 I2 **Hermannsburg** Germany
124 C7 **Hermanus** S. Africa
125 H5 **Hermes, Cape** S. Africa
71 G3 **Hermidale** Australia
138 C2 **Hermiston** U.S.A.
156 C9 **Hermite, Islas** *is* Chile
68 E2 **Hermit Islands** P.N.G.
80 E5 **Hermon, Mount** Lebanon/Syria
150 B1 **Hermosillo** Mex.
156 F3 **Hernandarias** Para.
108 F3 **Herne** Germany
105 I6 **Herne Bay** U.K.
103 J4 **Herning** Denmark
134 D1 **Heron Bay** Canada
150 D3 **Herradura** Mex.
111 D3 **Herrera del Duque** Spain
71 G8 **Herrick** Australia
109 I5 **Herrieden** Germany
146 E4 **Hershey** U.S.A.
105 G6 **Hertford** U.K.
125 F4 **Hertzogville** S. Africa
108 D4 **Herve** Belgium
69 F4 **Hervey Bay** Australia
161 I7 **Hervey Islands** Cook Is
109 K2 **Herzberg** *Brandenburg* Germany
109 L3 **Herzberg** *Brandenburg* Germany
108 F2 **Herzlake** Germany
109 I5 **Herzogenaurach** Germany
109 K1 **Herzsprung** Germany
81 L4 **Heşar** Iran
108 C4 **Hesbaye** *reg.* Belgium
108 F1 **Hesel** Germany
93 C6 **Heshan** China
92 C3 **Heshui** China
92 D2 **Heshun** China
140 D4 **Hesperia** U.S.A.
130 C2 **Hess** *r.* Canada
109 I5 **Heßdorf** Germany
109 I5 **Hesselberg** *h.* Germany
109 H4 **Hessen** *land* Germany
109 H3 **Hessisch Lichtenau** Germany
93 B6 **Het** *r.* Laos
140 B3 **Hetch Hetchy Aqueduct** *canal* U.S.A.
108 D3 **Heteren** Neth.
142 C2 **Hettinger** U.S.A.
104 E3 **Hetton** U.K.
109 J3 **Hettstedt** Germany
104 E3 **Hexham** U.K.
92 F4 **Hexian** China
92 B2 **Hexipu** China
124 C6 **Hex River Pass** S. Africa
92 D3 **Heyang** China
85 F4 **Ḥeydarābād** Iran
104 E3 **Heysham** U.K.
93 E6 **Heyuan** China
70 D7 **Heywood** Australia
104 E4 **Heywood** U.K.
134 C5 **Heyworth** U.S.A.
92 E3 **Heze** China
93 B5 **Hezhang** China
92 B3 **Hezheng** China
93 D5 **Hezhou** China
92 B3 **Hezuo** China
145 D7 **Hialeah** U.S.A.
142 E4 **Hiawatha** U.S.A.
134 A2 **Hibbing** U.S.A.
71 F9 **Hibbs, Point** Australia
145 D5 **Hickory** U.S.A.
72 G2 **Hicks Bay** N.Z.
151 G4 **Hicks Cays** *is* Belize
131 J2 **Hicks Lake** Canada
146 A4 **Hicksville** U.S.A.
143 D5 **Hico** U.S.A.
94 H3 **Hidaka-sanmyaku** *mts* Japan
151 E2 **Hidalgo** Mex.
151 E3 **Hidalgo** *state* Mex.
150 C2 **Hidalgo del Parral** Mex.
158 C2 **Hidrolândia** Brazil
95 C7 **Higashi-Hiroshima** Japan
94 G5 **Higashine** Japan
95 D7 **Higashi-ōsaka** Japan
95 A8 **Higashi-suidō** *sea chan.* Japan
147 F3 **Higgins Bay** U.S.A.
134 E3 **Higgins Lake** U.S.A.
138 B3 **High Desert** U.S.A.
134 C3 **High Falls Reservoir** U.S.A.
134 E3 **High Island** U.S.A.
93 □ **High Island Reservoir** *Hong Kong* China
134 D4 **Highland Park** U.S.A.
140 C2 **Highland Peak** *CA* U.S.A.
141 E3 **Highland Peak** *NV* U.S.A.
130 F3 **High Level** Canada
89 F5 **High Level Canal** India
145 E5 **High Point** U.S.A.
130 F3 **High Prairie** Canada
130 G4 **High River** Canada
145 E7 **High Rock** Bahamas
131 I3 **Highrock Lake** Canada
71 F9 **High Rocky Point** Australia
104 E3 **High Seat** *h.* U.K.
147 F4 **Hightstown** U.S.A.
105 G6 **High Wycombe** U.K.
150 B2 **Higuera de Zaragoza** Mex.
157 D2 **Higuerote** Venez.
103 M4 **Hiiumaa** *i.* Estonia
86 A4 **Hijaz** *reg.* Saudi Arabia
141 E3 **Hiko** U.S.A.
95 E7 **Hikone** Japan
72 G2 **Hikurangi** *mt.* N.Z.
141 F3 **Hildale** U.S.A.
109 I4 **Hildburghausen** Germany
109 I4 **Hilders** Germany
109 H2 **Hildesheim** Germany
89 G4 **Hili** Bangl.
81 J5 **Hillah** Iraq
142 D4 **Hill City** U.S.A.
141 H2 **Hill Creek** *r.* U.S.A.
108 C2 **Hillegom** Neth.
103 K5 **Hillerød** Denmark
142 D2 **Hillsboro** *ND* U.S.A.
147 H3 **Hillsboro** *NH* U.S.A.
146 B5 **Hillsboro** *OH* U.S.A.
143 D5 **Hillsboro** *TX* U.S.A.
134 B4 **Hillsboro** *WI* U.S.A.
146 C5 **Hillsboro** *WV* U.S.A.
134 E5 **Hillsdale** *MI* U.S.A.
147 G3 **Hillsdale** *NY* U.S.A.
146 E4 **Hillsgrove** U.S.A.
106 F4 **Hillside** U.K.
141 F4 **Hillside** U.S.A.
71 F4 **Hillston** Australia
146 C6 **Hillsville** U.S.A.
71 I5 **Hilltop** Australia
140 □2 **Hilo** U.S.A.
125 I4 **Hilton** S. Africa
146 E3 **Hilton** U.S.A.
135 F2 **Hilton Beach** Canada
145 D5 **Hilton Head Island** U.S.A.
81 G3 **Hilvan** Turkey
108 D2 **Hilversum** Neth.
88 D3 **Himachal Pradesh** *state* India
88 D2 **Himalaya** *mts* Asia
89 F3 **Himalchul** *mt.* Nepal
102 M2 **Himanka** Fin.
115 H4 **Himarë** Albania
88 C5 **Himatnagar** India
95 D7 **Himeji** Japan
94 G5 **Himekami-dake** *mt.* Japan
125 H4 **Himeville** S. Africa
95 E6 **Himi** Japan
Ḥimş Syria *see* **Homs**
97 C4 **Hinatuan** Phil.
68 E3 **Hinchinbrook Island** Australia
105 F5 **Hinckley** U.K.
134 A2 **Hinckley** *MN* U.S.A.
141 F2 **Hinckley** *UT* U.S.A.
147 F3 **Hinckley Reservoir** U.S.A.
88 D3 **Hindan** *r.* India
88 D4 **Hindaun** India
104 G3 **Hinderwell** U.K.
104 E4 **Hindley** U.K.
146 B6 **Hindman** U.S.A.
70 D6 **Hindmarsh, Lake** *dry lake* Australia
87 D1 **Hindola** India
85 G3 **Hindu Kush** *mts* Afgh./Pak.
87 B3 **Hindupur** India
130 F3 **Hines Creek** Canada
145 D6 **Hinesville** U.S.A.
88 D5 **Hinganghat** India
85 G5 **Hinglaj** Pak.
85 G5 **Hingol** *r.* Pak.
88 D6 **Hingoli** India
81 H2 **Hınıs** Turkey
140 D4 **Hinkley** U.S.A.
102 K1 **Hinnøya** *i.* Norway
97 B4 **Hinobaan** Phil.
111 D3 **Hinojosa del Duque** Spain
95 C7 **Hino-misaki** *pt* Japan
147 G3 **Hinsdale** U.S.A.
108 F1 **Hinte** Germany
91 B5 **Hinthada** Myanmar
130 F4 **Hinton** Canada
146 C6 **Hinton** U.S.A.
108 C2 **Hippolytushoef** Neth.
81 J2 **Hirabit Dağ** *mt.* Turkey
95 A8 **Hirado** Japan
95 A8 **Hirado-shima** *i.* Japan
87 C1 **Hirakud Reservoir** India
94 H3 **Hiroo** Japan
94 G4 **Hirosaki** Japan
95 C7 **Hiroshima** Japan
109 J5 **Hirschaid** Germany
109 J4 **Hirschberg** Germany
112 E7 **Hirschberg** *mt.* Germany
110 G2 **Hirson** France
103 J4 **Hirtshals** Denmark
88 C3 **Hisar** India
81 L3 **Hisar** Iran
85 G3 **Hisar, Koh-i-** *mts* Afgh.
80 D1 **Hisarönü** Turkey
81 J6 **Ḥisb, Sha'īb** *watercourse* Iraq
83 G5 **Hisor** Tajik.
149 J4 **Hispaniola** *i.* Caribbean Sea
89 F4 **Hisua** India
81 I5 **Hīt** Iraq
95 G6 **Hitachi** Japan
95 G6 **Hitachi-ōta** Japan
95 B8 **Hitoyoshi** Japan
102 J3 **Hitra** *i.* Norway
109 J1 **Hitzacker** Germany
95 C7 **Hiuchi-nada** *b.* Japan
67 J5 **Hiva Oa** *i.* Fr. Polynesia
130 E4 **Hixon** Canada
81 I2 **Hizan** Turkey
103 K4 **Hjälmaren** *l.* Sweden
131 H2 **Hjalmar Lake** Canada
103 J3 **Hjerkinn** Norway
103 K4 **Hjo** Sweden
103 J4 **Hjørring** Denmark
125 I4 **Hlabisa** S. Africa
125 I3 **Hlatikulu** Swaziland
117 E5 **Hlobyne** Ukr.
125 G4 **Hlohlowane** S. Africa
125 H4 **Hlotse** Lesotho
125 J4 **Hluhluwe** S. Africa
117 E5 **Hlukhiv** Ukr.
113 N4 **Hlusha** Belarus
116 C4 **Hlybokaye** Belarus
120 C4 **Ho** Ghana
93 B6 **Hoa Binh** Vietnam
98 C1 **Hoa Binh** Vietnam
123 B6 **Hoachanas** Namibia
98 C1 **Hoan Lao** Vietnam
71 G9 **Hobart** Australia
143 D5 **Hobart** U.S.A.
143 C5 **Hobbs** U.S.A.
145 D7 **Hobe Sound** U.S.A.
92 D1 **Hobor** China
103 J4 **Hobro** Denmark
122 E3 **Hobyo** Somalia
109 H5 **Höchberg** Germany
109 I3 **Hochharz** *nat. park* Germany
98 C3 **Ho Chi Minh City** Vietnam
112 G7 **Hochschwab** *mt.* Austria
109 G5 **Hockenheim** Germany
146 B5 **Hocking** *r.* U.S.A.
151 G3 **Hoctúm** Mex.
88 D4 **Hodal** India
104 E4 **Hodder** *r.* U.K.
105 G6 **Hoddesdon** U.K.
86 B7 **Hodeidah** Yemen

Column 4 and 5 continued:

Jingxian 185

141 G4 **Indian Wells** U.S.A.
77 P2 **Indigirka** *r.* Rus. Fed.
115 I2 **Indija** Serb. and Mont.
130 F2 **Indin Lake** Canada
140 D5 **Indio** U.S.A.
69 G3 **Indispensable Reefs** Solomon Is
91 D7 **Indonesia** *country* Asia
88 C5 **Indore** India
99 C4 **Indramayu, Tanjung** *pt* Indon.
99 B3 **Indrapura** Indon.
87 C2 **Indravati** *r.* India
110 E3 **Indre** *r.* France
88 B4 **Indus** *r.* China/Pak.
alt. **Shiquan He (China)**
88 A5 **Indus, Mouths of the** Pak.
162 I3 **Indus Cone** *sea feature* Indian Ocean
125 G5 **Indwe** S. Africa
117 E7 **Inebolu** Turkey
80 B1 **İnegöl** Turkey
146 B6 **Inez** U.S.A.
124 D7 **Infanta, Cape** S. Africa
150 D4 **Infiernillo, Presa** *resr* Mex.
98 B1 **Ing, Nam Mae** *r.* Thai.
134 D3 **Ingalls** U.S.A.
140 B2 **Ingalls, Mount** U.S.A.
131 I2 **Ingalls Lake** Canada
108 B4 **Ingelmunster** Belgium
159 C4 **Ingeniero Jacobacci** Arg.
135 G4 **Ingersoll** Canada
82 F5 **Ingichka** Uzbek.
104 E3 **Ingleborough** *h.* U.K.
129 K2 **Inglefield Land** *reg.* Greenland
104 E3 **Ingleton** U.K.
71 I2 **Inglewood** *Qld* Australia
70 E6 **Inglewood** *Vic.* Australia
105 H4 **Ingoldmells** U.K.
112 E6 **Ingolstadt** Germany
133 H4 **Ingonish** Canada
89 G4 **Ingraj Bazar** India
130 F2 **Ingray Lake** Canada
Ingushetia *aut. rep.* Rus. Fed. *see* **Ingushetiya, Respublika**
117 H7 **Ingushetiya, Respublika** *aut. rep.* Rus. Fed.
125 J3 **Ingwavuma** S. Africa
125 J2 **Inhaca** Moz.
125 J3 **Inhaca, Península** *pen.* Moz.
125 J2 **Inhaca e dos Portugueses, Ilhas da** *nature res.* S. Africa
123 D6 **Inhambane** Moz.
125 J1 **Inhambane** *prov.* Moz.
123 D5 **Inhaminga** Moz.
158 A3 **Inhanduízinho** *r.* Brazil
158 D1 **Inhaúmas** Brazil
157 C4 **Inírida** *r.* Col.
107 A4 **Inishark** *i.* Rep. of Ireland
107 A4 **Inishbofin** *i.* Rep. of Ireland
107 A3 **Inishkea North** *i.* Rep. of Ireland
107 A3 **Inishkea South** *i.* Rep. of Ireland
107 B4 **Inishmaan** *i.* Rep. of Ireland
107 B4 **Inishmore** *i.* Rep. of Ireland
107 C3 **Inishmurray** *i.* Rep. of Ireland
107 D2 **Inishowen** *pen.* Rep. of Ireland
107 E2 **Inishowen Head** Rep. of Ireland
107 D2 **Inishtrahull** *i.* Rep. of Ireland
107 D2 **Inishtrahull Sound** *sea chan.* Rep. of Ireland
107 A4 **Inishturk** *i.* Rep. of Ireland
82 E5 **Inkylap** Turkm.
72 D5 **Inland Kaikoura Range** *mts* N.Z.
129 L2 **Innaanganeq** *c.* Greenland
70 D1 **Innamincka** Australia
102 K2 **Inndyr** Norway
Inner Mongolia *aut. reg.* China *see* **Nei Mongol Zizhiqu**
106 C3 **Inner Sound** *sea chan.* U.K.
68 E3 **Innisfail** Australia
112 E7 **Innsbruck** Austria
107 D4 **Inny** *r.* Rep. of Ireland
122 B4 **Inongo** Dem. Rep. Congo
112 I4 **Inowrocław** Poland
120 C2 **In Salah** Alg.
116 H4 **Insar** Rus. Fed.
106 F3 **Insch** U.K.
76 H3 **Inta** Rus. Fed.
159 D2 **Intendente Alvear** Arg.
112 C7 **Interlaken** Switz.
142 E1 **International Falls** U.S.A.
95 G7 **Inubō-zaki** *pt* Japan
132 E2 **Inukjuak** Canada
128 E3 **Inuvik** Canada
106 C4 **Inveraray** U.K.
106 F4 **Inverbervie** U.K.
72 B7 **Invercargill** N.Z.
71 I2 **Inverell** Australia
106 D3 **Invergordon** U.K.
106 E4 **Inverkeithing** U.K.
133 H4 **Inverness** Canada
106 D3 **Inverness** U.K.
145 D6 **Inverness** U.S.A.
106 F3 **Inverurie** U.K.
162 K5 **Investigator Ridge** *sea feature* Indian Ocean
70 B5 **Investigator Strait** Australia
79 G1 **Inya** Rus. Fed.
139 C5 **Inyokern** U.S.A.
140 C3 **Inyo Mountains** U.S.A.
122 D4 **Inyonga** Tanz.
116 H4 **Inza** Rus. Fed.
82 D1 **Inzer** Rus. Fed.
117 G4 **Inzhavino** Rus. Fed.
115 I5 **Ioannina** Greece
91 G4 **Iō-jima** *i.* Japan
95 B9 **Iō-jima** *i.* Japan
143 E4 **Iola** U.S.A.
83 K2 **Iolgo, Khrebet** *mts* Rus. Fed.
106 B4 **Iona** *i.* U.K.
138 C1 **Ione** U.S.A.
134 E4 **Ionia** U.S.A.
115 H5 **Ionian Islands** Greece
114 G6 **Ionian Sea** Greece/Italy
Ionoi Nisoi *is* Greece *see* **Ionian Islands**
90 G1 **Iony, Ostrov** *i.* Rus. Fed.
81 K1 **Iori** *r.* Georgia
115 K6 **Ios** *i.* Greece
134 B5 **Iowa** *r.* U.S.A.
134 A4 **Iowa** *state* U.S.A.
134 B5 **Iowa City** U.S.A.
134 A4 **Iowa Falls** U.S.A.
142 E3 **Iowa Falls** U.S.A.
158 C2 **Ipameri** Brazil
154 D5 **Iparía** Peru
158 D2 **Ipatinga** Brazil
117 G6 **Ipatovo** Rus. Fed.
125 F3 **Ipelegeng** S. Africa
157 A4 **Ipiales** Col.
158 E1 **Ipiaú** Brazil
158 B4 **Ipiranga** Brazil
99 B2 **Ipoh** Malaysia
155 K5 **Ipojuca** *r.* Brazil
158 B2 **Iporá** Brazil
122 C3 **Ippy** Centr. Afr. Rep.
115 L4 **İpsala** Turkey
71 J1 **Ipswich** Australia
105 I5 **Ipswich** U.K.
129 L3 **Iqaluit** Canada
156 B2 **Iquique** Chile
154 D4 **Iquitos** Peru
85 F5 **Īrafshān** *reg.* Iran
95 E7 **Irago-misaki** *pt* Japan
115 K6 **Irakleia** *i.* Greece
Irakleio Greece *see* **Iraklion**
115 K7 **Iraklion** Greece
158 E1 **Iramaia** Brazil
84 D3 **Iran** *country* Asia
99 D2 **Iran, Pegunungan** *mts* Indon.
84 B2 **Īrānshāh** Iran
85 F5 **Īrānshahr** Iran
150 D3 **Irapuato** Mex.
81 I5 **Iraq** *country* Asia
147 G2 **Irasville** U.S.A.
158 B4 **Irati** Brazil
80 E5 **Irbid** Jordan
76 H4 **Irbit** Rus. Fed.
155 J6 **Irecê** Brazil
107 D4 **Ireland, Republic of** *country* Europe
122 C4 **Irema** Dem. Rep. Congo
82 E2 **Irgiz** Kazakh.
82 E2 **Irgiz** *r.* Kazakh.
91 F7 **Irian Jaya** Indon.
81 K2 **Īrī Dāgh** *mt.* Iran
97 B3 **Iriga** Phil.
120 B3 **Irigui** *reg.* Mali/Mauritania
123 D4 **Iringa** Tanz.
87 B4 **Irinjalakuda** India
155 H4 **Iriri** *r.* Brazil
104 B4 **Irish Sea** Rep. of Ireland
155 I4 **Irituia** Brazil
84 C5 **'Irj** *well* Saudi Arabia
90 C1 **Irkutsk** Rus. Fed.
80 D2 **Irmak** Turkey
163 G2 **Irminger Basin** *sea feature* N. Atlantic Ocean
70 B4 **Iron Baron** Australia
135 F2 **Iron Bridge** Canada
146 E3 **Irondequoit** U.S.A.
70 B4 **Iron Knob** Australia
134 C3 **Iron Mountain** *MI* U.S.A.
141 F3 **Iron Mountain** *mt. UT* U.S.A.
134 C2 **Iron River** U.S.A.
143 F4 **Ironton** *MO* U.S.A.
146 B5 **Ironton** *OH* U.S.A.
134 B2 **Ironwood** U.S.A.
147 F2 **Iroquois** Canada
134 D5 **Iroquois** *r.* U.S.A.
97 C3 **Irosin** Phil.
95 F7 **Irō-zaki** *pt* Japan
117 D5 **Irpin'** Ukr.
89 H5 **Irrawaddy** *r.* China/Myanmar
91 B5 **Irrawaddy, Mouths of the** Myanmar
88 C1 **Irshad Pass** Afgh./Pak.
116 I2 **Irta** Rus. Fed.
104 E3 **Irthing** *r.* U.K.
76 H3 **Irtysh** *r.* Kazakh./Rus. Fed.
83 H1 **Irtyshsk** Kazakh.
122 C3 **Irumu** Dem. Rep. Congo
111 F1 **Irún** Spain
106 D5 **Irvine** U.K.
140 D5 **Irvine** *CA* U.S.A.
146 B6 **Irvine** *KY* U.S.A.
143 D5 **Irving** U.S.A.
97 B5 **Isabela** Phil.
154 □ **Isabela, Isla** *i. Galapagos Is* Ecuador
150 H5 **Isabelia, Cordillera** *mts* Nicaragua
134 B2 **Isabella** U.S.A.
140 C4 **Isabella Lake** U.S.A.
134 D2 **Isabelle, Point** U.S.A.
102 B1 **Ísafjarðardjúp** *est.* Iceland
102 B1 **Ísafjörður** Iceland
95 B8 **Isahaya** Japan
88 B2 **Isa Khel** Pak.
116 G1 **Isakogorka** Rus. Fed.
157 C4 **Isana** *r.* Col.
106 □ **Isbister** U.K.
114 E4 **Ischia, Isola d'** *i.* Italy
159 C1 **Ischigualasto, Parque Provincial** *nature res.* Arg.
157 A4 **Iscuande** *r.* Col.
95 E7 **Ise** Japan
122 C3 **Isengi** Dem. Rep. Congo
110 H4 **Isère** *r.* France
109 F3 **Iserlohn** Germany
109 H2 **Isernhagen** Germany
114 F4 **Isernia** Italy
95 F6 **Isesaki** Japan
95 E7 **Ise-shima National Park** Japan
95 E7 **Ise-wan** *b.* Japan
120 C4 **Iseyin** Nigeria
Isfahan Iran *see* **Eşfahān**
83 G5 **Isfana** Kyrg.
83 G4 **Isfara** Tajik.
81 J5 **Isḥāq** Iraq
116 I4 **Isheyevka** Rus. Fed.
94 G3 **Ishikari-gawa** *r.* Japan
94 G3 **Ishikari-wan** *b.* Japan
83 F1 **Ishim** *r.* Rus. Fed.
83 F2 **Ishimskoye** Kazakh.
94 G5 **Ishinomaki** Japan
94 G5 **Ishinomaki-wan** *b.* Japan
95 G6 **Ishioka** Japan
95 C8 **Ishizuchi-san** *mt.* Japan
83 G5 **Ishkoshim** Tajik.
88 C1 **Ishkuman** Pak.
134 D2 **Ishpeming** U.S.A.
83 F5 **Ishtixon** Uzbek.
Ishtykhan Uzbek. *see* **Ishtixon**
89 G4 **Ishurdi** Bangl.
154 F7 **Isiboro Sécure, Parque Nacional** *nat. park* Bol.
80 B2 **Işıklı** Turkey
80 B2 **Işıklı Barajı** *resr* Turkey
76 I4 **Isil'kul'** Rus. Fed.
125 I4 **Isipingo** S. Africa
122 C3 **Isiro** Dem. Rep. Congo
85 G2 **Iskabad Canal** Afgh.
83 G4 **Iskandar** Uzbek.
80 F3 **İskenderun** Turkey
80 E1 **İskilip** Turkey
82 C3 **Iskine** Kazakh.
90 A1 **Iskitim** Rus. Fed.
115 K3 **Iskūr** *r.* Bulg.
130 C3 **Iskut** Canada
130 C3 **Iskut** *r.* Canada
80 F3 **Islahiye** Turkey
88 C2 **Islamabad** Pak.
88 C3 **Islam Barrage** Pak.
88 B4 **Islamgarh** Pak.
88 B4 **Islamkot** Pak.
145 D7 **Islamorada** U.S.A.
85 F3 **Islam Qala** Afgh.
97 A4 **Island Bay** Phil.
147 I1 **Island Falls** U.S.A.
70 B3 **Island Lagoon** *salt flat* Australia
131 K4 **Island Lake** Canada
131 K4 **Island Lake** *l.* Canada
134 A2 **Island Lake** *l.* U.S.A.
107 F3 **Island Magee** *pen.* U.K.
140 A1 **Island Mountain** U.S.A.
138 E2 **Island Park** U.S.A.
147 H2 **Island Pond** U.S.A.
72 E1 **Islands, Bay of** N.Z.
106 B5 **Islay** *i.* U.K.
146 E6 **Isle of Wight** U.S.A.
134 C2 **Isle Royale National Park** U.S.A.
81 L1 **İsmayıllı** Azer.
83 G5 **Ismoili Somoní, Qullai** *mt.* Tajik.
103 M3 **Isojoki** Fin.
123 D5 **Isoka** Zambia
102 N2 **Isokylä** Fin.
114 G5 **Isola di Capo Rizzuto** Italy
80 C3 **Isparta** Turkey
115 L3 **Isperikh** Bulg.
85 F5 **Ispikan** Pak.
81 H1 **İspir** Turkey
80 E5 **Israel** *country* Asia
116 H4 **Issa** Rus. Fed.
108 E3 **Isselburg** Germany
120 B4 **Issia** Côte d'Ivoire
81 J6 **Issin** *tourist site* Iraq
110 F4 **Issoire** France
Issyk-Kul' *salt l.* Kyrg. *see* **Ysyk-Köl**
81 I4 **Iṣṭablāt** *tourist site* Iraq
85 H3 **Istādeh-ye Moqor, Āb-e** *l.* Afgh.
80 B1 **İstanbul** Turkey (City Plan **54**)
İstanbul Boğazı *str.* Turkey *see* Bosporus
84 C3 **Istgāh-e Eznā** Iran
115 J5 **Istiaia** Greece
83 H5 **Istik** *r.* Tajik.
157 A3 **Istmina** Col.
145 D7 **Istokpoga, Lake** U.S.A.
Istra *pen.* Croatia *see* **Istria**
110 G5 **Istres** France
114 E2 **Istria** *pen.* Croatia
89 G5 **Iswaripur** Bangl.
82 D1 **Isyangulovo** Rus. Fed.
155 K6 **Itabaianinha** Brazil
155 J6 **Itaberaba** Brazil
158 D2 **Itabira** Brazil
158 D3 **Itabirito** Brazil
158 E1 **Itabuna** Brazil
155 G4 **Itacoatiara** Brazil
158 B3 **Itaguajé** Brazil
158 C3 **Itaí** Brazil
158 A4 **Itaimbey** *r.* Para.
155 G4 **Itaituba** Brazil
156 G3 **Itajaí** Brazil
158 D3 **Itajubá** Brazil
89 F5 **Itaki** India
103 J4 **Italy** *country* Europe
155 K7 **Itamaraju** Brazil
158 D2 **Itamarandiba** Brazil
158 E2 **Itambacuri** Brazil
158 E2 **Itambacuri** *r.* Brazil
158 D2 **Itambé, Pico de** *mt.* Brazil
123 E6 **Itampolo** Madag.
89 H4 **Itanagar** India
158 D1 **Itanguari** *r.* Brazil
158 C4 **Itanhaém** Brazil
158 E2 **Itanhém** Brazil
158 E2 **Itanhém** *r.* Brazil
158 E2 **Itaobím** Brazil
158 C2 **Itapajipe** Brazil
158 E1 **Itaparica, Ilha** *i.* Brazil
158 E1 **Itapebi** Brazil
158 D3 **Itapemirim** Brazil
158 E3 **Itaperuna** Brazil
158 E1 **Itapetinga** Brazil
158 C3 **Itapetininga** Brazil
158 C3 **Itapeva** Brazil
155 K6 **Itapicuru** *r. Bahia* Brazil
155 J5 **Itapicuru** *r.* Brazil
155 J4 **Itapicuru Mirim** Brazil
155 K4 **Itapipoca** Brazil
158 C4 **Itararé** Brazil
158 C3 **Itararé** *r.* Brazil
88 D5 **Itarsi** India
158 B2 **Itarumã** Brazil
97 B1 **Itbayat** *i.* Phil.
130 G1 **Itchen Lake** Canada
115 J5 **Itea** Greece
83 G1 **Itemgen, Ozero** *l.* Kazakh.
134 E4 **Ithaca** *MI* U.S.A.
146 E3 **Ithaca** *NY* U.S.A.
109 H2 **Ith Hils** *ridge* Germany
80 F6 **Ithrah** Saudi Arabia
Itihusa-yama *mt.* Japan *see* **Ichifusa-yama**
122 C3 **Itimbiri** *r.* Dem. Rep. Congo
158 E2 **Itinga** Brazil
158 A2 **Itiquira** Brazil
158 A2 **Itiquira** *r.* Brazil
82 C2 **Itmurinkol', Ozero** *l.* Kazakh.
95 F7 **Itō** Japan
95 E6 **Itoigawa** Japan
114 C4 **Ittiri** *Sardinia* Italy
158 C3 **Itu** Brazil
157 B3 **Ituango** Col.
154 E5 **Ituí** *r.* Brazil
158 D2 **Ituiutaba** Brazil
122 C4 **Itula** Dem. Rep. Congo
158 C2 **Itumbiara** Brazil
155 G2 **Ituni** Guyana
155 I5 **Itupiranga** Brazil
158 B2 **Iturama** Brazil
158 A4 **Iturbe** Para.
90 G2 **Iturup, Ostrov** *i.* Rus. Fed.
154 E5 **Ituxi** *r.* Brazil
112 D4 **Itzehoe** Germany
157 C4 **Iuaretê** Brazil
77 U3 **Iul'tin** Rus. Fed.
157 C4 **Iutica** Brazil
158 B3 **Ivaí** *r.* Brazil
102 N1 **Ivalo** Fin.
102 N1 **Ivalojoki** *r.* Fin.
117 C4 **Ivanava** Belarus
70 F4 **Ivanhoe** Australia
131 J2 **Ivanhoe** *r.* Canada
131 H2 **Ivanhoe Lake** *N.W.T.* Canada
135 F1 **Ivanhoe Lake** *Ont.* Canada
113 N5 **Ivankiv** Ukr.
117 C5 **Ivano-Frankivs'k** Ukr.
82 C1 **Ivanovka** Rus. Fed.
115 K3 **Ivanovo** *tourist site* Bulg.
116 G3 **Ivanovo** Rus. Fed.
116 G3 **Ivanovskaya Oblast'** *admin. div.* Rus. Fed.
141 E4 **Ivanpah Lake** U.S.A.
116 I4 **Ivanteyevka** Rus. Fed.
117 C4 **Ivatsevichy** Belarus
115 L4 **Ivaylovgrad** Bulg.
76 H3 **Ivdel'** Rus. Fed.
158 B3 **Ivinheima** Brazil
158 B3 **Ivinheima** *r.* Brazil
129 N3 **Ivittuut** Greenland
123 E6 **Ivohibe** Madag.
Ivory Coast *country* Africa *see* **Côte d'Ivoire**
114 B2 **Ivrea** Italy
115 L5 **İvrindi** Turkey
117 H7 **Ivris Ugheltekhili** *pass* Georgia
129 K3 **Ivujivik** Canada
113 M4 **Ivyanyets** Belarus
94 G5 **Iwaizumi** Japan
95 G6 **Iwaki** Japan
94 G4 **Iwaki-san** *vol.* Japan
95 C7 **Iwakuni** Japan
94 G3 **Iwamizawa** Japan
94 G5 **Iwate-san** *vol.* Japan
120 C4 **Iwo** Nigeria
Iwo Jima *i.* Japan *see* **Iō-jima**
116 C4 **Iwye** Belarus
108 C4 **Ixelles** Belgium
151 E3 **Ixmiquilpán** Mex.
125 I5 **Ixopo** S. Africa
150 C3 **Ixtlán** Mex.
151 E4 **Ixtlán** Mex.
105 H5 **Ixworth** U.K.
95 C8 **Iyo** Japan
95 C8 **Iyo-nada** *b.* Japan
151 G5 **Izabal, Lago de** *l.* Guat.
94 G3 **Izari-dake** *mt.* Japan
122 D4 **Izazi** Tanz.
117 H7 **Izberbash** Rus. Fed.
113 P3 **Izdeshkovo** Rus. Fed.
108 B4 **Izegem** Belgium
84 C4 **Īzeh** Iran
76 G4 **Izhevsk** Rus. Fed.
76 G3 **Izhma** Rus. Fed.
116 J1 **Izhma** *r.* Rus. Fed.
117 F4 **Izmalkovo** Rus. Fed.
117 D6 **Izmayil** Ukr.
115 L5 **İzmir** Turkey
115 L5 **İzmir Körfezi** *g.* Turkey
80 B1 **İznik Gölü** *l.* Turkey
117 G6 **Izobil'nyy** Rus. Fed.
95 F7 **Izu-hantō** *pen.* Japan
95 A7 **Izuhara** Japan
95 D7 **Izumisano** Japan
95 C7 **Izumo** Japan
160 E3 **Izu-Ogasawara Trench** *sea feature* N. Pacific Ocean
95 F7 **Izu-shotō** *is* Japan
117 C5 **Izyaslav** Ukr.
82 D3 **Izyndy** Kazakh.
117 F5 **Izyum** Ukr.

J

84 E3 **Jaba** *watercourse* Iran
121 F3 **Jabal, Bahr el** *r.* Sudan/Uganda *alt.* **Abiad, Bahr el,** *conv.* **White Nile**
84 C6 **Jabal Dab** Saudi Arabia
111 E3 **Jabalón** *r.* Spain
88 D5 **Jabalpur** India
80 F3 **Jabbūl** Syria
68 D3 **Jabiru** Australia
80 E4 **Jablah** Syria
114 G3 **Jablanica** Bos.-Herz.
155 L5 **Jaboatão** Brazil
158 C3 **Jaboticabal** Brazil
111 F1 **Jaca** Spain
155 J6 **Jacaré** *r.* Brazil
155 G5 **Jacareacanga** Brazil
158 C3 **Jacareí** Brazil
159 C1 **Jáchal** *r.* Arg.
109 K4 **Jáchymov** Czech Rep.
158 E2 **Jacinto** Brazil
154 F5 **Jaciparaná** *r.* Brazil
134 D1 **Jackfish** Canada
135 H3 **Jack Lake** Canada
147 H2 **Jackman** U.S.A.
143 D5 **Jacksboro** U.S.A.
143 G6 **Jackson** *AL* U.S.A.
140 B2 **Jackson** *CA* U.S.A.
146 B6 **Jackson** *KY* U.S.A.
134 E4 **Jackson** *MI* U.S.A.
142 E3 **Jackson** *MN* U.S.A.
143 F4 **Jackson** *MO* U.S.A.
143 F5 **Jackson** *MS* U.S.A.
146 B5 **Jackson** *OH* U.S.A.
145 B5 **Jackson** *TN* U.S.A.
138 E3 **Jackson** *WY* U.S.A.
73 B3 **Jackson, Mount** *mt.* Antarctica
72 B5 **Jackson Head** N.Z.
138 E2 **Jackson Lake** U.S.A.
134 D3 **Jacksonport** U.S.A.
143 E5 **Jacksonville** *AR* U.S.A.
145 D6 **Jacksonville** *FL* U.S.A.
134 B6 **Jacksonville** *IL* U.S.A.
145 E5 **Jacksonville** *NC* U.S.A.
143 E6 **Jacksonville** *TX* U.S.A.
145 D6 **Jacksonville Beach** U.S.A.
149 J5 **Jacmel** Haiti
88 B3 **Jacobabad** Pak.
155 J6 **Jacobina** Brazil
141 F3 **Jacob Lake** U.S.A.
124 F4 **Jacobsdal** S. Africa
133 H4 **Jacques-Cartier, Détroit de** *sea chan.* Canada
133 G4 **Jacques Cartier, Mont** *mt.* Canada
133 G4 **Jacquet River** Canada
159 G1 **Jacuí** *r.* Brazil
155 K6 **Jacuípe** *r.* Brazil
155 I4 **Jacunda** Brazil
158 C4 **Jacupiranga** Brazil
157 C2 **Jacura** Venez.
87 B2 **Jadcherla** India
85 F5 **Jaddi, Ras** *pt* Pak.
109 G1 **Jadebusen** *b.* Germany
114 G2 **Jadovnik** *mt.* Bos.-Herz.
121 D1 **Jādū** Libya
154 C5 **Jaén** Peru
97 B3 **Jaen** Phil.
111 E4 **Jaén** Spain
84 C3 **Ja'farābād** Iran
70 C6 **Jaffa, Cape** Australia
87 B4 **Jaffna** Sri Lanka
147 G3 **Jaffrey** U.S.A.
88 D3 **Jagadhri** India
87 B3 **Jagalur** India
87 C2 **Jagdalpur** India
125 F4 **Jagersfontein** S. Africa
88 D2 **Jaggang** China
85 E5 **Jagīn** *watercourse* Iran
87 C2 **Jagraon** India
109 H5 **Jagst** *r.* Germany
87 B2 **Jagtial** India
159 G2 **Jaguarão** Brazil
159 G2 **Jaguarão** *r.* Brazil/Uruguay
158 C4 **Jaguariaíva** Brazil
84 B5 **Jahām, 'Irq** *des.* Saudi Arabia
Jahanabad India *see* **Jehanabad**
81 L3 **Jahān Dāgh** *mt.* Iran
88 C4 **Jahazpur** India
81 J7 **Jahmah** *well* Iraq
84 D4 **Jahrom** Iran
89 E2 **Jainca** China
88 C4 **Jaipur** India
88 B4 **Jaisalmer** India
88 C4 **Jaisamand Lake** India
88 E5 **Jaisinghnagar** India
88 D5 **Jaitgarh** *h.* India
89 E3 **Jajarkot** Nepal
84 E2 **Jajarm** Iran
114 G2 **Jajce** Bos.-Herz.
89 G4 **Jakar** Bhutan
99 C4 **Jakarta** Indon. (City Plan **50**)
130 C2 **Jakes Corner** Canada
88 B5 **Jakhan** India
85 G4 **Jakin** *mt.* Afgh.
102 L2 **Jäkkvik** Sweden
Jakobshavn Greenland *see* **Ilulissat**
102 M3 **Jakobstad** Fin.
143 C5 **Jal** U.S.A.
85 H3 **Jalālābād** Afgh.
83 H4 **Jalal-Abad** Kyrg.
80 C7 **Jalālah al Baḥrīyah, Jabal** *plat.* Egypt
81 G6 **Jalāmīd, Ḥazm al** *ridge* Saudi Arabia
88 C3 **Jalandhar** India
151 G5 **Jalapa** Guat.
151 E4 **Jalapa** Mex.
150 H5 **Jalapa** Nicaragua
103 M3 **Jalasjärvi** Fin.
81 J4 **Jalawlā'** Iraq
89 G4 **Jaldhaka** *r.* Bangl.
87 B2 **Jaldrug** India
158 B3 **Jales** Brazil
89 F5 **Jaleshwar** India
88 C5 **Jalgaon** *Maharashtra* India
88 D5 **Jalgaon** *Maharashtra* India
81 K6 **Jalībah** Iraq
120 D4 **Jalingo** Nigeria
150 C4 **Jalisco** *state* Mex.
86 C5 **Jalna** India
85 F5 **Jālo** Iran
111 F2 **Jalón** *r.* Spain
150 D3 **Jalostotitlán** Mex.
150 D3 **Jalpa** Mex.
89 G4 **Jalpaiguri** India
151 E3 **Jalpan** Mex.
121 E2 **Jālū** Libya
85 F3 **Jām** *r.* Iran
85 F3 **Jām** *reg.* Iran
85 G3 **Jam, Minaret of** *tourist site* Afgh.
149 I5 **Jamaica** *country* Caribbean Sea
149 I5 **Jamaica Channel** Haiti/Jamaica
81 K3 **Jamalabad** Iran
84 C3 **Jamālābād** Iran
89 G4 **Jamalpur** Bangl.
89 F4 **Jamalpur** India
155 G5 **Jamanxim** *r.* Brazil
99 B3 **Jambi** Indon.
88 C4 **Jambo** India
99 B2 **Jambuair, Tanjung** *pt* Indon.
98 A4 **Jambuair, Tanjung** *pt* Indon.
97 A5 **Jambongan** *i. Sabah* Malaysia
81 J4 **Jambūr** Iraq
87 A1 **Jambusar** India
142 D2 **James** *r. ND* U.S.A.
146 D6 **James** *r. VA* U.S.A.
88 B4 **Jamesabad** Pak.
137 J1 **James Bay** Canada
145 E7 **James Cistern** Bahamas
159 D2 **James Craik** Arg.
129 P2 **Jameson Land** *reg.* Greenland
72 B6 **James Peak** N.Z.
73 B2 **James Ross Island** *i.* Antarctica
129 I3 **James Ross Strait** Canada
70 C4 **Jamestown** Australia
125 G5 **Jamestown** S. Africa
142 D2 **Jamestown** *ND* U.S.A.
146 D3 **Jamestown** *NY* U.S.A.
81 L4 **Jamīlābād** Iran
87 A2 **Jamkhandi** India
87 A2 **Jamkhed** India
87 B3 **Jammalamadugu** India
88 C2 **Jammu** Jammu and Kashmir
88 C2 **Jammu and Kashmir** *terr.* Asia
88 B5 **Jamnagar** India
88 D4 **Jamni** *r.* India
99 C4 **Jampang Kulon** Indon.
88 B3 **Jampur** Pak.
103 N3 **Jämsä** Fin.
103 N3 **Jämsänkoski** Fin.
89 F5 **Jamshedpur** India
89 G5 **Jamuna** *r.* Bangl.
158 D1 **Janaúba** Brazil
158 B2 **Jandaia** Brazil
84 D3 **Jandaq** Iran
88 B2 **Jandola** Pak.
140 B1 **Janesville** *CA* U.S.A.
134 C4 **Janesville** *WI* U.S.A.
85 E3 **Jangal** Iran
89 G4 **Jangipur** India
83 G4 **Jangy-Bazar** Kyrg.
81 K2 **Jānī Beyglū** Iran
109 L2 **Jänickendorf** Germany
100 C2 **Jan Mayen** *terr.* Arctic Ocean
82 C4 **Jaňňa** Turkm.
81 K5 **Jannah** Iraq
85 F3 **Jannatābād** Iran
124 F6 **Jansenville** S. Africa
158 D1 **Januária** Brazil
84 B4 **Janūbī, Al Fulayj al** *watercourse* Saudi Arabia
88 C5 **Jaora** India
94 G5 **Japan** *country* Asia
94 C4 **Japan, Sea of** Pacific Ocean
160 E3 **Japan Basin** *sea feature* Sea of Japan
160 E3 **Japan Trench** *sea feature* N. Pacific Ocean
154 E4 **Japurá** *r.* Brazil
89 H4 **Japvo Mount** India
150 J7 **Jaqué** Panama
80 G3 **Jarābulus** Syria
158 A3 **Jaraguari** Brazil
80 E5 **Jarash** Jordan
158 A3 **Jardim** Brazil
96 B2 **Jargalang** China
90 D2 **Jargalant** Mongolia
81 J4 **Jarmo** *tourist site* Iraq
103 L4 **Järna** Sweden
112 H5 **Jarocin** Poland
113 K5 **Jarosław** Poland
102 K3 **Järpen** Sweden
83 F5 **Jarqo'rg'o'n** Uzbek.
84 C4 **Jarrāhi** *watercourse* Iran
92 B2 **Jartai** China
154 F6 **Jarú** Brazil
103 N4 **Järvakandi** Estonia
103 N3 **Järvenpää** Fin.
67 I4 **Jarvis Island** *terr.* Pacific Ocean
88 B5 **Jasdan** India
85 E5 **Jāsk** Iran
82 D4 **Jasliq** Uzbek.
113 J6 **Jasło** Poland
156 D8 **Jason Islands** Falkland Is
73 B2 **Jason Peninsula** *pen.* Antarctica
130 F4 **Jasper** Canada
145 C5 **Jasper** *AL* U.S.A.
143 E4 **Jasper** *AR* U.S.A.
145 D6 **Jasper** *FL* U.S.A.
134 C4 **Jasper** *IN* U.S.A.
146 E3 **Jasper** *NY* U.S.A.
146 B5 **Jasper** *OH* U.S.A.
143 E6 **Jasper** *TX* U.S.A.
130 F4 **Jasper National Park** Canada
81 J5 **Jaṣṣān** Iraq
113 I6 **Jastrzębie-Zdrój** Poland
88 C4 **Jaswantpura** India
113 I7 **Jászberény** Hungary
158 B2 **Jataí** Brazil
155 G4 **Jatapu** *r.* Brazil
87 A2 **Jath** India
88 B4 **Jati** Pak.
88 B3 **Jatoi** Pak.
158 C3 **Jaú** Brazil
154 F4 **Jaú** *r.* Brazil
154 F4 **Jaú, Parque Nacional do** *nat. park* Brazil
157 E5 **Jauaperi** *r.* Brazil
157 D3 **Jaua Sarisariñama, Parque Nacional** *nat. park* Venez.
103 M4 **Jaunlutriņi** Latvia
103 N4 **Jaunpiebalga** Latvia
89 E4 **Jaunpur** India
85 F4 **Jauri** Iran
158 A2 **Jauru** Brazil
158 B2 **Jauru** *r.* Brazil
117 G7 **Java** Georgia
99 C4 **Java** *i.* Indon.
87 B3 **Javadi Hills** India
85 G3 **Javand** Afgh.
162 L5 **Java Ridge** *sea feature* Indian Ocean
90 D2 **Javarthushuu** Mongolia
Java Sea *sea* Indon. *see* **Jawa, Laut**
162 K5 **Java Trench** *sea feature* Indian Ocean
109 J2 **Jävenitz** Germany
Jawa *i.* Indon. *see* **Java**
99 D3 **Jawa, Laut** *sea* Indon.
88 C4 **Jawad** India
88 B4 **Jawai** *r.* India
81 F3 **Jawbān Bayk** Syria
88 C6 **Jawhar** India
122 E3 **Jawhar** Somalia
112 H5 **Jawor** Poland
91 F7 **Jaya, Puncak** *mt.* Indon.
91 G7 **Jayapura** Indon.
89 F4 **Jaynagar** India
80 F5 **Jayrūd** Syria
85 E5 **Jaz Mūrīān, Hāmūn-e** *salt marsh* Iran
81 L3 **Jazvān** Iran
134 D5 **J. C. Murphey Lake** U.S.A.
141 E4 **Jean** U.S.A.
130 E2 **Jean Marie River** Canada
133 G2 **Jeannin, Lac** *l.* Canada
84 E4 **Jebāl Bārez, Kūh-e** *mts* Iran
120 C4 **Jebba** Nigeria
82 C5 **Jebel** Turkm.
121 E3 **Jebel Abyad Plateau** Sudan
88 B4 **Jech Doab** *lowland* Pak.
106 F5 **Jedburgh** U.K.
86 A5 **Jeddah** Saudi Arabia
114 C6 **Jedeida** Tunisia
109 J1 **Jeetze** *r.* Germany
147 F3 **Jefferson** *NY* U.S.A.
134 C4 **Jefferson** *WI* U.S.A.
138 E2 **Jefferson** *r.* U.S.A.
140 D2 **Jefferson, Mount** U.S.A.
138 B2 **Jefferson, Mount** *vol.* U.S.A.
142 E4 **Jefferson City** U.S.A.
144 C4 **Jeffersonville** U.S.A.
124 F7 **Jeffreys Bay** S. Africa
89 F4 **Jehanabad** India
156 E2 **Jejuí Guazú** *r.* Para.
103 N4 **Jēkabpils** Latvia
112 G5 **Jelenia Góra** Poland
89 G4 **Jelep La** *pass* China
103 M4 **Jelgava** Latvia
146 A6 **Jellico** U.S.A.
98 C5 **Jemaja** *i.* Indon.
99 D4 **Jember** Indon.
83 K3 **Jeminay** Kazakh.
99 B2 **Jempang, Danau** *l.* Indon.
109 J4 **Jena** Germany
120 C1 **Jendouba** Tunisia
Jengish Chokusu *mt.* China/Kyrg. *see* **Pobeda Peak**
80 E5 **Jenin** West Bank
146 B6 **Jenkins** U.S.A.
140 A2 **Jenner** U.S.A.
143 E6 **Jennings** U.S.A.
131 J4 **Jenpeg** Canada
70 E6 **Jeparit** Australia
158 E1 **Jequié** Brazil
158 D2 **Jequitaí** Brazil
158 D2 **Jequitaí** *r.* Brazil
158 E2 **Jequitinhonha** Brazil
158 E2 **Jequitinhonha** *r.* Brazil
98 B5 **Jerantut** Malaysia
121 F4 **Jerbar** Sudan
149 J5 **Jérémie** Haiti
150 D3 **Jerez** Mex.
111 C4 **Jerez de la Frontera** Spain
111 C3 **Jerez de los Caballeros** Spain
Jergol Norway *see* **Jergol**
102 N1 **Jergol** Norway
115 I5 **Jergucat** Albania
80 E6 **Jericho** West Bank
109 K2 **Jerichow** Germany
71 F5 **Jerilderie** Australia
81 J2 **Jermuk** Armenia
138 D3 **Jerome** U.S.A.
110 C2 **Jersey** *i.* U.K.
147 F4 **Jersey City** U.S.A.
146 E4 **Jersey Shore** U.S.A.
144 B4 **Jerseyville** U.S.A.
155 J5 **Jerumenha** Brazil
80 E6 **Jerusalem** Israel/West Bank (City Plan **54**)
71 I5 **Jervis Bay** Australia
71 I5 **Jervis Bay** *b.* Australia
71 I5 **Jervis Bay Territory** *admin. div.* Australia
114 F1 **Jesenice** Slovenia
114 E3 **Jesi** Italy
109 K3 **Jessen** Germany
103 J3 **Jessheim** Norway
89 G5 **Jessore** Bangl.
109 H1 **Jesteburg** Germany
145 D6 **Jesup** U.S.A.
151 F4 **Jesús Carranza** Mex.
159 D1 **Jesús María** Arg.
88 B5 **Jetalsar** India
142 D4 **Jetmore** U.S.A.
109 F1 **Jever** Germany
89 F4 **Jha Jha** India
88 D3 **Jhajjar** India
88 C4 **Jhajju** India
88 A3 **Jhal** Pak.
89 G5 **Jhalakati** Bangl.
85 G5 **Jhal Jhao** Pak.
88 C3 **Jhang** Pak.
88 D4 **Jhansi** India
89 F5 **Jharia** India
89 F4 **Jharkhand** *state* India
87 D1 **Jharsuguda** India
88 B3 **Jhatpat** Pak.
88 C2 **Jhelum** Pak.
88 C2 **Jhelum** *r.* Pak.
89 G5 **Jhenaidah** Bangl.
88 B4 **Jhudo** Pak.
89 F4 **Jhumritilaiya** India
88 C3 **Jhunjhunun** India
92 C3 **Jiachuan** China
92 F4 **Jiading** China
93 D5 **Jiahe** China
93 B4 **Jiajiang** China
92 B3 **Jialing Jiang** *r.* China
94 B1 **Jiamusi** China
93 E5 **Ji'an** China
93 E5 **Ji'an** China
96 D3 **Ji'an** China
92 F1 **Jianchang** China
93 F4 **Jiande** China
93 C7 **Jianfeng** China
93 B4 **Jiang'an** China
93 A6 **Jiangcheng** China
93 B5 **Jiangchuan** China
Jiange China *see* **Pu'an**
93 C4 **Jiangjin** China
93 C5 **Jiangkou** China
93 E5 **Jiangle** China
92 B3 **Jiangluozhen** China
93 D6 **Jiangmen** China
93 E4 **Jiangshan** China
92 F3 **Jiangsu** *prov.* China
93 E5 **Jiangxi** *prov.* China
93 E4 **Jiangxia** China
92 D3 **Jiangxian** China
92 F3 **Jiangyan** China
92 F4 **Jiangyin** China
93 D5 **Jiangyong** China
92 B4 **Jiangyou** China
92 F3 **Jianhu** China
93 D6 **Jian Jiang** *r.* China
93 A5 **Jiankang** China
93 D4 **Jianli** China
93 E5 **Jianning** China
93 F5 **Jian'ou** China
92 F1 **Jianping** *Liaoning* China
92 F1 **Jianping** *Liaoning* China
92 E2 **Jianqiao** China
93 C4 **Jianshi** China
93 B6 **Jianshui** China
93 F5 **Jianyang** *Fujian* China
93 B4 **Jianyang** *Sichuan* China
92 D2 **Jiaocheng** China
96 D2 **Jiaohe** China
Jiaojiang China *see* **Taizhou**
96 A2 **Jiaolai He** *r. Nei Mongol* China
92 F2 **Jiaolai He** *r. Shandong* China
93 E5 **Jiaoling** China
92 F3 **Jiaonan** China
92 F2 **Jiaozhou** China
92 F2 **Jiaozhou Wan** *b.* China
92 D3 **Jiaozuo** China
96 D2 **Jiapigou** China
83 I5 **Jiashi** China
92 D2 **Jiaxian** China
92 F4 **Jiaxing** China
93 D4 **Jiayu** China
90 B3 **Jiayuguan** China
93 E6 **Jiazi** China
150 I7 **Jicarón, Isla** *i.* Panama
Jiddah Saudi Arabia *see* **Jeddah**
80 D6 **Jiddī, Jabal al** *h.* Egypt
96 F1 **Jidong** China
92 B2 **Jieheba** China
102 L1 **Jiehkkevárri** *mt.* Norway
Jiehkkevarri *mt.* Norway *see* **Jiehkkevárri**
93 E6 **Jieshi** China
93 E6 **Jieshi Wan** *b.* China
92 E3 **Jieshou** China
Ješjávri *l.* Norway *see* **Iešjávri**
93 E6 **Jiexi** China
92 D2 **Jiexiu** China
93 E6 **Jieyang** China
103 N5 **Jieznas** Lith.
82 E4 **Jigerbent** Turkm.
92 A3 **Jigzhi** China
112 G6 **Jihlava** Czech Rep.
85 F3 **Jija Sarai** Afgh.
122 E3 **Jijiga** Eth.
93 A4 **Jijū** China
121 E2 **Jilf al Kabīr, Haḍabat al** *plat.* Egypt
85 H3 **Jilga** *r.* Afgh.
122 E3 **Jilib** Somalia
96 D2 **Jilin** China
96 C2 **Jilin** *prov.* China
92 A2 **Jiling** China
96 C2 **Jilin Hada Ling** *mts* China
122 D3 **Jima** Eth.
150 C2 **Jiménez** Mex.
150 D1 **Jiménez** Mex.
151 E2 **Jiménez** Mex.
92 F2 **Jimo** China
147 F4 **Jim Thorpe** U.S.A.
92 E2 **Jinan** China
92 B2 **Jinchang** China
92 D3 **Jincheng** China
92 B4 **Jinchuan** China
88 D3 **Jind** India
71 H6 **Jindabyne** Australia
71 G5 **Jindera** Australia
112 G6 **Jindřichův Hradec** Czech Rep.
93 E4 **Jing'an** China
92 C2 **Jingbian** China
92 C3 **Jingchuan** China
93 F4 **Jingde** China
93 E4 **Jingdezhen** China
93 E5 **Jinggangshan** China
93 E4 **Jinggongqiao** China
92 E2 **Jinghai** China
83 J3 **Jinghe** China
92 C3 **Jing He** *r.* China
91 C4 **Jinghong** China
92 F3 **Jingjiang** China
92 D2 **Jingle** China
92 D4 **Jingmen** China
92 C3 **Jingning** China
92 E1 **Jingpeng** China
96 E2 **Jingpo** China
96 E2 **Jingpo Hu** *l.* China
92 B2 **Jingtai** China
93 C6 **Jingxi** China
93 F4 **Jingxian** China

Khuis 187

82 C2 Karakol' Kazakh.
83 H4 Kara-Köl Kyrg.
83 I4 Karakol Kyrg.
83 I4 Karakol Kyrg.
88 D2 Karakoram Pass China/Jammu and Kashmir
79 F3 Karakoram Range mts Asia
122 D2 Kara K'orē Eth.
83 G3 Karakoyyn, Ozero salt l. Kazakh.
Karakul' Uzbek. see Qorako'l
82 E1 Karakul'skoye Rus. Fed.
83 I3 Karakum Kazakh.
Karakum, Peski des. Kazakh. see Karakum Desert
82 C3 Karakum Desert Kazakh.
85 F2 Karakum Desert Turkm.
Karakumskiy Kanal canal Turkm. see Garagum Kanaly
Kara Kumy des. Turkm. see Garagum
Karakumy, Peski des. Turkm. see Karakum Desert
81 I1 Karakurt Turkey
103 M4 Karala Estonia
80 D3 Karaman Turkey
80 B3 Karamanlı Turkey
79 G2 Karamay China
88 C1 Karambar Pass Afgh./Pak.
72 D4 Karamea N.Z.
72 C4 Karamea Bight b. N.Z.
82 F2 Karamendy Kazakh.
Karamet-Niyaz Turkm. see Garamätnyýaz
89 F1 Karamiran China
89 F1 Karamiran Shankou pass China
80 B1 Karamürsel Turkey
116 D3 Karamyshevo Rus. Fed.
84 C5 Karān i. Saudi Arabia
88 D5 Karanja India
87 B2 Karanja r. India
89 F5 Karanjia India
88 C3 Karanpura India
83 I1 Karaoba Kazakh.
83 H3 Karaoy Almatinskaya Oblast' Kazakh.
83 H3 Karaoy Almatinskaya Oblast' Kazakh.
82 F3 Karaozek Kazakh.
80 D3 Karapınar Turkey
83 I4 Karaqi China
124 B3 Karas admin. reg. Namibia
124 B3 Karas watercourse Namibia
83 I4 Kara-Say Kyrg.
123 B6 Karasburg Namibia
76 I2 Kara Sea Rus. Fed.
83 H2 Karashoky Kazakh.
Kárášjohka Norway see Karasjok
102 N1 Karasjok Norway
83 H2 Karasor Kazakh.
83 H2 Karasor, Ozero salt l. Karagandinskaya Oblast' Kazakh.
83 H1 Karasor, Ozero salt l. Pavlodarskaya Oblast' Kazakh.
83 H3 Karasu Karagandinskaya Oblast' Kazakh.
82 F1 Karasu Kustanayskaya Oblast' Kazakh.
83 H1 Karasu r. Kazakh.
80 C1 Karasu Turkey
81 I2 Karasu r. Turkey
83 I1 Karasuk Rus. Fed.
83 H4 Kara-Suu Kyrg.
83 K3 Karatal Kazakh.
80 E3 Karataş Turkey
80 E3 Karataş Burun pt Turkey
83 G4 Karatau Kazakh.
83 F3 Karatau, Khrebet mts Kazakh.
Karatax Shan mts China see Karakax Shan
98 A3 Karathuri Myanmar
87 B4 Karativu i. Sri Lanka
82 C2 Karatobe Kazakh.
82 D3 Karatobe, Mys pt Kazakh.
82 D3 Karatogay Kazakh.
83 I3 Karatol r. Kazakh.
82 E1 Karatomarskoye Vodokhranilishche resr Kazakh.
82 C3 Karaton Kazakh.
89 G4 Karatoya r. Bangl.
95 A8 Karatsu Japan
95 C7 Karatung i. Indon.
82 F2 Kara-Turgay r. Kazakh.
83 I2 Karaul Kazakh.
Karaulbazar Uzbek. see Qorovulbozor
88 D4 Karauli India
81 I1 Karaurgan Turkey
99 C4 Karawang Indon.
83 J4 Karayulgan China
83 G2 Karazhal Kazakh.
82 B3 Karazhanbas Kazakh.
Karazhar Uzbek. see Qorajar
83 H3 Karazhingil Kazakh.
81 J5 Karbalā' Iraq
109 G4 Karben Germany
83 H2 Karbushevka Kazakh.
113 J7 Karcag Hungary
108 F4 Karden Germany
115 I5 Karditsa Greece
103 M4 Kärdla Estonia
125 G4 Karee S. Africa
124 D5 Kareeberge mts S. Africa
121 F3 Kareima Sudan
117 G7 K'areli Georgia
88 D5 Kareli India
116 E2 Kareliya, Respublika aut. rep. Rus. Fed.
90 D1 Karenga r. Rus. Fed.
88 D4 Karera India
102 M1 Karesuando Sweden
85 F5 Kārevāndar Iran
82 C2 Kargala Rus. Fed.
117 H7 Kargalinskaya Rus. Fed.
82 D2 Kargalinskoye Kazakh.
83 H2 Kargaly Karagandinskaya Oblast' Kazakh.
83 J2 Kargaly Vostochnyy Kazakhstan Kazakh.
81 H2 Kargapazarı Dağları mts Turkey
80 E1 Kargı Turkey
88 D2 Kargil Jammu and Kashmir
116 F2 Kargopol' Rus. Fed.
84 E5 Kargūshkī Iran
Karlholmsbruk Sweden see Karlholmsbruk
123 C5 Kariba Zimbabwe
123 C5 Kariba, Lake resr Zambia/Zimbabwe
94 F3 Kariba-yama vol. Japan
124 E6 Kariega r. S. Africa
102 N1 Karigasniemi Fin.
103 M3 Karijoki Fin.
72 D1 Karikari, Cape N.Z.
84 D3 Karīmābād Iran
99 C3 Karimata, Pulau-pulau is Indon.
99 C3 Karimata, Selat str. Indon.
87 B2 Karimnagar India
99 D4 Karimunjawa, Pulau-pulau is Indon.
122 E2 Karin Somalia
84 E3 Karit Iran
87 A2 Karjat India
89 F5 Karkai r. India
87 A3 Karkal India
83 H2 Karkaralinsk Kazakh.
97 C5 Karkaralong, Kepulauan is Indon.
68 E2 Karkar Island P.N.G.
84 C4 Karkheh, Rūdkhāneh-ye r. Iran
117 E6 Karkinits'ka Zatoka g. Ukr.
103 N3 Kärkölä Fin.
103 N4 Karksi-Nuia Estonia
103 L3 Karlholmsbruk Sweden
81 H2 Karlıova Turkey
117 E5 Karlivka Ukr.
Karl-Marx-Stadt Germany see Chemnitz
114 F2 Karlovac Croatia
115 K3 Karlovo Bulg.
112 F5 Karlovy Vary Czech Rep.
109 G6 Karlsbad Germany
103 K4 Karlsborg Sweden
103 K4 Karlshamn Sweden
103 K4 Karlskoga Sweden
103 K4 Karlskrona Sweden
109 G5 Karlsruhe Germany
103 K4 Karlstad Sweden
103 K4 Karlstad U.S.A.
142 D1 Karlstad U.S.A.
109 H5 Karlstadt Germany
116 D4 Karma Belarus
87 A2 Karmala India
Karmanovka Kazakh. see Kyrkopa
103 I4 Karmøy i. Norway
89 H5 Karnafuli Reservoir Bangl.
88 D3 Karnal India
89 E3 Karnali r. Nepal
87 A3 Karnataka state India
115 L3 Karnobat Bulg.
85 G5 Karodi Pak.
123 C5 Karoi Zimbabwe
89 G3 Karo La pass China
89 H4 Karong India
123 D4 Karonga Malawi
83 I4 Karool-Döbö Kyrg.
124 E6 Karoo National Park S. Africa
70 C5 Karoonda Australia
88 B3 Karor Pak.
122 D2 Karora Eritrea
109 K1 Karow Germany
115 L7 Karpathos i. Greece
115 L6 Karpathou, Steno sea chan. Greece
115 I5 Karpenisi Greece
116 H1 Karpogory Rus. Fed.
68 B4 Karratha Australia
84 C4 Karrī Iran
85 F3 Karrukh Afgh.
81 I1 Kars Turkey
103 N3 Kärsämäki Fin.
103 N4 Kārsava Latvia
Karshi Turkm. see Garşy
Karshi Uzbek. see Qarshi
89 G4 Karsiyang India
76 G3 Karskiye Vorota, Proliv str. Rus. Fed.
Karskoye More sea Rus. Fed. see Kara Sea
109 J1 Karstädt Germany
102 N3 Karstula Fin.
80 B1 Kartal Turkey
82 E1 Kartaly Rus. Fed.
102 N3 Karttula Fin.
84 C4 Karun, Kūh-e h. Iran
84 C4 Kārūn, Rūd-e r. Iran
87 B4 Karur India
103 M3 Karvia Fin.
102 N3 Karvianjoki r. Fin.
87 A3 Karwar India
90 D1 Karymskoye Rus. Fed.
82 D2 Karynzharyk, Peski des. Kazakh.
115 K5 Karystos Greece
80 B3 Kaş Turkey
132 C3 Kasabonika Canada
132 C3 Kasabonika Lake Canada
Kasai r. Dem. Rep. Congo see Kasaï
122 B4 Kasaï r. Dem. Rep. Congo
123 C5 Kasaji Dem. Rep. Congo
123 D5 Kasama Zambia
Kasan Uzbek. see Koson
123 C5 Kasane Botswana
122 B4 Kasangulu Dem. Rep. Congo
Kasansay Uzbek. see Kosonsoy
87 A3 Kasaragod India
131 I2 Kasba Lake Canada
120 B1 Kasba Tadla Morocco
95 B9 Kaseda Japan
81 K4 Kāseh Garān Iran
123 C5 Kasempa Zambia
123 C5 Kasenga Dem. Rep. Congo
122 C4 Kasese Dem. Rep. Congo
122 D3 Kasese Uganda
88 D4 Kasganj India
84 C3 Kāshān Iran
132 D3 Kashechewan Canada
Kashgar China see Kashi
83 I5 Kashi China
95 D7 Kashihara Japan
95 B8 Kashima Japan
95 G6 Kashima-nada b. Japan
116 F3 Kashin Rus. Fed.
88 D3 Kashipur India
95 F6 Kashiwazaki Japan
81 K5 Kashkan r. Iran
83 H3 Kashkanteniz Kazakh.
84 D4 Kashku'iyeh Iran
85 E3 Kāshmar Iran
88 C2 Kashmir, Vale of reg. India
88 B3 Kashmor Pak.
85 H3 Kashmund reg. Afgh.
122 C4 Kashyukulu Dem. Rep. Congo
116 G4 Kasimov Rus. Fed.
144 B4 Kaskaskia r. U.S.A.
131 K3 Kaskattama r. Canada
83 I4 Kaskelen Kazakh.
103 M3 Kaskinen Fin.
122 C4 Kasongo Dem. Rep. Congo
122 B4 Kasongo-Lunda Dem. Rep. Congo
115 L7 Kasos i. Greece
115 L7 Kasou, Steno sea chan. Greece
117 H7 Kaspi Georgia
117 H7 Kaspiysk Rus. Fed.
113 O3 Kasplya Rus. Fed.
121 F3 Kassala Sudan
115 J4 Kassandra pen. Greece
115 J4 Kassandras, Kolpos b. Greece
109 H3 Kassel Germany
120 C1 Kasserine Tunisia
134 A3 Kasson U.S.A.
80 D1 Kastamonu Turkey
108 F4 Kastellaun Germany
115 J7 Kastelli Greece
108 C3 Kasterlee Belgium
115 I4 Kastoria Greece
116 E4 Kastsyukovichy Belarus
95 E7 Kasugai Japan
122 D4 Kasulu Tanz.
95 D7 Kasumi Japan
95 G6 Kasumiga-ura l. Japan
117 I7 Kasumkent Rus. Fed.
123 D5 Kasungu Malawi
88 C3 Kasur Pak.
147 I2 Katahdin, Mount U.S.A.
88 D2 Kataklik Jammu and Kashmir
122 C4 Katako-Kombe Dem. Rep. Congo
88 D5 Katangi India
68 B5 Katanning Australia
85 H3 Katawaz Afgh.
122 C4 Katea Dem. Rep. Congo
115 J4 Katerini Greece
130 C3 Kate's Needle mt. Canada/U.S.A.
123 D5 Katete Zambia
87 C1 Katghora India
90 B4 Katha Myanmar
68 D3 Katherine r. Australia
88 B5 Kathiawar pen. India
87 C4 Kathiraveli Sri Lanka
Kathlehong S. Africa see Katlehong
89 F4 Kathmandu Nepal
124 E3 Kathu S. Africa
88 C2 Kathua Jammu and Kashmir
120 B3 Kati Mali
89 F4 Katihar India
72 E2 Katikati N.Z.
125 G6 Katikati S. Africa
Kati-Kati S. Africa see Katikati
123 C5 Katima Mulilo Namibia
120 B4 Katiola Côte d'Ivoire
124 D4 Katkop Hills S. Africa
125 H3 Katlehong S. Africa
115 I5 Kato Achaïa Greece
88 D5 Katol India
98 □ Katong Sing.
83 K2 Katon-Karagay Kazakh.
71 I4 Katoomba Australia
113 I5 Katowice Poland
89 G5 Katoya India
106 D4 Katrine, Loch l. U.K.
103 L4 Katrineholm Sweden
120 C3 Katsina Nigeria
120 C4 Katsina-Ala Nigeria
95 G7 Katsuura Japan
95 E6 Katsuyama Japan
133 G2 Kattaktoc, Cap c. Canada
Kattakurgan Uzbek. see Kattaqo'rg'on
82 F5 Kattaqo'rg'on Uzbek.
85 G3 Kattasang Hills Afgh.
103 J4 Kattegat str. Denmark/Sweden
83 K1 Katun' r. Rus. Fed.
88 B3 Katuri Pak.
108 C2 Katwijk aan Zee Neth.
109 H5 Katzenbuckel h. Germany
Kauai i. U.S.A. see Kaua'i
140 □2 Kaua'i i. U.S.A.
Kauai Channel U.S.A. see Kaua'i Channel
140 □2 Kaua'i Channel U.S.A.
109 F4 Kaub Germany
109 H3 Kaufungen Germany
102 M3 Kauhajoki Fin.
102 M3 Kauhava Fin.
102 N2 Kaukonen Fin.
140 □2 Ka'ula i. U.S.A.
Kaula i. U.S.A. see Ka'ula
140 □2 Kaulakahi Channel U.S.A.
133 H2 Kaumajet Mountains Canada
140 □2 Kaunakakai U.S.A.
103 M5 Kaunas Lith.
103 N4 Kaunata Latvia
82 C4 Kaundy, Vpadina depr. Kazakh.
120 C3 Kaura-Namoda Nigeria
93 □ Kau Sai Chau i. Hong Kong China
102 M3 Kaustinen Fin.
102 M1 Kautokeino Norway
98 A3 Kau-ye Kyun i. Myanmar
115 J4 Kavadarci Macedonia
80 F1 Kavak Turkey
115 K4 Kavala Greece
94 D2 Kavalerovo Rus. Fed.
87 C3 Kavali India
84 D4 Kavār Iran
87 A4 Kavaratti atoll India
115 M3 Kavarna Bulg.
87 B4 Kaveri r. India
Kavīr salt flat Iran see Daqq-e Sorkh, Kavīr-e
Kavīr salt flat Iran see Siāh Kūh, Kavīr-e
84 E3 Kavīr, Chāh-e well Iran
84 D3 Kavīr, Dasht-e des. Iran
95 F7 Kawagoe Japan
95 F7 Kawaguchi Japan
140 □2 Kawaihae U.S.A.
72 E2 Kawakawa N.Z.
123 C4 Kawambwa Zambia
132 E5 Kawartha Lakes Canada
95 F7 Kawasaki Japan
72 E2 Kawau Island N.Z.
133 G2 Kawawachikamach Canada
72 F3 Kawerau N.Z.
72 E3 Kawhia N.Z.
72 E3 Kawhia Harbour N.Z.
140 D3 Kawich Range mts U.S.A.
98 A1 Kawkareik Myanmar
98 A1 Kawludo Myanmar
84 E6 Kawr, Jabal mt. Oman
98 A3 Kawthaung Myanmar
83 I5 Kaxgar He r. China
83 J4 Kax He r. China
120 B3 Kaya Burkina
80 F2 Kayadibi Turkey
99 E2 Kayan r. Indon.
122 C4 Kayanza Burundi
87 B4 Kayankulam India
138 F3 Kaycee U.S.A.
82 D3 Kaydak, Sor dry lake Kazakh.
123 C4 Kayembe-Mukulu Dem. Rep. Congo
141 G3 Kayenta U.S.A.
120 A3 Kayes Mali
82 F2 Kayga Kazakh.
120 A4 Kayima Sierra Leone
83 H1 Kaymanachikha Kazakh.
83 I2 Kaynar Vostochnyy Kazakhstan Kazakh.
83 H4 Kaynar Zhambylskaya Oblast' Kazakh.
80 F2 Kaynar Turkey
80 F3 Kaypak Turkey
117 H5 Kaysatskoye Rus. Fed.
80 E2 Kayseri Turkey
99 B3 Kayuagung Indon.
76 J3 Kayyerkan Rus. Fed.
83 H4 Kayyngdy Kyrg.
77 O2 Kazach'ye Rus. Fed.
Kazakhdar'ya Uzbek. see Qozoqdaryo
83 G2 Kazakhskiy Melkosopochnik plain Kazakh.
82 C4 Kazakhskiy Zaliv b. Kazakh.
82 D3 Kazakhstan country Asia
83 G2 Kazalinsk Kazakh.
131 J2 Kazan r. Canada
116 I4 Kazan' Rus. Fed.
80 D3 Kazancı Turkey
116 I4 Kazanka r. Rus. Fed
115 K3 Kazanlŭk Bulg.
Kazan-rettō is Japan see Volcano Islands
117 G5 Kazanskaya Rus. Fed.
83 H4 Kazarman Kyrg.
82 D2 Kazatskiy Kazakh.
117 H7 Kazbek mt. Georgia/Rus. Fed.
115 L5 Kaz Dağı mts Turkey
84 C4 Kāzerūn Iran
116 I2 Kazhim Rus. Fed.
85 F5 Kazhmak r. Pak.
113 J6 Kazincbarcika Hungary
89 H4 Kaziranga National Park India
117 H7 Kazret'i Georgia
82 B2 Kaztalovka Kazakh.
94 G4 Kazuno Japan
83 G4 Kazygurt Kazakh.
76 H3 Kazymskiy Mys Rus. Fed.
115 K6 Kea i. Greece
107 E3 Keady U.K.
140 □2 Kealakekua Bay U.S.A.
141 G4 Keams Canyon U.S.A.
142 D3 Kearney U.S.A.
141 G5 Kearny U.S.A.
80 G2 Keban Turkey
80 G2 Keban Barajı resr Turkey
120 A3 Kébémèr Senegal
80 F4 Kebīr, Nahr al r. Lebanon/Syria
121 E3 Kebkabiya Sudan
102 L2 Kebnekaise mt. Sweden
106 B2 Kebock Head U.K.
122 E3 K'ebrī Dehar Eth.
99 C4 Kebumen Indon.
130 D3 Kechika r. Canada
80 C3 Keçiborlu Turkey
113 I7 Kecskemét Hungary
81 G2 K'eda Georgia
103 M5 Kėdainiai Lith.
88 D3 Kedar Kantha mt. India
89 F4 Kedarnath Peak India
133 G4 Kedgwick Canada
99 D4 Kediri Indon.
120 A3 Kédougou Senegal
130 D2 Keele r. Canada
130 C2 Keele Peak Canada
139 C4 Keeler U.S.A.
Keeling Is terr. Indian Ocean see Cocos Islands
106 F4 Keen, Mount h. U.K.
97 A5 Keenapusan i. Phil.
147 G3 Keene U.S.A.
71 I3 Keepit, Lake resr Australia
108 C3 Keerbergen Belgium
123 B6 Keetmanshoop Namibia
131 K6 Keewatin Canada
131 K5 Keewatin U.S.A.
Kefallonia i. Greece see Cephalonia
91 E7 Kefamenanu Indon.
102 B2 Keflavík Iceland
87 C5 Kegalla Sri Lanka
83 I4 Kegen Kazakh.
82 D4 Kegeyli Uzbek.
133 G2 Keglo, Baie de b. Canada
117 H6 Kegul'ta Rus. Fed.
103 N4 Kehra Estonia
104 F4 Keighley U.K.
103 N4 Keila Estonia
124 D4 Keimoes S. Africa
102 N3 Keitele Fin.
102 N3 Keitele l. Fin.
70 D6 Keith Australia
106 F3 Keith U.K.
130 E1 Keith Arm b. Canada
133 G5 Kejimkujik National Park Canada
140 □2 Kekaha U.S.A.
113 J7 Kékes mt. Hungary
88 C4 Kekri India
79 F6 Kelai i. Maldives
92 D2 Kelan China
Kelang Malaysia see Klang
98 B4 Kelantan r. Malaysia
108 E4 Kelberg Germany
83 G4 Keles Uzbek.
109 J6 Kelheim Germany
114 D6 Kelibia Tunisia
82 F5 Kelif Turkm.
Kelifskiy Uzboy marsh Turkm. see Kelif Uzboýy
82 E5 Kelif Uzboýy marsh Turkm.
109 G4 Kelkheim (Taunus) Germany
81 G1 Kelkit Turkey
80 F1 Kelkit r. Turkey
130 E2 Keller Lake Canada
83 G1 Kellerovka Kazakh.
146 B4 Kelleys Island U.S.A.
138 C2 Kellogg U.S.A.
102 O2 Kelloselkä Fin.
107 E4 Kells Rep. of Ireland
108 E4 Kelmis Belgium
121 D4 Kélo Chad
130 F5 Kelowna Canada
140 A2 Kelseyville U.S.A.
106 F5 Kelso U.K.
141 E4 Kelso CA U.S.A.
138 B2 Kelso WA U.S.A.
99 B2 Keluang Malaysia
131 I4 Kelvington Canada
116 E1 Kem' Rus. Fed.
116 E1 Kem' r. Rus. Fed.
81 G2 Kemah Turkey
81 G2 Kemaliye Turkey
80 B3 Kemalpaşa Turkey
130 D4 Kemano Canada
80 C3 Kemer Turkey
80 B3 Kemer Turkey
80 B3 Kemer Barajı resr Turkey
90 A1 Kemerovo Rus. Fed.
102 N2 Kemi Fin.
102 N2 Kemijärvi Fin.
102 N2 Kemijärvi l. Fin.
102 O2 Kemijoki r. Fin.
83 H4 Kemin Kyrg.
138 E3 Kemmerer U.S.A.
109 J5 Kemnath Germany
106 F3 Kemnay U.K.
143 D5 Kemp, Lake U.S.A.
102 N2 Kempele Fin.
108 C3 Kempen reg. Belgium
108 E3 Kempen Germany
73 D5 Kemp Land pen. Antarctica
73 C3 Kemp Peninsula pen. Antarctica
145 E7 Kemp's Bay Bahamas
71 J3 Kempsey Australia
132 F4 Kempt, Lac l. Canada
112 E7 Kempten (Allgäu) Germany
71 G9 Kempton Australia
125 H3 Kempton Park S. Africa
135 J3 Kemptville Canada
99 D4 Kemujan i. Indon.
88 E4 Ken r. India
128 C3 Kenai U.S.A.
128 C4 Kenai Mountains U.S.A.
85 F3 Kenār-e Kapeh Afgh.
104 E3 Kendal U.K.
71 J3 Kendall Australia
131 L2 Kendall, Cape Canada
134 E5 Kendallville U.S.A.
99 C4 Kendang, Gunung vol. Indon.
91 E7 Kendari Indon.
99 D3 Kendawangan Indon.
121 D3 Kendégué Chad
89 F5 Kendrapara India
138 C2 Kendrick U.S.A.
141 G4 Kendrick Peak U.S.A.
83 H4 Kendyktas mts Kazakh.
82 C4 Kendyrli-Kayasanskoye, Plato plat. Kazakh.
82 C4 Kendyrlisor, Solonchak salt l. Kazakh.
71 H3 Kenebri Australia
143 D6 Kenedy U.S.A.
120 A4 Kenema Sierra Leone
Keneurgench Turkm. see Köneürgenç
122 B4 Kenge Dem. Rep. Congo
82 D4 Keng-Peli Uzbek.
91 B4 Kengtung Myanmar
124 D4 Kenhardt S. Africa
120 A3 Kéniéba Mali
120 B1 Kénitra Morocco
92 F1 Kenli China
107 B6 Kenmare Rep. of Ireland
142 C1 Kenmare U.S.A.
107 A6 Kenmare River inlet Rep. of Ireland
108 E5 Kenn Germany
139 G5 Kenna U.S.A.
147 I2 Kennebec r. U.S.A.
147 H3 Kennebunk U.S.A.
147 H3 Kennebunkport U.S.A.
143 F6 Kenner U.S.A.
105 F6 Kennet r. U.K.
143 F4 Kennett U.S.A.
138 C2 Kennewick U.S.A.
Keno Canada see Keno Hill
135 G1 Kenogami Lake Canada
135 G1 Kenogamissi Lake Canada
130 B2 Keno Hill Canada
131 K5 Kenora Canada
134 D3 Kenosha U.S.A.
116 F2 Kenozero, Ozero l. Rus. Fed.
104 E3 Kent r. U.K.
147 G4 Kent CT U.S.A.
143 B6 Kent TX U.S.A.
138 B2 Kent WA U.S.A.
125 H6 Kentani S. Africa
83 G4 Kentau Kazakh.
71 G7 Kent Group is Australia
134 D5 Kentland U.S.A.
146 B4 Kenton U.S.A.
137 J4 Kentucky r. U.S.A.
146 A6 Kentucky state U.S.A.
145 B4 Kentucky Lake U.S.A.
133 H5 Kentville Canada
143 F6 Kentwood LA U.S.A.
134 E4 Kentwood MI U.S.A.
122 D3 Kenya country Africa
122 D3 Kenya, Mount Kenya
83 G2 Kenzharyk Kazakh.
140 □2 Kēōkea U.S.A.
Keokea U.S.A. see Kēōkea
134 B5 Keokuk U.S.A.
88 D4 Keoladeo National Park India
Keo Neua, Col de pass Laos/Vietnam see Keo Nưa, Đeo
98 C1 Keo Nưa, Đeo pass Laos/Vietnam
134 B5 Keosauqua U.S.A.
68 F4 Keppel Bay Australia
98 □ Keppel Harbour sea chan. Sing.
80 B2 Kepsut Turkey
85 E4 Kerāh Iran
87 A4 Kerala state India
70 E5 Kerang Australia
103 N3 Kerava Fin.
114 C6 Kerba Alg.
83 G4 Kerben Kyrg.
117 F6 Kerch Ukr.
68 E2 Kerema P.N.G.
130 F5 Keremeos Canada
117 E7 Kerempe Burun pt Turkey
122 D2 Keren Eritrea
84 B3 Kerend Iran
83 G2 Kerey watercourse Kazakh.
83 G2 Kerey, Ozero salt l. Kazakh.
82 D5 Kergeli Turkm.
162 I8 Kerguélen, Îles is Indian Ocean
162 I8 Kerguelen Plateau sea feature Indian Ocean
122 D4 Kericho Kenya
72 D1 Kerikeri N.Z.
103 O3 Kerimäki Fin.
99 B3 Kerinci, Gunung vol. Indon.
99 B3 Kerinci Seblat National Park Indon.
83 J5 Keriya He watercourse China
89 E2 Keriya Shankou pass China
108 E3 Kerken Germany
Kerki Turkm. see Atamyrat
Kerkichi Turkm. see Kerkiçi
82 F5 Kerkiçi Turkm.
115 J4 Kerkinitis, Limni l. Greece
115 H5 Kerkyra Greece
Kerkyra i. Greece see Corfu
121 F3 Kerma Sudan
67 H5 Kermadec Islands S. Pacific Ocean
160 H8 Kermadec Trench sea feature S. Pacific Ocean
84 E4 Kermān Iran
140 B3 Kerman U.S.A.
85 E4 Kermān, Bīābān-e des. Iran
Kermān Desert Iran see Kermān, Bīābān-e
84 B3 Kermānshāh Iran
84 D4 Kermānshāhān Iran
143 C6 Kermit U.S.A.
139 C5 Kern r. U.S.A.
140 C4 Kern, South Fork r. U.S.A.
133 G2 Kernertut, Cap c. Canada
140 C4 Kernville U.S.A.
115 K6 Keros i. Greece
116 J2 Keros Rus. Fed.
120 B4 Kérouané Guinea
108 E4 Kerpen Germany
73 B5 Kerr, Cape c. Antarctica
131 H4 Kerrobert Canada
143 D6 Kerrville U.S.A.
107 B5 Kerry Head Rep. of Ireland
98 B4 Kerteh Malaysia
103 J5 Kerteminde Denmark
Keryneia Cyprus see Kyrenia
116 H3 Kerzhenets r. Rus. Fed.
132 D3 Kesagami Lake Canada
103 O3 Kesälahti Fin.
117 C7 Keşan Turkey
80 G1 Keşap Turkey
94 G5 Kesennuma Japan
85 H2 Keshem Afgh.
85 G2 Keshendeh-ye Bala Afgh.
88 B5 Keshod India
81 L5 Keshvar Iran
80 D2 Keskin Turkey
116 E2 Keskozero Rus. Fed.
108 E3 Kessel Neth.
125 H4 Kestell S. Africa
102 O2 Kesten'ga Rus. Fed.
102 N2 Kestilä Fin.
135 H3 Keswick Canada
104 D3 Keswick U.K.
112 H7 Keszthely Hungary
76 J4 Ket' r. Rus. Fed.
120 C4 Keta Ghana
98 □ Ketam, Pulau i. Sing.
99 D3 Ketapang Indon.
130 C3 Ketchikan U.S.A.
108 D2 Ketelmeer l. Neth.
85 G5 Keti Bandar Pak.
83 J4 Ketmen', Khrebet mts China/Kazakh.
105 G5 Kettering U.K.
146 A5 Kettering U.S.A.
130 F5 Kettle r. Canada
134 A2 Kettle r. U.S.A.
146 E4 Kettle Creek r. U.S.A.
140 C3 Kettleman City U.S.A.
138 C1 Kettle River Range mts U.S.A.
146 E3 Keuka Lake U.S.A.
103 N3 Keuruu Fin.
134 C5 Kewanee U.S.A.
134 D3 Kewaunee U.S.A.
134 C2 Keweenaw Bay U.S.A.
134 C2 Keweenaw Peninsula U.S.A.
134 D2 Keweenaw Point U.S.A.
153 G2 Keweigek Guyana
107 C3 Key, Lough l. Rep. of Ireland
132 F3 Keyano Canada
135 G3 Key Harbour Canada
83 J4 Keyi China
145 D7 Key Largo U.S.A.
105 E6 Keynsham U.K.
146 D5 Keyser U.S.A.
146 D5 Keysers Ridge U.S.A.
141 G6 Keystone Peak U.S.A.
146 D6 Keysville U.S.A.
81 L4 Keytü Iran
145 D7 Key West FL U.S.A.
134 B4 Key West IA U.S.A.
147 H3 Kezar Falls U.S.A.
123 C6 Kezi Zimbabwe
113 J6 Kežmarok Slovakia
124 D2 Kgalagadi admin. dist. Botswana
124 D2 Kgalagadi Transfrontier Park nat. park Botswana/S. Africa
125 G2 Kgatleng admin. dist. Botswana
124 D1 Kgomofatshe Pan salt pan Botswana
124 F2 Kgoro Pan salt pan Botswana
125 G3 Kgotsong S. Africa
90 F2 Khabarovsk Rus. Fed.
83 I1 Khabary Rus. Fed.
81 H4 Khābūr, Nahr al r. Syria
81 I7 Khadd, Wādī al watercourse Saudi Arabia
84 B6 Khafs Daghrah Saudi Arabia
88 E4 Khaga India
89 G5 Khagrachari Bangl.
88 B3 Khairgarh Pak.
88 B4 Khairpur Pak.
85 H3 Khaja Du Koh h. Afgh.
88 D4 Khajuraho India
123 C6 Khakhea Botswana
Khakīr Afgh. see Dāykundī
85 G4 Khak-rēz Afgh.
85 G4 Khakriz reg. Afgh.
Khalach Turkm. see Halaç
84 C3 Khalajestan reg. Iran
88 D2 Khalatse Jammu and Kashmir
88 A3 Khalifat mt. Pak.
85 E3 Khalīlābād Iran
Khalkabad Uzbek. see Xalqobod
84 C2 Khalkhāl Iran
87 D2 Khallikot India
116 D4 Khalopyenichy Belarus
90 C1 Khamar-Daban, Khrebet mts Rus. Fed.
88 C5 Khambhat India
88 B5 Khambhat, Gulf of India
88 D5 Khamgaon India
84 D5 Khamīr Iran
98 C1 Khamkkeut Laos
84 B5 Khamma well Saudi Arabia
87 C2 Khammam India
77 M3 Khamra Rus. Fed.
84 C3 Khamseh reg. Iran
Khamza Uzbek. see Hamza
98 B1 Khan, Nam r. Laos
85 H2 Khānābād Afgh.
Khanabad Uzbek. see Xonobod
81 I5 Khān al Baghdādī Iraq
81 J5 Khān al Maḥāwīl Iraq
81 J5 Khān al Mashāhidah Iraq
81 J5 Khān al Muşallá Iraq
87 A3 Khanapur India
84 B2 Khānaqāh Iran
81 J4 Khānaqīn Iraq
81 J6 Khān ar Raḥbah Iraq
81 J2 Khanasur Pass Iran/Turkey
80 F6 Khān az Zabīb tourist site Jordan
88 C2 Khanbari Pass Jammu and Kashmir
71 H6 Khancoban Australia
88 B2 Khand Pass Afgh./Pak.
83 H5 Khandud Afgh.
88 D5 Khandwa India
77 O3 Khandyga Rus. Fed.
88 B3 Khanewal Pak.
Khanh Dương Vietnam see M'Đrak
88 D4 Khaniadhana India
84 D4 Khānī Yek Iran
81 J5 Khān Jadwal Iraq
94 C2 Khanka, Lake China/Rus. Fed.
88 C2 Khanki Weir Pak.
88 D3 Khanna India
88 B3 Khanpur Pak.
80 F4 Khān Shaykhūn Syria
83 H3 Khantau Kazakh.
76 K3 Khantayskoye, Ozero l. Rus. Fed.
83 J4 Khan-Tengri, Pik mt. Kyrg.
76 H3 Khanty-Mansiysk Rus. Fed.
80 E6 Khān Yūnis Gaza
98 A3 Khao Chum Thong Thai.
88 D5 Khapa India
117 H6 Kharabali Rus. Fed.
89 F5 Kharagpur India
84 E2 Kharakī Iran
84 E5 Khārān r. Iran
85 G4 Kharan Pak.
84 D3 Kharānoq Iran
88 B2 Kharbin Pass Afgh.
88 C6 Khardi India
88 D2 Khardung La pass India
85 F3 Kharez Ilias Afgh.
81 K6 Kharfiyah Iraq
84 C4 Khārg Islands Iran
88 C5 Khargon India
88 C4 Khari r. Rajasthan India
88 C4 Khari r. Rajasthan India
88 C2 Kharian Pak.
87 C1 Khariar India
121 F2 Khārijah, Wāḥāt al oasis Egypt
117 F5 Kharkiv Ukr.
115 K4 Kharmanli Bulg.
116 G3 Kharovsk Rus. Fed.
84 C3 Khar Rūd r. Iran
88 C3 Kharsia India
121 F3 Khartoum Sudan
Khasardag, Gora mt. Turkm. see Hasardag
117 H7 Khasavyurt Rus. Fed.
85 F4 Khash Afgh.
85 F4 Khāsh Iran
85 F4 Khash Desert Afgh.
85 F4 Khash Rūd r. Afgh.
117 G7 Khashuri Georgia
89 G4 Khasi Hills India
115 K4 Khaskovo Bulg.
77 L2 Khatanga Rus. Fed.
77 L2 Khatangskiy Zaliv b. Rus. Fed.
Khatmia Pass Egypt see Khutmīyah, Mamarr al
77 S3 Khatyrka Rus. Fed.
Khavast Uzbek. see Xovos
88 B5 Khavda India
85 H3 Khawak Pass Afgh.
84 E5 Khawr Fakkan U.A.E.
98 A2 Khayamnandi S. Africa
125 F5 Khayamnandi S. Africa
83 G5 Khaydarken Kyrg.
124 C7 Khayelitsha S. Africa
Khazarasp Uzbek. see Hazorasp
81 I3 Khāzir, Nahr al r. Iraq
Khê Bo Vietnam see Hoa Binh
87 A2 Khed India
88 C4 Khedbrahma India
85 E3 Khedrī Iran
88 E3 Khela India
111 H4 Khemis Miliana Alg.
98 C1 Khemmarat Thai.
120 C1 Khenchela Alg.
120 B1 Khenifra Morocco
84 D4 Kherāmeh Iran
Kherli India see Pathena
84 C4 Kherreh Iran
117 E6 Kherson Ukr.
84 C4 Khesht Iran
77 K2 Kheta r. Rus. Fed.
84 D4 Kheyrābād Iran
84 D2 Khezerābād Iran
88 D4 Khilchipur India
80 F4 Khirbat Isrīyah Syria
88 D2 Khitai Pass China/Jammu and Kashmir
Khiva Uzbek. see Xiva
84 B2 Khīyāv Iran
103 O3 Khiytola Rus. Fed.
98 B2 Khlong, Mae r. Thai.
117 C5 Khmel'nyts'kyy Ukr.
117 C5 Khmil'nyk Ukr.
98 C3 Khoai, Hon i. Vietnam
82 C2 Khobda Kazakh.
84 B2 Khodā Āfarīn Iran
Khodzhambaz Turkm. see Hojambaz
Khodzheyli Uzbek. see Xo'jayli
124 D2 Khokhowe Pan salt pan Botswana
88 B4 Khokhropar Pak.
116 G1 Kholmogory Rus. Fed.
90 G2 Kholmsk Rus. Fed.
113 P3 Kholm-Zhirkovskiy Rus. Fed.
81 L3 Khoman Iran
124 B1 Khomas admin. reg. Namibia
124 A1 Khomas Highland hills Namibia
84 C3 Khomeyn Iran
84 C3 Khomeynishahr Iran
81 L4 Khondāb Iran
117 G7 Khoni Georgia
84 D5 Khonj Iran
98 B1 Khon Kaen Thai.
77 P3 Khonuu Rus. Fed.
117 G5 Khoper r. Rus. Fed.
90 F2 Khor Rus. Fed.
90 F2 Khor r. Rus. Fed.
84 D3 Khorāsān, Chāh-e well Iran
Khordha India see Khurda
90 C1 Khorinsk Rus. Fed.
123 B6 Khorixas Namibia
94 C2 Khorol Rus. Fed.
117 E5 Khorol Ukr.
81 K2 Khoroslū Dāgh hills Iran
84 C3 Khorramābād Iran
81 L3 Khorram Darreh Iran
84 C4 Khorramshahr Iran
83 G5 Khorugh Tajik.
85 E3 Khosf Iran
117 H6 Khosheutovo Rus. Fed.
84 C4 Khosravī Iran
84 C4 Khosrowābād Iran
81 J4 Khosrowvī Iran
84 D4 Khowrjān Iran
84 D3 Khowrnag, Kūh-e mt. Iran
85 H3 Khowst Afgh.
81 I1 Khozap'ini, Tba l. Georgia
90 B1 Khrebtovaya Rus. Fed.
89 H5 Khreum Myanmar
89 G4 Khri r. India
116 H2 Khristoforovo Rus. Fed.
77 P2 Khroma r. Rus. Fed.
82 D2 Khromtau Kazakh.
77 P2 Khrustalnyy Rus. Fed.
113 N6 Khrystynivka Ukr.
85 G5 Khude Hills Pak.
124 F1 Khudumelapye Botswana
84 B5 Khuff Saudi Arabia
85 F5 Khuh Lab, Ra's pt Iran
124 D3 Khuis Botswana

188 Khŭjand

83 G4 **Khŭjand** Tajik.
98 C2 **Khu Khan** Thai.
85 G3 **Khulm** *r.* Afgh.
89 G5 **Khulna** Bangl.
81 I1 **Khulo** Georgia
125 G3 **Khuma** S. Africa
88 C2 **Khunjerab Pass** China/Jammu and Kashmir
84 C3 **Khunsar** Iran
89 F5 **Khunti** India
98 A1 **Khun Yuam** Thai.
85 E3 **Khūr** Iran
88 D4 **Khurai** India
84 D5 **Khūran** *sea chan.* Iran
85 G3 **Khurd, Koh-i-** *mt.* Afgh.
89 F5 **Khurda** India
88 D3 **Khurja** India
85 F3 **Khurmalik** Afgh.
81 I6 **Khurr, Wādī al** *watercourse* Saudi Arabia
88 C2 **Khushab** Pak.
81 L3 **Khūshāvar** Iran
85 E4 **Khushk Rud** Iran
85 F3 **Khuspas** Afgh.
117 B5 **Khust** Ukr.
80 D6 **Khutmīyah, Mamarr al** *pass* Egypt
125 G3 **Khutsong** S. Africa
85 G5 **Khuzdar** Pak.
85 F3 **Khvāf** Iran
116 I4 **Khvalynsk** Rus. Fed.
84 D3 **Khvor** Iran
84 E3 **Khvord Nārvan** Iran
84 C4 **Khvormūj** Iran
82 B1 **Khvorostyanka** Rus. Fed.
81 K3 **Khvosh Maqām** Iran
84 B2 **Khvoy** Iran
116 E3 **Khvoynaya** Rus. Fed.
98 A2 **Khwae Noi** *r.* Thai.
85 F4 **Khwaja Ali** Afgh.
85 H2 **Khwaja Muhammad Range** *mts* Afgh.
88 B2 **Khyber Pass** Afgh./Pak.
71 I5 **Kiama** Australia
97 C5 **Kiamba** Phil.
122 C4 **Kiambi** Dem. Rep. Congo
143 E5 **Kiamichi** *r.* U.S.A.
102 O2 **Kiantajärvi** *l.* Fin.
84 D2 **Kīāseh** Iran
129 L2 **Kiatassuaq** *i.* Greenland
88 D2 **Kibar** India
97 C5 **Kibawe** Phil.
122 D4 **Kibaya** Tanz.
123 D4 **Kibiti** Tanz.
122 C4 **Kibombo** Dem. Rep. Congo
122 D4 **Kibondo** Tanz.
115 I4 **Kičevo** Macedonia
116 H3 **Kichmengskiy Gorodok** Rus. Fed.
82 C5 **Kiçi Balkan Daglary** *h.* Turkm.
120 C3 **Kidal** Mali
105 E5 **Kidderminster** U.K.
122 D3 **Kidepo Valley National Park** Uganda
120 A3 **Kidira** Senegal
88 D2 **Kidmang** Jammu and Kashmir
72 F3 **Kidnappers, Cape** N.Z.
105 E4 **Kidsgrove** U.K.
112 E3 **Kiel** Germany
134 C4 **Kiel** U.S.A.
112 D3 **Kiel Canal** Germany
113 J5 **Kielce** Poland
104 E2 **Kielder Water** *resr* U.K.
112 E3 **Kieler Bucht** *b.* Germany
123 C5 **Kienge** Dem. Rep. Congo
108 F3 **Kierspe** Germany
117 D5 **Kiev** Ukr.
120 A3 **Kiffa** Mauritania
115 J5 **Kifisia** Greece
81 J4 **Kifrī** Iraq
122 D4 **Kigali** Rwanda
81 H2 **Kiğı** Turkey
133 H2 **Kiglapait Mountains** Canada
122 C4 **Kigoma** Tanz.
102 M2 **Kihlanki** Fin.
103 M3 **Kihniö** Fin.
83 H3 **Kiik** Kazakh.
102 N2 **Kiiminki** Fin.
95 D8 **Kii-sanchi** *mts* Japan
95 D8 **Kii-suidō** *sea chan.* Japan
115 I2 **Kikinda** Serb. and Mont.
85 F5 **Kikki** Pak.
116 H3 **Kiknur** Rus. Fed.
94 G4 **Kikonai** Japan
123 C4 **Kikondja** Dem. Rep. Congo
68 E2 **Kikori** P.N.G.
68 E2 **Kikori** *r.* P.N.G.
122 B4 **Kikwit** Dem. Rep. Congo
103 L3 **Kilafors** Sweden
87 B4 **Kilakkarai** India
88 D2 **Kilar** India
140 □2 **Kilauea** U.S.A.
140 □2 **Kilauea Crater** U.S.A.
106 C5 **Kilbrannan Sound** *sea chan.* U.K.
96 E3 **Kilchu** N. Korea
107 E4 **Kilcoole** Rep. of Ireland
107 D4 **Kilcormac** Rep. of Ireland
71 J1 **Kilcoy** Australia
107 E4 **Kildare** Rep. of Ireland
102 P1 **Kil'dinstroy** Rus. Fed.
122 B4 **Kilembe** Dem. Rep. Congo
106 C5 **Kilfinan** U.K.
143 E5 **Kilgore** U.S.A.
104 E2 **Kilham** U.K.
122 D4 **Kilifi** Kenya
122 D4 **Kilimanjaro** *vol.* Tanz.
122 D4 **Kilimanjaro National Park** Tanz.
69 F2 **Kilinailau Islands** P.N.G.
123 D4 **Kilindoni** Tanz.
103 N4 **Kilingi-Nõmme** Estonia
80 F3 **Kilis** Turkey
117 D6 **Kiliya** Ukr.
107 B5 **Kilkee** Rep. of Ireland
107 F3 **Kilkeel** U.K.
107 D5 **Kilkenny** Rep. of Ireland
105 C7 **Kilkhampton** U.K.
115 J4 **Kilkis** Greece
107 B3 **Killala** Rep. of Ireland
107 B3 **Killala Bay** Rep. of Ireland
107 C5 **Killaloe** Rep. of Ireland
135 I3 **Killaloe Station** Canada
131 G4 **Killam** Canada
71 J2 **Killarney** Australia
135 G3 **Killarney** Canada
107 B5 **Killarney** Rep. of Ireland
107 B6 **Killarney National Park** Rep. of Ireland
135 G2 **Killarney Provincial Park** Canada
107 B4 **Killary Harbour** *b.* Rep. of Ireland
143 D6 **Killeen** U.S.A.
107 D5 **Killenaule** Rep. of Ireland
107 C4 **Killimor** Rep. of Ireland
106 D4 **Killin** U.K.
107 F3 **Killinchy** U.K.
107 E5 **Killinick** Rep. of Ireland
133 H1 **Killiniq** Canada
133 H1 **Killiniq Island** Canada
107 B5 **Killorglin** Rep. of Ireland
107 E5 **Killurin** Rep. of Ireland
107 C3 **Killybegs** Rep. of Ireland
107 D2 **Kilmacrenan** Rep. of Ireland
107 B4 **Kilmaine** Rep. of Ireland
107 C5 **Kilmallock** Rep. of Ireland
106 B3 **Kilmaluag** U.K.
106 D5 **Kilmarnock** U.K.
106 C4 **Kilmelford** U.K.
116 I3 **Kil'mez'** Rus. Fed.
116 I3 **Kil'mez'** *r.* Rus. Fed.
107 C6 **Kilmona** Rep. of Ireland
70 F6 **Kilmore** Australia
107 E5 **Kilmore Quay** Rep. of Ireland
122 D4 **Kilosa** Tanz.
102 M1 **Kilpisjärvi** Fin.
102 P1 **Kilp"yavr** Rus. Fed.
107 E3 **Kilrea** U.K.
107 B5 **Kilrush** Rep. of Ireland
106 D5 **Kilsyth** U.K.
87 A4 **Kiltan** *atoll* India
107 C4 **Kiltullagh** Rep. of Ireland
123 C4 **Kilwa** Dem. Rep. Congo
123 D4 **Kilwa Masoko** Tanz.
106 D5 **Kilwinning** U.K.
123 D4 **Kimambi** Tanz.
70 B4 **Kimba** Australia
122 B4 **Kimba** Congo
142 C3 **Kimball** U.S.A.
68 F2 **Kimbe** P.N.G.
130 F5 **Kimberley** Canada
124 F4 **Kimberley** S. Africa
68 C3 **Kimberley Plateau** Australia
72 E4 **Kimbolton** N.Z.
96 E3 **Kimch'aek** N. Korea
96 E5 **Kimch'ŏn** S. Korea
103 M3 **Kimito** Fin.
96 D6 **Kimje** S. Korea
129 L3 **Kimmirut** Canada
115 K6 **Kimolos** *i.* Greece
116 F4 **Kimovsk** Rus. Fed.
122 B4 **Kimpese** Dem. Rep. Congo
116 F3 **Kimry** Rus. Fed.
122 B4 **Kimvula** Dem. Rep. Congo
99 E1 **Kinabalu, Gunung** *mt. Sabah* Malaysia
97 A5 **Kinabatangan** *r. Sabah* Malaysia
115 L6 **Kinaros** *i.* Greece
130 F4 **Kinbasket Lake** Canada
106 E2 **Kinbrace** U.K.
135 G3 **Kincardine** Canada
106 E4 **Kincardine** U.K.
70 E4 **Kinchega National Park** Australia
130 D3 **Kincolith** Canada
123 C4 **Kinda** Dem. Rep. Congo
89 H5 **Kindat** Myanmar
143 E6 **Kinder** U.S.A.
105 F4 **Kinder Scout** *h.* U.K.
131 H4 **Kindersley** Canada
120 A3 **Kindia** Guinea
122 C4 **Kindu** Dem. Rep. Congo
82 B1 **Kinel'** Rus. Fed.
116 G3 **Kineshma** Rus. Fed.
68 F4 **Kingaroy** Australia
140 B3 **King City** U.S.A.
73 C1 **King Edward Point** *research stn* Antarctica
146 E3 **King Ferry** U.S.A.
147 H2 **Kingfield** U.S.A.
143 D5 **Kingfisher** U.S.A.
73 B2 **King George Island** *i.* Antarctica
132 E2 **King George Islands** Canada
116 D3 **Kingisepp** Rus. Fed.
71 F8 **King Island** Australia
130 D4 **King Island** Canada
135 H1 **King Kirkland** Canada
70 F6 **Kinglake National Park** Australia
68 C3 **King Leopold Ranges** *hills* Australia
141 E4 **Kingman** *AZ* U.S.A.
143 D4 **Kingman** *KS* U.S.A.
147 I2 **Kingman** *ME* U.S.A.
67 I3 **Kingman Reef** *terr.* N. Pacific Ocean
130 D3 **King Mountain** Canada
70 A3 **Kingoonya** Australia
107 D5 **Kings** *r.* Rep. of Ireland
140 C3 **Kings** *r.* U.S.A.
105 D7 **Kingsbridge** U.K.
140 C3 **Kingsburg** U.S.A.
147 I2 **Kingsbury** U.S.A.
140 C3 **Kings Canyon National Park** U.S.A.
71 J2 **Kingscliff** Australia
70 B5 **Kingscote** Australia
107 E4 **Kingscourt** Rep. of Ireland
73 E2 **King Sejong** *research stn* Antarctica
134 C3 **Kingsford** U.S.A.
145 D6 **Kingsland** *GA* U.S.A.
134 E5 **Kingsland** *IN* U.S.A.
105 H5 **King's Lynn** U.K.
69 H2 **Kingsmill Group** *is* Kiribati
105 H6 **Kingsnorth** U.K.
68 C3 **King Sound** *b.* Australia
138 E3 **Kings Peak** U.S.A.
146 B6 **Kingsport** U.S.A.
135 I3 **Kingston** Canada
149 I5 **Kingston** Jamaica
72 B6 **Kingston** N.Z.
134 B6 **Kingston** *IL* U.S.A.
147 F4 **Kingston** *NY* U.S.A.
71 G9 **Kingston**
141 E4 **Kingston Peak** U.S.A.
70 C6 **Kingston South East** Australia
104 G4 **Kingston upon Hull** U.K.
149 L6 **Kingstown** St Vincent
143 D7 **Kingsville** U.S.A.
105 E6 **Kingswood** U.K.
105 D5 **Kington** U.K.
106 D3 **Kingussie** U.K.
129 I3 **King William Island** Canada
125 G6 **King William's Town** S. Africa
143 E6 **Kingwood** *TX* U.S.A.
146 D5 **Kingwood** *WV* U.S.A.
131 I4 **Kinistino** Canada
94 G5 **Kinka-san** *i.* Japan
72 B6 **Kinloch** N.Z.
106 E3 **Kinloss** U.K.
135 H3 **Kinmount** Canada
103 K4 **Kinna** Sweden
107 D4 **Kinnegad** Rep. of Ireland
87 C4 **Kinniyai** Sri Lanka
102 N3 **Kinnula** Fin.
131 I3 **Kinoosao** Canada
95 F5 **Kinpoku-san** *mt.* Japan
106 E4 **Kinross** U.K.
107 C6 **Kinsale** Rep. of Ireland
122 B4 **Kinshasa** Dem. Rep. Congo
142 D4 **Kinsley** U.S.A.
145 E5 **Kinston** U.S.A.
103 M5 **Kintai** Lith.
120 B4 **Kintampo** Ghana
106 F3 **Kintore** U.K.
106 C5 **Kintyre** *pen.* U.K.
130 F3 **Kinuso** Canada
121 F4 **Kinyeti** *mt.* Sudan
82 D2 **Kinzhaly** Kazakh.
109 H4 **Kinzig** *r.* Germany
135 H2 **Kiosk** Canada
132 E4 **Kipawa, Lac** *l.* Canada
147 F6 **Kiptopeke** U.S.A.
123 C5 **Kipushi** Dem. Rep. Congo
69 G3 **Kirakira** Solomon Is
87 C2 **Kirandul** India
116 D4 **Kirawsk** Belarus
109 G2 **Kirchdorf** Germany
109 G5 **Kirchheim-Bolanden** Germany
107 F3 **Kircubbin** U.K.
91 C1 **Kirenga** *r.* Rus. Fed.
90 C1 **Kirensk** Rus. Fed.
83 H4 **Kirghiz Range** *mts* Asia
67 H4 **Kiribati** *country* Pacific Ocean
81 H1 **Kırık** Turkey
80 F3 **Kırıkhan** Turkey
80 D2 **Kırıkkale** Turkey
116 F3 **Kirillov** Rus. Fed.
Kirinyaga *mt.* Kenya *see* **Kenya, Mount**
116 E3 **Kirishi** Rus. Fed.
95 B9 **Kirishima-yama** *vol.* Japan
67 I4 **Kiritimati** *atoll* Kiribati
80 A2 **Kırkağaç** Turkey
84 B2 **Kirk Bulāg Dāgi** *mt.* Iran
105 E4 **Kirkby** U.K.
105 F4 **Kirkby in Ashfield** U.K.
104 E3 **Kirkby Lonsdale** U.K.
104 E3 **Kirkby Stephen** U.K.
106 E4 **Kirkcaldy** U.K.
106 C6 **Kirkcolm** U.K.
106 D6 **Kirkcudbright** U.K.
103 K3 **Kirkenær** Norway
102 O1 **Kirkenes** Norway
135 H3 **Kirkfield** Canada
106 D5 **Kirkintilloch** U.K.
103 N3 **Kirkkonummi** Fin.
141 F4 **Kirkland** U.S.A.
141 F4 **Kirkland Junction** U.S.A.
135 G1 **Kirkland Lake** Canada
117 C7 **Kırklareli** Turkey
104 C3 **Kirk Michael** U.K.
104 E3 **Kirkoswald** U.K.
73 C5 **Kirkpatrick, Mount** Antarctica
142 E3 **Kirksville** U.S.A.
81 J4 **Kirkūk** Iraq
106 F2 **Kirkwall** U.K.
125 F6 **Kirkwood** S. Africa
140 B2 **Kirkwood** *CA* U.S.A.
142 F4 **Kirkwood** *MO* U.S.A.
80 C1 **Kırmır** *r.* Turkey
108 F5 **Kirn** Germany
116 E4 **Kirov** *Kaluzhskaya Oblast'* Rus. Fed.
116 I3 **Kirov** *Kirovskaya Oblast'* Rus. Fed.
Kirovabad Azer. *see* **Gäncä**
82 C2 **Kirovo** Kazakh.
116 I3 **Kirovo-Chepetsk** Rus. Fed.
117 E5 **Kirovohrad** Ukr.
81 L2 **Kirovsk** Azer.
116 D3 **Kirovsk** *Leningradskaya Oblast'* Rus. Fed.
102 P2 **Kirovsk** *Murmanskaya Oblast'* Rus. Fed.
116 I3 **Kirovskaya Oblast'** *admin. div.* Rus. Fed.
94 C2 **Kirovskiy** Rus. Fed.
82 D5 **Kirpili** Turkm.
106 E4 **Kirriemuir** U.K.
116 J3 **Kirs** Rus. Fed.
116 G4 **Kirsanov** Rus. Fed.
80 E2 **Kırşehir** Turkey
85 G5 **Kirthar Range** *mts* Pak.
109 H4 **Kirtorf** Germany
102 M2 **Kiruna** Sweden
122 C4 **Kirundu** Dem. Rep. Congo
116 H4 **Kirya** Rus. Fed.
95 F6 **Kiryū** Japan
103 K4 **Kisa** Sweden
122 C3 **Kisangani** Dem. Rep. Congo
122 B4 **Kisantu** Dem. Rep. Congo
99 A2 **Kisaran** Indon.
90 A1 **Kiselevsk** Rus. Fed.
89 F4 **Kishanganj** India
88 B4 **Kishangarh** *Rajasthan* India
88 C4 **Kishangarh** *Rajasthan* India
88 C2 **Kishen Ganga** *r.* India/Pak.
120 C4 **Kishi** Nigeria
95 B9 **Kishika-zaki** *pt* Japan
Kishinev Moldova *see* **Chişinău**
95 D7 **Kishiwada** Japan
83 H1 **Kishkenekol'** Kazakh.
89 G4 **Kishoreganj** Bangl.
Kishorganj Bangl. *see* **Kishoreganj**
88 C2 **Kishtwar** Jammu and Kashmir
Kisi Nigeria *see* **Kishi**
122 D4 **Kisii** Kenya
131 J4 **Kiskittogisu Lake** Canada
113 I7 **Kiskunfélegyháza** Hungary
113 I7 **Kiskunhalas** Hungary
117 G7 **Kislovodsk** Rus. Fed.
122 E4 **Kismaayo** Somalia
122 C4 **Kisoro** Uganda
95 E7 **Kiso-sanmyaku** *mts* Japan
120 A4 **Kissidougou** Guinea
145 D6 **Kissimmee** U.S.A.
145 D7 **Kissimmee, Lake** U.S.A.
122 D4 **Kisumu** Kenya
120 B3 **Kita** Mali
Kitab Uzbek. *see* **Kitob**
95 G6 **Kitaibaraki** Japan
94 G5 **Kitakami** Japan
94 G5 **Kitakami-gawa** *r.* Japan
95 F6 **Kitakata** Japan
95 B8 **Kita-Kyūshū** Japan
122 D3 **Kitale** Kenya
77 P5 **Kitami** Japan
139 G4 **Kit Carson** U.S.A.
135 G4 **Kitchener** Canada
102 O3 **Kitee** Fin.
122 D3 **Kitgum** Uganda
130 D4 **Kitimat** Canada
102 N2 **Kitinen** *r.* Fin.
83 F5 **Kitob** Uzbek.
122 B4 **Kitona** Dem. Rep. Congo
95 B8 **Kitsuki** Japan
70 C2 **Kittakittaooloo, Lake** *salt flat* Australia
146 D4 **Kittanning** U.S.A.
147 F4 **Kittatinny Mountains** U.S.A.
147 H3 **Kittery** U.S.A.
102 N2 **Kittilä** Fin.
145 F4 **Kitty Hawk** U.S.A.
122 D4 **Kitunda** Tanz.
130 D3 **Kitwanga** Canada
123 C5 **Kitwe** Zambia
112 F7 **Kitzbüheler Alpen** *mts* Austria
109 I5 **Kitzingen** Germany
109 K3 **Kitzscher** Germany
102 N3 **Kiuruvesi** Fin.
102 N3 **Kivijärvi** Fin.
103 N4 **Kiviõli** Estonia
122 C4 **Kivu, Lake** Dem. Rep. Congo/Rwanda
83 G2 **Kiyakty, Ozero** *salt l.* Kazakh.
83 G2 **Kiyevka** Kazakh.
94 C3 **Kiyevka** Rus. Fed.
115 M4 **Kıyıköy** Turkey
83 F2 **Kiyma** Kazakh.
76 G4 **Kizel** Rus. Fed.
116 H2 **Kizema** Rus. Fed.
83 J4 **Kizil** China
80 B3 **Kızılca Dağ** *mt.* Turkey
80 D1 **Kızılcahamam** Turkey
80 G2 **Kızıl Dağı** *mt.* Turkey
80 D1 **Kızılırmak** Turkey
80 D2 **Kızılırmak** *r.* Turkey
80 C3 **Kızılkaya** Turkey
80 D3 **Kızılören** Turkey
82 D1 **Kizil'skoye** Rus. Fed.
81 H3 **Kızıltepe** Turkey
117 H7 **Kizilyurt** Rus. Fed.
Kizil"yurt Rus. Fed. *see* **Kizilyurt**
117 H7 **Kizlyar** Rus. Fed.
Kizylayak Turkm. *see* **Gyzylaýak**
102 N1 **Kjøllefjord** Norway
102 L1 **Kjøpsvik** Norway
112 G5 **Kladno** Czech Rep.
112 G7 **Klagenfurt** Austria
141 H4 **Klagetoh** U.S.A.
103 M5 **Klaipėda** Lith.
102 □ **Klaksvík** Faroe Is
138 B3 **Klamath** *r.* U.S.A.
138 B3 **Klamath Falls** U.S.A.
138 B3 **Klamath Mountains** U.S.A.
99 B2 **Klang** Malaysia
103 K4 **Klarälven** *r.* Sweden
112 F6 **Klatovy** Czech Rep.
124 C5 **Klawer** S. Africa
130 C3 **Klawock** U.S.A.
108 E2 **Klazienaveen** Neth.
130 E4 **Kleena Kleene** Canada
124 D4 **Kleinbegin** S. Africa
124 C3 **Klein Karas** Namibia
124 F6 **Kleinpoort** S. Africa
124 D6 **Klein Roggeveldberge** *mts* S. Africa
124 B4 **Kleinsee** S. Africa
124 D6 **Klein Swartberg** *mt.* S. Africa
130 D4 **Klemtu** Canada
125 G3 **Klerksdorp** S. Africa
116 E4 **Kletnya** Rus. Fed.
117 G5 **Kletskaya** Rus. Fed.
108 E3 **Kleve** Germany
Klienpoort S. Africa *see* **Kleinpoort**
116 D4 **Klimavichy** Belarus
117 E4 **Klimovo** Rus. Fed.
116 F4 **Klimovsk** Rus. Fed.
116 F3 **Klin** Rus. Fed.
130 D4 **Klinaklini** *r.* Canada
109 H5 **Klingenberg am Main** Germany
109 K4 **Klingenthal** Germany
109 K1 **Klink** Germany
112 F5 **Klínovec** *mt.* Czech Rep.
103 L4 **Klintehamn** Sweden
117 I5 **Klintsovka** Rus. Fed.
116 E4 **Klintsy** Rus. Fed.
124 C5 **Kliprand** S. Africa
114 G2 **Ključ** Bos.-Herz.
112 H5 **Kłodzko** Poland
130 C3 **Klondike Gold Rush National Historical Park** *nat. park* U.S.A.
108 E2 **Kloosterhaar** Neth.
112 H6 **Klosterneuburg** Austria
132 F1 **Klotz, Lac** *l.* Canada
109 J2 **Klötze (Altmark)** Germany
130 A2 **Kluane Game Sanctuary** *nature res.* Canada
130 B2 **Kluane Lake** Canada
130 B2 **Kluane National Park** Canada
112 I5 **Kluczbork** Poland
88 B4 **Klupro** Pak.
116 C4 **Klyetsk** Belarus
77 R4 **Klyuchevskaya, Sopka** *vol.* Rus. Fed.
83 I1 **Klyuchi** Rus. Fed.
103 K3 **Knåda** Sweden
104 F3 **Knaresborough** U.K.
131 K3 **Knee Lake** Canada
109 I5 **Knetzgau** Germany
134 B1 **Knife Lake** Canada/U.S.A.
130 D4 **Knight Inlet** Canada
105 D5 **Knighton** U.K.
134 E6 **Knightstown** U.S.A.
114 G2 **Knin** Croatia
112 G7 **Knittelfeld** Austria
115 J3 **Knjaževac** Serb. and Mont.
107 C4 **Knock** Rep. of Ireland
107 B6 **Knockaboy** *h.* Rep. of Ireland
107 B5 **Knockacummer** *h.* Rep. of Ireland
107 C3 **Knockalongy** *h.* Rep. of Ireland
107 B5 **Knockalough** Rep. of Ireland
106 F3 **Knock Hill** U.K.
107 E2 **Knocklayd** *h.* U.K.
108 B3 **Knokke-Heist** Belgium
109 L1 **Knorrendorf** Germany
115 K7 **Knosos** *tourist site* Greece
105 F5 **Knowle** U.K.
73 B3 **Knowles, Cape** *c.* Antarctica
147 I1 **Knowles Corner** U.S.A.
147 G2 **Knowlton** Canada
134 D5 **Knox** U.S.A.
130 C4 **Knox, Cape** Canada
140 A2 **Knoxville** *CA* U.S.A.
134 B5 **Knoxville** *IL* U.S.A.
145 D4 **Knoxville** *TN* U.S.A.
106 C3 **Knoydart** *mts* U.K.
129 M1 **Knud Rasmussen Land** *reg.* Greenland
124 E7 **Knysna** S. Africa
95 B9 **Kobayashi** Japan
102 O1 **Kobbfoss** Norway
95 D7 **Kōbe** Japan
København Denmark *see* **Copenhagen**
120 B3 **Kobenni** Mauritania
108 F4 **Koblenz** Germany
116 I3 **Kobra** Rus. Fed.
91 F7 **Kobroör** *i.* Indon.
116 C4 **Kobryn** Belarus
117 G7 **K'obulet'i** Georgia
115 J4 **Kočani** Macedonia
80 B1 **Kocasu** *r.* Turkey
114 F2 **Kočevje** Slovenia
96 D6 **Kŏch'ang** S. Korea
96 D6 **Koch'ang** S. Korea
89 G4 **Koch Bihar** India
109 H5 **Kocher** *r.* Germany
Kochi India *see* **Cochin**
95 C8 **Kōchi** Japan
83 H4 **Kochkor** Kyrg.
116 H4 **Kochkurovo** Rus. Fed.
117 H6 **Kochubey** Rus. Fed.
117 G6 **Kochubeyevskoye** Rus. Fed.
87 B4 **Kodaikanal** India
87 D2 **Kodala** India
128 C4 **Kodiak** U.S.A.
128 C4 **Kodiak Island** U.S.A.
125 G1 **Kodibeleng** Botswana
116 F2 **Kodino** Rus. Fed.
121 F4 **Kodok** Sudan
117 G7 **Kodori** *r.* Georgia
117 D5 **Kodyma** Ukr.
115 K4 **Kodzhaele** *mt.* Bulg./Greece
124 D6 **Koedoesberg** *mts* S. Africa
124 D4 **Koegrabie** S. Africa
124 C5 **Koekenaap** S. Africa
89 E4 **Koel** *r.* India
108 D3 **Koersel** Belgium
123 B6 **Koës** Namibia
141 F5 **Kofa Mountains** U.S.A.
124 F4 **Koffiefontein** S. Africa
120 B4 **Koforidua** Ghana
95 F7 **Kōfu** Japan
132 E2 **Kogaluc** *r.* Canada
132 E2 **Kogaluc, Baie de** *b.* Canada
133 H2 **Kogaluk** *r.* Canada
71 I1 **Kogan** Australia
103 K5 **Køge** Denmark
82 F5 **Kogon** Uzbek.
85 G5 **Kohan** Pak.
88 B2 **Kohat** Pak.
103 N4 **Kohila** Estonia
89 H4 **Kohima** India
88 B3 **Kohlu** Pak.
85 F3 **Kohsan** Afgh.
103 N4 **Kohtla-Järve** Estonia
72 E2 **Kohukohunui** *h.* N.Z.
96 D6 **Kohŭng** S. Korea
95 F6 **Koide** Japan
130 A2 **Koidern** Canada
87 B3 **Koilkuntla** India
96 D3 **Koin** N. Korea
81 J3 **Koi Sanjaq** Iraq
96 E6 **Kŏje-do** *i.* S. Korea
94 F4 **Ko-jima** *i.* Japan
95 F8 **Ko-jima** *i.* Japan
98 A1 **Kok, Nam Mae** *r.* Thai.
147 I2 **Kokadjo** U.S.A.
82 F2 **Kokalat** Kazakh.
Kokand Uzbek. *see* **Qo'qon**
103 M4 **Kökar** Fin.
82 E3 **Kokaral** Kazakh.
83 H4 **Kök-Art** Kyrg.
83 H4 **Kök-Aygyr** Kyrg.
85 H2 **Kokcha** *r.* Afgh.
103 M3 **Kokemäenjoki** *r.* Fin.
124 C4 **Kokerboom** Namibia
113 N3 **Kokhanava** Belarus
116 G3 **Kokhma** Rus. Fed.
83 H4 **Kök-Janggak** Kyrg.
87 C4 **Kokkilai** Sri Lanka
102 M3 **Kokkola** Fin.
140 □1 **Koko Head** U.S.A.
134 D5 **Kokomo** U.S.A.
124 E2 **Kokong** Botswana
125 G3 **Kokosi** S. Africa
83 J2 **Kokpekti** Kazakh.
96 D4 **Koksan** N. Korea
83 G4 **Koksaray** Kazakh.
116 H3 **Koksharka** Rus. Fed.
83 G1 **Kokshetau** Kazakh.
133 G2 **Koksoak** *r.* Canada
125 H5 **Kokstad** S. Africa
83 I3 **Koksu** *Almatinskaya Oblast'* Kazakh.
83 G4 **Koksu** *Yuzhnyy Kazakhstan* Kazakh.
83 I3 **Koktal** Kazakh.
83 I3 **Kokterek** *Almatinskaya Oblast'* Kazakh.
82 B2 **Kokterek** *Zapadnyy Kazakhstan* Kazakh.
83 I2 **Koktobe** Kazakh.
82 D2 **Koktubek** Kazakh.
83 J3 **Koktuma** Kazakh.
83 I5 **Kokyar** China
83 J2 **Kokzhayyk** Kazakh.
102 P1 **Kola** Rus. Fed.
85 G5 **Kolachi** *r.* Pak.
88 C2 **Kolahoi** *mt.* India
91 E7 **Kolaka** Indon.
98 A4 **Ko Lanta** Thai.
76 E3 **Kola Peninsula** Rus. Fed.
87 B3 **Kolar** *Karnataka* India
88 E6 **Kolar** *Madhya Pradesh* India
88 D4 **Kolaras** India
87 B3 **Kolar Gold Fields** India
102 M2 **Kolari** Fin.
88 C4 **Kolayat** India
116 F3 **Kol'chugino** Rus. Fed.
120 A3 **Kolda** Senegal
103 J5 **Kolding** Denmark
122 C3 **Kole** Dem. Rep. Congo
122 C4 **Kole** Dem. Rep. Congo
111 H4 **Koléa** Alg.
102 M2 **Koler** Sweden
76 F3 **Kolguyev, Ostrov** *i.* Rus. Fed.
89 F5 **Kolhan** *reg.* India
87 A2 **Kolhapur** India
103 M4 **Kõljala** Estonia
103 M4 **Kolkasrags** *pt* Latvia
89 G5 **Kolkata** India
83 G5 **Kolkhozobod** Tajik.
Kollam India *see* **Quilon**
87 B3 **Kollegal** India
87 C2 **Kolleru Lake** India
108 E1 **Kollum** Neth.
Köln Germany *see* **Cologne**
112 G3 **Kołobrzeg** Poland
116 H3 **Kologriv** Rus. Fed.
120 B3 **Kolokani** Mali
69 F2 **Kolombangara** *i.* Solomon Is
116 F4 **Kolomna** Rus. Fed.
117 C5 **Kolomyya** Ukr.
120 B3 **Kolondiéba** Mali
68 C2 **Kolonedale** Indon.
Kolonkwane Botswana *see* **Kolonkwaneng**
124 D3 **Kolonkwaneng** Botswana
82 B2 **Kolovertnoye** Kazakh.
76 J4 **Kolpashevo** Rus. Fed.
117 F4 **Kolpny** Rus. Fed.
82 E4 **Ko'lquduq** Uzbek.
Kol'skiy Poluostrov *pen.* Rus. Fed. *see* **Kola Peninsula**
82 B1 **Koltubanovskiy** Rus. Fed.
86 B7 **Koluli** Eritrea
83 G2 **Koluton** Kazakh.
87 A2 **Kolvan** India
102 J2 **Kolvereid** Norway
102 N1 **Kolvik** Norway
85 G5 **Kolwa** *reg.* Pak.
123 C5 **Kolwezi** Dem. Rep. Congo
77 Q3 **Kolyma** *r.* Rus. Fed.
77 Q3 **Kolymskaya Nizmennost'** *lowland* Rus. Fed.
77 Q3 **Kolymskiy, Khrebet** *mts* Rus. Fed.
116 H4 **Kolyshley** Rus. Fed.
83 J4 **Kol'zhat** Kazakh.
115 J3 **Kom** *mt.* Bulg.
94 G3 **Komaga-take** *vol.* Japan
124 B4 **Komaggas** S. Africa
124 B4 **Komaggas Mountains** S. Africa
77 R4 **Komandorskiye Ostrova** *is* Rus. Fed.
112 I7 **Komárno** Slovakia
125 I2 **Komatipoort** S. Africa
95 E6 **Komatsu** Japan
95 D7 **Komatsushima** Japan
122 C4 **Kombe** Dem. Rep. Congo
120 B3 **Kombissiri** Burkina
99 B3 **Komering** *r.* Indon.
125 G6 **Komga** S. Africa
116 I2 **Komi, Respublika** *aut. rep.* Rus. Fed.
117 D6 **Kominternivs'ke** Ukr.
114 G3 **Komiža** Croatia
115 H1 **Komló** Hungary
122 B4 **Komono** Congo
95 F6 **Komoro** Japan
115 K4 **Komotini** Greece
124 D6 **Komsberg** *mts* S. Africa
82 E5 **Komsomol** Turkm.
77 K1 **Komsomolets, Ostrov** *i.* Rus. Fed.
82 C3 **Komsomolets, Zaliv** *b.* Kazakh.
116 G3 **Komsomol'sk** Rus. Fed.
Komsomol'sk Turkm. *see* **Komsomol**
117 E5 **Komsomol's'k** Ukr.
82 C3 **Komsomol'skiy** Kazakh.
117 H6 **Komsomol'skiy** Rus. Fed.
116 H4 **Komsomol'skiy** Rus. Fed.
90 F1 **Komsomol'sk-na-Amure** Rus. Fed.
Komsomol'sk-na-Ustyurte Uzbek. *see* **Kubla Ustyurt**
82 E2 **Komsomol'skoye** Kazakh.
81 I1 **Kömürlü** Turkey
141 F6 **Kom Vo** U.S.A.
116 F3 **Konakovo** Rus. Fed.
89 F6 **Konarka** India
89 F5 **Konar Reservoir** India
88 D4 **Konch** India
87 C2 **Kondagaon** India
135 I2 **Kondiaronk, Lac** *l.* Canada
122 D4 **Kondoa** Tanz.
116 E2 **Kondopoga** Rus. Fed.
116 E4 **Kondrovo** Rus. Fed.
Kondūz Afgh. *see* **Kunduz**
Kondūz *r.* Afgh. *see* **Kunduz**
82 D4 **Köneürgenç** Turkm.
98 B3 **Kŏng, Kaôh** *i.* Cambodia
98 C2 **Kông, Tônlé** *r.* Cambodia
98 C2 **Kong, Xé** *r.* Laos
129 O3 **Kong Christian IX Land** *reg.* Greenland
129 N3 **Kong Frederik VI Kyst** *coastal area* Greenland
96 D5 **Kongju** S. Korea
76 D2 **Kong Karls Land** *is* Svalbard
99 E2 **Kongkemul** *mt.* Indon.
122 C4 **Kongolo** Dem. Rep. Congo
129 P2 **Kong Oscars Fjord** *inlet* Greenland
120 B3 **Kongoussi** Burkina
103 J4 **Kongsberg** Norway
103 K3 **Kongsvinger** Norway
83 H5 **Kongur Shan** *mt.* China
122 D4 **Kongwa** Tanz.
129 P2 **Kong Wilhelm Land** *reg.* Greenland
83 G4 **Konibodom** Tajik.
109 J4 **Königsee** Germany
108 F4 **Königswinter** Germany
112 I4 **Konin** Poland
90 F1 **Konin** *r.* Rus. Fed.
115 G3 **Konjic** Bos.-Herz.
124 B3 **Konkiep** *watercourse* Namibia
120 B3 **Konna** Mali
109 J3 **Könnern** Germany
102 N3 **Konnevesi** Fin.
116 G2 **Konosha** Rus. Fed.
95 F6 **Kōnosu** Japan
117 E5 **Konotop** Ukr.
Kon Plong Vietnam *see* **Kon Plông**
98 D2 **Kon Plông** Vietnam
109 K5 **Konstantinovy Lázně** Czech Rep.
112 D7 **Konstanz** Germany
120 C3 **Kontagora** Nigeria
102 O3 **Kontiolahti** Fin.
102 N2 **Konttila** Fin.
98 C2 **Kon Tum** Vietnam
98 D2 **Kon Tum, Cao Nguyên** *plat.* Vietnam
Kontum, Plateau du Vietnam *see* **Kon Tum, Cao Nguyên**
80 D3 **Konya** Turkey
83 H3 **Konyrat** Kazakh.
83 I3 **Konyrolen** Kazakh.
82 C2 **Konystanu** Kazakh.
108 E5 **Konz** Germany
140 □1 **Ko'olau Range** *mts* U.S.A.
Koolau Range *mts* U.S.A. *see* **Ko'olau Range**
70 F5 **Koondrook** Australia
146 D5 **Koon Lake** U.S.A.
71 H5 **Koorawatha** Australia
138 C2 **Kooskia** U.S.A.
130 F5 **Kootenay** *r.* Canada/U.S.A.
130 F5 **Kootenay Lake** Canada
130 F4 **Kootenay National Park** Canada
124 D5 **Kootjieskolk** S. Africa
83 I3 **Kopa** Kazakh.
117 H6 **Kopanovka** Rus. Fed.
88 C6 **Kopargaon** India
102 C1 **Kópasker** Iceland
83 I3 **Kopbirlik** Kazakh.
114 E2 **Koper** Slovenia
82 D5 **Kopet Dag** *mts* Iran/Turkm.
103 L4 **Köping** Sweden
102 L3 **Köpmanholmen** Sweden
125 F2 **Kopong** Botswana
87 B3 **Koppal** India
103 J3 **Koppang** Norway
103 K4 **Kopparberg** Sweden
125 G3 **Koppies** S. Africa
124 D3 **Koppieskraal Pan** *salt pan* S. Africa
114 G1 **Koprivnica** Croatia
80 C3 **Köprü** *r.* Turkey
84 D4 **Kor, Rūd-e** *watercourse* Iran
116 G4 **Korablino** Rus. Fed.
85 G5 **Korak** Pak.
132 E1 **Korak, Baie** *b.* Canada
87 B2 **Korangal** India
85 G5 **Korangi** Pak.
87 C2 **Koraput** India
87 C1 **Korba** India
114 D6 **Korba** Tunisia
109 G3 **Korbach** Germany
98 B4 **Korbu, Gunung** *mt.* Malaysia
115 I4 **Korçë** Albania
83 J1 **Korchino** Rus. Fed.
114 G3 **Korčula** Croatia
114 G3 **Korčula** *i.* Croatia
114 G3 **Korčulanski Kanal** *sea chan.* Croatia
83 H4 **Korday** Kazakh.
81 L4 **Kord Khvord** Iran
84 D2 **Kord Kūy** Iran
85 F5 **Kords** *reg.* Iran
96 B4 **Korea Bay** *g.* China/N. Korea
95 A7 **Korea Strait** Japan/S. Korea
87 A2 **Koregaon** India
117 F6 **Korenovsk** Rus. Fed.
117 C5 **Korets'** Ukr.
80 B1 **Körfez** Turkey
73 C3 **Korff Ice Rise** *ice feature* Antarctica
83 G2 **Korgalzhyn** Kazakh.
83 J3 **Korgas** China
82 F2 **Korgasyn** Kazakh.
102 K2 **Korgen** Norway
120 B4 **Korhogo** Côte d'Ivoire
88 B5 **Kori Creek** *inlet* India
112 H7 **Kőris-hegy** *h.* Hungary
115 I3 **Koritnik** *mt.* Albania
95 G6 **Kōriyama** Japan
80 C3 **Korkuteli** Turkey
80 D4 **Kormakitis, Cape** Cyprus
112 H7 **Körmend** Hungary
83 H2 **Korneyevka** *Karagandinskaya Oblast'* Kazakh.
83 G1 **Korneyevka** *Severnyy Kazakhstan* Kazakh.
83 J1 **Kornilovo** Rus. Fed.
120 B4 **Koro** Côte d'Ivoire
69 H3 **Koro** *i.* Fiji
120 B3 **Koro** Mali
117 F5 **Korocha** Rus. Fed.
80 D1 **Köroğlu Dağları** *mts* Turkey
80 D1 **Köroğlu Tepesi** *mt.* Turkey
122 D4 **Korogwe** Tanz.
70 E7 **Koroit** Australia
70 E6 **Korong Vale** Australia
115 J4 **Koronia, Limni** *l.* Greece
69 H3 **Koro Sea** Fiji
117 D5 **Korosten'** Ukr.
117 D5 **Korostyshiv** Ukr.
121 D3 **Koro Toro** Chad
103 N3 **Korpilahti** Fin.
103 M3 **Korpo** Fin.
82 C3 **Korsak** Kazakh.
90 G2 **Korsakov** Rus. Fed.
116 I3 **Korshik** Rus. Fed.
102 M3 **Korsnäs** Fin.
103 J5 **Korsør** Denmark
117 D5 **Korsun'-Shevchenkivs'kyy** Ukr.
113 J3 **Korsze** Poland
102 M3 **Kortesjärvi** Fin.
116 I2 **Kortkeros** Rus. Fed.
108 B4 **Kortrijk** Belgium
116 G3 **Kortsovo** Rus. Fed.
71 F7 **Korumburra** Australia
120 D4 **Korup, Parc National de** *nat. park* Cameroon
102 N2 **Korvala** Fin.
88 D4 **Korwai** India
90 H1 **Koryakskaya, Sopka** *vol.* Rus. Fed.
77 R3 **Koryakskiy Khrebet** *mts* Rus. Fed.
116 H2 **Koryazhma** Rus. Fed.
96 E6 **Koryŏng** S. Korea
117 E5 **Koryukivka** Ukr.
82 C2 **Korzhyn** Kazakh.
115 L6 **Kos** *i.* Greece
82 E2 **Kosagal** Kazakh.
83 H1 **Kosagash** Kazakh.
96 D4 **Kosan** N. Korea
82 F2 **Kosay** Kazakh.
82 C3 **Koschagyl** Kazakh.
112 H4 **Kościan** Poland
143 F5 **Kosciusko** U.S.A.
130 C3 **Kosciusko Island** U.S.A.
71 H6 **Kosciuszko, Mount** Australia
71 H6 **Kosciuszko National Park** Australia
81 G1 **Köse** Turkey
80 F1 **Köse Dağı** *mt.* Turkey
87 B2 **Kosgi** India
79 G2 **Kosh-Agach** Rus. Fed.
82 B2 **Koshankol'** Kazakh.
83 H4 **Kosh-Döbö** Kyrg.
95 A9 **Koshikijima-rettō** *is* Japan
85 F3 **Koshkak** Iran
83 J3 **Koshkarkol', Ozero** *l.* Kazakh.
85 F3 **Koshk-e Kohneh** Afgh.
134 C4 **Koshkonong, Lake** U.S.A.
Koshkupyr Uzbek. *see* **Qo'shko'pir**
Koshoba Turkm. *see* **Goşoba**
Koshrabad Uzbek. *see* **Qo'shrabot**
88 D4 **Kosi** India
88 D3 **Kosi** *r.* India
125 J3 **Kosi Bay** S. Africa
113 J6 **Košice** Slovakia
87 B3 **Kosigi** India
82 D2 **Kos-Istek** Kazakh.
83 F2 **Koskol'** Kazakh.
83 I3 **Koskuduk** Kazakh.
102 M2 **Koskullskulle** Sweden
116 I2 **Koslan** Rus. Fed.
82 F5 **Koson** Uzbek.
96 E3 **Kosŏng** N. Korea
96 E4 **Kosŏng** N. Korea
83 G4 **Kosonsoy** Uzbek.
115 I3 **Kosovo** *prov. Srbija* Serb. and Mont.
115 I3 **Kosovska Mitrovica** Serb. and Mont.
67 F2 **Kosrae** *atoll* Micronesia
83 I5 **Kosrap** China
109 J5 **Kösseine** *h.* Germany
120 B4 **Kossou, Lac de** *l.* Côte d'Ivoire
82 E1 **Kostanay** Kazakh.
82 E1 **Kostanayskaya Oblast'** *admin. div.* Kazakh.
115 J3 **Kostenets** Bulg.
125 G2 **Koster** S. Africa
121 F3 **Kosti** Sudan
115 J3 **Kostinbrod** Bulg.
76 J3 **Kostino** Rus. Fed.
116 D1 **Kostomuksha** Rus. Fed.
117 C5 **Kostopil'** Ukr.
116 G3 **Kostroma** Rus. Fed.
116 G3 **Kostroma** *r.* Rus. Fed.

Lake City 189

116 G3 Kostromskaya Oblast' admin. div. Rus. Fed.
112 G4 Kostrzyn Poland
117 F5 Kostyantynivka Ukr.
112 H3 Koszalin Poland
112 H7 Kőszeg Hungary
87 C1 Kota Chhattisgarh India
88 C4 Kota Rajasthan India
99 B4 Kotaagung Indon.
88 C4 Kota Barrage India
99 D3 Kotabaru Indon.
99 E3 Kotabaru Indon.
99 B1 Kota Bharu Malaysia
99 B3 Kotabumi Indon.
88 C4 Kota Dam India
99 E1 Kota Kinabalu Sabah Malaysia
83 I3 Kotanemel', Gora mt. Kazakh.
87 C2 Kotaparh India
98 B5 Kotapinang Indon.
88 C4 Kotari r. India
99 B2 Kota Tinggi Malaysia
116 I3 Kotel'nich Rus. Fed.
117 G6 Kotel'nikovo Rus. Fed.
77 O2 Kotel'nyy, Ostrov i. Rus. Fed.
88 D3 Kotgarh India
109 J3 Köthen (Anhalt) Germany
88 E4 Kothi India
103 N3 Kotka Fin.
88 C3 Kot Kapura India
116 H2 Kotlas Rus. Fed.
88 C2 Kotli Pak.
128 B3 Kotlik U.S.A.
102 C3 Kötlutangi pt Iceland
103 O4 Kotly Rus. Fed.
114 G2 Kotor Varoš Bos.-Herz.
120 B4 Kotouba Côte d'Ivoire
117 H5 Kotovo Rus. Fed.
117 G4 Kotovsk Rus. Fed.
117 D6 Kotovs'k Ukr.
88 C4 Kotra India
88 E6 Kotri r. India
88 B4 Kotri Pak.
82 D2 Kotrtas Kazakh.
88 A5 Kot Sarae Pak.
87 C2 Kottagudem India
87 B4 Kottarakara India
87 B4 Kottayam India
87 B3 Kotturu India
Koturdepe Turkm. see Goturdepe
77 L2 Kotuy r. Rus. Fed.
128 B3 Kotzebue U.S.A.
128 B3 Kotzebue Sound sea chan. U.S.A.
109 K5 Kötzting Germany
120 A3 Koubia Guinea
120 B3 Koudougou Burkina
124 E6 Koueveldberge mts S. Africa
121 D3 Koufey Niger
115 L7 Koufonisi i. Greece
124 E6 Kougaberge mts S. Africa
80 D4 Kouklia Cyprus
122 B4 Koulamoutou Gabon
120 B3 Koulikoro Mali
69 G4 Koumac New Caledonia
120 A3 Koundâra Guinea
83 H3 Kounradskiy Kazakh.
120 B3 Koupéla Burkina
155 H2 Kourou Fr. Guiana
120 B3 Kouroussa Guinea
121 D3 Kousséri Cameroon
120 B3 Koutiala Mali
103 N3 Kouvola Fin.
102 O2 Kovdor Rus. Fed.
102 P2 Kovdozero, Ozero l. Rus. Fed.
117 C5 Kovel' Ukr.
116 G3 Kovernino Rus. Fed.
87 B4 Kovilpatti India
116 G3 Kovrov Rus. Fed.
116 G4 Kovylkino Rus. Fed.
116 F2 Kovzhskoye, Ozero l. Rus. Fed.
72 C5 Kowhitirangi N.Z.
93 □ Kowloon Peak h. Hong Kong China
93 □ Kowloon Peninsula Hong Kong China
96 D4 Kowŏn N. Korea
83 J5 Koxlax China
83 I5 Koxtag China
95 B7 Kōyama-misaki pt Japan
82 F1 Koybagar, Ozero l. Kazakh.
80 B3 Köyceğiz Turkey
116 I2 Koygorodok Rus. Fed.
Koymatdag, Gory hills Turkm. see Goýmatdag
87 A2 Koyna Reservoir India
116 H1 Koynas Rus. Fed.
128 C3 Koyukuk r. U.S.A.
80 F1 Koyulhisar Turkey
116 F3 Koza Rus. Fed.
95 A7 Kō-zaki pt Japan
80 E3 Kozan Turkey
115 I4 Kozani Greece
114 G2 Kozara mts Bos.-Herz.
117 D5 Kozelets' Ukr.
116 E4 Kozel'sk Rus. Fed.
Kozhikode India see Calicut
80 C1 Kozlu Turkey
116 H3 Koz'modem'yansk Rus. Fed.
83 G4 Kozmoldak Kazakh.
115 J4 Kožuf mts Greece/Macedonia
95 F7 Kōzu-shima i. Japan
117 D5 Kozyatyn Ukr.
120 C4 Kpalimé Togo
98 A3 Kra, Isthmus of Thai.
98 A3 Krabi Thai.
98 A3 Kra Buri Thai.
98 C2 Krâchéh Cambodia
102 L2 Kraddsele Sweden
103 J4 Kragerø Norway
108 D2 Kraggenburg Neth.
115 I2 Kragujevac Serb. and Mont.
109 G5 Kraichgau reg. Germany
99 C4 Krakatau i. Indon.
98 C2 Krâkôr Cambodia
113 I5 Kraków Poland
109 K1 Krakower See l. Germany
98 B2 Krâlănh Cambodia
157 C1 Kralendijk Neth. Antilles
117 F5 Kramators'k Ukr.
102 L3 Kramfors Sweden
108 C3 Krammer est. Neth.
115 J6 Kranidi Greece
114 F1 Kranj Slovenia
98 □ Kranji Reservoir Sing.
125 I4 Kranskop S. Africa
116 H2 Krasavino Rus. Fed.
76 G2 Krasino Rus. Fed.
94 B3 Kraskino Rus. Fed.
103 N5 Krāslava Latvia
109 K4 Kraslice Czech Rep.
113 O4 Krasnapollye Belarus
116 D4 Krasnaya Gora Rus. Fed.
83 H2 Krasnaya Polyana Kazakh.
117 H5 Krasnoarmeysk Rus. Fed.
117 F5 Krasnoarmiys'k Ukr.
116 H2 Krasnoborsk Rus. Fed.
117 F6 Krasnodar Rus. Fed.
117 F6 Krasnodarskiy Kray admin. div. Rus. Fed.
117 F5 Krasnodon Ukr.
116 D3 Krasnogorodskoye Rus. Fed.
117 G6 Krasnogvardeyskoye Rus. Fed.
117 E5 Krasnohrad Ukr.
117 E6 Krasnohvardiys'ke Ukr.
82 C2 Krasnokholm Rus. Fed.
113 Q2 Krasnomayskiy Rus. Fed.
117 E6 Krasnoperekops'k Ukr.
94 D2 Krasnorechenskiy Rus. Fed.
103 O3 Krasnosel'skoye Rus. Fed.
116 G4 Krasnoslobodsk Rus. Fed.
82 D1 Krasnousol'skiy Rus. Fed.
82 C5 Krasnovodsk, Mys pt Turkm.
Krasnovodskiy Zaliv b. Turkm. see Turkmenbashi, Zaliv
82 C4 Krasnovodskoye Plato plat. Turkm.
90 B1 Krasnoyarsk Rus. Fed.
113 O3 Krasnyy Rus. Fed.
116 H3 Krasnyye Baki Rus. Fed.
117 H6 Krasnyye Barrikady Rus. Fed.
116 F3 Krasnyy Kholm Rus. Fed.
117 H5 Krasnyy Kut Rus. Fed.
116 D3 Krasnyy Luch Rus. Fed.
117 F5 Krasnyy Lyman Ukr.
83 I3 Krasnyy Oktyabr' Kazakh.
83 G1 Krasnyy Yar Kazakh.
117 I6 Krasnyy Yar Astrakhanskaya Oblast' Rus. Fed.
82 B1 Krasnyy Yar Samarskaya Oblast' Rus. Fed.
117 H5 Krasnyy Yar Volgogradskaya Oblast' Rus. Fed.
117 C5 Krasyliv Ukr.
117 H7 Kraynovka Rus. Fed.
108 E3 Krefeld Germany
117 E5 Kremenchuk Ukr.
117 E5 Kremenchuts'ka Vodoskhovyshche resr Ukr.
117 G5 Kremenskaya Rus. Fed.
112 G6 Křemešník h. Czech Rep.
138 F3 Kremmling U.S.A.
112 G6 Krems an der Donau Austria
77 T3 Kresta, Zaliv g. Rus. Fed.
116 E3 Kresttsy Rus. Fed.
103 M5 Kretinga Lith.
108 E4 Kreuzau Germany
109 F4 Kreuztal Germany
113 M3 Kreva Belarus
120 C4 Kribi Cameroon
125 H3 Kriel S. Africa
115 I5 Krikellos Greece
94 H2 Kril'on, Mys c. Rus. Fed.
79 F5 Krishna r. India
79 G5 Krishna, Mouths of the India
87 B3 Krishnagiri India
89 G5 Krishnanagar India
87 B3 Krishnaraja Sagara l. India
103 I4 Kristiansand Norway
103 K4 Kristianstad Sweden
102 I3 Kristiansund Norway
Kristiinankaupunki Fin. see Kristinestad
103 K4 Kristinehamn Sweden
103 M3 Kristinestad Fin.
Kriti i. Greece see Crete
Krivoy Rog Ukr. see Kryvyy Rih
114 G1 Križevci Croatia
114 F2 Krk i. Croatia
102 K3 Krokom Sweden
102 J3 Krokstadøra Norway
102 K2 Krokstranda Norway
117 E5 Krolevets' Ukr.
109 J4 Kronach Germany
98 B3 Krŏng Kaôh Kŏng Cambodia
102 M3 Kronoby Fin.
129 O3 Kronprins Frederik Bjerge nunataks Greenland
98 A2 Kronwa Myanmar
125 G3 Kroonstad S. Africa
117 G6 Kropotkin Rus. Fed.
109 K3 Kropstädt Germany
113 J6 Krosno Poland
112 H5 Krotoszyn Poland
125 I2 Kruger National Park S. Africa
113 N3 Kruhlaye Belarus
99 B4 Krui Indon.
124 F7 Kruisfontein S. Africa
115 H4 Krujë Albania
115 K4 Krumovgrad Bulg.
Krung Thep Thai. see Bangkok
113 N3 Krupki Belarus
115 I3 Kruševac Serb. and Mont.
109 K4 Krušné Hory mts Czech Rep.
130 B3 Kruzof Island U.S.A.
116 D4 Krychaw Belarus
163 H4 Krylov Seamount sea feature N. Atlantic Ocean
117 F6 Krymsk Rus. Fed.
Kryms'kyy Pivostriv pen. Ukr. see Crimea
83 H3 Krypsalo Kazakh.
115 K6 Krytiko Pelagos sea Greece
117 E6 Kryvyy Rih Ukr.
120 B2 Ksabi Alg.
120 C1 Ksar el Boukhari Alg.
120 B1 Ksar el Kebir Morocco
117 F5 Kshenskiy Rus. Fed.
114 D7 Ksour Essaf Tunisia
116 H3 Kstovo Rus. Fed.
84 B5 Kū', Jabal al h. Saudi Arabia
98 A4 Kuah Malaysia
98 B4 Kuala Kangsar Malaysia
98 B4 Kuala Kerai Malaysia
98 B5 Kuala Kubu Baharu Malaysia
99 B2 Kuala Lipis Malaysia
99 B2 Kuala Lumpur Malaysia
98 B4 Kuala Nerang Malaysia
98 B5 Kuala Pilah Malaysia
98 B5 Kuala Rompin Malaysia
99 D3 Kualasampit Indon.
98 A4 Kualasimpang Indon.
99 B1 Kuala Terengganu Malaysia
97 A5 Kuamut Sabah Malaysia
96 C3 Kuandian China
93 F6 Kuanshan Taiwan
99 B2 Kuantan Malaysia
117 G6 Kuban' r. Rus. Fed.
81 G4 Kubār Syria
81 I5 Kubaysah Iraq
116 F3 Kubenskoye, Ozero l. Rus. Fed.
82 D4 Kubla Ustyurt Uzbek.
116 H4 Kubnya r. Rus. Fed.
115 L3 Kubrat Bulg.
88 C4 Kuchaman India
88 C4 Kuchera India
99 D2 Kuching Sarawak Malaysia
95 A10 Kuchino-shima i. Japan
83 I1 Kuchukskoye, Ozero salt l. Rus. Fed.
115 H4 Kuçovë Albania
87 A3 Kudal India
99 E1 Kudat Sabah Malaysia
87 B3 Kudligi India
87 A3 Kudremukh mt. India
99 D4 Kudus Indon.
112 F7 Kufstein Austria
129 J3 Kugaaruk Canada
83 I3 Kugaly Kazakh.
116 H3 Kugesi Rus. Fed.
128 G3 Kugluktuk Canada
128 E3 Kugmallit Bay Canada
84 E5 Kūh, Ra's-al- pt Iran
85 F5 Kūhak Iran
89 E3 Kuhanbokano mt. China
109 K1 Kuhbier Germany
84 E4 Kūhbonān Iran
84 B3 Kūhdasht Iran
81 L3 Kūhīn Iran
102 O2 Kuhmo Fin.
103 N3 Kuhmoinen Fin.
84 D3 Kūhpāyeh Iran
109 K3 Kühren Germany
98 A2 Kui Buri Thai.
124 B2 Kuis Namibia
124 A1 Kuiseb Pass Namibia
123 B5 Kuito Angola
130 C3 Kuiu Island U.S.A.
102 N2 Kuivaniemi Fin.
89 F5 Kujang India
96 C4 Kujang N. Korea
94 G4 Kuji Japan
95 B8 Kujū-san vol. Japan
135 F1 Kukatush Canada
115 I3 Kukës Albania
116 I3 Kukmor Rus. Fed.
98 B5 Kukup Malaysia
82 D5 Kükürtli Turkm.
84 D5 Kūl r. Iran
80 B2 Kula Turkey
82 B2 Kulagino Kazakh.
89 G3 Kula Kangri mt. Bhutan
82 B3 Kulaly, Ostrov i. Kazakh.
83 H4 Kulan Kazakh.
83 H4 Kulanak Kyrg.
82 D3 Kulandy Kazakh.
82 D3 Kulandy, Poluostrov pen. Kazakh.
85 F5 Kulaneh reg. Pak.
83 G2 Kulanotpes watercourse Kazakh.
83 I4 Kulansarak China
85 G4 Kulao r. Pak.
77 O2 Kular Rus. Fed.
97 B5 Kulassein i. Phil.
89 H4 Kulaura Bangl.
103 M4 Kuldīga Latvia
Kul'dzhuktau, Gory h. Uzbek. see Quljuqtov tog'lari
124 D1 Kule Botswana
116 G4 Kulebaki Rus. Fed.
98 C2 Kulen Cambodia
82 E1 Kulevchinskoye Rus. Fed.
116 H2 Kulikovo Rus. Fed.
98 B4 Kulim Malaysia
Kulkuduk Uzbek. see Ko'lquduq
70 F3 Kulkyne watercourse Australia
88 D3 Kullu India
109 J4 Kulmbach Germany
83 G5 Kŭlob Tajik.
81 H2 Kulp Turkey
88 D4 Kulpahar India
147 F4 Kulpsville U.S.A.
82 C3 Kul'sary Kazakh.
109 H5 Külsheim Germany
80 D2 Kulu Turkey
80 C3 Kulübe Tepe mt. Turkey
83 I1 Kulunda Rus. Fed.
83 J1 Kulunda r. Rus. Fed.
83 H1 Kulundinskaya Step' plain Kazakh./Rus. Fed.
83 I1 Kulundinskoye, Ozero salt l. Rus. Fed.
84 D4 Kūlvand Iran
70 E5 Kulwin Australia
117 H6 Kuma r. Rus. Fed.
95 F6 Kumagaya Japan
99 D3 Kumai, Teluk b. Indon.
94 F3 Kumaishi Japan
82 E2 Kumak Rus. Fed.
82 D2 Kumak r. Rus. Fed.
95 B8 Kumamoto Japan
95 E8 Kumano Japan
115 I3 Kumanovo Macedonia
120 B4 Kumasi Ghana
120 C4 Kumba Cameroon
87 B4 Kumbakonam India
80 C2 Kümbet Turkey
124 E1 Kumchuru Botswana
84 D3 Kumel well Iran
82 C1 Kumertau Rus. Fed.
96 D5 Kŭm-gang r. S. Korea
96 E4 Kumgang-san mt. N. Korea
96 E6 Kŭmho-gang r. S. Korea
96 D4 Kumhwa S. Korea
96 E5 Kumi S. Korea
103 K4 Kumla Sweden
109 L2 Kummersdorf-Alexanderdorf Germany
120 D3 Kumo Nigeria
96 D6 Kŭmŏ-do i. S. Korea
83 F3 Kumola watercourse Kazakh.
98 B1 Kumphawapi Thai.
124 C4 Kums Namibia
87 A3 Kumta India
117 H7 Kumukh Rus. Fed.
85 H3 Kunar r. Afgh.
90 G2 Kunashir, Ostrov i. Rus. Fed.
89 E2 Kunchuk Tso salt l. China
103 N4 Kunda Estonia
89 E4 Kunda India
87 A3 Kundapura India
88 B2 Kundar r. Afgh./Pak.
85 H2 Kunduz Afgh.
85 H2 Kunduz r. Afgh.
Künes China see Xinyuan
83 J4 Künes Chang China
83 J4 Künes He r. China
103 J4 Kungälv Sweden
83 I4 Kungei Alatau mts Kazakh./Kyrg.
130 C4 Kunghit Island Canada
Kungrad Uzbek. see Qo'ng'irot
82 E4 Kungradkol' Uzbek.
103 K4 Kungsbacka Sweden
103 J4 Kungshamn Sweden
122 B3 Kungu Dem. Rep. Congo
88 D6 Kuni r. India
95 B8 Kunimi-dake mt. Japan
89 F5 Kunjabar India
89 G4 Kunlui r. India/Nepal
79 F3 Kunlun Shan mts China
89 H2 Kunlun Shankou pass China
93 B5 Kunming China
88 D4 Kuno r. India
96 D6 Kunsan S. Korea
92 F4 Kunshan China
68 C3 Kununurra Australia
88 D4 Kunwari r. India
116 D3 Kun'ya Rus. Fed.
Kunyu Shan h. China see Taibo Ding
109 H5 Künzelsau Germany
109 J3 Künzels-Berg h. Germany
93 F4 Kuocang Shan mts China
103 N3 Kuohijärvi l. Fin.
102 O2 Kuolayarvi Rus. Fed.
102 N3 Kuopio Fin.
102 M3 Kuortane Fin.
114 2 Kupa r. Croatia/Slovenia
91 E8 Kupang Indon.
103 N5 Kupiškis Lith.
130 C3 Kupreanof Island U.S.A.
117 F5 Kup"yans'k Ukr.
83 J4 Kuqa China
81 L2 Kür r. Azer.
81 J1 Kura r. Azer./Georgia
117 G7 Kura r. Georgia/Rus. Fed.
83 H4 Kuragaty Kazakh.
117 H7 Kurakh Rus. Fed.
82 D2 Kurashasayskiy Kazakh.
95 C7 Kurashiki Japan
89 E5 Kurasia India
95 C7 Kurayoshi Japan
80 B1 Kurban Dağı mt. Turkey
117 E5 Kurchatov Rus. Fed.
83 J2 Kurchum Kazakh.
81 L1 Kürdämir Azer.
83 H4 Kurday Kazakh.
81 L2 Kür Dili pt Azer.
87 A2 Kurduvadi India
115 K4 Kŭrdzhali Bulg.
95 C7 Kure Japan
80 D1 Küre Turkey
67 G1 Kure Atoll U.S.A.
103 M4 Kuressaare Estonia
76 H4 Kurgan Rus. Fed.
117 G6 Kurganinsk Rus. Fed.
85 H2 Kuri Afgh.
88 B4 Kuri India
Kuria Muria Islands is Oman see Ḩalāniyāt, Juzur al
89 G4 Kuri Chhu r. Bhutan
102 M3 Kurikka Fin.
94 G5 Kurikoma-yama vol. Japan
160 E2 Kuril Basin sea feature Sea of Okhotsk
90 G2 Kuril Islands Rus. Fed.
82 B2 Kurilovka Rus. Fed.
90 G2 Kuril'sk Japan
Kuril'skiye Ostrova is Rus. Fed. see Kuril Islands
160 E3 Kuril Trench sea feature N. Pacific Ocean
82 B1 Kurmanayevka Rus. Fed.
121 F3 Kurmuk Sudan
87 B3 Kurnool India
80 E6 Kurnub tourist site Israel
95 E6 Kurobe Japan
94 G4 Kuroishi Japan
95 G6 Kuroiso Japan
109 I4 Kurort Schmalkalden Germany
95 A9 Kuro-shima i. Japan
116 F4 Kurovskoye Rus. Fed.
72 C6 Kurow N.Z.
88 B2 Kurram r. Afgh./Pak.
71 I4 Kurri Kurri Australia
117 F5 Kursk Rus. Fed.
117 H6 Kurskaya Rus. Fed.
117 F5 Kurskaya Oblast' admin. div. Rus. Fed.
80 D1 Kurşunlu Turkey
81 H3 Kurtalan Turkey
83 I3 Kurtty r. Kazakh.
80 G2 Kuruçay Turkey
88 D3 Kurukshetra India
90 A2 Kuruktag mts China
124 E3 Kuruman S. Africa
124 D3 Kuruman watercourse S. Africa
95 B8 Kurume Japan
90 D1 Kurumkan Rus. Fed.
87 C5 Kurunegala Sri Lanka
121 F2 Kurush, Jebel hills Sudan
83 J2 Kur'ya Rus. Fed.
82 B4 Kuryk Kazakh.
115 L6 Kuşadası Turkey
115 L6 Kuşadası Körfezi b. Turkey
130 B2 Kusawa Lake Canada
108 F5 Kusel Germany
80 A1 Kuş Gölü l. Turkey
117 F6 Kushchevskaya Rus. Fed.
95 B9 Kushikino Japan
95 D8 Kushimoto Japan
94 I3 Kushiro Japan
94 I3 Kushiro-Shitsugen National Park Japan
81 L5 Kūshkak Iran
82 F1 Kushmurun Kazakh.
87 B3 Kushtagi India
89 G5 Kushtia Bangl.
92 C2 Kushui He r. China
82 B2 Kushum Kazakh.
82 B2 Kushum r. Kazakh.
128 C3 Kuskokwim r. U.S.A.
128 B4 Kuskokwim Bay U.S.A.
128 C3 Kuskokwim Mountains U.S.A.
96 C4 Kusŏng N. Korea
94 I3 Kussharo-ko l. Japan
109 F1 Küstenkanal canal Germany
84 C4 Kut Iran
98 B3 Kut, Ko i. Thai.
81 L6 Kūt 'Abdollāh Iran
98 A5 Kutacane Indon.
80 B2 Kütahya Turkey
117 G7 K'ut'aisi Georgia
117 H6 Kutan Rus. Fed.
94 G3 Kutchan Japan
81 L5 Kūt-e Gapu tourist site Iran
114 G2 Kutina Croatia
114 G2 Kutjevo Croatia
113 I4 Kutno Poland
122 B4 Kutu Dem. Rep. Congo
89 G5 Kutubdia Island Bangl.
128 G2 Kuujjua r. Canada
133 G2 Kuujjuaq Canada
132 E2 Kuujjuarapik Canada
Kuuli-Mayak Turkm. see Guwlumaýak
102 O2 Kuusamo Fin.
103 N3 Kuusankoski Fin.
82 D2 Kuvandyk Rus. Fed.
123 B5 Kuvango Angola
116 E3 Kuvshinovo Rus. Fed.
81 K7 Kuwait country Asia
81 K7 Kuwait Kuwait
81 K7 Kuwait Jun b. Kuwait
95 E7 Kuwana Japan
116 G1 Kuya Rus. Fed.
76 I4 Kuybyshev Novosibirskaya Oblast' Rus. Fed.
Kuybyshev Samarskaya Oblast' Rus. Fed. see Samara
116 I4 Kuybyshevskoye Vodokhranilishche resr Rus. Fed.
92 D2 Kuye He r. China
83 H3 Kuygan Kazakh.
79 G2 Kuytun China
83 J3 Kuytun He r. China
115 M6 Kuyucak Turkey
82 F2 Kuyukkol', Ozero salt l. Kazakh.
83 K2 Kuyus Rus. Fed.
103 O3 Kuznechnoye Rus. Fed.
116 H4 Kuznetsk Rus. Fed.
94 F1 Kuznetsovo Rus. Fed.
117 C5 Kuznetsovs'k Ukr.
102 M1 Kvænangen sea chan. Norway
102 L1 Kvaløya i. Norway
102 M1 Kvalsund Norway
82 D1 Kvarkeno Rus. Fed.
114 F2 Kvarnerić sea chan. Croatia
128 C4 Kvichak Bay U.S.A.
130 D3 Kwadacha Wilderness Provincial Park Canada
93 □ Kwai Tau Leng h. Hong Kong China
160 G6 Kwajalein atoll Marshall Is
98 A5 Kwala Indon.
125 I4 KwaMashu S. Africa
125 H2 KwaMhlanga S. Africa
96 D5 Kwangch'ŏn S. Korea
96 D6 Kwangju S. Korea
122 B4 Kwango r. Dem. Rep. Congo
122 D4 Kwangwazi Tanz.
96 D6 Kwangyang S. Korea
96 E3 Kwanmo-bong mt. N. Korea
125 F6 Kwanobuhle S. Africa
125 F6 KwaNojoli S. Africa
125 G6 Kwanonqubela S. Africa
124 F5 Kwanonzame S. Africa
125 G6 Kwatinidubu S. Africa
125 H3 KwaZamokuhle S. Africa
124 F6 Kwazamukucinga S. Africa
124 F5 Kwazamuxolo S. Africa
125 H3 KwaZanele S. Africa
125 I4 Kwazulu-Natal prov. S. Africa
123 C5 Kwekwe Zimbabwe
124 F1 Kweneng admin. dist. Botswana
122 B4 Kwenge r. Dem. Rep. Congo
125 G5 Kwezi-Naledi S. Africa
113 I4 Kwidzyn Poland
128 B4 Kwigillingok U.S.A.
68 E2 Kwikila P.N.G.
122 B4 Kwilu r. Angola/Dem. Rep. Congo
91 F7 Kwoka mt. Indon.
93 □ Kwun Tong Hong Kong China
121 D4 Kyabé Chad
70 F6 Kyabram Australia
98 A1 Kya-in Seikkyi Myanmar
90 C1 Kyakhta Rus. Fed.
70 E5 Kyalite Australia
70 A4 Kyancutta Australia
116 F1 Kyanda Rus. Fed.
98 A1 Kyaukhnyat Myanmar
89 H6 Kyaukpyu Myanmar
89 H5 Kyauktaw Myanmar
103 M5 Kybartai Lith.
70 D6 Kybybolite Australia
93 C6 Ky Cung, Sông r. Vietnam
88 D2 Kyelang India
92 A2 Kyikug China
Kyiv Ukr. see Kiev
Kyklades is Greece see Cyclades
131 H4 Kyle Canada
106 C3 Kyle of Lochalsh U.K.
108 E5 Kyll r. Germany
115 J6 Kyllini mt. Greece
70 F6 Kyneton Australia
122 D3 Kyoga, Lake Uganda
95 D7 Kyōga-misaki pt Japan
71 J2 Kyogle Australia
98 A1 Kyondo Myanmar
96 E6 Kyŏngju S. Korea
95 D7 Kyōto Japan
115 I6 Kyparissia Greece
115 I6 Kyparissiakos Kolpos b. Greece
83 G2 Kypshak, Ozero salt l. Kazakh.
115 K5 Kyra Panagia i. Greece
80 D4 Kyrenia Cyprus
83 H4 Kyrgyzstan country Asia
109 K2 Kyritz Germany
82 B2 Kyrkopa Kazakh.
102 J3 Kyrksæterøra Norway
76 G3 Kyrta Rus. Fed.
116 H1 Kyssa Rus. Fed.
77 O3 Kytalyktakh Rus. Fed.
115 J6 Kythira i. Greece
115 K6 Kythnos i. Greece
98 A2 Kyungyaung Myanmar
82 D3 Kyushe Kazakh.
95 B8 Kyūshū i. Japan
160 E4 Kyushu-Palau Ridge sea feature N. Pacific Ocean
115 J3 Kyustendil Bulg.
71 G5 Kywong Australia
117 D5 Kyyivs'ke Vodoskhovyshche resr Ukr.
102 N3 Kyyjärvi Fin.
82 C3 Kyzan Kazakh.
90 B1 Kyzyl Rus. Fed.
83 G4 Kyzyl-Adyr Kyrg.
83 H5 Kyzylart Pass Kyrg.
83 H3 Kyzylbelen, Gora h. Kazakh.
83 G2 Kyzyldyykan Kazakh.
83 J3 Kyzylkesek Kazakh.
82 C2 Kyzylkoga Kazakh.
82 E2 Kyzylkol', Ozero l. Kazakh.
82 E4 Kyzylkum Desert Uzbek.
83 H4 Kyzyl-Kyya Kyrg.
82 F3 Kyzylorda Kazakh.
82 E3 Kyzylordinskaya Oblast' admin. div. Kazakh.
82 C4 Kyzylsay Kazakh.
83 I4 Kyzyl-Suu Kyrg.
83 H5 Kyzyl-Suu r. Kyrg.
83 H2 Kyzyltas Kazakh.
83 H3 Kyzyltau Kazakh.
82 F2 Kyzyluy Kazakh.
82 B3 Kyzylsor Kazakh.
82 C2 Kyzylzhar Aktyubinskaya Oblast' Kazakh.
83 G2 Kyzylzhar Karagandinskaya Oblast' Kazakh.

L

108 F4 Laacher See l. Germany
103 N4 Laagri Estonia
151 F5 La Angostura, Presa de resr Mex.
102 N1 Laanila Fin.
150 D3 La Ardilla, Cerro mt. Mex.
122 E3 Laascaanood Somalia
122 E2 Laasgoray Somalia
157 E2 La Asunción Venez.
120 A2 Laâyoune W. Sahara
117 G6 Laba r. Rus. Fed.
150 D1 La Babia Mex.
150 H4 La Bahía, Islas de is Hond.
132 F3 La Baleine, Grande Rivière de r. Canada
132 E2 La Baleine, Petite Rivière de r. Canada
133 G2 La Baleine, Rivière à r. Canada
156 D3 La Banda Arg.
138 E3 La Barge U.S.A.
69 H3 Labasa Fiji
110 C3 La Baule-Escoublac France
120 A3 Labé Guinea
132 F4 Labelle Canada
134 B5 La Belle U.S.A.
121 D4 La Bénoué, Parc National de nat. park Cameroon
130 B2 Laberge, Lake Canada
97 A5 Labian, Tanjung pt Sabah Malaysia
130 E2 La Biche r. Canada
131 G4 La Biche, Lac l. Canada
117 G6 Labinsk Rus. Fed.
98 B5 Labis Malaysia
97 B3 Labo Phil.
150 C2 La Boquilla Mex.
150 C2 La Boquilla, Presa de resr Mex.
120 B3 La Boucle du Baoulé, Parc National de nat. park Mali
80 F4 Laboué Lebanon
110 D4 Labouheyre France
159 D2 Laboulaye Arg.
133 H3 Labrador reg. Canada
133 G3 Labrador City Canada
129 M3 Labrador Sea Canada/Greenland
154 F5 Lábrea Brazil
99 E1 Labuan Malaysia
99 C4 Labuhan Indon.
99 B2 Labuhanbilik Indon.
98 A5 Labuhanruku Indon.
97 A5 Labuk r. Sabah Malaysia
99 E1 Labuk, Teluk b. Sabah Malaysia
91 E7 Labuna Indon.
70 A3 Labyrinth, Lake salt flat Australia
76 H3 Labytnangi Rus. Fed.
115 H4 Laç Albania
111 C1 La Cabrera, Sierra de mts Spain
159 D1 La Calera Arg.
159 B2 La Calera Chile
110 F2 La Capelle France
159 B4 Lácar, Lago l. Arg.
Lacar, Lago l. Arg. see Lácar, Lago
159 D2 La Carlota Arg.
111 E3 La Carolina Spain
115 L2 Lăcăuți, Vârful mt. Romania
147 I1 Lac-Baker Canada
78 F5 Laccadive Islands India
131 J4 Lac du Bonnet Canada
150 H5 La Ceiba Hond.
157 C2 La Ceiba Venez.
70 C6 Lacepede Bay Australia
157 D3 La Cerbatana, Sierra de mt. Venez.
147 E4 Laceyville U.S.A.
147 H1 Lac Frontière Canada
116 F2 Lacha, Ozero l. Rus. Fed.
109 I2 Lachendorf Germany
135 F3 Lachine U.S.A.
70 F5 Lachlan r. Australia
150 J6 La Chorrera Panama
132 F4 Lachute Canada
81 K2 Laçın Azer.
110 G5 La Ciotat France
150 C3 La Ciudad Mex.
146 D3 Lackawanna U.S.A.
131 G4 Lac La Biche Canada
130 E4 Lac La Hache Canada
Lac la Martre Canada see Wha Ti
131 H3 Lac La Ronge Provincial Park Canada
133 F4 Lac-Mégantic Canada
147 G2 Lacolle Canada
150 B1 La Colorada Mex.
130 G4 Lacombe Canada
120 B4 La Comoé, Parc National de nat. park Côte d'Ivoire
150 I6 La Concepción Panama
151 F4 La Concordia Mex.
114 C5 Laconi Sardinia Italy
147 H3 Laconia U.S.A.
135 I1 La Corne Canada
134 B4 La Crescent U.S.A.
134 B4 La Crosse U.S.A.
157 A4 La Cruz Col.
150 C3 La Cruz Sinaloa Mex.
151 E2 La Cruz Tamaulipas Mex.
150 H5 La Cruz Nicaragua
150 D1 La Cuesta Mex.
111 C2 La Culebra, Sierra de mts Spain
142 E4 La Cygne U.S.A.
88 D2 Ladakh Range mts India
98 A4 Ladang, Ko i. Thai.
111 E1 La Demanda, Sierra de mts Spain
80 E1 Ladik Turkey
124 D6 Ladismith S. Africa
85 F4 Lādīz Iran
88 C4 Ladnun India
157 B3 La Dorada Col.
Ladozhskoye Ozero l. Rus. Fed. see Lake Ladoga
89 H4 Ladu mt. India
116 E2 Ladva Rus. Fed.
116 E2 Ladva-Vetka Rus. Fed.
129 J2 Lady Ann Strait Canada
106 E4 Ladybank U.K.
125 G4 Ladybrand S. Africa
135 G2 Lady Evelyn Lake Canada
125 G5 Lady Frere S. Africa
125 G5 Lady Grey S. Africa
130 E5 Ladysmith Canada
125 H4 Ladysmith S. Africa
134 B3 Ladysmith U.S.A.
83 G2 Ladyzhenka Kazakh.
68 E2 Lae P.N.G.
98 B2 Laem Ngop Thai.
103 I3 Lærdalsøyri Norway
154 F8 La Esmeralda Bol.
157 D4 La Esmeralda Venez.
103 J4 Læsø i. Denmark
150 G5 La Esperanza Hond.
159 D1 La Falda Arg.
138 F4 Lafayette CO U.S.A.
134 D5 Lafayette IN U.S.A.
143 E6 Lafayette LA U.S.A.
145 C5 La Fayette U.S.A.
110 F5 La Fenille, Col de pass France
108 B5 La Fère France
108 B5 La-Ferté-Milon France
108 B6 La Ferté-sous-Jouarre France
84 C5 Laffān, Ra's pt Qatar
120 C4 Lafia Nigeria
110 D3 La Flèche France
146 A6 La Follette U.S.A.
135 H2 Laforce Canada
135 G2 Laforest Canada
133 F3 Laforge Canada
157 B2 La Fría Venez.
84 D5 Lāft Iran
114 C6 La Galite i. Tunisia
114 C6 La Galite, Canal de sea chan. Tunisia
117 H6 Lagan' Rus. Fed.
76 C4 Lagan Sweden
107 E3 Lagan r. U.K.
122 C3 La Garamba, Parc National de nat. park Dem. Rep. Congo
155 K6 Lagarto Brazil
109 G3 Lage Germany
103 J4 Lågen r. Norway
106 C5 Lagg U.K.
106 D3 Laggan U.K.
106 D4 Laggan, Loch l. U.K.
120 C1 Laghouat Alg.
89 F2 Lagkor Co salt l. China
157 B2 La Gloria Col.
157 A4 Lago Agrio Ecuador
158 D2 Lagoa Santa Brazil
81 K1 Lagodekhi Georgia
120 A2 La Gomera i. Canary Is
149 J5 La Gonâve, Île de i. Haiti
98 D5 Lagong i. Indon.
97 B3 Lagonoy Gulf Phil.
156 B7 Lago Posadas Arg.
159 B4 Lago Ranco Chile
120 C4 Lagos Nigeria
111 B4 Lagos Port.
150 D3 Lagos de Moreno Mex.
132 E3 La Grande r. Canada
138 C2 La Grande U.S.A.
132 E3 La Grande 2, Réservoir resr Canada
132 E3 La Grande 3, Réservoir resr Canada
132 F3 La Grande 4, Réservoir resr Canada
110 H4 La Grande Casse, Pointe de mt. France
68 C3 La Grange Australia
Lagrange Australia see La Grange
145 C5 La Grange GA U.S.A.
147 I2 La Grange ME U.S.A.
134 D5 La Grange MI U.S.A.
134 B5 La Grange MO U.S.A.
143 D6 La Grange TX U.S.A.
134 E5 Lagrange U.S.A.
157 E3 La Gran Sabana plat. Venez.
157 C1 La Guajira, Península de pen. Col.
156 G3 Laguna Brazil
140 D5 Laguna Beach U.S.A.
159 B3 Laguna de Laja, Parque Nacional nat. park Chile
150 I5 Laguna de Perlas Nicaragua
140 D5 Laguna Mountains U.S.A.
154 C5 Lagunas Peru
156 A7 Laguna San Rafael, Parque Nacional nat. park Chile
151 E5 Lagunas de Chacahua, Parque Nacional nat. park Mex.
157 C2 Lagunillas Venez.
La Habana Cuba see Havana
99 E1 Lahad Datu Sabah Malaysia
97 A5 Lahad Datu, Teluk b. Sabah Malaysia
110 D2 La Hague, Cap de c. France
140 □2 Lahaina U.S.A.
99 B3 Lahat Indon.
98 A5 Lahewa Indon.
86 B7 Laḩij Yemen
84 C2 Lāhījān Iran
140 □1 Lahilahi Point U.S.A.
109 F4 Lahn r. Germany
108 F4 Lahnstein Germany
103 K4 Laholm Sweden
140 C2 Lahontan Reservoir U.S.A.
88 C3 Lahore Pak.
157 E3 La Horqueta Venez.
149 J5 La Hotte, Massif de mts Haiti
88 B3 Lahri Pak.
103 N3 Lahti Fin.
150 C4 La Huerta Mex.
121 D4 Laï Chad
92 F3 Lai'an China
93 C6 Laibin China
71 J1 Laidley Australia
140 □1 Lā'ie U.S.A.
Laie U.S.A. see Lā'ie
140 □1 Lā'ie Point U.S.A.
Laie Pt U.S.A. see Lā'ie Point
93 C4 Laifeng China
110 E2 L'Aigle France
150 G5 La Iguala Hond.
102 M3 Laihia Fin.
89 H4 Laimakuri India
124 D6 Laingsburg S. Africa
102 M2 Lainioälven r. Sweden
120 C3 L'Aïr, Massif de mts Niger
106 D2 Lairg U.K.
97 C5 Lais Phil.
103 M3 Laitila Fin.
114 D1 Laives Italy
92 E2 Laiwu China
92 F2 Laiyang China
92 E2 Laiyuan China
92 F2 Laizhou China
92 F2 Laizhou Wan b. China
159 B3 Laja r. Chile
159 B3 Laja, Laguna de l. Chile
68 D3 Lajamanu Australia
155 K5 Lajes Brazil
156 F3 Lajes Brazil
150 C2 La Joya Mex.
139 G4 La Junta U.S.A.
149 H4 La Juventud, Isla de i. Cuba
138 E2 Lake U.S.A.
142 D3 Lake Andes U.S.A.
80 D6 Lake Bardawil Reserve nature res. Egypt
70 E6 Lake Bolac Australia
71 G4 Lake Cargelligo Australia
71 J3 Lake Cathie Australia
143 E6 Lake Charles U.S.A.
138 B1 Lake Chelan National Recreation Area park U.S.A.
145 D6 Lake City FL U.S.A.
134 E3 Lake City MI U.S.A.
134 A3 Lake City MN U.S.A.
145 E5 Lake City SC U.S.A.

Ludwigsfelde 191

106 C3 Liathach mt. U.K.
80 F4 Liban, Jebel mts Lebanon
157 B3 Libano Col.
138 D1 Libby U.S.A.
122 B3 Libenge Dem. Rep. Congo
143 C4 Liberal U.S.A.
112 G5 Liberec Czech Rep.
120 B4 Liberia country Africa
150 H6 Liberia Costa Rica
157 C2 Libertad Venez.
157 C2 Libertad Venez.
134 B6 Liberty IL U.S.A.
147 I2 Liberty ME U.S.A.
142 E4 Liberty MO U.S.A.
147 F4 Liberty NY U.S.A.
143 E6 Liberty TX U.S.A.
108 D5 Libin Belgium
97 B3 Libmanan Phil.
93 C5 Libo China
125 H5 Libode S. Africa
98 A4 Libong, Ko i. Thai.
110 D4 Libourne France
122 A3 Libreville Gabon
97 C5 Libuganon r. Phil.
121 D2 Libya country Africa
121 E2 Libyan Desert Egypt/Libya
121 E1 Libyan Plateau Egypt
159 B2 Licantén Chile
114 E6 Licata Sicily Italy
81 H2 Lice Turkey
109 G4 Lich Germany
105 F5 Lichfield U.K.
123 D5 Lichinga Moz.
109 J4 Lichte Germany
109 G3 Lichtenau Germany
125 G3 Lichtenburg S. Africa
109 J4 Lichtenfels Germany
108 E3 Lichtenvoorde Neth.
93 C4 Lichuan Hubei China
93 E5 Lichuan Jiangxi China
146 B5 Licking r. U.S.A.
116 C4 Lida Belarus
140 D3 Lida U.S.A.
124 C2 Lidfontein Namibia
103 K4 Lidköping Sweden
102 K2 Lidsjöberg Sweden
109 H2 Liebenau Germany
109 I2 Liebenburg Germany
109 L2 Liebenwalde Germany
68 D4 Liebig, Mount Australia
110 I3 Liechtenstein country Europe
108 D4 Liège Belgium
102 O3 Lieksa Fin.
113 L2 Lielupe r. Latvia
103 N4 Lielvārde Latvia
102 L3 Lien Sweden
122 C3 Lienart Dem. Rep. Congo
98 D3 Liên Nghia Vietnam
112 F7 Lienz Austria
103 M4 Liepāja Latvia
108 C3 Lier Belgium
108 D3 Lieshout Neth.
108 A4 Liévin France
135 J2 Lièvre r. Canada
112 G7 Liezen Austria
107 E4 Liffey r. Rep. of Ireland
107 D3 Lifford Rep. of Ireland
159 C4 Lifi Mahuida mt. Arg.
69 G4 Lifou i. New Caledonia
97 B3 Ligao Phil.
103 N4 Līgatne Latvia
71 G2 Lightning Ridge Australia
123 D5 Ligonha r. Moz.
134 E5 Ligonier U.S.A.
150 B2 Ligui Mex.
110 I5 Ligurian Sea France/Italy
68 F2 Lihir Group is P.N.G.
140 □2 Līhu'e U.S.A.
Lihue U.S.A. see Līhu'e
93 D5 Li Jiang r. China
92 F2 Lijin China
98 B1 Lik, Nam r. Laos
123 C5 Likasi Dem. Rep. Congo
130 E4 Likely Canada
116 E3 Likhoslavl' Rus. Fed.
99 C2 Liku Indon.
116 G3 Likurga Rus. Fed.
114 C3 L'Île-Rousse Corsica France
109 G1 Lilienthal Germany
93 D5 Liling China
88 C2 Lilla Pak.
103 K4 Lilla Edet Sweden
108 C3 Lille Belgium
110 F1 Lille France
Lille Bælt sea chan. Denmark see Little Belt
103 J3 Lillehammer Norway
108 A4 Lillers France
103 J4 Lillesand Norway
103 J4 Lillestrøm Norway
134 E4 Lilley U.S.A.
102 K3 Lillholmsjö Sweden
130 E4 Lillooet Canada
130 E4 Lillooet r. Canada
89 H4 Lilong India
123 D5 Lilongwe Malawi
97 B4 Liloy Phil.
70 C4 Lilydale S.A. Australia
71 G8 Lilydale Tas. Australia
154 C6 Lima Peru
(City Plan 64)
138 D2 Lima MT U.S.A.
146 A4 Lima OH U.S.A.
84 E5 Līmah Oman
117 H6 Liman Rus. Fed.
159 B1 Limari r. Chile
89 E2 Lima Ringma Tso salt l. China
80 D4 Limassol Cyprus
107 E2 Limavady U.K.
159 C3 Limay r. Arg.
159 C3 Limay Mahuida Arg.
103 N4 Limbaži Latvia
120 C4 Limbe Cameroon
99 E3 Limbungan Indon.
109 G4 Limburg an der Lahn Germany
98 □ Lim Chu Kang Sing.
98 □ Lim Chu Kang h. Sing.
124 E4 Lime Acres S. Africa
158 C3 Limeira Brazil
107 C5 Limerick Rep. of Ireland
134 A4 Lime Springs U.S.A.
147 J1 Limestone U.S.A.
102 K2 Limingen Norway
102 K2 Limingen l. Norway
147 H3 Limington U.S.A.
102 N2 Liminka Fin.
115 K5 Limnos i. Greece
147 F2 Limoges Canada
110 E4 Limoges France
Limón Costa Rica see Puerto Limón
150 H5 Limón Hond.
139 G4 Limon U.S.A.
80 E3 Limonlu Turkey
110 E4 Limousin reg. France
110 F5 Limoux France
125 J1 Limpopo r. Africa
125 H2 Limpopo prov. S. Africa
125 I1 Limpopo National Park S. Africa
84 A4 Linah well Saudi Arabia
102 O1 Linakhamari Rus. Fed.
93 F4 Lin'an China
97 A4 Linapacan i. Phil.
97 A4 Linapacan Strait Phil.
159 B2 Linares Chile
151 E2 Linares Mex.
111 E3 Linares Spain
90 C4 Lincang China
92 E2 Lincheng China
Linchuan China see Fuzhou
159 E2 Lincoln Arg.
105 G4 Lincoln U.K.
140 B2 Lincoln CA U.S.A.
134 C5 Lincoln IL U.S.A.
147 I2 Lincoln ME U.S.A.
135 F3 Lincoln MI U.S.A.
142 D3 Lincoln NE U.S.A.
147 H2 Lincoln NH U.S.A.
138 A2 Lincoln City U.S.A.
135 F4 Lincoln Park U.S.A.
105 G4 Lincolnshire Wolds hills U.K.
147 I2 Lincolnville U.S.A.
158 E1 Linda, Serra hills Brazil
109 K2 Lindau Germany
112 D7 Lindau (Bodensee) Germany
109 G4 Linden Germany
155 G2 Linden Guyana
145 C5 Linden AL U.S.A.
145 C5 Linden TN U.S.A.
134 A2 Linden Grove U.S.A.
Lindenow Fjord inlet Greenland see Kangerlussuatsiaq
109 F2 Lindern (Oldenburg) Germany
103 I4 Lindesnes c. Norway
122 C3 Lindi r. Dem. Rep. Congo
123 D4 Lindi Tanz.
Lindisfarne i. U.K. see Holy Island
125 G3 Lindley S. Africa
92 F1 Lindong China
115 M6 Lindos, Akra pt Greece
147 J1 Lindsay N.B. Canada
135 H3 Lindsay Ont. Canada
140 C3 Lindsay U.S.A.
67 I3 Line Islands S. Pacific Ocean
92 D2 Linfen China
87 A3 Linganamakki Reservoir India
97 B2 Lingayen Phil.
97 B2 Lingayen Gulf Phil.
92 D3 Lingbao China
92 E3 Lingbi China
93 D5 Lingchuan Guangxi China
92 D3 Lingchuan Shanxi China
125 G6 Lingelethu S. Africa
125 F6 Lingelihle S. Africa
108 F2 Lingen (Ems) Germany
99 B3 Lingga, Kepulauan is Indon.
96 A3 Linghai China
97 C5 Lingig Phil.
97 A5 Lingkabau Sabah Malaysia
138 F3 Lingle U.S.A.
122 C3 Lingomo Dem. Rep. Congo
92 E2 Lingqiu China
93 C6 Lingshan China
93 D6 Lingshui China
93 C7 Lingshui Wan b. China
87 B2 Lingsugur India
92 C3 Lingtai China
120 A3 Linguère Senegal
93 D5 Lingui China
92 C2 Lingwu China
92 F1 Lingyuan China
93 C5 Lingyun China
88 D2 Lingzi Thang Plains reg. China/Jammu and Kashmir
93 F4 Linhai China
158 E2 Linhares Brazil
Linh Cam Vietnam see Duc Tho
92 C1 Linhe China
147 H1 Linière Canada
81 I3 Linik, Chiyā-ē mt. Iraq
96 D3 Linjiang China
103 K4 Linköping Sweden
96 F1 Linkou China
93 D4 Linli China
106 E5 Linlithgow U.K.
92 D2 Linlü Shan mt. China
140 A1 Linn, Mount U.S.A.
106 C4 Linnhe, Loch inlet U.K.
108 E4 Linnich Germany
92 E2 Linqing China
92 F2 Linqu China
92 E3 Linquan China
158 C3 Lins Brazil
93 F3 Linshu China
93 C4 Linshui China
92 B3 Lintan China
92 B3 Lintao China
142 C2 Linton U.S.A.
92 C3 Lintong China
92 F1 Linxi China
92 B3 Linxia China
92 D2 Linxian China
93 D4 Linxiang China
92 E2 Linyi Shandong China
92 F3 Linyi Shandong China
92 D3 Linyi Shanxi China
92 E3 Linying China
112 G6 Linz Austria
92 A2 Linze China
110 F5 Lion, Golfe du g. France
135 G3 Lion's Head Canada
147 F4 Lionville U.S.A.
122 B3 Liouesso Congo
97 B3 Lipa Phil.
114 F5 Lipari Isole Lipari Italy
114 F5 Lipari, Isola i. Isole Lipari Italy
114 F5 Lipari, Isole is Italy
117 F4 Lipetsk Rus. Fed.
117 F4 Lipetskaya Oblast' admin. div. Rus. Fed.
116 F2 Lipin Bor Rus. Fed.
93 C5 Liping China
115 I1 Lipova Romania
94 B2 Lipovtsy Rus. Fed.
109 E3 Lippe r. Germany
109 G3 Lippstadt Germany
88 E3 Lipti Lekh pass Nepal
71 F7 Liptrap, Cape Australia
93 D5 Lipu China
122 D3 Lira Uganda
122 B4 Liranga Congo
97 C6 Lirung Indon.
82 E1 Lisakovsk Kazakh.
122 C3 Lisala Dem. Rep. Congo
123 E6 L'Isalo, Massif de mts Madag.
123 E6 L'Isalo, Parc National de nat. park Madag.
107 D3 Lisbellaw U.K.
Lisboa Port. see Lisbon
111 B3 Lisbon Port.
134 C5 Lisbon IL U.S.A.
147 H2 Lisbon ME U.S.A.
142 D2 Lisbon ND U.S.A.
147 H2 Lisbon NH U.S.A.
146 C4 Lisbon OH U.S.A.
107 E3 Lisburn U.K.
107 B5 Liscannor Bay Rep. of Ireland
107 B4 Lisdoonvarna Rep. of Ireland
93 F5 Lishan Taiwan
92 D2 Lishi China
96 C2 Lishu China
92 F4 Lishui Jiangsu China
93 F4 Lishui Zhejiang China
93 D4 Li Shui r. China
67 H2 Lisianski Island U.S.A.
110 E2 Lisieux France
105 C7 Liskeard U.K.
117 F5 Liski Rus. Fed.
108 A5 L'Isle-Adam France
110 G5 L'Isle-sur-la-Sorgue France
71 J2 Lismore Australia
107 D5 Lismore Rep. of Ireland
106 C4 Lismore i. U.K.
107 D3 Lisnarrick U.K.
107 D3 Lisnaskea U.K.
135 G4 Listowel Canada
107 B5 Listowel Rep. of Ireland
102 K3 Lit Sweden
93 C6 Litang Guangxi China
90 C3 Litang Sichuan China
155 H3 Litani r. Fr. Guiana/Suriname
Lītani r. Lebanon see Līṭānī, Nahr el
80 E5 Līṭānī, Nahr el r. Lebanon
140 B2 Litchfield CA U.S.A.
144 B4 Litchfield IL U.S.A.
137 H2 Litchfield MN U.S.A.
110 D4 Lit-et-Mixe France
71 I4 Lithgow Australia
103 M5 Lithuania country Europe
147 E4 Lititz U.S.A.
112 G5 Litoměřice Czech Rep.
145 E7 Little Abaco i. Bahamas
145 E7 Little Bahama Bank sea feature Bahamas
72 E2 Little Barrier i. N.Z.
134 D3 Little Bay de Noc U.S.A.
103 J5 Little Belt sea chan. Denmark
138 E2 Little Belt Mountains U.S.A.
149 H5 Little Cayman i. Cayman Is
141 H4 Little Colorado r. U.S.A.
141 F3 Little Creek Peak U.S.A.
135 G3 Little Current Canada
132 C3 Little Current r. Canada
105 D7 Little Dart r. U.K.
70 D6 Little Desert National Park Australia
147 F5 Little Egg Harbor inlet U.S.A.
145 F7 Little Exuma i. Bahamas
142 E2 Little Falls MN U.S.A.
147 F3 Little Falls NY U.S.A.
141 F3 Littlefield AZ U.S.A.
143 C5 Littlefield TX U.S.A.
142 E1 Little Fork U.S.A.
134 A1 Little Fork r. U.S.A.
89 F4 Little Gandak r. India
131 J4 Little Grand Rapids Canada
105 G7 Littlehampton U.K.
146 C5 Little Kanawha r. U.S.A.
124 C3 Little Karas Berg plat. Namibia
124 D6 Little Karoo plat. S. Africa
134 D2 Little Lake U.S.A.
146 A5 Little Miami r. U.S.A.
106 B3 Little Minch sea chan. U.K.
142 C2 Little Missouri r. U.S.A.
105 H5 Little Ouse r. U.K.
83 H5 Little Pamir mts Afgh.
134 D1 Little Pic r. Canada
88 B5 Little Rann marsh India
143 E5 Little Rock U.S.A.
134 D4 Little Sable Point U.S.A.
145 F7 Little San Salvador i. Bahamas
130 F4 Little Smoky r. Canada
139 F4 Littleton CO U.S.A.
147 H2 Littleton NH U.S.A.
146 C5 Littleton WV U.S.A.
134 E3 Little Traverse Bay U.S.A.
123 D5 Litunde Moz.
130 B3 Lituya Bay U.S.A.
92 C3 Liuba China
93 F6 Liuchiu Yü i. Taiwan
93 C5 Liuchong He r. China
96 B5 Liugong Dao i. China
92 F1 Liugu He r. China
96 C2 Liuhe China
96 B2 Liu He r. China
93 D4 Liujiachang China
92 B3 Liujiaxia Shuiku resr China
92 C3 Liupan Shan mts China
93 D4 Liuyang China
93 C5 Liuzhou China
94 C3 Livadiya Rus. Fed.
103 N4 Līvāni Latvia
140 B2 Live Oak CA U.S.A.
145 D6 Live Oak FL U.S.A.
68 C3 Liveringa Australia
140 B3 Livermore U.S.A.
143 B6 Livermore, Mount U.S.A.
147 H2 Livermore Falls U.S.A.
71 I4 Liverpool Australia
133 H5 Liverpool Canada
105 E4 Liverpool U.K.
129 K2 Liverpool, Cape Canada
128 E3 Liverpool Bay Canada
105 D4 Liverpool Bay U.K.
71 I3 Liverpool Plains Australia
71 I3 Liverpool Range mts Australia
150 G5 Livingston Guat.
106 E5 Livingston U.K.
140 B3 Livingston CA U.S.A.
138 E2 Livingston MT U.S.A.
145 C4 Livingston TN U.S.A.
143 E6 Livingston TX U.S.A.
143 E6 Livingston, Lake U.S.A.
123 C5 Livingstone Zambia
73 B2 Livingston Island i. Antarctica
114 G3 Livno Bos.-Herz.
117 F4 Livny Rus. Fed.
102 N2 Livojoki r. Fin.
135 F4 Livonia U.S.A.
114 D3 Livorno Italy
158 E1 Livramento do Brumado Brazil
84 E5 Liwā Oman
123 D4 Liwale Tanz.
92 B3 Lixian Gansu China
93 D4 Lixian Hunan China
92 B4 Lixian Sichuan China
92 E3 Lixin China
92 F4 Liyang China
105 B8 Lizard U.K.
105 B8 Lizard Point U.K.
108 B5 Lizy-sur-Ourcq France
114 F1 Ljubljana Slovenia
103 L4 Ljugarn Sweden
103 L3 Ljungan r. Sweden
103 L3 Ljungaverk Sweden
103 K4 Ljungby Sweden
103 L3 Ljusdal Sweden
103 L3 Ljusnan r. Sweden
103 L3 Ljusne Sweden
156 B5 Llaima, Volcán vol. Chile
105 C5 Llanbadarn Fawr U.K.
105 D5 Llanbister U.K.
159 C2 Llancanelo, Salina salt flat Arg.
105 D6 Llandeilo U.K.
105 C6 Llandissilio U.K.
105 D6 Llandovery U.K.
105 D5 Llandrindod Wells U.K.
105 D4 Llandudno U.K.
105 C5 Llandysul U.K.
105 C6 Llanegwad U.K.
105 C6 Llanelli U.K.
105 D5 Llanfair Caereinion U.K.
105 C4 Llangefni U.K.
105 D5 Llangollen U.K.
105 D5 Llangurig U.K.
105 D5 Llanidloes U.K.
105 C4 Llannerch-y-medd U.K.
105 C5 Llannor U.K.
143 D6 Llano U.S.A.
143 D6 Llano r. U.S.A.
143 C5 Llano Estacado plain U.S.A.
157 C3 Llanos plain Col./Venez.
159 B4 Llanquihue, Lago l. Chile
105 C5 Llanrhystud U.K.
105 D6 Llantrisant U.K.
105 D5 Llanuwchllyn U.K.
105 D5 Llanwnog U.K.
105 D4 Llay U.K.
111 G2 Lleida Spain
111 C3 Llerena Spain
111 F3 Llíria Spain
111 E1 Llodio Spain
128 F4 Lloyd George, Mount Canada
131 H3 Lloyd Lake Canada
131 G4 Lloydminster Canada
111 H3 Llucmajor Spain
156 C2 Llullaillaco, Volcán vol. Chile
Llyn Tegid l. U.K. see Bala Lake
Lô r. China/Vietnam see Lô, Sông
93 B6 Lô, Sông r. China/Vietnam
156 C2 Loa r. Chile
141 G2 Loa U.S.A.
116 I3 Loban' r. Rus. Fed.
111 D4 Lobatejo mt. Spain
123 C6 Lobatse Botswana
109 J3 Löbejün Germany
109 H3 Löbenberg h. Germany
159 E3 Loberia Arg.
123 B5 Lobito Angola
159 E2 Lobos Arg.
150 B2 Lobos, Isla i. Mex.
109 J2 Loburg Germany
106 D4 Lochaber reg. U.K.
106 C4 Lochaline U.K.
135 E1 Lochalsh Canada
106 A3 Lochboisdale U.K.
106 C3 Lochcarron U.K.
104 C1 Lochearnhead U.K.
108 E2 Lochem Neth.
110 E3 Loches France
106 E4 Lochgelly U.K.
106 C4 Lochgilphead U.K.
106 C2 Lochinver U.K.
106 E3 Loch Lomond and the Trossachs National Park U.K.
106 A3 Lochmaddy U.K.
106 E4 Lochnagar mt. U.K.
146 E5 Loch Raven Reservoir U.S.A.
106 D4 Lochy, Loch l. U.K.
70 A4 Lock Australia
106 E5 Lockerbie U.K.
71 G5 Lockhart Australia
143 D6 Lockhart U.S.A.
146 E4 Lock Haven U.S.A.
146 D3 Lockport U.S.A.
98 C3 Lôc Ninh Vietnam
146 B5 Locust Grove U.S.A.
80 E6 Lod Israel
70 E5 Loddon r. Australia
110 F5 Lodève France
116 E2 Lodeynoye Pole Rus. Fed.
138 F2 Lodge Grass U.S.A.
88 B3 Lodhran Pak.
114 C2 Lodi Italy
140 B2 Lodi CA U.S.A.
146 B4 Lodi OH U.S.A.
102 K1 Lødingen Norway
122 D3 Lodwar Kenya
113 I5 Łódź Poland
85 H3 Loe Dakka Afgh.
98 B1 Loei Thai.
124 C5 Loeriesfontein S. Africa
102 K1 Lofoten is Norway
117 G5 Log Rus. Fed.
71 J1 Logan r. Australia
139 G5 Logan NM U.S.A.
146 B5 Logan OH U.S.A.
138 E3 Logan UT U.S.A.
146 C6 Logan WV U.S.A.
130 A2 Logan, Mount Canada
130 D2 Logan Mountains Canada
134 D5 Logansport U.S.A.
114 F2 Logatec Slovenia
111 E1 Logroño Spain
89 H4 Logtak Lake India
124 E4 Lohatlha S. Africa
109 H4 Lohfelden Germany
102 N2 Lohiniva Fin.
103 M3 Lohjanjärvi l. Fin.
109 G2 Löhne Germany
109 G2 Lohne (Oldenburg) Germany
102 M2 Lohtaja Fin.
98 A1 Loikaw Myanmar
98 A1 Loi Lan mt. Myanmar/Thai.
103 M3 Loimaa Fin.
110 E3 Loire r. France
108 B5 L'Oise à l'Aisne, Canal de France
154 C4 Loja Ecuador
111 D4 Loja Spain
99 E1 Lokan r. Sabah Malaysia
102 N2 Lokan tekojärvi resr Fin.
108 C3 Lokeren Belgium
124 D2 Lokgwabe Botswana
122 D3 Lokichar Kenya
122 D3 Lokichokio Kenya
103 J4 Løkken Denmark
102 J3 Løkken Norway
113 O2 Loknya Rus. Fed.
120 C4 Lokoja Nigeria
120 C4 Lokossa Benin
117 E4 Lokot' Rus. Fed.
103 N4 Loksa Estonia
129 L3 Loks Land i. Canada
120 B4 Lola Guinea
140 B2 Lola, Mount U.S.A.
103 J5 Lolland i. Denmark
122 D4 Lollondo Tanz.
138 D2 Lolo U.S.A.
124 E3 Lolwane S. Africa
115 J3 Lom Bulg.
103 J3 Lom Norway
122 C4 Lomami r. Dem. Rep. Congo
85 G3 Lomar Pass Afgh.
159 E2 Lomas de Zamora Arg.
68 C2 Lomblen i. Indon.
99 E4 Lombok i. Indon.
99 E4 Lombok, Selat sea chan. Indon.
120 C4 Lomé Togo
122 C4 Lomela Dem. Rep. Congo
122 C4 Lomela r. Dem. Rep. Congo
108 A4 Lomme France
108 D3 Lommel Belgium
106 D4 Lomond, Loch l. U.K.
82 F1 Lomonosovka Kazakh.
164 M1 Lomonosov Ridge sea feature Arctic Ocean
116 G1 Lomovoye Rus. Fed.
91 D7 Lompobattang, Gunung mt. Indon.
140 B4 Lompoc U.S.A.
98 B1 Lom Sak Thai.
113 K4 Łomża Poland
98 D2 Lon, Hon i. Vietnam
88 D6 Lonar India
159 B3 Loncoche Chile
159 B3 Loncopue Arg.
135 G4 London Canada
105 G6 London U.K.
(City Plan 56)
146 A6 London KY U.S.A.
146 B5 London OH U.S.A.
107 D3 Londonderry U.K.
147 G3 Londonderry U.S.A.
68 C3 Londonderry, Cape Australia
156 B9 Londonderry, Isla i. Chile
158 B3 Londrina Brazil
140 C3 Lone Pine U.S.A.
98 A1 Long Thai.
106 D4 Long, Loch inlet U.K.
77 S2 Longa, Proliv sea chan. Rus. Fed.
93 C6 Long'an China
105 E6 Long Ashton U.K.
159 B3 Longaví, Nevado de mt. Chile
145 E5 Long Bay U.S.A.
72 C6 Longbeach N.Z.
140 C5 Long Beach CA U.S.A.
147 G4 Long Beach NY U.S.A.
147 F4 Long Branch U.S.A.
134 A6 Long Branch Lake U.S.A.
93 B4 Longchang China
93 E5 Longchuan China
105 F5 Long Eaton U.K.
96 D1 Longfengshan Shuiku resr China
107 D4 Longford Rep. of Ireland
93 E5 Longhai China
93 □ Long Harbour Hong Kong China
105 F2 Longhoughton U.K.
99 E3 Longiram Indon.
149 I4 Long Island Bahamas
132 E3 Long Island Canada
68 E2 Long Island P.N.G.
147 G4 Long Island U.S.A.
147 G4 Long Island Sound sea chan. U.S.A.
93 C5 Long Jiang r. China
89 H3 Longju China
92 F2 Longkou Gang b. China
132 C4 Longlac Canada
132 C4 Long Lake l. Canada
147 F3 Long Lake U.S.A.
147 I1 Long Lake l. ME U.S.A.
134 E3 Long Lake l. MI U.S.A.
135 F3 Long Lake l. MI U.S.A.
142 C2 Long Lake l. ND U.S.A.
147 F2 Long Lake l. NY U.S.A.
93 C5 Longli China
93 B5 Longlin China
105 H5 Long Melford U.K.
93 E6 Longmen China
92 B3 Longmen Shan mts China
138 F3 Longmont U.S.A.
93 E5 Longnan China
135 G4 Long Point Canada
72 B7 Long Point N.Z.
135 G4 Long Point Bay Canada
104 E3 Long Preston U.K.
93 F4 Longquan China
93 F4 Longquan Xi r. China
129 M5 Long Range Mountains Canada
133 I4 Long Range Mountains Canada
68 E4 Longreach Australia
92 B3 Longriba China
93 C4 Longshan China
93 D5 Longsheng China
93 D5 Longshi China
138 F3 Longs Peak U.S.A.
105 I5 Long Stratton U.K.
93 D4 Longtian China
104 E2 Longtown U.K.
132 F4 Longueuil Canada
108 D5 Longuyon France
140 A2 Longvale U.S.A.
141 F3 Long Valley Junction U.S.A.
143 E5 Longview TX U.S.A.
138 B2 Longview WA U.S.A.
94 C2 Longwangmiao Rus. Fed.
92 C3 Longxi China
92 C3 Longxian China
93 E5 Longxi Shan mt. China
98 C3 Long Xuyên Vietnam
93 E5 Longyan China
92 E2 Longyao China
93 C6 Longzhou China
109 F2 Löningen Germany
103 K4 Lönsboda Sweden
70 E6 Lonsdale, Lake Australia
110 G3 Lons-le-Saunier France
158 B3 Lontra r. Brazil
97 B3 Looc Phil.
134 E4 Looking Glass r. U.S.A.
147 F4 Lookout U.S.A.
132 D2 Lookout, Cape Canada
145 E5 Lookout, Cape U.S.A.
71 J1 Lookout, Point Australia
135 F3 Lookout, Point U.S.A.
140 C3 Lookout Mountain U.S.A.
134 C1 Loon Canada
130 F3 Loon r. Canada
131 H4 Loon Lake Canada
147 I1 Loon Lake l. U.S.A.
107 B5 Loop Head Rep. of Ireland
88 E1 Lop China
90 C1 Lopatina, Gora mt. Rus. Fed.
116 H4 Lopatino Rus. Fed.
98 B2 Lop Buri Thai.
97 B3 Lopez Phil.
147 E4 Lopez U.S.A.
90 B2 Lop Nur salt flat China
122 C3 Lopori r. Dem. Rep. Congo
102 M1 Lopphavet b. Norway
116 I2 Loptyuga Rus. Fed.
85 G4 Lora r. Afgh.
70 A2 Lora watercourse Australia
157 B2 Lora r. Venez.
85 G4 Lora, Hamun-i- dry lake Pak.
111 D4 Lora del Río Spain
146 B4 Lorain U.S.A.
88 B3 Loralai Pak.
88 B3 Loralai r. Pak.
146 A4 Loramie, Lake U.S.A.
111 F4 Lorca Spain
109 F4 Lorch Germany
97 A4 Lord Auckland sea feature Phil.
84 C4 Lordegān Iran
69 F5 Lord Howe Island Pacific Ocean
160 F7 Lord Howe Rise sea feature S. Pacific Ocean
141 H5 Lordsburg U.S.A.
109 F4 Loreley tourist site Germany
158 D3 Lorena Brazil
91 F7 Lorentz r. Indon.
151 E3 Lorenzo del Real Mex.
154 F7 Loreto Bol.
155 I5 Loreto Brazil
150 B2 Loreto Mex.
97 C4 Loreto Phil.
157 B2 Lorica Col.
110 C3 Lorient France
131 K1 Lorillard r. Canada
106 C4 Lorn, Firth of est. U.K.
70 E7 Lorne Australia
89 H3 Loro r. China
110 G2 Lorraine reg. France
109 G5 Lorsch Germany
109 F2 Lorup Germany
88 C4 Losal India
150 D2 Los Alamitos, Sierra de mt. Mex.
139 F5 Los Alamos U.S.A.
159 B3 Los Andes Chile
159 B3 Los Ángeles Chile
140 C5 Los Angeles U.S.A.
(City Plan 61)
140 C4 Los Angeles Aqueduct canal U.S.A.
140 B3 Los Banos U.S.A.
156 D2 Los Blancos Arg.
150 D1 Los Caballos Mesteños, Llano de plain Mex.
156 B7 Los Chonos, Archipiélago de is Chile
159 B4 Los Coronados, Golfo de b. Chile
140 D5 Los Coronados, Islas is Mex.
156 D8 Los Estados, Isla de i. Arg.
140 B3 Los Gatos U.S.A.
150 C1 Los Gigantes, Llanos de plain Mex.
156 B8 Los Glaciares, Parque Nacional nat. park Arg.
108 E5 Losheim Germany
114 F2 Lošinj i. Croatia
149 I4 Los Jardines de la Reina, Archipiélago de is Cuba
154 C2 Los Katios, Parque Nacional nat. park Col.
125 H2 Loskop Dam S. Africa
159 B4 Los Lagos admin. reg. Chile
139 F5 Los Lunas U.S.A.
151 E3 Los Mármoles, Parque Nacional nat. park Mex.
159 C4 Los Menucos Arg.
150 C1 Los Mexicanos, Lago de l. Mex.
150 B2 Los Mochis Mex.
140 A1 Los Molinos U.S.A.
150 I6 Los Mosquitos, Golfo de b. Panama
122 B3 Losombo Dem. Rep. Congo
150 D4 Los Reyes Mex.
159 D4 Los Riachos, Islas de is Arg.
157 D2 Los Roques, Islas is Venez.
108 E2 Losser Neth.
106 E3 Lossie r. U.K.
106 E3 Lossiemouth U.K.
109 K4 Lößnitz Germany
157 C2 Los Taques Venez.
157 D2 Los Teques Venez.
157 E2 Los Testigos is Venez.
140 C4 Lost Hills U.S.A.
138 D2 Lost Trail Pass U.S.A.
105 C7 Lostwithiel U.K.
159 B2 Los Vientos Chile
159 B1 Los Vilos Chile
159 B3 Lota Chile
82 D5 Lotfābād Iran
125 I3 Lothair S. Africa
122 D3 Lotikipi Plain Kenya
122 C4 Loto Dem. Rep. Congo
116 E3 Lotoshino Rus. Fed.
125 G1 Lotsane r. Botswana
102 O1 Lotta r. Fin./Rus. Fed.
109 F2 Lotte Germany
Louang Namtha Laos see Louangnamtha
91 C4 Louangnamtha Laos
91 C5 Louangphabang Laos
Louangphrabang Laos see Louangphabang
122 B4 Loubomo Congo
110 C2 Loudéac France
93 D5 Loudi China
122 B4 Loudima Congo
146 B4 Loudonville U.S.A.
120 A3 Louga Senegal
105 F5 Loughborough U.K.
105 C6 Loughor r. U.K.
107 C4 Loughrea Rep. of Ireland
105 H6 Loughton U.K.
146 B5 Louisa KY U.S.A.
146 E5 Louisa VA U.S.A.
107 B4 Louisburgh Rep. of Ireland
130 C4 Louise Island Canada
69 F3 Louisiade Archipelago is P.N.G.
143 E6 Louisiana state U.S.A.
Louis Trichardt S. Africa see Makhado
145 D5 Louisville GA U.S.A.
144 C4 Louisville KY U.S.A.
143 F5 Louisville MS U.S.A.
160 H8 Louisville Ridge sea feature S. Pacific Ocean
132 E3 Louis-XIV, Pointe pt Canada
76 E3 Loukhi Rus. Fed.
111 B4 Loulé Port.
131 K4 Lount Lake Canada
112 F5 Louny Czech Rep.
142 D3 Loup r. U.S.A.
132 F2 Loups Marins, Lacs des lakes Canada
112 C6 L'Our, Vallée de val. Germany/Lux.
133 I4 Lourdes Canada
110 D5 Lourdes France
111 B2 Lousã Port.
96 E1 Loushan China
71 F3 Louth Australia
105 G4 Louth U.K.
115 J5 Loutra Aidipsou Greece
Louvain Belgium see Leuven
124 B1 Louwater-Suid Namibia
125 I3 Louwsburg S. Africa
102 M2 Lövånger Sweden
116 D3 Lovat' r. Rus. Fed.
115 K3 Lovech Bulg.
138 F3 Loveland U.S.A.
138 E2 Lovell U.S.A.
140 C1 Lovelock U.S.A.
108 B3 Lovendegem Belgium
103 N3 Loviisa Fin.
146 D6 Lovingston U.S.A.
134 C6 Lovington IL U.S.A.
143 C5 Lovington NM U.S.A.
135 J3 Low Canada
131 L2 Low, Cape Canada
132 E3 Low, Lac l. Canada
122 C4 Lowa Dem. Rep. Congo
88 B2 Lowarai Pass Pak.
147 H3 Lowell MA U.S.A.
134 E4 Lowell MI U.S.A.
147 G2 Lowell VT U.S.A.
130 F5 Lower Arrow Lake Canada
Lower California pen. Mex. see Baja California
70 D7 Lower Glenelg National Park Australia
141 F4 Lower Granite Gorge U.S.A.
72 E4 Lower Hutt N.Z.
140 A2 Lower Lake U.S.A.
107 D3 Lower Lough Erne l. U.K.
98 □ Lower Peirce Reservoir Sing.
130 D3 Lower Post Canada
133 H5 Lower Sackville Canada
105 I5 Lowestoft U.K.
113 I4 Łowicz Poland
71 F9 Low Rocky Point Australia
106 E5 Lowther Hills U.K.
147 F3 Lowville U.S.A.
109 G1 Loxstedt Germany
70 D5 Loxton Australia
124 E5 Loxton S. Africa
146 E4 Loyalsock Creek r. U.S.A.
140 B2 Loyalton U.S.A.
69 G4 Loyauté, Îles is New Caledonia
117 D5 Loyew Belarus
115 H2 Loznica Serb. and Mont.
117 F5 Lozova Ukr.
83 I1 Lozovoye Kazakh.
123 C5 Luacano Angola
92 E4 Lu'an China
92 D3 Luanchuan China
123 B4 Luanda Angola
93 B7 Luang, Huai r. Thai.
98 A3 Luang, Khao mt. Thai.
98 B4 Luang, Thale lag. Thai.
123 D5 Luangwa r. Zambia
89 H2 Luanhaizi China
92 F1 Luan He r. China
92 F2 Luannan China
92 E1 Luanping China
123 C5 Luanshya Zambia
92 F2 Luanxian China
123 C4 Luanza Dem. Rep. Congo
99 D2 Luar, Danau l. Indon.
111 C1 Luarca Spain
123 C5 Luau Angola
151 G4 Lubaantun tourist site Belize
113 K5 Lubaczów Poland
103 N4 Lubānas ezers l. Latvia
97 B3 Lubang Phil.
97 B3 Lubang i. Phil.
97 A3 Lubang Islands Phil.
123 B5 Lubango Angola
122 C4 Lubao Dem. Rep. Congo
113 K5 Lubartów Poland
109 G2 Lübbecke Germany
124 C1 Lubbeskolk salt pan S. Africa
143 C5 Lubbock U.S.A.
109 I2 Lübbow Germany
109 I1 Lübeck Germany
96 A1 Lubei China
113 K5 Lubelska, Wyżyna hills Poland
82 C2 Lubenka Kazakh.
122 C4 Lubero Dem. Rep. Congo
112 H5 Lubin Poland
113 K5 Lublin Poland
117 E5 Lubny Ukr.
99 D2 Lubok Antu Sarawak Malaysia
109 J1 Lübstorf Germany
109 J1 Lübtheen Germany
97 B2 Lubuagan Phil.
123 C4 Lubudi Dem. Rep. Congo
99 B3 Lubuklinggau Indon.
98 A5 Lubukpakam Indon.
98 B2 Lubuksikaping Indon.
123 C5 Lubumbashi Dem. Rep. Congo
123 C5 Lubungu Zambia
122 C4 Lubutu Dem. Rep. Congo
109 K1 Lübz Germany
123 B4 Lucala Angola
107 E4 Lucan Rep. of Ireland
130 A2 Lucania, Mount Canada
123 C4 Lucapa Angola
145 E7 Lucaya Bahamas
114 D3 Lucca Italy
106 D6 Luce Bay U.K.
158 B3 Lucélia Brazil
97 B3 Lucena Phil.
111 D4 Lucena Spain
113 I6 Lučenec Slovakia
114 F4 Lucera Italy
112 D7 Lucerne Switz.
94 D1 Luchegorsk Rus. Fed.
93 D6 Luchuan China
93 B6 Lüchun China
70 D6 Lucindale Australia
123 B5 Lucira Angola
Luckeesarai India see Lakhisarai
109 L2 Luckenwalde Germany
124 F4 Luckhoff S. Africa
135 G4 Lucknow Canada
88 E4 Lucknow India
123 C5 Lucusse Angola
116 F1 Luda Rus. Fed.
108 F3 Lüdenscheid Germany
123 B6 Lüderitz Namibia
109 I1 Lüdersdorf Germany
88 C3 Ludhiana India
93 B5 Ludian China
134 D4 Ludington U.S.A.
105 E5 Ludlow U.K.
140 D4 Ludlow CA U.S.A.
147 I1 Ludlow ME U.S.A.
147 G3 Ludlow VT U.S.A.
115 L3 Ludogorie reg. Bulg.
103 K3 Ludvika Sweden
109 H6 Ludwigsburg Germany
109 L2 Ludwigsfelde Germany

192 Ludwigshafen am Rhein

109 G5 Ludwigshafen am Rhein Germany
109 J1 Ludwigslust Germany
103 N4 Ludza Latvia
122 C4 Luebo Dem. Rep. Congo
123 B5 Luena Angola
157 E3 Luepa Venez.
92 C3 Lüeyang China
93 E6 Lufeng China
143 E6 Lufkin U.S.A.
116 D3 Luga Rus. Fed.
116 D3 Luga r. Rus. Fed.
114 C1 Lugano Switz.
109 K4 Lugau Germany
109 H3 Lügde Germany
123 D5 Lugenda r. Moz.
105 D5 Lugg r. U.K.
114 D2 Lugo Italy
111 C1 Lugo Spain
115 I2 Lugoj Romania
83 H4 Lugovoy Kazakh.
97 B5 Lugus i. Phil.
117 F5 Luhans'k Ukr.
92 F3 Luhe China
109 I1 Luhe r. Germany
89 H4 Luhit r. India
123 D4 Luhombero Tanz.
117 D5 Luhyny Ukr.
123 C5 Luiana Angola
122 C4 Luilaka r. Dem. Rep. Congo
106 C4 Luing i. U.K.
114 C2 Luino Italy
102 N2 Luiro r. Fin.
150 D3 Luis Moya Mex.
122 C4 Luiza Dem. Rep. Congo
159 E2 Lujan r. Arg.
159 C2 Luján de Cuyo Arg.
92 E4 Lujiang China
115 H2 Lukavac Bos.-Herz.
122 C4 Lukenie r. Dem. Rep. Congo
141 F6 Lukeville U.S.A.
116 G3 Lukh r. Rus. Fed.
116 F4 Lukhovitsy Rus. Fed.
115 K3 Lukovit Bulg.
113 K5 Łuków Poland
116 H4 Lukoyanov Rus. Fed.
123 C5 Lukulu Zambia
123 D4 Lukumburu Tanz.
102 M2 Luleå Sweden
102 M2 Luleälven r. Sweden
80 A1 Lüleburgaz Turkey
93 B5 Luliang China
92 D2 Lüliang Shan mts China
143 D6 Luling U.S.A.
92 F2 Lulong China
89 F3 Lülung China
89 F3 Lumachomo China
99 D4 Lumajang Indon.
89 E2 Lumajangdong Co salt l. China
81 K5 Lümär Iran
123 C5 Lumbala Kaquengue Angola
123 C5 Lumbala N'guimbo Angola
145 E5 Lumberton U.S.A.
111 C2 Lumbrales Spain
89 H4 Lumding India
102 N2 Lumijoki Fin.
98 C2 Lumphăt Cambodia
72 B6 Lumsden N.Z.
99 C3 Lumut, Tanjung pt Indon.
87 B2 Luna Phil.
141 H5 Luna U.S.A.
106 F4 Lunan Bay U.K.
131 K2 Lunan Lake Canada
135 F5 Luna Pier U.S.A.
88 C5 Lunavada India
88 B4 Lund Pak.
103 K5 Lund Sweden
141 F2 Lund U.S.A.
131 J4 Lundar Canada
123 D5 Lundazi Zambia
105 C6 Lundy i. U.K.
Lundy Island U.K. see Lundy
104 E3 Lune r. U.K.
109 I1 Lüneburg Germany
109 I1 Lüneburger Heide reg. Germany
108 F3 Lünen Germany
110 H2 Lunéville France
123 C5 Lunga r. Zambia
89 E2 Lungdo China
89 E3 Lunggar China
120 A4 Lungi Sierra Leone
93 □ Lung Kwu Chau i. Hong Kong China
89 H5 Lunglei India
107 E5 Lungnaquilla Mountain Rep. of Ireland
123 C5 Lungwebungu r. Zambia
88 C4 Luni India
88 B4 Luni r. India
88 B3 Luni r. Pak.
140 C2 Luning U.S.A.
116 H4 Lunino Rus. Fed.
117 C4 Luninyets Belarus
88 C1 Lunkho mt. Afgh./Pak.
108 F2 Lünne Germany
120 A4 Lunsar Sierra Leone
125 H2 Lunsklip S. Africa
79 G2 Luntai China
93 C5 Luocheng China
92 C3 Luochuan China
93 C5 Luodian China
93 D6 Luoding China
93 D6 Luodou Sha i. China
92 E3 Luohe China
92 D3 Luo He r. Henan China
92 C3 Luo He r. Shaanxi China
92 D3 Luoning China
93 B5 Luoping China
92 E3 Luoshan China
93 E4 Luotian China
Luoto Fin. see Larsmo
92 D3 Luoyang China
93 F5 Luoyuan China
96 F2 Luozigou China
123 C5 Lupane Zimbabwe
93 B5 Lupanshui China
99 D2 Lupar r. Sarawak Malaysia
123 C4 L'Upemba, Parc National de nat. park Dem. Rep. Congo
115 J2 Lupeni Romania
123 D5 Lupilichi Moz.
97 C5 Lupon Phil.
141 H4 Lupton U.S.A.
92 B3 Luqu China
92 E2 Luquan Hebei China
93 B5 Luquan Yunnan China
81 J3 Lūrā Shīrīn Iran
123 B4 Luremo Angola
106 C2 Lurgainn, Loch l. U.K.
107 E3 Lurgan U.K.
123 E5 Lúrio Moz.
123 D5 Lurio r. Moz.
98 □ Lurudal Sing.
123 C5 Lusaka Zambia
122 C4 Lusambo Dem. Rep. Congo
68 F2 Lusancay Islands and Reefs P.N.G.
130 F4 Luscar Canada
131 H4 Luseland Canada
93 D4 Lushi China
115 H4 Lushnjë Albania
96 D2 Lushuihe China
96 A4 Lüshun China
125 H5 Lusikisiki S. Africa
138 F3 Lusk U.S.A.
85 E4 Lut, Dasht-e des. Iran
93 F6 Lü Tao i. Taiwan
135 G4 Luther Lake Canada
109 K3 Lutherstadt Wittenberg Germany
105 G6 Luton U.K.
99 D2 Lutong Sarawak Malaysia
131 G2 Łutselk'e Canada
117 C5 Luts'k Ukr.
108 D2 Luttelgeest Neth.
108 E2 Luttenberg Neth.
109 H5 Lützelbach Germany
73 E4 Lützow-Holm Bay b. Antarctica
124 D4 Lutzputs S. Africa
124 C5 Lutzville S. Africa
97 B5 Luuk Phil.
103 N3 Luumäki Fin.
122 E3 Luuq Somalia
123 D3 Luverne U.S.A.
122 C4 Luvua r. Dem. Rep. Congo
125 I1 Luvuvhu r. S. Africa
122 D3 Luwero Uganda
91 E7 Luwuk Indon.
108 E5 Luxembourg country Europe
108 E5 Luxembourg Lux.
110 H3 Luxeuil-les-Bains France
93 B5 Luxi Yunnan China
Luxi China see Wuxi
125 F5 Luxolweni S. Africa
121 F2 Luxor Egypt
92 E3 Luyi China
108 D3 Luyksgestel Neth.
116 H2 Luza Rus. Fed.
116 I2 Luza r. Rus. Fed.
Luzern Switz. see Lucerne
93 C5 Luzhai China
93 B5 Luzhi China
93 B4 Luzhou China
158 C2 Luziânia Brazil
155 J4 Luzilândia Brazil
97 B3 Luzon i. Phil.
97 B1 Luzon Strait Phil.
110 F3 Luzy France
117 C5 L'viv Ukr.
L'vov Ukr. see L'viv
116 D3 Lyady Rus. Fed.
116 C4 Lyakhavichy Belarus
130 G5 Lyall, Mount Canada
Lyangar Uzbek. see Langar
102 L2 Lycksele Sweden
105 H7 Lydd U.K.
73 C3 Lyddan Island i. Antarctica
125 I2 Lydenburg S. Africa
105 E6 Lydney U.K.
117 D5 Lyel'chytsy Belarus
140 C3 Lyell, Mount U.S.A.
130 C4 Lyell Island Canada
116 D4 Lyepyel' Belarus
146 E4 Lykens U.S.A.
138 E3 Lyman U.S.A.
105 E7 Lyme Bay U.K.
105 E7 Lyme Regis U.K.
105 F7 Lymington U.K.
146 D6 Lynchburg U.S.A.
147 H2 Lynchville U.S.A.
71 H4 Lyndhurst N.S.W. Australia
70 C3 Lyndhurst S.A. Australia
147 G2 Lyndonville U.S.A.
106 E2 Lyness U.K.
103 I4 Lyngdal Norway
147 H3 Lynn U.S.A.
130 B3 Lynn Canal sea chan. U.S.A.
141 F2 Lynndyl U.S.A.
131 I3 Lynn Lake Canada
105 D6 Lynton U.K.
131 H2 Lynx Lake Canada
110 G4 Lyon France
147 G2 Lyon Mountain U.S.A.
145 D5 Lyons GA U.S.A.
146 E3 Lyons NY U.S.A.
147 F3 Lyons Falls U.S.A.
116 D4 Lyozna Belarus
69 F2 Lyra Reef P.N.G.
103 J4 Lysekil Sweden
116 H3 Lyskovo Rus. Fed.
98 D2 Ly Son, Đao i. Vietnam
76 G4 Lys'va Rus. Fed.
117 F5 Lysychans'k Ukr.
104 D4 Lytham St Anne's U.K.
135 H3 Lytton Canada
116 D4 Lyuban' Belarus
117 C5 Lyubeshiv Ukr.
116 E4 Lyudinovo Rus. Fed.
116 H3 Lyunda r. Rus. Fed.

M

93 B6 Ma, Sông r. Laos/Vietnam
123 C5 Maamba Zambia
80 E6 Ma'ān Jordan
Ma'an Jordan see Ma'ān
102 N3 Maaninka Fin.
102 O2 Maaninkavaara Fin.
92 F4 Ma'anshan China
103 N4 Maardu Estonia
80 F4 Ma'arrat an Nu'mān Syria
108 D2 Maarssen Neth.
108 E3 Maas r. Neth.
alt. Meuse (Belgium/France)
108 D3 Maaseik Belgium
97 C4 Maasin Phil.
108 D4 Maasmechelen Belgium
108 D3 Maas-Schwalm-Nette nat. park Neth.
125 H1 Maasstroom S. Africa
108 D4 Maastricht Neth.
71 G9 Maatsuyker Group is Australia
97 B3 Mabalacat Phil.
123 D6 Mabalane Moz.
154 G2 Mabaruma Guyana
135 I3 Maberly Canada
93 B4 Mabian China
105 H4 Mablethorpe U.K.
125 H2 Mabopane S. Africa
123 D6 Mabote Moz.
97 B1 Mabudis i. Phil.
124 F2 Mabule Botswana
124 E2 Mabutsane Botswana
156 B7 Macá, Monte mt. Chile
159 D3 Macachín Arg.
158 E3 Macaé Brazil
97 C4 Macajalar Bay Phil.
71 G6 Macalister r. Australia
123 D5 Macaloge Moz.
128 H3 MacAlpine Lake Canada
125 J1 Macandze Moz.
155 H3 Macapá Brazil
154 C4 Macará Ecuador
158 E1 Macarani Brazil
157 B4 Macarena, Cordillera mts Col.
157 E2 Macareo, Caño r. Venez.
70 E7 Macarthur Australia
154 C4 Macas Ecuador
Macassar Strait str. Indon. see Makassar, Selat
155 K5 Macau Brazil
93 D6 Macau China
155 H6 Macaúba Brazil
158 D1 Macaúbas Brazil
157 B4 Macaya r. Col.
157 B4 Macayari Col.
125 J2 Maccaretane Moz.
105 E4 Macclesfield U.K.
68 C4 Macdonald, Lake salt flat Australia
68 D4 Macdonnell Ranges mts Australia
132 B3 MacDowell Lake Canada
106 F3 Macduff U.K.
111 C2 Macedo de Cavaleiros Port.
70 F6 Macedon mt. Australia
115 I4 Macedonia country Europe
155 K5 Maceió Brazil
120 B4 Macenta Guinea
114 E3 Macerata Italy
70 B4 Macfarlane, Lake salt flat Australia
107 B6 Macgillycuddy's Reeks mts Rep. of Ireland
88 A3 Mach Pak.
154 C4 Machachi Ecuador
158 D3 Machado Brazil
123 D6 Machaila Moz.
122 D4 Machakos Kenya
154 C4 Machala Ecuador
123 D6 Machanga Moz.
125 J2 Machatuine Moz.
108 C5 Machault France
92 E4 Macheng China
87 B2 Macherla India
87 C2 Machhakund Dam India
147 J2 Machias ME U.S.A.
146 D3 Machias NY U.S.A.
147 I1 Machias r. U.S.A.
87 C2 Machilipatnam India
157 B2 Machiques Venez.
106 C5 Machrihanish U.K.
154 D6 Machupicchu tourist site Peru
105 D5 Machynlleth U.K.
125 J2 Macia Moz.
115 M2 Măcin Romania
71 I2 Macintyre r. Australia
71 I2 Macintyre Brook r. Australia
141 H2 Mack U.S.A.
81 G1 Maçka Turkey
68 E4 Mackay Australia
138 D2 Mackay U.S.A.
68 C4 Mackay, Lake salt flat Australia
131 G2 MacKay Lake Canada
130 E3 Mackenzie B.C. Canada
134 C1 Mackenzie Ont. Canada
128 E3 Mackenzie r. Canada
73 E5 Mackenzie Bay b. Antarctica
128 E3 Mackenzie Bay Canada
130 F2 Mackenzie Bison Sanctuary nature res. Canada
128 G2 Mackenzie King Island Canada
130 C2 Mackenzie Mountains Canada
134 E3 Mackinac, Straits of lake channel U.S.A.
134 E3 Mackinac Island U.S.A.
134 C5 Mackinaw r. U.S.A.
134 E3 Mackinaw City U.S.A.
131 H4 Macklin Canada
71 J3 Macksville Australia
71 J2 Maclean Australia
125 H5 Maclear S. Africa
71 J3 Macleay r. Australia
68 B4 MacLeod, Lake dry lake Australia
130 C2 Macmillan r. Canada
134 B5 Macomb U.S.A.
114 C4 Macomer Sardinia Italy
110 G3 Mâcon France
145 D5 Macon GA U.S.A.
142 E4 Macon MO U.S.A.
123 C5 Macondo Angola
71 G3 Macquarie r. N.S.W. Australia
71 G8 Macquarie r. Tas. Australia
71 I4 Macquarie, Lake b. Australia
71 F9 Macquarie Harbour Australia
79 F7 Macquarie Island S. Pacific Ocean
71 G3 Macquarie Marshes Australia
71 H4 Macquarie Mountain Australia
160 F9 Macquarie Ridge sea feature S. Pacific Ocean
98 □ MacRitchie Reservoir Sing.
73 E5 Mac. Robertson Land reg. Antarctica
107 C6 Macroom Rep. of Ireland
157 C1 Macuira, Parque Nacional nat. park Col.
157 B4 Macuje Col.
68 D4 Macumba watercourse Australia
154 D6 Macusani Peru
151 F4 Macuspana Mex.
150 B2 Macuzari, Presa resr Mex.
147 I2 Macwahoc U.S.A.
80 E6 Mādabā Jordan
125 I3 Madadeni S. Africa
123 E6 Madagascar country Africa
162 H6 Madagascar i. Africa
162 H6 Madagascar Basin sea feature Indian Ocean
162 G7 Madagascar Ridge sea feature Indian Ocean
121 D3 Madagli Nigeria
125 I3 Madakasira India
121 D2 Madama Niger
115 K4 Madan Bulg.
87 B3 Madanapalle India
68 E2 Madang P.N.G.
120 C3 Madaoua Niger
89 G5 Madaripur Bangl.
135 I3 Madawaska Canada
135 I3 Madawaska r. Canada
147 I1 Madawaska U.S.A.
120 A1 Madeira terr. Atlantic Ocean
154 F5 Madeira r. Brazil
163 H3 Madeira, Arquipélago da is Port.
134 B2 Madeline Island U.S.A.
81 G2 Maden Turkey
83 I3 Madeniyet Kazakh.
148 C3 Madera Mex.
140 B3 Madera U.S.A.
87 A3 Madgaon India
89 F4 Madhepura India
87 C2 Madhira India
89 F4 Madhubani India
88 D5 Madhya Pradesh state India
125 F3 Madibogo S. Africa
154 E6 Madidi r. Bol.
70 B2 Madigan Gulf salt flat Australia
87 B3 Madikeri India
125 G2 Madikwe Game Reserve nature res. S. Africa
122 B4 Madingou Congo
Madini r. Bol. see Madidi
123 E5 Madirovalo Madag.
144 C4 Madison IN U.S.A.
147 I2 Madison ME U.S.A.
142 D2 Madison MN U.S.A.
142 D3 Madison NE U.S.A.
142 D2 Madison SD U.S.A.
134 C4 Madison WI U.S.A.
146 C5 Madison WV U.S.A.
138 E2 Madison r. U.S.A.
144 C4 Madisonville KY U.S.A.
143 E6 Madisonville TX U.S.A.
99 D4 Madiun Indon.
135 I3 Madoc Canada
122 D3 Mado Gashi Kenya
90 B3 Madoi China
103 N4 Madona Latvia
88 B4 Madpura India
115 L5 Madra Dağı mts Turkey
Madras India see Chennai
138 B2 Madras U.S.A.
151 E2 Madre, Laguna lag. Mex.
143 D7 Madre, Laguna lag. U.S.A.
97 B2 Madre, Sierra mt. Phil.
151 F4 Madre de Chiapas, Sierra mts Mex.
154 D6 Madre de Dios r. Peru
156 A8 Madre de Dios, Isla i. Chile
150 D4 Madre del Sur, Sierra mts Mex.
150 B1 Madre Occidental, Sierra mts Mex.
150 D2 Madre Oriental, Sierra mts Mex.
97 C4 Madrid Phil.
111 E2 Madrid Spain (City Plan 60)
97 B4 Madridejos Phil.
111 E3 Madridejos Spain
87 C2 Madugula India
99 D4 Madura i. Indon.
99 D4 Madura, Selat sea chan. Indon.
87 B4 Madurai India
88 D2 Madwas India
88 C2 Madyan Pak.
117 H7 Madzhalis Rus. Fed.
95 F6 Maebashi Japan
98 A1 Mae Hong Son Thai.
98 A1 Mae Sai Thai.
98 A1 Mae Sariang Thai.
98 A1 Mae Sot Thai.
149 I5 Maestra, Sierra mts Cuba
123 E5 Maevatanana Madag.
69 G3 Maéwo i. Vanuatu
131 I4 Mafeking Canada
125 G4 Mafeteng Lesotho
71 G6 Maffra Australia
123 D4 Mafia Island Tanz.
125 F2 Mafikeng S. Africa
123 D4 Mafinga Tanz.
158 C4 Mafra Brazil
125 I5 Magabeni S. Africa
77 Q4 Magadan Rus. Fed.
122 D4 Magadi Kenya
123 D5 Magaiza Moz.
97 B3 Magallanes Phil.
157 B2 Magangue Col.
80 D3 Mağara Turkey
117 H7 Magas Rus. Fed.
97 B2 Magat r. Phil.
159 F2 Magdalena Arg.
154 F6 Magdalena Bol.
157 B3 Magdalena r. Col.
148 B2 Magdalena Mex.
139 E6 Magdalena r. Mex.
139 F5 Magdalena U.S.A.
150 A2 Magdalena, Bahía b. Mex.
156 B6 Magdalena, Isla i. Chile
150 A2 Magdalena, Isla i. Mex.
97 A5 Magdaline, Gunung mt. Sabah Malaysia
109 J2 Magdeburg Germany
160 E4 Magellan Seamounts sea feature N. Pacific Ocean
102 N1 Magerøya i. Norway
95 B9 Mage-shima i. Japan
114 C2 Maggiorasca, Monte mt. Italy
114 C2 Maggiore, Lake Italy
120 A3 Maghama Mauritania
107 E3 Maghera U.K.
107 E3 Magherafelt U.K.
104 E4 Maghull U.K.
139 D3 Magna U.S.A.
114 F6 Magna Grande mt. Sicily Italy
73 E5 Magnet Bay b. Antarctica
68 E3 Magnetic Island Australia
102 P1 Magnetity Rus. Fed.
82 D1 Magnitogorsk Rus. Fed.
143 E5 Magnolia U.S.A.
133 F4 Magog Canada
151 E3 Magozal Mex.
133 H3 Magpie Canada
134 E1 Magpie r. Canada
133 H3 Magpie, Lac l. Canada
130 G5 Magrath Canada
140 D3 Magruder Mountain U.S.A.
120 A3 Magta' Laḥjar Mauritania
122 D4 Magu Tanz.
93 B6 Maguan China
155 I4 Maguarinho, Cabo c. Brazil
125 J2 Magude Moz.
131 J2 Maguse Lake Canada
89 H5 Magwe Myanmar
89 H5 Magyichaung Myanmar
84 B3 Mahābād Iran
87 A2 Mahabaleshwar India
89 F4 Mahabharat Range mts Nepal
123 E6 Mahabo Madag.
87 A2 Mahad India
88 D5 Mahadeo Hills India
122 D3 Mahagi Dem. Rep. Congo
88 C3 Mahajan India
123 E5 Mahajanga Madag.
99 E2 Mahakam r. Indon.
125 G1 Mahalapye Botswana
123 E5 Mahalevona Madag.
84 C3 Mahallāt Iran
88 D3 Maham India
84 E4 Māhān Iran
87 D1 Mahanadi r. India
123 E5 Mahanoro Madag.
88 C6 Maharashtra state India
87 C1 Mahasamund India
98 B1 Maha Sarakham Thai.
123 E6 Mahatalaky Madag.
80 F6 Maḥaṭṭat Dab'ah Jordan
123 E5 Mahavanona Madag.
123 E5 Mahavavy r. Madag.
87 C5 Mahaweli Ganga r. Sri Lanka
98 C1 Mahaxai Laos
87 C2 Mahbubabad India
87 B2 Mahbubnagar India
84 D5 Maḥḍah Oman
155 G2 Mahdia Guyana
114 D7 Mahdia Tunisia
119 I5 Mahé i. Seychelles
87 D2 Mahendragiri mt. India
88 C5 Mahesana India
88 C5 Maheshwar India
87 A2 Mahi r. India
85 E4 Māhī watercourse Iran
72 F3 Mahia Peninsula N.Z.
116 D4 Mahilyow Belarus
87 C5 Mahiyangana Sri Lanka
125 I4 Mahlabatini S. Africa
109 J2 Mahlsdorf Germany
Maḥmūd-e 'Erāqī Afgh. see Maḥmūd-e Rāqī
85 H3 Maḥmūd-e Rāqī Afgh.
81 L4 Mahnīān Iran
142 D2 Mahnomen U.S.A.
88 D4 Mahoba India
111 I3 Mahón Spain
146 D4 Mahoning Creek Lake U.S.A.
89 H5 Mahudaung mts Myanmar
88 B5 Mahuva India
115 L4 Mahya Dağı mt. Turkey
84 C3 Mahyār Iran
89 H4 Maibang India
157 B2 Maicao Col.
132 E4 Maicasagi, Lac l. Canada
93 C6 Maichen China
105 G6 Maidenhead U.K.
131 H4 Maidstone Canada
105 H6 Maidstone U.K.
121 D3 Maiduguri Nigeria
157 D3 Maigualida, Sierra mts Venez.
107 C5 Maigue r. Rep. of Ireland
88 E4 Maihar India
92 C3 Maiji Shan mt. China
89 F5 Maikala Range hills India
88 E3 Mailani India
109 F5 Main r. Germany
107 E3 Main r. U.K.
133 I3 Main Brook Canada
135 F3 Main Channel lake channel Canada
122 B4 Mai-Ndombe, Lac l. Dem. Rep. Congo
109 J5 Main-Donau-Kanal canal Germany
Maindong China see Coqên
135 I4 Main Duck Island Canada
147 I2 Maine state U.S.A.
120 D3 Maïné-Soroa Niger
98 A2 Maingy Island Myanmar
109 H5 Mainhardt Germany
97 C4 Mainit Phil.
97 C4 Mainit, Lake Phil.
106 E1 Mainland i. Orkney, Scotland U.K.
106 □ Mainland i. Shetland, Scotland U.K.
109 J4 Mainleus Germany
89 E5 Mainpat reg. India
88 D4 Mainpuri India
71 J1 Main Range National Park Australia
123 E5 Maintirano Madag.
109 G4 Mainz Germany
120 □ Maio i. Cape Verde
159 C2 Maipó, Volcán vol. Chile
159 F3 Maipú Arg.
159 C2 Maipú Arg.
157 D2 Maiquetía Venez.
89 G5 Maiskhal Island Bangl.
123 C6 Maitengwe Botswana
71 I4 Maitland N.S.W. Australia
70 B5 Maitland S.A. Australia
73 D3 Maitri research stn Antarctica
150 I5 Maíz, Islas del is Nicaragua
89 G3 Maizhokunggar China
95 D7 Maizuru Japan
115 H3 Maja Jezercë mt. Albania
87 B2 Majalgaon India
157 E4 Majari r. Brazil
80 E5 Majdel Aanjar tourist site Lebanon
99 E3 Majene Indon.
84 C6 Majhūd well Saudi Arabia
122 D3 Majī Eth.
92 E2 Majia He r. China
93 D6 Majiang China
111 H3 Major, Puig mt. Spain
111 H3 Majorca i. Spain
89 H4 Majuli Island India
Majuro atoll Marshall Is see Taongi
125 G4 Majwemasweu S. Africa
122 B4 Makabana Congo
Makaha U.S.A. see Mākaha
140 □1 Mākaha U.S.A.
91 D7 Makale Indon.
89 F4 Makalu mt. China
122 C4 Makamba Burundi
83 J3 Makanchi Kazakh.
140 □1 Makapu'u Head U.S.A.
116 I2 Makar-Ib Rus. Fed.
164 M1 Makarov Basin sea feature Arctic Ocean
114 G3 Makarska Croatia
99 E4 Makassar Indon.
99 E3 Makassar, Selat str. Indon.
82 C3 Makat Kazakh.
125 J3 Makatini Flats lowland S. Africa
120 A4 Makeni Sierra Leone
123 C6 Makgadikgadi depr. Botswana
117 H7 Makhachkala Rus. Fed.
125 H1 Makhado S. Africa
82 B3 Makhambet Kazakh.
80 G4 Makhfar al Ḥammām Syria
81 I4 Makhmūr Iraq
83 G1 Makhorovka Kazakh.
122 D4 Makindu Kenya
83 G1 Makinsk Kazakh.
117 F5 Makiyivka Ukr.
Makkah Saudi Arabia see Mecca
133 I2 Makkovik Canada
133 I2 Makkovik, Cape Canada
108 D1 Makkum Neth.
115 I1 Makó Hungary
122 B3 Makokou Gabon
123 D4 Makongolosi Tanz.
124 E2 Makopong Botswana
122 B4 Makotipoko Congo
85 F5 Makran reg. Iran/Pak.
88 C4 Makrana India
85 F5 Makran Coast Range mts Pak.
87 C2 Makri India
115 K6 Makronisi i. Greece
117 H6 Maksatikha Rus. Fed.
116 E3 Maksimovka Rus. Fed.
94 E1 Maksotag Iran
85 F4 Mākū Iran
84 B2 Makum India
89 H4 Makumbako Tanz.
123 D4 Makunguwiro Tanz.
123 D5 Makurazaki Japan
95 B9 Makurdi Nigeria
120 C4 Makūyeh Iran
84 D4 Makwassie S. Africa
125 F3 Malå Sweden
102 L2 Mala, Punta pt Panama
150 I7 Malabang Phil.
97 C5 Malabar Coast India
87 A3 Malabo Equat. Guinea
120 C4 Malabuñgan Phil.
97 A4 Malacca, Strait of Indon./Malaysia
99 A2 Malad City U.S.A.
138 D3 Maladzyechna Belarus
116 C4 Málaga Spain
111 D4 Malaga NJ U.S.A.
147 F5 Malaga NM U.S.A.
139 F5 Malaita i. Solomon Is
69 G2 Malakal Sudan
121 F4 Malakula i. Vanuatu
69 G3 Malakwal Pak.
88 C2 Malamala Indon.
91 E7 Malan, Ras pt Pak.
85 G5 Malang Indon.
99 D4 Malanje Angola
123 B4 Malanzán, Sierra de mts Arg.
159 C1 Malappuram India
87 B4 Mälaren l. Sweden
103 L4 Malargüe Arg.
159 C2 Malartic Canada
135 H1 Malartic, Lac l. Canada
135 H1 Malaspina Glacier U.S.A.
130 A3 Malatya Turkey
81 G2 Malaut India
88 C3 Malāvī Iran
81 K5 Malawali i. Sabah Malaysia
97 A5 Malawi country Africa
123 D5 Malawi, Lake l. Africa see Nyasa, Lake
116 E3 Malaya Vishera Rus. Fed.
97 C4 Malaybalay Phil.
84 C3 Malāyer Iran
83 I3 Malay Sary Kazakh.
99 C2 Malaysia country Asia
81 I2 Malazgirt Turkey
113 I3 Malbork Poland
108 E5 Malborn Germany
109 K1 Malchin Germany
109 K1 Malchiner See l. Germany
89 G4 Maldah India
108 B3 Maldegem Belgium
143 F4 Malden U.S.A.
67 I4 Malden Island Kiribati
74 C6 Maldives country Indian Ocean
105 H6 Maldon U.K.
159 F2 Maldonado Uruguay
74 C6 Male Maldives
115 J6 Maleas, Akra pt Greece
79 F6 Male Atoll Maldives
125 F4 Malebogo S. Africa
87 B2 Malegaon Maharashtra India
88 C5 Malegaon Maharashtra India
112 H6 Male Karpaty hills Slovakia
81 K3 Malek Kandī Iran
122 B4 Malele Dem. Rep. Congo
123 D5 Malema Moz.
88 C3 Maler Kotla India
85 G3 Mālestān Afgh.
117 H7 Malgobek Rus. Fed.
102 L2 Malgomaj l. Sweden
84 B5 Malham Saudi Arabia
138 C3 Malheur Lake U.S.A.
120 B3 Mali country Africa
122 C4 Mali Dem. Rep. Congo
120 A3 Mali Guinea
92 C3 Malian He r. China
88 E4 Malihabad India
85 F4 Malik Naro mt. Pak.
98 A2 Mali Kyun i. Myanmar
91 E7 Malili Indon.
97 D5 Malimping Indon.
122 E4 Malindi Kenya
107 D2 Malin Head Rep. of Ireland
107 D2 Malin More Rep. of Ireland
83 G2 Malinovka Kazakh.
94 D2 Malinovka r. Rus. Fed.
83 I2 Malinovoye Ozero Rus. Fed.
93 B6 Malipo China
114 F2 Mali Raginac mt. Croatia
97 C5 Malita Phil.
98 A3 Maliwun Myanmar
88 B5 Maliya India
81 K5 Malkaili Iran
87 C2 Malkangiri India
88 C5 Malkapur India
117 C7 Malkara Turkey
113 M4 Mal'kavichy Belarus
71 H6 Malko Tŭrnovo Bulg.
71 H6 Mallacoota Australia
71 H6 Mallacoota Inlet b. Australia
106 C4 Mallaig U.K.
70 C5 Mallala Australia
70 E5 Mallee Cliffs National Park Australia
131 J2 Mallery Lake Canada
Mallorca i. Spain see Majorca
107 C5 Mallow Rep. of Ireland
105 D5 Mallwyd U.K.
102 J2 Malm Norway
102 M2 Malmberget Sweden
108 E4 Malmédy Belgium
124 C6 Malmesbury S. Africa
105 E6 Malmesbury U.K.
103 K5 Malmö Sweden
116 I3 Malmyzh Rus. Fed.
69 G3 Malo i. Vanuatu
97 B3 Malolos Phil.
147 F2 Malone U.S.A.
93 B5 Malong China
123 C5 Malonga Dem. Rep. Congo
116 F2 Maloshuyka Rus. Fed.
103 I3 Måløy Norway
116 F4 Maloyaroslavets Rus. Fed.
154 B3 Malpelo, Isla de i. Col.
87 A3 Malprabha r. India
114 F7 Malta country Europe
103 N4 Malta Latvia
138 F1 Malta U.S.A.
114 F6 Malta Channel Italy/Malta
123 B6 Maltahöhe Namibia
105 F4 Maltby U.K.
104 H4 Maltby le Marsh U.K.
104 G3 Malton U.K.
Maluku is Indon. see Moluccas
91 E7 Maluku, Laut sea Indon.
103 K3 Malung Sweden
125 H4 Maluti Mountains Lesotho
69 G2 Malu'u Solomon Is
87 A2 Malvan India
143 E5 Malvern U.S.A.
117 D5 Malyn Ukr.
77 R3 Malyy Anyuy r. Rus. Fed.
Malyy Balkhan, Khrebet h. Turkm. see Kiçi Balkan Daglary
117 H6 Malyye Derbety Rus. Fed.
82 B1 Malyy Irgiz r. Rus. Fed.
Malyy Kavkaz mts Asia see Lesser Caucasus
77 P2 Malyy Lyakhovskiy, Ostrov i. Rus. Fed.
82 B2 Malyy Uzen' r. Kazakh./Rus. Fed.
77 P3 Mama r. Rus. Fed.
125 H3 Mamafubedu S. Africa
87 C3 Mamallapuram India
97 A5 Mambahenauhan i. Phil.
97 C4 Mambajao Phil.
122 C3 Mambasa Dem. Rep. Congo
122 B3 Mambéré r. Centr. Afr. Rep.
97 B3 Mamburao Phil.
125 H2 Mamelodi S. Africa
120 C4 Mamfe Cameroon
Mamfé Cameroon see Mamfe
83 F1 Mamlyutka Kazakh.
141 G5 Mammoth U.S.A.
144 C4 Mammoth Cave National Park U.S.A.
140 C3 Mammoth Lakes U.S.A.
154 E6 Mamoré r. Bol./Brazil
120 A3 Mamou Guinea
123 E5 Mampikony Madag.
120 B4 Mampong Ghana
159 B3 Mamuil Malal, Paso pass Arg./Chile
99 E3 Mamuju Indon.
124 D1 Mamuno Botswana
82 D2 Mamyt Kazakh.
120 B4 Man Côte d'Ivoire
104 C3 Man, Isle of terr. Irish Sea
157 B3 Manacacías r. Col.
154 F4 Manacapuru Brazil
111 H3 Manacor Spain
91 E6 Manado Indon.
150 H5 Managua Nicaragua
150 H5 Managua, Lago de l. Nicaragua
123 E6 Manakara Madag.
72 D5 Manakau mt. N.Z.
84 C5 Manama Bahrain
68 E2 Manam Island P.N.G.
157 E2 Mamo, Caño r. Venez.
140 □1 Mānana i. U.S.A.
Manana i. U.S.A. see Mānana
123 E6 Mananara r. Madag.
123 E5 Mananara, Parc National de nat. park Madag.
123 E5 Mananara Avaratra Madag.
70 E5 Manangatang Australia
123 E6 Mananjary Madag.
88 B4 Manantavadi India
88 D3 Mana Pass India
157 D2 Manapire r. Venez.
72 A6 Manapouri, Lake N.Z.
123 E5 Manarantsandry Madag.
89 G4 Manas r. Bhutan
90 A2 Manas Hu l. China
89 F3 Manaslu mt. Nepal
146 E5 Manassas U.S.A.
89 G4 Manas Wildlife Sanctuary nature res. Bhutan
91 E7 Manatuto East Timor
154 F4 Manaus Brazil
80 C3 Manavgat Turkey
72 E4 Manawatu r. N.Z.
97 C5 Manay Phil.
80 F3 Manbij Syria
104 E4 Manby U.K.
134 E3 Mancelona U.S.A.
105 E4 Manchester U.K.
140 A2 Manchester CA U.S.A.
147 G4 Manchester CT U.S.A.
134 B4 Manchester IA U.S.A.
146 B6 Manchester KY U.S.A.
134 E4 Manchester MI U.S.A.
147 H3 Manchester NH U.S.A.
146 B5 Manchester OH U.S.A.
145 C5 Manchester TN U.S.A.
147 G3 Manchester VT U.S.A.
88 A4 Manchhar Lake Pak.
80 F2 Mancılık Turkey
141 H3 Mancos U.S.A.
141 H3 Mancos r. U.S.A.
85 F5 Mand Pak.
84 D4 Mand, Rūd-e r. Iran
121 D4 Manda, Parc National de nat. park Chad
123 E6 Mandabe Madag.
99 B2 Mandah Indon.
98 □ Mandai Sing.
85 F3 Mandal Afgh.
88 C4 Mandal India
103 I4 Mandal Norway
91 G7 Mandala, Puncak mt. Indon.
91 B4 Mandalay Myanmar
90 C2 Mandalgovĭ Mongolia
81 J5 Mandalī Iraq
92 D1 Mandalt China
92 D1 Mandalt Sum China
142 C2 Mandan U.S.A.
97 B3 Mandaon Phil.
121 D3 Mandara Mountains Cameroon/Nigeria
114 C5 Mandas Sardinia Italy
122 E3 Mandera Kenya
141 F2 Manderfield U.S.A.
108 E4 Manderscheid Germany
149 I5 Mandeville Jamaica
72 B6 Mandeville N.Z.
88 B4 Mandha India
120 B3 Mandiana Guinea
98 B4 Mandi Angin, Gunung mt. Malaysia
88 C3 Mandi Burewala Pak.
123 D5 Mandié Moz.
123 D5 Mandimba Moz.
125 I4 Mandini S. Africa
89 F5 Mandira Dam India
88 E5 Mandla India
123 E5 Mandritsara Madag.
88 C4 Mandsaur India
97 A6 Mandul i. Indon.
68 B5 Mandurah Australia
114 G4 Manduria Italy
88 B5 Mandvi Gujarat India
88 C5 Mandvi Gujarat India
87 B3 Mandya India
82 E5 Mäne Turkm.
87 B2 Maner r. India
114 D2 Manerbio Italy
81 K5 Manesht Kūh mt. Iran
113 L5 Manevychi Ukr.

Mealhada 193

114 F4 **Manfredonia** Italy
114 G4 **Manfredonia, Golfo di** *g.* Italy
158 D1 **Manga** Brazil
120 B3 **Manga** Burkina
122 B4 **Mangai** Dem. Rep. Congo
67 I5 **Mangaia** *i.* Cook Is
72 E3 **Mangakino** N.Z.
87 C2 **Mangalagiri** India
89 H4 **Mangaldai** India
115 M3 **Mangalia** Romania
87 A3 **Mangalore** India
87 A2 **Mangalvedha** India
89 G4 **Mangan** India
87 C2 **Mangapet** India
97 C6 **Mangarang** Indon.
125 G4 **Mangaung** S. Africa
72 E3 **Mangaweka** N.Z.
89 G4 **Mangde Chhu** *r.* Bhutan
107 B6 **Mangerton Mountain** Rep. of Ireland
99 C3 **Manggar** Indon.
82 C3 **Mangistauskaya Oblast'** *admin. div.* Kazakh.
82 E4 **Mang'it** Uzbek.
Mangit Uzbek. *see* **Mang'it**
90 B3 **Mangnai** China
123 D5 **Mangochi** Malawi
91 E7 **Mangole** *i.* Indon.
105 E6 **Mangotsfield** U.K.
88 B5 **Mangral** India
111 C2 **Mangualde** Port.
85 G4 **Manguchar** Pak.
159 G2 **Mangueira, Lago** *l.* Brazil
158 B4 **Mangueirinha** Brazil
121 D2 **Manguéni, Plateau du** Niger
90 E1 **Mangui** China
97 C5 **Mangupung** *i.* Indon.
82 B3 **Mangyshlak, Poluostrov** *pen.* Kazakh.
82 B3 **Mangyshlakskiy Zaliv** *b.* Kazakh.
82 B4 **Mangystau** Kazakh.
142 D4 **Manhattan** *KS* U.S.A.
140 D2 **Manhattan** *NV* U.S.A.
123 D6 **Manhica** Moz.
125 J3 **Manhoca** Moz.
158 D3 **Manhuaçu** Brazil
158 E2 **Manhuaçu** *r.* Brazil
157 B3 **Mani** Col.
123 E5 **Mania** *r.* Madag.
114 E1 **Maniago** Italy
154 F5 **Manicoré** Brazil
133 G3 **Manicouagan** Canada
133 G3 **Manicouagan** *r.* Canada
133 G3 **Manicouagan, Petit Lac** *l.* Canada
133 G3 **Manicouagan, Réservoir** *resr* Canada
84 C5 **Manīfah** Saudi Arabia
67 I4 **Manihiki** *atoll* Cook Is
Manikgarh India *see* **Rajura**
88 E4 **Manikpur** India
97 B3 **Manila** Phil. (City Plan **50**)
138 E3 **Manila** U.S.A.
71 H4 **Manildra** Australia
71 I3 **Manilla** Australia
89 H4 **Manipur** *state* India
115 L5 **Manisa** Turkey
134 D3 **Manistee** U.S.A.
134 E3 **Manistee** *r.* U.S.A.
134 D3 **Manistique** U.S.A.
134 E2 **Manistique Lake** U.S.A.
132 B2 **Manitoba** *prov.* Canada
131 J4 **Manitoba, Lake** Canada
131 H4 **Manito Lake** Canada
131 J5 **Manitou** Canada
135 G3 **Manitou, Lake** Canada
146 E3 **Manitou Beach** U.S.A.
132 B3 **Manitou Falls** Canada
134 D2 **Manitou Island** U.S.A.
144 C2 **Manitou Islands** U.S.A.
135 F3 **Manitoulin Island** Canada
135 G3 **Manitowaning** Canada
134 E1 **Manitowik Lake** Canada
134 D3 **Manitowoc** U.S.A.
135 J2 **Maniwaki** Canada
157 B3 **Manizales** Col.
123 E6 **Manja** Madag.
125 J2 **Manjacaze** Moz.
87 B4 **Manjeri** India
96 D3 **Man Jiang** *r.* China
81 L3 **Manjil** Iran
87 B2 **Manjra** *r.* India
142 E2 **Mankato** U.S.A.
125 I3 **Mankayane** Swaziland
120 B4 **Mankono** Côte d'Ivoire
87 C4 **Mankulam** Sri Lanka
71 I4 **Manly** Australia
88 C5 **Manmad** India
99 B3 **Manna** Indon.
70 C4 **Mannahill** Australia
87 B4 **Mannar** Sri Lanka
87 B4 **Mannar, Gulf of** India/Sri Lanka
87 B3 **Manneru** *r.* India
109 G5 **Mannheim** Germany
107 A4 **Mannin Bay** Rep. of Ireland
130 F3 **Manning** Canada
145 D5 **Manning** U.S.A.
105 I6 **Manningtree** U.K.
114 C4 **Mannu, Capo** *c. Sardinia* Italy
70 C5 **Mannum** Australia
91 F7 **Manokwari** Indon.
122 C4 **Manono** Dem. Rep. Congo
98 A3 **Manoron** Myanmar
110 G5 **Manosque** France
129 K4 **Manouane, Lac** *l.* Canada
96 D3 **Manp'o** N. Korea
69 I2 **Manra** *i.* Kiribati
111 G2 **Manresa** Spain
88 C3 **Mansa** India
123 C5 **Mansa** Zambia
120 A3 **Mansa Konko** Gambia
88 C2 **Mansehra** Pak.
129 K3 **Mansel Island** Canada
71 G6 **Mansfield** Australia
105 F4 **Mansfield** U.K.
143 E5 **Mansfield** *LA* U.S.A.
146 B4 **Mansfield** *OH* U.S.A.
146 E4 **Mansfield** *PA* U.S.A.
130 E3 **Manson Creek** Canada
81 L6 **Manşūrī** Iran
80 E3 **Mansurlu** Turkey
154 B4 **Manta** Ecuador
154 B4 **Manta, Bahía de** *b.* Ecuador
97 A4 **Mantalingajan, Mount** Phil.
140 B3 **Manteca** U.S.A.
157 C3 **Mantecal** Venez.
109 K5 **Mantel** Germany
145 F5 **Manteo** U.S.A.
110 E2 **Mantes-la-Jolie** France
87 B2 **Manthani** India
141 G2 **Manti** U.S.A.
158 D3 **Mantiqueira, Serra da** *mts* Brazil
134 E3 **Manton** U.S.A.
Mantova Italy *see* **Mantua**
103 N3 **Mäntsälä** Fin.
103 N3 **Mänttä** Fin.
114 D2 **Mantua** Italy
116 H3 **Manturovo** Rus. Fed.
103 N3 **Mäntyharju** Fin.
102 N2 **Mäntyjärvi** Fin.
154 D6 **Manu, Parque Nacional** *nat. park* Peru
161 I7 **Manuae** *atoll* Fr. Polynesia
Manua Islands American Samoa *see* **Manu'a Islands**
67 H4 **Manu'a Islands** American Samoa
141 H4 **Manuelito** U.S.A.
159 F2 **Manuel J. Cobo** Arg.
158 E1 **Manuel Vitorino** Brazil
155 H5 **Manuelzinho** Brazil
91 E7 **Manui** *i.* Indon.
85 E5 **Manūjān** Iran
97 B4 **Manukan** Phil.
72 E2 **Manukau** N.Z.
72 E2 **Manukau Harbour** N.Z.
97 A5 **Manuk Manka** *i.* Phil.
70 C4 **Manunda** *watercourse* Australia
68 E2 **Manus Island** P.N.G.
87 B3 **Manvi** India
125 F2 **Manyana** Botswana
117 G6 **Manych-Gudilo, Ozero** *l.* Rus. Fed.
141 H3 **Many Farms** U.S.A.
122 D4 **Manyoni** Tanz.
80 D6 **Manzala, Lake** *lag.* Egypt
111 E3 **Manzanares** Spain
149 I4 **Manzanillo** Cuba
150 C4 **Manzanillo** Mex.
150 J6 **Manzanillo, Punta** *pt* Panama
84 C3 **Manzariyeh** Iran
90 D2 **Manzhouli** China
125 I3 **Manzini** Swaziland
121 D3 **Mao** Chad
Maó Spain *see* **Mahón**
92 D4 **Maocifan** China
92 C2 **Maojiachuan** China
91 F7 **Maoke, Pegunungan** *mts* Indon.
125 G3 **Maokeng** S. Africa
96 B3 **Maokui Shan** *mt.* China
96 B2 **Maolin** China
92 B2 **Maomao Shan** *mt.* China
93 D6 **Maoming** China
93 □ **Ma On Shan** *h. Hong Kong* China
123 D6 **Mapai** Moz.
88 E3 **Mapam Yumco** *l.* China
68 C2 **Mapane** Indon.
125 F5 **Maphodi** S. Africa
150 D2 **Mapimí** Mex.
150 C2 **Mapimí, Bolsón de** *des.* Mex.
97 A5 **Mapin** *i.* Phil.
123 D6 **Mapinhane** Moz.
157 D3 **Mapire** Venez.
134 E4 **Maple** *r.* U.S.A.
131 H5 **Maple Creek** Canada
160 G4 **Mapmakers Seamounts** *sea feature* N. Pacific Ocean
125 G4 **Mapoteng** Lesotho
155 G4 **Mapuera** *r.* Brazil
125 J2 **Mapulanguene** Moz.
123 D6 **Maputo** Moz.
125 J2 **Maputo** *prov.* Moz.
125 J3 **Maputo** *r.* Moz.
125 G4 **Maputsoe** Lesotho
81 H6 **Maqar an Na'am** *well* Iraq
92 B3 **Maqu** China
89 E3 **Maquan He** *r.* China
122 B4 **Maquela do Zombo** Angola
159 C4 **Maquinchao** Arg.
159 C4 **Maquinchao** *r.* Arg.
134 B4 **Maquoketa** U.S.A.
134 B4 **Maquoketa** *r.* U.S.A.
85 G5 **Mar** *r.* Pak.
158 D3 **Mar, Serra do** *mts* Brazil
131 H1 **Mara** *r.* Canada
89 E5 **Mara** India
125 H1 **Mara** S. Africa
154 E4 **Maraã** Brazil
155 I5 **Maraba** Brazil
155 H3 **Maracá, Ilha de** *i.* Brazil
157 C2 **Maracaibo** Venez.
157 C2 **Maracaibo, Lake** *inlet* Venez.
158 A3 **Maracaju** Brazil
158 A3 **Maracaju, Serra de** *hills* Brazil
158 E1 **Maracás, Chapada de** *hills* Brazil
157 D2 **Maracay** Venez.
121 D2 **Marādah** Libya
120 C3 **Maradi** Niger
84 B2 **Marāgheh** Iran
158 E1 **Maragogipe** Brazil
97 B3 **Maragondon** Phil.
157 D4 **Marahuaca, Cerro** *mt.* Venez.
155 I4 **Marajó, Baía de** *est.* Brazil
155 I3 **Marajó, Ilha de** *i.* Brazil
125 G2 **Marakele National Park** S. Africa
87 B3 **Marakkanam** India
122 D3 **Maralal** Kenya
88 C2 **Marala Weir** Pak.
81 I1 **Maralik** Armenia
68 D5 **Maralinga** Australia
69 G2 **Maramasike** *i.* Solomon Is
73 E2 **Marambio** *research stn* Antarctica
97 C5 **Marampit** *i.* Indon.
85 G4 **Maran** *mt.* Pak.
81 J4 **Marāna** Iraq
141 G5 **Marana** U.S.A.
84 B2 **Marand** Iran
98 B4 **Marang** Malaysia
98 A3 **Marang** Myanmar
158 C1 **Maranhão** *r.* Brazil
154 D4 **Marañón** *r.* Peru
125 K2 **Marão** Moz.
111 C2 **Marão** *mt.* Port.
157 D4 **Marari** *r.* Brazil
72 A6 **Mararoa** *r.* N.Z.
134 D1 **Marathon** Canada
145 D7 **Marathon** *FL* U.S.A.
143 C6 **Marathon** *TX* U.S.A.
158 E1 **Maraú** Brazil
99 D3 **Marau** Indon.
157 D4 **Marauiá** *r.* Brazil
97 C4 **Marawi** Phil.
81 L1 **Märäzä** Azer.
111 D4 **Marbella** Spain
68 B4 **Marble Bar** Australia
141 G3 **Marble Canyon** U.S.A.
141 G3 **Marble Canyon** *gorge* U.S.A.
125 H2 **Marble Hall** S. Africa
147 H3 **Marblehead** U.S.A.
131 K2 **Marble Island** Canada
125 I5 **Marburg** S. Africa
146 E5 **Marburg, Lake** U.S.A.
109 G4 **Marburg an der Lahn** Germany
112 H7 **Marcali** Hungary
105 H5 **March** U.K.
70 C4 **Marchant Hill** Australia
108 D4 **Marche-en-Famenne** Belgium
111 D4 **Marchena** Spain
154 □ **Marchena, Isla** *i. Galapagos Is* Ecuador
Mar Chiquita, Lago *l.* Arg. *see* **Mar Chiquita, Laguna**
159 D1 **Mar Chiquita, Laguna** *l.* Arg.
112 G6 **Marchtrenk** Austria
145 D7 **Marco** U.S.A.
108 B4 **Marcoing** France
132 E2 **Marcopeet Islands** Canada
159 D2 **Marcos Juárez** Arg.
147 G2 **Marcy, Mount** U.S.A.
88 C2 **Mardan** Pak.
159 F3 **Mar del Plata** Arg.
81 H3 **Mardın** Turkey
69 G4 **Maré** *i.* New Caledonia
106 C3 **Maree, Loch** *l.* U.K.
134 A5 **Marengo** *IA* U.S.A.
134 C4 **Marengo** *IL* U.S.A.
114 E6 **Marettimo, Isola** *i. Sicily* Italy
116 E3 **Marevo** Rus. Fed.
143 B6 **Marfa** U.S.A.
70 B2 **Margaret** *watercourse* Australia
68 B5 **Margaret River** Australia
157 E2 **Margarita, Isla de** *i.* Venez.
94 D3 **Margaritovo** Rus. Fed.
71 G9 **Margate** Australia
125 I5 **Margate** S. Africa
105 I6 **Margate** U.K.
Margilan Uzbek. *see* **Marg'ilon**
83 G4 **Marg'ilon** Uzbek.
Margo, Dasht-i *des.* Afgh. *see* **Mārgow, Dasht-e**
97 B5 **Margosatubig** Phil.
85 F4 **Mārgow, Dasht-e** *des.* Afgh.
108 D4 **Margraten** Neth.
134 E3 **Margrethe, Lake** U.S.A.
130 E4 **Marguerite** Canada
73 B2 **Marguerite Bay** *b.* Antarctica
89 G3 **Margyang** China
81 K5 **Marhaj Khalīl** Iraq
83 H4 **Marhamat** Uzbek.
81 I3 **Marhan Dāgh** *h.* Iraq
117 E6 **Marhanets'** Ukr.
161 I7 **Maria** *atoll* Fr. Polynesia
156 C2 **María Elena** Chile
159 E3 **María Ignacia** Arg.
71 H9 **Maria Island** Australia
68 D3 **Maria Island** Australia
160 E4 **Mariana Ridge** *sea feature* N. Pacific Ocean
160 E5 **Mariana Trench** *sea feature* N. Pacific Ocean
89 H4 **Mariani** India
130 F2 **Marian Lake** Canada
143 F5 **Marianna** *AR* U.S.A.
145 C6 **Marianna** *FL* U.S.A.
112 F6 **Mariánské Lázně** Czech Rep.
150 C3 **Marías, Islas** *is* Mex.
150 I7 **Mariato, Punta** *pt* Panama
72 D1 **Maria van Diemen, Cape** N.Z.
114 F1 **Maribor** Slovenia
141 F5 **Maricopa** *AZ* U.S.A.
140 C4 **Maricopa** *CA* U.S.A.
141 F5 **Maricopa Mountains** U.S.A.
121 E4 **Maridi** *watercourse* Sudan
73 B4 **Marie Byrd Land** *reg.* Antarctica
149 L5 **Marie-Galante** *i.* Guadeloupe
103 L3 **Mariehamn** Fin.
158 B1 **Mariembero** *r.* Brazil
109 L4 **Marienberg** Germany
108 F1 **Marienhafe** Germany
123 B6 **Mariental** Namibia
103 K4 **Mariestad** Sweden
145 C5 **Marietta** *GA* U.S.A.
146 C5 **Marietta** *OH* U.S.A.
110 G5 **Marignane** France
90 G1 **Marii, Mys** *pt* Rus. Fed.
90 A1 **Mariinsk** Rus. Fed.
82 E1 **Mariinskoye** Rus. Fed.
103 M5 **Marijampolė** Lith.
158 C3 **Marília** Brazil
151 D2 **Marín** Mex.
111 B1 **Marín** Spain
114 G5 **Marina di Gioiosa Ionica** Italy
116 D4 **Mar"ina Horka** Belarus
97 B3 **Marinduque** *i.* Phil.
134 D3 **Marinette** U.S.A.
158 B3 **Maringá** Brazil
111 B3 **Marinha Grande** Port.
144 B4 **Marion** *IL* U.S.A.
134 E5 **Marion** *IN* U.S.A.
147 J2 **Marion** *ME* U.S.A.
146 B4 **Marion** *OH* U.S.A.
145 E5 **Marion** *SC* U.S.A.
146 C6 **Marion** *VA* U.S.A.
145 D5 **Marion, Lake** U.S.A.
70 B5 **Marion Bay** Australia
157 D3 **Maripa** Venez.
140 C3 **Mariposa** U.S.A.
Mariscal Estigarribia Para. *see* **Mariscal José Félix Estigarribia**
156 D2 **Mariscal José Félix Estigarribia** Para.
110 H4 **Maritime Alps** *mts* France/Italy
115 K3 **Maritsa** *r.* Bulg.
116 I3 **Mari-Turek** Rus. Fed.
117 F6 **Mariupol'** Ukr.
157 E2 **Mariusa, Caño** *r.* Venez.
84 B3 **Marīvān** Iran
116 I3 **Mariy El, Respublika** *aut. rep.* Rus. Fed.
122 E3 **Marka** Somalia
83 K2 **Markakol', Ozero** *l.* Kazakh.
81 J2 **Mārkān** Iran
87 B3 **Markapur** India
103 K4 **Markaryd** Sweden
135 G3 **Markdale** Canada
125 H1 **Marken** S. Africa
108 D2 **Markermeer** *l.* Neth.
105 G5 **Market Deeping** U.K.
105 E5 **Market Drayton** U.K.
105 G5 **Market Harborough** U.K.
107 E3 **Markethill** U.K.
104 G4 **Market Weighton** U.K.
77 M3 **Markha** *r.* Rus. Fed.
135 H4 **Markham** Canada
Markhamet Uzbek. *see* **Marhamat**
83 I5 **Markit** China
117 F5 **Markivka** Ukr.
109 K3 **Markkleeberg** Germany
109 H2 **Marklohe** Germany
92 A3 **Markog Qu** *r.* China
77 S3 **Markovo** Rus. Fed.
109 K3 **Markranstädt** Germany
117 H5 **Marks** Rus. Fed.
109 H5 **Marktheidenfeld** Germany
112 E7 **Marktoberdorf** Germany
109 K4 **Marktredwitz** Germany
134 B6 **Mark Twain Lake** U.S.A.
108 F3 **Marl** Germany
147 H3 **Marlborough** U.S.A.
105 F6 **Marlborough Downs** *hills* U.K.
108 B5 **Marle** France
143 D6 **Marlin** U.S.A.
146 C5 **Marlinton** U.S.A.
71 H6 **Marlo** Australia
110 E4 **Marmande** France
80 B1 **Marmara, Sea of** *g.* Turkey
Marmara Denizi *g.* Turkey *see* **Marmara, Sea of**
80 B2 **Marmara Gölü** *l.* Turkey
80 B3 **Marmaris** Turkey
142 C2 **Marmarth** U.S.A.
146 C5 **Marmet** U.S.A.
132 B4 **Marmion Lake** Canada
114 D1 **Marmolada** *mt.* Italy
110 F2 **Marne-la-Vallée** France
81 J1 **Marneuli** Georgia
109 J1 **Marnitz** Germany
70 E6 **Marnoo** Australia
123 E5 **Maroantsetra** Madag.
109 I4 **Maroldsweisach** Germany
123 E5 **Maromokotro** *mt.* Madag.
123 D5 **Marondera** Zimbabwe
155 H2 **Maroni** *r.* Fr. Guiana
71 J1 **Maroochydore** Australia
67 I6 **Marotiri** *is* Fr. Polynesia
121 D3 **Maroua** Cameroon
123 E5 **Marovoay** Madag.
81 H4 **Marqādah** Syria
125 G4 **Marquard** S. Africa
67 J5 **Marquesas Islands** Fr. Polynesia
145 D7 **Marquesas Keys** *is* U.S.A.
134 D2 **Marquette** U.S.A.
108 B4 **Marquion** France
Marquises, Îles *is* Fr. Polynesia *see* **Marquesas Islands**
70 E3 **Marra** Australia
71 G3 **Marra** *r.* Australia
125 J2 **Marracuene** Moz.
120 B1 **Marrakech** Morocco
125 K2 **Marrangua, Lagoa** *l.* Moz.
121 E3 **Marra Plateau** Sudan
71 G5 **Marrar** Australia
71 F8 **Marrawah** Australia
70 C2 **Marree** Australia
143 F6 **Marrero** U.S.A.
123 D5 **Marromeu** Moz.
123 D5 **Marrupa** Moz.
121 F2 **Marsá al 'Alam** Egypt
121 D1 **Marsa al Burayqah** Libya
122 D3 **Marsabit** Kenya
114 E6 **Marsala** *Sicily* Italy
121 E1 **Marsá Maṭrūḩ** Egypt
109 G3 **Marsberg** Germany
114 E3 **Marsciano** Italy
71 G4 **Marsden** Australia
108 C2 **Marsdiep** *sea chan.* Neth.
110 G5 **Marseille** France
134 C5 **Marseilles** U.S.A.
102 K2 **Marsfjället** *mt.* Sweden
131 H4 **Marshall** Canada
143 E5 **Marshall** *AR* U.S.A.
144 C4 **Marshall** *IL* U.S.A.
134 E4 **Marshall** *MI* U.S.A.
142 E2 **Marshall** *MN* U.S.A.
142 E4 **Marshall** *MO* U.S.A.
143 E5 **Marshall** *TX* U.S.A.
71 G7 **Marshall Bay** Australia
67 F2 **Marshall Islands** *country* N. Pacific Ocean
142 E3 **Marshalltown** U.S.A.
134 B3 **Marshfield** U.S.A.
145 E7 **Marsh Harbour** Bahamas
147 J1 **Mars Hill** U.S.A.
143 F6 **Marsh Island** U.S.A.
130 C2 **Marsh Lake** Canada
81 L3 **Marshūn** Iran
138 C3 **Marsing** U.S.A.
103 L4 **Märsta** Sweden
89 F4 **Marsyangdi** *r.* Nepal
Martaban Myanmar *see* **Mottama**
Martaban, Gulf of Myanmar *see* **Mottama, Gulf of**
99 D3 **Martapura** Indon.
99 B3 **Martapura** Indon.
135 H2 **Marten River** Canada
131 H4 **Martensville** Canada
151 E2 **Marte R. Gómez, Presa** *resr* Mex.
147 H4 **Martha's Vineyard** *i.* U.S.A.
112 C7 **Martigny** Switz.
113 I6 **Martin** Slovakia
142 C3 **Martin** *SD* U.S.A.
145 B4 **Martin** *TN* U.S.A.
145 C5 **Martin, Lake** U.S.A.
151 E3 **Martínez** Mex.
141 E5 **Martinez Lake** U.S.A.
149 L6 **Martinique** *terr.* Caribbean Sea
73 B4 **Martin Peninsula** Antarctica
146 D4 **Martinsburg** *PA* U.S.A.
146 E5 **Martinsburg** *WV* U.S.A.
146 C4 **Martins Ferry** U.S.A.
146 D6 **Martinsville** U.S.A.
163 H7 **Martin Vas, Ilhas** *is* S. Atlantic Ocean
72 E4 **Marton** N.Z.
111 G2 **Martorell** Spain
111 E4 **Martos** Spain
82 D2 **Martuk** Kazakh.
81 J1 **Martuni** Armenia
85 F3 **Maruchak** Afgh.
95 C7 **Marugame** Japan
72 D5 **Maruia** *r.* N.Z.
155 K6 **Maruim** Brazil
117 G7 **Marukhis Ugheltekhili** *pass* Georgia/Rus. Fed.
71 H5 **Marulan** Australia
83 K1 **Marushka** Rus. Fed.
84 D4 **Marvast** Iran
110 F4 **Marvejols** France
141 G2 **Marvine, Mount** U.S.A.
131 G4 **Marwayne** Canada
85 F2 **Mary** Turkm.
69 F4 **Maryborough** *Qld* Australia
70 E6 **Maryborough** *Vic.* Australia
124 H3 **Marydale** S. Africa
116 I4 **Mar'yevka** Rus. Fed.
131 H2 **Mary Frances Lake** Canada
147 E5 **Maryland** *state* U.S.A.
104 D3 **Maryport** U.K.
133 I3 **Mary's Harbour** Canada
133 J4 **Marystown** Canada
141 F2 **Marysvale** U.S.A.
133 G4 **Marysville** Canada
140 B2 **Marysville** *CA* U.S.A.
142 D4 **Marysville** *KS* U.S.A.
146 B4 **Marysville** *OH* U.S.A.
142 E3 **Maryville** *MO* U.S.A.
145 C5 **Maryville** *TN* U.S.A.
109 K2 **Marzahna** Germany
150 H6 **Masachapa** Nicaragua
80 E6 **Masada** *tourist site* Israel
84 D4 **Masāhūn, Kūh-e** *mt.* Iran
122 D4 **Masaka** Uganda
125 G5 **Masakhane** S. Africa
81 L2 **Masallı** Azer.
68 C2 **Masamba** Indon.
96 E6 **Masan** S. Korea
147 I1 **Masardis** U.S.A.
123 D5 **Masasi** Tanz.
154 F7 **Masavi** Bol.
150 H6 **Masaya** Nicaragua
97 B3 **Masbate** Phil.
97 B4 **Masbate** *i.* Phil.
120 C1 **Mascara** Alg.
162 H6 **Mascarene Basin** *sea feature* Indian Ocean
162 H6 **Mascarene Plain** *sea feature* Indian Ocean
162 H5 **Mascarene Ridge** *sea feature* Indian Ocean
147 G2 **Mascouche** Canada
125 G4 **Maseru** Lesotho
125 H4 **Mashai** Lesotho
93 C6 **Mashan** China
88 D2 **Masherbrum** *mt.* Pak.
85 E2 **Mashhad** Iran
88 C4 **Mashi** *r.* India
81 K2 **Mashīrān** Iran
85 F4 **Mashkel, Hamun-i-** *salt flat* Pak.
85 F5 **Mashket** *r.* Pak.
85 F4 **Mashki Chah** Pak.
85 F5 **Māshkīd** *r.* Iran
102 M1 **Masi** Norway
150 B2 **Masiáca** Mex.
125 G5 **Masibambane** S. Africa
125 G4 **Masilo** S. Africa
122 D3 **Masindi** Uganda
97 A3 **Masinloc** Phil.
124 E5 **Masinyusane** S. Africa
Masīrah *i.* Oman *see* **Maşīrah, Jazīrat**
86 E5 **Maşīrah, Jazīrat** *i.* Oman
86 E6 **Maşīrah, Khalīj** *b.* Oman
81 J1 **Masis** Armenia
84 C4 **Masjed Soleymān** Iran
107 B4 **Mask, Lough** *l.* Rep. of Ireland
80 G3 **Maskanah** Syria
85 E5 **Maskūtān** Iran
85 G4 **Maslti** Pak.
123 E5 **Masoala, Parc National** Madag.
123 F5 **Masoala, Tanjona** *c.* Madag.
134 E4 **Mason** *MI* U.S.A.
140 C2 **Mason** *NV* U.S.A.
143 D6 **Mason** *TX* U.S.A.
72 A7 **Mason Bay** N.Z.
142 E3 **Mason City** *IA* U.S.A.
134 C5 **Mason City** *IL* U.S.A.
146 D5 **Masontown** U.S.A.
Masqaţ Oman *see* **Muscat**
114 D2 **Massa** Italy
147 G3 **Massachusetts** *state* U.S.A.
147 H3 **Massachusetts Bay** U.S.A.
141 H1 **Massadona** U.S.A.
114 G4 **Massafra** Italy
121 D3 **Massakory** Chad
114 D3 **Massa Marittimo** Italy
123 D6 **Massangena** Moz.
123 B4 **Massango** Angola
122 D2 **Massawa** Eritrea
147 G2 **Massawippi, Lac** *l.* Canada
147 F2 **Massena** U.S.A.
130 C4 **Masset** Canada
135 F2 **Massey** Canada
110 F4 **Massif Central** *mts* France
146 C4 **Massillon** U.S.A.
120 B3 **Massina** Mali
123 D6 **Massinga** Moz.
123 D6 **Massingir** Moz.
125 J1 **Massingir, Barragem de** *resr* Moz.
125 J2 **Massintonto** *r.* Moz./S. Africa
135 J3 **Masson** Canada
81 L1 **Maştağa** Azer.
83 G5 **Mastchoh** Tajik.
72 E4 **Masterton** N.Z.
115 L5 **Masticho, Akra** *pt* Greece
145 E7 **Mastic Point** Bahamas
88 C1 **Mastuj** Pak.
85 G4 **Mastung** Pak.
116 C4 **Masty** Belarus
95 B7 **Masuda** Japan
81 L3 **Masuleh** Iran
123 D6 **Masvingo** Zimbabwe
80 F4 **Maşyāf** Syria
135 G2 **Matachewan** Canada
150 C1 **Matachic** Mex.
157 D4 **Matacuni** *r.* Venez.
122 B4 **Matadi** Dem. Rep. Congo
150 H5 **Matagalpa** Nicaragua
132 E4 **Matagami** Canada
132 E4 **Matagami, Lac** *l.* Canada
143 D6 **Matagorda Island** U.S.A.
98 C5 **Matak** *i.* Indon.
83 H2 **Matak** Kazakh.
72 F2 **Matakana Island** N.Z.
123 B5 **Matala** Angola
87 C5 **Matale** Sri Lanka
120 A3 **Matam** Senegal
150 D2 **Matamoros** *Coahuila* Mex.
151 E2 **Matamoros** *Tamaulipas* Mex.
97 B5 **Matanal Point** Phil.
123 D4 **Matandu** *r.* Tanz.
133 G4 **Matane** Canada
88 B2 **Matanui** Pak.
149 H4 **Matanzas** Cuba
133 G4 **Matapédia** *r.* Canada
159 B2 **Mataquito** *r.* Chile
87 C5 **Matara** Sri Lanka
99 E4 **Mataram** Indon.
154 D7 **Matarani** Peru
68 D3 **Mataranka** Australia
111 H2 **Mataró** Spain
125 H5 **Matatiele** S. Africa
72 B7 **Mataura** N.Z.
72 B7 **Mataura** *r.* N.Z.
69 J3 **Matā'utu** Wallis and Futuna Is
157 C3 **Mataveni** *r.* Col.
72 F3 **Matawai** N.Z.
154 F6 **Mategua** Bol.
150 D3 **Matehuala** Mex.
123 D5 **Matemanga** Tanz.
114 G4 **Matera** Italy
114 C6 **Mateur** Tunisia
132 D4 **Matheson** Canada
143 D6 **Mathis** U.S.A.
70 F5 **Mathoura** Australia
88 D4 **Mathura** India
97 C5 **Mati** Phil.
89 G4 **Matiali** India
93 D5 **Matianxu** China
88 B4 **Matiari** Pak.
151 F4 **Matías Romero** Mex.
133 G3 **Matimekosh** Canada
135 F2 **Matinenda Lake** Canada
147 I3 **Matinicus Island** U.S.A.
89 G5 **Matla** *r.* India
125 G2 **Matlabas** S. Africa
125 G2 **Matlabas** *r.* S. Africa
88 B4 **Matli** Pak.
105 F4 **Matlock** U.K.
157 D3 **Mato** *r.* Venez.
157 D3 **Mato, Cerro** *mt.* Venez.
154 G7 **Mato Grosso** Brazil
158 A1 **Mato Grosso** *state* Brazil
158 A1 **Mato Grosso, Planalto do** *plat.* Brazil
158 A3 **Mato Grosso do Sul** *state* Brazil
125 J2 **Matola** Moz.
111 B2 **Matosinhos** Port.
86 E5 **Maţraḩ** Oman
124 C6 **Matroosberg** *mt.* S. Africa
95 C7 **Matsue** Japan
94 G4 **Matsumae** Japan
95 E6 **Matsumoto** Japan
95 E7 **Matsusaka** Japan
93 F5 **Matsu Tao** *i.* Taiwan
95 C8 **Matsuyama** Japan
132 D4 **Mattagami** *r.* Canada
135 H2 **Mattawa** Canada
147 I2 **Mattawamkeag** U.S.A.
112 C7 **Matterhorn** *mt.* Italy/Switz.
138 D3 **Matterhorn** *mt.* U.S.A.
67 G2 **Matthew Island** S. Pacific Ocean
157 E3 **Matthews Ridge** Guyana
149 J4 **Matthew Town** Bahamas
84 D6 **Maţţī, Sabkhat** *salt pan* Saudi Arabia
144 B4 **Mattoon** U.S.A.
87 C5 **Matugama** Sri Lanka
69 H3 **Matuku** *i.* Fiji
157 E2 **Maturín** Venez.
97 C5 **Matutuang** *i.* Indon.
125 G4 **Matwabeng** S. Africa
88 E4 **Mau** India
89 E4 **Mau Aimma** India
108 B4 **Maubeuge** France
110 E5 **Maubourguet** France
106 D5 **Mauchline** U.K.
163 J10 **Maud Seamount** *sea feature* S. Atlantic Ocean
155 G4 **Maués** Brazil
89 E4 **Mauganj** India
140 □2 **Maui** *i.* U.S.A.
109 G6 **Maulbronn** Germany
159 B2 **Maule** *admin. reg.* Chile
159 B2 **Maule** *r.* Chile
159 B4 **Maullín** Chile
107 B3 **Maumakeogh** *h.* Rep. of Ireland
146 B4 **Maumee** U.S.A.
146 B4 **Maumee** *r.* U.S.A.
135 F5 **Maumee Bay** U.S.A.
107 B4 **Maumturk Mountains** Rep. of Ireland
123 C5 **Maun** Botswana
140 □2 **Mauna Kea** *vol.* U.S.A.
140 □2 **Mauna Loa** *vol.* U.S.A.
Maunalua B. U.S.A. *see* **Maunalua Bay**
140 □1 **Maunalua Bay** U.S.A.
89 E4 **Maunath Bhanjan** India
125 G1 **Maunatlala** Botswana
72 E2 **Maungaturoto** N.Z.
89 H5 **Maungdaw** Myanmar
98 A2 **Maungmagan Islands** Myanmar
128 F3 **Maunoir, Lac** *l.* Canada
70 B5 **Maupertuis Bay** Australia
68 D4 **Maurice, Lake** *salt flat* Australia
108 D3 **Maurik** Neth.
120 A3 **Mauritania** *country* Africa
119 I6 **Mauritius** *country* Indian Ocean
134 B4 **Mauston** U.S.A.
157 D4 **Mavaca** *r.* Venez.
123 C5 **Mavinga** Angola
125 G5 **Mavuya** S. Africa
88 D3 **Mawana** India
122 B4 **Mawanga** Dem. Rep. Congo
93 D4 **Ma Wang Dui** *tourist site* China
98 A3 **Mawdaung Pass** Myanmar/Thai.
72 G3 **Mawhai Point** N.Z.
98 A1 **Mawlamyaing** Myanmar
73 E5 **Mawson** *research stn* Antarctica
73 D5 **Mawson Escarpment** Antarctica
73 B6 **Mawson Peninsula** Antarctica
98 A3 **Maw Taung** *mt.* Myanmar
142 C2 **Max** U.S.A.
151 G3 **Maxcanú** Mex.
114 C5 **Maxia, Punta** *mt. Sardinia* Italy
134 D5 **Maxinkuckee, Lake** U.S.A.
102 M3 **Maxmo** Fin.
135 F2 **Maxton** U.S.A.
140 A2 **Maxwell** U.S.A.
106 F4 **May, Isle of** *i.* U.K.
99 C3 **Maya** *i.* Indon.
90 F1 **Maya** *r.* Rus. Fed.
149 J4 **Mayaguana** *i.* Bahamas
149 K5 **Mayagüez** Puerto Rico
120 C3 **Mayahi** Niger
85 H2 **Mayakovskiy, Qullai** *mt.* Tajik.
83 G4 **Mayakum** Kazakh.
122 B4 **Mayama** Congo
84 D2 **Mayamey** Iran
151 G4 **Maya Mountains** Belize
93 C5 **Mayang** China
92 B3 **Mayanhe** China
94 F5 **Maya-san** *mt.* Japan
106 D5 **Maybole** U.K.
81 J4 **Maydān Sarāy** Iraq
Maydā Shahr Afgh. *see* **Meydān Shahr**
71 G9 **Maydena** Australia
108 F4 **Mayen** Germany
110 D2 **Mayenne** France
110 D2 **Mayenne** *r.* France
141 F4 **Mayer** U.S.A.
130 F4 **Mayerthorpe** Canada
72 C5 **Mayfield** N.Z.
144 B4 **Mayfield** U.S.A.
139 F5 **Mayhill** U.S.A.
96 E1 **Mayi He** *r.* China
83 H2 **Maykain** Kazakh.
83 I3 **Maykamys** Kazakh.
83 G5 **Maykhura** Tajik.
117 G6 **Maykop** Rus. Fed.
83 H4 **Mayluu-Suu** Kyrg.
82 E3 **Maylybas** Kazakh.
83 K1 **Mayma** Rus. Fed.
83 G4 **Maymak** Kazakh.
Maymyo Myanmar *see* **Pyin-U-Lwin**
90 B1 **Mayna** Rus. Fed.
87 A2 **Mayni** India
135 I3 **Maynooth** Canada
130 B2 **Mayo** Canada
97 C5 **Mayo Bay** Phil.
122 B4 **Mayoko** Congo
130 B2 **Mayo Lake** Canada
97 B3 **Mayon** *vol.* Phil.
159 D3 **Mayor Buratovich** Arg.
72 F2 **Mayor Island** N.Z.
156 D1 **Mayor Pablo Lagerenza** Para.
123 E5 **Mayotte** *terr.* Africa
97 B2 **Mayraira Point** Phil.
90 E1 **Mayskiy** Rus. Fed.
146 B5 **Maysville** U.S.A.
122 B4 **Mayumba** Gabon
89 E3 **Mayum La** *pass* China
87 B4 **Mayuram** India
135 F4 **Mayville** *MI* U.S.A.
142 D2 **Mayville** *ND* U.S.A.
146 D3 **Mayville** *NY* U.S.A.
134 C4 **Mayville** *WI* U.S.A.
142 C3 **Maywood** U.S.A.
159 D3 **Maza** Arg.
116 F3 **Maza** Rus. Fed.
123 C5 **Mazabuka** Zambia
155 H4 **Mazagão** Brazil
110 F5 **Mazamet** France
88 D1 **Mazar** China
85 G3 **Mazar, Koh-i-** *mt.* Afgh.
114 E6 **Mazara del Vallo** *Sicily* Italy
85 G2 **Mazār-e Sharīf** Afgh.
157 E3 **Mazaruni** *r.* Guyana
150 B1 **Mazatán** Mex.
151 G5 **Mazatenango** Guat.
150 C3 **Mazatlán** Mex.
141 G4 **Mazatzal Peak** U.S.A.
84 C3 **Mazdaj** Iran
103 M4 **Mažeikiai** Lith.
81 G2 **Mazgirt** Turkey
84 A5 **Maẓhūr, 'Irq al** *des.* Saudi Arabia
103 M4 **Mazirbe** Latvia
122 D4 **Mazomora** Tanz.
113 J4 **Mazowiecka, Nizina** *lowland* Poland
81 L3 **Mazr'eh** Iran
81 L5 **Māzū** Iran
123 C6 **Mazunga** Zimbabwe
117 D4 **Mazyr** Belarus
125 I3 **Mbabane** Swaziland
120 B4 **Mbahiakro** Côte d'Ivoire
122 B3 **Mbaïki** Centr. Afr. Rep.
123 D4 **Mbala** Zambia
122 D3 **Mbale** Uganda
120 D4 **Mbalmayo** Cameroon
122 B4 **Mbandaka** Dem. Rep. Congo
120 C4 **Mbanga** Cameroon
122 B4 **M'banza Congo** Angola
122 D4 **Mbarara** Uganda
122 C3 **Mbari** *r.* Centr. Afr. Rep.
125 J3 **Mbaswana** S. Africa
120 D4 **Mbengwi** Cameroon
123 D4 **Mbeya** Tanz.
123 D5 **Mbinga** Tanz.
123 D6 **Mbizi** Zimbabwe
122 B3 **Mbomo** Congo
120 D4 **Mbouda** Cameroon
120 A3 **Mbour** Senegal
120 A3 **Mbout** Mauritania
123 D4 **Mbozi** Tanz.
122 C4 **Mbuji-Mayi** Dem. Rep. Congo
122 D4 **Mbulu** Tanz.
122 D4 **Mbuyuni** Tanz.
147 J2 **McAdam** Canada
143 E5 **McAlester** U.S.A.
146 E4 **McAlevys Fort** U.S.A.
71 H5 **McAlister** *mt.* Australia
143 D7 **McAllen** U.S.A.
146 B5 **McArthur** U.S.A.
135 I3 **McArthur Mills** Canada
130 B2 **McArthur Wildlife Sanctuary** *nature res.* Canada
130 E4 **McBride** Canada
138 C2 **McCall** U.S.A.
143 C6 **McCamey** U.S.A.
138 D3 **McCammon** U.S.A.
130 C4 **McCauley Island** Canada
128 H2 **McClintock Channel** Canada
140 B3 **McClure, Lake** U.S.A.
128 F2 **McClure Strait** Canada
143 F6 **McComb** U.S.A.
142 C3 **McConaughy, Lake** U.S.A.
146 E5 **McConnellsburg** U.S.A.
146 C5 **McConnelsville** U.S.A.
142 C3 **McCook** U.S.A.
131 J4 **McCreary** Canada
141 E4 **McCullough Range** *mts* U.S.A.
130 D3 **McDame** Canada
138 C3 **McDermitt** U.S.A.
162 I8 **McDonald Islands** Indian Ocean
138 D2 **McDonald Peak** U.S.A.
70 C2 **McDonnell Creek** *watercourse* Australia
124 B4 **McDougall's Bay** S. Africa
141 G5 **McDowell Peak** U.S.A.
140 C4 **McFarland** U.S.A.
131 H3 **McFarlane** *r.* Canada
141 E2 **McGill** U.S.A.
128 C3 **McGrath** U.S.A.
130 E4 **McGregor** *r.* Canada
124 C6 **McGregor** S. Africa
134 A2 **McGregor** U.S.A.
135 G2 **McGregor Bay** Canada
138 D2 **McGuire, Mount** U.S.A.
123 D4 **Mchinga** Tanz.
147 G2 **McIndoe Falls** U.S.A.
142 C2 **McIntosh** U.S.A.
69 I2 **McKean** *i.* Kiribati
146 A6 **McKee** U.S.A.
146 D4 **McKeesport** U.S.A.
147 F3 **McKeever** U.S.A.
145 B4 **McKenzie** U.S.A.
128 C3 **McKinley, Mount** U.S.A.
143 D5 **McKinney** U.S.A.
140 C4 **McKittrick** U.S.A.
142 C2 **McLaughlin** U.S.A.
130 F3 **McLennan** Canada
130 F4 **McLeod** *r.* Canada
130 E3 **McLeod Lake** Canada
138 B3 **McLoughlin, Mount** U.S.A.
134 E2 **McMillan** U.S.A.
138 B2 **McMinnville** *OR* U.S.A.
145 C5 **McMinnville** *TN* U.S.A.
73 B5 **McMurdo** *research stn* Antarctica
141 H4 **McNary** U.S.A.
130 F4 **McNaughton Lake** Canada
141 H6 **McNeal** U.S.A.
142 D4 **McPherson** U.S.A.
71 J2 **McPherson Range** *mts* Australia
130 B2 **McQuesten** *r.* Canada
145 D5 **McRae** U.S.A.
130 E1 **McVicar Arm** *b.* Canada
125 G6 **Mdantsane** S. Africa
114 B6 **M'Daourouch** Alg.
98 D2 **M'Đrak** Vietnam
98 C1 **Mê, Hon** *i.* Vietnam
141 E3 **Mead, Lake** *resr* U.S.A.
143 C4 **Meade** U.S.A.
131 H4 **Meadow Lake** Canada
131 H4 **Meadow Lake Provincial Park** Canada
141 E3 **Meadow Valley Wash** *r.* U.S.A.
146 C4 **Meadville** U.S.A.
135 G3 **Meaford** Canada
94 I3 **Meaken-dake** *vol.* Japan
106 A2 **Mealasta Island** U.K.
111 B2 **Mealhada** Port.

194 Meall a' Bhuiridh

106 D4 Meall a' Bhuiridh mt. U.K.
133 I3 Mealy Mountains Canada
71 H1 Meandarra Australia
130 F3 Meander River Canada
97 C5 Meares i. Indon.
110 F2 Meaux France
122 B4 Mebridege r. Angola
86 A5 Mecca Saudi Arabia (City Plan 54)
147 H2 Mechanic Falls U.S.A.
146 B4 Mechanicsburg U.S.A.
134 B5 Mechanicsville U.S.A.
108 C3 Mechelen Belgium
108 D4 Mechelen Neth.
120 B1 Mecheria Alg.
108 E4 Mechernich Germany
80 E1 Mecitözü Turkey
108 F4 Meckenheim Germany
112 E3 Mecklenburger Bucht b. Germany
109 J1 Mecklenburgische Seenplatte reg. Germany
109 K1 Mecklenburg-Vorpommern land Germany
123 D5 Mecula Moz.
111 C2 Meda Port.
87 B2 Medak India
99 A2 Medan Indon.
159 D3 Médanos Arg.
156 C7 Medanosa, Punta pt Arg.
87 C4 Medawachchiya Sri Lanka
87 B2 Medchal India
147 J2 Meddybemps Lake U.S.A.
111 H4 Médéa Alg.
109 G3 Medebach Germany
157 B3 Medellín Col.
105 F4 Meden r. U.K.
120 D1 Medenine Tunisia
120 A3 Mederdra Mauritania
138 B3 Medford OR U.S.A.
134 B3 Medford WI U.S.A.
147 F5 Medford Farms U.S.A.
115 M2 Medgidia Romania
134 B5 Media U.S.A.
159 C2 Media Luna Arg.
113 L7 Mediaş Romania
138 C2 Medical Lake U.S.A.
138 F3 Medicine Bow U.S.A.
138 F3 Medicine Bow Mountains U.S.A.
138 F3 Medicine Bow Peak U.S.A.
131 G4 Medicine Hat Canada
143 D4 Medicine Lodge U.S.A.
158 E2 Medina Brazil
86 A5 Medina Saudi Arabia
146 D3 Medina NY U.S.A.
146 C4 Medina OH U.S.A.
111 E2 Medinaceli Spain
111 D2 Medina del Campo Spain
111 D2 Medina de Rioseco Spain
89 F5 Medinipur India
100 F5 Mediterranean Sea Africa/Europe
82 D2 Mednogorsk Rus. Fed.
110 D4 Médoc reg. France
116 H3 Medvedevo Rus. Fed.
117 H5 Medveditsa r. Rus. Fed.
114 F2 Medvednica mts Croatia
77 R2 Medvezh'i, Ostrova is Rus. Fed.
90 F2 Medvezh'ya, Gora mt. China/Rus. Fed.
116 E2 Medvezh'yegorsk Rus. Fed.
105 H6 Medway r. U.K.
68 B4 Meekatharra Australia
141 H1 Meeker U.S.A.
140 B2 Meeks Bay U.S.A.
133 I4 Meelpaeg Reservoir Canada
109 K4 Meerane Germany
108 E3 Meerlo Neth.
88 D3 Meerut India
138 E2 Meeteetse U.S.A.
122 D3 Mēga Eth.
99 B3 Mega i. Indon.
89 G4 Meghalaya state India
89 F5 Meghasani mt. India
89 G5 Meghna r. Bangl.
81 K2 Meghri Armenia
80 B3 Megisti i. Greece
102 N1 Mehamn Norway
85 G5 Mehar Pak.
68 B4 Meharry, Mount Australia
81 K4 Mehdīkhān Iran
88 D5 Mehekar India
89 G5 Meherpur Bangl.
146 E6 Meherrin r. U.S.A.
81 K2 Mehrābān Iran
84 D5 Mehrān watercourse Iran
81 K5 Mehrān Iraq
108 E4 Mehren Germany
84 D4 Mehrīz Iran
85 H3 Mehtar Lām Afgh.
158 C2 Meia Ponte r. Brazil
121 D4 Meiganga Cameroon
93 B4 Meigu China
96 C2 Meihekou China
93 E5 Mei Jiang r. China
106 D5 Meikle Millyea h. U.K.
91 B4 Meiktila Myanmar
93 D6 Meilu China
109 I2 Meine Germany
109 I3 Meinersen Germany
109 I4 Meiningen Germany
124 E6 Meiringspoort pass S. Africa
93 B4 Meishan China
112 F5 Meißen Germany
93 C5 Meitan China
92 C3 Meixian China
93 E5 Meizhou China
88 D4 Mej r. India
159 C3 Mejicana mt. Arg.
156 B2 Mejillones Chile
122 D2 Mek'elē Eth.
120 A3 Mékhé Senegal
88 B3 Mekhtar Pak.
114 C7 Meknassy Tunisia
120 B1 Meknès Morocco
98 C2 Mekong r. Asia
90 B3 Mekong r. China alt. Lancang Jiang
98 C3 Mekong, Mouths of the Vietnam
99 B2 Melaka Malaysia
160 F6 Melanesia is Oceania
160 F5 Melanesian Basin sea feature Pacific Ocean
97 A5 Melaut r. Malaysia
99 D3 Melawi r. Indon.
70 F6 Melbourne Australia (City Plan 50)
145 D6 Melbourne U.S.A.
106 □ Melby U.K.
151 G4 Melchor de Mencos Guat.
150 D2 Melchor Ocampo Mex.
103 D2 Meldorf Germany
135 F3 Meldrum Bay Canada
80 E2 Melendiz Dağı mt. Turkey
116 G4 Melenki Rus. Fed.
82 C1 Meleuz Rus. Fed.
133 F2 Mélèzes, Rivière aux r. Canada
121 D3 Mélfi Chad
114 F4 Melfi Italy
131 I4 Melfort Canada
102 J3 Melhus Norway
111 C1 Melide Spain
120 B1 Melilla Spain
159 E2 Melincué Arg.
99 E3 Melintang, Danau l. Indon.
159 B2 Melipilla Chile
108 B3 Meliskerke Neth.
131 I5 Melita Canada
117 E6 Melitopol' Ukr.
112 G6 Melk Austria
125 H1 Melkrivier S. Africa
105 E6 Melksham U.K.
102 N2 Mellakoski Fin.
102 L3 Mellansel Sweden
109 G2 Melle Germany
134 B2 Mellen U.S.A.
103 K4 Mellerud Sweden
109 I4 Mellrichstadt Germany
109 G1 Mellum i. Germany
125 I4 Melmoth S. Africa
159 F2 Melo Uruguay
70 C4 Melrose Australia
106 F5 Melrose U.K.
109 H3 Melsungen Germany
105 G5 Melton Mowbray U.K.
110 F2 Melun France
131 I4 Melville Canada
68 E3 Melville, Cape Australia
97 A5 Melville, Cape Phil.
133 I3 Melville, Lake Canada
68 D3 Melville Island Australia
128 G2 Melville Island Canada
129 J3 Melville Peninsula Canada
107 C3 Melvin, Lough l. Rep. of Ireland/U.K.
89 E2 Mêmar Co salt l. China
91 F7 Memberamo r. Indon.
125 H3 Memel S. Africa
109 I5 Memmelsdorf Germany
112 E7 Memmingen Germany
108 C5 Memmingen Germany
108 C5 Mémorial Américain tourist site France
99 C2 Mempawah Indon.
80 C7 Memphis tourist site Egypt
134 A5 Memphis MO U.S.A.
145 B5 Memphis TN U.S.A.
143 C5 Memphis TX U.S.A.
147 G2 Memphrémagog, Lac l. Canada
94 H3 Memuro-dake mt. Japan
117 E5 Mena Ukr.
143 E5 Mena U.S.A.
120 C3 Ménaka Mali
143 D6 Menard U.S.A.
134 C3 Menasha U.S.A.
99 D3 Mendawai r. Indon.
110 F4 Mende France
122 D2 Mendefera Eritrea
81 L3 Mendejīn Iran
164 M1 Mendeleyev Ridge sea feature Arctic Ocean
128 B4 Mendenhall, Cape U.S.A.
130 C3 Mendenhall Glacier U.S.A.
83 F2 Mendesh Kazakh.
151 E2 Méndez Mex.
122 D3 Mendī Eth.
68 E2 Mendi P.N.G.
105 E6 Mendip Hills U.K.
140 A2 Mendocino U.S.A.
138 A3 Mendocino, Cape U.S.A.
134 E4 Mendon U.S.A.
71 H3 Mendooran Australia
140 B3 Mendota CA U.S.A.
134 C5 Mendota IL U.S.A.
134 C4 Mendota, Lake U.S.A.
159 C2 Mendoza Arg.
159 C2 Mendoza prov. Arg.
159 C2 Mendoza r. Arg.
157 C2 Mene de Mauroa Venez.
157 C2 Mene Grande Venez.
115 L5 Menemen Turkey
92 E3 Mengcheng China
80 D1 Mengen Turkey
99 C3 Menggala Indon.
93 D5 Mengshan China
92 F3 Meng Shan mts China
92 E3 Mengyin China
93 B6 Mengzi China
133 G3 Menihek Canada
133 G3 Menihek Lakes Canada
70 E4 Menindee Australia
70 E4 Menindee, Lake Australia
70 C5 Meningie Australia
81 L4 Menjān Iran
77 N3 Menkere Rus. Fed.
110 F2 Mennecy France
134 D3 Menominee U.S.A.
134 D3 Menominee r. U.S.A.
134 C4 Menomonee Falls U.S.A.
134 B3 Menomonie U.S.A.
123 B5 Menongue Angola
Menorca i. Spain see Minorca
97 A6 Mensalong Indon.
99 A3 Mentawai, Kepulauan is Indon.
98 B5 Mentekab Malaysia
109 I3 Menteroda Germany
141 H4 Mentmore U.S.A.
99 C3 Mentok Indon.
110 H5 Menton France
146 C4 Mentor U.S.A.
120 C1 Menzel Bourguiba Tunisia
114 D6 Menzel Temime Tunisia
68 C4 Menzies Australia
73 D5 Menzies, Mount mt. Antarctica
150 C1 Meoqui Mex.
108 E2 Meppel Neth.
108 F2 Meppen Germany
125 J1 Mepuze Moz.
125 G4 Meqheleng S. Africa
116 G3 Mera r. Rus. Fed.
99 C4 Merak Indon.
102 J3 Meråker Norway
142 F4 Meramec r. U.S.A.
114 D1 Merano Italy
157 E3 Merari, Serra mt. Brazil
124 F1 Meratswe r. Botswana
99 E3 Meratus, Pegunungan mts Indon.
97 G7 Merauke Indon.
70 E5 Merbein Australia
140 B3 Merced U.S.A.
159 B1 Mercedario, Cerro mt. Arg.
159 E2 Mercedes Buenos Aires Arg.
156 E3 Mercedes Arg.
Mercedes Arg. see Villa Mercedes
159 E2 Mercedes Uruguay
146 A4 Mercer OH U.S.A.
134 B2 Mercer WI U.S.A.
130 F4 Mercoal Canada
72 E2 Mercury Islands N.Z.
129 L3 Mercy, Cape Canada
108 B4 Mere Belgium
105 E6 Mere U.K.
147 H3 Meredith U.S.A.
143 C5 Meredith, Lake U.S.A.
134 B6 Meredosia U.S.A.
117 F5 Merefa Ukr.
121 E3 Merga Oasis Sudan
82 B2 Mergenevo Kazakh.
Mergui Myanmar see Myeik
98 A3 Mergui Archipelago is Myanmar
70 D5 Meribah Australia
115 L4 Meriç r. Greece/Turkey
151 G3 Mérida Mex.
111 C3 Mérida Spain
157 C2 Mérida Venez.
157 C2 Mérida, Cordillera de mts Venez.
147 G4 Meriden U.S.A.
140 B2 Meridian CA U.S.A.
143 F5 Meridian MS U.S.A.
110 D4 Mérignac France
102 N3 Merijärvi Fin.
102 M3 Merikarvia Fin.
71 H6 Merimbula Australia
70 D5 Meringur Australia
70 D6 Merino Australia
83 H4 Merke Kazakh.
143 C5 Merkel U.S.A.
98 □ Merlimau, Pulau reg. Sing.
121 F3 Merowe Sudan
68 B5 Merredin Australia
106 D5 Merrick h. U.K.
135 J3 Merrickville Canada
134 C3 Merrill U.S.A.
134 D5 Merrillville U.S.A.
142 C3 Merriman U.S.A.
130 E4 Merritt Canada
145 D6 Merritt Island U.S.A.
71 I4 Merriwa Australia
71 H3 Merrygoen Australia
122 E2 Mersa Fatma Eritrea
108 E5 Mersch Lux.
109 J3 Merseburg (Saale) Germany
105 E4 Mersey est. U.K.
80 E3 Mersin Turkey
99 B2 Mersing Malaysia
103 M4 Mērsrags Latvia
88 C4 Merta India
105 D6 Merthyr Tydfil U.K.
122 D3 Merti Kenya
111 C4 Mértola Port.
82 C3 Mertvyy Kultuk, Sor dry lake Kazakh.
73 C6 Mertz Glacier glacier Antarctica
122 D4 Meru vol. Tanz.
85 F4 Merui Pak.
124 D6 Merweville S. Africa
80 E1 Merzifon Turkey
108 E5 Merzig Germany
73 B3 Merz Peninsula pen. Antarctica
141 G5 Mesa U.S.A.
134 A2 Mesabi Range hills U.S.A.
114 G4 Mesagne Italy
115 K7 Mesara, Ormos b. Greece
141 H3 Mesa Verde National Park U.S.A.
157 B4 Mesay r. Col.
109 G3 Meschede Germany
102 L2 Meselefors Sweden
132 F3 Mesgouez, Lac l. Canada
116 I2 Meshchura Rus. Fed.
82 E4 Meshekli Uzbek.
85 E2 Meshkān Iran
117 G5 Meshkovskaya Rus. Fed.
134 E3 Mesick U.S.A.
115 J4 Mesimeri Greece
115 I5 Mesolongi Greece
81 I4 Mesopotamia reg. Iraq
141 E3 Mesquite NV U.S.A.
143 D5 Mesquite TX U.S.A.
141 E4 Mesquite Lake U.S.A.
123 D5 Messalo r. Moz.
114 F5 Messina Sicily Italy
Messina S. Africa see Musina
114 F5 Messina, Strait of Italy
Messina, Stretta di str. Italy see Messina, Strait of
135 I2 Messines Canada
115 J6 Messini Greece
115 J6 Messiniakos Kolpos b. Greece
129 P2 Mesters Vig b. Greenland
109 J1 Mestlin Germany
115 K5 Meston, Akra pt Greece
114 E2 Mestre Italy
80 F1 Mesudiye Turkey
157 C3 Meta r. Col./Venez.
135 G2 Metagama Canada
129 K3 Meta Incognita Peninsula Canada
143 F6 Metairie U.S.A.
138 C2 Metaline Falls U.S.A.
156 C3 Metán Arg.
115 I6 Methoni Greece
147 H3 Methuen U.S.A.
106 E4 Methven U.K.
114 G3 Metković Croatia
130 C3 Metlakatla U.S.A.
123 D5 Metoro Moz.
99 C4 Metro Indon.
144 B4 Metropolis U.S.A.
108 C4 Mettet Belgium
109 F2 Mettingen Germany
140 C4 Mettler U.S.A.
87 B4 Mettur India
122 D3 Metu Eth.
110 H2 Metz France
108 D4 Meuse r. Belgium/France alt. Maas (Neth.)
109 K3 Meuselwitz Germany
105 C7 Mevagissey U.K.
92 B3 Mêwa China
143 D6 Mexia U.S.A.
148 A2 Mexicali Mex.
141 H3 Mexican Hat U.S.A.
141 H3 Mexican Water U.S.A.
150 C3 Mexico country Central America
151 E4 México state Mex.
147 H2 Mexico ME U.S.A.
142 F4 Mexico MO U.S.A.
147 E3 Mexico NY U.S.A.
151 F3 Mexico, Gulf of Mex./U.S.A.
151 E4 Mexico City Mex. (City Plan 64)
84 D3 Meybod Iran
85 H3 Meydān Shahr Afgh.
109 K1 Meyenburg Germany
85 G3 Meymaneh Afgh.
84 C3 Meymeh Iran
84 B3 Meymeh, Rūdkhāneh-ye r. Iran
151 F4 Mezcalapa Mex.
151 F4 Mezcalapa r. Mex.
115 J3 Mezdra Bulg.
76 F3 Mezen' Rus. Fed.
110 G4 Mézenc, Mont mt. France
90 A1 Mezhdurechensk Rus. Fed.
116 I2 Mezhdurechensk Respublika Komi Rus. Fed.
76 G2 Mezhdusharskiy, Ostrov i. Rus. Fed.
82 D1 Mezhozernyy Rus. Fed.
113 J7 Mezőtúr Hungary
150 C3 Mezquital Mex.
150 C3 Mezquital r. Mex.
150 D3 Mezquitic Mex.
103 N4 Mežvidi Latvia
123 C5 Mfuwe Zambia
87 A2 Mhasvad India
125 I3 Mhlume Swaziland
88 C5 Mhow India
89 H5 Mi r. Myanmar
151 E4 Miahuatlán Mex.
111 D3 Miajadas Spain
141 G5 Miami AZ U.S.A.
145 D7 Miami FL U.S.A.
143 E4 Miami OK U.S.A.
145 D7 Miami Beach U.S.A.
84 C4 Miān Āb Iran
85 F5 Mianaz Pak.
84 D3 Miāndarreh Iran
84 B2 Miāndowāb Iran
123 E5 Miandrivazo Madag.
84 B2 Mīāneh Iran
97 C5 Miangas i. Phil.
85 G5 Miani Hor b. Pak.
85 G3 Mianjoi Afgh.
93 B4 Mianning China
88 B2 Mianwali Pak.
92 C3 Mianxian China
92 B4 Mianyang China
92 B4 Mianzhu China
92 F2 Miao Dao i. China
92 F2 Miaodao Liedao is China
83 J3 Miao'ergou China
93 F5 Miaoli Taiwan
123 E5 Miarinarivo Madag.
76 H4 Miass Rus. Fed.
141 G5 Mica Mountain U.S.A.
92 C3 Micang Shan mts China
113 J6 Michalovce Slovakia
130 E4 Michel Canada
109 J4 Michelau in Oberfranken Germany
109 H5 Michelstadt Germany
109 L2 Michendorf Germany
134 C2 Michigamme Lake U.S.A.
134 C2 Michigamme Reservoir U.S.A.
134 D2 Michigan state U.S.A.
134 D4 Michigan, Lake U.S.A.
134 D5 Michigan City U.S.A.
134 E2 Michipicoten Bay Canada
134 E2 Michipicoten Island Canada
134 E1 Michipicoten River Canada
150 D4 Michoacán state Mex.
116 G4 Michurinsk Rus. Fed.
150 H5 Mico r. Nicaragua
160 E5 Micronesia is Pacific Ocean
66 F2 Micronesia, Federated States of country Pacific Ocean
99 C2 Midai i. Indon.
163 F4 Mid-Atlantic Ridge sea feature Atlantic Ocean
163 H8 Mid-Atlantic Ridge sea feature Atlantic Ocean
124 C6 Middelberg Pass S. Africa
108 B3 Middelburg Neth.
124 F5 Middelburg Eastern Cape S. Africa
125 H2 Middelburg Mpumalanga S. Africa
103 J5 Middelfart Denmark
108 C3 Middelharnis Neth.
124 D5 Middelpos S. Africa
125 G2 Middelwit S. Africa
138 C3 Middle Alkali Lake U.S.A.
161 M5 Middle America Trench sea feature N. Pacific Ocean
147 H4 Middleboro U.S.A.
146 E4 Middleburg U.S.A.
147 F3 Middleburgh U.S.A.
147 G2 Middlebury U.S.A.
72 C6 Middlemarch N.Z.
146 B6 Middlesboro U.S.A.
104 F3 Middlesbrough U.K.
151 G4 Middlesex Belize
140 A2 Middletown CA U.S.A.
147 G4 Middletown CT U.S.A.
147 F5 Middletown DE U.S.A.
147 F4 Middletown NY U.S.A.
146 A5 Middletown OH U.S.A.
134 E4 Middleville U.S.A.
105 G7 Midhurst U.K.
110 E5 Midi, Canal du France
162 J5 Mid-Indian Basin sea feature Indian Ocean
162 I6 Mid-Indian Ridge sea feature Indian Ocean
135 H3 Midland Canada
135 E4 Midland MI U.S.A.
143 C5 Midland TX U.S.A.
107 C6 Midleton Rep. of Ireland
160 F4 Mid-Pacific Mountains sea feature N. Pacific Ocean
102 □ Miðvágur Faroe Is
67 H2 Midway Islands terr. N. Pacific Ocean
138 F3 Midwest U.S.A.
143 D5 Midwest City U.S.A.
108 D2 Midwoud Neth.
81 H3 Midyat Turkey
106 □ Mid Yell U.K.
115 J3 Midzhur mt. Bulg./Serb. and Mont.
103 N3 Miehikkälä Fin.
102 N2 Miekojärvi l. Fin.
113 J5 Mielec Poland
123 D4 Miembwe Tanz.
71 G8 Miena Australia
102 N1 Mieraslompolo Fin.
113 L7 Miercurea-Ciuc Romania
111 D1 Mieres Spain
122 E3 Mī'ēso Eth.
109 J2 Mieste Germany
146 E4 Mifflinburg U.S.A.
146 E4 Mifflintown U.S.A.
92 C3 Migang Shan mt. China
125 B4 Migdol S. Africa
85 E4 Mighān Iran
89 H3 Miging India
89 G2 Migriggyangzham Co l. China
133 G4 Miguasha, Parc de nature res. Canada
151 E4 Miguel Alemán, Presa resr Mex.
150 D2 Miguel Auza Mex.
150 B2 Miguel Hidalgo, Presa resr Mex.
80 C2 Mihalıççık Turkey
95 C7 Mihara Japan
95 F7 Mihara-yama vol. Japan
111 F2 Mijares r. Spain
108 C2 Mijdrecht Neth.
135 F3 Mikado U.S.A.
113 M4 Mikashevichy Belarus
116 F4 Mikhaylov Rus. Fed.
83 I1 Mikhaylovka Kazakh.
94 C3 Mikhaylovka Primorskiy Kray Rus. Fed.
117 G5 Mikhaylovka Volgogradskaya Oblast' Rus. Fed.
83 I2 Mikhaylovskiy Rus. Fed.
73 E6 Mikhaytov Island i. Antarctica
89 H4 Mikir Hills India
103 N3 Mikkeli Fin.
103 N3 Mikkelin mlk Fin.
130 G3 Mikkwa r. Canada
122 D4 Mikumi Tanz.
116 I2 Mikun' Rus. Fed.
95 E6 Mikuni-sanmyaku mts Japan
95 F8 Mikura-jima i. Japan
142 E2 Milaca U.S.A.
87 A5 Miladhunmadulu Atoll Maldives
114 C2 Milan Italy (City Plan 60)
145 B5 Milan U.S.A.
70 C5 Milang Australia
123 D5 Milange Moz.
Milano Italy see Milan
80 A3 Milas Turkey
114 F5 Milazzo Sicily Italy
142 D2 Milbank U.S.A.
105 H5 Mildenhall U.K.
70 E5 Mildura Australia
93 B5 Mile China
138 F2 Miles City U.S.A.
107 C5 Milestone Rep. of Ireland
114 F4 Miletto, Monte mt. Italy
107 C5 Milford Rep. of Ireland
140 B1 Milford CA U.S.A.
147 G4 Milford CT U.S.A.
147 F5 Milford DE U.S.A.
134 D5 Milford IL U.S.A.
147 H3 Milford MA U.S.A.
147 I2 Milford ME U.S.A.
147 H3 Milford NH U.S.A.
147 F4 Milford NY U.S.A.
141 F2 Milford UT U.S.A.
105 B6 Milford Haven U.K.
72 A6 Milford Sound N.Z.
72 A6 Milford Sound inlet N.Z.
111 H4 Miliana Alg.
128 G5 Milk r. Canada
121 E3 Milk, Wadi el watercourse Sudan
77 Q4 Mil'kovo Rus. Fed.
111 G1 Millárs r. Spain
110 F4 Millau France
140 B1 Mill Creek r. U.S.A.
145 D5 Milledgeville GA U.S.A.
134 C5 Milledgeville IL U.S.A.
142 E2 Mille Lacs lakes U.S.A.
132 B4 Mille Lacs, Lac des l. Canada
70 A2 Miller watercourse Australia
142 D2 Miller U.S.A.
134 B3 Miller Dam Flowage resr U.S.A.
134 E1 Miller Lake Canada
117 G5 Millerovo Rus. Fed.
141 G6 Miller Peak U.S.A.
146 C4 Millersburg OH U.S.A.
146 E4 Millersburg PA U.S.A.
70 B3 Millers Creek Australia
146 E6 Millers Tavern U.S.A.
135 G2 Millerton Lake U.S.A.
106 C5 Milleur Point U.K.
70 D6 Millicent Australia
135 F4 Millington MI U.S.A.
145 B5 Millington TN U.S.A.
147 I2 Millinocket U.S.A.
73 D6 Mill Island i. Antarctica
71 I1 Millmerran Australia
104 D3 Millom U.K.
106 D5 Millport U.K.
147 F5 Millsboro U.S.A.
130 F2 Mills Lake Canada
146 C5 Millstone U.S.A.
135 H1 Milltown Canada
107 B5 Milltown Malbay Rep. of Ireland
147 J1 Millville Canada
147 F5 Millville U.S.A.
147 I2 Milo U.S.A.
94 D3 Milogradovo Rus. Fed.
115 K6 Milos i. Greece
116 F4 Miloslavskoye Rus. Fed.
70 D2 Milparinka Australia
146 E4 Milroy U.S.A.
135 H4 Milton Canada
72 B7 Milton N.Z.
145 C6 Milton FL U.S.A.
134 A5 Milton IA U.S.A.
146 E4 Milton PA U.S.A.
147 G2 Milton VT U.S.A.
146 C4 Milton, Lake U.S.A.
138 C2 Milton-Freewater U.S.A.
105 G5 Milton Keynes U.K.
93 D4 Miluo China
134 D4 Milwaukee U.S.A.
163 E4 Milwaukee Deep sea feature Caribbean Sea
82 E2 Mily Kazakh.
83 H2 Milybulabk Kazakh.
117 G5 Milyutinskaya Rus. Fed.
110 D4 Mimizan France
122 B4 Mimongo Gabon
150 D2 Mina Mex.
140 C2 Mina U.S.A.
84 E5 Mīnāb Iran
91 E6 Minahasa, Semenanjung pen. Indon.
84 D5 Mina Jebel Ali U.A.E.
131 K4 Minaki Canada
95 B8 Minamata Japan
95 E7 Minami Alps National Park Japan
99 B2 Minas Indon.
159 F2 Minas Uruguay
151 G5 Minas, Sierra de las mts Guat.
81 L7 Mīnā' Sa'ūd Kuwait
133 H4 Minas Basin b. Canada
159 F1 Minas de Corrales Uruguay
158 D2 Minas Gerais state Brazil
158 D2 Minas Novas Brazil
151 F4 Minatitlán Mex.
89 H5 Minbu Myanmar
89 H5 Minbya Myanmar
156 B6 Minchinmávida vol. Chile
114 D2 Mincio r. Italy
81 K2 Mincivan Azer.
97 C5 Mindanao i. Phil.
70 D5 Mindarie Australia
120 □ Mindelo Cape Verde
135 H3 Minden Canada
109 G2 Minden Germany
143 E5 Minden LA U.S.A.
140 C2 Minden NV U.S.A.
89 H6 Mindon Myanmar
70 E4 Mindona Lake imp. l. Australia
97 B3 Mindoro i. Phil.
97 A3 Mindoro Strait Phil.
122 B4 Mindouli Congo
82 D1 Mindyak Rus. Fed.
107 D6 Mine Head Rep. of Ireland
105 D6 Minehead U.K.
158 B2 Mineiros Brazil
143 E5 Mineola U.S.A.
140 B1 Mineral U.S.A.
140 C3 Mineral King U.S.A.
117 G6 Mineral'nyye Vody Rus. Fed.
134 B4 Mineral Point U.S.A.
143 D5 Mineral Wells U.S.A.
141 F2 Minersville U.S.A.
114 G4 Minervino Murge Italy
89 E1 Minfeng China
123 C5 Minga Dem. Rep. Congo
81 K1 Mingäçevir Azer.
81 K1 Mingäçevir Su Anbarı resr Azer.
133 H3 Mingan Canada
70 D4 Mingary Australia
Mingbulak Uzbek. see Mingbuloq
82 E4 Mingbuloq Uzbek.
92 E3 Minggang China
92 F3 Mingguang China
83 H4 Ming-Kush Kyrg.
111 F3 Minglanilla Spain
123 D5 Mingoyo Tanz.
93 B4 Mingshan China
90 E2 Mingshui China
93 E5 Mingteke China
106 A4 Mingulay i. U.K.
93 E5 Mingxi China
92 B2 Minhe China
93 F5 Minhou China
87 A4 Minicoy atoll India
70 B4 Minilya Australia
133 H3 Minipi Lake Canada
131 I4 Minitonas Canada
93 F5 Min Jiang r. Fujian China
92 B4 Min Jiang r. Sichuan China
92 A2 Minle China
120 C4 Minna Nigeria
103 G5 Minna Sweden
142 E2 Minneapolis U.S.A.
131 J4 Minnedosa Canada
137 G2 Minnesota r. U.S.A.
134 A2 Minnesota state U.S.A.
70 A4 Minnipa Australia
132 B4 Minnitaki Lake Canada
111 B2 Miño r. Port./Spain
134 C3 Minocqua U.S.A.
134 B2 Minong U.S.A.
134 C5 Minonk U.S.A.
111 I2 Minorca i. Spain
142 C1 Minot U.S.A.
92 B2 Minqin China
93 F5 Minqing China
92 B3 Min Shan mts China
89 H4 Minsin Myanmar
116 C4 Minsk Belarus
113 J4 Mińsk Mazowiecki Poland
105 E5 Minsterley U.K.
88 C1 Mintaka Pass China/Jammu and Kashmir
92 A3 Mintang China
133 G4 Minto Canada
132 F2 Minto, Lac l. Canada
128 G2 Minto Inlet Canada
139 F4 Minturn U.S.A.
80 C6 Minûf Egypt
90 B1 Minusinsk Rus. Fed.
89 I3 Minutang India
92 B3 Minxian China
70 E6 Minyip Australia
135 E3 Mio U.S.A.
132 E4 Miquelon Canada
133 I4 Miquelon i. N. America
157 A4 Mira r. Col.
85 F4 Mirabad Afgh.
147 F2 Mirabel Canada
158 D2 Mirabela Brazil
155 I5 Miracema do Tocantins Brazil
155 I5 Mirador, Parque Nacional de nat. park Brazil
151 G4 Mirador-Dos Lagunos-Río Azul, Parque Nacional nat. park Guat.
157 B4 Miraflores Col.
81 H5 Mirah, Wādī al watercourse Iraq/Saudi Arabia
158 D2 Miralta Brazil
159 E3 Miramar Arg.
151 G4 Miramar, Lago l. Mex.
110 G5 Miramas France
133 G4 Miramichi Canada
115 K7 Mirampelou, Kolpos b. Greece
88 B2 Miram Shah Pak.
158 A3 Miranda Brazil
158 A3 Miranda r. Brazil
140 A1 Miranda U.S.A.
111 E1 Miranda de Ebro Spain
111 C2 Mirandela Port.
114 D2 Mirandola Italy
158 B3 Mirandópolis Brazil
86 D6 Mirbāṭ Oman
110 E5 Mirepoix France
99 D2 Miri Sarawak Malaysia
85 F4 Miri mt. Pak.
87 B2 Mirialguda India
159 G2 Mirim, Lagoa l. Brazil
85 F4 Mīrjāveh Iran
73 D6 Mirny research stn Antarctica
116 G2 Mirnyy Arkhangel'skaya Oblast' Rus. Fed.
77 M3 Mirnyy Rus. Fed.
131 I3 Mirond Lake Canada
109 K1 Mirow Germany
88 C2 Mirpur Pak.
88 B4 Mirpur Batoro Pak.
88 B4 Mirpur Khas Pak.
88 A4 Mirpur Sakro Pak.
130 G4 Mirror Canada
93 □ Mirs Bay Hong Kong China
115 J6 Mirtoö Pelagos sea Greece
96 E6 Miryang S. Korea
84 D3 Mirzā, Chāh-e well Iran
89 E4 Mirzapur India
95 C8 Misaki Japan
83 J5 Misalay China
94 G4 Misawa Japan
133 H4 Miscou Island Canada
88 C1 Misgar Pak.
94 B2 Mishan China
84 C5 Mishāsh al Hādī well Saudi Arabia
134 D5 Mishawaka U.S.A.
134 E1 Mishibishu Lake Canada
95 B7 Mi-shima i. Japan
89 H3 Mishmi Hills India
68 F3 Misima Island P.N.G.
150 I5 Miskitos, Cayos is Nicaragua
113 J6 Miskolc Hungary
91 F7 Misoöl i. Indon.
134 B2 Misquah Hills U.S.A.
121 D1 Miṣrātah Libya
88 E4 Misrikh India
135 E1 Missanabie Canada
132 D3 Missinaibi r. Canada
135 F1 Missinaibi Lake Canada
131 I3 Missinipe Canada
130 E5 Mission Canada
142 C3 Mission SD U.S.A.
151 E2 Mission TX U.S.A.
132 D3 Missisa Lake Canada
135 F2 Mississagi r. Canada
135 H4 Mississauga Canada
134 E5 Mississinewa Lake U.S.A.
135 I3 Mississippi r. Canada
143 F6 Mississippi r. U.S.A.
143 F5 Mississippi state U.S.A.
143 F6 Mississippi Delta U.S.A.
138 D2 Missoula U.S.A.
142 C2 Missouri r. U.S.A.
134 A6 Missouri state U.S.A.
142 E3 Missouri Valley U.S.A.
129 K4 Mistassibi r. Canada
133 F4 Mistassini Canada
133 F4 Mistassini r. Canada
132 F3 Mistassini, Lac l. Canada
133 H2 Mistastin Lake Canada
112 H6 Mistelbach Austria
133 H2 Mistinibi, Lac l. Canada
132 F3 Mistissini Canada
130 C3 Misty Fiords National Monument Wilderness nat. park U.S.A.
150 C3 Mita, Punta de pt Mex.
68 E4 Mitchell Australia
71 J2 Mitchell r. N.S.W. Australia
68 E3 Mitchell r. Qld Australia
71 G6 Mitchell r. Vic. Australia
135 G4 Mitchell Canada
142 D3 Mitchell U.S.A.
134 E3 Mitchell, Lake U.S.A.
145 D5 Mitchell, Mount U.S.A.
107 C5 Mitchelstown Rep. of Ireland
80 C6 Mit Ghamr Egypt
88 B3 Mithankot Pak.
88 B4 Mithi Pak.
88 B4 Mithrani Can canal Pak.
115 L5 Mithymna Greece
130 C3 Mitkof Island U.S.A.
95 G6 Mito Japan
123 D4 Mitole Tanz.
72 E4 Mitre mt. N.Z.
69 H3 Mitre Island Solomon Is
71 I5 Mittagong Australia
71 G6 Mitta Mitta Australia
109 G2 Mittellandkanal canal Germany
109 K5 Mitterteich Germany
109 K4 Mittweida Germany
157 C4 Mitú Col.
157 C4 Mituas Col.
123 C5 Mitumba, Chaîne des mts Dem. Rep. Congo
122 C4 Mitumba, Monts mts Dem. Rep. Congo
122 B3 Mitzic Gabon
95 F7 Miura Japan
81 G4 Miyāh, Wādī al watercourse Syria
95 F7 Miyake-jima i. Japan
94 G5 Miyako Japan
95 B9 Miyakonojō Japan
82 C2 Miyaly Kazakh.
88 B5 Miyani India
95 B9 Miyanoura-dake mt. Japan
95 B9 Miyazaki Japan
95 D7 Miyazu Japan
93 B5 Miyi China
95 C7 Miyoshi Japan
92 E1 Miyun China
92 E1 Miyun Shuiku resr China
85 G3 Mīzāni Afgh.
122 D3 Mīzan Teferī Eth.
121 D1 Mizdah Libya
107 B6 Mizen Head Rep. of Ireland
117 B5 Mizhhir"ya Ukr.
92 D2 Mizhi China
89 H5 Mizoram state India
94 G5 Mizusawa Japan
103 K4 Mjölby Sweden
123 D4 Mkata Tanz.
122 D4 Mkomazi Tanz.
123 C5 Mkushi Zambia
112 G5 Mladá Boleslav Czech Rep.
115 I2 Mladenovac Serb. and Mont.
113 I4 Mława Poland
114 G3 Mljet i. Croatia
125 G5 Mlungisi S. Africa
113 L5 Mlyniv Ukr.
125 F2 Mmabatho S. Africa
125 G1 Mmamabula Botswana
125 F2 Mmathethe Botswana
103 I3 Mo Norway
141 H2 Moab U.S.A.
68 E3 Moa Island Australia
69 H3 Moala i. Fiji
84 D3 Mo'alla Iran
125 J2 Moamba Moz.
70 B1 Moanba, Lake salt flat Australia
141 E3 Moapa U.S.A.
107 D4 Moate Rep. of Ireland
122 C4 Moba Dem. Rep. Congo
95 G7 Mobara Japan
84 C3 Mobārakeh Iran
84 D4 Mobārakeh Iran
122 C3 Mobayi-Mbongo Dem. Rep. Congo
142 E4 Moberly U.S.A.
145 B6 Mobile AL U.S.A.
141 F5 Mobile AZ U.S.A.
145 B6 Mobile Bay U.S.A.
142 C2 Mobridge U.S.A.
155 I4 Mocajuba Brazil
123 E5 Moçambique Moz.
157 D2 Mocapra r. Venez.
93 B6 Môc Châu Vietnam
86 B7 Mocha Yemen
157 D2 Mochirma, Parque Nacional nat. park Venez.
123 C6 Mochudi Botswana
123 E5 Mocimboa da Praia Moz.
109 J2 Möckern Germany
109 H5 Möckmühl Germany
102 M2 Mockträsk Sweden
157 A4 Mocoa Col.
158 C3 Mococa Brazil
150 C2 Moctezuma Mex.
150 C3 Moctezuma Mex.
123 D5 Mocuba Moz.
110 H4 Modane France
88 C5 Modasa India
124 F4 Modder r. S. Africa
114 D2 Modena Italy
141 F3 Modena U.S.A.
140 B3 Modesto U.S.A.
125 H2 Modimolle S. Africa
71 G7 Moe Australia
105 D5 Moel Sych h. U.K.
103 J3 Moelv Norway

Murakami 195

102 L1 Moen Norway
141 G3 Moenkopi U.S.A.
72 C6 Moeraki Point N.Z.
108 E3 Moers Germany
106 E5 Moffat U.K.
88 C3 Moga India
122 E3 Mogadishu Somalia
146 C4 Mogadore Reservoir U.S.A.
125 H1 Mogalakwena r. S. Africa
125 H2 Moganyaka S. Africa
109 K2 Mögelin Germany
83 F5 Moghiyon Tajik.
158 C3 Mogi-Mirim Brazil
90 D1 Mogocha Rus. Fed.
114 C6 Mogod mts Tunisia
125 F2 Mogoditshane Botswana
90 B4 Mogok Myanmar
141 H5 Mogollon Mountains U.S.A.
141 G4 Mogollon Plateau U.S.A.
125 H1 Mogwadi S. Africa
125 G2 Mogwase S. Africa
115 H2 Mohács Hungary
72 F3 Mohaka r. N.Z.
125 G5 Mohale's Hoek Lesotho
131 I5 Mohall U.S.A.
85 E3 Mohammad Iran
111 G5 Mohammadia Alg.
88 E3 Mohan r. India/Nepal
141 E4 Mohave, Lake U.S.A.
141 F5 Mohawk U.S.A.
147 F3 Mohawk r. U.S.A.
141 F5 Mohawk Mountains U.S.A.
Moheli i. Comoros see Mwali
85 H5 Mohenjo Daro tourist site Pak.
107 D4 Mohill Rep. of Ireland
109 G3 Möhne r. Germany
141 F4 Mohon Peak U.S.A.
123 D4 Mohoro Tanz.
117 C5 Mohyliv Podil's'kyy Ukr.
103 I4 Moi Norway
125 G1 Moijabana Botswana
125 J2 Moine Moz.
113 M7 Moinești Romania
147 F2 Moira U.S.A.
102 K2 Mo i Rana Norway
89 H4 Moirang India
103 N4 Mõisaküla Estonia
159 E1 Moisés Ville Arg.
133 G3 Moisie Canada
133 G3 Moisie r. Canada
110 E4 Moissac France
140 C4 Mojave U.S.A.
140 D4 Mojave r. U.S.A.
140 D4 Mojave Desert U.S.A.
158 C3 Moji das Cruzes Brazil
158 C3 Moji-Guaçu r. Brazil
95 B8 Mojikō Japan
89 F4 Mokama India
Mokapu Pen. U.S.A. see Mōkapu Peninsula
140 □1 Mōkapu Peninsula U.S.A.
72 E3 Mokau N.Z.
72 E3 Mokau r. N.Z.
140 B2 Mokelumne r. U.S.A.
84 D4 Mokh, Gowd-e l. Iran
125 H4 Mokhoabong Pass Lesotho
125 H4 Mokhotlong Lesotho
114 D7 Moknine Tunisia
72 E1 Mokohinau Islands N.Z.
121 D3 Mokolo Cameroon
125 G2 Mokolo r. S. Africa
125 H2 Mokopane S. Africa
96 D6 Mokp'o S. Korea
116 G4 Moksha r. Rus. Fed.
116 H4 Mokshan Rus. Fed.
140 □1 Moku 'Āuia i. U.S.A.
Mokuauia I. U.S.A. see Moku 'Āuia
140 □1 Moku Lua is U.S.A.
Mokulua Is U.S.A. see Moku Lua
151 E3 Molango Mex.
111 F3 Molatón mt. Spain
Moldavia country Europe see Moldova
102 I3 Molde Norway
102 K2 Moldjord Norway
117 D6 Moldova country Europe
115 K2 Moldoveanu, Vârful mt. Romania
105 D7 Mole r. U.K.
120 B4 Mole National Park Ghana
123 C6 Molepolole Botswana
103 N5 Molėtai Lith.
114 G4 Molfetta Italy
111 F2 Molina de Aragón Spain
134 B5 Moline U.S.A.
103 K4 Molkom Sweden
81 L4 Mollā Bodāgh Iran
89 H4 Mol Len mt. India
109 L1 Möllenbeck Germany
154 D7 Mollendo Peru
109 I1 Mölln Germany
103 K4 Mölnlycke Sweden
116 F3 Molochnoye Rus. Fed.
102 P1 Molochnyy Rus. Fed.
73 E4 Molodezhnaya research stn Antarctica
83 G1 Molodogvardeyskoye Kazakh.
116 E3 Molodoy Tud Rus. Fed.
Molokai i. U.S.A. see Moloka'i
140 □2 Moloka'i i. U.S.A.
116 I3 Moloma r. Rus. Fed.
71 H4 Molong Australia
124 F2 Molopo watercourse Botswana/S. Africa
121 D4 Moloundou Cameroon
131 J4 Molson Lake Canada
91 E7 Moluccas is Indon.
Molucca Sea sea Indon. see Maluku, Laut
123 D5 Moma Moz.
70 E3 Momba Australia
122 D4 Mombasa Kenya
89 H4 Mombi New India
158 B2 Mombuca, Serra da hills Brazil
117 C7 Momchilgrad Bulg.
134 D5 Momence U.S.A.
157 B2 Mompós Col.
103 K5 Møn i. Denmark
141 G2 Mona U.S.A.
149 K5 Mona, Isla i. Puerto Rico
106 A3 Monach, Sound of sea chan. U.K.
106 A3 Monach Islands U.K.
110 H5 Monaco country Europe
163 H4 Monaco Basin sea feature N. Atlantic Ocean
106 D3 Monadhliath Mountains U.K.
107 E3 Monaghan Rep. of Ireland
143 C6 Monahans U.S.A.
149 K5 Mona Passage Dom. Rep./Puerto Rico
123 E5 Monapo Moz.
106 C3 Monar, Loch l. U.K.
130 D4 Monarch Mountain Canada
139 F4 Monarch Pass U.S.A.
130 F4 Monashee Mountains Canada
114 D7 Monastir Tunisia
113 O3 Monastyrshchina Rus. Fed.
117 D5 Monastyryshche Ukr.
94 H2 Monbetsu Japan
94 H3 Monbetsu Japan
114 B2 Moncalieri Italy
102 P2 Monchegorsk Rus. Fed.
108 E3 Mönchengladbach Germany
111 B4 Monchique Port.
145 E5 Moncks Corner U.S.A.
150 D2 Monclova Mex.
133 H4 Moncton Canada
111 C2 Mondego r. Port.
125 I3 Mondlo S. Africa
114 B2 Mondovì Italy
134 B3 Mondovi U.S.A.
114 E4 Mondragone Italy
115 J6 Monemvasia Greece
94 G1 Moneron, Ostrov i. Rus. Fed.
146 D4 Monessen U.S.A.
135 J1 Monet Canada
107 D5 Moneygall Rep. of Ireland
107 E3 Moneymore U.K.
114 E2 Monfalcone Italy
111 C1 Monforte Spain
122 C3 Monga Dem. Rep. Congo
93 C6 Mông Cai Vietnam
96 C4 Monggŭmp'o-ri N. Korea
98 A1 Mong Mau Myanmar
90 B2 Mongolia country Asia
88 C2 Mongora Pak.
123 C5 Mongu Zambia
147 I3 Monhegan Island U.S.A.
106 E5 Moniaive U.K.
140 D2 Monitor Mountain U.S.A.
140 D2 Monitor Range mts U.S.A.
107 C4 Monivea Rep. of Ireland
135 G4 Monkton Canada
89 F3 Mon La pass China
105 E6 Monmouth U.K.
134 B5 Monmouth IL U.S.A.
147 H2 Monmouth ME U.S.A.
130 E4 Monmouth Mountain Canada
105 E6 Monnow r. U.K.
120 C3 Mono r. Togo
140 C3 Mono Lake U.S.A.
147 H4 Monomoy Point U.S.A.
134 D5 Monon U.S.A.
134 B4 Monona U.S.A.
114 G4 Monopoli Italy
146 C5 Monorgahela r. U.S.A.
111 F2 Monreal del Campo Spain
114 E5 Monreale Sicily Italy
143 E5 Monroe LA U.S.A.
135 F5 Monroe MI U.S.A.
145 D5 Monroe NC U.S.A.
147 F4 Monroe NY U.S.A.
141 F2 Monroe UT U.S.A.
134 C4 Monroe WI U.S.A.
134 B6 Monroe City U.S.A.
145 C6 Monroeville U.S.A.
120 A4 Monrovia Liberia
108 B4 Mons Belgium
108 E4 Monschau Germany
114 D2 Monselice Italy
109 F4 Montabaur Germany
124 D6 Montagu S. Africa
134 D4 Montague U.S.A.
153 G7 Montagu Island S. Sandwich Is
114 F5 Montalto mt. Italy
114 G5 Montalto Uffugo Italy
115 J3 Montana Bulg.
138 E2 Montana state U.S.A.
150 H5 Montaña de Yoro nat. park Hond.
155 H3 Montanhas do Tumucumaque, Parque Nacional nat. park Brazil
110 F3 Montargis France
110 E4 Montauban France
147 G4 Montauk U.S.A.
147 H4 Montauk Point U.S.A.
125 H4 Mont-aux-Sources mt. Lesotho
110 G3 Montbard France
111 G2 Montblanc Spain
110 G4 Montbrison France
110 G3 Montceau-les-Mines France
108 C5 Montcornet France
110 D5 Mont-de-Marsan France
110 F2 Montdidier France
151 E4 Monte Albán tourist site Mex.
155 H4 Monte Alegre Brazil
158 C1 Monte Alegre de Goiás Brazil
158 D1 Monte Azul Brazil
132 E4 Montebello Canada
114 F6 Montebello Ionico Italy
114 E2 Montebelluna Italy
159 D2 Monte Buey Arg.
110 H5 Monte-Carlo Monaco
159 F1 Monte Caseros Arg.
Monte Christo S. Africa see Monte Cristo
159 C2 Monte Comán Arg.
149 J5 Monte Cristi Dom. Rep.
125 G1 Monte Cristo S. Africa
114 D3 Montecristo, Isola di i. Italy
149 I5 Montego Bay Jamaica
110 G4 Montélimar France
156 E2 Monte Lindo r. Para.
114 F4 Montella Italy
134 C4 Montello U.S.A.
151 E2 Montemorelos Mex.
111 B3 Montemor-o-Novo Port.
Montenegro aut. rep. Serb. and Mont. see Crna Gora
123 D5 Montepuez Moz.
114 D3 Montepulciano Italy
110 F2 Montereau-fault-Yonne France
140 B3 Monterey CA U.S.A.
146 D5 Monterey VA U.S.A.
140 B3 Monterey Bay U.S.A.
157 B2 Montería Col.
154 F7 Montero Bol.
151 D2 Monterrey Mex.
114 F4 Montesano sulla Marcellana Italy
155 K6 Monte Santo Brazil
158 D2 Montes Claros Brazil
114 F3 Montesilvano Italy
114 D3 Montevarchi Italy
159 F2 Montevideo Uruguay
142 E2 Montevideo U.S.A.
139 F4 Monte Vista U.S.A.
134 A5 Montezuma U.S.A.
141 G4 Montezuma Castle National Monument nat. park U.S.A.
141 H3 Montezuma Creek U.S.A.
140 D3 Montezuma Peak U.S.A.
108 D3 Montfort Neth.
105 D5 Montgomery U.K.
145 C5 Montgomery U.S.A.
112 C7 Monthey Switz.
143 F5 Monticello AR U.S.A.
145 D6 Monticello FL U.S.A.
134 B4 Monticello IA U.S.A.
134 D5 Monticello IN U.S.A.
147 J1 Monticello ME U.S.A.
134 B5 Monticello MO U.S.A.
147 F4 Monticello NY U.S.A.
141 H3 Monticello UT U.S.A.
134 C4 Monticello WI U.S.A.
159 E1 Montiel, Cuchilla de hills Arg.
110 E4 Montignac France
108 C4 Montignies-le-Tilleul Belgium
108 E5 Montigny-lès-Metz France
150 I7 Montijo, Golfo de b. Panama
111 D4 Montilla Spain
133 G4 Mont-Joli Canada
135 J2 Mont-Laurier Canada
133 G4 Mont Louis Canada
110 F3 Montluçon France
133 F4 Montmagny Canada
108 D5 Montmédy France
108 B6 Montmirail France
134 D5 Montmorenci U.S.A.
133 F4 Montmorency Canada
110 E3 Montmorillon France
108 B6 Montmort-Lucy France
68 F4 Monto Australia
138 E3 Montpelier ID U.S.A.
134 E5 Montpelier IN U.S.A.
146 A4 Montpelier OH U.S.A.
147 G2 Montpelier VT U.S.A.
110 F5 Montpellier France
132 F4 Montréal Canada (City Plan 62)
135 F2 Montreal r. Ont. Canada
135 G2 Montreal r. Ont. Canada
Montréal-Dorval Canada see Montréal-Trudeau
134 E2 Montreal Island Canada
131 H4 Montreal Lake Canada
131 H4 Montreal Lake l. Canada
147 F2 Montréal-Mirabel airport Canada
134 E2 Montreal River Canada
147 G2 Montréal-Trudeau airport Canada
112 C7 Montreux Switz.
124 D3 Montrose well S. Africa
106 F4 Montrose U.K.
139 F4 Montrose CO U.S.A.
135 F4 Montrose MI U.S.A.
147 F4 Montrose PA U.S.A.
133 G4 Monts, Pointe des pt Canada
149 L5 Montserrat terr. Caribbean Sea
133 F3 Montviel, Lac l. Canada
141 G3 Monument Valley reg. U.S.A.
90 B4 Monywa Myanmar
114 C2 Monza Italy
123 C5 Monze Zambia
111 G2 Monzón Spain
125 I4 Mooi r. S. Africa
124 B3 Mooifontein Namibia
125 I4 Mooirivier S. Africa
125 G1 Mookane Botswana
70 C2 Moolawatana Australia
71 H2 Moomin Creek r. Australia
70 A3 Moonaree Australia
71 I3 Moonbi Range mts Australia
71 I1 Moonie Australia
71 H2 Moonie r. Australia
70 B5 Moonta Australia
138 F2 Moorcroft U.S.A.
68 B4 Moore, Lake salt flat Australia
146 D5 Moorefield U.S.A.
145 E7 Moores Island Bahamas
147 J2 Moores Mills Canada
106 E5 Moorfoot Hills U.K.
142 D2 Moorhead U.S.A.
70 E4 Moornanyah Lake imp. l. Australia
70 D5 Moorook Australia
70 F6 Mooroopna Australia
124 C6 Moorreesburg S. Africa
132 D3 Moose r. Canada
132 D3 Moose Factory Canada
147 I2 Moosehead Lake U.S.A.
131 H4 Moose Jaw Canada
134 A2 Moose Lake U.S.A.
147 H2 Mooselookmeguntic Lake U.S.A.
132 D3 Moose River Canada
131 I4 Moosomin Canada
132 D3 Moosonee Canada
70 E3 Mootwingee Australia
71 E3 Mootwingee National Park Australia
125 H1 Mopane S. Africa
120 B3 Mopti Mali
85 G3 Moqor Afgh.
154 D7 Moquegua Peru
121 D3 Mora Cameroon
111 E3 Mora Spain
103 K3 Mora Sweden
159 B2 Mora, Cerro mt. Arg./Chile
88 A3 Morad r. Pak.
88 D3 Moradabad India
123 E5 Morafenobe Madag.
150 G5 Morales Guat.
87 B2 Moram India
123 E5 Moramanga Madag.
134 E3 Moran MI U.S.A.
138 E3 Moran WY U.S.A.
106 C4 Morar, Loch l. U.K.
88 D2 Morari, Tso l. India
87 B5 Moratuwa Sri Lanka
112 H6 Morava r. Austria/Slovakia
84 D2 Moraveh Tappeh Iran
147 E3 Moravia U.S.A.
106 E3 Moray Firth b. U.K.
108 F5 Morbach Germany
114 C1 Morbegno Italy
88 B5 Morbi India
110 D4 Morcenx France
90 E1 Mordaga China
81 J3 Mor Dağı mt. Turkey
131 J5 Morden Canada
70 F7 Mordialloc Australia
116 H4 Mordoviya, Respublika aut. rep. Rus. Fed.
117 G4 Mordovo Rus. Fed.
106 D2 More, Loch l. U.K.
142 C2 Moreau r. U.S.A.
104 E3 Morecambe U.K.
104 D3 Morecambe Bay U.K.
71 H2 Moree Australia
68 E2 Morehead P.N.G.
146 B5 Morehead U.S.A.
145 E5 Morehead City U.S.A.
88 D4 Morel r. India
150 D4 Morelia Mex.
111 F2 Morella Spain
151 G4 Morelos Mex.
151 E4 Morelos state Mex.
88 D4 Morena India
111 D3 Morena, Sierra mts Spain
141 H5 Morenci AZ U.S.A.
135 E5 Morenci MI U.S.A.
115 K2 Moreni Romania
159 E2 Moreno Arg.
150 B1 Moreno Mex.
140 D5 Moreno Valley U.S.A.
130 C4 Moresby Island Canada
124 F1 Moreswe Pan salt pan Botswana
71 J1 Moreton Bay Australia
105 F6 Moreton-in-Marsh U.K.
71 J1 Moreton Island Australia
108 A5 Moreuil France
80 D4 Morfou Cyprus
80 D4 Morfou Bay Cyprus
70 C5 Morgan Australia
140 C3 Morgan, Mount U.S.A.
143 F6 Morgan City U.S.A.
140 B3 Morgan Hill U.S.A.
147 F4 Morgantown PA U.S.A.
146 D5 Morgantown WV U.S.A.
125 H3 Morgenzon S. Africa
112 C7 Morges Switz.
89 F4 Morhar r. India
94 G3 Mori Japan
141 E2 Moriah, Mount U.S.A.
139 F5 Moriarty U.S.A.
71 F2 Moriarty's Range hills Australia
157 C4 Morichal Col.
157 E2 Morichal Largo r. Venez.
96 C2 Morihong Shan mt. China
125 G4 Morija Lesotho
109 H3 Moringen Germany
116 D3 Morino Rus. Fed.
94 G5 Morioka Japan
71 I4 Morisset Australia
94 G5 Moriyoshi-zan vol. Japan
102 M2 Morjärv Sweden
85 F4 Morjen r. Pak.
116 I3 Morki Rus. Fed.
110 C2 Morlaix France
104 F4 Morley U.K.
141 G4 Mormon Lake U.S.A.
156 A7 Mornington, Isla i. Chile
163 D9 Mornington Abyssal Plain sea feature S. Atlantic Ocean
68 D3 Mornington Island Australia
70 F7 Mornington Peninsula National Park Australia
88 A4 Moro Pak.
68 E2 Morobe P.N.G.
120 B1 Morocco country Africa
134 D5 Morocco U.S.A.
122 D4 Morogoro Tanz.
97 B5 Moro Gulf Phil.
125 G4 Morojaneng S. Africa
124 E3 Morokweng S. Africa
150 D3 Moroleón Mex.
123 E6 Morombe Madag.
149 I4 Morón Cuba
90 C2 Mörön Mongolia
123 E6 Morondava Madag.
111 D4 Morón de la Frontera Spain
123 E5 Moroni Comoros
91 E6 Morotai i. Indon.
122 D3 Moroto Uganda
117 G5 Morozovsk Rus. Fed.
135 G4 Morpeth Canada
104 F2 Morpeth U.K.
158 C2 Morrinhos Brazil
131 J5 Morris Canada
134 C5 Morris IL U.S.A.
142 E2 Morris MN U.S.A.
147 F2 Morrisburg Canada
134 C5 Morrison U.S.A.
141 F5 Morristown AZ U.S.A.
147 F4 Morristown NJ U.S.A.
147 F2 Morristown NY U.S.A.
145 D4 Morristown TN U.S.A.
147 F4 Morrisville PA U.S.A.
147 G2 Morrisville VT U.S.A.
156 B3 Morro, Punta pt Chile
140 B4 Morro Bay U.S.A.
157 C2 Morrocoy, Parque Nacional nat. park Venez.
150 D4 Morro de Petatlán hd Mex.
155 H4 Morro Grande h. Brazil
157 B2 Morrosquillo, Golfo de b. Col.
109 H3 Morschen Germany
134 D5 Morse Reservoir U.S.A.
116 G4 Morshanka Rus. Fed.
116 E2 Morskaya Masel'ga Rus. Fed.
114 C7 Morsott Alg.
110 E2 Mortagne-au-Perche France
110 D3 Mortagne-sur-Sèvre France
105 C6 Mortehoe U.K.
159 E1 Morteros Arg.
155 H6 Mortes, Rio das r. Brazil
145 F7 Mortimer's Bahamas
70 E7 Mortlake Australia
67 E2 Mortlock Islands Micronesia
105 G5 Morton U.K.
134 C5 Morton IL U.S.A.
138 B2 Morton WA U.S.A.
71 I5 Morton National Park Australia
71 G5 Morundah Australia
125 G1 Morupule Botswana
71 I5 Moruya Australia
106 C4 Morvern reg. U.K.
71 G7 Morwell Australia
109 H5 Mosbach Germany
105 F4 Mosborough U.K.
116 F4 Moscow Rus. Fed. (City Plan 55)
138 C2 Moscow U.S.A.
108 F4 Mosel r. Germany
124 F2 Moselebe watercourse Botswana
110 H2 Moselle r. France
109 J2 Möser Germany
140 D1 Moses, Mount U.S.A.
138 C2 Moses Lake U.S.A.
72 C6 Mosgiel N.Z.
124 E3 Moshaweng watercourse S. Africa
122 D4 Moshi Tanz.
134 C3 Mosinee U.S.A.
102 K2 Mosjøen Norway
102 K2 Moskenesøy i. Norway
116 F4 Moskovskaya Oblast' admin. div. Rus. Fed.
Moskva Rus. Fed. see Moscow
112 H7 Mosonmagyaróvár Hungary
157 A4 Mosquera Col.
139 F5 Mosquero U.S.A.
149 H5 Mosquitia reg. Hond.
158 E1 Mosquito r. Brazil
146 C4 Mosquito Creek Lake U.S.A.
131 I2 Mosquito Lake Canada
103 J4 Moss Norway
106 F3 Mossat U.K.
72 B6 Mossburn N.Z.
124 E7 Mossel Bay S. Africa
124 E7 Mossel Bay b. S. Africa
122 B4 Mossendjo Congo
70 F4 Mossgiel Australia
68 E3 Mossman Australia
155 K5 Mossoró Brazil
71 I5 Moss Vale Australia
112 F5 Most Czech Rep.
84 D3 Moşţafaabad Iran
120 C1 Mostaganem Alg.
114 G3 Mostar Bos.-Herz.
156 F4 Mostardas Brazil
131 G3 Mostoos Hills Canada
117 G6 Mostovskoy Rus. Fed.
99 E2 Mostyn Sabah Malaysia
81 I3 Mosul Iraq
103 J4 Møsvatnet l. Norway
151 G5 Motagua r. Guat.
103 K4 Motala Sweden
157 C2 Motatán r. Venez.
125 J2 Motaze Moz.
125 H2 Motetema S. Africa
88 D4 Moth India
106 E5 Motherwell U.K.
96 B3 Motian Ling h. China
89 F4 Motihari India
111 F3 Motilla del Palancar Spain
72 F2 Motiti Island N.Z.
124 E2 Motokwe Botswana
151 F5 Motozintla Mex.
111 E4 Motril Spain
115 J2 Motru Romania
98 A1 Mottama Myanmar
91 B5 Mottama, Gulf of Myanmar
151 G3 Motul Mex.
67 I5 Motu One atoll Fr. Polynesia
93 A5 Mouding China
120 A3 Moudjéria Mauritania
115 K5 Moudros Greece
103 M3 Mouhijärvi Fin.
122 B4 Mouila Gabon
70 F5 Moulamein Australia
70 F5 Moulamein Creek r. Australia
122 B4 Moulèngui Binza Gabon
110 F3 Moulins France
Moulmein Myanmar see Mawlamyaing
145 D6 Moultrie U.S.A.
137 K5 Moultrie, Lake U.S.A.
144 B4 Mound City IL U.S.A.
142 E3 Mound City MO U.S.A.
121 D4 Moundou Chad
146 C5 Moundsville U.S.A.
88 C4 Mount Abu India
145 C5 Mountain Brook U.S.A.
146 C6 Mountain City U.S.A.
143 E4 Mountain Grove U.S.A.
143 E4 Mountain Home AR U.S.A.
138 D3 Mountain Home ID U.S.A.
125 F6 Mountain Zebra National Park S. Africa
146 C6 Mount Airy U.S.A.
72 B6 Mount Aspiring National Park N.Z.
130 F4 Mount Assiniboine Provincial Park Canada
125 H5 Mount Ayliff S. Africa
142 E3 Mount Ayr U.S.A.
70 C5 Mount Barker Australia
71 G6 Mount Beauty Australia
107 C4 Mount Bellew Rep. of Ireland
71 G6 Mount Buffalo National Park Australia
147 J1 Mount Carleton Provincial Park Canada
141 F3 Mount Carmel Junction U.S.A.
134 C4 Mount Carroll U.S.A.
Mount Cook N.Z. see Aoraki
72 C5 Mount Cook National Park N.Z.
123 D5 Mount Darwin Zimbabwe
147 I2 Mount Desert Island U.S.A.
70 A1 Mount Dutton Australia
70 A3 Mount Eba Australia
71 G9 Mount Field National Park Australia
125 H5 Mount Fletcher S. Africa
135 G4 Mount Forest Canada
125 H5 Mount Frere S. Africa
70 D6 Mount Gambier Australia
146 B4 Mount Gilead U.S.A.
71 F4 Mount Hope N.S.W. Australia
70 A5 Mount Hope S.A. Australia
146 C6 Mount Hope U.S.A.
134 C4 Mount Horeb U.S.A.
68 D4 Mount Isa Australia
122 D3 Mount Kenya National Park Kenya
147 G4 Mount Kisco U.S.A.
70 C5 Mount Lofty Range mts Australia
135 G2 Mount MacDonald Canada
68 B4 Mount Magnet Australia
70 E4 Mount Manara Australia
140 B1 Mount Meadows Reservoir U.S.A.
107 D4 Mountmellick Rep. of Ireland
125 G5 Mount Moorosi Lesotho
70 E3 Mount Murchison Australia
134 B5 Mount Pleasant IA U.S.A.
144 C3 Mount Pleasant MI U.S.A.
146 D4 Mount Pleasant PA U.S.A.
145 E5 Mount Pleasant SC U.S.A.
143 E5 Mount Pleasant TX U.S.A.
141 G2 Mount Pleasant UT U.S.A.
134 C5 Mount Pulaski U.S.A.
138 B2 Mount Rainier National Park U.S.A.
130 F4 Mount Robson Provincial Park Canada
146 C6 Mount Rogers National Recreation Area park U.S.A.
105 B7 Mount's Bay U.K.
105 F5 Mountsorrel U.K.
134 B6 Mount Sterling IL U.S.A.
146 B5 Mount Sterling KY U.S.A.
146 D5 Mount Storm U.S.A.
146 E4 Mount Union U.S.A.
145 B6 Mount Vernon AL U.S.A.
134 B5 Mount Vernon IA U.S.A.
144 B4 Mount Vernon IL U.S.A.
146 A6 Mount Vernon KY U.S.A.
146 B4 Mount Vernon OH U.S.A.
138 B1 Mount Vernon WA U.S.A.
70 A4 Mount Wedge Australia
71 H8 Mount William National Park Australia
68 E4 Moura Australia
154 F4 Moura Brazil
121 E3 Mourdi, Dépression du depr. Chad
107 D3 Mourne r. U.K.
107 E3 Mourne Mountains U.K.
108 B4 Mouscron Belgium
121 D3 Moussoro Chad
91 E6 Moutong Indon.
108 A5 Mouy France
120 C2 Mouydir, Monts du plat. Alg.
108 D5 Mouzon France
84 C4 Moveyleh Iran
71 I1 Mowbullan, Mount Australia
145 E7 Moxey Town Bahamas
107 C4 Moy r. Rep. of Ireland
122 D3 Moyale Eth.
120 A4 Moyamba Sierra Leone
87 B4 Moyar r. India
120 B1 Moyen Atlas mts Morocco
125 G5 Moyeni Lesotho
107 E4 Moyer h. Rep. of Ireland
82 D4 Mo'ynoq Uzbek.
83 I5 Moyu China
83 H3 Moyynkum Kazakh.
83 F3 Moyynkum, Peski des. Karagandinskaya Oblast' Kazakh.
83 G3 Moyynkum, Peski des. Yuzhnyy Kazakhstan Kazakh.
83 H3 Moyynty Kazakh.
123 D6 Mozambique country Africa
123 E5 Mozambique Channel Africa
162 G6 Mozambique Ridge sea feature Indian Ocean
117 H7 Mozdok Rus. Fed.
85 F2 Mozdūrān Iran
116 F4 Mozhaysk Rus. Fed.
85 F3 Mozhnābād Iran
89 H5 Mozo Myanmar
122 C4 Mpala Dem. Rep. Congo
122 D4 Mpanda Tanz.
123 D5 Mpika Zambia
125 I4 Mpolweni S. Africa
123 D4 Mporokoso Zambia
125 H2 Mpumalanga prov. S. Africa
125 H5 Mqanduli S. Africa
89 H5 Mrauk-U Myanmar
114 G2 Mrkonjić-Grad Bos.-Herz.
120 D1 M'Saken Tunisia
116 D3 Mshinskaya Rus. Fed.
111 I5 M'Sila Alg.
116 E3 Msta r. Rus. Fed.
116 D4 Mstsislaw Belarus
116 F4 Mtsensk Rus. Fed.
125 J4 Mtubatuba S. Africa
125 I4 Mtunzini S. Africa
123 E5 Mtwara Tanz.
122 B4 Muanda Dem. Rep. Congo
93 B6 Muang Hiam Laos
98 B1 Muang Hôngsa Laos
Muang Khammouan Laos see Thakèk
98 C2 Muang Không Laos
98 C2 Muang Khôngxédôn Laos
93 B6 Muang Khoua Laos
98 A3 Muang Kirirath r. Thai.
98 C1 Muang Mok Laos
93 B6 Muang Ngoy Laos
98 C1 Muang Nong Laos
93 A6 Muang Ou Nua Laos
Muang Pakxan Laos see Pakxan
98 C1 Muang Phalan Laos
98 B1 Muang Phiang Laos
98 C1 Muang Phin Laos
98 B1 Muang Phôn-Hông Laos
98 B1 Muang Souy Laos
93 B6 Muang Va Laos
98 B1 Muang Vangviang Laos
Muang Xaignabouri Laos see Xaignabouli
Muang Xay Laos see Xay
93 B6 Muang Xon Laos
99 B2 Muar Malaysia
98 B5 Muar r. Malaysia
99 B3 Muarabungo Indon.
99 B3 Muaradua Indon.
99 A3 Muarasiberut Indon.
99 A2 Muarasipongi Indon.
99 B3 Muaratembesi Indon.
89 E4 Mubarakpur India
Mubarek Uzbek. see Muborak
81 H7 Mubarraz well Saudi Arabia
122 D3 Mubende Uganda
121 D3 Mubi Nigeria
82 F5 Muborak Uzbek.
157 E4 Mucajaí r. Brazil
157 E4 Mucajaí, Serra do mts Brazil
108 F4 Much Germany
123 D5 Muchinga Escarpment Zambia
93 B4 Muchuan China
106 B4 Muck i. U.K.
106 □ Muckle Roe i. U.K.
157 C3 Muco r. Col.
123 C5 Muconda Angola
157 E4 Mucucuaú r. Brazil
80 E2 Mucur Turkey
158 E2 Mucuri Brazil
158 E2 Mucuri r. Brazil
123 C5 Mucussueje Angola
98 B4 Muda r. Malaysia
87 A3 Mudabidri India
96 E1 Mudanjiang China
96 E1 Mudan Jiang r. China
80 B1 Mudanya Turkey
81 K7 Mudayrah Kuwait
146 C5 Muddlety U.S.A.
102 L2 Muddus nationalpark nat. park Sweden
141 G2 Muddy Creek r. U.S.A.
141 E3 Muddy Peak U.S.A.
85 E3 Mūd-e Dahanāb Iran
109 F4 Mudersbach Germany
71 H4 Mudgee Australia
87 A2 Mudhol India
88 C3 Mudki India
140 D3 Mud Lake U.S.A.
98 A1 Mudon Myanmar
80 C1 Mudurnu Turkey
116 F2 Mud'yuga Rus. Fed.
123 D5 Mueda Moz.
151 F4 Muerto, Mar lag. Mex.
116 H1 Muftyuga Rus. Fed.
123 C5 Mufulira Zambia
123 C5 Mufumbwe Zambia
93 E4 Mufu Shan mts China
147 J2 Mugaguadavic Lake Canada
81 L2 Muğan Düzü lowland Azer.
89 F2 Mugarripug China
89 E4 Mughal Sarai India
84 D3 Mūghār Iran
80 F7 Mughayrā' Saudi Arabia
83 G5 Mughsu r. Tajik.
80 B3 Muğla Turkey
82 D3 Mugodzhary, Gory mts Kazakh.
89 H2 Mug Qu r. China
89 E3 Mugu Karnali r. Nepal
89 H2 Mugxung China
121 F2 Muḥammad, Ra's pt Egypt
88 B4 Muhammad Ashraf Pak.
121 F2 Muhammad Qol Sudan
84 B5 Muḥayriqah Saudi Arabia
109 K3 Mühlanger Germany
109 L3 Mühlberg Germany
109 I3 Mühlhausen (Thüringen) Germany
102 N2 Muhos Fin.
122 C4 Muhulu Dem. Rep. Congo
Mui Dinh hd Vietnam see Ca Na, Mui
107 E5 Muine Bheag Rep. of Ireland
106 D5 Muirkirk U.K.
106 B2 Muirneag h. U.K.
106 D3 Muir of Ord U.K.
140 A3 Muir Woods National Monument nat. park U.S.A.
123 D5 Muite Moz.
84 D3 Mūjān, Chāh-e well Iran
151 H3 Mujeres, Isla i. Mex.
96 D6 Muju S. Korea
117 B5 Mukacheve Ukr.
99 D2 Mukah Sarawak Malaysia
86 C7 Mukalla Yemen
89 F3 Mükangsar China
98 C1 Mukdahan Thai.
68 B5 Mukinbudin Australia
99 B3 Mukomuko Indon.
82 F5 Mukry Turkm.
88 C3 Muktsar India
82 C3 Mukur Atyrauskaya Oblast' Kazakh.
83 J2 Mukur Vostochnyy Kazakhstan Kazakh.
131 J4 Mukutawa r. Canada
134 C4 Mukwonago U.S.A.
88 D5 Mul India
87 A2 Mula r. India
88 A3 Mula r. Pak.
83 I3 Mulaly Kazakh.
94 A2 Mulan China
97 B3 Mulanay Phil.
123 D5 Mulanje, Mount Malawi
84 B5 Mulayḩ Saudi Arabia
143 E5 Mulberry U.S.A.
159 B3 Mulchén Chile
109 K3 Mulde r. Germany
122 D4 Muleba Tanz.
141 H5 Mule Creek NM U.S.A.
138 F3 Mule Creek WY U.S.A.
150 A2 Mulegé Mex.
143 C5 Muleshoe U.S.A.
111 E4 Mulhacén mt. Spain
108 E3 Mülheim an der Ruhr Germany
110 H3 Mulhouse France
93 A5 Muli China
96 F1 Muling Heilong. China
96 F1 Muling Heilong. China
96 G1 Muling He r. China
106 C4 Mull i. U.K.
106 B4 Mull, Sound of sea chan. U.K.
81 L3 Mulla Ali Iran
107 B5 Mullaghareirk Mountains Rep. of Ireland
87 C4 Mullaittivu Sri Lanka
71 H3 Mullaley Australia
71 G3 Mullengudgery Australia
99 D2 Muller, Pegunungan mts Indon.
134 E3 Mullett Lake U.S.A.
68 B4 Mullewa Australia
106 F1 Mull Head U.K.
147 F5 Mullica r. U.S.A.
107 D4 Mullingar Rep. of Ireland
71 H4 Mullion Creek Australia
106 D6 Mull of Galloway c. U.K.
106 C5 Mull of Kintyre hd U.K.
106 B5 Mull of Oa hd U.K.
123 C5 Mulobezi Zambia
87 A2 Mulshi Lake India
88 D5 Multai India
88 B3 Multan Pak.
103 N3 Multia Fin.
108 A6 Multien reg. France
85 F5 Mūmān Iran
87 A2 Mumbai India (City Plan 54)
71 H4 Mumbil Australia
123 C5 Mumbwa Zambia
Mŭ'minobod Tajik. see Leningrad
117 H6 Mumra Rus. Fed.
98 C2 Mun, Mae Nam r. Thai.
68 C2 Muna i. Indon.
151 G3 Muna Mex.
77 M3 Muna r. Rus. Fed.
102 B1 Munaðarnes Iceland
82 C3 Munayly Kazakh.
82 C4 Munayshy Kazakh.
109 J4 Münchberg Germany
München Germany see Munich
109 G4 Münchhausen Germany
157 A4 Munchique, Cerro mt. Col.
130 D3 Muncho Lake Canada
130 D3 Muncho Lake Provincial Park Canada
96 D4 Munch'ŏn N. Korea
134 E5 Muncie U.S.A.
146 E4 Muncy U.S.A.
87 B5 Mundel Lake Sri Lanka
105 I5 Mundesley U.K.
105 H5 Mundford U.K.
68 C5 Mundrabilla Australia
88 C4 Mundwa India
87 C2 Muneru r. India
71 G2 Mungallala Creek r. Australia
88 D4 Mungaoli India
122 C3 Mungbere Dem. Rep. Congo
87 C1 Mungeli India
89 F4 Munger India
70 C2 Mungeranie Australia
98 D5 Munggursak, Tanjung pt Indon.
71 H2 Mungindi Australia
71 E4 Mungo National Park Australia
96 D5 Mun'gyŏng S. Korea
112 E6 Munich Germany
155 J4 Munim r. Brazil
134 D2 Munising U.S.A.
158 E3 Muniz Freire Brazil
102 O1 Munkebakken Norway
103 J4 Munkedal Sweden
Munkelva Norway see Munkebakken
103 K4 Munkfors Sweden
109 I4 Münnerstadt Germany
125 H1 Munnik S. Africa
71 H8 Munro, Mount Australia
96 D5 Munsan S. Korea
112 C7 Münsingen Switz.
109 G5 Münster Germany
109 I2 Münster Germany
108 F3 Münster Germany
108 F3 Münsterland reg. Germany
102 O2 Muojärvi l. Fin.
Mương Lam Vietnam see Xiêng Lam
93 B6 Mương Nhe Vietnam
Mương Nhie Vietnam see Mương Nhe
102 M2 Muonio Fin.
102 M2 Muonioälven r. Fin./Sweden
96 A5 Muping China
Muqdisho Somalia see Mogadishu
81 L1 Müqtädır Azer.
81 I2 Muradiye Turkey
98 □ Murai Reservoir Sing.
94 F5 Murakami Japan

198 Nueces

143 D6 **Nueces** *r.* U.S.A.
131 J2 **Nueltin Lake** Canada
150 G5 **Nueva Arcadia** Hond.
150 H5 **Nueva Armenia** Hond.
157 C2 **Nueva Florida** Venez.
159 F2 **Nueva Helvecia** Uruguay
159 B3 **Nueva Imperial** Chile
Nueva Loja Ecuador *see* Lago Agrio
156 B6 **Nueva Lubecka** Arg.
151 G5 **Nueva Ocotepeque** Hond.
150 D2 **Nueva Rosita** Mex.
151 G5 **Nueva San Salvador** El Salvador
149 I4 **Nuevitas** Cuba
159 D4 **Nuevo, Golfo** *g.* Arg.
148 C2 **Nuevo Casas Grandes** Mex.
150 C2 **Nuevo Ideal** Mex.
151 E2 **Nuevo Laredo** Mex.
151 E2 **Nuevo León** *state* Mex.
122 E3 **Nugaal** *watercourse* Somalia
72 B7 **Nugget Point** N.Z.
69 F2 **Nuguria Islands** P.N.G.
72 F3 **Nuhaka** N.Z.
69 H2 **Nui** *atoll* Tuvalu
98 C2 **Nui Ti On** *mt.* Vietnam
Nu Jiang *r.* China *see* Salween
70 A4 **Nukey Bluff** *h.* Australia
84 D3 **Nūklok, Chāh-e** *well* Iran
69 I4 **Nuku'alofa** Tonga
69 H2 **Nukufetau** *atoll* Tuvalu
67 J5 **Nuku Hiva** *i.* Fr. Polynesia
69 H2 **Nukulaelae** *atoll* Tuvalu
69 F2 **Nukumanu Islands** P.N.G.
Nukunono *i.* Pacific Ocean *see* Nukunonu
69 I2 **Nukunonu** *atoll* Pacific Ocean
82 D4 **Nukus** Uzbek.
68 C4 **Nullagine** Australia
68 C5 **Nullarbor Plain** Australia
92 F1 **Nulu'erhu Shan** *mts* China
70 F2 **Numalla, Lake** *salt flat* Australia
120 D4 **Numan** Nigeria
95 F6 **Numata** Japan
95 F7 **Numazu** Japan
103 J3 **Numedal** *val.* Norway
91 F7 **Numfoor** *i.* Indon.
71 F6 **Numurkah** Australia
133 H2 **Nunaksaluk Island** Canada
129 N3 **Nunakuluut** *i.* Greenland
Nunap Isua *c.* Greenland *see* Farewell, Cape
132 E2 **Nunavik** *reg.* U.S.A.
129 H3 **Nunavut** *admin. div.* Canada
146 E3 **Nunda** U.S.A.
71 I3 **Nundle** Australia
105 F5 **Nuneaton** U.K.
132 B3 **Nungesser Lake** Canada
128 B4 **Nunivak Island** U.S.A.
88 D2 **Nunkun** *mt.* India
77 T3 **Nunligran** Rus. Fed.
111 C2 **Nuñomoral** Spain
108 D2 **Nunspeet** Neth.
114 C4 **Nuoro** *Sardinia* Italy
69 G3 **Nupani** *i.* Solomon Is
86 B4 **Nuqrah** Saudi Arabia
157 A3 **Nuquí** Col.
88 E1 **Nur** China
84 D2 **Nur** *r.* Iran
83 H2 **Nura** Kazakh.
83 G2 **Nura** *r.* Kazakh.
84 C4 **Nūrābād** Iran
Nurata Uzbek. *see* **Nurota**
Nuratau, Khrebet *mts* Uzbek. *see* **Nurota tizmasi**
109 J5 **Nuremberg** Germany
81 I2 **Nurettin** Turkey
85 G4 **Nur Gama** Pak.
150 B1 **Nuri** Mex.
70 C5 **Nuriootpa** Australia
85 H3 **Nuristan** Afgh.
85 H3 **Nuristan** *reg.* Afgh.
116 I4 **Nurlaty** Rus. Fed.
102 O3 **Nurmes** Fin.
102 M3 **Nurmo** Fin.
Nürnberg Germany *see* Nuremberg
82 F4 **Nurota** Uzbek.
83 F4 **Nurota tizmasi** *mts* Uzbek.
71 G3 **Nurri, Mount** *h.* Australia
89 H1 **Nur Turu** China
81 H3 **Nusaybin** Turkey
85 G4 **Nushki** Pak.
133 H2 **Nutak** Canada
141 H5 **Nutrioso** U.S.A.
88 B3 **Nuttal** Pak.
164 U2 **Nuuk** Greenland
102 N2 **Nuupas** Fin.
129 M2 **Nuussuaq** Greenland
129 M2 **Nuussuaq** *pen.* Greenland
87 C5 **Nuwara Eliya** Sri Lanka
124 C5 **Nuwerus** S. Africa
124 D6 **Nuweveldberge** *mts* S. Africa
81 J4 **Nuzi** *tourist site* Iraq
125 I1 **Nwanedi Nature Reserve** S. Africa
76 H3 **Nyagan'** Rus. Fed.
70 E5 **Nyah West** Australia
89 G3 **Nyainqêntanglha Feng** *mt.* China
89 G3 **Nyainqêntanglha Shan** *mts* China
89 H2 **Nyainrong** China
102 L3 **Nyåker** Sweden
121 E3 **Nyala** Sudan
Nyalam China *see* **Congdü**
123 C5 **Nyamandhlovu** Zimbabwe
116 G2 **Nyandoma** Rus. Fed.
116 F2 **Nyandomskiy Vozvyshennost'** *hills* Rus. Fed.
122 B4 **Nyanga** *r.* Gabon
123 D5 **Nyanga** Zimbabwe
89 G3 **Nyang Qu** *r.* *Xizang* China
89 H3 **Nyang Qu** *r.* *Xizang* China
88 D3 **Nyar** *r.* India
123 D5 **Nyasa, Lake** Africa
116 C4 **Nyasvizh** Belarus
103 J5 **Nyborg** Denmark
102 O1 **Nyborg** Norway
103 K4 **Nybro** Sweden
129 M1 **Nyeboe Land** *reg.* Greenland
89 G3 **Nyêmo** China
122 D4 **Nyeri** Kenya
89 F3 **Nyima** China
90 B4 **Nyingchi** China
113 J7 **Nyíregyháza** Hungary
102 M3 **Nykarleby** Fin.
103 J5 **Nykøbing** Denmark
103 J5 **Nykøbing Sjælland** Denmark
103 L4 **Nyköping** Sweden
102 L3 **Nyland** Sweden
Nylstroom S. Africa *see* Modimolle
71 G4 **Nymagee** Australia
71 J2 **Nymboida** Australia
71 J2 **Nymboida** *r.* Australia
103 L4 **Nynäshamn** Sweden
71 G3 **Nyngan** Australia
113 K4 **Nyoman** *r.* Belarus/Lith.
112 C7 **Nyon** Switz.
89 F3 **Nyonni Ri** *mt.* China
110 G4 **Nyons** France
76 G3 **Nyrob** Rus. Fed.
112 H5 **Nysa** Poland
116 I2 **Nyuchpas** Rus. Fed.
94 F5 **Nyūdō-zaki** *pt* Japan
122 C4 **Nyunzu** Dem. Rep. Congo
77 M3 **Nyurba** Rus. Fed.
116 I2 **Nyuvchim** Rus. Fed.
117 E6 **Nyzhn'ohirs'kyy** Ukr.
122 D4 **Nzega** Tanz.
120 B4 **Nzérékoré** Guinea
122 B4 **N'zeto** Angola
125 I1 **Nzhelele Dam** S. Africa
123 E5 **Nzwani** *i.* Comoros

O

142 C2 **Oahe, Lake** U.S.A.
140 □1 **O'ahu** *i.* U.S.A.
140 □1 **O'ahu** *i.* U.S.A.
Oahu *i.* U.S.A. *see* **O'ahu**
70 D4 **Oakbank** Australia
141 F2 **Oak City** U.S.A.
143 E6 **Oakdale** U.S.A.
142 D2 **Oakes** U.S.A.
71 I1 **Oakey** Australia
105 G5 **Oakham** U.K.
138 B1 **Oak Harbor** U.S.A.
146 C6 **Oak Hill** U.S.A.
140 C3 **Oakhurst** U.S.A.
134 B2 **Oak Island** U.S.A.
140 A3 **Oakland** *CA* U.S.A.
146 D5 **Oakland** *MD* U.S.A.
142 D3 **Oakland** *NE* U.S.A.
138 B3 **Oakland** *OR* U.S.A.
71 G5 **Oaklands** Australia
134 D5 **Oak Lawn** U.S.A.
142 C4 **Oakley** U.S.A.
68 C4 **Oakover** *r.* Australia
138 B3 **Oakridge** U.S.A.
145 C4 **Oak Ridge** U.S.A.
70 D4 **Oakvale** Australia
135 H4 **Oakville** Canada
72 C6 **Oamaru** N.Z.
72 D5 **Oaro** N.Z.
97 B3 **Oas** Phil.
138 D3 **Oasis** U.S.A.
73 B6 **Oates Land** *reg.* Antarctica
71 G9 **Oatlands** Australia
141 E4 **Oatman** U.S.A.
151 E4 **Oaxaca** Mex.
151 E4 **Oaxaca** *state* Mex.
76 H3 **Ob'** *r.* Rus. Fed.
120 D4 **Obala** Cameroon
95 D7 **Obama** Japan
106 C4 **Oban** U.K.
94 G5 **Obanazawa** Japan
111 C1 **O Barco** Spain
132 F4 **Obatogamau, Lac** Canada
130 F4 **Obed** Canada
72 B6 **Obelisk** *mt.* N.Z.
109 H4 **Oberaula** Germany
109 I3 **Oberdorla** Germany
108 E3 **Oberhausen** Germany
142 C4 **Oberlin** *KS* U.S.A.
146 B4 **Oberlin** *OH* U.S.A.
109 F5 **Obermoschel** Germany
71 H4 **Oberon** Australia
109 K5 **Oberpfälzer Wald** *mts* Germany
109 H4 **Obersinn** Germany
109 H4 **Oberthulba** Germany
109 G4 **Obertshausen** Germany
109 H3 **Oberwälder Land** *reg.* Germany
91 E7 **Obi** *i.* Indon.
155 G4 **Óbidos** Brazil
83 G5 **Obigarm** Tajik.
94 H3 **Obihiro** Japan
117 H6 **Obil'noye** Rus. Fed.
157 C2 **Obispos** Venez.
90 F2 **Obluch'ye** Rus. Fed.
116 F4 **Obninsk** Rus. Fed.
122 C3 **Obo** Centr. Afr. Rep.
92 A2 **Obo** China
122 E2 **Obock** Djibouti
96 E3 **Ŏbŏk** N. Korea
122 C4 **Obokote** Dem. Rep. Congo
122 B4 **Obouya** Congo
117 F5 **Oboyan'** Rus. Fed.
116 G2 **Obozerskiy** Rus. Fed.
89 E4 **Obra** India
89 E4 **Obra Dam** India
150 B1 **Obregón, Presa** *resr* Mex.
115 I2 **Obrenovac** Serb. and Mont.
80 D2 **Obruk** Turkey
82 D2 **Obshchiy Syrt** *hills* Rus. Fed.
76 I2 **Obskaya Guba** *sea chan.* Rus. Fed.
120 B4 **Obuasi** Ghana
117 D5 **Obukhiv** Ukr.
116 I2 **Ob''yachevo** Rus. Fed.
145 D6 **Ocala** U.S.A.
157 D4 **Ocamo** *r.* Venez.
150 D2 **Ocampo** Mex.
157 B2 **Ocaña** Col.
111 E3 **Ocaña** Spain
154 E7 **Occidental, Cordillera** *mts* Chile
157 A4 **Occidental, Cordillera** *mts* Col.
154 C6 **Occidental, Cordillera** *mts* Peru
130 B3 **Ocean Cape** U.S.A.
147 F5 **Ocean City** *MD* U.S.A.
147 F5 **Ocean City** *NJ* U.S.A.
130 D4 **Ocean Falls** Canada
140 D5 **Oceanside** U.S.A.
143 F6 **Ocean Springs** U.S.A.
117 D6 **Ochakiv** Ukr.
117 G7 **Och'amch'ire** Georgia
106 E4 **Ochil Hills** U.K.
88 C1 **Ochili Pass** Afgh.
109 I5 **Ochsenfurt** Germany
108 F2 **Ochtrup** Germany
103 L3 **Ockelbo** Sweden
113 L7 **Ocolașul Mare, Vârful** *mt.* Romania
137 J5 **Oconee** *r.* U.S.A.
134 C4 **Oconomowoc** U.S.A.
134 D3 **Oconto** U.S.A.
151 F4 **Ocosingo** Mex.
150 H5 **Ocotal** Nicaragua
140 D5 **Ocotillo Wells** U.S.A.
150 D3 **Ocotlán** Mex.
68 C2 **Ocussi** *enclave* East Timor
120 B4 **Oda** Ghana
95 C7 **Ōda** Japan
102 C2 **Ódáðahraun** *lava field* Iceland
96 E3 **Ŏdaejin** N. Korea
94 G4 **Ōdate** Japan
95 F7 **Odawara** Japan
103 I3 **Odda** Norway
131 J3 **Odei** *r.* Canada
134 C5 **Odell** U.S.A.
111 B4 **Odemira** Port.
80 A2 **Ödemiş** Turkey
125 G3 **Odendaalsrus** S. Africa
103 J5 **Odense** Denmark
109 G5 **Odenwald** *reg.* Germany
109 I3 **Oder** *r.* Germany *alt.* **Odra (Poland)**
112 G3 **Oderbucht** *b.* Germany
117 D6 **Odesa** Ukr.
103 K4 **Ödeshog** Sweden
143 C6 **Odessa** U.S.A.
83 H1 **Odesskoye** Rus. Fed.
111 C4 **Odiel** *r.* Spain
120 B4 **Odienné** Côte d'Ivoire
116 F4 **Odintsovo** Rus. Fed.
98 C3 **Ŏdôngk** Cambodia
112 G4 **Odra** *r.* Poland *alt.* **Oder (Germany)**
155 J5 **Oeiras** Brazil
142 C3 **Oelrichs** U.S.A.
109 K4 **Oelsnitz** Germany
134 B4 **Oelwein** U.S.A.
108 D1 **Oenkerk** Neth.
81 H1 **Of** Turkey
114 G4 **Ofanto** *r.* Italy
109 G4 **Offenbach am Main** Germany
108 F6 **Offenburg** Germany
115 L6 **Ofidoussa** *i.* Greece
94 G5 **Ōfunato** Japan
94 F5 **Oga** Japan
122 E3 **Ogadēn** *reg.* Eth.
94 F5 **Oga-hantō** *pen.* Japan
95 E7 **Ōgaki** Japan
142 C3 **Ogallala** U.S.A.
Ogasawara-shotō *is* Japan *see* Bonin Islands
135 H2 **Ogascanane, Lac** *l.* Canada
120 C4 **Ogbomosho** Nigeria
Ogbomoso Nigeria *see* Ogbomosho
142 E3 **Ogden** *IA* U.S.A.
138 E3 **Ogden** *UT* U.S.A.
130 C3 **Ogden, Mount** Canada
147 F2 **Ogdensburg** U.S.A.
128 E3 **Ogilvie** *r.* Canada
128 E3 **Ogilvie Mountains** Canada
82 C5 **Oglanly** Turkm.
145 C5 **Oglethorpe, Mount** U.S.A.
114 D1 **Oglio** *r.* Italy
120 C4 **Ogoja** Nigeria
132 C3 **Ogoki** *r.* Canada
132 C3 **Ogoki Reservoir** Canada
115 J3 **Ogosta** *r.* Bulg.
103 N4 **Ogre** Latvia
114 F2 **Ogulin** Croatia
Ogurchinskiy, Ostrov *i.* Turkm. *see* **Ogurjaly Adasy**
82 C5 **Ogurjaly Adasy** *i.* Turkm.
81 K1 **Oğuz** Azer.
72 A6 **Ohai** N.Z.
72 E3 **Ohakune** N.Z.
94 G4 **Ōhata** Japan
72 B6 **Ohau, Lake** N.Z.
159 B2 **O'Higgins** *admin. reg.* Chile
156 B7 **O'Higgins, Lago** *l.* Chile
144 C4 **Ohio** *r.* U.S.A.
146 B4 **Ohio** *state* U.S.A.
109 G4 **Ohm** *r.* Germany
109 I4 **Ohrdruf** Germany
109 K4 **Ohře** *r.* Czech Rep.
109 J2 **Ohre** *r.* Germany
115 I4 **Ohrid** Macedonia
115 I4 **Ohrid, Lake** Albania/Macedonia
125 I2 **Ohrigstad** S. Africa
109 H5 **Öhringen** Germany
72 E3 **Ohura** N.Z.
155 H3 **Oiapoque** Brazil
106 D3 **Oich, Loch** *l.* U.K.
89 H3 **Oiga** China
108 A4 **Oignies** France
146 D4 **Oil City** U.S.A.
140 C4 **Oildale** U.S.A.
110 F2 **Oise** *r.* France
95 B8 **Ōita** Japan
115 J5 **Oiti** *mt.* Greece
140 C4 **Ojai** U.S.A.
159 D2 **Ojeda** Arg.
134 B3 **Ojibwa** U.S.A.
148 D3 **Ojinaga** Mex.
151 E4 **Ojitlán** Mex.
95 F6 **Ojiya** Japan
150 A2 **Ojo de Liebre, Lago** *b.* Mex.
156 C3 **Ojos del Salado, Nevado** *mt.* Arg.
116 G4 **Oka** *r.* Rus. Fed.
123 B6 **Okahandja** Namibia
72 E3 **Okahukura** N.Z.
123 B6 **Okakarara** Namibia
133 H2 **Okak Islands** Canada
130 F5 **Okanagan Falls** Canada
130 F4 **Okanagan Lake** Canada
138 C1 **Okanogan** *r.* Canada/U.S.A.
138 C1 **Okanogan** U.S.A.
138 B1 **Okanogan Range** *mts* U.S.A.
88 C3 **Okara** Pak.
Okarem Turkm. *see* **Ekerem**
123 B5 **Okaukuejo** Namibia
123 C5 **Okavango** *r.* Botswana/Namibia
123 C5 **Okavango Delta** *swamp* Botswana
95 F6 **Okaya** Japan
95 C7 **Okayama** Japan
95 E7 **Okazaki** Japan
145 D7 **Okeechobee** U.S.A.
145 D7 **Okeechobee, Lake** U.S.A.
145 D6 **Okefenokee Swamp** U.S.A.
105 C7 **Okehampton** U.K.
120 C4 **Okene** Nigeria
109 I2 **Oker** *r.* Germany
88 B5 **Okha** India
90 F1 **Okha** Rus. Fed.
89 F4 **Okhaldhunga** Nepal
88 B5 **Okha Rann** *marsh* India
77 P4 **Okhotka** *r.* Rus. Fed.
77 P4 **Okhotsk** Rus. Fed.
77 P4 **Okhotsk, Sea of** Rus. Fed.
Okhotskoye More *sea* Rus. Fed. *see* **Okhotsk, Sea of**
117 E5 **Okhtyrka** Ukr.
90 E4 **Okinawa** *i.* Japan
Okinawa-guntō *is* Japan *see* Okinawa-shotō
90 E4 **Okinawa-shotō** *is* Japan
95 B7 **Okino-shima** *i.* Japan
95 C6 **Oki-shotō** *is* Japan
143 D5 **Oklahoma** *state* U.S.A.
143 D5 **Oklahoma City** U.S.A.
143 D5 **Okmulgee** U.S.A.
122 B4 **Okondja** Gabon
130 G4 **Okotoks** Canada
116 E4 **Okovskiy Les** *for.* Rus. Fed.
122 B4 **Okoyo** Congo
83 J3 **Okpety, Gora** *mt.* Kazakh.
102 M1 **Øksfjord** Norway
116 F2 **Oksovskiy** Rus. Fed.
83 G5 **Oktyabr** Tajik.
116 I4 **Oktyabr'sk** Rus. Fed.
82 D4 **Oktyabr'sk** Turkm.
116 G2 **Oktyabr'skiy** Rus. Fed.
117 G6 **Oktyabr'skiy** Rus. Fed.
76 G4 **Oktyabr'skiy** Rus. Fed.
90 H1 **Oktyabr'skiy** Rus. Fed.
83 F5 **Oktyabr'skiy** Uzbek.
82 F1 **Oktyabr'skoye** Kazakh.
82 E1 **Oktyabr'skoye** Rus. Fed.
82 C1 **Oktyabr'skoye** Rus. Fed.
76 H3 **Oktyabr'skoye** Rus. Fed.
77 K2 **Oktyabr'skoy Revolyutsii, Ostrov** *i.* Rus. Fed.
Oktyah'sk Turkm. *see* **Oktyabr'sk**
116 E3 **Okulovka** Rus. Fed.
94 F3 **Okushiri-tō** *i.* Japan
124 E1 **Okwa** *watercourse* Botswana
102 B2 **Ólafsvík** Iceland
140 C3 **Olancha** U.S.A.
140 C3 **Olancha Peak** U.S.A.
150 H5 **Olanchito** Hond.
103 L4 **Öland** *i.* Sweden
102 O2 **Olanga** Rus. Fed.
70 D4 **Olary** Australia
70 D4 **Olary** *watercourse* Australia
142 E4 **Olathe** U.S.A.
159 E3 **Olavarría** Arg.
112 H5 **Oława** Poland
141 G5 **Olberg** U.S.A.
114 C4 **Olbia** *Sardinia* Italy
146 D3 **Olcott** U.S.A.
71 J3 **Old Bar** Australia
87 C2 **Old Bastar** India
107 D4 **Oldcastle** Rep. of Ireland
128 E3 **Old Crow** Canada
Oldeboorn Neth. *see* **Aldeboarn**
109 G1 **Oldenburg** Germany
112 E3 **Oldenburg in Holstein** Germany
108 E2 **Oldenzaal** Neth.
102 M1 **Olderdalen** Norway
147 F3 **Old Forge** *NY* U.S.A.
147 F4 **Old Forge** *PA* U.S.A.
104 E4 **Oldham** U.K.
107 C6 **Old Head of Kinsale** Rep. of Ireland
130 G4 **Oldman** *r.* Canada
106 F3 **Oldmeldrum** U.K.
147 H3 **Old Orchard Beach** U.S.A.
133 J4 **Old Perlican** Canada
130 G4 **Olds** Canada
147 I2 **Old Town** U.S.A.
115 I6 **Olduvai Gorge** *tourist site* Tanz.
131 H4 **Old Wives Lake** Canada
141 E4 **Old Woman Mountains** U.S.A.
146 D3 **Olean** U.S.A.
113 K3 **Olecko** Poland
77 N4 **Olekma** *r.* Rus. Fed.
77 N3 **Olekminsk** Rus. Fed.
117 E5 **Oleksandriya** Ukr.
116 H1 **Olema** Rus. Fed.
103 I4 **Ølen** Norway
116 E2 **Olenegorsk** Rus. Fed.
77 M3 **Olenek** Rus. Fed.
77 N2 **Olenek** *r.* Rus. Fed.
77 N2 **Olenekskiy Zaliv** *b.* Rus. Fed.
116 E3 **Olenino** Rus. Fed.
83 H1 **Olenti** *r.* *Pavlodarskaya Oblast'* Kazakh.
82 C2 **Olenti** *r.* *Zapadnyy Kazakhstan* Kazakh.
117 C5 **Olevs'k** Ukr.
94 D3 **Ol'ga** Rus. Fed.
111 C4 **Olhão** Port.
124 C2 **Olifants** *watercourse* Namibia
125 I1 **Olifants** S. Africa
124 C5 **Olifants** *r.* *W. Cape* S. Africa
124 D6 **Olifants** *r.* *W. Cape* S. Africa
124 E3 **Olifantshoek** S. Africa
124 C6 **Olifantsrivierberge** *mts* S. Africa
159 F2 **Olimar Grande** *r.* Uruguay
158 C3 **Olímpia** Brazil
151 E4 **Olinalá** Mex.
155 L5 **Olinda** Brazil
123 D5 **Olinga** Moz.
125 G2 **Oliphants Drift** Botswana
159 D2 **Oliva** Arg.
111 F3 **Oliva** Spain
156 C3 **Oliva, Cordillera de** *mts* Arg./Chile
159 C1 **Olivares, Cerro de** *mt.* Chile
146 B5 **Olive Hill** U.S.A.
158 D3 **Oliveira** Brazil
111 C3 **Olivenza** Spain
142 E2 **Olivia** U.S.A.
116 G4 **Ol'khi** Rus. Fed.
156 C2 **Ollagüe** Chile
159 B1 **Ollita, Cordillera de** *mts* Arg./Chile
159 B1 **Ollitas** *mt.* Arg.
83 G4 **Olmaliq** Uzbek.
154 C5 **Olmos** Peru
147 G3 **Olmstedville** U.S.A.
105 G5 **Olney** U.K.
144 C4 **Olney** U.S.A.
103 K4 **Olofström** Sweden
112 H6 **Olomouc** Czech Rep.
116 E2 **Olonets** Rus. Fed.
97 B3 **Olongapo** Phil.
110 D5 **Oloron-Ste-Marie** France
111 H1 **Olot** Spain
82 E5 **Olot** Uzbek.
90 D1 **Olovyannaya** Rus. Fed.
88 C5 **Olpad** India
109 F3 **Olpe** Germany
113 J4 **Olsztyn** Poland
112 C7 **Olten** Switz.
115 L2 **Oltenița** Romania
81 H1 **Oltu** Turkey
97 B5 **Olutanga** *i.* Phil.
115 I6 **Olympia** *tourist site* Greece
138 B2 **Olympia** U.S.A.
138 A2 **Olympic National Park** U.S.A.
80 C4 **Olympos** *tourist site* Turkey
115 J4 **Olympus, Mount** Greece
138 B2 **Olympus, Mount** U.S.A.
77 R3 **Olyutorskiy** Rus. Fed.
77 S4 **Olyutorskiy, Mys** *c.* Rus. Fed.
77 R4 **Olyutorskiy Zaliv** *b.* Rus. Fed.
89 E2 **Oma** China
94 G4 **Ōma** Japan
94 G5 **Ōmachi** Japan
95 F7 **Omae-zaki** *pt* Japan
107 D3 **Omagh** U.K.
142 E3 **Omaha** U.S.A.
124 C1 **Omaheke** *admin. reg.* Namibia
138 C1 **Omak** U.S.A.
86 E6 **Oman** *country* Asia
85 E5 **Oman, Gulf of** Asia
72 B6 **Omarama** N.Z.
123 B6 **Omaruru** Namibia
123 B5 **Omatako** *watercourse* Namibia
154 D7 **Omate** Peru
125 H2 **Omaweneno** Botswana
94 G4 **Ōma-zaki** *c.* Japan
122 A4 **Omboué** Gabon
114 D3 **Ombrone** *r.* Italy
89 F3 **Ombu** China
124 E5 **Omdraaisvlei** S. Africa
121 F3 **Omdurman** Sudan
114 C2 **Omegna** Italy
71 G6 **Omeo** Australia
150 H6 **Ometepe, Isla de** *i.* Nicaragua
122 D2 **Om Hajēr** Eritrea
84 C4 **Omīdīyeh** Iran
130 D3 **Omineca Mountains** Canada
124 C1 **Omitara** Namibia
95 F7 **Ōmiya** Japan
130 C3 **Ommaney, Cape** U.S.A.
108 E2 **Ommen** Neth.
92 B1 **Ömnögovĭ** *prov.* Mongolia
77 R3 **Omolon** Rus. Fed.
77 Q3 **Omolon** *r.* Rus. Fed.
122 D3 **Omo National Park** Eth.
94 G5 **Omono-gawa** *r.* Japan
76 I4 **Omsk** Rus. Fed.
77 Q3 **Omsukchan** Rus. Fed.
94 H2 **Ōmū** Japan
115 K2 **Omu, Vârful** *mt.* Romania
95 A8 **Ōmura** Japan
124 B1 **Omulaska** U.S.A.
147 F6 **Onancock** U.S.A.
132 D4 **Onaping Lake** Canada
150 B1 **Onavas** Mex.
135 E3 **Onaway** U.S.A.
98 A2 **Onbingwin** Myanmar
159 D1 **Oncativo** Arg.
105 E4 **Onchan** U.K.
123 B5 **Oncócua** Angola
123 B5 **Ondangwa** Namibia
124 B1 **Ondekaremba** Namibia
125 H3 **Onderstedorings** S. Africa
123 B5 **Ondjiva** Angola
120 C4 **Ondo** Nigeria
90 D2 **Öndörhaan** Mongolia
96 A1 **Ondor Had** China
92 B1 **Ondor Mod** China
92 D1 **Ondor Sum** China
116 E2 **Ondozero** Rus. Fed.
124 D1 **One Botswana** Botswana
116 F2 **Onega** Rus. Fed.
116 F2 **Onega** *r.* Rus. Fed.
116 E2 **Onega, Lake** Rus. Fed.
147 F3 **Oneida** U.S.A.
147 F3 **Oneida Lake** U.S.A.
142 D3 **O'Neill** U.S.A.
90 H2 **Onekotan, Ostrov** *i.* Rus. Fed.
147 F3 **Oneonta** U.S.A.
72 E2 **Oneroa** N.Z.
113 M7 **Onești** Romania
116 E1 **Onezhskaya Guba** *g.* Rus. Fed.
76 E3 **Onezhskoye Ozero** Rus. Fed. **Onezhskoye Ozero** *l.* Rus. Fed. *see* **Onega, Lake**
87 C1 **Ong** *r.* India
122 B4 **Onga** Gabon
72 F3 **Ongaonga** N.Z.
124 E4 **Ongers** *watercourse* S. Africa
96 C5 **Ongjin** N. Korea
87 C3 **Ongole** India
83 K2 **Onguday** Rus. Fed.
117 G7 **Oni** Georgia
123 E6 **Onilahy** *r.* Madag.
120 C4 **Onitsha** Nigeria
124 B1 **Onjati Mountain** Namibia
95 E7 **Ōno** Japan
69 I4 **Ono-i-Lau** *i.* Fiji
95 C7 **Onomichi** Japan
69 H2 **Onotoa** *atoll* Kiribati
130 G4 **Onoway** Canada
124 C4 **Onseepkans** S. Africa
68 B4 **Onslow** Australia
145 E5 **Onslow Bay** U.S.A.
96 F2 **Onsong** N. Korea
108 F1 **Onstwedde** Neth.
95 E7 **Ontake-san** *vol.* Japan
132 B3 **Ontario** *prov.* Canada
138 C2 **Ontario** U.S.A.
135 H4 **Ontario, Lake** Canada/U.S.A.
134 C2 **Ontonagon** U.S.A.
69 F2 **Ontong Java Atoll** Solomon Is
68 D4 **Oodnadatta** Australia
70 F5 **Oolambeyan National Park** Australia
143 E4 **Oologah Lake** *resr* U.S.A.
108 B3 **Oostburg** Neth.
Oostende Belgium *see* **Ostend**
108 D2 **Oostendorp** Neth.
108 C3 **Oosterhout** Neth.
108 B3 **Oosterschelde** *est.* Neth.
108 E2 **Oosterwolde** Neth.
108 A4 **Oostvleteren** Belgium
108 D1 **Oost-Vlieland** Neth.
130 D4 **Ootsa Lake** Canada
130 D4 **Ootsa Lake** *l.* Canada
146 E5 **Opal** U.S.A.
122 C4 **Opala** Dem. Rep. Congo
116 I3 **Oparino** Rus. Fed.
132 B3 **Opasquia** Canada
132 B3 **Opasquia Provincial Park** Canada
132 F3 **Opataca, Lac** *l.* Canada
112 H6 **Opava** Czech Rep.
145 C5 **Opelika** U.S.A.
143 E6 **Opelousas** U.S.A.
138 F1 **Opheim** U.S.A.
135 F2 **Ophir** Canada
99 B2 **Ophir, Gunung** *vol.* Indon.
72 C6 **Opihi** *r.* N.Z.
132 E3 **Opinaca** *r.* Canada
132 E3 **Opinaca, Réservoir** *resr* Canada
132 D3 **Opinnagau** *r.* Canada
81 J5 **Opis** *tourist site* Iraq
133 G3 **Opiscotéo, Lac** *l.* Canada
108 C2 **Opmeer** Neth.
116 D3 **Opochka** Rus. Fed.
112 H5 **Opole** Poland
111 B2 **Oporto** Port.
72 F3 **Opotiki** N.Z.
145 C6 **Opp** U.S.A.
102 J3 **Oppdal** Norway
72 D3 **Opunake** N.Z.
123 B5 **Opuwo** Namibia
82 B3 **Opytnoye** Kazakh.
82 D4 **Oqqal'a** Uzbek.
83 G5 **Oqsu** *r.* Tajik.
82 F5 **Oqtosh** Uzbek.
134 B5 **Oquawka** U.S.A.
147 H2 **Oquossoc** U.S.A.
82 D2 **Or'** *r.* Rus. Fed.
141 G5 **Oracle** U.S.A.
141 G5 **Oracle Junction** U.S.A.
113 J7 **Oradea** Romania
102 C2 **Öræfajökull** *glacier* Iceland
115 I3 **Orahovac** Serb. and Mont.
88 D4 **Orai** India
120 B1 **Oran** Alg.
156 D2 **Orán** Arg.
98 C2 **O Rang** Cambodia
96 E2 **Orang** N. Korea
71 H4 **Orange** Australia
110 G4 **Orange** France
124 B4 **Orange** *r.* Namibia/S. Africa
147 G3 **Orange** *MA* U.S.A.
143 E6 **Orange** *TX* U.S.A.
146 D5 **Orange** *VA* U.S.A.
155 H3 **Orange, Cabo** *c.* Brazil
145 D5 **Orangeburg** U.S.A.
163 J8 **Orange Cone** *sea feature* S. Atlantic Ocean
Orange Free State *prov.* S. Africa *see* **Free State**
135 G3 **Orangeville** Canada
141 G2 **Orangeville** U.S.A.
151 G4 **Orange Walk** Belize
97 B3 **Orani** Phil.
109 L2 **Oranienburg** Germany
124 B4 **Oranjemund** Namibia
125 F4 **Oranjestad** Aruba
107 C4 **Oranmore** Rep. of Ireland
123 C6 **Orapa** Botswana
97 C3 **Oras** Phil.
115 J2 **Orăștie** Romania
102 M3 **Oravais** Fin.
115 I2 **Oravița** Romania
82 E4 **Orba Co** *l.* China
114 D3 **Orbetello** Italy
111 C1 **Órbigo** *r.* Spain
71 H6 **Orbost** Australia
73 C2 **Orcadas** *research stn* S. Atlantic Ocean
141 H2 **Orchard Mesa** U.S.A.
157 D2 **Orchila, Isla** *i.* Venez.
140 B4 **Orcutt** U.S.A.
68 C3 **Ord** *r.* Australia
68 C3 **Ord, Mount** *h.* Australia
139 D4 **Orderville** U.S.A.
111 B1 **Ordes** Spain
140 D4 **Ord Mountain** U.S.A.
92 D2 **Ordos** China
80 F1 **Ordu** Turkey
81 K2 **Ordubad** Azer.
139 G4 **Ordway** U.S.A.
Ordzhonikidze Rus. Fed. *see* Vladikavkaz
117 E6 **Ordzhonikidze** Ukr.
140 C1 **Oreana** U.S.A.
103 K4 **Örebro** Sweden
134 C4 **Oregon** *IL* U.S.A.
134 B4 **Oregon** *OH* U.S.A.
134 C4 **Oregon** *WI* U.S.A.
138 B3 **Oregon** *state* U.S.A.
138 B2 **Oregon City** U.S.A.
116 F4 **Orekhovo-Zuyevo** Rus. Fed.
116 F4 **Orel** Rus. Fed.
90 F1 **Orel', Ozero** *l.* Rus. Fed.
141 G1 **Orem** U.S.A.
80 A2 **Ören** Turkey
115 L6 **Ören** Turkey
82 C2 **Orenburg** Rus. Fed.
82 C2 **Orenburgskaya Oblast'** *admin. div.* Rus. Fed.
159 E3 **Orense** Arg.
72 A7 **Orepuki** N.Z.
103 K5 **Öresund** *str.* Denmark
72 B7 **Oreti** *r.* N.Z.
72 E2 **Orewa** N.Z.
108 D4 **Oreye** Belgium
115 J4 **Orfanou, Kolpos** *b.* Greece
71 G9 **Orford** Australia
105 I5 **Orford** U.K.
105 I5 **Orford Ness** *hd* U.K.
141 F5 **Organ Pipe Cactus National Monument** *nat. park* U.S.A.
85 H3 **Orgūn** Afgh.
80 B2 **Orhaneli** Turkey
80 B1 **Orhangazi** Turkey
116 I3 **Orichi** Rus. Fed.
147 J2 **Orient** U.S.A.
154 E7 **Oriental, Cordillera** *mts* Bol.
157 B3 **Oriental, Cordillera** *mts* Col.
154 D6 **Oriental, Cordillera** *mts* Peru
159 E3 **Oriente** Arg.
111 F3 **Orihuela** Spain
117 E6 **Orikhiv** Ukr.
135 H3 **Orillia** Canada
103 N3 **Orimattila** Fin.
157 E2 **Orinoco** *r.* Col./Venez.
157 E2 **Orinoco Delta** Venez.
87 D1 **Orissa** *state* India
103 M4 **Orissaare** Estonia
114 C5 **Oristano** *Sardinia* Italy
103 N3 **Orivesi** Fin.
102 O3 **Orivesi** *l.* Fin.
155 G4 **Oriximiná** Brazil
151 E4 **Orizaba** Mex.
151 E4 **Orizaba, Pico de** *vol.* Mex.
102 J3 **Orkanger** Norway
103 K4 **Örkelljunga** Sweden
102 J3 **Orkla** *r.* Norway
125 G3 **Orkney** S. Africa
106 E1 **Orkney Islands** U.K.
143 C6 **Orla** U.S.A.
140 A2 **Orland** U.S.A.
158 C3 **Orlândia** Brazil
145 D6 **Orlando** U.S.A.
110 E3 **Orléans** France
147 I4 **Orleans** *MA* U.S.A.
147 G2 **Orleans** *VT* U.S.A.
116 I3 **Orlov** Rus. Fed.
116 F4 **Orlovskaya Oblast'** *admin. div.* Rus. Fed.
117 G6 **Orlovskiy** Rus. Fed.
85 G5 **Ormara** Pak.
85 G5 **Ormara, Ras** *hd* Pak.
97 C4 **Ormoc** Phil.
145 D6 **Ormond Beach** U.S.A.
104 E4 **Ormskirk** U.K.
147 G2 **Ormstown** Canada
110 D2 **Orne** *r.* France
102 K2 **Ørnes** Norway
102 L3 **Örnsköldsvik** Sweden
96 D4 **Oro** N. Korea
157 C3 **Orocué** Col.
120 B3 **Orodara** Burkina
138 C2 **Orofino** U.S.A.
139 F5 **Orogrande** U.S.A.
133 G4 **Oromocto** Canada
80 E6 **Oron** Israel
69 I2 **Orona** *atoll* Kiribati
147 I2 **Orono** U.S.A.
106 B4 **Oronsay** *i.* U.K.
97 B4 **Oroquieta** Phil.
155 K5 **Orós, Açude** *resr* Brazil
114 C4 **Orosei** *Sardinia* Italy
114 C4 **Orosei, Golfo di** *b.* *Sardinia* Italy
113 J7 **Orosháza** Hungary
141 G5 **Oro Valley** U.S.A.
140 B2 **Oroville** *CA* U.S.A.
138 C1 **Oroville** *WA* U.S.A.
140 B2 **Oroville, Lake** *resr* U.S.A.
70 C4 **Orroroo** Australia
103 K3 **Orsa** Sweden
116 D4 **Orsha** Belarus
82 D2 **Orsk** Rus. Fed.
103 I3 **Ørsta** Norway
111 C1 **Ortegal, Cabo** *c.* Spain
110 D5 **Orthez** France
111 C1 **Ortigueira** Spain
150 B1 **Ortiz** Mex.
157 D2 **Ortiz** Venez.
114 D1 **Ortles** *mt.* Italy
104 E3 **Orton** U.K.
114 F3 **Ortona** Italy
142 D2 **Ortonville** U.S.A.
77 N3 **Orulgan, Khrebet** *mts* Rus. Fed.
124 B1 **Orumbo** Namibia
Orūmīyeh Iran *see* **Urmia**
Orūmīyeh, Daryācheh-ye *salt l.* Iran *see* **Urmia, Lake**
154 E7 **Oruro** Bol.
114 E3 **Orvieto** Italy
146 C4 **Orwell** *OH* U.S.A.
147 G3 **Orwell** *VT* U.S.A.
103 J3 **Os** Norway
150 I6 **Osa, Península de** Costa Rica
134 A4 **Osage** U.S.A.
142 E4 **Osage** *r.* U.S.A.
95 D7 **Ōsaka** Japan
83 H2 **Osakarovka** Kazakh.
103 K4 **Osby** Sweden
143 F5 **Osceola** *AR* U.S.A.
142 E3 **Osceola** *IA* U.S.A.
109 I3 **Oschatz** Germany
109 J2 **Oschersleben (Bode)** Germany
114 C4 **Oschiri** *Sardinia* Italy
135 F3 **Oscoda** U.S.A.
116 F4 **Osetr** *r.* Rus. Fed.
95 A8 **Ōse-zaki** *pt* Japan
135 J3 **Osgoode** Canada
83 H4 **Osh** Kyrg.
123 B5 **Oshakati** Namibia
94 G3 **Oshamambe** Japan
135 H4 **Oshawa** Canada
94 G5 **Oshika-hantō** *pen.* Japan
94 F4 **Ō-shima** *i.* Japan
95 F7 **Ō-shima** *i.* Japan
142 C3 **Oshkosh** *NE* U.S.A.
134 C3 **Oshkosh** *WI* U.S.A.
84 B2 **Oshnovīyeh** Iran
120 C4 **Oshogbo** Nigeria
81 L5 **Oshtorān Kūh** *mt.* Iran
81 L5 **Oshtorīnān** Iran
122 B4 **Oshwe** Dem. Rep. Congo
115 H2 **Osijek** Croatia
114 E3 **Osimo** Italy
88 C4 **Osiyan** India
125 I3 **Osizweni** S. Africa
114 G2 **Osječenica** *mts* Bos.-Herz.
102 K3 **Ösjön** *l.* Sweden
142 E3 **Oskaloosa** U.S.A.
103 L4 **Oskarshamn** Sweden
135 J1 **Oskélanéo** Canada
117 F5 **Oskol** *r.* Rus. Fed.
103 J4 **Oslo** Norway
97 B4 **Oslob** Phil.
103 J4 **Oslofjorden** *sea chan.* Norway
87 B2 **Osmanabad** India
80 E1 **Osmancık** Turkey
80 B1 **Osmaneli** Turkey
80 F3 **Osmaniye** Turkey
103 O4 **Os'mino** Rus. Fed.
109 G2 **Osnabrück** Germany
115 J3 **Osogovska Planina** *mts* Bulg./Macedonia
159 B4 **Osorno** Chile
111 D1 **Osorno** Spain
159 B4 **Osorno, Volcán** *vol.* Chile
130 F5 **Osoyoos** Canada
103 I3 **Osøyri** Norway
68 E3 **Osprey Reef** Coral Sea Is Terr.
108 D3 **Oss** Neth.
71 G8 **Ossa, Mount** Australia
134 B3 **Osseo** U.S.A.
135 F3 **Ossineke** U.S.A.
147 H3 **Ossipee Lake** U.S.A.
109 J3 **Oßmannstedt** Germany
133 H3 **Ossokmanuan Lake** Canada
116 E3 **Ostashkov** Rus. Fed.
109 F2 **Ostbevern** Germany
109 H1 **Oste** *r.* Germany
108 A3 **Ostend** Belgium
113 O5 **Oster** Ukr.
109 J2 **Osterburg (Altmark)** Germany
103 K4 **Österbymo** Sweden
103 K3 **Österdalälven** *l.* Sweden
103 J3 **Østerdalen** *val.* Norway
109 J3 **Osterfeld** Germany
109 G1 **Osterholz-Scharmbeck** Germany
109 I3 **Osterode am Harz** Germany
102 K3 **Östersund** Sweden
109 I3 **Osterwieck** Germany
108 F1 **Ostfriesland** *reg.* Germany
103 L3 **Östhammar** Sweden
112 I6 **Ostrava** Czech Rep.
113 I4 **Ostróda** Poland
117 F5 **Ostrogozhsk** Rus. Fed.
109 K4 **Ostrov** Czech Rep.
116 D3 **Ostrov** Rus. Fed.
113 J5 **Ostrowiec Świętokrzyski** Poland
113 J4 **Ostrów Mazowiecka** Poland
112 H5 **Ostrów Wielkopolski** Poland
115 K3 **Osŭm** *r.* Bulg.
95 B9 **Ōsumi-kaikyō** *sea chan.* Japan
95 B9 **Ōsumi-shotō** *is* Japan
111 D4 **Osuna** Spain
147 F2 **Oswegatchie** U.S.A.
134 C5 **Oswego** *IL* U.S.A.
146 E3 **Oswego** *NY* U.S.A.
147 E3 **Oswego** *r.* U.S.A.
105 D5 **Oswestry** U.K.
95 F6 **Ōta** Japan
72 C6 **Otago Peninsula** N.Z.
72 E4 **Otaki** N.Z.
102 N2 **Otanmäki** Fin.
83 H4 **Otar** Kazakh.
157 B4 **Otare, Cerro** *h.* Col.
94 G3 **Otaru** Japan
72 B7 **Otatara** N.Z.
154 C3 **Otavalo** Ecuador
123 B5 **Otavi** Namibia
95 G6 **Ōtawara** Japan
83 I4 **Otegen Batyr** Kazakh.
72 C6 **Otematata** N.Z.
103 N4 **Otepää** Estonia
138 C2 **Othello** U.S.A.
150 C2 **Otinapa** Mex.
72 C5 **Otira** N.Z.
147 E3 **Otisco Lake** U.S.A.
133 F3 **Otish, Monts** *hills* Canada

200 Pee Dee

145 E5 Pee Dee r. U.S.A.
147 G4 Peekskill U.S.A.
71 I3 Peel r. Australia
128 E3 Peel r. Canada
104 C3 Peel U.K.
108 D3 Peer Belgium
130 F4 Peers Canada
70 E3 Peery Lake salt l. Australia
72 D5 Pegasus Bay N.Z.
109 J5 Pegnitz Germany
109 J5 Pegnitz r. Germany
91 B5 Pegu Myanmar
116 I2 Pegysh Rus. Fed.
159 E2 Pehuajó Arg.
93 F6 Peikang Taiwan
109 I2 Peine Germany
103 N4 Peipus, Lake Estonia/Rus. Fed.
109 J3 Peißen Germany
92 E3 Peitun China
155 I6 Peixe Brazil
158 B1 Peixe r. Goiás Brazil
158 B3 Peixe r. São Paulo Brazil
92 E3 Peixian China
158 A2 Peixo de Couro r. Brazil
125 G4 Peka Lesotho
99 C4 Pekalongan Indon.
98 B5 Pekan Malaysia
99 B2 Pekanbaru Indon.
134 C5 Pekin U.S.A.
Pelabuhan Kelang Malaysia see Pelabuhan Klang
98 B5 Pelabuhan Klang Malaysia
135 F5 Pelee Island Canada
135 F5 Pelee Point Canada
91 E7 Peleng i. Indon.
116 I2 Peles Rus. Fed.
134 A1 Pelican Lake MN U.S.A.
134 C3 Pelican Lake WI U.S.A.
131 I3 Pelican Narrows Canada
102 N2 Pelkosenniemi Fin.
124 C4 Pella S. Africa
131 H1 Pellatt Lake Canada
68 E2 Pelleluhu Islands P.N.G.
134 C4 Pell Lake U.S.A.
102 M2 Pello Fin.
130 B2 Pelly r. Canada
Pelly Bay Canada see Kugaaruk
130 B2 Pelly Crossing Canada
131 I1 Pelly Lake Canada
130 C2 Pelly Mountains Canada
159 G1 Pelotas Brazil
156 F3 Pelotas, Rio das r. Brazil
80 D6 Pelusium tourist site Egypt
110 H4 Pelvoux, Massif du mts France
147 I2 Pemadumcook Lake U.S.A.
99 C4 Pemalang Indon.
99 C2 Pemangkat Indon.
99 A2 Pematangsiantar Indon.
123 E5 Pemba Moz.
123 C5 Pemba Zambia
122 D4 Pemba Island Tanz.
130 F4 Pembina r. Canada
142 D1 Pembina U.S.A.
135 I3 Pembroke Canada
105 C6 Pembroke U.K.
147 J2 Pembroke U.S.A.
105 B5 Pembrokeshire Coast National Park U.K.
87 A2 Pen India
89 H5 Pen r. Myanmar
111 E2 Peñalara mt. Spain
151 E3 Peñamiller Mex.
151 E3 Peña Nevada, Cerro mt. Mex.
158 B3 Penápolis Brazil
111 D1 Peña Prieta mt. Spain
111 D2 Peñaranda de Bracamonte Spain
70 E5 Penarie Australia
111 F2 Peñarroya mt. Spain
111 D3 Peñarroya-Pueblonuevo Spain
105 D6 Penarth U.K.
111 D1 Peñas, Cabo de c. Spain
156 A7 Penas, Golfo de g. Chile
157 E2 Peñas, Punta pt Venez.
150 H6 Peñas Blancas Nicaragua
111 D1 Peña Ubiña mt. Spain
88 D5 Pench r. India
73 D6 Penck, Cape c. Antarctica
104 E4 Pendle Hill U.K.
138 C2 Pendleton U.S.A.
130 D4 Pendleton Bay Canada
138 C1 Pend Oreille r. U.S.A.
138 C2 Pend Oreille Lake U.S.A.
87 C1 Pendra India
135 H3 Penetanguishene Canada
92 C4 Peng'an China
88 D6 Penganga r. India
93 □ Peng Chau i. Hong Kong China
93 G5 P'enghu Ch'ün-tao i. Taiwan
122 C4 Penge Dem. Rep. Congo
125 I2 Penge S. Africa
93 F6 P'enghu Ch'üntao is Taiwan
93 F6 P'enghu Tao i. Taiwan
98 □ Peng Kang h. Sing.
92 F2 Penglai China
93 B4 Pengshan China
93 C4 Pengshui China
93 B4 Pengxi China
93 E4 Pengze China
125 G5 Penhoek Pass S. Africa
111 B3 Peniche Port.
106 E5 Penicuik U.K.
109 K4 Penig Germany
116 E2 Peninga Rus. Fed.
99 B2 Peninsular Malaysia Malaysia
81 J4 Penjwin Iraq
114 E3 Penne Italy
87 B3 Penner r. India
70 B5 Penneshaw Australia
104 E3 Pennines hills U.K.
125 I5 Pennington S. Africa
147 F5 Pennsville U.S.A.
146 D4 Pennsylvania state U.S.A.
146 E3 Penn Yan U.S.A.
129 L3 Penny Icecap Canada
147 I2 Penobscot r. U.S.A.
147 I2 Penobscot Bay U.S.A.
70 D6 Penola Australia
150 C2 Peñón Blanco Mex.
68 D5 Penong Australia
150 I6 Penonomé Panama
67 I4 Penrhyn atoll Cook Is
161 I6 Penrhyn Basin sea feature Pacific Ocean
104 E3 Penrith U.K.
145 C6 Pensacola U.S.A.
73 C4 Pensacola Mountains Antarctica
81 L2 Pensär Azer.
70 E6 Penshurst Australia
88 D2 Pensi La pass India
69 G3 Pentecost Island Vanuatu
130 F5 Penticton Canada
105 B7 Pentire Point U.K.
106 E2 Pentland Firth sea chan. U.K.
106 E5 Pentland Hills U.K.
134 D4 Pentwater U.S.A.
87 B3 Penukonda India
105 D5 Penygadair h. U.K.
104 E3 Pen-y-Ghent h. U.K.
131 H2 Penylan Lake Canada
116 H4 Penza Rus. Fed.
105 B7 Penzance U.K.
116 H4 Penzenskaya Oblast' admin. div. Rus. Fed.
77 R3 Penzhinskaya Guba b. Rus. Fed.
141 F5 Peoria AZ U.S.A.
134 C5 Peoria IL U.S.A.
98 B4 Perai Malaysia
98 A4 Perak i. Malaysia
98 B4 Perak r. Malaysia
111 F2 Perales del Alfambra Spain
87 B4 Perambalur India
133 H4 Percé Canada
147 H2 Percy U.S.A.
68 F4 Percy Isles Australia
135 I3 Percy Reach l. Canada
111 G1 Perdido, Monte mt. Spain
76 H3 Peregrebnoye Rus. Fed.
157 B3 Pereira Col.
158 B3 Pereira Barreto Brazil
116 D3 Perekhoda r. Rus. Fed.
117 G5 Perelazovskiy Rus. Fed.
82 B2 Perelyub Rus. Fed.
134 D4 Pere Marquette r. U.S.A.
82 B2 Peremetnoye Kazakh.
113 L6 Peremyshlyany Ukr.
116 F3 Pereslavl'-Zalesskiy Rus. Fed.
82 C2 Perevolotskiy Rus. Fed.
116 H4 Perevoz Rus. Fed.
117 D5 Pereyaslav-Khmel'nyts'kyy Ukr.
159 E2 Pergamino Arg.
98 B4 Perhentian Besar, Pulau i. Malaysia
102 N3 Perho Fin.
Péribonca, Lac l. Canada see Péribonka, Lac
133 F3 Péribonka, Lac l. Canada
156 C2 Perico Arg.
150 C2 Pericos Mex.
110 E4 Périgueux France
157 B2 Perijá, Parque Nacional nat. park Venez.
157 B2 Perija, Sierra de mts Venez.
156 B7 Perito Moreno Arg.
134 D3 Perkins U.S.A.
150 I5 Perlas, Laguna de lag. Nicaragua
150 I5 Perlas, Punta de pt Nicaragua
109 J1 Perleberg Germany
76 G4 Perm' Rus. Fed.
116 H3 Permas Rus. Fed.
Pernambuco Abyssal Plain sea feature S. Atlantic Ocean see Pernambuco Plain
163 H6 Pernambuco Plain sea feature S. Atlantic Ocean
70 B3 Pernatty Lagoon salt flat Australia
115 J3 Pernik Bulg.
110 F2 Péronne France
151 E4 Perote Mex.
110 F5 Perpignan France
105 B7 Perranporth U.K.
140 D5 Perris U.S.A.
110 C2 Perros-Guirec France
145 D6 Perry FL U.S.A.
145 D5 Perry GA U.S.A.
142 E3 Perry IA U.S.A.
143 D4 Perry OK U.S.A.
146 B4 Perrysburg U.S.A.
143 C4 Perryton U.S.A.
143 F4 Perryville U.S.A.
84 D4 Persepolis tourist site Iran
105 E5 Pershore U.K.
Persian Gulf g. Asia see The Gulf
81 G2 Pertek Turkey
68 B5 Perth Australia
135 I3 Perth Canada
106 E4 Perth U.K.
147 F4 Perth Amboy U.S.A.
147 J1 Perth-Andover Canada
162 L6 Perth Basin sea feature Indian Ocean
116 F1 Pertominsk Rus. Fed.
110 G5 Pertuis France
103 N3 Pertunmaa Fin.
114 C4 Pertusato, Capo c. Corsica France
154 C5 Peru country S. America
134 C5 Peru U.S.A.
161 M7 Peru Basin sea feature S. Pacific Ocean
161 N6 Peru-Chile Trench sea feature S. Pacific Ocean
114 E3 Perugia Italy
158 C4 Peruibe Brazil
108 B4 Péruwelz Belgium
116 G4 Pervomaysk Rus. Fed.
117 D5 Pervomays'k Ukr.
116 J2 Pervomayskaya Rus. Fed.
117 E6 Pervomays'ke Ukr.
83 J2 Pervomayskiy Kazakh.
82 C2 Pervomayskiy Orenburgskaya Oblast' Rus. Fed.
116 G4 Pervomayskiy Tambovskaya Oblast' Rus. Fed.
117 F5 Pervomays'kyy Ukr.
77 R3 Pervorechenskiy Rus. Fed.
114 E3 Pesaro Italy
140 A3 Pescadero U.S.A.
141 H4 Pescado U.S.A.
114 F3 Pescara Italy
114 F3 Pescara r. Italy
117 G6 Peschanokopskoye Rus. Fed.
82 B4 Peschanyy, Mys pt Kazakh.
98 □ Pesek, Pulau i. Sing.
88 B2 Peshawar Pak.
115 I4 Peshkopi Albania
115 K3 Peshtera Bulg.
134 D3 Peshtigo U.S.A.
134 C3 Peshtigo r. U.S.A.
83 F1 Peski Kazakh.
82 E5 Peski Turkm.
114 F1 Pesnica Slovenia
110 D4 Pessac France
109 K2 Pessin Germany
116 E3 Pestovo Rus. Fed.
116 G3 Pet r. Rus. Fed.
150 D4 Petacalco, Bahía de b. Mex.
80 E5 Petah Tiqwa Israel
103 N3 Petäjävesi Fin.
115 K5 Petalioi i. Greece
140 A2 Petaluma U.S.A.
108 D5 Pétange Lux.
99 E3 Petangis Indon.
157 D2 Petare Venez.
150 D4 Petatlán Mex.
123 D5 Petauke Zambia
135 I3 Petawawa Canada
151 G4 Petén Itzá, Lago l. Guat.
134 C3 Petenwell Lake U.S.A.
70 C4 Peterborough S.A. Australia
70 E7 Peterborough Vic. Australia
135 H3 Peterborough Canada
105 G5 Peterborough U.K.
106 F3 Peterculter U.K.
106 G3 Peterhead U.K.
73 B3 Peter I Island i. Antarctica
131 K2 Peter Lake Canada
104 F3 Peterlee U.K.
68 C4 Petermann Ranges mts Australia
159 B2 Peteroa, Volcán vol. Chile
131 H3 Peter Pond Lake Canada
133 F2 Peters, Lac l. Canada
109 H4 Petersberg Germany
130 C3 Petersburg AK U.S.A.
134 C6 Petersburg IL U.S.A.
146 E6 Petersburg VA U.S.A.
146 D5 Petersburg WV U.S.A.
105 G6 Petersfield U.K.
109 G2 Petershagen Germany
114 G5 Petilia Policastro Italy
147 J2 Petit Manan Point U.S.A.
133 H3 Petit Mécatina r. Canada
133 I3 Petit Mécatina r. Canada
130 E3 Petitot r. Canada
151 E4 Petlalcingo Mex.
151 G3 Peto Mex.
134 E3 Petoskey U.S.A.
80 E6 Petra tourist site Jordan
90 F2 Petra Velikogo, Zaliv b. Rus. Fed.
135 I4 Petre, Point Canada
115 J4 Petrich Bulg.
141 H4 Petrified Forest National Park U.S.A.
114 G2 Petrinja Croatia
115 J3 Petrokhanski Prokhod pass Bulg.
135 F4 Petrolia Canada
155 J5 Petrolina Brazil
83 J3 Petropavlovka Kazakh.
117 G5 Petropavlovka Rus. Fed.
83 G1 Petropavlovsk Kazakh.
90 H1 Petropavlovsk-Kamchatskiy Rus. Fed.
115 J2 Petroșani Romania
83 G1 Petrovka Kazakh.
82 B1 Petrovka Rus. Fed.
117 H4 Petrovsk Rus. Fed.
90 C1 Petrovsk-Zabaykal'skiy Rus. Fed.
117 H5 Petrov Val Rus. Fed.
116 E2 Petrozavodsk Rus. Fed.
125 H3 Petrus Steyn S. Africa
124 F5 Petrusville S. Africa
108 C2 Petten Neth.
107 D3 Pettigo U.K.
76 H4 Petukhovo Rus. Fed.
98 A4 Peureula Indon.
77 S3 Pevek Rus. Fed.
112 H6 Pezinok Slovakia
109 F5 Pfälzer Wald hills Germany
109 G6 Pforzheim Germany
112 D7 Pfullendorf Germany
109 G5 Pfungstadt Germany
125 H2 Phagameng Northern S. Africa
88 C3 Phagwara India
125 G4 Phahameng Free State S. Africa
Phahameng S. Africa see Phagameng
125 I1 Phalaborwa S. Africa
88 C4 Phalodi India
88 B4 Phalsund India
87 A2 Phaltan India
98 A1 Phan Thai.
98 B2 Phanat Nikhom Thai.
98 B3 Phangan, Ko i. Thai.
98 B1 Phang Hoei, San Khao mts Thai.
98 A3 Phangnga Thai.
93 B6 Phăng Xi Păng mt. Vietnam
98 C2 Phanom Dong Rak, Thiu Khao mts Cambodia/Thai.
Phan Rang Vietnam see Phan Rang-Thap Cham
98 D3 Phan Rang-Thap Cham Vietnam
Phan Ri Vietnam see Phan Ri Cua
98 D3 Phan Ri Cua Vietnam
98 D3 Phan Thiêt Vietnam
143 D7 Pharr U.S.A.
93 C6 Phat Diêm Vietnam
98 B4 Phatthalung Thai.
98 A1 Phayao Thai.
89 H4 Phek India
131 I3 Phelps Lake Canada
98 B1 Phen Thai.
145 C5 Phenix City U.S.A.
98 A2 Phet Buri Thai.
98 B1 Phetchabun Thai.
98 C1 Phiafai Laos
98 B1 Phichai Thai.
98 B1 Phichit Thai.
143 F5 Philadelphia MS U.S.A.
147 F2 Philadelphia NY U.S.A.
147 F5 Philadelphia PA U.S.A.
142 C2 Philip U.S.A.
108 C4 Philippeville Belgium
146 C5 Philippi U.S.A.
108 B3 Philippine Neth.
160 D4 Philippine Basin sea feature N. Pacific Ocean
97 Philippines country Asia
97 C2 Philippine Sea Phil.
160 D4 Philippine Trench sea feature N. Pacific Ocean
125 F5 Philippolis S. Africa
109 G5 Philippsburg Germany
146 D4 Philipsburg U.S.A.
125 G4 Philipsdam barrage Neth.
128 D3 Philip Smith Mountains U.S.A.
124 F5 Philipstown S. Africa
70 F7 Phillip Island Australia
147 H2 Phillips ME U.S.A.
134 B3 Phillips WI U.S.A.
142 D4 Phillipsburg KS U.S.A.
147 F4 Phillipsburg NJ U.S.A.
129 I1 Phillips Inlet Canada
146 D4 Phillipston U.S.A.
147 G3 Philmont U.S.A.
131 G3 Philomena Canada
146 C6 Philpott Reservoir U.S.A.
98 B2 Phimae tourist site Thai.
98 C2 Phimun Mangsahan Thai.
125 G3 Phiritona S. Africa
98 B1 Phitsanulok Thai.
98 C3 Phnom Penh Cambodia
Phnom Penh Cambodia see Phnom Penh
98 B4 Pho, Laem pt Thai.
141 F5 Phoenix U.S.A.
69 I2 Phoenix Islands Pacific Ocean
125 G3 Phomolong S. Africa
98 B2 Phon Thai.
91 C4 Phôngsali Laos
93 B6 Phong Thô Vietnam
98 B1 Phon Phisai Thai.
98 B1 Phon Thong Thai.
70 E7 Phoques Bay Australia
98 B2 Phrae Thai.
98 A1 Phrao Thai.
98 B2 Phra Phutthabat Thai.
98 A3 Phra Thong, Ko i. Thai.
98 C1 Phu Bai Vietnam
93 B6 Phuc Yên Vietnam
Phu Hôi Vietnam see Van Gia
98 A4 Phuket Thai.
98 A4 Phuket, Ko i. Thai.
88 C4 Phulera India
89 G5 Phultala Bangl.
93 B6 Phu Ly Vietnam
98 B2 Phumĭ Bânhchok Kon Cambodia
98 C3 Phumĭ Chhuk Cambodia
98 C2 Phumĭ Kâmpóng Trâlach Cambodia
98 B3 Phumĭ Kaôh Kŏng Cambodia
98 B2 Phumĭ Kiliêk Cambodia
98 C2 Phumĭ Mlu Prey Cambodia
98 B2 Phumĭ Moŭng Cambodia
98 B2 Phumĭ Prâmaôy Cambodia
98 B2 Phumĭ Sâmraông Cambodia
98 C2 Phumĭ Toêng Cambodia
98 D2 Phu My Vietnam
Phu Nhơn Vietnam see Chu Sê
98 C3 Phước Hai Vietnam
98 C3 Phước Long Vietnam
Phu Quôc Vietnam see Dương Đông
98 B3 Phu Quôc, Đao i. Vietnam
98 D3 Phu Quy, Đao i. Vietnam
125 H4 Phuthaditjhaba S. Africa
93 B6 Phu Tho Vietnam
98 B1 Phu Wiang Thai.
155 I5 Piaca Brazil
114 C2 Piacenza Italy
71 H3 Pian r. Australia
92 D3 Pianguan China
114 D3 Pianosa, Isola i. Italy
113 M7 Piatra Neamț Romania
155 J5 Piauí r. Brazil
114 E1 Piave r. Italy
121 F4 Pibor r. Sudan
121 F4 Pibor Post Sudan
134 D1 Pic r. Canada
141 F4 Pica U.S.A.
141 G5 Picacho AZ U.S.A.
140 D5 Picacho CA U.S.A.
110 F2 Picardy reg. France
145 B6 Picayune U.S.A.
150 C1 Picháchic Mex.
156 D2 Pichanal Arg.
159 C2 Pichi Ciego Arg.
159 B2 Pichilemu Chile
150 B2 Pichilingue Mex.
159 D3 Pichi Mahuida Arg.
88 D4 Pichor India
151 F4 Pichucalco Mex.
134 D1 Pic Island Canada
130 E4 Pickering U.K.
104 G3 Pickering, Vale of val. U.K.
134 E2 Pickford U.S.A.
132 B3 Pickle Lake Canada
120 □ Pico i. Azores
150 H5 Pico Bonito, Parque Nacional nat. park Hond.
157 D4 Pico da Neblina, Parque Nacional do nat. park Brazil
151 E4 Pico de Orizaba, Parque Nacional nat. park Mex.
155 J5 Picos Brazil
156 C7 Pico Truncado Arg.
134 D1 Pic River Canada
71 I5 Picton Australia
135 I4 Picton Canada
71 G9 Picton, Mount Australia
133 H4 Pictou Canada
134 D2 Pictured Rocks National Lakeshore nature res. U.S.A.
159 C3 Picún Leufú r. Arg.
85 F5 Pidarak Pak.
87 C5 Pidurutalagala mt. Sri Lanka
157 B3 Piedecuesta Col.
159 C1 Pie de Palo, Sierra mts Arg.
145 C5 Piedmont U.S.A.
146 C4 Piedmont Lake U.S.A.
159 F2 Piedras, Punta pt Arg.
150 D1 Piedras Negras Coahuila Mex.
151 E4 Piedras Negras Veracruz Mex.
134 C1 Pie Island Canada
102 N3 Pieksämäki Fin.
102 N3 Pielavesi Fin.
102 O3 Pielinen l. Fin.
125 H1 Pienaarsrivier S. Africa
134 E5 Pierceton U.S.A.
140 A2 Piercy U.S.A.
115 J4 Pieria mts Greece
106 F1 Pierowall U.K.
142 C2 Pierre U.S.A.
110 G4 Pierrelatte France
125 I4 Pietermaritzburg S. Africa
Pietersburg S. Africa see Polokwane
114 G5 Pietra Spada, Passo di pass Italy
125 I3 Piet Retief S. Africa
113 L7 Pietrosa mt. Romania
135 F4 Pigeon U.S.A.
135 F5 Pigeon Bay Canada
146 D6 Pigg r. U.S.A.
143 F4 Piggott U.S.A.
125 I2 Pigg's Peak Swaziland
159 D3 Pigüé Arg.
151 E3 Piguicas mt. Mex.
88 E4 Pihani India
92 E3 Pi He r. China
103 O3 Pihlajavesi l. Fin.
103 M3 Pihlava Fin.
102 N3 Pihtipudas Fin.
102 N2 Piippola Fin.
102 O2 Piispajärvi Fin.
151 F5 Pijijiapan Mex.
116 E3 Pikalevo Rus. Fed.
146 D3 Pike U.S.A.
135 G3 Pike Bay Canada
66 E2 Pikelot i. Micronesia
136 F4 Pikes Peak U.S.A.
124 C6 Piketberg S. Africa
146 B6 Pikeville U.S.A.
96 B4 Pikou China
159 E3 Pila Arg.
112 H4 Piła Poland
125 G2 Pilanesberg National Park S. Africa
159 E2 Pilar Arg.
156 E3 Pilar Para.
97 B5 Pilas i. Phil.
159 B4 Pilcaniyeu Arg.
156 E2 Pilcomayo r. Bol./Para.
97 B3 Pili Phil.
88 D3 Pilibhit India
71 H9 Pillar, Cape Australia
93 □ Pillar Pt Hong Kong China
71 H3 Pilliga Australia
159 E2 Pillo, Isla del i. Arg.
158 C2 Pilões, Serra dos mts Brazil
71 H6 Pilot, The mt. Australia
140 D2 Pilot Peak U.S.A.
143 F6 Pilottown U.S.A.
103 M4 Piltene Latvia
154 F6 Pimenta Bueno Brazil
88 C5 Pimpalner India
88 D4 Pin r. India
141 F6 Pinacate, Cerro del mt. Mex.
88 D4 Pinahat India
141 G5 Pinaleno Mountains U.S.A.
97 B3 Pinamalayan Phil.
159 F3 Pinamar Arg.
99 B1 Pinang i. Malaysia
80 F2 Pınarbaşı Turkey
149 H4 Pinar del Río Cuba
117 C7 Pinarhisar Turkey
97 B3 Pinatubo, Mount vol. Phil.
113 J5 Pińczów Poland
88 D3 Pindar r. India
155 I4 Pindaré r. Brazil
88 C2 Pindi Gheb Pak.
Pindos mts Greece see Pindus Mountains
89 E3 Pindu Pass China
115 I5 Pindus Mountains Greece
141 G4 Pine U.S.A.
134 E3 Pine r. MI U.S.A.
134 E4 Pine r. MI U.S.A.
134 C3 Pine r. WI U.S.A.
133 J4 Pine, Cape Canada
143 E5 Pine Bluff U.S.A.
138 F3 Pine Bluffs U.S.A.
134 A3 Pine City U.S.A.
68 D3 Pine Creek Australia
146 E4 Pine Creek r. U.S.A.
140 B2 Pinecrest U.S.A.
140 C3 Pinedale CA U.S.A.
138 E3 Pinedale WY U.S.A.
131 J4 Pine Falls Canada
140 C3 Pine Flat Lake U.S.A.
116 G1 Pinega Rus. Fed.
116 G1 Pinega r. Rus. Fed.
147 E4 Pine Grove U.S.A.
145 D6 Pine Hills U.S.A.
131 H3 Pinehouse Lake Canada
134 A3 Pine Island U.S.A.
73 B3 Pine Island Bay b. Antarctica
147 F3 Pine Lake U.S.A.
143 E6 Pineland U.S.A.
140 B4 Pine Mountain U.S.A.
141 F4 Pine Peak U.S.A.
130 G2 Pine Point Canada
140 C3 Pineridge U.S.A.
142 C3 Pine Ridge U.S.A.
114 B2 Pinerolo Italy
143 E6 Pines, Lake o' the U.S.A.
125 I5 Pinetown S. Africa
146 B6 Pineville KY U.S.A.
143 E6 Pineville LA U.S.A.
146 C6 Pineville WV U.S.A.
98 B2 Ping, Mae Nam r. Thai.
92 B2 Ping'an China
93 B6 Pingbian China
92 F3 Ping Dao i. China
92 D3 Pingding China
92 D2 Pingdingshan China
92 F2 Pingdu China
96 C2 Pinggang China
93 C6 Pingguo China
93 E5 Pinghe China
93 D4 Pingjiang China
93 D5 Pingle China
93 C5 Pingli China
92 C3 Pingliang China
92 D2 Pinglu China
92 C2 Pingluo China
93 F5 Pingnan Fujian China
93 D6 Pingnan Guangxi China
92 E3 Pingqiao China
92 F1 Pingquan China
92 E2 Pingshan China
93 D5 Pingshi China
93 F5 Pingtan China
93 C5 Pingtang China
93 F6 P'ingtung Taiwan
92 B3 Pingwu China
93 C6 Pingxiang Guangxi China
93 D5 Pingxiang Jiangxi China
93 F5 Pingyang China
92 D2 Pingyao China
92 E3 Pingyi China
92 E2 Pingyin China
92 E3 Pingyu China
93 E5 Pingyuan China
93 B6 Pingyuanjie China
93 □ Ping Yuen Ho r. Hong Kong China
93 C5 Pingzhai China
155 I4 Pinheiro Brazil
159 G1 Pinheiro Machado Brazil
105 D7 Pinhoe U.K.
99 A2 Pini i. Indon.
130 E3 Pink Mountain Canada
72 D4 Pinnacle mt. N.Z.
70 D5 Pinnaroo Australia
109 H1 Pinneberg Germany
140 C4 Pinos, Mount U.S.A.
151 E4 Pinotepa Nacional Mex.
69 G4 Pins, Île des i. New Caledonia
135 G4 Pins, Pointe aux pt Canada
117 C4 Pinsk Belarus
154 □ Pinta, Isla i. Galapagos Is Ecuador
141 F5 Pinta, Sierra h. U.S.A.
141 F3 Pintura U.S.A.
141 E3 Pioche U.S.A.
123 C4 Piodi Dem. Rep. Congo
76 J1 Pioner, Ostrov i. Rus. Fed.
113 J3 Pionerskiy Rus. Fed.
113 J5 Pionki Poland
72 E3 Piopio N.Z.
154 F4 Piorini, Lago l. Brazil
113 I5 Piotrków Trybunalski Poland
85 F5 Pip Iran
96 E2 Pipa Dingzi mt. China
88 C4 Pipar India
88 D5 Piparia India
115 K5 Piperi i. Greece
140 D3 Piper Peak U.S.A.
141 F3 Pipe Spring National Monument nat. park U.S.A.
132 B3 Pipestone r. Canada
142 D3 Pipestone U.S.A.
72 E3 Pipiriki N.Z.
88 C3 Pipli India
133 F4 Pipmuacan, Réservoir resr Canada
89 E4 Pipra Dam India
83 J4 Piqanlik China
146 A4 Piqua U.S.A.
158 A2 Piquiri r. Mato Grosso do Sul Brazil
158 B4 Piquiri r. Paraná Brazil
158 C2 Piracanjuba Brazil
158 C3 Piracicaba Brazil
158 D2 Piracicaba r. Minas Gerais Brazil
158 C3 Piracicaba r. São Paulo Brazil
158 C3 Piraçununga Brazil
155 J4 Piracuruca Brazil
115 J6 Piraeus Greece
158 C4 Piraí do Sul Brazil
158 C3 Piraju Brazil
88 C5 Piram Island India
158 B2 Piranhas Brazil
158 B2 Piranhas r. Goiás Brazil
155 K5 Piranhas r. Brazil
157 C4 Piraparaná r. Col.
158 C3 Pirapó r. Brazil
158 D2 Pirapora Brazil
159 G1 Piratini Brazil
159 G1 Piratini r. Brazil
88 D4 Pirawa India
159 C4 Pire Mahuida, Sierra mts Arg.
158 C2 Pires do Rio Brazil
89 G4 Pirganj Bangl.
155 J4 Piripiri Brazil
157 C2 Piritu Venez.
158 A2 Pirizal Brazil
108 F5 Pirmasens Germany
115 J3 Pirot Serb. and Mont.
88 C2 Pir Panjal Pass India
88 C2 Pir Panjal Range mts India/Pak.
157 A3 Pirre, Cerro mt. Panama
81 L2 Pirsaat Azer.
81 L1 Pirsaatçay r. Azer.
91 E7 Piru Indon.
114 D3 Pisa Italy
76 B6 Pisa, Mount N.Z.
156 B1 Pisagua Chile
147 F4 Piscataway U.S.A.
154 C6 Pisco Peru
154 C6 Pisco, Bahía de b. Peru
147 F3 Piseco Lake U.S.A.
112 G6 Písek Czech Rep.
83 I5 Pishan China
85 F5 Pīshīn Iran
88 A3 Pishin Pak.
85 G4 Pishin Lora r. Pak.
156 C3 Pissis, Cerro mt. Arg.
151 G3 Pisté Mex.
114 G4 Pisticci Italy
114 D3 Pistoia Italy
111 D1 Pisuerga r. Spain
138 B3 Pit r. U.S.A.
120 A3 Pita Guinea
133 G3 Pitaga Canada
151 G4 Pital Mex.
157 A4 Pitalito Col.
158 B4 Pitanga Brazil
158 D2 Pitangui Brazil
70 E5 Pitarpunga Lake imp. l. Australia
67 J7 Pitcairn Island S. Pacific Ocean
67 J7 Pitcairn Islands terr. Pacific Ocean
102 M2 Piteå Sweden
102 M2 Piteälven r. Sweden
117 H5 Piterka Rus. Fed.
115 K2 Pitești Romania
88 E5 Pithapuram India
139 D6 Pitiquito Mex.
116 D2 Pitkyaranta Rus. Fed.
106 E4 Pitlochry U.K.
151 H5 Pito Solo Hond.
159 B3 Pitrufquén Chile
125 F2 Pitsane Siding Botswana
106 F4 Pitscottie U.K.
130 D4 Pitt Island Canada
69 I6 Pitt Island Pacific Ocean
143 E4 Pittsburg U.S.A.
146 D4 Pittsburgh U.S.A.
134 B6 Pittsfield IL U.S.A.
147 G3 Pittsfield MA U.S.A.
147 I2 Pittsfield ME U.S.A.
147 H3 Pittsfield NH U.S.A.
147 G3 Pittsfield VT U.S.A.
71 I1 Pittsworth Australia
131 J2 Pitz Lake Canada
158 D3 Piumhi Brazil
154 B5 Piura Peru
140 C4 Piute Peak U.S.A.
89 E3 Piuthan Nepal
113 N6 Pivdennyy Buh r. Ukr.
114 F2 Pivka Slovenia
88 D1 Pixa China
151 G4 Pixoyal Mex.
112 E7 Piz Buin mt. Austria/Switz.
116 H3 Pizhma Rus. Fed.
116 H3 Pizhma r. Rus. Fed.
92 F3 Pizhou China
133 J4 Placentia Canada
133 J4 Placentia Bay Canada
97 B4 Placer Phil.
97 C4 Placer Phil.
140 B2 Placerville U.S.A.
149 I4 Placetas Cuba
98 B2 Plai Mat, Lam r. Thai.
147 H4 Plainfield CT U.S.A.
134 C5 Plainfield IL U.S.A.
134 C3 Plainfield WI U.S.A.
134 A3 Plainview MN U.S.A.
142 D3 Plainview NE U.S.A.
143 C5 Plainview TX U.S.A.
147 I1 Plaisted U.S.A.
135 J3 Plamondon Canada
99 E4 Plampang Indon.
109 K5 Planá Czech Rep.
140 B3 Planada U.S.A.
158 C1 Planaltina Brazil
159 B2 Planchón, Paso del pass Arg.
157 B2 Planeta Rica Col.
142 D3 Plankinton U.S.A.
134 C5 Plano IL U.S.A.
143 D5 Plano TX U.S.A.
145 D7 Plantation U.S.A.
143 F6 Plaquemine U.S.A.
111 C2 Plasencia Spain
82 E1 Plast Rus. Fed.
147 J1 Plaster Rock Canada
94 E2 Plastun Rus. Fed.
114 E6 Platani r. Sicily Italy
125 H4 Platberg mt. S. Africa
77 U4 Platinum U.S.A.
157 B2 Plato Col.
142 C3 Platte r. U.S.A.
134 B4 Platteville U.S.A.
109 K6 Plattling Germany
147 G2 Plattsburgh U.S.A.
142 E3 Plattsmouth U.S.A.
109 K1 Plau Germany
109 K4 Plauen Germany
109 K1 Plauer See l. Germany
116 F4 Plavsk Rus. Fed.
139 E6 Playa Noriega, Lago l. Mex.
154 B4 Playas Ecuador
131 J4 Playgreen Lake Canada
98 D2 Plây Ku Vietnam
150 B2 Playón Mex.
159 C3 Plaza Huincul Arg.
141 F5 Pleasant, Lake l. U.S.A.
147 I4 Pleasant Bay U.S.A.
141 G1 Pleasant Grove U.S.A.
141 H5 Pleasanton NM U.S.A.
143 D6 Pleasanton TX U.S.A.
72 C6 Pleasant Point N.Z.
141 H3 Pleasant View U.S.A.
147 F5 Pleasantville U.S.A.
144 C4 Pleasure Ridge Park U.S.A.
110 F4 Pleaux France
98 C2 Plei Doch Vietnam
98 C2 Plei Kân Vietnam
109 I5 Pleinfeld Germany
72 F2 Plenty, Bay of g. N.Z.
138 F1 Plentywood U.S.A.
116 G2 Plesetsk Rus. Fed.
133 F3 Plétipi, Lac l. Canada
108 F3 Plettenberg Germany
124 E7 Plettenberg Bay S. Africa
115 K3 Pleven Bulg.
115 H3 Pljevlja Serb. and Mont.
113 I4 Płock Poland
114 G3 Pločno mt. Bos.-Herz.
116 D2 Plodovoye Rus. Fed.
110 C3 Ploemeur France
115 L2 Ploiești Romania
113 O2 Ploskosh' Rus. Fed.
116 D3 Ploskoye Rus. Fed.
112 G4 Płoty Poland
110 C2 Ploudalmézeau France
110 B2 Plouzané France
115 K3 Plovdiv Bulg.
134 C3 Plover U.S.A.
134 C3 Plover r. U.S.A.
93 □ Plover Cove Reservoir Hong Kong China
147 G4 Plum Island U.S.A.
138 C2 Plummer U.S.A.
103 M5 Plungė Lith.
113 M3 Plyeshchanitsy Belarus
98 A1 Ply Huey Wati, Khao mt. Myanmar/Thai.
149 L5 Plymouth Montserrat
105 C7 Plymouth U.K.
140 B2 Plymouth CA U.S.A.
134 D5 Plymouth IN U.S.A.
147 H4 Plymouth MA U.S.A.
147 H3 Plymouth NH U.S.A.
144 F3 Plymouth PA U.S.A.
134 D4 Plymouth WI U.S.A.
147 H4 Plymouth Bay U.S.A.
105 D5 Plynlimon h. U.K.
112 F6 Plzeň Czech Rep.
120 B3 Pô Burkina
120 B3 Pô, Parc National de nat. park Burkina
163 P10 Pobeda Ice Island Antarctica
83 J4 Pobeda Peak China/Kyrg.
143 F4 Pocahontas U.S.A.
146 C5 Pocatalico r. U.S.A.
138 D3 Pocatello U.S.A.
117 C5 Pochayiv Ukr.
116 E4 Pochep Rus. Fed.
116 H4 Pochinki Rus. Fed.
116 E4 Pochinok Rus. Fed.
112 F6 Pocking Germany
104 G4 Pocklington U.K.
158 E1 Poções Brazil
147 F5 Pocomoke City U.S.A.
147 F6 Pocomoke Sound b. U.S.A.
158 A2 Poconé Brazil
147 F4 Pocono Mountains U.S.A.
147 F4 Pocono Summit U.S.A.
158 C3 Poços de Caldas Brazil
116 D3 Poddor'ye Rus. Fed.
117 F5 Podgorenskiy Rus. Fed.
115 H3 Podgorica Serb. and Mont.
76 J4 Podgornoye Rus. Fed.
87 B3 Podile India
77 K3 Podkamennaya Tunguska r. Rus. Fed.
82 A2 Podlesnoye Rus. Fed.
154 C4 Podocarpus, Parque Nacional nat. park Ecuador
116 F4 Podol'sk Rus. Fed.
116 E2 Podporozh'ye Rus. Fed.
114 G1 Podravina reg. Hungary
115 I3 Podujevo Serb. and Mont.
116 H2 Podvoloch'ye Rus. Fed.
116 I2 Podz' Rus. Fed.
124 C4 Pofadder S. Africa
135 G2 Pogamasing Canada
114 E4 Pogar Rus. Fed.
114 D3 Poggibonsi Italy
115 I4 Pogradec Albania
94 B2 Pogranichnyy Rus. Fed.
158 A2 Poguba r. Brazil
96 E5 P'ohang S. Korea
67 F2 Pohnpei atoll Micronesia
117 D5 Pohrebyshche Ukr.
88 D4 Pohri India
115 K2 Poiana Mare Romania
122 C4 Poie Dem. Rep. Congo
73 D6 Poinsett, Cape c. Antarctica
140 A2 Point Arena U.S.A.
135 J2 Point-Comfort Canada
149 L5 Pointe-à-Pitre Guadeloupe
135 G3 Pointe au Baril Station Canada
122 B4 Pointe-Noire Congo
128 B3 Point Hope U.S.A.
70 A4 Point Kenny Australia
130 G1 Point Lake Canada
71 J3 Point Lookout mt. Australia
Point Nepean National Park nat. park Australia see Mornington Peninsula National Park
135 F5 Point Pelee National Park Canada
147 F4 Point Pleasant NJ U.S.A.
146 B5 Point Pleasant WV U.S.A.
135 J3 Poisson Blanc, Lac du l. Canada
110 E3 Poitiers France
110 D3 Poitou reg. France
158 E1 Pojuca Brazil
88 B4 Pokaran India
71 H2 Pokataroo Australia
89 E3 Pokhara Nepal
82 C1 Pokhvistnevo Rus. Fed.
122 C3 Poko Dem. Rep. Congo
88 A4 Pokran Pak.
83 G2 Pokrovka Kazakh.
94 B3 Pokrovka Primorskiy Kray Rus. Fed.
94 C2 Pokrovka Primorskiy Kray Rus. Fed.
77 N3 Pokrovsk Rus. Fed.
117 F6 Pokrovskoye Rus. Fed.

Saavedra 203

70 D5 Renmark Australia
69 G3 Rennell i. Solomon Is
109 G4 Rennerod Germany
110 D2 Rennes France
73 B6 Rennick Glacier Antarctica
131 H2 Rennie Lake Canada
114 D2 Reno r. Italy
140 C2 Reno U.S.A.
146 E4 Renovo U.S.A.
92 E2 Renqiu China
93 B4 Renshou China
134 D5 Rensselaer IN U.S.A.
147 G3 Rensselaer NY U.S.A.
108 D2 Renswoude Neth.
138 B2 Renton U.S.A.
89 E4 Renukut India
72 D4 Renwick N.Z.
120 B3 Réo Burkina
91 E7 Reo Indon.
82 E5 Repetek Turkm.
138 C1 Republic U.S.A.
142 D3 Republican r. U.S.A.
129 J3 Repulse Bay Canada
154 D5 Requena Peru
111 F3 Requena Spain
80 F1 Reşadiye Turkey
81 I2 Reşadiye Turkey
158 B4 Reserva Brazil
156 E3 Resistencia Arg.
115 I2 Reşiţa Romania
129 I2 Resolute Canada
129 L3 Resolution Island Canada
72 A6 Resolution Island N.Z.
151 G5 Retalhuleu Guat.
98 □ Retan Laut, Pulau i. Sing.
105 G4 Retford U.K.
110 G2 Rethel France
109 H2 Rethem (Aller) Germany
115 K7 Rethymno Greece
94 C2 Rettikhovka Rus. Fed.
109 K2 Reuden Germany
119 I6 Réunion terr. Indian Ocean
111 G2 Reus Spain
109 K1 Reuterstadt Stavenhagen Germany
112 D6 Reutlingen Germany
140 D3 Reveille Peak U.S.A.
110 F5 Revel France
130 F4 Revelstoke Canada
148 B5 Revillagigedo, Islas is Mex.
130 C3 Revillagigedo Island U.S.A.
108 C5 Revin France
80 E6 Revivim Israel
88 E4 Rewa India
88 D3 Rewari India
138 E3 Rexburg U.S.A.
133 H4 Rexton Canada
140 A2 Reyes, Point U.S.A.
80 F3 Reyhanlı Turkey
102 B2 Reykir Iceland
163 G2 Reykjanes Ridge sea feature N. Atlantic Ocean
102 B3 Reykjanestá pt Iceland
102 B2 Reykjavík Iceland
151 E2 Reynosa Mex.
103 N4 Rēzekne Latvia
81 L3 Rezvānshahr Iran
105 D5 Rhayader U.K.
109 G3 Rheda-Wiedenbrück Germany
108 E3 Rhede Germany
108 E3 Rhein r. Germany alt. Rhin (France), conv. Rhine
108 F2 Rheine Germany
108 E4 Rheinisches Schiefergebirge hills Germany
108 F5 Rheinland-Pfalz land Germany
109 K1 Rheinsberg Germany
109 G6 Rheinstetten Germany
110 H2 Rhin r. France alt. Rhein (Germany), conv. Rhine
112 C5 Rhine r. Europe alt. Rhein (Germany), alt. Rhin (France)
147 G4 Rhinebeck U.S.A.
134 C3 Rhinelander U.S.A.
109 K2 Rhinkanal canal Germany
109 K2 Rhinluch marsh Germany
109 K2 Rhinow Germany
114 C2 Rho Italy
147 H4 Rhode Island state U.S.A.
115 M6 Rhodes Greece
115 M6 Rhodes i. Greece
138 D2 Rhodes Peak U.S.A.
115 K4 Rhodope Mountains Bulg./Greece
110 G4 Rhône r. France/Switz.
105 D4 Rhyl U.K.
158 E2 Riacho Brazil
158 E2 Riacho de Santana Brazil
158 C1 Rialma Brazil
158 C1 Rianópolis Brazil
88 C2 Riasi Jammu and Kashmir
99 B2 Riau, Kepulauan is Indon.
111 C1 Ribadeo Spain
111 D1 Ribadesella Spain
158 B3 Ribas do Rio Pardo Brazil
123 D5 Ribáuè Moz.
104 E4 Ribble r. U.K.
103 J5 Ribe Denmark
108 A5 Ribécourt-Dreslincourt France
158 C4 Ribeira r. Brazil
158 C3 Ribeirão Preto Brazil
108 B5 Ribemont France
110 E4 Ribérac France
154 E6 Riberalta Bol.
117 D6 Rîbniţa Moldova
112 F3 Ribnitz-Damgarten Germany
112 G6 Říčany Czech Rep.
141 E4 Rice U.S.A.
135 F2 Rice Lake l. Canada
134 B3 Rice Lake U.S.A.
134 A4 Riceville IA U.S.A.
146 D4 Riceville PA U.S.A.
125 J4 Richards Bay S. Africa
131 G3 Richardson r. Canada
143 D5 Richardson U.S.A.
147 H2 Richardson Lakes U.S.A.
128 E3 Richardson Mountains Canada
72 B6 Richardson Mountains N.Z.
141 F2 Richfield U.S.A.
147 F3 Richfield Springs U.S.A.
147 G2 Richford NY U.S.A.
147 G2 Richford VT U.S.A.
134 B5 Richland IA U.S.A.
136 C2 Richland WA U.S.A.
134 B4 Richland Center U.S.A.
146 C6 Richlands U.S.A.
71 I4 Richmond N.S.W. Australia
68 E4 Richmond Qld Australia
135 J3 Richmond Canada
72 D4 Richmond N.Z.
125 I4 Richmond Kwazulu-Natal S. Africa
124 E5 Richmond N. Cape S. Africa
104 F3 Richmond U.K.
134 E6 Richmond IN U.S.A.
146 A6 Richmond KY U.S.A.
147 I2 Richmond ME U.S.A.
135 F4 Richmond MI U.S.A.
146 E6 Richmond VA U.S.A.
147 G2 Richmond VT U.S.A.
72 D4 Richmond, Mount N.Z.
135 H4 Richmond Hill Canada
71 J2 Richmond Range hills Australia
124 B4 Richtersveld National Park S. Africa
146 B4 Richwood OH U.S.A.
146 C5 Richwood WV U.S.A.
135 J3 Rideau r. Canada
135 I3 Rideau Lakes Canada
140 D4 Ridgecrest U.S.A.
146 D4 Ridgway U.S.A.
131 I4 Riding Mountain National Park Canada
112 D6 Riedlingen Germany
108 D4 Riemst Belgium
109 L3 Riesa Germany
156 B8 Riesco, Isla i. Chile
124 D5 Riet watercourse S. Africa
103 M5 Rietavas Lith.
124 E6 Rietbron S. Africa
124 D3 Rietfontein S. Africa
114 E3 Rieti Italy
139 F4 Rifle U.S.A.
102 C1 Rifstangi pt Iceland
89 H3 Riga India
103 N4 Riga Latvia
103 M4 Riga, Gulf of Estonia/Latvia
85 E4 Rīgān Iran
147 F2 Rigaud Canada
138 C2 Riggins U.S.A.
133 I3 Rigolet Canada
106 E5 Rigside U.K.
84 E3 Rīgū Iran
89 E4 Rihand r. India
89 E4 Rihand Dam India
103 N3 Riihimäki Fin.
73 D3 Riiser-Larsen Ice Shelf ice feature Antarctica
73 E3 Riiser-Larsen Sea sea Southern Ocean
139 D5 Riito Mex.
114 F2 Rijeka Croatia
94 G5 Rikuzen-takata Japan
115 J3 Rila mts Bulg.
138 C3 Riley U.S.A.
110 G4 Rillieux-la-Pape France
113 J6 Rimavská Sobota Slovakia
130 G4 Rimbey Canada
114 E2 Rimini Italy
88 D2 Rimo Glacier India
133 G4 Rimouski Canada
109 H5 Rimpar Germany
106 D2 Rimsdale, Loch l. U.K.
89 G3 Rinbung China
150 D3 Rincón de Romos Mex.
88 E4 Rind r. India
102 J3 Rindal Norway
71 G8 Ringarooma Bay Australia
88 C4 Ringas India
89 G2 Ring Co salt l. China
108 E2 Ringe Germany
103 J3 Ringebu Norway
103 J4 Ringkøbing Denmark
107 E2 Ringsend U.K.
103 J5 Ringsted Denmark
Ringvassøy i. Norway see Ringvassøya
102 L1 Ringvassøya i. Norway
105 F7 Ringwood U.K.
159 B3 Riñihue Chile
159 B3 Riñihue, Lago l. Chile
99 E4 Rinjani, Gunung vol. Indon.
109 H2 Rinteln Germany
134 C4 Rio U.S.A.
154 C5 Río Abiseo, Parque Nacional nat. park Peru
158 A2 Rio Alegre Brazil
154 C4 Riobamba Ecuador
141 H2 Rio Blanco U.S.A.
154 E6 Rio Branco Brazil
157 E4 Rio Branco, Parque Nacional do nat. park Brazil
158 C4 Rio Branco do Sul Brazil
158 A3 Rio Brilhante Brazil
159 B4 Río Bueno Chile
157 E2 Río Caribe Venez.
159 D1 Río Ceballos Arg.
158 C3 Rio Claro Brazil
157 E2 Rio Claro Trin. and Tob.
159 D2 Río Colorado Arg.
159 D2 Río Cuarto Arg.
158 D3 Rio de Janeiro Brazil (City Plan 64)
158 D3 Rio de Janeiro state Brazil
150 I7 Río de Jesús Panama
156 G3 Rio do Sul Brazil
150 I6 Río Frío Costa Rica
156 C8 Río Gallegos Arg.
156 C8 Río Grande Arg.
159 G2 Rio Grande Brazil
150 D3 Río Grande Mex.
151 E2 Rio Grande r. Mex./U.S.A. alt. Bravo del Norte, Río
143 D7 Rio Grande City U.S.A.
163 G8 Rio Grande Rise sea feature S. Atlantic Ocean
157 B2 Ríohacha Col.
154 C5 Rioja Peru
151 G3 Río Lagartos Mex.
155 K5 Rio Largo Brazil
110 F4 Riom France
154 E7 Río Mulatos Bol.
159 C4 Río Negro prov. Arg.
158 C4 Rio Negro Brazil
159 F2 Río Negro, Embalse del resr Uruguay
117 G7 Rioni r. Georgia
159 G1 Rio Pardo Brazil
158 D1 Rio Pardo de Minas Brazil
159 D1 Río Primero Arg.
139 F5 Rio Rancho U.S.A.
141 G6 Rio Rico U.S.A.
159 D1 Río Segundo Arg.
157 A3 Riosucio Col.
159 D2 Río Tercero Arg.
154 C4 Río Tigre Ecuador
97 A4 Rio Tuba Phil.
158 B2 Rio Verde Brazil
151 E3 Río Verde Mex.
151 G4 Río Verde Mex.
158 A2 Rio Verde de Mato Grosso Brazil
140 B2 Rio Vista U.S.A.
158 A2 Riozinho r. Brazil
113 O5 Ripky Ukr.
104 F3 Ripley England U.K.
105 F4 Ripley England U.K.
146 B5 Ripley OH U.S.A.
145 B5 Ripley TN U.S.A.
146 C5 Ripley WV U.S.A.
111 H1 Ripoll Spain
104 F3 Ripon U.K.
140 B3 Ripon CA U.S.A.
134 C4 Ripon WI U.S.A.
105 D6 Risca U.K.
94 G2 Rishiri-tō i. Japan
80 E6 Rishon Le Ziyyon Israel
85 F5 Rish Pish Iran
103 J4 Risør Norway
102 J3 Rissa Norway
103 N3 Ristiina Fin.
102 O2 Ristijärvi Fin.
102 O1 Ristikent Rus. Fed.
124 F4 Ritchie S. Africa
73 D3 Ritscher Upland mts Antarctica
102 L2 Ritsem Sweden
140 C3 Ritter, Mount U.S.A.
109 G1 Ritterhude Germany
111 E2 Rituerto r. Spain
138 C2 Ritzville U.S.A.
159 D2 Rivadavia Buenos Aires Arg.
159 C2 Rivadavia Mendoza Arg.
156 D2 Rivadavia Arg.
159 B1 Rivadavia Chile
114 D2 Riva del Garda Italy
150 C2 Riva Palacio Mex.
150 H6 Rivas Nicaragua
85 E3 Rivash Iran
159 B3 Rivera Arg.
159 F1 Rivera Uruguay
120 B4 River Cess Liberia
147 G4 Riverhead U.S.A.
71 F5 Riverina reg. Australia
124 D7 Riversdale S. Africa
125 H5 Riverside S. Africa
140 D5 Riverside U.S.A.
70 C5 Riverton Australia
131 J4 Riverton Canada
72 B7 Riverton N.Z.
138 E3 Riverton U.S.A.
133 H4 Riverview Canada
110 F5 Rivesaltes France
145 D7 Riviera Beach U.S.A.
147 I1 Rivière Bleue Canada
133 G4 Rivière-du-Loup Canada
117 C5 Rivne Ukr.
72 D4 Riwaka N.Z.
86 C5 Riyadh Saudi Arabia
84 D3 Riza well Iran
81 H1 Rize Turkey
Rizhao China see Donggang
80 E4 Rizokarpason Cyprus
84 E4 Rīzū'īyeh Iran
103 J4 Rjukan Norway
103 I4 Rjuvbrokkene mt. Norway
120 A3 Rkîz Mauritania
103 J3 Roa Norway
105 G5 Roade U.K.
102 J3 Roan Norway
141 H2 Roan Cliffs ridge U.S.A.
110 G3 Roanne France
145 C5 Roanoke AL U.S.A.
134 C5 Roanoke IL U.S.A.
146 D6 Roanoke VA U.S.A.
144 E4 Roanoke r. U.S.A.
145 E4 Roanoke Rapids U.S.A.
141 H2 Roan Plateau U.S.A.
107 B6 Roaringwater Bay Rep. of Ireland
150 H4 Roatán Hond.
102 M3 Röbäck Sweden
85 F4 Robat r. Afgh.
84 E4 Robāţ Iran
84 E3 Robāţ-e Khān Iran
85 F4 Robat Thana Pak.
71 F8 Robbins Island Australia
70 C6 Robe Australia
107 B4 Robe r. Rep. of Ireland
70 D3 Robe, Mount h. Australia
109 K1 Röbel Germany
143 C6 Robert Lee U.S.A.
138 D3 Roberts U.S.A.
71 J2 Roberts, Mount Australia
140 D2 Roberts Creek Mountain U.S.A.
102 M2 Robertsfors Sweden
89 E4 Robertsganj India
143 E5 Robert S. Kerr Reservoir U.S.A.
124 C6 Robertson S. Africa
120 A4 Robertsport Liberia
70 C4 Robertstown Australia
133 F4 Roberval Canada
129 L1 Robeson Channel Canada/Greenland
104 G3 Robin Hood's Bay U.K.
93 □ Robin's Nest h. Hong Kong China
144 C4 Robinson U.S.A.
68 B4 Robinson Range hills Australia
70 E5 Robinvale Australia
141 G5 Robles Junction U.S.A.
141 G5 Robles Pass U.S.A.
131 I4 Roblin Canada
130 F4 Robson, Mount Canada
143 D7 Robstown U.S.A.
151 F4 Roca Partida, Punta pt Mex.
114 E6 Rocca Busambra mt. Sicily Italy
159 F2 Rocha Uruguay
104 E4 Rochdale U.K.
158 A2 Rochedo Brazil
108 D4 Rochefort Belgium
110 D4 Rochefort France
132 F2 Rochefort, Lac l. Canada
116 G2 Rochegda Rus. Fed.
134 C5 Rochelle U.S.A.
70 F6 Rochester Australia
105 H6 Rochester U.K.
134 D5 Rochester IN U.S.A.
134 A3 Rochester MN U.S.A.
147 H3 Rochester NH U.S.A.
146 E3 Rochester NY U.S.A.
105 H6 Rochford U.K.
109 K3 Rochlitz Germany
110 C2 Roc'h Trévezel h. France
130 D2 Rock r. Canada
134 B5 Rock r. U.S.A.
71 G5 Rock, The Australia
163 H2 Rockall Bank sea feature N. Atlantic Ocean
73 B4 Rockefeller Plateau plat. Antarctica
134 C4 Rockford U.S.A.
131 H5 Rockglen Canada
68 F4 Rockhampton Australia
134 C1 Rock Harbor U.S.A.
145 D5 Rock Hill U.S.A.
68 B5 Rockingham Australia
145 E5 Rockingham U.S.A.
147 G2 Rock Island Canada
134 B5 Rock Island U.S.A.
142 D1 Rocklake U.S.A.
147 F2 Rockland Canada
147 H3 Rockland MA U.S.A.
147 I2 Rockland ME U.S.A.
134 C2 Rockland MI U.S.A.
70 E6 Rocklands Reservoir Australia
141 H3 Rock Point U.S.A.
147 H3 Rockport U.S.A.
142 D3 Rock Rapids U.S.A.
138 F2 Rock Springs MT U.S.A.
138 E3 Rock Springs WY U.S.A.
143 C6 Rocksprings U.S.A.
146 D3 Rockton Canada
134 D6 Rockville IN U.S.A.
146 E5 Rockville MD U.S.A.
147 I2 Rockwood U.S.A.
139 G4 Rocky Ford U.S.A.
146 B5 Rocky Fork Lake U.S.A.
135 F2 Rocky Island Lake Canada
145 E5 Rocky Mount NC U.S.A.
146 D6 Rocky Mount VA U.S.A.
130 G4 Rocky Mountain House Canada
138 F3 Rocky Mountain National Park U.S.A.
136 D2 Rocky Mountains Canada/U.S.A.
130 F4 Rocky Mountains Forest Reserve nature res. Canada
108 B5 Rocourt-St-Martin France
108 C5 Rocroi France
103 I3 Rodberg Norway
103 J5 Rødbyhavn Denmark
133 I3 Roddickton Canada
106 B3 Rodel U.K.
108 E1 Roden Neth.
109 J4 Rödental Germany
159 C1 Rodeo Arg.
150 C2 Rodeo Mex.
141 H6 Rodeo U.S.A.
110 F4 Rodez France
109 K5 Roding Germany
83 J1 Rodino Rus. Fed.
85 G5 Rodkhan Pak.
116 G3 Rodniki Rus. Fed.
82 D2 Rodnikovka Kazakh.
Rodos Greece see Rhodes
Rodos i. Greece see Rhodes
162 I6 Rodrigues Island Mauritius
68 B4 Roebourne Australia
68 C3 Roebuck Bay Australia
125 H2 Roedtan S. Africa
108 D3 Roermond Neth.
108 B4 Roeselare Belgium
129 J3 Roes Welcome Sound sea chan. Canada
109 J2 Rogätz Germany
143 E4 Rogers U.S.A.
135 F3 Rogers City U.S.A.
140 D4 Rogers Lake U.S.A.
138 D3 Rogerson U.S.A.
146 B6 Rogersville U.S.A.
132 E3 Roggan r. Canada
161 N8 Roggeveen Basin sea feature S. Pacific Ocean
124 D6 Roggeveld plat. S. Africa
124 D6 Roggeveldberge esc. S. Africa
102 K2 Rognan Norway
138 A3 Rogue r. U.S.A.
140 A2 Rohnert Park U.S.A.
112 F6 Rohrbach in Oberösterreich Austria
108 F5 Rohrbach-lès-Bitche France
88 B4 Rohri Pak.
88 D3 Rohtak India
98 B1 Roi Et Thai.
67 J5 Roi Georges, Îles du is Fr. Polynesia
108 B5 Roisel France
103 M4 Roja Latvia
159 E2 Rojas Arg.
88 B3 Rojhan Pak.
151 E3 Rojo, Cabo Mex.
99 B2 Rokan r. Indon.
103 N5 Rokiškis Lith.
102 M2 Roknäs Sweden
117 C5 Rokytne Ukr.
158 B3 Rolândia Brazil
142 F4 Rolla U.S.A.
103 J3 Rollag Norway
72 D5 Rolleston N.Z.
135 H2 Rollet Canada
145 F7 Rolleville Bahamas
135 I2 Rolphton Canada
68 E4 Roma Australia
91 E7 Roma i. Indon.
Roma Italy see Rome
125 G4 Roma Lesotho
103 L4 Roma Sweden
145 E5 Romain, Cape U.S.A.
133 H3 Romaine r. Canada
113 M7 Roman Romania
163 H6 Romanche Gap sea feature S. Atlantic Ocean
115 K1 Romania country Europe
90 D1 Romanovka Rus. Fed.
117 G5 Romanovka Saratovskaya Oblast' Rus. Fed.
83 J1 Romanovo Rus. Fed.
110 G4 Romans-sur-Isère France
128 B3 Romanzof, Cape U.S.A.
110 H2 Rombas France
97 B3 Romblon Phil.
97 B3 Romblon i. Phil.
Rombo, Ilhéus Secos ou do i. Cape Verde see Secos, Ilhéus
114 E4 Rome Italy (City Plan 62)
145 C5 Rome GA U.S.A.
147 I2 Rome ME U.S.A.
147 F3 Rome NY U.S.A.
135 F4 Romeo U.S.A.
105 H6 Romford U.K.
110 F2 Romilly-sur-Seine France
Romitan Uzbek. see Romiton
82 F5 Romiton Uzbek.
146 D5 Romney U.S.A.
105 H6 Romney Marsh reg. U.K.
117 E5 Romny Ukr.
103 J5 Rømø i. Denmark
110 E3 Romorantin-Lanthenay France
99 B2 Rompin r. Malaysia
105 F7 Romsey U.K.
87 A3 Ron India
98 C1 Ron Vietnam
106 C1 Rona i. Scotland U.K.
106 C3 Rona i. Scotland U.K.
106 □ Ronas Hill U.K.
155 H6 Roncador, Serra do hills Brazil
69 F2 Roncador Reef Solomon Is
111 D4 Ronda Spain
103 J3 Rondane Nasjonalpark nat. park Norway
157 C3 Rondón Col.
157 E4 Rondon, Pico h. Brazil
158 A2 Rondonópolis Brazil
79 F3 Rondu Jammu and Kashmir
93 C5 Rong'an China
93 B4 Rongchang China
96 B5 Rongcheng China
96 B5 Rongcheng Wan b. China
89 G3 Rong Chu r. China
160 G6 Rongelap atoll Marshall Is
93 C5 Rongjiang China
93 C6 Rong Jiang r. China
89 H5 Rongklang Range mts Myanmar
72 E4 Rongotea N.Z.
93 C5 Rongshui China
93 D6 Rongxian Guangxi China
93 B4 Rongxian Sichuan China
103 K5 Rønne Denmark
103 K4 Ronneby Sweden
73 B3 Ronne Entrance str. Antarctica
73 B3 Ronne Ice Shelf ice feature Antarctica
109 H2 Ronnenberg Germany
108 B4 Ronse Belgium
108 E1 Roodeschool Neth.
Roodeshuizum Neth. see Reduzum
88 D3 Roorkee India
108 C3 Roosendaal Neth.
141 G5 Roosevelt AZ U.S.A.
141 G1 Roosevelt UT U.S.A.
130 D3 Roosevelt, Mount Canada
73 B5 Roosevelt Island i. Antarctica
130 E2 Root r. Canada
134 B4 Root r. U.S.A.
116 J2 Ropcha Rus. Fed.
110 D4 Roquefort France
157 E4 Roraima state Brazil
157 E3 Roraima, Mount Guyana
102 J3 Røros Norway
102 J2 Rørvik Norway
113 O6 Ros' r. Ukr.
Rosa, C. pt Ecuador see Rosa, Cabo
154 □ Rosa, Cabo c. Galapagos Is Ecuador
145 D2 Rosa, Lake Bahamas
150 B2 Rosa, Punta pt Mex.
140 C4 Rosamond U.S.A.
140 C4 Rosamond Lake U.S.A.
159 E2 Rosario Arg.
148 A2 Rosario Baja California Mex.
150 D2 Rosario Coahuila Mex.
150 C3 Rosario Sinaloa Mex.
150 B2 Rosario Sonora Mex.
97 B2 Rosario Phil.
97 B3 Rosario Phil.
157 B2 Rosario Venez.
159 E2 Rosario del Tala Arg.
159 F1 Rosário do Sul Brazil
158 A1 Rosário Oeste Brazil
150 A1 Rosarito Baja California Mex.
150 B2 Rosarito Baja California Sur Mex.
114 F5 Rosarno Italy
147 F4 Roscoe U.S.A.
110 C2 Roscoff France
107 C4 Roscommon Rep. of Ireland
134 E3 Roscommon U.S.A.
107 D5 Roscrea Rep. of Ireland
140 C2 Rose, Mount U.S.A.
149 L5 Roseau Dominica
131 J5 Roseau U.S.A.
71 F8 Rosebery Australia
133 I4 Rose Blanche Canada
138 B3 Roseburg U.S.A.
135 E3 Rose City U.S.A.
104 G3 Rosedale Abbey U.K.
121 F3 Roseires Reservoir Sudan
67 H4 Rose Island atoll American Samoa
143 E6 Rosenberg U.S.A.
103 I4 Rosendal Norway
125 G4 Rosendal S. Africa
112 F7 Rosenheim Germany
130 C4 Rose Point Canada
114 F3 Roseto degli Abruzzi Italy
131 H4 Rosetown Canada
131 I4 Rose Valley Canada
140 B2 Roseville CA U.S.A.
134 B5 Roseville IL U.S.A.
71 J1 Rosewood Australia
116 D2 Roshchino Leningradskaya Oblast' Rus. Fed.
94 D2 Roshchino Primorskiy Kray Rus. Fed.
85 E3 Roshkhvār Iran
124 B3 Rosh Pinah Namibia
83 G5 Roshtqal'a Tajik.
114 D3 Rosignano Marittimo Italy
115 K2 Roşiori de Vede Romania
103 K5 Roskilde Denmark
116 E4 Roslavl' Rus. Fed.
102 P1 Roslyakovo Rus. Fed.
71 G9 Ross Australia
130 C2 Ross r. Canada
72 C5 Ross N.Z.
72 E4 Ross, Mount h. N.Z.
114 G5 Rossano Italy
107 C3 Rossan Point Rep. of Ireland
143 F5 Ross Barnett Reservoir U.S.A.
133 G3 Ross Bay Junction Canada
107 B6 Ross Carbery Rep. of Ireland
73 A5 Ross Dependency reg. Antarctica
69 F3 Rossel Island P.N.G.
73 B5 Ross Ice Shelf ice feature Antarctica
133 H5 Rossignol, Lake Canada
73 B5 Ross Island i. Antarctica
107 E5 Rosslare Rep. of Ireland
105 A5 Rosslare Harbour Rep. of Ireland
109 K3 Roßlau Germany
135 I3 Rossmore Canada
120 A3 Rosso Mauritania
114 C3 Rosso, Capo c. Corsica France
105 E6 Ross-on-Wye U.K.
117 F5 Rossosh' Rus. Fed.
134 D1 Rossport Canada
130 C2 Ross River Canada
73 B5 Ross Sea sea Antarctica
109 I5 Roßtal Germany
102 K2 Røssvatnet l. Norway
134 D5 Rossville U.S.A.
109 L3 Roßwein Germany
130 D3 Rosswood Canada
81 J3 Rost Iraq
85 G3 Rostāq Afgh.
84 D5 Rostāq Iran
131 H4 Rosthern Canada
112 F3 Rostock Germany
116 F3 Rostov Rus. Fed.
117 F6 Rostov-na-Donu Rus. Fed.
117 G6 Rostovskaya Oblast' admin. div. Rus. Fed.
102 M2 Rosvik Sweden
145 C5 Roswell GA U.S.A.
139 F5 Roswell NM U.S.A.
91 G5 Rota i. N. Mariana Is
109 I5 Rot am See Germany
91 E8 Rote i. Indon.
109 H1 Rotenburg (Wümme) Germany
109 J4 Roter Main r. Germany
109 J5 Roth Germany
109 G4 Rothaargebirge hills Germany
104 F2 Rothbury U.K.
104 F2 Rothbury Forest U.K.
109 I5 Rothenburg ob der Tauber Germany
105 G7 Rother r. U.K.
73 E2 Rothera research stn Antarctica
72 D5 Rotherham N.Z.
105 F4 Rotherham U.K.
106 F3 Rothes U.K.
106 C5 Rothesay U.K.
134 C3 Rothschild U.S.A.
105 G5 Rothwell U.K.
71 F4 Roto Australia
72 C5 Rotomanu N.Z.
114 C3 Rotondo, Monte mt. Corsica France
72 D4 Rotoroa, Lake N.Z.
72 F3 Rotorua N.Z.
72 F3 Rotorua, Lake N.Z.
112 F6 Rott r. Germany
109 J5 Röttenbach Germany
109 I5 Rottendorf Germany
112 G7 Rottenmann Austria
108 C3 Rotterdam Neth.
109 I3 Rottleberode Germany
108 E1 Rottumeroog i. Neth.
108 E1 Rottumerplaat i. Neth.
112 D6 Rottweil Germany
69 H3 Rotuma i. Fiji
102 K3 Rötviken Sweden
109 K5 Rötz Germany
110 F1 Roubaix France
110 E2 Rouen France
72 B6 Rough Ridge N.Z.
Roulers Belgium see Roeselare
133 F3 Roundeyed Lake Canada
104 F3 Round Hill U.K.
71 J3 Round Mountain Australia
140 D2 Round Mountain U.S.A.
143 D6 Round Rock U.S.A.
138 E2 Roundup U.S.A.
106 E1 Rousay i. U.K.
147 G2 Rouses Point U.S.A.
110 F5 Roussillon reg. France
125 G5 Rouxville S. Africa
Rouyn Canada see Rouyn-Noranda
135 H1 Rouyn-Noranda Canada
102 N2 Rovaniemi Fin.
117 F5 Roven'ki Rus. Fed.
114 D2 Rovereto Italy
98 C2 Rôviĕng Tbong Cambodia
114 D2 Rovigo Italy
114 E2 Rovinj Croatia
117 H5 Rovnoye Rus. Fed.
71 H2 Rowena Australia
97 A4 Roxas Phil.
97 B2 Roxas Phil.
97 B3 Roxas Phil.
97 B3 Roxas Phil.
97 B4 Roxas Phil.
145 E4 Roxboro U.S.A.
72 B6 Roxburgh N.Z.
70 B3 Roxby Downs Australia
139 F4 Roy U.S.A.
107 E4 Royal Canal Rep. of Ireland
89 F4 Royal Chitwan National Park Nepal
134 C1 Royale, Isle i. U.S.A.
125 H4 Royal Natal National Park S. Africa
135 F4 Royal Oak U.S.A.
110 D4 Royan France
108 A5 Roye France
105 G5 Royston U.K.
117 D6 Rozdil'na Ukr.
117 E6 Rozdol'ne Ukr.
83 G2 Rozhdestvenka Kazakh.
117 F6 Rozivka Ukr.
84 C3 Rozveh Iran
117 G4 Rtishchevo Rus. Fed.
105 D5 Ruabon U.K.
123 B5 Ruacana Namibia
122 D4 Ruaha National Park Tanz.
72 F3 Ruahine Range mts N.Z.
72 E3 Ruapehu, Mount vol. N.Z.
72 B7 Ruapuke Island N.Z.
72 G2 Ruatoria N.Z.
116 D4 Ruba Belarus
86 C6 Rub' al Khālī des. Saudi Arabia
94 H3 Rubeshibe Japan
140 B2 Rubicon r. U.S.A.
117 F5 Rubizhne Ukr.
90 A1 Rubtsovsk Rus. Fed.
128 C3 Ruby U.S.A.
141 E1 Ruby Lake U.S.A.
141 E1 Ruby Mountains U.S.A.
93 D5 Rucheng China
146 D5 Ruckersville U.S.A.
88 E4 Rudauli India
85 F4 Rudbar Afgh.
81 L3 Rūdbār Iran
Rūd-i-Shur watercourse Iran see Shūr, Rūd-e
103 J5 Rudkøbing Denmark
90 F2 Rudnaya Pristan' Rus. Fed.
116 J3 Rudnichnyy Rus. Fed.
116 D4 Rudnya Rus. Fed.
82 E1 Rudnyy Kazakh.
94 D2 Rudnyy Rus. Fed.
76 G1 Rudol'fa, Ostrov i. Rus. Fed.
109 J4 Rudolstadt Germany
92 F3 Rudong China
134 E2 Rudyard U.S.A.
123 D4 Rufiji r. Tanz.
159 D2 Rufino Arg.
120 A3 Rufisque Senegal
123 C5 Rufunsa Zambia
92 F3 Rugao China
105 F5 Rugby U.K.
142 C1 Rugby U.S.A.
105 F5 Rugeley U.K.
112 F3 Rügen i. Germany
146 B4 Ruggles U.S.A.
109 I5 Rügland Germany
84 B5 Ruḩayyat al Ḩamr'ā' waterhole Saudi Arabia
122 C4 Ruhengeri Rwanda
103 M4 Ruhnu i. Estonia
108 F3 Ruhr r. Germany
93 F5 Rui'an China
139 F5 Ruidoso U.S.A.
93 E5 Ruijin China
131 M2 Ruin Point Canada
123 D4 Ruipa Tanz.
150 C3 Ruiz Mex.
157 B3 Ruiz, Nevado del vol. Col.
80 F5 Rujaylah, Ḩarrat ar lava field Jordan
103 N4 Rūjiena Latvia
84 C5 Rukbah well Saudi Arabia
89 E3 Rukumkot Nepal
122 D4 Rukwa, Lake Tanz.
84 E5 Rūl Ḑadnah U.A.E.
85 E3 Rūm Iran
106 B4 Rum i. U.K.
115 H2 Ruma Serb. and Mont.
84 B5 Rumāh Saudi Arabia
121 E4 Rumbek Sudan
145 F7 Rum Cay i. Bahamas
147 H2 Rumford U.S.A.
110 G4 Rumilly France
68 D3 Rum Jungle Australia
94 G3 Rumoi Japan
92 E3 Runan China
72 C5 Runanga N.Z.
72 F2 Runaway, Cape N.Z.
105 E4 Runcorn U.K.
123 B5 Rundu Namibia
102 L3 Rundvik Sweden
98 B3 Rŭng, Kaôh i. Cambodia
98 B3 Rŭng Sânlŏem, Kaôh i. Cambodia
92 E3 Runheji China
103 O3 Ruokolahti Fin.
90 A3 Ruoqiang China
89 H4 Rupa India
159 B4 Rupanco, Lago l. Chile
70 E6 Rupanyup Australia
99 B2 Rupat i. Indon.
132 E3 Rupert r. Canada
138 D3 Rupert U.S.A.
132 E3 Rupert Bay Canada
123 D5 Rusape Zimbabwe
115 K3 Ruse Bulg.
96 A5 Rushan China
105 G5 Rushden U.K.
134 B4 Rushford U.S.A.
134 C4 Rush Lake U.S.A.
89 H3 Rushon India
83 G5 Rushon Tajik.
134 B5 Rushville IL U.S.A.
142 C3 Rushville NE U.S.A.
70 F6 Rushworth Australia
143 E6 Rusk U.S.A.
145 D7 Ruskin U.S.A.
131 I4 Russell Man. Canada
147 F2 Russell Ont. Canada
72 E1 Russell N.Z.
142 D4 Russell U.S.A.
129 I2 Russell Island Canada
69 F2 Russell Islands Solomon Is
130 F2 Russell Lake Canada
145 C4 Russellville AL U.S.A.
143 E5 Russellville AR U.S.A.
144 C4 Russellville KY U.S.A.
109 G4 Rüsselsheim Germany
76 G3 Russian Federation country Asia/Europe
83 H1 Russkaya-Polyana Rus. Fed.
94 C3 Russkiy, Ostrov i. Rus. Fed.
81 J1 Rust'avi Georgia
125 G2 Rustenburg S. Africa
143 E5 Ruston U.S.A.
91 E7 Ruteng Indon.
141 E2 Ruth U.S.A.
109 G3 Rüthen Germany
135 H2 Rutherglen Canada
105 D4 Ruthin U.K.
116 H3 Rutka r. Rus. Fed.
147 G3 Rutland U.S.A.
105 G5 Rutland Water resr U.K.
131 G2 Rutledge Lake Canada
Rutög China see Dêrub
135 G2 Rutter Canada
102 N2 Ruukki Fin.
84 E5 Ru'us al Jibāl hills Oman
123 D5 Ruvuma r. Moz./Tanz.
80 F5 Ruwayshid, Wādī watercourse Jordan
84 D5 Ruweis U.A.E.
93 D5 Ruyuan China
83 F1 Ruzayevka Kazakh.
116 H4 Ruzayevka Rus. Fed.
92 D3 Ruzhou China
113 I6 Ružomberok Slovakia
122 C4 Rwanda country Africa
84 D2 Ryābād Iran
116 H2 Ryadovo Rus. Fed.
106 C5 Ryan, Loch b. U.K.
116 F4 Ryazan' Rus. Fed.
116 G4 Ryazanskaya Oblast' admin. div. Rus. Fed.
116 G4 Ryazhsk Rus. Fed.
76 E2 Rybachiy, Poluostrov pen. Rus. Fed.
82 D3 Rybachiy Poselok Uzbek.
83 J3 Rybach'ye Kazakh.
116 F3 Rybinsk Rus. Fed.
116 F3 Rybinskoye Vodokhranilishche resr Rus. Fed.
116 I4 Rybnaya Sloboda Rus. Fed.
113 I5 Rybnik Poland
116 F4 Rybnoye Rus. Fed.
130 F3 Rycroft Canada
103 K4 Ryd Sweden
73 B3 Rydberg Peninsula Antarctica
105 F7 Ryde U.K.
105 H7 Rye U.K.
104 G3 Rye r. U.K.
117 E5 Ryl'sk Rus. Fed.
71 H4 Rylstone Australia
82 B3 Ryn-Peski des. Kazakh.
95 F5 Ryōtsu Japan
90 E4 Ryukyu Islands Japan
162 M3 Ryukyu Trench sea feature N. Pacific Ocean
113 K5 Rzeszów Poland
117 G4 Rzhaksa Rus. Fed.
116 E3 Rzhev Rus. Fed.

S

84 E3 Sa'ābād Iran
84 D4 Sa'ādatābād Iran
84 D4 Sa'ādatābād Iran
109 J6 Saal an der Donau Germany
109 J3 Saale r. Germany
109 J4 Saalfeld Germany
108 F5 Saar r. Germany
108 E5 Saarbrücken Germany
103 M4 Saaremaa i. Estonia
102 N2 Saarenkylä Fin.
108 E5 Saargau reg. Germany
102 N3 Saarijärvi Fin.
102 N2 Saari-Kämä Fin.
102 M1 Saarikoski Fin.
108 E5 Saarland land Germany
108 E5 Saarlouis Germany
81 L2 Saatlı Azer.
159 D3 Saavedra Arg.

204 Sab' Ābār

80 F5 Şab' Ābār Syria
115 H2 Šabac Serb. and Mont.
111 H2 Sabadell Spain
95 E7 Sabae Japan
99 E1 Sabah state Malaysia
98 B5 Sabak Malaysia
81 K2 Sabalan, Kūhhā-ye mts Iran
99 E4 Sabalana, Kepulauan is Indon.
88 D4 Sabalgarh India
Sabamagrande Hond. see Sabanagrande
149 H4 Sabana, Archipiélago de is Cuba
150 H5 Sabanagrande Hond.
157 B2 Sabanalarga Col.
80 D1 Şabanözü Turkey
158 D2 Sabará Brazil
87 C2 Sabari r. India
88 C5 Sabarmati r. India
114 E4 Sabaudia Italy
85 E3 Sabeh Iran
124 E5 Sabelo S. Africa
121 D2 Sabhā Libya
84 B6 Şabḩā' Saudi Arabia
88 D3 Sabi r. India
125 J2 Sabie Moz.
125 J2 Sabie r. Moz./S. Africa
125 I2 Sabie S. Africa
150 D2 Sabinas Mex.
151 D2 Sabinas Hidalgo Mex.
143 E6 Sabine Lake U.S.A.
81 L1 Sabirabad Azer.
97 B3 Sablayan Phil.
129 L5 Sable, Cape Canada
145 D7 Sable, Cape U.S.A.
69 F3 Sable, Île de i. New Caledonia
129 M5 Sable Island Canada
135 F2 Sables, River aux r. Canada
73 C6 Sabrina Coast Antarctica
97 B1 Sabtang i. Phil.
111 C2 Sabugal Port.
134 B4 Sabula U.S.A.
86 B6 Şabyā Saudi Arabia
85 E2 Sabzevār Iran
115 M2 Sacalinul Mare, Insula i. Romania
115 K2 Săcele Romania
123 B5 Sachanga Angola
132 B3 Sachigo r. Canada
132 B3 Sachigo Lake Canada
88 C5 Sachin India
96 E6 Sach'on S. Korea
96 E6 Sach'ŏn S. Korea
88 D2 Sach Pass India
109 K3 Sachsen land Germany
109 J3 Sachsen-Anhalt land Germany
109 H6 Sachsenheim Germany
128 F2 Sachs Harbour Canada
147 E3 Sackets Harbor U.S.A.
109 G4 Sackpfeife h. Germany
133 H4 Sackville Canada
147 H3 Saco ME U.S.A.
138 F1 Saco MT U.S.A.
97 B5 Sacol i. Phil.
140 B2 Sacramento U.S.A.
140 B2 Sacramento r. U.S.A.
139 F5 Sacramento Mountains U.S.A.
138 B3 Sacramento Valley U.S.A.
125 G6 Sada S. Africa
111 F1 Sádaba Spain
84 C4 Sa'dābād Iran
80 F4 Şadad Syria
98 B4 Sadao Thai.
81 J5 Saddat al Hindīyah Iraq
125 I2 Saddleback pass S. Africa
98 C3 Sa Đec Vietnam
89 H3 Sadêng China
85 E5 Sadīj watercourse Iran
88 B3 Sadiqabad Pak.
88 C1 Sad Istragh mt. Afgh./Pak.
81 K5 Sa'dīyah, Hawr as imp. l. Iraq
84 D5 Sa'diyyat i. U.A.E.
84 E2 Sad-Kharv Iran
111 B3 Sado r. Port.
95 F6 Sadoga-shima i. Japan
90 F3 Sado-shima i. Japan
111 H3 Sa Dragonera i. Spain
103 J4 Sæby Denmark
81 K6 Safayal Maqūf well Iraq
85 H2 Safed Khirs mts Afgh.
85 G3 Safed Koh mts Afgh.
103 K4 Säffle Sweden
141 H5 Safford U.S.A.
105 H5 Saffron Walden U.K.
120 B1 Safi Morocco
84 C2 Safīd r. Iran
85 G2 Safīd, Daryā-ye r. Afgh.
84 D3 Safid Ab Iran
85 F4 Safidabeh Iran
81 L5 Safid Dasht Iran
80 F4 Şāfītā Syria
76 F3 Safonovo Arkhangel'skaya Oblast' Rus. Fed.
102 P1 Safonovo Murmanskaya Oblast' Rus. Fed.
116 E4 Safonovo Smolenskaya Oblast' Rus. Fed.
84 A5 Safrā' al Asyāḩ esc. Saudi Arabia
80 D1 Safranbolu Turkey
81 K6 Safwān Iraq
89 F3 Saga China
95 B8 Saga Japan
82 E2 Saga Kostanayskaya Oblast' Kazakh.
82 F2 Saga Kostanayskaya Oblast' Kazakh.
95 F7 Sagamihara Japan
95 F7 Sagami-nada g. Japan
95 F7 Sagami-wan b. Japan
157 B3 Sagamoso r. Col.
83 I4 Sagankuduk China
98 A2 Saganthit Kyun i. Myanmar
87 A3 Sagar Karnataka India
87 B2 Sagar Karnataka India
88 D5 Sagar Madhya Pradesh India
117 H7 Sagarejo Georgia
89 G5 Sagar Island India
77 N2 Sagastyr Rus. Fed.
84 D3 Saghand Iran
85 F3 Saghar Afgh.
87 B3 Sagileru r. India
135 F4 Saginaw U.S.A.
135 F4 Saginaw Bay U.S.A.
82 C2 Sagiz Kazakh.
133 H2 Saglek Bay Canada
114 C3 Sagone, Golfe de b. Corsica France
111 B4 Sagres Port.
89 H5 Sagu Myanmar
139 F4 Saguache U.S.A.
149 H4 Sagua la Grande Cuba
141 G5 Saguaro National Park U.S.A.
133 F4 Saguenay r. Canada
111 F3 Sagunto Spain
88 C5 Sagwara India
82 C2 Sagyz r. Kazakh.
157 B2 Sahagún Col.
111 D1 Sahagún Spain
81 K3 Sahand, Kūh-e mt. Iran
120 C2 Sahara des. Africa
88 D3 Saharanpur India
89 F4 Saharsa India
88 D3 Sahaswan India
84 C6 Sahbā', Wādī as watercourse Saudi Arabia
88 C3 Sahiwal Pak.
85 E3 Sahlābād Iran
81 K4 Şahneh Iran
81 J6 Şaḩrā al Ḩijārah reg. Iraq
150 B1 Sahuaripa Mex.
141 G6 Sahuarita U.S.A.
150 D3 Sahuayo Mex.
98 D2 Sa Huynh Vietnam
88 C5 Sahyadriparvat Range hills India
88 E4 Sai r. India
98 B4 Sai Buri Thai.
98 B4 Sai Buri, Mae Nam r. Thai.
Saïda Lebanon see Sidon
98 B2 Sai Dao Tai, Khao mt. Thai.
85 F5 Sa'īdī Iran
89 G4 Saidpur Bangl.
88 C2 Saidu Pak.
95 C6 Saigō Japan
Saigon Vietnam see Ho Chi Minh City
98 C3 Sai Gon, Sông r. Vietnam
Saigon, Sông r. Vietnam see Sai Gon, Sông
89 H5 Saiha India
92 D1 Saihan Tal China
92 A1 Saihan Toroi China
95 C8 Saijō Japan
95 B8 Saiki Japan
93 □ Sai Kung Hong Kong China
103 O3 Saimaa l. Fin.
80 F2 Saimbeyli Turkey
150 D3 Sain Alto Mex.
85 F4 Saindak Pak.
84 B2 Sa'īndezh Iran
106 F5 St Abb's Head U.K.
105 B7 St Agnes U.K.
105 A8 St Agnes i. U.K.
133 I4 St Alban's Canada
105 G6 St Albans U.K.
147 G2 St Albans VT U.S.A.
146 C5 St Albans WV U.S.A.
St Alban's Head hd U.K. see St Aldhelm's Head
130 G4 St Albert Canada
105 E7 St Aldhelm's Head U.K.
108 B4 St-Amand-les-Eaux France
110 F3 St-Amand-Montrond France
110 G3 St-Amour France
147 J2 St Andrews Canada
106 F4 St Andrews U.K.
149 I5 St Ann's Bay Jamaica
107 F6 St Ann's Head U.K.
133 I3 St Anthony Canada
138 E3 St Anthony U.S.A.
70 E6 St Arnaud Australia
72 D5 St Arnaud Range mts N.Z.
133 I3 St-Augustin Canada
145 D6 St Augustine U.S.A.
105 C7 St Austell U.K.
110 E3 St-Avertin France
108 E5 St-Avold France
149 L5 St-Barthélemy i. Guadeloupe
104 D3 St Bees U.K.
104 D3 St Bees Head U.K.
105 B6 St Bride's Bay U.K.
110 C2 St-Brieuc France
135 H4 St Catharines Canada
145 D6 St Catherines Island U.S.A.
105 F7 St Catherine's Point U.K.
110 E4 St-Céré France
147 G2 St-Césaire Canada
110 G4 St-Chamond France
138 E3 St Charles ID U.S.A.
146 E5 St Charles MD U.S.A.
134 A4 St Charles MN U.S.A.
142 F4 St Charles MO U.S.A.
135 F4 St Clair U.S.A.
135 F4 St Clair Shores U.S.A.
110 G3 St-Claude France
105 C6 St Clears U.K.
142 E2 St Cloud U.S.A.
133 G4 St Croix r. Canada
134 A2 St Croix r. U.S.A.
149 L5 St Croix i. Virgin Is (U.S.A.)
134 A3 St Croix Falls U.S.A.
141 G6 St David U.S.A.
107 F6 St David's U.K.
105 B6 St David's Head U.K.
108 A6 St-Denis France
110 H2 St-Dié France
110 G2 St-Dizier France
131 J5 Sainte Anne Canada
133 G3 Ste-Anne, Lac l. Canada
133 F4 Ste-Anne-de-Beaupré Canada
147 I1 Ste-Anne-de-Madawaska Canada
135 J2 Ste-Anne-du-Lac Canada
147 H1 Ste-Camille-de-Lellis Canada
110 G4 St-Égrève France
147 H1 Ste-Justine Canada
147 I1 St-Éleuthère Canada
130 B2 St Elias Mountains Canada
133 G3 Ste-Marguerite r. Canada
110 H5 Ste-Maxime France
110 D4 Saintes France
147 G2 Ste-Thérèse Canada
110 G4 St-Étienne France
147 F2 St Eugene Canada
147 G2 St-Eustache Canada
133 F4 St-Félicien Canada
107 F3 Saintfield U.K.
114 C3 St-Florent Corsica France
110 F3 St-Florent-sur-Cher France
122 C3 St Floris, Parc National nat. park Centr. Afr. Rep.
147 I1 St Francis r. Canada/U.S.A.
142 C4 St Francis KS U.S.A.
147 I1 St Francis ME U.S.A.
143 F4 St Francis r. U.S.A.
133 J4 St Francis, Cape Canada
147 I1 St Froid Lake U.S.A.
110 E5 St-Gaudens France
147 H2 St-Gédéon Canada
71 H2 St George Australia
147 J2 St George Canada
145 D5 St George SC U.S.A.
141 F3 St George UT U.S.A.
69 F2 St George, Cape P.N.G.
138 A3 St George, Point U.S.A.
145 C6 St George Island U.S.A.
133 F4 St-Georges Canada
149 L6 St George's Grenada
133 I4 St George's Bay Canada
68 F2 St George's Channel P.N.G.
105 A6 St George's Channel Rep. of Ireland/U.K.
112 D7 St Gotthard Pass pass Switz.
105 C6 St Govan's Head U.K.
134 E3 St Helen U.S.A.
118 D6 St Helena terr. Atlantic Ocean
140 A2 St Helena U.S.A.
124 C6 St Helena Bay S. Africa
124 C6 St Helena Bay b. S. Africa
71 H8 St Helens Australia
105 E4 St Helens U.K.
138 B2 St Helens U.S.A.
138 B2 St Helens, Mount vol. U.S.A.
71 H8 St Helens Point Australia
110 C2 St Helier U.K.
108 D4 St-Hubert Belgium
132 F4 St-Hyacinthe Canada
134 E3 St Ignace U.S.A.
134 C1 St Ignace Island Canada
105 C6 St Ishmael U.K.
105 B7 St Ives England U.K.
105 G5 St Ives England U.K.
147 I1 St-Jacques Canada
134 E3 St James U.S.A.
130 C4 St James, Cape Canada
133 F4 St-Jean, Lac l. Canada
110 D4 St-Jean-d'Angély France
110 C3 St-Jean-de-Monts France
132 F4 St-Jean-sur-Richelieu Canada
132 F4 St-Jérôme Canada
138 C2 St Joe r. U.S.A.
133 G4 Saint John Canada
147 J2 St John r. Canada/U.S.A.
141 F1 St John U.S.A.
149 L5 St John i. Virgin Is (U.S.A.)
149 L5 St John's Antigua and Barbuda
133 J4 St John's Canada
141 H4 St Johns AZ U.S.A.
134 E4 St Johns MI U.S.A.
145 D6 St Johns r. U.S.A.
147 H2 St Johnsbury U.S.A.
104 E3 St John's Chapel U.K.
134 D4 St Joseph MI U.S.A.
142 E4 St Joseph MO U.S.A.
134 E5 St Joseph r. U.S.A.
132 B3 St Joseph, Lake Canada
133 F4 St-Joseph-de-Beauce Canada
135 F2 St Joseph Island Canada
143 D7 St Joseph Island U.S.A.
132 F4 St-Jovité Canada
110 E4 St-Junien France
105 B7 St Just U.K.
108 A5 St-Just-en-Chaussée France
105 B7 St Keverne U.K.
149 L5 St Kitts and Nevis country Caribbean Sea
St-Laurent, Golfe du g. Canada/U.S.A. see St Lawrence, Gulf of
155 H2 St-Laurent-du-Maroni Fr. Guiana
133 J4 St Lawrence Canada
133 G4 St Lawrence inlet Canada
133 H4 St Lawrence, Gulf of Canada/U.S.A.
128 B3 St Lawrence Island U.S.A.
135 J3 St Lawrence Islands National Park Canada
147 F2 St Lawrence Seaway sea chan. Canada/U.S.A.
133 G4 St-Léonard Canada
133 I3 St Lewis Canada
133 I3 St Lewis r. Canada
110 D2 St-Lô France
120 A3 St-Louis Senegal
134 E4 St Louis MI U.S.A.
142 F4 St Louis MO U.S.A.
134 A2 St Louis r. U.S.A.
149 L6 St Lucia country Caribbean Sea
125 J3 St Lucia, Lake S. Africa
125 J4 St Lucia Estuary S. Africa
106 □ St Magnus Bay U.K.
110 D3 St-Maixent-l'École France
110 C2 St-Malo France
110 C2 St-Malo, Golfe de g. France
125 G6 St Marks S. Africa
149 L5 St-Martin i. Guadeloupe
124 B6 St Martin, Cape S. Africa
131 J4 St Martin, Lake Canada
134 D3 St Martin Island U.S.A.
105 A8 St Martin's i. U.K.
89 H5 St Martin's Island Bangl.
70 C3 St Mary Peak Australia
71 H8 St Marys Australia
135 G4 St Mary's Canada
106 F2 St Mary's U.K.
105 A8 St Mary's i. U.K.
146 A4 St Marys OH U.S.A.
146 D4 St Marys PA U.S.A.
146 C5 St Marys WV U.S.A.
146 A4 St Marys r. U.S.A.
133 J4 St Mary's, Cape Canada
128 A3 St Matthew Island U.S.A.
68 E2 St Matthias Group is P.N.G.
132 F4 St-Maurice r. Canada
105 B7 St Mawes U.K.
110 D4 St-Médard-en-Jalles France
133 I3 St Michael's Bay Canada
110 C3 St-Nazaire France
105 G5 St Neots U.K.
110 H2 St-Nicolas-de-Port France
110 F1 St-Omer France
147 I1 St-Pamphile Canada
133 G4 St-Pascal Canada
131 G4 St Paul Canada
134 A3 St Paul MN U.S.A.
142 D3 St Paul NE U.S.A.
146 B6 St Paul VA U.S.A.
162 J7 St Paul, Île i. Indian Ocean
137 H3 St Peter U.S.A.
110 C2 St Peter Port U.K.
116 D3 St Petersburg Rus. Fed. (City Plan 55)
145 D7 St Petersburg U.S.A.
110 G5 St-Pierre mt. France
133 I4 St-Pierre N. America
132 F4 St-Pierre, Lac l. Canada
129 M5 St Pierre and Miquelon terr. N. America
110 D4 St-Pierre-d'Oléron France
110 F3 St-Pierre-le-Moûtier France
108 A4 St-Pol-sur-Ternoise France
110 F3 St-Pourçain-sur-Sioule France
147 H1 St-Prosper Canada
110 F2 St-Quentin France
110 H5 St-Raphaël France
147 F2 St Regis r. U.S.A.
147 F2 St Regis Falls U.S.A.
147 G2 St-Rémi Canada
147 H2 St-Sébastien Canada
133 G4 St-Siméon Canada
145 D6 St Simons Island U.S.A.
147 J2 St Stephen Canada
145 E5 St Stephen U.S.A.
147 H2 St-Théophile Canada
131 K4 St Theresa Point Canada
135 G4 St Thomas Canada
110 H5 St-Tropez France
131 J5 St Vincent U.S.A.
71 F9 St Vincent, Cape Australia
70 B5 St Vincent, Gulf Australia
149 L6 St Vincent and the Grenadines country Caribbean Sea
108 E4 St-Vith Belgium
131 H4 St Walburg Canada
135 G4 St Williams Canada
110 E4 St-Yrieix-la-Perche France
92 C1 Sain Us China
111 F1 Saioa mt. Spain
88 E3 Saipal mt. Nepal
91 G5 Saipan i. N. Mariana Is
89 H5 Saitlai Myanmar
102 N2 Saittanulkki h. Fin.
154 E7 Sajama, Nevado mt. Bol.
84 B5 Sājir Saudi Arabia
124 D5 Sak watercourse S. Africa
98 B2 Sa Kaeo Thai.
95 D7 Sakai Japan
95 C7 Sakaide Japan
95 C7 Sakaiminato Japan
86 B3 Sakākah Saudi Arabia
85 G5 Saka Kalat Pak.
142 C2 Sakakawea, Lake U.S.A.
132 E3 Sakami Canada
132 F3 Sakami r. Canada
132 E3 Sakami Lake Canada
115 L4 Sakar mts Bulg.
Sakarya Turkey see Adapazarı
80 C1 Sakarya r. Turkey
94 F5 Sakata Japan
96 C3 Sakchu N. Korea
83 H2 Saken Seyfullin Kazakh.
98 B2 Sa Keo r. Thai.
120 C4 Sakété Benin
90 G2 Sakhalin i. Rus. Fed.
90 G1 Sakhalinskiy Zaliv b. Rus. Fed.
88 C3 Sakhi India
125 H3 Sakhile S. Africa
84 C2 Sakht-Sar Iran
81 K1 Şäki Azer.
103 M5 Šakiai Lith.
88 A3 Sakir mt. Pak.
90 E4 Sakishima-shotō is Japan
98 C1 Sakon Nakhon Thai.
98 □ Sakra, P. Sing.
88 B4 Sakrand Pak.
124 D5 Sakrivier S. Africa
82 E3 Saksaul'skiy Kazakh.
95 B9 Sakura-jima vol. Japan
117 E6 Saky Ukr.
103 M3 Säkylä Fin.
120 □ Sal i. Cape Verde
117 G6 Sal r. Rus. Fed.
150 H5 Sal, Punta pt Hond.
103 M4 Sala Latvia
103 L4 Sala Sweden
132 F4 Salaberry-de-Valleyfield Canada
103 N4 Salacgrīva Latvia
114 F4 Sala Consilina Italy
Salada, Laguna salt l. Mex. see Salade, Laguna
141 E5 Salade, Laguna dry lake Mex.
159 E2 Saladillo Arg.
159 D2 Saladillo r. Arg.
159 E2 Salado r. Buenos Aires Arg.
159 C2 Salado r. Mendoza/San Luis Arg.
159 D4 Salado r. Río Negro Arg.
159 E1 Salado r. Santa Fé Arg.
159 C3 Salado r. Arg.
151 E2 Salado r. Mex.
156 B3 Salado, Quebrada de r. Chile
120 B4 Salaga Ghana
124 F1 Salajwe Botswana
121 D3 Salal Chad
86 D6 Şalālah Oman
151 G5 Salamá Guat.
150 H5 Salamá Hond.
159 B1 Salamanca Chile
150 D3 Salamanca Mex.
111 D2 Salamanca Spain
146 D3 Salamanca U.S.A.
125 J3 Salamanga Moz.
84 B3 Salāmatābād Iran
157 B3 Salamina Col.
80 F4 Salamīyah Syria
134 E5 Salamonie r. U.S.A.
134 E5 Salamonie Lake U.S.A.
89 F5 Salandi r. India
103 M4 Salantai Lith.
92 D1 Salaqi China
111 C1 Salas Spain
103 N4 Salaspils Latvia
98 C2 Salavan Laos
82 C1 Salavat Rus. Fed.
91 F7 Salawati i. Indon.
88 B5 Salaya India
91 E7 Salayar i. Indon.
152 C5 Sala y Gómez, Isla i. S. Pacific Ocean
159 D3 Salazar Arg.
103 N5 Šalčininkai Lith.
105 D7 Salcombe U.K.
157 B4 Saldaña r. Col.
111 D1 Saldaña Spain
124 B6 Saldanha S. Africa
124 B6 Saldanha Bay S. Africa
159 E3 Saldungaray Arg.
103 M4 Saldus Latvia
71 G7 Sale Australia
81 K5 Şāleḩābād Iran
84 C3 Şāleḩābād Iran
76 H3 Salekhard Rus. Fed.
87 B4 Salem India
147 H3 Salem MA U.S.A.
143 F4 Salem MO U.S.A.
144 F4 Salem NJ U.S.A.
147 G3 Salem NY U.S.A.
146 C4 Salem OH U.S.A.
138 B2 Salem OR U.S.A.
144 D4 Salem VA U.S.A.
106 C4 Salen Scotland U.K.
106 C4 Salen Scotland U.K.
114 F4 Salerno Italy
114 F4 Salerno, Golfo di g. Italy
105 E4 Salford U.K.
155 K5 Salgado r. Brazil
113 I6 Salgótarján Hungary
155 K5 Salgueiro Brazil
85 F4 Salian Afgh.
97 C6 Salibabu i. Indon.
136 E4 Salida U.S.A.
110 D5 Salies-de-Béarn France
80 B2 Salihli Turkey
116 C4 Salihorsk Belarus
123 D5 Salima Malawi
123 D5 Salimo Moz.
142 D4 Salina KS U.S.A.
141 G2 Salina UT U.S.A.
114 F5 Salina, Isola i. Isole Lipari Italy
151 F4 Salina Cruz Mex.
158 D2 Salinas Brazil
154 B4 Salinas Ecuador
150 D3 Salinas Mex.
140 B3 Salinas r. CA U.S.A.
140 B3 Salinas r. U.S.A.
139 F5 Salinas Peak U.S.A.
143 E5 Saline r. AR U.S.A.
142 C4 Saline r. KS U.S.A.
140 D3 Saline Valley depr. U.S.A.
155 I4 Salinópolis Brazil
154 C6 Salinosó Lachay, Punta pt Peru
105 F6 Salisbury U.K.
147 F5 Salisbury MD U.S.A.
145 D5 Salisbury NC U.S.A.
105 E6 Salisbury Plain U.K.
155 J6 Salitre r. Brazil
80 F5 Şalkhad Syria
87 D1 Salki r. India
102 O2 Salla Fin.
159 D3 Salliqueló Arg.
143 E5 Sallisaw U.S.A.
129 K3 Salluit Canada
89 E3 Sallyana Nepal
84 B2 Salmās Iran
116 D2 Salmi Rus. Fed.
130 F5 Salmo Canada
138 D2 Salmon U.S.A.
138 D2 Salmon r. U.S.A.
130 F4 Salmon Arm Canada
147 F3 Salmon Reservoir U.S.A.
138 D2 Salmon River Mountains U.S.A.
108 E5 Salmtal Germany
103 M3 Salo Fin.
89 E4 Salon India
110 G5 Salon-de-Provence France
122 C4 Salonga Sud, Parc National de la nat. park Dem. Rep. Congo
113 J7 Salonta Romania
120 □ Sal Rei Cape Verde
159 D1 Salsacate Arg.
117 G6 Sal'sk Rus. Fed.
114 C2 Salsomaggiore Terme Italy
124 E5 Salt watercourse S. Africa
141 G5 Salt r. AZ U.S.A.
134 B6 Salt r. MO U.S.A.
156 C2 Salta Arg.
104 F4 Saltaire U.K.
105 C7 Saltash U.K.
106 D5 Saltcoats U.K.
146 B5 Salt Creek r. U.S.A.
107 E5 Saltee Islands Rep. of Ireland
102 K2 Saltfjellet Svartisen Nasjonalpark nat. park Norway
143 B6 Salt Flat U.S.A.
146 C4 Salt Fork Lake U.S.A.
150 D2 Saltillo Mex.
138 E3 Salt Lake City U.S.A.
159 E2 Salto Arg.
158 C3 Salto Brazil
159 F1 Salto Uruguay
158 E2 Salto da Divisa Brazil
158 A4 Salto del Guairá Para.
156 E4 Salto Grande, Embalse de resr Uruguay
141 E5 Salton Sea salt l. U.S.A.
88 C2 Salt Range hills Pak.
131 G2 Salt River Canada
146 B5 Salt Rock U.S.A.
145 D5 Saluda SC U.S.A.
146 E6 Saluda VA U.S.A.
88 C4 Salumbar India
87 C2 Salur India
114 B2 Saluzzo Italy
159 D1 Salvador Arg.
158 E1 Salvador Brazil
143 F6 Salvador, Lake U.S.A.
150 D3 Salvatierra Mex.
141 G2 Salvation Creek r. U.S.A.
84 C5 Salwah Qatar
84 C5 Salwah, Dawḩat b. Qatar/Saudi Arabia
90 4 Salween r. China
91 B5 Salween r. Myanmar
81 L2 Salyan Azer.
146 B6 Salyersville U.S.A.
124 B2 Salzbrunn Namibia
112 F7 Salzburg Austria
109 I2 Salzgitter Germany
109 I1 Salzhausen Germany
109 G3 Salzkotten Germany
109 J3 Salzmünde Germany
109 J2 Salzwedel Germany
88 B4 Sam India
93 B7 Sam, Nam r. Laos/Vietnam
98 B2 Samae San, Ko c. Thai.
84 B4 Samāh well Saudi Arabia
154 F7 Samaipata Bol.
97 C5 Samal i. Phil.
97 B5 Samales Group is Phil.
87 C2 Samalkot India
80 E3 Samandağı Turkey
94 H3 Samani Japan
80 C6 Samannūd Egypt
97 C4 Samar i. Phil.
82 B1 Samara Rus. Fed.
82 B1 Samara r. Rus. Fed.
157 D3 Samariapo Venez.
99 E3 Samarinda Indon.
83 H2 Samarka Kazakh.
94 D2 Samarka Rus. Fed.
Samarkand Uzbek. see Samarqand
83 F5 Samarqand Uzbek.
83 G5 Samarqand, Qullai mt. Tajik.
81 I4 Sāmarrā' Iraq
97 C4 Samar Sea g. Phil.
116 I4 Samarskaya Oblast' admin. div. Rus. Fed.
83 J2 Samarskoye Kazakh.
81 L1 Şamaxı Azer.
122 C4 Samba Dem. Rep. Congo
99 E2 Sambaliung mts Indon.
87 D1 Sambalpur India
99 D3 Sambar, Tanjung pt Indon.
99 C2 Sambas Indon.
123 F5 Sambava Madag.
89 G4 Sambha India
88 D3 Sambhal India
88 C4 Sambhar Lake India
117 B5 Sambir Ukr.
155 J5 Sambito r. Brazil
159 F2 Samborombón, Bahía b. Arg.
108 B4 Sambre r. Belgium/France
157 A3 Sambú r. Panama
96 E5 Samch'ŏk S. Korea
81 J3 Samdi Dag mt. Turkey
122 D4 Same Tanz.
Samirum Iran see Yazd-e Khvāst
96 E3 Samjiyŏn N. Korea
81 K1 Şämkir Azer.
96 E6 Samnangjin S. Korea
84 D3 Samnan va Damghan reg. Iran
69 I3 Samoa country Pacific Ocean
160 H7 Samoa Basin sea feature Pacific Ocean
114 F2 Samobor Croatia
116 G2 Samoded Rus. Fed.
115 J3 Samokov Bulg.
112 H6 Šamorín Slovakia
115 L6 Samos i. Greece
99 A2 Samosir i. Indon.
115 K4 Samothraki Greece
115 K4 Samothraki i. Greece
97 B3 Sampaloc Point Phil.
99 D3 Sampit Indon.
99 D3 Sampit, Teluk b. Indon.
123 C4 Sampwe Dem. Rep. Congo
143 E6 Sam Rayburn Reservoir U.S.A.
89 E3 Samsang China
93 B6 Sam Sao, Phou mts Laos/Vietnam
98 C1 Sâm Sơn Vietnam
80 F1 Samsun Turkey
117 G7 Samtredia Georgia
98 B3 Samui, Ko i. Thai.
117 I7 Samur r. Azer./Rus. Fed.
98 B2 Samut Prakan Thai.
98 B2 Samut Sakhon Thai.
98 B2 Samut Songkhram Thai.
89 G3 Samyai China
120 B3 San Mali
98 B1 San, Phou mt. Laos
98 C2 San, Tônlé r. Cambodia
86 B6 Şan'ā' Yemen
73 D3 Sanae research stn Antarctica
121 D4 Sanaga r. Cameroon
157 A4 San Agustín Col.
97 C5 San Agustin, Cape Phil.
84 B6 Sanām Saudi Arabia
161 N7 San Ambrosio, Isla i. S. Pacific Ocean
84 B3 Sanandaj Iran
140 B2 San Andreas U.S.A.
97 C3 San Andres Phil.
150 I5 San Andrés, Isla de i. Col.
139 F5 San Andres Mountains U.S.A.
151 F4 San Andrés Tuxtla Mex.
143 C6 San Angelo U.S.A.
150 G4 San Antonio Belize
159 B2 San Antonio Chile
97 B3 San Antonio Phil.
143 D6 San Antonio U.S.A.
140 B3 San Antonio r. U.S.A.
159 F3 San Antonio, Cabo c. Arg.
149 H4 San Antonio, Cabo c. Cuba
140 D4 San Antonio, Mount U.S.A.
111 G3 San Antonio Abad Spain
156 C2 San Antonio de los Cobres Arg.
157 D2 San Antonio de Tamanaco Venez.
159 D4 San Antonio Oeste Arg.
140 B4 San Antonio Reservoir U.S.A.
140 B3 San Ardo U.S.A.
159 E3 San Augustín Arg.
159 C1 San Augustín de Valle Fértil Arg.
88 D5 Sanawad India
151 D3 San Bartolo Mex.
114 E3 San Benedetto del Tronto Italy
148 B5 San Benedicto, Isla i. Mex.
143 D7 San Benito U.S.A.
140 B3 San Benito r. U.S.A.
140 B3 San Benito Mountain U.S.A.
140 D4 San Bernardino U.S.A.
139 C5 San Bernardino Mountains U.S.A.
159 B2 San Bernardo Chile
150 C2 San Bernardo Mex.
95 C7 Sanbe-san vol. Japan
150 C3 San Blas Nayarit Mex.
150 B2 San Blas Sinaloa Mex.
150 J6 San Blas, Archipiélago de is Panama
145 C6 San Blas, Cape U.S.A.
150 J6 San Blas, Cordillera de mts Panama
154 E6 San Borja Bol.
147 H3 Sanbornville U.S.A.
150 D2 San Buenaventura Mex.
159 C2 San Carlos Arg.
159 B3 San Carlos Chile
150 D1 San Carlos Coahuila Mex.
151 E2 San Carlos Tamaulipas Mex.
150 H6 San Carlos Nicaragua
97 B3 San Carlos Phil.
97 B4 San Carlos Phil.
159 F2 San Carlos Uruguay
141 G5 San Carlos U.S.A.
157 D4 San Carlos Venez.
157 C2 San Carlos Venez.
159 E1 San Carlos Centro Arg.
159 B4 San Carlos de Bariloche Arg.
159 E3 San Carlos de Bolívar Arg.
157 C2 San Carlos del Zulia Venez.
141 G5 San Carlos Lake U.S.A.
92 C2 Sancha Gansu China
92 D2 Sancha Shanxi China
93 C5 Sancha He r. China
83 I5 Sanchakou China
88 D5 Sanchi India
93 B6 San Chien Pau mt. Laos
88 B4 Sanchor India
92 D2 Sanchuan He r. China
116 H3 Sanchursk Rus. Fed.
151 E3 San Ciro de Acosta Mex.
159 B2 San Clemente Chile
140 D5 San Clemente U.S.A.
140 C5 San Clemente Island U.S.A.
110 F3 Sancoins France
159 E1 San Cristóbal Arg.
69 G3 San Cristobal i. Solomon Is
157 B3 San Cristóbal Venez.
154 □ San Cristóbal, Isla i. Galapagos Is Ecuador
151 F4 San Cristóbal de las Casas Mex.
141 F5 San Cristobal Wash watercourse U.S.A.
149 I4 Sancti Spíritus Cuba
125 H1 Sand r. S. Africa
94 D3 Sandagou Rus. Fed.
106 C5 Sanda Island U.K.
99 E1 Sandakan Sabah Malaysia
103 I3 Sandane Norway
115 J4 Sandanski Bulg.
109 K2 Sandau Germany
106 F1 Sanday i. U.K.
106 F1 Sanday Sound sea chan. U.K.
105 E4 Sandbach U.K.
103 J4 Sandefjord Norway
73 E4 Sandercock Nunataks Antarctica
141 H4 Sanders U.S.A.
109 J3 Sandersleben Germany
143 C6 Sanderson U.S.A.
71 J1 Sandgate Australia
106 D6 Sandhead U.K.
154 E6 Sandia Peru
140 D5 San Diego U.S.A.
156 C8 San Diego, Cabo c. Arg.
80 C2 Sandıklı Turkey
88 E4 Sandila India
134 B2 Sand Island U.S.A.
134 E2 Sand Lake Canada
103 I4 Sandnes Norway
102 K2 Sandnessjøen Norway
123 C4 Sandoa Dem. Rep. Congo
113 J5 Sandomierz Poland
157 A4 Sandoná Col.
114 E2 San Donà di Piave Italy
Sandoway Myanmar see Thandwè
105 F7 Sandown U.K.
124 C7 Sandown Bay S. Africa
102 □ Sandoy i. Faroe Is
138 C1 Sandpoint U.S.A.
106 A4 Sandray i. U.K.
113 M7 Şandrul Mare, Vârful mt. Romania
103 K3 Sandsjö Sweden
130 C4 Sandspit Canada
143 D4 Sand Springs U.S.A.
140 C2 Sand Springs Salt Flat U.S.A.
134 A2 Sandstone U.S.A.
141 F5 Sand Tank Mountains U.S.A.
93 C5 Sandu Guizhou China
93 D5 Sandu Hunan China
135 F4 Sandusky MI U.S.A.
146 B4 Sandusky OH U.S.A.
146 B4 Sandusky Bay U.S.A.
124 C5 Sandveld mts S. Africa
124 B3 Sandverhaar Namibia
103 J4 Sandvika Norway
102 K3 Sandvika Sweden
103 L3 Sandviken Sweden
133 I3 Sandwich Bay Canada
106 □ Sandwick U.K.
89 G5 Sandwip Channel Bangl.
147 H2 Sandy r. U.S.A.
131 I3 Sandy Bay Canada
69 F4 Sandy Cape Australia
71 F8 Sandy Cape Australia
146 B5 Sandy Hook U.S.A.
147 F4 Sandy Hook pt U.S.A.
Sandykachi Turkm. see Sandykgaçy
85 F2 Sandykgaçy Turkm.
82 E5 Sandykly Gumy des. Turkm.
132 B3 Sandy Lake Canada
132 B3 Sandy Lake l. Canada
147 E3 Sandy Pond U.S.A.
158 A4 San Estanislao Para.
97 B2 San Fabian Phil.
159 B2 San Felipe Chile
148 B2 San Felipe Baja California Mex.
150 C2 San Felipe Chihuahua Mex.
150 D3 San Felipe Guanajuato Mex.
157 C2 San Felipe Venez.
140 D5 San Felipe Creek watercourse U.S.A.
161 N7 San Félix, Isla i. S. Pacific Ocean
159 E2 San Fernando Arg.
159 B2 San Fernando Chile
151 E2 San Fernando Mex.
97 B2 San Fernando Phil.
97 B3 San Fernando Phil.
111 C4 San Fernando Spain
157 E2 San Fernando Trin. and Tob.
140 C4 San Fernando U.S.A.
157 D3 San Fernando de Apure Venez.
157 D3 San Fernando de Atabapo Venez.
145 D6 Sanford FL U.S.A.
147 H3 Sanford ME U.S.A.
145 E5 Sanford NC U.S.A.
134 E4 Sanford Lake U.S.A.
159 D1 San Francisco Arg.
150 I6 San Francisco Panama
140 A3 San Francisco U.S.A. (City Plan 62)
141 H5 San Francisco r. U.S.A.
156 C3 San Francisco, Paso de pass Arg.
140 A3 San Francisco Bay inlet U.S.A.
150 C2 San Francisco del Oro Mex.
150 D3 San Francisco del Rincón Mex.
149 J5 San Francisco de Macorís Dom. Rep.
156 C7 San Francisco de Paula, Cabo c. Arg.
151 E3 San Francisco el Alto Mex.
150 G5 San Francisco Gotera El Salvador
111 G3 San Francisco Javier Spain
157 A4 San Gabriel Ecuador
150 A1 San Gabriel, Punta pt Mex.
140 C4 San Gabriel Mountains U.S.A.
88 C6 Sangamner India
134 C6 Sangamon r. U.S.A.
85 G3 Sangan Afgh.
85 F4 Sangān Iran
Sangan, Koh-i- mt. Afgh. see Sangān, Kūh-e
85 G3 Sangān, Kūh-e mt. Afgh.
88 B3 Sangar r. Pak.
77 N3 Sangar Rus. Fed.
87 B2 Sangareddi India
114 C5 San Gavino Monreale Sardinia Italy
154 C4 Sangay, Parque Nacional nat. park Ecuador
85 E3 Sang Bast Iran
97 B5 Sangboy Islands Phil.
99 E4 Sangeang i. Indon.
92 B1 Sangejing China
140 C3 Sanger U.S.A.
109 J3 Sangerhausen Germany
92 E1 Sanggan He r. China
92 B3 Sanggarmai China
99 D2 Sanggau Indon.
96 B5 Sanggou Wan b. China
122 B3 Sangha r. Congo
88 B4 Sanghar Pak.
157 B3 San Gil Col.
114 G5 San Giovanni in Fiore Italy
114 F4 San Giovanni Rotondo Italy
97 C6 Sangir i. Indon.
91 E6 Sangir, Kepulauan is Indon.
96 E5 Sangju S. Korea
98 B2 Sângke, Stœ̆ng r. Cambodia
99 E2 Sangkulirang Indon.
87 A2 Sangli India
85 H2 Sanglich Afgh.
120 D4 Sangmélima Cameroon
88 D3 Sangnam India
89 H3 Sangngagqoiling China
96 E3 Sang-ni N. Korea
123 D6 Sango Zimbabwe
87 A2 Sangole India
140 D4 San Gorgonio Mountain U.S.A.
139 F4 Sangre de Cristo Range mts U.S.A.
157 E2 Sangre Grande Trin. and Tob.
88 C3 Sangrur India

South East Forests National Park 207

94 C2 Sibirtsevo Rus. Fed.
122 B4 Sibiti Congo
115 K2 Sibiu Romania
99 A2 Sibolga Indon.
98 A5 Siborongborong Indon.
89 H4 Sibsagar India
99 D2 Sibu *Sarawak* Malaysia
97 B5 Sibuco Phil.
97 B5 Sibuguey *r.* Phil.
97 B5 Sibuguey Bay Phil.
122 B3 Sibut Centr. Afr. Rep.
97 A5 Sibutu *i.* Phil.
97 A5 Sibutu Passage Phil.
97 B3 Sibuyan *i.* Phil.
97 B3 Sibuyan Sea Phil.
97 B2 Sicapoo *mt.* Phil.
98 A3 Sichon Thai.
93 B4 Sichuan *prov.* China
93 B4 Sichuan Pendi *basin* China
110 G5 Sicié, Cap *c.* France
Sicilia *i.* Italy *see* Sicily
114 E6 Sicilian Channel Italy/Tunisia
114 E6 Sicily *i.* Italy
154 D6 Sicuani Peru
88 C5 Siddhapur India
87 B2 Siddipet India
115 L7 Sideros, Akra *pt* Greece
124 E6 Sidesaviwa S. Africa
111 H5 Sidi Aïssa Alg.
111 G4 Sidi Ali Alg.
120 B1 Sidi Bel Abbès Alg.
114 C7 Sidi Bouzid Tunisia
114 D7 Sidi El Hani, Sebkhet de *salt pan* Tunisia
120 A2 Sidi Ifni Morocco
120 B1 Sidi Kacem Morocco
98 A5 Sidikalang Indon.
106 E4 Sidlaw Hills U.K.
73 B4 Sidley, Mount *mt.* Antarctica
105 D7 Sidmouth U.K.
130 E5 Sidney Canada
138 F2 Sidney *MT* U.S.A.
142 C3 Sidney *NE* U.S.A.
147 F3 Sidney *NY* U.S.A.
146 A4 Sidney *OH* U.S.A.
145 D5 Sidney Lanier, Lake U.S.A.
89 H5 Sidoktaya Myanmar
80 E5 Sidon Lebanon
116 G3 Sidorovo Rus. Fed.
158 A3 Sidrolândia Brazil
125 I3 Sidvokodvo Swaziland
Sidzhak Uzbek. *see* Sijjaq
110 F5 Sié, Col de *pass* France
113 K4 Siedlce Poland
109 G4 Siegen Germany
98 B2 Siĕmréab Cambodia
114 D3 Siena Italy
113 I5 Sieradz Poland
89 H3 Si'e>rdingka China
159 D4 Sierra, Punta *pt* Arg.
143 B6 Sierra Blanca U.S.A.
159 C4 Sierra Colorada Arg.
159 D4 Sierra Grande Arg.
120 A4 Sierra Leone *country* Africa
163 H5 Sierra Leone Basin *sea feature* N. Atlantic Ocean
163 H5 Sierra Leone Rise *sea feature* N. Atlantic Ocean
140 C4 Sierra Madre Mountains U.S.A.
150 D2 Sierra Mojada Mex.
157 C2 Sierra Nevada, Parque Nacional *nat. park* Venez.
157 B2 Sierra Nevada de Santa Marta, Parque Nacional *nat. park* Col.
140 B2 Sierraville U.S.A.
141 G6 Sierra Vista U.S.A.
112 C7 Sierre Switz.
102 N3 Sievi Fin.
93 C6 Sifang Ling *mts* China
115 K6 Sifnos *i.* Greece
111 F5 Sig Alg.
129 M2 Sigguup Nunaa *pen.* Greenland
113 K7 Sighetu Marmaţiei Romania
113 L7 Sighişoara Romania
87 C5 Sigiriya Sri Lanka
98 □ Siglap Sing.
99 A1 Sigli Indon.
102 C1 Siglufjörður Iceland
97 B4 Sigma Phil.
112 D6 Sigmaringen Germany
108 E4 Signal de Botrange *h.* Belgium
141 E5 Signal Peak U.S.A.
108 C5 Signy-l'Abbaye France
134 A5 Sigourney U.S.A.
115 K5 Sigri, Akra *pt* Greece
163 C4 Sigsbee Deep *sea feature* G. of Mexico
151 H5 Siguatepeque Hond.
111 E2 Sigüenza Spain
120 B3 Siguiri Guinea
103 N4 Sigulda Latvia
98 B3 Sihanoukville Cambodia
92 F3 Sihong China
88 E5 Sihora India
93 D6 Sihui China
102 N2 Siikajoki Fin.
102 N3 Siilinjärvi Fin.
81 H3 Siirt Turkey
83 G4 Sijjaq Uzbek.
99 B3 Sijunjung Indon.
88 B5 Sika India
130 E3 Sikanni Chief Canada
130 E3 Sikanni Chief *r.* Canada
88 C4 Sikar India
85 H3 Sikaram *mt.* Afgh.
120 B3 Sikasso Mali
83 K3 Sikeshu China
143 F4 Sikeston U.S.A.
90 F2 Sikhote-Alin' *mts* Rus. Fed.
115 K6 Sikinos *i.* Greece
89 G4 Sikkim *state* India
102 L2 Siksjö Sweden
96 B4 Sikuaishi China
99 E1 Sikuati *Sabah* Malaysia
111 C1 Sil *r.* Spain
97 C4 Silago Phil.
103 M5 Šilalė Lith.
150 D3 Silao Mex.
97 B4 Silay Phil.
109 H1 Silberberg *h.* Germany
89 H4 Silchar India
80 B1 Şile Turkey
87 C2 Sileru *r.* India
83 H1 Sileti *r.* Kazakh.
83 H1 Siletiteniz, Ozero *salt l.* Kazakh.
114 C6 Siliana Tunisia
80 D3 Silifke Turkey
89 G3 Siling Co *salt l.* China
115 L2 Silistra Bulg.
80 B1 Silivri Turkey
103 K3 Siljan *l.* Sweden
103 J4 Silkeborg Denmark
103 N4 Sillamäe Estonia
88 C5 Sillod India
125 I3 Silobela S. Africa
89 G3 Silong China
143 E6 Silsbee U.S.A.
102 N2 Siltaharju Fin.
85 F5 Sīlūp *r.* Iran
103 M5 Šilutė Lith.
81 H2 Silvan Turkey
88 C5 Silvassa India
134 B2 Silver Bay U.S.A.
139 E5 Silver City U.S.A.
134 C1 Silver Islet Canada
138 B3 Silver Lake U.S.A.
140 D4 Silver Lake *l. CA* U.S.A.
134 D2 Silver Lake *l. MI* U.S.A.
107 C5 Silvermine Mountains Rep. of Ireland
140 D3 Silver Peak Range *mts* U.S.A.
146 E5 Silver Spring U.S.A.
140 C2 Silver Springs U.S.A.
70 D3 Silverton Australia
105 D7 Silverton U.K.
135 F3 Silver Water Canada
151 G4 Silvituc Mex.
97 B3 Simara *i.* Phil.
135 H2 Simàrd, Lac *l.* Canada
81 K5 Şīmareh, Rūdkhāneh-ye *r.* Iran
89 F4 Simaria India
80 B2 Simav Turkey
80 B2 Simav Dağları *mts* Turkey
122 C3 Simba Dem. Rep. Congo
135 G4 Simcoe Canada
135 H3 Simcoe, Lake Canada
87 D1 Simdega India
122 D2 Simēn *mts* Eth.
Simēn Mountains Eth. *see* Simēn
99 A2 Simeulue *i.* Indon.
117 E6 Simferopol' Ukr.
89 E3 Simikot Nepal
157 B3 Simití Col.
140 C4 Simi Valley U.S.A.
139 F4 Simla U.S.A.
113 K7 Şimleu Silvaniei Romania
108 E4 Simmerath Germany
108 F5 Simmern (Hunsrück) Germany
140 C4 Simmler U.S.A.
141 F4 Simmons U.S.A.
145 F7 Simm's Bahamas
102 N2 Simojärvi *l.* Fin.
150 D2 Simon Mex.
130 F4 Simonette *r.* Canada
131 I4 Simonhouse Canada
112 D7 Simplon Pass Switz.
68 D4 Simpson Desert Australia
134 D1 Simpson Island Canada
140 D2 Simpson Park Mountains U.S.A.
103 K5 Simrishamn Sweden
97 A5 Simunul *i.* Phil.
90 H2 Simushir, Ostrov *i.* Rus. Fed.
87 A2 Sina *r.* India
99 A2 Sinabang Indon.
98 A5 Sinabung *vol.* Indon.
121 F2 Sinai *pen.* Egypt
108 C5 Sinai, Mont *h.* France
150 B2 Sinaloa *state* Mex.
114 D3 Sinalunga Italy
93 C5 Sinan China
96 C4 Sinanju N. Korea
89 H5 Sinbyugyun Myanmar
80 F2 Sincan Turkey
157 B2 Sincé Col.
157 B2 Sincelejo Col.
145 D5 Sinclair, Lake U.S.A.
130 E4 Sinclair Mills Canada
124 B2 Sinclair Mine Namibia
106 E2 Sinclair's Bay U.K.
88 D4 Sind *r.* India
97 B4 Sindañgan Phil.
99 C4 Sindangbarang Indon.
88 B4 Sindari India
112 D6 Sindelfingen Germany
87 B2 Sindgi India
88 B4 Sindh *prov.* Pak.
87 B3 Sindhnur India
80 B2 Sındırgı Turkey
88 D6 Sindkhed India
88 C5 Sindkheda India
96 C4 Sin-do *i.* China
116 I2 Sindor Rus. Fed.
89 F5 Sindri India
88 B3 Sind Sagar Doab *lowland* Pak.
116 I3 Sinegor'ye Rus. Fed.
115 L4 Sinekçi Turkey
111 B4 Sines Port.
111 B4 Sines, Cabo de *c.* Port.
102 N2 Sinettä Fin.
120 B4 Sinfra Côte d'Ivoire
121 F3 Singa Sudan
88 E3 Singahi India
88 D2 Singa Pass India
98 □ Singapore *country* Asia
98 B5 Singapore Sing. (City Plan 50)
98 □ Singapore, Strait of Indon./Sing.
99 E4 Singaraja Indon.
98 B2 Sing Buri Thai.
135 G3 Singhampton Canada
122 D4 Singida Tanz.
68 C2 Singkang Indon.
99 C2 Singkawang Indon.
98 A5 Singkil Indon.
71 I4 Singleton Australia
96 D4 Sin'gye N. Korea
87 C5 Sinharaja Forest Reserve *nature res.* Sri Lanka
96 D3 Sinhŭng N. Korea
114 C4 Siniscola *Sardinia* Italy
82 E2 Siniy-Shikhan Rus. Fed.
114 G3 Sinj Croatia
68 C2 Sinjai Indon.
81 H3 Sinjār Iraq
81 H3 Sinjār, Jabal *mt.* Iraq
81 J3 Sīnji Iran
121 F3 Sinkat Sudan
Sinkiang *aut. reg.* China *see* Xinjiang Uygur Zizhiqu
96 C4 Sinmi-do *i.* N. Korea
109 G4 Sinn Germany
155 H2 Sinnamary Fr. Guiana
115 M2 Sinoie, Lacul *lag.* Romania
117 E7 Sinop Turkey
96 D3 Sinp'a N. Korea
96 E3 Sinp'o N. Korea
96 D4 Sinp'yŏng N. Korea
96 D4 Sinsang N. Korea
109 G5 Sinsheim Germany
99 D2 Sintang Indon.
149 L5 Sint Eustatius *i.* Neth. Antilles
108 B3 Sint-Laureins Belgium
149 L5 Sint Maarten *i.* Neth. Antilles
108 C3 Sint-Niklaas Belgium
143 D6 Sinton U.S.A.
108 D4 Sint-Truiden Belgium
157 A2 Sinú *r.* Col.
96 C3 Sinŭiju N. Korea
108 F4 Sinzig Germany
97 B5 Siocon Phil.
112 I7 Siófok Hungary
112 C7 Sion Switz.
107 D3 Sion Mills U.K.
142 D3 Sioux Center U.S.A.
142 D3 Sioux City U.S.A.
142 D3 Sioux Falls U.S.A.
132 B3 Sioux Lookout Canada
151 G5 Sipacate Guat.
97 B4 Sipalay Phil.
96 C2 Siping China
131 J3 Sipiwesk Canada
131 J3 Sipiwesk Lake Canada
88 C5 Sipra *r.* India
145 C5 Sipsey *r.* U.S.A.
99 A3 Sipura *i.* Indon.
150 H5 Siquia *r.* Nicaragua
97 B4 Siquijor Phil.
97 B4 Siquijor *i.* Phil.
88 B5 Sir *r.* Pak.
87 B3 Sira India
103 I4 Sira *r.* Norway
84 D5 Şīr Abū Nu'āyr *i.* U.A.E.
98 B2 Si Racha Thai.
Siracusa *Sicily* Italy *see* Syracuse
130 E4 Sir Alexander, Mount Canada
81 G1 Şiran Turkey
85 G5 Siranda Lake Pak.
84 D5 Şīr Banī Yās *i.* U.A.E.
81 L3 Sīrdān Iran
83 G4 Sirdaryo Uzbek.
68 D3 Sir Edward Pellew Group *is* Australia
134 A3 Siren U.S.A.
84 E5 Sīrīk Iran
98 B1 Siri Kit Dam Thai.
84 D4 Sīrīz Iran
130 D2 Sir James MacBrien, Mount Canada
84 D4 Sīrjān Iran
84 D4 Sīrjān *salt flat* Iran
70 B5 Sir Joseph Banks Group *is* Australia
88 E4 Sirmour India
81 I3 Şırnak Turkey
87 C2 Sironcha India
88 D4 Sironj India
87 B2 Sirpur India
140 C4 Sirretta Peak U.S.A.
84 D5 Sīrrī, Jazīreh-ye *i.* Iran
88 C3 Sirsa *Haryana* India
89 E4 Sirsa *Uttar Pradesh* India
130 F4 Sir Sandford, Mount Canada
87 A3 Sirsi *Karnataka* India
88 D3 Sirsi *Uttar Pradesh* India
87 B2 Sirsilla India
121 D1 Sirte Libya
121 D1 Sirte, Gulf of Libya
87 A2 Sirur India
81 I2 Şirvan Turkey
103 N5 Širvintos Lith.
81 J4 Sīrwān *r.* Iraq
130 F4 Sir Wilfrid Laurier, Mount Canada
114 G2 Sisak Croatia
98 C2 Sisaket Thai.
151 G3 Sisal Mex.
124 E3 Sishen S. Africa
81 K2 Sisian Armenia
134 C2 Siskiwit Bay U.S.A.
98 B2 Sisŏphŏn Cambodia
140 B4 Sisquoc *r.* U.S.A.
142 D2 Sisseton U.S.A.
147 J1 Sisson Branch Reservoir Canada
85 F4 Sīstān *reg.* Iran
85 F4 Sīstan, Daryācheh-ye *marsh* Afgh.
71 F8 Sisters Beach Australia
85 E5 Sīt Iran
88 C5 Sitamau India
97 A5 Sitangkai Phil.
88 E4 Sitapur India
115 L7 Siteia Greece
125 I3 Siteki Swaziland
115 J4 Sithonia *pen.* Greece
158 C1 Sítio da Abadia Brazil
158 D1 Sítio do Mato Brazil
130 B3 Sitka U.S.A.
88 B3 Sitpur Pak.
108 D4 Sittard Neth.
89 H4 Sittaung Myanmar
109 H1 Sittensen Germany
105 H6 Sittingbourne U.K.
89 H5 Sittwe Myanmar
93 □ Siu A Chau *i. Hong Kong* China
150 H5 Siuna Nicaragua
89 F5 Siuri India
87 B4 Sivaganga India
87 B4 Sivakasi India
84 D4 Sivand Iran
80 F2 Sivas Turkey
80 B2 Sivaslı Turkey
81 G3 Siverek Turkey
81 G2 Sivrice Turkey
80 C2 Sivrihisar Turkey
125 H3 Sivukile S. Africa
121 E2 Sīwah Egypt
88 D3 Siwalik Range *mts* India/Nepal
89 F4 Siwan India
88 C4 Siwana India
110 G5 Six-Fours-les-Plages France
92 E3 Sixian China
134 E4 Six Lakes U.S.A.
107 D3 Sixmilecross U.K.
125 H2 Siyabuswa S. Africa
92 F3 Siyang China
82 A4 Siyäzän Azer.
92 C1 Siyitang China
84 D3 Sīyunī Iran
Sjælland *i.* Denmark *see* Zealand
115 I3 Sjenica Serb. and Mont.
103 K5 Sjöbo Sweden
102 L1 Sjøvegan Norway
117 E6 Skadovs'k Ukr.
102 C2 Skaftafell *nat. park* Iceland
102 C3 Skaftárós *r. mouth* Iceland
102 C1 Skagafjörður *inlet* Iceland
103 J4 Skagen Denmark
103 J4 Skagerrak *str.* Denmark/Norway
138 B1 Skagit *r.* Canada/U.S.A.
130 B3 Skagway U.S.A.
102 N1 Skaidi Norway
102 L1 Skaland Norway
102 K2 Skalmodal Sweden
103 J4 Skanderborg Denmark
147 E3 Skaneateles Lake U.S.A.
134 C2 Skanee U.S.A.
115 K5 Skantzoura *i.* Greece
103 K4 Skara Sweden
103 M4 Skärgårdshavets nationalpark *nat. park* Fin.
103 J3 Skarnes Norway
113 J5 Skarżysko-Kamienna Poland
102 M2 Skaulo Sweden
113 I6 Skawina Poland
130 D3 Skeena *r.* Canada
130 D3 Skeena Mountains Canada
105 H4 Skegness U.K.
102 M2 Skellefteå Sweden
102 M2 Skellefteälven *r.* Sweden
102 M2 Skelleftehamn Sweden
107 A6 Skellig Rocks *is* Rep. of Ireland
104 E4 Skelmersdale U.K.
107 E4 Skerries Rep. of Ireland
103 J4 Ski Norway
115 J5 Skiathos *i.* Greece
107 B6 Skibbereen Rep. of Ireland
102 M1 Skibotn Norway
104 D3 Skiddaw *h.* U.K.
103 J4 Skien Norway
113 J5 Skierniewice Poland
120 C1 Skikda Alg.
104 G4 Skipsea U.K.
70 E6 Skipton Australia
104 E4 Skipton U.K.
104 G4 Skirlaugh U.K.
103 J4 Skive Denmark
102 C2 Skjálfandafljót *r.* Iceland
103 J5 Skjern Denmark
103 I3 Skjolden Norway
83 H5 Skobeleva, Pik *mt.* Kyrg.
102 I3 Skodje Norway
Skoganvarre Norway *see* Skoganvarri
102 N1 Skoganvarri Norway
107 F6 Skokholm Island U.K.
134 D4 Skokie U.S.A.
82 E2 Skol' Kazakh.
105 B6 Skomer Island U.K.
115 J5 Skopelos *i.* Greece
116 F4 Skopin Rus. Fed.
115 I4 Skopje Macedonia
117 F5 Skorodnoye Rus. Fed.
103 K4 Skövde Sweden
147 I2 Skowhegan U.S.A.
103 M4 Skrunda Latvia
130 B2 Skukum, Mount Canada
125 I2 Skukuza S. Africa
140 D3 Skull Peak U.S.A.
134 B5 Skunk *r.* U.S.A.
103 M4 Skuodas Lith.
103 K5 Skurup Sweden
103 L3 Skutskär Sweden
117 D5 Skvyra Ukr.
106 B3 Skye *i.* U.K.
115 K5 Skyros Greece
115 K5 Skyros *i.* Greece
103 J5 Slagelse Denmark
102 L2 Slagnäs Sweden
99 C4 Slamet, Gunung *vol.* Indon.
107 E4 Slane Rep. of Ireland
107 E5 Slaney *r.* Rep. of Ireland
116 D3 Slantsy Rus. Fed.
117 G5 Slashchevskaya Rus. Fed.
134 D1 Slate Islands Canada
114 G2 Slatina Croatia
115 K2 Slatina Romania
131 G2 Slave *r.* Canada
120 C4 Slave Coast Africa
130 G3 Slave Lake Canada
83 I1 Slavgorod Rus. Fed.
113 N2 Slavkovichi Rus. Fed.
115 H2 Slavonia *reg.* Croatia
Slavonija *reg.* Croatia *see* Slavonia
115 H2 Slavonski Brod Croatia
117 C5 Slavuta Ukr.
117 D5 Slavutych Ukr.
94 B3 Slavyanka Rus. Fed.
117 F6 Slavyansk-na-Kubani Rus. Fed.
116 D4 Slawharad Belarus
112 H3 Sławno Poland
105 G4 Sleaford U.K.
70 A5 Sleaford Bay Australia
107 A5 Slea Head Rep. of Ireland
106 C3 Sleat *pen.* U.K.
106 C3 Sleat, Sound of *sea chan.* U.K.
132 E2 Sleeper Islands Canada
134 D3 Sleeping Bear Dunes National Lakeshore *nature res.* U.S.A.
134 D3 Sleeping Bear Point U.S.A.
117 H7 Sleptsovskaya Rus. Fed.
73 C3 Slessor Glacier Antarctica
143 F6 Slidell U.S.A.
107 A5 Slievanea *h.* Rep. of Ireland
107 D3 Slieve Anierin *h.* Rep. of Ireland
107 D5 Slieveardagh Hills Rep. of Ireland
107 C4 Slieve Aughty Mountains Rep. of Ireland
107 D3 Slieve Beagh *h.* Rep. of Ireland/U.K.
107 C5 Slieve Bernagh *hills* Rep. of Ireland
107 D4 Slieve Bloom Mountains Rep. of Ireland
107 B5 Slievecallan *h.* Rep. of Ireland
107 B3 Slieve Car *h.* Rep. of Ireland
107 F3 Slieve Donard *h.* U.K.
107 B4 Slieve Elva *h.* Rep. of Ireland
107 C3 Slieve Gamph *hills* Rep. of Ireland
107 C3 Slieve League *h.* Rep. of Ireland
107 B5 Slieve Mish Mountains Rep. of Ireland
107 B5 Slieve Miskish Mountains Rep. of Ireland
107 A3 Slieve More *h.* Rep. of Ireland
107 D4 Slieve na Calliagh *h.* Rep. of Ireland
107 D5 Slievenamon *h.* Rep. of Ireland
107 D2 Slieve Snaght *h.* Rep. of Ireland
106 B3 Sligachan U.K.
107 C3 Sligo Rep. of Ireland
107 C3 Sligo Bay Rep. of Ireland
103 L4 Slite Sweden
115 L3 Sliven Bulg.
116 H2 Sloboda Rus. Fed.
116 I2 Slobodchikovo Rus. Fed.
115 L2 Slobozia Romania
130 F5 Slocan Canada
108 E1 Slochteren Neth.
116 C4 Slonim Belarus
108 C2 Slootdorp Neth.
108 D2 Sloten Neth.
108 D2 Slotermeer *l.* Neth.
105 G6 Slough U.K.
113 I6 Slovakia *country* Europe
114 F1 Slovenia *country* Europe
114 F1 Slovenj Gradec Slovenia
117 F5 Slov"yans'k Ukr.
98 C3 S'Lung, B'Nom *mt.* Vietnam
112 H3 Słupsk Poland
102 L2 Slussfors Sweden
116 C4 Slutsk Belarus
107 A4 Slyne Head Rep. of Ireland
77 L4 Slyudyanka Rus. Fed.
147 I3 Small Point U.S.A.
133 H3 Smallwood Reservoir Canada
116 D4 Smalyavichy Belarus
113 M3 Smarhon' Belarus
124 E5 Smartt Syndicate Dam *resr* S. Africa
131 I4 Smeaton Canada
115 I2 Smederevo Serb. and Mont.
115 I2 Smederevska Palanka Serb. and Mont.
146 D4 Smethport U.S.A.
117 D5 Smila Ukr.
108 E2 Smilde Neth.
103 N4 Smiltene Latvia
83 G1 Smirnovo Kazakh.
130 G3 Smith Canada
140 C2 Smith U.S.A.
146 C6 Smith *r.* U.S.A.
128 C2 Smith Bay U.S.A.
130 D4 Smithers Canada
125 G5 Smithfield S. Africa
145 E5 Smithfield *NC* U.S.A.
138 E3 Smithfield *UT* U.S.A.
147 E5 Smith Island *MD* U.S.A.
147 F6 Smith Island *VA* U.S.A.
146 D6 Smith Mountain Lake U.S.A.
130 D3 Smith River Canada
135 I3 Smiths Falls Canada
129 K2 Smith Sound *sea chan.* Canada/Greenland
71 F8 Smithton Australia
140 C1 Smoke Creek Desert U.S.A.
130 F4 Smoky *r.* Canada
71 J3 Smoky Cape Australia
132 D3 Smoky Falls Canada
142 C4 Smoky Hill *r.* U.S.A.
142 D4 Smoky Hills U.S.A.
130 G4 Smoky Lake Canada
102 I3 Smøla *i.* Norway
82 B2 Smolenka Rus. Fed.
116 E4 Smolensk Rus. Fed.
116 E4 Smolenskaya Oblast' *admin. div.* Rus. Fed.
83 K1 Smolenskoye Rus. Fed.
115 K4 Smolyan Bulg.
94 C3 Smolyoninovo Rus. Fed.
132 D4 Smooth Rock Falls Canada
132 C3 Smoothrock Lake Canada
131 H4 Smoothstone Lake Canada
102 N1 Smørfjord Norway
147 F5 Smyrna *DE* U.S.A.
145 C5 Smyrna *GA* U.S.A.
146 C4 Smyrna *OH* U.S.A.
147 I1 Smyrna Mills U.S.A.
102 D2 Snæfell *mt.* Iceland
104 C3 Snaefell *h.* U.K.
130 A2 Snag Canada
138 D3 Snake *r.* U.S.A.
141 E2 Snake Range *mts* U.S.A.
138 D3 Snake River Plain U.S.A.
Snare Lakes Canada *see* Wekwetì
69 G6 Snares Islands N.Z.
102 K2 Snåsa Norway
108 D1 Sneek Neth.
107 B6 Sneem Rep. of Ireland
124 F6 Sneeuberge *mts* S. Africa
133 H3 Snegamook Lake Canada
105 H5 Snettisham U.K.
76 J3 Snezhnogorsk Rus. Fed.
114 F2 Snežnik *mt.* Slovenia
113 J4 Śniardwy, Jezioro *l.* Poland
117 E6 Snihurivka Ukr.
106 B3 Snizort, Loch *b.* U.K.
138 B2 Snohomish U.S.A.
138 B2 Snoqualmie Pass U.S.A.
102 K2 Snøtinden *mt.* Norway
131 I2 Snowbird Lake Canada
105 C4 Snowdon *mt.* U.K.
105 D5 Snowdonia National Park U.K.
141 G4 Snowflake U.S.A.
147 F5 Snow Hill *MD* U.S.A.
145 E5 Snow Hill *NC* U.S.A.
131 I4 Snow Lake Canada
70 C4 Snowtown Australia
138 D3 Snowville U.S.A.
71 H6 Snowy *r.* Australia
71 H6 Snowy Mountains Australia
71 G9 Snug Australia
133 I3 Snug Harbour *Nfld* Canada
135 G3 Snug Harbour *Ont.* Canada
98 C2 Snuŏl Cambodia
143 D5 Snyder *OK* U.S.A.
143 C5 Snyder *TX* U.S.A.
123 E5 Soalala Madag.
123 E5 Soanierana-Ivongo Madag.
96 D6 Soan-kundo *is* S. Korea
157 B3 Soata Col.
106 B3 Soay *i.* U.K.
96 D6 Sobaek-sanmaek *mts* S. Korea
121 F4 Sobat *r.* Sudan
109 F5 Sobernheim Germany
91 G7 Sobger *r.* Indon.
95 B8 Sobo-san *mt.* Japan
155 J6 Sobradinho, Barragem de *resr* Brazil
155 J4 Sobral Brazil
117 F7 Sochi Rus. Fed.
96 D5 Sŏch'ŏn S. Korea
67 I5 Society Islands Fr. Polynesia
158 C3 Socorro Brazil
157 B3 Socorro Col.
139 F5 Socorro U.S.A.
148 B5 Socorro, Isla *i.* Mex.
86 D7 Socotra *i.* Yemen
98 C3 Soc Trăng Vietnam
111 E3 Socuéllamos Spain
140 D4 Soda Lake U.S.A.
102 N2 Sodankylä Fin.
88 D2 Soda Plains China/Jammu and Kashmir
138 E3 Soda Springs U.S.A.
103 L3 Söderhamn Sweden
103 L4 Söderköping Sweden
103 L4 Södertälje Sweden
121 E3 Sodiri Sudan
122 D3 Sodo Eth.
103 L3 Södra Kvarken *str.* Fin./Sweden
125 H1 Soekmekaar S. Africa
108 D3 Soerendonk Neth.
109 G3 Soest Germany
108 D2 Soest Neth.
71 H4 Sofala Australia
115 J3 Sofia Bulg.
Sofiya Bulg. *see* Sofia
102 O2 Sofporog Rus. Fed.
95 G10 Sōfu-gan *i.* Japan
89 H3 Sog China
157 B3 Sogamoso Col.
81 G1 Soğanlı Dağları *mts* Turkey
108 F2 Sögel Germany
103 I4 Søgne Norway
103 I3 Sognefjorden *inlet* Norway
97 C4 Sogod Phil.
92 A1 Sogo Nur *l.* China
116 H2 Sogra Rus. Fed.
92 A3 Sogruma China
80 C1 Söğüt Turkey
96 D7 Sŏgwip'o S. Korea
88 D5 Sohagpur India
105 H5 Soham U.K.
88 B2 Sohan *r.* Pak.
69 F2 Sohano P.N.G.
87 C1 Sohela India
88 D3 Sohna India
96 E3 Sŏho-ri N. Korea
96 C6 Sohŭksan S. Korea
108 C4 Soignes, Forêt de *for.* Belgium
108 C4 Soignies Belgium
102 N3 Soini Fin.
110 F2 Soissons France
88 C4 Sojat India
97 B4 Sojoton Point Phil.
117 C5 Sokal' Ukr.
96 E4 Sokch'o S. Korea
115 L6 Söke Turkey
83 G5 Sokh Tajik.
117 G7 Sokhumi Georgia
120 C4 Sokodé Togo
93 □ Soko Islands *Hong Kong* China
116 G3 Sokol Rus. Fed.
113 K4 Sokółka Poland
120 B3 Sokolo Mali
109 K4 Sokolov Czech Rep.
94 C3 Sokolovka Rus. Fed.
113 K4 Sokołow Podlaski Poland
120 C3 Sokoto Nigeria
120 C3 Sokoto *r.* Nigeria
117 C5 Sokyryany Ukr.
88 D3 Solan India
72 A7 Solander Island N.Z.
87 A2 Solapur India
157 B2 Soledad Col.
140 B3 Soledad U.S.A.
157 E2 Soledad Venez.
151 E4 Soledad de Doblado Mex.
117 G6 Solenoye Rus. Fed.
102 K2 Solfjellsjøen Norway
81 H2 Solhan Turkey
116 G3 Soligalich Rus. Fed.
105 F5 Solihull U.K.
76 G4 Solikamsk Rus. Fed.
82 C2 Sol'-Iletsk Rus. Fed.
151 H4 Solimón, Punta *pt* Mex.
108 F3 Solingen Germany
124 A1 Solitaire Namibia
81 L1 Şollar Azer.
102 L3 Sollefteå Sweden
109 K3 Söllichau Germany
109 H3 Solling *hills* Germany
109 I3 Sollstedt Germany
109 G4 Solms Germany
116 F3 Solnechnogorsk Rus. Fed.
99 B3 Solok Indon.
151 G5 Sololá Guat.
69 G2 Solomon Islands *country* Pacific Ocean
68 F2 Solomon Sea P.N.G./Solomon Is
83 K2 Soloneshnoye Rus. Fed.
134 B2 Solon Springs U.S.A.
91 E7 Solor, Kepulauan *is* Indon.
112 C7 Solothurn Switz.
116 E1 Solovetskiye Ostrova *is* Rus. Fed.
116 H3 Solovetskoye Rus. Fed.
114 G3 Šolta *i.* Croatia
85 E2 Soltānābād Iran
85 E3 Solţānābād Iran
109 H2 Soltau Germany
116 D3 Sol'tsy Rus. Fed.
147 E3 Solvay U.S.A.
103 K4 Sölvesborg Sweden
106 E6 Solway Firth *est.* U.K.
123 C5 Solwezi Zambia
95 G6 Sōma Japan
80 A2 Soma Turkey
108 B4 Somain France
122 E3 Somalia *country* Africa
162 H5 Somali Basin *sea feature* Indian Ocean
123 C4 Sombo Angola
115 H2 Sombor Serb. and Mont.
150 D3 Sombrerete Mex.
88 C4 Somdari India
147 I2 Somerest Junction U.S.A.
103 M3 Somero Fin.
144 C4 Somerset *KY* U.S.A.
134 E4 Somerset *MI* U.S.A.
146 D5 Somerset *PA* U.S.A.
125 F6 Somerset East S. Africa
129 I2 Somerset Island Canada
147 G3 Somerset Reservoir U.S.A.
124 C7 Somerset West S. Africa
147 H3 Somersworth U.S.A.
143 D6 Somerville Reservoir U.S.A.
84 B3 Someydeh Iran
103 K4 Sommen *l.* Sweden
109 J3 Sömmerda Germany
133 G3 Sommet, Lac du *l.* Canada
88 B5 Somnath India
134 C5 Somonauk U.S.A.
150 H5 Somotillo Nicaragua
150 H5 Somoto Nicaragua
159 C4 Somuncurá, Mesa Volcánica de *plat.* Arg.
89 F4 Son *r.* India
150 I7 Soná Panama
83 G2 Sonaly *Karagandinskaya Oblast'* Kazakh.
83 G2 Sonaly *Karagandinskaya Oblast'* Kazakh.
89 F5 Sonamukhi India
89 G5 Sonamura India
87 C1 Sonapur India
88 D4 Sonar *r.* India
89 H4 Sonari India
96 C4 Sŏnch'ŏn N. Korea
116 E2 Sondaly Rus. Fed.
103 J5 Sønderborg Denmark
109 I3 Sondershausen Germany
114 C1 Sondrio Italy
87 B2 Sonepet India
88 B5 Songad India
92 E4 Songbu China
98 D2 Sông Câu Vietnam
123 D5 Songea Tanz.
96 D3 Sŏnggan N. Korea
96 D2 Songhua Hu *resr* China
96 C1 Songhuajiang China
94 B1 Songhua Jiang *r.* China
96 E2 Songjiang *Jilin* China
92 F4 Songjiang *Shanghai* China
96 D2 Songjianghe China
93 C4 Songkan China
98 B4 Songkhla Thai.
83 H4 Songköl *l.* Kyrg.
92 F1 Song Ling *mts* China
96 D5 Sŏngnam S. Korea
96 C4 Songnim N. Korea
122 B4 Songo Angola
123 D5 Songo Moz.
92 B3 Songpan China
89 G4 Songsak India
96 D7 Sŏngsan S. Korea
92 D3 Song Shan *mt.* China
96 D3 Songshuzhen China
93 C4 Songtao China
93 F5 Songxi China
92 D3 Songxian China
96 C1 Songyuan China
93 D4 Songzi China
98 D2 Sơn Ha Vietnam
98 D3 Sơn Hai Vietnam
88 D3 Sonipat India
102 N3 Sonkajärvi Fin.
93 B6 Sơn La Vietnam
85 G5 Sonmiani Pak.
85 G5 Sonmiani Bay Pak.
109 J4 Sonneberg Germany
158 D2 Sono *r. Minas Gerais* Brazil
155 I6 Sono *r.* Brazil
141 F6 Sonoita Mex.
141 F6 Sonoita *watercourse* Mex.
141 G6 Sonoita U.S.A.
150 B1 Sonora *r.* Mex.
150 B2 Sonora *state* Mex.
140 B3 Sonora *CA* U.S.A.
143 C6 Sonora *TX* U.S.A.
84 B3 Sonqor Iran
157 B3 Sonsón Col.
151 G5 Sonsonate El Salvador
93 B6 Sơn Tây Vietnam
125 H5 Sonwabile S. Africa
159 F1 Sopas *r.* Uruguay
121 E4 Sopo *watercourse* Sudan
115 K3 Sopot Bulg.
113 I3 Sopot Poland
112 H7 Sopron Hungary
83 H4 Sopu-Korgon Kyrg.
114 E4 Sora Italy
87 D2 Sorada India
103 L3 Söråker Sweden
96 E4 Sŏrak-san *mt.* S. Korea
132 F4 Sorel Canada
71 G9 Sorell Australia
71 G9 Sorell Lake Australia
80 E2 Sorgun Turkey
111 E2 Soria Spain
76 C2 Sørkappøya *i.* Svalbard
84 D3 Sorkh, Kūh-e *mts* Iran
84 D3 Sorkheh Iran
102 K2 Sørli Norway
89 F5 Soro India
117 D5 Soroca Moldova
158 C3 Sorocaba Brazil
82 C1 Sorochinsk Rus. Fed.
83 K1 Sorokino Rus. Fed.
91 G6 Sorol *atoll* Micronesia
91 F7 Sorong Indon.
122 D3 Soroti Uganda
102 M1 Sørøya *i.* Norway
111 B3 Sorraia *r.* Port.
102 L1 Sørreisa Norway
70 F7 Sorrento Australia
114 F4 Sorrento Italy
123 B6 Sorris Sorris Namibia
102 L2 Sorsele Sweden
97 C3 Sorsogon Phil.
116 D2 Sortavala Rus. Fed.
102 K1 Sortland Norway
116 I2 Sortopolovskaya Rus. Fed.
116 I3 Sorvizhi Rus. Fed.
96 D5 Sŏsan S. Korea
125 H2 Soshanguve S. Africa
117 F4 Sosna *r.* Rus. Fed.
159 C2 Sosneado *mt.* Arg.
116 J2 Sosnogorsk Rus. Fed.
83 I2 Sosnovka Kazakh.
116 H2 Sosnovka *Arkhangel'skaya Oblast'* Rus. Fed.
76 F3 Sosnovka *Murmanskaya Oblast'* Rus. Fed.
116 G4 Sosnovka *Tambovskaya Oblast'* Rus. Fed.
102 P2 Sosnovyy Rus. Fed.
103 O4 Sosnovyy Bor Rus. Fed.
113 I5 Sosnowiec Poland
117 F6 Sosyka *r.* Rus. Fed.
157 A4 Sotara, Volcán *vol.* Col.
102 O2 Sotkamo Fin.
159 D1 Soto Arg.
151 E3 Soto la Marina Mex.
151 G3 Sotuta Mex.
122 B3 Souanké Congo
120 B4 Soubré Côte d'Ivoire
147 F4 Souderton U.S.A.
115 L4 Soufli Greece
110 E4 Souillac France
108 D5 Souilly France
120 C1 Souk Ahras Alg.
Sŏul S. Korea *see* Seoul
110 D5 Soulom France
Soûr Lebanon *see* Tyre
111 H4 Sour el Ghozlane Alg.
131 I5 Souris *Man.* Canada
133 H4 Souris *P.E.I.* Canada
131 I5 Souris *r.* Canada/U.S.A.
155 K5 Sousa Brazil
120 D1 Sousse Tunisia
110 D5 Soustons France
124 E4 South Africa, Republic of *country* Africa
152 South America
135 G3 Southampton Canada
105 F7 Southampton U.K.
147 G4 Southampton U.S.A.
131 L2 Southampton Island Canada
146 E6 South Anna *r.* U.S.A.
105 F4 South Anston U.K.
133 H2 South Aulatsivik Island Canada
68 D5 South Australia *state* Australia
162 L7 South Australian Basin *sea feature* Indian Ocean
143 F5 Southaven U.S.A.
139 F5 South Baldy *mt.* U.S.A.
104 F3 South Bank U.K.
146 B4 South Bass Island U.S.A.
135 F3 South Baymouth Canada
134 D5 South Bend *IN* U.S.A.
138 B2 South Bend *WA* U.S.A.
145 E7 South Bight *sea chan.* Bahamas
146 D6 South Boston U.S.A.
72 D5 Southbridge N.Z.
147 G3 Southbridge U.S.A.
South Cape *pt* U.S.A. *see* Ka Lae
145 D5 South Carolina *state* U.S.A.
147 I2 South China U.S.A.
99 C1 South China Sea Pacific Ocean
142 C2 South Dakota *state* U.S.A.
147 G3 South Deerfield U.S.A.
105 G7 South Downs *hills* U.K.
125 F2 South-East *admin. dist.* Botswana
71 G9 South East Cape Australia
71 H6 South East Forests National Park Australia

208 Southeast Indian Ridge

162 J7 Southeast Indian Ridge sea feature Indian Ocean
161 L10 Southeast Pacific Basin sea feature S. Pacific Ocean
131 I3 Southend Canada
106 C5 Southend U.K.
105 H6 Southend-on-Sea U.K.
134 A5 South English U.S.A.
124 E2 Southern admin. dist. Botswana
72 C5 Southern Alps mts N.Z.
68 B5 Southern Cross Australia
131 J3 Southern Indian Lake Canada
121 E4 Southern National Park Sudan
160 E10 Southern Ocean
145 E5 Southern Pines U.S.A.
153 G7 Southern Thule Island S. Sandwich Is
106 D5 Southern Uplands hills U.K.
106 F4 South Esk r. U.K.
134 B6 South Fabius r. U.S.A.
160 G7 South Fiji Basin sea feature S. Pacific Ocean
139 F4 South Fork U.S.A.
South Fork South Branch r. U.S.A. see Potomac, South Fork South Branch
134 E3 South Fox Island U.S.A.
73 C5 South Geomagnetic Pole Antarctica
156 □ South Georgia terr. S. Atlantic Ocean
153 G7 South Georgia and South Sandwich Islands terr. Atlantic Ocean
106 A3 South Harris pen. U.K.
89 G5 South Hatia Island Bangl.
134 D4 South Haven U.S.A.
131 J2 South Henik Lake Canada
147 G2 South Hero U.S.A.
146 D6 South Hill U.S.A.
160 E3 South Honshu Ridge sea feature N. Pacific Ocean
131 J3 South Indian Lake Canada
147 G4 Southington U.S.A.
72 C6 South Island N.Z.
122 D3 South Island National Park Kenya
97 A4 South Islet rf Phil.
87 D1 South Koel r. India
96 D5 South Korea country Asia
140 B2 South Lake Tahoe U.S.A.
123 D5 South Luangwa National Park Zambia
73 C6 South Magnetic Pole Antarctica
134 D3 South Manitou Island U.S.A.
145 D7 South Miami U.S.A.
105 H6 Southminster U.K.
131 I4 South Moose Lake Canada
146 E5 South Mountains U.S.A.
130 D2 South Nahanni r. Canada
106 □ South Nesting Bay U.K.
163 G10 South Orkney Islands S. Atlantic Ocean
69 H5 South Pacific Ocean
147 H2 South Paris U.S.A.
138 G3 South Platte r. U.S.A.
73 C4 South Pole Antarctica
135 G1 South Porcupine Canada
71 J1 Southport Australia
104 D4 Southport U.K.
147 H3 South Portland U.S.A.
135 H3 South River Canada
106 F2 South Ronaldsay i. U.K.
147 G3 South Royalton U.S.A.
125 I5 South Sand Bluff pt S. Africa
163 H9 South Sandwich Islands S. Atlantic Ocean
163 H9 South Sandwich Trench sea feature S. Atlantic Ocean
131 H4 South Saskatchewan r. Canada
131 J3 South Seal r. Canada
73 B2 South Shetland Islands Antarctica
163 E10 South Shetland Trough sea feature S. Atlantic Ocean
104 F2 South Shields U.K.
134 A5 South Skunk r. U.S.A.
160 F6 South Solomon Trench sea feature Pacific Ocean
72 E3 South Taranaki Bight b. N.Z.
162 N8 South Tasman Rise sea feature Southern Ocean
141 G2 South Tent mt. U.S.A.
89 E4 South Tons r. India
132 E3 South Twin Island Canada
104 E3 South Tyne r. U.K.
106 A3 South Uist i. U.K.
71 G9 South West Cape Australia
72 A7 South West Cape N.Z.
162 G7 Southwest Indian Ridge sea feature Indian Ocean
133 G4 Southwest Miramichi r. Canada
71 G9 South West National Park Australia
161 I8 Southwest Pacific Basin sea feature S. Pacific Ocean
South-West Peru Ridge sea feature S. Pacific Ocean see Nazca Ridge
71 J3 South West Rocks Australia
134 E5 South Whitley U.S.A.
147 H3 South Windham U.S.A.
105 I5 Southwold U.K.
125 H1 Soutpansberg mts S. Africa
114 G5 Soverato Italy
116 B4 Sovetsk Kaliningradskaya Oblast' Rus. Fed.
116 I3 Sovetsk Kirovskaya Oblast' Rus. Fed.
90 G2 Sovetskaya Gavan' Rus. Fed.
76 H3 Sovetskiy Rus. Fed.
116 D2 Sovetskiy Leningradskaya Oblast' Rus. Fed.
116 I3 Sovetskiy Respublika Mariy El Rus. Fed.
125 G3 Soweto S. Africa
151 F4 Soyaló Mex.
94 G2 Sōya-misaki c. Japan
96 D4 Soyang-ho l. S. Korea
113 O4 Sozh r. Belarus
115 L3 Sozopol Bulg.
110 D4 Spa Belgium
111 D2 Spain country Europe
105 G5 Spalding U.K.
105 D6 Span Head h. U.K.
135 F2 Spanish Canada
135 G2 Spanish r. Canada
141 G1 Spanish Fork U.S.A.
149 I5 Spanish Town Jamaica
140 C2 Sparks U.S.A.
146 C6 Sparta NC U.S.A.
134 B4 Sparta WI U.S.A.
145 D5 Spartanburg U.S.A.
115 J6 Sparti Greece
114 G6 Spartivento, Capo c. Italy
130 G5 Sparwood Canada
116 E4 Spas-Demensk Rus. Fed.
116 E2 Spasskaya Guba Rus. Fed.
90 F2 Spassk-Dal'niy Rus. Fed.
115 J7 Spatha, Akra pt Greece
130 D3 Spatsizi Plateau Wilderness Provincial Park Canada
142 C2 Spearfish U.S.A.
143 C4 Spearman U.S.A.
147 F3 Speculator U.S.A.
142 E3 Spencer IA U.S.A.
138 D2 Spencer ID U.S.A.
146 C5 Spencer WV U.S.A.
70 B5 Spencer, Cape Australia
130 B3 Spencer, Cape U.S.A.
70 B5 Spencer Gulf est. Australia
130 E4 Spences Bridge Canada
104 F3 Spennymoor U.K.
107 D3 Sperrin Mountains U.K.
146 D5 Sperryville U.S.A.
109 H5 Spessart reg. Germany
115 J6 Spetses i. Greece
106 E3 Spey r. U.K.
109 G5 Speyer Germany
85 G4 Spezand Pak.
109 F1 Spiekeroog i. Germany
112 C7 Spiez Switz.
108 E1 Spijk Neth.
108 C3 Spijkenisse Neth.
114 E1 Spilimbergo Italy
105 H4 Spilsby U.K.
85 G4 Spīn Būldak Afgh.
88 B3 Spintangi Pak.
130 F3 Spirit River Canada
134 C3 Spirit River Flowage resr U.S.A.
131 H4 Spiritwood Canada
85 G3 Spirsang Pass Afgh.
113 J6 Spišská Nová Ves Slovakia
81 J1 Spitak Armenia
88 D3 Spiti r. India
76 C2 Spitsbergen i. Svalbard
112 F7 Spittal an der Drau Austria
114 G3 Split Croatia
131 J3 Split Lake Canada
131 J3 Split Lake l. Canada
138 C2 Spokane U.S.A.
114 E3 Spoleto Italy
Spong Cambodia see Spóng
98 C2 Spóng Cambodia
134 B3 Spooner U.S.A.
109 J1 Spornitz Germany
138 F2 Spotted Horse U.S.A.
135 F2 Spragge Canada
130 E4 Spranger, Mount Canada
91 D6 Spratly Islands S. China Sea
138 C2 Spray U.S.A.
109 K3 Spree r. Germany
108 D4 Sprimont Belgium
135 F3 Spring Bay Canada
124 B4 Springbok S. Africa
133 I4 Springdale Canada
143 E4 Springdale U.S.A.
109 H2 Springe Germany
139 F4 Springer U.S.A.
141 H4 Springerville U.S.A.
143 C4 Springfield CO U.S.A.
134 C6 Springfield IL U.S.A.
147 G3 Springfield MA U.S.A.
147 I2 Springfield ME U.S.A.
142 E2 Springfield MN U.S.A.
143 E4 Springfield MO U.S.A.
146 B5 Springfield OH U.S.A.
143 C4 Springfield OR U.S.A.
147 G3 Springfield VT U.S.A.
146 D5 Springfield WV U.S.A.
134 C6 Springfield, Lake U.S.A.
125 F5 Springfontein S. Africa
134 B4 Spring Green U.S.A.
134 B4 Spring Grove U.S.A.
133 H4 Springhill Canada
145 D6 Spring Hill U.S.A.
134 D4 Spring Lake U.S.A.
141 E3 Spring Mountains U.S.A.
72 D5 Springs Junction N.Z.
134 A4 Spring Valley U.S.A.
146 D3 Springville NY U.S.A.
141 G1 Springville UT U.S.A.
105 I5 Sprowston U.K.
130 G4 Spruce Grove Canada
146 D5 Spruce Knob-Seneca Rocks National Recreation Area U.S.A.
138 D3 Spruce Mountain U.S.A.
104 H4 Spurn Head U.K.
130 E5 Spuzzum Canada
130 E5 Squamish Canada
147 H3 Squam Lake U.S.A.
147 I1 Squapan Lake U.S.A.
147 I1 Square Lake U.S.A.
114 G5 Squillace, Golfo di g. Italy
115 I3 Srbija aut. rep. Serb. and Mont.
98 B3 Srê Âmběl Cambodia
114 H2 Srebrenica Bos.-Herz.
115 L3 Sredets Bulg.
77 Q4 Sredinnyy Khrebet mts Rus. Fed.
115 J3 Sredna Gora mts Bulg.
77 Q3 Srednekolymsk Rus. Fed.
Sredne-Russkaya Vozvyshennost' hills Rus. Fed. see Central Russian Upland
Sredne-Sibirskoye Ploskogor'ye plat. Rus. Fed. see Central Siberian Plateau
102 O2 Sredneye Kuyto, Ozero l. Rus. Fed.
115 K3 Srednogorie Bulg.
98 C2 Srêpok, Tônlé r. Cambodia
90 D1 Sretensk Rus. Fed.
99 D2 Sri Aman Sarawak Malaysia
87 C3 Sriharikota Island India
87 B5 Sri Jayewardenepura Kotte Sri Lanka
87 D2 Srikakulam India
87 B3 Sri Kalahasti India
88 D3 Srikanta mt. India
162 C5 Sri Lanka country Asia
88 D3 Srinagar India
88 C2 Srinagar Jammu and Kashmir
Sri Pada mt. Sri Lanka see Adam's Peak
87 B4 Srirangam India
98 B1 Sri Thep tourist site Thai.
87 B4 Srivaikuntam India
87 A2 Srivardhan India
87 B4 Srivilliputtur India
83 K1 Sroststi Rus. Fed.
87 C2 Srungavarapukota India
109 H1 Stade Germany
108 B3 Staden Belgium
108 E2 Stadskanaal Neth.
109 H4 Stadtallendorf Germany
109 H2 Stadthagen Germany
109 J4 Stadtilm Germany
108 E3 Stadtlohn Germany
109 H3 Stadtoldendorf Germany
109 J4 Stadtroda Germany
106 B4 Staffa i. U.K.
109 J4 Staffelberg h. Germany
109 I4 Staffelstein Germany
105 E5 Stafford U.K.
146 E5 Stafford U.S.A.
103 N4 Staicele Latvia
105 G6 Staines U.K.
117 F5 Stakhanov Ukr.
105 E7 Stalbridge U.K.
105 I5 Stalham U.K.
130 E3 Stalin, Mount Canada
Stalingrad Rus. Fed. see Volgograd
113 K5 Stalowa Wola Poland
115 K3 Stamboliyski Bulg.
105 G5 Stamford U.K.
147 G4 Stamford CT U.S.A.
147 F3 Stamford NY U.S.A.
123 B6 Stampriet Namibia
102 K1 Stamsund Norway
142 E3 Stanberry U.S.A.
108 C3 Standdaarbuiten Neth.
125 H3 Standerton S. Africa
135 F4 Standish U.S.A.
144 C4 Stanford U.S.A.
125 I4 Stanger S. Africa
145 E7 Staniard Creek Bahamas
113 L6 Staňkov Czech Rep.
71 F8 Stanley Australia
147 J1 Stanley Canada
93 □ Stanley Hong Kong China
156 E8 Stanley Falkland Is
104 F3 Stanley U.K.
138 D2 Stanley ID U.S.A.
142 C1 Stanley ND U.S.A.
134 B3 Stanley WI U.S.A.
71 F8 Stanley, Mount h. Australia
122 C3 Stanley, Mount Dem. Rep. Congo/Uganda
87 B4 Stanley Reservoir India
104 F2 Stannington U.K.
90 D1 Stanovoye Nagor'ye mts Rus. Fed.
90 E1 Stanovoy Khrebet mts Rus. Fed.
71 I2 Stanthorpe Australia
105 H5 Stanton U.K.
146 B6 Stanton KY U.S.A.
134 E4 Stanton MI U.S.A.
142 C3 Stapleton U.S.A.
113 J5 Starachowice Poland
Stara Planina mts Bulg./Serb. and Mont. see Balkan Mountains
116 H4 Staraya Kulatka Rus. Fed.
117 H5 Staraya Poltavka Rus. Fed.
116 D3 Staraya Russa Rus. Fed.
113 O2 Staraya Toropa Rus. Fed.
116 I4 Staraya Tumba Rus. Fed.
115 K3 Stara Zagora Bulg.
67 I4 Starbuck Island Kiribati
112 G4 Stargard Szczeciński Poland
116 F3 Staritsa Rus. Fed.
82 D2 Star Karabutak Kazakh.
145 D6 Starke U.S.A.
143 F5 Starkville U.S.A.
112 E7 Starnberger See l. Germany
83 J2 Staroaleyskoye Rus. Fed.
117 F5 Starobil's'k Ukr.
113 P4 Starodub Rus. Fed.
113 I4 Starogard Gdański Poland
117 C5 Starokostyantyniv Ukr.
117 F5 Starominskaya Rus. Fed.
117 F6 Staroshcherbinovskaya Rus. Fed.
82 D1 Starosubkhangulovo Rus. Fed.
140 C1 Star Peak U.S.A.
105 D7 Start Point U.K.
113 N4 Starya Darohi Belarus
77 L2 Staryy Kayak Rus. Fed.
117 F5 Staryy Oskol Rus. Fed.
109 J3 Staßfurt Germany
146 E4 State College U.S.A.
145 D5 Statesboro U.S.A.
145 D5 Statesville U.S.A.
164 W1 Station Nord Greenland
109 J3 Stauchitz Germany
109 G4 Staufenberg Germany
146 D5 Staunton U.S.A.
103 I4 Stavanger Norway
104 E4 Staveley U.K.
117 G6 Stavropol' Rus. Fed.
82 F1 Stavropolka Kazakh.
117 G6 Stavropol'skaya Vozvyshennost' hills Rus. Fed.
117 G6 Stavropol'skiy Kray admin. div. Rus. Fed.
70 E6 Stawell Australia
125 H4 Steadville S. Africa
140 C2 Steamboat U.S.A.
138 F3 Steamboat Springs U.S.A.
146 E4 Steelton U.S.A.
108 E2 Steenderen Neth.
125 I2 Steenkampsberge mts S. Africa
130 G3 Steen River Canada
138 C3 Steens Mountain U.S.A.
Steenstrup Gletscher glacier Greenland see Sermersuaq
108 A4 Steenvoorde France
108 E2 Steenwijk Neth.
128 H2 Stefansson Island Canada
109 I5 Steigerwald mts Germany
109 J5 Stein Germany
109 J4 Steinach Germany
131 J5 Steinbach Canada
109 G2 Steinfeld (Oldenburg) Germany
108 F2 Steinfurt Germany
123 B6 Steinhausen Namibia
109 H3 Steinheim Germany
109 H2 Steinhuder Meer l. Germany
102 J2 Steinkjer Norway
124 B4 Steinkopf S. Africa
141 H5 Steins U.S.A.
102 J2 Steinsdalen Norway
124 F3 Stella S. Africa
145 F7 Stella Maris Bahamas
124 C6 Stellenbosch S. Africa
114 C3 Stello, Monte mt. Corsica France
108 D5 Stenay France
109 J2 Stendal Germany
93 □ Stenhouse, Mount h. Hong Kong China
106 E4 Stenhousemuir U.K.
103 J4 Stenungsund Sweden
Stepanakert Azer. see Xankändi
117 H7 Step'anavan Armenia
131 J5 Stephen U.S.A.
70 D4 Stephens watercourse Australia
72 D4 Stephens, Cape N.Z.
70 D3 Stephens Creek Australia
134 D3 Stephenson U.S.A.
130 C3 Stephens Passage U.S.A.
133 I4 Stephenville Canada
143 D5 Stephenville U.S.A.
83 H1 Stepnogorsk Kazakh.
83 H4 Stepnoy Kyrg.
82 E1 Stepnoye Chelyabinskaya Oblast' Rus. Fed.
117 H5 Stepnoye Saratovskaya Oblast' Rus. Fed.
83 G1 Stepnyak Kazakh.
125 H4 Sterkfontein Dam resr S. Africa
125 G5 Sterkstroom S. Africa
82 C1 Sterlibashevo Rus. Fed.
124 E5 Sterling S. Africa
138 G3 Sterling CO U.S.A.
134 C5 Sterling IL U.S.A.
142 C2 Sterling ND U.S.A.
141 G2 Sterling UT U.S.A.
143 C6 Sterling City U.S.A.
134 D5 Sterling Heights U.S.A.
82 C1 Sterlitamak Rus. Fed.
109 J1 Sternberg Germany
130 G4 Stettler Canada
146 C4 Steuben U.S.A.
134 D4 Steubenville U.S.A.
105 G6 Stevenage U.K.
131 J4 Stevenson Lake Canada
134 C3 Stevens Point U.S.A.
128 D3 Stevens Village U.S.A.
130 D3 Stewart Canada
130 B2 Stewart r. Canada
130 B2 Stewart Crossing Canada
72 A7 Stewart Island N.Z.
69 G2 Stewart Islands Solomon Is
129 J3 Stewart Lake Canada
106 D5 Stewarton U.K.
134 A4 Stewartville U.S.A.
125 F5 Steynsburg S. Africa
112 G6 Steyr Austria
124 F6 Steytlerville S. Africa
108 D1 Stiens Neth.
130 C3 Stikine r. Canada/U.S.A.
130 C3 Stikine Plateau Canada
124 D7 Stilbaai S. Africa
134 A3 Stillwater MN U.S.A.
140 C2 Stillwater NV U.S.A.
143 D4 Stillwater OK U.S.A.
134 C4 Stillwater Range mts U.S.A.
105 G5 Stilton U.K.
115 J4 Štip Macedonia
70 C5 Stirling Australia
106 E4 Stirling U.K.
140 B2 Stirling City U.S.A.
70 B4 Stirling North Australia
102 J3 Stjørdalshalsen Norway
112 H6 Stockerau Austria
109 J4 Stockheim Germany
103 K4 Stockholm Sweden
147 I1 Stockholm U.S.A.
105 E4 Stockport U.K.
163 G6 Stocks Seamount sea feature S. Atlantic Ocean
140 B3 Stockton CA U.S.A.
142 D4 Stockton KS U.S.A.
141 F1 Stockton UT U.S.A.
134 B2 Stockton Island U.S.A.
143 E4 Stockton Lake U.S.A.
104 F3 Stockton-on-Tees U.K.
147 I2 Stockton Springs U.S.A.
103 L3 Stöde Sweden
98 C2 Stœng Trêng Cambodia
106 C2 Stoer, Point of U.K.
105 E4 Stoke-on-Trent U.K.
104 F3 Stokesley U.K.
71 E8 Stokes Point Australia
102 B3 Stokkseyri Iceland
102 K2 Stokkvågen Norway
102 K1 Stokmarknes Norway
115 G3 Stolac Bos.-Herz.
108 E4 Stolberg (Rheinland) Germany
83 K2 Stolboukha Kazakh.
117 C5 Stolin Belarus
109 K4 Stollberg Germany
109 H2 Stolzenau Germany
105 E5 Stone U.K.
135 I2 Stonecliffe Canada
147 F5 Stone Harbor U.S.A.
106 F4 Stonehaven U.K.
105 F6 Stonehenge tourist site U.K.
130 E3 Stone Mountain Provincial Park Canada
141 H3 Stoner U.S.A.
141 F3 Stone Ridge U.S.A.
131 J4 Stonewall Canada
146 C5 Stonewall Jackson Lake U.S.A.
135 F4 Stoney Point Canada
147 I2 Stonington U.S.A.
140 A2 Stonyford U.S.A.
147 E3 Stony Point U.S.A.
131 H3 Stony Rapids Canada
102 L2 Stora Lulevatten l. Sweden
102 L2 Stora Sjöfallets nationalpark nat. park Sweden
102 L2 Storavan l. Sweden
Store Bælt sea chan. Denmark see Great Belt
102 J3 Støren Norway
102 K2 Storforshei Norway
102 K2 Storjord Norway
128 H2 Storkerson Peninsula Canada
71 G9 Storm Bay Australia
125 G6 Stormberg S. Africa
125 G5 Stormberge mts S. Africa
142 E3 Storm Lake U.S.A.
106 B2 Stornoway U.K.
116 J2 Storozhevsk Rus. Fed.
117 C5 Storozhynets' Ukr.
147 G4 Storrs U.S.A.
102 L2 Storseleby Sweden
102 K3 Storsjön l. Sweden
103 J3 Storskrymten mt. Norway
102 M1 Storslett Norway
108 D1 Stortemelk sea chan. Neth.
102 L2 Storuman Sweden
102 L2 Storuman l. Sweden
103 L3 Storvik Sweden
103 J4 Storvorde Denmark
103 L4 Storvreta Sweden
105 G4 Stotfold U.K.
134 C4 Stoughton U.S.A.
105 F7 Stour r. England U.K.
105 F5 Stour r. England U.K.
105 H6 Stour r. England U.K.
105 I6 Stour r. England U.K.
105 E5 Stourbridge U.K.
105 E5 Stourport-on-Severn U.K.
131 K4 Stout Lake Canada
116 C4 Stowbtsy Belarus
147 F4 Stowe U.S.A.
105 H5 Stowmarket U.K.
107 D3 Strabane U.K.
107 D4 Stradbally Rep. of Ireland
105 I5 Stradbroke U.K.
114 C2 Stradella Italy
71 F9 Strahan Australia
141 G3 Straight Cliffs ridge U.S.A.
156 B8 Strait of Magellan Chile
112 F6 Strakonice Czech Rep.
112 F3 Stralsund Germany
124 C7 Strand S. Africa
102 I3 Stranda Norway
145 E7 Strangers Cay i. Bahamas
107 F3 Strangford U.K.
107 F3 Strangford Lough inlet U.K.
106 C6 Stranraer U.K.
110 H2 Strasbourg France
146 D5 Strasburg U.S.A.
71 G6 Stratford Australia
134 E4 Stratford Canada
72 E3 Stratford N.Z.
143 C4 Stratford TX U.S.A.
134 B3 Stratford WI U.S.A.
105 F5 Stratford-upon-Avon U.K.
70 C5 Strathalbyn Australia
106 D5 Strathaven U.K.
106 G3 Strathbeg, Loch of l. U.K.
106 D3 Strathcarron val. U.K.
130 D5 Strathcona Provincial Park Canada
106 D3 Strathconon val. U.K.
106 D3 Strath Dearn val. U.K.
106 D2 Strath Fleet val. U.K.
130 G4 Strathmore Canada
130 E4 Strathnaver Canada
106 D2 Strathnaver val. U.K.
106 E2 Strath of Kildonan val. U.K.
135 G4 Strathroy Canada
106 E3 Strathspey val. U.K.
106 E2 Strathy U.K.
106 D2 Strathy Point U.K.
105 C7 Stratton U.K.
147 H2 Stratton U.S.A.
109 K6 Straubing Germany
102 B1 Straumnes pt Iceland
134 B4 Strawberry Point U.S.A.
141 G1 Strawberry Reservoir U.S.A.
68 D5 Streaky Bay Australia
70 B5 Streaky Bay b. Australia
134 C5 Streator U.S.A.
105 E6 Street U.K.
115 K3 Strehaia Romania
109 L3 Strehla Germany
77 Q3 Strelka Rus. Fed.
103 N4 Strenči Latvia
109 K5 Stříbro Czech Rep.
106 F3 Strichen U.K.
115 J4 Strimonas r. Greece
159 D4 Stroeder Arg.
107 C4 Strokestown Rep. of Ireland
106 E2 Stroma, Island of i. U.K.
114 F5 Stromboli, Isola i. Isole Lipari Italy
106 E2 Stromness U.K.
142 D3 Stromsburg U.S.A.
103 J4 Strömstad Sweden
102 K3 Strömsund Sweden
146 C4 Strongsville U.S.A.
106 F1 Stronsay i. U.K.
71 I4 Stroud Australia
105 E6 Stroud U.K.
71 I4 Stroud Road Australia
147 F4 Stroudsburg U.S.A.
103 J4 Struer Denmark
115 I4 Struga Macedonia
116 D3 Strugi-Krasnyye Rus. Fed.
124 D7 Struis Bay S. Africa
109 I5 Strullendorf Germany
115 J4 Struma r. Bulg.
105 B5 Strumble Head U.K.
115 J4 Strumica Macedonia
115 K3 Stryama r. Bulg.
124 E4 Strydenburg S. Africa
103 I3 Stryn Norway
117 B5 Stryy Ukr.
70 D2 Strzelecki Creek watercourse Australia
71 H8 Strzelecki Peak h. Australia
145 D7 Stuart FL U.S.A.
146 C6 Stuart VA U.S.A.
130 E4 Stuart Lake Canada
146 D5 Stuarts Draft U.S.A.
71 H4 Stuart Town Australia
72 C6 Studholme Junction N.Z.
102 L3 Studsviken Sweden
143 C6 Study Butte U.S.A.
131 K4 Stull Lake Canada
116 F4 Stupino Rus. Fed.
73 B6 Sturge Island i. Antarctica
134 D2 Sturgeon r. U.S.A.
131 J4 Sturgeon Bay b. Canada
134 D3 Sturgeon Bay U.S.A.
134 E3 Sturgeon Bay b. U.S.A.
134 D3 Sturgeon Bay Canal lake channel U.S.A.
135 H2 Sturgeon Falls Canada
132 B3 Sturgeon Lake Canada
144 C4 Sturgis KY U.S.A.
134 E5 Sturgis MI U.S.A.
142 C2 Sturgis SD U.S.A.
70 D2 Sturt, Mount h. Australia
70 B5 Sturt Bay Australia
68 C3 Sturt Creek watercourse Australia
70 D2 Sturt National Park Australia
70 D2 Sturt Stony Desert Australia
125 G6 Stutterheim S. Africa
112 D6 Stuttgart Germany
143 F5 Stuttgart U.S.A.
102 B2 Stykkishólmur Iceland
113 L5 Styr r. Ukr.
158 D2 Suaçuí Grande r. Brazil
121 F3 Suakin Sudan
93 F5 Suao Taiwan
150 B1 Suaqui Grande Mex.
157 B3 Suárez r. Col.
113 L3 Subačius Lith.
89 H4 Subansiri r. India
89 F5 Subarnarekha r. India
81 G6 Subayhah Saudi Arabia
99 C2 Subi Besar i. Indon.
115 H1 Subotica Serb. and Mont.
113 M7 Suceava Romania
94 C3 Suchan r. Rus. Fed.
107 C4 Suck r. Rep. of Ireland
109 J1 Suckow Germany
154 E7 Sucre Bol.
157 B2 Sucre Col.
157 C3 Sucuaro Col.
158 B2 Sucuriú r. Brazil
69 G4 Sud, Grand Récif du rf New Caledonia
117 E6 Sudak Ukr.
121 E3 Sudan country Africa
116 G3 Suday Rus. Fed.
81 J6 Sudayr, Sha'īb watercourse Iraq
135 G2 Sudbury Canada
105 H5 Sudbury U.K.
121 E4 Sudd swamp Sudan
109 J1 Sude r. Germany
112 H5 Sudety mts Czech Rep./Poland
147 F5 Sudlersville U.S.A.
116 G4 Sudogda Rus. Fed.
80 D7 Sudr Egypt
102 □ Suðuroy i. Faroe Is
Sue watercourse Sudan
111 F3 Sueca Spain
121 F2 Suez Egypt
121 F2 Suez, Gulf of Egypt
121 F1 Suez Canal Egypt
146 E6 Suffolk U.S.A.
84 B2 Sūfīān Iran
134 C4 Sugar r. U.S.A.
147 H2 Sugarloaf Mountain U.S.A.
71 J4 Sugarloaf Point Australia
97 C4 Sugbuhan Point Phil.
83 I5 Sugun China
99 E1 Sugut r. Sabah Malaysia
97 A5 Sugut, Tanjung pt Sabah Malaysia
92 B2 Suhait China
86 E5 Şuḥār Oman
90 C1 Sühbaatar Mongolia
109 I4 Suhl Germany
109 I2 Suhlendorf Germany
80 C2 Şuhut Turkey
88 B3 Sui Pak.
94 B1 Suibin China
93 F4 Suichang China
93 E5 Suichuan China
92 D2 Suide China
96 F1 Suifenhe China
88 B4 Suigam India
90 E2 Suihua China
93 B4 Suijiang China
93 D5 Suining Hunan China
92 E3 Suining Jiangsu China
93 B4 Suining Sichuan China
92 E3 Suiping China
107 D5 Suippes France
107 D5 Suir r. Rep. of Ireland
92 E3 Suixi China
92 E3 Suixian China
93 C5 Suiyang Guizhou China
92 E3 Suiyang Henan China
92 F1 Suizhong China
92 D4 Suizhou China
92 C1 Suj China
88 C4 Sujangarh India
88 D3 Sujanpur India
88 B4 Sujawal Pak.
99 C4 Sukabumi Indon.
99 C3 Sukadana Indon.
95 G6 Sukagawa Japan
97 A5 Sukau Sabah Malaysia
96 C4 Sukchŏn N. Korea
116 E4 Sukhanovka Rus. Fed.
116 H2 Sukhinichi Rus. Fed.
116 H2 Sukhona r. Rus. Fed.
98 A1 Sukhothai Thai.
116 E2 Sukkozero Rus. Fed.
88 B4 Sukkur Pak.
87 C2 Sukma India
88 C4 Sukri r. India
116 F3 Sukromny Rus. Fed.
96 C4 Sukumo Japan
103 I3 Sula i. Norway
91 E7 Sula, Kepulauan is Indon.
88 B3 Sulaiman Range mts Pak.
117 H7 Sulak r. Rus. Fed.
84 C4 Sülār Iran
106 B1 Sula Sgeir i. U.K.
Sulawesi i. Indon. see Celebes
81 J4 Sulaymān Beg Iraq
84 C2 Suledeh Iran
106 D1 Sule Skerry i. U.K.
106 D1 Sule Stack i. U.K.
80 F3 Süleymanlı Turkey
120 A4 Sulima Sierra Leone
109 G2 Sulingen Germany
102 L2 Sulitjelma Norway
103 O3 Sulkava Fin.
154 B4 Sullana Peru
142 F4 Sullivan U.S.A.
131 G4 Sullivan Lake Canada
147 I1 Sully Canada
114 E3 Sulmona Italy
143 E6 Sulphur U.S.A.
143 E5 Sulphur Springs U.S.A.
135 F2 Sultan Canada
85 F4 Sultan, Koh-i- mts Pak.
80 C2 Sultan Dağları mts Turkey
80 D2 Sultanhanı Turkey
89 E4 Sultanpur India
97 B5 Sulu Archipelago is Phil.
83 G5 Sülüktü Kyrg.
80 F2 Sulusaray Turkey
97 A4 Sulu Sea Phil.
82 F3 Sulutobe Kazakh.
109 J5 Sulzbach-Rosenberg Germany
73 B5 Sulzberger Bay b. Antarctica
85 E6 Sumāil Oman
156 D3 Sumampa Arg.
157 B4 Sumapaz, Parque Nacional nat. park Col.
81 J5 Sūmār Iran
Sumatera i. Indon. see Sumatra
99 B3 Sumatra i. Indon.
112 F6 Šumava mts Czech Rep.
91 E7 Sumba i. Indon.
91 D7 Sumba, Selat sea chan. Indon.
82 C5 Sumbar r. Turkm.
99 E4 Sumbawa i. Indon.
99 E4 Sumbawabesar Indon.
123 D4 Sumbawanga Tanz.
123 B5 Sumbe Angola
106 □ Sumburgh U.K.
106 □ Sumburgh Head U.K.
88 D2 Sumdo China/Jammu and Kashmir
81 L3 Sume'eh Sarā Iran
99 D4 Sumenep Indon.
95 F9 Sumisu-jima i. Japan
81 I3 Summēl Iraq
132 C3 Summer Beaver Canada
133 J4 Summerford Canada
134 D3 Summer Island U.S.A.
106 C2 Summer Isles U.K.
133 H4 Summerside Canada
146 C5 Summersville U.S.A.
146 C5 Summersville Lake U.S.A.
130 E4 Summit Lake Canada
134 E5 Summit Lake l. U.S.A.
140 D2 Summit Mountain U.S.A.
88 D2 Sumnal China/India
72 D5 Sumner N.Z.
134 A4 Sumner U.S.A.
72 D5 Sumner, Lake N.Z.
130 C3 Sumner Strait U.S.A.
95 F6 Sumon-dake mt. Japan
95 D7 Sumoto Japan
112 H6 Šumperk Czech Rep.
82 A4 Sumqayıt Azer.
81 L1 Sumqayıt r. Azer.
88 B4 Sumrahu Pak.
145 D5 Sumter U.S.A.
117 E5 Sumy Ukr.
138 D2 Sun r. U.S.A.
116 I3 Suna Rus. Fed.
94 G3 Sunagawa Japan
89 G4 Sunamganj Bangl.
96 C4 Sunan N. Korea
106 C4 Sunart, Loch inlet U.K.
84 D6 Şunaynah Oman
81 J4 Sunbula Kuh mts Iran
138 E1 Sunburst U.S.A.
70 F6 Sunbury Australia
146 B4 Sunbury OH U.S.A.
146 E4 Sunbury PA U.S.A.
159 E1 Sunchales Arg.
96 C4 Sunch'ŏn N. Korea
96 D6 Sunch'ŏn S. Korea
125 G2 Sun City S. Africa
147 H3 Suncook U.S.A.
99 C4 Sunda, Selat str. Indon.
138 F2 Sundance U.S.A.
89 F5 Sundarbans coastal area Bangl./India
89 G5 Sundarbans National Park Bangl./India
87 D1 Sundargarh India
88 D3 Sundarnagar India
162 L4 Sunda Shelf sea feature Indian Ocean
Sunda Trench sea feature Indian Ocean see Java Trench
104 F3 Sunderland U.K.
109 G3 Sundern (Sauerland) Germany
80 C2 Sündiken Dağları mts Turkey
135 H3 Sundridge Canada
103 L3 Sundsvall Sweden
76 C3 Sundsvall commune Sweden
Sundukli, Peski des. Turkm. see Sandykly Gumy
125 I4 Sundumbili S. Africa
88 D4 Sunel India
98 B5 Sungaikabung Indon.
99 C3 Sungailiat Indon.
99 B3 Sungaipenuh Indon.
99 B1 Sungai Petani Malaysia
Sungei Petani Malaysia see Sungai Petani
98 □ Sungei Seletar Reservoir Sing.
80 E1 Sungurlu Turkey
83 H3 Sunkar, Gora mt. Kazakh.
89 F4 Sun Kosi r. Nepal
103 I3 Sunndal Norway
102 J3 Sunndalsøra Norway
103 K4 Sunne Sweden
138 C2 Sunnyside U.S.A.
140 A3 Sunnyvale U.S.A.
134 C4 Sun Prairie U.S.A.
140 □1 Sunset Beach U.S.A.
141 G4 Sunset Crater National Monument nat. park U.S.A.
77 M3 Suntar Rus. Fed.
85 F5 Suntsar Pak.
138 D3 Sun Valley U.S.A.
96 C5 Sunwi-do i. N. Korea
120 B4 Sunyani Ghana
102 O2 Suolijärvet l. Fin.
134 C1 Suomi Canada
102 O2 Suomussalmi Fin.
95 B8 Suō-nada b. Japan
Suonan China see Dongxiangzu
102 N3 Suonenjoki Fin.
98 C3 Suŏng Cambodia
93 B7 Suong r. Laos
116 E2 Suoyarvi Rus. Fed.
87 A4 Supa India
141 F3 Supai U.S.A.
157 E3 Supamo r. Venez.
89 F4 Supaul India
141 G5 Superior AZ U.S.A.
142 D3 Superior NE U.S.A.
134 A2 Superior WI U.S.A.
151 F4 Superior, Laguna lag. Mex.
134 C2 Superior, Lake Canada/U.S.A.
98 B2 Suphan Buri Thai.
81 I2 Süphan Dağı mt. Turkey
116 E4 Suponevo Rus. Fed.
96 C3 Supung N. Korea
81 K6 Sūq ash Shuyūkh Iraq
92 F3 Suqian China
Suquṭrā i. Yemen see Socotra
86 E5 Şūr Oman
140 B3 Sur, Point U.S.A.
159 F3 Sur, Punta pt Arg.
116 H4 Sura Rus. Fed.
116 H4 Sura r. Rus. Fed.
81 L1 Şuraabad Azer.
85 G4 Surab Pak.
99 D4 Surabaya Indon.
85 E5 Sūrak Iran
99 D4 Surakarta Indon.
71 H1 Surat Australia
88 C5 Surat India
88 C3 Suratgarh India
98 A3 Surat Thani Thai.
116 E4 Surazh Rus. Fed.
81 J4 Sūrdāsh Iraq
115 J3 Surdulica Serb. and Mont.
108 E5 Sûre r. Lux.
88 B5 Surendranagar India
150 I6 Suretka Costa Rica
140 B4 Surf U.S.A.
76 I3 Surgut Rus. Fed.
87 C2 Suriapet India
97 C4 Surigao Phil.
97 C4 Surigao Strait Phil.
98 B2 Surin Thai.
155 G3 Suriname country S. America
85 H3 Surkhab r. Afgh.
85 F3 Surkhandar'ya r. Uzbek.
88 E3 Surkhet Nepal
85 H2 Surkhob r. Tajik.
84 D4 Surmāq Iran
81 H1 Sürmene Turkey
117 G5 Surovikino Rus. Fed.
84 A6 Surrah, Nafūd as des. Saudi Arabia
146 E6 Surry U.S.A.
116 H4 Sursk Rus. Fed.
Surt Libya see Sirte
Surt, Khalīj g. Libya see Sirte, Gulf of
102 B3 Surtsey i. Iceland
85 E5 Sūrū Iran
80 G3 Suruç Turkey
95 F7 Suruga-wan b. Japan
99 B3 Surulangun Indon.
97 C5 Surup Phil.
108 F2 Surwold Germany
81 K2 Şuşa Azer.
95 B7 Susa Japan
95 C8 Susaki Japan
84 C4 Süsangerd Iran
116 G3 Susanino Rus. Fed.
140 B1 Susanville U.S.A.
80 G1 Suşehri Turkey
98 A4 Suso Thai.
93 E4 Susong China
147 E4 Susquehanna r. U.S.A.

210 Tcholliré

121 D4 **Tcholliré** Cameroon
113 I3 **Tczew** Poland
150 C3 **Teacapán** Mex.
72 A6 **Te Anau** N.Z.
72 A6 **Te Anau, Lake** N.Z.
151 F4 **Teapa** Mex.
72 G2 **Te Araroa** N.Z.
72 E2 **Te Aroha** N.Z.
72 E3 **Te Awamutu** N.Z.
104 E3 **Tebay** U.K.
131 J2 **Tebesjuak Lake** Canada
120 C1 **Tébessa** Alg.
114 B7 **Tébessa, Monts de** *mts* Alg.
156 E3 **Tebicuary** *r.* Para.
99 A2 **Tebingtinggi** Indon.
99 B3 **Tebingtinggi** Indon.
114 C6 **Tébourba** Tunisia
114 C6 **Téboursouk** Tunisia
117 H7 **Tebulos Mt'a** Georgia/Rus. Fed.
120 B4 **Techiman** Ghana
156 B6 **Tecka** Arg.
108 F2 **Tecklenburger Land** *reg.* Germany
151 E3 **Tecolutla** Mex.
150 D4 **Tecomán** Mex.
140 D4 **Tecopa** U.S.A.
150 B1 **Tecoripa** Mex.
150 D4 **Técpan** Mex.
113 M7 **Tecuci** Romania
135 F5 **Tecumseh** U.S.A.
Tedzhen Turkm. *see* **Tejen**
Tedzhen *r.* Turkm. *see* **Tejen**
85 F2 **Tedzhenstroy** Turkm.
141 H3 **Teec Nos Pos** U.S.A.
79 H1 **Teeli** Rus. Fed.
104 F3 **Tees** *r.* U.K.
104 E3 **Teesdale** *val.* U.K.
154 E4 **Tefé** *r.* Brazil
80 B3 **Tefenni** Turkey
99 C4 **Tegal** Indon.
109 L2 **Tegel** *airport* Germany
150 H5 **Tegucigalpa** Hond.
120 C3 **Teguidda-n-Tessoumt** Niger
140 C4 **Tehachapi** U.S.A.
139 C5 **Tehachapi Mountains** U.S.A.
140 C4 **Tehachapi Pass** U.S.A.
131 J2 **Tehek Lake** Canada
Teheran Iran *see* **Tehrān**
120 B4 **Téhini** Côte d'Ivoire
84 C3 **Tehrān** Iran (City Plan **54**)
88 D3 **Tehri** India
151 E4 **Tehuacán** Mex.
151 F5 **Tehuantepec, Gulf of** Mex.
151 F4 **Tehuantepec, Istmo de** *isth.* Mex.
161 M5 **Tehuantepec Ridge** *sea feature* N. Pacific Ocean
151 E4 **Tehuitzingo** Mex.
105 C5 **Teifi** *r.* U.K.
105 D7 **Teign** *r.* U.K.
105 D7 **Teignmouth** U.K.
82 E5 **Tejen** Turkm.
85 F2 **Tejen** *r.* Turkm.
111 **Tejo** *r.* Port. *alt.* **Tajo (Spain),** *conv.* **Tagus**
140 C4 **Tejon Pass** U.S.A.
150 D4 **Tejupan, Punta** *pt* Mex.
72 D1 **Te Kao** N.Z.
72 C5 **Tekapo, Lake** N.Z.
89 F4 **Tekari** India
151 G3 **Tekax** Mex.
83 H1 **Teke, Ozero** *salt l.* Kazakh.
82 E2 **Tekeli** *Aktyubinskaya Oblast'* Kazakh.
83 I3 **Tekeli** *Almatinskaya Oblast'* Kazakh.
83 J4 **Tekes** China
83 J4 **Tekes** Kazakh.
83 J3 **Tekes He** *r.* China
122 D2 **Tekezē Wenz** *r.* Eritrea/Eth.
88 E1 **Tekiliktag** *mt.* China
80 A1 **Tekirdağ** Turkey
87 D2 **Tekkali** India
81 H2 **Tekman** Turkey
89 H5 **Teknaf** Bangl.
134 E4 **Tekonsha** U.S.A.
72 E3 **Te Kuiti** N.Z.
87 C2 **Tel** *r.* India
150 H5 **Tela** Hond.
117 H7 **T'elavi** Georgia
80 E5 **Tel Aviv-Yafo** Israel
112 G6 **Telč** Czech Rep.
151 G3 **Telchac Puerto** Mex.
130 C3 **Telegraph Creek** Canada
158 B4 **Telêmaco Borba** Brazil
159 D3 **Telén** Arg.
99 E2 **Telen** *r.* Indon.
115 K2 **Teleorman** *r.* Romania
140 D3 **Telescope Peak** U.S.A.
155 G5 **Teles Pires** *r.* Brazil
105 E5 **Telford** U.K.
109 F3 **Telgte** Germany
150 H5 **Telica** Nicaragua
120 A3 **Télimélé** Guinea
130 D4 **Telkwa** Canada
128 B3 **Teller** U.S.A.
87 A4 **Tellicherry** India
108 D4 **Tellin** Belgium
81 K6 **Telloh** Iraq
151 E4 **Teloloapán** Mex.
159 C4 **Telsen** Arg.
103 M5 **Telšiai** Lith.
109 L2 **Teltow** Germany
Teluk Anson Malaysia *see* **Teluk Intan**
99 A2 **Telukdalam** Indon.
99 B2 **Teluk Intan** Malaysia
135 H2 **Temagami** Canada
135 G2 **Temagami Lake** Canada
99 D4 **Temanggung** Indon.
151 G3 **Temax** Mex.
125 H2 **Temba** S. Africa
77 K3 **Tembenchi** *r.* Rus. Fed.
99 B3 **Tembilahan** Indon.
125 H3 **Tembisa** S. Africa
122 B4 **Tembo Aluma** Angola
105 E5 **Teme** *r.* U.K.
140 D5 **Temecula** U.S.A.
80 D2 **Temelli** Turkey
99 B2 **Temerluh** Malaysia
81 L5 **Temīleh** Iran
82 D2 **Temir** Kazakh.
83 G4 **Temirlanovka** Kazakh.
83 H2 **Temirtau** Kazakh.
135 H2 **Témiscaming** Canada
Temiscaming Canada *see* **Témiscaming**
135 H2 **Témiscamingue, Lac** *l.* Canada
133 G4 **Témiscouata, Lac** *l.* Canada
71 F8 **Temma** Australia
102 N2 **Temmes** Fin.
116 G4 **Temnikov** Rus. Fed.
71 G5 **Temora** Australia
150 C1 **Temósachic** Mex.
141 G5 **Tempe** U.S.A.
109 L2 **Tempelhof** *airport* Germany
114 C4 **Tempio Pausania** *Sardinia* Italy
134 E3 **Temple** *MI* U.S.A.
143 D6 **Temple** *TX* U.S.A.
105 C5 **Temple Bar** U.K.
107 D5 **Templemore** Rep. of Ireland
97 A4 **Templer Bank** *sea feature* Phil.
104 E3 **Temple Sowerby** U.K.
109 L1 **Templin** Germany
151 E3 **Tempoal** Mex.
117 F6 **Temryuk** Rus. Fed.
159 B3 **Temuco** Chile
72 C6 **Temuka** N.Z.
154 C4 **Tena** Ecuador
140 D1 **Tenabo, Mount** U.S.A.
87 C2 **Tenali** India
151 E4 **Tenancingo** Mex.
98 A2 **Tenasserim** Myanmar
98 A2 **Tenasserim** *r.* Myanmar
105 E5 **Tenbury Wells** U.K.
105 C6 **Tenby** U.K.
135 F2 **Tenby Bay** Canada
122 E2 **Tendaho** Eth.
110 H4 **Tende** France
79 H6 **Ten Degree Channel** India
94 G5 **Tendō** Japan
81 I2 **Tendürek Dağı** *mt.* Turkey
120 B3 **Ténenkou** Mali
120 D3 **Ténéré** *reg.* Niger
120 D3 **Ténéré, Erg du** *des.* Niger
120 D2 **Ténéré du Tafassâsset** *des.* Niger
120 A2 **Tenerife** *i.* Canary Is
111 G4 **Ténès** Alg.
99 E4 **Tengah, Kepulauan** *is* Indon.
82 C4 **Tenge** Kazakh.
98 □ **Tengeh Reservoir** Sing.
92 B2 **Tengger Shamo** *des.* China
98 B4 **Tenggul** *i.* Malaysia
83 G2 **Tengiz, Ozero** *salt l.* Kazakh.
93 C7 **Tengqiao** China
120 B3 **Tengréla** Côte d'Ivoire
93 D6 **Tengxian** China
92 E3 **Tengzhou** China
82 F1 **Teniz, Ozero** *l.* Kazakh.
123 C5 **Tenke** Dem. Rep. Congo
77 P2 **Tenkeli** Rus. Fed.
120 B3 **Tenkodogo** Burkina
68 D3 **Tennant Creek** Australia
145 C5 **Tennessee** *r.* U.S.A.
146 B6 **Tennessee** *state* U.S.A.
139 F4 **Tennessee Pass** U.S.A.
102 L1 **Tennevoll** Norway
159 B2 **Teno** *r.* Chile
102 O1 **Tenojoki** *r.* Fin./Norway
151 G4 **Tenosique** Mex.
138 F2 **Ten Sleep** U.S.A.
68 C2 **Tenteno** Indon.
105 H6 **Tenterden** U.K.
71 J2 **Tenterfield** Australia
145 D7 **Ten Thousand Islands** U.S.A.
111 C3 **Tentudia** *mt.* Spain
158 B3 **Teodoro Sampaio** Brazil
158 E2 **Teófilo Otôni** Brazil
151 F4 **Teopisca** Mex.
151 E4 **Teotihuacán** *tourist site* Mex.
139 E6 **Tepache** Mex.
72 D1 **Te Paki** N.Z.
150 D4 **Tepalcatepec** Mex.
150 D3 **Tepatitlán** Mex.
81 H3 **Tepe** Turkey
81 I3 **Tepe Gawra** *tourist site* Iraq
150 C2 **Tepehuanes** Mex.
151 E4 **Tepeji** Mex.
115 I4 **Tepelenë** Albania
151 E4 **Tepelmeme de Morelos** Mex.
109 K5 **Tepelská Vrchovina** *hills* Czech Rep.
157 E4 **Tepequem, Serra** *mts* Brazil
150 C3 **Tepic** Mex.
72 C5 **Te Pirita** N.Z.
112 F5 **Teplice** Czech Rep.
116 J2 **Teplogorka** Rus. Fed.
116 F4 **Teploye** Rus. Fed.
72 F2 **Te Puke** N.Z.
151 F4 **Tequisistlán** Mex.
151 E3 **Tequisquiapán** Mex.
67 I3 **Teraina** *i.* Kiribati
88 D2 **Teram Kangri** *mt.* China/Jammu and Kashmir
114 E3 **Teramo** Italy
70 E7 **Terang** Australia
108 F2 **Ter Apel** Neth.
88 B3 **Teratani** *r.* Pak.
117 F4 **Terbuny** Rus. Fed.
81 H2 **Tercan** Turkey
100 A6 **Terceira** *i.* Azores
113 L6 **Terebovlya** Ukr.
117 H7 **Terek** Rus. Fed.
117 H7 **Terek** *r.* Rus. Fed.
83 G2 **Terekty** *Karagandinskaya Oblast'* Kazakh.
83 K2 **Terekty** *Vostochnyy Kazakhstan* Kazakh.
116 I4 **Teren'ga** Rus. Fed.
158 A3 **Terenos** Brazil
82 F3 **Terenozek** Kazakh.
82 D2 **Terensay** Rus. Fed.
157 C2 **Terepaima, Parque Nacional** *nat. park* Venez.
116 H4 **Tereshka** *r.* Rus. Fed.
155 J5 **Teresina** Brazil
158 D3 **Teresópolis** Brazil
108 B5 **Tergnier** France
83 F2 **Terisakkan** *r.* Kazakh.
80 F1 **Terme** Turkey
Termez Uzbek. *see* **Termiz**
114 E6 **Termini Imerese** *Sicily* Italy
151 G4 **Términos, Laguna de** *lag.* Mex.
83 F5 **Termiz** Uzbek.
114 F4 **Termoli** Italy
105 E5 **Tern** *r.* U.K.
91 E6 **Ternate** Indon.
108 B3 **Terneuzen** Neth.
94 E2 **Terney** Rus. Fed.
114 E3 **Terni** Italy
117 C5 **Ternopil'** Ukr.
70 C4 **Terowie** Australia
90 G2 **Terpeniya, Mys** *c.* Rus. Fed.
90 G2 **Terpeniya, Zaliv** *g.* Rus. Fed.
130 D4 **Terrace** Canada
134 D1 **Terrace Bay** Canada
124 E2 **Terra Firma** S. Africa
102 K2 **Terråk** Norway
114 C5 **Terralba** *Sardinia* Italy
133 J4 **Terra Nova National Park** Canada
143 F6 **Terrebonne Bay** U.S.A.
144 C4 **Terre Haute** U.S.A.
133 J4 **Terrenceville** Canada
138 F2 **Terry** U.S.A.
117 G5 **Tersa** *r.* Rus. Fed.
108 D1 **Terschelling** *i.* Neth.
83 I4 **Terskey Ala-Too** *mts* Kyrg.
114 C5 **Tertenia** *Sardinia* Italy
111 F2 **Teruel** Spain
102 N2 **Tervola** Fin.
114 G2 **Tešanj** Bos.-Herz.
122 D2 **Teseney** Eritrea
116 G4 **Tesha** *r.* Rus. Fed.
128 C2 **Teshekpuk Lake** U.S.A.
94 I3 **Teshikaga** Japan
94 G2 **Teshio** Japan
94 H3 **Teshio-dake** *mt.* Japan
94 G2 **Teshio-gawa** *r.* Japan
150 B2 **Tesia** Mex.
130 C2 **Teslin** Canada
130 C2 **Teslin** *r.* Canada
130 C2 **Teslin Lake** Canada
158 B1 **Tesouras** *r.* Brazil
158 B2 **Tesouro** Brazil
120 C3 **Tessaoua** Niger
105 F6 **Test** *r.* U.K.
114 C6 **Testour** Tunisia
156 B2 **Tetas, Punta** *pt* Chile
123 D5 **Tete** Moz.
72 F3 **Te Teko** N.Z.
113 O5 **Teteriv** *r.* Ukr.
109 K1 **Teterow** Germany
113 N6 **Tetiyiv** Ukr.
104 G4 **Tetney** U.K.
138 E2 **Teton** *r.* U.S.A.
138 E3 **Teton Range** *mts* U.S.A.
120 B1 **Tétouan** Morocco
115 I3 **Tetovo** Macedonia
88 B5 **Tetpur** India
116 I4 **Tetyushi** Rus. Fed.
156 D2 **Teuco** *r.* Arg.
124 B1 **Teufelsbach** Namibia
109 G1 **Teufels Moor** *reg.* Germany
94 G2 **Teuri-tō** *i.* Japan
109 G2 **Teutoburger Wald** *hills* Germany
103 M3 **Teuva** Fin.
Tevere *r.* Italy *see* **Tiber**
Teverya Israel *see* **Tiberias**
106 F5 **Teviot** *r.* U.K.
106 F5 **Teviotdale** *val.* U.K.
72 A7 **Te Waewae Bay** N.Z.
125 G1 **Tewane** Botswana
69 F4 **Tewantin** Australia
72 E4 **Te Wharau** N.Z.
105 E6 **Tewkesbury** U.K.
92 B3 **Têwo** China
130 E5 **Texada Island** Canada
143 E5 **Texarkana** U.S.A.
71 I2 **Texas** Australia
143 D6 **Texas** *state* U.S.A.
143 E6 **Texas City** U.S.A.
151 E4 **Texcoco** Mex.
108 C1 **Texel** *i.* Neth.
143 C4 **Texhoma** U.S.A.
143 D5 **Texoma, Lake** U.S.A.
125 G4 **Teyateyaneng** Lesotho
116 G3 **Teykovo** Rus. Fed.
85 G3 **Teyvareh** Afgh.
116 G3 **Teza** *r.* Rus. Fed.
151 E4 **Teziutlán** Mex.
89 H4 **Tezpur** India
89 I4 **Tezu** India
131 J2 **Tha-anne** *r.* Canada
125 H4 **Thabana-Ntlenyana** *mt.* Lesotho
125 G4 **Thaba Nchu** S. Africa
125 G4 **Thaba Putsoa** *mt.* Lesotho
125 H4 **Thaba-Tseka** Lesotho
125 G2 **Thabazimbi** S. Africa
98 B1 **Tha Bo** Laos
125 G3 **Thabong** S. Africa
84 B5 **Thādiq** Saudi Arabia
98 A2 **Thagyettaw** Myanmar
93 C6 **Thai Binh** Vietnam
98 A1 **Thailand** *country* Asia
98 B3 **Thailand, Gulf of** Asia
98 A3 **Thai Muang** Thai.
93 B6 **Thai Nguyên** Vietnam
84 C5 **Thaj** Saudi Arabia
98 C1 **Thakèk** Laos
88 E5 **Thakurtola** India
109 I4 **Thal** Germany
88 B2 **Thal** Pak.
114 C7 **Thala** Tunisia
98 A3 **Thalang** Thai.
88 B3 **Thal Desert** Pak.
109 J3 **Thale (Harz)** Germany
98 B1 **Tha Li** Thai.
71 H2 **Thallon** Australia
85 G4 **Thalo** Pak.
125 F2 **Thamaga** Botswana
84 B5 **Thāmām, 'Irq ath** *des.* Saudi Arabia
86 C7 **Thamar, Jabal** *mt.* Yemen
86 D6 **Thamarīt** Oman
105 G5 **Thame** *r.* U.K.
72 E2 **Thames** N.Z.
105 H6 **Thames** *est.* U.K.
105 G6 **Thames** *r.* U.K.
135 G4 **Thamesville** Canada
98 A2 **Thanbyuzayat** Myanmar
88 C5 **Thandla** India
91 B5 **Thandwè** Myanmar
87 A2 **Thane** India
88 B5 **Thangadh** India
Thăng Binh Vietnam *see* **Ha Lam**
98 C1 **Thanh Hoa** Vietnam
87 B4 **Thanjavur** India
98 B1 **Tha Pla** Thai.
98 A3 **Thap Put** Thai.
98 A3 **Thap Sakae** Thai.
88 B4 **Tharad** India
88 B4 **Thar Desert** India/Pak.
70 E1 **Thargomindah** Australia
81 I5 **Tharthār, Buḥayrat ath** *l.* Iraq
115 K4 **Thasos** *i.* Greece
141 H5 **Thatcher** U.S.A.
93 C6 **Thât Khê** Vietnam
91 B5 **Thaton** Myanmar
89 H4 **Thaungdut** Myanmar
98 A1 **Thaungyin** *r.* Myanmar/Thai.
98 C1 **Tha Uthen** Thai.
91 B5 **Thayetmyo** Myanmar
72 F2 **The Aldermen Islands** N.Z.
141 F5 **Theba** U.S.A.
149 I3 **The Bahamas** *country* Caribbean Sea
145 E7 **The Bluff** Bahamas
104 E2 **The Cheviot** *h.* U.K.
70 C5 **The Coorong** *inlet* Australia
138 B2 **The Dalles** U.S.A.
142 C3 **Thedford** U.S.A.
105 G5 **The Fens** *reg.* U.K.
147 I2 **The Forks** U.S.A.
120 A3 **The Gambia** *country* Africa
70 E6 **The Grampians** *mts* Australia
The Great Oasis *oasis* Egypt *see* **Khārijah, Wāḥāt al**
86 D4 **The Gulf** Asia
108 C2 **The Hague** Neth.
72 C6 **The Hunters Hills** N.Z.
98 A3 **Theinkun** Myanmar
72 A6 **The Key** N.Z.
131 H2 **Thekulthili Lake** Canada
131 I2 **Thelon** *r.* Canada
131 I2 **Thelon Game Sanctuary** *nature res.* Canada
109 I4 **Themar** Germany
124 F6 **Thembalesizwe** S. Africa
125 H3 **Thembalihle** S. Africa
106 C2 **The Minch** *sea chan.* U.K.
105 F7 **The Needles** *stack* U.K.
111 H4 **Thenia** Alg.
111 H5 **Theniet El Had** Alg.
154 F5 **Theodore Roosevelt** *r.* Brazil
141 G5 **Theodore Roosevelt Dam** U.S.A.
141 G5 **Theodore Roosevelt Lake** U.S.A.
142 C2 **Theodore Roosevelt National Park** U.S.A.
107 B5 **The Paps** *h.* Rep. of Ireland
131 I4 **The Pas** Canada
107 B6 **The Pocket** *h.* Rep. of Ireland
108 A5 **Thérain** *r.* France
147 F2 **Theresa** U.S.A.
115 J4 **Thermaïkos Kolpos** *g.* Greece
140 B2 **Thermalito** U.S.A.
138 E3 **Thermopolis** U.S.A.
108 A4 **Thérouanne** France
70 E3 **The Salt Lake** *salt l.* Australia
128 F2 **Thesiger Bay** Canada
105 F7 **The Solent** *str.* U.K.
135 F2 **Thessalon** Canada
115 J4 **Thessaloniki** Greece
106 B3 **The Storr** *h.* U.K.
105 H5 **Thet** *r.* U.K.
97 A4 **The Teeth** *mt.* Phil.
105 H5 **Thetford** U.K.
133 F4 **Thetford Mines** Canada
106 D4 **The Trossachs** *hills* U.K.
98 C1 **Theun** *r.* Laos
125 G4 **Theunissen** S. Africa
105 H5 **The Wash** *b.* U.K.
105 H6 **The Weald** *reg.* U.K.
143 F6 **Thibodaux** U.S.A.
131 J3 **Thicket Portage** Canada
142 D1 **Thief River Falls** U.S.A.
73 C4 **Thiel Mountains** *mts* Antarctica
110 F4 **Thiers** France
120 A3 **Thiès** Senegal
122 D4 **Thika** Kenya
Thiladhunmathee Atoll Maldives *see* **Thiladhunmathi Atoll**
87 A5 **Thiladhunmathi Atoll** Maldives
89 G4 **Thimphu** Bhutan
110 H2 **Thionville** France
115 K6 **Thira** *i.* Greece
115 K6 **Thirasia** *i.* Greece
104 F3 **Thirsk** U.K.
Thiruvananthapuram India *see* **Trivandrum**
103 J4 **Thisted** Denmark
70 B5 **Thistle Island** Australia
115 J5 **Thiva** Greece
131 J2 **Thlewiaza** *r.* Canada
131 H2 **Thoa** *r.* Canada
98 B3 **Thô Chu, Đao** *i.* Vietnam
125 I1 **Thohoyandou** S. Africa
108 C3 **Tholen** Neth.
108 F5 **Tholey** Germany
146 D5 **Thomas** U.S.A.
145 C5 **Thomaston** *GA* U.S.A.
147 I2 **Thomaston** *ME* U.S.A.
147 J2 **Thomaston Corner** Canada
107 D5 **Thomastown** Rep. of Ireland
145 D6 **Thomasville** U.S.A.
108 E4 **Thommen** Belgium
131 J3 **Thompson** Canada
130 E4 **Thompson** *r.* Canada
134 D3 **Thompson** *MI* U.S.A.
147 F4 **Thompson** *PA* U.S.A.
142 E3 **Thompson** *r.* U.S.A.
138 D2 **Thompson Falls** U.S.A.
145 D5 **Thomson** U.S.A.
Thôn Cư Lai Vietnam *see* **Thuân An**
112 C7 **Thonon-les-Bains** France
Thôn Sơn Hai Vietnam *see* **Sơn Hai**
139 E5 **Thoreau** U.S.A.
71 F2 **Thorlindah, Lake** *salt flat* Australia
108 D3 **Thorn** Neth.
104 F3 **Thornaby-on-Tees** U.K.
134 E4 **Thornapple** *r.* U.S.A.
105 E6 **Thornbury** U.K.
135 H2 **Thorne** Canada
104 G4 **Thorne** U.K.
140 C2 **Thorne** U.S.A.
130 C3 **Thorne Bay** U.S.A.
134 D5 **Thorntown** U.S.A.
134 B3 **Thorp** U.S.A.
73 D4 **Thorshavnheiane** *reg.* Antarctica
125 G4 **Thota-ea-Moli** Lesotho
110 D3 **Thouars** France
147 E2 **Thousand Islands** Canada
141 G2 **Thousand Lake Mountain** U.S.A.
140 C4 **Thousand Oaks** U.S.A.
115 L4 **Thrace** *reg.* Europe
115 K4 **Thrakiko Pelagos** *sea* Greece
138 E2 **Three Forks** U.S.A.
93 C4 **Three Gorges Dam Project** *resr* China
130 G4 **Three Hills** Canada
71 F8 **Three Hummock Island** Australia
72 D1 **Three Kings Islands** N.Z.
134 C3 **Three Lakes** U.S.A.
134 D5 **Three Oaks** U.S.A.
98 A2 **Three Pagodas Pass** Myanmar/Thai.
120 B4 **Three Points, Cape** Ghana
134 E5 **Three Rivers** *MI* U.S.A.
143 D6 **Three Rivers** *TX* U.S.A.
138 B2 **Three Sisters** *mt.* U.S.A.
Thrissur India *see* **Trichur**
143 D5 **Throckmorton** U.S.A.
Thu, Cu Lao *i.* Vietnam *see* **Phu Quy, Đao**
98 C1 **Thuân An** Vietnam
98 D1 **Thu Bôn, Sông** *r.* Vietnam
131 G2 **Thubun Lakes** Canada
98 C3 **Thu Dâu Môt** Vietnam
98 C3 **Thu Đuc** Vietnam
108 C4 **Thuin** Belgium
129 L2 **Thule** Greenland
123 C6 **Thuli** Zimbabwe
112 C7 **Thun** Switz.
134 C1 **Thunder Bay** Canada
134 C1 **Thunder Bay** *b.* Canada
135 F3 **Thunder Bay** *b.* U.S.A.
109 H5 **Thüngen** Germany
98 A3 **Thung Song** Thai.
98 A4 **Thung Wa** Thai.
109 I4 **Thüringen** *land* Germany
109 J3 **Thüringer Becken** *reg.* Germany
109 I4 **Thüringer Wald** *mts* Germany
107 D5 **Thurles** Rep. of Ireland
146 E5 **Thurmont** U.S.A.
112 F7 **Thurn, Pass** Austria
147 F2 **Thurso** Canada
106 E2 **Thurso** U.K.
106 E2 **Thurso** *r.* U.K.
73 A3 **Thurston Island** *i.* Antarctica
109 H2 **Thüster Berg** *h.* Germany
104 E3 **Thwaite** U.K.
103 J4 **Thyborøn** Denmark
92 A1 **Tiancang** China
92 F3 **Tianchang** China
93 C6 **Tiandeng** China
93 C6 **Tiandong** China
93 C5 **Tian'e** China
155 J4 **Tianguá** Brazil
92 E2 **Tianjin** China
92 E2 **Tianjin** *mun.* China
90 B3 **Tianjun** China
93 C5 **Tianlin** China
93 D4 **Tianmen** China
93 F4 **Tianmu Shan** *mts* China
96 E2 **Tianqiaoling** China
93 B4 **Tianquan** China
96 C3 **Tianshifu** China
92 B3 **Tianshui** China
88 D2 **Tianshuihai** China/Jammu and Kashmir
93 F4 **Tiantai** China
92 E1 **Tiantaiyong** China
93 C6 **Tianyang** China
92 B2 **Tianzhu** *Gansu* China
93 C5 **Tianzhu** *Guizhou* China
120 C1 **Tiaret** Alg.
120 B4 **Tiassalé** Côte d'Ivoire
158 B4 **Tibagi** *r.* Brazil
81 I5 **Tibal, Wādī** *watercourse* Iraq
121 D4 **Tibati** Cameroon
114 E3 **Tiber** *r.* Italy
80 E5 **Tiberias** Israel
Tiberias, Lake *l.* Israel *see* **Galilee, Sea of**
138 E1 **Tiber Reservoir** U.S.A.
121 D2 **Tibesti** *mts* Chad
Tibet *aut. reg.* China *see* **Xizang Zizhiqu**
79 G3 **Tibet, Plateau of** China
70 E2 **Tibooburra** Australia
89 E3 **Tibrikot** Nepal
103 K4 **Tibro** Sweden
150 A1 **Tiburón, Isla** *i.* Mex.
97 B3 **Ticao** *i.* Phil.
105 H6 **Ticehurst** U.K.
135 I3 **Tichborne** Canada
120 B3 **Tîchît** Mauritania
120 A2 **Tichla** W. Sahara
112 D7 **Ticino** *r.* Switz.
147 G3 **Ticonderoga** U.S.A.
151 G3 **Ticul** Mex.
103 K4 **Tidaholm** Sweden
89 H5 **Tiddim** Myanmar
120 C2 **Tidikelt, Plaine du** *plain* Alg.
120 A3 **Tidjikja** Mauritania
83 K3 **Tiechanggou** China
96 B2 **Tiefa** China
108 D3 **Tiel** Neth.
94 A1 **Tieli** China
96 B2 **Tieling** China
88 D2 **Tielongtan** China/Jammu and Kashmir
108 B4 **Tielt** Belgium
120 B4 **Tiémé** Côte d'Ivoire
108 C4 **Tienen** Belgium
79 F2 **Tien Shan** *mts* China/Kyrg.
Tientsin China *see* **Tianjin**
103 L3 **Tierp** Sweden
139 F4 **Tierra Amarilla** U.S.A.
151 E4 **Tierra Blanca** Mex.
151 E4 **Tierra Colorada** Mex.
156 C8 **Tierra del Fuego, Isla Grande de** *i.* Arg./Chile
111 D2 **Tiétar** *r.* Spain
111 D2 **Tiétar, Valle de** *val.* Spain
158 C3 **Tietê** Brazil
158 B3 **Tietê** *r.* Brazil
146 B4 **Tiffin** U.S.A.
Tiflis Georgia *see* **T'bilisi**
145 D6 **Tifton** U.S.A.
82 B3 **Tigen** Kazakh.
115 K3 **Tigheciului, Dealurile** *hills* Moldova
117 D6 **Tighina** Moldova
83 J2 **Tigiretskiy Khrebet** *mts* Kazakh./Rus. Fed.
89 F5 **Tigiria** India
121 D4 **Tignère** Cameroon
133 H4 **Tignish** Canada
154 C4 **Tigre** *r.* Ecuador/Peru
157 E2 **Tigre** *r.* Venez.
81 K5 **Tigris** *r.* Turkey *alt.* **Dicle (Turkey),** *alt.* **Dijlah, Nahr (Iraq/Syria)**
80 D7 **Tīh, Jabal at** *plat.* Egypt
86 B6 **Tihāmah** *reg.* Saudi Arabia
148 A2 **Tijuana** Mex.
158 C2 **Tijuco** *r.* Brazil
151 G4 **Tikal** *tourist site* Guat.
151 G4 **Tikal, Parque Nacional** *nat. park* Guat.
88 D4 **Tikamgarh** India
117 G6 **Tikhoretsk** Rus. Fed.
116 E3 **Tikhvin** Rus. Fed.
116 E3 **Tikhvinskaya Gryada** *ridge* Rus. Fed.
161 K7 **Tiki Basin** *sea feature* Pacific Ocean
72 F3 **Tikokino** N.Z.
69 G3 **Tikopia** *i.* Solomon Is
81 I4 **Tikrīt** Iraq
102 P2 **Tiksheozero, Ozero** *l.* Rus. Fed.
77 N2 **Tiksi** Rus. Fed.
89 E3 **Tila** *r.* Nepal
89 F4 **Tilaiya Reservoir** India
84 D2 **Tilavar** Iran
71 F1 **Tilbooroo** Australia
108 D3 **Tilburg** Neth.
105 H6 **Tilbury** U.K.
156 C2 **Tilcara** Arg.
70 D2 **Tilcha** Australia
89 H5 **Tilin** Myanmar
120 C3 **Tillabéri** Niger
138 B2 **Tillamook** U.S.A.
106 E4 **Tillicoultry** U.K.
135 G4 **Tillsonburg** Canada
106 F3 **Tillyfourie** U.K.
115 L6 **Tilos** *i.* Greece
70 F3 **Tilpa** Australia
117 F5 **Tim** Rus. Fed.
116 J1 **Timanskiy Kryazh** *ridge* Rus. Fed.
81 I2 **Timar** Turkey
72 C6 **Timaru** N.Z.
117 F6 **Timashevsk** Rus. Fed.
120 B3 **Timbedgha** Mauritania
68 D3 **Timber Creek** Australia
140 D3 **Timber Mountain** U.S.A.
146 D5 **Timberville** U.S.A.
70 E7 **Timboon** Australia
120 B3 **Timbuktu** Mali
120 B3 **Timétrine** *reg.* Mali
120 C2 **Timimoun** Alg.
83 F1 **Timiryazev** Kazakh.
82 F1 **Timiryazevo** Kazakh.
115 I2 **Timişoara** Romania
135 G1 **Timmins** Canada
116 F3 **Timokhino** Rus. Fed.
155 J5 **Timon** Brazil
91 E7 **Timor** *i.* Indon.
68 C3 **Timor Sea** Australia/Indon.
116 H3 **Timoshino** Rus. Fed.
159 D2 **Timote** Arg.
103 L3 **Timrå** Sweden
145 C5 **Tims Ford Lake** U.S.A.
83 G4 **Timur** Kazakh.
88 D5 **Timurni Muafi** India
157 C2 **Tinaco** Venez.
87 B3 **Tindivanam** India
120 B2 **Tindouf** Alg.
98 C5 **Tinggi** *i.* Malaysia
71 I2 **Tingha** Australia
93 E5 **Ting Jiang** *r.* China
89 F3 **Tingri** China
103 K4 **Tingsryd** Sweden
159 B2 **Tinguiririca, Volcán** *vol.* Chile
102 J3 **Tingvoll** Norway
106 E1 **Tingwall** U.K.
158 E1 **Tinharé, Ilha de** *i.* Brazil
98 C1 **Tinh Gia** Vietnam
91 G5 **Tinian** *i.* N. Mariana Is
156 C3 **Tinogasta** Arg.
115 K6 **Tinos** *i.* Greece
108 B5 **Tinqueux** France
120 C2 **Tinrhert, Plateau du** Alg.
89 H4 **Tinsukia** India
105 C7 **Tintagel** U.K.
70 D5 **Tintinara** Australia
106 E5 **Tinto** *h.* U.K.
146 E4 **Tioga** *r.* U.S.A.
99 B2 **Tioman** *i.* Malaysia
135 F1 **Tionaga** Canada
146 D4 **Tionesta Lake** U.S.A.
147 E3 **Tioughnioga** *r.* U.S.A.
111 H4 **Tipasa** Alg.
150 H5 **Tipitapa** Nicaragua
134 D5 **Tippecanoe** *r.* U.S.A.
134 E5 **Tippecanoe Lake** U.S.A.
107 C5 **Tipperary** Rep. of Ireland
89 F4 **Tiptala Bhanjyang** *pass* Nepal
134 B5 **Tipton** *IA* U.S.A.
134 D5 **Tipton** *IN* U.S.A.
141 E4 **Tipton, Mount** U.S.A.
134 E1 **Tip Top Hill** Canada
105 H6 **Tiptree** U.K.
157 C4 **Tiquié** *r.* Brazil
151 G5 **Tiquisate** Guat.
155 I4 **Tiracambu, Serra do** *hills* Brazil
115 H4 **Tirana** Albania
Tiranë Albania *see* **Tirana**
114 D1 **Tirano** Italy
117 D6 **Tiraspol** Moldova
124 B3 **Tiraz Mountains** Namibia
80 A2 **Tire** Turkey
106 B4 **Tiree** *i.* U.K.
88 B1 **Tirich Mir** *mt.* Pak.
87 B2 **Tirna** *r.* India
87 A3 **Tirthahalli** India
89 F5 **Tirtol** India
87 B4 **Tiruchchendur** India
87 B4 **Tiruchchirappalli** India
87 B4 **Tiruchengodu** India
87 B4 **Tirunelveli** India
87 B3 **Tirupati** India
87 B3 **Tiruppattur** India
87 B4 **Tiruppur** India
87 B4 **Tirutturaippundi** India
87 B3 **Tiruvannamalai** India
87 B4 **Tisaiyanvilai** India
131 I4 **Tisdale** Canada
87 C5 **Tissamaharama** Sri Lanka
111 G5 **Tissemsilt** Alg.
89 G4 **Tista** *r.* India
73 C4 **Titan Dome** *ice feature* Antarctica
77 N2 **Tit-Ary** Rus. Fed.
154 E7 **Titicaca, Lake** Bol./Peru
87 C1 **Titlagarh** India
114 G2 **Titov Drvar** Bos.-Herz.
135 E4 **Tittabawassee** *r.* U.S.A.
115 K2 **Titu** Romania
145 D6 **Titusville** *FL* U.S.A.
146 D4 **Titusville** *PA* U.S.A.
135 G3 **Tiverton** Canada
105 D7 **Tiverton** U.K.
114 E4 **Tivoli** Italy
151 G3 **Tixkokob** Mex.
151 E4 **Tixtla** Mex.
150 D3 **Tizapán el Alto** Mex.
111 H4 **Tizi El Arba** *h.* Alg.
151 G3 **Tizimín** Mex.
111 I4 **Tizi Ouzou** Alg.
157 D2 **Tiznados** *r.* Venez.
83 I5 **Tiznap He** *r.* China
120 B2 **Tiznit** Morocco
150 D2 **Tizoc** Mex.
125 I2 **Tjaneni** Swaziland
102 L2 **Tjappsåive** Sweden
108 D2 **Tjeukemeer** *l.* Neth.
103 I4 **Tjorhom** Norway
151 E4 **Tlacolula** Mex.
151 F4 **Tlacotalpán** Mex.
150 D2 **Tlahualilo** Mex.
151 E4 **Tlalnepantla** Mex.
151 E4 **Tlapa** Mex.
150 D3 **Tlaquepaque** Mex.
151 E4 **Tlaxcala** Mex.
151 E4 **Tlaxcala** *state* Mex.
151 E4 **Tlaxiaco** Mex.
120 B1 **Tlemcen** Alg.
124 E4 **Tlhakalatlou** S. Africa
125 H4 **Tlholong** S. Africa
125 F2 **Tlokweng** Botswana
98 C3 **Tnaôt, Prêk** *l.* Cambodia
130 D3 **Toad River** Canada
123 E5 **Toamasina** Madag.
98 □ **Toa Payoh** Sing.
159 D3 **Toay** Arg.
95 E7 **Toba** Japan
98 A5 **Toba, Danau** *l.* Indon.
88 A3 **Toba and Kakar Ranges** *mts* Pak.
154 F1 **Tobago** *i.* Trin. and Tob.
91 E6 **Tobelo** Indon.
135 G3 **Tobermory** Canada
106 B4 **Tobermory** U.K.
140 D1 **Tobin, Mount** U.S.A.
131 I4 **Tobin Lake** Canada
147 J1 **Tobique** *r.* Canada
94 F5 **Tobi-shima** *i.* Japan
99 C3 **Toboali** Indon.
82 E1 **Tobol** Kazakh.
76 H4 **Tobol** *r.* Kazakh./Rus. Fed.
Tô Bong Vietnam *see* **Hai Triêu**
155 I5 **Tocantinópolis** Brazil
155 I4 **Tocantins** *r.* Brazil
158 C1 **Tocantinzinha** *r.* Brazil
145 D5 **Toccoa** U.S.A.
88 B2 **Tochi** *r.* Pak.
103 J4 **Töcksfors** Sweden
156 B2 **Tocopilla** Chile
71 F5 **Tocumwal** Australia
157 C2 **Tocuyo** *r.* Venez.
114 E3 **Todi** Italy
112 D7 **Todi** *mt.* Switz.
83 J3 **Todog** China
94 H5 **Todoga-saki** *pt* Japan
94 G4 **Todohokke** Japan
154 E7 **Todos Santos** Bol.
150 B3 **Todos Santos** Mex.
140 D6 **Todos Santos, Bahía de** *b.* Mex.
130 G4 **Tofield** Canada
130 D5 **Tofino** Canada
106 □ **Toft** U.K.
134 B2 **Tofte** U.S.A.
69 I3 **Tofua** *i.* Tonga
91 E7 **Togian, Kepulauan** *is* Indon.
120 C4 **Togo** *country* Africa
134 A2 **Togo** U.S.A.
92 D1 **Togrog Ul** China
92 D1 **Togtoh** China
89 H2 **Togton He** *r.* China
82 E3 **Toguz** Kazakh.
141 H4 **Tohatchi** U.S.A.
102 N3 **Toholampi** Fin.
92 B1 **Tohom** China
89 G3 **Toiba** China
103 M3 **Toijala** Fin.
95 B9 **Toi-misaki** *pt* Japan
103 N3 **Toivakka** Fin.
140 D2 **Toiyabe Range** *mts* U.S.A.
83 G5 **Tojikobod** Tajik.
82 C1 **Tok** *r.* Rus. Fed.
128 D3 **Tok** U.S.A.
95 F6 **Tōkamachi** Japan
72 B7 **Tokanui** N.Z.
121 F3 **Tokar** Sudan
90 E4 **Tokara-rettō** *is* Japan
83 H2 **Tokarevka** Kazakh.
80 F1 **Tokat** Turkey
96 D5 **Tŏkchok-to** *i.* S. Korea
96 D4 **Tŏkch'ŏn** N. Korea
69 I2 **Tokelau** *terr.* Pacific Ocean
117 E6 **Tokmak** Ukr.
83 H4 **Tokmok** Kyrg.
72 G3 **Tokomaru Bay** N.Z.
72 E3 **Tokoroa** N.Z.
125 H3 **Tokoza** S. Africa
76 J5 **Toksun** China
83 H4 **Toktogul** Kyrg.
83 H4 **Toktogul Suu Saktagychy** *resr* Kyrg.
83 J3 **Tokty** Kazakh.
95 D7 **Tokushima** Japan
95 B7 **Tokuyama** Japan
95 F7 **Tōkyō** Japan (City Plan **52**)
95 F7 **Tōkyō-wan** *b.* Japan
85 G3 **Tokzār** Afgh.
72 G3 **Tolaga Bay** N.Z.
123 E6 **Tôlañaro** Madag.
82 C1 **Tolbazy** Rus. Fed.
150 I6 **Tolé** Panama
151 E3 **Toleant** *tourist site* Mex.
83 H4 **Tole Bi** Kazakh.
158 B4 **Toledo** Brazil
111 D3 **Toledo** Spain
134 A5 **Toledo** *IA* U.S.A.
146 B4 **Toledo** *OH* U.S.A.
111 D3 **Toledo, Montes de** *mts* Spain
143 E6 **Toledo Bend Reservoir** U.S.A.
159 B3 **Tolhuaca, Parque Nacional** *nat. park* Chile
83 J3 **Toli** China
123 E6 **Toliara** Madag.
157 B3 **Tolima, Nevado del** *vol.* Col.
91 E6 **Tolitoli** Indon.
76 J3 **Tol'ka** Rus. Fed.
109 L1 **Tollensesee** *l.* Germany
82 F5 **Tollimarjon** Uzbek.
116 D3 **Tolmachevo** Rus. Fed.
114 E1 **Tolmezzo** Italy
93 □ **Tolo Channel** *Hong Kong* China
93 □ **Tolo Harbour** *b. Hong Kong* China
111 E1 **Tolosa** Spain
96 D6 **Tolsan-do** *i.* S. Korea
135 F3 **Tolsmaville** Canada
106 B2 **Tolsta Head** U.K.
157 B2 **Tolú** Col.
151 E4 **Toluca** Mex.
102 O2 **Tolvand, Ozero** *l.* Rus. Fed.
116 I4 **Tol'yatti** Rus. Fed.
82 E2 **Tolybay** Kazakh.
134 B4 **Tomah** U.S.A.
134 C3 **Tomahawk** U.S.A.
94 G3 **Tomakomai** Japan
94 G2 **Tomamae** Japan
69 H3 **Tomanivi** *mt.* Fiji
157 E5 **Tomar** Brazil
111 B3 **Tomar** Port.
80 E2 **Tomarza** Turkey
159 F1 **Tomás Gomensoro** Uruguay
113 K5 **Tomaszów Lubelski** Poland
113 J5 **Tomaszów Mazowiecki** Poland
106 E3 **Tomatin** U.K.
150 C4 **Tomatlán** Mex.
145 B6 **Tombigbee** *r.* U.S.A.
122 B4 **Tomboco** Angola
158 D3 **Tombos** Brazil
Tombouctou Mali *see* **Timbuktu**
141 G6 **Tombstone** U.S.A.
123 B5 **Tombua** Angola
125 H1 **Tom Burke** S. Africa
82 F4 **Tomdibuloq** Uzbek.
159 B3 **Tomé** Chile
125 K1 **Tome** Moz.
103 K5 **Tomelilla** Sweden
111 E3 **Tomelloso** Spain
83 F4 **Tomenaryk** Kazakh.
135 H2 **Tomiko** Canada
71 H4 **Tomingley** Australia
91 E7 **Tomini, Teluk** *g.* Indon.
120 B3 **Tominian** Mali
106 E3 **Tomintoul** U.K.
114 G3 **Tomislavgrad** Bos.-Herz.
102 K2 **Tømmerneset** Norway
77 N4 **Tommot** Rus. Fed.
157 D4 **Tomo** Col.
157 C3 **Tomo** *r.* Col.
92 D1 **Tomortei** China
77 O3 **Tompo** Rus. Fed.
68 B4 **Tom Price** Australia
90 A1 **Tomsk** Rus. Fed.
103 K4 **Tomtabacken** *h.* Sweden
77 P3 **Tomtor** Rus. Fed.
94 H3 **Tomuraushi-yama** *mt.* Japan
117 G6 **Tomuzlovka** *r.* Rus. Fed.
151 F4 **Tonalá** Mex.

Ubundu 211

141 G3 Tonalea U.S.A.
154 E4 Tonantins Brazil
138 C1 Tonasket U.S.A.
105 H6 Tonbridge U.K.
91 E6 Tondano Indon.
103 J5 Tønder Denmark
105 E6 Tone r. U.K.
69 I4 Tonga country Pacific Ocean
125 I4 Tongaat S. Africa
70 F6 Tongala Australia
93 F5 Tong'an China
72 E3 Tongariro National Park N.Z.
69 I4 Tongatapu Group is Tonga
160 H7 Tonga Trench sea feature S. Pacific Ocean
92 D3 Tongbai China
92 D3 Tongbai Shan mts China
92 E4 Tongcheng Anhui China
93 D4 Tongcheng Hubei China
96 D4 T'ongch'ŏn N. Korea
92 C3 Tongchuan China
93 C5 Tongdao China
92 A3 Tongde China
96 D5 Tongduch'ŏn S. Korea
108 D4 Tongeren Belgium
93 E4 Tonggu China
93 D7 Tonggu Zui pt China
96 E5 Tonghae S. Korea
93 B5 Tonghai China
94 A2 Tonghe China
96 C3 Tonghua Jilin China
96 C3 Tonghua Jilin China
92 C4 Tongjiang China
96 B2 Tongjiangkou China
96 D4 Tongjosŏn-man b. N. Korea
93 C6 Tongking, Gulf of China/Vietnam
93 C4 Tongliang China
96 B2 Tongliao China
92 E4 Tongling China
93 F4 Tonglu China
96 E6 Tongnae S. Korea
93 B4 Tongnan China
70 E3 Tongo Australia
70 E5 Tongo Lake salt flat Australia
97 B5 Tongquil i. Phil.
93 B5 Tongren Guizhou China
92 A3 Tongren Qinghai China
93 E4 Tongshan Hubei China
92 E3 Tongshan Jiangsu China
Tongshi China see Wuzhishan
Tongtian He r. China see Yangtze
106 D2 Tongue U.K.
138 F2 Tongue r. U.S.A.
145 E7 Tongue of the Ocean sea chan. Bahamas
92 B3 Tongwei China
92 B3 Tongxin China
92 E4 Tongyanghe China
96 E4 T'ongyŏng S. Korea
96 B1 Tongyu China
96 B3 Tongyuanpu China
92 E2 Tongzhou Beijing China
92 F3 Tongzhou Jiangsu China
93 C4 Tongzi China
134 C5 Tonica U.S.A.
150 B1 Tónichi Mex.
88 C4 Tonk India
84 C2 Tonkābon Iran
93 B6 Tonkin reg. Vietnam
116 H3 Tonkino Rus. Fed.
98 C2 Tônlé Repou r. Laos
Tônlé Sab l. Cambodia see Tonle Sap
98 B2 Tonle Sap l. Cambodia
94 G5 Tōno Japan
140 D2 Tonopah U.S.A.
157 E2 Tonoro r. Venez.
150 I7 Tonosí Panama
88 D3 Tons r. India
103 J4 Tønsberg Norway
103 I4 Tonstad Norway
141 G5 Tonto National Monument nat. park U.S.A.
89 H5 Tonzang Myanmar
71 H2 Toobeah Australia
138 D3 Tooele U.S.A.
71 J1 Toogoolawah Australia
70 E5 Tooleybuc Australia
70 A4 Tooligie Australia
71 H6 Tooma r. Australia
71 G7 Toora Australia
71 H3 Tooraweenah Australia
124 F6 Toorberg mt. S. Africa
71 I1 Toowoomba Australia
141 G6 Topawa U.S.A.
140 C2 Topaz U.S.A.
83 J1 Topchikha Rus. Fed.
142 E4 Topeka U.S.A.
150 C2 Topia Mex.
130 D4 Topley Landing Canada
109 K2 Töplitz Germany
159 B2 Topocalma, Punta pt Chile
141 E4 Topock U.S.A.
112 I6 Topoľčany Slovakia
82 B3 Topoli Kazakh.
150 B2 Topolobampo Mex.
115 L3 Topolovgrad Bulg.
102 P2 Topozero, Ozero l. Rus. Fed.
138 B2 Toppenish U.S.A.
147 J2 Topsfield U.S.A.
141 F3 Toquerville U.S.A.
122 D3 Tor Eth.
115 L5 Torbalı Turkey
85 E3 Torbat-e Ḥeydarīyeh Iran
85 F3 Torbat-e Jām Iran
116 G4 Torbeyevo Rus. Fed.
134 E3 Torch Lake U.S.A.
111 D2 Tordesillas Spain
102 M2 Töre Sweden
111 H1 Torelló Spain
108 D2 Torenberg h. Neth.
109 K3 Torgau Germany
117 H5 Torgun r. Rus. Fed.
108 B3 Torhout Belgium
Torino Italy see Turin
95 G9 Tori-shima i. Japan
121 F4 Torit Sudan
158 B2 Torixoréu Brazil
Torixoreu Brazil see Torixoréu
81 K3 Torkamān Iran
85 F3 Torkestān, Band-e mts Afgh.
116 G3 Tor'kovskoye Vodokhranilishche resr Rus. Fed.
111 D2 Tormes r. Spain
102 M2 Torneälven r. Fin./Sweden
102 L1 Torneträsk Sweden
102 L1 Torneträsk l. Sweden
133 H2 Torngat Mountains Canada
102 N2 Tornio Fin.
159 D3 Tornquist Arg.
111 D2 Toro Spain
150 D2 Toro, Pico del mt. Mex.
90 F1 Torom r. Rus. Fed.
71 I4 Toronto Australia
135 H4 Toronto Canada (City Plan 62)
140 D5 Toro Peak U.S.A.
116 D3 Toropets Rus. Fed.
122 D3 Tororo Uganda
Toros Dağları mts Turkey see Taurus Mountains
106 F3 Torphins U.K.
105 D7 Torquay U.K.
140 C5 Torrance U.S.A.
111 B3 Torrão Port.
111 C2 Torre mt. Port.
111 G2 Torreblanca Spain
111 D1 Torrecerredo mt. Spain
114 F4 Torre del Greco Italy
111 D1 Torrelavega Spain
111 D4 Torremolinos Spain
70 B3 Torrens, Lake imp. l. Australia
111 F3 Torrent Spain
150 D2 Torreón Mex.
150 B1 Torres Mex.
69 G3 Torres Islands Vanuatu
111 B3 Torres Novas Port.
68 E2 Torres Strait Australia
111 B3 Torres Vedras Port.
111 G3 Torreta, Sierra h. Spain
111 F4 Torrevieja Spain
141 G2 Torrey U.S.A.
105 C7 Torridge r. U.K.
106 C3 Torridon, Loch b. U.K.
111 D3 Torrijos Spain
71 I2 Torrington Australia
147 G4 Torrington CT U.S.A.
138 F3 Torrington WY U.S.A.
111 H1 Torroella de Montgrí Spain
103 K3 Torsby Sweden
102 □ Tórshavn Faroe Is
83 G4 Tortkol' Kazakh.
82 E4 To'rtko'l Uzbek.
83 H2 Tortkuduk Kazakh.
114 C5 Tortolì Sardinia Italy
114 C2 Tortona Italy
111 G2 Tortosa Spain
150 I6 Tortuguero, Parque Nacional nat. park Costa Rica
81 H1 Tortum Turkey
83 I4 Toru-Aygyr Kyrg.
84 D3 Ţorūd Iran
81 G1 Torul Turkey
113 I4 Toruń Poland
107 C2 Tory Island Rep. of Ireland
107 C2 Tory Sound sea chan. Rep. of Ireland
116 E3 Torzhok Rus. Fed.
95 C8 Tosa Japan
95 C8 Tosashimizu Japan
102 K2 Tosbotn Norway
124 E2 Tosca S. Africa
114 C3 Toscano, Arcipelago is Italy
94 G4 Tōshima-yama mt. Japan
83 G4 Toshkent Uzbek.
116 D3 Tosno Rus. Fed.
156 D3 Tostado Arg.
109 H1 Tostedt Germany
95 B8 Tosu Japan
80 E1 Tosya Turkey
116 G3 Tot'ma Rus. Fed.
151 E4 Totolapan Mex.
82 C1 Totskoye Rus. Fed.
105 F7 Totton U.K.
95 D7 Tottori Japan
120 B4 Touba Côte d'Ivoire
120 A3 Touba Senegal
120 B1 Toubkal, Jbel mt. Morocco
92 D1 Toudaohu China
120 B3 Tougan Burkina
120 C1 Touggourt Alg.
120 A3 Tougué Guinea
110 G2 Toul France
93 F6 Touliu Taiwan
110 G5 Toulon France
110 E5 Toulouse France
120 B4 Toumodi Côte d'Ivoire
120 B2 Tounassine, Hamada des. Alg.
Toungoo Myanmar see Taung-ngu
93 D5 Toupai China
98 B1 Tourakom Laos
108 B4 Tourcoing France
108 B4 Tournai Belgium
110 G4 Tournon-sur-Rhône France
110 G3 Tournus France
155 K5 Touros Brazil
110 E3 Tours France
124 E6 Touwsrivier S. Africa
109 K4 Toužim Czech Rep.
157 C2 Tovar Venez.
105 F5 Tove r. U.K.
81 J1 Tovuz Azer.
94 G4 Towada Japan
94 G5 Towada-Hachimantai National Park Japan
94 G4 Towada-ko l. Japan
72 E1 Towai N.Z.
147 E4 Towanda U.S.A.
141 H3 Towaoc U.S.A.
105 G5 Towcester U.K.
107 C6 Tower Rep. of Ireland
134 A2 Tower U.S.A.
131 I5 Towner U.S.A.
140 D3 Townes Pass U.S.A.
138 E2 Townsend U.S.A.
71 H6 Townsend, Mount Australia
68 E3 Townsville Australia
91 E7 Towori, Teluk b. Indon.
146 E5 Towson U.S.A.
83 I4 Toxkan He r. China
94 G3 Tōya-ko l. Japan
95 E6 Toyama Japan
95 E6 Toyama-wan b. Japan
95 E7 Toyohashi Japan
95 E7 Toyokawa Japan
95 D7 Toyonaka Japan
95 D7 Toyooka Japan
95 E7 Toyota Japan
83 G4 To'ytepa Uzbek.
120 C1 Tozeur Tunisia
117 G7 Tqibuli Georgia
117 G7 Tqvarch'eli Georgia
108 F5 Traben Germany
Trâblous Lebanon see Tripoli
115 J4 Trabotivište Macedonia
81 G1 Trabzon Turkey
147 J2 Tracy Canada
140 B3 Tracy CA U.S.A.
142 E2 Tracy MN U.S.A.
134 A4 Traer U.S.A.
111 C4 Trafalgar, Cabo c. Spain
159 B3 Traiguén Chile
130 F5 Trail Canada
103 N5 Trakai Lith.
116 I2 Trakt Rus. Fed.
107 B5 Tralee Rep. of Ireland
107 B5 Tralee Bay Rep. of Ireland
157 E3 Tramán Tepuí mt. Venez.
107 D5 Tramore Rep. of Ireland
103 K4 Tranås Sweden
156 C3 Trancas Arg.
103 K4 Tranemo Sweden
106 F5 Tranent U.K.
98 A4 Trang Thai.
91 F7 Trangan i. Indon.
71 G4 Trangie Australia
159 F1 Tranqueras Uruguay
73 B5 Transantarctic Mountains Antarctica
131 G4 Trans Canada Highway Canada
131 J5 Transcona Canada
115 J2 Transylvanian Alps mts Romania
114 E5 Trapani Sicily Italy
71 G7 Traralgon Australia
Trashigang Bhutan see Tashigang
114 E3 Trasimeno, Lago l. Italy
111 E3 Trasvase, Canal de Spain
98 B2 Trat Thai.
112 F7 Traunsee l. Austria
112 F7 Traunstein Germany
70 E4 Travellers Lake imp. l. Australia
72 D5 Travers, Mount N.Z.
153 G7 Traversay Islands S. Sandwich Is
134 E3 Traverse City U.S.A.
98 C3 Tra Vinh Vietnam
143 D6 Travis, Lake U.S.A.
114 G2 Travnik Bos.-Herz.
114 F1 Trbovlje Slovenia
69 F2 Treasury Islands Solomon Is
109 L2 Trebbin Germany
112 G6 Třebíč Czech Rep.
115 H3 Trebinje Bos.-Herz.
113 J6 Trebišov Slovakia
114 F2 Trebnje Slovenia
109 G5 Trebur Germany
109 I3 Treffurt Germany
134 B3 Trego U.S.A.
106 D4 Treig, Loch l. U.K.
159 F2 Treinta y Tres Uruguay
156 C6 Trelew Arg.
103 K5 Trelleborg Sweden
108 C4 Trélon France
105 C5 Tremadog Bay U.K.
132 F4 Tremblant, Mont h. Canada
114 F3 Tremiti, Isole is Italy
138 D3 Tremonton U.S.A.
111 G1 Tremp Spain
134 B3 Trempealeau r. U.S.A.
105 B7 Trenance U.K.
112 I6 Trenčín Slovakia
109 H3 Trendelburg Germany
159 D2 Trenque Lauquén Arg.
104 G4 Trent r. U.K.
114 D1 Trento Italy
135 I3 Trenton Canada
142 E3 Trenton MO U.S.A.
147 F4 Trenton NJ U.S.A.
105 D6 Treorchy U.K.
133 J4 Trepassey Canada
159 F2 Tres Árboles Uruguay
159 E3 Tres Arroyos Arg.
105 A8 Tresco i. U.K.
158 D3 Três Corações Brazil
157 B4 Tres Esquinas Col.
106 B4 Treshnish Isles U.K.
158 B3 Três Irmãos, Represa resr Brazil
158 B3 Três Lagoas Brazil
156 B7 Tres Lagos Arg.
159 D3 Tres Lomas Arg.
158 D2 Três Marias, Represa resr Brazil
159 B4 Tres Picos mt. Arg.
151 F5 Tres Picos Mex.
159 E3 Tres Picos, Cerro mt. Arg.
139 F4 Tres Piedras U.S.A.
158 D3 Três Pontas Brazil
156 C7 Tres Puntas, Cabo c. Arg.
158 D3 Três Rios Brazil
151 E4 Tres Valles Mex.
151 F4 Tres Zapotes tourist site Mex.
103 J3 Tretten Norway
109 I6 Treuchtlingen Germany
109 K2 Treuenbrietzen Germany
103 J4 Treungen Norway
114 C2 Treviglio Italy
114 E2 Treviso Italy
105 B7 Trevose Head U.K.
109 J1 Triabunna Australia
115 L6 Tria Nisia i. Greece
115 M6 Trianta Greece
88 B2 Tribal Areas admin. div. Pak.
115 H5 Tricase Italy
87 B4 Trichur India
108 A5 Tricot France
71 F4 Trida Australia
108 E5 Trier Germany
114 E2 Trieste Italy
114 E1 Triglav mt. Slovenia
115 I5 Trikala Greece
80 D4 Trikomon Cyprus
91 F7 Trikora, Puncak mt. Indon.
107 E4 Trim Rep. of Ireland
87 C4 Trincomalee Sri Lanka
158 C2 Trindade Brazil
163 H7 Trindade, Ilha da i. S. Atlantic Ocean
154 F6 Trinidad Bol.
157 C3 Trinidad Col.
149 I4 Trinidad Cuba
154 F1 Trinidad i. Trin. and Tob.
159 F2 Trinidad Uruguay
139 F4 Trinidad U.S.A.
157 E2 Trinidad and Tobago country Caribbean Sea
133 J4 Trinity Bay Canada
128 C4 Trinity Islands U.S.A.
140 C1 Trinity Range mts U.S.A.
145 C5 Trion U.S.A.
113 J4 Tripkau Germany
115 J6 Tripoli Greece
80 E4 Tripoli Lebanon
121 D1 Tripoli Libya
87 B4 Tripunittura India
89 G5 Tripura state India
163 I8 Tristan da Cunha i. S. Atlantic Ocean
88 D3 Trisul mt. India
89 F4 Trisul Dam Nepal
109 I1 Trittau Germany
108 E5 Trittenheim Germany
87 B4 Trivandrum India
114 F4 Trivento Italy
113 I6 Trnava Slovakia
68 F2 Trobriand Islands P.N.G.
102 K2 Trofors Norway
114 G3 Trogir Croatia
114 F4 Troia Italy
108 F4 Troisdorf Germany
108 D4 Trois-Ponts Belgium
133 F4 Trois-Rivières Canada
82 E1 Troitsk Rus. Fed.
83 K1 Troitskoye Altayskiy Kray Rus. Fed.
82 C1 Troitskoye Orenburgskaya Oblast' Rus. Fed.
82 D1 Troitskoye Respublika Bashkortostan Rus. Fed.
117 H6 Troitskoye Respublika Kalmykiya - Khalm'g-Tangch Rus. Fed.
103 K4 Trollhättan Sweden
155 G3 Trombetas r. Brazil
119 I6 Tromelin, Île i. Indian Ocean
159 B3 Tromen, Volcán vol. Arg.
125 F5 Trompsburg S. Africa
102 L1 Tromsø Norway
140 D4 Trona U.S.A.
159 B3 Tronador, Monte mt. Arg.
102 J3 Trondheim Norway
102 J3 Trondheimsfjorden sea chan. Norway
89 G4 Trongsa Chhu r. Bhutan
80 D4 Troödos Cyprus
80 D4 Troödos, Mount Cyprus
106 D5 Troon U.K.
158 D1 Tropeiros, Serra dos hills Brazil
141 F3 Tropic U.S.A.
107 E2 Trostan h. U.K.
106 F3 Troup Head U.K.
130 E2 Trout r. Canada
135 H3 Trout Creek Canada
141 F2 Trout Creek U.S.A.
130 G3 Trout Lake Alta Canada
130 E2 Trout Lake l. N.W.T. Canada
132 B3 Trout Lake l. Ont. Canada
134 E2 Trout Lake U.S.A.
134 C2 Trout Lake l. U.S.A.
138 E2 Trout Peak U.S.A.
146 E4 Trout Run U.S.A.
105 E6 Trowbridge U.K.
71 F8 Trowutta Australia
145 C6 Troy AL U.S.A.
138 D1 Troy MT U.S.A.
147 G3 Troy NH U.S.A.
147 G3 Troy NY U.S.A.
146 A4 Troy OH U.S.A.
146 E4 Troy PA U.S.A.
115 K3 Troyan Bulg.
110 G2 Troyes France
140 D4 Troy Lake U.S.A.
141 E2 Troy Peak U.S.A.
115 I3 Trstenik Serb. and Mont.
117 E4 Trubchevsk Rus. Fed.
111 C1 Truchas Spain
116 E3 Trud Rus. Fed.
94 C3 Trudovoye Rus. Fed.
150 H5 Trujillo Hond.
154 C5 Trujillo Peru
111 D3 Trujillo Spain
157 C2 Trujillo Venez.
108 F5 Trulben Germany
147 G4 Trumbull U.S.A.
141 F3 Trumbull, Mount U.S.A.
99 A2 Trumon Indon.
71 G4 Trundle Australia
98 C2 Trung Hiệp Vietnam
93 C6 Trung Khanh China
133 H4 Truro Canada
105 B7 Truro U.K.
107 C3 Truskmore h. Rep. of Ireland
130 E3 Trutch Canada
139 F5 Truth or Consequences U.S.A.
112 G5 Trutnov Czech Rep.
115 L5 Truva tourist site Turkey
115 K7 Trypiti, Akra pt Greece
103 K3 Trysil Norway
112 G3 Trzebiatów Poland
90 A2 Tsagaannuur Mongolia
117 H6 Tsagan Aman Rus. Fed.
117 H6 Tsagan-Nur Rus. Fed.
117 G7 Ts'ageri Georgia
81 J1 Tsalka Georgia
123 E5 Tsaratanana, Massif du mts Madag.
115 L3 Tsarevo Bulg.
124 B2 Tsaris Mountains Namibia
117 H5 Tsatsa Rus. Fed.
124 A3 Tsaukaib Namibia
122 D4 Tsavo East National Park Kenya
117 G6 Tselina Rus. Fed.
123 B6 Tses Namibia
123 C6 Tsetseng Botswana
90 C2 Tsetserleg Mongolia
123 C6 Tshabong Botswana
123 C6 Tshane Botswana
117 F6 Tshchikskoye Vodokhranilishche resr Rus. Fed.
122 B4 Tshela Dem. Rep. Congo
122 C4 Tshibala Dem. Rep. Congo
122 C4 Tshikapa Dem. Rep. Congo
122 C4 Tshikapa r. Dem. Rep. Congo
125 G3 Tshing S. Africa
125 I1 Tshipise S. Africa
123 C4 Tshitanzu Dem. Rep. Congo
122 C4 Tshofa Dem. Rep. Congo
125 I2 Tshokwane S. Africa
122 C4 Tshuapa r. Dem. Rep. Congo
Tshwane S. Africa see Pretoria
117 G6 Tsimlyansk Rus. Fed.
117 G6 Tsimlyanskoye Vodokhranilishche resr Rus. Fed.
124 E3 Tsineng S. Africa
Tsing Shan Wan b. China see Castle Peak Bay
Tsing Shui Wan b. China see Clear Water Bay
Tsingtao China see Qingdao
93 □ Tsing Yi i. Hong Kong China
123 E6 Tsiombe Madag.
123 E5 Tsiroanomandidy Madag.
124 E6 Tsitsikamma Forest and Coastal National Park S. Africa
130 D4 Tsitsutl Peak Canada
116 H4 Tsivil'sk Rus. Fed.
117 G7 Ts'khinvali Georgia
116 G4 Tsna r. Rus. Fed.
88 D2 Tsokar Chumo l. India
Tsokr Chumo l. India see Tsokar Chumo
125 H5 Tsolo S. Africa
125 G6 Tsomo S. Africa
Tso Morari Lake India see Morari, Tso
117 G7 Tsqaltubo Georgia
95 E7 Tsu Japan
95 G6 Tsuchiura Japan
93 □ Tsuen Wan Hong Kong China
94 G4 Tsugarū-kaikyō str. Japan
123 B5 Tsumeb Namibia
123 B6 Tsumis Park Namibia
123 C5 Tsumkwe Namibia
89 G4 Tsunthang India
95 E7 Tsuruga Japan
95 D8 Tsurugi-san mt. Japan
94 F5 Tsuruoka Japan
95 A7 Tsushima is Japan
95 D7 Tsuyama Japan
124 D1 Tswaane Botswana
125 F4 Tswaraganang S. Africa
125 F3 Tswelelang S. Africa
113 L4 Tsyelyakhany Belarus
102 P1 Tsyp-Navolok Rus. Fed.
117 E6 Tsyurupyns'k Ukr.
91 F7 Tual Indon.
107 C4 Tuam Rep. of Ireland
72 D4 Tuamarina N.Z.
67 J5 Tuamotu Islands Fr. Polynesia
93 B6 Tuân Giao Vietnam
98 A5 Tuangku i. Indon.
117 F5 Tuapse Rus. Fed.
98 □ Tuas Sing.
72 A7 Tuatapere N.Z.
106 B2 Tuath, Loch a' b. U.K.
141 G3 Tuba City U.S.A.
99 D4 Tuban Indon.
156 G3 Tubarão Brazil
97 A4 Tubbataha Reefs Phil.
107 C3 Tubbercurry Rep. of Ireland
112 D6 Tübingen Germany
120 A4 Tubmanburg Liberia
97 B4 Tubod Phil.
121 E1 Tubruq Libya
161 J7 Tubuai i. Fr. Polynesia
67 I6 Tubuai Islands Fr. Polynesia
155 K6 Tucano Brazil
159 B3 Tucapel, Punta pt Chile
159 D3 Tucavaca Bol.
109 K1 Tüchen Germany
109 K2 Tucheim Germany
130 D2 Tuchitua Canada
147 F5 Tuckerton U.S.A.
141 G5 Tucson U.S.A.
141 G5 Tucson Mountains U.S.A.
139 G5 Tucumcari U.S.A.
157 E2 Tucupita Venez.
155 I4 Tucuruí Brazil
155 I4 Tucuruí, Represa resr Brazil
81 L5 Tū Dār Iran
111 F1 Tudela Spain
111 C2 Tuela r. Port.
93 □ Tuen Mun Hong Kong China
89 H4 Tuensang India
84 C5 Ţufayḩ Saudi Arabia
161 J2 Tufts Abyssal Plain sea feature N. Pacific Ocean
125 I4 Tugela r. S. Africa
97 C4 Tugnug Point Phil.
97 B2 Tuguegarao Phil.
77 O4 Tugur Rus. Fed.
83 K3 Tugyl Kazakh.
92 F2 Tuhai He r. China
98 A5 Tuhemberua Indon.
111 B1 Tui Spain
150 J6 Tuira r. Panama
82 D1 Tukan Rus. Fed.
91 E7 Tukangbesi, Kepulauan is Indon.
132 E2 Tukarak Island Canada
83 H5 Tŭkhtamish Tajik.
72 F3 Tukituki r. N.Z.
128 E3 Tuktoyaktuk Canada
103 M4 Tukums Latvia
151 E3 Tula Mex.
116 F4 Tula Rus. Fed.
89 H1 Tulagt Ar Gol r. China
151 E3 Tulancingo Mex.
140 C3 Tulare U.S.A.
140 C4 Tulare Lake Bed U.S.A.
139 F5 Tularosa U.S.A.
87 C2 Tulasi mt. India
124 C6 Tulbagh S. Africa
154 C3 Tulcán Ecuador
115 M2 Tulcea Romania
117 D5 Tul'chyn Ukr.
140 C3 Tule r. U.S.A.
84 D3 Tuleh Iran
89 G4 Tule La pass Bhutan
131 I2 Tulemalu Lake Canada
145 C5 Tulia U.S.A.
130 D2 Tulita Canada
80 E5 Ţūlkarm West Bank
107 C5 Tulla Rep. of Ireland
71 F8 Tullah Australia
145 C5 Tullahoma U.S.A.
71 G4 Tullamore Australia
107 D4 Tullamore Rep. of Ireland
110 E4 Tulle France
102 K3 Tulleråsen Sweden
71 G4 Tullibigeal Australia
143 E6 Tullos U.S.A.
107 E5 Tullow Rep. of Ireland
68 E3 Tully Australia
107 D3 Tully U.K.
147 E3 Tully U.S.A.
116 D2 Tulos Rus. Fed.
143 D4 Tulsa U.S.A.
116 F4 Tul'skaya Oblast' admin. div. Rus. Fed.
157 A3 Tuluá Col.
128 B3 Tuluksak U.S.A.
151 H3 Tulum tourist site Mex.
159 C1 Tulum, Valle de val. Arg.
90 C1 Tulun Rus. Fed.
99 D4 Tulungagung Indon.
89 H4 Tulung La pass China
97 A4 Tuluran i. Phil.
157 A4 Tumaco Col.
125 H4 Tumahole S. Africa
117 I6 Tumak Rus. Fed.
103 L4 Tumba Sweden
122 B4 Tumba, Lac l. Dem. Rep. Congo
99 D3 Tumbangsamba Indon.
97 C5 Tumbao Phil.
154 B4 Tumbes Peru
130 E3 Tumbler Ridge Canada
70 B5 Tumby Bay Australia
102 O2 Tumcha r. Fin./Rus. Fed.
96 E2 Tumen China
96 E2 Tumen Jiang r. China/N. Korea
92 B2 Tumenzi China
157 E3 Tumereng Guyana
97 A5 Tumindao i. Phil.
87 B3 Tumkur India
89 G3 Tum La pass China
106 E4 Tummel, Loch l. U.K.
90 G2 Tumnin r. Rus. Fed.
85 F5 Tump Pak.
98 B4 Tumpat Malaysia
120 B3 Tumu Ghana
155 G3 Tumucumaque, Serra hills Brazil
71 H5 Tumut Australia
71 H5 Tumut r. Australia
83 J4 Tumxuk China
105 H6 Tunbridge Wells, Royal U.K.
81 G2 Tunceli Turkey
93 D7 Tunchang China
71 J4 Tuncurry Australia
88 D4 Tundla India
123 D5 Tunduru Tanz.
115 L3 Tundzha r. Bulg.
87 B3 Tungabhadra r. India
87 A3 Tungabhadra Reservoir India
89 H3 Tunga Pass China/India
97 B5 Tungawan Phil.
93 □ Tung Chung Wan b. Hong Kong China
102 C2 Tungnaá r. Iceland
Tung Pok Liu Hoi Hap China see East Lamma Channel
130 D2 Tungsten Canada
116 E1 Tunguda Rus. Fed.
93 □ Tung Wan b. Hong Kong China
87 C2 Tuni India
120 D1 Tunis Tunisia
114 D6 Tunis, Golfe de g. Tunisia
120 C1 Tunisia country Africa
157 B3 Tunja Col.
92 D2 Tunliu China
102 K2 Tunnsjøen l. Norway
105 I5 Tunstall U.K.
102 O2 Tuntsa Fin.
133 G2 Tunulic r. Canada
133 H2 Tunungayualok Island Canada
159 C2 Tunuyán Arg.
159 C2 Tunuyán r. Arg.
92 D3 Tuo He r. China
92 F2 Tuoji Dao i. China
98 C3 Tuŏl Khpos Cambodia
140 B3 Tuolumne U.S.A.
136 B4 Tuolumne r. U.S.A.
140 C3 Tuolumne Meadows U.S.A.
93 B5 Tuoniang Jiang r. China
Tuotuo He r. China see Togton He
83 I4 Tüp Kyrg.
158 B3 Tupã Brazil
158 C2 Tupaciguara Brazil
125 F4 Tüp Āghāj Iran
156 F3 Tupanciretã Brazil
157 □ Tuparro r. Col.
143 F5 Tupelo U.S.A.
154 E8 Tupiza Bol.
147 F2 Tupper Lake U.S.A.
147 F2 Tupper Lake l. U.S.A.
159 C2 Tupungato Arg.
159 C2 Tupungato, Cerro mt. Arg./Chile
81 J7 Tuqayyid well Iraq
96 A1 Tuquan China
157 A4 Túquerres Col.
89 G4 Tura India
77 L3 Tura Rus. Fed.
86 B5 Turabah Saudi Arabia
157 D3 Turagua, Serranía mt. Venez.
72 E4 Turakina N.Z.
84 E3 Turan Iran
77 F1 Turana, Khrebet mts Rus. Fed.
72 E3 Turangi N.Z.
84 E2 Turan Lowland Asia
83 G4 Turar Ryskulov Kazakh.
Ţurayf Saudi Arabia see Ţurayf
80 G6 Ţurayf Saudi Arabia
87 C5 Ţurayf well Saudi Arabia
103 N4 Turba Estonia
157 B2 Turbaco Col.
85 F5 Turbat Pak.
157 A2 Turbo Col.
113 K7 Turda Romania
84 C3 Tureh Iran
Turfan China see Turpan
83 H2 Turgay Akmolinskaya Oblast' Kazakh.
82 E2 Turgay Kostanayskaya Oblast' Kazakh.
82 E3 Turgay r. Kazakh.
82 E2 Turgayskaya Dolina val. Kazakh.
82 E2 Turgayskaya Stolovaya Strana reg. Kazakh.
115 L3 Türgovishte Bulg.
80 C2 Turgut Turkey
80 A2 Turgutlu Turkey
80 F1 Turhal Turkey
103 N4 Türi Estonia
111 F3 Turia r. Spain
157 D2 Turiamo Venez.
114 B2 Turin Italy
94 B2 Turiy Rog Rus. Fed.
117 C5 Turiys'k Ukr.
122 D3 Turkana, Lake salt l. Eth./Kenya
115 L5 Türkeli Adası i. Turkey
83 G4 Turkestan Kazakh.
83 G5 Turkestan Range mts Asia
80 E2 Turkey country Asia
134 B4 Turkey r. U.S.A.
117 G5 Turki Rus. Fed.
Türkmenabat Turkm. see Türkmenabat
Türkmenabat
82 E5 Türkmenabat Turkm.
82 C5 Türkmen Aýlagy b. Turkm.
Turkmenbashi Turkm. see Türkmenbaşy
82 C5 Turkmenbashi, Zaliv b. Turkm.
82 C4 Türkmenbaşy Turkm.
80 C2 Türkmen Dağı mt. Turkey
82 E5 Türkmengala Turkm.
Turkmengala Turkm. see Türkmengala
82 C5 Turkmenistan country Asia
Turkmenskiy Zaliv b. Turkm. see Türkmen Aýlagy
80 F3 Türkoğlu Turkey
149 J4 Turks and Caicos Islands terr. Caribbean Sea
149 J4 Turks Islands Turks and Caicos Is
103 M3 Turku Fin.
122 D3 Turkwel watercourse Kenya
140 B3 Turlock U.S.A.
140 B3 Turlock Lake U.S.A.
72 F4 Turnagain, Cape N.Z.
106 D5 Turnberry U.K.
141 G5 Turnbull, Mount U.S.A.
151 H4 Turneffe Islands atoll Belize
135 F3 Turner U.S.A.
108 C3 Turnhout Belgium
131 H3 Turnor Lake Canada
115 K3 Turnu Măgurele Romania
71 H4 Turon r. Australia
116 G3 Turovets Rus. Fed.
90 A2 Turpan China
90 A2 Turpan Pendi depr. China
149 I4 Turquino, Pico mt. Cuba
106 F3 Turriff U.K.
81 J5 Tursāq Iraq
Turtkul' Uzbek. see To'rtko'l
134 B2 Turtle Flambeau Flowage resr U.S.A.
131 H4 Turtleford Canada
134 A3 Turtle Lake U.S.A.
83 H4 Turugart Pass China/Kyrg.
82 D3 Turush Kazakh.
158 B2 Turvo r. Goiás Brazil
158 C3 Turvo r. São Paulo Brazil
141 F4 Tusayan U.S.A.
145 C5 Tuscaloosa U.S.A.
146 C4 Tuscarawas r. U.S.A.
146 E4 Tuscarora Mountains U.S.A.
134 C6 Tuscola IL U.S.A.
143 D5 Tuscola TX U.S.A.
84 E3 Tusharīk Iran
145 C5 Tuskegee U.S.A.
146 D4 Tussey Mountains U.S.A.
81 I2 Tutak Turkey
116 F3 Tutayev Rus. Fed.
87 B4 Tuticorin India
142 D4 Tuttle Creek Reservoir U.S.A.
112 D7 Tuttlingen Germany
129 P2 Tuttut Nunaat reg. Greenland
69 I3 Tutuila i. Pacific Ocean
123 C6 Tutume Botswana
151 E4 Tututepec Mex.
96 D3 Tuun-bong mt. N. Korea
102 O3 Tuupovaara Fin.
102 O3 Tuusniemi Fin.
69 H2 Tuvalu country Pacific Ocean
84 B5 Tuwayq, Jabal hills Saudi Arabia
150 D4 Tuxpan Jalisco Mex.
151 E3 Tuxpan Veracruz Mex.
151 F4 Tuxtla Gutiérrez Mex.
157 D2 Tuy r. Venez.
98 C2 Tuy Đực Vietnam
93 B6 Tuyên Quang Vietnam
98 D2 Tuy Hoa Vietnam
84 C3 Tüysarkān Iran
83 I4 Tuyuk Kazakh.
80 D2 Tuz, Lake salt l. Turkey
Tuz Gölü salt l. Turkey see Tuz, Lake
141 F4 Tuzigoot National Monument nat. park U.S.A.
81 J4 Tuz Khurmātū Iraq
115 H2 Tuzla Bos.-Herz.
81 H2 Tuzla r. Turkey
117 F6 Tuzlov r. Rus. Fed.
103 J4 Tvedestrand Norway
116 E3 Tver' Rus. Fed.
116 E3 Tverskaya Oblast' admin. div. Rus. Fed.
135 I3 Tweed Canada
106 F5 Tweed r. U.K.
71 J2 Tweed Heads Australia
130 D4 Tweedsmuir Provincial Park Canada
124 C6 Tweefontein S. Africa
124 C2 Twee Rivier Namibia
108 E2 Twente reg. Neth.
140 D4 Twentynine Palms U.S.A.
133 J4 Twillingate Canada
138 D2 Twin Bridges U.S.A.
143 C6 Twin Buttes Reservoir U.S.A.
133 H3 Twin Falls Canada
138 D3 Twin Falls U.S.A.
130 F3 Twin Lakes Canada
147 H2 Twin Mountain U.S.A.
146 C6 Twin Oaks U.S.A.
140 B2 Twin Peak U.S.A.
70 A2 Twins, The Australia
109 G2 Twistringen Germany
72 C6 Twizel N.Z.
71 H6 Twofold Bay Australia
141 G4 Two Guns U.S.A.
134 B2 Two Harbors U.S.A.
131 G4 Two Hills Canada
138 D1 Two Medicine r. U.S.A.
134 D3 Two Rivers U.S.A.
89 H5 Tyao r. India/Myanmar
102 J3 Tydal Norway
146 D5 Tygart Lake U.S.A.
146 D5 Tygart Valley U.S.A.
90 E1 Tygda Rus. Fed.
143 E5 Tyler U.S.A.
143 F6 Tylertown U.S.A.
90 E1 Tynda Rus. Fed.
130 A2 Tyndall Glacier U.S.A.
106 F4 Tyne r. U.K.
104 F2 Tynemouth U.K.
103 J3 Tynset Norway
80 E5 Tyre Lebanon
73 B3 Tyree, Mount mt. Antarctica
102 N2 Tyrnävä Fin.
115 J5 Tyrnavos Greece
146 D4 Tyrone U.S.A.
70 E5 Tyrrell r. Australia
70 E5 Tyrrell, Lake dry lake Australia
131 H2 Tyrrell Lake Canada
114 D4 Tyrrhenian Sea France/Italy
77 P3 Tyubelyakh Rus. Fed.
82 B3 Tyub-Karagan, Mys pt Kazakh.
76 I4 Tyukalinsk Rus. Fed.
82 B2 Tyulen'i Ostrova is Kazakh.
82 D1 Tyul'gan Rus. Fed.
76 H4 Tyumen' Rus. Fed.
83 J1 Tyumentsevo Rus. Fed.
77 M3 Tyung r. Rus. Fed.
82 F1 Tyuntyugur Kazakh.
105 C6 Tywi r. U.K.
105 C5 Tywyn U.K.
125 I1 Tzaneen S. Africa

U

123 C5 Uamanda Angola
157 E4 Uatatás r. Brazil
155 K5 Uauá Brazil
157 D5 Uaupés Brazil
157 C4 Uaupés r. Brazil
151 G4 Uaxactún Guat.
84 B4 U'aywij well Saudi Arabia
81 I7 U'aywij, Wādī al watercourse Saudi Arabia
158 D3 Ubá Brazil
83 J2 Uba r. Kazakh.
82 F1 Ubagan r. Kazakh.
158 D2 Ubaí Brazil
158 E1 Ubaitaba Brazil
122 B3 Ubangi r. Centr. Afr. Rep./Dem. Rep. Congo
157 B3 Ubate Col.
81 I5 Ubayyiḑ, Wādī al watercourse Iraq/Saudi Arabia
95 B8 Ube Japan
111 E3 Úbeda Spain
158 C2 Uberaba Brazil
155 G7 Uberaba, Lagoa l. Bol./Brazil
158 C2 Uberlândia Brazil
98 □ Ubin, Pulau i. Sing.
98 B1 Ubolratna Reservoir Thai.
125 J3 Ubombo S. Africa
Ubonrat, Angkep Nam resr Thai. see Ubolratna Reservoir
98 C2 Ubon Ratchathani Thai.
109 G5 Ubstadt-Weiher Germany
122 C4 Ubundu Dem. Rep. Congo

212 Üçajy

82 E5 **Üçajy** Turkm.
81 K1 **Ucar** Azer.
154 D5 **Ucayali** *r.* Peru
88 B3 **Uch** Pak.
Uch-Adzhi Turkm. *see* **Üçajy**
82 D1 **Uchaly** Rus. Fed.
84 C2 **Üchān** Iran
83 J3 **Ucharal** Kazakh.
94 G3 **Uchiura-wan** *b.* Japan
Uchkuduk Uzbek. *see* **Uchquduq**
82 E4 **Uchquduq** Uzbek.
Uchsay Uzbek. *see* **Uchsoy**
82 D4 **Uchsoy** Uzbek.
109 G2 **Uchte** Germany
109 J2 **Uchte** *r.* Germany
90 F1 **Uchur** *r.* Rus. Fed.
105 H7 **Uckfield** U.K.
130 D5 **Ucluelet** Canada
141 H3 **Ucolo** U.S.A.
138 F2 **Ucross** U.S.A.
77 O4 **Uda** *r.* Rus. Fed.
117 H6 **Udachnoye** Rus. Fed.
77 M3 **Udachnyy** Rus. Fed.
87 B4 **Udagamandalam** India
88 C4 **Udaipur** *Rajasthan* India
89 G5 **Udaipur** *Tripura* India
89 E5 **Udanti** *r.* India/Myanmar
87 B3 **Udayagiri** India
103 J4 **Uddevalla** Sweden
106 D5 **Uddingston** U.K.
102 L2 **Uddjaure** *l.* Sweden
108 D3 **Uden** Neth.
87 B2 **Udgir** India
116 H2 **Udimskiy** Rus. Fed.
114 E1 **Udine** Italy
133 I2 **Udjuktok Bay** Canada
116 E3 **Udomlya** Rus. Fed.
98 B1 **Udon Thani** Thai.
90 F1 **Udskaya Guba** *b.* Rus. Fed.
87 B4 **Udumalaippettai** India
87 A3 **Udupi** India
90 F1 **Udyl', Ozero** *l.* Rus. Fed.
112 G4 **Ueckermünde** Germany
95 F6 **Ueda** Japan
68 C2 **Uekuli** Indon.
122 C3 **Uele** *r.* Dem. Rep. Congo
128 B3 **Uelen** Rus. Fed.
109 I2 **Uelzen** Germany
122 C3 **Uere** *r.* Dem. Rep. Congo
109 H1 **Uetersen** Germany
109 H5 **Uettingen** Germany
109 I2 **Uetze** Germany
76 G4 **Ufa** Rus. Fed.
109 I5 **Uffenheim** Germany
123 B6 **Ugab** *watercourse* Namibia
122 D4 **Ugalla** *r.* Tanz.
122 D3 **Uganda** *country* Africa
125 H5 **Ugie** S. Africa
90 G2 **Uglegorsk** Rus. Fed.
94 C3 **Uglekamensk** Rus. Fed.
116 F3 **Uglich** Rus. Fed.
114 F2 **Ugljan** *i.* Croatia
116 E3 **Uglovka** Rus. Fed.
94 C3 **Uglovoye** Rus. Fed.
83 J2 **Uglovskoye** Rus. Fed.
77 P3 **Ugol'noye** Rus. Fed.
77 S3 **Ugol'nyye Kopi** Rus. Fed.
116 E4 **Ugra** Rus. Fed.
83 H4 **Ügüt** Kyrg.
112 H6 **Uherské Hradiště** Czech Rep.
146 C4 **Uhrichsville** U.S.A.
106 B3 **Uig** U.K.
122 B4 **Uíge** Angola
96 D5 **Ŭijŏngbu** S. Korea
96 C3 **Ŭiju** N. Korea
82 C2 **Uil** Kazakh.
82 C2 **Uil** *r.* Kazakh.
102 O3 **Uimaharju** Fin.
141 F3 **Uinkaret Plateau** U.S.A.
138 E3 **Uinta Mountains** U.S.A.
123 B6 **Uis Mine** Namibia
107 D4 **Uisneach** *h.* Rep. of Ireland
96 E5 **Ŭisŏng** S. Korea
125 F6 **Uitenhage** S. Africa
108 C2 **Uithoorn** Neth.
108 E1 **Uithuizen** Neth.
133 H2 **Uivak, Cape** Canada
95 D7 **Uji** Japan
95 A9 **Uji-guntō** *is* Japan
88 C5 **Ujjain** India
Ujung Pandang Indon. *see* **Makassar**
125 H4 **uKhahlamba-Drakensberg Park** *nat. park* S. Africa
81 I5 **Ukhaydir** *tourist site* Iraq
89 H4 **Ukhrul** India
116 J2 **Ukhta** Rus. Fed.
116 J2 **Ukhta** *r.* Rus. Fed.
71 J2 **Uki** Australia
140 A2 **Ukiah** *CA* U.S.A.
138 C2 **Ukiah** *OR* U.S.A.
129 J3 **Ukkusiksalik National Park** Canada
129 M2 **Ukkusissat** Greenland
103 N5 **Ukmergė** Lith.
117 D5 **Ukraine** *country* Europe
83 J2 **Ukrainka** Kazakh.
116 I2 **Uktym** Rus. Fed.
95 A8 **Uku-jima** *i.* Japan
124 D1 **Ukwi** Botswana
124 D1 **Ukwi Pan** *salt pan* Botswana
Ulaanbaatar Mongolia *see* **Ulan Bator**
90 B2 **Ulaangom** Mongolia
71 H4 **Ulan** Australia
92 C2 **Ulan** China
90 C2 **Ulan Bator** Mongolia
83 G3 **Ulanbel'** Kazakh.
92 C1 **Ulan Buh Shamo** *des.* China
117 H6 **Ulan Erge** Rus. Fed.
90 E2 **Ulanhot** China
92 D1 **Ulan Hua** China
117 H6 **Ulan-Khol** Rus. Fed.
92 C1 **Ulansuhai Nur** *l.* China
92 A1 **Ulan Tohoi** China
90 C1 **Ulan-Ude** Rus. Fed.
89 G2 **Ulan Ul Hu** *l.* China
80 F2 **Ulaş** Turkey
69 G2 **Ulawa Island** Solomon Is
85 E4 **Ulāy, Kūh-e** *h.* Iran
83 J2 **Ul'ba** Kazakh.
96 E5 **Ulchin** S. Korea
103 J4 **Ulefoss** Norway
70 E2 **Ulenia, Lake** *salt flat* Australia
103 N4 **Ülenurme** Estonia
83 F2 **Ul'gili** Kazakh.
87 A2 **Ulhasnagar** India
90 D2 **Uliastai** China
90 B2 **Uliastay** Mongolia
108 C3 **Ulicoten** Neth.
102 P1 **Ulita** *r.* Rus. Fed.
91 F6 **Ulithi** *atoll* Micronesia
82 E2 **Ul'kayak** *r.* Kazakh.
83 H4 **Ul'ken Sulutor** Kazakh.
71 I5 **Ulladulla** Australia
106 C3 **Ullapool** U.K.
102 M3 **Ullava** Fin.
104 E3 **Ullswater** *l.* U.K.
96 F5 **Ullŭng-do** *i.* S. Korea
112 D6 **Ulm** Germany
71 J2 **Ulmarra** Australia
108 E4 **Ulmen** Germany
103 K4 **Ulricehamn** Sweden
108 E1 **Ulrum** Neth.
96 E6 **Ulsan** S. Korea
102 J3 **Ulsberg** Norway
107 D3 **Ulster Canal** Rep. of Ireland/U.K.
70 E5 **Ultima** Australia
151 G5 **Ulúa** *r.* Hond.
80 B1 **Ulubat Gölü** *l.* Turkey
80 C2 **Uluborlu** Turkey
80 B1 **Uludağ** *mt.* Turkey
98 B5 **Ulu Kali, Gunung** *mt.* Malaysia
80 E3 **Ulukışla** Turkey
125 I4 **Ulundi** S. Africa
90 A2 **Ulungur Hu** *l.* China
98 □ **Ulu Pandan** Sing.
68 D4 **Uluṟu** *h.* Australia
80 D1 **Ulus** Turkey
106 B4 **Ulva** *i.* U.K.
108 C3 **Ulvenhout** Neth.
104 D3 **Ulverston** U.K.
71 G8 **Ulverstone** Australia
103 K3 **Ulvsjön** Sweden
Ul'yanovo Uzbek. *see* **Dashtobod**
116 I4 **Ul'yanovsk** Rus. Fed.
116 H4 **Ul'yanovskaya Oblast'** *admin. div.* Rus. Fed.
83 H2 **Ul'yanovskiy** Kazakh.
143 C4 **Ulysses** U.S.A.
83 F2 **Ulytau** Kazakh.
83 F3 **Ulytau, Gory** *mts* Kazakh.
151 G3 **Umán** Mex.
117 D5 **Uman'** Ukr.
85 G4 **Umarao** Pak.
88 E5 **Umaria** India
88 D6 **Umarkhed** India
87 C2 **Umarkot** India
88 B4 **Umarkot** Pak.
138 C2 **Umatilla** U.S.A.
76 E3 **Umba** Rus. Fed.
147 H2 **Umbagog Lake** U.S.A.
68 E2 **Umboi** *i.* P.N.G.
102 M3 **Umeå** Sweden
102 L2 **Umeälven** *r.* Sweden
125 I4 **Umfolozi** *r.* S. Africa
81 K7 **Umgharah** Kuwait
Umhlanga S. Africa *see* **Umhlanga Rocks**
125 I4 **Umhlanga Rocks** S. Africa
129 N3 **Umiiviip Kangertiva** *inlet* Greenland
128 H3 **Umingmaktok** Canada
132 E2 **Umiujaq** Canada
125 I5 **Umkomaas** S. Africa
125 I4 **Umlazi** S. Africa
81 J6 **Umma** *tourist site* Iraq
84 D5 **Umm al Qaywayn** U.A.E.
84 C5 **Umm Bāb** Qatar
121 E3 **Umm Keddada** Sudan
81 K6 **Umm Qaṣr** Iraq
121 F3 **Umm Ruwaba** Sudan
121 E1 **Umm Sa'ad** Libya
84 C5 **Umm Sa'īd** Qatar
138 A3 **Umpqua** *r.* U.S.A.
123 B5 **Umpulo** Angola
88 D5 **Umred** India
88 C5 **Umreth** India
125 H5 **Umtata** S. Africa
125 I5 **Umtentweni** S. Africa
120 C4 **Umuahia** Nigeria
158 B3 **Umuarama** Brazil
125 H5 **Umzimkulu** S. Africa
125 I5 **Umzinto** S. Africa
114 G2 **Una** *r.* Bos.-Herz./Croatia
158 E1 **Una** Brazil
80 F6 **'Unāb, Wādī al** *watercourse* Jordan
158 C2 **Unaí** Brazil
85 H3 **Unai Pass** Afgh.
128 B3 **Unalakleet** U.S.A.
106 C2 **Unapool** U.K.
157 D2 **Unare** *r.* Venez.
80 E6 **'Unayzah** Jordan
86 B4 **'Unayzah** Saudi Arabia
81 G5 **'Unayzah, Jabal** *h.* Iraq
139 E4 **Uncompahgre Plateau** U.S.A.
125 H4 **Underberg** S. Africa
70 D5 **Underbool** Australia
142 C2 **Underwood** U.S.A.
116 E4 **Unecha** Rus. Fed.
71 G4 **Ungarie** Australia
70 B5 **Ungarra** Australia
132 F1 **Ungava, Péninsule d'** *pen.* Canada
133 G2 **Ungava Bay** Canada
96 F2 **Unggi** N. Korea
117 C6 **Ungheni** Moldova
82 E5 **Unguz, Solonchakovyye Vpadiny** *salt flat* Turkm.
82 D4 **Üngüz Angyrsyndaky Garagum** *des.* Turkm.
116 I3 **Uni** Rus. Fed.
158 B4 **União da Vitória** Brazil
157 B4 **Unilla** *r.* Col.
154 F4 **Unini** *r.* Brazil
158 A4 **Unión** Para.
147 I2 **Union** *ME* U.S.A.
145 D5 **Union** *SC* U.S.A.
146 C6 **Union** *WV* U.S.A.
141 F4 **Union, Mount** U.S.A.
134 E5 **Union City** *OH* U.S.A.
146 D4 **Union City** *PA* U.S.A.
145 B4 **Union City** *TN* U.S.A.
124 E6 **Uniondale** S. Africa
145 C5 **Union Springs** U.S.A.
146 D5 **Uniontown** U.S.A.
135 F4 **Unionville** U.S.A.
84 D6 **United Arab Emirates** *country* Asia
76 E3 **United Kingdom** *country* Europe
136 D4 **United States of America** *country* N. America
131 H4 **Unity** Canada
147 I2 **Unity** *ME* U.S.A.
138 C2 **Unity** *OR* U.S.A.
88 C5 **Unjha** India
109 F3 **Unna** Germany
88 E4 **Unnao** India
96 C4 **Ŭnp'a** N. Korea
96 C3 **Unsan** N. Korea
96 D4 **Ŭnsan** N. Korea
106 □ **Unst** *i.* U.K.
109 J3 **Unstrut** *r.* Germany
89 G2 **Unuli Horog** China
87 D1 **Upar Ghat** *reg.* India
157 E2 **Upata** Venez.
123 C4 **Upemba, Lac** *l.* Dem. Rep. Congo
97 C5 **Upi** Phil.
157 B3 **Upía** *r.* Col.
124 D4 **Upington** S. Africa
88 B5 **Upleta** India
102 O2 **Upoloksha** Rus. Fed.
69 I3 **'Upolu** *i.* Samoa
138 B3 **Upper Alkali Lake** U.S.A.
146 B4 **Upper Arlington** U.S.A.
130 F4 **Upper Arrow Lake** Canada
72 E4 **Upper Hutt** N.Z.
134 B4 **Upper Iowa** *r.* U.S.A.
147 J1 **Upper Kent** Canada
138 B3 **Upper Klamath Lake** U.S.A.
140 A2 **Upper Lake** U.S.A.
130 D2 **Upper Liard** Canada
107 D3 **Upper Lough Erne** *l.* U.K.
146 E5 **Upper Marlboro** U.S.A.
98 □ **Upper Peirce Reservoir** Sing.
133 I4 **Upper Salmon Reservoir** Canada
146 B4 **Upper Sandusky** U.S.A.
147 F2 **Upper Saranac Lake** U.S.A.
72 D4 **Upper Takaka** N.Z.
103 L4 **Uppsala** Sweden
132 B4 **Upsala** Canada
147 H2 **Upton** U.S.A.
81 K7 **Uqlat al 'Udhaybah** *well* Iraq
81 K6 **Ur** *tourist site* Iraq
157 A2 **Urabá, Golfo de** *b.* Col.
84 E4 **Ūrāf** Iran
94 H3 **Urakawa** Japan
71 G4 **Ural** *h.* Australia
82 B3 **Ural** *r.* Kazakh./Rus. Fed.
71 I3 **Uralla** Australia
76 G4 **Ural Mountains** Rus. Fed.
82 B2 **Ural'sk** Kazakh.
Ural'skiy Khrebet *mts* Rus. Fed. *see* **Ural Mountains**
122 D4 **Urambo** Tanz.
71 G5 **Urana** Australia
71 G5 **Urana, Lake** Australia
158 D1 **Urandi** Brazil
131 H3 **Uranium City** Canada
71 G5 **Uranquinty** Australia
157 E4 **Uraricoera** Brazil
157 E4 **Uraricoera** *r.* Brazil
157 E4 **Uraricoera** *r.* Brazil
157 E3 **Uraucaima, Serra** *mt.* Brazil
141 H2 **Uravan** U.S.A.
84 B5 **'Urayq ad Duḩūl** *des.* Saudi Arabia
117 F5 **Urazovo** Rus. Fed.
134 C5 **Urbana** *IL* U.S.A.
146 B4 **Urbana** *OH* U.S.A.
71 J2 **Urbenville** Australia
114 E3 **Urbino** Italy
154 D6 **Urcos** Peru
82 A2 **Urda** Kazakh.
116 I2 **Urdoma** Rus. Fed.
83 J3 **Urdzhar** Kazakh.
104 F3 **Ure** *r.* U.K.
116 H3 **Uren'** Rus. Fed.
76 I3 **Urengoy** Rus. Fed.
69 G3 **Uréparapara** *i.* Vanuatu
72 F3 **Urewera National Park** N.Z.
116 H4 **Urga** *r.* Rus. Fed.
82 E4 **Urganch** Uzbek.
Urgench Uzbek. *see* **Urganch**
80 E2 **Ürgüp** Turkey
83 F5 **Urgut** Uzbek.
102 N1 **Urho Kekkosen kansallispuisto** *nat. park* Fin.
157 B2 **Uribia** Col.
70 E2 **Urisino** Australia
103 M3 **Urjala** Fin.
108 D2 **Urk** Neth.
117 H7 **Urkarakh** Rus. Fed.
115 L5 **Urla** Turkey
107 D5 **Urlingford** Rep. of Ireland
83 G5 **Urmetan** Tajik.
84 B2 **Urmia** Iran
84 B2 **Urmia, Lake** *salt l.* Iran
93 □ **Urmston Road** *sea chan.* *Hong Kong* China
115 I3 **Uroševac** Serb. and Mont.
83 G5 **Ŭroteppa** Tajik.
89 F3 **Urru Co** *salt l.* China
92 A1 **Urt** Mongolia
150 B2 **Uruáchic** Mex.
158 C1 **Uruaçu** Brazil
150 D4 **Uruapan** Mex.
154 D6 **Urubamba** *r.* Peru
155 G4 **Urucara** Brazil
155 J5 **Uruçuí** Brazil
158 D2 **Urucuia** *r.* Brazil
155 J5 **Uruçui Preto** *r.* Brazil
155 G4 **Urucurituba** Brazil
156 E3 **Uruguaiana** Brazil
156 E4 **Uruguay** *r.* Arg./Uruguay
159 F2 **Uruguay** *country* S. America
90 A2 **Ürümqi** China
71 J3 **Urunga** Australia
117 G6 **Urup** *r.* Rus. Fed.
90 H2 **Urup, Ostrov** *i.* Rus. Fed.
117 H7 **Urus-Martan** Rus. Fed.
83 K2 **Uryl'** Kazakh.
117 G5 **Uryupinsk** Rus. Fed.
116 I3 **Urzhum** Rus. Fed.
115 L2 **Urziceni** Romania
95 B8 **Usa** Japan
116 I4 **Usa** *r.* Rus. Fed.
80 B2 **Uşak** Turkey
123 B6 **Usakos** Namibia
73 B6 **Usarp Mountains** *mts* Antarctica
156 E8 **Usborne, Mount** *h.* Falkland Is
76 I1 **Ushakova, Ostrov** *i.* Rus. Fed.
83 J2 **Ushanovo** Kazakh.
83 G4 **Usharal** Kazakh.
95 B8 **Ushibuka** Japan
83 I3 **Ushtobe** Kazakh.
156 C8 **Ushuaia** Arg.
109 G4 **Usingen** Germany
76 G3 **Usinsk** Rus. Fed.
105 E6 **Usk** U.K.
105 E6 **Usk** *r.* U.K.
89 E4 **Uska** India
116 C4 **Uskhodni** Belarus
109 H3 **Uslar** Germany
117 F4 **Usman'** Rus. Fed.
103 M4 **Usmas ezers** *l.* Latvia
116 I2 **Usogorsk** Rus. Fed.
90 C1 **Usol'ye-Sibirskoye** Rus. Fed.
83 I1 **Uspenka** Kazakh.
83 H2 **Uspenskiy** Kazakh.
110 F4 **Ussel** France
94 D1 **Ussuri** *r.* China/Rus. Fed.
90 F2 **Ussuriysk** Rus. Fed.
116 H3 **Usta** *r.* Rus. Fed.
77 L4 **Ust'-Barguzin** Rus. Fed.
117 G5 **Ust'-Buzulukskaya** Rus. Fed.
83 J1 **Ust'-Charyshskaya Pristan'** Rus. Fed.
117 G6 **Ust'-Donetskiy** Rus. Fed.
114 E5 **Ustica, Isola di** *i.* *Sicily* Italy
90 C1 **Ust'-Ilimsk** Rus. Fed.
90 C1 **Ust'-Ilimskiy Vodokhranilishche** *resr* Rus. Fed.
76 G3 **Ust'-Ilych** Rus. Fed.
112 G5 **Ústí nad Labem** Czech Rep.
112 H3 **Ustka** Poland
83 J1 **Ust'-Kalmanka** Rus. Fed.
77 R4 **Ust'-Kamchatsk** Rus. Fed.
83 J2 **Ust'-Kamenogorsk** Kazakh.
83 K2 **Ust'-Kan** Rus. Fed.
83 K2 **Ust'-Koksa** Rus. Fed.
90 C1 **Ust'-Kut** Rus. Fed.
77 O2 **Ust'-Kuyga** Rus. Fed.
117 F6 **Ust'-Labinsk** Rus. Fed.
103 O4 **Ust'-Luga** Rus. Fed.
77 O3 **Ust'-Maya** Rus. Fed.
76 G3 **Ust'-Nem** Rus. Fed.
77 P3 **Ust'-Nera** Rus. Fed.
116 I2 **Ust'-Ocheya** Rus. Fed.
77 M2 **Ust'-Olenek** Rus. Fed.
77 P3 **Ust'-Omchug** Rus. Fed.
90 C1 **Ust'-Ordynskiy** Rus. Fed.
76 J3 **Ust'-Port** Rus. Fed.
116 G2 **Ust'-Shonosha** Rus. Fed.
76 G3 **Ust'-Tsil'ma** Rus. Fed.
116 H2 **Ust'-Ura** Rus. Fed.
82 E1 **Ust'-Uyskoye** Kazakh.
116 G2 **Ust'-Vayen'ga** Rus. Fed.
116 H2 **Ust'-Vyyskaya** Rus. Fed.
116 G2 **Ust'ya** *r.* Rus. Fed.
116 F3 **Ust'ye** Rus. Fed.
116 F3 **Ust'ye** *r.* Rus. Fed.
82 C3 **Ustyurta** *esc.* Kazakh.
82 C3 **Ustyurt Plateau** Kazakh./Uzbek.
116 F3 **Ustyuzhna** Rus. Fed.
95 B8 **Usuki** Japan
150 G5 **Usulután** El Salvador
151 G4 **Usumacinta** *r.* Guat./Mex.
116 D4 **Usvyaty** Rus. Fed.
141 G2 **Utah** *state* U.S.A.
141 G1 **Utah Lake** U.S.A.
102 N2 **Utajärvi** Fin.
84 C5 **Utayyiq** Saudi Arabia
103 N5 **Utena** Lith.
98 B2 **Uthai Thani** Thai.
85 G5 **Uthal** Pak.
98 A2 **U Thong** Thai.
98 C2 **Uthumphon Phisai** Thai.
147 F3 **Utica** U.S.A.
111 F3 **Utiel** Spain
130 F3 **Utikuma Lake** Canada
150 H4 **Utila** Hond.
125 F3 **Utlwanang** S. Africa
89 E4 **Utraula** India
108 D2 **Utrecht** Neth.
125 I3 **Utrecht** S. Africa
111 D4 **Utrera** Spain
102 N1 **Utsjoki** Fin.
95 F6 **Utsunomiya** Japan
117 H6 **Utta** Rus. Fed.
98 B1 **Uttaradit** Thai.
88 D3 **Uttaranchal** *state* India
88 D4 **Uttar Pradesh** *state* India
105 F5 **Uttoxeter** U.K.
69 G3 **Utupua** *i.* Solomon Is
82 C2 **Utva** *r.* Kazakh.
Uummannaq Greenland *see* **Dundas**
129 M2 **Uummannaq Fjord** *inlet* Greenland
102 N3 **Uurainen** Fin.
103 M3 **Uusikaupunki** Fin.
157 C4 **Uva** *r.* Col.
143 D6 **Uvalde** U.S.A.
117 G5 **Uvarovo** Rus. Fed.
82 E1 **Uvel'ka** *r.* Rus. Fed.
122 D4 **Uvinza** Tanz.
125 I5 **Uvongo** S. Africa
90 B1 **Uvs Nuur** *salt l.* Mongolia
95 C8 **Uwajima** Japan
121 E2 **Uweinat, Jebel** *mt.* Sudan
105 G6 **Uxbridge** U.K.
92 C2 **Uxin Ju** China
151 G3 **Uxmal** *tourist site* Mex.
82 E1 **Uy** *r.* Rus. Fed.
82 E3 **Uyaly** Kazakh.
90 B1 **Uyar** Rus. Fed.
92 C1 **Üydzin** Mongolia
120 C4 **Uyo** Nigeria
83 G4 **Uyuk** Kazakh.
156 C2 **Uyuni** Bol.
154 E8 **Uyuni, Salar de** *salt flat* Bol.
116 H4 **Uza** *r.* Rus. Fed.
81 J4 **'Uẓaym, Nahr al** *r.* Iraq
82 E4 **Uzbekistan** *country* Asia
110 G4 **Uzès** France
117 B5 **Uzhhorod** Ukr.
115 H3 **Užice** Serb. and Mont.
116 F4 **Uzlovaya** Rus. Fed.
116 G3 **Uzola** *r.* Rus. Fed.
80 C3 **Üzümlü** Turkey
83 G5 **Uzun** Uzbek.
83 I4 **Uzunagach** Kazakh.
83 K3 **Uzunbulak** China
81 K3 **Ūzūn Darreh** *r.* Iran
117 C7 **Uzunköprü** Turkey
117 D5 **Uzyn** Ukr.
82 E3 **Uzynkair** Kazakh.
82 F1 **Uzynkol'** Kazakh.

V

103 N3 **Vaajakoski** Fin.
124 H3 **Vaal** *r.* S. Africa
102 N2 **Vaala** Fin.
124 F4 **Vaalbos National Park** S. Africa
125 H3 **Vaal Dam** S. Africa
125 H2 **Vaalwater** S. Africa
102 M3 **Vaasa** Fin.
Vabkent Uzbek. *see* **Vobkent**
113 I7 **Vác** Hungary
156 F3 **Vacaria** Brazil
158 A3 **Vacaria** *r.* *Mato Grosso do Sul* Brazil
158 D2 **Vacaria** *r.* *Minas Gerais* Brazil
158 A3 **Vacaria, Serra** *hills* Brazil
140 B2 **Vacaville** U.S.A.
116 G4 **Vad** *r.* Rus. Fed.
88 C6 **Vada** India
103 I4 **Vadla** Norway
88 C5 **Vadodara** India
102 O1 **Vadsø** Norway
112 D7 **Vaduz** Liechtenstein
102 K2 **Værøy** *i.* Norway
116 G2 **Vaga** *r.* Rus. Fed.
103 J3 **Vågåmo** Norway
114 F2 **Vaganski Vrh** *mt.* Croatia
102 □ **Vágar** *i.* Faroe Is
102 L2 **Vägsele** Sweden
102 □ **Vágur** Faroe Is
102 M3 **Vähäkyrö** Fin.
84 E4 **Vahhābī** Iran
69 H2 **Vaiaku** Tuvalu
103 N4 **Vaida** Estonia
87 B4 **Vaigai** *r.* India
141 G5 **Vail** U.S.A.
108 B5 **Vailly-sur-Aisne** France
69 H2 **Vaitupu** *i.* Tuvalu
83 H5 **Vakhan** Tajik.
83 G5 **Vakhsh** Tajik.
87 C5 **Valachchenai** Sri Lanka
135 J2 **Val-Barrette** Canada
103 L3 **Valbo** Sweden
159 C4 **Valcheta** Arg.
114 D2 **Valdagno** Italy
116 E3 **Valday** Rus. Fed.
116 E3 **Valdayskaya Vozvyshennost'** *hills* Rus. Fed.
111 D3 **Valdecañas, Embalse de** *resr* Spain
103 M4 **Valdemārpils** Latvia
103 L4 **Valdemarsvik** Sweden
110 G2 **Val-de-Meuse** France
111 E3 **Valdepeñas** Spain
110 E2 **Val-de-Reuil** France
159 D4 **Valdés, Península** *pen.* Arg.
135 J3 **Val-des-Bois** Canada
128 D3 **Valdez** U.S.A.
159 B3 **Valdivia** Chile
135 I1 **Val-d'Or** Canada
145 D6 **Valdosta** U.S.A.
103 J3 **Valdres** *val.* Norway
81 I1 **Vale** Georgia
138 C2 **Vale** U.S.A.
130 F4 **Valemount** Canada
158 E1 **Valença** Brazil
110 G4 **Valence** France
111 F3 **Valencia** Spain
111 F3 **Valencia** *reg.* Spain
157 D2 **Valencia** Venez.
111 G3 **Valencia, Golfo de** *g.* Spain
111 C3 **Valencia de Alcántara** Spain
111 D1 **Valencia de Don Juan** Spain
107 A6 **Valencia Island** Rep. of Ireland
110 F1 **Valenciennes** France
94 D3 **Valentin** Rus. Fed.
141 F4 **Valentine** *AZ* U.S.A.
142 C3 **Valentine** *NE* U.S.A.
143 B6 **Valentine** *TX* U.S.A.
97 B3 **Valenzuela** Phil.
103 J3 **Våler** Norway
157 C2 **Valera** Venez.
83 G1 **Valikhanovo** Kazakh.
115 H2 **Valjevo** Serb. and Mont.
103 N4 **Valka** Latvia
103 N3 **Valkeakoski** Fin.
108 D3 **Valkenswaard** Neth.
117 E5 **Valky** Ukr.
73 D4 **Valkyrie Dome** *ice feature* Antarctica
151 G3 **Valladolid** Mex.
111 D2 **Valladolid** Spain
111 F3 **Vall de Uxó** Spain
103 I4 **Valle** Norway
157 D2 **Valle de la Pascua** Venez.
150 D3 **Valle de Santiago** Mex.
157 B2 **Valledupar** Col.
159 C1 **Valle Fértil, Sierra de** *mts* Arg.
154 F7 **Valle Grande** Bol.
151 E2 **Valle Hermoso** Mex.
140 A2 **Vallejo** U.S.A.
151 E4 **Valle Nacional** Mex.
114 F7 **Valletta** Malta
105 C4 **Valley** U.K.
142 D2 **Valley City** U.S.A.
138 B3 **Valley Falls** U.S.A.
146 C5 **Valley Head** U.S.A.
130 F3 **Valleyview** Canada
111 G2 **Valls** Spain
131 H5 **Val Marie** Canada
103 N4 **Valmiera** Latvia
111 E1 **Valnera** *mt.* Spain
116 C4 **Valozhyn** Belarus
132 E4 **Val-Paradis** Canada
158 B3 **Valparaíso** Brazil
159 B2 **Valparaíso** Chile
159 B2 **Valparaíso** *admin. reg.* Chile
150 D3 **Valparaíso** Mex.
134 D5 **Valparaiso** U.S.A.
110 G4 **Valréas** France
91 F7 **Vals, Tanjung** *c.* Indon.
88 C5 **Valsad** India
124 F3 **Valspan** S. Africa
116 H1 **Val'tevo** Rus. Fed.
102 O3 **Valtimo** Fin.
117 G6 **Valuyevka** Rus. Fed.
117 F5 **Valuyki** Rus. Fed.
111 C4 **Valverde del Camino** Spain
98 C3 **Vam Co Tây** *r.* Vietnam
103 M3 **Vammala** Fin.
87 C2 **Vamsadhara** *r.* India
81 I2 **Van** Turkey
81 I2 **Van, Lake** *salt l.* Turkey
81 J1 **Vanadzor** Armenia
143 E5 **Van Buren** *AR* U.S.A.
147 J1 **Van Buren** *ME* U.S.A.
98 D2 **Vân Canh** Vietnam
147 J2 **Vanceboro** U.S.A.
146 B5 **Vanceburg** U.S.A.
130 E5 **Vancouver** Canada
138 B2 **Vancouver** U.S.A.
130 A2 **Vancouver, Mount** Canada/U.S.A.
130 D5 **Vancouver Island** Canada
144 B4 **Vandalia** *IL* U.S.A.
146 A5 **Vandalia** *OH* U.S.A.
125 G3 **Vanderbijlpark** S. Africa
134 E3 **Vanderbilt** U.S.A.
146 D4 **Vandergrift** U.S.A.
130 E4 **Vanderhoof** Canada
124 F5 **Vanderkloof Dam** *resr* S. Africa
68 D3 **Vanderlin Island** Australia
141 H4 **Vanderwagen** U.S.A.
68 D3 **Van Diemen Gulf** Australia
103 N4 **Vändra** Estonia
103 K4 **Vänern** *l.* Sweden
103 K4 **Vänersborg** Sweden
146 E3 **Van Etten** U.S.A.
123 E6 **Vangaindrano** Madag.
98 D2 **Van Gia** Vietnam
Van Gölü *salt l.* Turkey *see* **Van, Lake**
143 B6 **Van Horn** U.S.A.
135 J3 **Vanier** Canada
69 G3 **Vanikoro Islands** Solomon Is
68 E2 **Vanimo** P.N.G.
90 G2 **Vanino** Rus. Fed.
87 B3 **Vanivilasa Sagara** *resr* India
87 B3 **Vaniyambadi** India
83 G5 **Vanj** Tajik.
83 G5 **Vanj, Qatorkŭhi** *mts* Tajik.
77 U3 **Vankarem** Rus. Fed.
147 F2 **Vankleek Hill** Canada
Vanna *i.* Norway *see* **Vannøya**
102 L3 **Vännäs** Sweden
110 C3 **Vannes** France
102 L1 **Vannøya** *i.* Norway
91 F7 **Van Rees, Pegunungan** *mts* Indon.
124 C5 **Vanrhynsdorp** S. Africa
103 K3 **Vansbro** Sweden
103 N3 **Vantaa** Fin.
69 G3 **Vanua Lava** *i.* Vanuatu
69 H3 **Vanua Levu** *i.* Fiji
69 G3 **Vanuatu** *country* Pacific Ocean
146 A4 **Van Wert** U.S.A.
124 D5 **Vanwyksvlei** S. Africa
124 D5 **Vanwyksvlei** *l.* S. Africa
93 B6 **Văn Yên** Vietnam
124 E3 **Van Zylsrus** S. Africa
87 A3 **Varada** *r.* India
103 N4 **Varakļāni** Latvia
84 C3 **Varāmīn** Iran
89 E4 **Varanasi** India
102 O1 **Varangerfjorden** *sea chan.* Norway
102 O1 **Varangerhalvøya** *pen.* Norway
114 G1 **Varaždin** Croatia
103 K4 **Varberg** Sweden
87 B2 **Vardannapet** India
115 J4 **Vardar** *r.* Macedonia
103 J5 **Varde** Denmark
84 B1 **Vardenis** Armenia
102 O1 **Vardø** Norway
109 G1 **Varel** Germany
159 C2 **Varela** Arg.
103 N5 **Varėna** Lith.
114 C2 **Varese** Italy
94 C2 **Varfolomeyevka** Rus. Fed.
103 K4 **Vårgårda** Sweden
158 D3 **Varginha** Brazil
108 D3 **Varik** Neth.
102 N3 **Varkaus** Fin.
115 L3 **Varna** Bulg.
82 E1 **Varna** Rus. Fed.
103 K4 **Värnamo** Sweden
103 K3 **Värnäs** Sweden
116 H3 **Varnavino** Rus. Fed.
80 D4 **Varosia** Cyprus
102 N3 **Varpaisjärvi** Fin.
112 I7 **Várpalota** Hungary
85 H2 **Varsaj** Afgh.
81 H2 **Varto** Turkey
89 E4 **Varuna** *r.* India
146 D3 **Varysburg** U.S.A.
84 D3 **Varzaneh** Iran
158 D2 **Várzea da Palma** Brazil
116 H2 **Vashka** *r.* Rus. Fed.
116 H2 **Vasilevo** Rus. Fed.
103 N4 **Vasknarva** Estonia
113 M7 **Vaslui** Romania
135 F4 **Vassar** U.S.A.
103 L4 **Västerås** Sweden
103 K3 **Västerdalälven** *r.* Sweden
102 L2 **Västerfjäll** Sweden
103 L4 **Västerhaninge** Sweden
102 L3 **Västernorrland** *county* Sweden
103 L4 **Västervik** Sweden
114 F3 **Vasto** Italy
117 D5 **Vasyl'kiv** Ukr.
110 E3 **Vatan** France
106 A4 **Vatersay** *i.* U.K.
87 A2 **Vathar** India
115 L6 **Vathy** Greece
114 E4 **Vatican City** Europe
102 C2 **Vatnajökull** *ice cap* Iceland
113 L7 **Vatra Dornei** Romania
103 K4 **Vättern** *l.* Sweden
139 F5 **Vaughn** U.S.A.
108 B4 **Vaulx** *tourist site* Belgium
157 C4 **Vaupés** *r.* Col.
110 G5 **Vauvert** France
69 I3 **Vava'u Group** *is* Tonga
Vava'u Group *is* Tonga *see* **Vava'u Group**
120 B4 **Vavoua** Côte d'Ivoire
87 C4 **Vavuniya** Sri Lanka
116 C4 **Vawkavysk** Belarus
103 K4 **Växjö** Sweden
98 B3 **Vay, Đao** *i.* Vietnam
87 B3 **Vayalpad** India
116 H1 **Vazhgort** Rus. Fed.
123 E5 **Vazobe** *mt.* Madag.
98 B2 **Veal Vêng** Cambodia
109 G2 **Vechta** Germany
108 E2 **Vechte** *r.* Germany
109 H3 **Veckerhagen (Reinhardshagen)** Germany
87 B4 **Vedaranniyam** India
103 K4 **Veddige** Sweden
115 K3 **Vedea** *r.* Romania
117 H7 **Vedeno** Rus. Fed.
81 J2 **Vedi** Armenia
159 E2 **Vedia** Arg.
116 E2 **Vedlozero** Rus. Fed.
134 D5 **Veedersburg** U.S.A.
108 E1 **Veendam** Neth.
108 D2 **Veenendaal** Neth.
102 J2 **Vega** *i.* Norway
143 C5 **Vega** U.S.A.
131 G4 **Vegreville** Canada
103 N3 **Vehkalahti** Fin.
88 B3 **Vehoa** *r.* Pak.
88 B4 **Veirwaro** Pak.
109 H5 **Veitshöchheim** Germany
111 D4 **Vejer de la Frontera** Spain
103 J5 **Vejle** Denmark
87 B4 **Velanai Island** Sri Lanka
108 F3 **Velbert** Germany
115 J3 **Velbŭzhdki Prokhod** *pass* Macedonia
124 C6 **Velddrif** S. Africa
114 F2 **Velebit** *mts* Croatia
108 E3 **Velen** Germany
114 F1 **Velenje** Slovenia
115 I4 **Veles** Macedonia
157 B3 **Vélez** Col.
111 D4 **Vélez-Málaga** Spain
111 E4 **Vélez-Rubio** Spain
158 D2 **Velhas** *r.* Brazil
117 H6 **Velichayevskoye** Rus. Fed.
114 G2 **Velika Gorica** Croatia
115 I2 **Velika Plana** Serb. and Mont.
116 I3 **Velikaya** Rus. Fed.
77 S3 **Velikaya** *r.* Rus. Fed.
116 D3 **Velikaya** *r.* Rus. Fed.
116 E2 **Velikaya Guba** Rus. Fed.
94 E2 **Velikaya Kema** Rus. Fed.
115 L3 **Veliki Preslav** Bulg.
116 D3 **Velikiye Luki** Rus. Fed.
116 D3 **Velikiy Novgorod** Rus. Fed.
116 H2 **Velikiy Ustyug** Rus. Fed.
87 B3 **Velikonda Range** *hills* India
113 P2 **Velikooktyabr'skiy** Rus. Fed.
115 K3 **Veliko Tŭrnovo** Bulg.
116 F3 **Velikoye** Rus. Fed.
116 F3 **Velikoye, Ozero** *l.* Rus. Fed.
116 G4 **Velikoye, Ozero** *l.* Rus. Fed.
114 F2 **Veli Lošinj** Croatia
120 A3 **Vélingara** Senegal
113 O3 **Velizh** Rus. Fed.
112 H7 **Veľký Meder** Slovakia
69 F2 **Vella Lavella** *i.* Solomon Is
87 B4 **Vellar** *r.* India
109 H5 **Vellberg** Germany
109 H3 **Vellmar** Germany
87 B3 **Vellore** India
109 I2 **Velpke** Germany
116 G2 **Vel'sk** Rus. Fed.
109 L2 **Velten** Germany
108 D2 **Veluwe** *reg.* Neth.
108 E2 **Veluwezoom, Nationaal Park** *nat. park* Neth.
131 I5 **Velva** U.S.A.
163 J8 **Vema Seamount** *sea feature* S. Atlantic Ocean
162 I5 **Vema Trench** *sea feature* Indian Ocean
87 B4 **Vembanad Lake** India
106 D4 **Venachar, Loch** *l.* U.K.
159 E2 **Venado Tuerto** Arg.
114 F4 **Venafro** Italy
157 E3 **Venamo** *r.* Guyana/Venez.
157 E3 **Venamo, Cerro** *mt.* Venez.
158 C3 **Venceslau Bráz** Brazil
110 E3 **Vendôme** France
116 F4 **Venev** Rus. Fed.
Venezia Italy *see* **Venice**
157 C3 **Venezuela** *country* S. America
157 C2 **Venezuela, Golfo de** *g.* Venez.
163 E4 **Venezuelan Basin** *sea feature* S. Atlantic Ocean
87 A3 **Vengurla** India
114 E2 **Venice** Italy
145 D7 **Venice** U.S.A.
114 E2 **Venice, Gulf of** Europe
110 G4 **Vénissieux** France
87 B3 **Venkatagiri** India
87 C2 **Venkatapuram** India
108 E3 **Venlo** Neth.
103 I4 **Vennesla** Norway
108 D3 **Venray** Neth.
103 M4 **Venta** *r.* Latvia/Lith.
103 M4 **Venta** Lith.
159 D3 **Ventana, Sierra de la** *hills* Arg.
125 G4 **Ventersburg** S. Africa
125 G3 **Ventersdorp** S. Africa
125 F5 **Venterstad** S. Africa
105 F7 **Ventnor** U.K.
110 G4 **Ventoux, Mont** *mt.* France
103 M4 **Ventspils** Latvia
157 D3 **Ventuari** *r.* Venez.
140 C4 **Ventucopa** U.S.A.
140 C4 **Ventura** U.S.A.
70 F7 **Venus Bay** Australia
150 D2 **Venustiano Carranza** Mex.
156 D3 **Vera** Arg.
111 F4 **Vera** Spain
151 E4 **Veracruz** Mex.
151 E3 **Veracruz** *state* Mex.
88 B5 **Veraval** India
114 C2 **Verbania** Italy
114 C2 **Vercelli** Italy
102 J3 **Verdalsøra** Norway
159 D4 **Verde** *r.* Arg.
158 B2 **Verde** *r.* *Goiás* Brazil
158 C2 **Verde** *r.* *Goiás* Brazil
158 C2 **Verde** *r.* *Goiás/Minas Gerais* Brazil
158 B2 **Verde** *r.* *Mato Grosso do Sul* Brazil
136 E6 **Verde** *r.* Mex.
156 E2 **Verde** *r.* Para.
141 G4 **Verde** *r.* U.S.A.
159 D3 **Verde, Península** *pen.* Arg.
158 D1 **Verde Grande** *r.* Brazil
97 B3 **Verde Island Passage** Phil.
109 H2 **Verden (Aller)** Germany
143 E4 **Verdigris** *r.* U.S.A.
110 H5 **Verdon** *r.* France
110 G2 **Verdun** France
125 G3 **Vereeniging** S. Africa
159 G2 **Vergara** Uruguay
147 G2 **Vergennes** U.S.A.
111 C2 **Verín** Spain
82 D1 **Verkhne-Avzyan** Rus. Fed.
117 F6 **Verkhnebakanskiy** Rus. Fed.
113 P3 **Verkhnedneprovskiy** Rus. Fed.
76 J3 **Verkhneimbatsk** Rus. Fed.
102 O1 **Verkhnetulomskiy** Rus. Fed.
82 D1 **Verkhneural'sk** Rus. Fed.
77 N3 **Verkhnevilyuysk** Rus. Fed.
116 D1 **Verkhneye Kuyto, Ozero** *l.* Rus. Fed.
117 H5 **Verkhniy Baskunchak** Rus. Fed.
117 I5 **Verkhniy Kushum** Rus. Fed.
102 P2 **Verkhnyaya Pirenga, Ozero** *l.* Rus. Fed.
116 H2 **Verkhnyaya Toyma** Rus. Fed.
116 G2 **Verkhovazh'ye** Rus. Fed.
116 F4 **Verkhov'ye** Rus. Fed.
117 C5 **Verkhovyna** Ukr.
77 O3 **Verkhoyansk** Rus. Fed.
77 N3 **Verkhoyanskiy Khrebet** *mts* Rus. Fed.
83 J2 **Verkhuba** Kazakh.
108 B5 **Vermand** France
158 B1 **Vermelho** *r.* Brazil
131 G4 **Vermilion** Canada
134 C5 **Vermilion** *r.* U.S.A.
141 F3 **Vermilion Cliffs** U.S.A.
134 A2 **Vermilion Lake** U.S.A.
134 A2 **Vermilion Range** *hills* U.S.A.
142 D3 **Vermillion** U.S.A.
131 K5 **Vermillion Bay** Canada
147 G3 **Vermont** *state* U.S.A.
73 E2 **Vernadsky** *research stn* Antarctica
138 E3 **Vernal** U.S.A.
135 G2 **Verner** Canada
124 D5 **Verneuk Pan** *salt pan* S. Africa
130 F4 **Vernon** Canada
141 H4 **Vernon** *AZ* U.S.A.
147 G4 **Vernon** *CT* U.S.A.
143 D5 **Vernon** *TX* U.S.A.
141 F1 **Vernon** *UT* U.S.A.
145 D7 **Vero Beach** U.S.A.
115 J4 **Veroia** Greece
114 D2 **Verona** Italy
159 F2 **Verónica** Arg.
70 B4 **Verran** Australia
110 F2 **Versailles** France
109 G2 **Versmold** Germany
110 D3 **Vertou** France
125 I4 **Verulam** S. Africa
108 D4 **Verviers** Belgium
110 F2 **Vervins** France
108 C5 **Verzy** France
114 C3 **Vescovato** *Corsica* France
76 G4 **Veselaya, Gora** *mt.* Rus. Fed.
117 E6 **Vesele** Ukr.
117 G6 **Veselovskoye Vodokhranilishche** *resr* Rus. Fed.
83 J2 **Veseloyarsk** Rus. Fed.
82 F1 **Veselyy Podol** Kazakh.
117 G5 **Veshenskaya** Rus. Fed.
108 B5 **Vesle** *r.* France

Wattiwarriganna 213

110 H3 Vesoul France
94 D3 Vesselyy Yar Rus. Fed.
108 D3 Vessem Neth.
102 K1 Vesterålen *is* Norway
102 K1 Vesterålsfjorden *sea chan.* Norway
103 J4 Vestfjorddalen *val.* Norway
102 K2 Vestfjorden *sea chan.* Norway
102 □ Vestmanna Faroe Is
102 B3 Vestmannaeyjar Iceland
102 B3 Vestmannaeyjar *is* Iceland
102 I3 Vestnes Norway
102 D2 Vesturhorn *hd* Iceland
114 F4 Vesuvius *vol.* Italy
116 F3 Ves'yegonsk Rus. Fed.
112 H7 Veszprém Hungary
102 M3 Veteli Fin.
103 K4 Vetlanda Sweden
116 H3 Vetluga Rus. Fed.
116 H3 Vetluga *r.* Rus. Fed.
114 E3 Vettore, Monte *mt.* Italy
108 A3 Veurne Belgium
112 C7 Vevey Switz.
141 F3 Veyo U.S.A.
84 C4 Veys Iran
110 E4 Vézère *r.* France
80 E1 Vezirköprü Turkey
125 H1 Vhembe Dongola National Park S. Africa
159 B2 V. Hermosa, Paso de *pass* Chile
155 J4 Viana Brazil
111 B2 Viana do Castelo Port.
108 D3 Vianen Neth.
Viangchan Laos *see* Vientiane
158 C2 Vianópolis Brazil
114 D3 Viareggio Italy
103 J4 Viborg Denmark
114 G5 Vibo Valentia Italy
111 H2 Vic Spain
150 B2 Vicam Mex.
140 C5 Vicente, Point U.S.A.
150 D3 Vicente Guerrero Mex.
114 D2 Vicenza Italy
157 C3 Vichada *r.* Col.
116 G3 Vichuga Rus. Fed.
159 B2 Vichuquén Chile
110 F3 Vichy France
141 F5 Vicksburg *AZ* U.S.A.
143 F5 Vicksburg *MS* U.S.A.
158 D3 Viçosa Brazil
134 A5 Victor U.S.A.
73 D4 Victor, Mount *mt.* Antarctica
70 C5 Victor Harbor Australia
159 E2 Victoria Arg.
68 D3 Victoria *r.* Australia
70 F6 Victoria *state* Australia
130 E5 Victoria Canada
159 B3 Victoria Chile
150 H5 Victoria Hond.
114 F6 Victoria Malta
143 D6 Victoria U.S.A.
122 D4 Victoria, Lake Africa
70 D4 Victoria, Lake *N.S.W.* Australia
71 G6 Victoria, Lake *Vic.* Australia
89 H5 Victoria, Mount Myanmar
68 E2 Victoria, Mount P.N.G.
129 K2 Victoria and Albert Mountains Canada
123 C5 Victoria Falls Zambia/Zimbabwe
129 N1 Victoria Fjord *inlet* Greenland
93 □ Victoria Harbour *Hong Kong* China
128 G2 Victoria Island Canada
133 I4 Victoria Lake Canada
73 B6 Victoria Land *coastal area* Antarctica
122 D3 Victoria Nile *r.* Sudan/Uganda
72 D5 Victoria Range *mts* N.Z.
68 D3 Victoria River Downs Australia
133 F4 Victoriaville Canada
124 E5 Victoria West S. Africa
159 D3 Victorica Arg.
150 D3 Víctor Rosales Mex.
140 D4 Victorville U.S.A.
159 D2 Vicuña Mackenna Arg.
141 E4 Vidal Junction U.S.A.
115 K2 Videle Romania
115 J3 Vidin Bulg.
88 D5 Vidisha India
106 □ Vidlin U.K.
116 E2 Vidlitsa Rus. Fed.
113 M3 Vidzy Belarus
116 I2 Vidz'yuyar Rus. Fed.
109 K5 Viechtach Germany
159 D4 Viedma Arg.
156 B7 Viedma, Lago *l.* Arg.
109 J1 Vielank Germany
108 D4 Vielsalm Belgium
109 I3 Vienenburg Germany
112 H6 Vienna Austria
144 B4 Vienna *IL* U.S.A.
147 F5 Vienna *MD* U.S.A.
146 C5 Vienna *WV* U.S.A.
110 G4 Vienne France
110 E3 Vienne *r.* France
98 B1 Vientiane Laos
159 B3 Viento, Cordillera del *mts* Arg.
149 K5 Vieques *i.* Puerto Rico
102 N3 Vieremä Fin.
108 E3 Viersen Germany
112 D7 Vierwaldstätter See *l.* Switz.
110 F3 Vierzon France
150 D2 Viesca Mex.
103 N4 Viesīte Latvia
114 G4 Vieste Italy
102 L2 Vietas Sweden
98 Vietnam *country* Asia
93 B6 Viêt Quang Vietnam
93 B6 Viêt Tri Vietnam
97 B2 Vigan Phil.
114 C2 Vigevano Italy
151 H4 Vigía Chico Mex.
108 A4 Vignacourt France
110 D5 Vignemale *mt.* France
114 D2 Vignola Italy
111 B1 Vigo Spain
102 N2 Vihanti Fin.
88 C3 Vihari Pak.
103 N3 Vihti Fin.
102 N3 Viitasaari Fin.
88 C3 Vijainagar India
87 A2 Vijayadurg India
87 C2 Vijayawada India
102 C3 Vík Iceland
102 N2 Vikajärvi Fin.
115 K4 Vikhren *mt.* Bulg.
131 G4 Viking Canada
102 J2 Vikna *i.* Norway
103 I3 Vikøyri Norway
120 □ Vila da Ribeira Brava Cape Verde
Vila de Sal Rei Cape Verde *see* Sal Rei
Vila do Tarrafal Cape Verde *see* Tarrafal
111 B3 Vila Franca de Xira Port.
111 B1 Vilagarcía de Arousa Spain
125 J2 Vila Gomes da Costa Moz.
111 C1 Vilalba Spain
123 E5 Vilanandro, Tanjona *pt* Madag.
111 B2 Vila Nova de Gaia Port.
111 G2 Vilanova i la Geltrú Spain
120 □ Vila Nova Sintra Cape Verde
111 C2 Vila Real Port.
111 C2 Vilar Formoso Port.
87 B4 Vilavankod India
158 E3 Vila Velha Brazil
76 H1 Vil'cheka, Zemlya *i.* Rus. Fed.
102 L2 Vilhelmina Sweden
154 F6 Vilhena Brazil
103 N4 Viljandi Estonia
125 G3 Viljoenskroon S. Africa
103 M5 Vilkaviškis Lith.
103 M5 Vilkija Lith.
77 K2 Vil'kitskogo, Proliv *str.* Rus. Fed.
151 E4 Villa Alta Mex.
154 E6 Villa Bella Bol.
111 C1 Villablino Spain
159 E2 Villa Cañás Arg.
111 E3 Villacañas Spain
112 F7 Villach Austria
114 C5 Villacidro *Sardinia* Italy
159 E2 Villa Constitución Arg.
150 D4 Villa de Álvarez Mex.
150 D3 Villa de Cos Mex.
151 G4 Villa de Guadalupe Mex.
159 D1 Villa del Rosario Arg.
159 D1 Villa del Totoral Arg.
159 D1 Villa Dolores Arg.
151 F4 Villa Flores Mex.
159 F3 Villa Gesell Arg.
151 E2 Villagrán Mex.
159 E1 Villaguay Arg.
151 F4 Villahermosa Mex.
159 D2 Villa Huidobro Arg.
150 B2 Villa Insurgentes Mex.
159 D3 Villa Iris Arg.
Villajoyosa Spain *see* Villajoyosa-La Vila Joíosa
111 F3 Villajoyosa-La Vila Joíosa Spain
151 D2 Villaldama Mex.
159 D3 Villalonga Arg.
159 D2 Villa María Arg.
159 E1 Villa María Grande Arg.
159 D2 Villa Mercedes *San Luis* Arg.
154 F8 Villa Montes Bol.
125 H1 Villa Nora S. Africa
157 B2 Villanueva Col.
150 D3 Villanueva Mex.
111 D3 Villanueva de la Serena Spain
111 E3 Villanueva de los Infantes Spain
156 E3 Villa Ocampo Arg.
150 C2 Villa Ocampo Mex.
150 C2 Villa Orestes Pereyra Mex.
114 C5 Villaputzu *Sardinia* Italy
159 C3 Villa Regina Arg.
159 B3 Villarrica Chile
156 E3 Villarrica Para.
159 B3 Villarrica, Lago *l.* Chile
159 B3 Villarrica, Parque Nacional *nat. park* Chile
159 B3 Villarrica, Volcán *vol.* Chile
111 E3 Villarrobledo Spain
114 F5 Villa San Giovanni Italy
159 E2 Villa San José Arg.
159 C1 Villa Santa Rita de Catuna Arg.
156 C3 Villa Unión Arg.
150 D1 Villa Unión Mex.
150 C3 Villa Unión Mex.
150 C3 Villa Unión Mex.
159 D2 Villa Valeria Arg.
157 B3 Villavicencio Col.
154 E8 Villazon Bol.
110 F4 Villefranche-de-Rouergue France
110 G4 Villefranche-sur-Saône France
135 H2 Ville-Marie Canada
111 F3 Villena Spain
110 E4 Villeneuve-sur-Lot France
110 F2 Villeneuve-sur-Yonne France
143 E6 Ville Platte U.S.A.
108 B5 Villers-Cotterêts France
108 D5 Villerupt France
110 G4 Villeurbanne France
125 H3 Villiers S. Africa
112 D6 Villingen Germany
87 B4 Villupuram India
131 G4 Vilna Canada
103 N5 Vilnius Lith.
117 E6 Vil'nyans'k Ukr.
103 N3 Vilppula Fin.
109 J5 Vils *r.* Germany
108 C4 Vilvoorde Belgium
116 C4 Vilyeyka Belarus
77 N3 Vilyuy *r.* Rus. Fed.
77 L3 Vilyuyskoye Vodokhranilishche *resr* Rus. Fed.
103 K4 Vimmerby Sweden
108 A4 Vimy France
140 A2 Vina U.S.A.
159 B2 Viña del Mar Chile
147 I2 Vinalhaven U.S.A.
111 G2 Vinaròs Spain
144 C4 Vincennes U.S.A.
73 D6 Vincennes Bay *b.* Antarctica
102 L3 Vindelälven *r.* Sweden
102 L2 Vindeln Sweden
88 C5 Vindhya Range *hills* India
147 F5 Vineland U.S.A.
147 H4 Vineyard Haven U.S.A.
98 C1 Vinh Vietnam
Vinh Linh Vietnam *see* Hô Xa
98 C3 Vinh Long Vietnam
93 B6 Vinh Yên Vietnam
143 E4 Vinita U.S.A.
115 H2 Vinkovci Croatia
117 D5 Vinnytsya Ukr.
73 B3 Vinson Massif *mt.* Antarctica
103 J3 Vinstra Norway
134 A4 Vinton U.S.A.
87 B2 Vinukonda India
114 D1 Vipiteno Italy
109 K1 Vipperow Germany
97 C3 Virac Phil.
88 C5 Viramgam India
81 G3 Viranşehir Turkey
88 B4 Virawah Pak.
131 I5 Virden Canada
110 D2 Vire France
123 B5 Virei Angola
158 D2 Virgem da Lapa Brazil
141 F3 Virgin *r.* U.S.A.
135 H1 Virginatown Canada
107 D4 Virginia Rep. of Ireland
125 G4 Virginia S. Africa
134 A2 Virginia U.S.A.
146 D6 Virginia *state* U.S.A.
147 E6 Virginia Beach U.S.A.
140 C2 Virginia City U.S.A.
149 L5 Virgin Islands (U.K.) *terr.* Caribbean Sea
149 L5 Virgin Islands (U.S.A.) *terr.* Caribbean Sea
103 N3 Virkkala Fin.
98 C2 Virôchey Cambodia
134 B4 Viroqua U.S.A.
114 G2 Virovitica Croatia
103 M3 Virrat Fin.
108 D5 Virton Belgium
103 M4 Virtsu Estonia
87 B4 Virudhunagar India
122 C3 Virunga, Parc National des *nat. park* Dem. Rep. Congo
114 G3 Vis *i.* Croatia
103 N5 Visaginas Lith.
140 C3 Visalia U.S.A.
88 B5 Visavadar India
97 B4 Visayan Sea Phil.
109 G2 Visbek Germany
103 L4 Visby Sweden
128 G2 Viscount Melville Sound *sea chan.* Canada
108 D4 Visé Belgium
76 I2 Vise, Ostrov *i.* Rus. Fed.
115 H3 Višegrad Bos.-Herz.
155 I4 Viseu Brazil
111 C2 Viseu Port.
87 C2 Vishakhapatnam India
103 N4 Višķi Latvia
88 C5 Visnagar India
114 B2 Viso, Monte *mt.* Italy
115 H3 Visoko Bos.-Herz.
112 C7 Visp Switz.
109 H2 Visselhövede Germany
140 D5 Vista U.S.A.
158 A2 Vista Alegre Brazil
115 K4 Vistonida, Limni *lag.* Greece
113 I4 Vistula *r.* Poland
157 C3 Vita *r.* Col.
88 B3 Vitakri Pak.
114 E3 Viterbo Italy
114 G2 Vitez Bos.-Herz.
154 E8 Vitichi Bol.
111 C2 Vitigudino Spain
69 H3 Viti Levu *i.* Fiji
90 D1 Vitim *r.* Rus. Fed.
90 D1 Vitimskoye Ploskogor'ye *plat.* Rus. Fed.
158 E3 Vitória Brazil
158 E1 Vitória da Conquista Brazil
111 E1 Vitoria-Gasteiz Spain
163 G7 Vitória Seamount *sea feature* S. Atlantic Ocean
110 D2 Vitré France
108 A4 Vitry-en-Artois France
110 G2 Vitry-le-François France
116 D4 Vitsyebsk Belarus
102 M2 Vittangi Sweden
114 F6 Vittoria *Sicily* Italy
114 E2 Vittorio Veneto Italy
111 C1 Viveiro Spain
125 H1 Vivo S. Africa
70 B6 Vivonne Bay Australia
150 A2 Vizcaíno, Desierto de *des.* Mex.
150 A2 Vizcaíno, Sierra *mts* Mex.
117 C7 Vize Turkey
87 C2 Vizianagaram India
116 I2 Vizinga Rus. Fed.
108 C3 Vlaardingen Neth.
113 K7 Vlădeasa, Vârful *mt.* Romania
117 H7 Vladikavkaz Rus. Fed.
94 D3 Vladimir *Primorskiy Kray* Rus. Fed.
116 G3 Vladimir *Vladimirskaya Oblast'* Rus. Fed.
94 C3 Vladimiro-Aleksandrovskoye Rus. Fed.
82 F1 Vladimirovka *Kustanayskaya Oblast'* Kazakh.
82 B2 Vladimirovka *Zapadnyy Kazakhstan* Kazakh.
116 G4 Vladimirskaya Oblast' *admin. div.* Rus. Fed.
90 F2 Vladivostok Rus. Fed.
125 H2 Vlakte S. Africa
115 J3 Vlasotince Serb. and Mont.
124 D7 Vleesbaai *b.* S. Africa
108 C1 Vlieland *i.* Neth.
108 B3 Vlissingen Neth.
115 H4 Vlorë Albania
109 G2 Vlotho Germany
112 G6 Vltava *r.* Czech Rep.
82 F4 Vobkent Uzbek.
112 F6 Vöcklabruck Austria
116 F2 Vodlozero, Ozero *l.* Rus. Fed.
106 □ Voe U.K.
108 D4 Voerendaal Neth.
109 H4 Vogelsberg *hills* Germany
114 C2 Voghera Italy
109 K4 Vogtland *reg.* Germany
109 K5 Vohenstrauß Germany
123 E6 Vohimena, Tanjona *c.* Madag.
109 G3 Vöhl Germany
103 N4 Võhma Estonia
122 D4 Voi Kenya
120 B4 Voinjama Liberia
110 G4 Voiron France
103 J5 Vojens Denmark
115 H2 Vojvodina *prov. Srbija* Serb. and Mont.
116 H3 Vokhma Rus. Fed.
116 D1 Voknavolok Rus. Fed.
138 F2 Volborg U.S.A.
159 B1 Volcán, Cerro del *vol.* Chile
90 G4 Volcano Islands Japan
83 J1 Volchikha Rus. Fed.
103 I3 Volda Norway
108 D2 Volendam Neth.
117 H6 Volga *r.* Rus. Fed.
134 B4 Volga *r.* U.S.A.
117 G6 Volgodonsk Rus. Fed.
76 F5 Volgograd Rus. Fed.
117 H5 Volgogradskaya Oblast' *admin. div.* Rus. Fed.
112 G7 Völkermarkt Austria
116 E3 Volkhov Rus. Fed.
116 D3 Volkhov *r.* Rus. Fed.
108 E5 Völklingen Germany
125 H3 Volksrust S. Africa
94 B3 Vol'no-Nadezhdinskoye Rus. Fed.
117 F6 Volnovakha Ukr.
83 G1 Vol'noye Rus. Fed.
77 K2 Volochanka Rus. Fed.
117 C5 Volochys'k Ukr.
117 F6 Volodars'ke Ukr.
117 I6 Volodarskiy Rus. Fed.
113 N5 Volodars'k-Volyns'kyy Ukr.
113 M5 Volodymyrets' Ukr.
117 C5 Volodymyr-Volyns'kyy Ukr.
116 F3 Vologda Rus. Fed.
116 G3 Vologodskaya Oblast' *admin. div.* Rus. Fed.
117 F5 Volokonovka Rus. Fed.
115 J5 Volos Greece
116 D3 Volosovo Rus. Fed.
113 O2 Volot Rus. Fed.
117 F4 Volovo Rus. Fed.
117 H4 Vol'sk Rus. Fed.
120 B4 Volta, Lake *resr* Ghana
158 D3 Volta Redonda Brazil
114 F4 Volturno *r.* Italy
115 J4 Volvi, Limni *l.* Greece
116 I4 Volzhsk Rus. Fed.
82 B1 Volzhskiy *Samarskaya Oblast'* Rus. Fed.
117 H5 Volzhskiy *Volgogradskaya Oblast'* Rus. Fed.
123 E6 Vondrozo Madag.
116 G1 Vonga Rus. Fed.
102 D2 Vopnafjörður Iceland
102 D2 Vopnafjörður *b.* Iceland
116 B2 Vörå Fin.
113 L3 Voranava Belarus
116 I3 Vorchanka Rus. Fed.
116 E2 Vorenzha Rus. Fed.
163 J1 Voring Plateau *sea feature* N. Atlantic Ocean
76 H3 Vorkuta Rus. Fed.
103 M4 Vormsi *i.* Estonia
117 G5 Vorona *r.* Rus. Fed.
117 F5 Voronezh Rus. Fed.
117 F5 Voronezh *r.* Rus. Fed.
117 G5 Voronezhskaya Oblast' *admin. div.* Rus. Fed.
116 G3 Voron'ye Rus. Fed.
113 P3 Vorot'kovo Rus. Fed.
117 E5 Vorskla *r.* Rus. Fed.
103 N4 Võrtsjärv *l.* Estonia
103 N4 Võru Estonia
83 G5 Vorukh Tajik.
124 E5 Vosburg S. Africa
83 G5 Vose Tajik.
110 H2 Vosges *mts* France
82 D1 Voskresenskoye Rus. Fed.
103 I3 Voss Norway
Vostochno-Sibirskoye More *sea* Rus. Fed. *see* East Siberian Sea
Vostochnyy Chink Ustyurta *esc.* Uzbek. *see* Sharqiy Ustyurt Chink
83 J2 Vostochnyy Kazakhstan *admin. div.* Kazakh.
90 B1 Vostochnyy Sayan *mts* Rus. Fed.
73 C5 Vostok *research stn* Antarctica
94 D1 Vostok Rus. Fed.
67 I5 Vostok Island Kiribati
94 D2 Vostretsovo Rus. Fed.
76 G4 Votkinsk Rus. Fed.
158 C3 Votuporanga Brazil
108 C5 Vouziers France
110 E2 Voves France
116 I3 Voya *r.* Rus. Fed.
144 A1 Voyageurs National Park U.S.A.
102 O2 Voynitsa Rus. Fed.
116 F2 Vozhe, Ozero *l.* Rus. Fed.
116 G2 Vozhega Rus. Fed.
83 G1 Voznesenka Kazakh.
117 D6 Voznesens'k Ukr.
82 D3 Vozrojdenie Uzbek.
Vozrovdenye Uzbek. *see* Vozrojdenie
Vozrozhdeniya, O. *i.* Uzbek. *see* Vozrozhdenya Island
82 D3 Vozrozhdenya Island *pen.* Uzbek.
Vpadina Chagyllyshor *depr.* Turkm. *see* Çagyllyşor Çöketligi
94 C3 Vrangel' Rus. Fed.
Vrangelya, Ostrov *i.* Rus. Fed. *see* Wrangel Island
115 I3 Vranje Serb. and Mont.
115 L3 Vratnik *pass* Bulg.
115 J3 Vratsa Bulg.
114 G2 Vrbas *r.* Bos.-Herz.
115 H2 Vrbas Serb. and Mont.
125 H3 Vrede S. Africa
125 G3 Vredefort S. Africa
124 B6 Vredenburg S. Africa
124 C5 Vredendal S. Africa
108 C5 Vresse Belgium
87 B4 Vriddhachalam India
108 E1 Vries Neth.
103 K4 Vrigstad Sweden
115 I2 Vršac Serb. and Mont.
124 F3 Vryburg S. Africa
125 I3 Vryheid S. Africa
116 D2 Vsevolozhsk Rus. Fed.
115 I3 Vučitrn Serb. and Mont.
115 H2 Vukovar Croatia
76 G3 Vuktyl' Rus. Fed.
125 H3 Vukuzakhe S. Africa
114 F5 Vulcano, Isola *i. Isole Lipari* Italy
141 F5 Vulture Mountains U.S.A.
98 C3 Vung Tau Vietnam
103 N3 Vuohijärvi Fin.
102 N2 Vuolijoki Fin.
102 M2 Vuollerim Sweden
102 N2 Vuostimo Fin.
116 H4 Vurnary Rus. Fed.
82 E1 Vvedenka Kazakh.
123 D4 Vwawa Tanz.
88 C5 Vyara India
Vyatka Rus. Fed. *see* Kirov
116 I3 Vyatka *r.* Rus. Fed.
116 E4 Vyaz'ma Rus. Fed.
116 G3 Vyazniki Rus. Fed.
117 H5 Vyazovka *Astrakhanskaya Oblast'* Rus. Fed.
82 A1 Vyazovka *Saratovskaya Oblast'* Rus. Fed.
116 D2 Vyborg Rus. Fed.
116 I2 Vychegda *r.* Rus. Fed.
116 H2 Vychegodskiy Rus. Fed.
116 C4 Vyerkhnyadzvinsk Belarus
116 D4 Vyetryna Belarus
116 E2 Vygozero, Ozero *l.* Rus. Fed.
116 G4 Vyksa Rus. Fed.
117 D6 Vylkove Ukr.
113 K6 Vynohradiv Ukr.
116 E3 Vypolzovo Rus. Fed.
116 D3 Vyritsa Rus. Fed.
105 D5 Vyrnwy, Lake U.K.
117 F6 Vyselki Rus. Fed.
116 G4 Vysha Rus. Fed.
117 D5 Vyshhorod Ukr.
116 E3 Vyshnevolotskaya Gryada *ridge* Rus. Fed.
116 E3 Vyshniy-Volochek Rus. Fed.
112 H6 Vyškov Czech Rep.
117 D5 Vystupovychi Ukr.
116 F2 Vytegra Rus. Fed.

W

120 B3 Wa Ghana
108 D3 Waal *r.* Neth.
108 D3 Waalwijk Neth.
132 B3 Wabakimi Lake Canada
130 G3 Wabasca *r.* Canada
130 G3 Wabasca-Desmarais Canada
134 E5 Wabash U.S.A.
134 E5 Wabash *r.* U.S.A.
134 A3 Wabasha U.S.A.
135 E1 Wabatongushi Lake Canada
122 E3 Wabē Gestro *r.* Eth.
122 E3 Wabē Shebelē Wenz *r.* Eth.
131 J4 Wabowden Canada
132 C2 Wabuk Point Canada
133 G3 Wabush Canada
133 G3 Wabush Lake Canada
140 C2 Wabuska U.S.A.
145 D6 Waccasassa Bay U.S.A.
109 H4 Wächtersbach Germany
143 D6 Waco U.S.A.
85 G5 Wad Pak.
71 H6 Wadbilliga National Park Australia
121 D2 Waddān Libya
141 F5 Waddell Dam U.S.A.
108 C2 Waddenzee *sea chan.* Neth.
70 B4 Waddikee Australia
130 D4 Waddington, Mount Canada
108 C2 Waddinxveen Neth.
105 C7 Wadebridge U.K.
131 I4 Wadena Canada
142 E2 Wadena U.S.A.
108 E5 Wadern Germany
87 A2 Wadgaon India
108 E5 Wadgassen Germany
121 F2 Wadi Halfa Sudan
121 F3 Wad Medani Sudan
140 C2 Wadsworth U.S.A.
96 B4 Wafangdian China
109 G2 Wagenfeld Germany
109 I2 Wagenhoff Germany
129 J3 Wager Bay Canada
71 G5 Wagga Wagga Australia
88 C2 Wah Pak.
140 □1 Wahiawā U.S.A.
109 H3 Wahlhausen Germany
142 D3 Wahoo U.S.A.
142 D2 Wahpeton U.S.A.
141 F2 Wah Wah Mountains U.S.A.
87 A2 Wai India
140 □1 Wai'ale'e U.S.A.
140 □1 Waialua *reg.* U.S.A.
140 □1 Waialua Bay U.S.A.
140 □1 Wai'anae U.S.A.
140 □1 Wai'anae Range *mts* U.S.A.
72 D5 Waiau *r.* N.Z.
112 G7 Waidhofen an der Ybbs Austria
91 F7 Waigeo *i.* Indon.
72 E2 Waiharoa N.Z.
72 E2 Waiheke Island N.Z.
72 E2 Waihi N.Z.
72 E2 Waihou *r.* N.Z.
91 D7 Waikabubak Indon.
72 B6 Waikaia *r.* N.Z.
140 □1 Waikāne U.S.A.
72 D5 Waikari N.Z.
72 E2 Waikato *r.* N.Z.
72 F2 Waikawa Point N.Z.
70 C5 Waikerie Australia
140 □1 Waikīkī Beach U.S.A.
72 C6 Waikouaiti N.Z.
140 □2 Wailuku U.S.A.
72 D5 Waimakariri *r.* N.Z.
140 □1 Waimānalo U.S.A.
72 C4 Waimangaroa N.Z.
72 F3 Waimarama N.Z.
72 C6 Waimate N.Z.
140 □2 Waimea *HI* U.S.A.
140 □1 Waimea *HI* U.S.A.
88 D5 Wainganga *r.* India
91 E7 Waingapu Indon.
105 C7 Wainhouse Corner U.K.
131 G4 Wainwright Canada
128 C2 Wainwright U.S.A.
72 E3 Waiouru N.Z.
72 E3 Waipa *r.* N.Z.
72 B7 Waipahi N.Z.
140 □1 Waipahu U.S.A.
72 F3 Waipaoa *r.* N.Z.
72 B7 Waipapa Point N.Z.
72 D5 Waipara N.Z.
72 F3 Waipawa N.Z.
72 F3 Waipukurau N.Z.
72 F3 Wairakei N.Z.
72 E4 Wairarapa, Lake N.Z.
72 D4 Wairau *r.* N.Z.
72 F3 Wairoa N.Z.
72 F3 Wairoa *r.* N.Z.
72 E1 Wairoa *r.* N.Z.
72 F3 Waitahanui N.Z.
72 B6 Waitahuna N.Z.
72 E2 Waitakaruru N.Z.
72 C6 Waitaki *r.* N.Z.
72 E3 Waitara N.Z.
72 E2 Waitoa N.Z.
72 E2 Waiuku N.Z.
72 B7 Waiwera South N.Z.
93 F5 Waiyang China
95 E6 Wajima Japan
122 E3 Wajir Kenya
95 D7 Wakasa-wan *b.* Japan
72 B6 Wakatipu, Lake N.Z.
131 H4 Wakaw Canada
95 D7 Wakayama Japan
142 D4 WaKeeney U.S.A.
135 J3 Wakefield Canada
72 D4 Wakefield N.Z.
104 F4 Wakefield U.K.
134 C2 Wakefield *MI* U.S.A.
147 H4 Wakefield *RI* U.S.A.
146 E6 Wakefield *VA* U.S.A.
Wakeham Canada *see* Kangiqsujuaq
67 F2 Wake Island *terr.* N. Pacific Ocean
83 H5 Wakhan *reg.* Afgh.
94 G4 Wakinosawa Japan
94 G2 Wakkanai Japan
125 I3 Wakkerstroom S. Africa
70 F5 Wakool Australia
70 E5 Wakool *r.* Australia
133 G2 Wakuach, Lac *l.* Canada
112 H5 Wałbrzych Poland
71 I3 Walcha Australia
112 E7 Walchensee *l.* Germany
108 C4 Walcourt Belgium
112 H4 Wałcz Poland
147 F4 Walden U.S.A.
112 F6 Waldkraiburg Germany
105 C7 Waldon *r.* U.K.
146 E5 Waldorf U.S.A.
105 D5 Wales *admin. div.* U.K.
71 H3 Walgett Australia
122 C4 Walikale Dem. Rep. Congo
134 B4 Walker *IA* U.S.A.
142 E2 Walker *MN* U.S.A.
140 C2 Walker *r.* U.S.A.
124 C7 Walker Bay S. Africa
145 E7 Walker Cay *i.* Bahamas
140 C2 Walker Lake U.S.A.
140 C4 Walker Pass U.S.A.
135 G3 Walkerton Canada
142 C2 Wall U.S.A.
138 C2 Wallace U.S.A.
135 F4 Wallaceburg Canada
71 I2 Wallangarra Australia
70 B4 Wallaroo Australia
105 D4 Wallasey U.K.
71 G5 Walla Walla Australia
138 C2 Walla Walla U.S.A.
109 H5 Walldürn Germany
124 B5 Wallekraal S. Africa
71 H5 Wallendbeen Australia
147 F4 Wallenpaupack, Lake U.S.A.
105 F6 Wallingford U.K.
147 G4 Wallingford U.S.A.
69 I3 Wallis, Îles *is* Pacific Ocean
69 I3 Wallis and Futuna Islands *terr.* Pacific Ocean
71 J4 Wallis Lake *inlet* Australia
147 F6 Wallops Island U.S.A.
138 C2 Wallowa Mountains U.S.A.
106 □ Walls U.K.
131 H2 Walmsley Lake Canada
104 D3 Walney, Isle of *i.* U.K.
134 C5 Walnut U.S.A.
141 G4 Walnut Canyon National Monument *nat. park* U.S.A.
143 F4 Walnut Ridge U.S.A.
89 I3 Walong India
105 F5 Walsall U.K.
139 F4 Walsenburg U.S.A.
109 H2 Walsrode Germany
87 C2 Waltair India
145 D5 Walterboro U.S.A.
145 C6 Walter F. George Reservoir U.S.A.
70 F2 Walter's Range *hills* Australia
135 I3 Waltham Canada
144 C4 Walton *KY* U.S.A.
147 F3 Walton *NY* U.S.A.
123 B6 Walvis Bay Namibia
163 I8 Walvis Ridge *sea feature* S. Atlantic Ocean
122 C3 Wamba Dem. Rep. Congo
88 B2 Wana Pak.
70 F2 Wanaaring Australia
72 B6 Wanaka N.Z.
72 B6 Wanaka, Lake N.Z.
93 E5 Wan'an China
135 G2 Wanapitei Lake Canada
147 F4 Wanaque Reservoir U.S.A.
70 D5 Wanbi Australia
72 C6 Wanbrow, Cape N.Z.
70 D2 Wancoocha, Lake *salt flat* Australia
94 C2 Wanda Shan *mts* China
109 I4 Wandersleben Germany
109 L2 Wandlitz Germany
96 D6 Wando S. Korea
98 A1 Wang, Mae Nam *r.* Thai.
72 E3 Wanganui N.Z.
72 E3 Wanganui *r.* N.Z.
71 G6 Wangaratta Australia
70 A5 Wangary Australia
92 C3 Wangcang China
93 D4 Wangcheng China
109 F1 Wangerooge Germany
109 F1 Wangerooge *i.* Germany
96 A3 Wanghai Shan *h.* China
93 E4 Wangjiang China
93 C5 Wangmo China
96 E2 Wangqing China
88 B5 Wankaner India
122 E3 Wanlaweyn Somalia
109 G1 Wanna Germany
93 E4 Wannian China
93 D7 Wanning China
92 E1 Wanquan China
108 D3 Wanroij Neth.
93 D6 Wanshan Qundao *is* China
72 F4 Wanstead N.Z.
105 F6 Wantage U.K.
135 G2 Wanup Canada
93 C4 Wanxian China
92 C3 Wanyuan China
93 E4 Wanzai China
108 D4 Wanze Belgium
146 A4 Wapakoneta U.S.A.
134 B5 Wapello U.S.A.
132 C3 Wapikopa Lake Canada
130 F4 Wapiti *r.* Canada
143 F4 Wappapello Lake *resr* U.S.A.
134 A5 Wapsipinicon *r.* U.S.A.
92 B3 Waqên China
84 C6 Waqr *well* Saudi Arabia
88 A4 Warah Pak.
87 B2 Warangal India
70 F6 Waranga Reservoir Australia
88 E5 Waraseoni India
71 F8 Waratah Australia
71 F7 Waratah Bay Australia
109 H3 Warburg Germany
68 C4 Warburton Australia
70 B1 Warburton *watercourse* Australia
131 G2 Warburton Bay Canada
72 A6 Ward, Mount N.Z.
72 B5 Ward, Mount N.Z.
70 B5 Wardang Island Australia
125 H3 Warden S. Africa
109 G1 Wardenburg Germany
88 D5 Wardha India
88 D6 Wardha *r.* India
130 D3 Ware Canada
147 G3 Ware U.S.A.
105 E7 Wareham U.K.
147 H4 Wareham U.S.A.
108 D4 Waremme Belgium
109 K1 Waren Germany
109 F3 Warendorf Germany
71 I2 Warialda Australia
109 J1 Warin Germany
98 C2 Warin Chamrap Thai.
72 E2 Warkworth N.Z.
104 F2 Warkworth U.K.
108 A4 Warloy-Baillon France
131 H4 Warman Canada
124 C4 Warmbad Namibia
125 H2 Warmbad S. Africa
105 E6 Warminster U.K.
147 F4 Warminster U.S.A.
108 C2 Warmond Neth.
140 D2 Warm Springs *NV* U.S.A.
146 D5 Warm Springs *VA* U.S.A.
124 D6 Warmwaterberg *mts* S. Africa
147 H3 Warner U.S.A.
138 B3 Warner Mountains U.S.A.
145 D5 Warner Robins U.S.A.
154 F7 Warnes Bol.
71 J2 Warning, Mount Australia
88 D5 Warora India
71 I1 Warra Australia
70 E6 Warracknabeal Australia
71 I5 Warragamba Reservoir Australia
71 F7 Warragul Australia
70 C2 Warrakalanna, Lake *salt flat* Australia
70 A4 Warramboo Australia
71 G2 Warrambool *r.* Australia
68 E4 Warrego *r.* Australia
71 G3 Warren Australia
135 G2 Warren Canada
143 E5 Warren *AR* U.S.A.
135 F4 Warren *MI* U.S.A.
142 D1 Warren *MN* U.S.A.
146 C4 Warren *OH* U.S.A.
146 D4 Warren *PA* U.S.A.
146 C4 Warrendale U.S.A.
107 E3 Warrenpoint U.K.
142 E4 Warrensburg *MO* U.S.A.
147 G3 Warrensburg *NY* U.S.A.
124 F4 Warrenton S. Africa
146 E5 Warrenton U.S.A.
120 C4 Warri Nigeria
72 C6 Warrington N.Z.
105 E4 Warrington U.K.
145 C6 Warrington U.S.A.
70 C3 Warriota *watercourse* Australia
70 E7 Warrnambool Australia
142 E1 Warroad U.S.A.
70 A5 Warrow Australia
71 H3 Warrumbungle Range *mts* Australia
70 D2 Warry Warry *watercourse* Australia
113 J4 Warsaw Poland
134 E5 Warsaw *IN* U.S.A.
142 E4 Warsaw *MO* U.S.A.
146 D3 Warsaw *NY* U.S.A.
146 E6 Warsaw *VA* U.S.A.
109 G3 Warstein Germany
Warszawa Poland *see* Warsaw
112 G4 Warta *r.* Poland
109 I4 Wartburg, Schloss *tourist site* Germany
71 J2 Warwick Australia
105 F5 Warwick U.K.
147 F4 Warwick *NY* U.S.A.
147 H4 Warwick *RI* U.S.A.
139 E4 Wasatch Range *mts* U.S.A.
125 I4 Wasbank S. Africa
140 C4 Wasco U.S.A.
142 E2 Waseca U.S.A.
85 F5 Washap Pak.
134 C5 Washburn *IL* U.S.A.
147 I1 Washburn *ME* U.S.A.
142 C2 Washburn *ND* U.S.A.
134 B2 Washburn *WI* U.S.A.
88 D5 Washim India
146 E5 Washington *DC* U.S.A. (City Plan 62)
145 D5 Washington *GA* U.S.A.
134 B5 Washington *IA* U.S.A.
134 C5 Washington *IL* U.S.A.
144 C4 Washington *IN* U.S.A.
142 F4 Washington *MO* U.S.A.
145 E5 Washington *NC* U.S.A.
147 F4 Washington *NJ* U.S.A.
146 C4 Washington *PA* U.S.A.
141 F3 Washington *UT* U.S.A.
138 B2 Washington *state* U.S.A.
73 B5 Washington, Cape *c.* Antarctica
147 H2 Washington, Mount U.S.A.
146 B5 Washington Court House U.S.A.
134 D3 Washington Island U.S.A.
129 L1 Washington Land *reg.* Greenland
143 D5 Washita *r.* U.S.A.
85 G5 Washuk Pak.
84 B5 Wasī' Saudi Arabia
81 K5 Wasit *tourist site* Iraq
132 E3 Waskaganish Canada
131 J3 Waskaiowaka Lake Canada
150 H5 Waspán Nicaragua
108 C2 Wassenaar Neth.
124 C3 Wasser Namibia
109 H4 Wasserkuppe *h.* Germany
109 I5 Wassertrüdingen Germany
140 C2 Wassuk Range *mts* U.S.A.
132 E4 Waswanipi, Lac *l.* Canada
91 E7 Watampone Indon.
147 G4 Waterbury *CT* U.S.A.
147 G2 Waterbury *VT* U.S.A.
131 H3 Waterbury Lake Canada
107 D5 Waterford Rep. of Ireland
146 D4 Waterford U.S.A.
107 E5 Waterford Harbour Rep. of Ireland
107 C5 Watergrasshill Rep. of Ireland
108 C4 Waterloo Belgium
135 G4 Waterloo Canada
134 A4 Waterloo *IA* U.S.A.
147 H3 Waterloo *ME* U.S.A.
146 E3 Waterloo *NY* U.S.A.
134 C4 Waterloo *WI* U.S.A.
105 F7 Waterlooville U.K.
125 H1 Waterpoort S. Africa
134 C2 Watersmeet U.S.A.
130 G5 Waterton Lakes National Park Canada
147 E3 Watertown *NY* U.S.A.
142 D2 Watertown *SD* U.S.A.
134 C4 Watertown *WI* U.S.A.
125 I2 Waterval Boven S. Africa
Waterval-Boven S. Africa *see* Waterval Boven
70 C4 Watervale Australia
147 I2 Waterville U.S.A.
131 G3 Waterways Canada
135 G4 Watford Canada
105 G6 Watford U.K.
142 C2 Watford City U.S.A.
131 I3 Wathaman *r.* Canada
109 I2 Wathlingen Germany
146 E3 Watkins Glen U.S.A.
143 D5 Watonga U.S.A.
131 H4 Watrous Canada
122 C3 Watsa Dem. Rep. Congo
134 D5 Watseka U.S.A.
122 C4 Watsi Kengo Dem. Rep. Congo
131 I4 Watson Canada
130 D2 Watson Lake Canada
140 B3 Watsonville U.S.A.
106 E2 Watten U.K.
106 E2 Watten, Loch *l.* U.K.
131 I2 Watterson Lake Canada
70 A2 Wattiwarriganna *watercourse* Australia

Zadetkyi Kyun 215

93 D6 **Wuzhou** China
134 B5 **Wyaconda** *r.* U.S.A.
71 G4 **Wyalong** Australia
135 F4 **Wyandotte** U.S.A.
134 C5 **Wyanet** U.S.A.
71 H4 **Wyangala Reservoir** Australia
70 F2 **Wyara, Lake** *salt flat* Australia
70 E6 **Wycheproof** Australia
105 E6 **Wye** *r.* U.K.
105 F6 **Wylye** *r.* U.K.
105 I5 **Wymondham** U.K.
68 C3 **Wyndham** Australia
70 F6 **Wyndham-Werribee** Australia
143 F5 **Wynne** U.S.A.
128 G2 **Wynniatt Bay** Canada
71 F8 **Wynyard** Australia
131 I4 **Wynyard** Canada
134 C5 **Wyoming** *IL* U.S.A.
134 E4 **Wyoming** *MI* U.S.A.
138 E3 **Wyoming** *state* U.S.A.
138 E3 **Wyoming Peak** U.S.A.
71 I4 **Wyong** Australia
70 D5 **Wyperfeld National Park** Australia
104 E4 **Wyre** *r.* U.K.
147 E4 **Wysox** U.S.A.
113 J4 **Wyszków** Poland
105 F5 **Wythall** U.K.
146 C6 **Wytheville** U.S.A.
147 I2 **Wytopitlock** U.S.A.

X

122 F2 **Xaafuun** Somalia
82 A4 **Xaçmaz** Azer.
124 E1 **Xade** Botswana
89 H3 **Xagquka** China
88 D1 **Xaidulla** China
98 B1 **Xaignabouli** Laos
89 G3 **Xainza** China
123 D6 **Xai-Xai** Moz.
151 G3 **Xal, Cerro de** *h.* Mex.
82 D4 **Xalqobod** Uzbek.
92 C1 **Xamba** China
Xam Hua Laos *see* **Xam Nua**
91 C4 **Xam Nua** Laos
98 B1 **Xan** *r.* Laos
Xan, Xê *r.* Vietnam *see* **Pe Cô, Krông**
123 C6 **Xanagas** Botswana
92 B1 **Xangd** China
92 D1 **Xangdin Hural** China
89 E2 **Xangdoring** China
123 B5 **Xangongo** Angola
81 K2 **Xankändi** Azer.
115 K4 **Xanthi** Greece
154 E6 **Xapuri** Brazil
81 L2 **Xaraba Şähär Sayı** *sea feature* Azer.
81 L2 **Xärä Zirä Adası** *is* Azer.
89 F3 **Xarba La** *pass* China
92 D1 **Xar Moron** *r.* *Nei Mongol* China
92 F1 **Xar Moron** *r.* *Nei Mongol* China
111 F3 **Xátiva** Spain
123 C6 **Xau, Lake** Botswana
155 I6 **Xavantes, Serra dos** *hills* Brazil
Xa Vo Đat Vietnam *see* **Đưc Linh**
93 B6 **Xay** Laos
83 J4 **Xayar** China
83 I5 **Xekar** China
146 B5 **Xenia** U.S.A.
96 F1 **Xiachengzi** China
93 D6 **Xiachuan Dao** *i.* China
92 B3 **Xiahe** China
92 E2 **Xiajin** China
93 F5 **Xiamen** China
92 C3 **Xi'an** China
93 C4 **Xianfeng** China
92 D3 **Xiangcheng** *Henan* China
92 E3 **Xiangcheng** *Henan* China
92 D3 **Xiangfan** China
90 B4 **Xianggelila** China
98 B1 **Xiangkhoang** Laos
93 F4 **Xiangshan** China
93 D5 **Xiangtan** China
93 D5 **Xiangxiang** China
93 D4 **Xiangyin** China
93 F4 **Xianju** China
93 E4 **Xianning** China
93 D4 **Xiantao** China
93 E5 **Xianxia Ling** *mts* China
92 E2 **Xianxian** China
92 C3 **Xianyang** China
93 F5 **Xianyou** China
93 F4 **Xianyuan** China
92 D4 **Xiaochang** China
93 C6 **Xiaodong** China
93 D4 **Xiaogan** China
90 E1 **Xiao Hinggan Ling** *mts* China
92 B4 **Xiaojin** China
89 H2 **Xiaonanchuan** China
93 F4 **Xiaoshan** China
93 E5 **Xiaotao** China
92 E2 **Xiaowutai Shan** *mt.* China
92 E3 **Xiaoxian** China
93 B4 **Xiaoxiang Ling** *mts* China
Xiaoxita China *see* **Yiling**
92 D2 **Xiaoyi** China
93 F5 **Xiapu** China
96 A2 **Xiawa** China
92 D3 **Xiayukou** China
93 B5 **Xichang** China
92 B4 **Xichong** China
93 B6 **Xichou** China
92 D3 **Xichuan** China
93 B4 **Xide** China
157 D4 **Xié** *r.* Brazil
98 C1 **Xieng Lam** Vietnam
93 C6 **Xieyang Dao** *i.* China
92 E3 **Xifei He** *r.* China
92 B3 **Xifeng** *Gansu* China
93 C5 **Xifeng** *Guizhou* China
96 C2 **Xifeng** *Liaoning* China
79 G4 **Xigazê** China
92 C3 **Xihan Shui** *r.* China
92 B3 **Xihe** China
96 A3 **Xi He** *r.* China
92 A1 **Xi He** *watercourse* China
92 B3 **Xiji** China
93 D6 **Xi Jiang** *r.* China
89 G2 **Xijir** China
89 G2 **Xijir Ulan Hu** *salt l.* China
92 B2 **Xijishui** China
92 D1 **Xil** China
96 B2 **Xiliao He** *r.* China
93 B5 **Xilin** China
92 E1 **Xilinhot** China
92 A1 **Ximiao** China
92 C2 **Xin** China
93 F4 **Xin'anjiang** China
93 F4 **Xin'anjiang Shuiku** *resr* China
125 J2 **Xinavane** Moz.
96 C3 **Xinbin** China
92 D1 **Xin Bulag** China
92 E3 **Xincai** China
93 F4 **Xinchang** China
92 A2 **Xincheng** *Gansu* China
93 C5 **Xincheng** *Guangxi* China
92 C2 **Xincheng** *Ningxia* China
92 C2 **Xinchengbu** China
93 D6 **Xindu** *Guangxi* China
92 B4 **Xindu** *Sichuan* China
93 E5 **Xinfeng** *Guangdong* China
93 E5 **Xinfeng** *Jiangxi* China
93 E5 **Xinfengjiang Shuiku** *resr* China
93 E5 **Xingan** *Jiangxi* China
93 D5 **Xing'an** China
96 C4 **Xingangzhen** China
89 H3 **Xingba** China
92 F1 **Xingcheng** China
93 E5 **Xingguo** China
79 H3 **Xinghai** China
92 D1 **Xinghe** China
92 F3 **Xinghua** China
93 F5 **Xinghua Wan** *b.* China
94 C2 **Xingkai** China
Xingkai Hu *l.* China/Rus. Fed. *see* **Khanka, Lake**
93 E5 **Xingning** *Guangdong* China
93 D5 **Xingning** *Hunan* China
93 D4 **Xingou** China
92 C3 **Xingping** China
93 B5 **Xingren** China
92 A3 **Xingsagoinba** China
92 D4 **Xingshan** China
92 E2 **Xingtai** China
155 H4 **Xingu** *r.* Brazil
155 H6 **Xingu, Parque Indígena do** *res.* Brazil
93 B4 **Xingwen** China
92 D2 **Xingxian** China
92 D3 **Xingyang** China
93 C6 **Xingye** China
93 B5 **Xingyi** China
93 E4 **Xingzi** China
83 J4 **Xinhe** China
92 E1 **Xin Hot** China
93 D5 **Xinhua** China
92 B2 **Xinhuacun** China
93 C5 **Xinhuang** China
93 D6 **Xinhui** *Guangdong* China
92 F1 **Xinhui** *Nei Mongol* China
92 A2 **Xining** China
92 E2 **Xinji** China
93 E4 **Xinjian** China
92 D3 **Xinjiang** China
89 D1 **Xinjiang Uygur Zizhiqu** China
89 E1 **Xinjiang Uygur Zizhiqu** *aut. reg.* China
92 C2 **Xinjie** *Nei Mongol* China
93 B6 **Xinjie** *Yunnan* China
93 B4 **Xinjin** China
96 B1 **Xinkai He** *r.* China
96 B3 **Xinmin** China
93 D5 **Xinning** China
93 A5 **Xinping** China
93 E5 **Xinquan** China
93 D5 **Xinshao** China
92 E3 **Xintai** China
93 D5 **Xintian** China
92 E4 **Xinxian** China
92 D3 **Xinxiang** China
93 D6 **Xinxing** China
92 E3 **Xinyang** China
93 E3 **Xinye** China
93 D6 **Xinyi** *Guangdong* China
92 F3 **Xinyi** *Jiangsu* China
92 F3 **Xinyi He** *r.* China
93 C7 **Xinying** China
93 E5 **Xinyu** China
83 J4 **Xinyuan** China
92 D3 **Xinzhou** *Shanxi* China
92 D2 **Xinzhou** *Shanxi* China
111 C1 **Xinzo de Limia** Spain
96 B3 **Xiongyuecheng** China
93 D6 **Xiping** *Henan* China
92 E3 **Xiping** *Henan* China
92 A3 **Xiqing Shan** *mts* China
155 J6 **Xique Xique** Brazil
92 C1 **Xishanzui** China
93 C5 **Xishui** *Guizhou* China
93 E4 **Xishui** *Hubei* China
Xi Ujimqin Qi China *see* **Bayan Ul Hot**
93 F4 **Xiuning** China
93 C4 **Xiushan** China
93 E4 **Xiushui** China
93 E4 **Xiu Shui** *r.* China
93 C5 **Xiuwen** China
92 D3 **Xiuwu** China
96 B3 **Xiuyan** China
93 D6 **Xiuying** China
82 E4 **Xiva** Uzbek.
89 F3 **Xixabangma Feng** *mt.* China
92 D3 **Xixia** China
92 E3 **Xixian** *Henan* China
92 D2 **Xixian** *Shanxi* China
92 C3 **Xixiang** China
93 F5 **Xiyang Dao** *i.* China
93 B5 **Xiyang Jiang** *r.* China
89 G3 **Xizang Zizhiqu** *aut. reg.* China
96 A4 **Xizhong Dao** *i.* China
82 D4 **Xoʻjayli** Uzbek.
89 H3 **Xoka** China
Xom An Lôc Vietnam *see* **An Lôc**
Xom Duc Hanh Vietnam *see* **Đưc Bôn**
83 H4 **Xonobod** Uzbek.
83 G4 **Xovos** Uzbek.
93 F4 **Xuancheng** China
93 C4 **Xuan'en** China
92 C4 **Xuanhan** China
93 F4 **Xuanhepu** China
92 E1 **Xuanhua** China
98 C3 **Xuân Lôc** Vietnam
93 B5 **Xuanwei** China
Xuanzhou China *see* **Xuancheng**
92 D3 **Xuchang** China
82 A4 **Xudat** Azer.
122 E3 **Xuddur** Somalia
93 C5 **Xuefeng Shan** *mts* China
89 H2 **Xugui** China
89 F3 **Xungru** China
92 F3 **Xun He** *r.* China
93 D6 **Xun Jiang** *r.* China
93 E5 **Xunwu** China
92 E3 **Xunxian** China
92 E3 **Xunyang** China
92 C3 **Xunyi** China
93 D5 **Xupu** China
89 F3 **Xuru Co** *l.* China
92 E2 **Xushui** China
93 D6 **Xuwen** China
92 F3 **Xuyi** China
93 B4 **Xuyong** China
Xuzhou China *see* **Tongshan**

Y

93 B4 **Ya'an** China
70 E5 **Yaapeet** Australia
120 C4 **Yabassi** Cameroon
122 D3 **Yabēlo** Eth.
90 C1 **Yablonovyy Khrebet** *mts* Rus. Fed.
92 B2 **Yabrai Shan** *mts* China
92 B2 **Yabrai Yanchang** China
80 F5 **Yabrūd** Syria
96 E1 **Yabuli** China
157 C2 **Yacambu, Parque Nacional** *nat. park* Venez.
93 C7 **Yacheng** China
93 C5 **Yachi He** *r.* China
154 E6 **Yacuma** *r.* Bol.
87 B2 **Yadgir** India
137 J4 **Yadkin** *r.* U.S.A.
116 H4 **Yadrin** Rus. Fed.
92 B1 **Yagan** China
163 E9 **Yaghan Basin** *sea feature* S. Atlantic Ocean
94 G2 **Yagishiri-tō** *i.* Japan
82 C5 **Yagman** Turkm.
121 D3 **Yagoua** Cameroon
88 E3 **Yagra** China
89 H2 **Yagradagzê Shan** *mt.* China
159 F1 **Yaguari** *r.* Uruguay
98 B4 **Yaha** Thai.
80 D2 **Yahşihan** Turkey
80 E2 **Yahyalı** Turkey
85 H4 **Yahya Wana** Afgh.
95 F6 **Yaita** Japan
95 F7 **Yaizu** Japan
93 A4 **Yajiang** China
80 F3 **Yakacık** Turkey
85 G4 **Yakhehal** Afgh.
138 B2 **Yakima** U.S.A.
138 B2 **Yakima** *r.* U.S.A.
84 D3 **Yakinish** Iran
Yakkabag Uzbek. *see* **Yakkabogʻ**
83 F5 **Yakkabogʻ** Uzbek.
85 F4 **Yakmach** Pak.
120 B3 **Yako** Burkina
130 B3 **Yakobi Island** U.S.A.
94 C2 **Yakovlevka** Rus. Fed.
94 G3 **Yakumo** Japan
95 B9 **Yaku-shima** *i.* Japan
130 B3 **Yakutat** U.S.A.
130 B3 **Yakutat Bay** U.S.A.
77 N3 **Yakutsk** Rus. Fed.
117 E6 **Yakymivka** Ukr.
98 B4 **Yala** Thai.
135 F4 **Yale** U.S.A.
151 G3 **Yalkubul, Punta** *pt* Mex.
71 G7 **Yallourn** Australia
93 A5 **Yalong Jiang** *r.* China
80 B1 **Yalova** Turkey
117 F6 **Yalta** Ukr.
117 E6 **Yalta** Ukr.
96 C3 **Yalu Jiang** *r.* China/N. Korea
96 C4 **Yalujiang Kou** *r. mouth* N. Korea
80 C2 **Yalvaç** Turkey
94 G5 **Yamada** Japan
94 G5 **Yamagata** Japan
95 B9 **Yamagawa** Japan
95 B7 **Yamaguchi** Japan
Yamal, Poluostrov *pen.* Rus. Fed. *see* **Yamal Peninsula**
76 H2 **Yamal Peninsula** Rus. Fed.
71 J2 **Yamba** Australia
71 E7 **Yambacoona** Australia
131 G2 **Yamba Lake** Canada
157 C4 **Yambi, Mesa de** *hills* Col.
121 E4 **Yambio** Sudan
115 L3 **Yambol** Bulg.
76 I3 **Yamburg** Rus. Fed.
92 A2 **Yamenzhuang** China
95 G6 **Yamizo-san** *mt.* Japan
103 O4 **Yamm** Rus. Fed.
120 B4 **Yamoussoukro** Côte d'Ivoire
138 E3 **Yampa** *r.* U.S.A.
117 D5 **Yampil'** Ukr.
88 E4 **Yamuna** *r.* India
88 D3 **Yamunanagar** India
83 I2 **Yamyshevo** Kazakh.
89 G3 **Yamzho Yumco** *l.* China
77 O3 **Yana** *r.* Rus. Fed.
70 D6 **Yanac** Australia
87 C2 **Yanam** India
92 C2 **Yan'an** China
154 D6 **Yanaoca** Peru
86 A5 **Yanbu' al Baḥr** Saudi Arabia
92 F3 **Yancheng** China
68 B5 **Yanchep** Australia
92 C2 **Yanchi** China
92 D2 **Yanchuan** China
71 G5 **Yanco** Australia
70 D3 **Yanco Glen** Australia
71 F3 **Yanda** *watercourse* Australia
70 D3 **Yandama Creek** *watercourse* Australia
120 B3 **Yanfolila** Mali
89 H3 **Ya'ngamdo** China
89 G3 **Yangbajain** China
92 D3 **Yangcheng** China
93 D6 **Yangchun** China
96 B4 **Yangdok** N. Korea
92 D1 **Yanggao** China
92 E2 **Yanggu** China
92 E1 **Yang He** *r.* China
Yangiabad Uzbek. *see* **Yangiobod**
Yangikishlak Uzbek. *see* **Yangiqishloq**
Yangi-Nishan Uzbek. *see* **Yangi Nishon**
82 F5 **Yangi Nishon** Uzbek.
83 G4 **Yangiobod** Uzbek.
83 F4 **Yangiqishloq** Uzbek.
Yangirabad Uzbek. *see* **Yangirabot**
82 F4 **Yangirabot** Uzbek.
83 G4 **Yangiyoʻl** Uzbek.
Yangiyul' Uzbek. *see* **Yangiyoʻl**
93 D6 **Yangjiang** China
Yangôn Myanmar *see* **Rangoon**
92 D4 **Yangping** China
92 D2 **Yangquan** China
93 D5 **Yangshan** China
93 C5 **Yangshuo** China
98 D2 **Yang Sin, Chư** *mt.* Vietnam
89 H2 **Yangtze** *r.* *Qinghai* China
93 E4 **Yangtze** *r.* China
alt. **Chang Jiang,**
alt. **Jinsha Jiang,**
alt. **Tongtian He,**
alt. **Zhi Qu,**
long **Yangtze Kiang**
92 F4 **Yangtze, Mouth of the** China
122 E2 **Yangudi Rassa National Park** Eth.
93 D6 **Yangxi** China
92 C3 **Yangxian** China
96 E5 **Yangyang** S. Korea
92 E1 **Yangyuan** China
92 F3 **Yangzhou** China
93 C4 **Yanhe** China
92 D2 **Yan He** *r.* China
89 E2 **Yanhuqu** China
70 A4 **Yaninee, Lake** *salt flat* Australia
96 E2 **Yanji** China
93 B4 **Yanjin** China
120 C4 **Yankara National Park** Nigeria
142 D3 **Yankton** U.S.A.
93 D5 **Yanling** China
77 O2 **Yano-Indigirskaya Nizmennost'** *lowland* Rus. Fed.
87 C4 **Yan Oya** *r.* Sri Lanka
92 E1 **Yanqing** China
92 E2 **Yanshan** *Hebei* China
93 E4 **Yanshan** *Jiangxi* China
93 B6 **Yanshan** *Yunnan* China
92 E1 **Yan Shan** *mts* China
89 H2 **Yanshiping** China
96 E1 **Yanshou** China
77 O2 **Yanskiy Zaliv** *g.* Rus. Fed.
71 F2 **Yantabulla** Australia
96 A5 **Yantai** China
70 E2 **Yantara Lake** *salt flat* Australia
113 I3 **Yantarnyy** Rus. Fed.
96 D2 **Yantongshan** China
93 A5 **Yanyuan** China
92 E3 **Yanzhou** China
120 D4 **Yaoundé** Cameroon
92 C3 **Yaoxian** China
98 A3 **Yao Yai, Ko** *i.* Thai.
91 F6 **Yap** *i.* Micronesia
157 D4 **Yapacana, Cerro** *mt.* Venez.
91 F7 **Yapen** *i.* Indon.
91 F7 **Yapen, Selat** *sea chan.* Indon.
160 E5 **Yap Trench** *sea feature* N. Pacific Ocean
150 B1 **Yaqui** *r.* Mex.
157 C2 **Yaracuy** *r.* Venez.
68 E4 **Yaraka** Australia
116 H3 **Yaransk** Rus. Fed.
70 A4 **Yardea** Australia
80 C3 **Yardımcı Burnu** *pt* Turkey
81 L2 **Yardımlı** Azer.
105 I5 **Yare** *r.* U.K.
116 J2 **Yarega** Rus. Fed.
69 G2 **Yaren** Nauru
116 I2 **Yarensk** Rus. Fed.
157 B4 **Yarí** *r.* Col.
95 E6 **Yariga-take** *mt.* Japan
157 C2 **Yaritagua** Venez.
83 I5 **Yarkant He** *r.* China
135 I3 **Yarker** Canada
88 C1 **Yarkhun** *r.* Pak.
89 G4 **Yarlung Zangbo** *r.* Asia
alt. **Dihang (India),**
conv. **Brahmaputra**
133 G5 **Yarmouth** Canada
105 F7 **Yarmouth** U.K.
147 H4 **Yarmouth Port** U.S.A.
141 F4 **Yarnell** U.S.A.
116 F3 **Yaroslavl'** Rus. Fed.
116 F3 **Yaroslavskaya Oblast'** *admin. div.* Rus. Fed.
94 C2 **Yaroslavskiy** Rus. Fed.
70 F6 **Yarra** *r.* Australia
71 G7 **Yarram** Australia
71 I1 **Yarraman** Australia
89 H3 **Yartö Tra La** *pass* China
76 J3 **Yartsevo** Rus. Fed.
116 E4 **Yartsevo** *Smolenskaya Oblast'* Rus. Fed.
157 B3 **Yarumal** Col.
89 F5 **Yasai** *r.* India
69 H3 **Yasawa Group** *is* Fiji
117 F6 **Yasenskaya** Rus. Fed.
117 G6 **Yashalta** Rus. Fed.
83 H5 **Yashilkŭl** *l.* Tajik.
117 H6 **Yashkul'** Rus. Fed.
82 D2 **Yasnyy** Rus. Fed.
98 C2 **Yasothon** Thai.
71 H5 **Yass** Australia
71 H5 **Yass** *r.* Australia
84 C4 **Yāsūj** Iran
80 B3 **Yatağan** Turkey
69 G4 **Yaté** New Caledonia
143 E4 **Yates Center** U.S.A.
131 J2 **Yathkyed Lake** Canada
95 F7 **Yatsuga-take** *vol.* Japan
95 B8 **Yatsushiro** Japan
105 E6 **Yatton** U.K.
93 □ **Yau Tong** *b.* Hong Kong China
154 D5 **Yavari** *r.* Brazil/Peru
150 B2 **Yávaros** Mex.
88 D5 **Yavatmal** India
81 H2 **Yavi** Turkey
157 D3 **Yavi, Cerro** *mt.* Venez.
117 B5 **Yavoriv** Ukr.
95 C8 **Yawatahama** Japan
89 E1 **Yawatongguz He** *r.* China
89 H5 **Yaw Chaung** *r.* Myanmar
151 G4 **Yaxchilan** *tourist site* Guat.
84 D4 **Yazd** Iran
85 F3 **Yazdān** Iran
84 D4 **Yazd-e Khvāst** Iran
80 G2 **Yazıhan** Turkey
143 F5 **Yazoo** *r.* U.S.A.
143 F5 **Yazoo City** U.S.A.
103 J5 **Yding Skovhøj** *h.* Denmark
115 J6 **Ydra** *i.* Greece
98 A2 **Ye** Myanmar
70 F6 **Yea** Australia
105 D7 **Yealmpton** U.K.
83 I5 **Yecheng** China
150 B1 **Yécora** Mex.
145 D7 **Yeehaw Junction** U.S.A.
70 A5 **Yeelanna** Australia
116 F4 **Yefremov** Rus. Fed.
81 J2 **Yeghegnadzor** Armenia
83 I2 **Yegindybulak** Kazakh.
83 G2 **Yegindykol'** Kazakh.
117 G6 **Yegorlyk** *r.* Rus. Fed.
117 G6 **Yegorlykskaya** Rus. Fed.
94 E2 **Yegorova, Mys** *pt* Rus. Fed.
116 F4 **Yegor'yevsk** Rus. Fed.
121 F4 **Yei** Sudan
92 E4 **Yeji** China
76 H4 **Yekaterinburg** Rus. Fed.
117 G5 **Yelan'** Rus. Fed.
117 G5 **Yelan'** *r.* Rus. Fed.
71 I2 **Yelarbon** Australia
82 E5 **Yelbarsli** Turkm.
117 F4 **Yelets** Rus. Fed.
120 A3 **Yélimané** Mali
106 □ **Yell** *i.* U.K.
87 C2 **Yellandu** India
87 A3 **Yellapur** India
134 B3 **Yellow** *r.* U.S.A.
146 D4 **Yellow Creek** U.S.A.
128 G3 **Yellowknife** Canada
71 G4 **Yellow Mountain** *h.* Australia
92 E2 **Yellow River** *r.* China
96 B6 **Yellow Sea** Pacific Ocean
138 F2 **Yellowstone** *r.* U.S.A.
138 E2 **Yellowstone Lake** U.S.A.
138 E2 **Yellowstone National Park** U.S.A.
138 E2 **Yellowtail Reservoir** U.S.A.
106 □ **Yell Sound** *str.* U.K.
Yeloten Turkm. *see* **Yolöten**
117 D5 **Yel'sk** Belarus
83 J3 **Yel'tay** Kazakh.
129 J1 **Yelverton Bay** Canada
122 C7 **Yemen** *country* Asia
116 G2 **Yemetsk** Rus. Fed.
116 G2 **Yemtsa** Rus. Fed.
116 I2 **Yemva** Rus. Fed.
120 C2 **Yena** Rus. Fed.
117 F5 **Yenakiyeve** Ukr.
89 H5 **Yenangyat** Myanmar
89 H5 **Yenangyaung** Myanmar
89 H6 **Yenanma** Myanmar
93 B6 **Yên Bai** Vietnam
93 B6 **Yên Châu** Vietnam
71 G5 **Yenda** Australia
120 B4 **Yendi** Ghana
120 B3 **Yénéganou** Congo
81 K3 **Yengejeh** Iran
83 I5 **Yengisar** China
80 D1 **Yeniçağa** Turkey
80 E2 **Yenice** Turkey
115 L5 **Yenice** Turkey
80 D2 **Yeniceoba** Turkey
80 B1 **Yenişehir** Turkey
76 K4 **Yenisey** *r.* Rus. Fed.
76 K4 **Yeniseysk** Rus. Fed.
76 K4 **Yeniseyskiy Kryazh** *ridge* Rus. Fed.
76 I2 **Yeniseyskiy Zaliv** *inlet* Rus. Fed.
93 B6 **Yên Minh** Vietnam
117 H6 **Yenotayevka** Rus. Fed.
88 C5 **Yeola** India
Yeotmal India *see* **Yavatmal**
71 H4 **Yeoval** Australia
105 E7 **Yeovil** U.K.
150 B1 **Yepachi** Mex.
68 F4 **Yeppoon** Australia
82 D5 **Yerbent** Turkm.
77 L3 **Yerbogachen** Rus. Fed.
83 H2 **Yerementau, Gory** *hills* Kazakh.
81 J1 **Yerevan** Armenia
83 H2 **Yereymentau** Kazakh.
117 H6 **Yergeni** *hills* Rus. Fed.
140 C2 **Yerington** U.S.A.
80 E2 **Yerköy** Turkey
87 A2 **Yerla** *r.* India
164 A1 **Yermak Plateau** *sea feature* Arctic Ocean
150 C2 **Yermo** Mex.
140 D4 **Yermo** U.S.A.
117 I5 **Yershov** Rus. Fed.
116 G2 **Yertsevo** Rus. Fed.
Yerushalayim Israel/West Bank *see* **Jerusalem**
117 H5 **Yeruslan** *r.* Rus. Fed.
96 D5 **Yesan** S. Korea
83 I4 **Yesik** Kazakh.
82 F2 **Yesil'** Kazakh.
80 E2 **Yeşilhisar** Turkey
80 F1 **Yeşilırmak** *r.* Turkey
80 B3 **Yeşilova** Turkey
117 G6 **Yessentuki** Rus. Fed.
77 L3 **Yessey** Rus. Fed.
105 C7 **Yes Tor** *h.* U.K.
71 I2 **Yetman** Australia
Yeu Myanmar *see* **Ye-U**
90 B4 **Ye-U** Myanmar
110 C3 **Yeu, Île d'** *i.* France
81 K1 **Yevlax** Azer.
117 E6 **Yevpatoriya** Ukr.
92 D3 **Yexian** China
89 E1 **Yeyik** China
117 F6 **Yeysk** Rus. Fed.
116 H1 **Yezhuga** *r.* Rus. Fed.
116 D4 **Yezyaryshcha** Belarus
159 F2 **Yí** *r.* Uruguay
93 B4 **Yibin** China
89 F2 **Yibug Caka** *salt l.* China
93 D4 **Yichang** *Hubei* China
92 D4 **Yicheng** *Hubei* China
92 D3 **Yicheng** *Shanxi* China
92 D3 **Yichuan** China
90 E2 **Yichun** *Heilong.* China
93 E5 **Yichun** *Jiangxi* China
93 D4 **Yidu** China
93 E4 **Yifeng** China
92 D3 **Yi He** *r.* *Henan* China
92 D3 **Yi He** *r.* *Shandong* China
93 E5 **Yihuang** China
92 C3 **Yijun** China
94 A1 **Yilan** China
115 L4 **Yıldız Dağları** *mts* Turkey
80 F2 **Yıldızeli** Turkey
93 B5 **Yiliang** *Yunnan* China
93 B5 **Yiliang** *Yunnan* China
93 D4 **Yiling** *Hubei* China
92 C4 **Yilong** China
93 B6 **Yilong Hu** *l.* China
96 E1 **Yimianpo** China
92 F3 **Yinan** China
92 C2 **Yinchuan** China
96 C2 **Yingchengzi** China
93 D5 **Yingde** China
93 C7 **Yinggehai** China
92 E3 **Ying He** *r.* China
96 B3 **Yingkou** China
92 B2 **Yingpanshui** China
93 E4 **Yingshan** *Hubei* China
92 C4 **Yingshan** *Sichuan* China
92 E3 **Yingshang** China
93 E4 **Yingtan** China
92 D2 **Yingxian** China
83 J4 **Yining** China
93 C5 **Yinjiang** China
89 H5 **Yinmabin** Myanmar
96 C1 **Yinma He** *r.* China
92 C1 **Yin Shan** *mts* China
89 H3 **Yi'ong Zangbo** *r.* China
93 A5 **Yipinglang** China
122 D3 **Yirga Alem** Eth.
92 F2 **Yi Shan** *mt.* China
92 F3 **Yishui** China
98 □ **Yishun** Sing.
96 C2 **Yitong** China
96 C1 **Yitong He** *r.* China
90 B2 **Yiwu** China
96 A3 **Yiwulü Shan** *mts* China
93 E4 **Yixian** *Anhui* China
96 A3 **Yixian** *Liaoning* China
92 F4 **Yixing** China
93 D4 **Yiyang** *Hunan* China
93 E4 **Yiyang** *Jiangxi* China
93 D5 **Yizhang** China
93 C5 **Yizhou** China
103 M3 **Yläne** Fin.
103 M3 **Ylihärmä** Fin.
102 N2 **Yli-Ii** Fin.
102 N2 **Yli-Kärppä** Fin.
102 N2 **Ylikiiminki** Fin.
102 O2 **Yli-Kitka** *l.* Fin.
102 M3 **Ylistaro** Fin.
102 M2 **Ylitornio** Fin.
102 N2 **Ylivieska** Fin.
103 N3 **Ylöjärvi** Fin.
83 G2 **Yntaly** Kazakh.
143 D6 **Yoakum** U.S.A.
94 G3 **Yobetsu-dake** *vol.* Japan
99 D4 **Yogyakarta** Indon.
130 F4 **Yoho National Park** Canada
96 D5 **Yŏju** S. Korea
121 D4 **Yokadouma** Cameroon
95 E7 **Yokkaichi** Japan
121 D4 **Yoko** Cameroon
95 F7 **Yokohama** Japan
95 F7 **Yokosuka** Japan
94 G5 **Yokote** Japan
94 G4 **Yokotsu-dake** *mt.* Japan
121 D4 **Yola** Nigeria
82 E5 **Yolöten** Turkm.
151 E4 **Yoloxóchitl** Mex.
98 B2 **Yom, Mae Nam** *r.* Thai.
120 B4 **Yomou** Guinea
96 D5 **Yŏnan** N. Korea
95 G6 **Yonezawa** Japan
70 C4 **Yongala** Australia
96 D6 **Yŏng-am** S. Korea
93 E5 **Yong'an** China
92 A2 **Yongchang** China
92 E3 **Yongcheng** China
96 E6 **Yongch'ŏn** S. Korea
93 F5 **Yongchun** China
92 B2 **Yongdeng** China
93 E5 **Yongding** China
92 E2 **Yongding He** *r.* China
96 E5 **Yŏngdŏk** S. Korea
93 E5 **Yongfeng** China
93 C5 **Yongfu** China
96 D6 **Yŏnggwang** S. Korea
89 H3 **Yonggyap** *pass* India
96 D4 **Yŏnghŭng** N. Korea
96 D4 **Yŏnghŭng-man** *b.* N. Korea
96 D2 **Yongji** China
93 F4 **Yongjia** China
92 B3 **Yongjing** China
92 D2 **Yongjin Qu** *r.* China
96 E5 **Yŏngju** S. Korea
93 F4 **Yongkang** China
96 C3 **Yongling** China
92 E2 **Yongnian** China
93 C6 **Yongning** China
93 A5 **Yongren** China
96 D6 **Yŏngsan-gang** *r.* S. Korea
96 D6 **Yŏngsanp'o** S. Korea
93 C4 **Yongshun** China
93 F5 **Yongtai** China
96 E5 **Yŏngwol** S. Korea
93 D5 **Yongxing** *Hunan* China
93 E5 **Yongxing** *Jiangxi* China
93 E4 **Yongxiu** China
93 D5 **Yongzhou** China
96 D3 **Yŏnhwa-san** *mt.* N. Korea
147 G4 **Yonkers** U.S.A.
110 F2 **Yonne** *r.* France
157 B3 **Yopal** Col.
93 C5 **Yopurga** China
68 B5 **York** Australia
104 F4 **York** U.K.
142 D3 **York** *NE* U.S.A.
146 E5 **York** *PA* U.S.A.
145 D5 **York** *SC* U.S.A.
68 E3 **York, Cape** Australia
104 F3 **York, Vale of** *val.* U.K.
70 B5 **Yorke Peninsula** Australia
70 B5 **Yorketown** Australia
104 E3 **Yorkshire Dales National Park** U.K.
104 G4 **Yorkshire Wolds** *hills* U.K.
131 I4 **Yorkton** Canada
146 E6 **Yorktown** U.S.A.
150 H5 **Yoro** Hond.
120 B3 **Yorosso** Mali
140 C3 **Yosemite National Park** U.S.A.
140 C3 **Yosemite Village** U.S.A.
95 C8 **Yoshino-gawa** *r.* Japan
95 D7 **Yoshino-Kumano National Park** Japan
116 H3 **Yoshkar-Ola** Rus. Fed.
96 D6 **Yŏsu** S. Korea
80 E7 **Yotvata** Israel
107 D6 **Youghal** Rep. of Ireland
146 D5 **Youghiogheny River Lake** U.S.A.
93 C6 **You Jiang** *r.* China
71 H5 **Young** Australia
159 F2 **Young** Uruguay
70 B3 **Younghusband, Lake** *salt flat* Australia
70 C5 **Younghusband Peninsula** Australia
73 B6 **Young Island** *i.* Antarctica
146 C4 **Youngstown** U.S.A.
93 D4 **You Shui** *r.* China
120 B3 **Youvarou** Mali
93 F5 **Youxi** China
93 D5 **Youxian** China
93 C4 **Youyang** China
94 B1 **Youyi** China
92 D2 **Youyu** China
83 G5 **Yovon** Tajik.
71 F1 **Yowah** *watercourse* Australia
80 E2 **Yozgat** Turkey
158 E3 **Ypané** *r.* Para.
158 A3 **Ype-Jhú** Para.
Ypres Belgium *see* **Ieper**
138 B3 **Yreka** U.S.A.
Yr Wyddfa *mt.* U.K. *see* **Snowdon**
108 A4 **Yser** *r.* France
108 D3 **Ysselsteyn** Neth.
103 K5 **Ystad** Sweden
105 D5 **Ystwyth** *r.* U.K.
Ysyk-Köl Kyrg. *see* **Balykchy**
83 I4 **Ysyk-Köl** *salt l.* Kyrg.
106 F3 **Ythan** *r.* U.K.
77 O3 **Ytyk-Kyuyel'** Rus. Fed.
98 A1 **Yuam, Nam Mae** *r.* Myanmar/Thai.
92 D4 **Yuan'an** China
93 C5 **Yuanbao Shan** *mt.* China
93 D4 **Yuanjiang** *Hunan* China
93 A6 **Yuanjiang** *Yunnan* China
93 D4 **Yuan Jiang** *r.* *Hunan* China
93 B6 **Yuan Jiang** *r.* *Yunnan* China
93 F5 **Yüanli** Taiwan
93 D4 **Yuanling** China
93 A5 **Yuanmou** China
92 D2 **Yuanping** China
92 D3 **Yuanqu** China
140 B2 **Yuba** *r.* U.S.A.
140 B2 **Yuba City** U.S.A.
94 G3 **Yūbari** Japan
93 C4 **Yubei** China
151 G4 **Yucatán** *pen.* Mex.
151 G3 **Yucatán** *state* Mex.
148 G4 **Yucatan Channel** Cuba/Mex.
141 E4 **Yucca** U.S.A.
140 D3 **Yucca Lake** U.S.A.
140 D4 **Yucca Valley** U.S.A.
92 E2 **Yucheng** China
77 O4 **Yudoma** *r.* Rus. Fed.
93 E5 **Yudu** China
93 C4 **Yuechi** China
68 D4 **Yuendumu** Australia
93 □ **Yuen Long** *Hong Kong* China
93 F4 **Yueqing** China
93 E4 **Yuexi** *Anhui* China
93 B4 **Yuexi** *Sichuan* China
93 D4 **Yueyang** China
93 E4 **Yugan** China
76 H3 **Yugorsk** Rus. Fed.
Yugoslavia *country* Europe *see* **Serbia and Montenegro**
116 J2 **Yugydtydor** Rus. Fed.
93 F4 **Yuhuan** China
92 E2 **Yuhuang Ding** *mt.* China
93 E4 **Yujiang** China
93 D6 **Yu Jiang** *r.* China
77 Q3 **Yukagirskoye Ploskogor'ye** *plat.* Rus. Fed.
80 E2 **Yukarısarıkaya** Turkey
122 B4 **Yuki** Dem. Rep. Congo
128 C3 **Yukon** *r.* Canada/U.S.A.
130 B2 **Yukon Territory** *admin. div.* Canada
81 J3 **Yüksekova** Turkey
82 D1 **Yuldybayevo** Rus. Fed.
145 D6 **Yulee** U.S.A.
93 F6 **Yüli** Taiwan
93 D6 **Yulin** *Guangxi* China
93 C7 **Yulin** *Hainan* China
92 C2 **Yulin** *Shaanxi* China
141 E5 **Yuma** U.S.A.
141 E5 **Yuma Desert** U.S.A.
157 A4 **Yumbo** Col.
90 B3 **Yumen** China
83 J3 **Yumin** China
80 E3 **Yumurtalık** Turkey
80 C2 **Yunak** Turkey
93 D6 **Yunan** China
92 E3 **Yuncheng** *Shandong* China
92 D3 **Yuncheng** *Shanxi* China
93 D6 **Yunfu** China
93 B5 **Yungui Gaoyuan** *plat.* China
93 F4 **Yunhe** China
93 D5 **Yunkai Dashan** *mts* China
92 D4 **Yunmeng** China
93 A5 **Yunnan** *prov.* China
92 D4 **Yun Shui** *r.* China
70 C4 **Yunta** Australia
93 D6 **Yunwu Shan** *mts* China
93 D5 **Yunxi** China
92 D3 **Yunxian** China
93 E6 **Yunxiao** China
92 D3 **Yunyang** *Henan* China
92 C4 **Yunyang** *Sichuan* China
93 C5 **Yuping** China
93 F4 **Yuqian** China
92 E1 **Yuqiao Shuiku** *resr* China
93 C5 **Yuqing** China
71 J2 **Yuraygir National Park** Australia
90 A1 **Yurga** Rus. Fed.
154 C5 **Yurimaguas** Peru
157 E3 **Yuruán** *r.* Venez.
157 E3 **Yuruari** *r.* Venez.
157 C2 **Yurubi, Parque Nacional** *nat. park* Venez.
88 E1 **Yurungkax He** *r.* China
116 I3 **Yur'ya** Rus. Fed.
116 G3 **Yur'yevets** Rus. Fed.
116 F3 **Yur'yev-Pol'skiy** Rus. Fed.
150 H5 **Yuscarán** Hond.
93 F4 **Yushan** China
93 F6 **Yü Shan** *mt.* Taiwan
92 D2 **Yushe** China
116 E1 **Yushkozero** Rus. Fed.
96 D1 **Yushu** *Jilin* China
90 B3 **Yushu** *Qinghai* China
116 I3 **Yushut** *r.* Rus. Fed.
117 H6 **Yusta** Rus. Fed.
81 H1 **Yusufeli** Turkey
92 E3 **Yutai** China
89 E1 **Yutian** China
92 C2 **Yuwang** China
93 B5 **Yuxi** China
92 E2 **Yuxian** *Hebei* China
92 D2 **Yuxian** *Shanxi* China
93 F4 **Yuyao** China
94 G5 **Yuzawa** Japan
116 G3 **Yuzha** Rus. Fed.
90 D1 **Yuzhno-Muyskiy Khrebet** *mts* Rus. Fed.
90 G2 **Yuzhno-Sakhalinsk** Rus. Fed.
117 H6 **Yuzhno-Sukhokumsk** Rus. Fed.
117 D6 **Yuzhnoukrayinsk** Ukr.
82 E1 **Yuzhnoural'sk** Rus. Fed.
117 G6 **Yuzhnyy** Rus. Fed.
83 G4 **Yuzhnyy Kazakhstan** *admin. div.* Kazakh.
82 D1 **Yuzhnyy Ural** *mts* Rus. Fed.
92 B3 **Yuzhong** China
92 D3 **Yuzhou** China
Yuzkuduk Uzbek. *see* **Yuzquduq**
82 E4 **Yuzquduq** Uzbek.
112 C7 **Yverdon** Switz.
110 E2 **Yvetot** France
98 A1 **Ywathit** Myanmar
82 D4 **Yylanly** Turkm.

Z

Zaamin Uzbek. *see* **Zomin**
108 C2 **Zaandam** Neth.
81 I3 **Zāb al Kabīr, Nahr az** *r.* Iraq
81 I4 **Zāb aş Şaghīr, Nahr az** *r.* Iraq
90 D2 **Zabaykal'sk** Rus. Fed.
84 B2 **Zab-e Kuchek** *r.* Iran
86 B7 **Zabīd** Yemen
85 F4 **Zābol** Iran
85 F5 **Zāboli** Iran
82 B3 **Zaburun'ye** Kazakh.
151 G5 **Zacapa** Guat.
150 D4 **Zacapu** Mex.
150 D3 **Zacatecas** Mex.
150 D3 **Zacatecas** *state* Mex.
151 E4 **Zacatlán** Mex.
82 B2 **Zachagansk** Kazakh.
115 I6 **Zacharo** Greece
114 F2 **Zadar** Croatia
98 A3 **Zadetkale Kyun** *i.* Myanmar
98 A3 **Zadetkyi Kyun** *i.* Myanmar

ACKNOWLEDGEMENTS

Maps designed and created by
HarperCollins Reference, Glasgow

Additional work by Cosmographics, Watford and ML Design, Beckenham

Land cover map: Land Cover Center for Remote Sensing, Boston University, USA
Population map: Gridded Population of the World (GPW), Version 3. Palisades, NY: CIESIN,
Columbia University. Available at http://sedac.ciesin.columbia.edu/plue/gpw

IMAGES AND PHOTOS

pages 4–15
Remote Sensing Applications Consultants Ltd,
2 Prospect Place, Mill Lane, Alton, Hants. GU34 2SX, UK
pages 16–17
NRSC Ltd/Science Photo Library
pages 38–39
Fault lines: Digital image © 1996 CORBIS; Original image courtesy of NASA/CORBIS
Mount Bromo: Michael Pitts / naturepl.com
pages 40–41
Francois Suchel - Still Pictures
page 43
Tōkyō: U.S. Geological Survey, EROS Data Center, Sioux Falls, SD